MICROSOFT® ACCESS® 2010 PROGRAMMER'S REFERENCE

D0516713

Microsoft® Access® 2010

PROGRAMMER'S REFERENCE

Teresa Hennig
Rob Cooper
Geoffrey Griffith
Jerry Dennison

WILEY

Wiley Publishing, Inc.

Microsoft® Access® 2010 Programmer's Reference

Published by
Wiley Publishing, Inc.
10475 Crosspoint Boulevard
Indianapolis, IN 46256
www.wiley.com

Published by Wiley Publishing, Inc., Indianapolis, Indiana

Published simultaneously in Canada

ISBN: 978-0-470-59166-6

Manufactured in the United States of America

10 9 8 7 6 5 4 3 2 1

For general information on our other products and services please contact our Customer Care Department within the United States at (877) 762-2974, outside the United States at (317) 572-3993 or fax (317) 572-4002.

Wiley also publishes its books in a variety of electronic formats. Some content that appears in print may not be available in electronic books.

Library of Congress Control Number: 2010929738

To my family and incredible friends, you help me to realize that every day is filled with precious moments — sights, sounds, and emotions to be cherished. May we all remember to pause and savor the blessings that we have, especially the time that we share with those we love.

— TERESA

To my family, for all of the love and support you've shown me over the years.

— ROB

To my wife, Jamie, and my son, Ryan, I couldn't have been blessed with a better family and this would not have been possible without all of your love and support!

— GEOFF

To my wife Dianne, my son, Jeremy, my daughter, Amber, and my late parents, Clifford and Jeanette Dennison. You are my inspiration and my life. Thanks Dad, for instilling into me the insatiable appetite to explore and learn, without which I would not be where I am. To my grandchildren: Brianna, Fisher, and Huntlee. You are our future.

— JERRY

CREDITS

EXECUTIVE EDITOR
Robert Elliott

PROJECT EDITOR
Tom Dinse

CONTRIBUTING AUTHORS AND TECHNICAL EDITORS
Ben Clothier
Doug (Dagi) Yudovich

TECHNICAL EDITORS
Dr. Jeff Boyce
Albert D. Kallal
Armen Stein

TIP CONTRIBUTORS
Dane Miller
Garry Robinson
Steve Schapel
Larry Strange

PRODUCTION EDITOR
Kathleen Wisor

COPY EDITORS
Nancy Rapoport
Paula Lowell

EDITORIAL DIRECTOR
Robyn B. Siesky

EDITORIAL MANAGER
Mary Beth Wakefield

MARKETING MANAGER
Ashley Zurcher

PRODUCTION MANAGER
Tim Tate

VICE PRESIDENT AND EXECUTIVE GROUP PUBLISHER
Richard Swadley

VICE PRESIDENT AND EXECUTIVE PUBLISHER
Barry Pruett

ASSOCIATE PUBLISHER
Jim Minatel

PROJECT COORDINATOR, COVER
Lynsey Stanford

PROOFREADER
Nancy Carrasco

INDEXER
Robert Swanson

COVER DESIGNER
Michael E. Trent

COVER IMAGE
© Randolph Jay Braun/istockphoto

ABOUT THE AUTHORS

 TERESA HENNIG loves challenges, solving problems, and making things happen. So it is no surprise that she was immediately hooked on Access; by its tools for rapid development and the ability to quickly create intuitive, user-friendly applications. Within a month, she started her own company as an Access developer and business consultant (1997). With a strong background in business and project management, Teresa (and her company, Data Dynamics NW), focuses on using Access to provide cost-effective custom database solutions. In recognition of her expertise and dedication to the Access community, Teresa has been awarded as a Microsoft Access MVP (Most Valuable Professional) every year since 2006 . She continues to serve as President of both the Pacific Northwest Access Developers Group (PNWADG) and the Seattle Access Group. Her leadership, expertise, and service to the Access community have also earned her recognition as a National Community Champion from INETA. Being the lead author of several Access books has afforded Teresa the opportunity to work with esteemed colleagues and to invite others to share the experience of becoming published authors. Learn more at www.DataDynamicsNW.com and www.SeattleAccess.org.

 ROB COOPER is a Senior Test Lead at Microsoft. He started at Microsoft as a support engineer in Charlotte, North Carolina in 1998 and joined the Access 2003 test team in Redmond in 2001. During the Access 2010 release, he led the team that worked on exciting new features such as the Macro Designer, Navigation Control, Web Browser Control, and the design and migration of objects for Access Services. He also helped test the 64-bit version of VBA in Office 2010 and programmability and security in Access 2010. He is currently working on Microsoft Bing. Rob has spoken at user group meetings and conferences such as the Portland Access User Group conference and Office DevCon in Brisbane, Australia, and has written for the Microsoft Knowledge Base. Aside from writing code in Access and C#, he also enjoys spending time with his family cooking, watching movies, going to the zoo and aquarium, and hanging out in and around Seattle.

 GEOFFREY GRIFFITH is a professional software developer from Colorado, where he owns his own software consulting company. He holds a Bachelor of Science degree in Computer Science from the University of Colorado at Boulder, where he studied software engineering. He began his Access life working on various database systems, starting with Access 2.0, developed at GBS, Inc., a software development firm in Boulder, Colorado. An avid Access user, he worked on the Microsoft Access Team for the Access 2007 release. Today, Geoff continues his work with Access, by writing books about Access and building applications that use Access databases.

 JERRY DENNISON has over 18 years of professional experience designing and developing MS Access database applications beginning with Access v1.0. He has been awarded the Microsoft Office Access Most Valuable Professional Award for the past four years. Jerry is an active contributor and Administrator at UtterAccess.com, the premier MS Access forum on the Web. He is considered by many of his peers to be one of the foremost experts on the Forms of Data Normalization (a set of guidelines for relational databases developed by Dr. E. F. Codd). Jerry currently lives in Easley, South Carolina with his wife of 21 years and their two dogs, Duke and Duchess.

ABOUT THE CONTRIBUTING AUTHORS AND TECHNICAL EDITORS

 BEN CLOTHIER is an Access developer working as an independent contractor through development shops such as Advisicon and J Street Technology. He is also a certified MySQL developer, and has designed and supported Access front-end applications for corporate databases. In recognition of his contributions to the Access community, Ben is recognized as a Microsoft Access MVP (Most Valued Professional). Ben lives in San Antonio, Texas with his wife, Suzanne, and his son, Harry.

Suzanne, only with you could I have the time and energy to become a contributing author — you are the absolute best!

 DOUG (DAGI) YUDOVICH is the Director of Business Information Applications for UW Physicians in Seattle. The department's primary responsibilities range from developing enterprise-level Web-based reports and OLAP objects to developing database applications in support of various business needs for managing data. The applications vary in scope, from stop-gap applications, to bolt on tools, to mission critical–level applications that support up to 250 users. All of the database applications use Access for the FE, with some using Jet as the database platform, and some using SQL Server. Doug is also an Administrator on UtterAccess Forums and UtterAccess's Access Wiki. Joining UA in 2004, Doug progressed through the ranks (VIP, Editor, Administrator). UA is Doug's cyber home, where he shares his passion and knowledge of database design and information management with members who seek help, and with fellow developers discussing best practices. Doug is an active member of the Pacific Northwest Access Developer Group (PNWADG) and a presenter in the Seattle Access Group (SAG). Doug participated in two Developers' Kitchen events with the Microsoft Access Dev Team to work on early development versions of Access 2010. In acknowledgment of his contributions to the Access developers' community in UtterAccess and the user groups, and his work with the Access Dev Team, Doug was awarded as a Microsoft Access MVP in 2009 and 2010.

I'd like to thank my wife, Lisa, who patiently picks up my slack as I dive head-first into new adventures. I love you.

ABOUT THE TECHNICAL EDITORS

DR. JEFF BOYCE has been providing process and technology solutions to both public and private sectors for over 30 years. Jeff's approach focuses first on business need, emphasizing processes and practices before evaluating suitable technologies. Jeff has designed and developed over 25 applications. Most recently, his integrated Microsoft Office solutions provide data-based applications employing Access, Word, and SQL Server. The support he has provided in the Microsoft Access newsgroups has resulted in his recognition as a Microsoft Access MVP for the past eight years. When not working at his day job, consulting, or offering support in the newsgroups, Jeff enjoys wallyball, swimming, and recreational landscaping.

Jeff acknowledges and thanks his wife, Sue — her forbearance made his contribution possible.

ALBERT D. KALLAL is the owner of HCS consulting group and has been professionally developing software for more than 20 years. His first major project started while he was studying Computing Science at the University of Alberta. Albert was the original developer of a pilot project called Anat-sim, which was the basis for Omni-sim, the first successful commercial authoring system that allowed educators to create applications without having to write code. Albert's early success was an omen of great things to come. His software is currently used in more than six countries around the world with database platforms ranging from PDAs to server and mainframe systems. In recognition of Albert's contributions to the Access community, he received a Microsoft Most Valuable Professional award. Always seeking to stay on the leading edge, Albert was an early beta tester for the new Access 2010 Web Services that enables Access developers to build browser-neutral Web applications with Access 2010.

ARMEN STEIN is the president of J Street Technology, a Microsoft Gold Certified Partner with a team of database application developers near Seattle, Washington. J Street also offers CartGenie, a complete e-commerce Web storefront and shopping cart. Armen is a Microsoft Access MVP and MCP, has taught college-level database classes, and has also developed and taught one-day training classes on Access and Access/SQL Server development. Armen has spoken at various user groups and conferences, including Microsoft TechEd in the United States and Office DevCon in Australia, and is co-author of *Access 2007 VBA Programmer's Reference* (Wrox). His other interests include activities with his family, travel, backgammon, Mariners baseball, and driving his 1969 Ford Bronco in the sun.

Thanks to my wife, Lori, and to my kids, Lauren and Jonathan. I also would like to thank my great team at J Street Technology, who capably manage projects so that I can spend time on books like this.

ACKNOWLEDGMENTS

AS A TEAM, WE would like to express our respect and appreciation for all of the people who contributed to the editing and production of our book. Every book seems like a new adventure and we are fortunate to have the ongoing guidance from Wiley and Wrox to ensure that they are produced with the best standards. So we send a special thanks to Bob Elliott and Tom Dinse — is this our 5th book together? We'd also like to recognize some of the great behind-the-scenes players, Ashley Zurcher, Helen Russo, Mary Beth Wakefield, and Nancy Rapoport, and many others.

Of course, we wouldn't have anything to write about if it weren't for those incredible people on the Microsoft Access team. Their passion, dedication, and commitment to continuously expand and enhance Access are truly remarkable and inspiring. We see this, not only in the new features, but also in their support of the user community. And speaking of community, the Access community is a large part of what makes Access so special. Whether you are a novice or seasoned developer, if you have a problem, you can easily find assistance, guidance, and even friendship, from a variety of user groups and online forums.

We'll wrap up with a resounding round of appreciation for our five tech editors - and contributing authors. With the incredible new features and dramatic changes in Access, we have relied on their expertise to not only identify potential errors and omissions, but to question our content and writing to help ensure that it is both comprehensive and comprehensible. It is no wonder that they have each been recognized by Microsoft as Access MVPs. It is a pleasure to acknowledge you as an integral part of our team and to the success of this book.

— THE AUTHORS

FIRST AND FOREMOST, I want to thank my wonderful family who taught me to embrace life and to live each day with respect, integrity, and purpose. Thank you for helping me to recognize and celebrate the opportunities that life offers. I can rely on your encouragement and support as I dive into new adventures and projects such as this book.

I also want to thank my colleagues and great friends who continue to fuel my passion for helping others to learn about and use Access. In particular, I want to express my appreciation for the people in my user groups (Michka, Randy, Brandi, et al.) and the amazing people who are Access MVPs and community experts (Larry, Truitt, Arvin, George, our TEs, the list goes on) — friendships that are priceless!

One of my favorite aspects of being an author is the opportunity to involve and recognize contributions from people from around the world. In addition to our remarkable team of authors and editors, we have the benefit of sharing tips from our esteemed colleagues, Dane Miller, Garry Robinson, Steve Schapel, and Larry Strange. I especially want to recognize and thank Ben Clothier for his dedication, humor, and tenacity. Neither of us had any idea of what was to come when Ben became a contributing author. Even working into the wee hours of the morning, we were still having fun as we completed countless iterations of reviews. That epitomizes a great Access developer — passion, commitment, and collaboration. My thanks to everyone — a project of this magnitude is truly a team effort!

— Teresa

THANKS TO EVERYONE ON the Access team at Microsoft for their outstanding work during this release and in particular to the testers on my team for listening to my various ramblings about Access (and food): Nishant Kumar, Kevin Nickel, Michael Tucker, Sanghmitra Gite, Kevin Bell, and Rasika Chakravarthy. Thanks for all of your hard work on this release!

To Geoff Hollander, Jack Stockton, and everyone who's been a part of the Portland Access User Group conference the past few years. Thanks for the invite and for including me as a part of your family!

Last but not least, continued thanks to my wife, Sandi, and children, Isabel and Gillian, for their understanding while I was working evenings and weekends. To my oldest, Taryn, for coming to visit earlier in the year and indulging me with sushi. (Yup, still better on the left coast.)

— Rob

I'D LIKE TO THANK my wife, Jamie. Without all of your love and support, I would be nothing, and I appreciate everything you do for our family. I would like to thank my son, Ryan, and apologize for the time I missed in your life while I wrote this book. You two are the most important people in the world to me! I would like to thank my friends from GBS, Inc.: Andrei, Vladimir, Tianru, Steph, Mia, Richard, Bob, and Jeff. Without you, I would never have gotten my start on Access and the experience was invaluable to me. I would like to thank so many of my friends from the Access team who taught me so much about Access, and to call out a few specifically: Michael, Rob, Tosh, Tim, Shawn, and Sherri. Thanks for the knowledge and opportunities you gave me; the experience was invaluable. And, of course, I would like to thank all of my other friends, colleagues, and teachers that have meant to so much me over the years. You are all Rock Stars!

— Geoff

I'D LIKE TO THANK my wife, Dianne, a shining light guiding this lost soul into the sunshine. My son, Jeremy and daughter, Amber, no father could ask for better or brighter children to keep him humbled. I'd like to also acknowledge my online "family" at UtterAccess.com; especially Gord, Ricky, and George. You guys are the best. Most of all, I would like to thank Teresa Hennig for giving me the opportunity to work on this project with such a great team (thanks Rob and Geoff for being so patient with the "new kid").

— Jerry

CONTENTS

CHAPTER 7: USING VBA IN ACCESS

INTRODUCTION

Welcome to *Access 2010 Programmer's Reference*, your guide to the new features and opportunities that Access 2010 has to offer. With this release, Access has expanded its reach beyond the desktop and network to join the ranks in the cloud. In support of this new level of connectivity, you will find significant changes within the developer environment that require more decisions, different programming tools, and more options. With changes of this magnitude, you will want to leverage community resources to get up-to-speed quickly so that you are working smarter and more efficiently. That's where this book comes in.

What makes this book so special? In addition to the extensive coverage of subject matter, it is the unparalleled team of authors and tech editors who are as devoted to helping fellow developers as they are passionate about Access. Jerry and Teresa have both earned Access MVP status in recognition of their expertise and contributions to the Access community, and Rob and Geoff have worked on the Microsoft Access test team. They are joined by a team of five technical editors who are all Access MVPs; they are not only technical experts but also seasoned consultants and leading-edge developers. Their areas of focus and expertise cover the spectrum from VBA to macros, and from simple solutions to enterprise deployments to Web apps, and all areas in between.

Access 2010 builds on many of the new features that were introduced in Access 2007. Features such as templates, application parts, and Office themes will help you leverage existing resources to quickly create and tailor a custom application. To support the expanding use of macros, we have a new Macro Designer that makes it faster and easier to create and use macros. With their new functionality, you will want to learn how to utilize UI and Data macros in local solutions, not just Web applications.

For many of us, being able to take advantage of the new features, right out-of-the-box, is more than enough reason to upgrade. So although the primary focus of this book is to help you extend the power of Access, we will also discuss the new features of Access 2010. Because many of you are familiar with prior versions of Access, we also point out some of the major changes, particularly if they affect the way that you will be working.

The goal is for *Access 2010 Programmer's Reference* to be your primary resource and tool to help you leverage Access's built-in functionality along with VBA and other tools in a manner that helps you to create solid, robust applications. Access 2010 makes it easy to start working as soon as it's installed. With the new UI (user interface), people will be building complex applications using the tools and resources that ship with Access. And, with a little outside guidance, they can work a lot smarter, with more confidence, and avoid several pitfalls.

This book is for the typical Access user as well as the seasoned programmer. It will help you utilize the power of Microsoft Access more effectively and help you choose when to let the wizards do the work, as well as showing you how to modify and enhance the code that the wizards create. Access builds great forms and reports that can be customized on-the-fly by using VBA code to respond to a multitude of events. Interactive reports, Web apps, and new options for distributing applications exemplify the power and potential of Access.

With all the templates, macros, and built-in features, it is easier than ever to open the program and begin creating tables, forms, and reports with confidence. When you consider how easy it is to get started, you'll realize that it is doubly important to be working smart and in the right direction. Use this book and its online resources as your guide to better programming and more effective solutions.

WHY USE VBA?

Microsoft Visual Basic for Applications (VBA) enables programmers to develop highly customized desktop applications that integrate with a variety of Microsoft and non-Microsoft programs. For example, all of the Microsoft Office System products support VBA. In addition, many third-party programs, such as accounting software packages, mapping software, and drafting programs also support VBA. Those companies often provide an integration tool, or SDK (software development kit), which typically requires VB or VBA to work with it.

VBA is actually a subset of the Visual Basic programming language and is a superset of VB Script (another member of the Visual Basic family of development tools). VBA includes a robust suite of programming tools based on the Visual Basic development, arguably the world's most popular rapid application development system for desktop solutions. Developers can add code to tailor any VBA-enabled application to their specific business processes. Whether you are starting with a blank database or building on a template, you can build complex custom solutions. For example, a construction company can use VBA within Microsoft Access to develop a sophisticated system covering estimating, ordering, scheduling, costing, and inventory control. The look and operation of the system can be tailored for each group and it can easily limit what data a person can view or change.

You might wonder why you should develop in VBA rather than Visual Basic or .NET, which are also robust, popular, and capable programming languages. Using VBA within Access gives you a couple of key benefits. First, you can leverage the built-in Access Object Library, taking full advantage of a wide variety of Access commands, including executing any command from the Ribbon or custom toolbar in Access. And second, it's cost effective because VBA is included in all Microsoft Office System applications. Other languages and frameworks, such as .NET, require a separate tool such as Visual Studio and thus a purchase and license. And although they can be cost-effective tools if they are needed, they can also be an unnecessary burden on a project — both in time and money. But do not fear, the book discusses leveraging the power of .NET framework as well.

Access now includes another tool that is often an alternative to VBA — the new Macro Designer — so we have a chapter dedicated to a discussion of how to create and use macros. If you've worked with macros in other Office programs, you will be a step ahead. That is one of the benefits of working with tools that are an intrinsic part of Microsoft Office. If you learn how to program using VBA and macros in Access, your code and skills are transferable to other programs. Even if your primary focus is on Access, knowing VBA will make it much easier to integrate your solution with other applications.

WHAT DOES THIS BOOK COVER?

Access 2010 Programmer's Reference covers the key topics of greatest importance to Access developers. Although the premise is that most readers will have some familiarity with the VBA programming language, the book includes a brief introduction to VBA and to macros. And to help you leverage the new tools that Access provides, it also has a chapter that highlights the new features in Microsoft Office Access 2010. And, because many people will be faced with upgrading and converting programs from prior versions, a chapter is dedicated to discussing some of the key factors and issues associated with upgrading and running Access in mixed environments.

To help you build a strong foundation on the fundamentals for programming in VBA, the book discusses how to create and name variables, how to use Data Access Object (DAO) and ActiveX Data Object (ADO) to manipulate data both within Access and within other applications, proper error-handling techniques, and advanced functions, such as creating classes and using APIs. Key new areas, such as using macros, customizing the Ribbon, and working with Office Backstage are also explored.

Once the basics are covered, the focus turns to forms and reports, the two most powerful tools for working with and displaying data. Several examples demonstrate how all of the pieces fit together to create an application that not only meets your immediate needs, but is also easy to maintain and enhance.

Working with other applications is covered extensively both in general, and more specifically for Microsoft Office applications, Windows SharePoint Services, Access Services, and SQL Server. Of course, this book wouldn't be complete without discussing security issues. And, to supplement the chapters, it has a full compliment of appendixes that put helpful reference material conveniently at your fingertips.

The Chapters

Chapters 1–6 provide material that you need if you're new to Access, VBA, or macros. We start with an introduction to Access and then provide a review of Access 2010's new features. To help you make informed decisions about converting and upgrading, we'll discuss some of the major factors, processes, and options. After that, you learn about the 2010 macros, how to use them, and how they compare with using VBA. Chapters 5 and 6 discuss the VBA language, VBA Editor, and the building blocks of VBA, including variables, procedures, events, and properties.

The next two chapters are devoted to building a strong foundation on which you will build strong, versatile applications. Chapter 7 emphasizes the dynamics of an Access application — and the need to control what happens to the data and when. In this chapter, you will learn how do to that with a variety of tools and techniques, including using events, procedures, expressions, and Recordsets. In Chapter 8, we delve a bit deeper and examine VBA classes and class objects. You'll learn how to create, name, and use classes and objects.

The next step is working toward program integrations. Chapter 9 shows you how to use application programming interface (API) calls to work with and leverage libraries and objects from other sources, such as using Windows APIs. That leads you to the Win32 Registry. In Chapter 10, you will learn how the Registry is structured and how it works. Then we show you how to write basic VBA code to create, retrieve, edit, and delete Registry values.

Chapters 11 and 12 focus on using VBA to access data. Both DAO and ADO provide methods for accessing and working with data in Microsoft Access and other external data sources, which can be relational, such as Informix, SQL Server, or other RDBMSs (relational database management systems), as well as nonrelational, such as text files, spreadsheets, and XML, and a multitude of other possible sources including numerous accounting programs.

In Chapters 13 to 17, you will begin to use VBA within an Access application — or at least in demonstrations. You start by learning the structure for writing SQL statements, and we explain some critical techniques and nuances, such as the difference between using single and double quotes. As we focus on forms and reports, we'll provide real-world examples and techniques that you can incorporate directly into your solutions. From there, we'll move into more specialized areas, such as customizing the Ribbon and working with the new Office Backstage and manipulating XML for both Ribbon and Office Backstage.

Chapters 18–21 provide information about working with other Office applications, such as Word, Excel, Outlook, and PowerPoint. In addition to learning about the new Web applications, you'll also discover some new techniques for deploying database solutions and for sharing and securing data using SharePoint. We'll expand the discussion to focus on programming with .NET to automate Access 2010 and working with Visual Studio. We wrap up with a chapter on client-server development.

The final chapters discuss ways to create and deploy applications and some of the security options. Templates and application parts can provide an invaluable tool for quickly creating a solution. Chapter 22 explains how to find, create, and use templates and application parts. As you may have experienced, not everyone that wants to use your application has a copy of Microsoft Access, but that need not preclude them from using your solution. In Chapter 23, you learn how the Access Runtime enables developers to deploy solutions in a custom package that allows their application to run even though a complete version of Access is not installed on the machine. The last two chapters, 24 and 25, discuss database security and Access security features. You'll review options for locking the VBA project, using ACCDE files, and employing data encryption. With Access security, you'll learn about the trust center, disabled mode and macros, digital certificates, the sandbox mode, and some workarounds.

Although that brings you to the end of the chapters, it is far from the end of the book. There are still nine appendixes filled with reference material.

The Appendixes

As a developer, you can often spend hours going from source to source looking for reference material. The authors of this book have applied the principles of relational databases (doing the work once so it can be used many times in multiple ways) to the appendixes, and have created a compilation of data from a myriad of sources.

The first three appendixes document the Object Models for Access, DAO and ADO. In Appendix D, you will find a discussion on working with 64-bit Access. As mentioned in the discussions on upgrading in Chapter 3, there are significant issues to consider and specific steps to take if you are migrating to a 64-bit version of Access, particularly if you will be integrating with 32-bit applications.

Appendix E discusses references and is an invaluable resource when you are converting from or to different versions of Access or moving an application from one platform or environment to another.

The next three appendixes, F, G, and H, are about good practices, such as avoiding reserved words and special characters, implementing good naming conventions, and having a way to manage code, such as by using Source Code Control.

Appendix I, is like the extra topping on the cake. We share tips and techniques that will help you design polished and professional applications. We demonstrate the techniques and provide a working application so it can become part of your developer toolbox. In addition to our demo application, we also have tips and files from four of our esteemed colleagues, Dane Miller, UtterAccess VIP and database consultant; Garry Robinson, Access MVP and editor of www.vb123.com/kb; Steve Schapel, Access MVP; and Larry Strange, with www.AccessHosting.com.

HOW TO USE THIS BOOK

The initial chapters provide background information to help you build a strong foundation. They are written in a tutorial format with detailed examples. Subsequent chapters delve deeper into technical areas and demonstrate numerous techniques that will help you build robust solutions. Most chapters refer to online files that provide the code snippets and help demonstrate the scenarios. True to the Wrox *Programmer's Reference* format, the book includes numerous reference appendixes with details on the various Object Models, as well as guidelines and best practices that will help you to work with Access and to write VBA code.

Real-world examples are given for many, if not most, of the programming topics covered in this book. These are just of few of the topics and examples that are included:

➤ Creating intuitive, user-friendly forms to quickly find and work with data, and minimizing data entry errors

➤ Creating custom reports based on information entered on a form

➤ Leveraging report browse, the interactive report feature that enables drilling into data on reports

➤ Summarizing and graphically displaying data using cross-tab reports

➤ Using VBA to transfer data between Access and other Office programs such as Outlook, Word, and Excel

➤   Configuring custom Ribbons, toolbars, and menus for your Access database applications

➤   Creating custom Web apps and leveraging the features offered through SharePoint and Access Services

Throughout the book, we've also included tips and tricks discovered during the authors' programming experiences.

We recommend that as you go through the book, you also work with the code and sample databases provided in the companion download files on Wrox.com. Being able to run the code, see the effect of minor changes, and experiment on your own will reinforce the learning process. (See the "Source Code" section later in this Introduction for details on downloading the code.) By working with the code and examples, you will begin to take ownership of the concepts and learn how to incorporate them into your work and solutions.

OTHER ACCESS/VBA SOURCES

You've heard the saying that there are as many ways to build a solution as there are programmers. And that may only be a slight exaggeration. So, although this book is an excellent reference for all of your Access 2010 programming needs, there just isn't enough time and ink to cover everything — not to mention fixes, updates, and add-ons. That's where networking, newsgroups, and other information sites come in. Here are some of the authors' favorites for you to check out:

➤   **Microsoft Answers:** Microsoft provides a landing place for users to ask questions about their products, and Access is one of several products that are covered at the forums. To quickly get to the Access questions and answers, start with this URL: `http://social.answers.microsoft.com:80/Forums/en-US/addbuz/threads?filter=mf%3a6edab96e-a4cc-4ccb-ae44-7bcdb5ffa589`

➤   **The newsgroup** `comp.databases.ms-access`: An active community that can be accessed using an NNTP newsreader as well as by using `groups.google.com`. If you do not have NNTP access, free NNTP servers are available — for example, `eternal-september.org`.

➤   **Microsoft's Community website:** At (discussion groups) `www.microsoft.com/office/community/en-us/default.mspx`

➤   **MVPS.ORG** (`www.mvps.org/access`): Your jumping-off point to a number of interesting offerings provided by a few folks associated with the Microsoft Most Valuable Professional (MVP) program.

➤   **Microsoft Office Online — Access** (`http://office.microsoft.com/en-us/FX010857911033.aspx`): Provides quick tips, and direct links to Access resources such as downloads, templates, training, add-ins, and other pertinent information.

➤   **Utter Access** (`www.utteraccess.com`): Currently the leading independent forum for Microsoft Access questions and solutions.

➤ **The Access developer center:** Programming resources through Microsoft (`http://msdn.microsoft.com/en-us/office/aa905400.aspx`).

➤ **vb123 Knowledge Base:** A compilation of Access tips, tools, and articles. Hosted by Garry Robinson, Access MVP (`www.vb123.com/kb`).

CONVENTIONS

Several different styles of text are used in this book to help you understand different types of information. Some of those styles are illustrated here:

➤ We *highlight with italics* new terms and important words when we introduce them.

➤ We show keyboard strokes like this: Ctrl+A.

➤ We present notes, warnings, and sidebar information in shaded boxes:

 This is a note. It contains additional information about the subject under discussion.

 This is a warning. It provides information about how to avoid problems related to the subject under discussion.

> **THIS IS A SIDEBAR**
>
> It contains asides that provide information related to the subject under discussion.

➤ We show filenames, URLs, and code within the text like so: `sample.doc`, `persistence.properties`, and `www.microsoft.com`.

➤ We present code in two different ways:

```
We use a monofont type with no highlighting for most code examples.
We use bold to emphasize code that is particularly important in the present context
or to show changes from a previous code snippet.
```

SOURCE CODE

As you work through the examples in this book, you may choose either to type in all the code manually or to use the source code files that accompany the book. All the source code used in this book is available for download at www.wrox.com. When at the site, simply locate the book's title (use the Search box or one of the title lists) and click the Download Code link on the book's detail page to obtain all the source code for the book. Code that is included on the website is highlighted by the following icon:

Available for download on Wrox.com

Listings include the filename in the title. If it is just a code snippet, you'll find the filename in a code note such as this:

code snippet filename

> *Because many books have similar titles, you may find it easiest to search by ISBN; this book's ISBN is 978-0-470-59166-6.*

Once you download the code, just decompress it with your favorite compression tool. Alternately, you can go to the main Wrox code download page at www.wrox.com/dynamic/books/download .aspx to see the code available for this book and all other Wrox books.

ERRATA

We make every effort to ensure that there are no errors in the text or in the code. However, no one is perfect, and mistakes do occur. If you find an error in one of our books, like a spelling mistake or faulty piece of code, we would be very grateful for your feedback. By sending in errata, you may save another reader hours of frustration, and at the same time, you will be helping us provide even higher quality information.

To find the errata page for this book, go to www.wrox.com and locate the title using the Search box or one of the title lists. Then, on the book details page, click the Book Errata link. On this page, you can view all errata that has been submitted for this book and posted by Wrox editors. A complete book list, including links to each book's errata, is also available at www.wrox.com/ misc-pages/booklist.shtml.

If you don't spot "your" error on the Book Errata page, go to www.wrox.com/contact/techsupport .shtml and complete the form there to send us the error you have found. We'll check the information and, if appropriate, post a message to the book's errata page and fix the problem in subsequent editions of the book.

P2P.WROX.COM

For author and peer discussion, join the P2P forums at p2p.wrox.com. The forums are a Web-based system for you to post messages relating to Wrox books and related technologies and interact with other readers and technology users. The forums offer a subscription feature to e-mail you topics of interest of your choosing when new posts are made to the forums. Wrox authors, editors, other industry experts, and your fellow readers are present on these forums.

At http://p2p.wrox.com, you will find a number of different forums that will help you, not only as you read this book, but also as you develop your own applications. To join the forums, just follow these steps:

1. Go to p2p.wrox.com and click the Register link.

2. Read the terms of use and click Agree.

3. Complete the required information to join, as well as any optional information you wish to provide, and click Submit.

4. You will receive an e-mail with information describing how to verify your account and complete the joining process.

 You can read messages in the forums without joining P2P, but in order to post your own messages, you must join.

Once you join, you can post new messages and respond to messages other users post. You can read messages at any time on the Web. If you would like to have new messages from a particular forum e-mailed to you, click the Subscribe to this Forum icon by the forum name in the forum listing.

For more information about how to use the Wrox P2P, be sure to read the P2P FAQs for answers to questions about how the forum software works, as well as many common questions specific to P2P and Wrox books. To read the FAQs, click the FAQ link on any P2P page.

1

Introduction to Microsoft Access 2010

WHAT'S IN THIS CHAPTER?

➤ A short history of the Access product

➤ A discussion of when to use Access

➤ An introduction to Access 2010 and its main features

➤ A discussion of how to create each of the Access object types using the Access designers

Microsoft Office Access 2010 is the latest version of Microsoft Access, the world-class relational database management system (RDBMS) for the Microsoft Windows platform, designed for building small- to medium-scale database applications. Access 2010 provides a rich set of features and tools for designing, creating, storing, analyzing, and viewing data, as well as the capability to connect to a large variety of other data sources. Access combines ease-of-use features with software development capabilities to support a wide range of user skill sets. Access also provides a Primary Interop Assembly (PIA) to allow other development platforms, such as Microsoft Visual Studio .NET 2010, to manage data using an Access database or even incorporate Access functionality into an external application. Access 2010, simply put, is a database system that provides a wide variety of functionality and flexibility to build Windows-based applications.

If you're reading this book, you probably already know a good deal about Microsoft Office Access 2010 or a previous version. While this book presents the various aspects of programming Access applications using primarily VBA code, as well as a number of other methods, this chapter provides an overview of Access and discusses some of the basics. Although it's possible to create and administer a database application using only code, there are many tools for creating, designing, and editing database objects that do not require any code at all. If you've used

Access before and are familiar with the visual designers and other Access tools, you can easily skip ahead to the next chapter to begin learning about the new features included in Access 2010.

A BRIEF HISTORY OF ACCESS

Microsoft Access has been around for nearly 18 years. The first version, Microsoft Access 1.0, was released in November of 1992. Built on top of the Jet Database Engine, Access was designed to enable users to create and manipulate Jet-compatible database applications through a variety of visual designers and a scripting language called Access Basic. Access quickly became one of the most popular database development systems for Windows and the user base started growing rapidly.

With Microsoft Access 95, the fourth release, Access was adopted as a member of the Microsoft Office product line. This was the perfect move for the product because it allowed Access to integrate and leverage many great features shared among other Office applications, such as Spell Checking and the Format Painter. Access Basic was replaced with the integration of Visual Basic for Applications (VBA) across the Office applications to provide a common programming language for creating solutions using the core Office products.

By the time Access 2003 was released, there were over 100 million users based in over 80 countries around the world. Everyone from individual users to the United States government was using Access. Access 2003 included a number of feature enhancements, as well as new additions. XML support and data import and export were improved in a number of ways, and signed database projects and disabled mode were introduced for added security. The *Access 2003 VBA Programmer's Reference (Wrox, 2004, ISBN 978-0-764-55903-7)*, the original Access programmer's reference in this series, focused on this version, the eighth release of Access.

Fast-forward to the present, and you have Microsoft Office Access 2010, the tenth full release of Access. Now shipping in over 40 languages, Access is used throughout the world on Windows systems everywhere. For this release, there is a large focus on enhancing ease-of-use, and you'll notice major changes from the 2007 version as soon as you boot the program. There are a number of new features added to the ACCDB file format in this release, as well as a number of new builders, a completely overhauled Macro Designer, and the new SharePoint Web Application features, all of which will be covered more in Chapter 2. After trying out Access 2010, I'm sure you'll see that Microsoft Office Access 2010 is the absolute best release of Access ever.

WHEN TO USE ACCESS

Some may ask whether Access is the end-all to database systems. The simple answer is, "No." Access is not the only database product on the market, nor is it the only database product available from Microsoft or for Windows. There are times you might want to use a different type of database system, such as Microsoft SQL Server. If you've used only Microsoft Access for your database needs, you might be wondering why you'd ever need another database system. It could be argued that Access can connect to so many different types of data sources that there's no need for other front-end products. Moreover, developers could make a case that an Access database is a perfect solution for data storage for an application developed outside of the Access client, such as a .NET application that stores data in a back-end Access database. Still, there may be several reasons to use other database products, and the following sections discuss Access features, as well as other database system features, to help you choose which database system is best for your data storage needs.

Microsoft Office Access 2010

Microsoft Access is the perfect solution for single-user applications. Access provides many built-in features for quickly and easily building forms, reports, charts, and queries to view data. The user interface (UI) is designed to be simple and intuitive so that even novice users can accomplish their tasks. Developers have the ability to create macros and write VBA code to define application logic. Another key feature of an Access database that is often overlooked is the storage of all database objects in a single file, which makes the database easy to distribute to others. Access does not require that a server environment be running to work directly with the database file, and there are a number of different methods for connecting to and working with an Access database. And, although the maximum supported Access database size is 2GB that is usually ample space for almost any personal database.

Multipleuser applications are supported by Access, although there are a number of considerations you should be aware of. There are record-locking options that affect how data is accessed, and some operations require the database to be opened in exclusive mode, thus locking other users out of the application. The recommendation for multiuser Access applications is to create a distributable front-end database (for each user) that connects to a back-end database that stores the data. For example, a front-end application written in Visual Basic can take advantage of DAO or ADO to make calls to retrieve and modify data in the back-end Access database. This type of application, called a Client-Server application, works well in a single-user or multiuser environment, which is discussed more in Chapter 21, the chapter on Client-Server development. Even then, applications that have a large number of users or data transactions may encounter performance limitations in the ACE database engine. When the database application grows too large, Microsoft recommends moving the database to Microsoft SQL Server, which is specifically designed to handle larger loads.

SQL Server 2008 Express Edition

The Microsoft SQL Server 2008 Express Edition is a scaled-down version of SQL Server 2008. Microsoft provides this product for free and it can be distributed for free as one of many ways to integrate data with .NET applications. It is ideal as an embedded database for small desktop applications that call for a fully functional SQL Server database, but do not require a large number of users. SQL Server supports database triggers and stored procedures, which are database features not supported by the ACE database engine, although they can be used by Access in an Access Data Project (ADP) file. Also, Access can link to the tables in SQL Server Express, just as with full SQL Server. SQL Server Express is perfect for scenarios where a SQL database engine is needed, without a large number of user accounts.

However, database development using SQL Server Express requires a fair amount of knowledge and there is no built-in forms package. You would not be able to build a complete Windows database application using only SQL Server Express in the same way you could using Access. Probably the most common scenario for using SQL Server Express is when developing a front-end application using Microsoft .NET Framework technology, in a programming language such as C#, which connects to the SQL Server database engine, which is used by the application to manage data. It is worth noting that a fully functioning front-end database application (complete with forms, reports, and charts) easily could be created in Access and connected to a back-end SQL database on a machine running any version of SQL Server 2008 to enjoy the benefits of the SQL Server database engine.

SQL Server 2008

Full Microsoft SQL Server 2008 is the perfect solution for large-scale database applications. Typically, applications that require a large number of users, many concurrent connections, great amounts of data storage, data transactions, direct data security, or that need routine database backups are ideal for SQL Server. SQL Server is one of the most robust and scalable database systems available for Windows. But, as with SQL Server Express, SQL Server will require a front-end application to be developed that will allow users to access the data stored in the SQL database. And, all of this power comes with an associated cost. SQL Server is not free; in fact, it is quite expensive! Additionally, creating database applications with SQL Server also requires in-depth knowledge of database design and how to work with SQL Server. Although not the best choice for a small, end-user database solution, Microsoft SQL Server is ideal for enterprise systems used for storing critical and sensitive business data.

How Do You Choose?

If you're not sure which type of database to create for your application, ask yourself the following questions:

➤ Will your database realistically grow beyond 2GB?

➤ Are there security concerns for the data stored and used by your application?

➤ Is the data in your application critical or irreplaceable?

➤ Does your application require a large number of simultaneous transactions at any given time?

➤ Does your database need to be accessed by a large number of users simultaneously?

➤ How will users work with the data from the database in the application?

➤ Will the database need to provide user-level security?

Even answering these questions won't provide a definitive answer as to which type of database you should use for any given application. Every application's data storage mechanism should be evaluated on a separate basis by gathering storage requirements and researching the application's purpose to determine which type of database management system to use. For example, if the application will need to store 1.5GB of data, will store confidential data, and will need to be accessed by thousands of users at any given time you might consider employing SQL Server. However, if an application requires less than 1GB of data, needs to accommodate 20 users with relatively low traffic, and must maintain low development and support costs Microsoft Office Access 2010 is the perfect choice.

ACCESS DATABASE BASICS

The majority of this book is devoted to discussing how to write VBA code for Access database applications; however, many of the features that Access 2010 provides do not require any code whatsoever. In fact, Access is specifically designed to make it easy to build database applications without knowing how to write a lick of code. Although almost any operation in an Access database application can be created by writing and executing code, often there are simpler methods that Access provides, such as the various designers and wizards built into Access. Knowing when it is best to use code and when to use other tools is critical to building cost-effective database solutions, and fortunately, Access 2010 makes this very easy to do!

Getting Started in Access 2010

As soon as you start Access 2010, you will see immediate changes when compared to previous versions. Instead of seeing the Getting Started screen from Access 2007 or a blank window, as in prior versions of Access, you are taken to the new Office 2010 Backstage. The Backstage enables the user to quickly open an existing database, create a new blank database, or even create a new database template. If the computer has an Internet connection and is online, links to Office online and its content are also present to help keep you connected to the latest resources available. You may also notice that the Office button from Access 2007 has been replaced by the File Ribbon tab. The File Ribbon tab exposes all of the Access functionality for working with the database save and load options, the Access Options dialog box for database and applications settings, as well as many of the database analysis tools that Access 2010 provides. The new Backstage feature is the new launching point for all Access database sessions and will be discussed throughout this book.

Access 2010 Database Templates

The Access team has continued to leverage its database template features added in Access 2007 and has created a brand new set of templates for Access 2010. Many of the previous database template applications have been updated and a new slew of templates has been created, many of which are SharePoint Web Applications that work with the new features of SharePoint 2010. New to Access 2010 and Office online are Access database templates that have been submitted by the community. This allows developers from all over the world to share their database applications as part of the Microsoft community. Database templates are a great starting point for building a database solution.

To create a new database using a template, click on the New tab on the left panel of Access 2010 Backstage (the File Ribbon tab). Then click the Sample Templates category to show the built-in templates, or simply select one of the templates from the Office.com templates. Once the template is selected, the preview pane on the right side of the Backstage window will show the template's metadata details. If the template is from Office Online, you will see a Download button; otherwise, you see the Create button. Figure 1-1 provides an illustration of the Backstage with the Northwind template selected.

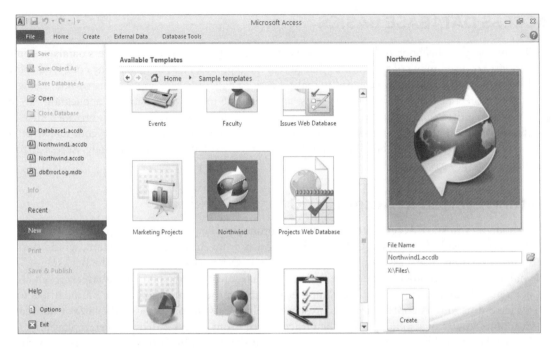

FIGURE 1-1

Clicking the Download or Create button will create a new database from the template—the Northwind template, in this example. Once you start the database creation process, you briefly see the Preparing Template dialog box and then the new database will be opened in the Access client window.

The Access Navigation Pane

Originally released in Access 2007, the Navigation Pane provides the user with the ability to see and open database objects. The Navigation Pane replaces its predecessor, the Database window, and provides a number of additional features not previously available. The Navigation Pane is found on the left side of the Access client window when a database is opened in a normal Access session. The Navigation Pane is the primary interface for working with database objects in Access 2010.

By default, when the Northwind database template is created, the Navigation Pane is collapsed. Click on the Navigation Pane to expand it and see the database objects contained in the Northwind database application. The Navigation Pane is highly customizable and provides a number of methods for grouping and filtering database objects. In the case of the Northwind database, a custom grouping, named Northwind Traders, has been created and is shown by that name at the top of the pane. Clicking the top of the pane displays the various object grouping options available in the database. If you choose the Object Type grouping option, the Navigation Pane will show all of the database objects, grouped by each object type, just as the Database window would have in versions of Access prior to 2007. If you are not familiar with the Navigation Pane, this view will be much more familiar and is comparable to the Database window.

The Access Ribbon

Introduced originally in Access 2007, the Access Ribbon is designed to be the primary interface for the majority of operations that Access 2010 provides. The Ribbon replaces the standard Windows style application menu bar and provides much more flexibility than its predecessor. The Ribbon is found at the top of the Access client window. The Access Ribbon is context driven, so certain Ribbons and functionality will only be available in certain modes. For example, the Access Form Design Tools Ribbon is only open when a form is open in Design View. Get to know the Ribbon well; it will be your primary method for working with the Access client functionality.

The Access Security Bar

The Access Security Bar was originally added in Access 2007 and is found directly below the Ribbon when a database is in disabled mode, which is the default mode for Access sessions. The Access Security Bar was added to provide a quick method to enable a database application to allow the execution of code, action queries, unsafe macros, and other operations that are deemed potentially dangerous. To enable a database application in Access 2010, simply click on the Enable Content button on the Access Security Bar.

ACCESS DATABASE OBJECTS

Now that you have a grasp of the basic components to the Access 2010 UI, it is good to have an overview of how to create database objects using the tools that Access 2010 provides. Access 2010 provides six basic object types: Tables, Queries, Forms, Reports, Macros, and Modules. These objects are used to build a database application and, if you are already familiar with Access, are most likely very familiar with each of these objects. Although any of these objects can be created by writing and executing code, often it is much simpler and faster to use the Access design tools to do so. The Create Ribbon is the primary location used for creating all of the major database objects, which will be discussed in this section.

Creating Tables

Tables are the backbone of any database. Tables store all of the data in an Access database application and designing them correctly the first time can save a lot of time and effort in the future, as any changes made to a table once it is already in use may also require substantial changes to all objects that depend on that table. Tables have columns, called Fields, and rows, called Records. The type of data you need to store in any given table field is dictated by its purpose in the application. For example, if you need to store the date on which some event occurred, you would use a Date/Time field data type. You could use a Text field type to store a date and there may be cases where that makes sense, but most of the time, the Date/Time type will be more beneficial because it enables you to leverage the comparison operations provided by the ACE (Access Connectivity Engine) database engine, which could not be done with the Text field type.

Creating tables through the Access 2010 UI is accomplished by choosing any of the options in the Tables group on the Create Ribbon. The Tables group contains three primary options for creating tables: a Table, a Table Design, and a SharePoint Lists option. The Table option opens a new table in the Table Layout designer. The Table Design option opens a new table in the standard Access Table designer. And the SharePoint Lists option enables you to create a new SharePoint Linked-Table from a selection of common list types or by selecting from an existing SharePoint list. Clicking on any of these Ribbon options will create the new table in the currently open Access database and open it in the main Access window.

Access 2010 Field Types

Access 2010 supports eleven field data types for building database tables. The field types supported by the ACE 2010 database engine are: Attachment, AutoNumber, Calculated, Currency, Date/Time, Hyperlink, Memo, Number, OLE Object, Text, and Yes/No.

The Table Designer has one new option available for ACCDB fields in Access 2010. New to Access 2010 is the Calculated field type, which is very similar to a calculated field in a query. This type allows the value of a field to be calculated based on the function supplied when the field is created. Although this is shown as a new field type and technically is its own field type, the data types that are stored in the field are still the basic data types. In itself, the Calculated field is not a new type of data, just a new option for tables.

The Access Table Designer also shows the Lookup field option as a separate option in the field type list. However, Lookup fields are nothing more than a Number or Text field type that defines a key value in another table, so Lookup field types are also not a separate data type.

Access 2010 also supports Complex Data fields for many data types, which were originally introduced in the Access 2007 release. The complex data field option allows multiple values to be selected from a value list for a field in a record. For example, one might have a field that allows selecting a fruit type and it list several kinds of fruit: an Apple, an Orange, and a Banana. If the Allow Multiple Values option is selected for this field, then the user would be able to select several options, instead of just a single option, such as Apples and Orange, instead of just one or the other. The data stored in a Complex Data field can be manipulated as a set of data or as single values. Although not really a different data type, complex data fields allow the Access data types to be used in a different fashion than allowed traditionally.

The following table provides a brief description of each data type's purpose and whether it supports complex data.

DATA TYPE	DESCRIPTION
Attachment	A field type to store a collection of files for a given record. Stored as a complex data field, the complex scalar fields expose three pieces of data: File Name, File Data (the file itself), and the File Type. Files stored as attachments are stored in a hidden system table.
AutoNumber	Stored as a 4-byte integer that is assigned automatically when the record is created. Can be assigned as consecutive or random values. If the AutoNumber is a Replication ID, it is stored as a 16-byte GUID, instead of an integer.
Currency	Stored as an 8-byte number allowing a numeric range of: −922,337,203,685,477.5808 to 922,337,203,685,477.5807. The type is a fixed-point number, providing 15 digits to the left and 4 digits to the right of the decimal place for numeric precision.

DATA TYPE	DESCRIPTION
Date/Time	Stored as IEEE 8-byte, floating-point number allowing a date range of 1 January 100 to 31 December 9999. The Date/Time field may also include a time value range of: 0:00:00 to 23:59:59.
Hyperlink	A combination of text and numbers stored in a Memo field type to be used as a hyperlink address. The hyperlink can have four parts: Text to Display, Address, Sub Address, and Screen Tip.
Memo	Stores any number of characters up to the limit on the size of the database, 2GB. However, text box controls and the datasheet only allow adding or editing up to the first 63,999 characters stored in the field. You need to use code to work with more than 64,000 characters in a Memo field. Only the first 255 of these characters can be indexed or searched.
Number	Provides several numeric data types dictated by the Field Size property for this type. A number field can be either an integer or floating type numbers. Supported data types are Byte (1-byte integer), Integer (2-byte integer), Long (4-byte integer), Single (2-byte scaled floating point), Double (4-byte scaled floating point), Replication ID (16-byte GUID), and Decimal (12-byte scaled floating point). Number fields can be complex data fields.
OLE Object	Stores up to 1GB of OLE object data (such as a bitmap image, Word document, an Excel spreadsheet, or some other binary data) linked to or embedded in the field.
Text	Stores up to 255 characters of text, where the field length is dictated by the Field Size property for the field. The field can be indexed and is fully searchable. Text data type fields can be complex data fields.
Yes/No	Stores a 1-bit value of −1 or 0, but can also be formatted as Yes/No, On/Off, or True/False. The size of this data type is 1 byte.

Each data type has its own unique purposes, some of which overlap, so be sure to choose the data types wisely. For example, both Text and Memo field types store text characters. Because both types are searchable up to 256 characters and the memo field can hold much more than 256 characters, one might assume that all strings should be stored in Memo fields. However, if that implementation were the case, database users might encounter performance issues when running queries against large sets of Memo field data, which could be avoided by using a Text field type instead. Be sure to completely analyze the data needs before creating a table so that required data types can be planned for appropriately.

Creating Queries

Queries can be created by selecting either option in the Queries group on the Create Ribbon. Queries can be used for a wide variety of purposes such as filtering data based on selection criteria, calculating values, joining records stored in different tables, deleting records from a table, updating records based upon specific criteria, creating new tables, and much, much more. If you have prior database development experience, you've probably had to write SQL statements and already know how complex they can be (and how difficult they can be to get correct). The Access Query Designer provides a graphical interface to help generate the correct SQL statement for many query types, often helping to reduce the complexity of creating accurate SQL statements. Access 2010 also continues to provide the Query Wizard, a tool specifically designed to walk the user through creating each of the pieces of the query in a step-by-step fashion. Switching any query to SQL View mode allows for direct modification of the SQL statement for the query. Access 2010 makes building queries extremely easy, whether you're using the Query Designer, using the Query Wizard, or writing the SQL statement from scratch.

Creating Forms

Forms are vital for allowing users to add, modify, and delete data in a database application. Access provides an extensive forms package and several designers for building robust Windows-style forms. The Create Ribbon provides the Forms group, which offers several options for creating new forms. There are 16 different options for creating various predefined form types, provided by Access to reduce development time by quickly creating common form types. It is important to remember that many options in the Forms group require that a database object be selected in the Navigation Pane, upon which the new form will be created when the option in the Ribbon is chosen. For example, selecting a query in the Navigation Pane and then clicking the Form button creates a new form based on that query. This rule applies for tables, queries, forms, and reports that are selected in the Navigation Pane. If you select any object that does not support the creation of one of the quick forms, such as a macro, many of the form options in the Ribbon will be disabled. It is important to note that any of the predefined form options can be created from any other form type by setting the correct set of form properties. Clicking on any of the form options on the Create Ribbon will create a new form and open it for editing in the Access window.

It should be noted that Access 2010 actually has two different form designers available. Originally introduced in the Access 2007 release, the Form Layout View mode designer allows the user to build the form while being able to see the actual data that will be shown in it. The original designer in Access 2010 is the classic Design View mode designer. Around since the beginning of Access, the Design View designer allows the user to build forms in a grid-based layout, where all of the sections of the form are broken up to show as separate parts. Both designers have their pros and cons, but you will probably find yourself using both to build forms in Access, depending on the specific task at hand.

Creating Reports

Reports are probably the most common way that users will view their data, and that's why it is one of the more robust features in Access. The Reports group of the Create Ribbon provides all of the options for creating reports through the Access UI. Much like forms, Access provides a number of different options for building predefined report types, many of which require an object to be selected in the Navigation Pane before the option is available. Clicking on any of these options will create a new report and open it in the main Access window.

Similar to forms, there are also two designers available for building reports in Access 2010: the classic Design View designer, and the newer Layout View designer. These designers operate in the same manner as they do with forms, but it is worth noting that the Layout View designer is extremely useful for reports because you can see the actual data that you are building the report for. The both Report designers provide two panes: the Grouping and Sorting pane, which greatly improves grouping, sorting, and filtering tasks in a report; and the Design Task pane, which provides the Property Sheet and the Field List. Finally, Access 2010 also provides two standard View modes for Reports: Report View and Print Preview modes. Report View is the default View mode for Reports and allows the user to interact directly with the data in the Report. Print Preview mode is a standard Windows Print Preview window that shows what the printed report will look like and provides options for actually printing the report. Reports in Access 2010 are extremely flexible and useful for any database application.

Creating Macros

The Access 2010 Create Ribbon provides only one option for creating macros, which is the Macro button. Clicking the Macro button option will create a new database-level Macro object and open it in the Access Macro Designer. Embedded macros can also be created via the Property Sheet. However, these macros live in the module for the host object and are not standalone database objects. Macros are often used as a simple alternative to writing VBA code to execute custom application functionality. Although Macros are discussed in depth in Chapter 4, this section will discuss a few of their basics.

Macros in Access are a set of one or more predefined actions that can be set to the events of objects to be executed when those events are triggered. One of the major new features of Access 2010 is that is provides a completely updated macros designer, as well as several new major features for macros. Macros come in two flavors: Safe and Unsafe. Safe macros can be executed when the database is in disabled mode, but unsafe macros cannot. Macros are extremely powerful because they are easy to create, can provide custom functionality just about anywhere in a database application, and provide a large number of common features. Chapter 4 of this book is devoted to discussing macros in Access 2010 and provides more in-depth information on the subject.

Creating Modules

Finally, the last database object type to discuss here, but certainly the most important database object type in terms of this book, is the Module object type. Modules provide storage for VBA code, which can be called in many places throughout a database application. There are three basic types of modules: Modules, class modules, and Form/report modules. While each of these module types has a slightly different purpose and design, they all provide basically the same functionality, which is a storage location for VBA code inside of the database file.

Modules and class modules are themselves individual database objects. Form/report modules are slightly different in that they are tied directly to the Form/Report that they live on. They are not shown as separate database objects in Access, although they are shown as separate modules in VBE (the Visual Basic Editor). Once any of these modules has been created, the user can begin writing VBA code within that module.

To create a new module in a database, simply click on any of the Module options on the Create Ribbon. The new module is created and VBE opens, with the module open for editing in the main window. A user can begin writing code and, when all changes have been completed, the Save button can be used to save the module to the database. In the case of Form/report modules, the module is created the first time the Code Builder or Macro Builder is invoked for a particular form or report. Any subsequent call to embedded code just re-uses that already created module. Regardless of the method chosen, creating modules in Access 2010 is a snap!

SUMMARY

This chapter discussed some of the basics of Microsoft Office Access 2010 and how to create database applications. You learned when it is appropriate to use an Access database to store your data and when it is appropriate to use other database systems. This chapter explored some of the benefits of using the designers to quickly build database objects without writing any code, as well as all of the major database objects that Access 2010 provides. And the Access 2010 UI makes it extremely easy to accomplish all of these database development tasks.

However, this book is about programming Access 2010 and you're probably wondering when you're going to write some code. Stay tuned — although Chapters 2 and 3 cover the new features of Access and upgrading to Access 2010 respectively, Chapter 4 kicks off the discussion of programming Access 2010 by discussing how to program macros. Chapter 5 and most of the subsequent chapters in this book discuss programming Access with VBA code to build high quality, robust database applications with the latest cutting-edge features available in Access 2010.

2

New Features

Access 2010 provides the most revolutionary changes to Access, arguably since Access was first released. Taking a giant step forward, it now offers you the capability to provide Web applications that rely on the Internet browser rather than requiring the user to have Access installed. These features can be combined with rich client applications to create robust hybrid solutions.

Access 2010 is built on the same platform as Access 2007, so you may be familiar with many of the features that provide a user interface that is functional and intuitive. The interactive display of commands and options is based on where you are in the interface, but you still retain control with the capability to resize, hide, and customize the display.

Most of the new features will be discussed in more detail in the chapters that follow, so this chapter will only briefly introduce those features to provide you with a quick overview. If you are migrating to Access 2010 directly from Access 2003 or older, you will appreciate the discussion about some of the 2007 new features that we've included in this chapter's download on Wrox.com.

NEW LOOK

You will immediately notice one change when you open Access and look at the first screen. Among the options, you can open a blank database or choose from online and offline files. If you are creating a new database, you can get a jump-start by selecting from the online templates that include an ever expanding list of files submitted by other users, as seen in Figure 2-1. If you click on the Recent tab you will have quick access to the list of files you've recently worked on. You can also click on the Open icon to browse to additional files that are not listed in the Recent window. If you are looking for a template, you can browse the templates that are grouped by topic, such as personal, business, and so on. When you choose a template, the pane on the right prompts and guides you through downloading the file or creating the database and linking it to a SharePoint site. We'll briefly talk about some of the new features for working with SharePoint in the section "Integration with SharePoint" later in this chapter. Chapter 19 discusses SharePoint in more detail.

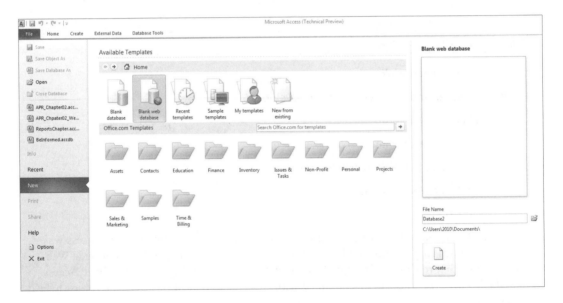

FIGURE 2-1

If you want to start a new, blank database, Access 2010 gives you the options of Blank Database and Blank Web Database. The Blank Database option enables you to build a client, desktop database file with all the features of Access 2010 available to you. Choosing the Blank Web Database option sets you on the path to creating a Web-enabled database application that can be published on Access Services on a SharePoint server. Due to the way Web applications are distributed and run, they restrict some of the features that we have come to expect in a robust Access solution. However, you will quickly learn how to create a rich Web interface that will meet most of your needs. You can also create a hybrid application by adding client objects to a Web application. However, you will need to keep in mind that although client applications can be distributed through SharePoint, they will not run on a browser. For more about this, we again refer you to Chapter 19.

DEVELOPMENT ENVIRONMENT

Access 2010 provides several new features and enhancements that will help developers work more efficiently and extend their capabilities and options. We will introduce some of the major enhancements and discuss their key benefits. As you read the remaining chapters, you will see how to incorporate these features into your solutions.

64-Bit

The Microsoft Office 2010 system, including Access 2010, is available in both 32-bit and 64-bit versions. The 64-bit version enables you to work more efficiently with much larger sets of data — especially when you are working with Excel 2010 to analyze large data sets. And, although an Access database file still has a 2GB limit, a 64-bit version can improve the performance on process-intense applications. We'll briefly cover some key differences and issues here, but we'll refer you to Chapter 3 and Appendix D to gain a better understanding of what is involved and the implications for both development and for working with mixed platform environments.

When installing Office 2010, the 32-bit version is the default version, even on 64-bit systems. To install Office 2010 64-bit, you must explicitly select that option. If you decide to use Access 2010 64-bit with existing 32-bit applications, you will need to update existing Windows application programming interface (API) `Declare` statements. And, you will also need to update the display Window Handles and the address pointers in any user-defined types used in the statements. You will encounter two major issues when you use the 64-bit version to run existing 32-bit solutions:

➤ The Office 2010 native 64-bit processes cannot load 32-bit binaries. You can expect the run into that issue if you have existing Microsoft ActiveX controls and existing add-ins.

➤ 32-bit VBA does not have a pointer data type and because of this, developers used 32-bit variables to store pointers and handles. These variables now truncate 64-bit values returned by API calls when using `Declare` statements.

While there are some benefits in installing the Office 2010 64-bit version, at this time they are not related to Access, so keeping the 32-bit version will not cause you to miss out on anything. Moreover, by using the 32-bit version, you will be able to use databases built in previous version of Access without modifications to the VBA code.

Office Backstage

In Access 2007, the file-level functionality was accessible by clicking the Office button. In Access 2010, as with the full suite of Microsoft Office 2010 programs, the Office button is replaced by a File tab. When you click the File tab, it opens the Microsoft Office Backstage view. In the Backstage view, you will have access to the features that are outside the features available in the Ribbon. You might think of it this way: The Ribbon and the Mini toolbar are there to help you work in your database, and the Backstage view helps you work with your database.

The Backstage view is fully extensible by developers, enabling you to customize the user interface (UI) to meet your needs. Even better, you can customize the Backstage UI using the same files, callbacks, and many of the controls used in the Ribbon. This means that if you are already familiar with customizing the Ribbon, you have the skills to customize the Backstage UI.

As you can see in Figures 2-2 (client database) and 2-3 (Web database), the Backstage view is different for each type of database you may develop in Access 2010. This difference is also seen in other features and objects throughout Access 2010.

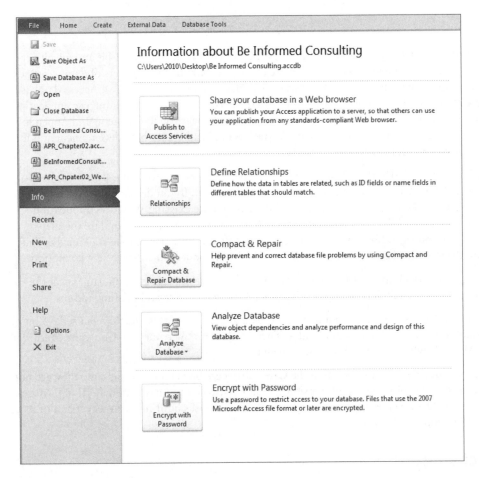

FIGURE 2-2

Calculated Columns

Access 2010 allows us to have calculated columns in tables. For those of you who worked with Microsoft SQL Server 2005 and later, this is not a new concept. Having a calculated column in an Access table enables you to store an expression at the table level — as a field. Every time there is a change in the underlying values, the expression will update the value that is stored.

The main benefit of calculated columns is achieving a cleaner database design by encapsulating the most common fields at the table level. For example, instead of having to calculate the full name of a client in multiple locations throughout your application, you can now maintain the expression in one location: the table.

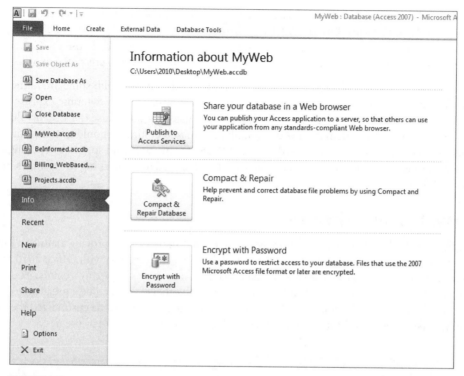

FIGURE 2-3

Another benefit is that calculated columns provide consistency with SharePoint. As you are learning, Access 2010 allows you to publish Web applications on SharePoint. Because the values in calculated columns are only recalculated when dependencies are updated, this feature optimizes performance and enables the server to respond faster to the users when sorting and/or filtering on the values in calculated columns.

To create a calculated column in a client database, open the table in design view and add the field. Set the Data Type of the new field to Calculated. The Expression Builder will pop up and let you create the expression (see Figure 2-4).

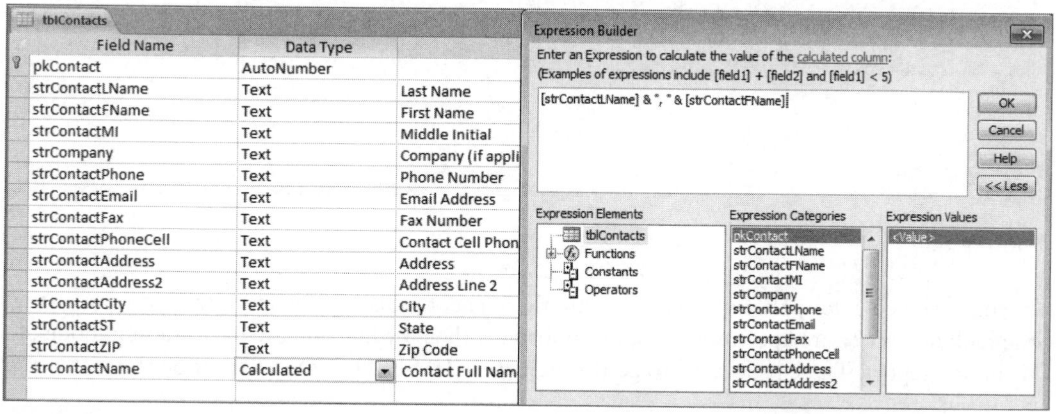

FIGURE 2-4

To create a calculated column in a Web database, open the table in browse view; then from the Ribbon, select Table Tools ⇨ Fields ⇨ Add & Delete ⇨ More Fields ⇨ Calculated Field. Alternatively, you can use the "Click to Add" option that is next to the last field in the table and choose the Calculated field type. As in the Client database, the Expression Builder will help you to create the expression.

It is important to realize that not all calculations are meant to be stored in a field; some are better left in queries. You cannot, and as a matter of best practice you should not, use dynamic expressions such as Date() and Now() in the calculated columns because they will cause the stored value to be inaccurate after the initial calculation. Additionally, calculated columns should not use functions that reference values outside of the record such as DCount(), DSum(), and so on. As you might anticipate, these can incur a costly performance impact when the system is checking for changes in the underlying values

Integration with Office Themes

Access 2010 integrates with Office themes to bring you rich color palettes and to provide a modern look to your application. In addition to choosing any of the available themes that come with Office 2010 as shown in Figure 2-5, you can create a customized theme to match a style or a company's colors. You can save the theme and use it in future applications or share it with others. This can be a great time saver if you work with a team of developers and would like everyone to use the same customized theme. Just send them the theme file or place it in a shared network folder so that anyone can use it.

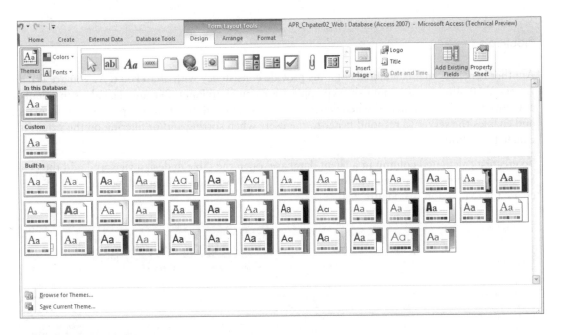

FIGURE 2-5

Beyond the rich color pallets you can use, another benefit of using a theme is that you can change the look of your entire application just by choosing a theme while you are in the design mode of a form or a report. There is no need to go through every UI object in the application to set the color scheme. The Theme Color Selection option allows you to quickly and easily change themes and to experiment with different colors.

Access 2010 ships with about 40 themes, but with the ability to customize and create your own themes, the possibilities are virtually endless. Of course, you can also look to the market place for more options, and perhaps the opportunity to share your own creations.

New Macro Designer

Access 2010 is sporting a new Macro Designer as shown in Figure 2-6. The new designer provides you with a richer interface with a lot of actions to manage your application.

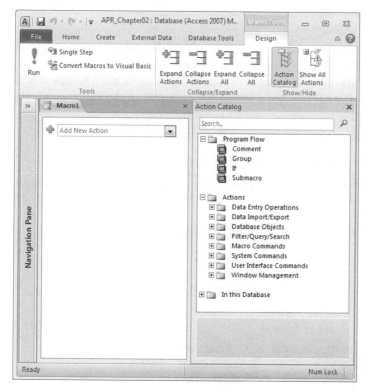

FIGURE 2-6

As you write a macro, you will notice that the new designer and actions have a closer resemblance to writing code than to using Macro Designers found in previous versions of Access. Features such as the Collapse/Expand actions in the Macro Tools ⇨ Design Ribbon will help you read your macro code better. The new designer also supports IntelliSense for the expressions as well as keyboard shortcuts and copy/paste functions. The new Macro Designer also supports complex logic, including ubiquitous nested IF-THEN-ELSE functions.

The search box in the Action Catalog allows you to search not only for action names but also for action descriptions. If you search for the word "query," the results will include OpenQuery, SetFilter, GoToRecord, and more (see Figure 2-7).

A significant feature, and one that may win over veteran VBA developers, is the ability to use error handling with the `On Error` macro action. Place it at the top of the macro and in combination with a `MessageBox` at the bottom of the macro you can get the error description when something goes wrong.

While macros cannot fully replace all VBA code, they can be leveraged to compliment VBA in client-server solutions and they are critical to Web-based applications.

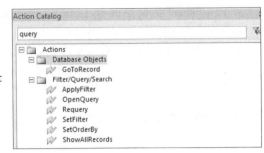

FIGURE 2-7

Expression Builder

The Expression Builder in Access 2010 introduces new features and a simplified interface. The new IntelliSense feature in the Expression Builder provides you with the information you need as you type, helping you to spend less time thinking about the syntax or looking for the available function or properties. Figure 2-8 illustrates what you might see using IntelliSense in the Expression Builder. You'll appreciate features such as:

➤ **AutoComplete:** Much like what's offered in the VBA Editor.

➤ **Quick Info:** The complete declaration for the function you selected is shown.

➤ **QuickTip:** Provides additional information about a UI component when you select a value using AutoComplete.

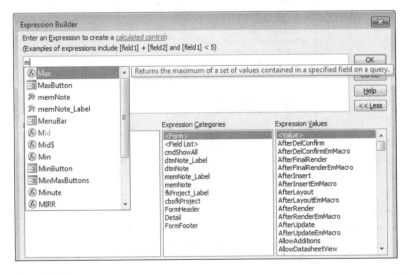

FIGURE 2-8

The Expression Builder dialog box uses what is referred to as Progressive Disclosure. It will show you only the expressions that are allowed in the context you are developing. So the controls, tables, and so on are specific to the database type — client or Web. You will also appreciate that the operator buttons have been removed to allow additional space for editing.

Web Service Expressions

When designing a client database, all the objects that use expressions share a single, common expression evaluation engine. This means that when adding an expression while working with a form or with a report, you will be able to access and use the same functions and operators. However, this will change when you start to build Web databases with Access 2010.

Web databases do not support the full suite of expressions that you can use in client databases. When an application is published to the SharePoint server, an expression could be evaluated in JavaScript, Excel calculation service, or SQL Server, depending on the object that it's being used in. The level of restriction varies based on the object that is holding the expression when developing the database application.

Using the Expression Builder and IntelliSense is the best way to know what expressions are available to you for the specific context that you are in. If you cannot create an expression in the Expression Builder, chances are it's not a valid expression for that specific context.

Application Parts

In addition to giving you access to full database templates both online and offline, Access 2010 also offers "Application Parts" which are essentially templates that provide a specific part of an application, from blank forms for dialogs or message boxes to a full set of objects to handle contacts or issues (see Figure 2-9).

For example, if you select the Contact application part, you will see that a table, a query (which allows you to search on all fields in one swoop), three forms, and four reports are added to your database. All objects are ready for you to use, or to modify as needed as illustrated in Figure 2-10.

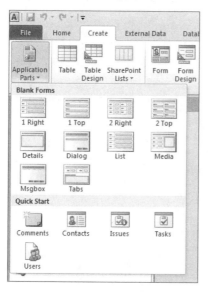

FIGURE 2-9

FIGURE 2-10

This feature enables you to develop basic database applications faster and more efficiently than before. By incorporating fully developed parts, you can focus your time and skills on refining your application to meet your specific business rules. Also, it saves you time by exposing some of the more frequently used forms as templates for you to customize.

FORMS

Access 2007 introduced some handy and creative new features that helped us to build a rich UI for our database applications, such as the Split Form, Date Picker, and Bound Image control. (You can read more about the other key features added in Access 2007 in this chapter's download on Wrox .com.) As Access 2010 builds on existing features and expands into a new era, the biggest enhancements to forms have to do with Web integration and navigation.

Web Browser Control

It is becoming more and more common, if not expected, for people to use content from the Web and data from Web services in their application. The new Web Browser control enables you to give your users a way to view and interact with Web content directly from within your application. By integrating with Business Connectivity Services (BCS), you can create read-only linked tables to SharePoint Line Of Business (LOB) Web services. This allows your users to use trusted and validated data provided by the IT department or other trusted sources.

When you add a Web Browser control to your form, the wizard appears and allows you to create the link and the properties (see Figure 2-11).

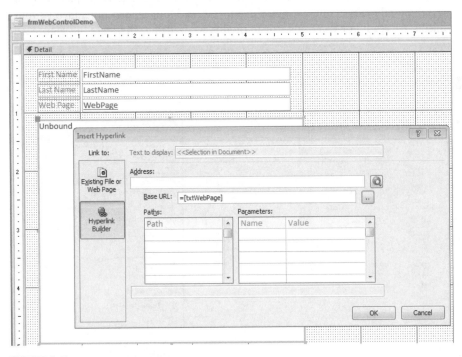

FIGURE 2-11

After you set the control's properties, you will present your users with the website you linked to directly in your application UI. By passing values to the parameters of the Web Browser object from other controls on the form, you can personalize the user's experience based on the data that they are viewing as shown in Figure 2-12. You will learn more about designing forms in Chapter 14.

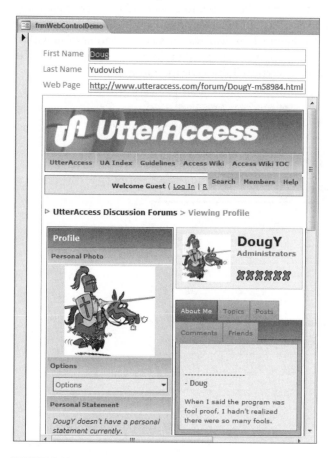

FIGURE 2-12

New Navigation Control

In Access 2010, the Switchboard form gives way to the new and improved navigation form. The new navigation control allows you to create tab style navigation forms, similar to many websites, without using any code.

You create the navigation form from the Create ➪ Forms ➪ Navigation Ribbon. As shown in Figure 2-13, there are six options so you can select the style that best fits your needs. Then, all you need to do is to drag the existing forms from the application Navigation Pane and drop them onto the navigation form, and you are good to go.

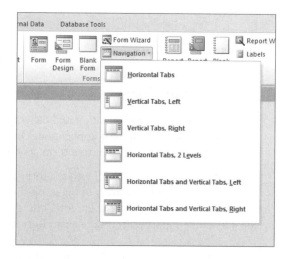

FIGURE 2-13

You can also nest navigation forms to create a rich user interface that neatly organizes and groups your forms. This is accomplished as easily as first creating the "child" navigation form; then, as you create the "parent" navigation form, you drag the child onto it to quickly add a layer of navigation. Although having the child form ready makes it easier to include as you are designing the parent, you can also do the process in the reverse order. Figure 2-14 displays a nested navigation form with the Sub-Navigation form (a Horizontal Tabs navigation form) nested in the Main Navigation form that was created using the Left Navigation form (a Vertical Tabs navigation form).

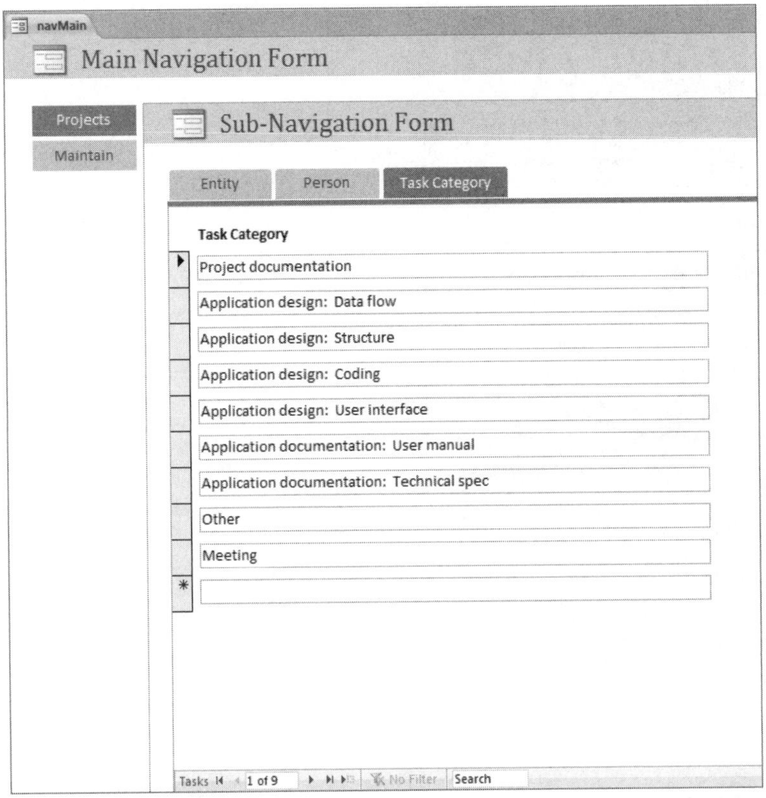

FIGURE 2-14

Subreports in Forms

Access 2010 focuses on integration and delivery of information so that you can provide users with a rich, content-focused database application. One of the new features that demonstrates that robustness is the ability to add a subreport to a form, as shown in Figure 2-15.

By adding a report (Total Paid) into the form you are able to show the user additional information related to the record they are looking at on the form, thus providing a richer information delivery interface. You can also use the Parent/Child property to link the subreport to the form thereby creating a dynamic report reflecting relevant information to the users as they navigate the form between different records. If you want to add more versatility to the UI, you can even change the subreport Source Object based on where in the record the user is editing/viewing. And, now that we have your interest piqued, we'll encourage you to learn more about Source Objects and how to leverage Parent/Child relationships in the chapters on forms and reports.

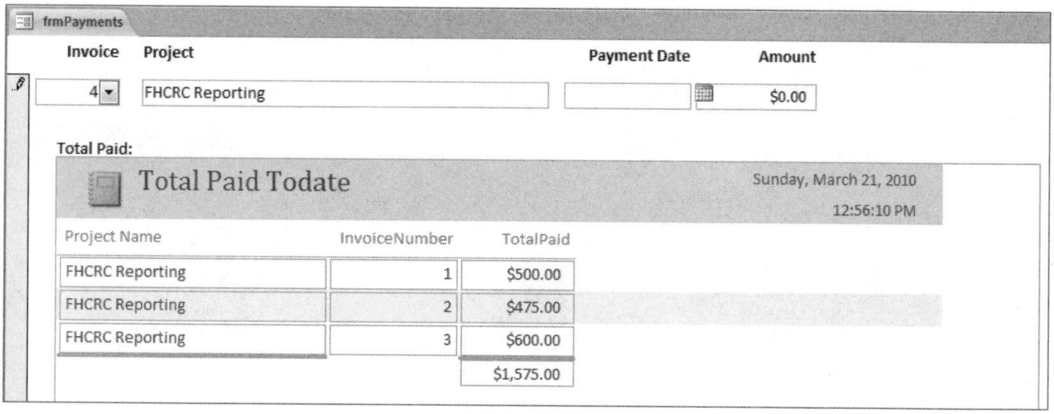

FIGURE 2-15

MACROS

One area with major changes in the new version of Access is macros. Not only did the macro interface get a facelift (as we mentioned earlier), but it was revamped and upgraded to include table-level triggers and a rich functionality previously available only through VBA coding. Access 2010 offers two types of macros: UI macros and Data macros. We discuss them briefly here and refer you to Chapter 4 for a more detailed explanation of how to use them.

UI Macros

UI macros are what we used to call macros in previous versions of Access. However, they not only have a new name, but they also feature a number of notable improvements.

The UI macro Editor, shown in Figure 2-16, provides an interface that resembles a code editor complete with complex logic, error handling, and looping through records. And, it provides the added convenience of collapsible segments. The redesigned UI macros allow you to create a rich and productive UI for your users to interact with the data. UI macros can be used in combination with Data macros to report back validation rule status and errors that may have occurred.

Data Macros

Data macros can serve as a convenient vehicle to help implement business rules in your application. Similar to using Triggers in SQL Server, (discussed in Chapter 21), you can use Data macros to attach logic to record events (also referred to as table events), centralizing the logic in one place, the table, where forms that are bound to the table inherit that logic. Data macros also enable you to manage calculated fields, ensuring that the current data stored is always the most accurate. The table events that can be used to set the macros are `BeforeChange`, `BeforeDelete`, `AfterInsert`, `AfterUpdate`, and `AfterDelete`. Figure 2-17 shows the available actions for the `AfterInsert` event. You can also set your macro as a Named macro and associate it with a table. The Named [Data] Macro can be called from other Data macros or UI macros and from VBA code so it can easily be leveraged and reused through the application.

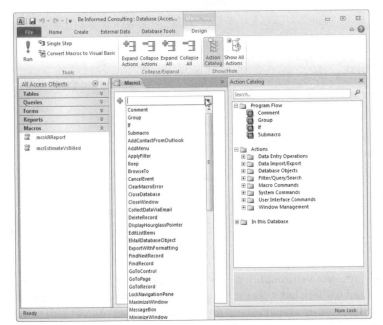

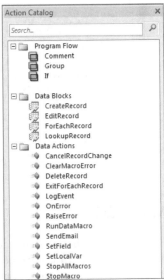

FIGURE 2-16

FIGURE 2-17

One key factor to remember is that Data macros do not have a user interface. So although you can interact with the Data macro and pass parameters to it from a UI macro, a Data macro cannot open a form or a report. However, you can use UI macros to process the errors returned by the Data macros and display the error to the user. The errors are also written to the `UsysApplicationLog` table in your database.

As we mentioned earlier, data macros can also be used to calculate and store de-normalized values in calculated fields in a table. Despite the apparent conflict with designing a fully normalized database, there are benefits to storing calculated values in a table, such as improved performance for data retrieval. Calculated columns and Data macros may prove to be invaluable functional alternatives to aggregate queries which are not supported Web databases.

INTEGRATION WITH SHAREPOINT

Access 2010 also enables you to publish your application on the Web using SharePoint. It gives you the tools to design a Web database application with a smooth interface that is familiar to your clients. The process for starting a Web database is similar to that of starting a new client database. When you select Blank Web Database, you will find a growing selection of templates to choose from, as shown in Figure 2-18. Keep in mind, that to deploy your database to SharePoint as a Web application, you will also need to have Access Services installed on the SharePoint server. As with website hosting, this service is also available from hosting companies.

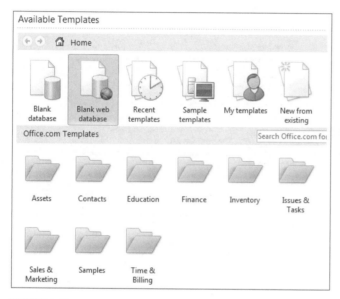

FIGURE 2-18

Working with Data on SharePoint

By selecting a Web database when you start Access 2010, you ensure that only the components that are Web-compatible will be available as you design the database. This minimizes the potential for compatibility issues when it comes time to publish the application. You will also want to consider approaches that will help the application work more efficiently with SharePoint. For example, SharePoint can leverage the use of lookup fields in your table; however, these are often discouraged in client databases.

Publish the Database to SharePoint

To publish your Web database to SharePoint, you will use the menu behind the File tab (Backstage). You can either click on Publish to Access Services, or select Share ⇨ Publish to Access Services. As shown in Figure 2-19, the Share screen contains the command to Run Compatibility Checker as well as the dialog to publish to Access Services.

Additional SharePoint Features

As mentioned in the "Web Service Expressions" sections earlier in this chapter, not all features and functionalities of a client database will be available to you when you design a Web database. One of the most significant "losses" that we might feel is not being able to use VBA code. SharePoint and Access Services do not support VBA. While it may seem like a show stopper for some of your applications, you will be able to use the robust Macro Designer to create macros that can perform many of the functions that you previously handled through code. As you can see in Figure 2-20, you can use VBA in a Web database, but only in a client object. That means that it will not be published to the SharePoint portal when you deploy your application; however, it will be available locally on the client copy.

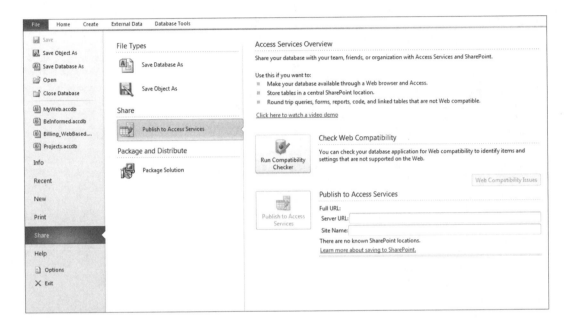

FIGURE 2-19

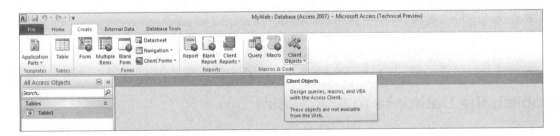

FIGURE 2-20

BROWSER INTERFACE/APPLICATIONS

As you have probably realized by now, the approach and tools for designing a Web database are a bit different from those used to design a client application. In order to accommodate the Web interface, you will need to allow for some considerations in your UI design that otherwise are not needed in a client application. Neither the forms nor the reports in a Web database can be opened in design view. You will have to design these types of objects in the layout view. And, you will quickly appreciate that forms and reports in a Web database don't support absolute positioning; because the final positioning will be determined when the object is rendered on the Web.

While each Web object designer is unique, they share some common traits and will feel somewhat similar as you develop the forms and the reports for your Web database application.

Introducing the Web Form Designer

When you start the Web form designer (see Figure 2-21), you will notice that the form is divided into rows and columns, similar to a table in Word. As you add controls to the form, they are aligned in a tabular format. This is important because the tabular format is essential for the form to render properly on SharePoint via Access Services.

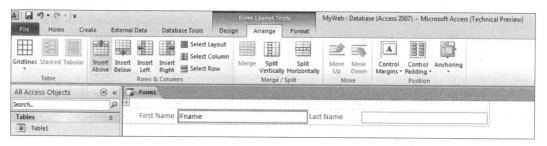

FIGURE 2-21

As you work with the controls, you will be able to work with the Arrange Ribbon to manage the cells to meet your layout needs.

Introducing Web Report Designer

Similar to the form designer, the report designer, shown in Figure 2-22, requires a tabular layout as well. However, you get a more expansive set of Ribbon tools to work with when designing reports. By splitting or merging cells you can create rich reports that will render beautifully in Access Services. Because Web databases do not support aggregate queries, you will also use reports as a preferred vehicle to deliver information that must be calculated or compiled.

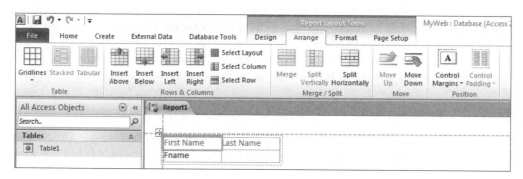

FIGURE 2-22

Feature Restrictions (Features Disabled in Web Applications)

As you've come to realize, because Web objects are dependant on the server (both SharePoint and Access Services), and are rendered in the browser, they do not have all of the functionality available to client database objects. To help you minimize and optimally avoid compatibility errors, Access provides development tools based on the type of object. So when you are working on a Web object, you will only see the options and features that are valid for Web objects. The following provides an overview of the restrictions:

> ➤ You cannot use design view to design Web tables. The tables must be designed in datasheet view and you will access the Web table properties through the Table Tools Ribbon.

> ➤ You cannot open a Web query in SQL view. That ensures that you can only use settings that are valid on the Web.

> ➤ You cannot use aggregated queries in a Web database. To aggregate values, you will need to use Data macros or summary reports.

> ➤ You cannot open Web forms and Web reports in design view; and neither object supports absolute positioning. However, the layout designers are expanded to include table layout tools, and when working on Web objects the property sheet will only show Web-legal settings.

Even with the best laid plans and practices, it is still important for you to run Compatibility Checker before attempting to publish your application. This will ensure that you will identify any issues that will cause an error when you publish the database application.

Chapters 14 and 15 discuss how to enhance forms and reports. You will dive deeper into the features and the properties of the object designers and learn how to leverage them to build robust applications.

WHAT'S GONE OR DEPRECATED

As we get excited about the new and improved features that Access 2010 has to offer, we would be remiss if we didn't review the features that did not make it from the previous version into Access 2010.

Calendar Control

The Calendar Control (`mscal.ocx`) is not included in Access 2010. If you have a Calendar Control on a form when you open it in Access 2010 you will see the following error: "Your Microsoft Office Access database or project contains a missing or broken reference to the file 'MSCAL.OCX'." To fix this, you will need to remove the Calendar Control from your form. As an alternative, you can use the built-in DatePicker, or use one of the third-party calendar controls.

ISAMs

With Access 2010, you will not be able to export, import, and/or link to data from ISAM (Indexed Sequential Access Method). If you try to do so, you may get the error "Installable ISAM not found."

Although this is not a common need, the following ISAMs are impacted:

➤ Paradox 3, 4, 5, 6, 7

➤ Lotus 1-2-3

➤ Access 1.0 and 2.0 (Red 2, or Jet 2)

If you are working with legacy files and you still need to maintain the connections, you'll need to use previous versions of Access in order to be able to export, import, or link to the data.

Replication Conflict Resolver

Previous versions of Access included a Line Of Business (LOB), which enabled users to graphically view replication conflicts and to resolve the conflicts. Access 2010 will not be shipped with this feature.

If you need to use this kind of functionality, you can write a custom function to mark the conflicts in the ReplicationConflictFunction property in the database replica set. For more information, we refer you to the Microsoft Knowledgebase article at http://support.microsoft.com/kb/158930.

Snapshot Format

As an alternative to the now deprecated snapshot format for reports in Access 2010, you can export your reports directly to PDF/XPS and Excel formats. Those formats are native to Access 2010 (and Office 2010), so they do not require users to download additional add-ons.

SUMMARY

This chapter provided you with a taste of what's to come in the subsequent chapters. It highlighted selected new features in Access 2010 — the rest of the book delves into the details and discusses how to incorporate the features into your database solutions. Access has always been one of the most powerful rapid development tools available for database applications, and Access 2010 has taken that to a new level to not only make it easier and faster to build robust and productive client solutions but now we can provide Web applications as well.

The changes in the application UI and the enhanced capability to easily integrate with Access Services to publish Web databases will help you break new ground by adding Web and hybrid solutions to your development skills The new in-the-box template solutions will not only save you development time, but will put you on the track to develop your own, richer solutions that leverage existing functionality and application parts. And the new Macro Designer will enable you to customize the UI and create an application for your users to manage and review their data.

Remember that most chapters in this book have sample databases and code available for download from this book's website on Wrox.com. Explore the files as you read through a chapter to help you get the most out of the book and out of Access 2010.

3

Upgrading and Converting to Access 2010

WHAT'S IN THIS CHAPTER?

➤ Considerations for upgrading

➤ Working with earlier versions of database file format

➤ Converting databases from earlier versions

➤ Working with 32-bit and 64-bit platforms.

With the most dramatic addition of features and power in more than a decade, Access 2010 is designed to appeal to a wide spectrum of users and developers, and it is moving full speed to bring Access's rapid application development to the Internet. As you learned from Chapter 2, the user interface (UI) is even more intuitive, and it offers many of the features and functionality that previously either required programming or weren't practical to accommodate.

The new features empower users to easily gather and analyze data from multiple sources, including SQL Server, Excel, e-mail, and websites. They make it easier for developers to automate processes and to provide unprecedented flexibility for user-customized reports. It is now feasible to include attachments in the database, and the new file format (ACCDB) offers security through encryption of the data file. One of the greatest extensions is the reach to the Web. Not only can you distribute an Access database to the Web using SharePoint 2010, you can also use Access Services to publish Web forms and reports. You can now offer Web solutions that do not require the user to have Access or even Office.

In the past, it was easier to be a slow adapter because the advantages of upgrading might not have compelled everyone to make the move. But the near revolutionary advances in both hardware and software will enable people to work faster and smarter and to make better decisions quicker. The ability to use Web applications and leverage online content gives Access an entirely new spectrum of opportunities for people to work with, integrate, and analyze data. With Web apps, you don't even need Access to use the application.

Because many of the new features are available only with the new ACCDB file format, there is a strong incentive for users to migrate their applications to the 2007 (2010) ACCDB file format. However, even with a uniform deployment of Access 2010 within a company, people may still need to work with files from prior versions. Whether it is to collaborate with others, to link to external data sources, or to incorporate custom code, there are a multitude of reasons to know how to safely open and use files that are generated or saved from previous versions and formats.

The integration issues are not limited to versions of Office and file formats. With the introduction of 64-bit operating systems and 64-bit software, you now need to factor in and be prepared to address compatibility issues associated with the hardware, the operating systems and the versions of Office that will (or might) come into play. With all of these factors to consider, individuals and businesses will be right alongside enterprises as they develop a plan to address the issues related to migrating to 2010 and potentially for working in a mixed environment.

That is what this chapter is all about. We will discuss various considerations for upgrading to 2010, working with older versions and maintaining compatibility between multiple versions. We will look at available options and provide information so you will be better equipped to make informed decisions with regards to integrating the new 2010 version into your environment. It is important to realize that you may experience different results and limitations based on the configuration of your computer, network, and the specific versions (including service packs) of Microsoft Office and Access.

TO CONVERT OR TO ENABLE

You have several things to consider when deciding whether to convert an application to the Access ACCDB file format. The primary reason to convert is to take advantage of the new features that require the ACCDB file format, such as the ability to work with complex data, the ease of collecting data from e-mail forms, linking to SharePoint Services, and creating Web applications.

To support some of the features added in Access 2007 and 2010, there are several new system tables that may or may not be used within an ACCDB file. Along with the new benefits, there are also limitations, such as the fact that the ACCDB file cannot be linked to by an MDB file, does not support replication, and does not support user-level security as was available in prior versions. However, Access 2010 continues to support MDB file format natively. Thus, an Access 2010 MDB will support several new features as long as the features do not depend on the file format — we'll discuss this shortly. If you are working in a mixed version environment, you will want to be mindful that although an ACCDB file can link to or import from an MDB file, the opposite is not true.

Common Terminology

Words such as "upgrade," "migrate," "convert," and "enable" are sometimes used interchangeably. To make the discussion easier, we'll establish a common meaning for the purposes of this chapter.

> ➤ **Upgrade:** You have Office and Access 2010 instead of some prior version. And, with purchases, "upgrade" is often associated with a discount based on owning a prior version. With this release, some of the documentation uses "upgrade" synonymously with "converting."

But that isn't uniformly applied, so to avoid confusion, we will avoid the use of the term "upgrade" for the rest of the chapter, using other terms as below.

➤ **Migrate:** The process of converting or moving applications from earlier versions so that they can be used with newer versions of Access — in this case, Access 2010. It applies to scenarios in which you will be using Access 2010 and have some Access applications that were created in previous versions.

➤ **Convert:** The specific process that Access runs to change the database format from one version to another. Obviously, this chapter focuses on converting to the Access 2007/2010 ACCDB format. Converting allows you to work with the database objects and to utilize the features of the specified version of Access, so by converting to the ACCDB format, your older applications can be enhanced to take advantage of new features.

➤ **Enable:** Enabling allows a newer version of Access to open a database created by a previous version of Access, but it does not change the file format. Access 2010 can work directly with Access 2000 and 2002–2003 file formats, and pre-95 formats must be converted, so only Access 95's or 97's format databases may be enabled. In some situations, the need to allow older versions of Access to use the database makes enabling the practical choice. For the purposes of this chapter, the term *enabling* refers to the fact that Access 2010 can open an Access 95 or 97 database without converting it. But once the Access 95 or 97 MDB file is "enabled," users can only view and update data; they cannot modify objects or create new database objects.

Key Decision Factors

Now that we have established some common terminology, we can focus on the key factors for making the decisions about whether, when, and how to enable and/or convert. A pivotal factor is whether the situation involves multiple versions of Access sharing the same data file or using the same application. Other key issues to consider include:

➤ Will any new features from Access 2010 be incorporated into the application and will they need to be instantly available to all users? This was specifically worded to prompt consideration for situations where migration may proceed in stages that allow strategically timed deployment of the Access 2010 version by groups or by selected individuals.

➤ What file types do you have and what do you need? Will those files be converted to newer formats or do you need to keep the current formats for compatibility with older versions? For example, if you have an MDE file, you will need to use the original MDB format to convert the file.

➤ Are you working with user and group level security and using an MDW file?

➤ If the database is split, what version is the original application in, and what version is the data file?

➤ What time and resources are required to test and convert the applications? A quick cost/benefit analysis can help determine if it is appropriate, let alone necessary, to convert.

For the most part, it is straightforward to either enable or convert a legacy Access database to an Access ACCDB format. However, the process may involve additional steps if you need to accommodate features that are no longer available in the ACCDB format, notably user-level security and replication. Moving to the ACCDB format may necessitate developing a new approach that replaces the functionality provided by either of those features. Some of the alternatives may provide significant benefits in other areas, such as when using Sharepoint Services to replace replication or using 2010 data encryption features for securing data instead of User-Level Security. We will refer you to other chapters to learn more about the powerful new features in these areas.

If the current approach to user-level security and/or replication is critical to the operation, Access 2010 still supports those features when working with MDB file formats. Chapters 24 and 25 discuss approaches for database security; and Chapter 19 is an excellent reference for working with Windows SharePoint Services. You will also find additional information online, such as through MSDN and Microsoft Access Online Help.

A few other features are not supported in Access 2010, such as the calendar control and Data Access Pages. Toolbars are not available unless specifically configured in the startup options. These types of issues are covered in more detail later.

Barring the reliance on the few features that are no longer supported by Access 2010, an evaluation of the tradeoffs typically endorses the effort to convert. If you are considering some of the costs and time associated with rolling out a new version over a large user base, you have several options that include a mix of status quo such as enabling (running applications unchanged as MDB format) and converting.

If you are involved with making the decisions about migrating or staying with earlier versions of Access, we recommend that you carefully evaluate the benefits that you will gain by using Access 2010's new features and weigh that against the functionality that you might loose if you are relying on features that are no longer supported in 2010. You will also need to look at the big picture, including the costs associated with the purchase and with converting files (both application and data files), and also consider the issues associated with file compatibility. There can be significant tradeoffs whether you convert, maintain legacy file formats, or use a combination of both.

Microsoft has also provided a tool to help evaluate and plan the migration process, the Office Migration Planning Manager (OMPM). The OMPM identifies and provides information about the databases on a network. It lists the files, their locations, format, size, and even the number of objects. If you are converting from Access 97, the OMPM will also identify some of the common issues that may be encountered. To get more information about the OMPM, visit Microsoft's TechNet site or search on Microsoft.com.

Feature Sets and File Extensions: What's New, What's Replaced, What Happens

Obviously, in a controlled environment where everyone will be using Access 2010, it would be a shame to not convert databases from earlier versions so that everyone can take advantage of the new features of the ACCDB file format as well the new features offered in Access 2010. Beyond the mentioned issues of replication, user level security, and Data Access Pages, even large complex applications with large amounts of VBA code should run without issues or problems when you convert these applications to the new ACCDB format.

Features such as embedded macros, the new picture control, and report layouts with live data will significantly empower and improve the productivity of users. If people are already using the new

Office Ribbon in Word and other programs, they will appreciate the consistency of using it in Access as well.

For applications heavily dependent upon user/group permissions or replication, it is best to establish and test a migration plan before attempting to convert in-service applications. Keep in mind that you will need to replace deprecated features such as Data Access Pages and the ActiveX calendar control.

 A brief discussion about deprecated features appears in the section "Features Not Available with ACCDB Files" later in this chapter.

In addition to Access 2010's capability to open and even make design changes to 2000 and 2002–2003 MDB file formats, it can also convert an ACCDB "back" to the earlier MDB file formats. With 2010, you can specify the file type so that it will work with the version of Access that will be opening it. However depending on which (new) features are present in the ACCDB file, Access will either convert and silently discard the unsupported features or it will provide an error message and abort the conversion process.

With dozens of new features, it is reassuring to know that MDB files will, for the most part, work as expected. The majority of the new features will be quietly ignored or will not appear when an Access 2010 MDB file is opened with an earlier version of Access. Chapter 2 provides a brief description of many key new features; our focus here is on the features that are available only with the ACCDB file format and how they may affect plans for moving to Access 2010.

File Extensions

Office Access 2010 supports and leverages the new file extensions that were introduced in Access 2007. For backward compatibility, Access 2010 continues to be able to use nearly all of the file extensions, including: .accdb, .accde, .accdt, .accdr, .laacdb, .ldb, .mdw, .mdb, .mde, and .adp. You probably recognize the meaning of each of these extensions, so we'll just mention two of the newer ones.

The .accdt file extension indicates a template. Developers can convert .accdb to .accdt. In 2007, developers had to download a separate add-in, Access Developer Extensions (ADE), but this is now included in 2010 natively. Changing an Access 2010 file's extension from .accdb to .accdr will cause the file to act as though it is in runtime mode — so users are unable to make design changes. However, all it takes is changing the extension back to .accdb and the design privileges are returned. So don't let this give you a false sense of protection. You can review the Access Help or MSDN for a complete list of file extensions and their effects on the file.

New Features Available Only with ACCDB File Format

The following features are available when using the ACCDB file format but are not accessible in an MDB file. If an MDB file is converted to an ACCDB file, these features become available:

➤ **Attachment data type:** New data type that provides efficient storage of binary streams which could be documents, pictures, or any kind of files.

➤ **Append -only memo fields:** Provides history of changes to memo field data; also integrates with the append-only text fields in a SharePoint list.

➤ **Built-in integration with Microsoft Office SharePoint Server:** Please see Chapter 19 for a detailed discussion.

➤ **Encrypt with database password:** Uses the Windows Crypto API to encrypt data.

➤ **Linked tables to files in an ACCDB format:** As in MDB format, we can link to other MDB files but not ACCDB files; ACCDB format allows us to link to both MDB and ACCDB formats.

➤ **Multi-valued lookup fields:** Also referred to as complex data fields.

➤ **TempVars:** Collection similar to global variables.

The following list details features that are available only in Access 2010 using the ACCDB file format. (Note that although the file will open in Access 2007, the features will not necessarily be available.)

➤ **Access Services:** Allows developers to author and publish Web applications (requires SharePoint 2010).

➤ **Data macros:** Create macros that runs based on when something changes in a table.

➤ **Image Gallery:** A pool of images that can be shared and used by several bound image controls.

➤ **Navigation control:** A new control that essentially combines a subform and tab control into a single control.

➤ **Web browser control:** Instead of using ActiveX control, we now have a native control that provides a frame into a Web browser and thus allows us to open a page right on the form.

➤ **Web style buttons:** Provide more formatting and customization options.

Access 2010 Is Based on 2007 File Format

As we mentioned earlier, Access 2007 and Access 2010 share the same file format (ACCDB). In fact, Access 2010 still refers to the .accdb file extension as "Access 2007 Database format" and there is no such thing as "Access 2010 Database format." However, Access 2010 has new features that are not available in Access 2007. The most significant change is that Access 2010 supports data macros and Web objects, and Access 2007 does not. If you attempt to open an ACCDB file that has Access 2010 data macros, Access 2007 (SP2 and later) will give you a message informing you that data macros are present, and the table will be opened as read-only in Access 2007. Because a data macro fires based on changes to the table, it will never fire for a read-only table.

Features Not Available with ACCDB Files

There are only a few features available in the MDB file format that the ACCDB file format does not support. Typically, this is because a more robust alternative has been provided. Although some of these features are still available if using an MDB format, others can be achieved only programmatically if at all. If you are relying on one of the deprecated features, it is likely that work-arounds are, or will become, available.

The following features are no longer available, as of Access 2007:

➤ Designing Data Access Pages (DAPs)

➤ Microsoft Office XP Web Components

➤ Replication

➤ The UI for import and export in older formats

➤ User-Level Security and Workgroup Administrator

The following features are no longer available as of Access 2010:

➤ Calendar control (`mscal.ocx`)

➤ ISAM support, including Paradox, Lotus 1-2-3, and Jet 2.*x* or older

➤ Opening Data Access Pages (DAPs)

➤ Replication Conflict Viewer

➤ Snapshot format for report output

What Happens When a 2007/2010 MDB Is Opened by Prior Versions

Access 2010 and 2007 introduced a multitude of new features available to both the MDB and ACCDB file formats. When working with multiple versions of Access, it can be confusing to keep track of what will work for each version. The following table lists the new features and how they will behave in prior versions of Access. New features for Access 2007 or 2010 MDB files are also available for ACCDB files, but the reverse is not always true. Features that are available for ACCDB files but not for 2007 or 2010 MDB files are denoted by the statement "Not available to MDB files; only available in ACCDB file format."

2007/2010 NEW FEATURE	BEHAVIOR IN ACCESS 2000, 2002, AND 2003
ACCDB file format	Cannot be opened.
Access security and the Trust Center	Prompts with security warnings and does not have the capability to trust a file based on its location.
Add Existing Fields task pane	Field list floating dialog box.
Add new fields in Datasheet view	New fields must be created in table Design view.
Alternating row color (alternate Back Color property)	All rows appear the same color as the first row. Alternate Back Color property is ignored.
Append-only memo fields	Not available to MDB files; available only in ACCDB file format.

continues

(continued)

2007/2010 NEW FEATURE	BEHAVIOR IN ACCESS 2000, 2002, AND 2003
Attachments	Not available to MDB files; available only in ACCDB file format.
Complex data	Not available to MDB files; available only in ACCDB file format.
Control auto-resize and anchoring	Controls do not automatically resize or move.
Control layouts (stacked and tabular)	Behave like independent controls.
Create data collection e-mail	Older versions have no option to create or manage data collection e-mail.
Custom groups in the Navigation Pane	Navigation Pane converts to the database window, but custom groups are lost.
Database templates	Cannot be opened.
Datasheet user interface enhancements	Record selectors and selection.
Date picker	Does not appear.
Design in browse mode for forms and reports	Design via the Property Sheet only.
Edit list items command for combo boxes and list boxes	Does not appear.
Editable value lists	Value lists do not have a user interface for editing and are not automatically inherited from the table.
Encrypt with database password	Not available to MDB files; available only in ACCDB file format.
Filtering and sorting improvements	Previous filtering and sorting user interface.
Getting Started experience	Getting Started task pane.
Gridlines on layouts	No gridlines appear.
Improved accessibility	Datasheet, forms, and reports do not have the same support for accessibility aides.
Linked tables to ACCDBs	Cannot link to ACCDB files. Available only in ACCDB file format.
Linked tables to Excel 12 files (.xslx)	Linked tables to Excel 12 cannot be opened.
Linked tables to Windows SharePoint Services V3	Not all data types are fully supported. Some columns may be read-only or might not appear.

2007/2010 NEW FEATURE	BEHAVIOR IN ACCESS 2000, 2002, AND 2003
Macros embedded in event properties	Event properties appear to be blank instead of showing "[Embedded Macro]" and will not function.
Manage data collection replies	Does not appear.
Navigation Pane	Database container.
New Sorting and Grouping task pane	Sorting and grouping dialog box.
Access Options via the Backstage	Separate dialog boxes for Options, Startup, and AutoCorrect.
Offline support for Linked Tables to Windows SharePoint Services	MDBs cannot link to SharePoint tables. This is available in ACCDB file format only.
Property Sheet task pane	Property sheet floating dialog box.
Report Browse mode	Print Preview only.
Ribbon	Command bars.
Ribbon customizations	Do not appear.
Rich text	Appears as plain text with HTML tags.
Save Database As	Can convert to and from older file formats, but cannot convert to the newer 2007 file format.
Saved imports and exports	Only the import and export specifications supported in the older format will be converted and available.
Search box in record navigation user interface	Does not appear.
Share database on SharePoint	Does not appear.
SharePoint Site Manager	Does not appear.
Split views	Appears as a single item form.
Tabbed document mode (SDI)	Multiple windows (MDI).
Tables and Views mode	Does not appear.
Upsize database to SharePoint	Does not appear.

What Happens When a 2010 ACCDB Is Opened by 2007

As noted previously, Access 2010 uses the same file format as 2007 does. However, 2010 introduces several new features that may not be accessible by 2007 — not even in the ACCDB format. Depending on what the ACCDB file contains, Access 2007 may either work seamlessly with all of the features and objects, not be able to open the file at all, or be able to open the database but not use specific objects that were new in Access 2010. Generally speaking, a published Web database is not available to Access 2007, so it should be expected that Web objects would not be backward compatible even though there are few instances where 2007 can still open unpublished Web objects.

2010 NEW FEATURE	BEHAVIOR OF THE DATABASE IF OPENED IN ACCESS 2007 SP2
Access 2010 Encryption Compliance	The database will not open in Access 2007 SP2.
Application navigation control	The database opens, but forms that contain the Application navigation control do not open in Access 2007 SP2.
Application published to Access Services	When you create a Web database application using Access 2010 and publish it to a website, the database will not open in Access 2007 SP2. However, the backup file that is created during the publication process can be opened in Access 2007 SP2. And it remains that some Web objects cannot be modified in Access 2007 SP2.
Calculated Column	The database opens, but tables that contain Calculated Columns will not open in Access 2007 SP2. Forms or reports that reference a table that contain Calculated Columns can be opened and modified in Design view only.
Data Macro	The database opens, but tables that contain data macros are read-only. The user cannot enter data or modify the table using Access 2007 SP2. Forms or reports that reference a table that contains data macros can be opened and modified in Layout or Design view; however, data drawn from the table cannot be modified.
Database with Web objects	If the database contains Web objects that have not been published, it opens in Access 2007 SP2. However, some Web objects (ie, published ones) cannot be modified in Access 2007 SP2.*
Linked tables with Connection strings that are longer than 512 characters	The database opens, but the linked tables with the long connection string cannot be opened in Access 2007 SP2.
New and updated database sort orders	The database will not open in Access 2007 SP2.
Web browser control	The database opens, but the forms that contain Web browser controls do not open in Access 2007 SP2.

* Documentation, functionality and compatibility issues will continue to change, especially with major releases and service packs.

When an ACCDB file contains any of the new 2010 features, it cannot be converted back into an MDB file. Similarly, even if an MDB file is opened in Access 2010, it will not be able to use new features that are specific to the ACCDB format.

Other Things to Consider

As with most projects, there are a lot of issues that you'll need to consider, such as converting a functional application, maintaining references, sharing data files, splitting databases, locking files, running multiple versions of Access, and new ways for working with various data sources.

Of course, there are situations that are not conducive to converting the file, such as when an application uses a feature that is not available with the ACCDB file format. If the replacement for the missing feature isn't an acceptable alternative, then the appropriate solution may be to enable the database. Keep in mind that it is acceptable to convert some applications and enable others. It is also feasible to use two versions of the same application; which allows some people to work with the converted file while others work with the original format. In that situation, the shared data files would need to remain in an MDB format compatible with the original application file. Regardless of other differences, you should compile the code before attempting to convert the file.

VBA References

Each version of Access has its own default VBA references. So when you change the file format, you should check the VBA references. By default, any Access applications will have at least four VBA references listed in the following order:

➤ Visual Basic for Applications

➤ Microsoft Access *n.n* Object Library

➤ OLE Automation

➤ Data Access Library(ies), as explained in the following list

Depending on which versions of Access the file was originally created under, the Data Access Libraries referenced may be:

➤ Microsoft Office *n.n* Access database engine Object Library

➤ Microsoft DAO *n.n* Object Library

➤ Microsoft ActiveX Data Objects *n.n* Library (aka ADO)

The *n.n* refers to the version of the library. For Microsoft Office libraries, the number will correspond to the version of Office. Thus, for an Access 2010 installation, the references will have "14.0" for *n.n*. Other libraries have different version numbering. For DAO and ADO, the latest versions are 3.6 and 6.0, respectively. You should also be aware that although Microsoft Office *n.n* Access database engine Object Library and Microsoft DAO *n.n* Object Library have different names, they are actually the same library, just a different version. You can choose either version, but you cannot have both versions; however, you can reference both DAO and ADO libraries within the same application. For simplicity, this section will refer to those libraries in general as the "Data Access Library."

Of the default references, the VBA and Microsoft Access Object Library can never be removed or modified by the user. And although you may remove the OLE Automation library and the data access library, doing so may break code, particularly if you remove the data access library. However, it may be desirable to change the data access library to the lowest version available to ensure that it will work uniformly across multiple versions of Access — given that all installations may not have the latest and newest version of the data access library. In a complex application, there may be additional references to extend the functionality — those will require the same care as working with data access libraries.

Normally, the VBA library and the Access Object Library will match the version of Access that is currently running. This is why having different versions of Access installed side-by-side on one computer will require a reconfiguration to update references each time a different version of Access is opened. Although all files inherit the applicable references from Access (see the previous list), the files retain their references to different versions of other libraries, including data access libraries.

When working with multiple versions of Office, it is a good practice to validate and, if needed, repair references and test the database on the oldest version of Access, Office, and Windows that will use it.

Be aware that Access may update the references for a file that was opened in a different version of Access to be compatible with the currently running instance of Access. So, if you are working in an environment with multiple versions, it is a good habit to take a quick look and verify that the references are what you expect to see for the file. Blindly accepting the default does not guarantee that the code will work. There are also third party tools that are designed to manage side-by-side installations and make it easier to work with multiple versions of Access on the same computer.

If an application contains references to both DAO and ADO libraries in VBA code, it may be necessary to check the references and ensure that DAO is listed above ADO so that DAO will take precedence over ADO and thus avoid compilation errors. ADO and DAO are covered extensively in Chapters 11 and 12 and there is additional reference material in the appendixes. You'll recall the benefits of including the Option Explicit statement at the beginning of your code modules to avoid ambiguity.

Shared Data Files

An ACCDB file can open and work with multiple data files and file formats, including those with ACCDB and MDB file formats. When linking to tables, it is important to remember that the data file must have the file format of the oldest version of Access that will open it. For MDB files that could be 2000, 2002–2003, or 2003 file formats — 95 and 97 are special cases. Access 2010 allows users to open previous files and save them in a specified file format.

Splitting a Database

Speaking of shared data files prompts a discussion of splitting the database, or moving the tables to their own file. It's not uncommon to initiate the database design with the tables in the same file as all the other objects. And although it works fine to keep it that way for small, single-user applications, it isn't advisable for larger applications or for multiple user applications. Although a combined (single-file) application can allow simultaneous use by multiple users, doing so can lead to significant performance and corruption issues. The easy way to avoid this is to split the database and have multiple front ends sharing one back-end data file.

Access 2010 can share files with earlier version of Access as long the file is saved as the earliest version's supported file formats. Be sure to create a copy of the file before initiating this process. The newly created back-end file will be in the same format as the original file, so if all users are moving to a newer version of Access, it can be helpful to convert the database first. However, if the data file will need to support an older version of Access, it is important to separate the tables before converting. The tables need to be in the format of the oldest version of Access that will use them. Splitting the database will not preserve password protection, so that would need to be added to the newly created back-end file if a password is desired.

Splitting your databases is strongly recommended under all but the most simplistic single-user situations.

After the database has been split, it is reassuring to confirm that the tables are correctly linked. Two of the more common ways to identify the source data for a linked table is to hover over the table's name in the Navigation Pane and read the path from the control tip, or to use the Linked Table Manager.

Now, if you want to create multiple versions of the database application, you will be converting only the front end. You can convert the front-end file to whatever versions of Access that users will need. All of the front-end files can be linked to the back-end (data) file that was just created. For steps on splitting a database, refer to Appendix I.

If multiple versions of Access will be linked to the data file, the data file should be created in or converted to the oldest file format. And, you will want to use that same older version to run the periodic compact and repair on the data file. The application file cannot be from an older format version than the data file.

The capability to support multiple users sharing the same data file is the basis for some of the most powerful benefits that Access has to offer. However, it is a best practice to not share the front-end applications. An application file should only be available to one user at a time. This is an important point that is worth reiterating. An application (the front-end file) with simultaneous users will suffer both in performance and reliability, and it has an increased risk of experiencing data corruption.

Working with SQL Server

As in the past, Access 2010 continues to support integration with SQL Server, both by linking to a SQL Server database or by creating Access Data Projects (ADP). Access 2007 and 2010 can connect to SQL Server data by linking and by using Access Data Projects (ADPs). Because both of the 2010 file formats (MDB and ACCDB) can create read/write linked tables to SQL Server tables or views, linking is typically the preferred method for connecting to SQL Server. Linking allows the full flexibility of using local tables and queries for record sources while leveraging the capacity of SQL Server.

As we discussed earlier, most of the new features for Access 2007 and 2010 are available in both MDB and ACCDB file formats; however, ADP files benefit from very few of the new features. So there are a few key factors to consider when determining whether to use linked tables or ADP files when you enable or convert. Linking provides the ability for one front-end file to connect to multiple data sources, including any combination of SQL Server, MDB, and ACCDB files; along with local tables and other data sources, such as SharePoint, Excel, or any ODBC-compliant databases. Linking also allows the use of local and ad hoc queries, which Jet will optimize so that SQL Server will do as much of the processing as possible. On the flip side, linking does not allow you to modify the linked table. You need to use an ADP file or SQL Server's Enterprise Manager to make schema or design changes to SQL Server files.

This discussion is intended only to highlight criteria for decision making. If you are working with SQL Server, you'll want to review Chapter 21 on client-server development.

Compiling the Code

Along with making a copy of the database, it is a good practice to be sure that code is compiled before initiating major changes. Not all applications or files have code, but most front-end applications do. Compiling will essentially clean up and compact the code. It identifies but does not fix errors. So if there are problems, you may need to debug the code before proceeding.

Use the Visual Basic Editor (VBE) to compact the code:

1. Open the VBE (press Alt+F11 or click the Visual Basic button on the Database Tools tab).

2. On the menu bar, click Debug.

3. Click the first option, which is Compile (*current filename*).

Ideally, everything works fine and there is nothing to debug. With small files it can be so fast that you don't know anything happened until you again click on the Debug menu and see that Compile is grayed out, indicating that the code is compiled.

INSTALLING MULTIPLE VERSIONS OF ACCESS ON ONE PC

As a developer, you are likely to need to work with multiple versions of Access at the same time and even for the same application. In the past, it was typical to use a different PC for each version. Although this avoided conflicts with Dynamic Linked Libraries (DLLs), it took a toll on resources and space. Thankfully, reliable options are now more affordable. Two of the popular options are to use virtualization software or to have side-by-side installations of selected programs.

LIBRARIES (DLL)

Complex applications and operating systems usually employ *libraries*, or files that contain common functions that are shared among the software. A *Dynamic Linked Library* (DLL) is a library that software loads on the fly. This helps reduce the application's install size and may use less system resources when it shares the libraries, but this comes at the price of being dependent on a specific version, which may not be available on other systems; and only one version can be registered at a time, which is why developers need to handle the dependency carefully. Referencing the libraries is an important concept, and you will touch on it again in Chapters 9 and 18 as well as in Appendix E, where we discuss managing references and troubleshooting problems.

With the new processors and hard drives, many machines have the space and capacity to run multiple versions of software. And, there are a growing number of options for creating virtual machines so that each version of software is running in its own operating environment. This can become resource intense, and each configuration requires individual maintenance but there are great benefits. For example, having virtual machines might allow you to design and test an application to run under multiple configurations, and it can allow you to emulate a client's environment to replicate their activities.

There are some general guidelines for installing multiple versions of Access directly onto one computer, also known as running side-by-side. First, be sure to install in order from oldest version to newest version. Second, if you are installing from an Office Suite instead of a standalone copy of Access, select a custom Office installation and install only Access — and while you're at it, install all of the features that might be used. It can be rather frustrating to have to stop in the middle of a process to get the CD and install more features.

 Be aware that because Access 2010 is brand new, there may be some challenges when in running it side-by-side with previous Access versions.

After installing the versions of Access that you need, you may want to set up shortcuts with icons that clearly denote which version it opens. Be aware that installing side-by-side comes with a price: Every time we switch the version, Office has to perform a reconfiguration to update the Registry to use the appropriate references for the version being opened. This occurs only the first time you open a certain version and doesn't happen again until you switch to the other version.

CHANGING FILE FORMATS

Before actually converting or enabling older files, it would be good to know how to work with the various file types in Access 2010. A good place to start is to specify the default file format. And, because we all agree that the data should not be in the front end or application file, we'll also tell you how to split the database. Given that legacy files could be MDE versions or runtime applications, we will also review the steps for creating these file types in the Access ACCDB format.

Selecting the Default File Format

For Access 2010, the default file format is ACCDB. But, if most of the files will be used by prior versions of Access, it might be best to specify a 2000 or 2002–2003 MDB as the default file format. It is easy to set the default file format, and it does not lock you into that selection. If you need to specify a different file type, it only takes a couple of extra clicks to override the default selection.

Setting the default file format is accomplished in a few easy steps:

1. Open Access 2010, but don't open a file.

2. If Backstage is not shown, click the File on the Ribbon. (Note: Backstage is a new feature or area in Office 2010. We discuss Access Backstage in Chapter 17.)

3. Click Options, a button on the left pane of the Backstage.

4. In the left pane of the Access Options dialog box, click General.

5. Under Creating Databases, in the Default File Format box, select the preferred format.

6. Click OK.

You can quickly confirm that the settings were saved as expected by initiating the process for creating a new database. That will open a pane on the right and provide a default name for the file. Then click the folder to the right of the filename to open the New Database File dialog box. The field "Save As Type" in the dialog box will display the default file format, including the version and extension, such as 2002–2003 format (*.mdb).

Overriding the Default File Format

As with other Office programs, you can easily save a file to a format other than the default format. However, changing the format of a database file may interfere with existing code and features, so it is best to select the desired format when you are first creating the database.

To override the default file format when creating a new database, choose New in the Backstage. The Backstage will then show a text box to enter a filename on the right.

1. Type a name for the new database in the File Name box.

2. Click the yellow folder next to the File Name box to open the New Database File dialog box.

3. Accept or select a different folder location and filename.

4. Select the file format that you want in the Save As Type drop-down list. You can specify 2000 MDB, 2002–2003 MDB, 2007 ACCDB, or ADP.

5. Click OK.

That's essentially all it takes to save a file in both the ACCDB and MDB file formats. Of course, when going from ACCDB to MDB, some features will not be available. And if the file has multi-value fields, SharePoint offline data, attachments, data macros, and/or Web objects, Access will either silently discard the unsupported features or provide an error message and not convert the file.

ACCDE and MDE Files

Access 2010 will create either a MDE or an ACCDE file, depending on which file type is open. Both files compile and lock down the code, so it cannot be viewed or modified. Any future changes have to be made to the originating MDB or ACCDB file and then a new ACCDE or MDE file will need to be created. Because the steps are essentially the same, this section will only provide the steps for creating an ACCDE file.

It takes just six steps to create an ACCDE file in Office Access 2010.

1. Use Access 2010 to open the database that you want to save as an ACCDE file.

2. Click File to access the Backstage.

3. Click Save & Publish.

4. On the middle pane, choose Save Database As.

5. On the right pane, choose Make ACCDE.

6. A Save As dialog box will appear. Type in the filename and click Save.

Steps for Converting or Enabling

For the most part, this section will focus on converting existing Access applications to Access 2010. However, if an Access 2010 application will be used by prior versions of Access, it will also be important to know how to create a compatible file. Access 2010 makes this relatively easy and straightforward. Note the qualifier, *relatively*, which is based on the inclination to include a caveat with regard to references and VBA.

The basic steps are typically adequate for simple files rather than complex applications. They do not check or fix broken references, test and debug code, replace custom menus and toolbars, or do a lot of other things that you will need to manage when converting your Access solutions. However, they do provide important guidance about the issues to consider, and they guide you through the steps for converting a database.

File Conversion Using Access 2010: A One-Stop Shop

Access 2010 has essentially one process to manage database conversion. You can quickly create a copy of a database so that it can be compatible with and used by multiple versions of Access. This is definitely a time to appreciate simplicity because the process is as easy as changing a picture from a 5MB BMP to a 300KB JPG.

In addition to converting to and from the ACCDB file format, Access 2007 will convert to and from MDB files with 2000 and 2002–2003 formats. As we previously mentioned, it requires extra steps and considerations to work with 95 and 97 file formats. Because Access creates and converts a copy of the original file, you will be ready to work with both the original and converted applications. An important, and seemingly obvious, item to note is that all database objects need to be closed when you are converting a file.

As always, we recommend that you compile the database and resolve issues related to deprecated features, references, and custom UI before you convert it. The investment at this point will quickly be rewarded by the reduced potential for errors and undue challenges during conversion. Keep in mind that conversion is a relatively low-risk process because Access creates a copy of the file. So the original is preserved, and you can quickly start again.

If you have an existing database that you want to convert to a different format, you can choose a format under the Save Database As command. Just follow these steps:

1. Use Access 2010 to open the database that you want to convert.
2. Click the File button to access backstage.
3. Click Save & Publish.
4. On the right pane, choose the desired format.
5. The Save As dialog box will appear. Type in the new filename and click Save. Depending on the size, this can take a few minutes.
6. When the conversion is completed, a dialog box advises you that the file cannot be shared with prior versions of Access. Click OK.
7. The new file opens in Access 2010.

Other Considerations When Converting

Keep in mind that saving a file to a different file format is only a small part of the process. As already discussed, there may be issues involving code, references, macros, security, and integration with other applications. For the most part, moving to newer versions is easier than moving backward. When converting to a prior version, some newer features may be lost or have only part of their functionality, and custom features may not be recognized or implemented as expected. Despite those concerns, it is certainly handy to have the ability to save a file in an older format when you want to.

But what about times when only some of objects are needed? Instead of converting an entire database, there is also the option to import database objects into an Access 2010 file, whether you need an MDB or ACCDB format. Importing objects does not automatically import or set the necessary references. So if you import VBA objects that depend on specific references, you may need to manually add the same references to the new file.

When converting a database that contains linked tables, it is a good practice to ensure that the linked tables are still in the location specified in the Connect *property. Using the Linked Table Manager to relink to the current tables is a fast, easy way to refresh or update the links. After the database has been converted, the tables can be moved and the Linked Table Manager can be used to relink to the tables in their new location.*

To convert a database, it must be closed, meaning that no users can be accessing the database, and you essentially need to have the equivalent of Administrator permissions for the database. Fortunately, the default mode for an unsecured database is for all users to have Admin permissions. There will be more about permissions in the section "Converting a Secured Database" later in this chapter.

Converting to Access 97 or Earlier Is a Two-Version Process

Rather than converting a 2010 file to work with Access 97, consider converting all Access 97 applications to the 2000 (or newer) file format if at all possible. If the situation demands that the files be converted to Access 97, keep in mind two important factors:

➤ Microsoft no longer supports Access 97.

➤ Access 97 does not support Unicode, so there will be issues if the databases contain Unicode data, including Asian and Complex Script languages.

To convert an Access 2007 database to Access 97, you first need to convert it to an intermediate version (2000 or 2002–2003) and then use that file and version to convert to an Access 97 file. Access 2010 will be able to open the new Access 97 database and users may enter data. However, you will have to have an installed copy of Access 97 in order to make any design changes. Additionally, the data file will also need to be converted to Access 95 (or newer) to be accessible to Access 2010.

CONVERTING A SECURED DATABASE

The Access ACCDB file format offers data encryption using a database password, but it does not support user-level security that uses the workgroup information manager (MDW) files. User-level security will be removed as the file is converted to the 2007 ACCDB file format. So, if the application has complex user-level security and permissions that you need to rely on, you may choose to keep the data in the MDB file. In that case, you're home free, at least for this part. Alternatively, you can implement a different approach to security and user permissions.

As security issues have become more critical and complex, new ways have been developed to protect the data and the application while making it easier for users to work with diverse and remote sources. To learn more about the new Access security features and options, please read Chapters 24 and 25 on database security and Access 2010 security.

After considering the options, let's say you decided to shed the user/group security (which is administered via a MDW file) and take advantage of the benefits offered by the ACCDB format. Switching to the new format removes user-level security and permissions from the file(s). Access will automatically remove the security settings so you can start clean when applying new security and interface controls to the new ACCDB or ACCDE file.

Keep in mind that if the application relied on user-level security to control who could enter, change, or view a specific date, those types of controls are not an inherent feature in the ACCDB format; so you will need to implement an alternative approach. As you are looking at options, you may find great value in some of the tips from Appendix I, which show you how to use TempVars and global variables to manage several aspects of user permissions.

> ### CONVERTING TO ACCDB FORMAT REMOVES USER-LEVEL SECURITY
>
> It's almost scary that it is so easy to remove user-level security which not only limited who could open a file, but also determined what data a user could see or change. It will be important to have a plan for replacing the security and control features before converting a database that relied on Access's user-level security (MDW) to a ACCDB format.

To convert the database, use Access 2010 to log in to the database as a user with full administrative permissions for all database objects. Then, follow the steps in the section "Changing File Formats" earlier in this chapter.

After the file is converted, close the application and Access. You will then be able to open the new ACCDB file without providing a password. However, if the application has custom user login features, those will still be enabled. And, if macros weren't already addressed, they will also need to be enabled. You may be quite surprised to realize a file is open but nothing shows up. If that occurs, you should look for an information bar — just under the Ribbon — that asks about enabling macros. One click may have everything working smoothly. In Chapter 4, we explain how to create a start-up form that uses macros to check whether the file is running in a trusted environment and then provides the users with a helpful message if it's not.

Converting a Password-Protected Database

If a database is password protected, the password protection must be removed before the database can be converted. You can use the following steps to remove the password:

1. Open Access 2010 and click the File button.

2. Click Open and browse to the target database.

3. Select the target database.

4. Click the drop-down arrow to the right of the Open button.

5. Select Open Exclusive.

6. In the Password Required dialog box, provide the database password and click OK. The database opens in exclusive mode, which enables you to remove the database password requirement.

7. Click the File button again and choose Info on the left pane.

8. Choose Unset Database Password on the right pane.

9. Type the password into the dialog box and click OK.

At this point, the password has been removed and the database can be converted using the same process discussed earlier in this chapter. Keep in mind that unless other measures have been implemented, the file will no longer have security so anyone who opens it will have full access to the data and the database objects.

Converting a Database with Password-Protected VBA

Password protection on the VBA does not affect opening the database itself, so the conversion process follows the same steps listed earlier in the section "File Conversion Using Access 2010: A One-Stop Shop." Unlike the experience using Access 2003 to convert a database with password-protected VBA, the password is not required to convert to 2010. With both 2010 and 2007, the file is converted and the password is preserved. The password will still be required to view or work with code. However, even if the VBA is secured, you (and others) will still be able to work with macros because they are in the Access file rather than the VBA project.

 There are mixed opinions about using a password to protect the code. Many developers think that using a password to protect the VBA is somewhat prone to corruption or being locked out of the code so they prefer to use an MDE or ACCDE file.

CONVERTING A REPLICATED DATABASE

Replication is not supported in the ACCDB file format. Instead, a more powerful and versatile alternative is offered using SharePoint services. But, if you need to preserve the benefits derived from replication, you can keep the Access 2000 and 2002–2003 MDB files. In some cases, however, the benefits of converting to the ACCDB file format will outweigh the benefits derived from replication. The following outlines the process for essentially creating a new database. And, as always, we recommend making copies of all files and data sets before embarking on the process.

 It's best to work with a copy of the Design Master after it has been fully synchronized, but the same process could be used with a replica. The issue is that only the data and objects that are in the file that you convert will be in the new ACCDB file. This alone should alert you to the importance of using the fully synchronized Design Master.

Here are some guidelines to note before you begin:

➤ Hidden and System objects in the replica must be visible so you can access the fields when you are re-creating the database.

➤ Create a copy of the database. This will require both Access 2010 and the version of Access that created the replica.

➤ Make interim copies as you proceed and allow plenty of time and patience for testing and adding features.

In general, the process is to use the original version of Access to display the hidden and system objects in the replica file, and then use Access 2010 to create the new application by importing the objects, except for the tables. The tables will be created using Make Table queries.

You will need to use the original version of Access to follow these steps.

1. Open the replica, preferably the Design Master.

2. Select Tools ➪ Options on the menu bar. The Options dialog box opens.

3. On the View tab, be sure Hidden Objects and System Objects are both selected (checked).

4. Click OK to save the changes.

5. Close the database and Access. The file is now ready for the objects to be imported into a new Database Container.

Open Access 2010 and ensure that the default file format is ACCDB. Follow these steps to create a copy of the replica:

1. Create a new blank database by selecting Blank Database and providing a filename. Be sure to accept or select the ACCDB format, and then click Create.

2. Delete the default Table1 by closing it.

3. In the Import group on the External Data tab, click Access. The Get External Data dialog box opens.

4. Browse to the folder containing the prepared replica file and select it by either double-clicking or selecting the file and then clicking Open. This returns you to the Get External Data dialog box.

5. Ensure that you have selected Import Tables, Queries, Forms Reports, Macros and Modules in the current database, and then click OK. The Import Objects window will then open.

6. On each tab, select the objects that you want to import. (If you want all of the objects, use the Select All button on each tab.) When all of the desired objects are selected, click OK. The wizard will import the objects and then offer the opportunity to save the import steps.

Selecting Yes enables you to give the process a name and description. If this import process will be repeated on a regular basis, it could even be scheduled as an Outlook task. After filling in the information, click Save Import. The Import Objects window will then close.

7. All the objects except for the tables are imported. Name and save the database.

8. Open another instance of Access 2010 and open the prepared replica database.

9. In the Macro & Codes group on the Create tab, click Query Design. This opens a new query in Design view.

10. Select the first table from the list, and click Add and then Close. The table is added to the query design window. Double-click the table's title bar to select all the fields, and then drag and drop the fields into the query grid. Although you don't want the s_Lineage and s_Generation fields in the new tables, the most efficient way to accomplish the task is to drag all of the fields into the query grid and then delete these two fields.

11. Click Make Table Query. In the Make Table dialog box, select the current table's name and then select Another Database. Browse to and select the newly created ACCDB. Click OK.

12. Click Run to create the table in the new database.

 If s_GUID is the primary key and it is referred to by the foreign keys in other tables, then s_GUID must be included in the new tables. If s_GUID is not used to establish relationships between tables, it is not needed in the new tables.

The new tables do not inherit the field properties or the primary key settings from the original database. Those need to be manually re-created:

1. Open a table in Design view. In the field list, select the field that should be the primary key, and then click Primary Key in the Tools group.

2. In the field list, select the field that requires an index. In the field's Properties pane, click the Indexed drop-down and select either YES (Duplicates OK) (if some values are repeated) or YES (No Duplicates). Continue this procedure through all the tables.

Finally, establish the table relationships as they were in the replica:

1. Click Relationships on the Database Tools tab.

2. Add the appropriate tables to the relationships window.

3. Drag a field from one table to another to create the relationship between the tables based on those two fields. The Edit Relationships dialog box enables you to enforce referential integrity and to specify a join type. When the relationships are established, click Close to close the window and return to the database objects.

4. Save and close the database. Make a copy and start testing.

As always, it is a good practice to split the database, either at this point or as soon as it is functioning properly.

ENABLING A DATABASE

As mentioned earlier, Access 2010 can work with Access 95 and 97 files. Basically, there are two options for working with the file: convert it or enable it. Converting creates a copy of the file in a newer format, as discussed earlier. However, in order to work with the file without converting it, you will need to enable the database.

There are some logical limitations when working with an enabled database. Considering that databases are not forward compatible, it makes sense that although you can use Access 2010 to work with an Access 95 or 97 file, you cannot use an Access 95 or 97 file to link to a table in an Access 2000 or newer database. Access 2010 will not convert a file to an Access 95 or 97 file format nor will it export the tables to an Access 95 or 97 file. However, you can move or copy (most) data from an Access 2010 table and paste it directly into a table in a legacy database.

Other concerns deal with the file format, mostly because many of the features of the new file formats were not available or supported in Access 95 or 97. For example, data that relies on Unicode compression may not convert correctly. And, Access 95 and 97 had a 256-character set, so they may not have equivalent characters for some of the characters in the new format. Additionally, in the 95 and 97 formats, `Number` fields do not have properties for `Decimal Places` and `Field Size`. These properties must be changed prior to conversion; the typical alternatives include `Single` or `Double` or changing the data type to `Currency`.

Enabling the Experience: Opening 95 or 97 Files with Access 2010

When Access 2010 opens an Access 95 or 97 file, it will display the Database Enhancement dialog box. This might be perceived as a polite way of encouraging users to convert (termed upgrade in this dialog box) the database so that it can take advantage of the new features. If you choose `Yes` (`Proceed With Enhancement`), Access 2010 will convert the file to the specified file format. Considering the age of the file, it is likely that it would benefit from a thorough review of the code and external dependencies. If the database is not enhanced, Access 2010 can still open the file and update records, but users will not be able to make any design changes. Remember that a data file should not be converted to a format that is newer than the oldest applications (front-end files) that will use it.

To enable the database, follow these steps:

1. Open Access 2010 and then click on a 95 or 97 `.mdb` file. The Database Enablement dialog box opens.

2. Click Yes, and the Save As dialog box opens.

3. Accept the default file location and filename or select the ones desired.

4. The enablement process will convert files to the default file format. However, the file format can easily be changed after the new file has been saved.

If errors are encountered, a message box will advise you that a table of conversion errors has been created. Here's an example of what you might see:

```
-3831: The current file format no longer supports user-level security. The
conversion or compaction process has removed any user-level permissions.
```

For those rare situations in which users still require a 95 or 97 file format, the only option is to enable the file. Enabling the database will let Access 2010 use the file, and the file will still be compatible with Access 95 and 97. It is remarkably quick and easy, using the following steps:

1. Open Access 2010 and select a 95 or 97 .mdb file. The Database Enablement dialog box opens.

2. Click No. The file will open in the Access 95 or 97 file format.

This works well for entering data and for connecting to a data file that is used by Access 95 or 97. The objects can be seen in Design view and the VBA Editor will display the code. Users can even make temporary modifications to objects, such as adding a text box to a form. However, when the object is closed, the design changes will not be saved.

ACCESS 2010: 64-BIT CONSIDERATIONS

As 64-bit systems become more mainstream, Microsoft has started to release both 32-bit and 64-bit versions of Office, providing you with an important decision to make at deployment. By default, Office 2010 will install the 32-bit version; which means that it requires an explicit choice and act to install a 64-bit version.

However, computers with 64-bit hardware must also have a 64-bit operating system in order to install the 64-bit version of Office. But that doesn't mean that just because a computer is running on a 64-bit hardware with a 64-bit operating system, that it is forced to run 64-bit applications. Indeed, it may be desirable to install 32-bit applications (software) on 64-bit systems.

64-bit Windows supports running 32-bit software in a special environment known as WOW64, or "Windows on Windows 64-bit." By installing 32-bit Office 2010 onto a 64-bit system, you can maintain compatibility with legacy databases that still depend on 32-bit components. This is especially important when the Access application uses ActiveX controls, COM Add-ins and objects, linked tables that depend on an ODBC driver, or API calls. Although there are 64-bit replacements available for ActiveX controls, COM Add-ins/objects, or ODBC drivers, you also need to consider that many users have not yet migrated to the 64-bit systems. Such factors could be very compelling arguments for choosing to stick to 32-bit Office 2010 even when you have a 64-bit system available. As you can see, switching to or integrating with 64-bit platforms and systems introduces numerous complex issues that will require further research if you are facing such a situation.

SharePoint 2010 requires a 64-bit system, and it is available only in 64-bit. This can be a significant factor to consider when moving to a new platform — especially if you might potentially host your own SharePoint site. Alternatively, you can use a hosted service and avoid the platform issues. Office 2010, both 32- and 64-bit, can publish to SharePoint with no restrictions. So from an Access perspective, you can use all of the new 2010 features without being concerned about whether it is 32- or 64-bit.

Practically speaking, the benefit of installing 64-bit Office distills down to this: You can make use of larger memory space, which is beneficial when you deal with large sets of data. The 32-bit system allows you to address 4GB of memory (less the amount needed by the operating system). Because the benefits of 64-bit become most evident when the processing requirements exceed 4GB, most of the databases may not realize much of a performance gain from being run within a 64-bit application, not even those with total records in the hundreds of thousands. This is another possible benefit, albeit indirect: The 64-bit Office enables Excel 2010 to handle much larger amount of data in its workbooks. So, if your Access database depends on automating Excel and dumping large amounts of data into Excel, you may see some benefits from using the 64-bit version of the Office.

It also should be noted that the decision to install a 32-bit or 64-bit Office is an either/or proposition; you cannot install both side-by-side. And, you may also encounter further restrictions based on other components present on the system. For example, if a 32-bit version of Excel Viewer or Access database engine (both available as a separate download from www.microsoft.com), is installed on the system, it may block 64-bit applications from being installed. Consult Appendix D for more information about 64-bit configurations.

Porting an Access Application to a 64-bit Platform

If a decision is reached that an application should be ported to or at least made available on a 64-bit platform, there are a few steps that may be required. For an ACCDB file that contains only Access objects and (most) VBA code, it is typically a simple matter of recompiling the VBA (which may be done automatically), and the file will be ready to use on a 64-bit platform. However, if an Access application links to an ODBC (or other) data source, you will need to provide drivers that match the bitness (32 or 64 bit) of the Access application.

In case of linked tables, the link may depend on ODBC drivers that are 32-bit. Generally speaking, the driver's bitness must match that of the client's. Therefore, there must be 64-bit drivers to replace 32-bit drivers. If no such drivers exist, then a 64-bit application will not be able to link to the source. In such situations, it may be best to remain on a 32-bit application. Fortunately, whenever a 64-bit version exists for the driver, there is usually no need to update the connection string of the linked tables.

Like the drivers, the bitness of the ActiveX controls and COM Add-ins must also match, so a suitable replacement should be found whenever an application uses any of those objects. You may contact the vendors who provided the tools for a 64-bit version, look for a replacement that is available in 64-bit, or, once again, stay with 32-bit applications.

Fortunately, API calls on VBA are fixable and do not require one to hope for the availability of 64-bit counterparts as Microsoft has already made most APIs available on the 64-bit platforms. However, there are two things you need to do to make the file acceptable on a 64-bit platform. First, you need to replace any references to a pointer data type from the usual Long data type to the LongPtr data type. Second, you need to mark the API calls as "safe." These two steps are necessary because, by convention, the data type of the pointer is dimensioned based on the platform it runs. So on a 32-bit platform, the pointer would be 4 bytes and likewise, on 64-bit, the same pointer would be 8 bytes. By design, Visual Basic aims to free developers from being concerned with managing pointers and manual memory management, a fruitful source for many bugs.

In the past, Visual Basic and VBA already had a 4-byte data type prior to transition from 16-bit to 32-bit so that was a non-issue for developers during that transition. However, you must now cope with the fact that VBA is introducing a pointer data type. So instead of using a Long data type, which would always be 4 bytes regardless of which platform it may run on, you should review API documentation and update the API declaration to use a LongPtr data type whenever a pointer or a handle is called out. For an example of how you would update your API declare, let's take a look at a type used by the ShellExecuteEx API function, SHELLEXECUTEINFO. Here's the declaration as you would have done in past:

```
Public Type SHELLEXECUTEINFO
    cbSize        As Long
    fMask         As Long
    Hwnd          As Long
    lpVerb        As String
    lpFile        As String
    lpParameters  As String
    lpDirectory   As String
    nShow         As Long
    hInstApp      As Long
    lpIDList      As Long
    lpClass       As String
    hkeyClass     As Long
    dwHotKey      As Long
    hIcon         As Long
    hProcess      As Long
End Type
```

It may be immediately obvious that the Hwnd parameter refers to a handle, which is a pointer, but there are also a few more. Here's the updated declaration for the same type:

```
Public Type SHELLEXECUTEINFO
    cbSize        As Long
    fMask         As Long
    Hwnd          As LongPtr
    lpVerb        As String
    lpFile        As String
    lpParameters  As String
    lpDirectory   As String
    nShow         As Long
    hInstApp      As LongPtr
    lpIDList      As LongPtr
    lpClass       As String
    hkeyClass     As LongPtr
    dwHotKey      As Long
    hIcon         As LongPtr
    hProcess      As LongPtr
End Type
```

So six parameters refer to a pointer data type and thus require you to use LongPtr instead. Note that you don't change other integer data types, even though VBA supports a new 8-byte integer data type, LongLong. Recall that the pointer data type is dimensioned based on the platform it runs. That does not happen for a plain integer data type so you should continue to use the same dimension as declared in the API at least until the API is revised explicitly to run only on the 64-bit platform. Also, if you look at the documentation, cbSize is of DWORD type, which is always 4 bytes regardless of the platform it is on. Therefore, using a LongPtr would not have been appropriate for this parameter, so you can't just replace every Long with a LongPtr.

There is one more aspect to consider: the cbSize parameter is used to determine the size of the structure and traditionally you have done this by using the Len() function, which will calculate the data types' size to provide the complete size for the SHELLEXECUTEINFO type as whole. On a 64-bit platform, this will no longer be reliable because of how the type has a Long followed by a LongPtr and this happens twice in the type. The members are aligned by an 8-byte boundary on a 64-bit platform and thus 4-byte padding is added to each Long parameter. Doing a Len() upon the SHELLEXECUTEINFO type would give you 104, which is 8 bytes too short. Thus, you should take care to use the LenB() function which counts bytes instead of characters and thus will account for the padding created and return the correct 112-byte length required for the cbSize parameter.

After you've accounted for all pointer data types, you will need to determine if the API needs to know the structure size. If so, you need to replace the Len() function with the LenB() function in those instances. That brings you to the final step, which is relatively easy: you'll need to mark the API calls as safe for pointers. For example, if you use the ShellExecuteEx function (which requires the type), the function would have been declared as follows in a 32-bit platform:

```
Declare Function ShellExecuteEx Lib "shell32.dll" Alias "ShellExecuteEx" _
    (SEI As SHELLEXECUTEINFO) As Long
```

You would add the PtrSafe keyword as shown here:

```
Declare PtrSafe Function ShellExecuteEx Lib "shell32.dll" Alias "ShellExecuteEx" _
    (SEI As SHELLEXECUTEINFO) As Long
```

Now the Declare statement is compatible for 64-bit. Note that you do not change the return value to LongPtr because it does not return a handle. Had you used the ShellExecute function instead, which does return a handle, you would have to change the return data type in the declaration.

Working in Mixed Bitness

It is possible that in some situations, you have some users who have 64-bit Office installed working beside others who are using 32-bit Office. Microsoft has provided some tools for you to develop applications that can be compatible across different platforms. A 64-bit ACCDB file with some VBA and no external dependencies can be seamlessly ported to 32-bit platforms and vice versa.

However, as discussed in the previous section, accommodations must be made for the file that has external dependencies. Microsoft has provided two compilation flags to use in helping to support both 32-bit and 64-bit platforms, WIN64 and VBA7. Within an environment where Access 2010 is used exclusively, you can make use of the WIN64 flag to help the application use the correct ActiveX control where the 64-bit replacements exist. With regard to drivers that are used to manage linked tables, if a 64-bit counterpart exists, the connection string need not be changed or updated as the new 64-bit driver will appear to have the same identity as its 32-bit counterpart; thus, it will be used correctly on both platforms. If, for whatever reasons, the 64-bit driver is not a direct replacement of its 32-bit driver and thus it is identified differently, you might prefer to treat it in the same way as ActiveX controls, using the WIN64 flag to determine which drivers to use and manually re-link the tables via VBA code or using different DSNs to support both configurations.

Regarding API calls, PtrSafe keyword is required for the 64-bit platform. With that in mind, we strongly encourage you to take time to update all API declarations within the application to use the new pointer data type and thus make it compatible for both the 32-bit and 64-bit platforms for

Access 2010. Thus, the modified ShellExecuteEx function sample discussed previously will run on both platforms.

In cases where you must support mixed bitness and mixed versions, however, you must also make use of the VBA7 flag to rectify the fact that earlier VBA versions do not support either the new PtrSafe keyword or the LongPtr data type. If you go back to the ShellExecuteEx function example, you would have to keep both declarations separated out by the VBA7 flag. Refer to Appendix D for a complete explanation and examples of how to use the new compilation flags.

For ACCDE files, you must create a version that is compatible with the target system. You can create only a 32-bit version ACCDE on a 32-bit machine, and create only a 64-bit version ACCDE on a 64-bit machine. This means you cannot interchange the ACCDE version between 32- and 64-bit systems as you can with ACCDB files. So, if you intend to deploy ACCDE files to both platforms, you must maintain two ACCDE files for each of the platforms. It should also be noted that while Office 2010 supports converting MDB files to MDE files, the 32-bit version of Access cannot run a MDE created by 64-bit Access 2010.

SUMMARY

This chapter discussed the major factors that need to be considered when you plan an upgrade to Access 2010. In addition to evaluating the benefits of the new features, you'll also need to consider the compatibility with other versions of Office and with the operating system. You'll need to determine whether you want to work on a 32- or 64-bit operating system, or if it might be a mixed environment. On top of that, you may be forced to address additional compatibility issues if 64-bit environment is added to the equation.

As we talked about the compatibility between different versions, we explained features that will be affected by upgrading to, converting from, or running on a different platform. We also provided the steps for converting and working with files from prior versions, including ways to address special configurations, such as using the user and group security or replication.

Now that you've had an introduction to Access, the new features, and how Access 2010 works with files from prior versions, you are ready to start delving deeper into the program itself and learn how to leverage the power of Access to create powerful and flexible database solutions. A great place to start is in Chapter 4, where we show you how to create and leverage macros.

Macros in Access 2010

WHAT'S IN THIS CHAPTER?

➤ When to use Macros in an Access application

➤ An in depth look at the new Macro Designer in Access 2010

➤ How to leverage data macros that add logic to tables and enable new scenarios that don't require VBA code

For many years, Access has supported two different ways of accomplishing programming tasks — Visual Basic for Applications (VBA) and macros. The term "macro" as it relates to other Office applications such as Word or Excel, typically refers to VBA. In Access, however, the term "macro" means something else entirely.

Compared with VBA, a macro in Access provides a reduced set of functionality for achieving certain tasks. These tasks might be as simple as opening a form or report, or something more complex such as running a series of queries in a particular order and then exporting the data to Excel. In some situations, one of these tasks may also include calling into VBA code.

This chapter starts out by covering some of the basic differences between VBA and macros in Access 2010. We'll take a look at scenarios in which using macros may be more interesting than using VBA and review some of the many new features that are available related to macros in Access 2010. Finally, we take a look at some common scenarios in which you might use macros in Access and how to write these macros. These examples will be in the Access 2010 macro format, and not in VBA code.

VBA VERSUS MACROS IN ACCESS

The majority of this book takes a look at using VBA in Access 2010. You are probably eager to get started and to keep reading! Before doing so, however, you might also consider one alternative to using VBA code: macros. Like VBA, an Access macro allows you to perform a variety of operations in response to some event such as the click of a button or the loading of a form or report.

If you've programmed in Word or Excel, you know that you can create a macro by starting the macro recorder and performing the desired steps. When you stop the macro recorder, all of the operations you've performed — from mouse clicks to keyboard strokes to menu selections — are recorded and saved in VBA code. You can then run the macro at a later time by selecting it from the Macros dialog box or in response to a keyboard or Ribbon command. After you've recorded your macro, you can examine the VBA code behind the macro by simply choosing Edit from the Macros dialog box. This is one of the easiest ways to learn some VBA code within Word or Excel. For example, if you want to know the VBA code to insert three lines of text at the end of your Word document, just create a Word document, start recording a macro, and type your three lines of text. You'll end up with code that looks similar to the following:

```
Sub InsertNames()
'
' InsertNames Macro
'
    Selection.TypeText Text:="Rob Cooper"
    Selection.TypeParagraph
    Selection.TypeText Text:="Senior Test Lead"
    Selection.TypeParagraph
    Selection.TypeText Text:="Microsoft Corporation"
End Sub
```

As you can see, you need to know some keywords before you can program Word to do what you want in VBA. Recording a macro in Word first, then perusing the commands, can help you to figure out how to write more sophisticated code directly in the VBA Editor. TypeText, for example, is the method of the Selection object that allows you to enter your own text in the document. TypeParagraph inserts a carriage return in the document. These are just two of the many methods you can use with the Selection object. While few programmers ever need to use every method of an object, you can write better VBA code by familiarizing yourself with some of the most frequently used methods of the objects you'll deal with.

Although Word and Excel provide the capability to record macros, Access does not. To write VBA code in Access, you just jump right in and code. However, if you aren't quite ready for VBA code, you can still create detailed macros using the Macro Designer in Access. The only limitation is that you can't record a macro; you must create it yourself step-by-step.

Before going deeper into macros in Access 2010, let's take a look at some of the advantages of using VBA versus macros.

Benefits of Using VBA

While macros are perfectly acceptable and even recommended in certain situations, there are some advantages to using VBA for many scenarios. The following is a list of some of the advantages you'll enjoy by using VBA instead of a macro.

➤ **Speed:** A one-action macro may execute faster than the equivalent VBA code. However, running a complex macro with 10 or 12 actions usually takes significantly longer than the equivalent code. VBA code is fast. If you're designing an end-user application, you definitely need to be concerned with speed. If your users see the hourglass for even more than 5 or 6 seconds, their perception will be that your application is slow.

➤ **Functionality:** Although macros enable you to do many things, there are also things that you *cannot* do natively in macros. For example, how would you play a sound other than the default "beep" or open an HTML file in response to a button click? The types of applications that can be written using VBA are pretty much limited only by imagination (or perhaps by budget). By using external references and libraries, you can interact with other applications such as Word and Excel, or other non-Microsoft products. You could open a Web browser and navigate to a particular website, or open almost any file stored on your computer or a network drive.

➤ **Control:** With VBA, you can exercise almost complete control over your code. Instead of having to let macro actions perform the work, you can control each step of the process in VBA. Some tasks — such as dynamically creating an ADO connection based on user input — simply cannot be accomplished using macros. Some tasks are possible, but considerably more difficult. Asking for a variety of variables to input into an equation, for instance, can be easily accomplished using VBA, but is rather difficult using a macro. (Macros would require a `TempVar` or hidden form to store the data.) Macros cannot easily run a different set of actions for each user of your application. VBA can accomplish this task with ease.

➤ **Interaction with other applications:** When using VBA in Access, you're not limited to merely programming Microsoft Access. You can add references to other object libraries such as Word, Excel, Outlook, and even non-Microsoft programs including accounting packages, drafting programs, and graphics programs.

Benefits of Using Macros

VBA has been the de facto standard for programming Access applications for a number of years. That said, there are some compelling reasons to consider using macros in Access 2010:

➤ **Access Services:** If you're building an application to run in the browser using Access Services, one of the things you'll notice is that VBA is not available on the SharePoint server. Logic running on the server needs to be predictable and must protect the server itself at all costs. As a result, macros provide a nice way to extend applications that run in the browser, while attempting to maintain security and reliability on the server.

➤ **Disabled mode:** By default, beginning with Access 2007, databases are opened in a mode where VBA code does not run for security reasons. We call this disabled mode, to indicate that VBA code is disabled. Changes were required to macros to make applications relatively functional without running code. Together, these two features make macros more viable than in previous versions, and the templates in Access were designed with Disabled mode in mind. As mentioned in Chapter 1, most of the new templates run using safe macro actions and without code.

➤ **Easy to write:** With macros becoming first-class citizens for Access Services applications, the authoring experience also needed to be improved. As you'll see later in this chapter, the new Macro Designer makes it even easier to write macros.

➤ **Embedded macros:** It is possible to have a macro that is embedded as part of the properties for a control. This means that you can copy a control such as a command button, and the macro code behind the button will be pasted along with the button itself.

➤ **Variables are not reset:** In VBA, unhandled errors will reset public variables. This causes many problems in an application where you may depend on the values of these variables downstream. With macros, variables that are set using a `TempVar` keep their values even when an error occurs in the macro because the `TempVars` collection is an in-memory collection that exists until Access is closed or you call either the `RemoveTempVar` or `RemoveAllTempVars` actions. We'll take a closer look at variables in macros later in this chapter.

Does that mean that you shouldn't use VBA for your solutions? Of course not! But it does mean that in certain scenarios such as a situation in which you might not want code to run, or you are looking for simple lightweight solutions, macros might provide a reasonable alternative.

TYPES OF MACROS

There are three different types of macros in Access 2010 that you should be familiar with. These are discussed in the following sections.

Macro Objects

Access macros that are listed as objects in the Navigation Pane are referred to as standalone macros or simply as macro objects. This is because they exist as their own distinct objects and are not associated with any controls. Macro objects are often used to carry out a reusable series of commands such as running several queries in succession or exporting data.

Because this type of macro is not associated with a particular control, they are also often created when they will need to be reused from multiple forms or reports.

Embedded Macros

An embedded macro is a macro object that is stored directly in an event property for a form, report, or control. These macros have two advantages over VBA and macro objects. First, if you have ever copied a control that had code behind it and then wished that the code also was duplicated, this feature is for you! Because these macros are part of a control's properties, the macro that is associated with a control event is also copied.

Second, you no longer need separate macro objects that perform small, simple one-off tasks. These macros can be associated directly with an event property.

 Embedded macros cannot be referenced from other macros. If you need to re-use the actions that are defined by a macro you should create a separate macro object.

To create an embedded macro, choose Macro Builder from an event property's Choose Builder dialog box. Once you create the macro, the event property changes to `[Embedded Macro]`.

To take advantage of these benefits, the wizards in Access 2010 are updated to create embedded macros in the new format database (ACCDB). This is because VBA code is not allowed to execute in Disabled mode, meaning that wizard-generated code would not run unless a database is trusted. By using macros, the wizards now allow the application to run as much as possible in Disabled mode without failing. For backward compatibility, VBA code is still created using the wizards in the previous file formats (MDB and ADP), but they have been updated to use the `RunCommand` method where appropriate. That's right — the wizards no longer create code that calls `DoMenuItem`! For more information about safe macros, please read the section titled "Additional Macro Changes" later in this chapter.

Data Macros

Access 2010 introduces a new type of macro called a *data macro*. A data macro is similar to a trigger in SQL Server in the sense that you can run a series of actions when a record in a table is inserted, updated, or deleted. These actions are associated with the table itself, meaning that regardless of how the record is inserted, updated, or deleted, the data macro will run.

Data macros are available for databases running in Access 2010, but are also designed to run for applications running in the browser with Access Services. We take a closer look at data macros later in this chapter.

CREATING MACROS IN ACCESS 2010

You can use macros for a variety of tasks in Access. Although most developers prefer to write code than to create macros, that's not always the easiest method of automation. For example, how many times have you written the following code?

```
Private Sub CommandButton_Click
    DoCmd.OpenForm "FormName"
End Sub
```

Any code in your database is code that you have to maintain. Chances are that nothing will go wrong with this code, but the code still needs to be maintained as a part of the overall application. Using a single macro with submacros, you could create one place in your application that is responsible for opening forms or reports. This might look something like the macro shown in Figure 4-1.

Access 2010 includes 86 built-in macros. Many have additional arguments that you can use to extend their functionality. For example, the `OpenForm` macro action requires you to select an existing form in your database. You can also choose whether to open the form in Form view or Design view. Other macro actions have similar required and optional arguments.

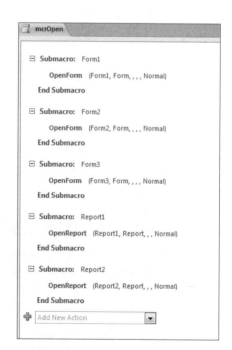

FIGURE 4-1

To create a new macro in Access 2010, click the Macro button on the Create tab of the Ribbon. Access displays the new Macro window, as shown in Figure 4-2.

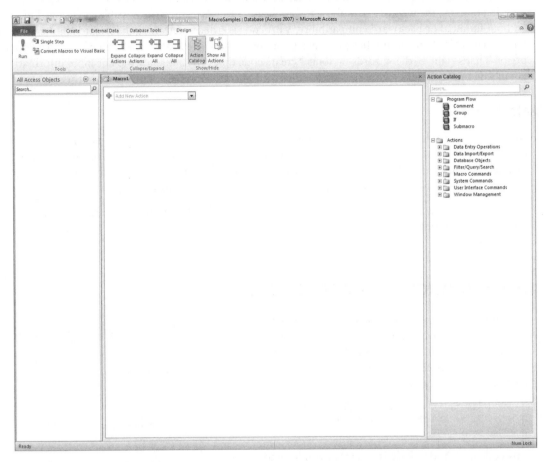

FIGURE 4-2

MACRO EXAMPLES IN THIS CHAPTER

This chapter will show examples using macros in Access 2010 containing macro constructs, actions, and arguments. The general format we will use to illustrate these examples is as follows:

```
ActionName1
    ArgumentName1: ArgumentValue1
    ArgumentName2: ArgumentValue2

ActionName2
    ArgumentName1: ArgumentValue1
```

Arguments for an action will be indented below the action and the value for the argument will follow the name. For readability, we will separate actions with a blank line.

For macro actions that are defined in a construct, the construct will appear at the first level and actions and arguments will be indented from there as follows:

```
MacroConstruct

    ActionName1
        ArgumentName1: ArgumentValue1
        ArgumentName2: ArgumentValue2

    ActionName2
        ArgumentName1: ArgumentValue1

End MacroConstruct
```

This is intended to mirror how macros will appear in the Macro Designer in Access 2010.

New Macro Designer

When you open the Macro Designer in Access 2010 for the first time, you'll immediately notice that things are a bit different. Access macros are first-class citizens for programming and adding logic to applications that run with Access Services. As such, the Macro Designer was re-written to make writing macros easier than ever.

If you wrote macros in earlier versions of Access, you may have noticed that the previous Macro Designer was a bit difficult to use. More specifically, the Macro Designer in Access 2010 addresses the following issues:

➤ Arguments are contained within their actions such that when you write a macro, you don't need to switch between different parts of the screen. This makes writing macros in Access 2010 feel more like writing code.

➤ The `If...Else...Else If` construct makes it easier to read and write conditional blocks of macros.

➤ Macro actions have been renamed and categorized to make them easier to find. A new macro action catalog was added to make finding them easier as well.

➤ Certain arguments of the `RunCommand` action such as `SaveRecord` and `Refresh` have been promoted to appear as actions because they are commonly used.

➤ The F5 keyboard shortcut was added to run a macro.

➤ Context menu items were added to wrap actions in an If block, Group, or Submacro.

➤ A new XML format was created for macros to be able to share them in e-mail or on websites via copy and paste.

Let's take a closer look at the new Macro Designer and how you can start using it to design macros in your applications.

Adding Actions

There are a few ways to add actions to a macro. The easiest way is to use the drop-down box at the bottom of the Macro Designer, as shown in Figure 4-3.

This drop-down also appears at the bottom of a macro construct, such as the `If...End If` construct, as shown in Figure 4-4.

In addition to the Add New Action drop-down, the Macro Designer includes a new feature called the Action Catalog. As the name suggests, the Action Catalog contains all the macros that can be used in a macro. Macros are categorized as shown in Figure 4-5 to make them easier to find. To add a macro using the Action Catalog, simply drag it to the macro surface.

If there were existing macros in the database, they would appear in the Action Catalog under the item called In This Database. Using the context menu for the items in this folder allows you to copy an existing macro into the current macro, or to add the `RunMacro` action to call the existing macro. The Action Catalog also has a search box at the top that enables searching for a macro action. The search functionality searches for text using the name or description of a macro, as well as the name of the macro as it existed in Access 2007. For example, the `MsgBox` macro action was renamed to `MessageBox` in the Macro Designer in Access 2010 for improved readability. You can still search for `MsgBox` and find it using the Action Catalog.

Another way to add macros to the new Macro Designer is by simple copy and paste. Actions and arguments in the Macro Designer are represented using an XML format, which is discussed later in this chapter in the section "Sharing Macros Using Access 2010."

FIGURE 4-3

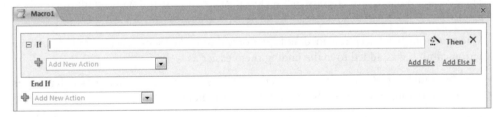

FIGURE 4-4

Macro Constructs

Macros in earlier versions of Access provided simple constructs such as conditions and macro names. These constructs have been made easier in Access 2010, and a couple of new constructs have been added.

If...Else...Else If

The Macro Designer in Access 2007 and earlier versions included a column named Conditions that allowed you to conditionally execute a macro action. If you wanted to repeat the condition, you could either repeat the entire expression, or use ellipses (. . .) in the row below the expression. The use of the ellipses was not discoverable, so the Macro Designer in Access 2010 includes an `If...End If` macro block, as shown in Figure 4-6.

As you can see in Figure 4-6, you enter an expression in the space following the `If` statement. You can type this expression directly, or use the Expression Builder.

In addition to the `If` statement, you can easily add an `Else` statement or one or more `Else If` statements. The Macro Designer will show additional statements in the `If` block, as shown in Figure 4-7.

FIGURE 4-5

FIGURE 4-6

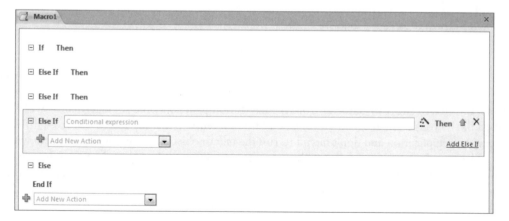

FIGURE 4-7

Macros that include the `Else If` *or* `Else` *constructs in Access 2010 are not compatible with Access 2007 or earlier. Running or designing these macros from within Access 2007 or earlier will result in an error.*

Submacros

Submacros are named macros within a single macro object. These were previously defined using the Macro Names column in Access 2007 and earlier. Because they are named, they can be called as distinct macros themselves using the following syntax:

```
MacroName.SubmacroName
```

Submacros are useful for creating related functionality in a single macro object. Some examples of this might include:

➤ Opening forms and reports

➤ Running groups of queries in succession

➤ Exporting tables or queries to Excel

Submacros are great because they allow you to create multiple macros without cluttering the navigation pane with many different macro objects. That said, there are a couple of things to be aware of when using submacros. First, there is no way to call a submacro inside an embedded macro. You can define a submacro in an embedded macro, but it can only be called from the OnError macro action within the same embedded macro. Second, if you run a macro object that contains submacros, only the first submacro will run. For example, consider the following macro, which contains two submacros:

Available for download on Wrox.com

```
Submacro: Sub1
    MessageBox
        Message: This is submacro Sub1
End Submacro

Submacro: Sub2
    MessageBox
        Message: This is submacro Sub2
End Submacro
```

code snippet MacroSamples

If you run this macro either by name or from the navigation pane, only the submacro Sub1 will run. Most likely, you're using submacros to add additional reuse to macros and to call from different places in an application and don't intend to run the macro object directly. In this scenario, we tend to add a MessageBox action followed by a StopMacro action at the top of the macro before the first submacro as shown in the following code. This way, if the macro is run on its own, a message appears that indicates this was unintended.

Available for download on Wrox.com

```
MessageBox
    Message: This macro defines Submacros only and is not intended for direct use.

StopMacro

Submacro: Sub1
    MessageBox
        Message: This is submacro Sub1
```

```
End Submacro

Submacro: Sub2
    MessageBox
        Message: This is submacro Sub2
End Submacro
```

code snippet MacroSamples

The StopMacro action is not required as macro execution stops at the first submacro, but it makes it clear as to the intention of the macro so we like to include it.

Groups

The Group construct is new to macros in Access 2010 and provides a simple mechanism for grouping actions together so that they may be collapsed and expanded for readability. They do not affect macro execution. If you run a macro that contains groups, all actions will run regardless of whether they are in a group.

Macros with the Group construct in Access 2010 can be executed in Access 2007 but not designed.

Comments

The Comment construct in macro replaces the Description column in macros from Access 2007 and earlier. Comments are represented using a syntax found in the C/C++ languages as follows:

```
/* This is a comment */
```

Comments improve the readability of your macros and also make the macro feel more like code, as shown in Figure 4-8.

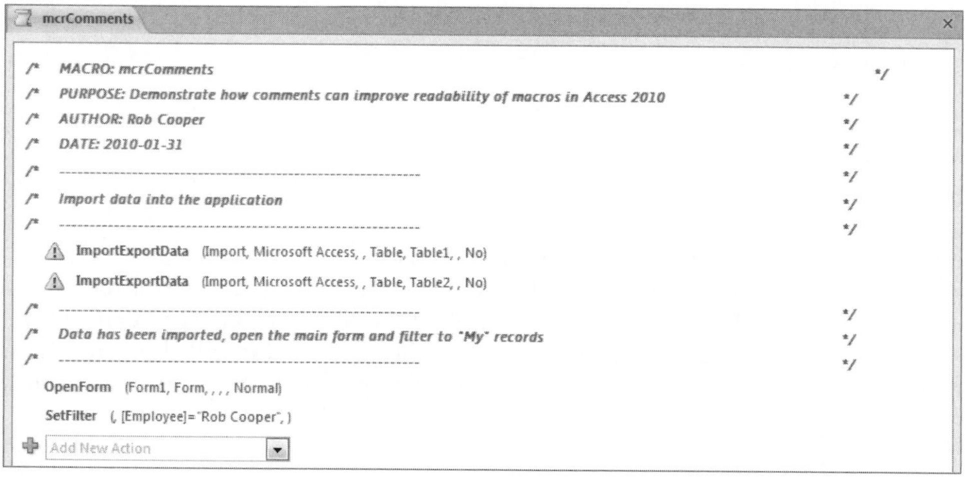

FIGURE 4-8

You can create comments by typing or choosing Comment in the Add New Action drop-down, by selecting Comment under Program Flow in the Action Catalog, or by typing comment characters directly in the Add New Action drop-down as follows:

```
' You can enter a VBA comment character to add a comment
// You can enter C-style single-line comments
```

Carriage returns in comments are not displayed using line breaks so we've used multiple comments to display comments on separate lines. The actions are also collapsed for readability.

Parameters

Parameter queries are a powerful technique for creating dynamic forms and reports with varying data. When Access encounters either an implicit or explicit parameter, it will prompt with the familiar Enter Parameter Value dialog box. Because this dialog box does not exist in Access Services, there needed to be some way to provide parameter values to forms and reports that use parameter queries. To accommodate parameter queries, you can supply parameters to certain macro actions, as shown in Figure 4-9.

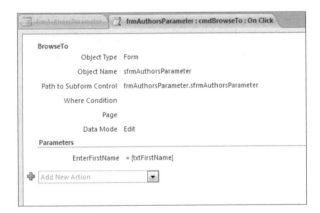

FIGURE 4-9

The names of the parameters are supplied when you choose the `BrowseTo`, `OpenForm`, `OpenReport`, or `OpenQuery` actions. If you change the name of the parameters after creating the macro, you can click the Update Parameters link in the Macro Designer to update the names of the parameters. Be cautious when doing this however — this will clear the data in the parameters as well, so you should copy the expression passed to the parameter if you will need it later.

EXPLICIT VS. IMPLICIT PARAMETERS

An explicit parameter is one that appears in the Parameters dialog box for a query. An implicit parameter does not appear in this dialog box. Generally speaking, if you see unexpected parameter prompts in Access, it means that there was something that Access did not recognize. These are treated as implicit parameters.

It is good practice to use explicit parameters. First, using explicit parameters allows you to specify the data type of the parameter. This creates the PARAMETERS statement in the SQL behind the query. Next, when you define an explicit parameter, Access 2010 will provide AutoComplete support in the Expression Builder, making them easier to use. Lastly, explicit parameters are supported by Access Services whereas implicit parameters are not.

Additional Macro Changes

By default, Access 2010 shows only those macro actions that have been deemed *safe*. Generally speaking, a safe action is one that does not perform any of the following tasks:

➤ Change data

➤ Create or delete objects

➤ Update or alter the Access user interface

➤ Access the Windows file system

➤ Run a SQL statement

➤ Send e-mail

Actions that fall under these categories include ImportExportData (formerly TransferText, creates a file), CopyObject (creates a new object), DeleteObject (removes an object), or RunSQL (can be used to add or remove objects, or update or delete data).

To see the list of all possible actions, click the Show All Actions button in the Ribbon. All actions and RunMenuCommand action arguments are then available for choosing. When an unsafe action is selected, the Macro Designer displays a warning icon in the column next to the action name, as shown in Figure 4-10.

It is important to note that some actions can be deemed safe until you change one of their action arguments. In

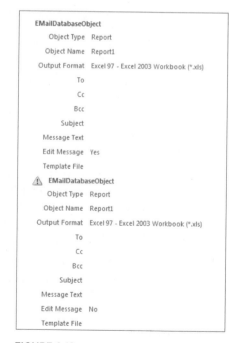

FIGURE 4-10

the example in Figure 4-9, the `EMailDatabaseObject` (formerly `SendObject`) action is deemed safe until you change the `Edit Message` action argument to `No`. That's because it is safe to send e-mail when the e-mail message is opened first because the person running the macro has the chance to cancel the message if sending it was unexpected.

> *The Show All Actions item in the Ribbon has no effect for Web macros in a Web database. This is because Access Services will not run those actions that are considered unsafe in Access 2010.*

Sharing Macros Using Access 2010

It's common practice to share VBA code using e-mail, newsgroups, or community websites. VBA code lends itself well to copy and paste by using the Visual Basic Editor (VBE). If you copied a macro to the clipboard in Access 2007 or earlier, the only place where it could be pasted was in Access. There was no text-based format that could be pasted for sharing. Access 2010 addresses this by creating a new XML-based format for macros in the Macro Designer.

If you copy the `MessageBox` action from the Macro Designer and paste it into Notepad, you should see something like this:

```xml
<?xml version="1.0" encoding="UTF-16" standalone="no"?>
<UserInterfaceMacros xmlns="http://schemas.microsoft.com/office/accessservices/
    2009/04/application">
  <UserInterfaceMacro>
    <Statements>
      <Action Name="MessageBox">
        <Argument Name="Message">This is in Group1</Argument>
      </Action>
    </Statements>
  </UserInterfaceMacro>
</UserInterfaceMacros>
```

Details about this format are beyond the scope of this book, but as you can see, by having a text-based format you can now share macros with coworkers and others in the Access community via e-mail, newsgroups, community websites, Facebook, Twitter, and so on.

If you copy this XML to the clipboard and paste it into the Macro Designer, you should have a new macro action, as shown in Figure 4-11.

FIGURE 4-11

Running Macros

You've already seen one way to run a macro from the navigation pane, but there are a few other ways as well. One of the common uses for a macro is in response to the click event of a command button on a form. To associate a macro with the click event of a command button, use the following steps:

1. Add a command button to the design of a new form, or choose a command button on an existing form.

2. Click the Property Sheet button on the Ribbon button to display the Property Sheet for the command button.

3. Click the Event tab of the Property Sheet.

4. Click in the `OnClick` property of the Property Sheet to display the drop-down list.

5. From the drop-down list, choose the name of your macro. (All macros including submacros in your database are included in the drop-down list.)

6. Save and open your form. Clicking the command button runs each action in the macro sequentially.

You can also call macros from within your code. You might wonder why you would ever do that. After all, you're already writing code — why not just write code to accomplish the steps in the macro? Well, there's no definitive answer to that question, except to say that if you already have a perfectly good macro that does what you need, why not use it? You can run an existing macro in code using the following method:

```
DoCmd.RunMacro MacroName, [RepeatCount], [RepeatExpression]
```

The `RepeatCount` argument specifies the number of times to run the macro, and the `RepeatExpression` argument specifies the expression to evaluate when running the macro. The macro will run until the expression evaluates to `False`, or until the `RepeatCount` argument is hit, whichever comes first.

Debugging Macros

You can debug your macros by enabling Single Step in the macro in question. Single step was available in macros in previous versions of Access but was added as an action in Access 2007. By using the `SingleStep` action, you can conditionally step through macros using the Macro Single Step dialog box, as shown in Figure 4-12.

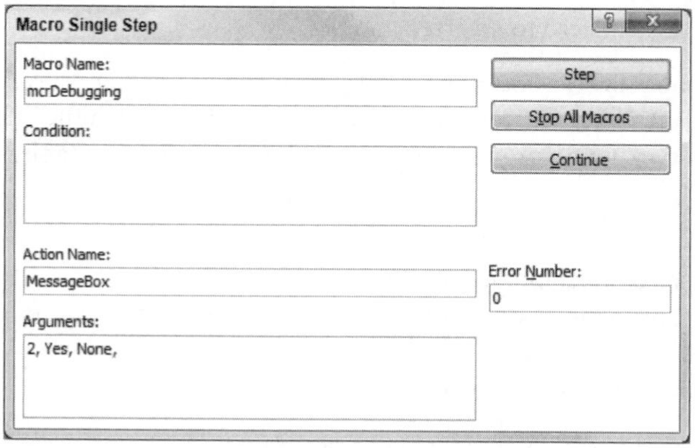

FIGURE 4-12

The SingleStep *method is available on the* DoCmd *object in VBA but this has no effect when running VBA code.*

The Single Step dialog box contains the following information:

➤ Name of the macro

➤ Condition, if any

➤ Name of the action and argument values

➤ Error number

Unfortunately the SingleStep macro action will only enable debugging — it will not disable it — so what do you do if you want to turn off debugging in the same macro? Well, it turns out you can use the RunMenuCommand action with the SingleStepCommand argument to do this.

Now that you've gone into the basics of how to create, run, and debug macros in Access 2010, let's take a closer look at the different types of macros and the types of things you can do with them.

MACRO OBJECTS AND EMBEDDED MACROS

As you have learned, macro objects can start to replace some of the VBA code in your database in certain scenarios. Let's start looking at how you can begin using macros as a part of your applications to accomplish tasks in the user interface. Of course, this is still a book about VBA, but by using new features that were added to macros in Access 2007, macros may become more attractive and feasible than they were in the past. These new features include error handling, embedded macros, and TempVars.

Error Handling

Error handling is often the primary reason that developers have steered clear from Access macros. In previous versions of Access, error handling in macros was simply not possible. When a macro encountered an error, there was no way to redirect the macro to an error handler.

Macros in Access 2010 include error handling using the OnError, SingleStep, and ClearMacroError macro actions, and the MacroError object. The OnError statement defines the error-handling behavior for a macro action and includes two action arguments described in the following table.

ARGUMENT	DESCRIPTION
Go to	Determines how errors are propagated by an action. Next: Moves to the next line in the macro. This is similar to On Error Resume Next. Macro Name: Jumps to the named macro. Fail: Aborts the macro and throws the macro error.
Macro Name	Name of a macro in the current macro group that handles errors.

The `MacroError` object is similar to the Error object in VBA, with the difference being that it is only available in a macro. Figure 4-13 shows the new macro error handling features in action.

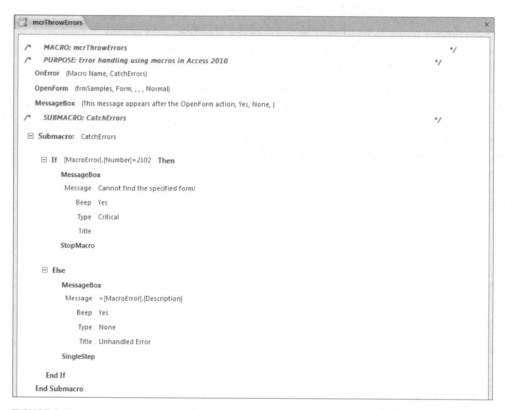

FIGURE 4-13

In this example, the `OnError` action redirects macro errors to the macro named `CatchErrors` in this macro group. This macro tests the `Number` property of the `MacroError` object to display a custom error message, and then clears the error and exits the macro. If we receive an error other than `2102`, the `Description` property of the `MacroError` object is displayed so we can do additional troubleshooting.

Variables

Variables were another reason that many Access developers have traditionally avoided using macros. Prior to Access 2007, there was no way to create a variable that could be used in a macro, let alone between macros. Access 2007 introduced the `TempVars` collection, which was the first step toward making variables available to macros. However, there are now two new ways to use variables in macros in Access 2010 — `LocalVars` and `ReturnVars`. Each type of variable is defined in the following sections.

TempVars

Access 2007 added a new object called `TempVar` that is contained in the `TempVars` collection. A `TempVar` object is simply a name/value pair that can be referenced in macros.

You can use three macro actions to work with `TempVars`. The first, `SetTempVar`, is used to create a new `TempVar`. To remove a `TempVar`, you can use the `RemoveTempVar` action. Finally, you can clear the `TempVars` collection by calling the `RemoveAllTempVars` action.

`TempVars` are pretty cool on their own, but you can also work with them in expressions in queries, forms, and reports. You can even work with them in VBA, meaning that you can now pass data between your macros and your VBA code. Where you might have used a hidden form or global variables in the past, you can now use `TempVar`. Once you create some `TempVar` objects, you can use the following code to list the `TempVar` objects from VBA:

```
' Demonstrates communication between macros
' and VBA using TempVars
Function ShowTempVars()
    Dim tv      As TempVar
    Dim strVars As String

    ' Build the TempVars string
    For Each tv In Application.TempVars
        strVars = strVars & tv.Name & " = " & tv.Value & vbCrLf
    Next

    ' display
    MsgBox strVars, vbInformation
End Function
```

LocalVars

The name `TempVars` suggests that the variables defined in this collection are temporary, but this is not the case. Variables in the `TempVars` collection exist in memory until the database is closed or until they are removed. In order to have a variable that was only in scope until the macro completed, a new collection was needed. Macros can now define local variables called a `LocalVar` as a part of the `LocalVars` collection. These exist in the memory for a given macro, meaning that two macros can define the same name of a `LocalVar` with different values.

Scope of TempVars and LocalVars

To see how `TempVars` and `LocalVars` work, let's consider two macros: `mcrVariables1` and `mcrVariables2`. These macros are defined as follows:

MCRVARIABLES1

```
SetTempVar
    Name: TempVar1
    Expression: "This is TempVar1"

SetLocalVar
    Name: LocalVar1
```

```
        Expression: "FIRST MACRO"

    RunMacro
        Macro Name: mcrVariables2

    MessageBox
        Message: =[TempVars]![TempVar1]
        Title: Read TempVar AFTER RemoveTempVar

    MessageBox
        Message: =[LocalVars]![LocalVar1]
        Title: Read LocalVar - Should be FIRST MACRO
```

code snippet MacroSamples

MCRVARIABLES2

Available for
download on
Wrox.com

```
    MessageBox
        Message: =[TempVars]![TempVar1]
        Title: Read TempVar

    RemoveTempVar
        Name: TempVar1

    SetLocalVar
        Name: LocalVar1
        Expression: ="SECOND MACRO"

    MessageBox
        Message: =[LocalVars]![LocalVar1]
        Title: LocalVar1, from mcrVariables2
```

code snippet MacroSamples

The first macro defines a TempVar named TempVar1 and a LocalVar named LocalVar1, and then calls the second macro, which reads the variable in the MsgBox before removing it with the RemoveTempVar action.

The second macro then sets a LocalVar using the name LocalVar1, which was also defined by the first macro. The second macro then displays the value of LocalVar1, which was set in the second macro.

When the second macro completes, the first macro continues to run and displays the value of TempVar1. This value is now Null because it was removed by the second macro. Lastly, it reads the value of LocalVar1, which was defined earlier in the first macro.

ReturnVars

There are many times in an application when you want to read a value from a table and use it somewhere else. This is true for applications running in Access itself and in the browser. For example, you might receive an input from a text box on a form, and need to retrieve the ID number that matches the input. Another place where you might want to return a value is from a data macro that performs some calculation across a set of data.

To return a value, you can use the SetReturnVar action, which adds to the ReturnVars collection. The SetReturnVar action is used in a data macro to return a value from a table to a macro object or embedded macro. The overall workflow goes something like this.

1. The macro object calls the RunDataMacro action to execute the specified data macro.

2. The data macro in question performs some calculation or retrieves a value. It then calls SetReturnVar to the value to return.

3. The macro object then uses the ReturnVars collection to retrieve the value.

There are a couple of things to be aware of with the ReturnVars collection. First, the values in the collection are only available in macros that run in the user interface — that is, macro objects or embedded macros. These values cannot be used in expressions on forms or reports. Second, the return value can only be used in the macro that called it. In other words, you cannot call RunDataMacro from one macro and use the ReturnVar in another macro. Even with these limitations, ReturnVars are still a valuable tool for developing using macros and data macros.

Macro Actions and Arguments

There are 86 macro actions in Access 2010, including those that are unsafe and do not run in Access Services. When you add in the arguments that can be used with the RunMenuCommand action, hundreds of different actions can be defined in a macro. The following table shows some of the macro actions that are most commonly used.

ACTION NAME ACCESS 2010	ACTION NAME ACCESS 2007	DESCRIPTION	NEW?	WEB?
ApplyFilter	ApplyFilter	Applies a filter to the currently open object.	No	No
BrowseTo	N/A	Navigates to the specified form or report.	Yes	Yes
CloseDatabase	CloseDatabase	Closes the database.	No	No
CloseWindow	Close	Closes the specified object window.	No	Yes
DeleteRecord	RunCommand DeleteRecord	Deletes the current record.	No	Yes
DisplayHourglassPointer	Hourglass	Sets or clears the hourglass cursor.	No	No

ACTION NAME ACCESS 2010	ACTION NAME ACCESS 2007	DESCRIPTION	NEW?	WEB?
EMailDatabaseObject	SendObject	Sends an object in the database as an attachment in an e-mail.	No	No
ExportWithFormatting	OutputTo	Exports an object in the database in the specified format.	No	No
GoToControl	GoToControl	Moves focus to the specified control.	No	Yes
GoToRecord	GoToRecord	Moves to the specified record as an offset of the current record.	No	Yes
ImportExportData	TransferDatabase	Imports or exports data or objects from another Access database.	No	No
ImportExportSpreadsheet	TransferSpreadsheet	Imports or exports data or objects from Excel.	No	No
ImportExportText	TransferText	Imports or exports data from text files.	No	No
ImportSharePointList	TransferSharePointList	Imports or links data from SharePoint.	No	No
MessageBox	MsgBox	Displays a message to users.	No	Yes
OnError	N/A	Defines behavior for error handling.	No	Yes
OpenForm	OpenForm	Opens the specified form.	No	Yes
OpenReport	OpenReport	Opens the specified report.	No	Yes
PrintPreview	RunCommand PrintPreview	Opens Print Preview for the current object.	No	No

continues

(continued)

ACTION NAME ACCESS 2010	ACTION NAME ACCESS 2007	DESCRIPTION	NEW?	WEB?
QuitAccess	Quit	Exits Access.	No	No
RemoveAllTempVars	RemoveAllTempVars	Clears the TempVars collection.	No	Yes
RemoveTempVar	RemoveTempVar	Removes the specified TempVar from the TempVars collection.	No	Yes
Requery	Requery	Re-executes the query for the current object.	No	Yes
RunCode	RunCode	Runs the specified VBA user-defined function.	No	No
RunDataMacro	N/A	Runs the specified data macro.	Yes	Yes
RunMacro	RunMacro	Runs the specified macro.	No	Yes
RunMenuCommand	RunCommand	Runs the specified command.	No	Yes
RunSavedImportExport	RunSavedImportExport	Runs the specified import or export specification.	No	No
SaveRecord	RunCommand SaveRecord	Saves the current record.	No	Yes
SearchForRecord	SearchForRecord	Searches for the specified record using a SQL WHERE clause.	No	No
SetFilter	N/A	Applies a filter to the specified control or current object.	Yes	Yes
SetLocalVar	N/A	Creates or sets a local variable.	Yes	Yes

ACTION NAME ACCESS 2010	ACTION NAME ACCESS 2007	DESCRIPTION	NEW?	WEB?
SetOrderBy	N/A	Applies a sort to the specified control or current object.	Yes	Yes
SetProperty	SetProperty	Sets a property value for the specified control.	No	Yes
SetTempVar	SetTempVar	Creates or sets a TempVar.	No	Yes
StopAllMacros	StopAllMacros	Stops all currently active macros.	No	Yes
StopMacro	StopMacro	Stops the current macro from running.	No	Yes

 For some of the macro actions listed as being available on the Web in Access Services, only a subset of arguments or argument values are available. For example, the OpenForm *action is available in Access Services, but the* View *and* Filter Name *arguments are not. Also, the* Window Mode *argument supports only the value* Dialog *in a Web macro.*

We looked at some of the new macro actions related to variables in the previous section, so let's take a look at some of the other new macro actions in Access 2010.

BrowseTo

One of the more powerful new macro actions in Access 2010 is the BrowseTo action. This action is used to navigate to the specified form or report, but let's take a look at the arguments defined by this action to understand what that means.

ARGUMENT NAME	DESCRIPTION
Object Type	Specifies the type of object to navigate to.
Object Name	Specifies the name of the object to navigate to.
Path to Subform Control	Specifies the subform control to host the specified object.
Where Condition	A filter loaded with the specified object.
Page	Page number of a form to navigate to in Access Services.
Data Mode	The mode used to view data on the object that is opened.

The most interesting argument to the `BrowseTo` action and possibly the hardest to understand is the `Path to Subform Control` argument. This argument is used to specify a subform to receive the form or report that you open. That's correct — you can now host reports in forms in Access 2010! In the past, you may have set the `SourceObject` property of a `Subform` object using VBA to change the subform at runtime. This macro action provides the same functionality for macros.

The syntax for this argument is as follows:

```
FormName.NameOfSubformControl>SubformName.NameOfSubformControl
```

In this path, `FormName` refers to the name of the main form, while the first `NameOfSubformControl` part of the path refers to the name of the subform control on `FormName`. Remember that this is not necessarily the name of the subform.

This syntax supports a single-level of nesting for subforms — that is, a single subform on a main form. But what if you wanted to target a nested subform? In other words, you want to replace the subform of a subform on a main form. You can do that as well by repeating the syntax beginning with the > character. In other words:

```
FormName.NameOfSubformControl>
SubformName.NameOfSubformControl>
SubformName.NameOfSubformControl
```

This functionality is cool because using macros, you can now affect the `SourceObject` property of a subform and build some interesting navigation for applications in either Access 2010 or Access Services. By combining the `Where Condition` argument of the `BrowseTo` action, you can also open filtered forms or reports in a subform.

As powerful as the `Path to Subform Control` argument is, it so happens that the argument is actually optional. If you leave the argument blank, the current window that called the macro will be replaced with the specified form or report. This is really powerful in Access Services. With a Web form running in the browser, you can replace the current top-level form using the `BrowseTo` with an empty `Path to Subform Control` argument, all without having to worry about hyperlinks or how the browser works — you can write all of this just within a macro in Access.

SetFilter

Another new macro action that is bound to get a lot of use is `SetFilter`. Previous versions of Access have the `ApplyFilter` action. These actions are very similar in that they both apply a filter but there are subtle differences in the context in which they execute. The `ApplyFilter` action acts upon the object that receives the focus — that is, the context moves to the object that is opened. Consider the following macro that opens a form called `frmFoods`.

```
OpenForm
    Form Name: frmFoods
    View: Form
    Window Mode: Normal

ApplyFilter
    Where Condition: =[display_name] LIKE "*cheese*"
```

code snippet MacroSamples

When you run this macro, the form named `frmFoods` will open and a filter will be applied to the form in the `display_name` field.

The `SetFilter` action, on the other hand, sets the filter on the object that called the action. Let's take a look at the same macro using `SetFilter` instead of `ApplyFilter`.

Available for download on Wrox.com

```
OpenForm
    Form Name: frmFoods
    View: Form
    Window Mode: Normal

SetFilter
    Where Condition: =[display_name] LIKE "*cheese*"
```

code snippet MacroSamples

In this case, `SetFilter` tries to set the filter to the object where the macro is defined. If the form that called `SetFilter` is unbound, an error occurs, as shown in Figure 4-14. If the form that calls the action does not define this field, Access will prompt for a parameter value.

FIGURE 4-14

SetOrderBy

The `SetOrderBy` action in Access 2010 lets you apply a sort order to an object, much as you could use `SetFilter` to apply a filter. The context of the `SetOrderBy` action works the same way as `SetFilter` — the action is applied to the object that called the action.

Macro Scenarios

So far you've seen how to use the new Macro Designer in Access 2010, as well as learned about the different types of macros that are available. With these things in mind, let's dig deeper into macros and look at some examples. The following examples show some common things that you might want to do with macros in the user interface. These macros are intended to run in Access 2010, but many will run in Access Services as well.

Testing for Disabled Mode

One of the first things to think about doing with macros is to test for disabled mode. If you ran Access 2007 and saw that your code didn't run the first time a database was opened, this macro is for you.

The following macro tests the `CurrentProject.IsTrusted` property to determine if the database has been opened with trust enabled. If the database is trusted, we'll call the `RunCode` action to run an initialization routine in VBA. Otherwise, we'll display a message to the user to indicate that the database is disabled.

```
If [CurrentProject].[IsTrusted] Then
    RunCode
        FunctionName: =Init()
Else
    MessageBox
        Message: The application is opened in disabled mode.
        Title: Cannot Launch Application
End If
```

code snippet MacroSamples

Opening Objects

When opening objects, there are advantages to using macros instead of VBA. Think about how much code in your database needs to be maintained that simply opens or closes objects. Chances are there's quite a bit. Using macros, you can create one macro using submacros that is responsible for opening objects. If anything changes, there is only one place to look.

The following macro includes submacros that are used to open forms and reports in a database.

```
MessageBox
    Message: This macro is intended to be run from the submacros

StopMacro

SubMacro Form1
    OpenForm
        Form Name: Form1
End Submacro

SubMacro Form2
    OpenForm
        Form Name: Form2
End Submacro

SubMacro Report1
    OpenReport
        Report Name: Report2
        View: Report
End Submacro

SubMacro Report2
    OpenReport
        Report Name: Report2
        View: Report
End Submacro
```

code snippet MacroSamples

Now let's say that you want to provide an easy way to view reports in your application. One way to do this is to create a table that stores names of reports in your application, and then use a combo box (named cboReports in this example) to display the reports to users. The combo box could be part of a main form that is always visible, and you could have a subform control to display the reports. An example of such a form is shown in Figure 4-15.

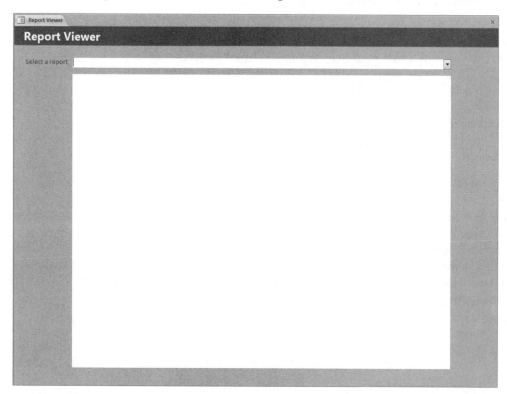

FIGURE 4-15

To change the subform to the selected report, you use the BrowseTo action as follows:

```
BrowseTo
    Object Type: Report
    Object Name: =[cboReports]
    Path to Subform Control: frmReportViewer.sfrmReport
```

code snippet MacroSamples

This is good, but now let's say that you want to clear the combo box after a selection is made. You can add the following SetProperty action to do that by leaving the Value argument blank:

```
SetProperty
    Control Name: cboReports
    Property: Value
Value:
```

code snippet MacroSamples

Opening a Report Based on a Parameter Query

It's pretty common to have a report based on a parameter query. For example, you might be interested in viewing customers who haven't paid in a specified amount of time, where the amount of time is defined in a parameter value; you might want to view orders for a particular customer, or sales for a given region or country.

Fortunately the Macro Designer allows you to pass parameter values directly in the macro. Start out with a report bound to a parameter query. In this example, I'm looking for the name of a particular author that is specified by a value in a combo box named `cboAuthors`.

Available for download on Wrox.com

```
OpenReport
     Report Name: rptChapters
     View: Report
     Window Mode: Normal
Parameters
     SelectedAuthor: =[cboAuthors]
```

code snippet MacroSamples

This macro uses the `OpenReport` action to open the report in a new window; however, you could just as easily use the `BrowseTo` action to display the report in a subform control on a form, as shown in the next example. Notice in this case that the `BrowseTo` action appears twice because a form may or may not be hosted inside a navigation control in Access 2010. An error occurs if the `Path to Subform Control` argument is invalid, so we're using the `OnError` action to allow the case where the action fails.

Available for download on Wrox.com

```
OnError
     Go to: Next

/* Try to load the report in the host form (frmAuthorsParameters) */
BrowseTo
     Object Type: Report
     Object Name: rptChapters
     Path to Subform Control: frmAuthorsParameters.sfrmChild
     Data Mode: Edit
Parameters
     SelectedAuthor: =[cboAuthor]

/* If this fails, try to load it in the navigation subform */
BrowseTo
     Object Type: Report
     Object Name: rptChapters
     Path to Subform Control: frmMain.sfrmNav>frmAuthorsParameters.sfrmChild
     Data Mode: Edit
Parameters
     SelectedAuthor: =[cboAuthor]
```

code snippet MacroSamples

While you cannot pass an expression to the `Path to Subform Control` argument, you might be able to add a little flexibility to your macros by using some error handling.

Working with Controls

One of the more versatile macro actions is the SetProperty action. This action allows you to set a property from a predefined list on the specified control name. The properties you can set using this action are:

➤   BackColor

➤   Caption

➤   Enabled

➤   ForeColor

➤   Height

➤   Left

➤   Locked

➤   Top

➤   Value

➤   Visible

➤   Width

The ability to set the Value property of a control is new in Access 2010.

The Value argument of the SetProperty action specifies the value of the property to set. This argument is effectively a Variant, meaning that it can be Null or can accept any value. If you set the BackColor or ForeColor properties, you can specify the color in either a decimal value, or in a hex value. In other words, if you wanted to set the BackColor property of a control to red, you could use the value 255 or #FF0000. The following macro shows you how to toggle the visibility of a control using the SetProperty action:

Available for download on Wrox.com

```
SetProperty
    Control Name: MyTextbox
    Property: Visible
    Value: =Not [MyTextbox].[Visible]
```

code snippet MacroSamples

Working with Records

Another area where macros might have some advantage over VBA is in simple functionality such as deleting or saving records. This is important functionality in an application, but is straightforward enough that this is another nice opportunity to use macros. The following macro shows you how to save a record.

```
RunMenuCommand
    Command: SaveRecord
```

Alternatively, you can simply type **SaveRecord** in the Add New Action drop-down to add this action.

Return to the Previous Record Following a Requery

The Requery action is used to re-execute the query for the bound form or report. Because the query runs again, the record position is moved back to the first record. Using VBA, you can use the Bookmark property of the Form object to find the previous record you were on and move back to it after the Requery action completes.

The goal of this macro is to provide similar functionality. There isn't a bookmark that you can use, and without a Recordset object or property available in macros or Access Services, you need to use a different approach. The technique shown uses a TempVar, an If block, and the RunMacro action to run the specified macro in a loop until some condition is met. The condition we want to evaluate is whether or not the current record on the form matches the ID value of the record we were on before the Requery. As you can imagine, we're going to move the records one at a time.

Pulling this off will actually require two macros. The first macro is an embedded macro that will issue the Requery action and call the second macro, which does most of the work. Start off by adding a command button to a bound form. Add the following macro to the Click event of the button:

```
/* Store the old ID value */
SetTempVar
    Name: MyOldID
    Expression: [ID]

/* Requery the form */
Requery

/* Find the old ID value by calling the second macro */
RunMacro
    Name: FindIDValue
```

Once the embedded macro has been created, we need to create the FindIDValue macro. Let's create that now as follows:

```
If [ID]=[TempVars]![MyOldID] Then

    /* Found the matching ID, stop */
    StopAllMacros

Else

    /* Did not find a match, move next, run again */
    GoToRecord

    RunMacro
        Macro Name: FindIDValue

End If
```

As you can see, the first thing we do is test the value of the ID control. If it matches the value we saved earlier in the TempVar, we're done. Otherwise, we need to move to the next record and call the macro again.

Note that Next *is the default argument for the* GoToRecord *action so we've omitted it from the listing.*

Running Macro Actions in Access or Access Services

If your application is going to run in the Web browser using Access Services, you may want to add additional functionality when the application is running in Access. For example, you may have a macro that opens a form in both Access and Access Services, but when the database is opened in Access you might want to run some additional VBA code using the RunCode action.

To accomplish these scenarios, there is a new expression called IsClient that determines whether the macro is running in Access or Access Services. When running in Access, the IsClient expression returns True; otherwise, it returns False.

The following example shows you how to use IsClient to call additional VBA code before opening a form. There are a few subtleties to point out here. First, the expression must be written using the brackets as shown: [IsClient]. If you begin to type "IsClient" in the Macro Designer, autocomplete for expressions in Access 2010 will add a parenthesis following the name of the expression. IsClient is effectively a property, not a function, so the macro will not run. Second, the RunCode action is not available in a Web macro so we're using the RunMacro action to call another macro, which will call the RunCode action. We've used the prefix cmcr to indicate that this is a client macro, or one that we expect to only run in Access 2010. Lastly, the form is opened outside of the IsClient check so the form will be opened in the Web browser as well. With these points in mind, here is the macro:

```
If [IsClient] Then
    RunMacro
        Macro Name: cmcrInitialize
End If

OpenForm
    Form Name: wfrmAuthors
    Window Mode: Dialog
```

DATA MACROS

As mentioned earlier in this chapter, data macros are an exciting new feature in Access 2010 that allows you to add a macro to tables themselves. For many years, Access developers have been asking for a way to add logic in the data layer that didn't require VBA code. This is important for several reasons:

➤ **Centralized business logic:** By putting business logic on the table, the logic is called regardless of the form that is used. In addition, this logic is also enforced when data is updated through other means such as when using linked tables, action queries, or VBA code. If you run code that updates a record, the data macros are still enforced.

➤ **Logic runs in disabled mode:** Remember that macros are a great way to provide functionality to applications, even when the application is disabled. If business logic is implemented in VBA, the application must be enabled to run. By adding data macros to a table, this logic will run in disabled mode, meaning that the logic is always enforced.

➤ **Runs in Access Services:** Data macros provide one mechanism for writing business logic for the client or the server.

Macro objects and embedded macros execute in response to some user-interface action such as the click of a button. Similarly, data macros execute in response to a *data* action, such as when a record is added, updated, or deleted.

Data macros are created using the Ribbon when a table is open, as shown in Figure 4-16.

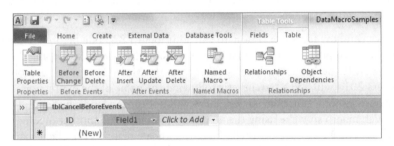

FIGURE 4-16

Data macros are only available in the ACCDB file format, and because they are defined directly on a table, they are not compatible with previous versions of Access.

Types of Data Macros

Similar to macro objects, a data macro can also exist as a named object, or associated with certain events on tables. You can think of these in three distinct categories: *Before* data macros, *After* data macros, and *Named* data macros. We'll describe the first two types in terms of how they are implemented — via events.

Before Events

As the name suggests, a Before data macro runs before something happens. There are two Before events for data macros, `Before Change`, and `Before Delete`. The `Before Change` event executes before a record is updated, whereas the `Before Delete` event is fired before a record is deleted.

Much like Before events in Access forms, the Before events in data macros can be canceled, making them the event of choice for data validation. We'll show you how to do that later in this section.

After Events

There are three After events for data macros: `After Insert`, which fires after a record has been added; `After Update`, which fires when a record has been updated; and `After Delete`, which fires after a record has been deleted. The `After Update` event does not fire when a new record is added.

If multiple records are affected at once, the After events will fire for each one. For example, let's say that you copy five records and paste them into a table that has the `After Insert` event defined. The `After Insert` event will fire once for each insert, or five times. Similarly, if you were to delete five records, the `After Delete` event fires for each record.

Named Data Macros

A named data macro is one that you can call directly as you can call a standalone macro object for the user interface. Named data macros can accept input via defined parameters, and are called using the `RunDataMacro` action in a macro object, embedded macro, or another data macro. Named data macros cannot be called from the Before event of a table, only from an After event or from another named data macro. Named data macros are called using the following syntax:

```
TableName.DataMacroName
```

Running Data Macros

In a client (non-Web) database, or a Web database that has not been published, data macros are executed by the Access Database Engine. When you publish a Web database to Access Services, data macros are executed by the server. This is also true when the published database is opened in Access 2010. To fire the data macro, you simply need to execute a data-related operation: insert, update, or delete.

Data Macro Blocks

A new type of construct is available in data macros called a *data block*. A data block acts upon a single record or a set of records, and contains actions that are applied to one or more records in the block. There are four different data blocks, but they are not available in all data macros.

CreateRecord

As you might imagine, the `CreateRecord` block is used to create a new record. This block is available in After events and named data macros — it is not available in Before events. The block defines two parameters: the name of the table to create the record in and an alias. We'll go into more details about aliasing at the end of this section. The following actions are available in the `CreateRecord` block and are defined in the next section:

➤ `CancelRecordChange`

➤ `SetField`

➤ `SetLocalVar`

There are some pretty cool scenarios for the `CreateRecord` block. For example, let's say that you have a database that tracks equipment for an office such as a copier or fax machine. The table containing the equipment stores information such as the serial number, manufacturer, and purchase date. This same application might also track service requests for the equipment over time. When the equipment is ordered, it will also need to be installed, which may be handled by a service request. When you add a record to the equipment table, you could use the `CreateRecord` block in the `After Insert` event of the table to automatically schedule the service request in the service request table.

Another scenario in which you might use the `CreateRecord` block is the change tracking scenario, also called the *audit trail*. The change tracking scenario is used when you want to track inserts, updates, and deletes for records in a table. An example of implementing this scenario appears later in this chapter.

EditRecord

The `EditRecord` block is used to edit an existing record. This block is also available in After events and named data macros, but not Before events. The `EditRecord` block includes the `Alias` parameter, and can contain the following actions:

➤   `CancelRecordChange`

➤   `SetField`

➤   `SetLocalVar`

Keeping with our equipment and service request scenario, let's say that the service request table also has a field that tracks the expected completion date. When a request is assigned to a technician, we'd like to automatically update the expected completion date. Using the `EditRecord` block in the `After Update` event of the table, you could update the value of this field. You could also determine whether the assigned to field is being cleared, and if so, clear the value of the expected completion date field.

ForEachRecord

The `ForEachRecord` block is used to iterate over records and apply the actions to each record that is returned by in the block. This block accepts a `Where Condition` argument that can be used to limit the amount of records that are returned by the block. Similar to `CreateRecord` and `EditRecord`, the `ForEachRecord` block is only available in After events and named data macros. All data macro actions are available in the `ForEachRecord` block. You can also use the `EditRecord`, `ForEachRecord`, or `LookupRecord` blocks inside a `ForEachRecord` block, but you cannot use the `CreateRecord` block inside the `ForEachRecord` block.

The `ForEachRecord` block is helpful for doing custom calculations across a set of data.

LookupRecord

Actions inside the `LookupRecord` block apply to each record that meets the specified query for the block. This block includes three arguments: the name of the table, a where condition, and an alias. The following actions are available in the `LookupRecord` block when the block is used in a Before event:

➤   `ClearMacroError`

➤   `OnError`

➤   `RaiseError`

➤   `SetField`

➤ SetLocalVar

➤ StopMacro

In an After event, all data macro actions and blocks are available in the LookupRecord block.

We've come this far with our service request example, so let's stick with it. Remember that our service request table stores the name of the technician assigned to the request. Using the LookupRecord action in the Before Change event, we can raise an error if someone tries to assign a request to a technician who already has a request assigned that has not been completed.

Aliasing

Several of the data macro blocks have an Alias argument. The Alias argument is used to refer to the records returned by a query in the specified data block.

For example, in the LookupRecord and ForEachRecord data blocks, the Alias is used to distinguish records returned by the Where Condition argument from those in the table itself. In the CreateRecord and EditRecord blocks, the Alias argument will refer to the new record that is being created or edited in the block. Think of this argument as providing context or scope for records.

Sometimes the Alias is essential. For example, let's say that you are using the LookupRecord block in the Before Change event to check another value in the same table. The values in the record you are editing are referred to using the name of the table directly such as TableName. FieldName. This will return the current value of the field before the update occurs. The Alias argument of the LookupRecord block can be used to refer to values for other records that are returned by the data block.

You will see an example of using an alias in this manner in the section "Canceling a Before Event."

Data Macro Properties

There are three members that are only available in data macros that help you determine how data has been affected by a data macro. These are described in the subsections that follow.

Updated Function

The Updated function accepts the name of a field as a string, and returns True if the specified field was updated. Unfortunately, Access 2010 does not have a mechanism that lets you iterate through fields (only records), so there may be times when you want to test that a specific field was updated.

Old Property

The [Old] property is an alias for the table that provides the original value of the specified field for a record in the After Update and After Delete events of a table. This is the data macro equivalent of the OldValue property of a control on a form in VBA. Old appears as a table name in autocomplete in Access 2010, as shown in Figure 4-17.

FIGURE 4-17

You can use the `Old` property of the table to test for previous values in a Before event to determine if a record should be updated or deleted. For example, let's say that you have an employee in a table whose record is being deleted. Before the employee record is deleted, you want to make sure there are no outstanding projects assigned to the employee. So, in the `Before Delete` event, you might use the `LookupRecord` data block to check a Projects table for a record that matches the employee's ID value that has not been completed. Using the `Old` property of the employees table, you can pass the original value of the ID field as part of the criteria to `LookupRecord`. If a match is found for the specified ID, you would call `RaiseError` to cancel the delete operation.

IsInsert Property

The `IsInsert` property of the table indicates that a new record is being added. When you add a record, both the `Before Change` and `After Insert` events fire for the new record, so to know which operation actually occurred, you should check the `IsInsert` property of the table in the `Before Change` event. The property returns `True` if the record is being added; otherwise, it returns `False` if the record is being updated.

Data Macro Actions and Arguments

Because data macros are intended to run in a Web browser using Access Services, all actions for data macros are inherently legal for use on the Web. The following table describes the actions that you can define in a data macro.

ACTION NAME	DESCRIPTION
CancelRecordChange	Exits the `CreateRecord` or `EditRecord` block. Does not save the record.
ClearMacroError	Clears the `MacroError` object.
DeleteRecord	Deletes a record.
ExitForEachRecord	Exits the `ForEachRecord` block.
LogEvent	Logs a record to the `USysApplicationLog` table. This table is described in more detail later in this chapter.
OnError	Begins error handling for the macro.
RaiseError	Notifies the application of an error. This action is used to cancel the Before events.
RunDataMacro	Runs a named data macro in the current database.
SendEmail	Sends e-mail to the specified recipient.
SetField	Sets the value of a field.
SetLocalVar	Creates or updates a local variable.

ACTION NAME	DESCRIPTION
SetReturnVar	Sets a return variable for macros calling the current data macro.
StopAllMacros	Stops all currently running macros.
StopMacro	Stops the currently running macro.

Error Handling

Error handling in data macros works much like error handling in regular macros with a couple of exceptions. The first difference is that the OnError action in a data macro cannot hand-off errors to another submacro. The only arguments available to this action in a data macro are Next and Fail. The other difference is that there are two additional actions that are used to help with error handling.

The first action is the RaiseError action. This action is used to notify callers that an error has occurred in the data macro. When used in an After event, the action does not display a message to the user unless it has been called from a user interface macro, either named or embedded. It will, however, display a message when called from a Before event in a table, and therefore is used to cancel the Before event.

The other action you can use to help with error handling is the LogEvent action. This action is used for logging and can help when debugging and error handling. The LogEvent action logs a record to a system table called USysApplicationLog. The fields in this table are shown in the table that follows.

FIELD NAME	DATA TYPE	DESCRIPTION
ID	AutoNumber	Primary key for the table.
SourceObject	Text	Object that logged the event. For a data macro event, this appears in the form: TableName.EventName.
Data Macro Instance ID	Text	GUID that identifies a unique running instance of a data macro. Multiple instance IDs for the same action indicates a possible recursion issue.
Error Number	Long Integer	Error number for the event. May be specified in the RaiseEvent action.
Category	Text	Specifies the category of the event. Possible entries are: Execution — Error raised by RaiseError action. User — Added by LogEvent action.
Object Type	Text	Type of object that logged the event.
Description	Memo	Description of the event.
Context	Text	Provides the name of the block or action where the error occurred.
Created	Date/Time	Timestamp of the event.

Because this table has the USys prefix, you'll need to show system objects for it to appear in the navigation pane. When there are new messages to display, a message will appear in the status bar that says "New Application Errors." Click on this message to view the table. In addition to the status bar notification, the table will display messages in the Office Backstage, as shown in Figure 4-18.

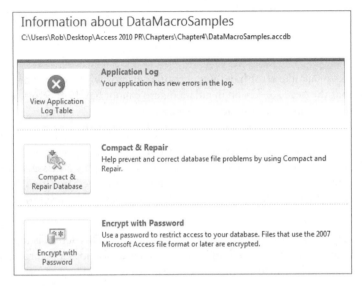

FIGURE 4-18

Click on the button to view the USysApplicationLog table. The notifications will not appear until the next time an event is logged. Until this happens, you'll see a message in the Office Backstage that indicates there are no new errors, as shown in Figure 4-19.

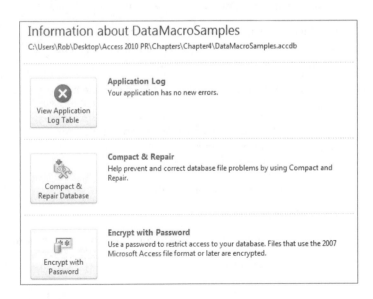

FIGURE 4-19

The integration with the Office Backstage makes this an easy way to add event logging for your own applications. For more information about the Office Backstage, please refer to Chapter 17.

Variables

Two types of variables are available in data macros: local variables and return variables. Local variables are stored in the `LocalVars` collection, and are available to the macro that defines them.

Return variables are stored in the `ReturnVars` collection and are used to return values from a data macro to calling macros. You create a return variable by using the `SetReturnVar` action. Because they are stored in a collection, it is possible for a data macro to return more than one value.

In a data macro, you refer to a local variable by its name only. An error is added to the `USysApplicationLog` *table if you use the* `LocalVars` *collection when referring to a local variable in an expression. For example, the following expression would cause an error in a data macro:*

```
LogEvent
    Description: ="The value is: " & LocalVars!VarName
```

Instead, you should use the following:

```
LogEvent
    Description: ="The value is: " & VarName
```

Data Macro Scenarios

Now that you've seen some of what goes into a data macro, let's take a look at some scenarios in which you might use data macros in your applications.

Aggregating Data

One common reason for using `ForEachRecord` in a data macro is to create custom calculations or aggregates for data in a table. Aggregate functions such as `Count` and `Sum` are available in reports, but unfortunately totals queries (i.e., aggregate functions) are not supported in Access Services. As a result, there may be many times where you'll need to create this functionality by hand. This is where the `ForEachRecord` block comes in.

To use the aggregates on a form in an Access Services application, you'll need to store the aggregate value in a separate table. This table might maintain additional statistics for the application that allows for other calculations as well. To populate the statistics table, let's examine the following named macro. The first thing we'll do is initialize three `LocalVars`. The last variable is the name of the table in question. It will be used later to do a lookup into the totals table.

```
SetLocalVar
    Name: lngTotalCost
    Expression: 0
SetLocalVar
    Name: fFoundTotal
    Expression: False
```

```
SetLocalVar
    Name: strTableName
    Expression: "tblEquipment"
```

Next, we calculate the total using the `ForEachRecord` block and store it in `lngTotalCost`. The expression used in the code that follows will accumulate the `lngTotalCost` local variable to add the value of the Cost field in the `tblEquipment` table. Notice that the `Nz` function works in the data macro. This is because the `Nz` function was added to the Access Database Engine itself in Access 2010.

Available for
download on
Wrox.com

```
For Each Record in tblEquipment
        Where Condition:
        Alias:

    SetLocalVar
        Name: lngTotalCost
        Expression: [lngTotalCost]+Nz([Cost], 0)
```

Now that we've got the aggregate value, we need to update the totals table, called `tblTotals`. Our totals table contains the name of the table that has the total so that we can have one place to store aggregates. You could extend this further to include the name of the field that defines the aggregate, but for the sake of this example we're only tracking the name of the table. If the name of the table does not exist in `tblTotals`, we'll create a new record for the aggregate value; otherwise, we'll edit the existing record. To determine if the aggregate already exists, we'll use the `LookupRecord` block.

Available for
download on
Wrox.com

```
Look Up A Record In: tblTotals
        Where Condition: =T.[TableName]=strTableName
        Alias: T

    SetLocalVar
        Name: fFoundTotal
        Expression: =True

    EditRecord
        Alias: T

        SetField
            Name: TotalCost
            Value: =[lngTotalCost]

    End EditRecord

If Not [fFoundTotal] Then
    Create a Record In: tblTotals
            Alias: T

    SetField
        Name: TotalCost
        Value: =[lngTotalCost]
```

```
        SetField
            Name: TableName
            Value: =[strTableName]


    End If
```

Because we've defined this macro as a named data macro, we can call it whenever totals need to be calculated. More specifically, this will be called from the `After Insert`, `After Update`, and `After Delete` events because these are the operations where values are affected. Call the macro using the `RunDataMacro` action in the data macros for the events.

Canceling a Before Event

Like the Before events on Access forms, the `Before Change` and `Before Delete` events for a table can be canceled. To cancel one of these events, use the `RaiseError` action in the data macro. You could use this to make sure that a value is present, or is not present in another table. For example, let's take a look at the service request example we created earlier.

One of the fields in the service request table is a column that indicates the actual completion date. When this field is null, the service request is still active as it has not yet been completed. Let's say that we only want to assign a service request to someone who does not have one outstanding. We can use the `Before Change` event to check for these criteria.

The first thing we'll do is to look up the name of the technician from the `tblTechnicians` table and store it in a local variable so that we can display the name of the technician instead of the ID later on.

```
/* Get the name of the technician */
Look Up A Record In: tblTechnicans
        Where Condition: =[tblTechnicians].[ID]=[tblServiceRequests].[AssignedTo]
    SetLocalVar
        Name: TechName
        Expression: [tblTechnicians].[FirstName] & " " & [tblTechnicians].[LastName]
/* End LookupRecord */
```

Next, we need to determine whether the specified technician for the request has an active request. To do this, we'll look for technicians that match the current technician, where the ID of the request is not the one we're currently on, and where the actual completion date is `Null`.

```
If Updated("AssignedTo") Then
    Look Up A Record In: tblServiceRequests
        Where Condition: SR.[AssignedTo]=tblServiceRequests.[AssignedTo] And
            SR.[ID]<>tblServiceRequests.[ID] And IsNull(SR.[ActualCompletionDate])
        Alias: SR
```

```
RaiseError
    Error Number: 1234
    Error Description: ="Cannot assign a request to the specified
                        technician: " & [TechName]

End If
```

code snippet DataMacroSamples

Single Checkbox Value for Records

There are certain scenarios where you might want to have a checkbox bound to a Yes/No field but allow only one of the values to be set to True across a set of records. For example, consider an application that tracks contact information for customers. Your customers might have more than one method of contact: e-mail, cell phone, work phone, or home phone. Of these options, only one of them may be preferred, so the table that stores the contact information for a customer may also have a field called Preferred to indicate that one method should be the primary means of contact.

To do this in VBA, you would reset each of the other Boolean values to False except for the one that is being updated. Because this is a business rule, it might be a good practice to put this directly on the table using a data macro, as shown here. Create the following data macro in the After Update event of a table. This macro assumes there is a field named ID in the table that is the primary key of the table.

Available for download on Wrox.com

```
SetLocalVar
    Name: TempID
    Expression: =[ID]

If Updated("Preferred") And [Preferred]=True Then
    For Each Record In: tblCustomerContactInfo
        Where Condition: =[ID]<>TempID

        EditRecord
            SetField
                Name: Preferred
                Value: =False
        End EditRecord
End If
```

code snippet DataMacroSamples

Because this macro will run in the After Update event, it will only run when the record is saved. As a result, the previously preferred value will appear True until you commit the record. You can force the record to save using the following macro for the After Update event of the checkbox control on a form:

```
RunMenuCommand
    Command: SaveRecord
```

Custom Sort Order for Displaying Records

I wrote an application one time where I tracked the work I did over the course of a week. This database also had a feature where I could send my manager an e-mail that displayed these items under category headings. For example, customer-related activities such as responding to questions or attending user group meetings were included under my Customer heading, while coaching or mentoring were included under a heading called People Management.

This database worked well for me, and for my headings, but I wanted to make it a bit more generic. So, the database was also able to customize the category headings, as well as the order in which they appeared in the e-mail. One person might choose to show the People Management category at the top of the e-mail, while another might choose to show Customer activity at the top.

To accomplish this, I added a field to the categories table called `SortOrder`. This field stored the order in which the category should appear in the e-mail, and when the e-mail was created, a query that looked at the categories would sort by this field. Once the sort order was defined, you could move items up and down in a list box using code behind the form, as shown in Figure 4-20.

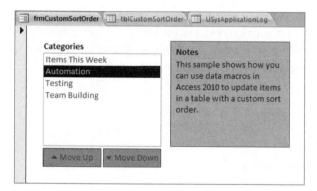

FIGURE 4-20

Before we go into the bulk of the logic, let's take care of some housekeeping. First, make sure that you have a table that has a field named `SortOrder` that is a number. For the purpose of this example, the name of the table will be `tblCustomSortOrder`, which appears in the sample database for this book. Fill in the sort order in the table sequentially. Next, let's take a quick look at the macros we'll create and then dive in to each one.

MACRO TYPE	MACRO NAME	DESCRIPTION
Named data macro	`tblCustomSortOrder` `.MoveCategory`	Determines the old and new values of the `SortOrder` field.
Named data macro	`tblCustomSortOrder` `.SwapSortOrder`	Updates the values of the `SortOrder` field for the old and new values.

continues

(continued)

MACRO TYPE	MACRO NAME	DESCRIPTION
Embedded macro	`cmdMoveUp.Click`	Calls the named data macro in the table to move an item up in the sort order.
Embedded macro	`cmdMoveDown.Click`	Calls the named data macro to move an item down in the sort order.
Named macro object	`mcrEnableMoveButtons`	Enables or disables the move up and move down buttons on the form. This macro is also called by the After Update event of the list box on the form.

Now that you know which macros we're going to create, let's take a closer look.

MoveCategory Named Data Macro

The `MoveCategory` named data macro defines two parameters: `prmSelectedItem` and `prmDirection`. The `prmSelectedItem` parameter is the ID (or primary key) value of the item that is being moved. The `prmDirection` parameter indicates which direction we'll move. Valid values for `prmDirection` are 1 and −1. Start by defining the parameters and validation for the `prmDirection` parameter as follows:

```
Parameters
    Name              Description
    prmSelectedItem   ID value of the currently selected item.
    prmDirection      Integer value indicating the direction to move.

/* Input Validation */
If  [prmDirection]<>1 And [prmDirection]<>-1 Then
    RaiseError
        Error Number: &H80070057
        Error Description: Invalid argument: prmDirection
End If
```

code snippet DataMacroSamples

 The error number `&H80070057` *used in the* `RaiseError` *action is the Invalid Argument error value in Windows. You could use any error number you like here.*

Next, you need to retrieve the value of the `SortOrder` field for the selected item using the `Lookup-Record` block, as shown here:

```
/* Get the sort order for the selected item */
Look Up A Record In: tblCustomSortOrder
```

```
          Where Condition: =[ID]=CDbl([prmSelectedItem])

     SetLocalVar
          Name: lngOldOrder
          Expression: =[SortOrder]
 /* End LookupRecord */
```

Once you have the original sort order, you need to get the sort order that will be changed. This is where the `prmDirection` parameter comes into play. Remember that valid values for this parameter are `1` and `-1`. By adding this to the original sort order, you can determine which item also needs to be moved. The value `1` will effectively move the sort order down the list because you'll add 1 to the sort order. The value `-1` therefore will move an item up in the sort order by subtracting 1. Add the following `LookupRecord` block to determine the new sort order value.

```
 /* Look up the sort order for the other item to move.
 Look Up A Record In: tblCustomSortOrder
          Where Condition: =[SortOrder]=CDbl([lngOldOrder])+CDbl([prmDirection])

     SetLocalVar
          Name: lngNewOrder
          Expression: =[SortOrder]
 /* End LookupRecord */
```

Once you've retrieved the sort order values, you'll need to call the `SwapSortOrder` data macro, which is defined in the next section. If the item being moved is at the beginning or end of the sort order, the `lngNewOrder` local variable will be `Null`. We'll skip any errors that may occur in this condition with an `OnError` action.

```
 OnError
      Go To: Next

 RunDataMacro
      Macro Name: tblCustomSortOrder.SwapSortOrder
 Parameters
      prmOldOrder: =[lngOldOrder]
      prmNewOrder: =[lngNewOrder]
```

You'll need to update the parameters for the `RunDataMacro` *action after creating the* `SwapSortOrder` *data macro.*

SwapSortOrder Named Data Macro

The `SwapSortOrder` data macro implements a simple swap routine for two records. The first item is saved in a local variable while it is updated to a known value. Then, the old sort order is updated to the new sort order, and finally the new sort order is updated to the old sort order. Create the `SwapSortOrder` named data macro as follows:

```
Parameters
    Name                Description
    prmOldOrder         Original sort order
    prmNewOrder         New sort order

/* Cache the original sort order */
SetLocalVar
    Name: Temp
    Expression: =[prmOldOrder]

/* Set the new sort order to -1 temporarily */
Look Up A Record In: tblCustomSortOrder
      Where Condition: =[SortOrder]=[prmNewOrder]

    EditRecord
        SetField
            Name: SortOrder
            Value: -1
    End EditRecord
/* End LookupRecord

/* Update the old sort order to the new sort order */
Look Up A Record In: tblCustomSortOrder
      Where Condition: =[SortOrder]=[prmOldOrder]

    EditRecord
        SetField
            Name: SortOrder
            Value: =[prmNewOrder]
    End EditRecord
/* End LookupRecord

/* Update the new sort order to the old sort order */
Look Up A Record In: tblCustomSortOrder
      Where Condition: =[SortOrder]=-1
    EditRecord
        SetField
            Name: SortOrder
            Value: =[prmOldOrder]
    End EditRecord
/* End LookupRecord
```

code snippet DataMacroSamples

Embedded Macros

Now that you've written the data macros, you need some way to call them. To do this, we'll use embedded macros behind controls on the form. There are two embedded macros to write. The first will call the `MoveCategory` data macro to move an item up in the list box, and the second will call `MoveCategory` to move an item down. Add two command buttons named `cmdMoveUp` and `cmdMoveDown`, and a list box named `lstCategories`, as shown earlier in Figure 4-20. Behind the `cmdMoveUp` command button, add the following macro for the `Click` event to move items up:

Available for download on Wrox.com

```
RunDataMacro
    Macro Name: tblCustomSortOrder.MoveCategory
Parameters
    prmSelectedItem: =[lstCategories]
    prmDirection: =-1

Requery
    Control Name: lstCategories
```

code snippet DataMacroSamples

Next, add the following macro behind the `cmdMoveDown` button to move items down in the list box:

Available for download on Wrox.com

```
RunDataMacro
    Macro Name: tblCustomSortOrder.MoveCategory
Parameters
    prmSelectedItem: =[lstCategories]
    prmDirection: =1

Requery
    Control Name: lstCategories
```

code snippet DataMacroSamples

mcrEnableMoveButtons Named Macro

To add some polish to the form and make it function professionally, you want to enable or disable the command buttons when the first or last items are selected in the list box. When the first item is selected, we'll disable the `cmdMoveUp` command button, and when the last item is selected, we'll disable the `cmdMoveDown` button. Create a new named macro object called `mcrEnableMoveButtons` as follows:

Available for download on Wrox.com

```
If [lstCategories].[ListIndex]=0 Then
    SetProperty
        Control Name: cmdMoveUp
        Property: Enabled
        Value: False
Else
    SetProperty
        Control Name: cmdMoveUp
        Property: Enabled
```

```
        Value: True
End If

If [lstCategories].[ListIndex]=[lstCategories].[ListCount]-1 Then
    SetProperty
        Control Name: cmdMoveDown
        Property: Enabled
        Value: False
Else
    SetProperty
        Control Name: cmdMoveDown
        Property: Enabled
        Value: True
End If
```

code snippet DataMacroSamples

There are three places to call this macro. First, set the `AfterUpdate` event property of the `lstCategories` list box to `mcrEnableMoveButtons` to call the macro when an item is selected. Next, add the following macro action to both Click events for the `cmdMoveUp` and `cmdMoveDown` command buttons to enable or disable the buttons as items are moved:

Available for download on Wrox.com

```
RunMacro
    Macro Name: mcrEnableButtons
```

code snippet DataMacroSamples

That's it! To test this functionality, open the form in Form view and select items in the list box to move up and down. With each move, the `SortOrder` field in the table should be updated.

Returning Values from a Data Macro

There are many times when you might want to look for a value in a table. For example, searching for records is a common scenario in many databases so you might have a form where you build complex search criteria, or you might need to return a related value from a table based on some other value. In an Access Services application, you might have a named data macro that performs a calculation and subsequently returns the value of the calculation.

Values are returned from data macros using the `SetReturnVar` macro action. Calling this action creates a new variable in the `ReturnVars` collection. This collection is only available to macros that run in the user interface.

In our service request scenario, let's say that you have a technicians form that shows information about technicians who respond to service requests. On the form, you'd like to show a custom string that shows their current service request. Remember that the service request table has a lookup field that tracks the equipment that needs servicing. Because this is a lookup field, you'll need to retrieve the name of the equipment from the equipment table. Fortunately, you can use a SQL statement in the `LookupRecord` block, as shown here. This example also demonstrates using a parameter in a named data macro.

```
Parameters
    Name: prmAssignedTo

SetLocalVar
    Name: fFoundMatch
    Expression: =False

Look Up A Record In: SELECT * FROM tblServiceRequests AS SR INNER JOIN tblEquipment
                     AS EQ ON SR.Equipment=EQ.EquipmentID;

    Where Condition: QRY.AssignedTo=[prmAssignedTo]
    Alias: QRY

    SetReturnVar
        Name: CurrentServiceRequest
        Expression: "Service requested for " & [EquipmentType] & " (Serial # " &
                    [SerialNumber] & ") on " & [ServiceRequestDate] & "."

    SetLocalVar
        Name: fFoundMatch
        Expression: =True
/* End LookupRecord */

If Not [fFoundMatch] Then
    SetReturnVar
        Name: CurrentServiceRequest
        Expression: ="None"
End If
```

code snippet DataMacroSamples

Now that the data macro has been written, we need to retrieve the value from the `ReturnVars` collection. This is done with another macro behind the form. In the `OnCurrent` event of the technicians form, we'll call this data macro and set the value from the `ReturnVars` collection to a text box.

```
RunDataMacro
    Macro Name: tblServiceRequests.dmGetCurrentServiceRequest

Parameters
    prmAssignedTo: =[ID]

SetProperty
    Control Name: txtCurrentSR
    Property: Value
    Value: =[ReturnVars]![CurrentServiceRequest]
```

code snippet DataMacroSamples

The end result appears in Figure 4-21. Notice that our custom string appears in the text box at the bottom of the form.

Sending E-mail

Another interesting thing you can do with a data macro is send e-mail. This is very handy. Consider our service request scenario again. Using the `SendEmail` action in a data macro you could send the technician an e-mail when a new request is assigned.

Remember that Access 2010 runs the data macros for client databases as well as non-published Web databases. When a database is published to Access Services, the server runs the data macros. This is important when it comes to sending e-mail. When Access is running the data macros, e-mail is sent using a default MAPI e-mail client such as Outlook. This is also the case with `DoCmd.SendObject` in VBA. Sending e-mail with Access Services must be configured on the server. Note that no error is displayed in Access if the e-mail is not sent. You should check the `USysApplicationLog` table to make sure there are no errors when using the `SendEmail` action.

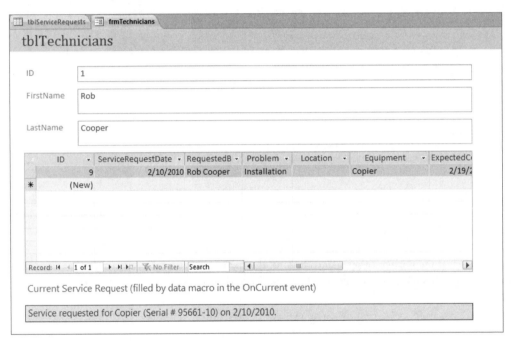

FIGURE 4-21

In this example, we're sending an e-mail from the `After Insert` event of the table, `tblServiceRequests`. The data macro first looks up the equipment type to use in the body of the e-mail.

```
SetLocalVar
    Name: strEquipment
    Expression: "UNKNOWN"

Look Up A Record In: tblEquipment
        Where Condition: =EQ.[EquipmentID]=[tblServiceRequests].[Equipment]
        Alias: EQ

    SetLocalVar
        Name: strEquipment
```

```
        Expression: [EQ].[EquipmentType]
/* End LookupRecord */

SendEmail
        To: <EnterEmailAddress>
        Subject: ="New Service Request: " & [ID]
        Body: = "A new service request for a " & [strEquipment] &
                " has been assigned to you. Thank you."
```

code snippet DataMacroSamples

Tracking Change History

Certain types of applications may require change tracking. This is commonly referred to as an *audit trail*. This scenario is important when you need to capture all the information about changes made to data in the database. For example, you might want to track the change in price for a product over time. By using an audit trail, you can log whenever the value of the field changes and then track changes over time.

This scenario has typically been implemented using VBA because Access has not had anything like triggers in the past. This leads to a lot of code in the database that needs to be maintained. If you create a new form bound to a table that requires auditing, the code will also need to be added to the new form. By using data macros, you can centralize the logic where it belongs — in the data layer of the application.

The basic audit trail table typically consists of a few fields. For our example, we will create a new table called tblAuditTrail with the following fields:

FIELD NAME	DATA TYPE	DESCRIPTION
ID	AutoNumber	Primary key for the table.
TableName	Text (255)	Name of the table where the change occurred.
FieldName	Text (255)	Name of the field where the change occurred.
Action	Text (255)	Data operation: Insert/Update/Delete.
OldValue	Memo	Original value of the field.
NewValue	Memo	New value of the field.
Timestamp	Date/Time	Date/time of the field change. Set the Default Value property of this field to the expression =Now().

The purpose of the audit trail is to show previous and current values for a given field. There are three operations that need to be tracked, and conveniently enough, these operations are also available in data macro events: Insert, Update, and Delete.

The logic for the audit trail should be generic enough that it can be reused for any action in any field in any table. As a result, we'll use a named data macro that we can call from anywhere. This data macro will be defined on the `tblAuditTrail` table itself and will include parameters. This macro is actually pretty simple — it only needs to add a record to the audit trail using the parameter values.

Create a new named data macro on the `tblAuditTrail` table named `dmAudit`, defined as follows:

```
Parameters
    Name                Description
    prmTableName        Name of the table
    prmFieldName        Name of the field
    prmAction           Data action: insert, update, delete
    prmOldValue         Original value of the specified field
    prmNewValue         New value of the specified field

Create a Record In: tblAuditTrail
    Alias:

    SetField
        Name: TableName
        Value: =[prmTableName]

    SetField
        Name: FieldName
        Value: =[prmFieldName]

    SetField
        Name: Action
        Value: =[prmAction]

    SetField
        Name: OldValue
        Value: =[prmOldValue]

    SetField
        Name: NewValue
        Value: =[prmNewValue]
/* End CreateRecord */
```

code snippet DataMacroSamples

Next, we need to call this macro for each data action for a table. In other words, it will need to be called from the `After Insert`, `After Update`, and `After Delete` events of any given table. To minimize the logic that goes into each event, however, we're first going to define a named data macro on the table that will be audited. This is so that we can abstract the operation for each event as a parameter in the macro. For this example, we're using a simple Tasks table named `tblTasks`. Create a new table with the following fields:

FIELD NAME	DATA TYPE (FIELD SIZE)
ID	AutoNumber
AssignedTo	Text (255)
Task	Text (255)

FIELD NAME	DATA TYPE (FIELD SIZE)
DueDate	Date/Time
EstHours	Number (Long Integer)
ActualHours	Number (Long Integer)

Once you've created the table, create a new named data macro named dmAuditTasks. Unfortunately there is no way to refer to a field in a data macro using a collection, so we're calling the Updated function for each field. Notice that we're calling the tblAuditTrail.dmAudit data macro for each field so that we get a new record in the audit trail for each field change in the table. Also notice that the OldValue field in the audit trail is supplied using the [Old] property of the table, as described earlier in this chapter.

```
Parameters
    Name        Description
    prmAction   Action to pass to the audit trail macro

/* Define a constant for the name of the table */
SetLocalVar
    Name: CON_TABLENAME
    Expression: "tblTasks"

/* Update the audit trail for each field */
If Updated("ActualHours") Then
    RunDataMacro
        Macro Name: tblAuditTrail.dmAudit
        Parameters
            prmTableName: =[CON_TABLENAME]
            prmFieldName: ="ActualHours"
            prmAction: =[prmAction]
            prmOldValue: =[Old].[ActualHours]
            prmNewValue: =[ActualHours]
End If

If Updated("EstHours") Then
    RunDataMacro
        Macro Name: tblAuditTrail.dmAudit
        Parameters
            prmTableName: =[CON_TABLENAME]
            prmFieldName: =" EstHours"
            prmAction: =[prmAction]
            prmOldValue: =[Old].[EstHours]
            prmNewValue: =[EstHours]
End If

If Updated("Task") Then
    RunDataMacro
        Macro Name: tblAuditTrail.dmAudit
        Parameters
            prmTableName: =[CON_TABLENAME]
            prmFieldName: ="Task"
```

```
            prmAction: =[prmAction]
            prmOldValue: =[Old].[Task]
            prmNewValue: =[Task]
    End If

    If Updated("AssignedTo") Then
        RunDataMacro
            Macro Name: tblAuditTrail.dmAudit
        Parameters
            prmTableName: =[CON_TABLENAME]
            prmFieldName: ="AssignedTo"
            prmAction: =[prmAction]
            prmOldValue: =[Old].[AssignedTo]
            prmNewValue: =[AssignedTo]
    End If

    If Updated("DueDate") Then
        RunDataMacro
            Macro Name: tblAuditTrail.dmAudit
        Parameters
            prmTableName: =[CON_TABLENAME]
            prmFieldName: ="DueDate"
            prmAction: =[prmAction]
            prmOldValue: =[Old].[DueDate]
            prmNewValue: =[DueDate]
    End If
```

code snippet DataMacroSamples

So far so good. You've got one named data macro that will handle the creation of records in the audit trail table, and another named data macro on the table to be audited. The last thing you need to do is to call this last data macro from each After event for the table. Add the following data macro for the `After Insert` event of the `tblTasks` table:

```
RunDataMacro
    Macro Name: tblTasks.dmAuditTasks
Parameters
    prmAction: "Insert"
```

code snippet DataMacroSamples

Next, add the following data macro for the `After Update` event of `tblTasks`:

```
RunDataMacro
    Macro Name: tblTasks.dmAuditTasks
Parameters
    prmAction: "Update"
```

code snippet DataMacroSamples

Finally, add the following data macro for the After Delete event of tblTasks.

```
RunDataMacro
    Macro Name: tblTasks.dmAuditTasks
Parameters
    prmAction: "Delete"
```

code snippet DataMacroSamples

To test these macros, add, update, or delete records from tblTasks. After each operation, you should have new records in tblAuditTrail showing the changes that were made. There you have it. An audit trail implemented without VBA code that will run regardless of how an update is made!

> *This audit trail does not currently enable you to track who made a change. There are a couple of ways to do this. If you're using an Access Services application, the best way to track a change is to use the* Modified By *field in SharePoint. This field is present on each SharePoint list and is used primarily for change tracking.*
>
> *If you're using a client database, you can still use VBA in a user-defined function in an expression in the data macro. For example, you might use the following function to return the name of the user:*
>
>
> ```
> Public Function GetUserName() As String
>     GetUserName = Environ$("USERNAME")
> End Function
> ```
> *code snippet DataMacroSamples*
>
> *Then, you could pass this as a parameter value for a field in the* tblAuditTrail *table as you could with other values or expressions.*

SUMMARY

Macros are an important feature in Access 2010. This chapter compared some of the differences between VBA and macros and how you can use the new Macro Designer in Access 2010 to create macros more efficiently. It also looked at other new features for macros in both Access 2007 and Access 2010, including data macros, which add the ability to include logic directly in tables.

Although there are several reasons to start considering using macros in Access 2010, there are still many reasons to use VBA. If you're going to use VBA, you'll need to understand the various components of VBA programming. Chapter 5 explores the VBA editor, Chapter 6 goes into VBA basics, and Chapter 7 covers execution of VBA code including properties, methods, and events. If you're an experienced VBA programmer, you may consider skipping ahead to Chapter 8, which shows you how to use class modules in VBA.

5

Using the VBA Editor

WHAT'S IN THIS CHAPTER?

➤ Learn about the VBA Editor's components and how to use them to write and test code.

➤ How to use the Object Browser to explore and work with different database objects and their properties

➤ Learn different techniques for testing and debugging code

You will write VBA code almost solely using the VBA Editor. In this chapter you explore the major components of the VBA Editor and learn how to use them to properly structure and debug your code. This chapter also provides some basic debugging techniques to help you save development time while you are at it.

 The topics in Chapters 5 and 6 are so interconnected that deciding which chapter to put first was difficult. If you get the sense that you are jumping into the middle without having covered the basics, what you think you're missing is likely in Chapter 6.

ANATOMY OF THE VBA EDITOR

You can access the VBA Editor in several ways. From anywhere in Microsoft Access, press Alt+F11 or choose from several places on Access's new Ribbon: Create, Macros, Modules, Database Tools, or Visual Basic. You can also open the VBA Editor by double-clicking a module name in the Navigation Pane or from any form or report. From the Properties dialog box, click the Events tab, select the event that you're interested in, click the Ellipses button

(. . .), and choose Code Builder. When you first view the VBA Editor, you might be a little over-whelmed by the number of components on the screen. Take a look at the VBA Editor within a user-created module, as shown in Figure 5-1.

The VBA Editor has the following components:

➤ **Three types of modules:** Form or report modules, listed under the Microsoft Access Class Objects, class modules, and standard modules. Each type of component has its own icon. The Project Explorer, shown in Figure 5-1, contains a class module, five standard modules, and two source forms. The VBA project carries the same name as the current database. If the Project Explorer isn't visible when you display the VBA Editor, press Ctrl+R to display it.

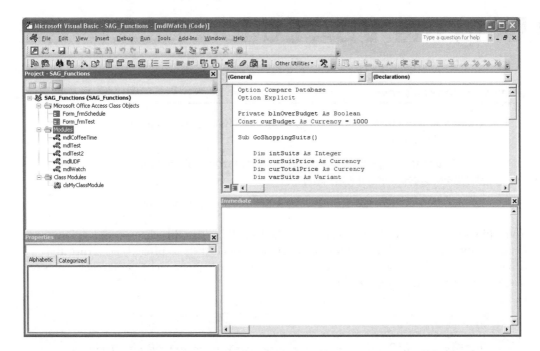

FIGURE 5-1

➤ **The Properties window:** Typically shown in the bottom-left corner of the VBA Editor, the Properties window lists all properties for the currently selected object. The object could be a module or a class module. Although the Properties window is quite helpful for working with user forms in Visual Basic, chances are you won't use it very often when coding in Access. However, it is a handy way to see all the properties for an object, so it's worth checking out — you may find it useful. By clicking the drop-down list you can scroll through the alpha-betical listing of the properties for that object.

➤ **The Code window:** This is where you write your code. The Code window displays by default all the subs and functions within the current module. You can limit the display of the code window to only the currently selected procedure by selecting Tools ➪ Options and, in the Window Settings frame of the Editor tab, clearing the Default to Full Module View checkbox. Click OK to save your changes. Several components are in the Code window, such as the Object list on the upper left and the Procedure list on the upper right.

➤ **The Object list box:** Provides you with the options to choose from different objects. When you're writing code inside a standard module, the list box contains only the (General) option. When you're writing code in a class module associated with a form or report, the Object list box contains an entry for every object (text box, combo box, label, and so on) within that form or report.

➤ **The Procedure list box:** Displays the items corresponding to the type of module you're viewing. When you're viewing a class module associated with a form or report, the Procedure list box shows every event associated with the selected object. For example, if you choose a text box on your form, you will see in the Procedure list box entries for events such as the Click, Enter, Keydown, and Undo, among others.

If you're viewing a standard module, the list box displays an entry for every sub or function in your module, even the ones that you write or rename. Using the drop-down list is a quick way to select the specific procedure you need to edit. You can then click on the name to open the procedure in the Code window to edit the code behind it.

When working with a module with lots of objects and procedures, scrolling through the Code window to find the desired procedure can be a time-consuming task. Selecting the object and then clicking the Procedure drop-down box will allow you to quickly navigate to that procedure. Although your code may not list the subs and/or functions alphabetically, you will see that they are listed in ascending order in the drop-down box. You can also use the Procedure drop-down list to jump directly to the General Declaration section.

In addition to these visible components, you can display a number of other components that will help you to write your code and to work with the Access 2010 objects. Most of these components are available under the VBA Editor's View menu.

YOUR DATABASE AND VBA PROJECT — BETTER TOGETHER

You might wonder about the correlation between a VBA project and your database. Quite simply, the database with forms and reports is what you see, and the VBA project contains the instructions to make it work. Although you won't see a separate file, a VBA project exists for every database created in Access. The objects in the Project Explorer shown in Figure 5-1 are present no matter where the code is used in your database. Whether you are writing code behind a form or report or in a module, you see the same objects listed in the Project Explorer.

USING THE OBJECT BROWSER

The Object Browser is probably one of the most powerful tools you'll use when writing VBA code. You can display it in the VBA Editor by selecting View ➪ Object Browser or by clicking F2. The Object Browser, shown in Figure 5-2, has a number of components.

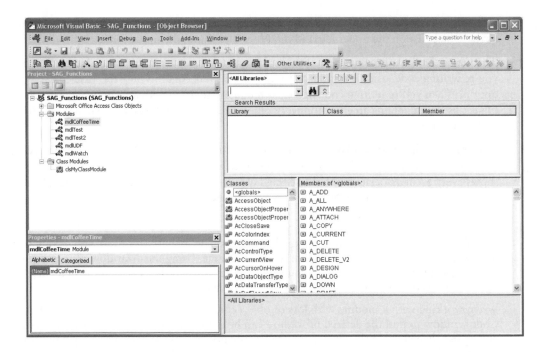

FIGURE 5-2

Object Browser Components

When you load the Object Browser, you can still view the Project Explorer and the Properties window. The Object Browser appears directly over the Code window. You can return to the Code window at any time by selecting View ➪ Code. When multiple Code windows are open, you can navigate to the desired window by choosing Window from the menu and then selecting the Code window that you want, or press F7 to move the cursor to the Code window. The following are some of the most commonly used components of the Object Browser:

➤ **The Project/Library box:** Shows all the available type libraries. You can choose All Libraries or a specific type library from the drop-down box. The type library you choose impacts which objects you can browse with the Object Browser. You'll see how to add a type library to your project later in this chapter.

➤ **The Search box:** Use the Search box to search for selected type libraries. After you've entered the search terms click the Search button (the binoculars icon). The results of your search are displayed in the Search Results pane.

➤ **The Search Results pane:** The results of your search are listed in the Search Results pane. You can show or hide it by clicking the Show/Hide icon (two up or down arrows) next to the Search button. The Search Results pane lists the relevant library, class, and member of any object returned by your search. If you click on the object, the full information will be displayed in the Details pane.

➤ **The Classes list:** All the objects, enumerations (enums), and collections in the currently referenced library are displayed in the Classes list. Scrolling through the Classes list you can click to select any of the listed items. After you make the selection, its details appear in the Members Of list and in the Details pane. You learn more about objects, collections, and enums in Chapter 6.

➤ **The Members of *classname* list:** Displays the properties, methods, events, and constants associated with the object currently selected in the Classes list. See the details of a member by selecting it in the Members of *classname* list.

➤ **The Details pane of the Object Browser:** Information such as the type of object, its data type, the arguments it needs, and the parent library or collection is shown in the Details pane. For example, in Figure 5-3, the Details pane informs you that the constant vbOKOnly is a member of the enum vbMsgBoxStyle, which is a member of the VBA Object Library. Its value is 0; the other members of the enum vbMsgBoxStyle include vbInformation, vbOKCancel, and vbYesNo.

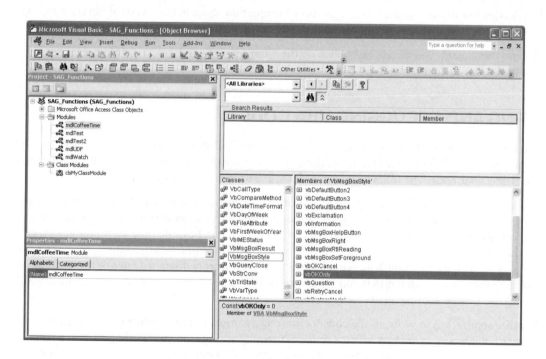

FIGURE 5-3

When a Help file is associated with the currently selected object, you can display a Help topic by selecting the item in either the Classes or Members list, and then pressing F1 or clicking the Help button in the upper-right corner of the Object Browser.

Use the buttons next to the Project/Library box to scroll through the previous or next members of the current collection.

One of the advantages of the Object Browser is that you can actually use it to take you to anywhere in the code that the current object is declared. For example, in Figure 5-3 the current database's Object Library (SAG_Functions) is searched for the procedure CoffeeTime. The Search Results pane lists the library, class, and member for the CoffeeTime sub. You can click the View Definition button (the fourth button from the left, next to the Project Library drop-down box) to return to the Code window and display the CoffeeTime sub.

The rest of this chapter delves into the other components of the VBA Editor that will help you to write and debug VBA code.

Show Hidden Members

You can show the hidden members in the Object Browser by right-clicking on the Object Browser and selecting Show Hidden Members. When listed, the Hidden Members will appear in a light gray text (as shown in Figure 5-4) because they are not intended for you to use within your code. However, when you want or need to know more about them, the Object Browser can be a convenient resource. By selecting one of the objects, you can get more information about it, such as what library it belongs to, the members of the class, and the argument and data type (listed in the bottom of the window).

To hide them again, you merely right-click on the Object Browser, and deselect Show Hidden Members from the pop-up menu.

TESTING AND DEBUGGING VBA CODE

The Code window is where you actually write your code, including the subroutines, functions, and declarations. In addition to the Code window, you'll use other components of the VBA Editor to test and debug your code. The following sections look at each of those components.

Like other things in database design, there is not one definitive right answer for when to debug your VBA code; it's also normal for developers to use different approaches depending on the situation. You could debug as you write, testing every few lines. That can be quite time-consuming, as you would have to run your code every few lines (possibly with incomplete procedures) and make heavy use of tools such as the Immediate window and Watch statements discussed later in this section. The advantage of this approach is that you always know the value of your variables, and the likelihood of making or perpetuating a mistake is reduced.

Another approach is to write all the code for your application and then debug it. Although this approach might seem tempting because it doesn't require you to stop your coding to debug your application, you can easily end up with numerous errors — some of which could require you to make major changes to your code. Using that technique can be like peeling an onion, particularly as the code becomes more complex and interdependent, with one function calling another function.

The best debugging approach falls somewhere between those two options. Debugging as you go — testing and debugging your code at the end of each procedure — enables you to be confident that each procedure produces the appropriate and expected values. If you are writing particularly long procedures, you may want to debug the procedure more frequently. Otherwise, this approach should be sufficient to ensure you're not in too deep with too many errors.

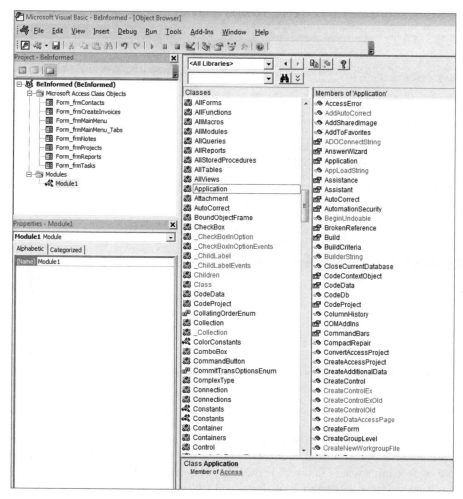

FIGURE 5-4

Immediate Window

The Immediate window in the Visual Basic Editor enables you to enter commands and view the contents of variables while your code is in break mode. Press Ctrl+G or select View ➪ Immediate Window to open the window, as shown in Figure 5-5.

You can display the value of a variable in the Immediate window by either using the ? *<Variable Name>* or the `Debug.Print` *<Variable Name>* in the window. Just type ? along with the variable name and press Enter. VBA Editor displays the contents of the variable in the Immediate window. For example, typing the following and pressing Enter displays the value of `intNumEmployee` in the Immediate window:

```
? intNumEmployees
```

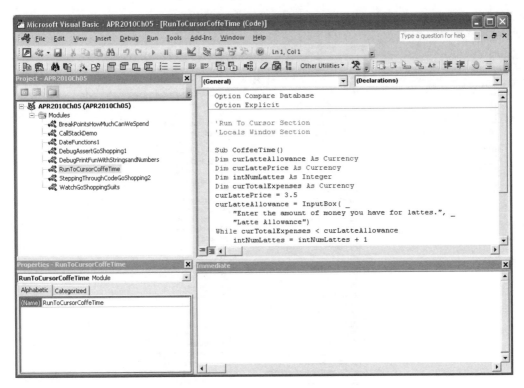

FIGURE 5-5

Seeing the current value of a variable can help you troubleshoot code if you're encountering unexpected results. Simply set a breakpoint in your code and test the value of a variable at any time. This enables you to determine where in the code the value is being incorrectly calculated. Using the question mark in the Immediate window is shorthand for typing `Debug.Print`. So typing `? intNumEmployees` or `Debug.Print intNumEmployees` produces the same results when you press Enter.

In addition to displaying the value of variables, you can also execute VBA commands in the Immediate window. Just eliminate the `?` character and type the entire command, and then press Enter. Typing `msgbox("Coffee or Tea?")` and pressing Enter displays the message shown in Figure 5-6.

FIGURE 5-6

You can even perform calculations in the Immediate window such as:

```
? intTotalEmployees = intTempEmployees + intFullTimeEmployees.
```

The Immediate window is also a powerful debugging tool for your applications. For more information about the Immediate window, see Chapter 7.

USING THE MSGBOX AS A TOOL TO DEBUG CODE

Using the Immediate window along with other aspects of the VBA Editor detailed in this chapter, such as breakpoints and stepping through code, is the most common way that most developers test and debug code. However, there are other effective approaches. One technique that is often used by beginning developers is to place MsgBox *<Variable Name>* code throughout the code to test the values of selected variables or calculations. Although there is nothing that is technically wrong with this technique, it has the potential to become cumbersome and cluttered. Keep in mind that when you're done debugging the code, you must remove (or comment out) all the message box calls, which can be a lot of unnecessary work.

The Debug.Print Statement

We previously mentioned using statements in the Immediate window, they are also useful in other places. The following module demonstrates how to use Debug.Print in your code. In looking at this example, you might imagine how Debug.Print can be helpful for testing and debugging.

Available for download on Wrox.com

```
Sub FunWithStringsAndNumbers()
    Dim strBikes As String
    Dim strCost As String
    Dim strCustomerName As String
    Dim intBikes As Integer
    Dim curCost As Currency

    strBikes = "19"
    strCost = "74"
    strCustomerName = "The Space Needle Seattle, WA"
    intBikes = 19
    curCost = 74

    Debug.Print strBikes + strCost
    Debug.Print intBikes + curCost
    Debug.Print strCustomerName
End Sub
```

code snippet CS 1 in ch5_VBAEditor_Code.txt

This code will show the following output in the Immediate window when you run it:

```
1974
93
The Space Needle Seattle, WA
```

Displaying the results of calculations or values of variables in the Immediate Window is one of the ways you can test your procedure. If the results aren't what you expect, you know that you have a problem somewhere; you may need to determine if it is in the initial data provided, the code, or the underlying logic.

The Debug.Assert Statement

In addition to `Debug.Print`, you can also use `Debug.Assert` to pause the code execution when a Boolean value passed to the statement evaluated to `False`. For example, the following code stops the code execution when a `blnUnderBudget` is `False`:

Available for download on Wrox.com

```
Option Compare Database
Private blnUnderBudget As Boolean
Const curBudget = 1000

Sub GoShopping()
    Dim intSuits As Integer
    Dim curSuitPrice As Currency
    Dim curTotalPrice As Currency
    Dim curBudget As Currency
    Dim i as Integer

    curBudget = 1000
    curSuitPrice = 100
    intSuits = InputBox("Enter the desired number of suits", "Suits")

    For i=1To intSuits
        curTotalPrice = curTotalPrice + curSuitPrice
        If curTotalPrice > curBudget Then
            blnUnderBudget = False
        Else
            blnUnderBudget = True
        End If
        Debug.Assert blnUnderBudget
    Next
End Sub
```

code snippet CS 2 in ch5_VBAEditor_Code.txt

The code breaks every time you go over budget on your shopping trip. You can use this statement when testing for specific conditions within your code. Although `Debug.Assert` is a good debugging tool, you should not use it in live code because it's a rather abrupt way to stop an application. The user would get no warning, and because the code stops, you do not get to exit gracefully by providing him with a friendly message or explanation. However, the `Debug.Assert` statement is essentially ignored in an MDE or ACCDE. That said, we also caution you that you will need to use a conditional compilation to essentially wrap the specified code in If, Then, and Else statements and stipulate that they will be ignored. You can find additional guidance about conditional compilations online by searching the Access communities and help resources. It seems much easier to search and comment out or remove the lines.

Breakpoints

Breakpoints are essentially places in your code where you want to pause the execution of the code. For example, if you want to check the value of the variable `curTotalCost` midway through the following procedure, you can use the `Debug.Print` statement as shown in the following code snippet or set a breakpoint, which we will demonstrate shortly.

```
Sub HowMuchCanWeSpend()
    Dim curTotalPrice As Currency
    Dim curUnitPrice As Currency
    Dim intNumSocks As Integer
    Dim i As Integer

    curUnitPrice = 3.5
    intNumSocks = InputBox( _
        "Please enter the number of pairs of socks you want.", _
        "Pairs of Socks")

    For i=1 To intNumSocks
        curTotalPrice = curTotalPrice + curUnitPrice
    Next

    Debug.Print curTotalPrice
End Sub
```

code snippet CS 3 in ch5_VBAEditor_Code.txt

This code uses the Immediate window to display the amount you'll spend for the total sock purchase (using the line, `Debug.Print curTotalPrice`). That's great for a single transaction, but what if you want to see the total accumulating as you go? One option is to add a `Debug.Print` statement within the `For...Next` loop. Alternatively, you can set a breakpoint anywhere in the loop. When the breakpoint is reached, the code stops running and you can use the Immediate window to obtain the value of any variable of interest (`? <VariableName>`). You can set a breakpoint on any line of code except for `Dim` statements and comments.

Setting a breakpoint is as simple as clicking in the left margin of the Code window. A brick-colored dot appears in the margin and the corresponding line of code is highlighted. To clear a breakpoint, just click on the dot in the left margin. You can also set and clear a breakpoint by placing the cursor in the desired line of code and selecting Debug ➪ Toggle Breakpoint or by pressing F9. When you run code that has breakpoints, every time the breakpoint is reached, the code execution stops and waits for you to decide (and tell it) what to do next. At that point, you basically have four options:

➤ Check the value of variables in the Immediate window. When your code reaches a breakpoint, the value of all variables is retained. You can check the value of any variable by using the `Debug.Print` statement or the `?` character within the Immediate window (as we discussed it earlier in the chapter)..

➤ Use your mouse to hover over any variable in the current procedure. The value of the variable appears close to the mouse cursor. Keep in mind that variables will show no value when you hover over them if a value was not assigned to them before you reached the break point,

➤ Press F5 or select Run ➪ Continue to continue code execution. The code will run until it reaches the next breakpoint or the end of the procedure.

➤ Press F8 to step through the code (explained in the following section). When you press F8, the code execution stops at the next line of code — even if it does not have a breakpoint. This enables you to step through the code and identify missed steps or other errors. As you step through the code, you can continue to check the value of the variables or press F5 to resume code execution.

BREAKPOINTS

When VBA encounters a breakpoint, it pauses execution immediately before the line of code executes. The line of code that contains the breakpoint is not executed unless or until you choose to step through the code using the F8 key (or continue running the code).

Stepping through Code

In most cases, you design code to run with little or no user intervention. However, when testing the code, it is often helpful or even necessary to do more than insert a couple of breakpoints or include some Debug.Print statements. If your code has several variable changes and/or some intricate looping, it can help clarify the process to step through the code line-by-line. This allows you to validate the value of variables after each line of code has executed, and it can help you pinpoint any errors or mistakes in the underlying logic.

To start stepping through your code, place the cursor at the point that you want to initiate the process and press F8 (you can also press F8 after the code has entered break mode to step through the remaining code). When you press F8 to begin code execution, the name of the sub or function will be highlighted in yellow. Pressing the F8 key moves the code execution from line to line, sequentially highlighting the next executable line. Much like with breakpoints, comment lines and Dim statements are skipped when stepping through code. As you press F8, the highlighted line executes.

STEPPING THROUGH CODE

Stepping through code is an important tool so it is worth reiterating how the process works. The first pressing of F8 highlights the next executable code; the subsequent pressing of F8 executes the highlighted code. If nothing is highlighted, pressing F8 highlights code; if something is highlighted, pressing F8 runs it.

If the current procedure calls another sub or function, F8 also executes the called procedure line-by-line. If you already tested the called procedure and are confident it doesn't contain any errors, you can execute the entire called procedure and then return to line-by-line execution of the calling procedure by pressing Shift+F8. This is called *stepping over* the procedure.

Stepping over the called procedure executes the entire procedure and then returns to the calling procedure to continue with code execution one step at a time. If you're within a called procedure, you can press Ctrl+Shift+F8 to *step out* of the current procedure. This may sound like nothing more than semantics. And indeed, if you're already in the called procedure, stepping out has the same effect as stepping over. But, the two actions will not always provide the same results. We'll use the following example to illustrate the difference and to give you some practice with code. Assume you're stepping through the following code (which is in the Chapter 5 download material):

Available for download on Wrox.com

```vba
Option Compare Database
Private blnUnderBudget As Boolean
Const curBudget As Currency = 1000

Private Sub GoShopping()
    Dim intSuits As Integer
    Dim curSuitPrice As Currency
    Dim curTotalPrice As Currency
    Dim curBudget As Currency
    Dim i As Integer

    curBudget = 1000
    curSuitPrice = 100
    intSuits = InputBox("Enter the desired number of suits", "Suits")

    For i=1To intSuits
        curTotalPrice = curTotalPrice + curSuitPrice
        If curTotalPrice > curBudget Then
            blnUnderBudget = False
        Else
            blnUnderBudget = True
        End If
    Next

    If blnUnderBudget = False Then
        OverBudget
    End If
End Sub

Private Sub OverBudget()
    Debug.Print "You've gone over budget."
    Debug.Print "You need to work some overtime."
    Debug.Print "Remember to pay your taxes."
End Sub
```

code snippet CS 4 in ch5_VBAEditor_Code.txt

Use the F8 key to step through the code until you reach the last If...Then loop (If blnUnderBudget = False Then). When the OverBudget line is highlighted in yellow (meaning it hasn't yet been executed), stepping over the OverBudget procedure returns execution to the line after the OverBudget call (in this case the End If line). If you step out of the procedure, the OverBudget procedure runs, and your code returns to the GoShopping procedure and completes the procedure. If, however, you use the F8 key to step through the code until you reach the first line of the OverBudget procedure, stepping out of the procedure returns you to the line after the OverBudget called (the End If line).

You can use the following table as a cheat sheet and create some simple procedures to help you test and understand the differences between the various debugging techniques shown in this chapter.

DEBUGGING TECHNIQUE	DESCRIPTION	KEYBOARD SHORTCUT
Step Into	Executes the next line of code in your procedure (highlights the line in yellow).	F8
Step Over	Executes code one line at a time within the current procedure. If a second procedure is called from within the first, the entire second procedure is executed at once.	Shift+F8
Step Out	VBA executes the remainder of the current procedure. If you are within the second procedure and then Step Out, the entire second procedure is executed and code execution continues in the first procedure — on the line following the line that called the second procedure.	Ctrl+Shift+F8

Call Stack

The Call Stack dialog box displays a list of the current active procedure(s) when you are stepping through code. An active procedure is one that is started but has not completed — and as you are beginning to realize, the list can grow rather quickly. You can access the Call Stack dialog box in several ways — you can press Ctrl+L or use the menu bar (View ⇨ Call Stack). Because the call stack is available only in break mode, access to the call stack is grayed out (disabled) when you are in Design mode.

> **THE CALL STACK**
>
> The Call Stack dialog box is a modal window and therefore cannot be left open when stepping through code. So, after you review the list of active procedures, you will need to close the dialog box in order to continue running the code.

The Call Stack dialog box is most beneficial when one procedure is calling another or if your code has nested procedures, whether they are in the same module or being called by other modules. When one procedure is called from another procedure, the dialog box displays the new procedure at the top of the list with the original (calling) procedure under it, thus the stacking effect. Figure 5-7 illustrates this stacking process. You will see that OverBudget was called by GoShopping, so OverBudget is listed first, and it is highlighted because it is the procedure being run. After a procedure is finished, it is removed from the stack. In this case, after OverBudget is run, GoShopping will be the only procedure in the stack.

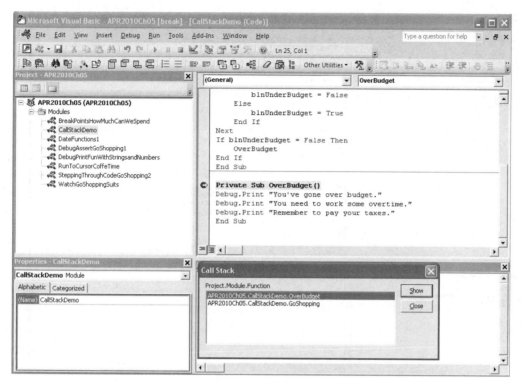

FIGURE 5-7

When you step through multiple procedures from different modules, or even from the same module, it can be a bit challenging to figuring out where a particular procedure is being called. To help find the start of any active procedure in the call stack, select the active (top) procedure in the list and either double-click the item or click the Show button. In the current example, the call stack was opened when OverBudget was called, so two procedures are listed.

To find out what line called OverBudget, you can double-click on GoShopping, the calling procedure. This puts a green pointer at the line in GoShopping, which called OverBudget. Figure 5-8 shows OverBudget still highlighted, because that's the current point in stepping through the code, and the green pointer at the call to OverBudget.

As you can see, the call stack is helpful when you are working with multiple procedures and trying to determine where errant data may be originating. It is also a handy tool to be used in conjuction with the other debugging tools when you need to decipher and work with someone else's application or modules.

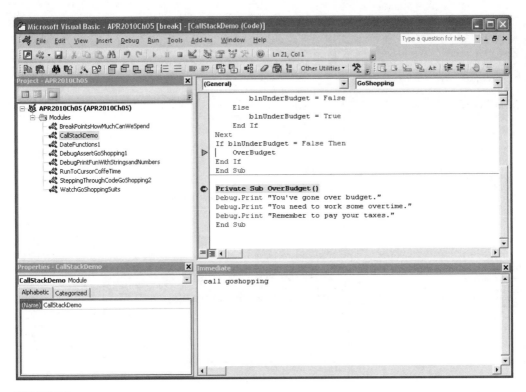

FIGURE 5-8

Run to Cursor

When testing your code, you will likely have many times that you don't want to run every line of code line-by-line, but executing the entire procedure at once isn't conducive to isolating and identifying the source of a problem. And, if the code includes loops, it can be very tedious to execute every line of the loop each time it needs to run. For example, consider the loop (`While ... Wend`) in the following code:

```
Sub CoffeeTime()
    Dim curLatteAllowance As Currency
    Dim curLattePrice As Currency
    Dim intNumLattes As Integer
    Dim curTotalExpenses As Currency

    curLattePrice = 3.5
    curLatteAllowance = InputBox( _
        "Enter the amount of money you have for lattes.", _
        "Latte Allowance")

    If curLattePrice <= curLatteAllowance Then
        curTotalExpenses = curTotalExpenses + curLattePrice
    Else
        MsgBox "You do not have enough funds to buy a latte", _
```

```
                vbOKOnly, "Total Lattes"
            Exit Sub
        End If

        While curTotalExpenses < curLatteAllowance
            intNumLattes = intNumLattes + 1
            curTotalExpenses = curTotalExpenses + curLattePrice
        Wend

        Debug.Print intNumLattes
        MsgBox "You can purchase " & intNumLattes & " lattes.", _
            vbOkOnly, "Total Lattes"
    End Sub
```

code snippet CS 5 in ch5_VBAEditor_Code.txt

If you have $350 to spend on lattes, the While...Wend loop will run 100 times. You do not want to have to press F8 to step through the loop that many times. Thankfully, you have other options. If you know that the loop is producing correct data, you can place your cursor in the Debug.Print intNumLattes line and press Ctrl+F8 to invoke the Run to Curser. Pressing Ctrl+F8, will cause your procedure to run until it reaches the Debug.Print line; at that point, it will halt and the line will be highlighted. You can then press F8 to step through and execute just the highlighted line of code or press F5 to continue execution until the end of the procedure.

Locals Window

You may also find situations when testing the value of every variable when your code enters break mode that would be utterly mind-numbing — but you still need to know the values. If you're stepping through code and need to test the value of seven different variables every step of the way, that's a lot of Debug.Print statements to type and keep track of in the Immediate window. The Locals window comes to the rescue by displaying all the variables in a procedure along with their values. You can observe the changes in the values of the variable as you step through the code. To display the Locals window, select View ⇨ Locals Window. Figure 5-9 shows the Locals window while stepping through the procedure CoffeeTime.

As you step through the procedure, you see the up-to-date values of all variables showing in the Locals window. The Locals window retains the values until the last line of code has executed. In this example, it will retain the values until you see a message box stating, "You can purchase 100 lattes."

Watch Window

The next tool that we'll examine is the Watch window. The Watch window enables you to watch a variable within your procedure. When the value of the variable changes or when the variable is True, your code enters break mode. To open the Watch window, select View ⇨ Watch Window.

To see how the Watch window works, we will use WatchGoShoppingSuits, which is a modified version of the GoShopping module. Recall that it uses a Boolean expression and message box to let you know if (when) you're over budget. We will add a watch on the variable blnOverBudget. You start by right-clicking in the Watch window and choosing Add Watch. The Add Watch dialog box opens (see Figure 5-10).

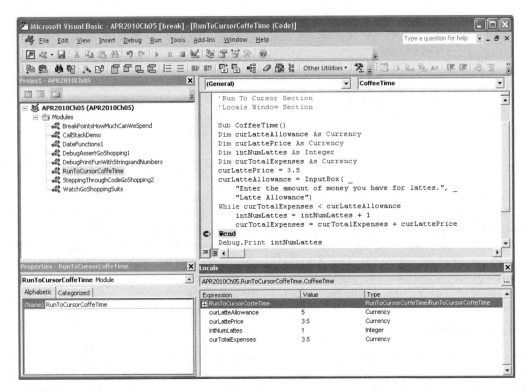

FIGURE 5-9

Enter `blnOverBudget` in the Expression text box. In the Watch Type you can select one of three options: Watch Expression (the default selection), Break When Value is True, or Break When Value Changes. For this example, choose Break When Value Is True, and then click OK to save your watch. When you run the `SteppingThroughCodeGoShopping2` procedure, the procedure will enter the break mode when the value of `blnOverBudget` becomes `True`. As soon as the loop executes for the eleventh time, the watch expression is triggered and the code enters break mode.

If you choose to simply watch the expression (rather than break), the Watch window behaves almost

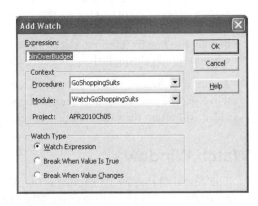

FIGURE 5-10

exactly like the Locals window except that only the selected watched variables are shown.

DELETE WATCH

If you have a rather long loop to execute and you no longer need your watch, you can delete it while your code is in break mode. Simply right-click the watch and select Delete Watch. You can then press F5 to continue code execution.

A shortcut for adding a watch is to right-click the variable and select Add Watch. The variable name is filled in automatically, which is a great way to avoid the risk of typos.

Edit and Continue

The last tool that we'll cover here is Edit and Continue. In the VBA Editor options (choose Tools ⇨ Options ⇨ General), you can set a feature called Edit and Continue. With only a few limitations, this feature allows you to make changes to the code while the program is in break mode and to apply those changes without requiring you to end the debug session and execute the program again.

When your code halts because of an error or a breakpoint, the VBA Editor displays the problem line or breakpoint line with an arrow pointing to it. You may identify the issue on that line and make the appropriate changes. When you execute that line (by pressing F8), the line may execute correctly (as intended). However, there will be times when you determine that the problem lies several lines before the current break location. Fortunately, you can make the correction and then restart the code from a location other then where it stopped. To change the starting point, just click on the original arrow (pointer) and drag it to the line where you want to start executing the code.

Be aware that depending on what code was executed, you may still not get valid results, particularly if the results are dependent on earlier code or values. So if you think you've corrected the problem but the code still isn't displaying the expected values, it is typically best to rerun the entire procedure, module, or function.

You should also keep in mind that code changes made during execution may not always be saved when the program ends. Regretfully, there is no definitive list of all the scenarios that might trigger a loss of changes to the code, but you can expect the changes to be lost if running the new code causes the application to shut down. Presumably, the logic is that you would not want to save modifications that caused the application to crash. But it doesn't differentiate between desired and undesired changes. So, to minimize the extent of potential losses, we recommend that you save changes as you go, a prudent move in most tasks associated with computers.

USING OPTION STATEMENTS

The first time you open the VBA Editor, you should set the Require `Variable Declaration`. If you have any doubts, it's a good idea to double check that it is set. It is in the Options dialog box, which you can get to by selecting Tools ⇨ Options from the toolbar of the VBA Editor.

The option to Require Variable Declaration adds one line of code to every new module as it is added to the database: `Option Explicit`. It means that you must declare every variable that is used in your code. This practice goes a long ways towards preventing ghost errors (errors in the data values that will not cause the application to raise an error message) that can be caused by having a typo in a variable name in your code. `Option Explicit` will not be added to existing modules, so you will need to add the code if it's not in the module.

Take a look at the following code:

Available for download on Wrox.com

```
Dim intQty As Integer
Dim curPrice As Currency
Dim curTotal As Currency

<...snip...>

CurTotals = intQty * curPrice

MsgBox curTotal
```

code snippet CS 6 in ch5_VBAEditor_Code.txt

Without the `Option Explicit` line, the code will execute, and the value of `curTotal` will remain 0. The value of `curTotals`, however, will be the result of the multiplication, but you will never see it in the message box. With `Option Explicit`, the code will not compile as written. It generates an error message (see Figure 5-11) and highlights the offending variable (curTotals) in your code.

The `Option Compare` is another statement that you should become familiar with. By default, it appears on the top of every module with the `Database` option (`Option Compare Database`). You can modify the `Option` statement so that it will use either a binary or text comparison. To change the `Option` statement, replace the `Option Compare Database` with either `Option Compare Binary` or `Option Compare Text`. The different `Option Compare` statements affect the way the database compares text. The `Database` option uses the values defined in the New Database Sort Order in the Options dialog box.

FIGURE 5-11

For example, when evaluating the expression `"a" > "Z"`, the code returns `True` if you use `Option Compare Binary` because the ASCII value of `"a"` is greater than the ASCII value of `"Z"`. The code returns `False` if you use `Option Compare Text`, because "Z" comes after "a" in the alphabet. If you use `Option Compare Database` combined with the New Database Sort Order set to US-English, the code will also return `False`.

The `Option Compare` statement also impacts the results you get when using the `Instr()` function. For example, in the following function, the results vary based on the option you selected:

Available for download on Wrox.com

```
Function FindTheD(strMyText As String) As Long
    'this function will find the position of the upper case 'D'
    FindTheD = InStr(1, strMyText, "D")
End Function
```

code snippet CS 7 in ch5_VBAEditor_Code.txt

Passing the string `"1 asdASD"` as an argument, the function returns the following values based on the setting used for `Option Compare`:

```
?FindTheD("1 asdACD")
Option Compare Database: 5
Option Compare Binary: 8
Option Compare Text: 5
```

INSTR([START,]STRING1, STRING2[, COMPARE])

The last argument for the `InStr()` function is `compare`. It's an optional argument that defaults to `Binary`. When you declare `Option Compare` in your module (Binary or Text), the omitted `[compare]` argument defaults to the value that you set in the statement.

The third `Option` statement that we'll discuss is `Option Base`. This is used on a module level to declare the default lower bound for an array. The statement has two possible values: 0 or 1. In Access it's an optional statement, and when the statement is omitted, the value will default to 0.

If used, the `Option` statement must appear in a module before any procedures or array declarations. `Option Base` can be declared only once in each module and it affects only the arrays in that module.

SUMMARY

This chapter explored the VBA Editor and showed you how to use some of the tools and numerous windows that it provides. Knowing how to debug your code to identify and fix those pesky bugs enables you to produce a smooth application. As you work with applications and projects, you will find the Immediate window to be an invaluable tool.

Understanding the fundamentals and the basic tools available to you will make going through the rest of the book easier and more fun. Many new features and tools are available to create powerful and professional forms and reports and to make working with other applications a breeze.

Remember that you can download the code, databases, and other materials from the book's website. At a minimum, the sample files make it easier for you to follow along with the chapters. And, by using the code snippets that we provide, you can minimize the potential for making typos, misreading characters, or making formatting errors.

6

VBA Basics

WHAT'S IN THIS CHAPTER?

➤ Laying the foundation for writing solid, reusable VBA code

➤ Understanding the basic components of a VBA procedure

➤ Naming and using variables

➤ Using other VBA components

➤ Working with VBA objects, properties, and methods

➤ Writing code in modules and behind forms and reports

➤ A few, easy-to-follow examples

Now that you know a bit about automating Access, using the various types of macros, and how VBA fits into the Access automation picture, you are almost ready to write some code. But before you launch into that, we will review some VBA basics to help ensure that we have a strong foundation to build on.

This chapter contains vital information that will help you to better understand and utilize what you'll learn in subsequent chapters. Veteran programmers may find a refresher helpful, but the chapter is mostly geared for those who are just delving into VBA, including those who may have experience with another programming language or VBScript. We'll examine the basic VBA programming objects, learn about variables and how to declare them, and review some of the VBA structures that you'll use in your code. Along the way, you'll build a few procedures, and you will soon gain the skill and confidence to modify those procedures as well as to create your own from scratch. All of the code snippets are provided on Wrox.com in the companion file for this chapter, ch6_VBABasics_Code.txt.

THE MINDSET OF A PROGRAMMER

Let's start by establishing a frame of reference as to what we should expect when we are writing code. Consider the scenario where you command a child to "open the door." Think about all the individual actions that it takes to accomplish that one statement. The child has to approach the door, align the hand with the knob, move the hand and grasp it around the knob, and then twist and pull the knob while swinging the arm in an arc. We don't have to command each specific step, and indeed life would be very tedious if we constantly had to issue commands at such a minute level of detail. However, somewhere along the line, the child had to learn what it meant and all the steps in the process to open a door. The child didn't have to be told for each step and probably figured it out by observing others and by bumping into themselves a few times.

When working on a computer, it is helpful to remember that computers have to be instructed on how you want it to do things. And the first thing to remember about computers is that they can't do what you didn't tell them to do. Therefore, to ask the computer to open the door is meaningless until you actually define the exact steps required to accomplish the task. You can't rely on the computer to observe and understand the act of opening the door as a child would. Fortunately, you can build upon the work done by other programmers. So, for example, when you want to display a little message box saying, "Hello, World!" you can use a single line of code or instructions as shown below. This combines programming done by others with something you want said.

```
MsgBox "Hello, World!"
```

Behind the scenes, the instruction (command) MsgBox goes through several steps; it instructs the computer how to draw the box, how to position it, what button to put on it, and how to style it. All of those details are abstracted away from us, which makes our task so much easier. Knowing that the computer needs every step to be defined, you can appreciate the benefit of being able to leverage existing programming and commands to write your own code. But it's still upon you to supply the missing pieces, like the actual message "Hello, World!" Remembering the general rule that it can't do what you didn't tell it to do is invaluable in programming.

When writing code, you are working with a type of program called a *compiler*, which is responsible for translating the VBA language into machine language that the computer can understand and execute. As you write code, the compiler provides feedback on whether statements are valid and free of syntax errors. When discussing how the computer will react, we will often refer to the compiler or VBA Editor.

ANATOMY OF VBA PROCEDURES

The *procedures* are the basic building blocks you use to assemble together individual steps, or *statements*, for a specific task. You can then assemble a series of procedures to generate a complex output. To start with, there are basically three types of procedures: *Sub*, *Function*, and *Property*. The Property procedure is a more advanced topic that will be discussed later in the book. For now, we'll focus on Functions and Subs, which you will find throughout most applications.

We'll start by looking at a simple procedure and explaining the different parts and how they are constructed.

```
Sub SayHello()
    MsgBox "Hello, World!"
End Sub
```

code snippet EXAMPLES - Say Hello in ch6_VBABasics_Code.txt

Procedures always have a *signature* statement (typically the first line), which itself must contain at a minimum: type of procedure, *identifier*, or the name of the procedure and *parameters* (or also *arguments*). SayHello is a Sub procedure; although it displays a message box, it does not return a value. Because this example does not require a parameter, the () is empty. The final line is the End <procedure> statement that is required at the end of every procedure. Let's change this a bit by introducing a parameter:

```
Sub SayHello(strMessage As String)
    MsgBox strMessage
End Sub
```

code snippet EXAMPLES - Say Hello in ch6_VBABasics_Code.txt

The new SayHello procedure requires a string parameter. Thus, it is now more flexible than the first procedure, which would always say "Hello, World!" The second procedure can accept and display any message supplied in the parameter during execution.

> **COMPILE TIME VS. RUN TIME**
>
> Developers frequently talk about "compile time" and "run time." This is an essential distinction that is especially important for error handling and during design and testing. "Compile time" refers to the moment when the code is compiled (typically during development stages), whereas "runtime" occurs during the program's execution — when it is deployed and with the end user. You'll learn more about compiling and testing code in Chapter 7.

Now let's look at a Function procedure:

```
Function AddIt() As Long
    AddIt = 1 + 1
End Function
```

code snippet EXAMPLES - Say Hello - Message Box in ch6_VBABasics_Code.txt

You can quickly notice two major differences between the structure of the Function and the Sub. You see the As <data type> after the parameter list; telling the Function that the value will be a Long integer data type. And, you also see how we set the result (1+1) to the name of the function — that is how you tell it to return a value back to the procedure that calls the AddIt function.

Obviously, `AddIt` is not very flexible, so you will want to consider how you might make it work for any numbers. One way to do this is to add a parameter, as we did in the previous example:

```
Function AddIt(intInput As Integer) As Long
    AddIt = intInput + 1
End Function
```

code snippet EXAMPLES - AddIt Function in ch6_VBABasics_Code.txt

The new `AddIt` will return a number one bigger than whatever number you passed to the function. So whenever you want to increment a number by one, you just need to call the `AddIt` function. You'll learn more in Chapter 7, when we revisit the differences between the types of procedures. We will also discuss creating and calling custom procedures later in this chapter, in the section, "Writing Code in Modules."

All procedure signatures, as well as certain statements, can accept certain kinds of *modifiers*. Think of a modifier as instructions that tell the compiler what kind of characteristic this procedure should have. Controlling how a procedure is defined or used will help you leverage your code and programming techniques — as you will see in later discussions. For now, let's look at one kind of modifier.

There will be times where you may also want to control where a procedure can be used. You can do that by including a modifier that determines *accessibility* of a procedure. We will focus on the access modifiers: `Public` and `Private`. When we prefix a signature with either of those modifiers, we are describing where it can be called.

The primary goal of the next two procedures is to demonstrate these concepts, so don't worry about what each term means — we will discuss this later. For now, we just want to provide an overview and general understanding about the different types of procedures, how they are constructed, and how they are used and controlled or limited. Be sure to note the keywords `Public` and `Private` that are contained in each procedure's signature.

```
Public Function WhoAmI() As String
    WhoAmI = GetUserName & ": " & Application.CurrentUser
End Function

Private Function GetUserName() As String
    GetUserName = Environ("UserName")
End Function
```

code snippet EXAMPLES - WhoAmI in ch6_VBABasics_Code.txt

As you can see, we have two functions: `GetUserName`, which basically asks Windows OS for the username that was used to log in on Windows, and `WhoAmI`, which calls the `GetUserName` function and then also asks another question by asking Access who the current user is, which in most cases will be "Admin." The function then pieces together both a Windows OS login and an Access username. So if the Windows login is `Bob`, the result will be `Bob: Admin`.

Note that the `WhoAmI` function is able to call the `GetUserName` function. This will work even though `GetUserName` is marked as `Private` because they are in the same module. If `GetUserName` is moved to another module, the `WhoAmI` function will fail because it can't access `Private` procedures in *other* modules. On the other hand, any procedures from any module can call a `Public` procedure. As mentioned, the access modifier is optional, but when we omit it, the compiler will assume that it is `Public` by default. It is desirable to be explicit and add the access modifier to help others and yourself understand the code. We'll talk about `Public` and `Private` again in the section "Variables" and have a more in-depth discussion in Chapter 7.

VBA KEYWORDS

Keywords have specific meanings to a program and are used to tell it what to do in a given situation — much like a command. In the preceding section, you saw a few of the important VBA *keywords*, which are used to form a complete statement. The following are a few of the keywords that are frequently used. You'll learn more about these words as you see them throughout this chapter and the rest of the book.

Public	If	Select Case	Do	Dim
Private	Then	Case	Until	Static
Friend	End If	End Select	Loop	Global

Like the English language, VBA has syntax rules and expects certain constructs in a specific order. For example, you cannot have a `Then` keyword without a preceding `If` keyword. It is also important to remember that a keyword may have more than one meaning, and it usually helps a lot to remember what context you are looking at. Think about the English word, "right," which could mean an adjective denoting a certain direction, a noun for one's entitlement, or an adverb for whether one guessed correctly. VBA language has similar constructs and thus it is very important to remember in which context we are using a given keyword. Consider the `Date` keyword. It has three possible uses: as a data type, as a function returning today's date, and as a statement. The following snippet shows how the `Date` keyword is used in each of these constructs:

Available for download on Wrox.com

```
Dim dteDay As Date 'Date keyword is used as a data type
dteDay = Date() 'Date keyword is used as a function
' Date = dteDay 'Date keyword is used as a statement. See warning.
' You MUST retain apostrophe before 'Date = dteDay.
' WARNING: Example Only! Do not execute the Date statement.
' The Date statement will change the system date!
```

code snippet DEMO - Date Keyword in ch6_VBABasics_Code.txt

As you write code, you will find the VBA help files to be an indispensable resource for learning about additional keywords — how they can be used and in what context. When you look at the preceding `Dim` statement, you can see that, in addition to the keywords `Dim` and `As`, and the data type, it uses other keywords to form a complete statement. Omitting any one of those would be considered to be a syntax error.

You will use keywords to describe the expected logic and tell the computer what to do. Fortunately, once you become familiar with the syntax, most of the logic will be fairly easy to interpret and even write. You're probably familiar with if . . . then logic from math and routine activities. The following snippet, albeit incomplete, is an introductory example of how you might write an `If...Then` statement in VBA.

```
If blnResult = True Then
   MsgBox "The test result is positive."
Else
   MsgBox "The test result is negative."
End If
```

code snippet EXAMPLE - If Then in ch6_VBABasics_Code.txt

The keywords `If` and `Then`, along with `Loop`, `Select`, and `Case` belong to a family of "conditional branch" constructs. They represent important concepts that are discussed and demonstrated in Chapter 7.

VBA OPERATORS

As you saw in the preceding section, it is very common to perform some kind of operation within a given statement. You may have inferred that we used an addition *operator* in the `AddIt` procedures, and you may have noted that we used another operator, `&`, in the `WhoAmI` function. Indeed, operators are an important part of any statement. Here's a partial list of VBA operators and what they do.

OPERATOR	NAME	EXPLANATION
&	Concatenation	Used to splice strings together.
*	Multiplication	Multiply two numbers.
+	Addition	Add two numbers together; can also splice strings together*.
−	Subtraction	Subtract two numbers.
/	Floating Division	Divides two numbers and returns a floating result.
\	Integer Division	Divides two numbers and returns an integer, truncating the fraction.
^	Power	Raises a number to the *n*th power.
=	Equality	Compares two operands for equality.
Is	Object Comparison	Determines if an *object*** is a certain type of object.
Not	Negation	Logical inversion of Boolean result.
Mod	Modulo	Returns the remainder of a division for two numbers.
And	Logical And	Returns `true` only when both Boolean results are `true`.
Or	Logical Or	Returns `true` whenever either one of the Boolean results is `true`.

*The differences between & and + operators for string concatenation are discussed in Chapter 7.

**Object has a special meaning and is explained later.

It is important to note that some operators require one operand (*unary operator*) while others may require two (*binary operator*). For the most part, this is no different from what you may be already familiar with typical math operations. It should also be noted that VBA has some logical operators that expect Boolean results. However, VBA is capable of implicitly converting an operand into a Boolean result, which is explained in greater detail in Chapter 7.

The operators and operands together form an *expression*. An expression can in turn contain other expressions which may be separated with a () just like you did in Algebra class way back in school. Here's an example of a complex expression combining a few operators:

```
"Hello" & ", " & "World!"
"Todayís date is " & Date() & ". Tomorrowís date will be " & (Date() + 1)
```

code snippet EXAMPLE - Expression using Hello World in ch6_VBABasics_Code.txt

Note that VBA is flexible enough to allow you to perform operations on items that may not be strictly perceived as a number such as adding 1 to today's date to get tomorrow's date. But be aware that flexibility can also have its pitfalls and lessons that can be frustrating for novice programmers. Some of the more common pitfalls will be addressed later in this chapter and in the next chapter. For now, we'll continue exploring the basics with a discussion of variables.

VARIABLES AND VBA SYNTAX

This section gives you a brief introduction to some important factors about variables and VBA syntax that will help you to successfully program in VBA. The brief explanations will provide a foundation for the material covered in subsequent chapters, but they are not intended to be an exhaustive tutorial on VBA. We encourage you to explore the material that is offered through the Access and VBA help features as well as other online resources, such as MSDN. You might also want to purchase a beginner's guide to VBA programming, such as *VBA For Dummies*, by John Paul Mueller (Jan 2007 Wiley Publishing, Inc., ISBN 978-0-470-04650-0).

Variables

One of the most important concepts in programming is the use of variables. A *variable* is a named location in memory where you can store a value while your code is running. One advantage of using a variable is that the stored value can be changed as required by your program. For example, you can create a variable called strState, which will hold the value of a state, e.g., Washington. Once you've assigned a value to that variable — strState — you can use it repeatedly in your code without having to specify the state each time. When the variable appears, the code will retrieve the stored value, Washington, from its location in memory. If you later need to use California instead of Washington, you only have to find the one place in your code where you have assigned the value to the strState variable, instead of searching for all of the code that refers to state or writing separate blocks of code to handle each possible state. Later in this section, we'll provide additional details about how to create variables and assign values to them.

Using variables can also make your code easier for others to interpret because each variable is defined with a specific data type — that is, it states what type of data the variables can contain: for example, string, number, object, or date. As you'll see, a string variable is basically any combination of alphanumeric data, such as a phrase or name. Although a string can store numbers, the numbers will function as text rather than as numbers on which you can perform mathematical operations. Some common examples of numbers that might be stored in a string are Social Security Numbers (in the U.S.), telephone numbers, and postal codes. We'll go into more detail a little later in the chapter. A number data type is used to store values that can be used in mathematical operations. Objects, including specific database objects and collections, can be any type of data.

Properly defining variables is one of the most important tasks you need to master to program in VBA. It's not hard, but it is a critical skill. As you saw in the earlier examples, one key aspect is to match the variable with the contents. The variable to hold a number was `Long`, and the variable to hold text was `String`. In the next few sections, we will explore some of the major rules and recommendations for variables.

Variable Data Types

As you've seen, you can declare variables as many different data types. And it is a best practice for the name to indicate the type of data. We'll briefly mention naming conventions and reserved words in the next section. They are covered in more detail in Appendixes F and G, so for now our focus is to ensure that the variable is declared with the correct data type. Doing so will help your code run as efficiently as possible; and if it does generate an error, having the correct data type will typically provide a more descriptive and specific error message. If you don't declare a data type, the variable is created as a `Variant`. Variables defined as variant data types require more memory allocation (the system needs to prepare for the largest possible data type), and they often result in slower performance than with explicitly defined data types because the appropriate data type of a variant must be determined at runtime.

The following table lists the more commonly used variable data types, the amount of memory they take, and the range of values that they can store. You can find more comprehensive lists from MSDN and other sites.

DATA TYPE	SIZE IN MEMORY	POSSIBLE VALUES
`Byte`	1 byte	0 to 255.
`Boolean`	2 bytes	True or False
`Integer`	2 bytes	–32,768 to 32,767.
`Long` (long integer)	4 bytes	–2,147,483,648 to 2,147,483,647.
`LongLong` (big integer)	8 bytes	–9,223,372,036,854,775,808 to +9,223,372,036,854,775,807.
`LongPtr`	Scalable	On 32-bit platform, same as `Long`; On 64-bit platform, same as `LongLong`.
`Single` (single-precision real)	4 bytes	Approximately –3.4E38 to 3.4E38.
`Double` (double-precision real)	8 bytes	Approximately –1.8E308 to 4.9E324.

DATA TYPE	SIZE IN MEMORY	POSSIBLE VALUES
`Currency` (scaled integer)	8 bytes	Approximately −922,337,203,685,477.5808 to 922,337,203,685,477.5807.
`Decimal*`	14 bytes	With no decimal places, the range is +/−79,228,162,514,264, 337,593,543,950,335. With decimal places, the range is +/− 1E−28 (one to the 28th power). The smallest possible non-zero number is 0.000,000,000,000,000,000,000,000,000,1 written +/−1E-28.
`Date`	8 bytes	1/1/100 to 12/31/9999.
`GUID**`	16 bytes	Approximately 3.40 * 10^{38} possible distinct values.
`Object`	4 bytes	Any object reference.
`String`	10 bytes + string length	Variable length: ≤ about 2 billion.
`String * N`	String length	N of bytes, up to 65,400 maximum.
`Variant` (holding a number)	16 bytes for numbers	Same as double.
`Variant` (holding a string)	22 bytes + string length	Same as string.
User-defined	Varies	Defined by user.

*The Decimal data type is included in this table although it cannot be used as a variable in a Dim statement. Rather, the Decimal data type can be a Variant subtype using the `CDec()` function.

**Likewise, GUID is not an actual data type in VBA but is available as an Access database engine data type and will be represented as a string in VBA.

Although the data types in Access tables and variables in VBA are different sets of data types, you will notice a partial parallel between them. Two of the main differences are that there is no equivalent to the variant or object data types in Access data types, and the Access `Number` data type has a field size property that enables you to specify the field as `Byte`, `Integer`, `Long`, `Single`, `Decimal`, or `Double`. If you are accustomed to using variables in other programming languages, such as C or C#, you should pay close attention to any differences in how those programming languages handle variables.

Naming Your Variables

When naming your variables, following a few rules and guidelines can avoid conflicts within your code and when integrating with other programs. They can also make it easier for you and others to interpret your code. Some of the basic rules include:

➤ Use only letters, numbers, and the underscore symbol (_). No other symbols are allowed.

➤ Variable names must start with a letter.

➤ Do not use a reserved word for your variable name (see the sidebar that follows).

➤ Variable names must be less than 255 characters.

SPECIAL CHARACTERS, RESERVED WORDS AND NAMING CONVENTIONS

In addition to the rules that you must follow when naming your variables, best practices suggest that you follow a naming convention, avoid special characters, and avoid using a reserved word (including those recognized by other programs that are involved) as the name of an object. In that line, you may want to review the Reddick naming convention (see the following sidebar), as it is arguably the most popular among Access developers.

Appendix F explains and lists the reserved words and special characters associated with Access and VBA for Access. Appendix G explains the basic naming conventions, and provides some guidance to help you create your own. Depending on your work environment, you may have the latitude to implement, modify, or even ignore conventions. However, we strongly recommend that you at least create meaningful variable names. Meaningful names will make it easier to read through the code, and they will help to minimize conflicts and facilitate debugging. If you create variables with names such as `var1`, `var2`, and `var3`, you and anyone who works on your code will face undue challenges in tracking which variable is used in which statement.

REDDICK NAMING CONVENTIONS

This book sticks pretty closely to the Reddick naming conventions. The names of variables include a prefix that indicates the data type. String variables, for example, usually have the `str` prefix, such as `strSQL` and `strMsg`, whereas Boolean variables will have a `bln` prefix, such as `blnUnderBudget` and `blnCurrentMeeting`.

In addition (or as an alternative) to the Reddick naming conventions, some developers use other conventions to make their code easier to interpret by adding a leading prefix to variable names to denote whether the variable is a global, private, or local variable. The following table describes the prefixes used to denote variable scope and lifetime. You'll also note that these examples use CamelCase, instead of an underscore or space between words. CamelCase essentially capitalizes the first letter of each word and removes all spaces.

PREFIX	VARIABLE SCOPE	EXAMPLES	USAGE
g	Global variable	`gobj; gcurPrice`	Variables declared with the `Public` keyword
m	Private (module-level) variables	`mSalesTotal`	Variables declared with the `Private` keyword
s	Static variables	`sintWhileCount`	Local variables declared with the `Static` keyword

Variable Scope and Lifetime

The scope of a variable defines the visibility and accessibility for that variable. The *lifetime* of a variable describes how long it will exist in memory.

Unless you indicate otherwise, when you declare a variable within a sub or function, the variable's scope is limited to that specific sub or function, meaning that the variable is visible and accessible only within that sub or function, and it is destroyed when the routine is exited. That's why you don't need to worry about conflict between variables with the same name being used in different subs or functions. The lifetime of that variable is the period of time when the sub or function is in the computer memory — the variable is in memory only while the sub or function is running. As soon as the procedure ends, the variable is destroyed and the memory allocated to it is released. A subsequent call of the procedure creates a new instance of the variable and it has no memory of the previous instance.

You use a `Dim` statement to define a variable, as shown in this snippet.

Available for download on Wrox.com

```
Private Sub SayHello()
  Dim strMessage As String
  strMessage = "Hello, World!"
  Msgbox strMessage
End Sub
```

code snippet EXAMPLE - SayHello in ch6_VBABasics_Code.txt

The variable `strMessage` is a *local variable* and is not accessible outside of the `SayHello` sub. The variable basically lives and dies within that procedure.

At times you may want a particular variable to exist outside of the scope of a sub or function. In that case, you can use a module-level variable. By declaring the variable in the General Declarations section at the top of the module, the variable will have the scope and lifetime of the module (declaring a module-level variable anywhere else outside the General Declarations section may cause a compile error). Similar to procedures, the module-level variable can be declared as `Private` or `Public`.

➤ Use the `Private` keyword to limit visibility of the variable only to procedures within the current module.

➤ Use the `Public` keyword to make the variable available anywhere in the entire application.

The following code sample illustrates how both the declaration and its location affect a variable's scope (visibility and use) and lifetime. The first four lines would typically be located at the top of a module. We'll discuss this more after looking at the examples.

Available for download on Wrox.com

```
Option Explicit 'Used to require variable declaration
  Public gtxtCustomerName As String 'Public sets the scope as the entire application
  Private mtxtVendor As String ' Private sets the scope to within the module
  Dim mtxtSupplier As String ' set within a module, the scope is the current module

Private Sub GetCustomerName()
  Dim txtCustomer As String ' set within a sub, the scope is limited to that sub
End Sub
```

Code DEMO - Setting Variable Scope in Snippet ch6_VBABasics_Code.txt

Notice that the two statements that begin with `Dim` have different scopes. Just like the Private declaration, use of the `Dim` keyword in the General Declarations section, as with `mtxtSupplier`, sets the scope of the variable to the module so it can be used by any procedure in that module. Declaring the variable within the procedure, as we did above with `txtCustomer`, limits the scope of the variable to only that procedure. In the previous listing, `mtxtVendor` and `mtxtSupplier` are both module-level variables. They can be used anywhere within the module and anytime the module is loaded. However, `gtxtCustomerName` was declared with the keyword `Public`, so it is a global variable and can be used anywhere within any procedure in the application.

This brings us to another keyword that merits discussing; `Static`. It has two meanings — depending on whether it is being used as a modifier for a procedure or as a modifier for a variable's declaration. In both cases, the modifier extends the variable's lifetime and allows the value to persist even after the procedure is completed and is no longer in scope. Because we are working with variables, we will start by discussing how `Static` is used with a variable. We can declare a variable as `Static`, as shown in this snippet:

```
Public Function IncrementIt() As Integer
   Static sintIncrement As Integer
   sintIncrement = sintIncrement + 1
   IncrementIt = sintIncrement
End Function
```

code snippet EXAMPLES - Using Static in ch6_VBABasics_Code.txt

There are several reasons why you might want to mark a local variable as `Static`. For example, you may need to know how many times a particular procedure was run. In that case, you could simply declare a global variable and increment this variable every time the procedure runs. However, sometimes it's easier to track the use of variables when they are declared within the procedure in which they're used.

There's one big difference between using the `Static` keyword within the procedure and using the `Public` keyword in the General Declarations section to declare your variables. Declaring the variable with the `Public` keyword in the General Declarations section allows you to use the variable anywhere within your application. Using the `Static` keyword within a procedure restricts the variable to use within that procedure. Keep in mind that in the latter case, the static variable is still dedicated to the one procedure, so you cannot use the `Static` keyword to create a variable within Procedure A and then use the variable within Procedure B.

The second use for the `Static` keyword is to include it within the procedure's signature. We'll modify the previous example to move `Static` from the variable level to the signature, as shown here:

```
Public Static Function IncrementIt()
   Dim sintIncrement As Integer
   sintIncrement = sintIncrement + 1
   IncrementIt = sintIncrement
End Function
```

code snippet EXAMPLES - Using Static in ch6_VBABasics_Code.txt

By marking a procedure itself as `Static`, all of the variables that are declared within that procedure will be static even if they are declared using a `Dim` statement. Although it is legal (meaning that the compiler will allow it) to declare a local variable using `Static` within a `Static` procedure, it is redundant. If you have a procedure where you only want to retain the value between calls for certain variables but not all variables, then the `Static` keyword should not be used in the procedure's signature. Instead, you should selectively declare each variable as either `Static` or `Dim`.

Overlapping Variables

When writing code, you should ensure that you give each variable a unique name. If you declare a public variable with the name `strString` and then declare a variable within your procedure also named `strString`, VBA will always use the local variable. Because local variables take precedence over global variables, this might return unexpected results in a procedure that calls a routine that uses a variable that has the same name as a public variable. This is an important concept, and it can be easy to grasp with the following code.

Available for download on Wrox.com

```
Option Compare Database
Option Explicit
    'this module demonstrates that local variables
    'take precedence over public variables.
Public intQuantity As Integer
Public curPrice As Currency

Private Sub FindTotals()
Dim intQuantity As Integer
Dim curTotalPrice As Currency
    'this sub declares the local variable intQuantity
    'but does not give it a value, so the value is 0.

    curPrice = InputBox("Please enter the bike price.", _
    "Enter Bike Price")
    curTotalPrice = intQuantity * curPrice
    MsgBox curTotalPrice, vbOKOnly, "Total Price"
End Sub

Private Sub EnterValues()
    'this is storing the value into the global variable.
    intQuantity = InputBox("Please enter the number of bikes", _
    "you want to buy.", "Total Bikes")
End Sub

Private Sub CalculatePrice()
    'This sub runs the two subs listed below.
    'Although Enter Values stores a quantity in the
    'global Variable, intQuantity, the FindTotals sub will
    'use the local variable intQuantity to calculate curTotalPrice.
    EnterValues
    FindTotals
End Sub
```

code snippet EXAMPLES - Overlapping Variables in ch6_VBABasics_Code.txt

These three procedures illustrate how variables can overlap. If you run the `CalculatePrice` procedure, Access VBA will run the other two procedures, `EnterValues` and `FindTotals`. When that code is run, the `EnterValues` procedure asks you for the total number of bikes you want to buy. This stores the value into the public variable, `intQuantity`. The `FindTotals` procedure asks you for the bike price and calculates the total purchase price (quantity of bikes multiplied by the purchase price). However, there's a problem here. The line in the `FindTotals` procedure — `Dim intQuantity as Integer` — causes the calculation to return zero. This one line tells Access VBA to create a local procedure-level variable with the same name as the public variable declared in the General Declarations section of the module. Because there is no input for this local variable, it uses the default value of 0. And, because local variables have precedence, the procedure uses the local variable, `intQuantity`, instead of the global variable, `intQuantity`. So the result of the equation `curTotalPrice` is 0.

If you want Access VBA to use the public variable, you can prefix the public variable in accordance with Reddick VBA naming convention with an `m`. The following code will work as intended:

```
Option Compare Database
Option Explicit
   'this module demonstrates that by explicitly naming a variable with
   'both the public and variable name, the value of the public variable
   'will be used. You can also use a specific prefix such as mintQuantity.

Public mintQuantity As Integer
Public mcurPrice As Currency

Private Sub FindTotals()
Dim intQuantity As Integer
Dim curTotalPrice As Currency
   'This sub declares the local variable intQuantity
   'but it does not give it a value, so the value is 0.

curPrice = InputBox("Please enter the bike price.", _
   "Enter Bike Price")
   curTotalPrice = mintQuantity * curPrice
   MsgBox curTotalPrice, vbOKOnly, "Total Price"

End Sub

Private Sub EnterValues()
   'this is storing the value into the public variable.
   mintQuantity = InputBox("Please enter the number of bikes", _
   "you want to buy.", "Total Bikes")
End Sub

Private Sub CalculatePrice()
   'This sub runs the two subs listed below.
   'Although Enter Values stores a quantity in the public Variable, intQuantity,
   'the FindTotals uses the local variable intQuantity to calculate curTotalPrice.
   EnterValues
   FindTotals
End Sub
```

code snippet EXAMPLE - Public Variables (1) in ch6_VBABasics_Code.txt

If you want Access VBA to use the public variable, you can explicitly name the variable by adding the prefix m before the variable's name. The same approach also applies to module variables. However, it is typically best to avoid this situation entirely. A best practice is to utilize naming conventions and to declare variables with the narrowest scope practical. If you don't need to declare a public variable, it is generally better to use a local variable.

To illustrate why local variables may be desirable — let us pretend for a moment that we have nothing but public variables as shown here:

```
Public strCustomerName As String

Private Sub WhoReferredWhom()
   FindCustomer 1 'Traci DeVine
   GetReferral 1  'Brandi Whine
   MsgBox gstrCustomerName & _
      " was referred by " & _
      gstrCustomerName
End Sub

Private Sub FindCustomer(lngCustomerID As Long)
   gstrCustomerName = DLookup( _
      "CustomerName", _
      "tblCustomers", _
      "CustomerID=" & lngCustomerKey)
End Sub

Private Sub GetReferral(lngCustomerID As Long)
   gstrCustomerName = DLookup( _
      "CustomerName", _
      "tblCustomers", _
      "ReferredBy=" & lngCustomerID)
End Sub
```

code snippet EXAMPLE - Public Variables (2) in ch6_VBABasics_Code.txt

Suppose gstrCustomerName was given a value Traci DeVine when FindCustomer is executed. Then GetReferral runs and needs to look up another customer, and puts in Brandi Whine in the gstrCustomerName. Do we know whether we are really done with Traci DeVine or could it be needed again by another procedure? Do you want to check for the current value every time you call a procedure, or risk having it stomped upon in the course of normal execution?

In our example, WhoReferredWhom will end up displaying Brandi Whine was referred by Brandi Whine because when GetReferral ran, it overwrote Traci DeVine and inserted Brandi Whine in its place. While this is a simplistic and obvious example, it demonstrates one of the things that can easily be missed in production code that has complex logic. By restricting the variable to the procedure where it is needed, you greatly minimize the overhead (and associated risks) of maintaining different variables. You'll also have confidence that each procedure can use its own local variable, strCustomerName, and have the correct value.

For even more robust programming, you will find it beneficial to use parameters in conjunction with local variables. By passing in Traci DeVine to a procedure's strCustomerName parameter, you do not need to declare a public gstrCustomerName variable or even a local strCustomerName variable, and you remove the chance of issues related to a procedure that is attempting to look up "Traci DeVine" returning "Brandi Whine" instead.

For your convenience, we have included these two modules in this chapter's sample file so that you can easily experiment and run some tests.

Very quickly, it should become apparent that having too many public variables gets unwieldy and difficult to manage. By carefully determining and setting the appropriate scope of a variable you can avoid the risks and challenges associated with overlapping variables.

OTHER VBA COMPONENTS

There are a few other VBA components that you'll frequently use within your code: option statements, comments, constants, and to a lesser extent, enums. Some were mentioned in Chapter 5, and they will be covered in more detail later in this book, so our intent here is to provide a brief discussion of the more common components along with a demonstration of how they can be helpful within your code.

Option Statements

Modules can have option statements that are used to govern specific default modes for that module. There are four kinds of option statements: `Compare`, `Explicit`, `Base`, and `Private`. Out of the box, Access's VBA Editor will only insert `Option Compare Database`. This determines how to compare strings; specifically, should the comparison be case sensitive or not? The `Database` directs the compiler to follow the same rules of string comparison as the database has adopted — this is governed by the database's Sort Order, which is established when you create a new database. Alternatively, we can choose `Text` (`Option Compare Text`), which is not case sensitive, or `Binary` (`Option Compare Binary`), which is case sensitive. We talk more about String comparisons in Chapter 7.

The option `Explicit` is not on by default, but we strongly recommend that you turn it on as it can be an enormous help in reducing mistakes due to typos, misspelling, or incorrect variables. `Explicit` instructs the compiler to require you to declare all variables. Without this option, the compiler will silently create a new variable (of type Variant) for every unknown identifier it comes across in the code. So, if you named a variable `strCustomerName` and inadvertently typed `strCsutomerName` in another place (within the code), you would end up with two variables. Not only would they have different values, but the variable that you correctly defined will not be used where the "new" variable was created. Using `Option Explicit` helps to prevent this type of scenario.

The other two options, `Base` and `Private`, are rarely used so we will only mention their most common uses. `Base` is used to specify what number is the first (or base) number in an array. The normal convention is for the first element to be indexed at zero. It is best to not change `Base` as that can cause more confusion than it is worth. `Private` is useful when you do not want another project to see the module. This can be useful in a library or reference database. You can explore these more on MSDN and through other online resources.

Comments

VBA programming consists of writing statements (that affect the code) and comments (that do not affect the code). Although comments are not required, they are highly recommended as they make it much easier to read the code and to figure out what it is intended to do. As you may have noticed, uncommented code is often hard to read and can be quite difficult to understand.

Comments are invaluable tools for the developer, the tester, and anyone trying to interpret or modify the code. You can use them to document business rules that are enforced by a specific function, and they are particularly helpful in a production file to record when, why, and by whom code is modified. You will find that the comments in well-documented code can be especially helpful if you need to quickly get up-to-speed on a previous project — whether it is something you worked on recently, several years ago, or in a project that you inherit. Comments offer an excellent way to provide convenient documentation explaining why something is handled in a particular way and not another.

As you saw in our earlier examples, you can add comments by placing an apostrophe in front of the text. Any text that appears on the same line and to the right of an apostrophe is a comment and will be ignored by the compiler, regardless of where the apostrophe is in the line. That means that you can also place a comment at the front of a line of otherwise-normal code to prevent it from running. This is commonly called "commenting out" the code.

The default setting is for comments to appear in green, so they are quickly recognized when you are looking through code. Although you can insert comments at the end of a line of code, to improve readability they are commonly placed on separate lines and used before or after a procedure or function. As comments are ignored during code execution, you can have as few or many lines of comments as seem helpful in any procedure. Comments don't slow down the execution of your code so you can use them liberally. However, a good practice is not to overburden your code with unnecessary comments — for example, you don't need to interpret every line of simple VBA code into its English equivalent.

Line Continuation

Strategic line breaks also help make code more readable and easier to understand. Many VBA statements can be quite long. Take the following If...Then statement that is used to fill a variable with a value:

Available for download on Wrox.com

```
If (txtCustomerState = "CA" And txtCustomerZip = "95685") Or _
   (txtCustomerState = "WA" And txtCustomerZip = "89231") Then
   txtCustomerRegion = "Western US"
End If
```

---

code snippet EXAMPLES - Line Continuation in ch6_VBABasics_Code.txt

As you can see, this code is a bit long. When printed in this book, even the conditional portion of the statement takes up several lines. VBA does not impose word wrapping, so the default is for all of the code to go on one very long line — that often continues beyond the screen display. Having to scroll horizontally can make it unduly challenging to view the entire procedure in order to read and interpret code.

A line continuation character (an underscore preceded by a space) is used to break long lines of code into shorter lines that are understandable and easy-to-read. Although you are inserting characters into the code, they are only to control the appearance and do not impact the meaning of the code. The space/underscore at the end of a code line indicates that the next line is a continuation of the current line. As you can see from the following example, just by strategically inserting line breaks, the code becomes easier to interpret.

```
If (txtCustomerState = "CA" And _
    txtCustomerZip = "95685") Or _
    (txtCustomerState = "WA" _
    And txtCustomerZip = "89231") Then
    txtCustomerRegion = "Western US"
End If
```

code snippet EXAMPLES - Line Continuation in ch6_VBABasics_Code.txt

Line breaks not only keep the code within the viewing pane, but they also make it easier to recognize individual steps within a procedure. But we also need to be cautious about breaking a string within a line, as we cannot just insert a line continuation and expect the string to continue on the next line. For example, we might have a very long SQL statement to include all of the fields and data you need from your table. The statement might read something like the following:

```
strSQL = "SELECT [CustomerName], [CustomerCode], [CustomerAddress1],
[CustomerCity], [CustomerState], [CustomerZip] FROM Customers WHERE [CustomerState]
Is Not Null;"
```

code snippet EXAMPLES - Line Continuation in ch6_VBABasics_Code.txt

You can use the line continuation character (_) along with the concatenation operator (&) and string delimiters (") to format the previous example into a display that is much easier to read and interpret, as shown here:

```
strSQL = "SELECT [CustomerName], [CustomerCode]" _
    & ", [CustomerAddress1], [CustomerCity]" _
    & ", [CustomerState], [CustomerZip] FROM" _
    & " Customers WHERE [CustomerState] Is Not Null;"
```

code snippet EXAMPLES - Line Continuation in ch6_VBABasics_Code.txt

In addition to breaking the code lines to delineate actions, you should also break lines any time they are longer than a standard screen width. In addition to the line-continuation characters, you will also need to include a space to separate words within the literal string. The space can be placed after the last character at the end of the line just before the underscore, or it can be inserted between the quotation mark and the first character at the beginning of the next line (as shown above). Without the appropriate spaces, words can run together. In the preceding example, you might end up with a senseless term such as FROMCustomers, as shown here:

```
... [CustomerZip] FROMCustomers WHERE ...
```

The result of this error is invalid SQL syntax, which will cause an error when you try to execute that SQL statement.

Constants

In general, a constant is exactly what the name implies — something that doesn't change. It can be a string or numeric value. Constants can be literal, symbolic, or built-in.

Literal constants are numbers, strings, and dates that are hard-coded within the procedure. They are often used to improve clarity and consistency. For example, the following line of code shows how to use a literal constant. By assigning a literal value to the variable dteStartDate, you know that the "start date" will always be October 23, 2007 unless, of course, the value of variable dteStartDate is subsequently changed.

```
Dim dteStartDate As Date    'Declare the variable
dteStartDate = #10/23/2007# 'Assign the literal constant
```

code snippet EXAMPLE - Literal Constant in ch6_VBABasics_Code.txt

A symbolic constant is an identifier that is used to store fixed values that won't change in your code. They are usually declared at the beginning of the procedure (or at the module level) by using the Const keyword instead of the Dim keyword. Specifying a constant for the width of a page is an example of a symbolic constant. Often, the constant name is typed in all capital letters, as in this example: Const PAGE_WIDTH = 80

> As you're reading and working through the examples, you may want to start your own list of conventions that will provide structure and consistency to the format and layout of your code. Of course, we encourage you to do as many developers have and adopt the Reddick conventions — and continue to expand them to meet your needs.

You can declare literal and symbolic constants in several ways, such as in the General Declarations section or within a procedure. As with variables, you can also stipulate the scope by declaring them as Public or Private. While Constants follow many of the same rules as variables, they also have a couple of rules of their own. Their name must be unique throughout the application, including both the names that you create and the built-in constants. And once a constant is created, you cannot change its value while the program is running.

Built-in constants are defined within VBA, either by a program or by the system. They help you code faster by enabling you to use the constant's name rather than the value associated with the constant. For example, VBA provides constants for such uses as defining the types of buttons you see on a message box. One that is commonly used to format text in a message box is vbNewline, which as the name suggests inserts line breaks into the text. Because the constant has a somewhat intuitive name, it is easier to remember than its value (some special ASCII characters). A built-in constant can be used by simply typing its name. All built-in constants in VBA begin with the letters vb.

There are approximately 700 built-in constants in VBA, and more in Access itself (beginning with ac). Thankfully, you don't need to learn all of them. In fact, you will typically use only a few of them.

The following table describes some of VBA's built-in constants. As you can see, there are constants to specify values for a wide range of VBA operations. As with our list, many of the Access and VBA constants can also be categorized as Enums, which we will explain shortly. You can find more extensive lists of Access and VBA constants through their respective Help files and on MSDN. You can also view a list of VBA constants in the Object Browser. From the VBA window, you can simply use the shortcut key F2 or you can select View ⇨ Object Browser.

CONSTANT NAME	LITERAL VALUE OR CHARACTER VALUE	PURPOSE
vbBack	Chr(8)	Represents a backspace character.
vbCrLf	Chr(13) & Chr(10)	Represents two characters: a carriage return and then a line feed.
vbLf	Chr(10)	Represents a line feed character.
vbNullChar	Chr(0)	Represents a null character (not to be confused with database null).
vbNewLine	Varies	Returns either vbCrLf on Windows or vbLf on Macintosh.
vbNullString	" "	Returns a zero-length string, which appears as a blank field.
vbObjectError	-2147221504	Used to mark the start for custom error numbering.
vbTab	Chr(9)	Inserts a tab character.

Each Object Library (these will be explained in the upcoming section on objects) that is referenced within your code contains its own set of built-in constants. Additionally, each Object Library typically has its own prefix; all built-in constants in Access use the prefix ac; in Outlook the prefix is ol; and in Word the prefix is wd. A few examples will quickly clarify what we mean, so here are a few built-in constants from Access: acDataErrAdded, acFormatXLS, and acSave. You may also use several constants from VBA, such as vbCrLf, vbTab, and vbNullString. As mentioned previously, it is a lot easier to use the built-in constants in your code than it is to remember the actual value the constant represents.

Enums

Both Access and VBA have another way to group constants — that is, by using an enumeration, commonly known as an enum. An enum allows you to group logically related constants under a meaningful group name, and it also allows you to specify a meaningful name and an integer value for each constant within the group. As you saw when we were reviewing the Access and VBA constants, this serves multiple purposes. First, it specifies the possible values that can be in the enum (the group), and it essentially provides a shorthand for identifying the members within the enum. You'll also appreciate that the names of the enums and members are accessible through IntelliSense as you write your code, a feature that we'll demonstrate shortly.

Your code won't actually contain the enum itself; rather, you'll use the constants that are declared in the enum instead of using their intrinsic values. As you can imagine, Access has many built-in enums. For example, the following enum lists the constants that can be used to specify a specific view of a form.

```
Enum acFormView
   acNormal = 0
   acDesign = 1
   acPreview = 2
   acFormDS = 3
   acFormPivotTable = 4
   acFormPivotChart = 5
   acFormLayout = 6
End Enum
```

You can browse any of the Access or VBA enums in the Object Browser, which you learned about in Chapter 5.

VBA OBJECTS

In order to program efficiently in VBA you need to understand how the various VBA components work together. As shown earlier, VBA code comprises individual statements. Those statements take objects and manipulate their properties, call their methods, and perform their events. This section introduces the concepts of objects, properties, methods, and events.

VBA is a language with many object-oriented programming (OOP) features. In general, OOP is a type of programming that allows developers to define a data structure, and to specify both the data types and the operations that can be applied to the data structure. Programmers can create an entire object that contains both data (properties) and the operations that the object can perform (methods). They can also create relationships between different objects.

The collection of objects that is exposed by a particular application is called an *Object Library*. You can incorporate and simultaneously work with multiple Object Libraries in VBA. For example, you can use VBA to manipulate the Access Object Library (aka the Access Object Model) and to work with objects such as tables, queries, forms, and reports. You can also set references to Object Libraries from other applications such as Microsoft Outlook, Adobe Acrobat, or Microsoft Word. Appendix E provides an in-depth discussion of how to set and use references. Every time you set a reference to the Object Library of another application, you have access to public objects within that library. This ability to reference numerous Object Libraries gives VBA the ability to work with a remarkably large number of objects.

One way to conceptualize the idea of an object is to compare it to a familiar physical thing, such as an automobile. If you could set a reference to a car's Object Library, you could then use all of the objects that make up the car, such as its tires, engine, carpet, and steering wheel. We'll expand on this example as we discuss properties.

Properties

A *property* is an attribute of an object. Each property can take on one of several possible values. For example, the properties for a Car object include color (values of color can be silver or blue, and so on), doors (it can have two or four, or more), and cylinders (it can typically have four, six, or eight). Similar to a form (object), the Car object has objects of its own, such as tire and seat. The car's tire object has a brand property (Yuko). A particular car's seat object might have properties such as style (bucket) and clean (true).

Some properties of an object can be easily changed. If you want to change the value for the car's property color, you can take it to an auto detailer and have them paint it. With one spilled coffee, the carpet's property clean must be changed to False. Of course, you can't easily change the number of doors on the car. And, short of completely replacing the engine, you can't change the number of cylinders. Likewise, objects in VBA have some properties that can be changed and some that cannot.

Similar to VBA objects, every object in Access also has properties. The form object, for instance, has numerous properties including Border Style, Width, Height, and Caption. Each of these properties has a range of possible values. The Border Style property, for example, can be set to None, Thin, Sizable, and Dialog — each choice presents the form object with a slightly different look, and it can significantly affect the functionality.

Before manipulating properties in VBA code, you should take a look at the object and examine some of its properties. In the case of a form, you can launch the form in Design mode and change some of its properties. Then run the form to see how the changes can affect not only the display but also the operation of the form. Forms and controls generally have dozens of properties and options; fortunately they're relatively logical and you typically work with only a few. You'll learn more about forms in Chapter 14.

Methods

A *method* is an action that can be performed by, or on, an object. When you're in your car, you can invoke the start method of the engine, invoke the release method of the parking break, invoke the shift method of the transmission, and invoke the press method of the gas pedal. Each of these methods causes something to happen. If you've programmed things correctly, the car goes forward (which can be described as causing the accelerate method to be executed on the car itself). Generally, an action or event that happens (such as driving) is made up of many other methods performed on multiple objects.

Objects in VBA have methods as well. For example, you can invoke the LoadPicture method on an ActiveX control within an Access form to cause a picture to be displayed within that control. One of the frequently used methods moves the cursor to the next record in a DAO Recordset by using rst.MoveNext. You'll see a wide range of events, methods, and commands as we move forward in this chapter and throughout the book.

Events

An *event* is something that *happens* in response to a change in the state of an object. The car turns (the event) when you turn the steering wheel (you change its state). The horn blares when you press it. The seats heat when the seat heater is turned on. Turning, blaring, and heating are all events that can *happen* for the car. Most events happen when the user does something — in other words, when the user invokes a method on the object. The act is the method, or another way of stating it is that the action that is taken when the event is fired is the Event method. When you invoke the move method on the wheel, the car's turn event happens. It can be difficult to understand the difference between a method and an event with a real-world analogy of a car, but the distinction will become clearer as you take a look at the relationship between the methods and events of an Access form.

When you open an Access form, the OnOpen event will fire — meaning it will automatically be initiated; and when you close the form, the OnClose event will fire. You can also invoke the Open method of the form in code, which, under the correct circumstances, will cause the OnOpen event to fire. This means that invoking a method will often cause one or more events to fire. The next section will go into event creation.

Now that you know a bit more about properties, methods, and events, you're ready for a brief overview of the fundamentals for writing VBA code.

USING CODE BEHIND FORMS AND REPORTS

Now that you're becoming familiar with code in general, we'll move on to talk about how to include VBA code behind forms and reports, so that they will be the high performance tools that you can use to manage your business information. Throughout our discussion, we will refer to forms, but the same concepts also apply to reports.

The first step is to open the VBA Editor. When you look at a form or report in Design view, you can open the VBA editor by selecting View Code from the Design Ribbon (see Figure 6-1).

FIGURE 6-1

Clicking View Code on a new form will give you a blank module. However, it may be more interesting to see how you can create an event that will be raised in (called by) VBA. Let's start by creating a blank form:

1. In Access 2010, click the Create tab of the Ribbon.

2. Click Blank Form.

3. Switch to Design view.

4. Click Property Sheet in the Tools group of the Ribbon.

5. On the Property Sheet on the right-hand side, verify that Form is selected in the combo box.

6. Select the Event tab.

7. Scroll down to find the event "On Open."

8. Select the text box to the right of On Open; two buttons should then appear, as shown in Figure 6-2.

9. Click the drop-down button and choose [Event Procedure] from the list.

10. Click the ellipsis button. This will then take you to the VBA Editor, which opens to the Form_ Open event, as shown in Figure 6-3.

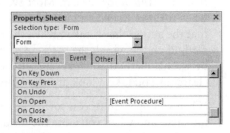

FIGURE 6-2

Notice how the procedure signature is automatically added. You might also take note of the two combo boxes containing Form and Open — they will be discussed later. Also, note how the Form_Open procedure has a Cancel parameter — another important item that we'll discuss shortly. You can use these same steps when you are working with Reports, just substitute "Report" for "Form."

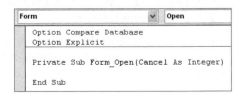

FIGURE 6-3

With the structure for the event all set up, the next step is to write the code that will describe and implement your custom logic. By placing it between the Private Sub and End Sub lines it will run whenever this event fires. We'll use one of our earlier examples to illustrate this; Figure 6-4 shows you the code to display a message box that will say "Hello, World!"

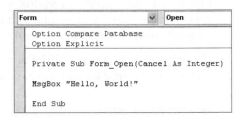

FIGURE 6-4

Now, every time this form opens, a message box will pop up and display "Hello, World!" This is a simplistic example that is intended to illustrate how to use events to do something automatically.

Now, suppose you want to say "Goodbye, World!" when the form closes. You would repeat the preceding steps but select the form's Close event (On Close line) and revise the text for "Hello, World." With that, you will end up with a module that looks like this:

```
Option Compare Database
Option Explicit

Private Sub Form_Close()
    MsgBox "Goodbye, World!"
End Sub

Private Sub Form_Open(Cancel As Integer)
    MsgBox "Hello, World!"
End Sub
```

code snippet EXAMPLES - Modify and Reuse Code in ch6_VBABasics_Code.txt

Maybe you noticed that both procedures do something similar — display a message box — but with different text. A good programmer would recognize this as an opportunity to reuse code. This provides us with an opportunity to show you how to create a custom procedure to receive a parameter and display it. We'll aptly name our procedure `DisplayIt`. To use this approach, you can type this on the bottom of the module, after the `End Sub` statement.

```
Private Sub DisplayIt(strMessage As String)
   MsgBox strMessage
End Sub
```

code snippet EXAMPLES - Modify and Reuse Code in ch6_VBABasics_Code.txt

The next step is to update the event procedures to use the new custom procedure. To do that, we call our custom procedure by typing out the identifier and filling the parameters, if there's any. The revised module is as follows:

```
Private Sub Form_Close()
   DisplayIt "Goodbye World!"
End Sub

Private Sub Form_Open(Cancel As Integer)
   DisplayIt "Hello, World!"
End Sub

Private Sub DisplayIt(strMessage As String)
   MsgBox strMessage
End Sub
```

code snippet EXAMPLES - Modify and Reuse Code in ch6_VBABasics_Code.txt

Now you have a custom procedure that accepts a string and displays it in a message box. One advantage of this approach is that if you later decided to change the message box display, you would only have to change the code in one place. Let's say that you want the message box's title to say "My Application." In the first version, you would have to specify the title twice, once in each event procedure; but in the second version you only need to go to the `DisplayIt` procedure and revise it once. Programmers often call this the One Definition Rule, and that is a very good rule to keep in mind.

You will delve much deeper into writing code in Chapter 7, and into using code to enhance forms and reports in Chapters 14 and 15.

USING VBA CODE TO CALL MACROS

You can call both data macros and named macros from within your VBA code. So after you have designed and created the macros, you can refer to them using the `DoCmd` commands, as shown in the following two examples. The first line provides the syntax for each type of macro, and the second line is an example of what it might look like in an application.

```
DoCmd.RunMacro("MacroName", [RepeatCount], [RepeatExpression])
DoCmd.RunMacro("mcrNewHireForm", 1, 0)

DoCmd.RunDataMacro("MacroName")
DoCmd.RunDataMacro("mcrGetEmployeeName")
```

code snippet Examples Using Code to Call Macros in ch6_VBABasics_Code.txt

The `DoCmd.RunMacro` arguments are just like they were in previous versions of Access. You pass the macro name followed by the optional arguments of:

➤ `[RepeatCount]`: Specifies the number of times the macro will run.

➤ `[RepeatExpression]`: A numeric expression that evaluates each time the macro repeats. When it evaluates to `False`, the macro stops.

You can specify either `RepeatCount` or `RepeatExpression`, or both. Whichever condition is reached first (repeat count or repeat expression) will stop the macro. You'll learn more about SQL statements in Chapter 13.

The `DoCmd.RunDataMacro`, like data macros themselves, is a new command as of Access 2010. You may recall that forms, reports, and other objects have events. And as of Access 2010, you now can attach events to tables, albeit in a slightly different way. You can now use data macros to handle the events for tables; however, you still cannot use VBA to create an event on a table. The arguments are pretty straightforward; you provide the name of the data macro to the `RunDataMacro`. Some named data macros may have parameters which you may have to supply. In Macro Designer, you can click "Update Parameters" to have Access enumerate them for you to fill in. In VBA, you must run `DoCmd.SetParameter` for each parameter before you can run the `DoCmd.RunDataMacro`.

As you are beginning to appreciate, the ability to call macros from code allows you to harness the new powers of the macros in combination with the existing flexibility of VBA. When you read Chapter 4, you will find some excellent explanations and examples for using data and named macros.

WRITING CODE IN MODULES

In Access, code is written and stored in modules. These can be specific to an object, such as a form or a control on a form, or they can be more general and apply to multiple objects. We'll talk about code behind forms and reports in the next section and focus on writing more general code for now.

To write code, you will need to open the VBA Editor, which you toured in Chapter 5. You may recall that you can start a new module by clicking on the Create Ribbon and selecting Module or Class Module (see Figure 6-5). This will open the VBA Editor with a new module, ready for you to start coding.

FIGURE 6-5

You can create your own function — known as a UDF, or User-Defined Functions — to accommodate various business rules and logic. You can also create a procedure that you can call from other procedures and events from within your application.

As you saw earlier in Anatomy of VBA Procedures, you can actually create two types of procedures: Functions and Subs. One of the key distinguishing differences between a Function and a Sub is that a Function will return a value in place of its own name but a Sub will not. Another way to think of this is that a Function *is* something, whereas a Sub *does* something. Functions and Subs are otherwise the same. They both execute instructions to perform actions such as validating user input or manipulating data in forms and reports.

You may often need to create a UDF to address specific business rules. And since a UDF is not limited in length, it can be as long and complex as necessary to handle complicated processes.

Once the UDF is defined, it can be used in queries, forms or reports. With this in mind, you can see that creating a UDF can provide considerable flexibility and control for working with your data.

Fortunately, VBA code provides some tools to help you write and manage that logic. Using the following code sample, we'll show you how to use a UDF to simplify formulas that are used in queries. This demonstrates how to use a UDF instead of writing a lengthy or complex formula directly in the SQL. The code will pass the arguments from the query to the UDF, and then return the resulting value back to the query. For example, let's say you need to find the last business date of the previous month. You can use a formula in our query to find it, such as:

```
LastBusinessDate: IIf(Weekday(DateSerial(Year(Date()),Month(Date()),0))-1,
    DateAdd("d",-2, DateSerial(Year(Date()), Month(Date()),0)),
    IIf(Weekday(DateSerial(Year(Date()),Month(Date()),0))=7,
    DateAdd("d",-1,DateSerial(Year(Date()),Month(Date()),0)),
    DateSerial(Year(Date()),Month(Date()),0)))
```

code snippet EXAMPLE - User Defined Function in ch6_VBABasics_Code.txt

As you can see, this is fairly long, and if you need to use it throughout your application, it would be tedious to copy and maintain. However, by using the UDF that follows, you can maintain the code in one place but still use it where needed by typing the following statements as indicated:

In Query Design view in place of a field name:

```
LastBusinessDate: EndOfBusinessMonth()
```

In Forms/Reports Design view as a controls' ControlSource:

```
=EndOfBusinessMonth()
```

In VBA code:

```
EndOfBusinessMonth()
```

code snippet EXAMPLE - User Defined Function in ch6_VBABasics_Code.txt

One of the key benefits of using a UDF is the ease of maintenance that is the result of having a central place to incorporate modifications to the code. For example, if the business rule changes to include Saturday as a business day, all you need is to modify the UDF in just one place rather than changing every query and other location that relies on the rule. The code in the queries will remain the same.

The following example provides the UDF that calculates the end of the business month. Although it uses Case statements, which we haven't yet discussed, it provides a real example that you will find fairly easily to interpret. Case statements are discussed in more detail in Chapter 7, and you'll see them in examples throughout the book.

```
Public Function EndOfBusinessMonth() As Date
'---------------------------------------------
' Function    : EndOfBusinessMonth
' Author      : Doug Yudovich
' Date        : 7/09/2010
```

```
' Purpose   : Returns the last date of the previous month sans weekends
'---------------------------------------------
Dim dtmLastDay As Date
'find the last date of the month
dtmLastDay = DateSerial(Year(Date), Month(Date), 0)

'check for weekend days (Sun, Sat)
Select Case Weekday(dtmLastDay)
Case 1   'sunday
  EndOfBusinessMonth = DateAdd("d", -2, dtmLastDay)
Case 7   'Saturday
  EndOfBusinessMonth = DateAdd("d", -1, dtmLastDay)
Case Else 'other weekdays
  EndOfBusinessMonth = dtmLastDay
End Select
End Function
```

code snippet EXAMPLE - CASE Statement in ch6_VBABasics_Code.txt

If you find yourself coding the same actions or process in multiple parts of your application, you will most likely benefit from writing a separate procedure to encompass the actions, and call that procedure from the various locations in your application. Although our current discussion is limited to the basics, we wanted to encourage your interest by showing you some real-world uses. You will find detailed instructions and examples for writing, modifying, and leveraging VBA throughout the rest of this book.

During our earlier discussion about methods, properties, enums and constants, you may have wondered how you could possibly remember them all. Although you can look them up in the Object Browser, there is a much easier way to find the right one when you need it — use IntelliSense. IntelliSense is one of the great advantages that VBA offers. In most cases, once you start typing, the VBA Editor will prompt you with the correct syntax and it will offer a selection of available options for many objects and commands. An important factor to remember is that although in some cases you can use either dot (.) or bang (!) to refer to object names (such as controls on a form), Intelli-Sense will only work if you use the dot (.), not the bang (!). But if you want to use bang, you can easily start with the dot, use the prompts, and then change the . to !. And once again, we will refer you to Chapter 7 for a more thorough explanation.

For example, when you start typing the message box function, VBA prompts you to choose the proper constant for the type of buttons you need, as shown in Figure 6-6.

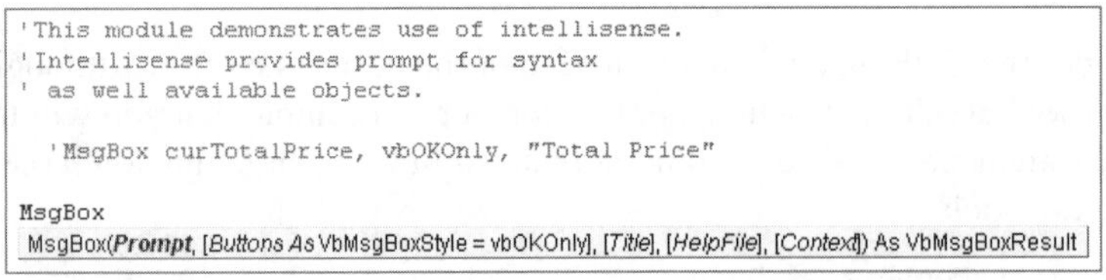

```
'This module demonstrates use of intellisense.
'Intellisense provides prompt for syntax
' as well available objects.

  'MsgBox curTotalPrice, vbOKOnly, "Total Price"

MsgBox
MsgBox(Prompt, [Buttons As VbMsgBoxStyle = vbOKOnly], [Title], [HelpFile], [Context]) As VbMsgBoxResult
```

FIGURE 6-6

As you can see, when you are working with commands and objects, IntelliSense will indicate the appropriate syntax and the available commands, objects, and arguments. So when you type the period (dot) after DoCmd — DoCmd. — a drop-down list will display the available actions; the list is context sensitive and will update based on the letters that you type. Similarly, as soon as you type the period after forms (so that is, forms.),

you will get prompts specific to the forms collections, a listing of all methods, properties, events, and collections. And, when you type a period after form you will see the list of members for the active form, as shown in Figure 6-7. In later chapters in this book, you learn how and when you can use Me. to reference the current object.

```
Private Sub Form_Open(Cancel As Integer)
'Demo of Intellisense providing the list of
'Form Properties and Events.
'Start by typing form. Intellisense kicks in with the .

form.
    ActiveControl
    AfterDelConfirm
End AfterFinalRender
    AfterInsert
    AfterLayout
    AfterRender
    AfterUpdate
```

FIGURE 6-7

There are some important keystrokes that are particularly helpful when using IntelliSense. Pressing the spacebar moves the cursor to the next prompt; pressing Enter ends the IntelliSense session and moves the cursor to a new blank line; pressing Ctrl+Space will prompt for all names that match what you've typed so far; and using the Tab key will accept the selected IntelliSense value.

We've provided this brief tutorial about using IntelliSense because it is an invaluable tool to leverage while you are writing code. We also refer you to Chapter 5, to learn more about the VBA Editor in general.

EXAMPLE: USER-DEFINED FUNCTION

As mentioned, you can create a User-Defined Function to address specific business rules and complex formulas. The following code snippet provides a few VBA code samples that will give you a better understanding of what you can accomplish. You'll find many more samples and styles in the remaining chapters and in the book's download files.

Let's build on the example used in the section "Writing Code in Modules" where we made a function named EndOfBusinessMonth(). This will provide the last business date of the current month. However, if you want to find the last business date of a month based on a specific date rather than the date the function is run, you can modify the function and pass the specified date as an argument. In the following example, we've modified the EndOfBusinessMonth() function to calculate the response based on a date provided in an argument.

Available for download on Wrox.com

```
Public Function EndOfBusinessMonth_Any(MyDate) As Date
'------------------------------------------------------
' Purpose   : Returns the last (work) date of the month based
'             on a specified date (ignoring weekends)
'------------------------------------------------------

Dim dtmLastDay As Date

    'use DateSerial() to find the last day of the month
    'prior to the date you selected
dtmLastDay = DateSerial(Year(MyDate), Month(MyDate), 0)
```

```
Select Case Weekday(dtmLastDay)
Case 1  'sunday
  EndOfBusinessMonth_D = DateAdd("d", -2, dtmLastDay)
Case 7  'Saturday
  EndOfBusinessMonth_D = DateAdd("d", -1, dtmLastDay)
Case Else
  EndOfBusinessMonth_D = dtmLastDay
End Select

End Function
```

code snippet EXAMPLE SECTION in ch6_VBABasics_Code.txt

Much as we did before, you will use the function in a query, but this time, you will also have to include the date as an argument, as shown here:

```
LastBusDay:EndOfBusinessMonth_Any(#7/1/2009#).
```

Similarly, you can also use this in the `ControlSource` of a report or form, by typing:
```
=EndOfBusinessMonth_Any(#7/1/2009#).
```

To reinforce this concept, we will look at another example. This time, we will calculate a bus/train schedule. If the business rules identify the start time, the frequency (in minutes in our case), and the end time, you can return the schedule as a string, such as the following: `12:00:00 PM, 12:30:00 PM, 1:00:00 PM`. This example uses a Loop statement, which repeats a block of code until a certain condition is met. We explain more about how to create and use Loop statements in Chapter 7, but for now, we will focus on our limited example.

```
Public Function MySchedule(STime, Freq, ETime) As String

'---------------------------------------------------------
' Purpose   : Returns a string with the times of the bus schedule
' based on the start time, frequency (in minutes), and the end time
'---------------------------------------------------------

Dim strMySchedule As String 'the schedule
Dim dtmLoop As Date  'current schedule value
Dim lngLoop As Long  'how many time points the \ will return an integer value

lngLoop = DateDiff("n", STime, ETime) \ Freq
strMySchedule = CStr(STime)
dtmLoop = STime

For lngLoop = lngLoop To 1 Step -1

  'add the number of minutes to find the next scheduled bus
dtmLoop = DateAdd("n", Freq, dtmLoop)
strMySchedule = strMySchedule & ", " & CStr(dtmLoop)
```

```
Next    'lngloop

MySchedule = strMySchedule

End Function
```

code snippet EXAMPLE SECTION in ch6_VBABasics_Code.txt

You can also use the output of this UDF as the row source for a list box so that the times can be displayed in a form. So, we will assume that we have a form that has three text boxes that are used to collect the values that are needed for the arguments (`txtFrom`, `txtFreq`, and `txtTo`), a list box to display the schedule (`lstSchedule`), and a command button to trigger the function. With that in place, we can use the following code to fill the list box with the bus or train schedule.

Available for download on Wrox.com

```
Me.lstSchedule.RowSourceType = "Value List"
Me.lstSchedule.RowSource = MySchedule(CDate(txtFrom), txtFreq, CDate(txtTo))
```

code snippet EXAMPLE SECTION in ch6_VBABasics_Code.txt

To help you learn and experiment with UDFs, the examples used in this chapter are in the text file that can be downloaded with the other chapter files for this book.

SUMMARY

In this chapter, you reviewed the basics of VBA, which also reinforced some of the material that was discussed in Chapters 4 and 5. You now have some of the essential tools and are starting to learn how to write code. As you proceed through the book, you'll learn about DAO and ADO, about leveraging the powerful tools that Access provides for customizing forms and reports, and about interfacing with other programs and applications.

Remember that this is a multipurpose reference book that is intended to be used in many ways. It's a great tool for becoming familiar with fundamental concepts, as well as for learning about advanced techniques. You'll find examples that will not only help you learn about the features and how to create solid solutions, but that can also be modified and incorporated into your applications. Although there is a logical progression for going through the chapters in order, we encourage you to also use the book as a reference, to leverage the content and examples that are most relevant to your needs at any given moment.

Chapters 5 and 6 are intended to help you build solid foundations of the basics and to provide a common understanding of the terms, processes, and structure associated with writing code. The next chapter helps you make the transition from concepts to practice. By the time you get to the subsequent chapters, such as those that cover enhancing forms and reports, you will be ready to focus on the features and examples, without stumbling on terms and structure. Keep in mind that you can always return for a refresher.

7

Using VBA in Access

WHAT'S IN THIS CHAPTER?

➤ Using events

➤ Employing good practices with VBA procedures

➤ How to evaluate expressions in VBA

➤ Using recordsets

➤ Using multiple recordsets

➤ Coding behind forms and reports

➤ The VBA debugging environment

➤ Determining the value of variables

➤ Handling common VBA challenges

➤ Concatenating strings

➤ Handling VBA errors

In the early days of programming, procedural languages ruled, meaning that the overall program execution was very structured and code was generally run in a very specific order. The main body of any of these programs had to cover every possibility: Display a screen to the user, gather input, perform edit checking, display messages, update the database (or simple files in those days), and close when everything was done. The main program also had to deal with every option or side request that the user might make. This made it difficult to understand the entire program, and it was tough to make changes because everything had to be retested when a modification was made. Those lumbering beasts included FORTRAN, COBOL, RPG, Pascal, and earlier forms of Basic. Millions of lines of code were written in these languages.

Fortunately, those days are over for VBA programmers. VBA is an *event-driven* language. In every Access form and report, a variety of events are waiting for you to use. They are available when the form opens and closes, when records are updated, even when individual fields on the screen are changed. They're all there at your fingertips. Each event can contain a procedure, which is where we get back to the procedural roots of standard programming. Although each procedure runs from top to bottom, just like in the old days, it only runs when the event *fires*. Until then, it sleeps quietly, not complicating your logic or slowing down your program.

Event-driven programming makes it much easier to handle complex programming tasks. Because your code will only run when an event occurs, each procedure is simpler and easier to debug.

In this chapter, you'll explore the nature of VBA events and see how the most common events are used, and you'll look at how two different sections of your VBA code can run at the same time. The chapter provides some guidelines about when and how to use Public and Private procedures, and data types, and also outlines structural guidelines for procedures, shows some common string and date handling techniques, and explains how to prevent rounding errors in your calculations. Class procedures, a powerful and useful tool, are covered in great detail in Chapter 8.

WHEN EVENTS FIRE

Events are at the heart of event-driven programming — which is no surprise. What can be surprising to novice programmers is the sheer number of events available to use. They all beg to have some code behind them. In reality, however, very few events are used on a consistent basis. Most of them have absolutely no code behind them, and never will in normal usage. The trick is to know which ones are important and commonly used, and which ones are obscure and rarely ever used. They all appear equally important in Access Help.

Common Form Events

The following table provides a list of common events and how you might want to use them. By knowing how to use this basic set of events, you're most of the way there to understanding event-driven programming in Access VBA.

FORM EVENT	DESCRIPTION
On Open	Fires before the On Load event (so you can't reference any bound controls on your form yet because they haven't been instantiated) and before the recordset is evaluated for the form. This means you can use this event to change the recordset (by changing the WHERE or ORDER BY clause) before the form continues to load. Cancel this event by setting its intrinsic parameter Cancel = True, so the form will close without continuing to the On Load event.
On Load	Fires after the recordset for the form has been evaluated but before the form is displayed to the user. This offers you an opportunity to make calculations, set defaults, and change visual attributes based on the data from the recordset.

FORM EVENT	DESCRIPTION
Before Update	To perform some data edits before the user's changes are updated in the database, use this event. All the field values are available to you, so you can do multiple field edits (such as `HireDate` must be greater than `BirthDate`). If something doesn't pass your validity checks, you can display a message box and cancel this event by setting the intrinsic parameter `Cancel = True`. This event also fires before a new record is inserted, so you can place edits for both new and changed records here.
On Double Click	A non-intuitive, special-purpose event. If you build a continuous form to display records in a read-only format, your users may expect to drill down to the detail of the record by double-clicking anywhere on the row. But what if they double-click the record selector (the gray arrow at the left side of each row)? The event that fires is the form's `On Double Click` event. By using this event, you can run the code that opens your detail form. This gives your user a consistent experience and the confidence that your applications work no matter what.
On Unload	This event can be used to check data validity before your form closes. It can be canceled, which redisplays your form without closing it. It also has another useful behavior. If it is canceled during an unload that occurred because the user is closing Access (using the X button in the window heading), canceling the `Unload` event also cancels all other form closures and the closure of Access itself. This allows you to prompt the user with an "Are you sure?" message box when the user tries to close Access.
On Current	This is one of the most overused events by novice programmers, but it does have some good uses. It fires every time your form's "current" record changes. The current record is the one that the record selector (the gray arrow on the left side of each record) points to. It also fires when your form initially loads and positions to the first record in your recordset. One good place to use `On Current` is on a continuous form where one of the buttons below is valid for some records but not for others. In the `On Current` event, you can test the current record and set the Enabled property of the button to `True` or `False` as appropriate. Because this event fires so often, it can be hard to control and may cause performance issues. Use it only when you need to.
On Delete	Fires after each record is deleted, but before the delete is actually finalized, enabling you to display an "Are you sure?" message. Then the user has an opportunity to decide whether or not to delete this individual record. Use this in conjunction with the `Before Delete Confirm` event.
Before Delete Confirm	Fires before a group of deletes is finalized. If you cancel this event, none of the records in the group is actually deleted. This event also has a `Response` parameter; it can be used to suppress the normal Access message asking the user if he wants to delete the group of records.
On Activate	Fires after the form's `On Open` and `On Load` events, just before the form is displayed. It also fires whenever the form regains the focus, so it can be used to refresh or requery the data on the form after the user has returned from another form.

Common Control Events

The following table lists some commonly used events for controls on forms (such as text boxes, combo boxes, command buttons, and so on).

CONTROL EVENT	DESCRIPTION
On Click	This one is obvious; it fires when the control (most likely a command button) is clicked. This is where you put the code to run when the user clicks a button.
Before Update	Useful for controls whose value or state can change, such as checkboxes, text boxes, and combo boxes. It fires just before a change to the control is committed, so you have a chance to validate the new value of the control. If this event is canceled, the control reverts to its previous value. You can ask the user a question in this event using a message box, such as "Are you sure you want to change the Invoice Number?" You can then continue normally or set Cancel = True based on the response.
After Update	Fires after a change to the control is made. This is a good time to control the next field to receive the focus, manipulate other fields in response to this one, or perform other actions (these techniques are used in Chapter 14).
On Double Click	Fires when a control is double-clicked. Useful when you want to provide a method of drilling down to a detail form from a read-only index form. Make sure you add the code to open the detail form to every double-click event of every field in the detail section. If your record selector arrow is visible, include your drill-down code to the form's On Double Click event (see previous section).

Common Report Events

The following table lists some commonly used report events. These events can run code to customize and add flexibility for your users when displaying reports.

REPORT EVENT	DESCRIPTION
On Open	Fires before the recordset is evaluated for the report. As with forms, you can use this event to change the recordset (by changing the WHERE or ORDER BY clause) before the report continues to load. This can be especially helpful when you use a form to prompt the user for selection criteria before the report continues to load (described in detail in Chapter 15). This event can be canceled by setting the Cancel parameter to True, which will prevent the report from continuing to open.

REPORT EVENT	DESCRIPTION
On Activate	Fires after the On Open event and just as the report window is displayed to the user. The main thing this event is used for is to maximize the Access windows using DoCmd.Maximize. This allows the user to see more of the report. However, you'll probably want to restore the Access windows to their previous sizes when the report closes, which brings us to the On Close event.
On Close	Fires when the report closes. A common line of code to include here is DoCmd .Restore to restore the sizes of your form windows that were maximized in the On Activate event.
On No Data	Fires after the On Open event when the report evaluates the recordset and discovers that there are no records. This can easily happen if you allow users to specify the criteria for the report and they choose a combination of values that doesn't exist in the database. You can display a friendly message box to the user, and then set the intrinsic Cancel parameter to True, which closes the report.
On Load	Introduced in Access 2007. The On Load event fires after the On Open event. In this event, the recordset for the report has already been evaluated and data from the first record is available.

Asynchronous Execution

Sometimes, Access runs two areas of your VBA code simultaneously, even though you've placed the code into different events or even in different forms and reports. This ability for Access to start running one procedure of code before another one is finished is called *asynchronous execution*. Most of the time asynchronous execution happens without you (or your user) really noticing, but it can sometimes cause problems, so you should know when it happens and how to work with it.

OpenForm

The most common asynchronous execution you'll encounter is when you open a form using the OpenForm method. Most of the time you won't notice it, but here's what really happens: When the OpenForm statement runs, the form you ask for starts to open, along with all of its On Open, On Load, and On Current events. However, any code after the OpenForm command also continues to run at the same time. Usually, not much happens at this point, so there's no harm done.

However, there are times when you would like the execution of the code in the calling form to stop until the user is done with the newly opened form. This is often the case when you are prompting the user for selection criteria during the Open event of a report (see Chapter 14), or when you open a form to add a new record from an index form.

In this latter case, you normally want to requery the index form to show the newly added record, but you must wait for the user to finish adding it. If you perform a requery right after the OpenForm, your code will continue merrily along and requery your first form, only within milliseconds after your second form has started to open. No matter how fast your user is, that's not enough time for them to add the new record. So your requery runs before the new record is added, and the new record will not appear on your index form.

There is a simple solution to the normal asynchronous execution of the `OpenForm` command. It's called Dialog mode.

Dialog Mode to the Rescue

To prevent asynchronous execution when a form opens, use Dialog mode. Instead of:

```
DoCmd.OpenForm FormName:="frmMyForm"
```

specify this:

```
DoCmd.OpenForm FormName:="frmMyForm", WindowMode:=acDialog
```

code snippet Prevent Asynchronous Execution When A Form Opens in ch07_CodeSnippets.txt

 Note the use of named parameters in these examples — `FormName:="frmMyForm"`, *for instance. Functions and subroutines in VBA can receive parameters (often called arguments) using either positions or names. If the names are not specified, VBA assigns parameters based on their position: first, second, and so on. When you see extra commas indicating missing parameters, you know that positional parameters are being used. Named parameters are much clearer to read and understand, and experienced programmers often use them.*

Dialog mode accomplishes two things:

➤ It opens the form in Modal mode, which prevents the user from clicking on any other Access windows until they are done with this form. Modal forms are hierarchical in nature, meaning they can be opened one after the other with the most currently open form the only one accessible. As you close the current Modal form, the one opened immediately before it is now the only one accessible and so on. All Modal forms must be closed before you can navigate to any other database object.

➤ It stops the execution of the calling code until the newly opened form is either closed or hidden.

This second feature of Dialog mode is what is so helpful in preventing Access from trying to run two areas of your code at once.

Notice that the code stops until the form is closed or hidden. This is the basis for many clever uses of Dialog mode where values from the called form are used elsewhere. If you just hide the form (by setting its `Visible` property to `False`), the values on the form are still there and ready for you to reference, even though the code in the calling form now continues to run. This is the technique for gathering selection criteria and building SQL statements, which is described in Chapter 14.

There is a disadvantage to using Dialog mode. While a form is open and visible in Dialog mode, any report that is opened will appear behind the form and won't be accessible. If you encounter this problem, you can use another technique to control the timing of form requeries. One technique is to open the second form normally and allow the code in the first form to complete. Then, put your requery code in the first form's On Activate *event to fire when the focus returns to the first form.*

VBA PROCEDURES

VBA code can be structured clearly and efficiently by breaking up sections of code into logical "chunks" called *procedures*. In this section, you'll see how to use the different types of VBA procedures and to employ good practices in their design.

Function or Sub?

A common area of confusion among novice VBA programmers is whether to write a function or a sub (short for "subroutine"). Some developers create functions for every procedure they write, in the belief that they are better in some way. They aren't. Functions and subs are just two kinds of procedures, and they both have their purposes. A quick way to determine which one is more appropriate is to ask this question: Does my procedure *do* something or *return* something?

If the purpose of your procedure is to compute or retrieve a value and return it to the calling procedure, then of course you should use a function. After all, functions are designed to return a single value to the calling procedure. They do it efficiently and easily, and they can be used directly in queries and calculated controls on forms and reports. They can even be used directly in macros.

Functions tend to have names that are nouns, like LastDayOfMonth or FullAddress. For example, a control on a report might have this Control Source property value:

```
=LastDayOfMonth(Date())
```

The field would display the results of calling some function called LastDayOfMonth with the parameter value of today's date.

On the other hand, if the main purpose of your procedure is to do some action and there is no clear-cut value to return, use a sub. Many programmers think that they must return something, even if they have to make up some artificial return code or status. This practice can make your code harder for others to understand. However, if you really need a return code or status after the procedure finishes, it is perfectly okay to make it a function.

Subs tend to have names that are verbs like LoadWorkTable or CloseMonth. In practice, the code looks like this:

```
LoadWorkTable
```

Pretty easy, right? Any developer looking at this line of code can see the obvious: A sub called LoadWorkTable is being called, and it doesn't return a value.

It is possible to call a function as if it were a sub, without parentheses around the parameters. In that case, the function runs, but the return value is discarded. This usually is not a good coding practice, but you may encounter it in existing code.

Public or Private?

Another decision that you have to make when you create procedures is whether to make them Public or Private. By default, Access makes procedures you create Public, but that's not necessarily what you want.

If you are working in a standalone module (those that appear in the Modules area of the Access Navigation Pane), the rules are a little different than if you are working in code that resides in a form or report. Form and report modules are intrinsically encapsulated as class modules so their Public procedures aren't as public as you might expect. Let's take a look at procedures in stand-alone modules first.

Public and Private Procedures in Modules

Public functions and subs in standalone modules are just that — public property. Every area of your application can see them and use them. To do that, Public procedures in modules must have unique names. Otherwise, how would your code know which procedure to run? If you have two Public procedures with the same name, you'll get a compile error.

Private procedures in modules are very shy — they can't be seen or referenced by any code outside their own module. If you try to reference a Private procedure from a different module or another form or report, Access insists (at compile time) that no such procedure exists.

The hidden nature of Private procedures is their best feature. Because they are hidden, their names need to be unique only within their own module. Therefore, you can name them whatever you want — you don't have to worry about them conflicting with other procedures in your application.

This feature really comes into play when you reuse code by importing modules into other data-bases, maybe even ones you didn't create. If most of your module procedures are Private, you'll have a minimum of naming conflicts because the rest of the application can't see them. The Public procedures still need to have a unique name, which is why many procedures that are meant to be imported have interesting prefixes such as the author's initials or the company name.

Public and Private Procedures in Forms and Reports

Private procedures in forms and reports behave just like Private procedures in modules. They can't be seen or referenced from outside the form or report. The event procedures that Access auto-matically builds behind your forms and reports are automatically set to Private. This makes sense because Form_Open and OnClick events are useful only inside that particular form or report. Also, these procedures need to have standard names, which could result in a big mess of duplicate names if they were Public.

In reality, this problem wouldn't occur. The code behind your forms and reports isn't like the code in normal modules. Access calls them class objects, but they behave like class modules, which are covered in Chapter 8. You can see this in the Visual Basic Editing window, as shown in Figure 8-1. Note the three headings: Microsoft Access Class Objects, Modules, and Class Modules.

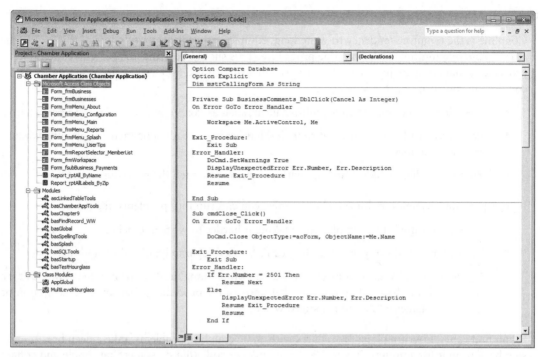

FIGURE 7-1

It turns out that even a `Public` procedure that you build in the code behind a form can be named the same as a procedure in another form. That's because class objects require that you specify the name of the class object (in this case, the form name) before the name of the procedure if you want to call it from outside the form. However, this is rarely needed. One possible situation might be some form initialization code that you want to run from outside the form, such as `InitializeForm`. If you want to do it, here's the syntax:

Available for download on Wrox.com

```
Form_frmMyFormName.InitializeForm
```

code snippet Initialize Form in ch07_CodeSnippets.txt

Notice that the prefix `Form_` and the name of the form qualify the `InitializeForm` procedure name. Because many forms could have the same procedure name, you need to tell the code which form's procedure you want to run.

Coupling and Cohesion

The design of your procedures is important to delivering understandable, readable code. Two principles that guide the logical design of procedures (functions or subs) are *coupling* (bad) and *cohesion* (good). This topic is not specific to VBA, but it bears mentioning since we're working with procedures.

Uncouple Procedures

Coupling is the tempting tendency to write long, complex procedures that do lots of things; in other words, *coupling* multiple tasks into one procedure. This should be avoided. As a guideline, write procedures that compute just one value or perform a single task. Some signs that you might have coupling in your procedures include:

➤ Procedure names that include multiple ideas, such as `ComputeValuesAndReloadWorkTables`

➤ Procedures with large blocks of code that have section header comments explaining what each section does

➤ Procedures that include "modes," with parameters that tell the procedure what to do

If your procedure couples multiple tasks together, you can run into problems like these:

➤ Your procedure is too complicated, making it harder to write and debug.

➤ The different tasks in your procedure can't be used separately; it's all-or-nothing.

➤ If you make a change to your procedure, the whole thing needs to be retested. You can't trust that your little change didn't affect other parts of the procedure. Remember the common programmer's lament: "But all I changed was . . ."

If you find yourself writing long procedures with these coupling problems, take a deep breath and step back from it for a minute. Try to identify chunks of code that do something simple and cohesive. As a rule, procedures should do or calculate one thing, and should do so independently using parameters that are passed to them.

You may wonder how to build procedures that must be complex. Sometimes there is no way to avoid complexity, but you can hide a lot of complexity by breaking your logic into smaller functions and subs, then calling them where appropriate. That way, each one of your procedures can be written and debugged separately. If you are working as a team, the procedures can even be written by different developers.

Adhere to Cohesion

Cohesion means that each procedure should perform one function, and should be able to do its thing without a lot of help or knowledge from outside the procedure. It shouldn't rely on global variables or other objects to exist when the procedure is invoked. Some signs of a poor cohesion are:

➤ Procedures that include duplicate blocks of code

➤ Procedures that expect forms or reports with specific names

➤ Use of global variables, especially when they are expected to retain their value for a long time

➤ Hard coding of system environment information such as file paths

➤ Hard coding or special handling of certain records or values in tables

Hard coding is the practice of using values in code that would be more appropriate in a configurable lookup table or some other easy-to-change place. For example, many poorly written applications hard code paths to files. The moment those applications are moved to another computer, they break. Another more insidious example is the use of values lists for combo boxes in forms. These seem so easy to set up, but they are just another instance of hard coding that makes your application less robust and more difficult to change over time. A better approach for a list of values that you don't think will change (or that you need to code against) is to put them in a table that doesn't have a maintenance form. This prevents your user from adding or removing the critical values your code depends on, but allows you flexibility over time. If you like, you can use a specific naming convention (as an extension of Reddick naming conventions) for these value list tables, such as `tval` instead of `tlkp` or `tbl`.

To improve cohesion, think of the old black-box principle of programming: You should need no knowledge of how a procedure produces its result, only that given valid input, it will produce the correct output. Along the same lines, the procedure should need little knowledge of the world outside to do its job. Each procedure you write should perform one task or calculation and need a minimum of special knowledge from outside its own boundaries. The best way to send information into a procedure is through parameters, not by using global variables or referring to specific forms or reports.

All this being said, cohesion is a spectrum, not a final black-or-white goal. Using VBA in Access sometimes calls for the use of global variables in controlled scenarios, or referring to an open form, or duplicating some code. It's best to be aware of coupling and cohesion principles so that you can make good coding decisions.

Error Handling

All of your procedures should have at least a minimum level of error handling. There are easy ways to implement simple error handling that can help you debug your code and protect your users from errors (both expected and unexpected). This topic is covered in much greater detail later in this chapter.

Using Variables

When using variables in your VBA code, there are several things to remember to ensure that your code runs smoothly. Choosing the appropriate data type for each variable is critical, and it's also important to use global variables correctly.

Naming conventions for variables are important. The Reddick naming conventions for variables are described in Appendix G. If you get into the habit of naming your variables consistently, your code will be easier to maintain over time, faster to debug, and look more professional.

Using Appropriate Data Types and Sizes

First, make sure that your variable types will handle the size of data they are expected to store. Many overflow errors occur because an attempt was made to store an `AutoNumber` key value from a table in a variable defined as an Integer. This may work fine during testing because an integer can store numbers with values up to 32,767. Then, when a user starts adding more data, the application breaks on an overflow error.

It's a good idea to define variables with the maximum size that is possible to occur. AutoNumber fields should be stored in variables defined as Long (which is the same as the Long Integer in Access tables). Defining a variable as String allows it to store very long strings, whether they are defined as Text or Memo in a table.

If a variable can possibly contain a Null, then you must define it as a Variant, in which case it will be able to store just about anything that you throw into it — a messy approach, and one that takes Access a bit longer to process. It's usually better to decide what kind of data each variable is going to hold; then set the appropriate data type so that Access doesn't have to figure out what's in there every time it uses the variable. Sometimes, however, it's useful to allow a variable to contain a Null, especially when there might not always be data to load into the field. If you do use a Variant data type, use it because there's a specific reason that it might be passed a Null, not because you don't know what type it should be.

If you don't specify a variable's data type, it is a Variant by default. A common error is to define more than one variable on a single line of code, like this:

```
Dim strCallingForm, strReportTitle as String
```

Many novice VBA programmers think that both variables in this example are defined as Strings — they won't be. VBA requires that each variable have its data type explicitly defined. In this example, strCallingForm will be defined as a Variant because its data type wasn't specified.

You can define the two string variables on one line like this:

```
Dim strCallingForm as String, strReportTitle as String
```

code snippet Define Two Strings On One Line Of Code in ch07_CodeSnippets.txt

This style is technically correct (both variables are defined as Strings), but the second variable is easy to miss when you are looking at your code. The clearest and most consistent style for defining variables is to give each one its own line:

```
Dim strCallingForm as String
Dim strReportTitle as String
```

This may take an extra line of code, but it is much easier to read and understand.

Using Global Variables

Global variables are variables that retain their value until they are changed or until the application stops. They can be handy, but they should be used in specific ways to avoid problems. To define a global variable, simply use Global instead of Dim, like this:

```
Global gstrCallingForm As String
```

code snippet Dimensioning A Global Variable in ch07_CodeSnippets.txt

Notice the naming convention: g for Global, str for String, and then the variable name.

A global can be defined in any standalone module; it doesn't matter which one. You can refer to it and set its value from anywhere in your application (that's why it's called global). However, you probably want to designate a module to store all your main reusable application code, which is where you should define your global variables. You could name this module basGlobal or something similar.

Global variables, however, have a problem. If your code is interrupted — after an error, for example — the global variables are cleared out. There are two ways to reduce the impact of this little problem. The best way is to use the value in global variables for a very short time, perhaps a few milliseconds. Globals can be used like parameters for objects that don't accept true parameters, such as forms. For example, the form daisy-chaining logic given in Appendix I uses a single global variable to pass the name of the calling form to the called form, but the called form immediately stores the name in a local module variable for safekeeping.

Another way to work around the problem with global variables is to create a wrapper function that first checks whether the variable has a value. If it does, it merely returns it. If it doesn't have a value (which will happen the first time the function is called, or if the value has been reset), the function then computes or retrieves the value, sets the global variable, and returns the value. This can be a good way to retrieve or compute values that take some time, such as connection string properties or other application-wide values that are retrieved from tables. You get the speed of a global variable and the reliability of computing the values when necessary.

Access 2007 introduced a new way of storing global values: TempVars. This is a collection of values that you can define and maintain, and it won't be reset if you stop your code during debugging. The values are retained as long as the current database is open. TempVars is explained in detail in Appendix I.

EVALUATING EXPRESSIONS IN VBA

Expressions are one of the basic building blocks of any programming language. There are several ways to evaluate expressions in VBA that allow you to control the flow of your procedural logic.

If ... Then

Almost every programming language has some way of asking If, and VBA is no exception. The If..Then structure is one of the most commonly used in VBA. Its usage is straightforward, but there are a couple of issues that warrant extra attention. First, the expression you are using needs to be formed correctly and completely. One common mistake is to use an expression like this:

```
If intOrderStatus = 1 Or 2 Then
  `some interesting code here
End If
```

The problem here is that a complete Boolean (True or False) expression needs to be on both sides of the Or. The literal way to interpret this expression is "if intOrderStatus = 1 or if 2 is True, then," which, of course, makes no sense. The constant 2 will always evaluate to True. In fact, the only value that evaluates to False is 0. All other values are True. Internally, Access will store -1 as True, but any value other than 0 evaluates to True.

The correct way to write this line of code is as follows:

```
If intOrderStatus = 1 Or intOrderStatus = 2 Then
   `some interesting code here
End If
```

code snippet Correct 'If...Then' Syntax in ch07_CodeSnippets.txt

It's repetitive, but you have to tell VBA exactly what you want to do.

> *Instead of using multiple* Or *operators in SQL statements, you can use a much easier syntax: the* In *operator. In SQL, the equivalent to* Where OrderStatus = 1 or OrderStatus = 2 *is merely* Where OrderStatus In (1,2). *That's much easier to read and understand, and it only gets better the more values you have to compare.*

Checking for Nulls

Another common area of confusion is checking for Null. The following statement is incorrect:

```
If varCustomerKey = Null Then
   `even more interesting code here
End If
```

An interesting fact about Null: It is, by definition, unknown and undefined. A variable containing a Null can't "equal" anything, including Null. In this example, the interesting code will never run, no matter how null the customer key field is.

To check for a Null in a field, you must use the IsNull function, like this:

```
If IsNull(varCustomerKey) Then
   `even more interesting code here
End If
```

code snippet Checking For Nulls in ch07_CodeSnippets.txt

The IsNull function is the only way VBA can evaluate a variable or recordset field and determine if it is Null. The = just can't do it. By the way, this is true in Access SQL, too — you need to use IsNull to test for Nulls in the WHERE clauses of queries and recordsets, or you can use the SQL specific syntax WHERE [FieldName] IS NULL.

Sometimes, you want to check to see if a field is either Null or contains an empty string (also known as a *zero-length string*). Empty strings can creep into your tables if you specify Yes to Allow Zero Length in the field definition during table design. To ensure that you are checking for both, use code such as this:

```
If IsNull(BusinessName) or BusinessName = `" Then
```

What a hassle — you have to type the name of the field twice, and the line is confusing to read. There's a much easier way:

```
If BusinessName & "" = "" Then
```

code snippet Checking For Null Or Empty String -- Two Ways in ch07_CodeSnippets.txt

This technique uses the concatenation behavior of the & operator. The & concatenates two strings, even if one of them is Null (see the section "String Concatenation Techniques" later in this chapter). In this case, it concatenates an empty string ("") onto the end of BusinessName. If BusinessName is Null, the result is an empty string. If BusinessName has any string value in it, it remains unchanged by tacking on an empty string. This behavior enables you to quickly check if a field has a Null or an empty string.

Notice that this example uses the & operator to concatenate strings. The + operator also concatenates strings, but there's an important difference: + propagates Null. That is, if either side (operand) is Null, the result is also Null. Concatenation of strings is discussed in more detail later in this chapter.

On the subject of Nulls, the nz() function converts a Null value to 0 (zero). It's built into VBA and can be helpful in math calculations when you don't want a Null to wipe out the whole result. For example, to calculate a price with a discount, you could use this code:

```
NetPrice = ItemPrice - (ItemPrice * DiscountPercent)
```

This works fine as long as DiscountPercent has a value. If it is Null, the NetPrice will also be set to Null, which is an error. The following code works correctly:

```
NetPrice = ItemPrice - (ItemPrice * nz(DiscountPercent))
```

Now, if DiscountPercent is Null, it is converted to 0 by the NZ function, and the NetPrice will be set to the full ItemPrice.

The nz() function will accept two parameters separated by a comma. The second parameter is optional and allows you to define the replacement value if the first parameter is null. The syntax is: nz(TestValue, ReplacementValue). The default replacement value is 0 except when used in a query where the default value (unless otherwise specified) is an empty string. When specifying the replacement value it must be treated as text. When using a literal replacement value, enclose the value in quotes. For example, if you would like to replace a null field value for a text field with the word "Unknown," use the following syntax:

```
CurrentStatus = nz([StatusField], "Unknown")
```

Select Case

Another way to evaluate expressions and run code based on them is the often under-utilized `Select Case` structure. It enables you to test for multiple values of a variable in a clean, easy-to-understand structure, and then run blocks of code depending on those values. Here's an example of a `Select Case` structure:

Available for download on Wrox.com

```
Select Case intOrderStatus
Case 1, 2
    `fascinating code for status 1 or 2
Case 3
    `riveting code for status 3
Case Else
    `hmm, it's some other value, just handle it
End Select
```

code snippet The Select Case in ch07_CodeSnippets.txt

Notice that there is no need for nested and indented `If` statements, and each `Case` block of code doesn't need a beginning or ending statement. Just to show the difference, the equivalent code using plain old `If` statements looks like this:

```
If intOrderStatus = 1 Or intOrderStatus = 2 Then
    `fascinating code for status 1 or 2
Else
    If intOrderStatus = 3 Then
        `riveting code for status 3
    Else
        `hmm, it's some other value, just handle it
    End If
Endif
```

This code is harder to read and understand. If you need to choose among multiple blocks of code depending on an expression's value, then `Select Case` is the preferred method.

USING RECORDSETS

Recordset operations are one of the cornerstones of Access VBA, enabling you to directly read, update, add, and delete records in Access tables and queries. You explore all of this in the following sections.

Opening Recordsets

Opening a recordset is easy, using either DAO or ADO (for more details about DAO and ADO, refer to Chapters 11 and 12). To open a recordset, you first need a reference to the current database, usually named db, and a `recordset` object. Here's how to accomplish that using DAO:

```
Dim db as DAO.Database
Set db = CurrentDB
Dim rst as DAO.Recordset
```

Now you need to actually open the recordset. There are three basic ways to open a recordset: by table, by query, and by SQL statement. Here's how to use a table directly:

```
Set rst = db.OpenRecordset(`tblMyTableName")
```

code snippet Opening A Recordset Using An Existing Table Or Query in ch07_CodeSnippets.txt

If you have a query that already has some joined tables, selection criteria, or sort order, you can use it to open the recordset instead of using a table.

```
Set rst = db.OpenRecordset(`qryMyQueryName")
```

code snippet Opening A Recordset Using An Existing Table Or Query in ch07_CodeSnippets.txt

Finally, you can open a recordset using your own SQL statement instead of using a preexisting query. Access evaluates and runs the query string on-the-fly.

```
Set rst = db.OpenRecordset(`Select * From tblMyTableName")
```

code snippet Opening A Recordset Using A SQL Statement in ch07_CodeSnippets.txt

Now, you're probably thinking, "why is that last way any better than opening the table directly?" Your question is justified in this simple example. But using a recordset based on a SQL statement is much more flexible than using a table or query directly because you can modify the SQL statement in VBA code — like this:

```
Set rst = db.OpenRecordset(`Select * From tblMyTable Where MyKey = ` & Me!MyKey)
```

code snippet Opening A Recordset Using SQL Statement With Filter in ch07_CodeSnippets.txt

Now you're seeing some flexibility. This example opens a recordset limited to only those records that match the MyKey field on the form that contains this code. You can use values from your open forms or other recordsets as selection criteria, set flexible sort fields, and so on.

Looping through Recordsets

When your recordset opens, it automatically points to the first record. One of the most common uses for a recordset is to loop through the records, top to bottom, and perform some action for each one. The action could be sending an e-mail, copying records across child tables, or whatever you need to do. Following is some example code to loop through all of the records in tblBusiness:

```
Dim db As DAO.Database
Dim rstBusiness As DAO.Recordset
```

```
Set db = CurrentDb

Set rstBusiness = db.OpenRecordset("tblBusiness")

Do While Not rstBusiness.EOF
    `do some code here with each business
    rstBusiness.MoveNext
Loop
```

code snippet Looping Through Recordsets in ch07_CodeSnippets.txt

Notice that the EOF (end of file) property of the recordset object is True when there are no more records in the recordset. It begins with a True value if there are no records in the recordset at all.

Remember to include the .MoveNext method before the Loop statement. If you omit it, your code drops into an infinite loop, repeatedly processing the first record, and not moving to the next one.

> *Don't use recordset looping and updating to simply update a group of records in a table. It is much more efficient to build an update query with the same selection criteria to modify the records as a group.*

> *If you need to perform an action on some of the records in a recordset, limit the recordset using a* Where *clause when you open it. Avoid testing the records with* If *statements inside your loop to determine which record(s) to perform the action against. It is much more efficient to exclude them from the recordset to begin with, rather than ignoring certain records in your loop.*

Adding Records

To add a record using a recordset, the recordset type needs to be capable of updates. Most recordsets for Access (Access Control Entry, or ACE) tables , such as the one previously described, can be updated. However, if you need an updatable recordset for a SQL Server table opened via ODBC, you may need to also specify the dbOpenDynaset parameter value for the type. There's no harm in specifying it, even if it is an ACE table.

Available for download on Wrox.com

```
Set rst = db.OpenRecordset("tblMyTable", dbOpenDynaset)

With rst
  .AddNew
  !MyField1 = "A"
  !MyField2 = "B"
  .Update

End With
```

code snippet Adding Records in ch07_CodeSnippets.txt

The .AddNew method of the recordset object instantiates the new record in the table, and if the table is in ACE, also immediately assigns a new AutoNumber value to the record if the table contains one. Don't forget the final .Update, because without it, your record won't actually be added.

If the table is linked using ODBC (such as SQL Server), the AutoNumber/Identity value is not generated immediately when the .AddNew method runs. Instead, the Identity value is set after the .Update. This is discussed in the section "Copying Trees of Parent and Child Records" later in this chapter.

Finding Records

To find a record in a recordset, use the FindFirst method. This is really just a way to reposition the current record pointer (cursor) to the first record that meets some criteria you specify. The criteria is specified like a WHERE clause in a SQL statement, except you omit the word WHERE. It looks like this:

```
rst.FindFirst `CustomerKey = ` & Me!CustomerKey
```

code snippet Finding Records Using FindFirst in ch07_CodeSnippets.txt

After you perform a FindFirst, you can check the NoMatch property of the recordset to determine whether you successfully found at least one matching record. You can also use the FindNext, FindPrevious, and FindLast methods to navigate to other records.

 In general, you shouldn't need to use the Seek method of a recordset. It may be slightly faster than FindFirst, but it won't work on a linked table without extra programming to open the table in a separate Workspace.

Updating Records

The code for updating records in a recordset is almost the same as for adding them. You may also need to find the correct record to update using FindFirst. If you find it successfully, you can update it. Here's an example:

```
Set rst = db.OpenRecordset(`tblMyTable`)

With rst
  .FindFirst `CustomerKey = ` & Me!CustomerKey
  If Not .NoMatch Then `we found the record

    .Edit
    !CustomerName = `ABC Construction`
    !CustomerStatus = 1
    .Update

  End If
End With
```

code snippet Updating Records in ch07_CodeSnippets.txt

The With *statement is purely a programming convenience. Instead of typing the name of the object every single time, you can use* With <objectname>. *After that, and until you use* End With, *any references with no object name, just a dot (.) or bang (!), are assumed to belong to the* With *object. You may want to improve the clarity of your code by not using it when you are trying to keep track of multiple recordsets.*

USING MULTIPLE RECORDSETS

You can easily keep track of multiple open recordsets at once. Each one needs to be defined with a Dim statement and opened using the OpenRecordset method, and they are kept completely separate by Access. Each recordset has its own current record pointer (often called a cursor), end of file (EOF) and beginning of file (BOF) values, and so on.

This technique is necessary to perform the following trick: Copy a parent record and all of its child records into the same tables.

Copying Trees of Parent and Child Records

Here's a task that can stump an Access programmer trying to tackle it for the first time. The problem is as follows: There are two tables, tblPC and tblSpecification. Each (parent) PC has many (child) Specifications. Many PCs have almost identical Specifications, but with slight variations. You need to write some code to copy one PC to another, along with all of its Specifications. The user will then manually update the copied PC's Specifications.

At first, you might think that this seemingly simple problem can be performed using only queries. However, you soon run into a problem — you need to know the key of the newly copied PC so that you can assign the copied Specifications to it.

You can solve the problem by using multiple recordsets. Let's say that you have a continuous form showing a list of PCs and a Copy button at the bottom of the form. The desired functionality is to copy the PC record (with `Copy of ` as a prefix of the new PC) and also copy over all of its Specification records to the new PC:

Available for download on Wrox.com

```
On Error GoTo Error_Handler
Dim db As Database
Dim rstPC As DAO.Recordset
Dim rstSpecFrom As DAO.Recordset
Dim rstSpecTo As DAO.Recordset
Dim lngPCKey as Long

Set db = CurrentDb

If Not IsNull(Me.PCKey) Then

    Set rstPC = db.OpenRecordset(`tblPC`, dbOpenDynaset)

    `copy the parent record and remember its key
    rstPC.AddNew
    rstPC!PCName = `Copy of` & Me!PCName
```

```
    rstPC.Update
    rstPC.Bookmark = rstPC.LastModified
    lngPCKey = rstPC!PCKey

    rstPC.Close
    Set rstPC = Nothing

    Set rstSpecTo = db.OpenRecordset("tblSpecification", dbOpenDynaset)
    Set rstSpecFrom = db.OpenRecordset _
    ("Select * From tblSpecification Where PCKey = " & Me!PCKey)

    Do While Not rstSpecFrom.EOF

      rstSpecTo.AddNew
      rstSpecTo!PCKey = lngPCKey `set to the new parent key
      rstSpecTo!SpecificationName = rstSpecFrom!SpecificationName
      rstSpecTo!SpecificationQty = rstSpecFrom!SpecificationQty
      rstSpecTo.Update

      rstSpecFrom.MoveNext
    Loop

    rstSpecTo.Close
    Set rstSpecTo = Nothing
    rstSpecFrom.Close
    Set rstSpecFrom = Nothing

    Me.Requery
  End If

Exit_Procedure:
  On Error Resume Next
  Set db = Nothing
  Exit Sub

Error_Handler:
  DisplayUnexpectedError Err.Number, Err.Description
  Resume Exit_Procedure
  Resume
```

code snippet Copying Trees Of Parent And Child Records in ch07_CodeSnippets.txt

It's important to understand the following key points about the preceding code:

➤ The variable lngPCKey stores the key of the newly created copy of the PC record. It's defined as a Long because this example assumes you are using AutoNumber keys, which are Long Integers.

➤ To find the record that was just created, you can use the LastModified property of the recordset. It returns a Bookmark to the record that was added. You can use this to find the new key.

➤ Setting the Bookmark property of a recordset positions it to that record.

➤ Use Me.Requery to requery the form's recordset so that the newly added record will be shown.

If your back-end database is Access (ACE), there's a simpler way to find the AutoNumber key of a newly added record. Anywhere between the `.AddNew` and the `.Update`, the AutoNumber key field of the table has already been set, so you can save it into a variable. Using this method, you don't need the `Bookmark` or `LastModified` properties. But be careful: If your back-end database is SQL Server or another ODBC database, the key won't be set until after the `.AddNew`, and your code won't work. The technique shown here is more flexible because it works for both ACE and ODBC databases.

Some developers are tempted to find the AutoNumber key with the highest value immediately after adding a record, thinking that this is a good way to find the new record. Don't do it! There are two problems with this approach. First, it fails in a multiuser environment if another user just happens to add a record in the fraction of a second after your code adds a new record but before it finds the "highest" value. Second, you shouldn't write code that depends on an AutoNumber key to have a certain value or sequence. If your database is ever switched to random keys (which can happen if it is replicated), this technique fails.

Using Bookmark and RecordsetClone

In the previous example, there's one annoying behavior. After the form is requeried, the record selector is repositioned to the top of the list. That's disconcerting and can make it difficult to find the record that was just created.

It's easy to reposition the form to the new record — after all, you already know its key. Just after the `Me.Requery`, you add some code to find the new record in the just-requeried recordset and reposition the form to it.

To reposition the form, you use a `RecordsetClone`. This is a strange concept to developers when they first use it. Think of a `RecordsetClone` as a "twin" of the main recordset that the form is bound to. The nice thing about a `RecordsetClone` is that it has its own record cursor (with separate `FindFirst`, `EOF`, and so on), but it uses the exact same set of records as the form. You synchronize the "twin" recordsets with a `Bookmark`, which is essentially a pointer to an exact record in both recordsets.

If you find a record using a form's `RecordsetClone`, you can use the `Bookmark` to instantly reposition the form to that record. Here's the same code, with the extra repositioning section:

Available for download on Wrox.com

```
On Error GoTo Error_Handler
Dim db As Database
Dim rstPC As DAO.Recordset
Dim rstSpecFrom As DAO.Recordset
Dim rstSpecTo As DAO.Recordset
Dim lngPCKey as Long

Set db = CurrentDb

If Not IsNull(Me.PCKey) Then

    Set rstPC = db.OpenRecordset("tblPC", dbOpenDynaset)

    `copy the parent record and remember its key
    rstPC.AddNew
    rstPC!PCName = "Copy of " & Me!PCName
    rstPC.Update
```

```
rstPC.Bookmark = rstPC.LastModified
lngPCKey = rstPC!PCKey

rstPC.Close
Set rstPC = Nothing

Set rstSpecTo = db.OpenRecordset("tblSpecification", dbOpenDynaset)
Set rstSpecFrom = db.OpenRecordset _
("Select * From tblSpecification Where PCKey = " & Me!PCKey)

Do While Not rstSpecFrom.EOF

  rstSpecTo.AddNew
  rstSpecTo!PCKey = lngPCKey 'set to the new parent key
  rstSpecTo!SpecificationName = rstSpecFrom!SpecificationName
  rstSpecTo!SpecificationQty = rstSpecFrom!SpecificationQty
  rstSpecTo.Update

  rstSpecFrom.MoveNext
Loop

rstSpecTo.Close
Set rstSpecTo = Nothing
rstSpecFrom.Close
Set rstSpecFrom = Nothing

Me.Requery

'reposition form to new record
Set rstPC = Me.RecordsetClone
rstPC.FindFirst "PCKey = " & lngPCKey
If Not rstPC.EOF Then
  Me.Bookmark = rstPC.Bookmark
End If
rstPC.Close
Set rstPC = Nothing

End If

Exit_Procedure:
  On Error Resume Next
  Set db = Nothing
  Exit Sub

Error_Handler:
  DisplayUnexpectedError Err.Number, Err.Description
  Resume Exit_Procedure
  Resume
```

code snippet Using Bookmark And RecordsetClone in ch07_CodeSnippets.txt

You can reuse the rstPC recordset object for the repositioning logic because you are finished using it from earlier in the code, it has already been dimensioned, and it has an appropriate name. Of course, you need to close it and set it to Nothing again when you're done.

Cleaning Up

Although Access VBA is supposed to automatically clean up local objects when a procedure ends, there is a history of errors and exceptions to this. So, programmers have learned that the safest practice is to clean up everything themselves. It's boring, but it shows an attention to detail that is missing in many novice applications. To clean up recordsets, make sure that you:

➤ Close the recordset using the `.Close` method.

➤ Release the recordset object by setting it to `Nothing`.

These two easy steps may prevent strange problems and, more importantly, help you gain the respect of your peers.

USING VBA IN FORMS AND REPORTS

Much of the power and flexibility of applications built using Access comes from the VBA code that you can use behind your forms and reports. Although code-less forms and reports can provide a lot of good functionality, they really shine when VBA coding techniques are added.

Access wizards provide a first look at VBA code behind forms and reports. However, wizard-built code is just scratching the surface. The following sub-sections offer some guidelines and techniques that will help you build extra functionality into your Access applications.

All about Me

`Me` is a very special word in Access VBA. It is a reference to the form or report that your code is running in. For example, if you have some code behind the form `frmBusiness`, anytime you use `Me` in that code, you get a reference to the form object of `frmBusiness`.

This is a beautiful thing because there are many times that you need a reference to your own form or report, such as when you need to make it visible. You could refer to it directly, like this:

```
Forms!frmBusiness.Visible = True
```

Or, you can use the `Me` reference instead:

```
Me.Visible = True
```

Obviously, the `Me` reference is much shorter and easier to type. But there is a far greater reason to use `Me`: It enables you to move code from one form or report to another, where it automatically adapts to its new home.

The `Me` object is a full reference to a form object. Not only can you refer to it, but you can also pass it to other functions as a parameter. Simply define a function with a parameter with a `Form` data type, and you can pass the `Me` reference to it. You can see that used in the Better Record Finder technique shown in Appendix I.

It's good that you can pass `Me` as a parameter because it doesn't work outside the code of the form or report. Remember that `Me` refers to the form or report that it lives in, not the form or report that is currently active. So `Me` will not work in a standalone module (a module not behind a form or report).

Referring to Controls

A control is any object that is placed on a form or report, such as a label, text box, combo box, image, checkbox, and so on. To refer to a control (for example, a bound text box named BusinessName) from the code behind a form or report, you use the following:

```
Me!BusinessName
```

So, if you want to clear out the BusinessName control, you use the following:

```
Me!BusinessName = Null
```

There has long been confusion in the VBA world about when to use a ! (bang) and when to use a . (dot). There are more technical ways to describe it, but for the average VBA programmer there's a quick rule that works most of the time: If you (or any programmer) named it, you can use a bang. If Access named it, you use a dot. (Now, before all the VBA experts reading this get upset, please realize that it's only a general guideline. However, it does help.)

With that said, here's an exception. In the last few versions of Access, you can use either a bang or a dot when referring to controls on forms or reports, even though you named them. That's because of a little trick Access does: It turns all of your controls into properties of the form or report so they can be referred to with dots. This has a handy benefit: Access uses IntelliSense to prompt you with the possible properties and methods that are available for an object. So, in the Me!BusinessName, for example, you type **Me** and then . (dot); Access can then prompt you with every method and property for the object Me, including your control BusinessName.

> That little trick about using a dot instead of a bang for controls on forms and reports does not extend to fields in a recordset. To refer to them directly, you still need to use a bang, like this: rstMyRecordset!BusinessName. Or you can use other ways, such as the Fields collection: rstMyRecordset .Fields("BusinessName"). It is for that reason you should ensure that your control names are not the same as your field names. By default, a control bound to a field assumes the name of the field. A good programming practice is to immediately rename these controls using a Reddick naming convention prefix (txt for Text Box, cbo for combo box, and so on, depending on the type of control being used).

Referring to Subforms and Subreports

One of the most common questions about subforms and subreports is how to refer to their controls from the main form or report. Let's say that you have a form named frmBusiness, and on it you have a continuous subform named fsubPayments. Each Business record may have many Payments. You need to refer to a value of the calculated control txtSumPaymentAmount on the subform, but you want to do it from the main form frmBusiness.

The correct way to refer to `txtSumPaymentAmount` from `frmBusiness` is:

```
Me!fsubPayments.Form!txtSumPaymentAmount
```

The following table shows what each of the parts refers to:

COMPONENT	DESCRIPTION
`Me`	The parent form where the code is running, which in this example is `frmBusiness`.
`!fsubPayments`	The control that contains the subform (its name usually defaults to the name of the subform object itself, but some programmers rename it).
`.Form`	This is the tricky piece. You need to drill down into the form that's in the control because that's where the controls in the subform live. The control on the main form named `fsubPayments` is just a Container — it doesn't contain the control you're looking for, but it does have this `Form` reference to use to get down into the subform itself.
`!txtSumPaymentAmount`	The control you want. You can even refer to controls that are on subforms on subforms (two levels down).

Remember that you need to use the `Form` reference to get into the form that's in the subform control Container. For example, `frmA` contains subform `fsubB` contains subform `fsubC`, which has control `txtC`. The full reference looks like this:

```
Me!fsubB.Form!fsubC.Form!txtC
```

You can also shift into reverse and refer to controls above a subform, using the `Parent` property. If some code in `fsubC` (at the bottom) needed to refer to control `txtA` on `frmA` (at the top), it would look like this:

```
Me.Parent.Parent!txtA
```

Note that you don't need the `Form` reference here because the `Parent` reference is already a `Form` reference.

Closing Forms

Most of us will use the built-in Access wizards when creating certain types of buttons — one for closing your forms, for example. When you do, Access will create an Embedded Macro to perform this action. Often, you may not wish to use the macro but would like to use code so that you can run certain types of data validation or other operations before the form closes. While you could allow Access to convert the form's macros to code for you, you may just want to create the code yourself from scratch. The basic way to do that is with the following code:

```
DoCmd.Close
```

This method of the `DoCmd` object closes the active object, like your form. It doesn't get much simpler than that. Unfortunately, there is an obscure situation that will cause this code to fail to close the correct form. If you read the help documentation on `DoCmd.Close`, you'll see that if you don't provide any parameters, it closes the active form. You might assume that the active form is the one containing this code; after all, you just clicked the Close button, so the form must be active. However, there are situations where another form is the active one.

You may, for example, have a hidden form on a timer that periodically does something. This is a technique that is often used in automatic log-off functionality, where a hidden form uses a timer to periodically check a table to determine whether it should shut down the application. The problem is that, when that timer fires and the code in the form checks the table, it becomes the active form. If you're unlucky enough for that to happen right when the Close button is clicked, the wrong form (the hidden one) will close instead of the form you intended.

Another situation is when the code in your closing routine reaches out and runs code in another form; this can make the other form active at that moment. The solution is to clarify the `DoCmd` `.Close` statement, like this:

```
DoCmd.Close ObjectType:=acForm, ObjectName:=Me.Name
```

This specifies that a form be closed, specifically the form to which this code belongs. If you get into the habit of using this syntax, the proper form will always close correctly.

DEBUGGING VBA

Programming in VBA isn't easy. No matter how skilled you are there are times when you need help figuring out what the code is actually doing. Fortunately, VBA provides a rich and powerful debugging environment. You can stop the code at various times and for various reasons, view values of variables (and even change them), and step through your code line-by-line until you understand what's going on.

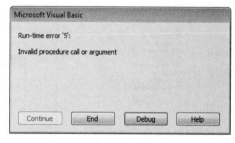

FIGURE 7-2

The main reason you need to debug your code is that Access has displayed an error message. (Hopefully you've put error handling in your code, which can make this activity easier.) Let's say you've coded a cool copy routine like the one shown earlier in this chapter. However, when you try it, Access displays an error. If you don't have error handling, a message box displays, as shown in Figure 7-2.

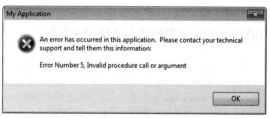

FIGURE 7-3

If you do have error handling, good job! Your error handling message box will display, as shown in Figure 7-3.

When Access displays your handled error message box, your code execution is suspended. To debug your code, press Ctrl+Break to interrupt code execution and display the dialog box shown in Figure 7-4.

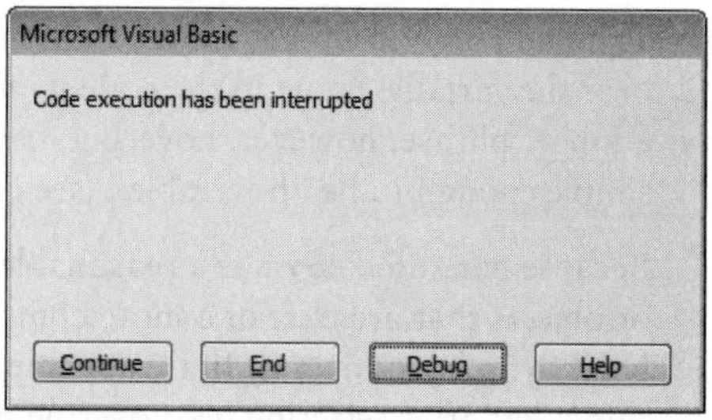

FIGURE 7-4

Whichever way you get there, you can finally click the Debug button. When you do, your code appears in the VBA code window. If you are not using error handling, the line of code that caused the error is indicated by an arrow and highlighted in yellow. If you are using error handling with the centralized Msgbox text and an extra Resume statement detailed later in this chapter, press F8 to step back to the procedure that contains the error. Then you can reposition to the specific line that caused the error, as shown in Figure 7-5.

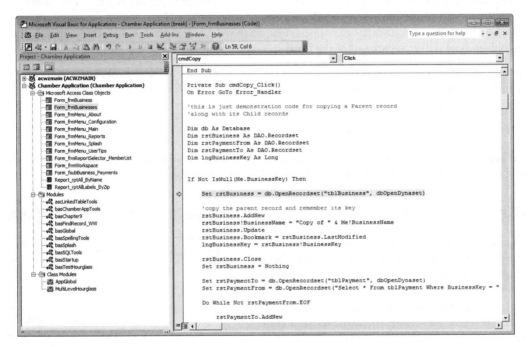

FIGURE 7-5

INVESTIGATING VARIABLES

Now that you can see your code and the line that might be causing the problem, it's time to investigate. The error message — Object variable or With block variable not set — is a clue, but it doesn't tell you exactly what the problem is. The first step is to check the current values of the variables near the line that caused the error. Remember that your code is suspended, so all your variables are intact and able to report their values.

The quickest and easiest way to determine the value of a variable is to hover your mouse pointer over the variable name in the code window when your code is suspended. If the variable is part of a longer phrase, however, hovering may not work. For example, the variable Me.BusinessKey is simple enough to be "hoverable" (see Figure 7-6).

Because BusinessKey has a reasonable value, it doesn't seem to be the problem. To check variables or objects that are part of a more complex statement, highlight the portion you are interested in before you hover over it. In this example, just hovering over the object name db doesn't display anything, but after selecting db, hovering provides a value, as shown in Figure 7-7.

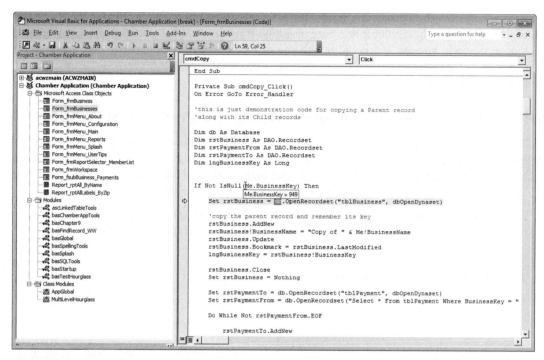

FIGURE 7-6

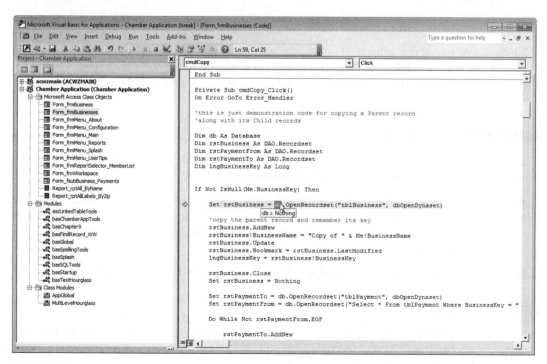

FIGURE 7-7

By checking the value of db, you can see that it is currently set to Nothing. This is Access's way of telling you that the db object reference hasn't been set to any value yet. Sure enough, when you look at the code, you can see that although you defined db using the line Dim db As Database, you forgot to include the line Set db = CurrentDb. Adding this line before the OpenRecordset line resolves the problem.

When Hovering Isn't Enough — Using the Immediate Window

There are times when having the value of a variable pop up by hovering over it isn't sufficient. Perhaps the value doesn't fit in the pop-up, or maybe you need to copy the value to use it somewhere else. Or maybe you just want to look at it longer than the limited time the pop-up value displays. In those cases, you can use the Immediate window (instead of hovering) to view variable values.

If the Immediate window isn't already displayed, select View ➪ Immediate Window or press Ctrl+G to open it. Then you can ask Access to display the value of a variable using ?, like this:

```
?Me.BusinessKey
```

When you press Enter, Access returns the value:

```
?Me.BusinessKey
949
```

 The ? *in the Immediate window is just a quick way of specifying* Debug.Print.

No matter how long this value is (it could be a very long string, for example), Access displays it here so that you can study it or even copy it into the clipboard to use somewhere else. This comes in handy when the variable contains a long SQL string that you want to try out by pasting it into a new query.

Setting Breakpoints

Sometimes your code doesn't actually produce an error, but it still doesn't work correctly. In those cases, you need to stop the code yourself using breakpoints.

The easiest way to set a breakpoint is to click the gray area to the left of a line of code where you would like the code to suspend execution. This places a red dot to remind you where the breakpoint is set. Just before that line runs, your code will suspend and the code window will be displayed with that line highlighted in yellow, as shown in Figure 7-8.

At this point, you can investigate variable values as discussed previously in this chapter.

Setting Watch Values

Sometimes you have no clue where the problem lies, so you don't know where to set the breakpoint. However, you may want to suspend your code and investigate whenever a certain variable is set to a certain value. To do this, you can use a watch value.

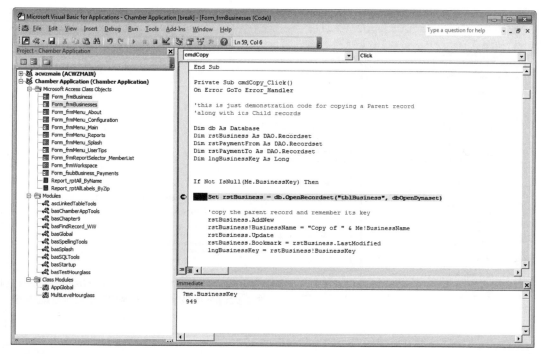

FIGURE 7-8

A watch value enables you to suspend execution of your code whenever a variable or object (or expression using a variable or object) changes or has a certain value. This is especially powerful in complex code scenarios where you are having trouble finding where your logic is going wrong. You create watch values using the Add Watch window (see Figure 7-9), which you can request using Debug...Add Watch or by right-clicking in the Watches window.

You can watch a single field, or you can type in an expression that uses multiple variables or values. Also, you can widen the context; it defaults to the procedure you are in, but you can expand on this to

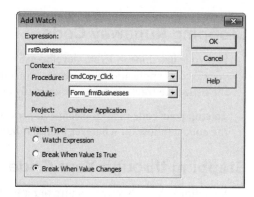

FIGURE 7-9

include all procedures. Finally, you can choose to merely watch the expression, to break (suspend your code execution) when the expression becomes True (for example, when BusinessKey = 949), or to break every time your expression changes. After you add your watch, it appears in the Watches window, as shown in Figure 7-10.

When the break condition you specify occurs, your code is displayed in the window. However, now you have an additional window, the Watches window. You can add more watch expressions here, if needed, and if you specify an object to watch (such as a form, report, recordset, and so on), you can even drill down to all of its properties using the plus sign (+) next to the object name.

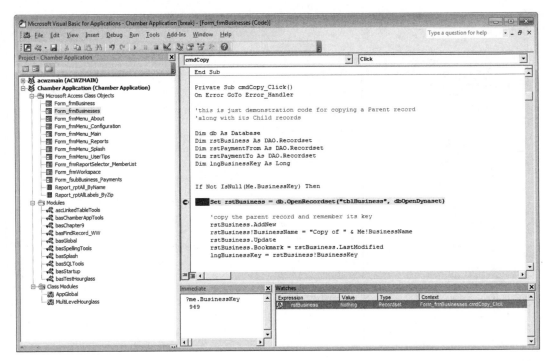

FIGURE 7-10

Stopping Runaway Code

Everyone has done it. Every developer has created code that created an infinite loop. That's where your Access application just freezes, consuming all available computer power while it runs around the little race track that you accidentally created.

To stop your code in mid-execution, press Ctrl+Break. This suspends your code and drops you into the code window on whatever line that happens to be executing at that moment.

Stepping through Your Code

Sometimes the only way to figure out a problem in your code is to actually run it line-by-line until you see where it goes wrong. You can use any of the preceding methods to stop your code, but there's nothing like getting your mind right into the logic by stepping through the code one line at a time.

You step through code by selecting Debug ➪ Step Into (or pressing F8). This debug command is the most common one to use because it's so basic. It runs the line of code that is highlighted, displays the next line that will be run, and awaits your next command. The Step Into and other Step commands are shown in Figure 7-11.

Sometimes the basic nature of Step Into is a problem. If the highlighted line of code is a call to another procedure (either a function or a sub), Step Into will do just that — it will dive into that procedure and highlight its first line.

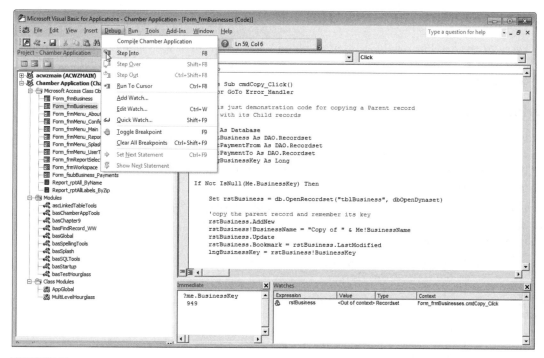

FIGURE 7-11

Now, maybe that's just what you want. But if you are following good programming practices, such as the coupling and cohesion guidelines presented earlier in this chapter, you have lots of small, fully tested functions that will be supremely boring and laborious to step through. After all, you know the error isn't in one of those, right?

The answer to this little problem is to use a cousin of Step Into called Step Over (Shift+F8). Its name isn't quite accurate, because when you use it, the highlighted line of code isn't really stepped over — it's actually stepped through. The line of code that's highlighted will run, even if it is a call to one of your functions or subs, and then the next line will be highlighted. The entire function or sub will run without stopping, so you don't have to step through all that boring code.

Also note that Step Over works exactly the same as Step Into for a normal line of code (not a call to another procedure). This means that you can get into the habit of leaning on the Shift key when you use F8, and you'll never need to step through called procedures unless you want to.

What if you accidentally use Step Into when you meant to use Step Over? Hope is not lost. By using the often-forgotten Step Out (Ctrl+Shift+F8), you can run the remainder of the current procedure without stopping, and automatically stop on the next line after your code returns to the calling procedure.

COMMON VBA TECHNIQUES

Every Access developer will face some common VBA challenges at some point. There are simple and easy ways to handle drilling down to detail records, date math, rounding issues, and tricky string concatenation problems.

Drilling Down with Double-Click

It's a good design practice to use read-only continuous forms to display multiple records and then allow your user to drill down to the detail of a single selected record. This action should have a button at the bottom of the form (called Detail, for example) that opens the detail form for the currently selected record.

For convenience and to compliment Windows standard behavior, it's also good to allow the user to drill down using double-click. Because you already have code behind the Detail button that opens the detail form, you can easily reuse that code:

Available for download on Wrox.com

```vba
Private Sub cmdDetail_Click()
On Error GoTo Error_Handler
    Dim stLinkCriteria As String
    If IsNull(Me!BusinessKey) Then
        EnableDisableControls
        GoTo Exit_Procedure
    End If

    gstrCallingForm = Me.Name
    stLinkCriteria = "[BusinessKey]= " & Me![BusinessKey]
    DoCmd.OpenForm FormName:="frmBusiness", _
        wherecondition:=stLinkCriteria
    Me.Visible = False

Exit_Procedure:
    On Error Resume Next
    Exit Sub
Error_Handler:
    DisplayUnexpectedError Err.Number, Err.Description
    Resume Exit_Procedure
    Resume

End Sub
```

code snippet Drilling Down With Double-Click in ch07_CodeSnippets.txt

Because this code is already written and tested, you only need to call it by name (`cmdDetail_Click`) when the user double-clicks a record. This is quite simple to do: You just add a double-click event to each text box on your detail form and add one line of code to each double-click procedure:

Available for download on Wrox.com

```vba
Private Sub txtBusinessName_DblClick(Cancel As Integer)
On Error GoTo Error_Handler

    cmdDetail_Click

Exit_Procedure:
    On Error Resume Next
    Exit Sub
```

```
Error_Handler:
    DisplayUnexpectedError Err.Number, Err.Description
    Resume Exit_Procedure
    Resume
End Sub
```

code snippet Calling Code In Another Procedure in ch07_CodeSnippets.txt

Here's a case where your actual code (1 line) is a lot shorter than all the error handling, but that line allows you to reuse the code you already have behind the Detail button.

Just because Access creates and names an event procedure (cmdDetail_Click in this case) doesn't mean you can't use it yourself. Just call it by typing its name as a statement in VBA.

To support double-click all the way across your row, you need to add the same code to each field's Double-Click event. That way, whichever field your user double-clicks, they'll drill down to the detail record.

Now, there's only one more thing to add. Users will often double-click the Record Selector itself (the arrow to the left of the current record) when they want to drill down to the record's detail. Surprisingly, the event that fires in this case is not related to the detail section of the continuous form; instead, the Form's double-click event will fire. To support double-click of the Record Selector, you can use this code behind the Form's On Double Click event:

```
Private Sub Form_DblClick(Cancel As Integer)
On Error GoTo Error_Handler

    cmdDetail_Click

Exit_Procedure:
    On Error Resume Next
    Exit Sub

Error_Handler:
    DisplayUnexpectedError Err.Number, Err.Description
    Resume Exit_Procedure
    Resume
End Sub
```

Date Handling

The way Access stores and manipulates dates can be a source of confusion to developers, especially those who remember the older database methods of storing days, months, and years in date fields. Access handles dates in an elegant, easy-to-use manner.

How Access Stores Dates and Times

Access stores a particular date as the number of days that have elapsed since an arbitrary starting "zero date" (December 30, 1899). You can prove this to yourself by typing the following in the Immediate window (you can bring up the Immediate window in Access using Ctrl+G).

```
?CLng(#12/31/1899#)
1
```

The CLng function converts an expression to a Long Integer. To this question, Access will answer with 1, meaning that 1 day elapsed since December 30, 1899. Of course, Access can handle dates before this date; they're stored as negative integers. If you want to see how many days have elapsed since that special zero date, try this:

```
?CLng(Date)
```

Access can perform date math very easily because internally it doesn't store a date as days, months, and years. It just stores the number of days since the zero date and converts that value to an understandable date format only when the date needs to be displayed. But the date storage technique that Access uses goes even farther. Access can also store the time of day in the same date field. To do this, Access uses the decimal portion (the numbers after the decimal point) to store a fraction of a day. For example, 12:00 noon is stored as .5 (half way through the day), and 6 a.m. is stored as .25. Again, you can see this for yourself by typing this into the Immediate window:

```
?CDbl(Now)
```

There are a couple of things to note here. The first is that you now need to use CDbl (Convert to Double Precision Number) so that you can see the decimal portion (the time portion) that is returned by the Now function. The other is that each time you run this command, you'll see that the decimal portion changes because time is elapsing.

When you're storing the current date in a table, be sure to use the Date function. If you use Now, you'll also get a time component, which may cause incorrect results when you use dates in your query criteria. For example, if your query selects records where a date field is <=4/28/2007, then any records with a date of 4/28/2007 should be returned. However, if they were stored with a decimal time component (by using Now instead of Date), the value will be fractionally greater than 4/28/2007 and that date won't be returned.

Simple Date Math

To add or subtract calendar time from a date field, use the DateAdd function. For example, to add 1 month to today's date, use:

```
?dateadd("m",1,Date)
```

To subtract, use a negative number for the second parameter, Number. You can use different units of calendar time for the Interval parameter, such as "d" for days, "ww" for weeks, "q" for quarters, and so on. Be careful when adding or subtracting years; you have to use "yyyy", not just "y". The interval of "y" is day of year, which acts just like day in the DateAdd function.

Here's an example of date math. It computes the last day of a month by finding the first day of the next month, and then subtracting 1 day.

```
Public Function LastDateofMonth(StartDate As Date)

On Error GoTo Error_Handler

  Dim dtNextMonth As Date
  Dim dtNewDate As Date

  `add a month to the start date
  dtNextMonth = DateAdd(`m", 1, StartDate)

  `build a date
  dtNewDate = CDate((DatePart(`m", dtNextMonth)) & _
  "/01/" & (DatePart(`yyyy", dtNextMonth)))

  `subtract a day
  LastDateofMonth = dtNewDate -1

Exit_Procedure:
  Exit Function
Error_Handler:
  DisplayUnexpectedError Err.Number, Err.Description
  Resume Exit_Procedure
  Resume

End Function
```

code snippet Function To Find Last Date Of Month in ch07_CodeSnippets.txt

Note the use of CDate, which converts any expression that can be interpreted as a date into an actual date data type. You can use IsDate to check whether an expression can be interpreted as a date. Also note how the DatePart function is used to break up a date into string components for Month, Year, and so on.

Handling Rounding Issues

Rounding problems are among the most difficult to understand and debug. They usually occur when adding up money values, but they can also happen in any math where a series of values is expected to add up correctly.

Rounding of Sums

One basic issue is not Access-related at all, but rather an issue whenever you add up a list of rounded numbers. For example, take a list of numbers that each represent one third of a dollar. If you add them up, you'll get 99 cents because the value of each portion (.33333333...) was truncated to .33.

```
.33
.33
.33
.99
```

A common place for this to show up is in a list of percentages that are supposed to total 100 percent. They often don't because some precision was lost in the list. Then, you are faced with a decision — add up the actual numbers and show a total that's not 100, or just hard-code 100 percent so that it looks right. Most of the time, you will want to ensure that your final value is correct and eliminate an accumulated rounding error. This can be accomplished by eliminating rounding of the individual components of your formula and reserving rounding to the final outcome. For display purposes, each component can be formatted in the displayed control to the number of decimal places you wish to show but the underlying control will still contain the full value it represents.

Rounding Errors Caused by Floating Point Numbers

Another kind of rounding error comes from the way Access stores numbers in floating-point fields. These fields cannot store certain numbers without losing some precision, so totals based on them may be slightly wrong. The best way to avoid this kind of rounding error is to use the Currency data type for fields when they need to hold money values (as you might expect), or the Decimal type for any other numeric values that you want to use in calculations. The Currency data type is somewhat misnamed; it really can hold any decimal value.

Access uses the word "Currency" for both a data type and a format. This is unfortunate because they really are two different things. The Currency data type is a method of storing the numeric values in a table. The Currency format affects only the display of numeric data. The two can be used independently or together.

Access Rounding Functions

Access has a built-in function (Round) to round numbers, but it may not work the way you expect. Most people think that any decimal ending in 5 should round up to the next higher number. However, Access uses a form of scientific rounding that works like this:

➤ If the digit to be rounded is 0 through 4, round down to the lower number.

➤ If the digit to be rounded is 6 through 9, round up to the higher number.

➤ If the digit to be rounded is 5, round up if digit to the left is odd, and round down if the digit to the left is even.

This last rule is what surprises a lot of developers. Using this rule, Round gives the following results:

```
?round(1.5)
2
?round(2.5)
2
```

Yes, that's right. Both 1.5 and 2.5 round to 2 using the built-in Round function in Access VBA, because 1 is odd (round up) and 2 is even (round down). Here's another example:

```
?round(1.545,2)

1.54
?round(1.555,2)

1.56
```

In this example, .545 rounds down, but .555 rounds up, for the same reason. Because this can cause some trouble in business applications, developers have taken to writing their own rounding functions that behave the way business people expect. Here's an example of a function that rounds a trailing 5 upward to a specified number of decimal places:

Available for download on Wrox.com

```
Public Function RoundCurr(OriginalValue As Currency, Optional _
NumberOfDecimals As Integer) As Currency
On Error GoTo Error_Handler

`returns a currency value rounded to the specified number of decimals of
`the Original Value

If IsMissing(NumberOfDecimals) Then
  NumberOfDecimals = 0
End If

RoundCurr = Int((OriginalValue * (10 ^ NumberOfDecimals)) + 0.5) _
  / (10 ^ NumberOfDecimals)

Exit_Procedure:
  Exit Function
Error_Handler:
  DisplayUnexpectedError Err.Number, Err.Description
  Resume Exit_Procedure

End Function
```

code snippet Substitute Rounding Function in ch07_CodeSnippets.txt

This function can be placed in any module in your application and used whenever you want the business-style rounding that most users expect. Note that if you don't specify the number of decimals you would like, the function will assume that you want none and will return a whole number.

STRING CONCATENATION TECHNIQUES

Sooner or later, you'll need to join (concatenate) two strings together. The operator for performing concatenation is &. You may be tempted to say "and" when you see this symbol, but it really means "concatenate with." A classic example is joining First Name with Last Name, like this:

```
strFullName = FirstName & " " & LastName
```

This results in the first name and last name together in one string, as in "Tom Smith."

The Difference between & and +

There are times when you may need to concatenate something to a string, but only if the string actually has a value. For example, you may want to include the middle initial in a person's full name. If you write code like this:

```
strFullName = FirstName & " " & MiddleInitial & " " & LastName
```

you will have a small problem. People with no middle name (Null in the table) will have two spaces between their first and last names, like this:

```
Tom   Smith
```

Fortunately, there is another concatenation operator: +. The technical explanation of this operator is "concatenation with Null propagation." That's a great phrase to impress your friends with at parties, but an easier explanation is that it concatenates two strings just as the & operator does, but only if both strings have a value. If either one is Null, the result of the whole concatenation operation is Null.

Using the FullName example, the goal is to have only one space separating first and last names if there is no middle initial. Using +, you can tack on the extra space only if the middlenName is not null:

```
MiddleName + " "
```

The whole thing looks like this:

```
strFullName = FirstName & " " & (MiddleInitial + " ") & LastName
```

As shown, you can use parentheses to ensure that the operations happen in the correct order. In this case, the inner phrase — (MiddleInitial + " ") — will evaluate to the middle initial plus a space, or to Null (if there is no middle initial). Then, the rest of the statement will be performed.

String Concatenation Example

Here is another example that you can use in your code. It concatenates the city, state, postal code (ZIP Code), and nation into one text field. This can be handy if you want to show a simulation of an address label on a form or report.

Available for download on Wrox.com

```
Function CityStZIPNat(City As Variant, State As Variant, ZIP As Variant, _
    Nation As Variant) As Variant
On Error GoTo Error_Handler

CityStZIPNat = City & (", " + State) & (" " + ZIP) & _
(IIf(Nation = "US" Or Nation = "CA", Null, (" " + Nation)))

Exit_Procedure:
  Exit Function
Error_Handler:
  MsgBox Err.Number & ", " & Err.Description
  Resume Exit_Procedure
  Resume

End Function
```

code snippet String Concatenation Function in ch07_CodeSnippets.txt

You can try it out by calling it in the Immediate window like this:

```
?CityStZIPNat("Seattle", "WA", "98011", "US")

Seattle, WA 98011
```

Notice that this code also tacks on the Nation at the end of the string, but only if it isn't US or CA (the ISO standard nation codes for USA and Canada, respectively). This enables you to use this function for both domestic and foreign addresses.

VBA ERROR HANDLING

When programmers use the term "error handling," they really mean graceful or planned error handling. After all, Access takes some kind of action for any error that it encounters in your code. *Graceful* error handling includes the following:

➤ Quietly absorbing expected errors so the user never sees them

➤ Displaying a "friendly" message to the user for unexpected errors, and closing the procedure properly

Error handling in Access VBA involves adding code to every procedure — both subroutines and functions — to take specific actions when Access encounters an error. This is called handling or trapping the error. (Some developers call the encounter with an error: *throwing* an error. Error handling is the code that *catches* the error and handles it properly, either by hiding it from the users or by explaining it to them.)

This section provides techniques to handle several types of expected and unexpected errors so that your applications look and feel more professional to your users. But first, you'll explore why you should use error handling at all. Many Access developers see it as a mundane chore, but there are good reasons for including error handling in every procedure you write.

Why Use Error Handling?

Without error-handling code, Access treats all errors equally, displaying unfriendly or vague error messages and abruptly ending procedures. Even worse, if you are using the runtime mode of Access, the entire application closes. This is not what you want users to experience.

Figure 7-12 shows an example of an error message that Access displays if you attempt to divide a number by zero in your application. Sure, technically it indicates what happened, but what is the user supposed to do about it? And what if he clicks the Debug button? If he's running an MDB/ACCDB instead of an MDE/ACCDE, he'll be looking at your code!

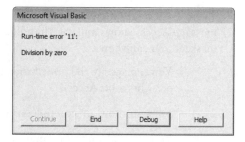

When Access encounters an error, it abruptly ends the procedure. It does not run another line of code; it just terminates the function or sub that contains the error.

FIGURE 7-12

So, it can often leave things hanging — open objects, open forms, the mouse pointer in hourglass mode, warnings turned off, and so on.

Amateur or pro? When your code is being evaluated by another programmer, one of the easiest things for him to check is whether you have proper error handling. No matter how good your code is, without error handling you may look like a beginner. It's worth making sure that every procedure has error handling.

Now for the good news: Error handling isn't difficult. By using some easy techniques and code templates, you can make sure that your application never suffers an unhandled error. If you establish a standard way to handle errors, you can make it easy to implement in every procedure you write. It may not be fun or glamorous, but it will certainly make your application better.

Two Kinds of Errors: Unexpected and Expected

All errors that your Access application may encounter fall into one of two categories: unexpected and expected. The following sections explain these two categories and what your application should do when errors occur in each of them.

Handling Unexpected Errors

Unexpected errors are ones that you have no way of predicting, and that under normal circumstances should not occur. When your application encounters an unexpected error (for example, divide by zero or a missing object), and no error handling is in effect, Access displays an error message like the one shown earlier and abruptly ends the procedure.

The goal of error handling in this case is not to solve the problem the error is indicating — there's nothing you can do about that now. Your code has tripped on an error and fallen down. The only thing you can do is let the user know what happened calmly and in plain language. Figure 7-13 is an example of what your error message might look like.

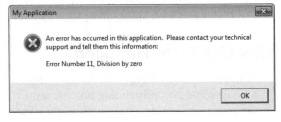

FIGURE 7-13

There are several differences between the error message Access shows and the "handled" error message you can show:

➤ You can specify the title of the message box instead of displaying "Microsoft Visual Basic" or "Microsoft Access."

➤ You can show an icon to have a stronger impact.

➤ You can add a text explanation. You can even mention your phone number or other contact information.

➤ You can format the error message with blank lines, commas, and so on.

➤ Your user can't enter debug mode and look at your code.

Absorbing Expected Errors

Some errors can be expected during normal operation. One such error happens in your application whenever the On Open event of a report is canceled. This occurs when you display a form to prompt the user for selection criteria during the On Open event, and the user decides to cancel the report. This report criteria technique is described in Chapter 14.

There are other errors that you can expect. Maybe you expect a certain file to be on the hard drive, but it isn't. Maybe you expect a form to be open, but somehow it has been closed. These kinds of errors can usually be absorbed by your application, never allowing the user to see them.

In these situations, your code should just ignore the error and keep going. Whenever Access encounters an error, it makes an error number available to your code. To absorb an expected error, you add an `If` statement to check if the error number matches the number you expect. If it matches, you can just `Resume Next` to continue to the next line of code without bothering the user with an error dialog box. If it doesn't match, you can drop into your normal error handling.

Next, we explore some basic error-handling code that can be used to handle both expected and unexpected errors in your application. Then we'll look more specifically at expected errors in the section "More on Absorbing Expected Errors."

Basic Error Handling

Let's start with the basics. Here's some code that you could add to every procedure to build in easy, no-frills error handling:

Available for download on Wrox.com

```
Public Function MyFunction
On Error GoTo Error_Handler

    `your function code goes here

Exit_Procedure:
  Exit Function

Error_Handler:
  MsgBox "An error has occurred in this application. " _
  & "Please contact your technical support and " _
  & "tell them the following information:" _
  & vbCrLf & vbCrLf & "Error Number " & Err.Number & ", " _
  & Err.Description, _
  Buttons:=vbCritical

  Resume Exit_Procedure
End Function
```

code snippet Basic Error Handling in ch07_CodeSnippets.txt

Let's take a look at some important lines in the code, beginning with the following:

```
On Error GoTo Error_Handler
```

The `On Error GoTo` statement in VBA tells the code to jump to a particular line in the procedure whenever an error is encountered. It sets up this directive, which remains in effect until it is replaced by another `On Error` statement or until the procedure ends. In this example, when any error is encountered, the code execution jumps to the line named `Error_Handler`.

 In the early days of Basic and other procedural languages, lines were numbered, not named. For example, your code might have a line GOTO 1100. In VBA, you still have the GoTo statement, but instead of numbering the lines, you can give them meaningful names like Exit_Procedure.

If no error occurs throughout the main body of the procedure, the execution of the code falls through to this point:

```
Exit_Procedure:
    Exit Function
```

and the `Exit Function` will run. As its name implies, the `Exit Function` statement exits this function immediately, and no lines after it will be executed. Note that if this procedure is a sub instead of a function, you use `Exit Sub` instead.

This same `Exit_Procedure` line is also executed after any unexpected errors are handled:

```
Error_Handler:
    MsgBox "An error has occurred in this application. " _
    & "Please contact your technical support and " _
    & "tell them this information:" _
    & vbCrLf & vbCrLf & "Error Number " & Err.Number & ", " _
    & Err.Description, _
    Buttons:=vbCritical
```

If an error occurs, execution jumps to the `Error_Handler` line, and a message box is displayed to the user. When the user clicks OK (her only choice), the code execution is redirected back to the `Exit_Procedure` line:

```
Resume Exit_Procedure
```

and your code exits the procedure.

With this technique, execution of the code falls through to the `Exit_Procedure` code and the function exits normally, as long as no errors are encountered. However, if an error is encountered, the execution is redirected to the error-handling section.

> *In early versions of Access, the labels for the* `Exit_Procedure` *and* `Error_Handler` *sections had to be unique in the entire module. This forced programmers to use labels such as* `Exit_MyFunction` *and* `Error_MyFunction`. *In recent versions of Access, these labels may be duplicated in different procedures. This is a great improvement because now you can copy and paste error-handling code into each procedure with almost no modification.*

This is the most basic error handling you can include in your code. However, there's one word that you can add to make your code much easier to debug: `Resume`. Yes, it's just one word, but it can work wonders when you are trying to make your code easier to debug.

Basic Error Handling with an Extra Resume

One of the problems with basic error handling is that when an error does occur, you have no easy way of knowing the exact line that caused the error. After all, your procedure may have dozens or hundreds of lines of code. When you see the error message, the execution of your code has already jumped to your error handler routine and displayed the message box; you may not be able to tell which line caused the problem. Many programmers rerun the code, using debug mode, to step through the code to try to find the offending line.

But there is a much easier way to find that error-producing line of code: Just add a `Resume` line after the `Resume Exit_Procedure`.

You're probably thinking, "Why would you add an extra `Resume` right after another `Resume Exit_Procedure`? The extra `Resume` will never run!" You're right. It will never run under *normal* circumstances. But it will run if you ask it to. If your application encounters an error, you can override the next line that will run. In debug mode, you can just change the next line to be executed to your extra `Resume`. The `Resume Exit_Procedure` statement is skipped entirely. The following code is identical to the basic code shown previously, but with that one extra `Resume`.

```
Public Function MyFunction()
On Error GoTo Error_Handler

    Dim varReturnVal As Variant

    `your function code goes here

Exit_Procedure:
    Exit Function `or Exit Sub if this is a Sub

Error_Handler:
    MsgBox "An error has occurred in this application. " _
    & "Please contact your technical support and tell them this information:" _
    & vbCrLf & vbCrLf & "Error Number " & Err.Number & ", " _
    & Err.Description, _
    Buttons:=vbCritical, title:="My Application"
    Resume Exit_Procedure
    Resume

End Function
```

code snippet Basic Error Handling With An Extra Resume in ch07_CodeSnippets.txt

Under normal operation, the extra `Resume` never runs because the line before it transfers execution of the code elsewhere. It comes into play only when you manually cause it to run. To do this, you can do something that is rarely done in debug mode: Move the execution point in the code to a different statement.

Here's how the extra `Resume` works. Say your code is supposed to open a report, but there's a problem: The report name you specified doesn't exist. Your code might look like this:

```
Private Sub cmdPreview_Click()
On Error GoTo Error_Handler

    If Me!lstReport.Column(3) & "" <> "" Then
      DoCmd.OpenReport ReportName:=Me!lstReport.Column(3),
      View:=acViewPreview
    End If

    `Update the Last Run Date of the report
    DoCmd.SetWarnings False
    DoCmd.RunSQL "UPDATE tsysReport " _
    & "SET tsysReport.DtLastRan = Date() " _
    & "WHERE tsysReport.RptKey = " & Me.lstReport
    DoCmd.SetWarnings True
```

```
Exit_Procedure:
  On Error Resume Next
  DoCmd.SetWarnings True
  Exit Sub

Error_Handler:
  MsgBox "An error has occurred in this application. " _
  & "Please contact your technical support and " _
  & "tell them the following information:" _
  & vbCrLf & vbCrLf & "Error Number " & Err.Number & ", " &
  Err.Description, _
  Buttons:=vbCritical, title:="My Application"
  Resume Exit_Procedure
  Resume

End Sub
```

When you run your code, an error message appears, as shown in Figure 7-14.

Instead of clicking OK as your user would do, press Ctrl+Break on your keyboard. A Visual Basic dialog box appears, as shown in Figure 7-15.

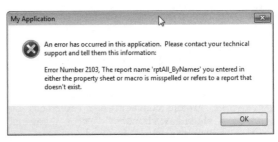

FIGURE 7-14

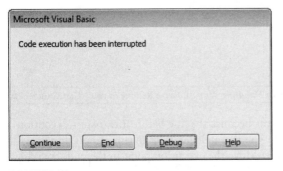

FIGURE 7-15

 This extra Resume *technique won't work in an Access runtime application because in runtime versions no design modes are allowed, including the VBA code editor. It also won't work in an Access MDE or ACCDE because all VBA source code is not accessible from within those applications.*

Now click the Debug button. The code displays in the Code window, as shown in Figure 7-16.

The Resume Exit_Procedure statement will be indicated by an arrow and highlighted in yellow. This is the statement that will execute next if you continue normally. But instead of letting it run, you take control, using your mouse to drag the yellow arrow down one line to the extra `Resume` line. By doing this, you indicate that you want the `Resume` line to run next.

 Instead of using the mouse, you can click or arrow down to the `Resume` *line, and then use* `Debug...Set Next` *statement (Ctrl+F9 on your keyboard). As usual in Access, there are several ways to do the same thing.*

Now, the yellow arrow will be pointed at the `Resume` statement, as shown in Figure 7-17.

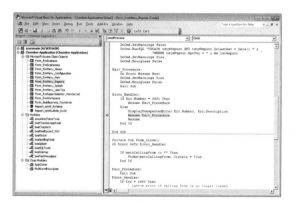

FIGURE 7-16

FIGURE 7-17

Now, you want the `Resume` statement to run in order to retry the statement that caused the error. Press F8 to run the next line of code (your `Resume`) and stop. Or, you can choose `Debug...Step Into` from the menu.

The exact line that caused the error will now be indicated by an arrow, as shown in Figure 7-18. That was easy, wasn't it?

Now, admittedly, this is a simple example. You probably could have determined which line caused the error just by looking at the error description. However, when your procedures contain pages of code, often with coding

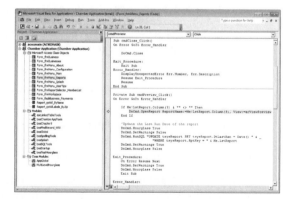

FIGURE 7-18

loops, complex logic, and similar statements, this extra `Resume` technique comes in handy. It can save you many hours of time while you are debugging your VBA code.

The extra `Resume` doesn't cause any harm in your code, so you can leave it in every procedure even when you deliver your application. Also, if a technically savvy client encounters an unexpected error and she's running an MDB or ACCDB (not an MDE or ACCDE), you can walk the client through this process to help determine what caused the problem in the client's environment. As you know, what works on your PC doesn't always work when your user is running it.

Basic Error Handling with a Centralized Message

There's one more thing you can do to make your error-handling code even easier to maintain. Instead of repeating the code to display the message box in every procedure, you can move it to a reusable function that handles it consistently every time.

The following code basically tells the user that an unexpected error occurred. It is needed in every procedure in your application.

```
MsgBox "An error has occurred in this application. " _
& "Please contact your technical support and " _
& "tell them this information:" _
& vbCrLf & vbCrLf & "Error Number " & Err.Number & ", " &
Err.Description, _Buttons:=vbCritical, title:="My Application"
```

Instead, you can centralize this in a function that's called using one line:

```
DisplayUnexpectedError Err.Number, Err.Description
```

Much cleaner! This mundane bit of business is handled with just one line. Now you just need the function that it calls, `DisplayUnexpectedError`. Here it is:

```
Public Sub DisplayUnexpectedError(ErrorNumber As String, _
ErrorDescription As String)
'Note: since this is a universal error handling procedure,
'it does not have error handling

MsgBox "An error has occurred in this application. " _
& "Please contact your technical support and " _
& "tell them this information: " _
& vbCrLf & vbCrLf & "Error Number " & ErrorNumber & ", " &
ErrorDescription, _Buttons:=vbCritical, title:="My Application"

End Sub
```

code snippet Error Handling With A Centralized Message in ch07_CodeSnippets.txt

In this code, `Err.Number` is replaced with `ErrorNumber`, and `Err.Description` with `ErrorDescription`. That's necessary because you're calling a different function and sending in those two values as parameters.

This technique cleans up and shortens your code a lot, but there is an even better reason to use it. If you ever want to change the text of the message displayed to the user, you have only to change it in one place — the `DisplayUnexpectedError` function — instead of searching and replacing it throughout all your procedures.

Note that if you use this centralized message technique, you'll have one more step in your code when you debug using the extra `Resume` statement shown earlier. After you click Debug, the `End Sub` statement in the subroutine `DisplayUnexpectedError` will be highlighted. Press F8 (Step Into) once to get back to the procedure that caused the error. (This is a minor inconvenience compared to the benefit of the centralized error message.)

Cleaning Up after an Error

Errors often occur in the middle of a lengthy procedure, when all kinds of things are happening. Many settings or values persist after an error occurs, and it's up to you to make sure they are reset back to their appropriate values. For example, these situations may be true when an unexpected error occurs in your procedure:

➤ Objects are open.

➤ The hourglass is on.

➤ You have set the status bar text or a progress meter.

➤ Warnings are off.

➤ You are in a transaction that should be rolled back if an error occurs.

Although your code may clean up all these settings under normal circumstances, a common mistake is to leave a mess when your code encounters an error. You don't want to leave a mess, do you?

Neglecting to clean up can cause problems, ranging in severity from annoying to serious. For example, if you don't turn the hourglass off, it will remain on while your users continue their work in Access. That's just annoying.

More seriously, if you don't turn `DoCmd.SetWarnings` back to `True`, any action queries (such as an `Update` or `Delete` query) will modify or delete data without any warning. Obviously, that can cause some serious problems that neither you nor your users will appreciate.

> *Have you ever seen an Access application that won't close? Even when you click the X button, or run a* `DoCmd.Quit` *in your code, Access just minimizes instead of closing. This can be quite mysterious. Many reasons have been identified for this behavior, but one of them is related to cleaning up. Normally, Access automatically closes and releases objects when they fall out of scope, typically when your procedure ends. However, some versions of Access have issues where this normal cleanup doesn't occur. Because Access won't close if it thinks that some of its objects are still needed, it just minimizes instead. To prevent this, make sure you close the objects you open, and then set them equal to Nothing. Although later versions of Access, including Access 2010, do a better job of automatically releasing each object when its procedure ends, it is good practice to clean them up explicitly.*

To prevent these issues, make sure your code cleans everything up even if it encounters an error. Even as it is failing and exiting the procedure, its last actions can save you some trouble. Here's an example:

```
Public Function MyFunction

On Error GoTo Error_Handler

   Dim varReturnVal as Variant

   `your function code goes here
```

```
Exit_Procedure:
  Exit Function

Error_Handler:
  On Error Resume Next
  DoCmd.Hourglass False
  DoCmd.SetWarnings True
  varReturnVal = SysCmd(acSysCmdClearStatus)

  DisplayUnexpectedError Err.Number, Err.Description

  Resume Exit_Procedure
  Resume

End Function
```

Note that the first line in the `Error_Handler` section is `On Error Resume Next`. This overrides the normal error handling and forces the code to continue even if an error is encountered.

Programmers have different styles and preferences for cleaning up after an error. For example, some programmers prefer to put all the cleanup code in the `Exit_Procedure` section because they know that section will run whether the procedure ends normally or abnormally. Other programmers prefer to clean everything up as they go along in the main body of the code and then add additional cleanup code in the `Error_Handler` section. Either style is fine. The important thing to remember is that your procedure won't necessarily end normally. Look through your code to see what will happen if an error occurs, and make sure it is cleaned up.

One last point: Don't let your error handling trigger an infinite error loop. When your code is already in an error-handling situation, or if it is just trying to finish the procedure, set your error trapping to `On Error Resume Next`. That way, your code continues, ignoring any errors that occur. If you don't add that statement, you might end up in an infinite loop where an error in your error handler triggers the error handler again and again.

More on Absorbing Expected Errors

As stated earlier in this chapter, sometimes a normal activity in your application results in Access encountering an error. For example, if the code behind a report cancels the `On Open` event, Access displays an error message. Because this is a normal event, it isn't necessary for your user to see an error message. Your application should continue as though nothing happened.

The code in the `Open` event of the report looks something like this:

```
Private Sub Report_Open(Cancel As Integer)
On Error GoTo Error_Handler

  Me.Caption = "My Application"

  DoCmd.OpenForm FormName:="frmReportSelector_MemberList", _
  WindowMode:=acDialog

  'Cancel the report if 'cancel' was selected on the dialog form.

  If Forms!frmReportSelector_MemberList!txtContinue = "no" Then
    Cancel = True
    GoTo Exit_Procedure
  End If

  Me.RecordSource = ReplaceWhereClause(Me.RecordSource,
```

```
    Forms!frmReportSelector_MemberList!txtWhereClause)

Exit_Procedure:
  Exit Sub

Error_Handler:
  DisplayUnexpectedError Err.Number, Err.Description

  Resume Exit_Procedure
  Resume

End Sub
```

An open selection criteria form is shown in Figure 7-19.

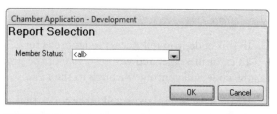

FIGURE 7-19

If the user clicks OK, the form is hidden and the report's On Open code continues. It adds the selection criteria to the report's RecordSource property and displays the report. However, if the user clicks Cancel, the form sets a hidden Continue text box to no before it is hidden. If the report sees a "no" in this text box, it cancels itself by setting Cancel = True.

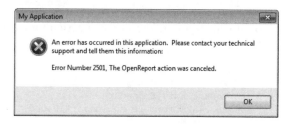

FIGURE 7-20

If you set the Cancel parameter to True in a report's On Open procedure, an error is returned to the calling code, and if it isn't handled, you see an error, as shown in Figure 7-20.

Now that is one unnecessary error message! For Access to continue without inflicting it on your poor user, you must check for this particular error (in this case, 2501) and absorb it by doing nothing but exiting the procedure. The following code shows how to absorb the error:

```
Private Sub cmdPreview_Click()
On Error GoTo Error_Handler

  If Me!lstReport.Column(3) & `" <> `" Then
    DoCmd.OpenReport ReportName:=Me!lstReport.Column(3), _
    View:=acViewPreview
  End If

  `Update the Last Run Date of the report
  DoCmd.Hourglass True
  DoCmd.SetWarnings False
  DoCmd.RunSQL _
  `UPDATE tsysReport SET tsysReport.DtLastRan = Date() ` & _
  `WHERE tsysReport.RptKey = ` & Me.lstReport
  DoCmd.SetWarnings True
  DoCmd.Hourglass False

Exit_Procedure:
  Exit Sub
```

```
Error_Handler:
  If Err.Number = 2501 Then
    Resume Exit_Procedure
  Else
    On Error Resume Next
    DoCmd.SetWarnings True
    DoCmd.Hourglass False
    DisplayUnexpectedError Err.Number, Err.Description
    Resume Exit_Procedure
    Resume

  End If
End Sub
```

In this code, you tell Access to ignore error 2501, should it be encountered. Access will not display an error message, and will instead exit the procedure immediately. If errors other than 2501 occur, the code will continue through to the `Else` statement and use your normal error-handling logic.

If you have several expected error codes that you want to quietly absorb, you can either add them to the `If` statement using `Or`, like this:

```
If Err.Number = 2501 Or Err.Number = 2450 Then
```

or, if you want to take a different action for each error, you can use a `Select Case` statement, like this:

```
Select Case Err.Number
Case 2501 `report was cancelled
  Resume Exit_Procedure
Case 2450 `form is no longer loaded
  Resume Next
Case Else
  ...normal error handling
End Select
```

In this example, when the report is canceled (error 2501), Access will jump directly to `Exit_Procedure`, but if it encounters a form that is not loaded (error 2450), it will use `Resume Next` to ignore the error and continue with the next line of code.

While you are becoming familiar with including error handling in every procedure, or if you aren't sure which error numbers need special handling, just include the basic error handling with the extra `Resume`. As specific expected errors pop up during your development and testing, you can add the code to quietly handle and absorb them.

Issues in Error Handling

Some developers try to enhance their error handling with writing log files or sending e-mail. There are some issues involved with these error-handling techniques, as explained in the following sections.

Don't Use Error Handling with Logging

Some developers write code to insert an error log record into a table or text file when an error occurs. The idea is to be able to analyze when and where errors have occurred by querying this table long after the errors happened. However, this technique has some issues.

➤ Access does not provide a way to determine the name of the procedure that is currently running. Because any error logging routine needs to know which procedure caused the error, you need to manually code the name of the current procedure into each error routine. That is labor intensive and prone to errors.

➤ The benefit of error logging is questionable because few errors should be happening after your code has been tested and delivered. Errors should be rare enough that your users will let you know when they happen. You can always ask them to capture a screenshot if you want to see the details.

➤ Some types of errors cause the attempt to log them to fail. Examples include loss of network connectivity, and disconnected storage hardware. Your user may see additional unrelated errors, or you could be lulled into thinking that all errors are logged, when they may not be.

If your code is running in a managed environment, it may be beneficial to log errors to the System Event Log. For more information on this, refer to Chapter 20. The bottom line is that spending the time to log unexpected errors to a table or text file is not recommended. This is one of those cases where the benefits usually don't outweigh the costs.

Don't Use Error Handling That Sends E-Mail

Another interesting way to track the errors that are occurring in an application is to add code to the error-handling routines that "phone home" when an error occurs. Specifically, the application builds and sends an e-mail to you (the developer) whenever an unexpected error occurs. This is usually done with the SendObject method, although there are other ways to utilize MAPI (mail application programming interface) directly.

This approach has the same problems listed in the preceding section, plus a few more:

➤ Your code needs to be able to send an e-mail using an installed e-mail client. There is always a possibility that there is no e-mail client installed, or it is not compatible with your e-mailing code.

➤ Some e-mail clients (for example, Microsoft Outlook) have code to protect against viruses using the e-mail program to propagate themselves to other computers. If an outside program (in this case, yours) tries to send an e-mail, a warning message displays, alerting the user that a virus may be attempting to send e-mail. That isn't what you want your user to see when your application is running.

As with error handling with logging, this technique is probably more trouble than it is worth.

SUMMARY

The only way to really learn how to execute VBA in your Access applications is to jump in there and try it. Using the techniques explained in this chapter — how to prevent problems with asynchronous execution, how to use recordsets and recordset clones, how to debug VBA, and more — you can tackle many of the common programming tasks that your users will need.

Every procedure you write in Access VBA should have error handling. Keep error handling simple and easy to implement, with one basic copy-and-paste code block. Then do a few quick steps if necessary to adapt the error handling to your procedure:

➤   Change `Exit Function` to `Exit Sub` if the procedure is a sub.

➤   Add code to quietly absorb expected errors, if any.

➤   Make sure you perform any necessary cleanup if an error occurs.

By following these error-handling guidelines, you'll build VBA code that is easier to debug and maintain, so you can focus on building great features into your application.

8

Creating Classes in VBA

WHAT'S IN THIS CHAPTER?

➤ Introduction to principles of using class modules in Access such as naming and organization

➤ The pieces that make up a class module including properties, methods, enumerations, and events

➤ Subclassing Access forms to extend them using your own code

➤ Writing collection classes to help you group similar objects together

➤ Core principles of object-oriented programming and how they translate to writing class modules in VBA

In object-oriented programming (OOP), an *object* is a unique *instance* of a data structure, called a *class*, that has both *properties* (which define its characteristics) and procedures called *methods* (which define its behavior).

Classes have been likened to rubber stamps, cookie-cutters, and several other everyday items in an attempt to make the concept more understandable. Because you are reading a book on software development, it seems fairly safe to assume that you understand the concept of a template, such as a Microsoft Word template. Templates are a good way to think about the distinction between a class module and a class instance. The class module is equivalent to a Word template and an instance of the class would be equivalent to a Word document that is based on that template. In other words, the class module defines the definition of an object, while the object itself is an instance of a class. The class module is used to define properties, methods, and events, which collectively make up the object's interface to the programming environment.

This chapter examines VBA classes and class objects. You learn what a class actually is and the difference between it and a class object. Then you create your first class and figure out how it works. After that, you learn to identify classes and then how to get them to communicate with the rest of your application. Then you dive into the more advanced topics, such as building collection classes. Some object-oriented theory concludes the chapter.

Classes are not as daunting as you might first think, and it's my hope that after reading this chapter, you will cast off any fears you may have had and happily find many uses for your newfound skills.

WHY USE CLASSES?

From a coding perspective, the only real difference between using the built-in Access or VBA objects and the ones you write yourself is that you have to *instantiate* your custom objects. Other than that, there's no difference at all.

There is a learning curve associated with creating your own class objects, but once learned, the primary benefit is much simpler and more manageable code. Let's say you are using Application Programming Interface (API) functions in your application. A class module is a great tool to create your own interface and to hide the complexity of the API functions. By this same token, classes are also very useful if you are writing code that will be used by other developers.

Admittedly, if you've never written classes before, using them requires a different way of thinking at first. Once you become familiar with the concepts however, you may find great benefit in their use. Once written, classes provide increased reusability and a layer of abstraction that enables you to focus more on business logic or rules defined by the application. This can result in code that is easier to use. The `Recordset` class in Data Access Objects (DAO) is an example of a class that is used quite frequently. So why not write your own?

Despite having just expounded the virtues of adopting modern OOP techniques, I still recommend using the right tool for the right job. You shouldn't rush out and write a full-blown collection class if a simple array would suffice. If a standard module is all you need, use one! In other words, don't over-engineer a project, just so you can use the latest technology.

A TOUCH OF CLASS

Each unique instance of a class will be exactly the same as the class module it was based on, except of course for the data it contains. In fact, the class module itself never gets instantiated and never contains any data. Instead, you can create as many instances of the class as you'd like, each of which is identified by a different address in memory. To make a change to all the class objects, you need change only the class module. Probably the easiest way to describe a class is to compare it to a standard VBA module.

Let's say that you have a VBA module called `modClassroom` that contains procedures to implement a single property of a classroom — the number of students in the class. The module is defined as follows:

```
Option Compare Database
Option Explicit

Private mintStudents As Integer

Public Sub AddStudent()
```

```
    mintStudents = mintStudents + 1
End Sub

Public Function GetStudents() As Integer
    GetStudents = mintStudents
End Function
```

Your property, the number of students, is stored in a module-level variable called mintStudents which is marked Private. To add a student to the classroom, you call the AddStudent() procedure, and to retrieve the current count you call the GetStudents() function.

But, what would happen if you had another module somewhere that also used the AddStudent() procedure? It would change the value of mintStudents. To ensure you can change the number of students for different classrooms, you would have to either create multiple AddStudent procedures, or implement some other way of doing it, such as by using an array or adding a parameter to the procedure.

This is where class modules come in. Now let's take a look at the following code, which is for a class module called clsClassroom.

```
Option Compare Database
Option Explicit

Private mintStudents As Integer

Public Sub AddStudent()
    mintStudents = mintStudents + 1
End Sub

Public Property Get Students() As Integer
    Students = mintStudents
End Property
```

This class is effectively the same as modClassroom. The cool part about it is that the code used to define the class is actually a template that you can use to create as many classroom objects as you wish. Furthermore, if you had two different procedures that each called the AddStudent() procedure on different instances of the clsClassroom class, they would each operate on a different copy, or instance, of the clsClassroom class.

To see how this works, the following VBA module contains two procedures, each of which creates a classroom object called myClassroom. The first one, TestClassroom1, adds one student to the classroom and then calls TestClassroom2, which creates a second classroom instance and adds two students.

```
Option Compare Database
Option Explicit

Public Sub TestClassroom1()
    Dim MyClassroom As clsClassroom
    Set MyClassroom = New clsClassroom

    MyClassroom.AddStudent
    MsgBox "I have " & MyClassroom.Students & " student in my class."
    TestClassroom2
```

```
        MsgBox "I still have only " & MyClassroom.Students & " student in my class."
    End Sub

    Public Sub TestClassroom2()
        Dim MyClassroom As clsClassroom
        Set MyClassroom = New clsClassroom

        MyClassroom.AddStudent
        MyClassroom.AddStudent
        MsgBox "I have " & MyClassroom.Students & " students in my class."
    End Sub
```

Both instances of the `clsClassroom` class are exactly the same in form and function, but are completely different entities. Thus, the properties of each are completely distinct from each other.

CREATING A CLASS MODULE

Many people learn best by doing, so to learn the basics of creating a class module, you'll create one now. The class module that we'll create here will model a classroom at a school. You'll see this example throughout the chapter, showing the different parts of a class module and how to model its relationships with other classes.

Adding a Class Module to the Project

The easiest way to add a new class module to your project is to press Alt+F11 to open the Visual Basic Editor. Then, in the Visual Basic designer window, select Insert ➪ Class Module. You can also right-click anywhere in the Project Explorer window and select Insert ➪ Class Module from the context menu. In addition, you can also create a class module from within Access by selecting Class Module under the Macros & Code group on the Ribbon's Create tab.

VBA opens a new class module and adds a reference to it in the Project Explorer window. Copy the `clsClassroom` code into the module as shown here:

```
    Private mintStudents As Integer

    Public Sub AddStudents()
        mintStudents = mintStudents + 1
    End Sub

    Public Property Get Students() As Integer
        Students = mintStudents
    End Property
```

That's it! You've created your first class module!

A Brief Word on Naming the Class

All things have names, and class modules are no different. The name you give a class module, however, is the name that is shown in both the Project Explorer window and the Object Browser, so it should be something relevant and meaningful. A more in-depth discussion on naming objects comes later in this chapter.

To name your class, display the Properties window by selecting it from the View menu, or by pressing F4. Then enter a name in the (Name) property. Access also enables you to create a hidden class (or module) by prefixing the name of your module with an underscore. Class modules are also displayed in the Navigation Pane with all code modules. Class modules can therefore be renamed like other objects in the Navigation Pane by highlighting the object and pressing the F2 key.

Another property in the Properties window has not been covered: `Instancing`. There are several other concepts to introduce first, but later in the chapter, you explore `Instancing` and look at a trick that uses `Instancing` to enable additional reusability.

Instantiating Class Objects

In Chapter 6, you saw how to declare and instantiate object variables, such as the `Recordset` object, using the `Set` keyword. Class objects are brought into existence in exactly the same way. The following code segment demonstrates how to declare and instantiate an object variable.

```
Dim myClassroom As clsClassroom
Set myClassroom = New clsClassroom
```

As mentioned earlier, once you instantiate a class, it is referred to as an *instance* of that class.

If you were declaring a variable to hold an integer value, you would declare it as an Integer data type using the `Dim intMyVariable As Integer` construct. But because you are declaring a variable to contain an *instance* of a class object, you declare it as an object, but more specifically as an object of the `clsSomeClass` type, where `clsSomeClass` is the name you gave to your class. So when you declare a variable of that type, Access allocates sufficient memory to hold a *pointer* to an *instance* of your object. That's right — when you instantiate the class object, the variable doesn't contain the object itself, just a pointer to it.

Of course, you could save a line of code by instantiating the object on one line using the `New` keyword, but it's not the recommended way of doing things. For example:

```
Dim myClassroom As New clsClassroom
```

Although you might save a line of code, using the `New` keyword isn't a good idea because programmers often need to know exactly when an object is instantiated, particularly when debugging someone else's code. By using one line to declare the variable and one to instantiate the object, it is quite clear when things happen. The performance impact is negligible.

Using the `Dim myObject As New clsSomeClass` construct, the object is not actually instantiated until the first property or method of the object is accessed. Given the following example, the object is instantiated on the call to `AddStudent`.

```
Dim myClassroom As New clsClassroom
myClassroom.AddStudent
```

Creating Class Methods

Class modules have subs and functions, but when referred to in the context of a class module, they're called *methods*. It makes some sense when you consider that a class's procedures carry out actions on its properties, and therefore, constitute the *method* by which those actions are executed.

In the same way that methods are executed against objects in the Access Object Model, class methods are executed against class objects. For example, to move a DAO recordset cursor to the next record, you are actually using a method exposed by the `Recordset` class.

There are three types of methods: sub(routine)s, functions, and properties. Subs and functions you know about, but properties, which are introduced a little later, are special types of methods that can exhibit the characteristics of both.

> *Subs, functions, and properties of a class are also known as members of the class.*

To create an external interface for your class, you need to add subs, functions, and properties. Let's take a closer look at the `clsClassroom` class:

Available for download on Wrox.com

```
Option Compare Database
Option Explicit

Private mintStudents As Integer

Public Sub AddStudents(intHowMany As Integer)
    'Make sure we don't receive a negative number
    If intHowMany > 0 Then
        mintStudents = mintStudents + intHowMany
    End If
End Sub

Public Function GiveTest() As Boolean
    'Code to implement the GiveTest action.
    If AllStudentsPresent() = True Then
        'code to administer a test
        GiveTest = True
    End If
End Function

Private Function AllStudentsPresent() As Boolean
    'Code to determine if all students are present.
    'For our example, we'll just return True.
    AllStudentsPresent = True
End Function

Public Property Let Students(intNewValue As Integer)
    mintStudents = intNewValue
End Property

Public Property Get Students() As Integer
    Students = mintStudents
End Property
```

code snippet ClassExamples

In this class module, you have a private integer variable called `mintStudents` declared at module-level so all your procedures can access it. You also have a public sub procedure called `AddStudents`, a public function called `GiveTest()`, a private function called `AllStudentsPresent()`, and two `Property Procedures`, both called `Students` (I'll explain in a moment).

The `AddStudents` method takes a single integer argument that specifies the number of students to add to your classroom. Nothing special there. The `GiveTest` method takes no arguments, but returns a `Boolean` value indicating success or failure. You might also notice that `GiveTest` executes some code to actually administer the test, but only if the `AllStudentsPresent()` function returns `True`. Once the students have had their test, `GiveTest` returns `True` to the code that called it.

You've probably already noticed that there appear to be duplicate procedure names. That's true, but property procedures are a special type of procedure for which duplicate names are allowed. Before you explore property procedures, you should first understand a term that is often used to describe the object properties and methods that are visible and accessible to the VBA code that instantiated the object: the interface.

Simply put, an *interface* is the set of `Public` properties and methods in a class. Much like any VBA procedure, the `Public` members of the class are available to other code running outside the class, whereas `Private` members are only available inside the class. In the example shown in the preceding section, the interface is defined by those methods and procedures declared as `Public`. Code outside the class cannot see private members, and therefore, cannot execute them. Therefore, properties and methods declared as `Private` are not part the interface of your class.

In the following example, the `PrintPayraise()` procedure is part of the object's interface, whereas `GivePayraise()` is not. It's that simple!

```
Public Sub PrintPayraise()
    `Public methods are part of the object's interface.
End Sub

Private Sub GivePayraise()
    `Private methods are not part of the object's interface.
End Sub
```

When creating classes, it is very important that you maintain the integrity of its interface. That is, you should avoid changing the names of properties, methods, or any arguments. Also, avoid changing the number of arguments or their data types. Programmers go to a great deal of trouble to write VBA code to instantiate and use a class object that has a specific interface, so if you change that interface, you *break* the very thing that VBA code needs to make it all work.

The rule in most software development houses is *"never break an interface!"* If you need to make changes that will result in the need to change large sections of VBA code, either create a new class or add new methods to the existing one. Existing code continues to use the existing interface, whereas newer code that needs to take advantage of any new or modified functionality can use the new ones.

Creating Property Procedures

Property procedures come in three flavors that define the characteristics of an object: `Property Get`, `Property Let`, and `Property Set`. These procedures provide a standardized way of setting and retrieving the property values of an object, and also enable you to perform additional validation.

 Property procedures are the only procedures that can share the same name within the same module.

In the `clsClassroom` class example, `mintStudents` is the actual property, and the two `Students` methods are its property procedures. The property itself is declared as `Private`, to ensure that VBA code must access the property through one of the defined property procedures. This way, your class can always be assured of controlling how students are added to the classroom and knowing when a property changes.

Using Property Get

The `Property Get` procedure retrieves the value of a class property. Its declaration is much the same as a standard VBA function, but with the addition of the `Get` keyword. As with a function, you declare its return data type to that of the class property it returns. Whatever receives the return value of the procedure must be declared with the same data type.

For example, the following code is a `Property Get` procedure called `Students` from the `clsClassroom` class example.

```
Public Property Get Students() As Integer
    Students = mintStudents
End Property
```

The name `Students` defines the name of the property of the class and its return data type is declared as an `Integer`. To call this property, you would use code similar to:

```
intNumberOfStudents = myClassroom.Students
```

VBA calls the procedure just as any standard function, and the code inside returns the privately declared variable `mintStudents`. Property procedures can do anything a standard procedure can do, even accept arguments, but in practice, that is rarely done. Because methods act on data in ways that often depend on other values or conditions, they tend to be used to accept arguments. Referring to an argument declared in a `Property Get` procedure is simple enough. For example, if you declare your procedure like so:

```
Public Property Get Students(strStreet As String) As Integer
    ` Code that uses the strStreet argument
    Students = mintStudents
End Property
```

you can refer to it like this:

```
intSomeVariable = myClassroom.Students("Main Street")
```

Using Property Let

Whereas the `Property Get` retrieves the value of a class property, the `Property Let` procedure sets the value. For example, the following code is the `Students Property Let` procedure from the `clsClassroom` class example. It is constructed similarly to the `Property Get` procedure, but using the `Let` keyword.

Available for download on Wrox.com

```
Public Property Let Students(intNewValue As Integer)
    If intNewValue > 0 Then
        mintStudents = intNewValue
    End If
End Property
```

code snippet ClassExamples

You can declare the data types of its arguments according to your needs, and you can even rename the argument as you would with any other procedure argument. In fact, you can declare more than one argument if you need to — just as with any other procedure.

`Property Let` procedures work differently than standard procedures, and it may take a little getting used to. When VBA code assigns a value to the property, like so:

```
myClassroom.Students = intSomeVariable
```

the code inside passes the argument to the privately declared property `mintStudents`. As with the `Property Get` procedure, you can declare more than one argument in `Property Let`. For example, if you declare your procedure like so:

```
Public Property Let Students(strStreet As String, intNewValue As Integer)
    ` Code that uses the strStreet argument
    mintStudents = intNewValue
End Property
```

you can refer to it like this:

```
myClassroom.Students("Main Street") = intSomeVariable
```

Notice that the property value being passed must be the last argument in the list.

Using Property Set

The `Property Set` procedure is similar to `Property Let` in that it sets the value of properties. But where `Property Let` populates scalar properties (integer, date, string, and so on), `Property Set` populates *object properties* — that is, properties that are actually pointers to other objects.

For example, in the following `clsClassroom` class module, the `Property Set` procedure sets the value of the `Teacher` property so the `Property Get` procedure can return a new `clsTeacher` object (for clarity, the other properties and methods have been removed):

```
Option Compare Database
Option Explicit

`Private variable that will contain a reference
`to an instance of the clsTeacher object.
Private mobjTeacher As clsTeacher

Public Property Get Teacher() As clsTeacher
    `Return an instance of the mobjTeacher object that
    `was instantiated by the Property Set procedure
    Set Teacher = mobjTeacher
End Property

Public Property Set Teacher(objTeacher As clsTeacher)
    `Instantiate the module-level object variable
    `using the object passed to the procedure
    Set mobjTeacher = objTeacher
End Property
```

code snippet ClassExamples

To use this construct, external VBA code must pass the `clsTeacher` object to the `Property Set` procedure in a `Set` statement, after which it can access its properties and methods through `myClassroom`'s `Teacher` property.

```
Set myClassroom.Teacher = New clsTeacher
myClassroom.Teacher.Name = "Rob Cooper"
myClassroom.Teacher.GiveHomework
```

Although `Teacher` is a property of the `myClassroom` object, it has been instantiated as a `clsTeacher` object. `clsTeacher` has its own properties and methods, they can now be accessed through the object chain just created. This facility enables you to create a basic Object Model.

 The data type you pass as the argument to the `Property Let` *or* `Property Set` *procedure must be the same as the data type returned by* `Property Get`.

Declaring Property Read-Write Attributes

To declare an object's property as readable (as far as external VBA code is concerned), you expose its associated `Property Get` procedure to the interface of the class using the `Public` access modifier. This makes the procedure visible and accessible to VBA once the object is instantiated.

To declare the property writable, you expose its `Property Let` or `Property Set` procedures to the interface in a similar fashion. If you want to make a property read-only, declare its `Property Let` or `Property Set` procedures as `Private`, or simply eliminate those procedures entirely. To make a property write-only, do the same thing to the `Property Get` procedure.

A balance on a bank account is a good example of a read-only property. You could create a `Property Let` procedure that performs the necessary validation on the account, but using the `Property Let` procedure, you would have to pass a positive number to deposit money into the account and a negative number to withdraw funds. In this example, separate methods such as `Withdraw` or `Deposit` might be a more natural approach to carry out these actions.

A password is a good example of when you might consider a write-only property. It is common practice to be able to set a password using code, but not read it.

Using Enumerated Types with Properties and Methods

You often need to create a set of related constants, and Chapter 6 discussed using enumerated types, or *enums*, for that purpose. In class modules, you often use enumerated types in property procedures and methods.

Recall that in the `clsClassroom` class, provision was made for a `clsTeacher` class — after all, it wouldn't be much of a classroom if it didn't have a teacher. To assign the grade level that a teacher will teach and to provide some measure of automation and consistency in the assignment process, you'd set up some enumerated types for specifying the grades to which you may want to assign the teachers.

```
Public Enum GradeLevel
    glFreshman
    glSophomore
    glJunior
    glSenior
End Enum
```

Notice that in the previous example, no values were specified for any of the constants. This works because VBA automatically assigns a Long Integer value to each of them starting at zero and incrementing by one for each member specified. Therefore, `glFreshman` will have a value of 0, `glSophomore` a value of 1, and so on. If you want to explicitly declare values, you can, like so:

```
Public Enum GradeLevel
    glFreshman = 0
    glSophomore = 1
    glJunior
    glSenior = 3
End Enum
```

code snippet ClassExamples

In this code, the constants for which a value is specified will have that value, but notice that one of them (`glJunior`) has no value specified. Its value is determined by the value of its preceding member, so in this case, `glJunior` will have a value of 2. Try changing the value of `glSophomore` to 123 and test it to see what `glJunior`'s value will be. Once you've defined the constants you need, simply use the `Enum` as you would any other data type.

Because VBA allows you to specify values other than those listed by IntelliSense, your code needs to account for that possibility as well, as shown here.

```
Public Property Let GradeLevel(lngLevel As GradeLevel)
    Select Case lngLevel
        Case glFreshman, glSophomore, glJunior, glSenior
            mlngLevel = lngLevel
        Case Else
            ` Do something when the wrong grade is assigned
    End Select
End Property
```

Because Enum values are numbers, you can also perform numeric comparisons using named values. For example:

```
Public Property Let GradeLevel(lngLevel As GradeLevel)
    If lngLevel >= glFreshman And lngLevel <= glSenior Then
        mlngLevel = lngLevel
    Else
        ` Do something when the wrong grade is assigned
    End If
End Property
```

Creating Flags

Let's say that you are designing a class named clsAccount to model a bank account. In this class, you want to know whether an account has certain features. For example, you might want to know whether an account has overdraft protection, includes free checks, includes a debit card, or offers direct deposit. You can use separate Boolean properties for each of these or you can use *flags*.

A flag is a combination of numeric values that can be used to determine whether one or more attributes is set. Because these values are numbers, enumerations provide an excellent mechanism for working with flags. The trick is to use a power of 2 for the flag values. For example:

```
Private mlngFeatures As AccountFeatures

Public Enum AccountFeatures
    None = 0                     ` no flags set
    OverdraftProtection = 1      ` 2 ^ 0
    FreeChecks = 2               ` 2 ^ 1
    DebitCard = 4                ` 2 ^ 2
    DirectDeposit = 8            ` 2 ^ 3
End Enum
```

code snippet ClassExamples

Let's add a property that uses this Enum:

```
Public Property Get Features() As AccountFeatures
    Features = mlngFeatures
```

```
End Property

Public Property Let Features(lngFeatures As AccountFeatures)
    mlngFeatures = lngFeatures
End Property
```

code snippet ClassExamples

To determine whether a flag has been set in the Enum value, use the And operator. To set a flag in an Enum value, use the Or operator. To remove a flag from an Enum value, use the And Not operators. The following example demonstrates:

```
Public Sub TestAccountFeatures()
    ` Create a clsAccount object
    Dim myAccount As clsAccount
    Set myAccount = New clsAccount

    ` Set some features on the account
    myAccount.Features = (myAccount.Features Or OverdraftProtection)
    myAccount.Features = (myAccount.Features Or FreeChecks)

    ` Determine whether the account offers direct deposit
    If (myAccount.Features And DirectDeposit) = DirectDeposit Then
        Debug.Print "The account offers direct deposit"
    Else
        Debug.Print "This account does not offer direct deposit"
    End If

    ` Remove the free checking feature
    myAccount.Features = (myAccount.Features And Not FreeChecks)

    ` Verify that it was removed
    If (myAccount.Features And FreeChecks) = FreeChecks Then
        Debug.Print "The account offers free checking"
    Else
        Debug.Print "This account does not offer free checking"
    End If

    ` cleanup
    Set myAccount = Nothing
End Sub
```

code snippet ClassExamples

Because flags are simply enums, which are simply Long Integer values, you might use a helper routine in a standard module to determine whether a flag is set:

```
Function IsFlagSet(Flag As Long, Flags As Long) As Boolean
    IsFlagSet = ((Flags And Flag) = Flag)
End Function
```

code snippet ClassExamples

If you're working with many flags, you could create a wrapper function to set flag values as well:

```
Sub SetFlag(Flag As Long, Flags As Long)
    Flags = (Flags Or Flag)
End Sub
```

code snippet ClassExamples

And, to remove a flag:

```
Sub RemoveFlag(Flag as Long, Flags As Long)
    Flags = Flags And Not Flag
End Sub
```

code snippet ClassExamples

Another approach would be to combine the use of flags and Boolean properties. You can use Boolean properties to determine whether a feature is included on the account, but use the value in `mlngFeatures` to make the determination. Here's what that might look like:

```
Public Property Get HasOverdraftProtection() As Boolean
    HasOverdraftProtection = IsFlagSet(OverdraftProtection, mlngFeatures)
End Property

Public Property Let HasOverdraftProtection(blnProtect As Boolean)
    If blnProtect Then
        SetFlag OverdraftProtection, mlngFeatures
    Else
        RemoveFlag OverdraftProtection, mlngFeatures
    End If
End Property
```

As you can see, you can design a lot of flexibility into your classes. Thinking about how you would want to use the class can be helpful when you are designing your classes.

Exiting Property Procedures

In Chapter 5, you exited a procedure using the `Exit Sub` and `Exit Function` constructs. Similarly, you can exit a `For..Next` loop or `Do..While` loop, using the `Exit For` and `Exit Do` constructs respectively. When your property procedure has done what it was supposed to do, there is no need to continue executing any more code. You can use the `Exit Property` construct to immediately stop processing any more code and exit the property procedure.

As with other procedures, it is always better to have a single point of exit, so use `Exit Property` sparingly.

Procedure Attributes

When declaring class properties and procedures, you can set a number of attributes that modify the procedure's behavior. These attributes are declared on the same line as the property or procedure declaration. The following examples demonstrate the possible declarations:

```
[Public | Private | Friend] [Static] Sub name [(arglist)]
[Public | Private | Friend] [Static] Function name [(arglist)] [As type]
[Public | Private | Friend] [Static] Property Get name [(arglist)] [As type]
[Public | Private | Friend] [Static] Property Let name ([arglist,] value)
[Public | Private | Friend] [Static] Property Set name ([arglist,] reference)
```

The `Static` keyword ensures that all the procedure-level variables retain their values between calls. Variables declared outside the procedure are unaffected. For more information on `Static`, refer to Chapter 6.

You're already familiar with `Public` and `Private` attributes, so the following section focuses on `Friend` attributes.

Friendly Procedures

Let's say you wanted to create a teacher management system that others will reference in their databases. Of course, you want your own database to be able to see and execute its own class properties and methods, but you don't want consumers of your database to execute them directly.

To protect the properties and methods of your class, you can declare them using the `Friend` keyword. Procedures declared as `Friend` are public within the project in which they are defined but invisible to other projects. The `Friend` keyword can only be used in class modules, and can't be late bound. Because modules behind Access forms and reports are also class modules, you can use the `Friend` keyword there as well.

For example, suppose you want to prevent other databases from changing the salary for your teachers; the following code illustrates the principle. The `mcurSalary` property is accessible to all consumers of the class; any procedure that instantiates the object can read the property's value, but only code within the project can assign a value to it.

Available for download on Wrox.com

```
Private mcurSalary As Currency

Public Property Get Salary() As Currency
    Salary = mcurSalary
End Property

Friend Property Let Salary(curNewValue As Currency)
    mcurSalary = curNewValue
End Property
```

code snippet ClassExamples

NAMING AND IDENTIFYING OBJECTS

The name you assign to *any* database object will have an impact on its perceived purpose, and ultimately, its usability. It doesn't much matter whether it's a form, table, control, or class method; programmers will respond differently to it according to the name you give it. Ultimately it's up to you, but this section seeks to provide a few guidelines to help in the decision-making process.

What Does the Object Do?

One of the most important aspects of naming an object is to describe what it is or what it does. For example, Access has many built-in objects that are, in my opinion, aptly named. These include the `Database` object, `TableDef`, `Collection`, `Error`, and so on. These names unambiguously describe the object to which they refer.

It is always good practice to keep the names as short as possible while still being descriptive. Long class and object names are difficult to read and can make for difficult and painstaking coding. You can make good use of abbreviations, acronyms, numbers, and so on, but ensure they are meaningful, rather than cryptic. What may be meaningful or obvious to you, may not mean a thing to someone else.

> *In practice, I frequently do not use the `cls` prefix when naming a class object. Because the classes you create become part of the Object Model for the database, leaving off the prefix seems more natural.*

Naming Techniques

Using names that describe an object's purpose and function is arguably the best strategy, but the decision about whether to use verbs, nouns, or adjectives is equally important.

Most programmers use nouns and adjectives to describe properties, and use verbs to describe functions and methods. For example, typical properties might be called `Color`, `Name`, and `Width`, whereas functions and methods might have names like `Add`, `Calculate`, `Show`, and so on.

Naming variables is often a confusing decision, but they should follow the same naming strategy as property names. An exception might be variables of the `Boolean` data type. Because they denote a true or false condition, you could use one of two strategies You can prefix them with "Is" or "Has" (for example, `IsOpen` or `HasPermissions`), or where they are used to indicate an authority to carry out some action, use verbs — for example, `ShowDialog`.

Events are often named in two ways. First, name events by using verbs to denote the fact that some action has or is about to occur — for example, `BeforeUpdate` or `Finished`. Second, as is done in web applications, name events by prefixing the name with `on`, as in `onupdate` or `onopen`.

Whichever strategy you choose, try to be consistent throughout the application.

Case

The judicious use of case can be a highly effective means of naming an object. Traditionally, many objects or members are named with sentence case; that is, the first character of every word is capitalized. For example:

```
AddNewObject
```

Often to distinguish them from other objects, constants are named using all uppercase — for example:

```
ERR_NOT_FOUND
```

Plurality

In code, and particularly with regard to classes, plural object names are typically used for collections, such as the `TableDefs` collection. Singular objects are therefore named in the singular, as with the `TableDef` object. This strategy unambiguously describes the *actual* state of the object.

Except in the case of collections, applying plural names to some objects and singular to others of the same type is a definite no-no. Consistency is important, as object names are sometimes all a programmer has to determine the purpose and function of objects in the applications you create.

Identifying a Class Instance

Let's say that you want to compare two instances of a class, but need some way to uniquely identify each instance. There are a few ways you could go about this. For example, you might create your own automatically incrementing value by keeping track of the next available number in a regular module, or you could generate a random number and use that as the identifier for the class.

Fortunately, another way is built into VBA itself — using the `ObjPtr` function. `ObjPtr` is a function in VBA that returns the memory address of an object variable. Because class instances are assigned an address in memory when they are created, this function can be used to uniquely identify an instance of a class. You'll see this function used again later in the section "Creating a Clone Method."

USING CLASS EVENTS

Unlike standard modules, class modules can raise their own events. This is a very powerful feature of VBA because it not only gives your code the ability to know what's going on inside the class instance, but it provides the opportunity to take whatever actions you deem necessary based on those events.

Another very important benefit of using class events is that that you can keep User Interface (UI) functionality separate from the class implementation, making the class truly independent and reusable. You can then use your class in many places without worrying about specific UI implementation. This section focuses on getting your class to talk to the rest of your application through events.

Initialize and Terminate Events

Every class module has two built-in events that fire automatically: `Initialize` and `Terminate`. The `Initialize` event fires when the class instance is first created. You can use the `Initialize` event to set default property values and create references to other objects. The `Terminate` event fires before the object is destroyed, and is normally used to clean up local object references.

To define code for these events, select Class from the Object drop-down and then select the event from the Procedure drop-down.

The following example shows what the `Initialize` and `Terminate` events might look like for the `clsClassroom` class:

Available for download on Wrox.com

```
Option Compare Database
Option Explicit

`Declare the Teacher object
Private mobjTeacher As clsTeacher

`Declare the Student object
Private mobjStudent As clsStudent

`Declare the room number
Private mlngRoomNumber As Long

Public Property Get RoomNumber() As Long
    RoomNumber = mlngRoomNumber
End Property

Private Sub Class_Initialize()
    mlngRoomNumber = 302

    Set mobjTeacher = New clsTeacher
    Set mobjStudent = New clsStudent
End Sub

Private Sub Class_Terminate()
    Set mobjTeacher = Nothing
    Set mobjStudent = Nothing
End Sub
```

code snippet ClassExamples

Creating Custom Class Events

You can, of course, create your own events. Once you've decided on the specific events you want to expose, you declare them in the class's declarations section. Let's say you have a class called `clsTest` that implements a test given by the teacher. You may want to provide events that notify your code before and after a test is given.

Available for download on Wrox.com

```
Public Event BeforeTest(Cancel As Integer)
Public Event AfterTest()
Public Event Pass(Score As Byte)
Public Event Fail(Score As Byte)
```

code snippet ClassExamples

Events are declared `Public` by default, but for clarity, you might want to explicitly declare scope. Event names can be alphanumeric, but must begin with a non-numeric character, and they can only be raised in the module that declared them.

To fire an event in your class, you issue the `RaiseEvent` keyword. For example, the following code demonstrates a typical use.

```
Private Const PASSING_SCORE As Byte = 70

Public Sub SubmitTest()
    Dim bytScore As Byte

    ' fire the AfterTest event
    RaiseEvent AfterTest

    ' calculate the test score
    ' for demo purposes, this returns a random number
    bytScore = TestScore

    ' determine pass/fail and return the test score
    If bytScore >= PASSING_SCORE Then
        RaiseEvent Pass(bytScore)
    Else
        RaiseEvent Fail(bytScore)
    End If
End Sub

Private Property Get TestScore() As Byte
    ' get a random score between 0 and 100
    Const MIN_SCORE = 0
    Const MAX_SCORE = 100

    TestScore = CInt(Int((MAX_SCORE - MIN_SCORE + 1) * Rnd() + MIN_SCORE))
End Property
```

code snippet ClassExamples

Just like VBA procedures, you can declare event arguments using the `ByVal` and `ByRef` keywords. By default, event arguments are passed `ByRef`, which means that the code that's listening for the event can change its value, and that change is passed back to the class procedure.

Responding to Events

Now that you know how to create custom events in your object, you might want to know how to listen and respond to them in your code. It's actually quite simple. All you need to do is declare the object variable using the `WithEvents` keyword. Note, however, that you can only use `WithEvents` for object variables declared at module-level and only in class modules.

Because the code behind forms and reports are class modules, too, you can also use the `WithEvents` keyword in forms. The following declaration example demonstrates.

```
Private WithEvents myTest As clsTest
```

Once you declare an object variable using the `WithEvents` keyword, select the object from the Object drop-down, and the event becomes available from the Procedure drop-down. VBA creates the procedure stub based on the arguments you supplied when you defined the event.

Defining custom class events enables you to implement different behavior for different scenarios based on the same outcome. In the `clsTest` example, for instance, the class defines an event named `Fail`, which is raised if the passing score is less than 70 percent. If you have two applications that use this class, you might choose to format a text box in one to indicate that the student did not pass the test. In the other application, you might choose to send an e-mail to the student with the results. By raising an event, the `clsTest` class separates user-interface code from business logic code.

 An example database is included in the download code for this chapter.

The only thing that might be considered a drawback to class events is that the object that raises the event must wait until the event code is responded to before it can continue processing.

Now let's see how you might be able to use the `WithEvents` keyword in a way that makes practical sense in your day-to-day application development. Let's say you have several text boxes on several different forms whose `BeforeUpdate` and `AfterUpdate` events contain exactly the same code. Normally, you would simply write the same code over and over in the event procedures for each control. But what if you were able to write the code once and have *every* control implement that code. You can accomplish this using a technique known as *subclassing*.

You start by creating your class module (`clsTBox` in this example). Notice that you set the `BeforeUpdate` and `AfterUpdate` properties of the text box. This is because Access won't respond to an event unless the corresponding event property is set to the string `[Event Procedure]`. To simplify this, set the event property when the `Textbox` object property is set.

```
`Declare the class instance
Private WithEvents mtxtTextbox As TextBox

Public Property Get MyTextbox() As TextBox
    Set MyTextbox = mtxtTextbox
End Property

Public Property Set MyTextbox(objTextbox As TextBox)
    Set mtxtTextbox = objTextbox

    ` Access requires that event properties are set
    ` to [Event Procedure] to respond to events.
    ` Set the event properties when the textbox object is set.
    mtxtTextbox.BeforeUpdate = "[Event Procedure]"
    mtxtTextbox.AfterUpdate = "[Event Procedure]"
```

```
End Property

Private Sub mtxtTextbox_AfterUpdate()
    `Set the text to normal weight.
    Me.MyTextbox.FontBold = False
End Sub

Private Sub mtxtTextbox_BeforeUpdate(Cancel As Integer)
    `Test for the textbox's value.
    Select Case Me.MyTextbox.Value
        Case "Fred", "Mary"
            `The value is OK.
            `Change the text to black.
            Me.MyTextbox.ForeColor = vbGreen
        Case Else
            `Wrong value! Undo the changes,
            `and change the text to bold red.
            Cancel = True

            Me.MyTextbox.ForeColor = vbRed
            Me.MyTextbox.FontBold = True
    End Select
End Sub
```

code snippet ClassExamples

As you can see, this code implements the `BeforeUpdate` and `AfterUpdate` events for text boxes that can be anywhere in the project. The `BeforeUpdate` event checks the value of the text box and turns its text green if it equals "Fred" or "Mary"; otherwise, it turns it bold red. The `AfterUpdate` event only fires (setting the text weight to normal) if the text is correct.

Now let's create the form, as shown in Figure 8-1.

Add two text boxes named `txtFirst` and `txtLast` (it doesn't really matter what their captions read), and then add the following code to the form's module.

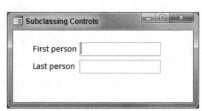

FIGURE 8-1

```
`Declare a reference to the class module
Public FirstTB As New clsTBox
Public LastTB As New clsTBox

Public Sub Form_Load()
    `Instantiate the class object for each control
    Set FirstTB.myTextbox = Me.txtFirst
    Set LastTB.myTextbox = Me.txtLast
End Sub

Private Sub Form_Unload(Cancel As Integer)
    `Clean up
    Set FirstTB = Nothing
    Set LastTB = Nothing
End Sub
```

code snippet ClassExamples

Open the form and type **Fred** into the first text box. It turns green. Now enter **John** into the second text box and the text should change to red.

Quite simply, here's how it works:

1. When the form class module is instantiated, `clsTBox` is immediately instantiated into `FirstTB` and `LastTB`. When the form loads, the two text box instances are created in separate instances of `clsTBox` through the `MyTextBox` property.

2. The `mtxtTextbox` variable stores the instance of the text box object on the form. When the property is set, you set the event property to `[Event Procedure]` to let Access know that the text box will respond to events.

3. Once that happens, the linking is complete, and all the text box events that are exposed in the form are now available in `clsTBox`.

4. When the `BeforeUpdate` or `AfterUpdate` events occur for either text box, they actually fire in the instance of `clsTBox` created for it.

5. Try placing breakpoints in the form's `Load` event, and `clsTBox`'s `BeforeUpdate` and `AfterUpdate` events to see what happens.

This is just a small example of how to subclass form controls using the `WithEvents` keyword. You can do the same thing with other controls and events, and also with forms and report events (with the exception of the `Open` event). This is a very powerful technique to provide consistent behavior on a large number of controls or objects throughout an application.

Handling Errors in Classes

A large part of developing software is trapping and handling errors, and all but the simplest procedure should include some form of error handling. Much of the error handling that we do as programmers is to either respond to status conditions generated by other objects, or to protect data from users.

Because errors are often unexpected and undesirable, not only should you trap and respond to them, but you should also understand how to work with them in class modules.

Trapping VBA Errors

Chapter 7 discusses trapping errors in standard modules, including using the `On Error` and `If Err` constructs.

You might recall that when there is no error handler in the procedure in which the error occurs, VBA passes the error to the next highest procedure in the call stack. VBA continues passing the error up the call stack until it either finds an error handler or reaches the top level, in which case it then displays the standard runtime error dialog box. If you don't handle the errors, VBA will, and when it does, it will reset all your variables.

Error trapping in class modules is exactly the same, but you also need to consider the runtime `Error Trapping` setting in the IDE's Options dialog box, as shown in Figure 8-2.

The Error Trapping settings control how Access handles runtime errors. The default setting, Break on Unhandled Errors, causes Access to display the standard Windows run-time error dialog box in the absence of any error handlers in the call stack. This is the desired behavior because it enables your error handlers to do their job.

Break on All Errors causes Access to override all your error handlers and display the runtime error dialog box whenever an error occurs in any module (including class modules). Finally, the Break in Class Module option overrides your class module error handlers, but not those in standard modules.

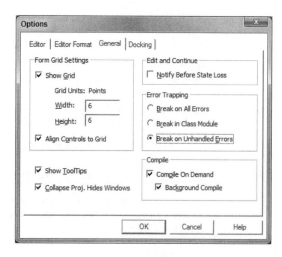

FIGURE 8-2

Raising Custom-Defined Errors

Error messages sometimes have a tendency not to describe a problem or its resolution. Raising your own errors provides the flexibility to display more user-friendly or user-specific error messages.

The VBA Err object provides a Raise method, which enables you to construct and to fire your own custom errors. You must supply everything the Err object needs to return anything useful, which includes the error number, description, source, optional path to a help file and the ContextID, which identifies a specific topic in the help file.

The syntax for the Err.Raise method is as follows:

```
Err.Raise Number, Source, Description, HelpFile, HelpContext
```

To avoid conflicts with errors that are built in to Access or other components, you should add vbObjectError to your error number. The system reserves errors through vbObjectError + 512, so by convention user-defined errors in class modules should begin with vbObjectError + 513.

For example, the following procedure demonstrates the typical method for trapping errors and raising your own:

```
Const MyContextID = 1010407 ' Define a constant for ContextID

Private Sub ErrorTest()
    Dim xlApp As Object
    On Error Goto ErrorTest_Err

    ` If Excel is already open, get a handle to
    `the existing instance.
    Set xlApp = GetObject(, "Excel.Application")

    ` Other code

ErrorTest_Exit:
    On Error Resume Next
```

```
        xlApp.Quit
        Set xlApp = Nothing
        Exit Sub

ErrorTest_Err:
    Select Case Err.Number
        Case 429 ` ActiveX component can't create object
            ` Raise the error.
            strErrDescr = "Unable to open Excel. It may not be installed."

            Err.Raise vbObjectError + 513, TypeName(Me), _
                strErrDesc, _
                "c:\MyProj\MyHelp.Hlp", MyContextID
        Case Else
            ` Something else went wrong.
            Err.Raise Err.Number, Err.Source, Err.Description
    End Select
End Sub
```

You might have noticed the TypeName function in the preceding code. Given any variable, the TypeName function returns the name of the data type used for the variable. When passed an instance of a class object, it returns the name of the class module.

Passing Errors in Class Modules

Although class objects can respond to errors that occur within them, they should not because doing so forever binds the object to a specific implementation.

Class objects don't spontaneously leap into existence; they must be instantiated by other code. The code that creates the class is typically part of a broader function that only consumes or instantiates the class instance. It calls the class only for a smaller part of it, and so *this code* should be what responds to errors that occur within the class object. By definition, any error in the class object is an error in the broader function.

So what do you do? Your class must pass the error back to the calling code using the Err.Raise method. Whether it's a VBA error or a custom-defined error, your class procedures must trap it and pass it along. All the calling code has to do is test for it. The following examples show how to do this.

EXAMPLE 1

```
Public sub TestErrors()
    Dim obj As clsMyClass

    On Error Resume Next
    Set obj = New clsMyClass
    Obj.SomeMethod

    If Err <> 0 Then
        ` Handle the error
    End If
    On Error Goto 0
End Sub
```

EXAMPLE 2

```
Public sub TestErrors()
    Dim obj As clsMyClass
    On Error Goto TestErrors_Err

    Set obj = New clsMyClass
    Obj.SomeMethod 'Error occurs in here

TestErrors_Exit:
    On Error Resume Next
    Set Obj = Nothing
    Exit Sub

TestErrors_Err:
    'Handle the error
    Resume TestErrors_Exit
End Sub
```

FORMS AND REPORTS AS OBJECTS

By now you should have a fair grasp of how to create classes and class objects in Access 2010. Because form and report modules are also class modules, you can instantiate and use them in exactly the same way as you would any other class object. The greatest benefits of this are that you can create and operate on more than one instance of the object at any one time, and you can use its events by declaring their object variables using the WithEvents keyword.

Let's say you have a form called Form1. You would, of course, be familiar with the tried and true method of displaying a standard form.

```
DoCmd.OpenForm "Form1"
DoCmd.Close acForm, "Form1"
```

Copy the following code into a standard module and try stepping through it using the F8 key.

```
Public Sub TestFormClass()
    Dim frm As Form_Form1
    Set frm = New Form_Form1

    frm.Visible = True
    Set frm = Nothing
End Sub
```

Then try the same thing with a report:

```
Public Sub TestReportClass()
    Dim rpt As Report_Report1
    Set rpt = New Report_Report1

    rpt.Visible = True
    Set rpt = Nothing
End Sub
```

> *In order to instantiate a Form or Report as an object, it must be a heavyweight form. That is, it must have a class module behind it, and the* HasModule *property of the Form or Report must be set to Yes.*

Often, you may want to display a data selection dialog box while editing data in a form, and to return the selected value from the dialog box to the original form. Here is a mechanism for returning the value selected by the user from the dialog box to the form whose code instantiates it. More often than not, the data selection dialog box must be used in different places throughout the application, so it must be completely independent of specific UI implementation. Past techniques for passing a value to another form included using the OpenForm method's OpenArgs argument:

```
DoCmd.OpenForm "Form1", , , , , , strSomeValue
```

Passing multiple values involved stuffing OpenArgs with multiple values separated by some arbitrary character such as the vertical bar (|), and parsing Me.OpenArgs when the data selection dialog box opened, as shown in the following code:

```
Private Sub Form_Open()
    Dim varArgs As Variant
    Dim intCounter As Long

    `Extract all the values from OpenArgs that are separated
    `by the vertical bar character, and put them into varArgs.
    varArgs = Split(Me.OpenArgs, "|", -1, vbTextCompare)

    `Print out the resulting array.
    For intCounter = LBound(varArgs) To UBound(varArgs)
        Debug.Print varArgs(intCounter)
    Next
End Sub
```

Passing values back to the calling form usually involved either setting a global variable with the name of the calling form or adding the form name to OpenArgs so the dialog box can pass the value directly to the calling form, which meant hard-coding the value-passing code into the dialog box itself. None of this could be classified as a professional, object-oriented approach.

In the following example, you create a reusable data selection dialog box that is completely independent of other forms. You use the techniques discussed in this chapter, including form properties and events. Yes that's right — forms can have custom property procedures and expose their events to the VBA environment.

1. Create a new form, and set its properties, as shown in the following table.

PROPERTY	VALUE
Name	DlgMyDialog
Caption	My Dialog

PROPERTY	VALUE
BorderStyle	Dialog
RecordSelectors	No
NavigationButtons	No
DividingLines	No
Modal	Yes

2. Add the following controls, and set their properties, as shown in this table:

CONTROL TYPE	PROPERTY	VALUE
Combo box	Name	cboCombo1
	RowSourceType	Value List
	RowSource	"Value 1"; "Value 2"; "Value 3"
	Enabled	No
Combo box	Name	cboCombo2
	RowSourceType	Value List
	RowSource	"Value 4"; "Value 5"; "Value 6"
	Enabled	No
Command button	Name	CmdOK
	Caption	OK
Command button	Name	CmdCancel
	Caption	Cancel

Figure 8-3 shows how the form should look.

FIGURE 8-3

3. Copy the following code to the form's class module:

```
`Declare the event to notify the calling form
`that the dialog has finished
`We could also have used the dialog's Close or
`Unload events
Public Event Finished(varReturn As Variant)

`Declare the dialog properties
Private varValueSelected As Variant
Private intWhichOne As Integer

Private Sub cboCombo1_Change()
    varValueSelected = Me.cboCombo1
End Sub

Private Sub cboCombo2_Change()
    varValueSelected = Me.cboCombo2
End Sub

Private Sub cmdCancel_Click()
    varValueSelected = Null
    DoCmd.Close acForm, Me.Name
End Sub

Public Property Get WhichOne() As Integer
    WhichOne = intWhichOne
End Property

Public Property Let WhichOne(ByVal iNewValue As Integer)
    intWhichOne = iNewValue

    `Enable the appropriate combo
    Me.cboCombo1.Enabled = (intWhichOne = 1)
    Me.cboCombo2.Enabled = (intWhichOne = 2)
End Property

Private Sub cmdOK_Click()
    DoCmd.Close acForm, Me.Name
End Sub

Private Sub Form_Unload(Cancel As Integer)
    `Raise the Finished event so the calling
    `form knows what's happened
    RaiseEvent Finished(varValueSelected)
End Sub
```

code snippet ClassExamples

4. Create a new form and set its properties, as shown in the following table.

PROPERTY	VALUE
Name	frmMyMainForm
Caption	My Main Form
BorderStyle	Sizable
Modal	Yes

5. Add the following controls, and set their properties, as shown in the following table.

CONTROL TYPE	PROPERTY	VALUE
Option group	Name	optMyOptionGroup
Option button	Name	[Default]
	OptionValue	1
	Caption (of the associated label)	Select from combo 1
Option button	Name	[Default]
	OptionValue	2
	Caption (of the associated label)	Select from combo 2
Text box	Name	txtMyTextBox
	Caption (of the associated label)	Value selected
Button	Name	cmdSelect
	Caption	Select
Button	Name	cmdClose
	Caption	Close

Figure 8-4 shows how the form should look.

FIGURE 8-4

6. Copy the following code to the form's class module:

```
`Declare the object variable using WithEvents
Private WithEvents dlg As Form_dlgMyDialog

Private Sub cmdClose_Click()
    DoCmd.Close acForm, Me.Name
End Sub

Private Sub cmdSelect_Click()
    `Instantiate the dialog
    Set dlg = New Form_dlgMyDialog

    `Enable the appropriate combo
    dlg.WhichOne = Me.optMyOptionGroup

    `If we had declared dialog properties, we
    `could pass their values here:
    `dlg.Property1 = 123
    `dlg.Property2 = "some value"
    `etc…

    `Show the dialog
    dlg.Visible = True
End Sub

Private Sub dlg_Finished(varReturn As Variant)
    Me.txtMyTextBox.Enabled = (Not IsNull(varReturn))

    If Not IsNull(varReturn) Then
        Me.txtMyTextBox = varReturn
    End If
End Sub

Private Sub Form_Unload(Cancel As Integer)
    `Clean up
    Set dlg = Nothing
End Sub
```

code snippet ClassExamples

7. Now open `frmMyMainForm`, select one of the options, and click Select. Pick a value from the combo box, and click OK.

Figure 8-5 shows the main form in action.

You can call this dialog box from anywhere in your application, without having to specify the name of the form that calls it, and you can also keep all the form-specific functionality in the main form where it belongs.

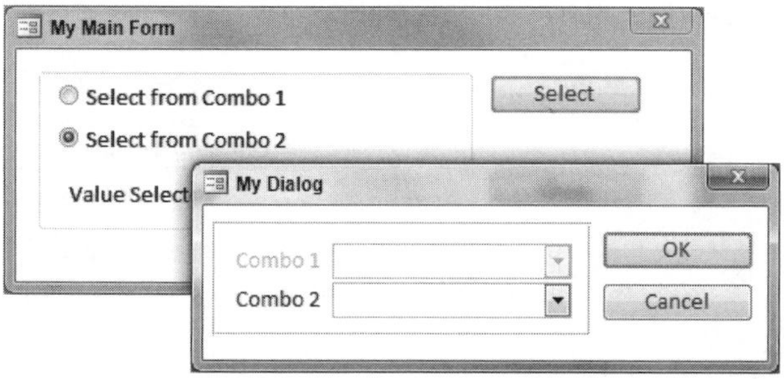

FIGURE 8-5

VARIABLE SCOPE AND LIFETIME

Variables declared within class modules exhibit the same scope and lifetime as those declared within standard modules. For example, Private module-level variables are only available to procedures within the same module, and are destroyed when the class instance is destroyed. Public module-level variables are visible to any code that has access to the class instance. Public variables in a class are an easy way to create properties for the class but lack the ability to perform validation.

Class variables declared at procedure-level remain accessible only to code within that procedure and are destroyed when the procedure exits — unless of course the variable is declared using the Static keyword. In such a case, the variable is destroyed along with the module-level variables when the object is destroyed.

Although the variables used to hold pointers to objects obey the normal scope and lifetime rules as described previously, they demand special consideration, as you will soon see.

To see how variable scope and lifetime work, create the following two class modules.

CLSCLASS1

Available for
download on
Wrox.com

```
Private obj As clsClass2

Public Property Set Link(objMyObject As clsClass2)
    `Create a link from this object to the other one
    Set obj = objMyObject
    Debug.Print "Creating reference to clsClass2 from clsClass1"
End Property

Private Sub Class_Initialize()
    Debug.Print "Instantiating clsClass1"
End Sub

Private Sub Class_Terminate()
```

```
        Debug.Print "Terminating clsClass1 instance"
    End Sub
```

CLSCLASS2

```
    Private obj As clsClass1

    Public Property Set Link(objMyObject As clsClass1)
        `Create a link from this object to the other one
        Set obj = objMyObject
        Debug.Print "Creating reference to clsClass1 from clsClass2"
    End Property

    Private Sub Class_Initialize()
        Debug.Print "Instantiating clsClass2"
    End Sub

    Private Sub Class_Terminate()
        Debug.Print "Terminating clsClass2 instance"
    End Sub
```

Then add the following procedure to a standard module.

```
    Public Sub TestClassLifetime()
        Dim objMyObject1 As clsClass1
        Dim objMyObject2 As clsClass2

        `Instantiate the two object variables
        Set objMyObject1 = New clsClass1
        Set objMyObject2 = New clsClass2

        `Create a link to one object from the other
        Set objMyObject2.Link = objMyObject1

        `Destroy the local object references
        Set objMyObject1 = Nothing
        Set objMyObject2 = Nothing
    End Sub
```

Take a look at the `TestClassLifetime` procedure. If you step through the procedure line by line (by successively pressing F8), the debug window tells the real story.

The procedure begins by creating the two class objects, objMyObject1 and objMyObject2. The code then sets a second pointer to objMyObject1 in objMyObject2, as shown in Figure 8-6.

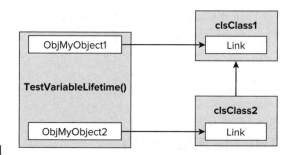

Despite the fact that the first local pointer to clsClass1 (objMyObject1) is then set to Nothing, you see that the object itself is not destroyed until after objMyObject2 is destroyed. Why? Because the second pointer still exists after the demise of the first pointer, so the object itself remains alive.

FIGURE 8-6

When the pointer to clsClass2 is destroyed, its pointer to clsClass1 is also destroyed, thereby releasing the clsClass1 object. But that's not the worst that can happen! If you change TestClassLifetime() by setting a reference to clsClass2 from clsClass1, a circular reference is created.

```
`Create a link to one object from the other
Set objMyObject2.Link = objMyObject1
Set objMyObject1.Link = objMyObject2
```

code snippet ClassExamples

Run the procedure to see what happens. Neither object is destroyed! Why? Because each object maintains a reference to the other, as shown in Figure 8-7. Once such code is executed, both objects remain in memory until the application is shut down; there is no way to programmatically terminate them.

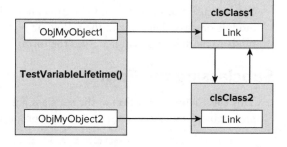

So how do you avoid such circular references? You must explicitly terminate each inner reference before destroying the outer reference. You can do so by adding the following method to each class:

FIGURE 8-7

```
Public Sub TerminateLink()
    `If the object exists, destroy it
    If Not obj Is Nothing Then
        Set obj = Nothing
    End If
End Sub
```

code snippet ClassExamples

Then you add the following two lines to `TestClassLifetime()`:

```
objMyObject1.TerminateLink
objMyObject2.TerminateLink
```

code snippet ClassExamples

THE ME PROPERTY

The `Me` keyword is an implicitly declared variable that is automatically available to every procedure in a class module. When a class can have more than one instance, `Me` provides a way to refer to the specific instance of the class where the code is executing. Using `Me` is particularly useful for passing information about the currently executing instance of a class to a procedure in another module.

The `Me` keyword contains an object reference to the current class instance, and can be used by code written in forms, reports, and user-defined classes. It returns faster than a fully qualified object reference, and is useful when you have several instances of a class. For example, either of the following code fragments can be executed from the Employees form to refer to the value of the LastName text box on that form.

```
strLastName = Forms!Employees.LastName
strLastName = Me!LastName
```

You can also use `Me` to pass information about the current class instance to a procedure in another module or class. The code in the following sections demonstrates a class that subclasses a form, and binds to the subclass instance from the form.

Subclassing the Form

This class defines a portion of the subclass named `clsFormSubclassed`. Because the subclass stores an instance of an Access `Form` object, all properties of the form are available in the subclass.

```
Private WithEvents mfrmMyForm As Form

Public Property Get FormObject() As Form
    Set FormObject = mfrmMyForm
End Property

Public Property Set FormObject(objForm As Form)
    Set mfrmMyForm = objForm
    Debug.Print "clsFormSubclassed is bound to the form: " & _
        mfrmMyForm.Name
End Property
```

code snippet ClassExamples

Creating the Subclassed Form

The following code represents a form named `frmSubclasedForm` that is subclassed by `clsFormSub?classed`. Note the use of the `Me` keyword that is passed to the `FormObject` property.

```
Private objSubclass As clsFormSubclassed

Private Sub Form_Open(Cancel As Integer)
    `Create an instance of the class
    Set objSubclass = New clsFormSubclassed

    `Use the Me keyword to pass the current form
    `to the subclass
    Set objSubclass.FormObject = Me
End Sub
```

code snippet ClassExamples

Creating a Parent Property

To create a relationship between a parent class and a child class, the parent class needs code such as this:

```
Option Compare Database
Option Explicit

Private mobjTeacher As clsTeacher

Private Sub Class_Initialize()
    `Create a new instance of the derived class
    Set mobjTeacher = New clsTeacher

    `Create the relationship between the parent and child classes
    Set mobjTeacher.Parent = Me
End Sub
```

code snippet ClassExamples

Of course, you would also need to define the `Parent` property procedures in the child class:

```
Option Compare Database
Option Explicit

Private mobjClassroom As clsClassroom

Public Property Set Parent(objClassroom As clsClassroom)
    `Check that the property hasn´t already been set
    If mobjClassroom Is Nothing Then
```

```
            Set mobjClassroom = objClassroom
        End If
    End Property
```

In these examples, the child class has one property procedure, `Property Set`. This procedure accepts an object (of the type `clsClassroom`) as its argument, and uses it to store the instance of the parent object.

The parent object instantiates the child object and simply passes itself (`Me`) to the derived `Parent` property procedure of the object.

>
> *If the `Instancing` property of the parent class is `Private`, you cannot pass it as an argument to the child class. You must set `Instancing` to `PublicNotCreatable` to successfully compile the `Parent` property.*

CREATING A CLONE METHOD

Let's say you want to create a separate copy of a class object. It might be tempting to write something like this:

Available for download on Wrox.com

```
Dim objTeacher1 As clsTeacher
Dim objTeacher2 As clsTeacher

Set objTeacher1 = New clsTeacher
Set objTeacher2 = objTeacher1
```

On the surface, this looks as if it would create a new object named `objTeacher2` that has the same property values as `objTeacher2`, and that is true. However, these objects actually point to the same data. If you change a property for `objTeacher2`, `objTeacher1` also reflects the same value as illustrated in the following code:

Available for download on Wrox.com

```
Sub TestCopy()
    Dim objTeacher1 As clsTeacher
    Dim objTeacher2 As clsTeacher

    ` create the first instance
    Set objTeacher1 = New clsTeacher
    objTeacher1.Name = "Steven Buchanan"
    Debug.Print "Before: " & objTeacher1.Name

    ` create the second instance
```

```
        Set objTeacher2 = objTeacher1

        ` set the second name, then print the first
        objTeacher2.Name = ""Nancy Davolio"
        Debug.Print "After: " & objTeacher1.Name

        ` Verify that the objects point to different locations
        Debug.Assert ObjPtr(objTeacher1) <> ObjPtr(objTeacher2)

        ` cleanup
        Set objTeacher1 = Nothing
        Set objTeacher2 = Nothing
    End Sub
```

code snippet ClassExamples

The first time the Name is printed, the code prints Steven Buchanan. Then after changing the name of objTeacher2, objTeacher1 has been changed to Nancy Davolio.

 Note that I'm using the ObjPtr *function in a* Debug.Assert *statement to make sure that the two objects are not equal. If the* Assert *fails, then the two objects are pointing to the same location in memory.*

To create a proper Clone method, you need to create a new instance of the class and then copy the private data in the first instance to the new instance. Add the following code to the clsTeacher class to add a Clone method:

Available for download on Wrox.com

```
Public Function Clone() As clsTeacher
    Set Clone = New clsTeacher

    ` Copy individual property values to the cloned instance
    With Clone
        .Name = Me.Name
        .GradeLevel = Me.GradeLevel
        .Salary = Me.Salary
        Set .Parent = Me.Parent
    End With
End Function
```

code snippet ClassExamples

Change the test code that creates the copy to:

```
Set objTeacher2 = objTeacher1.Clone()
```

Now, the Debug.Assert should succeed and you should have a new clsTeacher object that has the same initial properties as objTeacher1. Furthermore, changing the name of objTeacher2 does not change the name of objTeacher1.

CREATING AND USING COLLECTION CLASSES

So far, this chapter has dealt with situations where the relationship between objects is one-to-one. Although that's often the case in real-world programming, it is also quite often the case where the relationship is one-to-many. A group of related objects is called a *collection*, and a collection class is simply a class that contains a list, or collection of related classes. VBA provides a neat little object for creating and handling object collections, oddly enough called a `Collection` object.

The Collection Object

You are probably already familiar with using object collections; VBA is full of them. The `TableDefs` and `QueryDefs` collections are examples that you use almost every day. These collections maintain a list of pointers to the individual objects that they contain.

To access an individual object within an object collection, you refer to its collection name and either the name of one of the objects it contains, or its ordinal position within the collection. For example, to check the date a table was created, you could use either of the following constructs.

```
Debug.Print CurrentDb.TableDefs("Table1").DateCreated
Debug.Print CurrentDb.TableDefs(1).DateCreated
```

Most collection objects implement the `Add`, `Remove`, and `Item` methods, and the `Count` property. Depending on the name and the design of the class, the name given to the `Add` method can vary from application to application, and even from object to object. For example, to add a worksheet to an Excel workbook, you use the `Add` method of the `Worksheets` collection. By contrast, to add a table to the Access `TableDefs` collection, you create the new table object using `CreateTableDef()` and append it to the collection using the collection's `Append` method.

The VBA `Collection` object uses the `Add` method, as shown in the next section.

The Add Method

The `Add` method of the `Collection` object adds a member to the collection, and has the following syntax:

```
object.Add Item, [Key], [Before], [After]
```

The method parameter arguments are:

➤ `Item`: The `Item` parameter is an expression of any type (`Variant`) that represents the member to add to the collection. In the case of object collections, this is where you supply a pointer to the object instance.

➤ `Key`: An optional unique string expression that specifies a key that can be used to identify the collection member, instead of using its ordinal position in the collection. The `Key` parameter must be a unique string; otherwise, an error occurs.

➤ `Before`: An optional parameter that enables you to specify that the new member is to be added at the position immediately preceding an existing member in the collection. The parameter you supply can be the ordinal numeric position of the existing member, or the `Key` that the existing member was saved with when it was added to the collection. If specifying a number, it must be in the range between 1 and the collection's `Count` property. You can specify a `Before` or `After` position, but not both.

➤ `After`: Similar to the `Before` parameter, the `After` parameter specifies that the new member is to be added at the position immediately following an existing collection member. The parameter you supply can be either the ordinal numeric position of the existing member, or the `Key` that the existing member was saved with when it was added to the collection. If specifying a number, it must be in the range between 1 and the collection's `Count` property. You can specify a `Before` or `After` position, but not both.

 Note that the VBA.Collection object is a 1-based collection; that is, the ordinal of the first item in the collection is 1, not 0 as is the case for collections in Access and DAO.

The Remove Method

The `Remove` method allows you to remove a member from the collection, and uses the following syntax.

```
object.Remove index
```

The `Index` argument specifies the position of an existing collection member. The argument you supply can be the ordinal numeric position of the existing member, or the `Key` that the existing member was saved with when it was added to the collection. If specifying a number, it must be in the range between 1 and the collection's `Count` property.

The Item Method

The `Item` method provides a way for you to specify an object by its ordinal position in the collection. It uses the following syntax:

```
object.Item(index)
```

The `Index` argument specifies the position of an existing collection member. The argument you supply can be either the ordinal numeric position of the existing member, or the `Key` that the existing member was saved with when it was added to the collection. If specifying a number, it must be in the range between 1 and the collection's `Count` property.

As you add and remove members from the middle of the collection, the Item numbers of all the members around it are renumbered to maintain continuity. For example, if you remove item 2 from a four-member collection, item 3 is renumbered to 2, and item 4 is renumbered to 3. It is for this reason that you should not rely on an object's ordinal position in the collection.

The Count Property

The Count property returns a Long Integer containing the number of objects in a collection, and is read-only.

Collection Class Basics

To demonstrate the basic concepts and techniques used to create a collection class, you extend the classroom example to add students. You create an interface that mirrors the members provided by the VBA Collection object, but by creating your own collection class, you can create an object that is strongly typed. Your collection class can be used to create students and only students.

First, let's flush out a few members of a class that represents a student.

clsStudent

Start by creating a class named clsStudent. This class will represent a student that you'll store in a collection of clsStudent objects.

```
Option Compare Database
Option Explicit

Private mstrName      As String
Private mdatDOB       As Date
Private lngStudentID As Long

Private Sub Class_Initialize()
    `Generate the unique key for this object.
    lngStudentID = CLng(Rnd * (2 ^ 31))
End Sub

Public Property Get ID() As Long
    `Return the object's unique key.
    ID = lngStudentID
End Property

Public Property Get Name() As String
    Name = mstrName
End Property

Public Property Let Name(strName As String)
    mstrName = strName
End Property

Public Property Get DOB() As Date
    DOB = mdatDOB
End Property

Public Property Let DOB(datDOB As Date)
    mdatDOB = datDOB
```

```
End Property

Public Sub TakeTest()
    ` Code to implement taking a test
End Sub
```

code snippet ClassExamples

Let's stop for a minute and talk about the ID property. The calculation in the Initialize event of the class returns a random number between 215 and 2,147,483,433. This is the largest number that will fit into a Long Integer data type, and offers sufficient range to minimize the risk of duplicates. You'll see why you are generating the random number in a few minutes.

clsStudents

The Collection object is declared at module-level and instantiated in the Initialize event. Following best practice, the Terminate event destroys the Collection instance and any objects it may still contain.

Available for download on Wrox.com

```
Option Compare Database
Option Explicit

Private mcol As Collection 'Declare the collection object

Private Sub Class_Initialize()
    `Instantiates the collection object.
    Set mcol = New Collection
End Sub

Private Sub Class_Terminate()
    `Destroys the collection object.
    Set mcol = Nothing
End Sub
```

code snippet ClassExamples

The Add method adds a pointer to a new clsStudent object to the collection class clsStudents. You'll get to the actual implementation of the Add method in a moment, but first take a look at the usage. There are a couple ways you can implement this method depending on how you want to use it. The Add method of the VBA Collection object is a Sub procedure — that is, it does not return a value. If you choose this implementation, you might pass a clsStudent object to the method like this:

```
` Sample usage for the Add method as a Sub
Dim myStudents As clsStudents
Dim myStudent  As clsStudent

` Create the collection class
Set myStudents = New clsStudents

` Create and add a student
```

```
Set myStudent = New clsStudent
myStudent.Name = "Rob Cooper"
myStudents.Add myStudent
```

Some implementations of the `Add` method are created as `Function` procedures to return the instance of the object they are adding. In this case, you would need to pass the minimum amount of information, such as the name, to the `Add` method to create the student.

```
`   Sample usage for the Add method as a Function
Dim myStudents As clsStudents
Dim myStudent As clsStudent

`  Create the collection class
Set myStudents = New clsStudents

`  Create and add the student
Set myStudent = myStudents.Add("Rob Cooper")
```

code snippet ClassExamples

Whichever approach you choose, you should be consistent in your designs and choose the approach that is best suited for your application. Often, the amount of input you have and when you elect to create the object are deciding factors.

> *Add methods, when implemented as function procedures, are known in OOP parlance as Factory methods. They create an instance of the object they encapsulate.*

Okay, time to implement the `Add` method. For this example, you use the factory method approach and implement `Add` as a function. One benefit is that you have less test code as a result.

As mentioned, the `Add` method adds a pointer to a new `clsStudent` object and then returns it. Because you are creating a collection of `clsStudent` objects, you use the `ID` property that was defined in `clsStudent`. If an optional `Before` or `After` parameter is included in the call, the `Add` method inserts the object before or after the object that occupies the position specified by the `varBefore` or `varAfter` parameter.

The following examples use a routine named `ThrowError` to display error messages coming from the collection class. The routine is defined later.

```
Public Function Add(strStudentName As String, _
      Optional varBefore As Variant, _
      Optional varAfter As Variant) As clsStudent
   `Adds a member to the collection.

   `  create a temporary student object
   Dim objStudent As clsStudent
   Set objStudent = New clsStudent

   `  set the student name
```

```
        objStudent.Name = strStudentName

        If Not IsMissing(varBefore) Then
            mcol.Add objStudent, CStr(objStudent.ID), varBefore
        ElseIf Not IsMissing(varAfter) Then
            mcol.Add objStudent, CStr(objStudent.ID), , varAfter
        Else
            mcol.Add objStudent, CStr(objStudent.ID)
        End If

        ` return the object
        Set Add = objStudent
        On Error Resume Next
        If Err.Number <> 0 Then
            ThrowError Err.Number, Err.Description, Err.Source
        End If
        OnError Goto 0

    End Function
```

code snippet ClassExamples

The following procedure removes the member specified by strKey from the collection, but does not return anything to the calling code.

Available for download on Wrox.com

```
    Public Sub Remove(strKey As Variant)
        `Removes a member from the collection.

        mcol.Remove strKey

        On Error Resume Next
        If Err.Number <> 0 Then
            ThrowError Err.Number, Err.Description, Err.Source
        End If
        On Error Goto 0
    End Sub
```

code snippet ClassExamples

The Item property is interesting (you'll see why shortly), but for the moment the explanation is that it returns a pointer to the object whose Key matches that supplied by the strKey parameter.

Available for download on Wrox.com

```
    Public Property Get Item(strKey As String) As clsStudent
        Set Item = mcol(strKey)
    End Property
```

code snippet ClassExamples

The following procedure simply returns a number that represents the number of objects contained in the collection.

```
`Returns the number of items in the collection
Public Property Get Count() As Long
    Count = mcol.Count
End Property
```

code snippet ClassExamples

The `ThrowError` method takes all the errors that occur within the class and packages them up before passing them back up the error chain to the calling procedure.

```
Private Sub ThrowError(lngError As Long, strDescr As String, strSource As String)
    `Procedure used to return errors
    Dim strMsg As String

    Select Case lngError
        Case 5: strMsg = "Member not found."
        Case 9: strMsg = "Subscript out of range."
        Case 457: strMsg = "Duplicate member."
        Case Else: strMsg = "Error " & lngError & vbCrLf & strDescr
    End Select

    Err.Raise vbObjectError + lngError, strSource, strMsg
End Sub
```

code snippet ClassExamples

Because you're writing your own collection class, you can also extend the functionality of the VBA `Collection` object! What follows is only a subset of the additional functionality you could add to your collection classes. For example, you might also choose to add methods that search or sort items in the collection.

The `FirstStudent` property returns a pointer to the object that occupies the first position in the collection, but it doesn't remove it from the collection. Remember that you use 1 for the first item in a VBA `Collection`, not 0 as in Access collections such as `TableDefs`.

```
Public Property Get FirstStudent() As clsStudent
    `Returns the first member added to the collection,
    `but does NOT remove it from the collection.

    'Get the first member.
    Set FirstStudent = mcol(1)

    If Err.Number <> 0 Then
        ThrowError Err.Number, Err.Description, Err.Source
    End If
End Property
```

code snippet ClassExamples

Similarly, the `LastStudent` property returns a pointer to the object that occupies the last position in the collection.

```
Public Property Get LastStudent() As clsStudent
    `Returns the last member added to the collection,
    `but does NOT remove it from the collection.

    `Get the last member.
    Set LastStudent = mcol(mcol.Count)

    If Err.Number <> 0 Then
        ThrowError Err.Number, Err.Description, Err.Source
    End If
End Property
```

code snippet ClassExamples

The `Clear` method destroys the collection and thus all objects it contains, and then re-instantiates the collection. Although you could have iterated through the collection, removing and destroying objects as you went, destroying the `Collection` object is faster.

```
Public Sub Clear()
    `Clears the collection and destroys all its objects.
    `This is the fastest way.
    Set mcol = Nothing
    Set mcol = New Collection
End Sub
```

code snippet ClassExamples

Setting Unique Object Keys

The `Collection` object requires that each Key value is unique in the collection. Setting unique `Collection` object keys is not always easy. You can't easily use incrementing numbers because the `Key` parameter requires a `String` data type, and once you set it, it can't be changed without removing the object and reinserting it.

The best method is to use a property of the object being added (if it has one), but isn't hard to implement. This is the approach you used in your `Add` method, where you used the `ID` property of the Student object, but there are other ways to generate unique values as well:

➤ Timestamp values (current date and time)

➤ Network MAC addresses

➤ Telephone numbers

➤ Combination of name and date of birth

➤ Cryptographic random numbers

Okay, perhaps that last one might be a bit of overkill. The point is that you can use whatever means you like to generate a key, but however you do it, ensure the key is unique in the collection.

Testing the clsStudents Class

To test the functionality of the `clsStudents` class, you can run the following code in a standard module. This test code adds four `clsStudent` objects to the `clsStudents` object (the `Collection` class), and then starts removing them using two different methods, `Remove` and `Clear`, all the while accessing the `clsStudent` object's `ID` property through the collection object. The first `Debug.Print` statement shows how to access the `clsStudent` object's `Name` property through the `Students Collection` class instance. To begin, create the collection:

```
Public Sub TestCollectionClass()
    Dim myStudents As clsStudents
    Dim obj As clsStudent
    Dim strKey1 As String
    Dim strKey As String

    On Error Resume Next
    Debug.Print "Begin test"

    ` Create the collection
    Set myStudents = New clsStudents
```

Now add code to add a student to the collection using the `Add` method:

```
    ` Add a student to the collection
    Set obj = myStudents.Add("Teresa Hennig")
    strKey1 = CStr(obj.ID)
    Set obj = Nothing
```

Do the same thing three more times, to add another three students:

```
    ` Add another student to the collection
    Set obj = myStudents.Add("Jerry Dennison")
    Set obj = Nothing

    ` And another one…
    Set obj = myStudents.Add("Geoff Griffith")
    strKey = CStr(obj.ID)
    Set obj = Nothing

    ` And the final student
    Set obj = myStudents.Add("Rob Cooper")
    Set obj = Nothing
```

Now print the Name of the student that occupies the first position in the collection:

```
    Debug.Print "The student with ID [" & strKey1 & "] = " & _
        myStudents.Item(strKey1).Name
```

To start removing students from the collection, use the `Remove` method:

```
    'Start removing objects from the collection
    Debug.Print , "There are now " & myStudents.Count & " students."
    Debug.Print , "Removing student: " & strKey1
```

Available for
download on
Wrox.com

```
myStudents.Remove strKey1

Debug.Print , "There are now " & myStudents.Count & " students."
Debug.Print , "Removing student: " & strKey
myStudents.Remove strKey

Debug.Print , "There are now " & myStudents.Count & " students."
```

Take advantage of the fact that you issued the On Error Resume Next line to trap an error:

```
`Create an error (key was already removed)
myStudents.Remove strKey
If Err <> 0 Then Debug.Print ,"***ERROR " & Err.Number
```

Now, remove the remaining students from the collection without causing any errors:

```
`Now do it properly
myStudents.Clear
Debug.Print , "There are now " & myStudents.Count & " students."
Debug.Print "End test"

Set myStudents = Nothing
End Sub
```

code snippet ClassExamples

Specifying the Default Procedure

By default, Access treats your collection class as a normal object rather than a true collection. As such, you do not have the ability to refer to a default property or procedure for the class. For example, using VBA, the following two statements are equivalent.

```
Debug.Print Forms.Item(0).Name
Debug.Print Forms(0).Name
```

The default property of the Forms collection in Access is the Item property, which means if you want to, you can omit the Item keyword.

Using a custom Collection class, you are forced to explicitly use the Item property, as you did in the previous example. But all is not lost! There is a way to tell VBA which procedure to use as the default, but of course, things are never straightforward.

You have to export the procedure to a file, manually add a line of code to the procedure definition and then import it back into Access. The procedure for doing so is as follows:

1. From the Project Explorer window in code view, right-click the module and select Remove.

2. When asked if you want to export the module before removing it, click Yes. The Export File dialog box is displayed.

3. Browse to a convenient folder and change the filename to *modulename*.txt, where *modulename* is the name of the module you're exporting.

4. Click Save. The class is removed from the project and saved to disk as a text file.

5. Using Windows Explorer, browse to the appropriate folder and double-click the text file to open it in Notepad.

6. Locate the procedure (in this case the `Item` property), and add the single line of text that begins with the word `Attribute`, as shown here:

```
Public Property Get Item(strKey As String) As clsStudent
Attribute Item.VB_UserMemId = 0
    Set Item = mcol(strKey)
End Property
```

7. Ensure the procedure or property name appears in the attribute statement and that the attribute is set to zero.

8. Save the file and exit Notepad.

9. In Access code view, right-click anywhere in the Project Explorer window and select Import File from the context menu. The Import File dialog box is displayed.

10. Browse to the appropriate folder, select the file you just edited, and click Open. The class is added to the Project Explorer window.

You can check the Object Browser to see that a small blue ball is shown above the procedure's icon, indicating that it is now the default procedure.

The test code previously accessed the `clsStudent` object's `Name` property through the `myStudents` object like this:

```
myStudents.Item(strKey1).Name
```

It can now be accessed like this:

```
myStudents(strKey1).Name
```

Enumerating Collection Classes

A second drawback to using custom `Collection` objects is that you can't enumerate through its members using the `For Each` construct. For example, consider the following code.

```
Public Sub TestEnumeration()
    Dim tdf As TableDef

    For Each tdf In CurrentDb.TableDefs
        Debug.Print tdf.Name
    Next tdf
End Sub
```

This code enables you to enumerate, or iterate, through the collection by declaring an object variable. To accomplish the same thing with your custom `Collection` class, you need to go back to Notepad as you did to specify the default procedure, only this time, add an entire public procedure.

Export the class as before and open it in Notepad. Now add the procedure *exactly* as shown here (the only change you can make is the name of the `Collection` object you're using — in this case, `mcol`):

```
Public Function NewEnum() As IUnknown
Attribute NewEnum.VB_UserMemId = -4
    Set NewEnum = mcol.[_NewEnum]
End Function
```

Save the file and re-import it into Access as you did before. Now you can enumerate the collection objects as you can with other Access collections.

```
Dim mbr As Object `or clsStudent
For Each mbr In myStudents
    Debug.Print mbr.ID
Next mbr
```

Pretty cool stuff, huh?

THE THREE PILLARS

So far, you've examined how to create class modules that define their own properties and methods. You've seen how to instantiate them as objects, link them to other objects in different types of relationships, and finally, use them in the application. For most cases, this is all you need to know.

But if you want to create a lot of related classes, and do it in the most efficient way, then you need to understand a few principles of object-oriented programming.

The three pillars of object-oriented theory are:

➤ Encapsulation

➤ Inheritance

➤ Polymorphism

These things may have different meanings to different people, and the extent to which they apply to an object-oriented language differs according to which language you happen to prefer.

Encapsulation

A major advantage of object-oriented programming is the capability to *encapsulate* the private data for an object in the object itself. When you create a set of properties and methods to define the interface for a class, external code can use that interface to implement its behavior without ever knowing what goes on inside. This allows you to hide the internal data and even change the internal algorithms in the class.

Once the interface to a class is defined, you can improve the performance of the class, or provide additional information as long as you don't break the interface of the class. If you break the interface of the class (its properties, methods, and events), you run the risk of breaking applications that call into the class.

A side benefit of encapsulation is that it also offers a way of hiding specific business rules and behavior from other developers. For example, suppose you have created a class that determines certain properties of a proprietary chemical formula. You wouldn't want your employees knowing the details of the formula, so you encapsulate it in a custom class and expose only the interface to it.

Inheritance

In a nutshell, inheritance is the capability to create new classes from existing ones. A derived class, or subclass, inherits the properties and methods of the class that instantiated it (called the base class, or superclass), and may add new properties and methods. New methods can be defined with the same name as those in the superclass, in which case, they override the original one.

There are two types of inheritance: *interface* and *implementation inheritance.* Interface inheritance has been available to Access since VBA 6 introduced the `Implements` keyword. Implementation inheritance is available in Visual Basic .NET through the `Inherits` keyword, but unfortunately not in Access 2010.

The essential difference between the two forms of inheritance is that interface inheritance specifies only the interface. It doesn't actually provide any corresponding implementation code. For example, suppose you have a `Bike` object that wants to ask the `Wheel` object for its part number. The `Wheel` object wants to borrow the functionality from its superclass, `Parts`. The `Bike` object might implement the following functionality:

```
Private myWheel As Wheel

Private Function GetPartNo() As String
    GetPartNo = myWheel.PartNo()
End Function
```

The implementation of this behavior is in `Part`'s `PartNo()` method. Because VBA doesn't support implementation inheritance, you would need to put some code into the `Wheel` class.

```
Implements Part
Private MyPart As New Part

Private Function Part_PartNo() As String
    Part_PartNo = myPart.PartNo()
End Function
```

VBA allows the interface, in this case `Part`, to implement the actual behavior. `Wheel` retains an instance of `Part` (a behavior called *containment*), and then asks that reference to carry out some action for it (called *delegation*). This isn't true interface inheritance because it allows you to add code to `Wheel` to provide the actual behavior, but it's close enough.

Polymorphism

Polymorphism is the capability for different object types to implement the same method, thereby allowing you to write VBA code without concerning yourself about what type of object you're using at the time. Another way of looking at it is that objects can be more than one type of thing.

There are two types of polymorphism: *ad-hoc* polymorphism (called *overloading* in VB.NET) and *parametric* polymorphism. Parametric polymorphism is not implemented in Access 2010, and is thus beyond the scope of this book.

Ad-hoc polymorphism provides the capability to use the same calling syntax for objects of different types. For example, say you have `bikes` and `cars` classes, each having its own methods to implement its own unique properties and behaviors, but because both need their tires pumped up occasionally, they would both have a `pump_tires` method. The actual code to implement this behavior would perhaps differ, but as long as their interface remained the same, your VBA code could simply call the `pump_tires` method for both, confident that each class knows how to pump up its own tires.

Okay, it's true that VBA doesn't demonstrate some of the characteristics of a true object-oriented language like C#, but it doesn't pretend to. Applications where you would need polymorphism or inheritance would not be written in VBA but instead in a language such as VB.NET, C#, or Java.

Inheriting Interfaces

Inheritance is an object-oriented concept that allows one class to *inherit* the public properties and methods (the interface) of another class. This section illustrates how you can implement that in your own Access Object Models.

The `Implements` keyword in VBA allows you to implement interface inheritance, giving programmers access to a form of polymorphism.

For example, suppose you have two objects: `Object1` and `Object2`. If `Object1` inherits the interface exposed by `Object2`, you can say that `Object1` *is a kind of* `Object2`, which is polymorphism in a nutshell.

Often interfaces are referred to as a *contract* because there is an agreement between the creator of the object and its user that the object will provide all the properties and methods that make up its interface. The internal implementation may vary, but the object's signatures (its property and method names, parameters and data types) must not.

You can use interfaces and polymorphism in any number of ways, but to understand how it all works, let's examine the most common — categorizing objects on the basis of common traits. Employees are a good example because you can implement different types, such as Programmer, Tester, or Manager.

Each employee has his or her own attributes and behaviors, such that they each merit their own class. They all share common traits — such as the fact that they all work for the same company, have a date of birth, hire date, salary, and so on. All do work, take lunch, and take telephone calls. If you put all the common traits into a single interface (`IEmployee`), you have a generic way of dealing with all employees at once. For example, you can pay each employee like so:

```
Dim Employee As IEmployee

For Each Employee In Company
    Employee.Pay
Next Employee
```

Although all employees receive pay, they all receive different amounts of pay and may receive pay in different ways. For example, some employees may receive paychecks, whereas others may receive payment through direct deposit. Therefore, the code to pay each employee must be in that employee's class, and will certainly differ from employee to employee.

Additionally, the members of an implemented interface do not automatically become part of the default interface for a class. That is, if a `Manager` had only one public method, `GivePayRaise`, you would have to get at the `GivePayRaise` method like this:

```
Dim Employee As clsManager

Set Employee = new clsManager
Employee.GivePayRaise
```

Traditionally, interface class names are distinguished from other types of class by prepending their names with an uppercase I.

You could copy the `IEmployee` interface into the default interface, and have both point to a common private procedure that contains the code that makes the employee give a raise. You could also make it simple and just use the `Implements` keyword in each employee's class:

```
Implements IEmployee
```

By so doing, every employee whose class definition included the `Implements` keyword would inherit the public properties and methods exposed by the `IEmployee` interface. So that you can begin to understand how interface inheritance works, start by defining two `Employee` classes based on the type of employee: Programmers and Managers. Before you do that, create an interface class that defines the characteristics that all employees have in common (naturally, you call this class `IEmployee`):

```
Option Compare Database
Option Explicit

Public Property Get Salary() As Currency
End Property

Public Property Let Salary(curSalary As Currency)
End Property

Public Property Get Name() As String
End Property

Public Property Let Name(strName As String)
End Property

Public Property Get HireDate() As Date
End Property

Public Property Let HireDate(datHireDate As Date)
End Property

Public Sub DoWork()
End Sub

Public Sub TakeLunch()
```

```
End Sub

Public Sub Pay()
End Sub
```

The first thing you notice is that it doesn't have any code to implement an employee's attributes or behavior. That's because you're inheriting the *interface*, not the *implementation*. As discussed at the beginning of the chapter, a class module is like a template. An implementation class is also like a template, but where the template provided by "standard" classes includes interface and implementation, an interface class only provides an interface template.

Next you can create your new `Employee` classes, the first being the `Programmer` class. The `Programmer` class might have some specific properties and methods of its own. For the sake of example, let's add one property and method as follows:

```
Option Compare Database
Option Explicit

Public Property Get KnowsVBA() As Boolean
    ` Code to determine whether the programmer knows VBA
End Property

Public Sub DoCodeReview()
    ` Code to perform a code review
End Property
```

Now you add the `Implements` keyword, after which you can select the `IEmployee` class from the `Object` drop-down list.

Selecting all the `IEmployee` class's interface procedures from the Procedure drop-down list, you can see that they've all been inherited as Private members. This is because, although all `IEmployee`'s public properties and procedures are inherited (in fact, an error is generated if you don't inherit all of them), you may not want to expose all of them to consumers of the `Programmer` class.

```
Private Sub IEmployee_Pay()

End Sub

Private Sub IEmployee_DoWork()

End Sub

Private Property Let IEmployee_HireDate(RHS As Date)

End Property
```

You can now implement the unique behavior for this employee, without affecting the implementation of any other employee. Add a local variable to store the employee's salary and you end up with the following class definition. First, you declare the objects and variables you need, and issue the `Implements` keyword.

```
Option Compare Database
Option Explicit

Implements IEmployee

Private mcurSalary As Currency
```

Then, create some custom procedures to perform a range of employee-specific actions:

```
Private Sub IEmployee_DoWork()
    ` Code to implement doing work
End Sub

Private Sub IEmployee_Pay()
    ` Code to implement paying a Programmer
End Sub
```

code snippet ClassExamples

Finally, add a property and a sub procedure to carry out what might be deemed standard operations for all employees.

```
Private Property Let IEmployee_Salary(RHS As String)
    mcurSalary = RHS
End Property

Private Sub IEmployee_TakeLunch()
    ` Code to implement a Programmer taking lunch
End Sub
```

code snippet ClassExamples

You can then create any number of classes for any number of employees, to which you can link an unlimited number of `Employee` classes, to track individual employees.

Interface inheritance isn't terribly difficult; making sure it doesn't get out of hand is the hard part!

Instancing

Earlier, you were introduced to the `Instancing` property. Now it's time to explore it. Figure 8-8 shows the available values for the `Instancing` property for a class module in Access.

A class's `Instancing` property defines whether the class is private or public, and whether it can be created from external code.

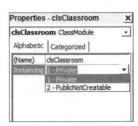

FIGURE 8-8

Setting a class's `Instancing` property to `Private` means that the class can be used only within the application in which it is defined. As you saw earlier in the section "Creating a Parent Property," it can also determine whether instances of the class can be passed as arguments.

Setting it to `PublicNotCreatable` means that although other applications can access type library information about the class, they can use it only after your application has created it first; they can't create instances of it. This can be accomplished by using helper methods in standard modules, such as:

Available for download on Wrox.com

```
Public Function GetNotCreatableInstance() As clsPublicNotCreatable
    Set GetNotCreatableInstance = New clsPublicNotCreatable
End Function
```

code snippet InstancingExample

Classes that have their `Instancing` property set to `PublicNotCreatable` are referred to as *dependent objects* and typically form part of more complex objects. Using the Classroom/Teacher/Student example, you might want to allow an external application to create multiple `clsClassroom` objects but only allow `clsStudent` objects to exist as a part of a `clsClassroom`. To do that, you make the `clsStudent` class `PublicNotCreatable` and let the user add new `Students` by adding a `Students` collection to the `clsClassroom` class. That way, they can only create new `Students` using the collection's `Add` method.

There are situations where you might want to be able to create new instances of a class from another application. The classic example is where you are developing a class library in a database and would like to use it in multiple applications. For this, there is one additional value you can use for the `Instancing` property that does not appear in the Properties window.

Remember that VBA has its roots in VB, which actually supports *six* values for the `Instancing` property! Access supports one of these values called `GlobalMultiUse`, the value of which is 5. Setting the `Instancing` property to 5 allows you to create new instances of your classes, even when used as a reference in another application. To set the property, run this code in the Immediate window:

```
VBE.ActiveVBProject.VBComponents("clsMyClass").Properties("Instancing") = 5
```

Remember to select the correct VBA project in the Project Explorer window before running this code.

SUMMARY

This chapter took you on a whirlwind tour of the object-oriented programming techniques that are available in Access 2010. If you had any trouble understanding the concepts, just remember that it may just take a little practice. Before long, you'll be writing quite complex OOP code that will make your application development and maintenance a joy to behold.

Specifically in this chapter, you looked at class modules, how they differ from object instances, and when you would use OOP techniques in your applications. You created several classes of your own, designed their properties and methods, and instantiated the classes as objects to investigate how they work and how to use them.

You learned about the object naming strategy, and then you examined class events and errors, to understand how classes communicate with the outside world. You also practiced using forms and reports as objects, and explored collection classes, which are the basis for building your own Object Models. Finally, you looked at some basic OOP theory and saw how to implement some of it in code.

You have now gone as far as standard VBA can take you. Chapter 9 starts you on the next leg of your programming journey by introducing the Windows API and the many built-in functions that the Windows operating system can offer in terms of advanced programming functionality.

Extending VBA with APIs

WHAT'S IN THIS CHAPTER?

➤ Using the Windows API to add functionality to Access applications

➤ Converting API Function Declarations from C++ to VBA

➤ Writing API declarations that will work on 32-bit and 64-bit Office 2010, as well as in previous versions of Office

Microsoft Visual Basic for Applications (VBA) is a full-featured software development language that offers a vast array of built-in functions such that many Access developers never require anything else.

However, when you start developing more and more complex applications in Access, you may find yourself needing to do things for which VBA does not have a built-in function. Moreover, you'll sometimes need to do things that VBA simply can't do. That's not to say that VBA is incomplete, but, like every other programming language, it does not include every function you're ever likely to need.

The Windows operating system provides a large library of functions that you can access using VBA to extend what you're able to do in your applications. But because the Application Programming Interface (API) is primarily geared toward C/C++ developers and thereby VBA-unfriendly, you must first understand what it is, and what special considerations you must take into account to use it from VBA.

This chapter explores what the Windows API is, and why you might want to use it. It describes the libraries that make up the API and how to declare API functions to use them with VBA. You'll examine the differences between the data types used in APIs and those used in VBA, learning techniques to convert between them. The chapter also introduces the VBA LastDLLError property for dynamic-link library (DLL) error handling. Finally, the chapter will provide examples of some API functions that are commonly used in Access applications.

INTRODUCING THE WINDOWS API

An API — application programming interface — is a group of standard functions that are packaged together and made available to application programmers. There are quite a few APIs, but the one that you've probably heard the most about is the Win32 API, also known as the 32-bit Windows API. The Windows API consists of many DLLs that make up the Windows operating system and helps ensure that every application that runs under Windows behaves in a consistent manner.

In addition to the Win32 API, 64-bit versions of Windows include what is known as the Win64 API. The Win64 API is made up of many of the same functions as the Win32 API, but there is a difference in how pointers are treated between the two systems. We will take a closer look at 64-bit pointers to API functions in the section "Pointers in 64-Bit Windows." Beginning with Office 2010, Office and Access are now available in 64-bit versions.

What this actually means is that standard Windows operations such as saving files, opening forms, managing dialog boxes, and so on are all handled by the Windows APIs. For example, the standard Windows File Open dialog box is an API function called `GetOpenFileName` found in `comdlg32.dll`. Similarly, the `GetTempPath` function in `Kernel32.dll` returns the name of the folder where temporary files are stored.

The File dialog boxes found in Office applications are customized versions of the Windows dialog boxes. To use these dialog boxes, use the `FileDialog` object in the Office 14.0 Object Library.

All Windows-based applications interact with the Windows APIs in some way, whether they are opening a file, displaying time, putting text on the screen, or managing computer memory.

When you program in Microsoft Access, you use built-in libraries such as VBA, Access, and Data Access Objects (DAO), which you could loosely refer to as an API. Similarly, when you use the Access Add-in Manager or References dialog box to link to an external DLL, OCX, MDB, and so on, you are linking to something that is essentially an API.

Finding API Functions

Despite the fact that the API has a reputation of being highly complex, there's really no need to feel intimidated by the API. Because the Windows APIs are written in C/C++, VB programmers must be aware of certain rules, but other than that, the APIs can pretty much be used in the same way as any other function.

Let's start from the beginning. With so many libraries available to developers on Windows, how do you know where to find API functions? Furthermore, how do you know what the functions do? The following table describes just a few of the DLLs that contain APIs to use in VBA applications.

API	BASIC DESCRIPTION
`KERNEL32.DLL`	Low-level operating system functions, such as memory and task management, resource handling, and so on.
`USER32.DLL`	Window management functions, including messages, menus, cursors, timers, communications, and most of the non-display functions.
`GDI32.DLL`	The Graphics Device Interface library. Device output, including most drawing functions, and display context, metafile, coordinate, and font functions.
`COMDLG32.DLL`	Windows common dialog boxes.
`LZ32.DLL`	File compression.
`VERSION.DLL`	Version control.
`MAPI32.DLL`	Electronic mail.
`COMCTL32.DLL`	Implements a new set of Windows controls and dialog boxes, including the tree view and rich text edit controls.
`NETAPI32.DLL`	Network access and control.
`ODBC32.DLL`	Implements ODBC (Open Database Connectivity), providing functions to work with databases.
`WINMM.DLL`	Multimedia.
`ADVAPI32.DLL`	Advanced Win32 Base API. Includes functions to read and write to the Windows Registry, and to retrieve the username.

Before we move into how to use an API function, let's take a look at why the API is helpful in Access applications.

Why You Need the API

VBA is a powerful language, but you can control only a small part of the operating system with its built-in functions. One of the best features of VBA is its extensibility; that is, you can extend its capabilities in a variety of ways — one of which is by using the API.

For example, VBA provides several built-in functions for manipulating the Windows Registry, but these functions let you use only one small part of the Registry set aside for VBA. To access the remainder of the Registry, you need to use the API.

Similarly, to retrieve and manipulate a disk drive, printer, or system resource settings, you need the API. If you want your Access applications to do more than just beep, the `sndPlaySound` API function enables you to play sound effects or music. You can even control the transparency of your Access forms by combining several API functions.

Here's an example that puts an icon in a form's title bar; something you can't do using standard VBA. Place the following code into a standard module:

```
Public Declare Function LoadImage Lib `user32" _
  Alias `LoadImageA" (ByVal hInst As Long, _
  ByVal lpsz As String, ByVal un1 As Long, _
  ByVal n1 As Long, ByVal n2 As Long, _
  ByVal un2 As Long) As Long

Public Declare Function SendMessage Lib `user32" _
  Alias `SendMessageA" (ByVal hWnd As Long, _
  ByVal wMsg As Long, ByVal wParam As Long, _
  LParam As Any) As Long

`Image type constants
Public Const IMAGE_ICON = 1

`un2 Flags
Public Const LR_LOADFROMFILE = &H10

`Message parameters
Public Const WM_SETICON = &H80
Public Const ICON_SMALL = 0

`Default image size for the Access Titlebar
Public Const IMG_DEFAULT_HEIGHT = 16
Public Const IMG_DEFAULT_WIDTH = 16

Public Sub SetFormIcon(hWnd As Long, strIcon As String)
  Dim hIcon As Long
  Dim lngReturn As Long

  hIcon = LoadImage(0&, strIcon, IMAGE_ICON, IMG_DEFAULT_WIDTH, _
    IMG_DEFAULT_HEIGHT, LR_LOADFROMFILE)

  If hIcon <> 0 Then
    lngReturn = SendMessage(hWnd, WM_SETICON, ICON_SMALL, ByVal hIcon)
  End If
End Sub
```

To try this out, create a new form and add the following code to the form's Load event, making sure to change the C:\myIcons\myIco.ico path to that of an icon file that exists on your computer. You may also have to change the Document Window Options setting to Overlapping Windows in the Current Database group of the Access Options dialog box.

```
Private Sub Form_Load()
  SetFormIcon Me.hWnd, `C:\myIcons\myIcon.ico"
End Sub
```

Now open the form to see the icon appear in the form's title bar.

With the APIs at your disposal, you can control a significant portion of the Windows operating system and almost everything within it. Let's begin by discussing how the API works.

If you're running the 64-bit version of Office 2010, the preceding code will not compile. We'll take a closer look at this later on in this chapter in the section "Pointers in 64-Bit Windows."

INTRODUCING LINKING

As previously mentioned, function libraries can be linked or incorporated into applications when required. Libraries are linked using a tool called a *linker*. It takes objects created by a compiler and puts them together into a single executable file. There are two types of linking: *static* and *dynamic*. Static linking occurs at design time, when you create the application. Dynamic linking occurs at runtime.

Static Linking

Most programming languages provide the capability to access some operating system functions. They also usually enable you to create and store your own custom functions, which you can compile into library (`*.lib`) files and then merge into your applications.

When an executable program is compiled, the linker scans the application for references to external functions and libraries, and then copies them into the final executable, thereby linking them to your application. This is called *static linking* because the addresses your program uses to access these functions are fixed into the executable and remain unchanged (static) when the program runs.

Although newer compilers enable you to copy individual functions, older ones typically copied the entire module to the application when linking a library. This meant that all the library's functions were merged into the executable, regardless of whether they were needed.

Of course, copying the entire module to the application increased the resulting file size. While the size increase was usually small, it started to actually mean something if there were 20 executables, each containing a copy of the same library. In a multitasking environment such as Windows, all 20 programs could conceivably be running simultaneously, so a great deal of memory would be in use at any one time.

Dynamic Linking

Instead of grouping functions into libraries, later versions of Windows grouped these functions into a special type of executable called a DLL. When you link a DLL, you specify which function you want to include in your application, and instead of copying in the entire contents of the DLL, the linker/compiler records the name of each externally referenced function along with the name of the DLL in which it resides.

When your application runs, Windows loads the required library so that all its functions are exposed, and it is then that the address of each function is resolved and dynamically linked to the application. With dynamic linking, only one copy of the library needs to be stored on disk. All the applications that use its functions access the same physical copy.

Dynamic linked libraries typically have the same file extension (*.dll), but that isn't an absolute requirement. Custom controls such as those created in Visual Basic and C++ can have file extensions like *.ocx. Device drivers and some Windows system libraries sometimes use file extensions such as *.drv and *.exe.

DECLARING APIS

Now that you've seen a little of the background behind API functions and linking, let's take a look at how you can use them. In VBA, the way that you declare an API function is to use the Declare keyword. The Declare statement consists of several parts, and supports both functions and sub-procedures. You can only declare a procedure at module level in the declarations section.

Declare Syntax for a Sub Procedure

```
[Public | Private] Declare [PtrSafe] Sub name Lib "libname" [Alias "aliasname"]
[([arglist])]
```

Declare Syntax for a Function Procedure

```
[Public | Private] Declare [PtrSafe] Function name Lib "libname" [Alias "aliasname"]
[([arglist])] [As type]
```

The Declare Keyword

The Declare keyword tells VBA that what follows is the definition for a procedure stored in a DLL. The Declare statement also defines the type of procedure being declared: Function or Sub.

As you've already discovered, you can specify that the procedure be either Public or Private, depending on whether you want the procedure to be available to the entire project or only to the module in which it appears. Declare statements made in class modules can only be Private. In fact, you will get a compile error if you omit the Private keyword in a class module.

In order for a function to be available for use in VBA as an API function, it must be exported from the library in question. The way this is done may vary by compiler, but either way the function must provide an entry point for use outside of the library. It turns out that in Windows, functions can be exported from libraries other than DLLs. They can also be exported from EXEs. There are a couple of ways to find the functions that are exported from a given library. You can use the depends.exe tool or the dumpbin command-line tool with the /exports option specified. Dumpbin is included with Visual Studio and depends.exe can be downloaded from http://www.dependencywalker.com.

The PtrSafe Keyword

There are a few considerations to take into account when developing for 64-bit Windows. As far as VBA goes, one of the larger considerations is around the use of Windows API functions. Many of the functions in Windows return one or more types of pointers or handles. The PtrSafe keyword added in Office 2010, tells VBA that the Declare statement in question will work in 64-bit Windows. Without specifying the PtrSafe keyword, arguments to API functions are not guaranteed to work on 64-bit Windows. As such, the PtrSafe keyword is required on 64-bit versions of Office 2010 — the code will not compile without it.

> *The* PtrSafe *keyword is optional on 32-bit Office 2010. If you are developing for Office 2010 and will not have users running earlier versions, you can safely include the keyword without issue.*

Naming the Procedure

The name that follows Declare Function or Declare Sub is the name you use to call the procedure from VBA. There is a degree of flexibility here because the name need not be the actual name of the procedure in the DLL.

As in the following example, you can rename the procedure to almost anything, provided you use the Alias keyword to specify the actual name of the API procedure.

```
Private Declare Function MyProcedureName Lib `advapi32.dll` _
Alias `GetUserNameA` (ByVal lpBuffer As String, _
nSize As Long) As Long
```

The Alias keyword specifies the actual name of the procedure as it appears in the API. You cannot change this, but as you've seen, you can change the Name argument in the procedure declaration.

There are several reasons for renaming an API procedure:

➤ Some API procedures begin with an underscore character (_), which is illegal in VBA. To get around this, rename the procedure and use the Alias keyword.

➤ API procedure names are case sensitive, and terribly intolerant of programmers who forget that. VBA, on the other hand, doesn't care one way or the other, so by renaming the procedure, you build in a level of forgiveness.

➤ Several API procedures have arguments that can accept different data types. Supplying a wrong data type to such a procedure is a good way to get the API angry because VBA does not check the data types of the arguments you supply. The kind of response you are likely to get by using a wrong data type can range from erroneous data, unexpected application behavior, application hang, or system crash. To avoid type problems, declare several versions of the same procedure, each with a different name and each using arguments of different data types.

➤ Some Windows APIs have names that share the same as something in Access, such as `SetFocus` and `GetObject`. Using those keywords results in a compile error. Because you can't rename the Access keywords, you can give the API a unique name in the `Declare` statement and use the `Alias` keyword to refer to the API as defined by Windows.

➤ Most API procedures that can take string arguments come in two flavors: one for ANSI and one for Unicode. The ANSI version is suffixed by an `A`, as in the `GetUserNameA` example. The Unicode flavor has a `W` suffix (for wide). VBA uses Unicode internally and converts all strings to ANSI before calling a DLL procedure, so you generally use the ANSI version. But if you need to use both versions in the same project, renaming one or both of them makes sense.

➤ Finally, you can create procedure names that conform to your object naming standards.

WHAT IS UNICODE?

Unicode is one of the three distinct character sets supported by the Windows API:

➤ **Single-byte:** 8 bits wide, and provides for 256 characters. The ANSI character set is a single-byte character set.

➤ **Double-byte (DBCS):** Also 8 bits wide, but some of its byte values are called DBCS lead bytes, which are combined with the byte that follows them to form a single character. DBCSs provide a sufficient number of characters for languages such as Japanese, which have hundreds of characters.

➤ **Unicode:** 16 bits, which provides for up to 65,535 characters; enough to support all the characters in all the languages around the world.

If you make a mistake when declaring the `Alias`, VBA won't find the procedure in the DLL and will present runtime error 453, which your error-handling code can trap.

Specifying the Lib(rary) and Argument List

The `Lib` keyword specifies the filename of the library that contains the procedure you're declaring. This keyword can point to a full path, or to a file name only that is in the search path for VBA which will include both the current directory and the system directory. If VBA can't find the file, it generates a runtime error 53 (`File not found`), which your error handler can also trap.

The API argument list is specified in much the same way as it is in standard VBA subs and functions. However, there are a few rules that you must understand and adhere to when calling API procedures, including knowing when to pass arguments `ByRef` or `ByVal`, how to translate data types, and how to use values that are returned from an API. You'll get a closer look at data types you might encounter when reading API documentation in the "Understanding C Parameters" section later in the chapter.

Passing Values

To understand how to pass values to an API function, take a look at the declaration of the GetUserName function as defined on MSDN. This declaration is defined in C++:

```
BOOL GetUserName(
  LPTSTR lpBuffer,
  LPDWORD lpnSize
);
```

Two arguments are passed to the GetUserName function: lpBuffer, a fixed-width string storage area that contains the value returned by the procedure, and lpnSize, which is the length of the string. Here's how the GetUserName arguments work in VBA:

Available for download on Wrox.com

```
Private Declare Function GetUserName Lib "advapi32.dll" Alias "GetUserNameA" _
(ByVal lpBuffer As String, nSize As Long) As Long

Private Const MAXLEN = 255

Function GetLoginName() As String
    Dim strUserName As String
    Dim lngSize As Long
    Dim lngReturn As Long

    lngSize = 256

    strUserName = Space(MAXLEN) & Chr(0)

    If GetUserName(strUserName, lngSize) <> 0 Then
        GetLoginName = left(strUserName, lngSize -1)
    Else
        GetLoginName = ""
    End If
End Function
```

code snippet APISamples.accdb

The function is declared with two arguments: ByVal lpBuffer As String and nSize As Long. You might be thinking, "Hang on, ByRef passes a pointer, not ByVal." Normally that's true, but VBA is inconsistent here when it comes to strings. By default, VBA passes variables ByRef; that is, it passes a pointer to the value's location in memory, allowing the procedure to modify the actual value. To test this behavior in VBA, create the following two procedures in a standard module.

TestByRef Procedure

```
Public Sub TestByRef()
    Dim intMyValue As Integer
    intMyValue = 1
```

```
        Debug.Print `Initial value: ` & intMyValue
        ChangeMyValue intMyValue
        Debug.Print `New value: ` & intMyValue
    End Sub
```

ChangeMyValue Procedure

```
    Private Sub ChangeMyValue(ByRef intSomeValue As Integer)
        intSomeValue = 3
    End Sub
```

Run `TestByRef` and you'll see that the value of `intMyValue` changes. If you modify the `ChangeMyValue` procedure to pass `intSomeValue ByVal`, and re-run `TestByRef`, the value doesn't change. In VBA, this is true of strings as well. But when you pass strings to an API, the reverse happens. Because a string variable is itself a pointer, passing it to an API `ByRef` actually passes a pointer to an OLE 2.0 string (a `BSTR` data type). Generally, the only APIs to use this type of string are those that are part of the OLE 2.0 API. Other APIs don't take too kindly to it. Windows API procedures expect strings to be passed as a pointer to a *null-terminated string* — that is, the string ends with an ASCII zero character. This is a C language convention. When you pass a string `ByVal`, VBA converts the string to C language format by appending a null-termination character. Because the value is a pointer, the DLL can modify the string even though the `ByVal` keyword is used.

If you fail to specify the `ByVal` or `ByRef` keyword, you run the risk of an error 49, `Bad DLL calling convention`. Also, if you pass a value `ByRef` when `ByVal` is expected, or vice versa, the procedure can overrun memory that it shouldn't, and the system can crash.

Returning Values

Even sub-procedure APIs can return values, and the values returned by many API procedures can be quite different from those returned by VBA procedures. You may have noticed that the `GetUserName` function defined earlier returns a `Long Integer`, not a `String`. This is commonplace with many API functions, particularly those declared in Windows. There are two main reasons for this. First, API functions were initially designed to be used by C programmers who are accustomed to checking for an error code after calling a function.

Second, strings in C and C++ are different from those in VBA. VBA has a native data type called `String` that you can use to assign or refer to character data. C and C++ do not have this intrinsic type; their strings are usually created as an array of characters. As a result, DLLs often cannot return strings directly. Instead, they modify strings that you pass as one of their parameters. When you pass a string parameter to an API that will modify it, you often must initialize the string with sufficient characters to take the value that will be returned. The API function provides another parameter to accept a number that represents the length of the string. You initialize the string using the VBA `Space` function, and the `Len(strMyString)+1` construct can be used to specify its length. The +1 accounts for the terminating null character in the return string.

> *What all of this really means is that strings in VBA are not really strings. The actual storage for a String in VBA is in an array of bytes. As a result, you can directly assign a string value to a variable that is declared as a Byte array and vice versa.*

The other set of rules that must be followed when passing values to or receiving values from API procedures is that of data types, which are discussed in the next section.

UNDERSTANDING C PARAMETERS

Most APIs were written by C programmers, so most APIs are written for the C language. Consequently, there are many APIs that are completely unusable by VBA because VBA does not support some of the data types required by those APIs. Of those APIs that are accessible to VBA, most require consideration with regard to the data types used. Use a wrong data type and your computer will quickly let you know all about it.

The following sections describe the C data types often specified for API parameters, the VBA data types that should be used with them, the recommended calling conventions, and, where applicable, the technique that converts signed integer values from unsigned integer values and vice versa.

Signed and Unsigned Integers

First, the C language uses something that is largely unknown to VBA: *unsigned numbers.* VBA mostly uses *signed numbers.* An unsigned number is a positive number; that is, it does not have a sign. A signed number can be either positive or negative because of the sign. VBA does actually support one unsigned data type: Byte. For example, Figure 9-1 shows an 8-bit byte. Having a binary 1 in the most significant bit (the eighth bit) signifies that the number contained within the byte is a negative number. A 0 in the same position indicates that the number is positive.

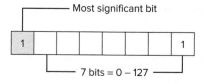

FIGURE 9-1

Sometimes you'll run across numeric parameters that require an unsigned value. The general algorithm for supplying that value is to convert the value to its next highest data type, subtract the maximum value that the data type can carry, and then convert it back to the original data type.

The following table shows how to convert values from unsigned to signed, and vice versa, for the bit widths of values supported by VBA.

TYPE	CONVERT UNSIGNED TO SIGNED	CONVERT SIGNED TO UNSIGNED
8-bit	signed = CByte(unsigned - 255)	unsigned = (CInt(signed) And 255)
16-bit	signed = CInt(unsigned - 65535)	unsigned = (CLng(signed) And 65535)
32-bit	signed = CLng(unsigned - 1.79769313486232E308)	unsigned = (CDbl(signed) And 1.79769313486232E308)

Numeric Parameters

As with VBA, there are many types of numeric data you might come across when working with APIs. The following table outlines the numeric types defined in C/C++ along with their VBA equivalents. Also included are the data type prefixes often found in Windows API declarations on MSDN.

SIZE (BITS)	DATA TYPE	PREFIX	DESCRIPTION	VBA EQUIVALENT
8	char	ch	8-bit signed integer	Byte
8	byte, uchar	ch	8-bit unsigned integer	Byte
8	TCHAR	ch	8-bit or 16-bit signed (depending on whether you're using ANSI or Unicode)	Byte or Integer
16	Short	c	16-bit signed integer	Integer
16	unsigned short, WORD	w	16-bit unsigned integer	Integer
16	TCHAR	ch	8-bit or 16-bit signed (depending on whether you're using ANSI or Unicode)	Byte or Integer
32	int	n	32-bit signed integer	Long
32	long	l	32-bit signed integer	Long
32	unsigned int, UINT	n	32-bit unsigned integer	Long
32	unsigned long, DWORD	dw	32-bit unsigned integer (also referred to as a double-word)	Long
64	INT64, LONG64	qw	64-bit signed integer	LongLong
64	DWORD64, UINT64, ULONG64	qw	64-bit unsigned integer	LongLong

Let's take a closer look at these types of parameters.

8-Bit Numeric Parameters

The 8-bit (1-byte) parameter types are char, uchar, BYTE, and (if using the ANSI character set) 8-bit TCHAR. Although it is unlikely that you will run across them under Win32, they should be explained just in case.

Signed 8-bit values range between –128 and 127, whereas unsigned values range between 0 and 255. VBA supports only unsigned Byte values, regardless of size.

If you do ever have to use unsigned 8-bit parameters, the VBA Byte data type works just fine. Supplying 8-bit signed values is not as straightforward and requires a small algorithm (explained in the preceding section) to produce the required value.

16-Bit Numeric Parameters

The 16-bit (2-byte) numeric parameter types are short, unsigned short, WORD, and, if using the Unicode character set, 16-bit TCHAR. Beginning with 32-bit versions of Windows, you won't likely run into these parameters often, but they are worth explaining. The VBA Integer data type can be used to supply values for the signed parameters (short and 16-bit TCHAR) because VBA Integer values range from –32,768 to 32,767.

To supply unsigned values to unsigned short and WORD parameters, you must first convert the value to something that the API will recognize as an unsigned value. (Refer to the conversion formula shown earlier in the section "Signed and Unsigned Integers.")

32-Bit Numeric Parameters

The five 32-bit (4-byte) numeric parameters are int, unsigned int, long, unsigned long, and DWORD.

The range for the Long Integer data type in VBA is between –2,147,483,648 and 2,147,483,647 and is equivalent to the signed C Integer types (int and long). As such, it can be used anywhere they appear. The unsigned type must be converted; see the conversion formula in the section "Signed and Unsigned Integers."

64-Bit Numeric Parameters

The five 64-bit (8-byte) numeric parameters are int64, DWORD64, LONG64, unsigned int64, and unsigned long64.

To accommodate theses larger data types, VBA in Office 2010 introduces a new data type: LongLong. The LongLong data type is only available in 64-bit versions of Office. This data type does not compile on 32-bit versions of Office.

The range for the LongLong data type in VBA is between –9,223,372,036,854,775,808 and 9,223,372,036,854,775,807 and is equivalent to signed C integer types INT64 or LONG64. This data type can be used anywhere they appear.

Currency Parameters

The Win32 API does not use a Currency data type. You should generally not use this data type when using API functions.

Floating-Point Parameters

A few APIs use the Single (float in C/C++) or Double data types.

Single values are 32 bits (4 bytes) wide and range between –3.402823E38 and –1.401298E–45 for negative values, and from 1.401298E–45 to 3.402823E38 for positive values. Double values are 64 bits (8 bytes) wide, and range from –1.79769313486231E308 to –4.94065645841247E–324 for negative values and from 4.94065645841247E–324 to 1.79769313486232E308 for positive values.

If you are supplying values to DLLs that use floating-point parameters, you must ensure that those functions are compatible with VBA because not all are.

Boolean Parameters

The VBA Long Integer data type can be used to supply a value for the BOOL parameter type. However, both C++ and VBA define the Boolean False as 0. By default, that means all nonzero values must not be false, and are thereby true.

The C++ language defines a Boolean True to be 1, whereas VBA defines True as -1.

Supplying a VBA True value can sometimes lead to problems when using some API functions because of the way in which Boolean values are interpreted in the C++ language — some APIs return any nonzero value as True.

The C++ language includes both logical and bitwise operations. A logical operation is a standard Boolean operation that you're familiar with, such as AND, OR, and NOT. A bitwise operation is performed on the individual bits in a number. C++'s bitwise not operation is distinguished by a tilde preceding the number or variable (~myvar). The logical not operator is distinguished by an exclamation mark (!myvar).

If you perform a logical NOT operation on the True value (~1) in C++, you get 0. If you do the same thing for the VBA True (~-1), you get 0. No problem, as long as both values are nonzero. Because VBA doesn't have a logical Not operator, performing a NOT against both values returns -2 and 0, respectively.

To get around that problem, specify Abs(booMyVar) when supplying a Boolean parameter, and Not (booMyVar = False) when checking a return value.

The C/C++ BOOL data type is a 32-bit Boolean value; 0 is false and 1 is true (although any nonzero VBA value equates to true). Prefixes are b and f — you'll see both used in C/C++.

Handle Parameters

On 32-bit Windows, a handle is a 32-bit (4-byte) number that identifies the memory location where the definition of a Windows object, such as a window, can be found. On 64-bit Windows, a handle is a 64-bit (8-byte) number. Handles come in different flavors, including HANDLE, HWND, and hDC. More specifically, HWND refers to a handle to a window, and hDC refers to a handle to a device context.

For example, the hwnd of the Access application is a window handle that can be discovered using VBA code. The following table illustrates how to find the hwnd for familiar Access objects.

FOR ACCESS OBJECT	DO THIS
Application	`Application.hWndAccessApp`
Form	`Me.Hwnd`

User control on a form	`Private Declare Function GetFocus Lib "user32" () As Long`
	
	`Function GetCtrlhWnd(ctrl As Control) As Long`
	  `'Set the focus to the control`
	  `ctrl.SetFocus`
	
	  `'Get the hwnd from the API`
	  `GetCtrlhWnd = GetFocus`
	`End Function`

With the introduction of the 64-bit version of Office, a data type that scales between 4 and 8 bytes depending on the platform begins to present some challenges. In the past, you would use the Long data type in VBA to represent a handle. Because you can no longer guarantee that a handle is 4 bytes, this is not reliable and will lead to unintended behavior — often a crash.

To address this, VBA introduced another new data type called `LongPtr`. The `LongPtr` data type should be used as arguments to API functions that expect or return pointers or handles. Since members of user-defined types can also contain pointers or handles, you should consider the use of the `LongPtr` data type when writing Type statements for 64-bit Windows.

 VB and VBA do a fair amount of implicit type coercion on your behalf. This means that for the `Variant` *data type, VB will actually coerce the type into the appropriate type at runtime. The same thing occurs for the scalable* `IntPtr` *data type in VB.NET or C#. Using the Watch or Locals windows, a variable defined as* `LongPtr` *will be coerced to a* `Long` *in the 32-bit version of Office 2010 and coerced to a* `LongLong` *in the 64-bit version.*

Object Parameters

As far as the Windows API is concerned, the `Object` data type has no meaning. However, the OLE 2.0 API set does support parameters of this type, namely, `LPUNKNOWN` and `LPDISPATCH`, which are pointers to COM interfaces.

Therefore, if you ever have to specify an `Object` pointer, use the VBA `Object` data type. The following table describes these data types.

DATA TYPE	PREFIX	DESCRIPTION	VBA EQUIVALENT
`LPUNKNOWN`	`lp`	Pointer to an IUnknown OLE 2.0 interface	`Object`
`LPDISPATCH`	`lp`	Pointer to an IDispatch OLE 2.0 interface	`Object`

String Parameters

There are several different data types used to represent strings in C/C++. One of the most common is the LPWSTR data type, which is a pointer to the memory location where the string begins. Most DLLs require null-terminated strings, which VBA can pass ByVal. Some C-language DLLs might return LPSTR pointers that can be copied to VBA strings using API functions. Only those APIs that were specifically written for VB (like APIGID32.dll) actually accept or return VBA strings.

A null-terminated string is one that ends in an ASCII Null character. To form such a string, append an ASCII zero or use the vbNullChar constant. These two lines of code are equivalent:

```
param = `abc" & Chr$(0)
param = `abc" & vbNullChar
```

A null string, on the other hand, is an empty string, which is formed using a pair of quotes or the vbNullString constant. The following lines of code are equivalent:

```
param = `"
param = vbNullString
```

The following table shows some of the more common string data types used by APIs.

DATA TYPE	PREFIX	DESCRIPTION
LPWSTR	Lpsz	Long pointer to a C null-terminated wide string. A wide string is typically a double-byte character.
LPSTR	Lpsz	Long pointer to a C null-terminated string.
LPCSTR	Lpsz	Long pointer to a constant C null-terminated string.
LPTSTR	Lpsz	Long pointer to a C null-terminated string.
LPCWSTR	Lpsz	Long pointer to a constant C null-terminated wide string.

Variant Parameters

The VBA Variant data type is not supported under the core Windows API. The only APIs that use it are those of the OLE 2.0 specification, in which case the VBA Variant data type can be used without conversion.

Pointers to Numeric Values

Pointers are used frequently in the C language. A pointer is simply a memory address that points to a piece of data. Pointers to numeric values, such as LPINT and LPSHORT, can be passed by VBA simply by using the ByRef keyword (or just by omitting the ByVal keyword).

You must ensure, however, that the data type you pass matches what is required. For example, if a 32-bit data type is required, pass a Long Integer, not an Integer (16-bit). If you pass an Integer when a Long Integer is required, the DLL will write not only into the 16 bits of the Integer, but also into the next 16 bits, which can cause all sorts of problems, from erroneous data to a system crash.

The following table shows some of the common pointers to numeric data.

DATA TYPE	PREFIX	DESCRIPTION
LPSHORT	Lps	16-bit (short) pointer to a 16-bit signed integer
LPINT	Lpi	32-bit (long) pointer to a 32-bit signed integer
LPUSHORT	Lpu	16-bit (short) pointer to a 16-bit unsigned integer
LPUINT	Lpu	32-bit (long) pointer to a 32-bit unsigned integer

Pointers to C Structures

A structure in the C language is essentially the same as a user-defined type (UDT) in VBA, which was described in Chapter 6. When you pass a UDT as a parameter to an API function, it must be passed ByRef — they cannot be passed ByVal. When you declare the UDT itself, you must also ensure that all the members of the UDT consist of data types that are compatible with the API, as described in this chapter.

For example, the following is the RECT structure as defined in C. This structure is frequently used by API functions to refer to a rectangle on the screen.

```
typedef struct _RECT {
  LONG left;
  LONG top;
  LONG right;
  LONG bottom;
} RECT, *PRECT;
```

And here's the VBA equivalent:

```
Public Type RECT
    Left As Long
    Top As Long
    Right As Long
    Bottom As Long
End Type
```

Pointers to Arrays

Passing arrays to APIs not specifically written for VBA is accomplished by ByRef because those APIs expect a pointer to the first element in the array. Such APIs also often expect a parameter that indicates the number of elements in the array.

There are three issues you should be aware of when passing arrays:

➤ You cannot pass entire string arrays. You can only pass a single array element.

➤ To pass an entire array, specify the first array element in the call as follows: myArray(0)

➤ When denoting the number of elements in an array, you must specify `UBound(strMyArray)+1` because `UBound` returns only the maximum numeric bound of the array, not the actual count of its elements. Remember also that specifying `Option Base 1` will affect the number returned by `UBound`. You can, of course, specify a number; just make sure it reflects the actual number of array elements.

C-style APIs don't care much about whether you're telling the truth about the number of elements in the array. If you tell it you have ten elements when you have only five, C happily writes to the space required for ten, regardless of whether they actually exist. Naturally this is going to have interesting side effects, which you may not be too happy about.

You can also pass array elements either singly or as a subset of the array. For example, if you have an array that contains a number of `xy` coordinates, you can get the `hwnd` of the window within which a specific `xy` coordinate exists by calling the `WindowFromPoint` API like this:

```
Myhwnd = WindowFromPoint(lngPtArray(2), lngPtArray(3))
```

Arrays that were written specifically with VBA in mind (and they are rare) expect an OLE 2.0 `SAFEARRAY` structure, including a pointer that is itself a pointer to the array. Therefore, you simply pass the VBA array. That makes sense if you consider a string variable as a single-element array.

Pointers to Functions

The C/C++ languages also allow developers to pass a pointer to a function, which allows for more dynamic programming. For Windows API functions, you may see types defined as `FARPROC` and `DLGPROC`, which are examples of pointers to functions. These pointers are supplied so the API can execute a function as part of its own functionality. Such functions are referred to as *callback functions*.

You specify the memory address of a callback function using the VBA `AddressOf` operator, which has certain limitations:

➤ It can only be specified in a standard module — you can't use it in a class module.

➤ It must precede an argument in an argument list, and the argument it precedes must be the name of a procedure (sub, function, or property).

The procedure whose location it returns must exist in the same project, so it can't be used with external functions declared with the `Declare` keyword, or with functions referenced from type libraries.

You can pass a function pointer to an `As Any` parameter (discussed later in this chapter) and also create your own callback functions in DLLs compiled in Visual Basic or C++. To work with `AddressOf`, these functions must use the `_stdcall` calling convention when working with C or C++.

`FARPROC` and `DLGPROC` are 32-bit (far) pointers to functions or procedures in VBA. Their prefix is often `lpfn`, which reads as "long pointer to a function."

 Because the `AddressOf` operator returns a function pointer, it also scales between 4 and 8 bytes on 32-bit and 64-bit versions of Office 2010, respectively.

Pointers in 64-Bit Windows

As mentioned earlier in the chapter, pointers on 32-bit Windows are 4 bytes, and are 8 bytes on 64-bit Windows. If you're running the 64-bit version of Office 2010, you may need to account for this fact when working with API functions. It is also possible to run the 32-bit version of Office on 64-bit Windows, in which case pointers are 32-bits, or 4 bytes.

Versions of Office beginning with Office 2000 included VBA6 as the version of VBA. The version of VBA included with Office 2010 is now called VBA7.

Defining Type Statements

Function parameters are not the only aspect of API programming in VBA that may need updating for 64-bit. Members of user-defined types may also contain pointers or handles and as a result, are also potentially affected by the change.

User-defined types often include a member that defines the size of the structure. These sizes will increase as a result of the move toward 64-bit platforms, however the increase in size may not necessarily add up to what you expect. For example, let's consider the SHELLEXECUTEINFO structure in Windows which is used with the ShellExecuteEx common dialog function. The following code is the type definition for 32-bit versions of VBA:

```
Public Type SHELLEXECUTEINFO
    cbSize        As Long
    fMask         As Long
    Hwnd          As Long
    lpVerb        As String
    lpFile        As String
    lpParameters  As String
    lpDirectory   As String
    nShow         As Long
    hInstApp      As Long
    lpIDList      As Long
    lpClass       As String
    hkeyClass     As Long
    dwHotKey      As Long
    hIcon         As Long
    hProcess      As Long
End Type
```

Internally, the String data type is a pointer to a string. The size of the type is 4 bytes. As a result, the size of the structure in 32-bit VBA is 60 (15 members @ 4 bytes each). When you convert this structure to 64-bit VBA, it should look something like the following:

```
Public Type SHELLEXECUTEINFO
    cbSize        As Long
    fMask         As Long
    Hwnd          As LongPtr
    lpVerb        As String
    lpFile        As String
```

```
        lpParameters  As  String
        lpDirectory   As  String
        nShow         As  Long
        hInstApp      As  LongPtr
        lpIDList      As  LongPtr
        lpClass       As  String
        hkeyClass     As  LongPtr
        dwHotKey      As  Long
        hIcon         As  LongPtr
        hProcess      As  LongPtr
    End Type
```

Here, the members in the structure that are handles have been changed to use the new `LongPtr` data type, which, as we've seen, is 8-bytes on 64-bit Windows. Since strings are also pointers internally, it would appear that the size of the user-defined type is now 104. However, that is incorrect. The reason for this is due to *padding*. On 64-bit Windows, variables are aligned on 8-byte boundaries. This means that all variables in memory will start at an offset that is divisible by 8. The first two members of the type, `cbSize` and `fMask`, are both a `Long`, and are 4-bytes each. Since these add up to 8 bytes, there are no problems. Now look at the `nShow` member. This is also a `Long` integer, but it is followed by a `LongPtr`. Since the 4-byte member is followed by an 8-byte member, Windows adds 4-bytes of padding in memory after the `nShow` member. This also happens with the `dwHotKey` member. The correct size of the structure is actually 112, not 104.

We typically use the `Len` function in VBA to determine the size of a user-defined type, however in this case, the `Len` function returns 104, not 112. This is because `Len` does not take padding into account when it calculates the size. The correct way to determine the size of a type when writing for 64-bit Windows is to use the `LenB` function in VBA. This function will calculate the size needed in bytes for all members, and will include the padding.

 Use the LenB *function in VBA when you need to determine the size of a user-defined Type for a Windows API function in the 64-bit version of Office 2010.*

Portability of Code between Platforms

It's fairly common to want to run an Access database in multiple versions of Access. For example, you and a few others may have already upgraded to Access 2010, while others you work with or develop databases for are still running Access 2007.

There are some considerations to keep in mind when it comes to API functions if you find yourself in this scenario. The first is that the `PtrSafe` keyword that you used to get the function to compile is not available in previous versions of VBA. The second consideration is that the `LongPtr` data type is not available in previous versions as well. To accommodate this issue and have code work across platforms and versions, you will need to use *conditional compilation.*

Conditional Compilation

As the name suggests, conditional compilation is used to conditionally compile certain blocks of code. If you're familiar with C, C++, or C#, you may already be familiar with this concept through the use of the `#if` directive. VBA has the same functionality. To use conditional compilation in VBA, you use the `#If...#ElseIf...#Else...#End If` construct. If the expression in the `#If` block evaluates to `True`, the code in the block will be compiled; otherwise it will not.

Built-in Conditional Compilation Constants

In order to know how to compile the code, you must know two things: the platform you are running on and the version of VBA. Fortunately, both of these are available to you using built-in conditional compilation constants. To determine the platform, you use the `Win64` or `Win32` constants. To determine the version of VBA, you use the `VBA6` or `VBA7` constants. The following code demonstrates the pattern you should use:

```
#If Win64 = 1 And VBA7 = 1 Then
    ' This block of code compiles for 64-bit Office 2010
#Else If Win32=1 Then
    ' This block of code compiles for any version of 32-bit Office
#End If
```

On 64-bit versions of Office, both `Win32` and `Win64` constants evaluate to `1`. On 32-bit versions of Office, the `Win32` constant will evaluate to `1`, but the `Win64` constant will evaluate to `0`. As a result, you should check the `Win64` constant first to determine if you are running 64-bit. The same is true for the `VBA6` constant. This constant returns `1` even on Office 2010.

Compilation of API Functions

Now that you know how to use the conditional compilation constants, let's take a look at the `LoadImage` and `SendMessage` APIs that you used earlier. More specifically, let's see how you could write these so they will run in Access 2010, as well as in Access 2007 or earlier.

Here are their respective declarations in C according to MSDN:

```
HANDLE LoadImage(HINSTANCE hinst,
    LPCTSTR lpszName,
    UINT uType,
    int cxDesired,
    int cyDesired,
    UINT fuLoad
);

LRESULT SendMessage(HWND hWnd,
    UINT Msg,
    WPARAM wParam,
    LPARAM lParam
);
```

There are a few arguments here that will present issues for portability. For `LoadImage`, the `HINSTANCE` parameter is a "handle to an instance." Because it's a handle, it has the same issue as pointers between the two platforms where a handle is 4-bytes on 32-bit versions of Windows and 8-bytes on 64-bit versions of Windows. The `LoadImage` function also returns a `HANDLE`. The `SendMessage` function accepts an `HWND`, which is a "handle to a window."

Given these issues, the following code provides an example of how to write these for portability between versions and platforms:

```
#If Win64 = 1 And VBA7 = 1 Then

    Public Declare PtrSafe Function LoadImage Lib `user32" Alias `LoadImageA" _
        (ByVal hInst As LongPtr, ByVal lpsz As String, _
        ByVal un1 As Long, ByVal n1 As Long, _
        ByVal n2 As Long, ByVal un2 As Long) As LongPtr

    Public Declare PtrSafe Function SendMessage Lib `user32" Alias `SendMessageA" _
        (ByVal hWnd As LongPtr, ByVal wMsg As Long, _
        ByVal wParam As LongPtr, LParam As Any) As Long

#ElseIf VBA6 = 1 Then

    Public Declare Function LoadImage Lib `user32" Alias `LoadImageA" _
        (ByVal hInst As Long, ByVal lpsz As String, _
        ByVal un1 As Long, ByVal n1 As Long, _
        ByVal n2 As Long, ByVal un2 As Long) As Long

    Public Declare Function SendMessage Lib `user32" Alias `SendMessageA" _
        (ByVal hWnd As Long, ByVal wMsg As Long, _
        ByVal wParam As Long, LParam As Any) As Long

#End If
```

code snippet APISamples.accdb

Though not used here, the code that compiles when the condition VBA6=1 is true will also be true for the condition Win32=1 on both 32-bit and 64-bit versions of Windows.

The Any Data Type

Some DLL function parameters can accept different data types. Such parameters are declared using the As Any data type. Calling a DLL function with parameters declared As Any is inherently dangerous because VBA doesn't perform any type checking on it. That is, VBA doesn't check that the data type you supply matches that which is required by the function. Therefore, you need to be absolutely certain that the data type you are supplying to the function is correct.

To avoid the hazards of passing such arguments, declare several versions of the same DLL function, giving each a unique name and a different parameter data type. You can give each version the same Alias to point to the same function in the DLL.

ERR.LASTDLLERROR

Like the VBA procedures you write, API procedures can also generate errors. These can be the result of bad or missing data, invalid data type assignments, or a variety of other conditions or failures. This section describes how to trap and retrieve API-generated errors so you can take remedial or other action to shield the user from their adverse effects.

LastDLLError is a property of the VBA Err object. It returns the error code produced by a call to a DLL, and always contains zero on systems that don't have DLLs.

DLL functions usually return a code that indicates whether the call succeeded or failed. Your VBA code should check the value returned after a DLL function is called and, on detecting a failure code, should immediately check the LastDLLError property and take whatever action you deem necessary. The DLL's documentation will indicate which codes to check for.

Because no exception is raised when the LastDLLError property is set, you cannot use the On Error Goto construct, so use On Error Resume Next.

The Err object's Description property will be empty because the error is DLL-specific. However, for many error messages you can use the FormatMessage API to get the error message returned by a DLL. Add this code to the module containing the SetFormIcon procedure:

Available for download on Wrox.com

```
Private Const FORMAT_MESSAGE_FROM_SYSTEM = &H1000

Private Declare Function FormatMessage Lib "kernel32" Alias _
    "FormatMessageA" (ByVal dwFlags As Long, lpSource As Long, _
    ByVal dwMessageId As Long, ByVal dwLanguageId As Long, _
    ByVal lpBuffer As String, ByVal nSize As Long, Arguments As Any) _
    As Long

Public Function GetAPIErrorMessage(lngError As Long) As String
    Dim strMessage As String
    Dim lngReturn  As Long
    Dim nSize      As Long

    strMessage = Space(256)
    nSize = Len(strMessage)
    lngReturn = FormatMessage(FORMAT_MESSAGE_FROM_SYSTEM, 0, _
        lngError, 0, strMessage, nSize, 0)

    If lngReturn > 0 Then
        GetAPIErrorMessage = Replace(Left(strMessage, lngReturn), vbCrLf, "")
    Else
        GetAPIErrorMessage = "Error not found."
    End If
End Function
```

code snippet APISamples.accdb

Next, modify the SetFormIcon procedure to generate a DLL error by passing an empty string as the icon path (this shows the LastDLLError property in action):

Available for download on Wrox.com

```
Public Sub SetFormIcon(hWnd As Long, strIcon As String)
Dim hIcon As Long
Dim lngReturn As Long

On Error Resume Next

'Pass an empty string as the icon path
hIcon = LoadImage(0&, "", IMAGE_ICON, IMG_DEFAULT_WIDTH, _
IMG_DEFAULT_HEIGHT, LR_LOADFROMFILE)

'Now check for an error
```

```
If hIcon <> 0 Then
lngReturn = SendMessage(hWnd, WM_SETICON, ICON_SMALL, ByVal hIcon)

Else
`Display the error
MsgBox `The last DLL error was: ` & GetAPIErrorMessage(Err.LastDllError)

End If
End Sub
```

code snippet APISamples.accdb

The `FormatMessage` API will not return error messages defined by applications.

DISTRIBUTING APPLICATIONS THAT REFERENCE TYPE LIBRARIES AND CUSTOM DLLS

It is a bit trickier to deploy applications if they contain references to some type libraries and DLLs. You can't always just drop a database file onto a disk and expect it to work because the target system may not already contain the required type libraries and DLLs.

To ensure that the database functions correctly on every platform, you may have to include additional libraries or DLLs in an installation package you create using the Package and Deployment Wizard that comes with the Access Developer Extensions (ADE).

The Package and Deployment Wizard scans the application for external references and includes the referenced files in the setup package it creates. When run on the target system, the setup program copies all the required files onto the hard disk, and usually registers the type libraries and DLLs. For more information about the ADE, refer to Chapter 23.

USEFUL API FUNCTIONS

Apart from the `SetFormIcon` function described earlier, this section shows how to use some useful API functions. The `PtrSafe` keyword has been included here to compile for Office 2010.

Returning the Path to the Windows Folder

To find the Windows folder (the one that contains most of the Windows application and initialization files), use the following code:

Available for download on Wrox.com

```
'Declare the function
Private Declare PtrSafe Function GetWindowsDirectory _
Lib `kernel32" Alias "GetWindowsDirectoryA" ( _
ByVal lpBuffer As String, _
ByVal nSize As Long) As Long

Private Const MAXLEN = 255

Public Function WindowsDir() As String
```

```
        Dim strDirectory As String
        Dim lngSize As Long
        Dim lngReturn As Long

        `Pre-initialize the string
        strDirectory = Space(MAXLEN) & Chr(0)
        `Initialize the string length
        lngSize = MAXLEN + 1

        `Retrieve the length of the string returned by the function
        lngReturn = GetWindowsDirectory(strDirectory, lngSize)

        If lngReturn <> 0 Then
            `Return the string containing the Windows directory,
            `using lngReturn to specify how long the string is.
            WindowsDir = left(strDirectory, lngReturn)
        Else
            WindowsDir = `"
        End If
    End Function
```

code snippet APISamples.accdb

Determining Whether the System Processor Is 32-Bit or 64-Bit

Now that you're starting to see some of the changes as Office moves toward the new platform, you may be wondering how to determine whether the processor in the computer is a 32-bit or the 64-bit processor. Fortunately, there is an API to do this called GetSystemInfo. The GetSystemInfo function is used to determine information about the processor in a system, including its architecture.

Here is the declaration:

Available for download on Wrox.com

```
Type SYSTEM_INFO
    wProcessorArchitecture As Integer
    wReserved As Integer
    dwPageSize As Long
    lpMinimumApplicationAddress As Long
    lpMaximumApplicationAddress As Long
    dwActiveProcessorMask As Long
    dwNumberOrfProcessors As Long
    dwProcessorType As Long
    dwAllocationGranularity As Long
    wProcessorLevel As Integer
    wProcessorRevision As Integer
End Type

Declare PtrSafe Sub GetNativeSystemInfo Lib "kernel32" (lpSystemInfo As SYSTEM_INFO)
```

code snippet APISamples.accdb

Given the declaration, here's how to determine the processor architecture:

```
Public Function Is64BitProcessor() As Boolean
    Const PROCESSOR_ARCHITECTURE_AMD64 As Integer = 9
    Const PROCESSOR_ARCHITECTURE_IA64  As Integer = 6

    Dim si As SYSTEM_INFO

    ' call the API
    GetNativeSystemInfo si

    ' check the struct
    Is64BitProcessor = (si.wProcessorArchitecture = PROCESSOR_ARCHITECTURE_AMD64 _
                        Or _
                        si.wProcessorArchitecture = PROCESSOR_ARCHITECTURE_IA64)
End Function
```

code snippet APISamples.accdb

Determining Whether Windows Is 32-Bit or 64-Bit

Determining whether Windows itself is running 32-bit or 64-bit can be accomplished by checking for the ProgramW6432 environment variable, as shown here:

```
Public Function IsWin64() As Boolean
    IsWin64 = (Len(Environ$("ProgramW6432")) > 0)
End Function
```

code snippet APISamples.accdb

Determining Whether Office Is 32-Bit or 64-Bit

In addition to knowing whether Windows is running on a 32-bit or 64-bit processor, it may be useful to know if the running version of Office is the 32-bit or 64-bit version. It is also possible to run 32-bit Office 2010 on 64-bit Windows. This is known as Windows 32 on Windows 64, or WOW64.

To determine this, you'll need to know two things — first, whether or not the process is a WOW64 process, and second, whether Windows itself is running 64-bit. To determine whether the running process is running under WOW64, you'll use the IsWow64Process API function as shown here:

```
Declare PtrSafe Function IsWow64Process Lib "kernel32" (ByVal hProcess As LongPtr, _
    ByRef Wow64Process As Long) As Long
```

code snippet APISamples.accdb

This function expects the handle to a process, which you can obtain using the `GetCurrentProcess` API:

```
Declare PtrSafe Function GetCurrentProcess Lib "kernel32" () As Long
```

code snippet APISamples.accdb

Then, using the `IsWin64` function you wrote earlier to determine whether the computer is running a 64-bit version of Windows, you can use the following code to determine whether the current process is a 64-bit process:

```
Public Function Is64BitProcess() As Boolean
    Dim pIsWow64 As Long
    Dim rc       As Long

    ' determine if the process is running in WOW64
    rc = IsWow64Process(GetCurrentProcess(), pIsWow64)

    ' this will return False for 64-bit processes, so let's determine if
    ' Windows is 64-bit
    Is64BitProcess = (pIsWow64 = 0 And IsWin64())
End Function
```

code snippet APISamples.accdb

Displaying the Windows Open Dialog Box

One of the more commonly used API functions in Access applications is the `GetOpenFileName` function. This function is used to display an open file dialog box to retrieve a filename. The function accepts a user-defined type as a parameter, which contains several pointers and handles. As such, let's look at the type definition for both 32-bit and 64-bit. The type is wrapped in a conditional compilation block for portability.

```
#If Win64 = 1 Then
Type OPENFILENAME
    lStructSize As Long
    hwndOwner As LongPtr
    hInstance As LongPtr
    lpstrFilter As String
    lpstrCustomFilter As String
    nMaxCustFilter As Long
    nFilterIndex As Long
    lpstrFile As String
    nMaxFile As Long
    lpstrFileTitle As String
    nMaxFileTitle As Long
```

```
        lpstrInitialDir As String
        lpstrTitle As String
        flags As Long
        nFileOffset As Integer
        nFileExtension As Integer
        lpstrDefExt As String
        lCustData As LongPtr
        lpfnHook As LongPtr
        lpTemplateName As String

    End Type
#Else
Type OPENFILENAME
        lStructSize As Long
        hwndOwner As Long
        hInstance As Long
        lpstrFilter As String
        lpstrCustomFilter As String
        nMaxCustFilter As Long
        nFilterIndex As Long
        lpstrFile As String
        nMaxFile As Long
        lpstrFileTitle As String
        nMaxFileTitle As Long
        lpstrInitialDir As String
        lpstrTitle As String
        flags As Long
        nFileOffset As Integer
        nFileExtension As Integer
        lpstrDefExt As String
        lCustData As Long
        lpfnHook As Long
        lpTemplateName As String
    End Type
#End If
```

code snippet APISamples.accdb

Now that the UDT has been defined, let's take a look at the function declaration. It, too, is wrapped in a conditional compilation block for portability. The only difference here is the presence of the `PtrSafe` keyword.

```
#If Win64 = 1 And VBA7 = 1 Then

Declare PtrSafe Function GetOpenFileName Lib "comdlg32.dll" Alias _
    "GetOpenFileNameA" (pOpenfilename As OPENFILENAME) As Long

#Else

Declare Function GetOpenFileName Lib "comdlg32.dll" Alias "GetOpenFileNameA" _
    (pOpenfilename As OPENFILENAME) As Long

#End If
```

code snippet APISamples.accdb

Here's how to use it to return a filename from the user:

```
Public Function GetFileName() As String
    Dim ofn As OPENFILENAME
    Dim rc  As Long

    ' set parameters
    ofn.lStructSize = LenB(ofn)
    ofn.lpstrFile = String(260, 0)
    ofn.nMaxFile = LenB(ofn.lpstrFile) - 1
    ofn.hwndOwner = Application.hWndAccessApp()
    ofn.lpstrTitle = "Select a file to open"

    ' call the function
    rc = GetOpenFileName(ofn)

    ' if the return code is > 0,
    If (rc > 0) Then
        GetFileName = left(ofn.lpstrFile, InStr(ofn.lpstrFile, vbNullChar) - 1)
    End If
End Function
```

code snippet APISamples.accdb

Finding the Position of a Form

The `Form` object in Access includes four properties that would appear to give an indication as to the location of a form onscreen: `WindowHeight`, `WindowLeft`, `WindowTop`, and `WindowWidth`. These properties actually return values based on the client workspace within the Access application window. Because these values can change based on the location of the Access window itself, there is no built-in mechanism to expose the current `xy` position of a form. The following example demonstrates how to use the `GetWindowRect` API to return the form's screen position in pixels.

Create a small form containing a single command button, and add the following code:

```
Option Compare Database
Option Explicit

Private Type RECT
    left As Long
    top As Long
    right As Long
    bottom As Long
End Type

Private Declare PtrSafe Function GetWindowRect Lib `user32` _
(ByVal hwnd As Long, lpRect As RECT) As Long

Private Sub cmdShow_Click()
    Dim FormDims As RECT

    If GetWindowRect(Me.hwnd, FormDims) Then
        MsgBox `The form is located at:" & _
```

```
                    vbCrLf & `Left: ` & vbTab & FormDims.left & _
                    vbCrLf & `Top: ` & vbTab & FormDims.top & _
                    vbCrLf & `Right: ` & vbTab & FormDims.right & _
                    vbCrLf & `Bottom: ` & vbTab & FormDims.bottom
        End If
    End Sub
```

code snippet APISamples.accdb

Now open the form and click the button. A message box displays the form's location. You could use this information to store the last location of a form based on where the user moved it onscreen.

Finding the Temp Directory

The Temp directory (typically C:\Windows\Temp) is the place where Windows stores temporary files. The GetTempPath function returns the path of the Temp directory on the computer. You can also use the Environ function in VBA to read the TEMP environment variable to return the Temp directory.

Available for download on Wrox.com

```
Private Declare PtrSafe Function GetTempPath _
    Lib `kernel32` Alias `GetTempPathA` ( _
    ByVal nBufferLength As Long, _
    ByVal lpBuffer As String) As Long

Private Const MAXLEN = 255

Public Function TempPath() As String
    Dim strPath As String
    Dim lngSize As Long
    Dim lngReturn As Long

    strPath = Space(MAXLEN) & Chr(0)
    lngSize = MAXLEN + 1

    lngReturn = GetTempPath(lngSize, strPath)
    If lngReturn <> 0 Then
        TempPath = left(strPath, lngReturn)
    Else
        TempPath = `"
    End If
End Function
```

code snippet APISamples.accdb

Generating a Unique Temp Filename

The GetTempFileName function generates a unique temporary filename with a .tmp extension:

Available for download on Wrox.com

```
Private Declare PtrSafe Function GetTempFileName _
    Lib `kernel32` Alias `GetTempFileNameA` ( _
    ByVal lpPathName As String, _
```

```
        ByVal lpPrefixString As String, _
        ByVal uUnique As Long, _
        ByVal lpTempFileName As String) As Long

Private Const MAXLEN = 255

Public Function GetTemporaryFile( _
  Optional strDirectory As String, _
  Optional strPrefix As String) As String

    Dim strPath As String
    Dim lngReturn As Long

    strPath = Space(255)

    ` Default to the folder where the database resides
    If Len(strDirectory) = 0 Then
        strDirectory = CurrentProject.Path
    End If

    lngReturn = GetTempFileName(strDirectory, strPrefix, 0, strPath)
    If lngReturn <> 0 Then
        GetTemporaryFile = Left(strPath, InStr(strPath, Chr(0)) - 1)
    Else
        GetTemporaryFile = ``"
    End If
End Function
```

code snippet APISamples.accdb

Finding the Login Name of the Current User

The `GetUserName` function returns the name of the user currently logged on to the computer. It returns only the login name for the user — it does not return the name of the domain.

```
Private Declare PtrSafe Function GetUserName _
    Lib `advapi32.dll" Alias `GetUserNameA" _
    (ByVal lpBuffer As String, _
    nSize As Long) As Long

Private Const MAXLEN = 255

Function GetLoginName() As String
    Dim strUserName As String
    Dim lngSize As Long

    strUserName = Space(MAXLEN) & Chr(0)
    lngSize = MAXLEN + 1

    If GetUserName(strUserName, lngSize) <> 0 Then
        GetLoginName = Left(strUserName, lngSize -1)
    Else
```

```
            GetLoginName = ""
        End If
End Function
```

Finding the Computer Name

The `GetComputerName` function returns the name of the computer. It does not return the fully qualified domain name (FQDN) for computers that are joined to a domain.

```
Private Declare PtrSafe Function GetComputerName _
    Lib "kernel32.dll" Alias "GetComputerNameA" _
    (ByVal lpBuffer As String, _
     nSize As Long) As Long

Private Const MAX_COMPUTERNAME_LENGTH = 31

Function GetMachineName() As String
    Dim strComputerName As String
    Dim lngSize As Long

    strComputerName = Space(MAX_COMPUTERNAME_LENGTH) & Chr(0)
    lngSize = MAX_COMPUTERNAME_LENGTH + 1

    If GetComputerName(strComputerName, lngSize) <> 0 Then
        GetMachineName = Left(strComputerName, lngSize)
    Else
        GetMachineName = ""
    End If
End Function
```

Opening or Printing Any File

The following procedure enables you to open or print any file, without your needing to know what its executable program is. For example, this same procedure can be used to open or print a Word or PDF document, an Excel spreadsheet, or an ASCII text file. It can even be used to generate e-mail with the default e-mail client if you use the `mailto:` protocol followed by an e-mail address, or to open a Web page with the default Internet browser if you specify a Web address that includes the HTTP protocol.

```
Public Const SW_HIDE            As Long = 0
Public Const SW_MINIMIZE        As Long = 6
Public Const SW_RESTORE         As Long = 9
Public Const SW_SHOW            As Long = 5
Public Const SW_SHOWMAXIMIZED   As Long = 3
Public Const SW_SHOWMINIMIZED   As Long = 2
Public Const SW_SHOWMINNOACTIVE As Long = 7
Public Const SW_SHOWNA          As Long = 8
```

```
Public Const SW_SHOWNOACTIVATE  As Long = 4
Public Const SW_SHOWNORMAL      As Long = 1

Public Declare PtrSafe Function ShellExecute Lib ``shell32.dll" Alias ``ShellExecuteA" _
    (ByVal hWnd As Long, ByVal lpOperation As String, ByVal lpFile As String, _
    ByVal lpParameters As String, ByVal lpDirectory As String, _
    ByVal nShowCmd As Long) As Long

Public Sub ExecuteFile(sFileName As String, sAction As String)
    Dim vReturn As Long
    `sAction can be either `Open" or `Print".

    If ShellExecute(Access.hWndAccessApp, sAction, _
            sFileName, vbNullString, `", SW_SHOWNORMAL) < 33 Then
        DoCmd.Beep
        MsgBox `File not found."
    End If
End Sub
```

code snippet APISamples.accdb

Delaying Code Execution

The following procedure enables you to make your code pause for a specified amount of time.
Appropriately enough, the API used is called Sleep.

Available for download on Wrox.com

```
Declare PtrSafe Sub Sleep Lib `kernel32.dll" (ByVal lngMilliseconds As Long)

Public Sub Pause(lngSeconds As Long)
    `Convert seconds to milliseconds
    Sleep lngSeconds * 1000
End Sub
```

code snippet APISamples.accdb

Getting the Path to a Special Folder

There are many folders that have special meaning to Windows, such as the My Documents and My
Pictures folders. Collectively, these are often referred to as *special folders*. Let's say that your database includes a setup program that places images in a subfolder under the My Pictures directory.
Users can change the location of this folder, so how do you know where the images are? The answer
is to use a Windows Shell API called SHGetFolderPath. This function is defined as follows:

Available for download on Wrox.com

```
Public Declare PtrSafe Function SHGetFolderPath Lib "shell32.dll" _
    Alias "SHGetFolderPathA" _
    (ByVal hwndOwner As Long, _
    ByVal nFolder As Long, _
    ByVal hToken As Long, _
    ByVal dwFlags As Long, _
    ByVal pszPath As String) As Long
```

code snippet APISamples.accdb

Special folders are identified in Windows using an ID value called a CSIDL. The ones you can use with this function are:

```
Public Enum CSIDL
    CSIDL_ADMINTOOLS = &H30
    CSIDL_COMMON_ADMINTOOLS = &H2F
    CSIDL_APPDATA = &H1A
    CSIDL_COMMON_APPDATA = &H23
    CSIDL_COMMON_DOCUMENTS = &H2E
    CSIDL_COOKIES = &H21
    CSIDL_HISTORY = &H22
    CSIDL_INTERNET_CACHE = &H20
    CSIDL_LOCAL_APPDATA = &H1C
    CSIDL_MYPICTURES = &H27
    CSIDL_PERSONAL = &H5
    CSIDL_PROGRAM_FILES = &H26
    CSIDL_PROGRAM_FILES_COMMON = &H2B
    CSIDL_SYSTEM = &H25
    CSIDL_WINDOWS = &H24
End Enum
```

code snippet APISamples.accdb

The following function shows you how to use the API:

```
Public Function GetSpecialFolderPath(id As CSIDL) As String
    Dim rc     As Long
    Dim stPath As String

    ' allocate some space for the path
    stPath = Space(MAX_PATH)

    ' call the API
    rc = SHGetFolderPath(0, id, 0, 0, stPath)
    If (rc = 0) Then
        GetSpecialFolderPath = Left(stPath, InStr(stPath, vbNullChar) - 1)
    End If
End Function
```

code snippet APISamples.accdb

 The MAX_PATH constant appears frequently in Windows API functions. The value for this constant is 260 which includes the drive letter such as C:\, *the null termination character at the end of a string, and a file name of 256 characters.*

Locking the Computer

It can be a good practice to lock the computer when you step away from it. However, because not everyone does this, you might want to do this when the application exits, or when the computer is idle.

To lock the computer, use the LockWorkStation API, as shown here:

```
Declare PtrSafe Function LockWorkStation Lib "user32.dll" () As Long
```

Available for download on Wrox.com

code snippet APISamples.accdb

SUMMARY

In this chapter, you looked at what APIs and DLLs are, and why you might want to use them. You explored the concept of static versus dynamic linking and learned how to reference APIs in Access projects. You also tackled the anatomy of an API call, learning how to use the correct data types when calling API functions. You learned how to write code that uses API functions that is portable between computers running both the 32-bit version of Office 2010 and the 64-bit version. Finally, you learned how to define some commonly used Windows API functions for use in your Access databases.

10

Working with the Windows Registry

➤ Registry basics such as what it does and how it is organized

➤ Frequently used functions in the Registry API that you can use to add personalization scenarios to your applications

➤ Advanced Registry functions that allow you to enumerate keys and values on a local or remote computer

The Registry is the heart and soul of the Windows operating system. It maintains information about the hardware and software installed on a computer, configuration settings, user settings, and information that the system needs to function. In fact, Windows can't operate without it.

The ability to read and write the information in the Registry is essential to all but the most basic software developer. As you move toward doing more and more serious programming, understanding the Registry is critical.

As you'll see, VBA includes four built-in Registry functions, which allow you to store, retrieve, and delete values from one specific area of the Registry. To do anything more advanced, you need to use the Windows Registry APIs. If you don't feel confident with API programming, you should first read Chapter 9, which provides the background you'll need to understand the more advanced topics in this chapter.

Although you can't damage anything by simply reading the Registry, making changes to Registry entries when you don't know what you're doing is a bit like randomly pressing buttons in the control room of your local nuclear power station — press the wrong button and everything will melt into a bubbling fluorescent ooze at your feet.

This chapter is not intended to provide highly detailed information about every key, subkey, and value in the Registry; to do so would require a book far larger than you could carry. Instead, the intent is to provide you with enough information so you can confidently find your way around the Registry and can write basic VBA code to create, read, write, and delete Registry values. To get started, here's a basic look at what the Registry is, what's in it, how it is structured, how it works, and, finally, how programmers can make best use of it.

ABOUT THE REGISTRY

Needless to say, the Registry has evolved quite a bit over time. It first appeared in Windows 3.1, in a file called `Reg.dat`, and was used mainly to store OLE object information. At that time, several additional files — namely, `Win.ini`, `System.ini`, and other application-specific INI files carried out the bulk of what is handled by today's Registry.

Beginning with Windows 95, the Registry's role was expanded to include all the operating system and application settings and preferences, thereby doing away with the need for INI files.

As it is today, the Registry consists of a set of files called *hives*, which control all aspects of the operating system and how it interacts with the hardware and software that operate within it. It brings together all the information previously held in `Reg.dat` and all the INI files. With the exception of the hive that controls hardware (which is re-created each time you log on), you can find a list of hive files in the following Registry key:

```
HKEY_LOCAL_MACHINE\System\CurrentControlSet\Control\hivelist
```

What the Registry Does

Without the Registry, Windows does not have enough information to run. It doesn't have enough information to control devices, applications, or to respond to user input. The Registry essentially performs the following functions:

➤ **Hardware and device driver information:** For the operating system to access a hardware device, it gets the location and settings of the driver from the Registry, even if the device is a basic input/output system (BIOS)–supported device. Drivers are independent of the operating system, but Windows still needs to know where to find them and how to use them. So information such as their filename, location, version, and configuration details must be accessed; otherwise they would be unusable.

➤ **Application information:** When you launch an application, the Registry supplies all the information the operating system needs in order to run it and manage it.

The Registry also contains configuration information for applications such as file locations, menus and toolbars, window status, and other details. The operating system also stores file information in the Registry, such as installation date, the user who installed it, version number, add-ins, and so on.

Often, applications store temporary or runtime information in the Registry, such as the current position of a window, the last document opened by a user, or the value of a "Don't display this" checkbox.

What the Registry Controls

The Registry doesn't control anything on its own, but it does contain information that is used by the operating system and applications to control almost everything. Within the Registry, there are two basic types of information that is stored: information that pertains to users and information pertaining to computers (machines). As a result, there are only two persistent Registry hives called: `HKEY_LOCAL_MACHINE` and `HKEY_USERS`.

Every entry in the Registry controls either user functionality or computer-wide functionality. User functionality may include things such as customizable options, while functionality for the computer includes items that are common to all users, such as the printers and the software installed on a computer.

Other examples of user functionality controlled by the Registry include:

➤ Control panel

➤ Desktop appearance

➤ Network preferences

➤ Explorer functionality and features

Computer-related items are based on the computer name, without regard to the specific user. For example, when you install an application, the ability to launch the application is available to several users, while icons used to launch the application can be specified by the user. Both pieces of information are stored in the Registry. Network protocol availability and priority are specified for the computer, but current connections are based on user information.

Some examples of computer-based functionality in the Registry include:

➤ Access control

➤ Log-in validation

➤ File and print sharing

➤ Network card settings and protocols

➤ System performance and virtual memory settings

The remainder of this chapter is devoted to diving into the Registry and learning about how you can use it in your applications.

Accessing the Registry

You can access the Registry with a built-in Windows utility called the Registry Editor. There are two flavors of the Registry Editor: `RegEdit.exe` and `Regedt32.exe`.

RegEdit.exe

The name of the executable that contains the Registry Editor is `regedit.exe`. On 64-bit versions of Windows, you will find both a 32-bit version and a 64-bit version of `regedit.exe`. The 64-bit version is the one that is launched by default. To launch the 32-bit version of `regedit.exe` on 64-bit based versions of Windows, type **`%windir%\SYSWOW64\regedit`** in the Run dialog box.

Regedt32.exe

Prior to Windows XP and Windows Server 2003, there was another version of the Registry Editor called `Regedt32.exe`. Since Windows XP, however, `regedt32.exe` is a simple wrapper program that runs `regedit.exe`.

Launching and Using the Registry Editor

You won't find the Registry Editor on the Start menu because it is possible to damage the machine by editing values unknowingly. The only way to launch it is via the Run dialog box. Here's how:

1. Click the Start button and select Run, or press the key combination Windows+R. The Run dialog box displays.

2. Type **`regedit`** and then click OK.

 Launching the Registry Editor requires administrator privileges on Windows Vista, Windows Server 2008, and Windows 7.

Figure 10-1 shows the Registry Editor with the `HKEY_CURRENT_USER` hive expanded to show some of its keys, subkeys, and values.

You can think of keys and subkeys as being like the hierarchy of folders and subfolders in the Windows file system. As its name suggests, a value is a named container for a single piece of information, such as the width of a menu. The Registry Editor's right pane shows the values contained within the subkey selected in the left pane. With the exception of a default value that is present in every subkey, each value has its own unique name. The icon to the left of each value indicates its data type.

Registry Organization

The Registry tree is divided into five sections:

➤ HKEY_CLASSES_ROOT

➤ HKEY_CURRENT_USER

➤ HKEY_LOCAL_MACHINE

➤ HKEY_USERS

➤ HKEY_CURRENT_CONFIG

These major sections are called Root Keys, much like C:\ is the root directory of your hard disk. Because the Registry can differ greatly from one operating system version to another, you'll examine the most common keys, and for the sake of simplicity, they're listed in the order in which they appear in the Registry Editor (see Figure 10-2).

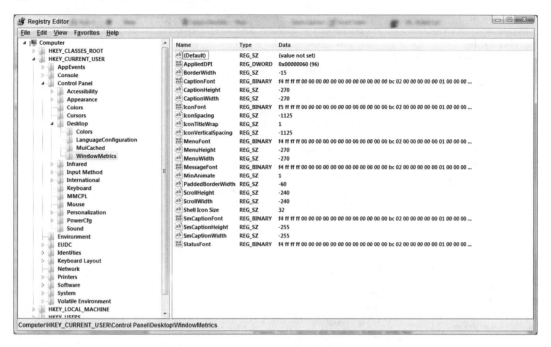

FIGURE 10-1

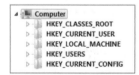

The following sections examine each of the Root Keys.

HKEY_CLASSES_ROOT

FIGURE 10-2

The HKEY_CLASSES_ROOT branch of the Registry tree is actually an alias for HKEY_LOCAL_MACHINE\ Software\Classes, and contains information about file associations, documents, and OLE objects. It is a very large branch, containing several thousand entries at the first level alone.

The first level contains subkeys that define file associations and programmatic identifiers such as Access.Application. The data for the file associations includes the following information:

> ➤ A descriptive name for the document type as you might see in the type column in Windows Explorer (see Figure 10-3).

> ➤ A pointer to the default icon.

> ➤ Information about how the application handles the documents as OLE objects.

> ➤ Information about how the documents are manipulated from the Windows shell (what context menu actions can be taken). See Figure 10-4.

HKEY_CLASSES_ROOT is updated every time an application is installed or removed.

Name	Date modified	Type	Size
esent.dll	7/13/2009 6:40 PM	Application extens...	2,505 KB
esentprf.dll	7/13/2009 6:40 PM	Application extens...	39 KB
esentutl.exe	7/13/2009 6:39 PM	Application	136 KB
esrb.rs	7/13/2009 4:55 PM	RS File	51 KB
eudcedit.exe	7/13/2009 6:39 PM	Application	352 KB
EULA.Microsoft.Application.Verifier.rtf	1/26/2009 12:21 PM	Rich Text Format	119 KB
eventcls.dll	7/13/2009 6:40 PM	Application extens...	16 KB
eventcreate.exe	7/13/2009 6:39 PM	Application	44 KB
EventViewer_EventDetails.xsl	6/10/2009 1:57 PM	XSL Stylesheet	18 KB
eventvwr.exe	7/13/2009 6:39 PM	Application	80 KB
eventvwr.msc	6/10/2009 1:58 PM	Microsoft Commo...	142 KB
evr.dll	7/13/2009 6:40 PM	Application extens...	616 KB
expand.exe	7/13/2009 6:39 PM	Application	64 KB
ExplorerFrame.dll	7/13/2009 6:40 PM	Application extens...	1,820 KB
extrac32.exe	7/13/2009 6:39 PM	Application	61 KB
f3ahvoas.dll	7/13/2009 6:27 PM	Application extens...	34 KB
Faultrep.dll	7/13/2009 6:40 PM	Application extens...	347 KB
fc.exe	7/13/2009 6:39 PM	Application	24 KB

FIGURE 10-3

FIGURE 10-4

HKEY_CURRENT_USER

The HKEY_CURRENT_USER branch is built during logon and is an alias for the current user's subkey in the HKEY_USERS branch; it contains user-specific information. Twelve major subkeys are in this branch, but depending on your system setup and what's installed, you might find some extra ones.

The following table describes the major subkeys.

SUBKEY	DESCRIPTION
AppEvents	Contains information about the sound files that are specified for individual system and application events, such as the Windows Logon sound and the MailBeep sound. It has two subkeys of its own: EventLabels, which contains the event names, and Schemes, which contains references to the actual sound files organized by the application.
Console	Contains all the user options for the MS-DOS Windows, including layout, screen color, and font settings.
Control Panel	Contains many other subkeys for all the Control Panel settings, such as color schemes, screen savers, keyboard repeat rate, mouse speed, and so on.
Environment	Contains the environment settings, specifically the temporary file locations. It contains the environment variables that you would see in DOS when you typed SET at the command line. Much of the information contained in this key is connected to the System applet in the Control Panel.
Identities	Is present only if Outlook Express 5.x (or later) is installed. It contains sub-keys for an Outlook Express account, e-mail, and newsgroup settings, and the MSN Messenger, if installed.
Keyboard Layout	Contains three subkeys that hold information about the current keyboard layout, which you can set using the Control Panel's Keyboard properties. The Preload subkey contains a value for each installed keyboard layout. These values point to keys in HKEY_LOCAL_MACHINE\System\CurrentControlSet\Control\Keyboard Layouts, which contains references to the keyboard drivers.
Network	Contains two subkeys that describe the mapped network drives, including persistent connections and recent connections. These subkeys contain values for the connection type and the provider name of each connection.
Printers	This subkey contains information about the current user's installed printers. There may also be a subkey for each remote printer, if installed.
RemoteAccess	Contains address and profile subkeys for the user's dial-up and networking connections. The subkey itself contains global connection details, such as the area code and the number of redial attempts, whereas the Address and Profile subkeys contain settings for specific connections.
SessionInformation	Contains the number of programs currently running on the computer.

continues

(continued)

SUBKEY	DESCRIPTION
Software	Easily the largest key in the Registry, and one of the two Registry keys intended to be used for applications (the other is HKEY_LOCAL_MACHINE\ Software). It contains vendor-specific subkeys that describe the current user's software settings and a raft of application-specific information that was previously stored in the Win.ini or custom vendor INI files under Windows 3.*x*. Each vendor subkey contains a separate subkey for each software application supplied by that vendor. The subkeys and values below them are completely determined by the vendor, but typically contain user preferences, histories, and so on.
Volatile Environment	Contains environment variables related to the current logon session.

Of particular interest to VB and VBA programmers is the Registry key HKEY_CURRENT_USER\ Software\VB and VBA Program Settings. This key is used by the built-in functions in VBA, which are discussed later in this chapter.

HKEY_LOCAL_MACHINE

The HKEY_LOCAL_MACHINE hive contains all the computer-specific settings, including hardware configuration and any computer-specific settings for installed software. There are five major subkeys under this hive, which are described in the following table.

SUBKEY	DESCRIPTION
Hardware	Contains profiles for all the hardware that has been installed on the computer, such as device drivers, resources such as IRQ assignments, and other details. All the information contained is built during startup and deleted during shutdown. That being the case, use this subkey only for viewing, not for writing.
SAM	Contains all the user and group account information for the Security Account Manager (SAM). The information in its subkeys is maintained in User Manager. It is also mapped to HKEY_LOCAL_MACHINE\Security, so changes to either are immediately reflected in the other. Do not attempt to change anything in here unless you want to reformat your hard disk afterward.
Security	Contains all the security information for the computer, such as password policies, user rights and permissions, and the groups to which each user belongs. The information in its subkeys is maintained in User Manager. Do not attempt to change anything in here either.

SUBKEY	DESCRIPTION
`Software`	Contains configuration information about the software installed on the computer. The entries under this subkey apply to all users, not just the current user. In here you would find information about the software that is installed, as well as file associations and OLE information. This key has a subkey called `Classes`, which is an alias for `HKEY_CLASSES_ROOT`. In 64-bit versions of Windows, there is a subkey called `WOW6432Node`, which stores 32-bit program settings on 64-bit Windows. Organization of the Registry on 64-bit versions of Windows is discussed later in this chapter.
`System`	Contains other subkeys that contain the persistent information about devices and parameters that the system needs to start up, including control sets that contain information such as the computer name, subsystems that need to be started, hardware configuration for devices and drivers that the operating system loads, specific hardware profile information when multiple hardware profiles are configured, file system services, and so on.

HKEY_USERS

The `HKEY_USERS` hive contains the settings for all registered users and the default user. The number of subkeys depends on the number of users registered on the system. The following sections briefly explain the two major kinds of subkeys: `.DEFAULT` and security identifiers.

.DEFAULT

The settings in the `.DEFAULT` key constitute the default template that is applied when new users are added to the system, and includes user profiles, environment, screen, sound, and other user-related settings. If you change any of the settings in this subkey, those changes will take place for all new users because they inherit the same settings. Existing users will retain their existing settings, however.

Security Identifier Keys

You may also see several subkeys such as this:

```
S-1-5-21-1475383443-718524000-196120627-1006
```

Each represents a user who has logged on to the system. The number is the user's SID (security identifier). Every user on the network is assigned a unique SID by User Manager for domains. The information thus changes depending on who is currently logged on.

The information for the key is gleaned from the `NTUSER.DAT` file, found in the user's profile directory. This subkey carries the same data as `HKEY_CURRENT_USER\Software\Classes`:

```
S-1-5-21-1475383443-718524000-196120627-1006_Classes
```

HKEY_CURRENT_CONFIG

The HKEY_CURRENT_CONFIG branch contains all of the details for the profiles that are current in the system, and is taken from HKEY_LOCAL_MACHINE at system startup.

Registry Organization on 64-Bit Windows

With the introduction of 64-bit Windows, a separate view was added to the Registry for 32-bit applications to prevent data in 64-bit Registry keys from being overwritten by keys and values installed by 32-bit programs. Program settings for 64-bit programs are still stored in HKEY_LOCAL_MACHINE\Software, while settings for 32-bit programs run are now stored in a new key called HKEY_LOCAL_MACHINE\Software\WOW6432Node.

 The Microsoft documentation frequently uses the term "WOW64" which stands for "Windows32-on-Windows 64-bit."

Let's take a look at some important aspects of the Registry on 64-bit Windows.

Registry Redirection

When a call is made to the Registry, it is forwarded to either the 32-bit Registry branch or the 64-bit Registry branch, depending on whether a 32-bit or 64-bit application is making the request. This process is known as *Registry redirection*. For example, if you run a 32-bit application that attempts to read a value from HKEY_LOCAL_MACHINE\Software\MyApplication, the value is actually read from HKEY_LOCAL_MACHINE\Software\WOW6432Node\MyApplication. A 64-bit application that reads this key does not require redirection.

 For more information about Registry Redirection, please see the "Registry Redirection" article in the Platform SDK, which is available at http://msdn .microsoft.com/en-us/library/aa384232%28VS.85%29.aspx

The following keys participate in redirection by default:

- ➤ HKEY_LOCAL_MACHINE\Software\Classes
- ➤ HKEY_LOCAL_MACHINE\Software\COM3
- ➤ HKEY_LOCAL_MACHINE\Software\EventSystem
- ➤ HKEY_LOCAL_MACHINE\Software\Ole
- ➤ HKEY_LOCAL_MACHINE\Software\Rpc
- ➤ HKEY_USERS*\Software\Classes
- ➤ HKEY_USERS*_Classes

(An asterisk (*) indicates that redirection occurs for all user security identifiers (SID) under HKEY_USERS.)

Registry Reflection

Naturally, certain keys and values should be available to both 32-bit and 64-bit applications. A good example of such a key is the registration for a COM application. Imagine that you have a 32-bit COM library that was registered on 64-bit Windows. In order for a 64-bit application to use the library, it needs to be registered in both the 32-bit and 64-bit Registry branches. This is accomplished using Registry reflection.

As the name suggests, *Registry reflection* is a process used by Windows to maintain a mirror between certain 64-bit and 32-bit Registry settings. This mirroring keeps the settings synchronized in real time. On 64-bit Windows, there are Registry API functions that enable you to define how keys are reflected.

> *For more information about Registry reflection, please see the white paper "Registry Reflection in Microsoft Windows," which is available at* `http://microsoft.com/whdc/system/platform/64bit/RegReflect.mspx`. *Also note, however, that Registry Reflection has been removed on Windows Server 2008 R2 and Windows 7. Many of the keys that were previously reflected in Windows Vista are now shared under Windows 7.*

USING THE BUILT-IN VBA REGISTRY FUNCTIONS

Many programmers use global variables to hold values that are used throughout the application. There are two problems with this approach. First, if an unhandled error occurs, all your global variables are reset. Second, you have to reassign their values every time the application is launched. An alternative is to store this type of value in the database, but if you're storing the connection string to the remote data store, it might be a little difficult to get at if your application doesn't know where to look.

Another alternative, one that is used in many professional applications, is to store such information in the Registry. You can store all sorts of information in the Registry, from simple values that your applications use from time to time, to connection strings, to user preferences, such as the position and color of forms, and so on.

VBA provides four built-in functions for manipulating the Registry. The only drawback to these functions is that they operate on only one part of the Registry — one that has been specifically allocated to VB and VBA.

The `HKEY_CURRENT_USER\Software\VB and VBA Program Settings` key has been set aside for use by VB and VBA applications. This key is created the first time you call the `SaveSetting` function, as shown in the next section.

As application-specific Registry entries are stored using the *application-name*, *section*, *key* construct, it makes sense that VBA should do the same. This section describes the built-in VBA Registry functions and how to use them.

SaveSetting

The `SaveSetting` procedure enables you to store a single value in the `HKEY_CURRENT_USER\ Software\VB and VBA Program Settings` hive. The syntax is as follows:

```
SaveSetting AppName, Section, Key, Setting
```

The arguments — all of which are required — are described in the following table.

ARGUMENT	DESCRIPTION
AppName	A string that specifies the name of the application or project whose key is being set
Section	A string that specifies the name of the section under which the key is to be set
Key	A string that specifies the name of the key you are setting
Setting	An expression of any data type that specifies the value to which the key will be set

You can store as many values as you like, in as many keys and subkeys as you like. All VB/VBA applications will have access to the values you store, as long as they know the correct `AppName`, `Section`, and `Key` names.

To standardize your Registry entries, you might use either the `AppTitle` property if it is set or the `CurrentProject.Name` property as the `AppName` argument, although you are free to use any expression you like.

The following code demonstrates two calls to the `SaveSetting` procedure:

```
SaveSetting CurrentDb.Properties("AppTitle"), "Settings", "myStringKey", "123"
SaveSetting CurrentDb.Properties("AppTitle"), "Settings", "myNumericKey", 123
```

Notice that a string value `123` is used in the first example and a numeric example in the second. This is acceptable; however, you must remember that `GetSetting` always returns `String` and `GetAllSettings` always returns `Variant`.

You can set the `Application Title` property in the Current Database page in the Access Options dialog box.

GetSetting

You can use the `GetSetting` function to retrieve a string value from a single Registry key that you have previously saved. It returns the value specified by the default argument if the key is empty or doesn't exist. `GetSetting` has the following syntax:

```
GetSetting(AppName, Section, Key, [Default])
```

The function arguments are explained in the following table.

ARGUMENT	DESCRIPTION
AppName	A required string expression that contains the name of the application or project whose key is being sought.
Section	A required string expression that contains the name of the section under which the key is found.
Key	A required string expression that contains the name of the requested key.
Default	An optional default expression to be returned if the key is empty. If you omit this argument, it is assumed to be a zero-length string (" ").

The following code demonstrates the GetSetting function:

```
?GetSetting(CurrentDb.Properties("AppTitle"), "Settings", i
"SomeSetting","myDefault")
```

GetAllSettings

The GetAllSettings function retrieves all the key values that exist under the specified section, as a two-dimensional variant array. It has the following syntax:

```
GetAllSettings(AppName, Section)
```

The GetAllSettings function returns an uninitialized (empty) variant if either AppName or Section does not exist. The arguments are described in the following table.

ARGUMENT	DESCRIPTION
AppName	A required string expression that contains the name of the application or project whose key is being sought
Section	A required string expression that contains the name of the section under which the key is found

To use this function, you must declare a standard variable that will hold the return values. That's right, a standard variable — not an array. If there are values to return, the function redimensions the variable as an array. For example, the following code segment saves several values to the Registry using SaveSetting and retrieves them into a variant using GetAllSettings:

```
Dim varMySettings As Variant
Dim intCtr As Integer

SaveSetting "myapp", "mysection", "mykey1", "my first setting"
SaveSetting "myapp", "mysection", "mykey2", "my second setting"
SaveSetting "myapp", "mysection", "mykey3", "my third setting"

varMySettings = GetAllSettings("myapp", "mysection")

For intCtr = LBound(varMySettings, 1) To UBound(varMySettings, 1)
```

```
        Debug.Print varMySettings(intCtr, 0) & "-" & varMySettings(intCtr, 1)
    Next intCtr

    DeleteSetting "myapp", "mysection"
```

Notice that the first dimension contains the key name, and the second contains the actual value.

DeleteSetting

The last of the native VBA Registry functions is `DeleteSetting`. As its name suggests, `DeleteSetting` deletes a section or key, depending on whether the optional key is supplied. It has the following syntax:

```
DeleteSetting AppName, [Section], [Key]
```

The `DeleteSetting` arguments are described in the following table.

ARGUMENT	DESCRIPTION
AppName	A required string expression that contains the name of the application or project whose key is being sought.
Section	A string expression that contains the name of the section where the key is being deleted. If only `appname` and section are provided, the specified section is deleted, along with its keys. If omitted, all sections for a given `AppName` are deleted.
Key	An optional string expression that contains the name of the key to be deleted.

The following code demonstrates using the `DeleteSetting` function to delete the specified key:

```
DeleteSetting CurrentDb.Properties("AppTitle"), "Settings", _
    "myKey"
```

Similarly, the following `DeleteSetting` call deletes the entire specified section and all its keys:

```
DeleteSetting CurrentDb.Properties("AppTitle"), "Settings"
```

Typical Uses for the Built-In VBA Registry Functions

Now that you have a fundamental understanding of the Registry, you might still be wondering how you would use it and what values you would want to store there. In short, why bother?

It all comes down to functionality. As programmers, we are already disciplined enough to know not to use a particular technology, function, or facility unless it is necessary. For example, you wouldn't build a complex procedure where a built-in one exists. But by the same token, you should employ things that enable you to provide the functionality the application requirements demand.

Implementing a Daily Reminders Screen

A typical example might be the humble daily reminders screen implemented in many applications. This screen usually pops up when the application starts up, to remind users of overdue accounts, tasks they need to perform that day, or any number of things of which they need to be made aware.

Having such a facility can be of great benefit to both the organization and the user, but some users prefer to display this screen when they want to. Having the screen pop up every time they start the application can be a real nuisance, particularly if it takes some time to process and sort the information that's displayed. The resolution here is to offer the user the capability to have the screen pop up or not.

To do this, you need to store a Boolean value somewhere. You can store it in a table, but if your database is built on a client-server model, with the tables stored on a server share, the setting may affect all users. Storing the value in a local table would mean all users of that particular computer would similarly share the same setting. The answer is to store the value in the Registry so each user can set his or her own preferences.

To implement that behavior, start by creating a new form called frmOverdueAccounts containing a list box, command button, and checkbox, as shown in Figure 10-5. (This example simply adds the company names and amounts to the list box's RowSource property, but a real form would probably populate it using a recordset or table.)

FIGURE 10-5

Then, add the following code to the checkbox's Click event.

Available for
download on
Wrox.com

```
Private Sub chkShowAtStartup_Click()
    Dim strApp As String

    ' Assuming you have set the Application Title property
    ' in the Access Options dialog
    strApp = CurrentDb.Properties("AppTitle")

    'Save the new checkbox setting.
    SaveSetting strApp, "Settings", "Show at Startup", _
        Me.chkShowAtStartup
End Sub
```

code snippet RegistrySamples.accdb

In this code, it doesn't matter if the user doesn't click the checkbox because the form displays whether the setting exists or not. But if he does click it, the appropriate setting will be immediately saved to the Registry.

Of course, you need to set the initial value of the checkbox when the form displays, so add the following code to the form's Load event.

Available for
download on
Wrox.com

```
Private Sub Form_Load()
    Dim strApp As String

    ' Assuming you have set the Application Title property
    ' in the Access Options dialog
    strApp = CurrentDb.Properties("AppTitle")

    'Set the checkbox value.
```

```
          'If the setting doesn't exist, assume a default True.
          Me.chkShowAtStartup = GetSetting(strApp, "Settings", "Show at Startup", True)
      End Sub
```

Then all you have to do is modify your startup code to decide whether to show this form:

```
Dim strApp As String
Dim fShowForm As Boolean

'Assuming you have set the Application Title property in the Access Options dialog
strApp = CurrentDb.Properties("AppTitle")

fShowForm = GetSetting(strApp, "Settings", "Show at Startup", True)

'If the setting doesn't exist, it is probably the
'first time the user has launched the application,
'so show the form.
If fShowForm = True Then
    DoCmd.OpenForm "frmOverDueAccts"
End If
```

Storing and Retrieving Connection Strings

Sometimes an application may need to switch between one or more sets of connection strings. Examples of this might include when switching the application between a test and production environment, when running connected or disconnected to the primary network, or in failover situations where additional resiliency is needed.

Where multiple databases, spreadsheets, or files are frequently connected, you may choose to store their connection strings in the Registry to save time and prevent potential code changes in the application. For example, the following function retrieves the connection string for a named data source that may be passed to the function. This function would subsequently be used at runtime to relink tables in the application.

```
Public Function GetConnString(strConnectionSource As String) As String
    Dim strApp As String
    Dim strCon As String

    strApp = CurrentDb.Properties("AppTitle")

    strCon = GetSetting(strApp, "Settings", strConnectionSource, "")
    GetConnString = strCon
End Function
```

Storing User Preferences

The VBA Registry functions are often used to store user preferences, such as the following:

- ➤ Default values, such as the default date to enter into a text box
- ➤ Sort orders, such as whether to display the delinquent customers' list by value or by due date
- ➤ Menus, toolbars, or ribbons that the user wants displayed
- ➤ Form colors
- ➤ Sound effects on/off
- ➤ The name of the report that was last opened
- ➤ The last five customer ID records that were retrieved
- ➤ Language settings

Storing a Last Used List

Like the Documents list on the Windows Start menu (stored in `HKEY_CURRENT_USER\Software\ Microsoft\Windows\CurrentVersion\Explorer\RecentDocs`), you can store your own lists in the Registry. For example, you might want to store a list of the last ten forms or reports that a user visited, the last six files that were opened, or the primary key values for the last several records that were viewed or modified. As you can see, because the Registry is a persistent location controlled by Windows, it may also be possible to add additional resiliency to your applications.

USING THE WINDOWS REGISTRY APIs

This section describes the Windows Registry API functions you can use to access and manipulate a wider range of Registry keys than you can with the built-in VBA functions. Before attempting this section, however, we strongly advise that you read Chapter 9.

The Windows API provides all the functions you need to access the Registry. This section provides real-world examples of how to use these functions. For example, if you wanted to add your company name under the `HKEY_CURRENT_USER\Software` key instead of storing Registry settings under `Software\VB and VBA Program Settings`, you could use the Registry APIs to do so.

To make sense of all the information presented in the preceding sections, you need to see how the Registry APIs are used. To do that, you'll create a module that performs some of the most widely used functionality: Create a key, set a key value, read that value, delete the value, and, of course, delete the key.

Getting Started

Before we get into the actual API functions, you'll need to add some constants and API declarations. Create a new standard module and add the constants described in the subsections that follow.

Windows Registry Hive Constants

Before you can read data from the Registry using the Windows API, you'll need to be able to specify the hive where the key exists. This is accomplished with one of the constants defined in the following code:

```
'Key declarations
Public Const HKEY_CLASSES_ROOT As Long = &H80000000
Public Const HKEY_CURRENT_CONFIG As Long = &H80000005
Public Const HKEY_CURRENT_USER As Long = &H80000001
Public Const HKEY_DYN_DATA As Long = &H80000006
Public Const HKEY_LOCAL_MACHINE As Long = &H80000002
Public Const HKEY_PERF_ROOT As Long = HKEY_LOCAL_MACHINE
Public Const HKEY_PERFORMANCE_DATA As Long = &H80000004
Public Const HKEY_USERS As Long = &H80000003
```

code snippet RegistrySamples.accdb

Windows Registry Data Types

In the same way that fields in a table, variables, and other API parameters require data of specific types, the kind of data the Registry can store is also defined in terms of data types. The data types in the table that follows are supported under Windows 2000, Windows XP, Windows Vista, and Windows 7.

DATA TYPE	DESCRIPTION
REG_BINARY	Specifies raw binary data. Most hardware information is stored with this data type, which can be displayed and entered in binary or hexadecimal format.
REG_DWORD	A 32-bit (4-byte) number, which is used to store Boolean or other numeric values and information about many device drivers and services. REG_DWORD values can be displayed and edited as binary, hexadecimal, or decimal format.
REG_DWORD_LITTLE_ENDIAN	Same as REG_DWORD, a 32-bit number, but it is used to store values in a specific way. In REG_DWORD_LITTLE_ENDIAN, the most significant byte is stored in the rightmost address. This is the format used for storing numbers in Windows.
REG_DWORD_BIG_ENDIAN	The only difference between this data type and REG_DWORD_ LITTLE_ENDIAN is that this data type stores the most-significant byte in the leftmost address.
REG_EXPAND_SZ	A variable-length text string used to store variables that are resolved when an application or service uses the data. For example, some values include the variable System root. When a service or application references the data in this data type, it is replaced by the name of the directory containing the Windows system files.

DATA TYPE	DESCRIPTION
REG_LINK	Stores a symbolic link between system or application data, and a Registry value. REG_LINK supports both ANSI and Unicode characters.
REG_MULTI_SZ	Stores multiple strings that are formatted as an array of null-terminated strings, the last of which is terminated by an extra null character. This means the entire array is terminated by two null characters. The values in this data type can be separated by spaces, commas, or other characters.
REG_QWORD	A 64-bit (8-byte) number that's used to store Boolean or other numeric values and information about many device drivers and services. REG_QWORD values can be displayed and edited as binary, hexadecimal, or decimal format.
REG_QWORD_LITTLE_ENDIAN	The same as REG_QWORD, a 64-bit number.
REG_SZ	A null terminated string. Boolean values and short-text strings are usually stored with this data type.

The constants that specify these data types are defined as follows:

```
'Key value types
Public Const REG_BINARY As Long = 3
Public Const REG_DWORD As Long = 4
Public Const REG_DWORD_BIG_ENDIAN As Long = 5
Public Const REG_DWORD_LITTLE_ENDIAN As Long = 4
Public Const REG_EXPAND_SZ As Long = 2
Public Const REG_LINK As Long = 6
Public Const REG_MULTI_SZ As Long = 7
Public Const REG_NONE As Long = 0
Public Const REG_RESOURCE_LIST As Long = 8
Public Const REG_SZ As Long = 1
```

code snippet RegistrySamples.accdb

For convenience, I sometimes define these constants in an Enum. *This allows you to use the* Enum *type as an argument to a* Sub *or* Function *procedure.* Enum *statements were discussed in Chapter 8.*

Other Windows Registry Constants

Once you've defined the basic constants to specify the Registry hive or data types, add the following constants. These constants specify things such as security access, operations, and some return codes from the API functions.

```
'Parameter declarations
Public Const REG_CREATED_NEW_KEY As Long = &H1
Public Const REG_OPENED_EXISTING_KEY As Long = &H2
Public Const REG_OPTION_BACKUP_RESTORE As Long = 4
Public Const REG_OPTION_VOLATILE As Long = 1
Public Const REG_OPTION_NON_VOLATILE As Long = 0
Public Const STANDARD_RIGHTS_ALL As Long = &H1F0000
Public Const SYNCHRONIZE As Long = &H100000
Public Const READ_CONTROL As Long = &H20000
Public Const STANDARD_RIGHTS_READ As Long = (READ_CONTROL)
Public Const STANDARD_RIGHTS_WRITE As Long = (READ_CONTROL)
Public Const KEY_CREATE_LINK As Long = &H20
Public Const KEY_CREATE_SUB_KEY As Long = &H4
Public Const KEY_ENUMERATE_SUB_KEYS As Long = &H8
Public Const KEY_NOTIFY As Long = &H10
Public Const KEY_QUERY_VALUE As Long = &H1
Public Const KEY_SET_VALUE As Long = &H2
Public Const MAX_VALUE_NAME As Long = 16383

Public Const KEY_READ As Long = (( _
    STANDARD_RIGHTS_READ _
    Or KEY_QUERY_VALUE _
    Or KEY_ENUMERATE_SUB_KEYS _
    Or KEY_NOTIFY) _
    And (Not SYNCHRONIZE))

Public Const KEY_WRITE As Long = (( _
    STANDARD_RIGHTS_WRITE _
    Or KEY_SET_VALUE _
    Or KEY_CREATE_SUB_KEY) _
    And (Not SYNCHRONIZE))

Public Const KEY_EXECUTE As Long = (KEY_READ)

Public Const KEY_ALL_ACCESS As Long = (( _
    STANDARD_RIGHTS_ALL _
    Or KEY_QUERY_VALUE _
    Or KEY_SET_VALUE _
    Or KEY_CREATE_SUB_KEY _
    Or KEY_ENUMERATE_SUB_KEYS _
    Or KEY_NOTIFY _
    Or KEY_CREATE_LINK) _
    And (Not SYNCHRONIZE))
```

code snippet RegistrySamples.accdb

Next, add the following constants which are used to test success or failure of each API function. In your applications, you may want to test for a specific error, but this example tests only for success or failure.

```
'API return codes
Public Const ERROR_SUCCESS As Long = 0
Public Const ERROR_NO_MORE_ITEMS As Long = 259
```

code snippet RegistrySamples.accdb

Windows Registry API Function Declarations

Next, add the following API declarations. Note that this is not the complete list; it includes only those declarations that are needed by the procedures that will follow. These declarations include the conditional compilation checks required to compile the code on both the 32-bit and 64-bit versions of Office 2010.

```
#If Win64 = 1 And VBA7 = 1 Then

Public Declare PtrSafe Function RegCloseKey Lib "advapi32.dll" _
    (ByVal hKey As LongPtr) As Long

Public Declare PtrSafe Function RegCreateKeyEx Lib "advapi32.dll" _
    Alias "RegCreateKeyExA" ( _
    ByVal hKey As LongPtr, _
    ByVal lpSubKey As String, _
    ByVal Reserved As Long, _
    ByVal lpClass As String, _
    ByVal dwOptions As Long, _
    ByVal samDesired As Long, _
    ByVal lpSecurityAttributes As Long, _
    phkResult As LongPtr, _
    lpdwDisposition As Long) As Long

Public Declare PtrSafe Function RegDeleteKey Lib "advapi32.dll" _
    Alias "RegDeleteKeyA" ( _
    ByVal hKey As LongPtr, _
    ByVal lpSubKey As String) As Long

Public Declare PtrSafe Function RegDeleteValue Lib "advapi32.dll" _
    Alias "RegDeleteValueA" ( _
    ByVal hKey As LongPtr, _
    ByVal lpValueName As String) As Long

Public Declare PtrSafe Function RegOpenKeyEx Lib "advapi32.dll" _
    Alias "RegOpenKeyExA" ( _
    ByVal hKey As LongPtr, _
    ByVal lpSubKey As String, _
    ByVal ulOptions As Long, _
    ByVal samDesired As Long, _
    phkResult As LongPtr) As Long

Public Declare PtrSafe Function RegQueryValueEx Lib "advapi32.dll" _
    Alias "RegQueryValueExA" ( _
    ByVal hKey As LongPtr, _
    ByVal lpValueName As String, _
    ByVal lpReserved As Long, _
    lpType As Long, _
    lpData As Any, _
    lpcbData As Long) As Long

Public Declare PtrSafe Function RegSetValueEx Lib "advapi32.dll" _
    Alias "RegSetValueExA" ( _
    ByVal hKey As LongPtr, _
    ByVal lpValueName As String, _
```

```
    ByVal Reserved As Long, _
    ByVal dwType As Long, _
    lpData As Any, _
    ByVal cbData As Long) As Long

#Else

Private Declare Function RegCloseKey Lib "advapi32.dll" _
    (ByVal hKey As Long) As Long

Private Declare Function RegCreateKeyEx Lib "advapi32.dll" _
    Alias "RegCreateKeyExA" ( _
    ByVal hKey As Long, _
    ByVal lpSubKey As String, _
    ByVal Reserved As Long, _
    ByVal lpClass As String, _
    ByVal dwOptions As Long, _
    ByVal samDesired As Long, _
    ByVal lpSecurityAttributes As Long, _
    phkResult As Long, _
    lpdwDisposition As Long) As Long

Private Declare Function RegDeleteKey Lib "advapi32.dll" _
    Alias "RegDeleteKeyA" ( _
    ByVal hKey As Long, _
    ByVal lpSubKey As String) As Long

Private Declare Function RegDeleteValue Lib "advapi32.dll" _
    Alias "RegDeleteValueA" ( _
    ByVal hKey As Long, _
    ByVal lpValueName As String) As Long

Private Declare Function RegOpenKeyEx Lib "advapi32.dll" _
    Alias "RegOpenKeyExA" ( _
    ByVal hKey As Long, _
    ByVal lpSubKey As String, _
    ByVal ulOptions As Long, _
    ByVal samDesired As Long, _
    phkResult As Long) As Long

Private Declare Function RegQueryValueEx Lib "advapi32.dll" _
    Alias "RegQueryValueExA" ( _
    ByVal hKey As Long, _
    ByVal lpValueName As String, _
    ByVal lpReserved As Long, _
    lpType As Long, _
    lpData As Any, _
    lpcbData As Long) As Long

Private Declare Function RegSetValueEx Lib "advapi32.dll"
    Alias "RegSetValueExA" ( _
    ByVal hKey As Long, _
    ByVal lpValueName As String, _
    ByVal Reserved As Long, _
```

```
          ByVal dwType As Long, _
          lpData As Any, _
          ByVal cbData As Long) As Long

     #End If
```

Now add the following variable declaration, which is used to store the result of the API function calls. You could declare this variable in each procedure that uses it, but for the purposes of a convenient example, it's declared at module level.

```
     'Return value for most procedures
     Private lngReturn As Long
```

With the constants and declarations added, let's dive into the functions that will do the work of manipulating the Registry. Add the following procedures to the same module as the preceding declarations. Some of them may look a bit complicated, but if you strip out the error handling, you see they are actually quite simple.

Creating a Registry Key

The first procedure, CreateKey, wraps the RegCreateKeyEx function to create a new subkey. After the call, it checks that the call completed successfully, and if not, raises a custom error. If the call is successful, it returns the name of the newly created subkey.

```
Public Function CreateKey(lngRootKey As Long, _
        strSubKey As String, _
        lngValueType As Long) As String

    Dim hKey As Long
    Dim hSubKey As LongPtr
    Dim strClass As String
    Dim lngSize As Long
    Dim lngDisposition As Long

    On Error GoTo CreateKey_Err

    'Create the key
    lngReturn = RegCreateKeyEx(lngRootKey, _
                               strSubKey, _
                               0&, _
                               vbNullString, _
                               0&, _
                               KEY_WRITE, _
                               0&, _
                               hSubKey, _
                               lngDisposition)

    'Check that the call succeeded
```

```
        If lngReturn <> ERROR_SUCCESS Then
            Err.Raise vbObjectError + 1, , "Could not create key."
        End If

        'If successful, return the name of the new subkey
        CreateKey = strSubKey

CreateKey_Exit:
        On Error Resume Next
        'Close the key
        lngReturn = RegCloseKey(hKey)
        Exit Function

CreateKey_Err:
        CreateKey = ""
        DoCmd.Beep
        MsgBox "Error " & Err.Number & vbCrLf & _
            Err.Description, vbOKOnly + vbExclamation, _
            "Could not save the key value"

        Resume CreateKey_Exit
End Function
```

code snippet RegistrySamples.accdb

Setting the Value for a Key

The next procedure, `SetKeyValue`, wraps the `RegOpenKeyEx` and `RegSetValueEx` functions to open the subkey and set its value, respectively. After each function call, it checks that the call completed successfully, and if not, raises a custom error and returns `False`. If the call completes successfully, it returns `True`.

```
Public Function SetKeyValue(lngRootKey As Long, _
        strSubKey As String, _
        strValueName As String, _
        strNewValue As String) As Boolean

    Dim hKey As LongPtr
    Dim lngSize As Long

    On Error GoTo SetKeyValue_Err

    'Open the key and get its handle
    lngReturn = RegOpenKeyEx(lngRootKey, strSubKey, _
        0&, KEY_WRITE, hKey)
    'Check that the call succeeded
    If lngReturn <> ERROR_SUCCESS Then
        Err.Raise vbObjectError + 2, , "Could not open key."
    End If

    'Initialize the size variable
    lngSize = Len(strNewValue)

    'Set the key value
```

```
        lngReturn = RegSetValueEx(hKey, _
                                  strValueName, _
                                  0&, _
                                  REG_SZ, _
                                  ByVal strNewValue, _
                                  lngSize)

    'Check that the call succeeded
    If lngReturn <> ERROR_SUCCESS Then
        Err.Raise vbObjectError + 3, , "Could not save value."
    End If

SetKeyValue_Exit:
    On Error Resume Next

    'Return success or failure
    SetKeyValue = (lngReturn = ERROR_SUCCESS)

    'Close the key
    lngReturn = RegCloseKey(hKey)
    Exit Function

SetKeyValue_Err:
    DoCmd.Beep
    MsgBox "Error " & Err.Number & vbCrLf & _
        Err.Description, vbOKOnly + vbExclamation, _
        "Could not save the key value"

    Resume SetKeyValue_Exit
End Function
```

code snippet RegistrySamples.accdb

Getting the Value for a Key

The `GetKeyValue` procedure wraps the `RegOpenKeyEx` and `RegQueryValueEx` functions, which open the subkey and retrieve its value, respectively. Again, after each function call, we ensure that the call completed successfully and if not, raises a custom error and returns a `Null` value. If the call does complete successfully, it returns the current value.

```
Public Function GetKeyValue(lngRootKey As LongPtr, _
        strSubKey As String, _
        strValueName As String) As Variant

    Dim hKey As LongPtr
    Dim strBuffer As String
    Dim lngSize As Long

    On Error GoTo GetKeyValue_Err

    'Open the key and get its handle
    lngReturn = RegOpenKeyEx(lngRootKey, strSubKey, _
        0&, KEY_READ, hKey)

    'Check that the call succeeded
```

```
        If lngReturn <> ERROR_SUCCESS Then
            Err.Raise vbObjectError + 2, , "Could not open key."
        End If

        'Initialize the variables
        strBuffer = Space(255)
        lngSize = Len(strBuffer)

        'Read the key value
        lngReturn = RegQueryValueEx(hKey, _
                                    strValueName, _
                                    0&, _
                                    REG_SZ, _
                                    ByVal strBuffer, _
                                    lngSize)

        'Check that the call succeeded
        If lngReturn <> ERROR_SUCCESS Then
            Err.Raise vbObjectError + 4, , "Could not read value."
        End If

        'Return the key value
        GetKeyValue = Left(strBuffer, lngSize -1)

    GetKeyValue_Exit:
        On Error Resume Next
        'Close the key
        lngReturn = RegCloseKey(hKey)
        Exit Function

    GetKeyValue_Err:
        GetKeyValue = Null
        DoCmd.Beep

        MsgBox "Error " & Err.Number & vbCrLf & _
            Err.Description, vbOKOnly + vbExclamation, _
            "Could not retrieve the key"

        Resume GetKeyValue_Exit
    End Function
```

code snippet RegistrySamples.accdb

Deleting a Registry Value

The `DeleteValue` function wraps the `RegOpenKeyEx` and `RegDeleteValue` functions to open the subkey and delete the value that you created in the previous example.

```
    Public Function DeleteValue(lngRootKey As Long, _
        strSubKey As String, strValueName As String) As Boolean

        Dim hKey As LongPtr

        On Error GoTo DeleteValue_Err
```

```
        'Open the key and get its handle
        lngReturn = RegOpenKeyEx(lngRootKey, strSubKey, _
            0&, KEY_ALL_ACCESS, hKey)

        'Check that the call succeeded
        If lngReturn <> ERROR_SUCCESS Then
            Err.Raise vbObjectError + 2, , "Could not open key."
        End If

        'Delete the key value
        lngReturn = RegDeleteValue(hKey, strValueName)

DeleteValue_Exit:
    On Error Resume Next

        'Return success or failure
        DeleteValue = (lngReturn = ERROR_SUCCESS)

        'Close the key
        lngReturn = RegCloseKey(hKey)
    Exit Function

DeleteValue_Err:
    DoCmd.Beep
    MsgBox "Error " & Err.Number & vbCrLf & _
        Err.Description, vbOKOnly + vbExclamation, _
        "Could not retrieve the key"

    Resume DeleteValue_Exit
End Function
```

code snippet RegistrySamples.accdb

Deleting a Registry Key

The DeleteKey function is the last of this example's action procedures. It wraps the RegOpenKeyEx and RegDeleteKey functions to open the subkey and delete it. If both calls complete successfully, a Boolean True is returned; otherwise a Boolean False is returned.

```
Public Function DeleteKey(lngRootKey As Long, strSubKey As String, _
    strKillKey As String) As Boolean

    Dim hKey As LongPtr

    On Error GoTo DeleteKey_Err

    'Open the key and get its handle
    lngReturn = RegOpenKeyEx(lngRootKey, strSubKey, _
        0&, KEY_ALL_ACCESS, hKey)

    'Check that the call succeeded
    If lngReturn <> ERROR_SUCCESS Then
        Err.Raise vbObjectError + 2, , "Could not open key."
    End If
```

```
        'Delete the subkey
        lngReturn = RegDeleteKey(hKey, strKillKey)

DeleteKey_Exit:
    On Error Resume Next

    'Return success or failure
    DeleteKey = (lngReturn = ERROR_SUCCESS)

    'Close the key
    lngReturn = RegCloseKey(hKey)
    Exit Function

DeleteKey_Err:
    DoCmd.Beep
    MsgBox "Error " & Err.Number & vbCrLf & _
        Err.Description, vbOKOnly + vbExclamation, _
        "Could not retrieve the key"

    Resume DeleteKey_Exit
End Function
```

code snippet RegistrySamples.accdb

Testing the Function Wrappers

Finally, the following procedure is the one you can use to test the preceding API function wrappers.
Copy this code to a standard module and step through it using the F8 key.

```
Public Sub TestReg()
    Dim strBaseKey As String
    Dim strSubKey As String
    Dim strMsg As String
    Dim varReturn As Variant

    'For convenience only, initialize variables with
    'the subkey names.
    strBaseKey = "Software\VB and VBA Program Settings\myapp\Settings"
    strSubKey = "Software\VB and VBA Program Settings\myapp\Settings\myNewKey"

    '=== Create a new subkey.
    varReturn = CreateKey(HKEY_CURRENT_USER, strSubKey, REG_SZ)

    'Check for success or failure.
    'If success, continue with the remaining procedures.
    If Not IsNull(varReturn) Then
        strMsg = "Created a new key '" & varReturn & "'."
        MsgBox strMsg, vbOKOnly + vbInformation, "Test Registry functions"

        '=== Set a new subkey value.
        varReturn = SetKeyValue(HKEY_CURRENT_USER, strSubKey, _
            "myValue", "11123")

        'Check success or failure.
```

```
        If varReturn = True Then
            strMsg = "Set a new key value to '11123'."
        Else
            strMsg = "Failed to set new key value."
        End If

        MsgBox strMsg, vbOKOnly + vbInformation, "Test Registry functions"

        '=== Retrieve the value we just set.
        varReturn = GetKeyValue(HKEY_CURRENT_USER, strSubKey, _
            "myValue")

        'Check success or failure.
        If Len(varReturn) > 0 Then
            strMsg = "The current value of key '" & strSubKey & _
                "' is '" & varReturn & "'"
        Else
            strMsg = "Failed to read key value."
        End If

        MsgBox strMsg, vbOKOnly + vbInformation, "Test Registry functions"

        '=== Now delete the key value
        varReturn = DeleteValue(HKEY_CURRENT_USER, strSubKey, "myValue")

        'Check success or failure.
        If varReturn = True Then
            strMsg = "Deleted the key value."
        Else
            strMsg = "Failed to delete the key value."
        End If

        MsgBox strMsg, vbOKOnly + vbInformation, "Test Registry functions"

        '=== Lastly, delete the subkey itself
        varReturn = DeleteKey(HKEY_CURRENT_USER, strBaseKey, "myNewKey")

        'Check success or failure.
        If varReturn = True Then
            strMsg = "Deleted the key."
        Else
            strMsg = "Failed to delete the key."
        End If

        MsgBox strMsg, vbOKOnly + vbInformation, "Test Registry functions"
    Else
        strMsg = "Failed to create the new key."
        MsgBox strMsg, vbOKOnly + vbInformation, "Test Registry functions"
    End If
End Sub
```

code snippet RegistrySamples.accdb

Opening an Existing Registry Key

In several of the preceding examples, you used the `RegOpenKeyEx` API function to open an existing Registry key. Because this function will be used quite often, the following code offers another way to write this function. In this example, you return the handle to the Registry key as the return value of the wrapper function. Add the following code to the module:

```vba
#If Win64 = 1 And VBA7 = 1 Then

Public Function OpenKey(lngRootKey As Long, _
    strKeyName As String, _
    Optional lngKeyAccess As Long = KEY_READ) As LongPtr

    Dim hKey As LongPtr

#Else

Public Function OpenKey(lngRootKey As Long, _
    strKeyName As String, _
    Optional lngKeyAccess As Long = KEY_READ) As Long

    Dim hKey As Long

#End If

    ' open the registry key
    lngReturn = RegOpenKeyEx(lngRootKey, strKeyName, 0, lngKeyAccess, hKey)

    ' return the handle to the specified key
    ' callers should call the CloseKey API to close the handle
    OpenKey = hKey
End Function
```

code snippet RegistrySamples.accdb

To use this function, you would simply call it before calling any of the other Registry API functions. Because this function will call the `RegOpenKeyEx` API, you'll need to remember to call the `RegCloseKey` API when you're done with the handle. For example:

```vba
Dim hKey As LongPtr
hKey = OpenKey(HKEY_CLASSES_ROOT, ".accdb")
```

> *We're using the `LongPtr` data type for the return value of the function because handles on 64-bit Windows are also 64-bit values. Using conditional compilation, you can change the declaration of your function in VBA to conditionally change the return type, as shown here. This allows you to share code in a single function while only changing the `Function` statement. As an alternative, you could also put the entire function in conditional compilation blocks. Conditional compilation was discussed in more detail in Chapter 9.*

Connecting to the Registry on a Remote Computer

The larger an application grows, the more necessary it may be to communicate with other computers. This also applies to the Registry, and as such, there is a Windows API that allows you to connect to the Registry on another computer. The API in question is called `RegConnectRegistry` and requires administrator privileges to connect. Here is the declaration:

```
#If Win64 = 1 And VBA7 = 1 Then

Public Declare PtrSafe Function RegConnectRegistry Lib "advapi32.dll" _
    Alias "RegConnectRegistryA" ( _
    ByVal lpMachineName As String, _
    ByVal hKey As Long, _
    phkResult As LongPtr) As Long

#Else

Public Declare Function RegConnectRegistry Lib "advapi32.dll" _
    Alias "RegConnectRegistryA" ( _
    ByVal lpMachineName As String, _
    ByVal hKey As Long, _
    phkResult As Long) As Long

#End If
```

code snippet RegistrySamples.accdb

The following code demonstrates how to use this API function. Call this function by passing the name of a remote computer for which you have administrative rights.

```
Public Sub ConnectToRemoteRegistry(strRemoteComputer As String)
    #If Win64 = 1 And VBA7 = 1 Then
        Dim phKey As LongPtr
    #Else
        Dim phKey As Long
    #End If

    Dim vValue As Variant

    ' connect to the remote machine
    ' strRemoteComputer can be a computer name or IP address
    lngReturn = RegConnectRegistry(strRemoteComputer, HKEY_USERS, phKey)

    Stop

    ' were we able to connect?
    If lngReturn <> ERROR_SUCCESS Then
        MsgBox "Unable to connect to remote registry"
        Exit Sub
    End If

    ' We should now be connected to HKLM on the remote machine.
    ' The key handle that is returned by RegConnectRegistry is that
```

```
    ' of a ROOT key.
    vValue = GetKeyValue(phKey, ".DEFAULT\Environment", "TEMP")

    If (IsNull(vValue)) Then
        MsgBox "Cannot read the specified value"
    Else
        MsgBox "The value of the remote key is: " & vValue
    End If

    ' close the key
    If phKey <> 0 Then RegCloseKey phKey
End Sub
```

code snippet RegistrySamples.accdb

> The hKey parameter of the `RegConnectRegistry` function must be one of the
> following predefined key values: `HKEY_LOCAL_MACHINE`, `HKEY_USERS`, `HKEY_`
> `PERFORMANCE_DATA`. The handle that is returned by the function is that of the
> root key on the remote machine.

Enumerating Registry Keys and Values

If you are managing a set of keys and values for your application, you might want to display
them or save them in some manner. Two functions will help you enumerate Registry keys and values — `RegEnumExKey` and `RegEnumValue` respectively. They are defined as follows, along with the
`FILETIME` user-defined type which is the data type for one of the arguments to the functions:

**Available for
download on
Wrox.com**

```
Public Type FILETIME
    dwLowDateTime  As Long
    dwHighDateTime As Long
End Type

#If Win64 = 1 And VBA7 = 1 Then

Public Declare PtrSafe Function RegCloseKey Lib "advapi32.dll" _
    (ByVal hKey As LongPtr) As Long

Public Declare PtrSafe Function RegOpenKeyEx Lib "advapi32.dll" _
    Alias "RegOpenKeyExA" ( _
    ByVal hKey As LongPtr, _
    ByVal lpSubKey As String, _
    ByVal ulOptions As Long, _
    ByVal samDesired As Long, _
    phkResult As LongPtr) As Long

Public Declare PtrSafe Function RegEnumKeyEx Lib "advapi32.dll" _
    Alias "RegEnumKeyExA" ( _
    ByVal hKey As LongPtr, _
    ByVal dwIndex As Long, _
```

```vba
    ByVal lpName As String, _
    lpcbName As LongPtr, _
    ByVal lpReserved As LongPtr, _
    ByVal lpClass As String, _
    lpcbClass As LongPtr, _
    lpftLastWriteTime As FILETIME) As Long

Public Declare PtrSafe Function RegEnumValue Lib "advapi32.dll" _
    Alias "RegEnumValueA" ( _
    ByVal hKey As LongPtr, _
    ByVal dwIndex As Long, _
    ByVal lpValueName As String, _
    lpcbValueName As LongPtr, _
    ByVal lpReserved As LongPtr, _
    lpType As LongPtr, _
    lpData As Any, _
    lpcbData As LongPtr) As Long

#Else

Public Declare Function RegCloseKey Lib "advapi32.dll" _
    (ByVal hKey As Long) As Long

Public Declare Function RegOpenKeyEx Lib "advapi32.dll" _
    Alias "RegOpenKeyExA" ( _
    ByVal hKey As Long, _
    ByVal lpSubKey As String, _
    ByVal ulOptions As Long, _
    ByVal samDesired As Long, _
    phkResult As Long) As Long

Public Declare Function RegEnumKeyEx Lib "advapi32.dll" _
    Alias "RegEnumKeyExA" ( _
    ByVal hKey As Long, _
    ByVal dwIndex As Long, _
    ByVal lpName As String, _
    lpcbName As Long, _
    ByVal lpReserved As Long, _
    ByVal lpClass As String, _
    lpcbClass As Long, _
    lpftLastWriteTime As FILETIME) As Long

Public Declare Function RegEnumValue Lib "advapi32.dll" _
    Alias "RegEnumValueA" ( _
    ByVal hKey As Long, _
    ByVal dwIndex As Long, _
    ByVal lpValueName As String, _
    lpcbValueName As Long, _
    ByVal lpReserved As Long, _
    lpType As Long, _
    lpData As Any, _
    lpcbData As Long) As Long

#End If
```

code snippet RegistrySamples.accdb

The following code recursively calls these functions to enumerate all subkeys and values under the specified key. The Registry API functions return the error code ERROR_NO_MORE_ITEMS when you reach the last item from one of these functions. This constant is also defined in the code that follows.

Note that this code also requires the RegOpenKeyEx and RegCloseKey functions that were defined earlier.

```vb
Public Sub EnumKeysAndValues(lRootKey As Long, strStartingKey As String)
    ' data for registry keys
    Dim lngKeyIndex     As Long      ' index of the key
    Dim strKeyName      As String    ' name of the key
    Dim lngKeyNameLen   As LongPtr   ' length of the key name

    ' data for registry values
    Dim lngValueIndex   As Long      ' index of the value
    Dim strValueName    As String    ' name of the value
    Dim lngValueNameLen As LongPtr   ' length of the value name
    Dim lngValueType    As LongPtr   ' registry data type

    ' other locals
    Dim lngKeyResult    As Long      ' return variable for RegEnumKeyEx
    Dim lngValueResult  As Long      ' return variable for RegEnumValue
    Dim hKey            As LongPtr   ' handle to a reg key
    Dim ft              As FILETIME  ' last write time for the key

    Debug.Print strStartingKey

    ' loop until there are no more items
    Do
        'open the key
        If RegOpenKeyEx(lRootKey, strStartingKey, 0, _
                        KEY_READ, hKey) <> ERROR_SUCCESS Then
            MsgBox "Unable to open the specified key: " & _
                    strStartingKey, vbExclamation
            Exit Sub
        End If

        ' hKey should be non-zero
        Debug.Assert hKey <> 0

        ' print the values for the current registry key
        Do
            ' data for the value names needs to be initialized each time
            lngValueNameLen = MAX_VALUE_NAME
            strValueName = Space(MAX_VALUE_NAME)

            ' get the value name without the data
            lngValueResult = RegEnumValue(hKey, lngValueIndex, strValueName, _
                                lngValueNameLen, 0, lngValueType, ByVal 0, 0)

            ' print the value
            If lngValueResult = ERROR_SUCCESS And Len(Trim(strValueName)) > 0 Then
                Debug.Print Left(strValueName, InStr(strValueName, vbNullChar) - 1)
            End If

            ' get the next value
```

```
            lngValueIndex = lngValueIndex + 1
        Loop While lngValueResult <> ERROR_NO_MORE_ITEMS

        ' data for the key names needs to be initialized each time
        strKeyName = Space(MAX_KEY_LENGTH)
        lngKeyNameLen = MAX_KEY_LENGTH

        ' enumerate the keys
        lngKeyResult = RegEnumKeyEx(hKey, lngKeyIndex, strKeyName, lngKeyNameLen, _
                            0, vbNullString, 0, ft)

        ' ERROR CHECKING.
        ' If the function returns something other than success, or that there are
        ' more items, then display the error
        If lngKeyResult <> ERROR_SUCCESS And _
           lngKeyResult <> ERROR_NO_MORE_ITEMS Then
            MsgBox "Cannot enumerate the specified key. Error = " & lngKeyResult, _
                    vbExclamation
            Exit Sub
        End If

        ' Get the next key index
        lngKeyIndex = lngKeyIndex + 1

        ' recurse
        If lngKeyResult <> ERROR_NO_MORE_ITEMS Then
            EnumKeysAndValues lRootKey, _
                        strStartingKey & "\" & Left(strKeyName, _
                        CLng(lngKeyNameLen))
        End If

        ' We're done with the current key, close it
        RegCloseKey hKey

    Loop While lngKeyResult <> ERROR_NO_MORE_ITEMS
End Sub
```

code snippet RegistrySamples.accdb

SUMMARY

In this chapter, you considered the evolution of the Windows Registry, what it does, how it works, and how it is used, and looked at the tools you can use to examine and modify the Registry.

You explored the Windows Registry structure and perused the built-in VBA functions you can use to manipulate that portion of the Registry specifically set aside for VBA programmers. Finally, you built your own modest Registry module.

Having reached the end of this chapter, you've now acquired enough information and experience to develop some fairly sophisticated database applications. From here, we'll move into exploring data access using DAO in Chapter 11.

11

Using DAO to Access Data

WHAT'S IN THIS CHAPTER?

➤ A look at new features available in DAO in Access 2007 and Access 2010

➤ In-depth descriptions of objects you'll use in DAO to help create objects and work with data

As you've seen in previous chapters, VBA is the programming language you use to programmatically interact with the Access Object Model. You use VBA to manipulate Access-specific objects, such as forms, reports, and so on. But because Access is a relational database management system, you will undoubtedly find yourself also needing to programmatically interact with the data it contains, and indeed with the database design, or schema. Microsoft Access employs two data access Object Models: Data Access Objects (DAO) and ActiveX Data Objects (ADO).

Chapter 12 covers ADO; this chapter is solely concerned with the DAO model. It begins with a brief history of DAO and an indication of when it might be most appropriate to use DAO in preference to ADO. You'll see the new features in DAO before examining the three most important objects in the DAO object hierarchy: the DBEngine, Workspace, and Database objects. Then you'll explore database properties and how to use them.

Before you start working with DAO objects to access your data, you'll take an in-depth look at how to use DAO to create and modify your database structure, including tables, fields, indexes, and relations. Finally, you'll look at data access in detail using QueryDefs and Recordsets.

DATA ACCESS OBJECTS

DAO is the programmatic interface between VBA and the Access database engine databases, ODBC (Open Database Connectivity) data stores, and installable ISAM (indexed sequential access method) data sources, such as Excel and Text. DAO was first released as a part of Visual Basic 2.0 and later released with Access 1.0 in November 1992. Over the years, many changes have been made to both DAO and to the Microsoft Jet database engine to reflect technologies at the time. There were even versions of Access (2000 and XP/2002) that de-emphasized the importance of DAO and led to conjecture that support for DAO was waning. Since then, however, the support for DAO has increased. Now, support for 32-bit operating systems, ODBC data sources, and Unicode languages is included in current versions of DAO, and for the first time, there is a 64-bit version of DAO for use with the 64-bit version of Access 2010.

The most recent version of DAO is 14.0, which ships with Access 2010. This version was written for use with the Access database engine (also known as ACE), which is an updated version of the Microsoft Jet database engine. New features were added to the Access database engine in both Access 2007 and Access 2010. We'll explore these new features shortly. The file names for DAO and the Access database engine for these components are `ACEDAO.DLL` and `ACECORE.DLL` respectively.

WHY USE DAO?

Applications written in other programming languages, such as Visual Basic.NET, C#, and the like, must explicitly connect to the data source they intend to manipulate. That's because, unlike Access, these environments do not have an inherent connection to the data source. When used in Access, DAO enables you to manipulate data and schema through an implicit connection that Access maintains to whichever Access database engine, ODBC, or ISAM data source it happens to be connected to.

DAO has evolved right alongside Jet and the Access database engine, and is often the best model for accessing and manipulating Access database engine objects and structure. Because of its tight integration with Access, DAO also provides better access to Access databases than ADO or the Jet Replication Objects (JRO). Here are some of the advantages of using DAO:

➤ ADO connections can be applied to only one database at a time, whereas DAO enables you to link (connect) to multiple databases simultaneously.

➤ Using the `OpenRecordset` method's `dbDenyWrite` option, DAO enables you to open a table while preventing other users from opening the same table with write access. The ADO `Connection` object's `adModeShareDenyWrite` constant operates at connection level — not at table level.

➤ Using the `OpenRecordset` method's `dbDenyRead` option, DAO enables you to open a table while preventing other users from opening the table at all. The ADO `Connection` object's `adModeShareDenyRead` constant can only be set at connection level.

➤ You can dynamically link an updatable ODBC table in DAO, but not in ADO.

➤ DAO enables you to create replica databases that prevent users from deleting records; JRO does not.

➤ In DAO, you can return information about Exchange and Outlook folders and columns using the `TableDef` and `Field Attributes` properties. ADO does not pass this information through to Access.

➤ Using the DBEngine's GetOption and SetOption methods, DAO enables you to set and change Access database engine options without requiring you to make Registry changes.

➤ DAO enables you to create, change, and delete custom database properties.

➤ You can force the database-locking mode with the DAO.LockTypeEnum constants against CurrentDb, but you can't do the same thing in ADO using ADO.LockTypeEnum against CurrentProject.Connection.

➤ DAO enables you to run a separate session of the Access database engine, using PrivDBEngine; ADO does not.

➤ DAO enables you to create multi-value lookup fields using new complex data types. A multi-value lookup field is a single field that can store multiple values in an embedded Recordset. You explore this new field type in more detail later in this chapter.

➤ DAO enables you to create and insert data in an Attachment field. Attachment fields are a new data type in the Access database engine and will be examined in more detail later in this chapter.

The current version of DAO is a very mature, well-documented, and easy-to-use Object Model for accessing database services. You can use DAO from any VBA environment such as Word, Excel, and so on, and a variety of other programming languages such as Visual Basic, C++, and even managed languages such as C#.

Finally, it's fairly safe to say that DAO will be around as long as Access or Jet databases are used.

NEW FEATURES IN DAO

As mentioned earlier, several new features were introduced to DAO in Access 2007 that are also available in Access 2010. These features are multi-value lookup fields, attachment fields, append-only memo fields, and database encryption. Access 2010 adds calculated fields to the list of new features in DAO. Each of these features is only available in the ACCDB file format so as not to break backward compatibility with the MDB file format.

All of these features, with the exception of database encryption, have been available on Windows SharePoint Services, and were added to Access for feature parity with that platform. (You can find out more about SharePoint in Chapter 19.)

Multi-Value Lookup Fields

When you create a lookup field in Access 2007 or Access 2010, you can optionally choose to allow that field to store multiple values. For example, say you have a table of students, and you want to track their favorite colors. Traditionally, you accomplish this by using three tables: one for Students, one for Colors, and a table in between these two called a junction table. *Multi-value lookup fields*, also known as *complex* fields, can also be used to store the favorite colors for a particular student as a single field in the Students table. A multi-value lookup field can store many related records in a single field value. You can think of them as an embedded or nested Recordset in a field for a particular record. In fact, that's exactly how you work with multi-value lookup fields in DAO. Access displays them using a list of values, as shown in Figure 11-1.

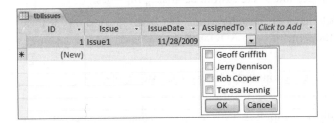

FIGURE 11-1

You might look at that list and think to yourself, "Isn't that denormalized?" Well, not to worry — the values for multiple-value fields are stored behind the scenes in related tables. Since these values are stored behind the scenes, they are not available for viewing or querying directly. However, Access does all of the work to maintain these relationships and lets you, as the developer, focus on data manipulation in a natural manner — by using DAO or SQL.

> *While it is possible to use SQL to query multi-value fields, it may be easier to use DAO.*

Multi-value lookup fields can be useful for simple one-to-many relationships, but they have one major limitation. The nested Recordset for a multi-value lookup field contains only one column called `Value`. This is true whether the lookup field is created using the Access interface or DAO. To extend the example a little, it might be nice to know the semester in which a student attended a particular class, and even the grade he received for the class. That is not possible using a multi-value lookup field because those fields store only one field per record.

Attachment Fields

Access has had a means for storing files in the database for some time with the `OLE Object` data type. However, there are a few problems with this type. The first is that Access stores a wrapper around the data, which can often result in a database that grows unexpectedly. This unexpected growth is called *database bloat*. This is even true for linked OLE Objects. Once the data was stored in the database, it wasn't easy to retrieve outside of Access. Frequently, a form was required to display data in the field, and using DAO against OLE Object fields was not easy.

Microsoft has solved this problem by adding a new data type called *Attachment*. Attachment fields are a special type of multi-valued field that allow for both multiple fields and multiple values in the nested Recordset. The file itself is compressed by Access and stored in the database. As such, Access can store an attachment field without the additional space required by an OLE Object. No more database bloat! A new Attachment control is also available for working with the data inside of Access.

Append-Only Fields

Have you ever wanted to track the history for a particular field in a table? As requirements for maintaining data over time become more and more common, scenarios such as this may become more important. Access now enables you to store a history of the data in a memo field, using a new property called `Append Only`. When this property is set, Access automatically stores the previous version of text in the field as part of the data along with a timestamp. As you might imagine, this data is also stored using a multi-valued field.

Database Encryption

In previous versions of Access, you could assign a password to your database to require users to enter a password when opening a database, but that did not encrypt the data in the file. Database encryption in Access 2007 and Access 2010 now uses Windows encryption technologies to encrypt a database when you assign a database password. This feature also replaces the *encoding* feature that was available in Jet.

The database encryption feature is covered in more detail in Chapter 24.

Calculated Fields

For many years, we've created calculated columns using an expression in a query. In many cases, calculating the value each time in a query is desired as values in a row may change. In this case, each time you run the query, the expression is reevaluated for all rows. Since the expression is evaluated every time, this may slow down the query depending on the number of rows and the complexity of the calculation.

In Access 2010, a new type of field was added called a calculated field. In a calculated field, the expression for the calculation is defined in the field, and the calculated values are stored in the table. These values are updated only when a field used in the expression is updated, making calculated fields nearly as fast as other fields.

At first glance, it appears that storing calculated values would violate database normalization rules. This is true. However, there are scenarios when data may not change very often where this type of denormalization is valuable. For example, first and last name are often concatenated to form a person's full name. Names may not change very often, so this example is a good candidate for using the new calculated field type.

Also, calculated fields can be indexed if desired, allowing faster retrieval and sorting of records based on the calculated value.

REFERRING TO DAO OBJECTS

You might recall from earlier discussion that a collection is a container for a group of objects of the same type. Many DAO collections contain other collections, so it is sometimes necessary to drill down through several collections before you get to the object that you want to operate on. This provides a highly structured and predictable method for accessing data and schema.

With the exception of the `DBEngine` object, all DAO objects are contained within their own collections. For example, the `TableDef` object is part of a `TableDefs` collection, and the `Index` object is part of an `Indexes` collection. Collections provide an easy way to enumerate their members by allowing you to refer to them by their name or ordinal position. The examples in the following table show how you can refer to the same object in different ways.

SYNTAX	DESCRIPTION	EXAMPLE
`Collection("name")`	Literal string	`DBEngine.Workspaces(0).Databases("myDB")`
`Collection(position)`	Ordinal collection position	`DBEngine.Workspaces(0).Databases(0)`
`Collection(variable)`	String or variant variable	`strVar = "myDB"DBEngine.Workspaces(0)` `.Databases(strVar)`
`Collection![Name]`	Object name	`DBEngine.Workspaces(0).Databases!myDB`

Where the object name contains nonstandard characters, such as spaces, you must enclose the object name in square brackets ([]).

Let's say you wanted to retrieve the `DefaultValue` property for a field called `PaymentDate` in a table called `tblPayments`. This is the long way of doing it:

```
DBEngine.Workspaces(0).Databases(0).TableDefs!tblPayments.Fields!PaymentDate
.DefaultValue
```

As you can see, referring to objects, properties, and methods can result in pretty long lines of code. This can get tedious after a while, so you can also refer to objects by their parent collection's default item. Assuming `tblPayments` is the first table in the `TableDefs` collection, and `PaymentDate` is the first field in that table's `Fields` collection, here is the shortened version:

```
DBEngine(0)(0)(0)(0).DefaultValue
```

Collections in DAO and Access are 0-based, meaning that the first item in the collection is at ordinal position 0. This is in contrast to collections in VBA which are 1-based.

Although the syntax shown above is valid and will return a `Field` object, this type of syntax is seldom used.

The following table lists examples of the two ways you can refer to DAO collection members.

COLLECTION	DEFAULT MEMBER	EXAMPLE
Containers	Documents	DBEngine.Workspaces(0).Databases(0) .Containers(0).Documents(0) DBEngine(0)(0).Containers(0)(0)
Databases	TableDefs	DBEngine.Workspaces(0).Databases(0) .TableDefs(0)DBEngine(0)(0)(0)
DBEngine	Workspaces	DBEngine.Workspaces(0)DBEngine(0)
QueryDefs	Parameters	DBEngine.Workspaces(0).Databases(0) .QueryDefs(0).Parameters(0) DBEngine(0)(0).QueryDefs(0)(0)
Recordsets	Fields	DBEngine.Workspaces(0).Databases(0) .Recordsets(0).Fields(0) DBEngine(0)(0).Recordsets(0)(0)
Relations	Fields	DBEngine.Workspaces(0).Databases(0) .Relations(0).Fields(0) DBEngine(0)(0).Relations(0)(0)
TableDefs	Fields	DBEngine.Workspaces(0).Databases(0) .TableDefs(0).Fields(0) DBEngine(0)(0)(0)(0)
Workspaces	Databases	DBEngine.Workspaces(0) DBEngine(0)

THE DBENGINE OBJECT

The DBEngine object is a property of the Access Application object, and represents the top-level object in the DAO model. The DBEngine object contains all the other objects in the DAO object hierarchy, yet unlike many of the other DAO objects, you can't create additional DBEngine objects.

The DBEngine object contains two major collections — Workspaces and Errors — which are described in the following subsection.

The Workspaces Collection

A *workspace* is a named user session that contains open databases and provides the facility for transactions and (depending on the database format) user-and group-level security. As you can have more than one workspace active at any time, the Workspaces collection is the repository for all the workspaces that have been created.

You use the Microsoft Access workspace to access Microsoft Access database engine databases (ACCDB files created in Access 2007 or Access 2010), Microsoft Jet databases (MDB files created in previous versions), and ODBC or installable ISAM data sources through the Microsoft Access database engine. For a list of the collections, objects, and methods supported by Microsoft Access workspaces, refer to Appendix B.

ODBCDirect

In addition to the Microsoft Access workspace, previous versions of DAO supported a second type of `Workspace` object called ODBCDirect. ODBCDirect workspaces are used against ODBC data sources such as SQL Server. Beginning with Office 2007, Microsoft is no longer shipping RDO that enabled this type of workspace. As a result, ODBCDirect is no longer supported in DAO. You will see a runtime error if you try to create an ODBCDirect workspace using the `CreateWorkspace` method in DAO.

Subsequently, because you cannot create ODBCDirect workspaces, calling the `OpenConnection` method will cause a runtime error, and the `Connections` collection of the `DBEngine` object will not contain any `Connection` objects.

With the removal of ODBCDirect workspaces, all DAO code in this chapter will use a Microsoft Access workspace.

Creating a Workspace

If you have Microsoft Jet databases that use Jet user-level security (ULS) to help secure objects, there may be times when you need to access them from unsecured databases. In such cases, you can create a new `Workspace` object to provide the username and password for the secured database.

You don't have to do anything to begin using a Microsoft Access workspace; Access creates one by default. The default workspace is given the name #Default Workspace#. In the absence of user- and group-level security, the default workspace's `UserName` property is set to `Admin`. If security is implemented, the `UserName` property is set to the name of the user who logged in to Access (not the Windows user).

You can use a workspace without appending it to the `Workspaces` collection, but you must refer to it using the object variable to which it was assigned. You will not be able to refer to it through the `Workspaces` collection until it is appended.

The following example demonstrates how to create a Microsoft Access workspace, and print the `Name` property:

```
Dim wsAccess As DAO.Workspace
Dim strUserName As String
Dim strPassword As String

'Set the user name and password
strUserName = "Admin"
strPassword = ""

'Create a new Microsoft Access workspace
Set wsAccess = DBEngine.CreateWorkspace( _
    "myAccessWS", strUserName, strPassword, dbUseJet)

'Append the workspaces to the collection
Workspaces.Append wsAccess

'Print the name of the workspace
```

```
Debug.Print "wsAccess.Name: " & wsAccess.Name 'myAccessWS

'Clean up
wsAccess.Close
Set wsAccess = Nothing
```

To use the default workspace, you can either refer to it as `DBEngine(0)`, or create a reference to it in the same way you create references to other Access or DAO objects:

```
'Create a reference to the default workspace
Set wsAccess1 = DBEngine(0)
Debug.Print "wsAccess1.Name: " & wsAccess1.Name '#Default Workspace#
```

Because you're not creating a new workspace object, there is no need to append it to the `Workspaces` collection.

Finally, there is one other way to create a new workspace. To maintain compatibility with previous versions of DAO, Access 2010 still provides the `DefaultWorkspaceClone` method.

```
'Create a clone of the default workspace
Set wsAccess2 = Application.DefaultWorkspaceClone
Debug.Print "wsAccess2.Name: " & wsAccess.Name '#CloneAccess#
```

The `DefaultWorkspaceClone` method creates an identical copy of the default workspace, whatever it happens to be. The cloned workspace takes on properties identical to those of the original, with the exception of its `Name` property, which is set to #CloneAccess#. You can change this name if you choose.

You would use the `DefaultWorkspaceClone` method where you want to operate two independent transactions simultaneously without needing to prompt the user again for the username and password.

Using Transactions

A *transaction* is defined as a delimited set of changes that are performed on a database's schema or data. They increase the speed of actions that change data, and enable you to undo sets of changes that have not yet been committed as a group.

Transactions offer a great deal of data integrity insurance for situations where an entire series of actions must complete successfully, or not complete at all. This is the all-or-nothing principle that is employed in most financial transactions.

For example, when your employer transfers your monthly salary from their bank to yours, two actions actually occur. The first is a withdrawal from your employer's account, and the second is a deposit into yours. If the withdrawal completes, but for some reason, the deposit fails, you can argue until you're blue in the face, but your employer can prove that they paid you, and are not likely to want to do so again. Similarly, your bank will not be too impressed if the withdrawal fails, but the deposit succeeds. The reality is that the bank will take the money back, and you still end up with no salary. If, however, the two actions are enclosed in a single transaction, they must both complete successfully, or the transaction is deemed to have failed, and both actions are rolled back (reversed).

You begin a transaction by issuing the `BeginTrans` method against the `Workspace` object. To write the transaction to disk, you issue the `CommitTrans` method, and to cancel, or roll back the transaction, you use the `Rollback` method.

Typically, transactions are cached, and not immediately written to disk. But if you're in a real hurry to get home at five o'clock, and immediately switch off your computer before the cache is written to disk, your most recent changes are lost. In Microsoft Access workspaces, you can force the database engine to immediately write all changes to disk, instead of caching them. You do this by including the `dbForceOSFlush` constant with `CommitTrans`. Forcing immediate writes may affect your application's performance, but the data integrity benefits may outweigh any performance hit in certain situations.

The following code segment demonstrates a typical funds transfer transaction.

> *In this and in other examples in this chapter, the code shortens the name of* `Workspace`, `Database`, *and* `Recordset` *object variables and therefore deviates from the Reddick naming convention for brevity.*

Available for download on Wrox.com

```
Public Sub TransferFunds()
    Dim wrk As DAO.Workspace
    Dim dbC As DAO.Database
    Dim dbX As DAO.Database

    Set wrk = DBEngine(0)
    Set dbC = CurrentDb
    Set dbX = wrk.OpenDatabase("c:\Temp\myDB.mdb")

    On Error GoTo trans_Err

    'Begin the transaction
    wrk.BeginTrans

    'Run a SQL statement to withdraw funds from one account table
    dbC.Execute "UPDATE Table1.....", dbFailOnError

    'Run a SQL statement to deposit funds into another account table
    dbX.Execute "INSERT INTO Table22.....", dbFailOnError

    'Commit the transaction
    wrk.CommitTrans dbForceOSFlush

trans_Exit:
    'Clean up
    wrk.Close
    Set dbC = Nothing
    Set dbX = Nothing
    Set wrk = Nothing
    Exit Sub

trans_Err:
    'Roll back the transaction
```

```
        wrk.Rollback
        Resume trans_Exit
End Sub
```

code snippet Chapter 11 - DAO Samples

In this example, changes to both databases will complete as a unit, or will be rolled back as a unit. Also note that if a complete system error occurs before the transaction is committed (say the PC's power is switched off), the uncommitted transaction will be rolled back the next time the database is opened, even though the Rollback method never had a chance to run.

You don't need to use transactions, but if you do, they can be nested up to five levels. It is also important to understand that transactions are global to the workspace — not the database. For example, if you make changes to two databases in the same workspace, and you roll back the changes to one of those databases, the changes made to the other database will also be rolled back.

The Errors Collection

The first thing to remember about the DAO Errors collection is that it is not the same as the VBA.Err object. The VBA.Err object is a single object that stores information about the last VBA error. The DAO Errors collection stores information about the last DAO error.

Any operation performed on any DAO object can generate one or more errors. The DBEngine.Errors collection stores all the Error objects that are added as the result of an error that occurs during a single operation. The lowest level error is stored in the collection first, followed by the higher level errors. Enumerating the Errors collection enables your error-handling code to more precisely determine the cause of the problem, and to take the most appropriate action. When a subsequent DAO operation generates an error, the Errors collection is cleared and a new set of Error objects is added to the collection.

One last point to note is that an error that occurs in an object that has not yet been added to its collection is not added to the DBEngine.Errors collection because the "object" is not considered to be an object until it is added to a collection. In such cases, the error information will be available in the VBA.Err object.

To fully account for all errors, your error handler should verify that the error number returned by both the VBA.Err object and the last member of the DBEngine.Error object are the same. The following code demonstrates a typical error handler:

Available for download on Wrox.com

```
intDAOErrNo = DBEngine.Errors(DBEngine.Errors.Count -1).Number

If VBA.Err <> intDAOErrNo Then
    DBEngine.Errors.Refresh
End If

For intCtr = 0 To DBEngine.Errors.Count -1
    Select Case DBEngine.Errors(intCtr).Number
        Case 1
            'Code to handle error
```

```
            Case 2
            'Code to handle error
            '
            'Other Case statements
            '
            Case 99
            'Code to handle error
            End Select
    Next intCtr
```

code snippet Chapter 11 - DAO Samples

THE DATABASE OBJECT

Using DAO, you can have more than one database open at any time. If you're using an .accdb or .mdb database file, you already have one database open (called the *current* database). Using the Workspace object's OpenDatabase method as shown earlier, you can open more than one database, and operate on them under the same workspace. Indeed, if you were to define more than one Workspace object, you could have several databases open, each operating under a different workspace. The Databases collection contains and manages all databases currently open in the workspace.

The Default (Access) Database

Unless you're working with an Access Data Project (ADP), when you create a database in Access, it is automatically added to the Databases collection.

Among its properties and methods, the Database object contains five collections: TableDefs, Containers, QueryDefs, Recordsets, and Relations. Each of these collections and their respective objects and properties are discussed in later sections. In most cases, you will be working with the default Microsoft Access database, which you can refer to using any of the following syntaxes:

```
DBEngine.Workspaces("#Default Workspace#").Databases(0)
DBEngine.Workspaces(0).Databases(0)
DBEngine(0).Databases(0)
DBEngine(0)(0)
CurrentDb()
```

The current user's default database is an object that you will use quite a lot. Although you can work with it using any of the reference methods listed, in most cases it is often more convenient to assign it to an object variable.

```
Dim dbs As DAO.Database
Set dbs = DBEngine(0)(0)
```

But far and away the most common method is to use the CurrentDb() function, described in the following section.

The CurrentDb Function

Access always maintains a reference to the current database. The first member of the Databases collection is populated with a reference to the current database at startup. This reference, pointed to by DBEngine(0)(0), is fine under most circumstances, but when, for example, you are working on wizards, it may not always be the database you expect. In these circumstances it is possible for the first database in the collection to point to something other than the current database. Although the chance of this occurring in *normal* databases is negligible, there is a way to ensure that you are always working with the current database.

The solution that Microsoft came up with was to provide the CurrentDb function. CurrentDb is a method of the Access Application object that provides a reference to the currently open database. Although CurrentDb and DBEngine(0)(0) usually refer to the same database, it is essential that you understand some important concepts.

First, CurrentDb and DBEngine(0)(0) are not the same objects internally. Access maintains a reference to the current database, but CurrentDb temporarily creates a new object internally — one in which the collections are guaranteed to be up-to-date. When CurrentDb is executed, Access creates a new internal object that recreates the hierarchy and refers to the current database. After CurrentDb executes and returns, the internal object is destroyed. As a result, the following code generates an error because the reference to the current database is lost immediately after the line containing CurrentDb executes:

```
Dim fld As DAO.Field
Set fld = CurrentDb.TableDefs(0).Fields(0)
Debug.Print fld.Name
```

This is the case for most DAO objects. One notable exception to this is the Recordset object, for which Access tries to maintain the database reference. To use CurrentDb effectively, it is always wiser to assign the reference to an object variable, as shown here:

```
Dim dbs As DAO.Database
Dim fld As DAO.Field

Set dbs = CurrentDb
Set fld = dbs.TableDefs(0).Fields(0)

Debug.Print fld.Name
dbs.Close
Set dbs = Nothing
```

Of course, nothing is free, and CurrentDb is no exception. The price you pay for the convenience and reliability of a function like CurrentDb is a performance hit. So why would you use it?

There are two reasons you would use CurrentDb instead of DBEngine(0)(0). First, you can rely on its collections being up-to-date, and second, it is guaranteed to return the database that is currently open in Access. For the majority of cases, the performance hit experienced using CurrentDb is not an issue because it is unlikely that you will ever call it in a loop where performance issues often manifest themselves. The recommended method for setting a reference to the current database is as follows:

```
Private dbC As DAO.Database

Public Property Get CurrentDbC() As DAO.Database
    If (dbC Is Nothing) Then Set dbC = CurrentDb()
    Set CurrentDbC = dbC
End Property
```

This `Property` procedure can be used in both class modules and standard modules, and relies on the existence of a `Database` object variable declared at the module level. If you want, you can change it to a function instead; it will work just the same. The property first checks the `dbC` variable because variables can be erased (and thus the reference lost) when an error occurs somewhere in your application, or if someone hits Stop in the IDE (integrated development environment).

 The technique in which the `dbC` variable is set on first use is called lazy initialization.

Opening an External Database

Sometimes you need to work with data in another Access database, Text file, or Excel spreadsheet, but don't want a permanent link. You can do so by opening a temporary connection to the external file or database with the `OpenDatabase` method of the `DBEngine` object. Although the connection to the external database is temporary, the new `Database` object is still added to the `Databases` collection.

The `OpenDatabase` method is fairly straightforward:

```
Set dbs = DBEngine.OpenDatabase(dbname, options, read-only, connect)
```

The following table describes the arguments for the `OpenDatabase` method.

ARGUMENT	DESCRIPTION
dbname	A string value that represents the full path and filename of the database you want to open.
options	An optional Boolean `True` (-1) or `False` (0) that indicates whether to open the database in exclusive (`True`) or shared mode (`False`).
Read-only	An optional Boolean `True` (-1) or `False` (0) that indicates whether to open the database as read-only.
Connect	Specifies connection information such as passwords.

The following code demonstrates how to open several different databases using various techniques. After opening each database, you'll notice that the code prints the name of the database and a count of the respective `Databases` collection.

Specifically, it opens the following databases from the following sources:

➤ Microsoft Access database

➤ dBase IV database using the Access database engine

➤ SQL Server database using ODBC through the Access database engine

```vba
Public Sub OpenSeveralDatabases(strUsrName As String, strPwd As String)
    Dim wsAccess As Workspace
    Dim dbAccess As DAO.Database
    Dim dbdBase As DAO.Database
    Dim dbODBC As DAO.Database

    'Create the Access workspace
    Set wsAccess = DBEngine(0)

    'Print the details for the default database
    Debug.Print "Access Database "; wsAccess.Databases.Count & _
        "-"& CurrentDb.Name

    'Open a Microsoft Access database -shared -read-only
    Set dbAccess = wsAccess.OpenDatabase("C:\Temp\db1.accdb", False, True)
    Debug.Print "Access Database "; wsAccess.Databases.Count & _
        "-"& dbAccess.Name

    'Open a dBase IV database -exclusive -read-write
    Set dbdBase = wsAccess.OpenDatabase( _
        "C:\Temp", True, False, "dBASE IV")
    Debug.Print "Database"; wsAccess.Databases.Count & _
        "-"& dbdBase.Name

    'Open an ODBC database using a DSN -exclusive -read-only
    Set dbODBC = wsAccess.OpenDatabase( _
        "", dbDriverComplete, True, "ODBC;DATABASE=myDB;DSN=myDSN")
    Debug.Print "Access Database "; wsAccess.Databases.Count & _
        "-"& dbODBC.Name

    'Clean up
    wsAccess.Close
    Set dbAccess = Nothing
    Set dbdBase = Nothing
    Set dbODBC = Nothing
    Set cn = Nothing
    Set wsAccess = Nothing
End Sub
```

code snippet Chapter 11 - DAO Samples

DAO OBJECT PROPERTIES

As you're no doubt already aware from previous chapters, every Access object (such as forms and reports) has a collection of properties. This section examines some of those properties, and describes how to use them to change Access and DAO object behavior.

All the properties associated with an Access object exist from the moment you create the object. DAO object properties, however, exhibit quite different behavior. In DAO, depending on the object, some of its properties don't exist until you set their values. It is quite important, therefore, that you understand the differences between the types of properties used in DAO.

DAO Property Types

There are three types of object properties in DAO: built-in, system-defined, and user-defined:

➤ Built-in properties exist when the object is created, and like most of their Access counterparts, define the characteristics of the object itself. For example, `Name` and `Type` are examples of built-in properties.

➤ System-defined properties are those that Access adds to the object's `Properties` collection when it needs the property in order to work its magic. These are not Access database engine properties, but are created and used by Access.

➤ A user-defined property can be added to an object's `Properties` collection when you explicitly set a value to it. For example, the `Description` property of a field is a user-defined property. Although you can set a value to it when you define the table, this property is not available in Access or DAO until after you've done so. Because the property is user-defined, after you've set its value, it will appear in the field's `Properties` collection, but not in the `Object Browser`.

Creating, Setting, and Retrieving Properties

Without even thinking about it, you've been setting and retrieving properties for as long as you've been programming. Whenever you check the value of a `TextBox`, or set the `Enabled` state of a command button, you are working with properties. This section explores how to manipulate Access properties, object properties, and user-defined properties.

You can refer to built-in properties either directly through the object to which they belong or through the object's `Properties` collection. User-defined properties, on the other hand, do not form part of an object's type library, and thus are not available via that route, so you have to refer to them through the object's `Properties` collection.

Setting and Retrieving Built-In Object Properties

The built-in properties that you would be most familiar with are those that affect the way form and report controls work. Even DAO objects have properties that can be manipulated in the same way. For example, to change a `TextBox`'s `Enabled` property, you can refer to it in either of the following two ways:

```
Me!TextBox1.Enabled = False
Me!TextBox1.Properties("Enabled") = False
```

To check the name of a Recordset's `Field` object, you retrieve its `Name` property. The following two examples are equivalent ways to check this property:

```
Debug.Print rst.Fields(0).Name
Debug.Print rst.Fields(0).Properties("Name")
```

All objects have a default property, which is the property that is referenced when you call the object itself. For example, when you test a `Field` object directly, you are actually referring to its `Value` property. The following lines of code all refer to the `Field` object's `Value` property:

```
rst.Fields(0)
rst.Fields(0).Properties("Value")
rst.Fields(0).Properties(0)
rst.Fields(0).Value
```

Creating Object Properties

You can create user-defined properties for persistent DAO objects, such as tables and queries. You can't create properties for nonpersistent objects, such as Recordsets. To create a user-defined property, you must first create the property, using the `Database`'s `CreateProperty` method. You then append the property using the `Properties` collection's `Append` method. That's all there is to it.

The following code uses a field's `Description` property to demonstrate just how easy it is:

```
Public Sub SetFieldDescription(strTableName As String, _
    strFieldName As String, _
    varValue As Variant)

    Dim dbs As DAO.Database
    Dim prop As DAO.Property

    Set dbs = CurrentDb

    'Create the property
    Set prop = dbs.CreateProperty("Description", dbText, varValue)

    'Append the property to the object Properties collection
    dbs(strTableName)(strFieldName).Properties.Append prop
    Debug.Print dbs(strTableName)(strFieldName).Properties("Description")

    'Clean up
    Set prop = Nothing
    Set dbs = Nothing
End Sub
```

You could even create a special user-defined property for a table in the same way, as the following code shows. This approach can be used with all persistent objects.

```
Public Sub CreateSpecialTableProp(strTableName As String, _
    strPropName As String, _
    lngPropType As DataTypeEnum, _
    varValue As Variant)

    Dim dbs As DAO.Database
```

```
        Dim prop As DAO.Property

        Set dbs = CurrentDb

        'Create the property
        Set prop = dbs.CreateProperty(strPropName, lngPropType, varValue, False)

        'Append the property to the object Properties collection
        dbs(strTableName).Properties.Append prop

        Debug.Print dbs(strTableName).Properties(strPropName)

        'Clean up
        Set prop = Nothing
        Set dbs = Nothing
    End Sub
```

For another example, let's say you wanted to create a Yes/No field, but tell Access to make the field a checkbox instead of a text box. You can create the `DisplayControl` property to specify the type of control for Access.

```
    Public Sub CreateYesNoField(strTableName As String, _
            strFieldName As String)

        Dim dbs As DAO.Database
        Dim tdf As DAO.TableDef
        Dim fld As DAO.Field
        Dim prop As DAO.Property

        Set dbs = CurrentDb
        Set tdf = dbs.TableDefs(strTableName)

        'Create and append the field
        Set fld = tdf.CreateField(strFieldName, dbBoolean)
        tdf.Fields.Append fld

        'Create the property
        Set prop = dbs.CreateProperty("DisplayControl", _
            dbInteger, acCheckBox)

        'Append the property to the object Properties collection
        fld.Properties.Append prop

        'Clean up
        Set prop = Nothing
        Set fld = Nothing
        Set tdf = Nothing
        Set dbs = Nothing
    End Sub
```

Setting and Retrieving SummaryInfo Properties

When you select View and edit database properties from the File menu, Access opens the Properties dialog box. It displays several built-in properties — some you can change, and some you can't. The

General tab displays information about the database, including its file location and size, creation date, and the dates it was last modified and accessed. The Summary tab enables you to enter your own properties, such as the document Title (which is different from the Application Title), Subject, Author, Manager, and so on. These two tabs contain the information that Windows Search uses when you want to find a specific file.

In DAO code, you can set and retrieve the value of any of these properties from the `SummaryInfo` document of the `Databases` Container for the current database. Of course, you don't have to create these properties before using them. Access creates them automatically when you launch the database. The following code line illustrates how to access the `Subject` property shown in the Properties dialog box.

```
dbs.Containers("Databases").Documents("SummaryInfo").Properties("Subject")
```

Setting and Retrieving User-Defined Properties

You can also create and use user-defined properties for other purposes. A lot of developers often use a custom database property to record the database version. As with the example of a field's `Description` property, there are two ways to create a user-defined property: using the user interface, and through code.

To create such a property with the user interface, click the File menu and select View and edit database properties in the Info place. Select the Custom tab, as shown in Figure 11-2. Enter the property name into the Name box, select the appropriate data type, give it a value, and click Add.

FIGURE 11-2

The following example shows how you can create the same property in code, and retrieve its value using `Debug.Print`:

```
Public Sub SetVersion(strVersion As String)
    Dim prop As DAO.Property
    Dim dbs As DAO.Database

    On Error Resume Next

    Set dbs = CurrentDb

    'Set the property's value
    'If it doesn't exist, an error 3270 "Property not found" will occur
    dbs.Containers("Databases")("UserDefined").Properties("Version") = _
        strVersion

    If Err <> 0 Then
        'If the property doesn't exist, create it
        Set prop = dbs.CreateProperty("Version", dbText, strVersion)

        'Append it to the collection
        dbs.Containers("Databases")("UserDefined").Properties.Append prop
    End If

    'Now read the property
    Debug.Print _
        dbs.Containers("Databases")("UserDefined").Properties("Version")

    'Clean up
    Set prop = Nothing
    Set dbs = Nothing
End Sub
```

First you must test that the property exists. In this example, you test it by attempting to set its value. If all goes well, the property must already exist, and its value is set. If an error occurs, you have to create the property — again by using the `CreateProperty` method at database level, and then appending it to the appropriate collection.

CREATING SCHEMA OBJECTS WITH DAO

Sometimes you need to create data access objects on-the-fly. Much of DAO's power lies in its capability to create things such as tables and queries programmatically.

Let's say you inherit a copper-plated widget manufacturing company from an uncle. He never actually sold any because of the absence of an invoicing system, so you decide to implement one. Naturally you'll want to create a database schema to record the details of the invoices you issue to your customers: one table for the invoice header, and one for the line items. Here are the basics steps:

➤ Create the header table (`tblInvoice`), including its fields.

➤ Create the line items table (`tblInvItem`), including its fields.

➤ Create the indexes for both tables.

➤ Create the relationship between the two tables.

Creating Tables and Fields

For the invoicing system, you have two tables to create. The basic procedure for creating a table in code is as follows:

1. Check if the table already exists, and if so, rename it. You could also choose to delete the table instead of renaming it.

2. Create the table using the `CreateTableDef` method of the `Database` object.

3. Create the `Field` objects in memory, using the `TableDef`'s `CreateField` method, setting each field's attributes as appropriate.

4. Append each `Field` object to the `TableDef`'s `Fields` collection.

5. Append the `TableDef` object to the `Database`'s `TableDefs` collection.

6. Refresh the `TableDefs` collection to ensure it is up-to-date, and optionally call `Application.RefreshDatabaseWindow` to refresh the Navigation Pane.

The header table stores the basic high-level information about each invoice, such as the invoice number, date, and the customer ID. The following example demonstrates how to create a new table called `tblInvoice` and add four fields to it. First, declare all the objects needed to create the table:

```
Public Sub CreateInvoiceTable()
    Dim dbs As DAO.Database
    Dim tdf As DAO.TableDef
    Dim fldInvNo As DAO.Field
    Dim fldInvDate As DAO.Field
    Dim fldCustID As DAO.Field
    Dim fldComments As DAO.Field

    Set dbs = CurrentDb
    On Error Resume Next

    'If the table already exists, rename it
    If IsObject(dbs.TableDefs("tblInvoice")) Then
        DoCmd.Rename "tblInvoice_Backup", acTable, "tblInvoice"
    End If
    On Error GoTo 0

    'Create the table definition in memory
    Set tdf = dbs.CreateTableDef("tblInvoice")
```

At this point, you have created the new `TableDef`, but it only exists in memory. It won't become a permanent part of the database until you add it to the `TableDefs` collection. Before you do that, however, you need to add one or more fields to the table, because you can't save a table that has no fields. Add the fields like this:

```
    'Create the field definitions in memory
    Set fldInvNo = tdf.CreateField("InvoiceNo", dbText, 10)
```

```
fldInvNo.AllowZeroLength = False
fldInvNo.Required = True

Set fldInvDate = tdf.CreateField("InvoiceDate", dbDate)
fldInvDate.Required = True

Set fldCustID = tdf.CreateField("CustomerID", dbLong)
fldCustID.Required = True

Set fldComments = tdf.CreateField("Comments", dbText, 50)
fldComments.AllowZeroLength = True
fldComments.Required = False

'Append the fields to the TableDef's Fields collection
tdf.Fields.Append fldInvNo
tdf.Fields.Append fldInvDate
tdf.Fields.Append fldCustID
tdf.Fields.Append fldComments
```

The fields have been added, but the table still needs to be added to the `TableDefs` collection to make it part of the database. Once you've done that, refresh the `TableDefs` collection to ensure it is up-to-date, because in a multiuser application, the new table may not be immediately propagated to other users' collections until you do. Then clean up by setting all the objects to Nothing.

```
'Append the TableDef to the Database's TableDefs collection
dbs.TableDefs.Append tdf

'Refresh the TableDefs collection
dbs.TableDefs.Refresh
Application.RefreshDatabaseWindow

Set fldInvNo = Nothing
Set fldInvDate = Nothing
Set fldCustID = Nothing
Set fldComments = Nothing
Set tdf = Nothing
Set dbs = Nothing
End Sub
```

code snippet Chapter 11 - DAO Samples

Next, you need to create a table to store the invoice line items, including the product ID, the number of items sold, and their individual unit price. The following code creates a new table called `tblInvItem`, and adds five fields to it. It is based on the same basic technique for creating tables, but includes an additional attribute definition, `dbAutoIncrField`, to create an `AutoNumber` field.

```
Public Sub CreateInvItemTable()
    Dim dbs As DAO.Database
    Dim tdf As DAO.TableDef
    Dim fldInvItemID As DAO.Field
    Dim fldInvNo As DAO.Field
    Dim fldProductID As DAO.Field
```

```vba
Dim fldQty As DAO.Field
Dim fldUnitPrice As DAO.Field

Set dbs = CurrentDb
On Error Resume Next

'If the table already exists, rename it
If IsObject(dbs.TableDefs("tblInvItem")) Then
    DoCmd.Rename "tblInvItem_Backup", acTable, "tblInvItem"
End If

'Create the table definition in memory
Set tdf = dbs.CreateTableDef("tblInvItem")

'Create the field definitions in memory
Set fldInvItemID = tdf.CreateField("InvItemID", dbLong)

'Make the field an AutoNumber datatype
fldInvItemID.Attributes = dbAutoIncrField
fldInvItemID.Required = True

Set fldInvNo = tdf.CreateField("InvoiceNo", dbText, 10)
fldInvNo.Required = True
fldInvNo.AllowZeroLength = False

Set fldProductID = tdf.CreateField("ProductID", dbLong)
fldProductID.Required = True

Set fldQty = tdf.CreateField("Qty", dbInteger)
fldQty.Required = True

Set fldUnitPrice = tdf.CreateField("UnitCost", dbCurrency)
fldUnitPrice.Required = False

'Append the fields to the TableDef's Fields collection
tdf.Fields.Append fldInvItemID
tdf.Fields.Append fldInvNo
tdf.Fields.Append fldProductID
tdf.Fields.Append fldQty
tdf.Fields.Append fldUnitPrice

'Append the TableDef to the Database's TableDefs collection
dbs.TableDefs.Append tdf

'Refresh the TableDefs collection
dbs.TableDefs.Refresh
Application.RefreshDatabaseWindow

Set fldInvItemID = Nothing
Set fldInvNo = Nothing
Set fldProductID = Nothing
Set fldQty = Nothing
Set fldUnitPrice = Nothing
```

```
        Set tdf = Nothing
        Set dbs = Nothing
    End Sub
```

Creating Indexes

Just creating the tables and fields isn't enough. Eventually the tables are going to get pretty big, and querying against them will take some time. To improve performance, you need to create indexes because without them, the Access database engine must scan the entire table to find the records you want. Here's the basic procedure for creating an index:

1. Create the `Index` object using the `TableDef`'s `CreateIndex` method.

2. Set the index's properties as appropriate.

3. Create the index's `Field` objects using its `CreateField` method.

4. Append each `Field` object to the index's `Fields` collection.

5. Append the index to the `TableDef`'s `Indexes` collection.

Before you create your first index, you should be aware of the following:

➤ Once an index is appended to its collection, its properties are read-only. Therefore, if you want to change an index's property after you've created it, you must delete the index and re-create it with the new properties.

➤ Although you can give an index any name you like, when you create a primary key using the Access Table Designer, it is automatically named PrimaryKey. For consistency, it is a good idea to give code-created primary keys the same name.

➤ Access databases do not support clustered indexes, so the `Clustered` property of the `Index` object is ignored.

Start the process of creating indexes by creating the primary key. When you create a primary key, Access automatically creates an index for it. The following procedure creates a primary key index for the specified table, which includes the fields supplied in the `ParamArray` argument. In the case of the invoice tables, that'll be only one field in each.

```
Public Sub CreatePKIndexes(strTableName As String, ParamArray varPKFields())
    Dim dbs As DAO.Database
    Dim tdf As DAO.TableDef
    Dim idx As DAO.Index
    Dim fld As DAO.Field
    Dim strPKey As String
    Dim strIdxFldName As String
    Dim intCounter As Integer

    Set dbs = CurrentDb
```

```
Set tdf = dbs.TableDefs(strTableName)

'Check if a Primary Key exists.
'If so, delete it.
strPKey = GetPrimaryKey(tdf)

If Len(strPKey) > 0 Then
    tdf.Indexes.Delete strPKey
End If

'Create a new primary key
Set idx = tdf.CreateIndex("PrimaryKey")
idx.Primary = True
idx.Required = True
idx.Unique = True
```

At this point, the index exists in memory, and remains so until it is added to the `TableDef`'s `Indexes` collection. But before you do that, you must add the fields that make up the key to the index's `Fields` collection. Then, you can refresh the collection and clean up.

Available for download on Wrox.com

```
'Append the fields
For intCounter = LBound(varPKFields) To UBound(varPKFields)
    ' get the field name
    strIdxFldName = varPKFields(intCounter)

    ' get the field object and append it to the index
    Set fld = idx.CreateField(strIdxFldName)
    idx.Fields.Append fld
Next intCounter

'Append the index to the Indexes collection
tdf.Indexes.Append idx

'Refresh the Indexes collection
tdf.Indexes.Refresh

Set fld = Nothing
Set idx = Nothing
Set tdf = Nothing
Set dbs = Nothing
End Sub
```

code snippet Chapter 11 - DAO Samples

The following function is called from the `CreatePKIndexes` procedure, and returns the name of the primary key if one exists, and an empty string if there isn't one:

Available for download on Wrox.com

```
Public Function GetPrimaryKey(tdf As DAO.TableDef) As String
    'Determine if the specified Primary Key exists
    Dim idx As DAO.Index

    For Each idx In tdf.Indexes
        If idx.Primary Then
```

```
            'If a Primary Key exists, return its name
            GetPrimaryKey = idx.Name
            Exit Function
        End If
    Next idx

    'If no Primary Key exists, return empty string
    GetPrimaryKey = vbNullString
End Function
```

code snippet Chapter 11 - DAO Samples

The next step is to create the relationship between the `tblInvoice` and `tblInvItem` tables. Later on we'll show you how to put all this together to create the schema for the invoices database.

Creating Relations

The basic procedure for creating a relation is as follows:

1. Create the `Relation` object using the `Database`'s `CreateRelation` method.

2. Set the `Relation` object's attributes as appropriate.

3. Create the fields that participate in the relationship, using the `Relation` object's `CreateField` method.

4. Set the `Field` object's attributes as appropriate.

5. Append each field to the `Relation`'s `Fields` collection.

6. Append the `Relation` object to the `Database`'s `Relations` collection.

The following code creates a relationship whose name is specified by the `strRelName` argument, specifies its attributes, and adds the tables and fields that make up the relationship. You can name a relationship any way you like, but when you create a relationship using the Relationships window, Access names the relationship according to the names of the tables involved. For example, if you were to create a relationship between `tblInvoice` and `tblInvItem`, Access would name it `tblInvoicetblInvItem`.

```
Public Sub CreateRelation(strRelName As String, _
    strSrcTable As String, strSrcField As String, _
    strDestTable As String, strDestField As String)

    Dim dbs As DAO.Database
    Dim fld As DAO.Field
    Dim rel As DAO.Relation
    Dim varRel As Variant

    Set dbs = CurrentDb
    On Error Resume Next

    'Check if the relationship already exists.
    'If so, delete it.
```

```
        If IsObject(dbs.Relations(strRelName)) Then
            dbs.Relations.Delete strRelName
        End If
        On Error Goto 0

        'Create the relation object
        Set rel = dbs.CreateRelation(strRelName, strSrcTable, strDestTable)
```

The Relation object now exists in memory, but as with the TableDef and Index objects, it won't be a part of the database until you append it to the Database's Relations collection.

The following code segment defines the relationship's attributes. It combines three Relation attribute enum values using the Or operator: dbRelationLeft, dbRelationUpdateCascade, and dbRelationDeleteCascade. These, of course, define a LEFT JOIN relationship with referential integrity set to Cascade Update and Cascade Delete.

```
        'Set this relationship to:
        ' LEFT JOIN
        ' Referential integrity = Cascade Update and Cascade Delete
        rel.Attributes = dbRelationLeft Or _
                         dbRelationUpdateCascade Or _
                         dbRelationDeleteCascade
```

Once the Relation object has been created and its attributes specified, you then add all the fields that form the relationship. Finally, you add the new relationship to the Database's Relations collection and refresh it.

Available for download on Wrox.com

```
        'Append the field(s) involved in the relationship
        'The Field object represents the left side of the relationship,
        'where the right side of the relationship is set with the
        'ForeignName property.
        Set fld = rel.CreateField(strSrcField)
        fld.ForeignName = strDestField

        'Append the field to the relation's Fields collection
        rel.Fields.Append fld

        'Append the relation to the Database's Relations collection
        dbs.Relations.Append rel

        'Refresh the Relations collection
        dbs.Relations.Refresh

        Set rel = Nothing
        Set fld = Nothing
        Set dbs = Nothing
    End Sub
```

code snippet Chapter 11 - DAO Samples

When you create your own relationships in code, they will not automatically appear in the Relationships window. To display the Relationships window, click the Relationships button from the Database Tools tab in the Access Ribbon.

To display the new relationships you've created in code, either add the related tables to the Relationships window, or click Show All from the Relationships group.

Putting It All Together

When writing your own procedures to create DAO objects, you should include sufficient error-handling code, and perhaps even wrap the whole lot in a transaction, so if any part of it fails, you don't have orphaned or partially built objects that you will have to delete manually.

You can use the following procedure to manage all the code you just created, to test the creation of invoice tables, indexes, and relationships:

```
Public Sub CreateInvoiceSchema()
    CreateInvoiceTable
    CreatePKIndexes "tblInvoice", "InvoiceNo"
    CreateInvItemTable
    CreatePKIndexes "tblInvItem", "InvItemID"
    CreateRelation "Relation1", "tblInvoice", _
        "InvoiceNo", "tblInvItem", "InvoiceNo"
End Sub
```

code snippet Chapter 11 - DAO Samples

Creating Multi-Value Lookup Fields

There are new data types in DAO that are used to define a multi-value lookup field. The names of these types begin with dbComplex and contain the name of a type that can be used for the lookup field. In other words, if the related field for the lookup is an Integer, you can use dbComplexInteger for a multi-value lookup field. The valid field types are:

➤ dbComplexByte

➤ dbComplexDecimal

➤ dbComplexDouble

➤ dbComplexGUID

➤ dbComplexInteger

➤ dbComplexLong

➤ dbComplexSingle

➤ dbComplexText

Let's say that you have a database that tracks students and their favorite colors, with tables named tblStudents and tblColors. The tblColors table defines a ColorID field, which is an AutoNumber field and the primary key. The tblStudents table includes a field that is defined as dbComplexLong that is the multi-value lookup field for the tblColors table. To create a multi-valued field, you must use the new Field2 object defined in DAO.

This code also demonstrates an alternate technique you can use when executing the CreateField method:

```
tdf.Fields.Append tdf.CreateField("FirstName", dbText, 50)
```

Because `CreateField` returns a `DAO.Field2` object, it is passed as the argument to the `Append` method of the `Fields` property on the `TableDef` object. Using this approach reduces the amount of code you have to write and maintain.

Here's the code:

```vba
' Creates the Colors table
Sub CreateColorsTable()
    Dim dbs As DAO.Database
    Dim tdf As DAO.TableDef
    Dim idx As DAO.Index
    Dim fld As DAO.Field2

    'Get the database
    Set dbs = CurrentDb

    'Create the colors table
    Set tdf = dbs.CreateTableDef("tblColors")

    'Create the ColorID field
    Set fld = tdf.CreateField("ColorID", dbLong)
    fld.Attributes = dbAutoIncrField
    tdf.Fields.Append fld

    'Create the Primary Key index using ColorID
    Set idx = tdf.CreateIndex("PrimaryKey")
    idx.Primary = True
    idx.Fields.Append tdf.CreateField("ColorID")
    idx.Fields.Refresh

    'Append the index and refresh
    tdf.Indexes.Append idx
    tdf.Indexes.Refresh

    'Create and append the ColorCode field using the abbreviated syntax
    tdf.Fields.Append tdf.CreateField("ColorCode", dbLong)

    'Create and append the ColorName field
    tdf.Fields.Append tdf.CreateField("ColorName", dbMemo)
    tdf.Fields.Refresh

    'Append the table to the database
    dbs.TableDefs.Append tdf

    'Cleanup
    Set fld = Nothing
    Set tdf = Nothing
    Set dbs = Nothing
End Sub

'Creates the students table
Sub CreateStudentsTable()
    Dim dbs As DAO.Database
    Dim tdf As DAO.TableDef
    Dim idx As DAO.Index
```

```
Dim fld As DAO.Field2

'Get the database
Set dbs = CurrentDb

'Create the Students table
Set tdf = dbs.CreateTableDef("tblStudents")

'Create the StudentID field
Set fld = tdf.CreateField("StudentID", dbLong)
fld.Attributes = dbAutoIncrField
tdf.Fields.Append fld

'Create the Primary Key (Student - AutoNumber)
Set idx = tdf.CreateIndex("PrimaryKey")
idx.Primary = True
idx.Fields.Append tdf.CreateField("StudentID")
idx.Fields.Refresh

'Append the index and refresh
tdf.Indexes.Append idx
tdf.Indexes.Refresh

'Create and append the following fields:
'FirstName, LastName, Address, City, StateOrProvince, Region, PostalCode, Country
tdf.Fields.Append tdf.CreateField("FirstName", dbText, 50)
tdf.Fields.Append tdf.CreateField("LastName", dbText, 50)
tdf.Fields.Append tdf.CreateField("Address", dbText, 50)
tdf.Fields.Append tdf.CreateField("City", dbText, 50)
tdf.Fields.Append tdf.CreateField("StateOrProvince", dbText, 50)
tdf.Fields.Append tdf.CreateField("Region", dbText, 50)
tdf.Fields.Append tdf.CreateField("PostalCode", dbText, 50)
tdf.Fields.Append tdf.CreateField("Country", dbText, 50)

'Ok, now for the multi-value lookup field.
'For this, define the field as dbComplexLong since it will
'perform a lookup to a Long Integer field (ColorID) in the Colors table
Set fld = tdf.CreateField("Colors", dbComplexLong)

'Append the field
tdf.Fields.Append fld

'Append the table to the database
dbs.TableDefs.Append tdf

'Set Access properties to use the combo box control
'- DisplayControl: ComboBox
'- ColumnCount: 2
'- ColumnWidths: "0"
'- RowSource: tblColors - This is the lookup table
With fld
    .Properties.Append .CreateProperty("DisplayControl", dbInteger, acComboBox)
    .Properties.Append .CreateProperty("RowSource", dbText, "tblColors")
```

```
        .Properties.Append .CreateProperty("ColumnCount", dbInteger, 2)
        .Properties.Append .CreateProperty("ColumnWidths", dbText, "0")
    End With

    'Cleanup
    Set fld = Nothing
    Set tdf = Nothing
    Set dbs = Nothing
End Sub
```

code snippet Chapter 11 - DAO Samples

Creating Calculated Fields

To create a calculated field using DAO, set the new `Expression` property of a `Field2` object to an expression to use for the calculated field. The following example shows how to create a table with first and last name, as well as a calculated field for full name that concatenates these two fields.

```
Sub CreateCalculatedField()
    Dim dbs As DAO.Database
    Dim tdf As DAO.TableDef
    Dim fld As DAO.Field2

    ' get the database
    Set dbs = CurrentDb()

    ' create the table
    Set tdf = dbs.CreateTableDef("tblContactsCalcField")

    ' create the fields: first name, last name
    tdf.Fields.Append tdf.CreateField("FirstName", dbText, 20)
    tdf.Fields.Append tdf.CreateField("LastName", dbText, 20)

    ' create the calculated field: full name
    Set fld = tdf.CreateField("FullName", dbText, 50)
    fld.Expression = "[FirstName] & "" "" & [LastName]"
    tdf.Fields.Append fld

    ' append the table and cleanup
    dbs.TableDefs.Append tdf

Cleanup:
    Set fld = Nothing
    Set tdf = Nothing
    Set dbs = Nothing
End Sub
```

code snippet Chapter 11 - DAO Samples

DATA ACCESS WITH DAO

Accessing data is the reason you use databases, and a large proportion of your programming will usually revolve around manipulating those objects that deal with data: queries and Recordsets. In this section, you take a detailed look at how to access and manipulate the data in your database using DAO.

Working with QueryDefs

When you build a query with the graphical Query Designer, you are building a QueryDef object. When you save the query, you are also appending a reference to it in the QueryDefs collection. You can also build a QueryDef in code, which is one of the purposes of this section.

You can think of permanent QueryDef objects as SQL statements that are compiled the first time they are executed. This is similar in concept to the way code is compiled. Once compiled, permanent queries run marginally faster than their temporary, unsaved counterparts, because Access does not need to compile them before execution. Temporary QueryDef objects are useful when you don't need to save them, as when you create their SQL statements during runtime. You would normally build and run SQL statements in line with your code when you need to change its clauses depending on current operating conditions or the value of some variable.

Creating a QueryDef

To create a QueryDef, execute the CreateQueryDef method against the Database object.

If you set a QueryDef's Name property to something other than a zero-length string, it is automatically appended to the QueryDefs collection, and saved to disk. Omitting the Name property, or explicitly setting it to a zero-length string, results in a temporary (unsaved) QueryDef.

The following code demonstrates how to create a QueryDef object:

```
Public Sub CreateQuery (strName As String, strSQL As String)
    Dim dbs As DAO.Database
    Dim qdf As DAO.QueryDef

    Set dbs = CurrentDb

    'Create the QueryDef
    'If the user supplies a name, the QueryDef will be
    'automatically appended to the QueryDefs collection
    Set qdf = dbs.CreateQueryDef(strName, strSQL)

    'If the user supplies a name, refresh the Navigation Pane
    If vbNullString <> strName Then Application.RefreshDatabaseWindow

    Set qdf = Nothing
    Set dbs = Nothing
End Sub
```

You can create a pass-through query to an ODBC data source by setting the QueryDef's Connect property to a valid connection string, after the query has been created. Pass-through queries enable you to run SQL statements directly on another database such as SQL Server or Oracle.

```
qdf.Connect = strConnectionString
```

Parameters

Although you can't append parameters to a `QueryDef` using DAO, you can create them by declaring them in the SQL, as shown in the following code:

```
Sub CreateQueryWithParameters()

    Dim dbs As DAO.Database
    Dim qdf As DAO.QueryDef
    Dim strSQL As String

    Set dbs = CurrentDb
    Set qdf = dbs.CreateQueryDef("myQuery")
    Application.RefreshDatabaseWindow

    strSQL = "PARAMETERS Param1 TEXT, Param2 INT; "
    strSQL = strSQL & "SELECT * FROM [Table1] "
    strSQL = strSQL & "WHERE [Field1] = [Param1] AND [Field2] = [Param2];"
    qdf.SQL = strSQL

    qdf.Close
    Set qdf = Nothing
    Set dbs = Nothing
End Sub
```

You can also specify a query parameter's value in order to specify the value of criteria to filter the query's output, or the selected records on which the query operates. For example, the following procedure sets a reference to an existing query called `myActionQuery`, sets the value of its parameter (`Organization`), and then executes the query:

```
Public Sub ExecParameterQuery()
    Dim dbs As DAO.Database
    Dim qdf As DAO.QueryDef

    Set dbs = CurrentDb
    Set qdf = dbs.QueryDefs("myActionQuery")

     'Set the value of the QueryDef's parameter
    qdf.Parameters("Organization").Value = "Microsoft"

     'Execute the query
    qdf.Execute dbFailOnError

     'Clean up
    qdf.Close
    Set qdf = Nothing
    Set dbs = Nothing

End Sub
```

Executing Queries

Queries that insert (append), update, or delete records are known as *action queries*. While these types of queries do not return records, it is common to run them using code.

There are three ways to programmatically execute a query: using the `DoCmd.RunSQL` method, the `object.Execute` method, and the `OpenRecordset` method. Let's take a look at all three.

DoCmd.RunSQL

Although not part of the DAO Object Model, you can execute the `RunSQL` method of the `DoCmd` object to run an action query:

```
DoCmd.RunSQL "UPDATE Table1 SET Field1 = 123"
```

Running a query this way displays a message box to confirm that you want to make changes to the database. To eliminate that message box, use the `DoCmd` object's `SetWarnings` method prior to calling `DoCmd.RunSQL`, but remember to set it back when you've finished, or all warning messages will thereafter be disabled.

```
DoCmd.SetWarnings False
DoCmd.RunSQL "UPDATE Table1 SET Field1 = 123"
DoCmd.SetWarnings True
```

Any errors that are raised while executing the query will still display the message box. By default, the query is included in an existing transaction, but you can exclude it by setting the `UseTransaction` property to `False`:

```
DoCmd.RunSQL "UPDATE Table1 SET Field1 = 123", False
```

object.Execute

You can also use the `Execute` method of the `QueryDef` object or the `Database` object to run an action query:

```
qdf.Execute options
dbs.Execute "UPDATE Table1 SET Field1 = 123", options
```

With the `Execute` method, there is no need to call the `SetWarnings` method to disable message boxes because none are displayed. The `Execute` method operates directly on its parent object.

There are several major benefits to using the `Execute` method rather than the `DoCmd.RunSQL` method:

➤   `Execute` runs marginally faster than `DoCmd.RunSQL`.

➤   `Execute` can be included in an existing transaction, like any other DAO operation, without needing to specify an option to do so.

➤   You can specify several options that change the way the method works.

The following table lists the various constants that can be supplied as options for the `Execute` method.

CONSTANT	DESCRIPTION
dbDenyWrite	Denies write permission to other users.
dbInconsistent	Executes inconsistent updates.

CONSTANT	DESCRIPTION
dbConsistent	Executes consistent updates.
dbSQLPassThrough	Executes a SQL pass-through query, which passes the query to an ODBC database for processing.
dbFailOnError	Rolls back updates if an error occurs.
dbSeeChanges	Generates a runtime error if another user is changing data that you are editing.

OpenRecordset

Finally, you can execute a query when you open a Recordset. To do so, specify the query name in the Database object's OpenRecordset method to run a select or action query:

```
Set rst = dbs.OpenRecordset("SELECT * FROM Table1")
```

Similarly, you can open a Recordset based on a query, like so:

```
Set qdf = dbs.QueryDefs("qryMyQuery")
Set rst = qdf.OpenRecordset(dbOpenDynaset)
```

The following section on Recordsets describes this in greater detail.

Working with Recordsets

When you need to access and manipulate data one record at a time, you must use a Recordset object. For this reason, Recordsets are the workhorses of database programming. As you've already seen, four types of Recordsets are available in DAO. The one you use depends on where the data comes from, and what you want to do with it.

Creating a Recordset

You can create a Recordset by using the OpenRecordset method of the Database, TableDef, or QueryDef objects:

```
Set rst = dbs.OpenRecordset( Source, Type, Options, LockEdits )
Set rst = object.OpenRecordset( Type, Options, LockEdits )
```

The Source argument specifies the name of a table or query, or a string expression that is a SQL query. For Recordsets opened using the dbOpenTable type argument, the Source argument can only be the name of a table.

The default Recordset type that is opened if you omit the Type argument depends on the type of table you're trying to open. If you open a Microsoft Access Recordset on a local table, the default type of Recordset is dbOpenTable. If you open a Microsoft Access Recordset against a linked table or query, the default type is dbOpenDynaset. The following code examples demonstrate how to open different types of Recordsets.

Opening a Recordset Based on a Table or Query

To open a table type Recordset or dynaset-type Recordset, use code such as the following:

```
Dim dbs As DAO.Database
Dim rsTable As DAO.Recordset
Dim rsQuery As DAO.Recordset

Set dbs = CurrentDb

'Open a table-type Recordset
Set rsTable = dbs.OpenRecordset("Table1", dbOpenTable)

'Open a dynaset-type Recordset using a saved query
Set rsQuery = dbs.OpenRecordset("qryMyQuery", dbOpenDynaset)
```

Opening a Recordset Based on a Parameter Query

Parameter queries accept criteria based on a parameter prompt. The parameter prompt can be a hard-coded name such as the prompt shown in Figure 11-3, or you can supply its value based on a control on a form, as illustrated in Figure 11-4.

FIGURE 11-3

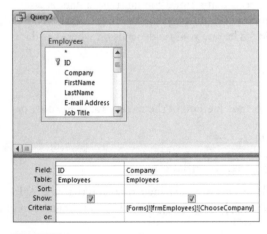

FIGURE 11-4

You must provide the parameter values before opening a Recordset based on this type of query. To do so, you can use the Parameters collection of the QueryDef object:

```
Dim dbs As DAO.Database
Dim qdf As DAO.QueryDef
```

```
Dim rst As DAO.Recordset

Set dbs = CurrentDb

'Get the parameter query
Set qdf = dbs.QueryDefs("qryMyParameterQuery")

'Supply the parameter values
qdf.Parameters("EnterStartDate") = Date
qdf.Parameters("EnterEndDate") = Date + 7

'Open a Recordset based on the parameter query
Set rst = qdf.OpenRecordset()
```

Opening a Recordset Based on a SQL Statement

The following code shows you how to open a snapshot-type Recordset based on a SQL statement:

```
Dim dbs As DAO.Database
Dim rsSQL As DAO.Recordset
Dim strSQL As String

Set dbs = CurrentDb

'Open a snapshot-type Recordset based on an SQL statement
strSQL = "SELECT * FROM Table1 WHERE Field2 = 33"
Set rsSQL = dbs.OpenRecordset(strSQL, dbOpenSnapshot)
```

Opening a Recordset That Locks Out All Other Users

The following code opens a dynaset-type Recordset using a saved query and specifies the dbDenyRead argument to prevent other users from reading the same table. Use this with caution!

```
Dim dbs As DAO.Database
Dim rsSQL As DAO.Recordset

Set dbs = CurrentDb

'Open a dynaset-type Recordset based on a saved query
Set rsSQL = dbs.OpenRecordset("qryMyQuery", _
    dbOpenDynaset, dbDenyRead)
```

Filtering and Ordering Recordsets

Whenever you work on records in a database, it is rare that you want to carry out an action on the entire table. If you did, you would be best served by using an action query because queries operate much faster on large numbers of rows than do row processing methods using Recordsets. It is more likely that you'll want to do something with a subset of records, and that means you would need to filter your query to select only those records that you wanted to work on.

With Recordsets, you have the additional opportunity to sort the records, so you can operate on them in a specific order. This section illustrates how to filter your Recordsets and order their output.

> *Sorting can be a slow operation. With larger amounts of data, opening a Recordset that is sorted may take longer than a Recordset that is not sorted, so sort only when you need to. Also, be sure to consider which fields you may want to sort by frequently when designing tables and indexes.*

Filtering Records

Filtering is simply a way of restricting the number of rows returned by a Recordset so that you can minimize the amount of data you have to wade through. The additional benefit of filtering is that it potentially reduces the amount of data that is sent across a network, thereby minimizing bandwidth usage.

As you've already seen, you can filter a Recordset using a WHERE clause in a query on which the Recordset can be based, or in its Source argument. For example:

```
Set rst = dbs.OpenRecordset( _
    "SELECT * FROM tblCustomers WHERE CustomerNo > 1234")
```

This filters the Recordset as it is being created. Of course, you can't do this on table-type Recordsets because they load the entire table. You can, however, filter dynaset- and snapshot-type Recordsets.

Another method of filtering a Recordset as it is being created is to use the Recordset object's Filter property. You can't filter an existing Recordset once it's been created, so the filter won't take effect until you create a new Recordset that is based on the first. The Filter property is the WHERE clause of a SQL query, without the word WHERE. For example:

```
rst.Filter = "[CustName] LIKE '*parts*'"
```

Once the Filter property has been set, create a new Recordset that will be based on a subset of the rows in the first Recordset such as this:

```
Set rstFiltered = rst.OpenRecordset
```

After doing so, rstFiltered contains only those rows from rst whose CustName rows contain the word *parts*. You might think that this is a rather inefficient way of doing things, and under normal circumstances you'd be right; however, there are circumstances in which this approach might be the better way to go.

For example, say you want your sales representatives to visit all the customers in a certain city, based solely on when that city that was last visited. You don't know which city that might be, so the following example code creates a Recordset that returns rows for all customers who were last visited between 30 and 60 days ago. Once you have the record for the last customer visited within that time frame, you then extract the name of the city in which they reside, and create another filtered Recordset (based on the first), and set their ToBeVisited flag to True. This lets the sales representatives know to visit them. Of course, there's nothing here that couldn't be done in an action query, but this example demonstrates how you could use this feature.

```
Dim dbs As DAO.Database
Dim rst As DAO.Recordset
Dim rstFiltered As DAO.Recordset
```

```
Dim strCity As String

Set dbs = CurrentDb
'Create the first filtered Recordset, returning customer records
'for those visited between 30-60 days ago.

Set rst = dbs.OpenRecordset( _
"SELECT * FROM Customers WHERE LastVisitDate BETWEEN Date()-60 " & _
"AND Date()-30 ORDER BY LastVisitDate DESC")

'Begin row processing
Do While Not rst.EOF

    'Retrieve the name of the first city in the selected rows
    strCity = rst!City

    'Now filter the Recordset to return only the customers from that city
    rst.Filter = "City = '" & strCity & "'"
    Set rstFiltered = rst.OpenRecordset

    'Process the rows
    Do While Not rstFiltered.EOF
        rstFiltered.Edit
        rstfiltered!ToBeVisited = True
        rstFiltered.Update
        rstFiltered.MoveNext
    Loop

    'We've done what was needed. Now exit.
    Exit Do
    rst.MoveNext
Loop

'Cleanup
rstFiltered.Close
rst.Close

Set rstFiltered = Nothing
Set rst = Nothing
```

Notice the ORDER BY clause in this example? It's explained in the next section.

Ordering Records

Ordering is a way of defining how the data returned in the Recordset is to be sorted. For example, you might want to see, in descending order of amount, a list of customers who owe you money.

There are three ways to sort Recordsets: using the ORDER BY clause in a query on which the Recordset is based; using the Index property; or using the Sort property. You can only use the Index property on table-type Recordsets, whereas the ORDER BY clause and Sort property work only with dynaset- and snapshot-type Recordsets.

Ordering Using the ORDER BY Clause

When you specify the SQL statement on which a Recordset is based, you can include an ORDER BY clause. This clause specifies three things: the columns on which the sort will be based, the order of precedence for the sorting of those columns, and the actual order in which the data in those columns will be sorted. For example:

```
SELECT * FROM tblCustomers ORDER BY CustomerNo DESC, CustName
```

In this query, the records returned will be ordered according to the criteria set up for both the CustomerNo and CustName columns. As a result of their relative positions in the clause, the Recordset will first be sorted according to the criteria for CustomerNo, and then by CustName. As you can see, CustomerNo will be sorted in descending order. The default order is ascending, so although you can specify ASC, there's no need to explicitly declare it.

Ordering Using the Index Property

Setting the Index property of a table-type Recordset is quite simple; however, you are restricted to the sort order already specified by the table's index. For example, the following code will immediately reorder the Recordset in CustomerNo order. If the idxCustomerNo index is defined in ascending order, that is how the Recordset will be sorted.

```
rst.Index = "idxCustomerNo"
```

Ordering Using the Sort Property

As with the Filter property discussed previously, setting the Sort property does not affect the current Recordset. Rather, it affects only a new Recordset that is based on the current one.

For instance, if you create a Recordset, filtered on CustomerNo, you set the Recordset's Sort property by specifying the ORDER BY clause of a SQL query, without the words ORDER BY. For example:

```
Set rst = dbs.OpenRecordset( _
    "SELECT * FROM tblCustomers WHERE CustomerNo > 1234")
rst.Sort = "[CustomerNo] DESC, [CustName]"
```

Then you create a new Recordset whose sort order is defined by the Sort property, such as this:

```
Set rstOrdered = rst.OpenRecordset
```

Navigating Recordsets

Once you've opened a Recordset, you'll probably want to get at its data and you'll probably want to move from record to record.

DAO provides five methods and five properties to help you navigate through your Recordsets. The methods are Move, MoveFirst, MovePrevious, MoveNext, and MoveLast. The properties are AbsolutePosition, PercentPosition, RecordCount, BOF (beginning of file), and EOF (end of file).

Navigational Methods

The Recordset object's Move method enables you to move the *cursor* (the virtual "pointer" to a particular record) to another position relative to either the current position, or that specified by a bookmark. The Move method provides two arguments:

```
rst.Move rows[, start]
```

The rows argument specifies the number of rows to move, and the direction: Greater than zero indicates forward, less than zero means backward. The optional start argument specifies where to start the move. When you supply a bookmark (discussed later in this chapter) for the start argument, DAO moves the cursor the appropriate number of rows from the position specified by the bookmark. If you omit the start argument, DAO moves the cursor from the current position.

MoveFirst, MovePrevious, MoveNext, and MoveLast are the workhorses of Recordset navigation, particularly MoveNext and MovePrevious. As their names suggest, they allow you to move the cursor forward and backward one record from the current position.

AbsolutePosition, PercentPosition

The AbsolutePosition and PercentPosition methods enable you to move the cursor to a specific row in the Recordset. For example, if you wanted to move to the 127th row, you could issue the following method call:

```
rst.AbsolutePosition = 127
```

Similarly, to move to (roughly) half-way through the Recordset, you could issue this:

```
rst.PercentPosition = 50
```

AbsolutePosition does not equate to a row number, and although it does return the cursor's current position in the Recordset, the position can change as you add or delete rows, or change your filtering and sorting. You can't use AbsolutePosition with table-type Recordsets.

RecordCount

Given its name, you might assume that the RecordCount property actually indicates the number of records returned by a Recordset. That assumption is not quite accurate.

Recordsets do not always return their entire data set immediately. They can take quite some time to populate; the more rows they have to return, the longer they take. DAO returns a pointer to the Recordset early, so you can get on with doing whatever it is you want to do, assuming that the later rows will have been returned by the time you get to them.

The RecordCount property actually returns the number of rows that the Recordset has accessed so far.

If you issue the MoveLast method before checking RecordCount, the Recordset does not return until all the records have been accessed, in which case RecordCount then reports the correct number of rows. In fact, that's how you get an accurate record count, by issuing a MoveLast, followed by checking the RecordCount property, as the following example shows.

```
Set rst = dbs.OpenRecordset("SELECT * FROM Table1", dbOpenDynaset)

If rst.AbsolutePosition > -1 Then
    'Move to the last row
    rst.MoveLast

    'Now get the count
    lngCount = rst.RecordCount

    'If you want, you can now move again
```

```
rst.MoveFirst

' - -
'Continue processing
' - -

End If
```

> `RecordCount` *always returns the correct number of rows for table-type Recordsets.*

In a single-user environment, once `RecordCount` has the correct number of rows, it stays synchronized when rows are added or deleted. In a multiuser environment, however, things get a little trickier.

For example, if two users are modifying records in the same table, additions or deletions made by one user will not be reflected on the other user's computer until they access *that* record (or the place where a deleted record *used* to be). To ensure you have an accurate record count in a multiuser environment, do one of the following:

➤ Use the Recordset's `Requery` method (see the following note).

➤ Use the `MoveLast` method again.

> *The* `Requery` *method is not supported on table-type Recordsets. The* `RecordCount` *property for snapshot-type Recordsets will not change once it has been created, and it certainly won't reflect changes made by other users.*

BOF, EOF

If you try to move beyond the boundaries of a Recordset, an error will occur. To avoid this rather unpleasant side effect, you should test to see whether you have reached the beginning or end of the Recordset by checking the value of BOF and EOF. For example:

```
If Not rst.BOF Then rst.MovePrevious
```

or

```
If Not rst.EOF Then rst.MoveNext
```

To help you understand the behavior of these properties, consider the following scenarios:

➤ You issue `MoveNext` while the cursor is on the last row, and EOF returns True. You then issue `MoveNext` again, EOF remains True, and an error occurs.

➤ You issue `MovePrevious` while the cursor is on the first row, and BOF returns True. You then issue `MovePrevious` again, BOF remains True, and an error occurs.

➤ BOF and EOF are widely used when looping through Recordsets, when you don't know how many records have been returned. Usually, row processing begins at the first row, and continues until all the rows have been processed. Sometimes, however, processing begins at the last record, and continues backward until the beginning of the Recordset. BOF and EOF allow you to do this.

For example, the following code shows a standard forward looping construct:

```
Set rst = dbs.OpenRecordset("SELECT * FROM Table1", dbOpenDynaset)

Do While Not rst.EOF
    'Process the rows
    rst.MoveNext
Loop
```

The following example demonstrates a typical reverse-direction loop:

```
Set rst = dbs.OpenRecordset("SELECT * FROM Table1", dbOpenDynaset)
rst.MoveLast

Do While Not rst.BOF
    'Process the rows
    rst.MovePrevious
Loop
```

Testing for an Empty Recordset

As mentioned in the previous section, if you attempt to move beyond a Recordset's boundaries, an error occurs. Similarly, if you attempt to execute any other Recordset method on an empty Recordset (one that has not returned any records), an error occurs.

Whenever you open a Recordset, you usually want to do something with the data it returns, so the first thing you need to know is whether it returned any records. If the data is there, you can confidently take whatever actions you had planned. But if, for whatever reason, the Recordset doesn't return any records, you have to take some alternative action such as displaying a message to the user or simply exiting the routine.

Testing for an empty Recordset can be accomplished in several ways:

➤ Test for BOF and EOF together. If BOF and EOF are both True, the Recordset is empty. For example:

```
Set rst = dbs.OpenRecordset("SELECT * FROM Table1", dbOpenDynaset)
If Not (rst.BOF And rst.EOF) Then
    'The Recordset returned records
End If
```

➤ If you need to loop through the Recordset, create a condition test that can't be met in the event of an empty Recordset. For example:

```
Set rst = dbs.OpenRecordset("SELECT * FROM Table1", dbOpenDynaset)
Do Until rst.EOF
    'The Recordset returned records
Loop
```

➤ Check the Recordset's RecordCount property. If it is zero, you know there aren't any records. For example:

```
Set rst = dbs.OpenRecordset("SELECT * FROM Table1", dbOpenDynaset)
If rst.RecordCount > 0 Then
```

```
            'The Recordset returned records
    End If
```

Navigating Recordsets with Multi-Value Lookup Fields

You've seen the `Recordset` and `Field` objects for accessing data in a table or query. There are, how-ever, new objects in DAO that are used to manipulate and navigate multi-value lookup fields. These objects are appropriately named `Recordset2` and `Field2`. In fact, if you declare a `Recordset` or `Field` object in an ACCDB file, you are actually using a `Recordset2` or `Field2` object. This happens regardless of whether you open a Recordset that contains a multi-value lookup field.

Because a multi-value lookup field can store many values, the value of the field is actually a Record-set. In other words, you can navigate through the values in a multi-value lookup field in the same manner as other Recordsets.

For example, say you are an administrator at a small college and would like to track students and the classes that those students take. You have already created the table of classes that contains infor-mation about each class. You start by creating the Students table and adding a multi-value lookup field named `Classes` to store all of the classes taken by a particular student. The following code shows how to print the list of students and the classes they take:

```
Sub PrintStudentsAndClasses()
    Dim dbs As DAO.Database
    Dim rsStudents As DAO.Recordset2    'Recordset for students
    Dim rsClasses  As DAO.Recordset2    'Recordset for classes
    Dim fld As DAO.Field2

    'open the database
    Set dbs = CurrentDb()

    'get the table of students
    Set rsStudents = dbs.OpenRecordset("tblStudents")

    'loop through the students
    Do While Not rsStudents.EOF

        'get the classes field
        Set fld = rsStudents("Classes")

        'get the classes Recordset
        'make sure the field is a multi-valued field before
        'getting a Recordset object
        If fld.IsComplex Then
            Set rsClasses = fld.Value
        End IF

        'access all records in the Recordset
        If Not (rsClasses.BOF And rsClasses.EOF) Then
            rsClasses.MoveLast
            rsClasses.MoveFirst
        End If

        'print the student and number of classes
        Debug.Print rsStudents("FirstName") & " " & rsStudents("LastName"), _
```

```
            "Number of classes: " & rsClasses.RecordCount

        'print the classes for this student
        Do While Not rsClasses.EOF
            Debug.Print , rsClasses("Value")
            rsClasses.MoveNext
        Loop

        'close the Classes Recordset
        rsClasses.Close

        'get the next student
        rsStudents.MoveNext
    Loop

    'cleanup
    rsStudents.Close

    Set fld = Nothing
    Set rsStudents = Nothing
    Set dbs = Nothing
End Sub
```

Because the related class data is stored as a Recordset, you can use the following line to retrieve the classes for a student:

```
Set rsClasses = fld.Value
```

This creates a `Recordset2` object that contains one field named `Value`. This field contains the value of the bound column as displayed in the multi-valued combo box or list box in Access.

Bookmarks and Recordset Clones

A Recordset bookmark is a special marker in a Recordset that can be used to quickly return to a particular location. For example, to move from your current position in the Recordset to check or change a value in some other part of the same Recordset, you could set a bookmark, move to the other spot, make your changes, and then return to where you were in the first place.

In terms of Recordsets, a clone is a functional replica of the original. A clone of a Recordset points to the same data as the Recordset it was copied from. Changes made to the data in the clone are reflected in the original Recordset. The difference is primarily in navigation. A cloned Recordset has its own cursor, so you can navigate or search for data without moving the cursor in the original Recordset. For example, you might want to search for data in a form without changing the record position of the form. Using a clone, you can perform the search, and then when you find the data you're looking for, save the current bookmark for the clone. Once the bookmark has been set, you can then set the bookmark in the original Recordset to move its cursor (and therefore the record selector on the form).

Using Bookmarks

When you open a Recordset, every row is automatically assigned a unique internal bookmark, and as you will soon see, creating a reference to a bookmark is simply a matter of setting the value of a variable. So there is really no practical limit to the number of bookmarks you can set. When you close the Recordset, the internal bookmarks are lost, and any bookmarks you have set become invalid.

Although Recordsets based entirely on Access tables always support bookmarks, not all Recordset types do. Recordsets based on external data sources may not allow them. For that reason, you should always check the `Recordset` object's `Bookmarkable` property before attempting to use bookmarks on non-Access Recordsets.

Using bookmarks is much faster than using the other Recordset navigation methods. The following procedure demonstrates how to use bookmarks for record navigation:

```
Public Sub UsingBookmarks()
    Dim dbs As DAO.Database
    Dim rst As DAO.Recordset
    Dim varBookmark As Variant

    Set dbs = CurrentDb
    Set rst = dbs.OpenRecordset("SELECT * FROM Table1", dbOpenDynaset)

    If rst.AbsolutePosition > -1 Then
        'Force the entire Recordset to load
        rst.MoveLast
        rst.MoveFirst

        'Move to the middle of the Recordset, and print
        'the current cursor position, for reference
        rst.PercentPosition = 50
        Debug.Print "Current position: " & rs.AbsolutePosition

        'Set the bookmark
        varBookmark = rst.Bookmark

        'Move to the last record, and print its position
        rst.MoveLast
        Debug.Print "Current position: " & rs.AbsolutePosition

        '
        'Do whatever you came here to do
        '

        'Now move back, and verify the position
        rst.Bookmark = varBookmark
        Debug.Print "Current position: " & rs.AbsolutePosition
    End If

    rst.Close
    Set rst = Nothing
    Set dbs = Nothing

End Sub
```

Now What about Those Clones?

As mentioned earlier, a clone is a functional replica of the original, with its own cursor. Now let's take a closer look at how to use clones. There are two clone methods: `Clone` and `RecordsetClone`. `Clone` is a method of the `Recordset` object, whereas `RecordsetClone` is a property of the Access

Form object. Both are identical in function, except that you can't set the Filter or Sort properties for Recordsets created using the RecordsetClone property.

If you use the Clone or RecordsetClone method to create a copy of the original Recordset, all the bookmarks are identical. Rather than creating a new Recordset from scratch, the two clone methods simply point an object variable at the original set of rows. The clone operates on exactly the same data as the original, so any changes made in one are reflected in the other. Although the data and bookmarks are identical, you can navigate the clone independent of the original; that is, you can change the cursor position in the clone and have no effect on the cursor position in the original.

Let's say you are designing a data entry form for customers and that you want to allow the users to type in a customer number, and have the form immediately display the record for the customer with that number. There are several ways to do this, not all of them satisfactory.

You could use DoCmd.ApplyFilter or reopen the form using a WHERE condition with DoCmd .OpenForm, but at best, they would return only one record, and your form navigation buttons would be useless. At worst, they would return an empty Recordset. The solution is to use a bookmark and Recordset clone together. In the AfterUpdate event of your Customer Number text box, you could add something like:

```
Private Sub txtEnterCustNo_AfterUpdate()
    Dim rstClone As DAO.Recordset
    Dim strCustNo As String

    'Remove leading and trailing spaces
    strCustNo = Trim(Me.txtEnterCustNo)

    'Check that the text box contains a value
    If strCustNo <> "" Then
        'Create a clone of the form's Recordset
        Set rstClone = Me.RecordsetClone

        'Search for the customer's record
        rstClone.FindFirst "[CustNo] = """ & strCustNo & """"

        'The FindFirst method is explained in the following section
        'Test the result of the search
        If rstClone.NoMatch Then
            'NoMatch returned True (not a match)
            MsgBox "Customer not found."
        Else
            'NoMatch returned False (found)
            'The clone's bookmark is now set to its current position
            'which is the row returned by the FindFirst method
            '
            'Move the form's current cursor position
            'to the one pointed to by the clone's bookmark
            Me.Bookmark = rstClone.Bookmark
        End If
    End If

    'Clean up
    On Error Resume Next
```

```
    rstClone.Close
    Set rstClone = Nothing

End Sub
```

Examining the code, you can see that the real work is done in no more than four lines.

1. Create a clone of the form's Recordset.

```
Set rsClone = Me.RecordsetClone
```

2. Search for the record using the clone (leaves the original Recordset untouched).

```
rsClone.FindFirst "[CustNo] = """ & strCustNo & """"
```

3. Check if the search failed. If so, you return a message box to inform the user. If the search passes, you execute line 4.

```
If rsClone.NoMatch Then
```

4. Change the form's `Bookmark`.

```
Me.Bookmark = rsClone.Bookmark
```

Finding Records

As you saw in the preceding section, you often need a way to find a specific record when working with Recordsets. DAO provides two ways to find a specific record: `Seek` and `Find`. The one you choose to use depends entirely on the type of Recordset you want to use it on.

The Seek Method

The `Seek` method is the fastest way to find a specific record, but it can be used only on table-type Recordsets because it specifically relies on the table's indexes. Naturally, the table must have at least one index for it to search on. Trying to call `Seek` against a non–table-type Recordset will earn you a runtime error. `Seek` uses the following syntax:

```
rst.Seek comparison, key1, key2. . .key13
```

To use `Seek`, you must specify three things: the name of the index to use (you can specify only one index at a time), a comparison operator string (which can be <, <=, =, =>, or >), and one or more values that correspond to the value of the key you're looking for. You can specify up to 13 different key values.

 A runtime error occurs if the name of the index cannot be found when using the Seek method. If you rename or delete an index in a table that is searched using the Seek method the code will break.

For example, the following code shows you how to search the `tblCustomers` table to find a customer whose `CustomerNo` is `123`:

```
Set rst = dbs.OpenRecordset("tblCustomer", dbOpenTable)
rst.Index = "CustomerNo"
rst.Seek "=", 123
```

You might recall from the section on creating table indexes that the primary key index is called PrimaryKey by default, although you can name it anything you like. If you want to use the table's primary key index, you must know its name.

To use Seek effectively, you need to understand how it works. If you specify =, =>, or > as the comparison operator, Access starts its search at the beginning of the Recordset and works its way to the end. If you use any of the other operators, Access starts at the end of the Recordset, and moves toward the beginning. With that knowledge, you can see that using Seek within a loop is essentially pointless.

You must specify a key value for each column in the index, particularly if you're using the = comparison operator. The reason is that some of the key fields may default to Null, and because nothing can "equal" Null, your Seek method will usually not find what you're looking for.

The Seek method is not supported for linked tables, but all is not lost; the following code demonstrates how to use Seek on a linked table:

```
Sub TestSeek()
    Dim strMyExternalDatabase As String
    Dim dbs    As DAO.Database
    Dim dbsExt As DAO.Database   ' External database
    Dim rst    As DAO.Recordset
    Dim tdf    As DAO.TableDef

    ' Get the path to the external database that contains
    ' the tblCustomers table we're going to search.
    Set dbs = CurrentDb()
    Set tdf = dbs.TableDefs("tblCustomers")
    strMyExternalDatabase = Mid(tdf.Connect, 11)

    'Open the database that contains the table that is linked
    Set dbsExt = OpenDatabase(strMyExternalDatabase)

    'Open a table-type Recordset against the external table
    Set rst = dbsExt.OpenRecordset("tblCustomers", dbOpenTable)

    'Specify which index to search on
    rst.Index = "PrimaryKey"

    'Specify the criteria
    rst.Seek "=", 123

    'Check the result
    If rst.NoMatch Then
        MsgBox "Record not found."
    Else
        MsgBox "Customer name: " & rst.CustName
    End If

    ' // Cleanup code goes here.
End Sub
```

What this does is open the external database that contains the table that is linked in the current database. It then creates a table-type Recordset on the table in that database, so that you are operating directly on the table you want to search. The code searches the table and, finally, checks to see if the search failed. Never assume that the search is successful; instead, always use the Recordset's NoMatch property to determine the result.

Even doing things this way, in most circumstances, the Seek method is still faster than the Find methods. But it is more complex to use on linked tables, and it relies on specifically named indexes to exist.

The Find Methods

There are four Find methods: FindFirst, FindPrevious, FindNext, and FindLast. Their purpose is self-evident, given their names, and you can use them on all Recordset types.

Because the Find methods enable you to specify any field in the criteria, they may not be capable of using a table's indexes to execute a search. Compare this to the Seek method, which always uses a table's indexes to execute the search. Without an indexed field, the Find methods can just as easily use a table scan to find the right record; it just depends on the type of search, and amount of data being searched. Not surprisingly then, the Find methods can be slower than using Seek. You can help the Find methods run faster by making sure you have indexes on the fields you are searching.

In a table scan, the database engine must read each record as a part of a search. This often results in a query or operation that is significantly slower than methods such as Seek.

The Find methods can be used on filtered dynaset and snapshot Recordsets, which minimizes the number of records that have to be searched.

In addition, because you have FindNext and FindPrevious methods at your disposal, you don't have to start at the beginning or end of the Recordset to find subsequent matches; you can just keep searching until you find the record you want.

All four methods use the same syntax:

```
rs.[FindFirst | FindPrevious | FindNext | FindLast] criteria
```

The criteria argument can be any valid SQL WHERE clause, without the word WHERE. For example, the following code demonstrates how to find all instances of a customer having the word *parts* in his or her name.

```
Sub FindOrgName()
    Dim dbs As DAO.Database
    Dim rst As DAO.Recordset

    'Get the database and Recordset
    Set dbs = CurrentDb
    Set rst = dbs.OpenRecordset("tblCustomers")

    'Search for the first matching record
    rst.FindFirst "[OrgName] LIKE '*parts*'"

    'Check the result
    If rst.NoMatch Then
        MsgBox "Record not found."
        GoTo Cleanup
    Else
```

```
            Do While Not rs.NoMatch
                MsgBox "Customer name: " & rst!CustName
                rs.FindNext "[OrgName] LIKE '*parts*'"
            Loop

            'Search for the next matching record
            rst.FindNext "[OrgName] LIKE '*parts*'"
        End If

Cleanup:
    rst.Close
    Set rst = Nothing
    Set dbs = Nothing
End Sub
```

Once a matching record is found, any subsequent search begins from the *current* cursor position, not the start or end of the Recordset, as in the Seek method. Again, always follow the search with a check of the Recordset's NoMatch property to determine the result of the search.

Working with Recordsets

So far you've looked at navigating through Recordsets, setting and using bookmarks, creating Recordset clones, and finding specific records. All this has been done so that you can get to the exact record that you intend to do something with.

So what can you do with Recordsets? The following sections answer that question.

Retrieving Field Values

On an open Recordset, you return a field value by simply referring to it. There are, of course, several ways to do this.

The first method is to refer to the field by name, as in the following code:

```
Set rst = dbs.OpenRecordset("tblMyTable")
MsgBox rst!CustomerNo
'or
MsgBox rst("CustomerNo")
```

Don't forget that the field name you use depends entirely on the table or query on which the Recordset is based. For example, if the customer number is contained in the CustomerNo field, and the Recordset gets its data directly from tblCustomers, then rs!CustomerNo would suffice. However, if the Recordset gets its data from a query in which the CustomerNo field is renamed (using the As keyword) to CustNo:

```
SELECT CustomerID, CustomerNo As CustNo, CustName FROM tblCustomers
```

you would use rs!CustNo.

You can also refer to a field by the Recordset's Field object, as in the following example:

```
MsgBox rst.Fields!CustomerNo
MsgBox rst.Fields("CustomerNo")
MsgBox rst.Fields(2)
```

Adding, Editing, and Deleting Rows

Not all Recordsets are editable, and the same can be said about some rows. Snapshot Recordsets are never editable, and user permissions and record locks can result in Recordsets or individual rows that you cannot edit. In addition, joins in some Recordsets that are based on multiple tables or totals (aggregate) queries can render the entire Recordset uneditable.

Adding Rows

The procedure for adding rows to a Recordset is quite simple: Open the Recordset, issue the Recordset's `AddNew` method, make the additions, and then issue the `Update` method. Here's an example:

```
'Open the Recordset
Set rst = dbs.OpenRecordset("tblCustomers", dbOpenynaset)
With rst

    'Begin the editing session

    .AddNew
    'Make the additions
    !CustName = "Fred Nurk"
    !DOB = DateSerial(1956, 11, 5)
    !LastVisited = Date()
    '
    'Make other additions if you wish
    '
    'Commit the changes

    .Update
End With
```

If using an Autonumber field, there is no need to specify it as Access will automatically calculate and enter it for you. In fact, if you try to specify it, an error will be generated.

Editing Rows

The procedure for editing Recordset data is also quite simple: Move to the row you want to edit, issue the Recordset's `Edit` method, make the changes, and then issue the `Update` method. The following example demonstrates how:

```
'Open the Recordset
Set rst = dbs.OpenRecordset("tblCustomers", dbOpenDynaset)
With rst
    'Find the record you want to edit
    .FindFirst "[CustomerNo] = 123"

    If Not .NoMatch Then
        'Begin the editing session
        .Edit

        'Make the change(s)
        !LastVisited = Date()
        '
        'Make other changes if you wish
        '

        'Commit the changes
```

```
            .Update
        Else

            MsgBox "Record not found."
        End If
End With
```

Deleting Rows

Deleting rows is even simpler; you just move to the row you want to delete and issue the `Delete` method.

```
'Open the Recordset
Set rst = dbs.OpenRecordset("tblCustomers", dbOpenynaset)
With rst

    'Find the record you want to edit
    .FindFirst "[CustomerNo] = 123"

    If Not .NoMatch Then
        'Delete the row
        .Delete
    Else
        MsgBox "Record not found."
    End If
End With
```

An important point to note when deleting rows is that as soon as you delete one, all the rows above it shift down one position. This is of real consequence only if you are moving down through the Recordset (from beginning to end), deleting rows as you go. For example, if you wanted to delete a contiguous set of rows, you could end up deleting every second row because when you delete the current row, the cursor does not move, but the rows above it move down one position to compensate. So, as Figure 11-5 shows, if you were on row 6 when you deleted it, the cursor hasn't changed position, but you will then be on row 7.

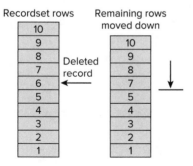

FIGURE 11-5

The recommended procedure for deleting contiguous rows is to move up (from the end to the beginning) through the rows, rather than up.

```
rst.MoveLast
Do Until rst.BOF
```

```
        rst.Delete
        rst.MovePrevious
Loop
```

Canceling an Edit

If you change your mind and decide not to continue adding or editing records, you can cancel the update using the `CancelUpdate` method. You can only cancel changes between the `AddNew...Update` or `Edit...Update` methods. For example:

```
With rst
    .AddNew
    !OrgName = strOrgName
    !Address = strAddress

    'If some criteria is met, update the record
    If IsFinancial(lngOrgID) Then
        .Refund = curRefundAmt
        .Update
    Else
        'If the criteria test fails, cancel the update
    .CancelUpdate
    End If
End With
```

Using Arrays with Recordsets

Sometimes you may choose to populate an array with data from a Recordset. Perhaps you're intending to pass the array to a Windows API, and because APIs do not accept Recordsets as parameters, this is the only way you can do it. Typically, you would define the array and then loop through the rows, appending data to the array as you went, as the following code illustrates:

```
Dim varMyArray() As Variant
Dim varField As Variant

Set rst = dbs.OpenRecordset("Table1", dbOpenSnapshot)

rst.MoveLast
ReDim varMyArray(rst.RecordCount, rst.Fields.Count)
rst.MoveFirst

Do While Not rst.EOF
    For Each varField In rst.Fields
        varMyArray(rst.AbsolutePosition, varField.OrdinalPosition) = varField
    Next varField
    rst.MoveNext
Loop
```

But DAO provides a handy method to do all this for you called `GetRows`. `GetRows` returns a two-dimensional array containing all the column data for the specified number of rows, with the first element specifying the row and the second specifying the column.

```
Dim varMyArray As Variant
Set rst = dbs.OpenRecordset("SELECT Field1, Field2 FROM Table1", dbOpenSnapshot)
varMyArray = rst.GetRows(120)
```

You don't have to define the array's rows; in fact, you don't even have to declare it as an array; just define it as a variant. Access takes care of the rest.

After you call `GetRows`, the Recordset's cursor position is set to the next unread row. You can specify the number of rows to return, but if you specify more rows than exist, Access returns only the number of rows actually present in the Recordset.

Be a little judicious when using this technique because Access returns all the Recordset columns in the query, regardless of their data type. You could end up with Memo and OLE (Object Linking and Embedding) data in your array. It is a good idea to specify specific fields, and to filter the Recordset, so you only have the data you actually need.

Working with Attachment Fields

As mentioned previously, Access 2007 included a new data type — Attachment — that you can use with the new ACCDB file format. This type can store zero or more files that are associated with an individual record. Remember the students and classes example? Say that you want to store the class syllabus and homework assignments with the class. The Attachment data type enables you to save the file as part of the database without the bloat of an OLE Object.

Attachment fields are a special type of multi-valued field in which multiple fields are included in the nested Recordset. The fields defined by the Attachment data type are described in the following table:

FIELD NAME	DESCRIPTION
FileData	The file itself is stored in this field.
FileFlags	Reserved for future use.
FileName	The name of the file in the attachment field.
FileTimeStamp	Reserved for future use.
FileType	The file extension of the file in the attachment field.
FileURL	The URL for the file for a linked SharePoint list. Will be `Null` for local Access tables.

Navigating Attachments

Because attachment fields are a type of multi-valued field, you can navigate them by enumerating through the nested Recordset for the field. The following code shows how to print a list of attachments that are included with each record in a table.

```
Sub ListAttachments()
    Dim dbs As DAO.Database
    Dim rst As DAO.Recordset2
    Dim rsA As DAO.Recordset2
    Dim fld As DAO.Field2

    'Get the database, Recordset, and attachment field
    Set dbs = CurrentDb
    Set rst = dbs.OpenRecordset("tblAttachments")
    Set fld = rst("Attachments")

    'Navigate through the table
    Do While Not rst.EOF

        'Print the first and last name
        Debug.Print rst("FirstName") & " " & rst("LastName")

        'Get the Recordset for the Attachments field
        Set rsA = fld.Value

        'Print all attachments in the field
        Do While Not rsA.EOF
            Debug.Print , rsA("FileType"), rsA("FileName")

            'Next attachment
            rsA.MoveNext
        Loop

        'Next record
        rst.MoveNext
    Loop

    rst.Close
    dbs.Close
    Set fld = Nothing
    Set rst = Nothing
    Set dbs = Nothing
End Sub
```

code snippet Chapter 11 - DAO Samples

Adding, Saving, and Deleting Attachments

In the past, to load binary data in an Access database, you could either use the OLE Object
data type and automate a form by using the Bound OLE Object control, or you could use the
AppendChunk method of the Field object. Attachment fields make this much more elegant and
save space because they are compressed in the database.

Adding Attachments

Using the Field2 object, you can insert or save attachment fields. The Field2 object makes it easy
to insert an attachment into a field using a new method called LoadFromFile.

The following code demonstrates how to insert a file into an attachment field. The strPattern
argument in the function enables you to add all files in the directory specified by strPath that

match a given pattern. This might be useful for loading all .bmp files in a folder, but not the .gif files.

```
Public Function LoadAttachments(strPath As String, Optional strPattern As i
String = "*.*") As Long
    Dim dbs As DAO.Database
    Dim rst As DAO.Recordset2
    Dim rsA As DAO.Recordset2
    Dim fld As DAO.Field2
    Dim strFile As String

    'Get the database, Recordset, and attachment field
    Set dbs = CurrentDb
    Set rst = dbs.OpenRecordset("tblAttachments")
    Set fld = rst("Attachments")

    'Navigate through the table
    Do While Not rst.EOF

        'Get the Recordset for the Attachments field
        Set rsA = fld.Value

        'Load all attachments in the specified directory
        strFile = Dir(strPath & "\*.*")

        rst.Edit
        Do While Len(strFile) > 0
            'Add a new attachment that matches the pattern.
            'Pass "" to match all files.
            If strFile Like strPattern Then
                rsA.AddNew
                rsA("FileData").LoadFromFile strPath & "\" & strFile
                rsA.Update

                'Increment the number of files added
                LoadAttachments = LoadAttachments + 1
            End If
            strFile = Dir
        Loop
        rsA.Close

        rst.Update
        'Next record
        rst.MoveNext
    Loop
    rst.Close
    dbs.Close

    Set fld = Nothing
    Set rsA = Nothing
    Set rst = Nothing
    Set dbs = Nothing
End Function
```

code snippet Chapter 11 - DAO Samples

Saving Attachments

In the past, to save an OLE Object field value to the computer required writing code for the Bound OLE Object control on a form. Using an Attachment field, you can now save your attachments to the computer without the need for a form. The Field2 object includes a new method named SaveToFile that makes this easier. The following code demonstrates saving an attachment to a specified location.

```vb
Public Function SaveAttachments(strPath As String, Optional strPattern As _
String = "*.*") As Long
    Dim dbs As DAO.Database
    Dim rst As DAO.Recordset2
    Dim rsA As DAO.Recordset2
    Dim fld As DAO.Field2
    Dim strFullPath As String

    'Get the database, Recordset, and attachment field
    Set dbs = CurrentDb
    Set rst = dbs.OpenRecordset("tblAttachments")
    Set fld = rst("Attachments")

    'Navigate through the table
    Do While Not rst.EOF

        'Get the Recordset for the Attachments field
        Set rsA = fld.Value

        'Save all attachments in the field
        Do While Not rsA.EOF
            If rsA("FileName") Like strPattern Then
                strFullPath = strPath & "\" & rsA("FileName")

                'Make sure the file does not exist and save
                If Dir(strFullPath) = "" Then
                    rsA("FileData").SaveToFile strFullPath
                End If

                'Increment the number of files saved
                SaveAttachments = SaveAttachments + 1
            End If

            'Next attachment
            rsA.MoveNext
        Loop
        rsA.Close

        'Next record
        rst.MoveNext
    Loop

    rst.Close
    dbs.Close

    Set fld = Nothing
    Set rsA = Nothing
```

```
            Set rst = Nothing
            Set dbs = Nothing
      End Function
```

code snippet Chapter 11 - DAO Samples

Deleting Attachments

The following code shows you how to delete an attachment from a table. The strRemoveFile argument is the name of the file to remove. Specify the strFilter argument to add a filter to the table prior to deleting attachments.

```
Function RemoveAttachment(strRemoveFile As String, Optional strFilter As i
String) As Long
      Dim dbs As DAO.Database
      Dim rst As DAO.Recordset2
      Dim rsA As DAO.Recordset2
      Dim fld As DAO.Field2

      'Get the database
      Set dbs = CurrentDb

      'Open the Recordset. If the strFilter is supplied, add it to the WHERE
      'clause for the Recordset. Otherwise, any files matching strFileName
      'will be deleted
      If Len(strFilter) > 0 Then
          Set rst = dbs.OpenRecordset("SELECT * FROM tblAttachments WHERE " i
 & strFilter)
      Else
          Set rst = dbs.OpenRecordset("tblAttachments")
      End If

      'Get the Attachment field
      Set fld = rst("Attachments")

      'Navigate through the Recordset
      Do While Not rst.EOF

          'Get the Recordset for the Attachments field
          Set rsA = fld.Value

          'Walk the attachments and look for the file name to remove
          Do While Not rsA.EOF
              If rsA("FileName") Like strRemoveFile Then
                  rsA.Delete

                  'Increment the number of files removed
                  RemoveAttachment = RemoveAttachment + 1
              End If
              rsA.MoveNext
          Loop

          'Cleanup the Attachments Recordset
```

```
        rsA.Close
        Set rsA = Nothing

        'Next record
        rst.MoveNext
    Loop

    rst.Close
    dbs.Close
    Set fld = Nothing
    Set rst = Nothing
    Set dbs = Nothing
End Function
```

code snippet Chapter 11 - DAO Samples

APPEND-ONLY FIELDS

As mentioned previously, you can create an append-only field by setting the `AppendOnly` property of a Memo field to `True`. When this property is enabled, the memo field keeps its previous values as the data in the field is changed. This happens regardless of whether you change the value in the Access interface or in DAO. In the Access interface only the current value is displayed.

This can be useful in many scenarios such as:

➤   Call centers tracking correspondence with a customer

➤   Keeping a maintenance history for an asset

➤   Content tracking for a small content management system

While this feature is very powerful, there isn't a way to retrieve the history data for the field using DAO. Fortunately, the Access `Application` object has a method named `ColumnHistory` to retrieve this data. This, however, requires that Access is installed to retrieve this information. External applications will not be able to retrieve this data.

There are some limitations to the `ColumnHistory` method. First, the combined history is returned as a single string value. That means you have to parse the value to get something meaningful. You'll see an example of parsing this value shortly. Second, all rich formatting is removed. Finally, the date/time value in the string is localized, making it more difficult to write generic parsing code.

For tracking purposes, the column history also includes the date and time that the change was made. This data is stored in the order in which the changes were made and appears in the following format:

```
[Version:  Date Time ] History Data
```

You can also view the column history for a memo field using the Access interface (see Figure 11-6).

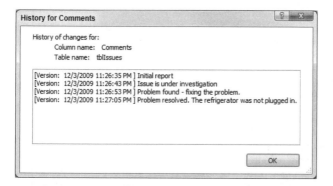

FIGURE 11-6

Let's say that in the issue tracking example you would like to see the data sorted in descending order. The following code uses the ColumnHistory method in Access to retrieve the values that were in the column and add them to a list box named lstHistory:

```
Private Sub ShowColumnHistory(strTableName As String, strFieldName As String)
    'History data is in this format:
    '[Version:  Date Time ] History Data
    Const VERSION_PREFIX As String = "[Version:  "

    Dim strHistory      As String
    Dim strHistoryItem  As String
    Dim astrHistory()   As String
    Dim lngCounter      As Long
    Dim datDate         As Date
    Dim datTime         As Date
    Dim strData         As String

    'Get the column history
    strHistory = Application.ColumnHistory(strTableName, strFieldName, "")

    'Make sure there is history data
    If Len(strHistory) > 0 Then
        'Parse the column history into separate items.
        'Each item in the history is separated by a vbCrLf, but
        'if there are carriage-returns in the memo field data
        'you will get unexpected results. Split on the VERSION string
        'in the history data.
        astrHistory = Split(strHistory, VERSION_PREFIX)

        'Adding these lines ensures this code works regardless of
        'how the control is configured on the form
        Me.lstHistory.RowSourceType = "Value List"
        Me.lstHistory.ColumnCount = 3
        Me.lstHistory.ColumnHeads = True

        'Add column headings to the list box
```

```
        Me.lstHistory.AddItem "Date;Time;History"

    'Enumerate the history data in reverse
    'to fill the list box in descending order
    For lngCounter = UBound(astrHistory) To LBound(astrHistory) Step -1
        'Parse the history data
        strHistoryItem = astrHistory(lngCounter)

        If Len(strHistoryItem) > 0 Then

            'Parse the date from the history data.
            'This example parses the default US date format.
            datDate = CDate(Left(strHistoryItem, InStr(strHistoryItem, " ") - 1))
            strHistoryItem = Mid(strHistoryItem, InStr(strHistoryItem, " ") + 1)

            'Parse the time from the history data
            datTime = CDate(Left(strHistoryItem, InStr(strHistoryItem, " ] ") - 1))
            strHistoryItem = Mid(strHistoryItem, InStr(strHistoryItem, " ] ") + 3)

            'Add the history item to the list box.
            Me.lstHistory.AddItem datDate & ";" & datTime & ";" & strHistoryItem
        End If
    Next
    Else
        MsgBox "There is no history information for the specified field"
    End If
End Sub
```

code snippet Chapter 11 - DAO Samples

The form with the list box is shown in Figure 11-7.

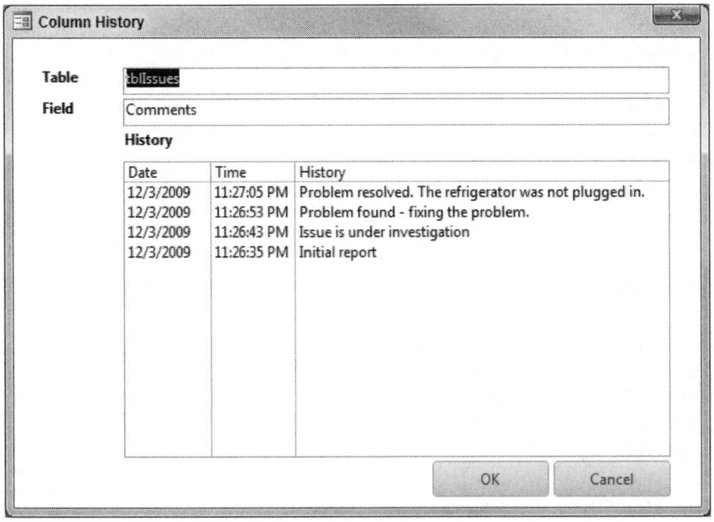

FIGURE 11-7

SUMMARY

In this chapter, you took a detailed look into the world of DAO including powerful new features that have been added in Access 2007 and Access 2010. By now you should have a fairly good understanding of when to use DAO and how to refer to its objects. You should have a good working knowledge of the main objects in the hierarchy, such as the `DBEngine`, `Workspace`, `Error`, `Database`, and `Recordset` objects, and their associated collections. Although very few people can remember every single property and method of every object, you should have gained enough exposure to them by now to be able to start writing some reasonably sophisticated software. In any case, IntelliSense can help you out when you're unsure.

Now that you've mastered DAO, you're ready to tackle a whole new Object Model — ActiveX Data Objects.

12

Using ADO to Access Data

WHAT'S IN THIS CHAPTER?

- ➤ Using ActiveX Data Objects (ADO) in an Access database application
- ➤ Adding a reference to ADO for a VBA code project
- ➤ Creating connection strings to ADO data sources
- ➤ Setting cursor types
- ➤ Using ADO transactions
- ➤ Adding/Modifying/Deleting Data in an ADO data source
- ➤ Executing SQL statements against an ADO data source
- ➤ Creating and manipulating ADO Recordset objects
- ➤ Creating and executing ADO events
- ➤ Working with data source schema using ADOX

ActiveX Data Objects (ADO) was created by Microsoft to provide a standardized Object Model for connecting to a wide variety of external data sources, as part of the Universal Data Access (UDA) plan. UDA refers to a plan in which there is a single, standardized object that can be implemented to retrieve data from any type of data source. Specifically, the "Object Linking and Embedding Databases" (OLE DB) is the UDA interface that enables providers to implement data access to their data source. ADO is the API that sits on top of OLE DB, providing the code functionality. Essentially, ADO is a code library that allows developers to work with data from all different types of data sources.

Appendix C provides a detailed description of the ADO Object Model and should be used in conjunction with this chapter.

INTRODUCTION TO ADO IN ACCESS

When you use Access 2010 to create a new database, by default, Access uses the ACE OLE DB provider for the connection to the `CurrentProject`. That means any functionality that uses the `CurrentProject` object will go through the OLE DB provider. To confirm this, enter the following line of code into the Visual Basic Editor's Immediate window:

```
?CurrentProject.Connection
```

The return connection string begins with the following:

```
Provider=Microsoft.ACE.OLEDB.12.0;
```

Similarly, Access uses the Access OLE DB provider when you create an Access Data Project (ADP) against the SQL Server. For example, running the code:

```
?CurrentProject.AccessConnection
```

returns a connection string that begins with the string:

```
Provider=Microsoft.Access.OLEDB.10.0;
```

Although ADPs use the Access OLE DB provider for the `CurrentProject` object, the data provider for an ADP is the SQLOLEDB provider because an ADP is connected to a SQL data source. This chapter explores ADO and how it applies to Access database solutions.

ADDING ADO REFERENCES

Before you can start using the ADO Object Model, there must be a reference to ADO in the code project for the database. By default, new ACCDB databases in Access 2010 do not have a reference to an ADO library. However, some older versions of Access do create a reference to ADO by default in new databases, which can be confusing; we discuss this shortly.

The easiest way to know if your database has a reference to ADO is to check the References dialog box in the Visual Basic Editor. If there is a reference to ADO, it will be something like "Microsoft Office ActiveX Data Objects 2.8 Library." If not, simply add it by finding the reference in the list and clicking the checkbox to add it to the code project. Once an ADO reference is present in the VBA code project, the ADO library can be used in the VBA code for the Access database application.

Referring to ADO Objects

Writing unambiguous VBA code will help avoid confusion between DAO and ADO objects. The VBA language makes it very easy to write code that does not reference a specific Object Library. Consider the following code:

```
Dim db As Database
Dim rs As Recordset
```

Nothing is terribly strange in this code, but there are two things to consider: First, only DAO has a `Database` object — ADO has none. Second, both DAO and ADO have a `Recordset` object. This begs the question: to which library does the `Recordset` object refer? If only one library is referenced, Access chooses the only possible `Recordset` object. However, if both ADO and DAO are referenced, Access chooses the first (highest) object in the reference list.

To ensure that both Access and you know which object refers to which Object Library, simply prefix the name of the Object Library to the class being declared. The following code illustrates how to explicitly reference both ADO and DAO objects:

```
Dim db     As DAO.Database
Dim cn     As ADODB.Connection
Dim rsDAO  As DAO.Recordset
Dim rsADO  As ADODB.Recordset
```

By prefixing the type library onto the class name, VBA is forced to use the Object Library that is explicitly specified. Clarifying references also makes the code run slightly faster, because Access doesn't have to examine the reference list to decide which library to use.

CONNECTING TO ADO DATA SOURCES

The `Connection` object is considered the top-level object in the ADO Object Model. Although it doesn't encompass all the other ADO objects, a connection must be specified and opened before commands can be executed against a data source. The `Connection` object is used to represent a single connection to an OLE DB data source, via the ADO provider. There are essentially two ways to create a connection: implicitly and explicitly.

Creating an Implicit Connection

Probably the simplest method for opening a connection to an ADO data source is to create an implicit connection. For example, by supplying the `CurrentProject` object's connection string, a `Recordset` object can be quickly opened containing data from the current database.

Available for download on Wrox.com

```
Function CreateImplicitAdoConnection() As ADODB.Recordset

    ' Define Variables
    Dim strSQL As String
    Dim rs     As New ADODB.Recordset

    ' Set the SQL for the Recordset
    strSQL = "SELECT [CONTACTS].* FROM [CONTACTS]"

    ' Open the Recordset using to Contacts connection
    rs.Open strSQL, CurrentProject.AccessConnection
```

```
    ' Return the Recordset
    Set CreateImplicitAdoConnection = rs

End Function
```

module SampleCode in Ch12_Sample.accdb

In this example, the `Recordset` object created that connection automatically, with the given connection string. This creates a connection that will remain open until the `Recordset` is closed. But, obviously, there are many cases where you want to create connections to data sources other than the current database, which is really the entire purpose of using ADO. In that case, we can easily create an explicit connection.

Creating an ADO Connection Object

ADO `Connection` objects are by far the most flexible method for connecting to external data sources outside of Access, since the point of ADO is to be able to connect to all kinds of different data sources, not just the current database. To create an ADO `Connection` object, you must declare it, instantiate it, supply it with the various properties it needs, and then open it. The following function creates an ADO connection to the current database and returns a `Connection` object to the caller.

Available for download on Wrox.com

```
Function CreateConnection() As ADODB.Connection

    ' Define Variables
    Dim strConnectionString As String
    Dim cn                   As New ADODB.Connection

    ' Set the Connection Settings
    With cn
        .ConnectionString = CurrentProject.Connection
        .CursorLocation = adUseClient
        .Attributes = .Attributes Or adXactCommitRetaining
    End With

    ' Open the Connection
    cn.Open

    ' Return the Connection
    Set CreateConnection = cn

End Function
```

module SampleCode in Ch12_Sample.accdb

> The `Open` *method for the* `Connection` *will fail to open an Access database if it is already opened in Exclusive mode by another source, such as the current instance of Access that is running the code. This could easily be the case with the previous code sample because it creates the new connection with* `CurrentProject.Connection`.

Again, this example created a connection to the current database, but you would generally use an explicit connection when connecting to an external data source from an ACCDB, MDB, or ADP. You may have also noticed that the `CursorLocation` property was set above, setting the cursor location for the connection. The `CurrentProject.Connection` property, as used in the above code, can also be called in the VBE Immediate window to provide the exact connection string for the current Access session. The following sections will discuss creating custom connections to ADO data sources, setting the cursor type for the connection, and working with ADO transactions.

Creating a Connection String

Building a custom connection string is the most common and the most useful way to create an ADO connection. To see an example of a connection string, create the Access 2010 Northwind sample database from the template and execute the following command in the VBE Immediate window:

```
?CurrentProject.Connection
```

The output connection string will be similar to the following example (the file paths have been changed in this example):

```
Provider=Microsoft.ACE.OLEDB.12.0;
User ID=Admin;
Data Source=C:\Databases\Northwind2010.accdb;
Mode=Share Deny Read|Share Deny Write;
Extended Properties="";
Jet OLEDB:System database=C:\Databases\System.mdw;
Jet OLEDB:Registry Path=
    Software\Microsoft\Office\14.0\Access\Access Connectivity Engine;
Jet OLEDB:Database Password="";
Jet OLEDB:Engine Type=6;
Jet OLEDB:Database Locking Mode=0;
Jet OLEDB:Global Partial Bulk Ops=2;
Jet OLEDB:Global Bulk Transactions=1;
Jet OLEDB:New Database Password="";
Jet OLEDB:Create System Database=False;
Jet OLEDB:Encrypt Database=False;
Jet OLEDB:Don't Copy Locale on Compact=False;
Jet OLEDB:Compact Without Replica Repair=False;
Jet OLEDB:SFP=False;
Jet OLEDB:Support Complex Data=True
```

 The `Jet OLEDB:Support Complex Data=True` *option requires that the connection provider support the complex data for* `Multi-valued` *and* `Attachment` *field types in Access 2007 and higher.*

When creating a connection string, only the following five parameters need to be supplied: the provider (including version), the user id, the password or database password (if applicable), the data source, and the system database (if applicable). In the case of an ADP, the requirements for the connection string are slightly different: the provider, the security option, the data source, the integrated security option, the initial catalog, and the data provider. The following is an example of an ADP connection string:

```
Provider=Microsoft.Access.OLEDB.10.0;
Persist Security Info=False;
Data Source=<SQL machine name>;
Integrated Security=SSPI;
Initial Catalog=SampleDB;
Data Provider=SQLOLEDB.1
```

To actually write the code to create an ADO connection with a custom connection string, simply supply the `Connection` object's `ConnectionString` property with the string data.

Available for download on Wrox.com

```
Function CreateConnectionFromString() As ADODB.Connection

    ' Define Variables
    Dim cn As New ADODB.Connection

    ' The paths have been truncated in this example.
    ' For this to work properly, the developer need to
    ' specify the correct Database and MDW file paths.
    cn.ConnectionString = _
        "Provider=Microsoft.ACE.OLEDB.12.0;" & _
        "User ID=Admin;" & _
        "Data Source=D:\Sample.accdb;" & _
        "Mode=Share Deny None;" & _
        "Jet OLEDB:System database=D:\System.mdw;" & _
        "Jet OLEDB:Database Password=""""";" & _
        "Jet OLEDB:Support Complex Data=True"

    ' Open the Connection
    cn.Open

    ' Return the Connection
    Set CreateConnectionFromString = cn

End Function
```

module SampleCode in Ch12_Sample.accdb

Creating a custom connection string is very common because it is very easy for the developer to manipulate the connection properties. But in common practice, once a data source has been established, it tends not to change very often. That is why there is another option for creating an ADO connection — using a Data Link connection.

Creating a Data Link Connection

A Data Link connection is basically a file that specifies the connection information to the data source. The Data Link file is type UDL and can be specified as a parameter of the `Connection` object. To create a UDL file, follow these steps:

1. Open Windows Explorer and create a text file (right click in any blank area): New ➪ Text Document.

2. Rename the file to something meaningful, and change its file extension to .UDL. (File extensions must be displayed to rename a .TXT file to .UDL) Click Yes in the message box that Windows subsequently displays to rename the extension.

3. Double-click the new UDL file and the Data Link Properties dialog box opens.

4. On the Provider tab, select Microsoft Office 12.0 Access Database Engine OLE DB Provider, and click the Next button.

5. In the Data Source text box, type the name and path to your Access database. For example:

```
C:\Databases\Northwind2010.accdb
```

6. Click the Test Connection button. If all went well, you will get a message that says "Test Connection Succeeded."

7. Go to the Advanced tab and examine the permissions that can be set for this link. For this demonstration, accept the default settings. If you want, the ALL tab can be selected to change the settings manually.

8. Click OK.

The UDL file is now created and should be working properly. The UDL file can be specified in the connection string by supplying the filename and path to the Data Link file.

Available for download on Wrox.com

```
Function CreateConnectionUDL() As ADODB.Connection

    ' Define Variables
    Dim strConnectionString As String
    Dim cn                  As New ADODB.Connection

    ' Open the Conection from the UDL file
    cn.Open "File Name=C:\MyConnection.UDL"

    ' Return the Connection
    Set CreateConnectionUDL = cn

End Function
```

module SampleCode in Ch12_Sample.accdb

In all of the examples so far, a connection has been opened to the specified data source via each different method. But no matter which method is used to create the `Connection` object, they can be used in the same manner. The general formula for working with ADO connections in VBA code is: Create the connection, operate on that connection, and then close the connection.

Closing a Connection

Once a connection is opened, it will remain in an "open" state until the connection has been closed. Before closing a connection, it is always a good idea to check the `Errors` collection to ensure that there were no unhandled errors during the connection's lifetime. To close the `Connection` object, simply call the `Close` method.

```
Connection.Close
```

Once a connection has been closed, it has not been destroyed. The connection can be reopened at any time; and in different connection modes as well. To destroy the `Connection` object, set it to `Nothing`:

```
Set Connection = Nothing
```

And, of course, it is easy to make a function do all of this work.

```
Function DestroyAdoConnection(Connection As ADODB.Connection)

    ' Check the Errors collection
    If Connection.Errors.Count > 0 Then
        ' Do some error handling
    End If

    ' Close the Connection
    Connection.Close

    ' Destroy the Connection
    Set Connection = Nothing

End Function
```

module SampleCode in Ch12_Sample.accdb

It is always a good practice to close connections once they are no longer in use. Closing the connection will help reduce the risk of locking out other connections to the same data source.

Working with Cursors

When creating an ADO connection, a *cursor* type will be specified. A cursor is a database element that controls record navigation, data updatability, and the tracking of changes made by other users. There are two types of cursor: client side and server side. To choose the cursor to use, set the `Connection` (or `Command` or `Recordset`) object's `CursorLocation` property to one of the following constants before opening the connection:

```
cn.CursorLocation = adUseClient ' Use a client-side cursor
cn.CursorLocation = adUseServer ' Default. Use a server-side cursor
```

When setting `CursorLocation` at the `Connection` object level, you are specifying the location that will be used by default when creating or opening `Recordset` or `Command` objects against that connection. However, this can be overridden at the `Recordset` or `Command` level by setting the `CursorLocation` for the object explicitly.

Server-Side Cursors

When using a server-side cursor (the default in ADO), the records contained in the `Recordset` are cached on the server. The major benefit is significantly reduced network traffic, which can greatly improve overall application performance. The downside is that server resources are consumed for every active client — the more clients and data, the more server resources are consumed. Server-side cursors allow the use of both keyset and dynamic cursors, and also support direct positional updates, which are fast and will help avoid record update collisions. Additionally, each connection can be used for more than one operation. Server-side cursors are best for inserting, updating, and deleting records, and they have the ability to have multiple active statements on the same connection.

Client-Side Cursors

Some data sources support client-side cursors only. With non-keyset client-side cursors, the server sends the entire data set to the client across the network. Because the client must now provide and manage the resources necessary to cache the records, this can place a significant load on both the network and the client and can greatly reduce an application's performance.

However, one benefit of using client-side cursors is that, once the data is cached, subsequent access to the data is much faster than with server-side cursors because the data resides locally. A second benefit is that the application is generally more scalable because the resources required to run the application are distributed among many clients, rather than loading down a single server. Although client-side cursors have some performance drawbacks, they also provide some benefits when used properly.

Using Transactions

A *transaction* is a delimited set of changes that are performed on a database's schema or data as a single unit. Transactions can increase the speed of actions that change data, have the ability to undo changes that have not yet been committed, and allow a large set of changes to be completed as a specific unit.

Transaction Support in ADO

Not all providers support transactions, so you need to verify that the provider-defined property Transaction DDL is one of the Connection object's properties. The following function determines if transactions are supported for a given ADO connection:

Available for download on Wrox.com

```
Public Function SupportsAdoTransactions(Conn As ADODB.Connection) As Boolean

' If an error occurs, the Connection doesn't support transactions
On Error GoTo Exit_False

    ' Check to see if the Connection supports Transactions
    If Conn.Properties("Transaction DDL") Then
        SupportsAdoTransactions = True
    Else
        SupportsAdoTransactions = False
    End If
    Exit Function

Exit_False:

    ' Error, the property does not exit, set to False
    SupportsAdoTransactions = False

End Function
```

module SampleCode in Ch12_Sample.accdb

Creating a Transaction

In ADO, transactions operate under the context of a `Connection`. A transaction is started by calling the `BeginTrans` method against the `Connection` object. To write the transaction to disk, call the `CommitTrans` method. To undo a transaction, call the `RollbackTrans` method.

```
Public Sub UseTransactions()

    ' Define Variables
    Dim cn As New ADODB.Connection

    ' Open a connection to the current database
    cn.ConnectionString = CurrentProject.AccessConnection
    cn.Open

    'Begin the Transaction
    cn.BeginTrans

' Set error handling to rollback the transaction if there is an error
On Error GoTo Transaction_Error

    ' Try to complete the transaction.
    cn.Execute "UPDATE Table1..."       ' Execute some command
    cn.Execute "INSERT INTO Table2..."  ' Execute another command
    cn.CommitTrans                      ' Commit the transaction

Transaction_Exit:

    ' Clean up
    cn.Close
    Set cn = Nothing
    Exit Sub

Transaction_Error:

    'Do some error handling and rollback the transaction
    cn.RollbackTrans
    Resume Transaction_Exit

End Sub
```

module SampleCode in Ch12_Sample.accdb

In this example, changes to both tables are either completed as a unit or rolled back as a unit. If an error occurs, the error handling routine ensures no changes occurred to the data source by rolling back the transaction.

Nesting Transactions

ADO transactions can be nested, but in contrast with DAO transactions, the ADO transaction's nesting position can be returned when it is created. A return value of 1 indicates the transaction occupies the top-level position in a virtual collection. A value of 2 indicates the transaction is a second-level transaction, and so on.

When calling CommitTrans or RollbackTrans for nested transactions, the most recently opened transaction is being operated upon. Additional calls to CommitTrans or RollbackTrans will operate on the previous higher-level transactions, if they exist. By calling CommitTrans or RollbackTrans, the appropriate action is taken and the transaction is closed.

Also note that if you set the Connection object's Attributes property to adXactCommitRetaining, a new transaction is automatically created after calling CommitTrans. If you set it to adXactAbort-Retaining (you can set both), the same occurs after calling RollbackTrans.

DATA ACCESS WITH ADO

Storing and retrieving data is the reason databases are employed, and a large proportion of programming usually revolves around manipulating those objects that deal with data: views, stored procedures, and recordsets. Data manipulation is quite easy to do in ADO, especially if you are already familiar with the SQL language.

Overview of the ADO Object Model

The ADO Object Model contains six main objects: Connection, Command, Recordset, Record, Field, and Stream. Table 12-1 provides a short description of each of these objects:

TABLE 12-1: The Major ADO Object Types

OBJECT	DESCRIPTION
Connection	Provides the ability to connect to an ADO data source.
Command	Provides the ability to manipulate and execute commands against a given data source.
Recordset	Provides the ability to read, write, and update records for a given data set.
Record	Provides the ability to manipulate a single row of data.
Field	Provides the ability to manipulate a table column.
Stream	Provides the ability to read, write, and update data from a stream.

Although we've already explored some examples that use the `Connection` object to execute actions on a data source, that's really just the beginning of the ADO functionality. These other ADO objects provide much of the rich and powerful functionality of the ADO library.

 The complete ADO Object Model is far too extensive to discuss every property, object, method, and event it provides in this chapter. However, Appendix C of this book provides an in-depth description of most of the ADO Object Model. Also, the Access help files and the MSDN library provide hundreds of pages describing the various aspects of the model and examples for working with those objects.

Using the Execute Method

The most common method used in the ADO Object Library is, by far, the `Execute` method. The `Execute` method is used to perform actions, usually SQL statements, against the data source. Both the `Connection` and `Command` objects expose an `Execute` method to explicitly execute commands. These methods vary slightly depending on the object, but are essentially the same.

The Connection.Execute Method

The `Connection` object's `Execute` method takes three parameters and returns a `Recordset` object containing any records the command may have returned. The `CommandText` argument can be a SQL statement, the name of a table or a stored procedure, or a provider-specific text or command. The `RecordsAffected` is a `ByRef` parameter which returns the number of records affected by the operation. The `Options` argument can be a bitwise combination of any of the `CommandTypeEnum` and/or `ExecuteOptionEnum` member values.

 Appendix C provides a detailed description of the `Execute` method, each of the parameters, and all of the `CommandTypeEnum` and `ExecuteOptionEnum` members.

To use the `Connection.Execute` method, simply instantiate a connection and call `Execute` with the desired SQL statement, as shown in this code:

Available for download on Wrox.com

```
Function ExecuteFromConnection(strSQL As String) As ADODB.Recordset

    ' Define Variables
    Dim cn As New ADODB.Connection

    ' Open the connection
    cn.ConnectionString = CurrentProject.Connection
    cn.CursorLocation = adUseClient
    cn.Open

    ' Execute the command and return the Recordset
    Set ExecuteFromConnection = cn.Execute(strSQL)
```

```
    ' Clean up
    Set cn = Nothing

End Function
```

module SampleCode in Ch12_Sample.accdb

The preceding function returns a `Recordset` object containing the results from the SQL operation specified in the parameter of this function.

The Command.Execute Method

The `Command.Execute` method provides a little more functionality for executing ADO commands. Specifically, the `Command.Execute` method allows parameters for the SQL statement to be specified. The `Command.Execute` method takes three parameters and returns a `Recordset` object, if the command supports returning records. Calling `Execute` from the `Command` object is slightly different; the `CommandText` parameter is not passed because it is a property of the `Command` object itself. The `Command.Execute` object takes the `RecordsAffected`, `Parameters`, and `Options` parameters.

 Appendix C provides a detailed description of this `Execute` *method and each of these parameters.*

A common way to execute a command from the `Command` object is to simply set the `Command` object's `CommandText`, `CommandType`, and `ActiveConnection` properties; then call the `Execute` method without any parameters. The following code illustrates how this can be done.

Available for download on Wrox.com

```
Function ExecuteFromCommand(strSQL As String) As ADODB.Recordset

    ' Define Variables
    Dim cmd As New ADODB.Command

    ' Set the required properties
    With cmd
        .CommandText = strSQL
        .CommandType = adCmdUnknown
        .ActiveConnection = CurrentProject.AccessConnection
    End With

    ' Execute the command and return the Recordset
    Set ExecuteFromCommand = cmd.Execute(strSQL)

    ' Clean up
    Set cmd = Nothing

End Function
```

module SampleCode in Ch12_Sample.accdb

The preceding function returns a `Recordset` object containing the results from the SQL operation specified in the parameter of this function.

Specifying Command Parameters

Instead of specifying the `Command` object's parameters in the SQL statement, the `Parameter` object can be used to set the parameters on the `Command` object. For example, the following function retrieves the price of a specified item by calling a `Select` query in the current database and providing the name of the item for the price to retrieve.

```
Public Function GetPrice(strName As String) As Double

    ' Define Variables
    Dim cmd As New ADODB.Command
    Dim rs  As ADODB.Recordset

    ' Build the Command object
    With cmd
        ' Set the connection
        .ActiveConnection = CurrentProject.AccessConnection

        ' Set other properties
        .CommandText = "qryGetPrice"
        .CommandType = adCmdTable

        ' To be able to refer to parameters by name,
        ' you must refresh the parameters collection
        .Parameters.Refresh

        ' Supply the parameter for the query
        .Parameters("[strItemName]") = strName
    End With

    ' Execute the Query and return the price
    Set rs = cmd.Execute

    ' Set the Price
    If rs.RecordCount < 1 Then
        MsgBox "There was no record for the Item Specified"
        GetPrice = 0
    Else
        GetPrice = rs("Price").Value
    End If

    ' Clean up
    Set rs = Nothing
    Set cmd = Nothing

End Function
```

module SampleCode in Ch12_Sample.accdb

Creating Parameters Dynamically

It's quite simple to create parameters for a query on-the-fly with ADO code. To create the parameter for a given query, call the CreateParameter method from the Command object. The benefit here is that you can specify a SQL statement in code and create the parameters for that statement when the code is run. Here's an example of creating parameters using the Command object:

```
Public Function GetPriceByCustomParameter(strName As String) As Double

    ' Define Variables
    Dim cmd As New ADODB.Command
    Dim rs  As New ADODB.Recordset

    ' Setup the Command object
    With cmd
        ' Set the connection
        .ActiveConnection = CurrentProject.AccessConnection

        ' Set the CommandText
        .CommandText = "SELECT [Prices].* FROM [Prices] " & _
                       "WHERE [Prices].[ItemName]=[strItemName]"
        .CommandType = adCmdUnknown

        ' Create the parameter and set the value
        .Parameters.Append cmd.CreateParameter( _
                    "[strItemName]", adVarChar, adParamInput, 100)
        .Parameters("[strItemName]") = strName
    End With

    ' Execute the Query and return the price
    Set rs = cmd.Execute

    ' Set the Price
    If rs.RecordCount < 1 Then
        MsgBox "There was no record for the Item specified"
        GetPriceByCustomParameter = 0
    Else
        GetPriceByCustomParameter = rs("Price").Value
    End If

    ' Clean up
    Set rs = Nothing
    Set cmd = Nothing

End Function
```

module SampleCode in Ch12_Sample.accdb

To pass parameters to a stored procedure in an ADP, you need to do two things: Specify the CommandType as adCmdStoredProc, and prefix field names with the @ symbol. Based on the code from our last example, specifying the parameters for a stored procedure would be something like this:

```
'Build the Command object for an ADP Stored Procedure
With cmd
    .ActiveConnection = CurrentProject.AccessConnection
    .CommandText = "GetPricesProc"
    .CommandType = adCmdStoredProc
    .Parameters.Refresh
    .Parameters("@ItemName") = strName
End With
```

Creating Recordsets

The examples provided so far have returned Recordset objects that were created implicitly as a result of the actions executed on the data source. The Open method of the Recordset object is used to retrieve the records from a data source and store them in the Recordset object. This method takes five parameters: Source, ConnectionString, CursorType, LockType, and Options. The Open method can be used in several different ways and this section will discuss a couple of examples for creating Recordset objects.

> *Appendix C provides a detailed description of the Recordset.Open method and each of these parameters and their specific enumeration objects.*

Creating a Recordset from a SQL Statement

A very common way to create a Recordset object is to open it directly from a SQL statement. Simply call the Open method with the SQL statement string and the connection and a new Recordset will be created.

Available for download on Wrox.com

```
Public Function OpenRecordsetFromSql() As ADODB.Recordset

    ' Define Variables
    Dim rs As New ADODB.Recordset

    ' Open the Recordset using a SQL statement
    rs.Open "SELECT [CONTACTS].* FROM [CONTACTS]", CurrentProject.AccessConnection

    ' Return the Recordset
    Set OpenRecordsetFromSql = rs

End Function
```

module SampleCode in Ch12_Sample.accdb

In this case, the CurrentProject connection was supplied, but we could have easily created a Connection object to the desired source and supplied that instead.

Creating a Recordset from a Table or View

Another common way to create a `Recordset` object is to open it as a table or view. Simply call the `Open` method with the table or view name string and a new `Recordset` will be created for that object:

```
Public Function OpenRecordsetFromTable() As ADODB.Recordset

    ' Define Variables
    Dim rs As New ADODB.Recordset

    ' Open the Recordset using a SQL statement
    rs.Open "Contacts", CurrentProject.AccessConnection

    ' Return the Recordset
    Set OpenRecordsetFromView = rs

End Function
```

module SampleCode in Ch12_Sample.accdb

The SQL statement used here is pretty run-of-the-mill, but ADO also provides a lot of flexibility for very complex statements and record types, as we will show next.

Creating a Shaped Recordset

A powerful feature of ADO is the ability to create shaped `Recordset` objects using the SQL language. *Data shaping* enables the developer to define the columns of a recordset, the relationships between them, and the manner in which the recordset is populated with data. This only works with providers that support MSDataShape, such as SQL Server.

The next example uses two tables with a parent-child relationship: `Orders` and `Order Details`. These tables are included in the `Ch12_Sample.accdb` file, included in the sample files for this chapter, but this code sample must be executed against a provider that supports the SQL Shape statement, like the SQL Server provider. Closely examine the following code, paying particular attention to the SQL statement:

```
Public Function OpenShapedRecordset() As ADODB.Recordset
    ' Define Variables
    Dim strSQL As String
    Dim cn     As New ADODB.Connection
    Dim rs     As New ADODB.Recordset

    ' Set the connection and open
    cn.ConnectionString = "<Your SQL Server Connection String>"
    cn.Provider = "MSDataShape"      ' We are using the MS Shape provider
    cn.CursorLocation = adUseClient
    cn.Open

    ' Create the SQL statement that builds the shaped Recordset
    strSQL = _
        "SHAPE" & _
            "{SELECT DISTINCT OrderID, CustomerID, OrderDate " & _
```

```
                    "FROM Orders " & _
                    "WHERE OrderID BETWEEN 50 AND 70 " & _
                    "ORDER BY OrderDate DESC} " & _
                "APPEND(" & _
                    "{SELECT OrderID, ProductID, UnitPrice, Quantity " & _
                    "FROM [Order Details]} AS CustomerOrders " & _
                    "RELATE OrderID TO OrderID)"

        ' Open the Shaped Recordset
        rs.Open strSQL, cn

        ' Return the Recordset
        Set OpenShapedRecordset = rs

    End Function
```

In this SQL statement, the parent record is selected and then the child records are appended as a child Recordset object. Shaped Recordsets such as this are called *hierarchical Recordsets*. They exhibit a parent-child relationship in which the parent Recordset is the container in which the child Recordset is contained.

Creating a Recordset Containing Multiple Recordsets

There are many cases in which a command will generate a result containing multiple Recordset objects. When the Recordset object is returned, the first Recordset is already referenced by default. Each additional Recordset can be accessed by calling the NextRecordset method, which will return the next Recordset if it exists.

```
Public Function CreateMultiRecordset() As ADODB.Recordset

    ' Define Variables
    Dim rs     As New ADODB.Recordset
    Dim rsTemp As New ADODB.Recordset
    Dim strSQL As String

    ' Create the Multi Recordset SQL Statement and open the Recordset
    strSQL = "SELECT Prices.* FROM Prices; SELECT Contacts.* FROM Contacts"
    rs.Open strSQL, "<Provider that supports commands returning multi Recordsets>"

    ' Get the Next Recordset returned from the command
    Set rsTemp = rs.NextRecordset

    ' Return the Recordset
    Set CreateMultiRecordset = rs

End Function
```

Note that this example requires that the provider support commands that return multiple `Recordset` objects as a result, which the Access 2010 data provider does not. However, this type of result is very common in standard SQL statements, and the SQL Server provider often returns multiple `Recordset` objects in views and stored procedures.

Verifying Recordset Options

The `Supports` method is used to verify the features (`Recordset` methods) that a specific ADO data provider supports for a `Recordset` object, which is determined by the provider and cursor type. The `Supports` method takes one parameter: `CursorOptions`, which is specified as a member of the `CursorOptionEnum` object. The method returns `True` if the option is supported, otherwise `False`. Consider the following code:

```
Public Function SupportsFind() As Boolean

    ' Define Variables
    Dim rs As New ADODB.Recordset

    ' Open the Recordset using to Contacts connection
    rs.Open "Contacts", CurrentProject.Connection

    ' Return whether or not the Find method is supported
    SupportsFind = rs.Supports(adFind)

End Function
```

module SampleCode in Ch12_Sample.accdb

In this case, the function should return `True` because the `Find` method is supported by the provider, which is Access.

Appendix C provides a detailed description of the `Recordset.Supports` *method and the* `CursorOptionEnum` *object.*

Navigating Recordsets

`Recordset` objects are a collection of `Record` objects. The current record cursor defines the `Record` object that the `Recordset` is currently pointing at. Therefore, navigating through the records is necessary to gather the data from any given `Record`. A number of methods are available in the `Recordset` object to complete this task.

The Move Methods

When a `Recordset` object is created, and it has records, the current record cursor is automatically moved to the first record. To move forward (and backward, if supported by the cursor) through the records in the `Recordset`, there are five basic methods, each of which is listed and described in Table 12-2 below.

TABLE 12-2: The Move Methods of a Recordset Object

METHOD	DESCRIPTION
Move	Moves the cursor to the specified record.
MoveFirst	Moves the cursor to the first record.
MoveNext	Moves the cursor to the next record.
MovePrevious	Moves the cursor to the previous record.
MoveLast	Moves the cursor to the last record.

The following code provides an example of navigating records:

Available for download on Wrox.com

```
Public Sub NavigateRecords()

    ' Define Variables
    Dim rs       As New ADODB.Recordset
    Dim results As String

    ' Get a Recordset from one of our previous example functions
    Set rs = OpenRecordsetFromSql

    ' Move through the Recordset
    results = results & "Name: " & rs(3).Value & vbNewLine
    rs.MoveNext
    results = results & "Name: " & rs(3).Value & vbNewLine
    rs.MovePrevious
    results = results & "Name: " & rs(3).Value & vbNewLine
    rs.MoveLast
    results = results & "Name: " & rs(3).Value & vbNewLine
    rs.MoveFirst
    results = results & "Name: " & rs(3).Value & vbNewLine

    ' Show the results
    MsgBox results

End Sub
```

module SampleCode in Ch12_Sample.accdb

If the cursor is moved before the first record or after the last record, the BOF and EOF properties are set, respectively.

Appendix C provides a detailed description of these methods.

The Seek Method

The Seek method is the fastest way to find a specific record, but it can only be used with server-side cursors on tables that have been opened as `adCmdTableDirect` because it specifically relies on the table's indexes (and the indexes reside on the server — not on the client). Naturally, the table must have at least one index for it to search on. And, unfortunately, it is not supported by all providers.

To use the ADO Seek method, three items must be specified: The name of the index key to use, a variant array whose members specify the values to be compared with the key columns, and a SeekEnum constant that defines the kind of Seek to execute. The Recordset object's Index property must be set prior to calling the Seek method.

Available for download on Wrox.com

```
Public Sub SeekRecord()

    ' Define Variables
    Dim rs      As New ADODB.Recordset
    Dim strSQL As String

    ' Open the Recordset
    strSQL = "SELECT [CONTACTS].* FROM [CONTACTS]"
    rs.Open strSQL, "<Connection to Seek Supported Provider>"

    ' Seek to the record we want
    rs.Index = "ID"
    rs.Seek 4, adSeekFirstEQ

    ' Show the results
    MsgBox "Name: " & rs(3).Value

End Sub
```

module SampleCode in Ch12_Sample.accdb

If the method finds a record that matches the criteria, the Recordset object's cursor is moved to that row, and if not, to the end of the recordset. So, if no matching record is found, the Recordset object's EOF property is set to True.

Appendix C provides a detailed description of the Recordset.Seek method, its parameters, and the SeekEnum object.

The Find Method

The `Recordset.Find` method can also be used to navigate to a specific record. The `Find` method takes four parameters: `Criteria`, `SkipRows`, `SearchDirection`, and `Start`, but only the `Criteria` is required. Unless otherwise specified, all searches begin at the current row.

```
Public Sub FindRecord()

    ' Define Variables
    Dim rs As New ADODB.Recordset

    ' Open the Recordset
    rs.Open "Contacts", CurrentProject.Connection

    ' Find the record we want
    rs.Find "[Last Name] = 'Griffith'"

    ' Show the results
    MsgBox "Name: " & rs("First Name").Value

End Sub
```

module SampleCode in Ch12_Sample.accdb

Once the record is found, the current record cursor is moved to the record, as shown in the last example.

There are two other interesting points to note about the `Find` method. First, literal string values for the `Criteria` parameter can be specified either within single quotes or within hash characters. For example:

```
"State = 'NY'" or "State = #NY#"
```

Also, the use of the asterisk as a wildcard character in the `Criteria` parameter is restricted. It be can specified at the end of the criteria string, or at the beginning *and* end. But, the asterisk cannot be at the beginning only (without one also being at the end), or in the middle. Table 12-3 illustrates this point.

TABLE 12-3: Use of the Asterisk Operator for the Criteria Parameter

EXAMPLE	VALIDITY
State LIKE '*York'	Illegal
State LIKE 'New*'	OK
State LIKE '*ew Yor*'	OK
State LIKE 'New *ork'	Illegal

Appendix C provides a detailed description of the Recordset.Find *method, its parameters, and the associated enumeration objects.*

The AbsolutePosition Property

Assuming the provider supports absolute positioning, the AbsolutePosition property enables you to move the cursor to a specific row in the Recordset. For example, to move to the 127ᵗʰ row, issue the following call:

```
rs.AbsolutePosition = 127
```

ADO provides three constants in the CursorPositionEnum to verify the cursor position:

➤ adPosUnknown: The recordset is empty, or the provider doesn't support absolute positioning.

➤ adPosBOF: True if the current cursor position is before the first record.

➤ adPosEOF: True if the current cursor position is after the last record.

The AbsolutePosition property will be set to one of these values if the current record cursor does not point to a valid record.

Working with Data in Recordsets

The primary purpose of the Recordset is to work with the data stored within. There are several methods for working with this data, as we discuss in this section.

Appendix C provides a detailed description of the all of the objects, properties, methods, and their parameters, and the associated enumerations discussed in this section.

Referring to Fields

The ADO Recordset object cursor points to a Record that contains a collection of Field objects (columns). Those fields can be referred to in a variety of ways. The field can be specified by the field name or ordinal index directly from the Recordset object:

```
rs("myField")
rs(1)
rs!myField
```

Or, it could be referred to as a member of the `Fields` collection:

```
rs.Fields(1)
rs.Fields("myField")
rs.Fields!myField
```

Retrieving Data

Gathering the data values from within the `Field` is quite easy to do, once the correct `Record` is selected. To get the data from the `Field`, simply call the `Value` property, as shown in the following code:

```
Public Function RetrievingData() As String

    ' Define Variables
    Dim rs      As New ADODB.Recordset
    Dim result As String

    ' Open the Recordset
    rs.Open "Contacts", CurrentProject.Connection

    ' Get the data from the Record
    result = rs("ID").Value
    result = result & " - " & rs("First Name").Value & " " & rs("Last Name").Value

    ' Return the data
    RetrievingData = result

End Function
```

module SampleCode in Ch12_Sample.accdb

Modifying Data

In ADO, changes are (usually) immediately committed to the `Recordset` when moving away from the record, depending upon the `Recordset` lock type, cursor mode, connection mode, and other connections to the `Recordset`. This is completely opposite of DAO, so be sure not to get the two libraries confused! The `Supports` method can be used to determine if `Update` is supported, and if not, the data cannot be modified. The following code illustrates just how easily data can be modified:

```
Public Sub ModifyData()

    ' Define Variables
    Dim rs As New ADODB.Recordset

    ' Open the Recordset using adLockOptimistic
    rs.Open "Contacts", CurrentProject.Connection, , adLockOptimistic

    ' Modify the Data
    If rs("Last Name").Value = "Lincoln" Then
        rs("Last Name").Value = "Washington"
```

```
     Else
         rs("Last Name").Value = "Lincoln"
     End If

     ' Move away from the Record to commit the value
     rs.MoveNext

     ' Clean up
     rs.Close
     Set rs = Nothing

End Sub
```

module SampleCode in Ch12_Sample.accdb

It is important to note that, in this example, it is not required to call the `Update` method to actually update the data in the data source because it was implicitly called when the `Recordset` object was destroyed. However, it is a best practice to always explicitly call the `Update` method when modifying a `Record` to persist changes to the `Recordset`. Also, the `Close` method should always be called after completing all tasks on a `Recordset` to persist the changes and ensure that the data source objects have been released.

Creating Batch Updates

ADO allows multiple records to be edited and then committed as a single operation, by calling the `UpdateBatch` method. To use this feature, the cursor type must be client-side and the lock type must be `adLockBatchOptimistic`.

Available for download on Wrox.com

```
Public Sub ModifyDataBatch(CommitChanges As Boolean)

    ' Define Variables
    Dim rs As New ADODB.Recordset

    ' Open the Recordset using adLockBatchOptimistic
    rs.Open "Contacts", CreateConnection, , adLockBatchOptimistic

    ' Modify the Data as a Batch Operation
    While rs.EOF = False
        If rs("Company").Value = "ABC Corp" Then
            rs("Company").Value = "XYZ Inc"
        Else
            rs("Company").Value = "ABC Corp"
        End If

        ' Move to the Next Record without commiting changes
        rs.MoveNext
    Wend

    ' Commit or Deny the changes as a Batch update
    If CommitChanges Then
        rs.UpdateBatch
    Else
```

```
            rs.CancelBatch
        End If

        ' Clean up
        rs.Close
        Set rs = Nothing

    End Sub
```

module SampleCode in Ch12_Sample.accdb

A benefit to using batch updating is that you can also reverse any changes made to the `Recordset` by calling `CancelUpdate`. Always call the `Close` method to persist all updates to the `Recordset` and ensure that the data source objects have been released.

Adding New Data

To add a new `Record` to a `Recordset`, the `Recordset` must support the `AddNew` method, which can be verified with the `Supports` method. To add a new `Record`, simply call the `AddNew` method with an array of `Field` names and an array of values for each corresponding field.

Available for download on Wrox.com

```
    Public Sub AddNewRecord()

        ' Define Variables
        Dim rs              As New ADODB.Recordset
        Dim fieldsArray(1) As Variant
        Dim valuesArray(1) As Variant

        ' Open the Recordset using adLockOptimistic
        rs.Open "Contacts", CreateConnection, , adLockOptimistic

        ' Add a new record
        fieldsArray(0) = "First Name"
        fieldsArray(1) = "Last Name"
        valuesArray(0) = "John"
        valuesArray(1) = "Adams"
        rs.AddNew fieldsArray, valuesArray

        ' Commit the Record and clean up
        rs.Update
        rs.Close
        Set rs = Nothing

    End Sub
```

module SampleCode in Ch12_Sample.accdb

Always call the `Close` method to persist all updates to the `Recordset` and ensure that the data source objects have been released.

Deleting Data

To delete a Record from a Recordset, the Recordset must support the Delete method, which can be verified with the Supports method. To delete the Record, simply navigate to it and call the Delete method:

```
Public Sub DeleteRecord()

    ' Define Variables
    Dim rs As New ADODB.Recordset

    ' Open the Recordset using adLockOptimistic
    rs.Open "Contacts", CreateConnection, , adLockOptimistic

    ' Move to the last record and delete it
    rs.MoveLast
    rs.Delete

    ' Commit the Record and clean up
    rs.Update
    rs.Close
    Set rs = Nothing

End Sub
```

module SampleCode in Ch12_Sample.accdb

Always call the Close method to persist all updates to the Recordset and ensure that the data source objects have been released.

Closing Recordsets

The Close method of the Recordset object is used to close a recordset once you have finished working with its data. It is always a best practice to close Recordsets once you have finished with them to ensure all changes are persisted to the data source. Also, Update, UpdateBatch, Cancel, or CancelBatch should be called before closing to ensure all changes to the Recordset have been committed or rolled back. If all changes are not committed and the Recordset is closed, an error occurs. The following code illustrates an example of a function to close Recordsets:

```
Public Sub CloseRecordset(rs As ADODB.Recordset)

    ' Check the Mode to call update
    If rs.LockType = adLockBatchOptimistic Then
        rs.UpdateBatch
    Else
        rs.Update
    End If

    ' Close and clean up
```

```
        rs.Close
        Set rs = Nothing

    End Sub
```

Saving Recordset Data to a File

ADO also provides methods to save a `Recordset` to a file on the disk. This means that it can later be reopened at any time, and it will not be connected to any other source, such as the database the data came from. To do this, use the `Recordset` object's `Save` method to save the `Recordset` to a file. The `PersistFormat` parameter specifies which of the two possible save formats to use: Advanced Data TableGram (ADTG), which is a proprietary Microsoft format, or the Extensible Markup Language (XML) format.

```
    Public Sub SaveRecordsetToFile()

        ' Define Variables
        Dim rs As New ADODB.Recordset

        ' Open the Recordset
        rs.Open "Prices", CreateConnection

        ' Save the Recordset to disk
        rs.Save "C:\temp\MyRecordset.xml", adPersistXML

        ' Clean up
        rs.Close
        Set rs = Nothing

    End Sub
```

You can continue to work with the `Recordset` after saving it to disk, but all changes to the `Recordset` data will be reflected in the database, not in the file. Any data that needs to be saved to a file must be explicitly saved to the file — remember `Recordset` objects are bound to the database by the connection.

Loading Recordset Data from a File

The `Recordset.Open` method can also reload `Recordsets` that have been saved to a file. To do this, simply call the `Open` method with the file path to the data file as the parameter.

```
    Public Function LoadRecordsetFromFile() As ADODB.Recordset

        ' Define Variables
        Dim rs As New ADODB.Recordset

        ' Open the Recordset from File
```

```
      rs.CursorLocation = adUseClient
      rs.Open "C:\temp\MyRecordset.xml"

      ' Return the Recordset
      Set LoadRecordsetFromFile = rs

  End Function
```

module SampleCode in Ch12_Sample.accdb

Recordset objects opened from a file can be used like any other Recordset, except that these Recordset objects are not connected to any data source, which we will discuss shortly. It is important to note that changes made to this Recordset are not persisted to the original data file implicitly.

Disconnected Recordsets

When opening a Recordset from a file, the Recordset is put into a disconnected state and it is not connected to any data source; it is known as a *disconnected recordset*. As mentioned, they can be used like any other Recordset objects, but the Recordset has no ActiveConnection setting value. This means that persisting changes to the data source is different than normal Recordset objects that have a valid ActiveConnection. But, this fact is not to be confused with persisting changes to the data contained in the Recordset object itself. Remember that the data in a disconnected Recordset can be modified in the same way as with any other Recordset object, in that it is just not persisted to any other data source by default. To manually disconnect a Recordset from the data source, simply set the ActiveConnection property to Nothing:

Available for download on Wrox.com

```
  Public Function DisconnectRecordset() As ADODB.Recordset

      ' Create a new Recordset
      Dim rs As New ADODB.Recordset

      ' Set a Client side cursor required for disconnection
      rs.CursorLocation = adUseClient

      ' Open the Recordset
      rs.Open "Prices", CurrentProject.Connection

      ' Now disconnect the Recordset
      Set rs.ActiveConnection = Nothing

      ' Return the Recordset
      Set DisconnectRecordset = rs

  End Function
```

module SampleCode in Ch12_Sample.accdb

Disconnected Recordset objects have two basic options for persisting data to a data source. The first option is simply saving the Recordset object back to a file, but if the file exists, it should be deleted first; otherwise, the Save method will throw a runtime error. The second method is to actually establish a connection to an ADO data source. This can be either the original data source or a brand new data source. To connect a disconnected `Recordset` to a data source, simply set the `ActiveConnection` property to a valid ADO data source.

```
Public Function ReconnectRecordset() As ADODB.Recordset

    ' Define Variables
    Dim rs As New ADODB.Recordset

    ' Re-open the Recordset from File
    rs.CursorLocation = adUseClient
    rs.Open "C:\temp\MyRecordset.xml", , , adLockOptimistic

    ' Now set the Recordset's ActiveConnection to reconnect to the source
    rs.ActiveConnection = CurrentProject.Connection

    ' Return the Recordset
    Set ReconnectRecordset = rs

End Function
```

module SampleCode in Ch12_Sample.accdb

Disconnected `Recordsets` can be extremely handy when trying to take snapshots of data and storing that data in a location other than the data source.

USING ADO EVENTS

The ADO `Connection` and `Recordset` objects support several events for a variety of operations. Capturing these events and having the chance to run custom code when the event occurs can be very useful, especially for asynchronous `Recordset` operations. There are several things that need to be done when working with ADO events.

Declaring WithEvents

To use the ADO events for either the `Connection` or the `Recordset` object, the `Connection` must be declared with the `WithEvents` keyword. The important thing to understand about the `WithEvents` keyword is that it can be used only within a *class module* in VBA. It will generate the compile error "Only valid in object module" in a regular VBA code module. The code sample for this chapter has a specific class module file for this section, called `ADOEventsExample`. Also, this `Connection` variable must be declared as a global member of the `Class` object. At the top of the class module file, this `Connection` object can be declared as follows:

```
' The Connection is declared as a class member, using the WithEvents keyword
Public WithEvents cn As ADODB.Connection
Public WithEvents rs As ADODB.Recordset
```

module ADOEventsExample in Ch12_Sample.accdb

Once the `Connection` variable has been defined, you can begin implementing the various events for the `Connection` object. All of these rules apply to the `Recordset` object when implementing its events as well.

Implementing ADO Event Methods

To implement a specific ADO event for the `Connection` (or `Recordset`) object, create an event subroutine. This subroutine is required to have the name format of the variable name, then the underscore character, and then the event name with its given parameters. For example, the `ConnectComplete` event could be implemented for the `Connection` as follows:

Available for download on Wrox.com

```
Public Sub cn_ConnectComplete( _
    ByVal pError As ADODB.Error, _
    adStatus As ADODB.EventStatusEnum, _
    ByVal pConnection As ADODB.Connection)

    ' Do something when the ConnectComplete event fires
    MsgBox "The ConnectComplete event fired!"

    ' Set the event aruguments
    If adStatus = adStatusOK Then
        Set pError = Nothing
        Set pConnection = cn
    End If

End Sub
```

module ADOEventsExample in Ch12_Sample.accdb

It is a best practice to set the event's parameter values to return error information to the caller about the execution status of this event, if there is a failure. These types of subroutines are called *event handlers* and are one of the powerful features supported by both ADO and VBA.

Implicitly Triggering Events

The true power of creating event handlers is that they are automatically called any time that an event occurs for the object. That is, your code is run implicitly whenever that event happens. For example, we can create the following method in our class:

Available for download on Wrox.com

```
Public Function GetConnection() As ADODB.Connection

    ' Set the Connection
    Set cn = New ADODB.Connection
    cn.ConnectionString = CurrentProject.Connection
    cn.CursorLocation = adUseClient
    cn.Mode = adModeShareDenyNone

    ' Open the Connection - the ConnectComplete event will be fired
    cn.Open

    ' Return the Connection
```

```
        Set GetConnection = cn

    End Function
```

Because this function opens a `Connection` object with the `Connection` member variable we created earlier, it triggers the `ConnectComplete` event automatically when the connection has been established. We can see the event being triggered by creating a subroutine to call our `GetConnection` method like this:

```
Public Sub ImplicitlyCallAdoEvent()

    ' Define Variables
    Dim aee As New ADOEventsExample
    Dim cn  As New ADODB.Connection

    ' Call the Class to Trigger the ConnectComplete event
    Set cn = aee.GetConnection

End Sub
```

Running this code will implicitly fire the `ConnectComplete` event implemented for the `ADOEventExample` class because the `GetConnection` method triggers the event.

Explicitly Calling Events

One other feature is the ability to also call events explicitly. This is done exactly the same as any other method call, and only requires the proper code access level.

```
Public Sub ExplicitlyCallAdoEvent()

    ' Define Variables
    Dim aee As New ADOEventsExample
    Dim cn  As Adodb.Connection
    Dim errors As Adodb.Error

    ' Call the event directly from the Class object
    aee.cn_ConnectComplete errors, adStatusOK, cn

End Sub
```

It is a best practice to check the `pError` parameter of the event to ensure that no errors occurred when the event completed.

Testing the State Property

It is worth mentioning that the `Connection` and `Recordset` objects' `State` property can be tested to determine the current status of the object, particularly for asynchronous operations. The following code checks the state of the `Connection` to see if it is open:

```
Public Sub CheckConnectionState()

    ' Define Variables
    Dim cn As Adodb.Connection

    ' Get the connection
    Set cn = CreateConnection

    ' Test the state
    If cn.State = adStateOpen Then
        MsgBox "The Connection is Open"
    Else
        MsgBox "The Connection in not Open yet"
    End If

End Sub
```

module SampleCode in Ch12_Sample.accdb

The `State` property and the `ObjectStateEnum` options are described in depth in Appendix C.

SCHEMA RECORDSETS WITH ADO

Another useful feature of ADO is that it allows the creation of schema `Recordsets`. Schema `Recordsets` are `Recordset` objects that contain information about the data sources' tables and views. This information can also be procured using ADOX, which is designed specifically for this task, but some details are more readily accessed using ADO schema Recordsets.

ADO Schema Recordsets

To open a schema `Recordset`, call the `OpenSchema` method from the `Connection` object. The `OpenSchema` method takes three parameters: `Schema`, `Restrictions`, and `SchemaID`. The following example function returns the schema for the tables in the current database:

```
Public Function OpenSchemaRecordset() As ADODB.Recordset

    ' Return Schema for the Tables in the current database
    Set CreateSchemaRecordset = _
            CurrentProject.Connection.OpenSchema(adSchemaTables)

End Function
```

module SampleCode in Ch12_Sample.accdb

> *Appendix C provides a detailed description of the* OpenSchema *method, its parameters, the associated enumerations, and a detailed constraint column–mapping table.*

Specifying Constraint Columns

To restrict the output of the OpenSchema method, supply an array of values from the restrictions list. In other words, where the preceding code returns a list of all the tables and views in the database, the constraint columns for the adSchemaTables option are: TABLE_CATALOG, TABLE_SCHEMA, TABLE_NAME, and TABLE_TYPE. The array values must be specified in that order, so that the OpenSchema method handles them correctly:

```
Array(TABLE_CATALOG, TABLE_SCHEMA, TABLE_NAME, TABLE_TYPE)
```

To restrict the output to a single table with a TABLE_NAME of Contacts and a TABLE_TYPE of Table, the resulting array would be:

```
Array(TABLE_CATALOG, TABLE_SCHEMA, "Contacts", "Table")
```

So, the final code would be written as follows:

Available for download on Wrox.com

```
Public Function OpenSchemaWithConstraints() As ADODB.Recordset

    ' Return Schema for the "Contacts" table only
    Set OpenSchemaWithConstraints = _
            CurrentProject.Connection.OpenSchema( _
                adSchemaTables, _
                Array(Empty, Empty, "Contacts", "Table"))

End Function
```

module SampleCode in Ch12_Sample.accdb

This code would produce a Recordset object containing information about the properties of the Contacts table.

Using ACE Specific Schemas

The ACE provider also supplies eight provider-specific schema Recordset objects. The following is a list of each and their GUIDs:

```
'Access object security GUIDs
Public Const JET_SECURITY_FORMS = _
"{c49c842e-9dcb-11d1-9f0a-00c04fc2c2e0}"
Public Const JET_SECURITY_REPORTS = _
"{c49c8430-9dcb-11d1-9f0a-00c04fc2c2e0}"
Public Const JET_SECURITY_MACROS = _
"{c49c842f-9dcb-11d1-9f0a-00c04fc2c2e0}"
```

```
Public Const JET_SECURITY_MODULES = _
"{c49c8432-9dcb-11d1-9f0a-00c04fc2c2e0}"

'Jet OLE DB provider-defined schema rowsets
Public Const JET_SCHEMA_REPLPARTIALFILTERLIST = _
"{e2082df0-54ac-11d1-bdbb-00c04fb92675}"
Public Const JET_SCHEMA_REPLCONFLICTTABLES = _
"{e2082df2-54ac-11d1-bdbb-00c04fb92675}"
Public Const JET_SCHEMA_USERROSTER = _
"{947bb102-5d43-11d1-bdbf-00c04fb92675}"
Public Const JET_SCHEMA_ISAMSTATS = _
"{8703b612-5d43-11d1-bdbf-00c04fb92675}"
```

Interestingly enough, the `JET_SCHEMA_USERROSTER` option provides a `Recordset` containing a list of all of the users logged on. The following code illustrates an example of how to get this list of users:

Available for download on Wrox.com

```
Public Function WhoIsLoggedOn() As ADODB.Recordset

    ' Create the list of users logged on in a Recordset
    Set WhoIsLoggedOn = _
            CurrentProject.Connection.OpenSchema( _
            adSchemaProviderSpecific, , _
            "{947bb102-5d43-11d1-bdbf-00c04fb92675}") 'JET_SCHEMA_USERROSTER

End Function
```

module SampleCode in Ch12_Sample.accdb

CREATING SCHEMA WITH ADOX

The ADOX library is used to work with the schema of the data source objects, such as tables, views (queries), indexes, and so on. ADOX is quite simple to use and can be incredibly useful for working with and creating new objects, as well as setting security options. This last section describes the more common features of ADOX.

Adding References to ADOX

To implement ADOX, a reference to the ADOX library needs to be added to the code project. Select the "Microsoft ADO Ext. 2.8 for DDL and Security" option in the References dialog box. Once this reference has been added to the code project, you should be able to begin using the ADOX library.

The ADOX Object Model

The ADOX model contains one top-level object, `Catalog`, which contains five collections: `Tables`, `Groups`, `Users`, `Procedures`, and `Views`.

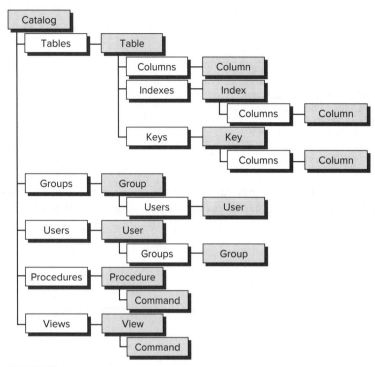

FIGURE 12-1

In addition to this model, each of the `Table`, `Index`, and `Column` objects also contains a standard ADO `Properties` collection.

Working with Tables

ADOX provides a number of methods for working tables in the data source. Specifically, ADOX provides the capability to create, modify, and delete `Table` objects. This functionality is contained in the `Catalog.Tables` object. This section outlines several examples of working with the `Tables` object to accomplish these tasks.

Creating a Table

It is very easy to create a new `Table` object in the data source. Simply create a new `Table` object, append the desired columns, and then append the new table to the `Catalog`. The following code provides an example of creating a new `Table` object.

Available for download on Wrox.com

```
Public Sub CreateTable()

    ' Define Variables
    Dim cat As New ADOX.Catalog
    Dim tbl As New ADOX.Table

    ' Set the Connection to the Current Database
    cat.ActiveConnection = CurrentProject.Connection

    ' Set the table name and create the columns with common Access types
```

```
        tbl.Name = "TempTable"
        tbl.Columns.Append "ID", adInteger              ' Long type
        tbl.Columns.Append "Title", adVarWChar, 100     ' Text type
        tbl.Columns.Append "Cost", adCurrency           ' Currency type
        tbl.Columns.Append "Notes", adLongVarWChar      ' Memo type
        tbl.Columns.Append "Size", adDouble             ' Double type
        tbl.Columns.Append "IsValid", adBoolean         ' Boolean type
        tbl.Columns.Append "Created", adDate            ' DateTime type

        ' Set some Access Field Properties
        tbl.Columns("ID").ParentCatalog = cat
        tbl.Columns("ID").Properties("AutoIncrement") = True     ' Set Autonumber

        ' Append the new table to the Tables collection
        cat.Tables.Append tbl
        cat.Tables.Refresh

    End Sub
```

module SampleCode in Ch12_Sample.accdb

The preceding code also sets the `AutoIncrement` field property to make the `ID` field an `AutoNumber` field. Many of the Access-specific field properties can be set using the `Properties` object on the `Columns` collection. However, there are several field types and properties that cannot be set through ADOX, such as `Hyperlink`, `Multi Value`, and `Attachment` field types.

Deleting a Table

Deleting a table can be completed by calling the `Delete` method from the `Catalog.Tables` collection and supplying the name of the table, as shown in the following code.

Available for download on Wrox.com

```
Public Sub DeleteTable()

    ' Define Variables
    Dim cat As New ADOX.Catalog

    ' Set the Connection to the Current Database
    cat.ActiveConnection = CurrentProject.Connection

    ' Delete the table from the Tables collection
    cat.Tables.Delete "TempTable"
    cat.Tables.Refresh

End Sub
```

module SampleCode in Ch12_Sample.accdb

Working with Views (Queries)

ADOX provides a number of methods for working views in the data source. Specifically, ADOX provides the capability to create, modify, and delete these objects. This functionality is contained in the `Catalog.Views` object. This section outlines several examples of working with the `Views` object to accomplish these tasks.

Creating a Query

To create a new query, simply supply a `Command` object and a name, and it will be created by appending it to the `Catalog.Views` object. The following code is an example of creating a new view from a simple SQL command in the current database.

```
Public Sub CreateQuery()

    ' Define Variables
    Dim cat As New ADOX.Catalog
    Dim cmd As New ADODB.Command

    ' Open the Catalog
    cat.ActiveConnection = CurrentProject.Connection

    ' Create the Command object that represents the View
    cmd.CommandText = "SELECT [Contacts].* FROM [Contacts]"

    ' Provide the Name and Create the View
    cat.Views.Append "AllContacts", cmd

End Sub
```

module SampleCode in Ch12_Sample.accdb

Modifying a Query

To modify an existing query, simply provide a new `Command` object with the desired values. The following code provides an example.

```
Public Sub ModifyQuery()

    ' Define Variables
    Dim cat As New ADOX.Catalog
    Dim cmd As New ADODB.Command

    ' Open the Catalog
    cat.ActiveConnection = CurrentProject.Connection

    ' Create the Command object that represents the View
    cmd.CommandText = "SELECT [Contacts].[First Name] FROM [Contacts]"

    ' Set the View Command
    cat.Views("AllContacts").Command = cmd

End Sub
```

module SampleCode in Ch12_Sample.accdb

Deleting a Query

Deleting a query can be completed by calling the `Delete` method on the `Catalog.View` object, as shown in the following code.

Available for download on Wrox.com

```
Public Sub DeleteQuery()

    ' Define Variables
    Dim cat As New ADOX.Catalog
    Dim cmd As New ADODB.Command

    ' Open the Catalog
    cat.ActiveConnection = CurrentProject.Connection

    ' Delete the Query
    cat.Views.Delete "AllContacts"

End Sub
```

module SampleCode in Ch12_Sample.accdb

Managing Security with ADOX

Finally, one very powerful feature ADOX provides is the capability to manage database security. ADOX can set a database password and manage user and group permissions (when supported). Chapter 24 provides more information about working with Access security features and it is recommended to review this material to learn more about managing security using ADO.

SUMMARY

This chapter discussed working with the ADO Object Model, which included both the ADODB library, for manipulating data, and the ADOX library, for manipulating database schema. By now, you should have a good knowledge of the following topics:

- ➤ The purpose of ADO
- ➤ How to create `Connection` objects
- ➤ How to execute commands
- ➤ How to work with `Recordset` objects
- ➤ How to create transactions
- ➤ How to work with batch operations
- ➤ How to create and work with ADO events
- ➤ How to manipulate the data source schema

If you haven't had a chance, we recommend that you review Appendix C, the ADO Object Model reference that accompanies the material in this chapter. It is our sincerest hope that you find ADO to be easy and convenient to use in your Access database applications.

13

Using SQL with VBA

WHAT'S IN THIS CHAPTER?

➤ Working with SQL strings in VBA

➤ Using SQL when opening Forms and Reports

➤ The ReplaceOrderByClause and ReplaceWhereClause Functions

You may be familiar with SQL; after all, it's inside every query you create. SQL (Structured Query Language) is the language of queries and Recordsets; it's how you retrieve, update, insert, and delete records in your database tables.

When you use the Query Design View in Access, you are actually building a SQL statement. Most of the time, you won't actually need to look at the SQL code, but you can see it using the SQL view if you're curious.

Conversely, you can take most SQL statements, paste them into the SQL view of a new query, and then switch over to Design view to see how they work. There are a few types of SQL statements for which this won't work — union queries and pass-through queries, for example, cannot be viewed using Design view.

Even if you're comfortable using SQL in queries, you may not be familiar with building SQL statements in VBA. If you're not, you're missing out! Using SQL in VBA is a powerful technique that can enable many great features in your Access applications. By using VBA, you can build custom SQL statements for combo boxes, forms, and reports. For example, you'll be able to change the sorting and selecting of records on continuous forms, control the record selection on reports, and limit the drop-down lists of combo boxes based on other combo boxes.

Let's begin by exploring how to build SQL statements using string variables in VBA.

WORKING WITH SQL STRINGS IN VBA

To build SQL statements in VBA, you usually load them into string variables by concatenating various phrases. Some of the phrases are exact SQL text that you supply, while others are the contents of variables in VBA or controls on forms or reports. When the SQL statement is complete, you can use it in queries, in the RecordSource of forms or reports, or in the RowSource of combo boxes or list boxes. This enables you to deliver power and flexibility in your Access applications.

Building SQL Strings with Quotes

The first thing to learn about building SQL statements in VBA is how to handle concatenation and quotes. They may seem simple, but many programmers have stared at VBA strings with multiple nested quotes and struggled to make them work.

Consider a SQL string that selects a record for a particular business from a table of businesses:

```
Select * From tblBusiness Where BusinessKey = 17
```

In actual usage, you replace the 17 in this statement with the BusinessKey that the user is currently working with. To build this SQL statement in VBA with the BusinessKey from the current form, you would use something like this:

```
strSQL = `Select * From tblBusiness Where BusinessKey = ` _
& Me!BusinessKey
```

One reason this is so simple is that BusinessKey is a numeric value. In SQL, numeric values are just stated, without quotes around them. This is great for primary key values, which are often AutoNumbers (that use the Long Integer data type).

However, consider a SQL statement that selects businesses in a particular city:

```
Select * from tblBusiness Where BusinessCity = `Seattle"
```

This is where it starts to get complicated. As you can see, Seattle must be in quotes because SQL expects quotes around text values. The VBA to create this statement, again assuming that BusinessCity is on the current form, is as follows:

```
strSQL = `Select * From tblBusiness Where BusinessCity = `"" _
& Me!BusinessCity & `""`
```

At first glance, all those quotation marks seem a little extreme. But if you break them down, they make sense. The first thing to remember is that to have a quotation mark (`) inside a string, you need to type two quotation marks in a row. That lets VBA know that you aren't closing the string with a quotation mark — you actually want a quotation mark *inside* the string. So, the string

```
`Select * From tblBusiness Where BusinessCity = `""
```

results in a string that contains:

```
Select * From tblBusiness Where BusinessCity = `
```

Notice that last quotation mark It's a result of the two quotation marks after the equal sign (=) "collapsing" into just one quotation mark. The idea of *collapsing quotes* in the interior of your strings is crucial to understanding how to build complex SQL strings in VBA. You may even want to print out your VBA code and circle the interior quote pairs with a pen. Each of these circles represents a quotation mark that will be included inside your string.

Now, for the rest of this simple example . . . After the first phrase (the one that ends with a quotation mark), you tack on the value of `BusinessCity` (Seattle) and then finish it off with a final quotation mark. Concatenating the `BusinessCity` is easy:

```
& Me!BusinessCity
```

But what about that final quotation mark? Here's how it is added:

```
& """"
```

Yes, that's four quotation marks in a row. Remember that the interior pairs of quotation marks are collapsed into a quotation mark inside the string. In this case, the result is a string containing merely one quotation mark, which is exactly what you need at the end of `Seattle` in your final SQL string:

```
Select * from tblBusiness Where BusinessCity = "Seattle"
```

In quote collapsing, remember that whenever you see three quotation marks in a row, you can be sure that one quotation mark is being included at the beginning or end of some other text, like this:

```
"Select * From tblBusiness Where BusinessCity = """
```

And whenever you see four quotation marks in a row, you are seeing just one quotation mark being concatenated to the string, as in this example:

```
Me!BusinessCity & """"
```

Now that you know how to build SQL strings with text, values from variables and forms, and double quotation marks, there's one little side topic to cover: the use of single quotation marks (`'`) instead of double quotation marks (`"`).

Using Single Quotation Marks instead of Double Quotation Marks

Some programmers use a mixture of single quotation marks (`'`) and double quotation marks (`"`) when they are building SQL strings. This can be a good technique because you don't need to do any "quotation mark collapsing" as described previously. However, to some people it can be confusing to see the different types of quotes mixed together. It's a style thing — there isn't a right or wrong way.

VBA remembers what kind of quotation mark started a string, so if you use the other kind in the middle of the string, it won't get confused and try to close the string. Access Wizards often use this technique to build SQL strings. For example, here's how the Access Wizard generates the `WhereCondition` phrase when you ask to open a form filtered to a specific value:

```
stLinkCriteria = "[City]=" & "'" & Me![txtCity] & "'"
DoCmd.OpenForm stDocName, , , stLinkCriteria
```

Notice the mixture of single and double quotation marks in the string loaded into `stLinkCriteria`. The double quotation marks are used to indicate to VBA where the text phrases start and stop. The single quotation marks are built into the `stLinkCriteria` field itself. The single quotation marks work because the Access query processor recognizes either single or double quotation marks around text values. Therefore, the following two statements are identical to Access SQL:

```
Where City = 'Seattle'
Where City = "Seattle"
```

Also notice that the technique to build the string is a little more complicated than necessary. To generically handle either text values (with quotation marks) or numeric values (without quotation marks), the Access Wizard concatenates the first single quotation mark separately. If you are building it yourself, you can tack the single quotation mark right after the equal sign, like this:

```
stLinkCriteria = "[City]='" & Me![txtCity] & "'"
```

> *If you build SQL strings to use in SQL Server, remember that only single quotation marks are valid there — double quotes will not work. This isn't an issue if you're querying linked tables in Access because Access translates the syntax for you. But you must use SQL Server syntax if you're using a pass-through query or are opening a SQL Server Recordset directly in code.*

The rest of the examples in this chapter use the "collapsing quotation marks" method described previously. That method works whether you use all single quotation marks (`'`) or all double quotation marks (`"`).

Concatenating Long SQL Strings

To keep your VBA readable, break your long statements onto multiple lines. While this is true any time, it's especially helpful when building long SQL strings. If you do not break them into multiple VBA lines, you have to scroll far to the right to read it all. There are two ways to break up those long statements: by building up the string variable in multiple steps, or by using the VBA line continuation character.

Many programmers still use the build-up method for storing long SQL strings into a string variable. It might just be habit left over from the days when there wasn't a line continuation character, or maybe they just like the way it looks. Here's what the method looks like:

```
strSQL = "Select * From tblBusiness"
strSQL = strSQL & " Where BusinessCity = """ & Me!BusinessCity & """"
strSQL = strSQL & " And BusinessActiveFlag = True"
```

Notice how the second and third lines concatenate more text to the same variable, which is why it's called "building up" the string. This method has a slight advantage during debugging because you can see your string's value step-by-step as it is being built.

The VBA line continuation character is a space and underscore together, right at the end of the code line:

```
strSQL = "Select * From tblBusiness" & _
" Where BusinessCity = """ & Me!BusinessCity & """" & _
" And BusinessActiveFlag = True"
```

Some developers indent the subsequent lines for clarity:

```
strSQL = "Select * From tblBusiness" & _
    " Where BusinessCity = """ & Me!BusinessCity & """" & _
    " And BusinessActiveFlag = True"
```

This method runs the entire concatenation as one line in VBA, even though it is visually spread across multiple lines in your code.

Breaking your VBA onto multiple lines is another area that's really a style choice — all these methods work just fine. The build-up method offers slightly slower performance than using line continuation characters, but on modern PCs it isn't noticeable. Whichever method you choose, break the statement where it makes sense. Start each new VBA line with a keyword such as `Where`, `And`, `Or`, or `Join`, so that others can read along more easily.

Be careful to add the extra spaces around the keywords like `Where` and `And`. If you don't, your words will run together in the final string, the syntax will be incorrect, and the SQL statement won't run. Many programmers add spaces to the beginning of each section of text instead of the end so that they really stand out, as shown in the preceding examples. Remember that extra spaces between words aren't a problem in SQL; they're ignored by both Access and SQL Server.

Now you're ready to use quotes and build long SQL strings in VBA to enhance Access forms and reports.

USING SQL WHEN OPENING FORMS AND REPORTS

Whenever you use the Access Wizard to build a command button to open a form or report with a filter to limit the records that are displayed, you are actually using SQL in VBA. The wizard builds VBA code to open the form with a `WhereCondition`, like this:

```vba
Private Sub cmdCityBusinesses_Click()
    On Error GoTo Err_cmdCityBusinesses_Click
    Dim stDocName As String
    Dim stLinkCriteria As String
    stDocName = `frmBusiness"
    stLinkCriteria = `[City]=" & ```` & Me![txtCity] & ````
    DoCmd.OpenForm stDocName, , , stLinkCriteria
Exit_cmdCityBusinesses_Click:
    Exit Sub
Err_cmdCityBusinesses_Click:
    MsgBox Err.Description
    Resume Exit_cmdCityBusinesses_Click
End Sub
```

code snippet Using Sql When Opening Forms and Reports (in CodeSnippets.txt)

The `WhereCondition` on the `OpenForm` command (it's the fourth parameter, using a variable named `stLinkCriteria`) is used to filter the form being opened to a set of records that meet some criteria. It's usually used to drill down to a specific single record, so the criterion is merely the primary key value of the record. As in this example, however, it can be used to open a form to a set of multiple records that meet the specified criterion (in this case, the City).

 In Access 2010, the wizard will actually create a macro but the syntax is still the same. Convert the macro to code to follow along with this chapter. When you use the `WhereCondition`, you don't include the word `Where` at the beginning of the string. It's assumed, so you'll see an error if you specify it.

This is a simple example of using a fragment of SQL in your code; after all, the wizard will build it for you. The wizard to open a report works much the same way. However, there are many other more compelling reasons to use SQL in your VBA code.

USING SQL TO ENHANCE FORMS

Using SQL, you can enhance your forms in many ways. You can allow quick and easy record sorting, the capability to narrow a list of records by applying selections, and the use of combo box values to limit the drop-down lists for other combo boxes. These are all powerful tools that help your user get more value from your application.

Sorting on Columns

Users often expect the capability to sort on columns, in much the same way as you can with other Windows applications such as Outlook and Excel. For example, if you have a continuous form of businesses, your user may want to sort on either the Business Name or Contact Name column, as shown in Figure 13-1.

FIGURE 13-1

 When using a form in Datasheet view, you automatically have the option to sort on any column using the column header (exactly like an Excel spreadsheet).

The two toggle buttons (Business Name and Contact Name) are in an option group control called optSort, which has an After Update event that contains the following code:

```
Private Sub optSort_AfterUpdate()
    On Error GoTo Error_Handler

    Dim strOrderBy As Variant
    strOrderBy = Null

    Select Case Me!optSort
        Case 1 `Business Name
            strOrderBy = " tblBusiness.BusinessName," &_
            "tblBusiness.LastName, tblBusiness.FirstName"
        Case 2 `Contact information
            strOrderBy = "tblBusiness.LastName," &_
            "tblBusiness.FirstName, tblBusiness.BusinessName"
    End Select

    strOrderBy = " ORDER BY " + strOrderBy

    Me.RecordSource = ReplaceOrderByClause(Me.RecordSource, strOrderBy)
    `Me.Requery `may be needed for earlier versions of Access

Exit_Procedure:
    On Error Resume Next
    Exit Sub

Error_Handler:
    MsgBox Err.Number & ": " & Err.Description
    Resume Exit_Procedure
    Resume

End Sub
```

code snippet Sorting on Columns (in CodeSnippets.txt)

This technique takes advantage of the fact that you can change the record source of a form while it is already open, and then re-query the form. When you do, the form is reloaded with the records from the new record source, including the sort order.

You build a new Order By clause based on the button that is clicked. To swap the new Order By clause into the RecordSource, you use a function named ReplaceOrderByClause. The code for this function and its cousin ReplaceWhereClause are at the end of this chapter. For now, just assume that the Order By clause will be magically "cut and pasted" into the SQL string in the RecordSource property of the form.

> *To replace part of the SQL string in a* RecordSource *property, start with a SQL string! To use this technique, you can't have just the name of a query or table in the* RecordSource. *It needs to be a real SQL statement. To make one, just take the query name, say* qryBusinesses, *and turn it into a SQL string such as* `Select * From qryBusinesses`. *Then you can manipulate it with new* Where *and* Order By *clauses.*

When your user clicks a column heading, the records are instantly re-sorted by that column. This is much more intuitive and Windows-standard than right-clicking or selecting menu options. Your user will appreciate how easy it is to sort records this way. If you want to get extra fancy, see if you can work out how to alternate the sort order depending on if the control is clicked more than two times in a row.

Note the Me.Requery in the preceding code. Recent versions of Access automatically requery the form if you change its RecordSource property. If you are using an older version of Access and you don't see the form reflect your sort and select changes, try uncommenting the Me.Requery to force Access to do it.

Sorting isn't the end of the story. You can also provide instant record selection.

Selections on Index Forms

One of the most effective features you can offer your users is the capability to narrow a set of records so that they can more easily find the information they're looking for, often using a read-only "index" form. By enhancing your index forms with selection criteria, you add a lot of power to your application with only a little work.

Easy Selection Criteria on an Index Form

Simple selections are the most common. Your user would like to narrow the Recordset by selecting a criterion for a particular field. However, you also need to provide the capability to open the selection up again to include all records, as shown in Figure 13-2.

First of all, the default selection criterion for a field is <all>. To include this in the drop-down list for your criteria combo box, you must use a UNION query. An easy way to understand a Union query is to think of it joining tables vertically instead of horizontally; a Union query adds records to the result instead of columns. In this case, you just want to add one additional record: the <all> value.

A UNION query cannot be built directly using the Query Designer, but fortunately it isn't difficult to create it using SQL. In this case, the RowSource for the combo box looks like this:

```
SELECT tblMemberStatus.MemberStatusKey, tblMemberStatus.MemberStatusName
FROM tblMemberStatus
UNION
SELECT `<all>`, `<all>` FROM tblMemberStatus
ORDER BY tblMemberStatus.MemberStatusName;
```

Note that UNION is really just patching together two SELECT statements. The first one returns the actual member statuses from tblMemberStatus. The second one is "fake" — it just returns the values `<all>` and `<all>`. The field names of the resulting set of records will be those from the first SELECT statement in your UNION query.

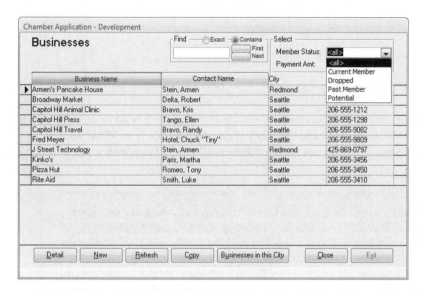

FIGURE 13-2

To more easily create your UNION query, build the first part (which retrieves records from a table) using the Query Designer. Then, switch to SQL view and add the UNION and second SELECT phrase. In fact, whenever you are building a UNION query, you can use the Query Designer to build each SELECT statement, and then copy its SQL code from SQL view and paste it into your query. Just "glue" each SELECT statement together with the UNION keyword. Make sure each SELECT statement has the exact same number of fields represented.

The Order By clause specifies that the records should be sorted in an ascending order by MemberStatusName, so the <all> value appears at the top of the list because < is a lower value than any alphabet letter. The code to process the user's criteria selection is in the After Update event of the Combo box:

Available for download on Wrox.com

```
Private Sub cboMemberStatusKey_AfterUpdate()
    On Error GoTo Error_Handler

    SelectRecords
 `   cboMemberStatusKey.Requery   `needed for Access versions prior to 2007
```

```
Exit_Procedure:
    On Error Resume Next
    Exit Sub

Error_Handler:
    MsgBox Err.Number & ": " & Err.Description
    Resume Exit_Procedure
    Resume

End Sub
```

code snippet Easy Selection Criteria on an Index Form Afterupdate Event Code (in CodeSnippets.txt)

This code calls another procedure in this form: `SelectRecords`. You don't want to actually rebuild the SQL statement here because you may add other selection criteria fields later. By rebuilding the `Where` clause in a central procedure, you can easily add the new criteria fields with a simple procedure just like this one.

> *Notice that there is a `Requery` of the combo box after `SelectRecords` runs, but it is commented out. That's there to handle a little bug that was in the last several versions of Access, including Access 2003, but was fixed in Access 2007 and higher. The bug causes the text in an unbound combo box to become invisible if the Recordset of the form contains no records. Requerying the combo box (just the control itself, not the whole form) causes the mysterious invisible text to appear again.*

The `SelectRecords` procedure is where the SQL statement is rebuilt and the form is requeried:

Available for download on Wrox.com

```
Public Sub SelectRecords()
    On Error GoTo Error_Handler

    Dim varWhereClause As Variant
    Dim strAND As String

    varWhereClause = Null
    strAND = " AND "

    If cboMemberStatusKey & "" <> "<all>" Then

        varWhereClause = (varWhereClause + strAND) & _
        "tblBusiness.MemberStatusKey = """ & _
        cboMemberStatusKey & """"

    End If

    varWhereClause = " WHERE " + varWhereClause

    Me.RecordSource = ReplaceWhereClause(Me.RecordSource,
    varWhereClause)
    Me.Requery

EnableDisableControls
```

```
Exit_Procedure:
    On Error Resume Next
    Exit Sub

Error_Handler:
    MsgBox (Err.Number & ": " & Err.Description)
    Resume Exit_Procedure
    Resume

End Sub
```

code snippet Select Records Procedure to Rebuild SQL and Requery Form (in CodeSnippets.txt)

If the combo box contains `<all>`, no Where clause is built. The ReplaceWhereClause function is designed to just remove the Where clause (and therefore return all records) if a Null is passed in for the WhereClause parameter.

All this code runs immediately when the user chooses a different criterion in the drop-down list, and the records meeting the criteria are displayed. If there are any records that match the selection criteria, they are displayed and the command buttons are enabled, as shown in Figure 13-3.

Using some simple techniques, you can handle multiple selections of different types on the same form.

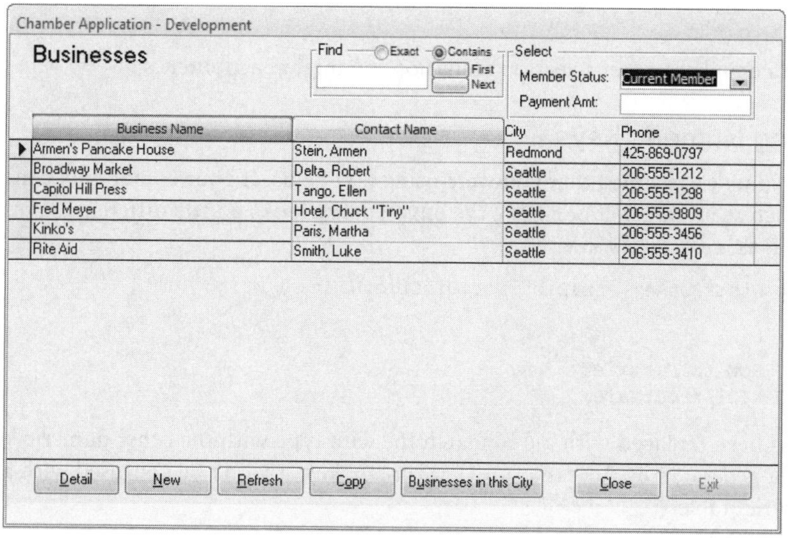

FIGURE 13-3

The Amazing Expandable SelectRecords Procedure

The code in SelectRecords to build the Where clause may seem overly complex, but there are good reasons: expandability and flexibility. The code is ready for you to add more criteria fields. For example, to add another selection for District, you just need to add the following:

```
If cboDistrictKey & "" <> "<all>" Then

    varWhereClause = (varWhereClause + strAND) & _
```

```
    `tblBusiness.DistrictKey = `"` & _
    cboDistrictKey & `"`"

End If
```

The key to this expandability is the concatenation of varWhereClause and strAND. When the procedure starts, varWhereClause is Null, and it continues like that until the code discovers a specified selection criterion. When it does, the phrase (varWhereClause + strAND) performs its magic. The first time it runs, varWhereClause is still Null, so the null-propagating + operator (see Chapter 7) does not add the word AND.

However, the second time it runs (because the user has specified another selection criterion), things are different. Now, varWhereClause has a value in it, so the + operator successfully concatenates the AND onto the string before the next part of the Where clause is added.

When all the pieces have been built, the final step is to add the word WHERE onto the front of the newly built Where clause. However, you don't need it if there are no selection criteria, so it's + to the rescue again. If varWhereClause is still Null, you have the following statement:

```
varWhereClause = ` WHERE ` + varWhereClause
```

That appends WHERE to the front of varWhereClause, but only if varWhereClause has a value. If it doesn't, it will remain Null. Regardless of the order in which you build the parts of the Where clause, this logic works. This extra effort up front makes the SelectRecords procedure easy to change and expand later.

Now let's take a look at a couple of other selection scenarios you might encounter.

Selection Criteria Using Numeric Keys

The previous selection examples assumed that you were using text fields. If your combo box contains a numeric value (such as an AutoNumber key), the UNION query looks a little different. Say the DistrictKey is an AutoNumber primary key:

```
SELECT tblDistrict.DistrictKey, tblDistrict.DistrictName
FROM tblDistrict
UNION
SELECT 0, `<all>" FROM tblDistrict
ORDER BY tblDistrict.DistrictName;
```

The first <all> value has been replaced with a 0 to match the data type with the other numeric key values. Because 0 is never generated by Access as an AutoNumber key, it won't be confused with a real record from the District table.

The code in the SelectRecords procedure is a little different, too:

```
If cboDistrictKey <> 0 Then
    varWhereClause = (varWhereClause + strAND) & _
    `tblBusiness.DistrictKey = ` & cboDistrictKey
End If
```

Note that you are checking to see if the combo box value is 0 instead of <all>. Also, with a numeric value you don't need all the nested quotes — you can just concatenate that number right after the equal sign.

Selection Criteria in Child Records

Sometimes, your users want to search for records that contain a value not in those records, but in their child records. In the example, they might want to find all Businesses that made one or more Payments of a certain amount, say $150, as shown in Figure 13-4.

FIGURE 13-4

In this case, you do not want to apply selection criteria to the Business records themselves. Instead, you want to display all Businesses that have one or more records in the Payment table that are for the desired dollar amount. To perform that kind of selection, you use a *subquery*. A subquery is a query inside another query, and in this example it is used to select Businesses that appear in another query: a list of payments of a certain dollar amount. As with Union queries, subqueries cannot be represented directly in the graphical Design view. However, they are easy to build using SQL view.

For example, when you want the Businesses that have made one or more payments of $150, the desired WHERE clause would be:

```
WHERE tblBusiness.BusinessKey IN (Select BusinessKey

From tblPayment Where PaymentAmount = 150)
```

The key thing is the SQL operator IN, which enables you to determine if a value appears anywhere in a Recordset from another Select statement. Here you want all Businesses with BusinessKeys that appear in a list of Payments that equal $150.

The code in the SelectRecords procedure looks like this:

```
If Not IsNull(txtPaymentAmt) Then

    varWhereClause = (varWhereClause + strAND) & _
    `tblBusiness.BusinessKey IN (` & _
```

```
        `Select BusinessKey From tblPayment Where" & _
        " PaymentAmount = " & Me!txtPaymentAmt & ")"

    End If
```

Because the Payment Amount is a numeric value, you don't need the nested quotes. However, you do need to build the inner subquery with its own `Select` statement and wrap it in its own set of parentheses: `" () "`.

With all these selections going on, you should take a look at what happens if the user specifies criteria that omit all of the records.

Disabling Buttons if No Records Are Displayed

When you give your users the capability to narrow a list of records, they might figure out a way to omit all of them! The subroutine `EnableDisableControls` is called just in case no records meet the criteria. Otherwise, users would get an error if they clicked the Detail button because there wouldn't be a key with which to open the detail record. To prevent that, the Detail button is disabled, as shown in Figure 13-5.

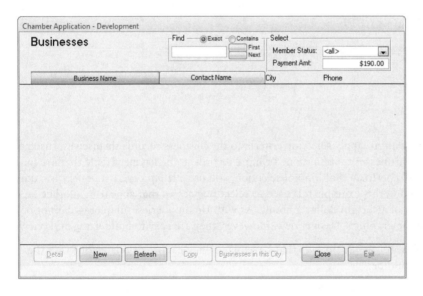

FIGURE 13-5

The code to disable or enable the appropriate buttons looks like this:

```
Public Sub EnableDisableControls()
    On Error GoTo Error_Handler

    If Me.RecordsetClone.RecordCount = 0 Then
        Me!cmdDetail.Enabled = False
        Me!cmdCityBusinesses.Enabled = False
        Me!cmdCopy.Enabled = False
```

```
        Else
            Me!cmdDetail.Enabled = True
            Me!cmdCityBusinesses.Enabled = True
            Me!cmdCopy.Enabled = True

        End If

    Exit_Procedure:
        On Error Resume Next
        Exit Sub

    Error_Handler:
        MsgBox Err.Number & ": " & Err.Description
        Resume Exit_Procedure
        Resume

    End Sub
```

---

code snippet Disabling Buttons If No Records Are Displayed (in CodeSnippets.txt)

The next section explains how to enhance forms with cascading combo boxes.

Cascading Combo Boxes

Sometimes you want your users to choose a value of a combo box and then use that value to limit the selections in another combo box. Because the upper combo box affects the lower, this is sometimes called *cascading* the combo boxes.

To accomplish this, you need the SQL statement building techniques described earlier in this chapter. Say that you have two combo boxes, one for County and one for City. Each County can have many Cities and each City is in one County. The table design would look something like this:

```
tblCounty
CountyKey AutoNumber
CountyName Text 255

tblCity
CityKey AutoNumber
CityName Text 255
CountyKey Long Integer
```

When you present the selection form, you want the County to be selected first, and then the City list to be limited to those found in that County.

The control `cboCounty` will start off enabled in Design view, but `cboCity` will be disabled. In the `After Update` event for `cboCounty`, you'll include the following code:

Available for download on Wrox.com

```
Me!cboCity = Null

If IsNull(cboCounty) Then
    Me!cboCounty.SetFocus

    Me!cboCity.Enabled = False
```

```
Else
  Me!cboCity.Enabled = True
  Me!cboCity.Rowsource = ReplaceWhereClause(Me!cboCity.Rowsource, _
  `Where CountyCode = ` & Me!cboCounty)
  Me!cboCity.Requery
End If
```

code snippet Cascading Combobox (Place In Afterupdate Event Of Combobox) (in CodeSnippets.txt)

Let's examine this code section by section.

First, you clear out the City combo box by setting it to Null:

```
Me!cboCity = Null
```

You do that because you are in the After Update event of the County combo box, so you know it's just been changed. If the whole County has been changed, then any value that was in the City combo box is no longer valid, so you just wipe it out.

Now, if the user just deleted the value for County (setting it to Null), you need to disable the City combo box because the user must choose a County before he can select a City.

Disabling the City combo box won't be possible if it has the focus. Just in case it does, you set the focus back to cboCounty:

```
If IsNull(cboCounty) Then
  Me!cboCounty.SetFocus
  Me!cboCity.Enabled = False
```

Alternatively, if the user changed the County to another value, the City combo box can be enabled so the user can select a City:

```
Else
  Me!cboCity.Enabled = True
```

But now you need to limit the cities in the drop-down list to those that are in the selected County. To do this, you modify the Rowsource property for the City combo box using your old friend ReplaceWhereClause:

```
Me!cboCity.Rowsource = ReplaceWhereClause(Me!cboCity.Rowsource, _
`Where CountyCode = ` & Me!cboCounty)
```

Although you have changed the Rowsource property of the City combo box, it won't take effect until you requery it:

```
  Me!cboCity.Requery
End If
```

At this point, the user can select from a list of cities that are in the selected County. The cascading selection is complete.

Using SQL for Report Selection Criteria

Many developers build Access reports so that their users can quickly view and print out their data. Consider a report to list businesses from the database, as shown in Figure 13-6.

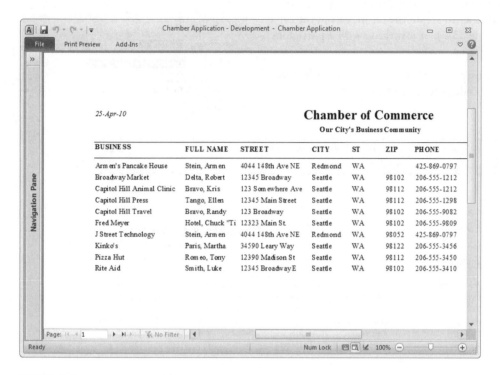

FIGURE 13-6

Some reports are designed to show all the records in a table or query. However, your user will often want to print only some of the records, based on selection criteria. You can create a different report for each selection criteria, but that approach will result in duplication of report code and difficulty in handling combinations of selection criteria.

When novice Access developers want to allow their users to specify the selection criteria for reports, they often use parameter queries to prompt the user to enter the values. Unfortunately, parameter queries have a few problems:

➤ They prompt the user with a separate dialog box for each value.

➤ They don't allow any formatting or validation of the values.

➤ They often require the user to know key values instead of descriptions for lookups.

➤ They are awkward in handling `Null` or `<all>` values.

A better way to prompt for report selection criteria is to display a form to gather them in easy-to-use fields and combo boxes. This way, you can handle `null` values, multiple criteria, and validation checking.

For the business list report, your user wants to select whether to see all the businesses in the table (as in Figure 13-7), or just those with a particular Member Status.

After the user makes his selection and clicks OK, the report is displayed (see Figure 13-8).

FIGURE 13-7

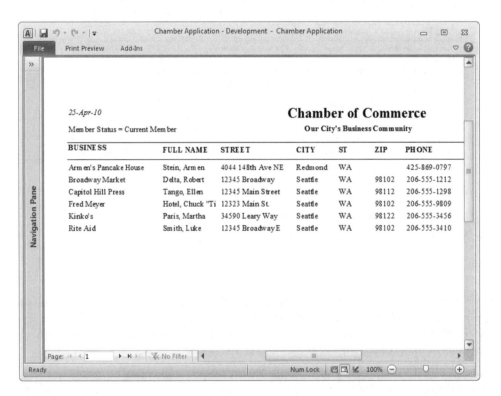

FIGURE 13-8

The first thing to note is that the order of events might be different than you expect. Many programmers would think that the selection form is opened first, which then opens the report when the OK button is clicked. In fact, it's just the opposite. First, the report is opened. During its `On Open` event (before the report is displayed to the user), the report calls the selection form in Dialog mode, which halts the report code until the selection form is hidden. Here is the code in the `On Open` event of the report:

```
Private Sub Report_Open(Cancel As Integer)

    On Error GoTo Error_Handler

    Me.Caption = `My Application"

    DoCmd.OpenForm FormName:="frmReportSelector_MemberList", _
    Windowmode:=acDialog

    `Cancel the report if `cancel" was selected on the dialog form.

    If Forms!frmReportSelector_MemberList!txtContinue = `no" Then
        Cancel = True
        GoTo Exit_Procedure
    End If
    Me.RecordSource = ReplaceWhereClause(Me.RecordSource, _
      Forms!frmReportSelector_MemberList!txtWhereClause)

Exit_Procedure:
    Exit Sub

Error_Handler:
    MsgBox Err.Number & `: ` & Err.Description
    Resume Exit_Procedure
    Resume

End Sub
```

code snippet Using SQL For Report Criteria Selection (in CodeSnippets.txt)

During the report's Open event, its Recordset has not been evaluated yet, so you still have a chance to change it.

Now it's time to see what the selection form really does. It has a few fields that are normally hidden, as shown in Figure 13-9.

The extra fields above the OK button are normally set to Visible = No. They hold three pieces of information:

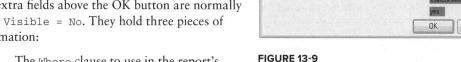

FIGURE 13-9

➤ The Where clause to use in the report's RecordSource

➤ Some selection title text to use in the report's heading

➤ A field to indicate whether the report should continue (OK was clicked) or not (Cancel was clicked)

> It's a good idea to mark normally invisible fields in some special way so that you can easily see them if you forget to hide them. One technique is to make the background color of a hidden field red (BackColor = 255). That way, you'll notice it if you forget to hide it!

Here's the code in the form that builds the Where clause and the selection title, both stored in the hidden fields:

```
Sub RebuildWhereClause()
On Error GoTo Err_RebuildWhereClause

`This subroutine builds an SQL WHERE clause based on the choices
`made by the user on the form. It can be used as the WHERE parameter
`in the OpenReport command. The invisible text box Me![txtWhereClause]
`displays the completed WHERE clause.
`
`SelectionTitle string that contains a title to place at the top
` of the report, which specifies the selection made.
` Stored on form in invisible text box
Me![txtSelectionTitle].

Dim varWhereClause As Variant
Dim strWhereAnd As String
Dim strSelectionTitle As String
Dim strComma As String

varWhereClause = Null
strWhereAnd = ""
strSelectionTitle = ""
strComma = ""

`Member Status Combo Box
If Not (Me!cboMemberStatus & "" = "") And Not _
  (Me!cboMemberStatus = 0) Then

  varWhereClause = (varWhereClause + strWhereAnd) _
  & " (tblBusiness.MemberStatusKey = "" & _
  Me!cboMemberStatus.Column(0) & "") "
  strWhereAnd = " AND "
  strSelectionTitle = strSelectionTitle & strComma _
  & "Member Status = " & Me!cboMemberStatus.Column(1)
  strComma = ", "

End If

If strWhereAnd = "" Then
  varWhereClause = Null
Else
  varWhereClause = " WHERE " + varWhereClause
End If
```

```
Me![txtWhereClause] = varWhereClause
Me![txtSelectionTitle] = strSelectionTitle

Exit_RebuildWhereClause:
  Exit Sub

Err_RebuildWhereClause:
  MsgBox (Err.Number & ": " & Err.Description)
  Resume Exit_RebuildWhereClause
  Resume

End Sub
```

code snippet Code to Provide Where Clause for Preceding Code (in CodeSnippets.txt)

Because it contains the key value, `Column(0)` of the combo box is used to build the `Where` clause. However, to build the selection title, you use `Column(1)` because it contains the more friendly description of the Member Status record from the lookup table.

This code runs when OK is clicked. It rebuilds the `Where` clause and tells the report to proceed:

Available for download on Wrox.com

```
Sub cmdOK_Click()
On Error GoTo Err_cmdOK_Click

RebuildWhereClause
Me!txtContinue = "yes"
Me.Visible = False

Exit_cmdOK_Click:
  Exit Sub

Err_cmdOK_Click:
  MsgBox (Err.Number & ": " & Err.Description)
  Resume Exit_cmdOK_Click
  Resume

End Sub
```

code snippet OK Command Code for Using Preceding Code (in CodeSnippets.txt)

After the `RebuildWhereClause` procedure builds the first two hidden fields, only two more things have to happen. First, the third hidden field, `txtContinue`, is set to `Yes`. It's the field that the report will check to see if it should continue to open or just cancel.

Finally, the current form's `Visible` property is set to `False`. Remember that this form was opened in Dialog mode, so hiding it causes the report code to continue running.

 Because the selection form is always hidden, not closed, the selection criteria are retained each time the form is used while the Access database remains open. That makes it easier for your user to re-run reports with the same selection criteria or to adjust the criteria slightly instead of typing it all again each time.

If the user clicks Cancel, the following code runs instead. It tells the report to stop opening.

```
Sub cmdCancel_Click()

On Error GoTo Err_cmdCancel_Click

Me!txtContinue = `no"
Me.Visible = False

Exit_cmdCancel_Click:
   Exit Sub

Err_cmdCancel_Click:
   MsgBox (Err.Number & `: ` & Err.Description)
   Resume Exit_cmdCancel_Click
   Resume

End Sub
```

code snippet Cancel Command Code for Using Preceding Code (in CodeSnippets.txt)

The only difference between this code and the OK code is that you don't bother to rebuild the Where clause because the user is canceling anyway, and you set txtContinue to No so that the report will cancel itself before it even gets a chance to display anything.

When the report is canceled, it generates Error 2501, which you should handle so that your user doesn't see an ugly error message. See Chapter 7 for a description of how to handle expected errors like this one.

By adding more fields to your selection form and building the Where clause to apply them to the report's Recordset, you can deliver a report to your user that is both flexible and easy to use.

Altering the SQL inside Queries

Sometimes it can be advantageous to alter the SQL inside a saved query. That's especially common when you are using pass-through queries to another database like SQL Server, but it can also come in handy when you need to nest Access queries several layers deep. Because the queries a few layers down can't be modified in a report or form's RecordSource, you may need to change them directly.

Remember that if you use this technique for a pass-through query, you must use the SQL Server syntax of the back-end database, not Access syntax. For example, the wildcard in SQL Server is %, not *. Also, SQL Server expects string values to be surrounded by single quotes (`), whereas Access doesn't care whether you use single quotes (`) or double quotes (").

First, realize that this technique will work only if your user is using the front-end application database exclusively. Because you're changing an actual saved query in the application, you must make sure that you aren't causing problems for other users. The best practice is to have each user run a copy of the front-end application on their local computer, not share it on the network. If you follow this recommendation, altering saved queries in your front-end Access application will work just fine.

To change the `Where` clause in a saved query, use code like the following:

```
Dim qdf as QueryDef
Dim db as Database
Set db = CurrentDB
Set qdf = db.QueryDefs(`YourQueryName")
qdf.SQL = ReplaceWhereClause(qdf.SQL, strYourNewWhereClause)
set qdf = Nothing
set db = Nothing
```

code snippet Altering SQL Inside Queries (in CodeSnippets.txt)

The SQL property of the query definition contains the actual SQL statement of the query; it's the same SQL statement that you see in the SQL view in the Query Designer. You don't have to do anything else to change it; the SQL is replaced instantly.

Will this bloat your database? Database bloating is a problem because Access doesn't reclaim unused space until the database is compacted, so the database size can increase dramatically if you (or your code) creates and deletes objects in the front-end database. However, merely replacing the SQL statement inside an existing query doesn't cause significant bloating.

THE REPLACEORDERBYCLAUSE AND REPLACEWHERECLAUSE FUNCTIONS

It's often necessary to "cut and replace" the `Where` and `Order By` clauses of a SQL string using VBA. Throughout this chapter, the `ReplaceWhereClause` and `ReplaceOrderByClause` functions are used to do that. This section shows you the code that's been doing all that hard work!

This first procedure, `ParseSQL` (shown in the following code), does the "heavy lifting" of the SQL handling functions. It breaks up the original SQL string into components, so that individual pieces can be replaced. Although `ParseSQL` is `Public`, it's rarely called from anywhere other than the `ReplaceWhereClause` and `ReplaceOrderByClause` functions that follow it.

Please note that you don't have to type all this code into your application! It's in the Chamber Application file included with this chapter's download code.

```
Option Compare Database
Option Explicit
Public Sub ParseSQL(strSQL As Variant, strSELECT As Variant, strWhere A
Variant, strOrderBy As Variant, strGROUPBY As Variant, strHAVING As Variant)
```

```
On Error GoTo Error_Handler
`
`This subroutine accepts a valid SQL string and passes back separated
`SELECT, WHERE, ORDER BY, and GROUP BY clauses.

`
`INPUT:

` strSQL valid SQL string to parse

`OUTPUT:
` strSELECT  SELECT portion of SQL (includes JOIN info)
` strWHERE   WHERE portion of SQL
` strORDERBY ORDER BY portion of SQL
` strGROUPBY GROUP BY portion of SQL
` strHAVING  HAVING portion of SQL
```

 Access queries have a semicolon (;) at the end of their SQL statements. While the subroutine accepts the trailing ; character in strSQL, *there is no ; character passed back at any time.*

This subroutine takes in only one parameter (the original SQL string), but modifies and outputs five parameters — one for each portion of the parsed SQL string.

```
Dim intStartSELECT As Integer
Dim intStartWHERE As Integer
Dim intStartORDERBY As Integer
Dim intStartGROUPBY As Integer
Dim intStartHAVING As Integer
Dim intLenSELECT As Integer
Dim intLenWHERE As Integer
Dim intLenORDERBY As Integer
Dim intLenGROUPBY As Integer
Dim intLenHAVING As Integer
Dim intLenSQL As Integer
```

The following code determines the starting location of each clause in the SQL statement by finding the position in the string of the corresponding keywords:

```
intStartSELECT = InStr(strSQL, `SELECT `)

intStartWHERE = InStr(strSQL, `WHERE `)

intStartORDERBY = InStr(strSQL, `ORDER BY `)

intStartGROUPBY = InStr(strSQL, `GROUP BY `)

intStartHAVING = InStr(strSQL, `HAVING `)

`if there´s no GROUP BY, there can´t be a HAVING
```

```
    If intStartGROUPBY = 0 Then

        intStartHAVING = 0
    End If

    If InStr(strSQL, ";") Then `if it exists, trim off the `;'
        strSQL = Left(strSQL, InStr(strSQL, ";") -1)
    End If

    intLenSQL = Len(strSQL)
```

Next, the code calculates the length of the Select clause of the SQL statement. Basically, it starts by assuming that the Select clause is the entire remaining length of the SQL statement and then tries shorter and shorter lengths by testing against the starting positions of the other SQL clauses:

```
` find length of Select portion

If intStartSELECT > 0 Then
    ` start with longest it could be
    intLenSELECT = intLenSQL -intStartSELECT + 1
    If intStartWHERE > 0 And intStartWHERE > intStartSELECT _
        And intStartWHERE < intStartSELECT + intLenSELECT Then

        `we found a new portion closer to this one

        intLenSELECT = intStartWHERE -intStartSELECT
    End If
    If intStartORDERBY > 0 And intStartORDERBY > intStartSELECT _
        And intStartORDERBY < intStartSELECT + intLenSELECT Then

        `we found a new portion closer to this one

        intLenSELECT = intStartORDERBY -intStartSELECT
    End If
    If intStartGROUPBY > 0 And intStartGROUPBY > intStartSELECT _
        And intStartGROUPBY < intStartSELECT + intLenSELECT Then

        `we found a new portion closer to this one

        intLenSELECT = intStartGROUPBY -intStartSELECT
    End If
    If intStartHAVING > 0 And intStartHAVING > intStartSELECT _
        And intStartHAVING < intStartSELECT + intLenSELECT Then

        `we found a new portion closer to this one
        intLenSELECT = intStartHAVING -intStartSELECT
    End If
End If
```

Then the code does the same thing for the Group By clause, determining its length by finding the beginning of the next clause:

```
` find length of GROUPBY portion

If intStartGROUPBY > 0 Then
    ` start with longest it could be
```

```
      intLenGROUPBY = intLenSQL -intStartGROUPBY + 1
      If intStartWHERE > 0 And intStartWHERE > intStartGROUPBY _
        And intStartWHERE < intStartGROUPBY + intLenGROUPBY Then

        `we found a new portion closer to this one

        intLenGROUPBY = intStartWHERE -intStartGROUPBY
      End If
      If intStartORDERBY > 0 And intStartORDERBY > intStartGROUPBY _
        And intStartORDERBY < intStartGROUPBY + intLenGROUPBY Then

        `we found a new portion closer to this one

        intLenGROUPBY = intStartORDERBY -intStartGROUPBY
      End If
      If intStartHAVING > 0 And intStartHAVING > intStartGROUPBY _
        And intStartHAVING < intStartGROUPBY + intLenGROUPBY Then

        `we found a new portion closer to this one
        intLenGROUPBY = intStartHAVING -intStartGROUPBY
      End If
    End If
```

The following code does the same thing for the Having clause:

```
` find length of HAVING portion

If intStartHAVING > 0 Then
  ` start with longest it could be
  intLenHAVING = intLenSQL -intStartHAVING + 1
  If intStartWHERE > 0 And intStartWHERE > intStartHAVING _
    And intStartWHERE < intStartHAVING + intLenHAVING Then

    `we found a new portion closer to this one

    intLenHAVING = intStartWHERE -intStartHAVING
  End If
  If intStartORDERBY > 0 And intStartORDERBY > intStartHAVING _
    And intStartORDERBY < intStartHAVING + intLenHAVING Then

    `we found a new portion closer to this one

    intLenHAVING = intStartORDERBY -intStartHAVING
  End If
  If intStartGROUPBY > 0 And intStartGROUPBY > intStartHAVING _
    And intStartGROUPBY < intStartHAVING + intLenHAVING Then

    `we found a new portion closer to this one
    intLenHAVING = intStartGROUPBY -intStartHAVING
  End If
End If
```

And this code does the same thing for the `Order By` clause:

```
` find length of ORDERBY portion

If intStartORDERBY > 0 Then
  ` start with longest it could be
  intLenORDERBY = intLenSQL -intStartORDERBY + 1
  If intStartWHERE > 0 And intStartWHERE > intStartORDERBY _
    And intStartWHERE < intStartORDERBY + intLenORDERBY Then

    `we found a new portion closer to this one

    intLenORDERBY = intStartWHERE -intStartORDERBY
  End If
  If intStartGROUPBY > 0 And intStartGROUPBY > intStartORDERBY _
    And intStartGROUPBY < intStartORDERBY + intLenORDERBY Then

    `we found a new portion closer to this one

    intLenORDERBY = intStartGROUPBY -intStartORDERBY
  End If
  If intStartHAVING > 0 And intStartHAVING > intStartORDERBY _
    And intStartHAVING < intStartORDERBY + intLenORDERBY Then

    `we found a new portion closer to this one
    intLenORDERBY = intStartHAVING -intStartORDERBY
  End If
End If
```

Finally, the length of the `Where` clause is determined:

```
` find length of WHERE portion

If intStartWHERE > 0 Then
  ` start with longest it could be
  intLenWHERE = intLenSQL -intStartWHERE + 1

  If intStartGROUPBY > 0 And intStartGROUPBY > intStartWHERE _
    And intStartGROUPBY < intStartWHERE + intLenWHERE Then
    `we found a new portion closer to this one
    intLenWHERE = intStartGROUPBY -intStartWHERE

  End If
  If intStartORDERBY > 0 And intStartORDERBY > intStartWHERE _
    And intStartORDERBY < intStartWHERE + intLenWHERE Then

    `we found a new portion closer to this one

    intLenWHERE = intStartORDERBY -intStartWHERE
  End If
  If intStartHAVING > 0 And intStartHAVING > intStartWHERE _
```

```
      And intStartHAVING < intStartWHERE + intLenWHERE Then

        `we found a new portion closer to this one
        intLenWHERE = intStartHAVING -intStartWHERE
      End If
   End If
```

Now that all the starting positions and lengths of the five SQL clauses have been determined, the output parameters can be set:

```
   `  set each output portion
   If intStartSELECT > 0 Then
     strSELECT = Mid$(strSQL, intStartSELECT, intLenSELECT)
   End If
   If intStartGROUPBY > 0 Then
     strGROUPBY = Mid$(strSQL, intStartGROUPBY, intLenGROUPBY)
   End If
   If intStartHAVING > 0 Then
     strHAVING = Mid$(strSQL, intStartHAVING, intLenHAVING)
   End If
   If intStartORDERBY > 0 Then
     strOrderBy = Mid$(strSQL, intStartORDERBY, intLenORDERBY)
   End If
   If intStartWHERE > 0 Then
     strWhere = Mid$(strSQL, intStartWHERE, intLenWHERE)
   End If

   Exit_Procedure:
     Exit Sub

   Error_Handler:
     MsgBox (Err.Number & `: ` & Err.Description)
     Resume Exit_Procedure

   End Sub
```

---

code snippet ParseSQL Subroutine (in CodeSnippets.txt)

The next two functions merely use the `ParseSQL` procedure to break up the SQL statement into its five clauses, and then they replace the appropriate clause with the new clause that was passed in:

```
Public Function ReplaceWhereClause(strSQL As Variant, strNewWHERE As Variant)
On Error GoTo Error_Handler

`This subroutine accepts a valid SQL string and Where clause, and
`returns the same SQL statement with the original Where clause (if any)
`replaced by the passed in Where clause.
`
`INPUT:
`  strSQL valid SQL string to change
`OUTPUT:
`  strNewWHERE New WHERE clause to insert into SQL statement
`
```

```
Dim strSELECT As String, strWhere As String
Dim strOrderBy As String, strGROUPBY As String, strHAVING As String

Call ParseSQL(strSQL, strSELECT, strWhere, strOrderBy, _
strGROUPBY, strHAVING)

ReplaceWhereClause = strSELECT &`"& strNewWHERE &`"_
& strGROUPBY &`"& strHAVING &`"& strOrderBy

Exit_Procedure:
  Exit Function

Error_Handler:
  MsgBox (Err.Number & `: ` & Err.Description)
  Resume Exit_Procedure

End Function
```

code snippet ReplaceWhereClause Function (in CodeSnippets.txt)

```
Public Function ReplaceOrderByClause(strSQL As Variant, strNewOrderBy As Variant)
On Error GoTo Error_Handler
`
`This subroutine accepts a valid SQL string and Where clause, and
`returns the same SQL statement with the original Where clause (if any)
`replaced by the passed in Where clause.
`
`INPUT:
` strSQL valid SQL string to change
`OUTPUT:
` strNewOrderBy New OrderBy clause to insert into SQL statement
`
Dim strSELECT As String, strWhere As String
Dim strOrderBy As String, strGROUPBY As String, strHAVING As String

Call ParseSQL(strSQL, strSELECT, strWhere, strOrderBy, _
strGROUPBY, strHAVING)

ReplaceOrderByClause = strSELECT &`"& strWhere &`"& strNewOrderBy

Exit_Procedure:
  Exit Function

Error_Handler:
  MsgBox (Err.Number & `: ` & Err.Description)
  Resume Exit_Procedure

End Function
```

code snippet RepelaceOrderByClause Function (in CodeSnippets.txt)

These SQL handling procedures can be added to all of your Access applications in their own module, such as basSQLTools. By using ReplaceWhereClause and ReplaceOrderByClause, you can take a lot of the hassle out of manipulating SQL strings in your VBA code.

SUMMARY

VBA and SQL are both powerful tools for you to use in your Access applications, and they work very well together. The techniques explained in this chapter enable you to add instant sorting to column headings, provide easy record selection on continuous forms, build smart cascading combo boxes that change their drop-down lists based on other selections, prompt your user for report selection criteria without using parameter queries, and change the SQL statement inside saved queries. With these features, your Access applications will be more flexible and easy to use.

14

Using VBA to Enhance Forms

➤ Fundamental VBA concepts

➤ Creating Forms the 2010 way

➤ Using the TreeView and ListView controls

A first impression is lasting, so be sure that your forms make it a great one. In the solution you provide for a client, the forms you create are the first things that people see and use. So forms should be as attractive as they are effective and intuitive.

Access 2010's out-of-the box features and controls replace many of the common tools and functions that required testing, error trapping, and add-ins. These features are more than just time savers; they build in consistency and motivate you to deliver better solutions. You can dress up forms with subtle shading, colorful lines, and sleek image controls.

Users like being able to scroll through data sheets, instantly see the details, and even update the record. They also appreciate how easy assigning a task to several people is, particularly because they can add a person to the list without missing a beat. Unlimited opportunities exist for including attachments right in the database.

Those are just some of the features that you'll explore in this chapter.

If something already looks and works this good, then imagine how great your solution will be when you leverage it with VBA. That's what this chapter is all about. In addition to seeing how to use VBA with some of the enhanced features, you'll also examine some of the important mainstays such as working with combo boxes, creating multiple instances of a form, and building a tree view control.

VBA BASICS

Before you dive into the wonderful world of forms, take a minute to review the following table, which shows the concepts that are fundamental to working with VBA.

CONCEPT	DEFINITION	EXAMPLES
Object	An entity that can be manipulated with code	`Form, Report, TextBox, ComboBox, CommandButton, DoCmd, Debug`
Method	Any intrinsic (built-in) functionality already assigned to an object	`Form.Requery, Report.Print, TextBox.SetFocus, ComboBox.Dropdown, DoCmd.OpenForm, Debug.Print`
Event	An action associated to an object that executes when triggered by the user	`Form.Open, Report.NoData, TextBox.AfterUpdate, ComboBox.NotInList, CommandButton.Click`
Property	An attribute of an object that defines its characteristics (such as size, color, or screen location) or an aspect of its behavior (such as whether it is hidden)	`Form.BackColor, TextBox.ControlSource, ComboBox.RowSource, CommandButton.Picture, Report.Recordsource`

Properties

Forms have properties and so do the controls on a form. Although a few properties exist that can only be read or set in VBA, the majority of an object's properties are listed on the Property Sheet. The main four categories of properties are format, data, event, and other. The needs of the customer and users dictate which of these properties you set and when. Setting the properties in the Property Sheet may be all that is needed for some; however, the majority of your forms will have some kind of programmatic interaction with the user. Being able to respond to user input relies heavily on setting the properties using VBA. Of course, some of the routine functionality can now be provided by embedded macros. But this chapter focuses on VBA, particularly on how to utilize the event properties.

The following table provides examples of properties. Appendix G provides a more extensive list in discussing the Access Object Model, and it is complemented by the Appendices on ADO and DAO.

OBJECT	PROPERTY	DESCRIPTION
Form	`Caption`	A string expression that appears in the title bar of the form
	`RecordSource`	A string expression that defines the source of the form's bound data
	`AllowEdits`	Boolean value that specifies whether the user can edit records on the form

OBJECT	PROPERTY	DESCRIPTION
Text box	ControlSource	A string expression identifying the name of the field in the form's RecordSource into which the text box should push or pull data; or an expression evaluated to display a calculation or text result
	Visible	Boolean value that specifies whether the control is visible to the user
	InputMask	A string expression that defines the way data is entered
	StatusBarText	A string expression displayed at the bottom of the Access window while the cursor is in the control
Combo box	RowSource	A string expression that defines the source of data
	LimitToList	Boolean value that restricts the user's selection to only values that already exist in the combo box's RowSource data set
	TabIndex	Numerical value that specifies the order in which the cursor should travel from one field to the next

Event Properties: Where Does the Code Go?

The power of a form is often derived from responding to the user. Typically, a response is based on intentional input. But VBA can also respond to ancillary or inadvertent actions. The most common place to use code is in the event properties of the form or control. This code is frequently referred to as the code behind the form.

Having the code right isn't enough; the code also has to be behind the right event or it may not be triggered. Time and again, the problem of code that "just doesn't work" is solved by moving the code to a different event. So, in addition to being able to write VBA, being familiar with the timing or order of events, as well as what triggers them, is important. After all, the best code in the world isn't going to help if it doesn't get to run. The following table describes what triggers some of the events most commonly used in a form and in the form's objects.

 In code, events have no spaces with the first letter of each word capitalized: Open *and* BeforeUpdate.

EVENTS	TRIGGERS WHEN
Open	The form is opened (can be canceled).
Close	The form is closing, but before it is removed from the screen.
Load	The form loads.
Unload	The form unloads before it deactivates and is closed, so criteria in this event can determine whether the form should remain open. Because the Close event cannot be canceled, this is the stage in which to include a way to abort the process of closing the form.
Click	A section of the form or a control is clicked once by the mouse.
DblClick	A section of the form or a control is double-clicked by the mouse.
Current	A record gets the focus when a form is opened or focus moves to a different record.
Dirty	The user makes any modification to the current record.
BeforeInsert	User types the first character in a new record of a bound form. This actually occurs before the record is created; it can also be canceled.
BeforeUpdate	Before the update (new data or change) is committed to the form or control — so the update can be canceled.
AfterUpdate	A form record or an individual control has been updated.
AfterInsert	The record updated is a new record.
Change	A value on a control is modified. Note that this applies only to a text box or the text portion of a combo box and to moving between pages on a tab control.
Timer	Regular intervals specified by the TimerInterval property are reached.
NotInList	The user enters a value that is not in a combo box.
MouseMove	The user moves the mouse over a section of the form or a control.
Enter	The user physically places the edit cursor into the control. This can be done with the Tab or Enter key or by a mouse click.

As you can see, events are fired or triggered by a specific action or circumstance. Some events occur in sequence, such as when opening or closing a form, and others — Click and NotInList, for example — occur when certain conditions are met. (To understand more about event firing, see Chapter 7.)

Although there isn't a comprehensive list of events and their firing order (Access 2010 has 50 form events), you can use Access 2010 Help to get information about a specific event. Office Online typically lists three to five related events, giving a brief explanation. For example, when a user opens a form, the events occur in this order: Open ⇨ Load Resize ⇨ Activate ⇨ Current. And events closely related to closing a form occur as follows: Unload ⇨ Deactivate ⇨ Close. The Close event can be the mechanism for such things as opening another form or creating a log of who used the form.

Naming Conventions

As you know by now, adopting and consistently applying naming conventions is important. In addition to making your code more readable, a good naming convention minimizes the potential for the same name to be given to more than one object. The following table shows some of the more common ways to name objects and controls.

 Appendix G provides a more extensive list of tags for forms, subforms, and the objects that might be used on them. Note that some items have more than one common tag. A subform, for example, might be represented by fsub, sfrm, *or* sfr.

TAG	OBJECT	EXAMPLE
frm	Form	frmContacts
sfr	Subform	sfrContactDetails
cbo	Combo box	cboClientNames
lst	Listbox	lstClientNames
txt	Text box	txtFName
cmd	Command Button	cmdOpenContacts
qry	Query	qryFavoriteContacts

If your first programming language is VBA, you were probably taught to use cmd for command buttons. When you get into other languages such as VB.NET, ASP.NET, and C#, *command* takes on a different meaning and refers to commands that talk to a database (OLE DB or SQL Server). With ADO, it was often suggested that Cmd (uppercase C) be used for *command* and cmd (lowercase) be used for *command button*. btn has also been used as a generic tag for a button. And now, using btn may become popular as a way to differentiate between command buttons on the Ribbon and controls on a form or report, which use cmd as a tag. That isn't to underplay the benefits of explicit naming, such as tgl for a toggle button, opt for an option button, and, yes, cmd for a command button.

Now let's move on to building custom forms.

CREATING FORMS THE 2010 WAY

When you are ready to create a new form, you'll probably have a good idea about its general look and function based on the record source and purpose. Access 2010 gives developers a huge jumpstart on form design by providing a good selection of form options on the Ribbon (see Figure 14-1). You can select an item from the Navigaton Pane, which will become the record source of the new form, and then click on one of the Ribbon's form buttons to initiate the process. Thanks to a Form Wizard, the new form (instantly) appears in Layout view so that you can begin adding more features and functionality.

FIGURE 14-1

With the introduction of Access 2007 and the Ribbon, new types of forms were added to the library of available predefined forms. You generate most of the forms automatically by selecting a record source (that is, a table or query) before clicking on the form generation button found under Create ➪ Forms on the Ribbon. The most commonly used types of forms are placed first on the Ribbon. These include: Form, Form Design, and Blank Form. Less prominent on the Ribbon, but significantly more useful are Form Wizard, Navigation, and More Forms. The following table lists these forms and their expected usage.

RIBBON COMMAND BUTTON	TYPICAL USAGE
Form	Automatically generated Columnar form (uses all fields from underlying record source).
Form Design	Creates a blank form in Design view with no record source. A field list and all tables/queries are available.
Blank Form	Creates a blank form in Layout view with no record source, no controls, or format. A field list and all tables/queries are available.
Form Wizard	The most versatile form generation method. Allows selection of included fields and type of form from a choice of the four most common form types: Columnar, Tabular, Datasheet, and Justified.
PivotTable	PivotTable (located under More Forms).
PivotChart	PivotChart (located under More Forms).
Modal Dialog	This form is intended as a custom dialog form and is generally not bound to a record source. (It is located under More Forms.)
Split Form	This special form displays a datasheet and, below that, a standard form of the same record source at the same time. This allows easy browsing through records while allowing the currently selected datasheet record to be edited in the form below. (It is located under More Forms.)

RIBBON COMMAND BUTTON	TYPICAL USAGE
Datasheet	Spreadsheet style form that displays one record per row (can be created using the wizard and is also found under More Forms).
Multiple Items	This form is also referred to as a *continuous form*. It displays multiple records. Unlike with the datasheet, you can arrange the controls any way you want. (Can be created using the wizard and is also found under More Forms. Using the wizard it is called Tabular.)
Navigation	This feature is new for Access 2010. These forms allow you to add Access objects to create customizable navigation forms, making it easy to create logical groupings of your forms, queries, tables, and reports into an easy-to-navigate series of forms. It provides similar functionality to the Switchboard of earlier Access versions.

You may be wondering why the Form Wizard is still around even though a button seems to exist on the Ribbon for each of the form layouts. At this point, the biggest benefits of the wizard are that it enables you to specify which fields to include from the selected record source and that it makes using the new styles (AutoFormats) so easy. When you create a form by clicking one of the layouts on the Ribbon, the form includes all the underlying fields — which means you'll likely spend extra time deleting and repositioning fields.

Columnar and Tabular Layouts

Understanding tabular and columnar (stacked) layouts is important because of the effect they have on moving controls when you're designing a form. You'll see some examples in a moment, but for now, you might envision that columnar layout is used for what is known as *single form view,* and tabular layout is a *continuous view* that essentially looks like a datasheet. In Access 2010, using a wizard to create a form almost always results in a columnar layout when you're working in Design view. The normal process for creating a form is to select a record source from the Navigation Pane and then use the Ribbon's Create tab to select the desired form. The form opens in Layout view and includes all the fields in the record source (except, obviously, when you choose a blank form, Form Design, or the Form Wizard). Logically, selecting the layout for Multiple Items creates a form with a stacked layout. But selecting one of the other formats, such as Form, places all the fields on the form in columnar layout. Even the Pivot Chart has a columnar layout if you look at the form in Design view.

One of the key benefits of columnar and tabular layouts is that the controls are pre-grouped, so they move together and stay in alignment. The grouping enables you to reorder or remove fields and have controls automatically reposition themselves to the proper spacing and alignment. You can remove the grouping from all controls or from selected controls, and you can even use a combination of columnar and tabular groups along with independent fields all on the same form. The grouping can be changed in Design or Layout view by using the control layout options on the Ribbon's Arrange tab (see Figure 14-2). That's where you can also specify the margins within the control (the distance between the control border and the control contents) as well as the padding (space between controls).

FIGURE 14-2

Right-click a control within a group to access the shortcut menu for Layout, as shown in Figure 14-3. This menu enables you to quickly remove one control from the group or to work with an entire column or row of controls. (If you can't adapt to working with grouped controls, you can remove the grouping using the same shortcut menu; merely select the group and then right-click to use the shortcut menu and then choose Layout ➪ Remove.)

The Gridlines option on the shortcut menu is a slick way to add vertical and horizontal lines to a form.

Anchoring

Anchoring ties a control or group of controls to a position. Specify the position — top, bottom, side, or corner — and the control moves into place. You do this by using two of the properties for controls: Horizontal Anchor and Vertical Anchor. (Note — these two properties apply only to controls on forms and are not available on reports.) If two stacks of controls are anchored to opposite sides or corners of a form and the form is resized, the controls automatically move in accordance with their anchor points. Anchoring includes several options that you can select from the shortcut menu by right-clicking a control. But a better way to see what the options do is to check out the Anchoring section of the Ribbon's Arrange tab as shown in Figure 14-4. You can also find these options under the right-click menu.

FIGURE 14-3

The stretch options enable you to maximize the use of available space by expanding the control or group of controls vertically or horizontally, and you can stretch labels as well. For example, you can use stretch across the top to position a heading so that the width of the label grows as the form gets wider. With two stacks of controls, you can anchor the group on the right to the right, put the cursor in a text box of the stack on the left, and select Stretch Down and Across. Then as the form grows, the fields in the left stack get wider and taller. Or, if you know that the data is going to be a fixed width, but would like to give the labels more room, you could designate that column of the stack as the portion to stretch. Knowing that you can set only one control in a tabular layout to stretch horizontally and that you can set only one control in a stacked layout to stretch vertically is important.

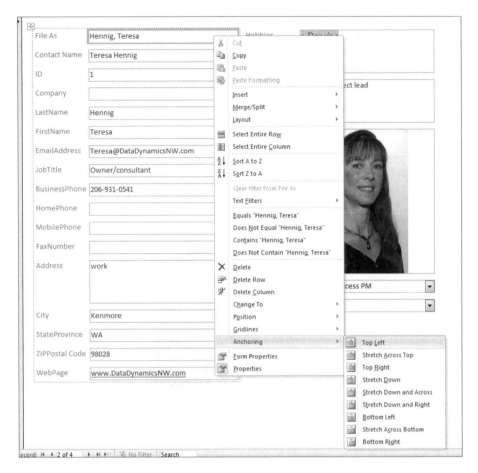

FIGURE 14-4

As in past versions of Access, perfecting a form's design has several subtleties. For one thing, controls that are not in a group may end up overlapping if the form is stretched. A good illustration is two controls, side-by-side — as they stretch with the form, the control on the left will eventually encroach upon the space for the control on the right. This is also a good example of the type of issues to be alert to, in addition to issues from your other experiences with form design.

You can use the gridline options mentioned earlier in conjunction with groups and anchoring so you can have horizontal and vertical lines that grow and move with the controls.

 If you make design changes to a form that has the `AutoResize` *property set to* `NO` *and the* `AutoCenter` *property set to* `YES`, *switch to Form view before saving the form. Otherwise, the right and bottom edges might be trimmed the next time the form opens.*

The Modal Dialog Box Mode

The Modal Dialog form opens as a modal window, which means that the user must respond to and close the form before any other object can have the focus. These are often referred to as modal dialog forms because they typically have the sole purpose of receiving a specific input or feedback from the user. After the user has provided the required response, he can close the form and the application can continue its process, whereas a modal form merely needs to be closed before the user can proceed with other processes.

If you have ever created dialog forms, you know how tedious the process can be — setting the same form properties and adding the same command buttons to every form. The Modal Dialog Wizard now does the work and saves you a lot of time. The new form will be essentially blank, except for two command buttons (one labeled OK and the other, Cancel). Both buttons have the `Close` method for their `On Click` event, so you will most likely want to change or remove one of the buttons. Because the buttons use an embedded macro, they run in disabled mode. The best part of using the wizard to create a modal dialog form is that the wizard correctly sets the appropriate properties such as the formatting (border style and navigation) and the settings for pop-up and modal mode.

Creating a new modal form is great, but simple dialog forms aren't the only ones that you may want to open in modal mode. You can set any form or report to open in modal dialog mode by setting the `Modal` property to `Yes` or by using code to specify the view as the form is opened. Here are two examples of code that opens a modal form in a modal window:

```
Docmd.OpenForm "frmMyModalForm" , acNormal, ,, acFormEdit, acWindowNormal

Docmd.OpenForm "frmMyModalForm" , acNormal, ,, acFormEdit, acDialog
```

Available for download on Wrox.com

code 59166_ch14_CodeSnippets.txt Open A Form In Dialog Mode -- Two Ways

The first line works only when the form properties specify that the form is modal. The second line can be used to open any form in a modal window — providing that you put the correct form name in the quotes. The difference between the two is the last parameter. It is an optional parameter named `WindowMode` that specifies the window mode in which the form will open. IntelliSense prompts you through the process of writing the command line and shows the options as the cursor gets to each parameter. `WindowMode` has the options to use the Access keywords `acDialog`, `acHidden`, `acIcon`, and `acWindowNormal`, but only two apply to modal forms. `acWindowNormal` opens the form to whatever the form properties state as the default view and style. Stipulating `acDialog` overrides the property settings and opens the form in a modal window.

Control Wizards — Creating Command Buttons Using VBA or Macros

Control wizards provide a fast, easy process for adding controls, or command buttons, to a form. Wizards provide consistency and write the code. Right? Well, not necessarily anymore — at least as far as writing code. Access 2010 relies heavily on embedded macros. So, instead of code, the control wizards now generate macros when you are working with an ACE database (ACCDB) file. Be assured that the wizards support backward compatibility and will continue to create VBA code in MDB and ADP files. After you complete the wizard process, you can open the Property Sheet (see Figure 14-5) to see the embedded macro listed for the event. You can click the builder button [...] to the right of the property to view or edit the embedded macro. However, if instead of using the newly created macro, you choose something else from the drop-down list (such as Event Procedure), you cannot subsequently select the original embedded macro. The builder button allows you to select the Macro Builder, Expression Builder, or Code Builder. The drop-down list enables you to select Event Procedure or one of the previously created named macros.

If you choose to have the wizard create a macro, you still have the option to change the property from using an embedded macro to using an event procedure. One of the easiest ways to convert a macro to VBA code is to use Convert Form's Macros to Visual Basic found in the Tools group on the Design tab of the Form

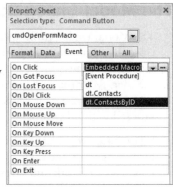

FIGURE 14-5

Design Tools Ribbon. Keep in mind that this process deletes the macro; however, it preserves the functionality by creating the appropriate VBA code.

 You also must be aware that if you merely use the control's Property Sheet to select Event Procedure from the drop-down list, it will erase the macro and leave your event procedure blank.

Command Button Properties

Beginning with Access 2007 several new command button properties are available, including two that provide fun features that are worth mentioning. Although they aren't specifically called out in the examples in the book, they are used in the sample databases for this chapter. I'm sure you'll want to use them as well:

`Cursor On Hover`: Enables your cursor to change to the hyperlink hand (little hand pointing a finger) when hovering over the button.

`Picture Caption Arrangement`: Enables you to add a caption with a picture and then arrange the caption — well, arrange within the limited options of No Picture Caption, General, Top, Bottom, Left, and Right.

And yes, `Picture Caption Arrangement` means that you can include a caption with an image on a command button. For example, navigation buttons might have Previous and Next juxtaposed with double arrows. As you'll see later, the command buttons that navigate through the attachments on a record in Figure 14-6 display both a caption and an image.

Each new version of Access offers more properties for each object. The following table describes a few of the properties related to the exciting new features for forms.

```
    Else
        Me.txtFileName.Value = Null
        Me.txtFileCount.Value = Null
        Me.txtFileType.Value = Null
    End If

End Sub
```

code snippet59166_ch14_CodeSnippets.txt Attachment Controls -- Displaying Values

With this code, you can now view the attachment filenames and file types (extension) as you browse through the attachments. Explicitly retrieving the file type may seem redundant because it typically shows up in the filename, but the purpose here is to demonstrate how to retrieve the information.

This example code starts by retrieving the values for the attachment only if the form is not displayed in Datasheet view (you already learned that lesson). You may have issues or unexpected results when trying to obtain these values from other form views, so the value is set to `Null` for other cases. When specifying the values, the left side of the equation identifies the text box that will display the value retrieved. The right side identifies the source of the data; in this case, it is looking at the control called `MyAttachment`. Because it's an attachment control, it has some special properties, including `FileName`, `FileType`, and `AttachmentCount`.

➤ `FileName`: The actual name of the file (`MyPicture.jpeg` will display as `MyPicture.jpeg`).

➤ `FileType`: This refers to file extension or type (JPEG, TXT, BMP, PDF).

➤ `AttachmentCount`: This is the number of attachments stored for that record.

The event `AttachmentCurrent` works similarly to the form's `OnCurrent` event in that it fires when the focus moves from one attachment to another. Within this event you can both extract information and specify the way that attachments will be represented. As the preceding code demonstrated, you can use the `AttachmentCount` property to list the number of attachments. Using this count in conjunction with the icon and image displays is helpful because they do not indicate the number of attachments. The attachment control uses an image and has the following three display options:

➤ `acDisplayAsIcon`: Displays the default icon for that file.

➤ `acDisplayAsImageIcon`: Displays icons for TXT files and the actual picture for JPEGs and BMPs.

➤ `acDisplayAsPaperclip`: The default setting. Although this does not indicate the file type, it is the only option that, by default, displays the `AttachmentCount`.

In the next example, an option group demonstrates the three different views to display the image. The option group is added to the form, and Figure 14-7 uses the `DisplayAsImageIcon` option in showing the same record and attachment shown in Figure 14-6.

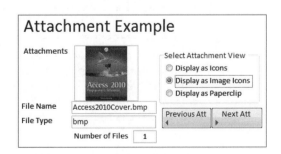

FIGURE 14-7

The following code allows the user to choose whether the attachment control will display as an icon, icon/image, or paper clip.

```
Private Sub grpAttachView_Click()
Dim OptSelect as Integer
OptSelect = Me.grpAttachView.Value
Select Case OptSelect
    Case 1
        With Me.MyAttachment
            .ControlTipText = "This option displays file Icons only."
            .DisplayAs = acDisplayAsIcon
            .Height = "450"
        End With
    Case 2
        With Me.MyAttachment
            .ControlTipText = "This option displays file Images and Icons."
            .DisplayAs = acDisplayAsImageIcon
            .Height = "1440"
        End With
    Case 3
        With Me.MyAttachment
            .ControlTipText = "This option displays files as a Paperclip."
            .DisplayAs = acDisplayAsPaperclip
        End With
End Select
End Sub
```

code snippet 59166_ch14_CodeSnippets.txt Changing Attachment Icon Type

For options `acDisplayAsIcon` and `acDisplayAsImageIcon`, you add the `Height` property and set it to `"450"` twips and `"1440"` twips (1 inch), respectively. Why specify the height? Because the default height for an attachment control that is set to `acDisplayAsPaperclip` is only 0.1667 inches. By specifying the height in code, the control can grow or shrink as appropriate for the display type.

 I don't know about you, but I certainly am not accustomed to calculating in twips. So, if you are trying to specify image heights, you may appreciate knowing that a twip is 1/1440 of an inch, which is the equivalent of 1/567 of a centimeter or 1/20 of a point.

 When using code to specify the height and width in twips, do not use commas because regional settings may cause the comma to be interpreted as a decimal point. Notice that the code uses 1440, not 1,440, and that the numbers are enclosed in double quotes.

While you are at it, you may also want to use the Property Sheet Format tab and change the Picture Size Mode to `Zoom` to preserve the image proportions. If you are concerned about space or presenting a compact look, you may also want to adjust the cell padding around images and icons. Figure 14-8 illustrates the effects of several of these settings.

The attachment control has its own pop-up menu for adding, removing, opening, saving, and moving through attachments. This little control is powerful because it works like the OpenFile dialog box but saves the collections of files within the record rather than in a separate table, streamlining the process of saving or attaching files to a record. However, with the built-in control, you must select working with none, one, or all attachments. Although the built-in selection dialog box allows for fully functional multi-select capability (using Shift-click and/or Control-click, it does not have an option to "select all" attachments.

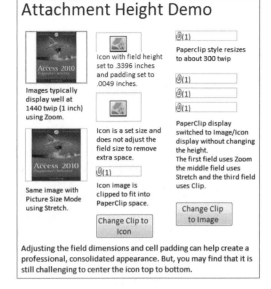

Attachment Height Demo

Images typically display well at 1440 twip (1 inch) using Zoom.

Same image with Picture Size Mode using Stretch.

Icon with field height set to .3396 inches and padding set to .0049 inches.

Icon is a set size and does not adjust the field size to remove extra space.

Icon image is clipped to fit into PaperClip space.

Change Clip to Icon

Paperclip style resizes to about 300 twip

PaperClip display switched to Image/Icon display without changing the height.
The first field uses Zoom the middle field uses Stretch and the third field uses Clip.

Change Clip to Image

Adjusting the field dimensions and cell padding can help create a professional, consolidated appearance. But, you may find that it is still challenging to center the icon top to bottom.

FIGURE 14-8

Combo Boxes

The combo box is a potent control that can combine the processes to search, select, and populate data into fields (or other objects), as well as limit the values that a user may enter. Many nuances affect how combo boxes work; this section addresses some of the more common ones. It also covers some new features added with Access 2007, including two properties: Allow Value List Edits and List Items Edit Form. Earlier versions of Access required extensive programming on the developer's part to provide the functionality of these new properties. They are real time savers.

The combo box and list box have a lot of the same properties and functionality. The primary difference is that the contents of the list box are always displayed on the form, so the list box takes more space. List box values are also limited to the list, which you can update programmatically by adding values to the row source, but not directly by the user. Combo boxes, on the other hand, generally use the space of a normal text box and employ a drop-down list to display the number of rows specified in the properties. You can set the row source to be updatable or to allow only existing values.

Before continuing, you should know the difference between control source and row source. The *control source* is specified if the value selected in the combo box will automatically (rather than programmatically) be stored in a field. The last question in the Combo Box Wizard, for instance, is about remembering or storing the selected value. If you choose to store the selected value in a field, that field becomes the control source. The *row source* provides the values that are displayed and used by the combo box. It can be a table, a query, a value list, or a field list. The row source value can even be an empty string when the form opens and then be set programmatically. For the most part, the row source consists of multiple columns with only one column visible to the user when the control does not have the focus. The other columns can be used to populate other fields or as the link to other record sources and are visible when the control has the focus and is expanded. For example, one column could be the field that links the current form to a subform. Again, referring to the wizard provides a quick demonstration of some of the properties related to the row source.

When you tell the Combo Box Wizard, for instance, that the combo box will look up values in a table or query, you are specifying the row source. The wizard then goes through the process of selecting the fields for the columns and allowing you to specify the column widths. The wizard automatically adds the primary key if one is available.

The other main element that you'll work with is controlling the values that the user can use or add. But first, you'll tackle an easy example of using a combo box to display existing data.

Combo Box as a Lookup

An excellent use for the combo box control is to display descriptive information for the user even though the data that's actually stored in the database is the value of some sort of key (primary or foreign). For example, you may have a form in which users allocate sales and you want the users to identify a department. If that form (or even just the combo box) is bound to a table that stores the Department ID rather than the name of the department, you don't want to force the user to remember or figure out which Department ID to enter. Instead, you can use a combo box to display a list of departments (field name `Department`) and let the form manage how the Department ID is stored. The following table lists the combo box settings for this scenario. You can also find an example of using a combo box as a lookup in `frmContactsComboLookUp` in this chapter's database file (available on Wrox.com) named `ComboBox.accdb`.

PROPERTY	VALUE
Control Source	Department (this is from the table Contacts)
Row Source	Select DepartmentID and Department from tblDepartment
Row Source Type	Table/Query
Bound Column	1
Limit To List	Yes
Allow Value List Edits	No
List Items Edit Form	No value (leave blank)
Column Count	2
Column Width	0";2"

Two of the properties that are crucial to selecting the value that will be stored in the database are `Bound Column` and `Column Width`. Setting `Bound Column` to 1 means the data for the field that will be stored in the database is in the first column of the `Row Source`. Setting the `Column Width` of the bound column to 0 means that the bound column will not be displayed in the combo box.

If you are familiar with coding combo boxes, you probably noticed the new Access 2010 Combo Box properties `Allow Value List Edits` and `List Items Edit Form`. These properties enable you to let users maintain their own set of valid values for the field without requiring you to write code. The following sections examine those properties.

As in prior versions of Access, if the `Limit To List` property is set to `No`, the user is allowed to type whatever he wants as many times as he wants. The combo box only helps the user select previously defined values without restricting him to only those values, and it allows the user to enter the same value multiple times and with myriad variations. When `Limit To List` is set to `Yes`, the user can select only the values in the list. However, if the user enters a value that isn't in the list, it can trigger a response depending on whether you've captured bad data entry using the `On Not In List` event and/or based on the settings for the `Allow Value List Edits` property along with the `List Items Edit Form` property. Be aware that the `On Not In List` event occurs before the settings of the other two properties are even considered.

It may seem as though this section is concentrating on just a few properties, but slight variations in how they are combined can have a big impact on results.

Auto Expand

By default, the `Auto Expand` property is set to `yes`. This is the behavior that you will want your users to experience. It allows them to type a few characters and the first matching item in the list will be displayed. This behavior is generally expected and very convenient.

Allow Value List Edits

The `Allow Value List Edits` property provides a simple way for you to allow the user to change the contents of the list without requiring the user to go into Design view to change the row source or you (the developer) to write code to change the row source. Keep in mind that this property is intended for combo boxes where the `Row Source Type` property is set to `Value List` — meaning that it is not designed to work with other row source types, so don't be tempted to misapply this feature.

If `Allow Value List Edits` is set to `No` and the user enters a value that isn't in the list, the user will see the standard Access message (see Figure 14-9) advising him to select an item from the list.

If `Allow Value List Edits` is set to `Yes` and the user enters a value that isn't in the list, the

FIGURE 14-9

user will see a message box that asks whether he wants to edit the items in the list, as shown in the left image in Figure 14-10. You'll also notice the extra question at the bottom of the message box, "Was this information helpful?" That message appears if the user has enabled "Help Improve Access." Responding to this query clears that message without closing the message box, as shown in the right image Figure 14-10.

FIGURE 14-10

If the user chooses Yes, to edit the list, the default Access Edit List Items form displays (see Figure 14-11). This default form is clearly designed to capture only a simple list of values, and it is intended to be used only when the combo box `Row Source Type` is set to `Value List`, `Inherit Value List` is set to `Yes`, and both the `Bound Column` and `Column Count` are set to `1`. Keep in mind that this form provides no means for you to control the values that the user might enter, so terms may be entered multiple times with different spellings. In Figure 14-11, you can see that Dance has been added to the list from the combo box labeled "`Value List With Edit:`" even though "Dancing" was already in the list. If you want more control over what the user enters for the list or if you want to provide a multicolumn list, you should set the `Row Source Type` to be `Table/Query` and use the `List Items Edit Form` property to specify a custom form (covered shortly).

FIGURE 14-11

One thing to note about using this approach to allow value list edits is that the `Row Source` property of the combo box is actually updated, which in turn causes Access to respond as if the design of the form has changed. Because of this, when the user closes the form that contains the (updated) combo box, Access displays a message box to ask whether the user wants to "…save changes to the design of the form [*form name*]." This is not a good message for users to see, so you may want to use the `DoCmd.Save acForm, Me.Name` statement to save the form in the `Form_AfterUpdate` event.

 When allowing value list edits by using the default Access `Edit Items List` form, ensuring that the `Row Source Type` is `Value List` and `Inherit Value List` is set to `Yes` is critical. This allows Access to properly handle the update. Even with these property configurations, users may get a warning and be asked whether they want to save changes to the design of the form. After all, a change to a value list behind a control is a change to the form's design.

List Items Edit Form

As mentioned earlier, the big advantages of the `Allow Value List Edits` property is that you don't have to write code in the `On Not In List` event to capture the new value, and it provides a method that allows the user to include the values he wants in the list. But please remember (and this is worth repeating) that the `Allow Value List Edits` property is intended only for combo boxes and list boxes with a `Row Source Type` of `Value List`. If you are using the `Row Source Type` of `Table/Query`, you can use the new `List Items Edit Form` property to display an alternate form that allows the user to edit the list.

First you must create a form that will maintain the data that is displayed from the `row source` of the combo box. Then you set the `List Items Edit Form` property to the name of that form. You could get a little fancy with your form by programmatically taking the invalid value that the user entered in the combo box and loading it into the appropriate field on your edit form. That kind of defeats the concept of using this new feature to avoid writing code, but then this book is about code and creating solutions that save time and prevent errors. Coming up is one example of using code to optimize use of a couple of the "no code required" features.

> *Because users can use the Navigation Pane, programmatically restricting the capability to open your edit forms, such as by using the* Is Loaded *event (see discussion later in this chapter) might be beneficial. After all, you don't want users to get an error message if they open a form from the Navigation Pane. (In the database for this section, EditValueList.accdb, the form frmMayorUpdate includes a method to prevent the form from being opened from the Navigation Pane.)*

This example uses a form called frmContactMayor with combo box cboCity, which uses a lookup table to capture the city for the contact, storing the data in the field named City in tblContacts. For this exercise, assume that the application needs to capture the mayor of every city. Basically, this means that if a user enters a new city, you want the application, through a form, to require him to enter the name of that city's mayor. To accomplish this, the example uses a table of mayors called tblMayors and a frmMayorUpdate form to update that table. You also want to think about creating an index on city/state and requiring it to have a unique value.

This example is provided in the chapter download file, EditValueList.accdb. To get the process started, you'll create (or modify) the combo box, cboCity, to have the key property values shown in the following table.

PROPERTY	VALUE
Control Source	City
Row Source	tblMayors
Row Source Type	Table/Query
Bound Column	2
Limit To List	Yes
Allow Value List Edits	Yes
List Items Edit Form	frmMayorUpdate
Column Count	2
Column Widths	0";2"

To ensure that the mayor's name is provided, the form should use one of the other techniques you've learned in this book. For instance, you could use the Form_BeforeUpdate event to see whether the mayor's name field has a value. The example uses Form_Open to check for the value.

Additionally, set the frmMayorUpdate form Pop Up property to Yes, set the Modal property to Yes, and set Cycle to Current Record (found on the Other tab of the Property Sheet). You do this so that the Form_Open code in the form frmMayorUpdate always executes. One reason for making this a modal form is to force the user to close the form before he can enter additional data in the frmContactMayor form (or before he can work with other objects, for that matter). If the user is allowed to leave frmMayorUpdate open while continuing to enter data on frmContactMayor, the next invalid entry in cboCity won't fire the Form_Open event in frmMayorUpdate.

At this point, you're about ready to put the following code in the Open event for frmMayorUpdate. Establish a constant to be used for the "calling form." That makes this snippet more portable. Instead of replacing the name of the calling form throughout the code, you merely change the value for the constant, cFormUsage.

```
Const cFormUsage = "frmContactMayor"
Private Sub Form_Open(Cancel As Integer)
Dim strText As String
Dim rs As Recordset

' Don't let this form be opened from the Navigator
If Not CurrentProject.AllForms(cFormUsage).IsLoaded Then
    MsgBox "This form cannot be opened from the Navigation Pane.", _
        vbInformation + vbOKOnly, "Invalid form usage"
    Cancel = True
    Exit Sub
End If

strText = Forms(cFormUsage)!cboCity.Text
If strText = "" Then
    ' If the City is empty, the user may have opened the form from the navigator
    ' while the other form is opened (thus it passed the above test)
    MsgBox "This form is intended to add Cities for the '" & i
Forms(cFormUsage).Caption & "' form.", _
        vbInformation + vbOKOnly, "Invalid form usage"
    Cancel = True
    Exit Sub
End If

' If you use the following syntax to insert the new value,
' make sure that the user hasn't entered an apostrophy (') in his text.
' Of course there are many ways to add the record
DoCmd.SetWarnings False
DoCmd.RunSQL "INSERT INTO tblMayors (City) VALUES ('" & strText & "')"
Me.Requery
DoCmd.SetWarnings True

' Now point to the row just added and set the filter so the user can't scroll
Set rs = Me.RecordsetClone
rs.FindFirst "City = '" & strText & "'"
If Not rs.EOF Then
    Me.Bookmark = rs.Bookmark
    Me.Filter = "[ID] = " & Me.ID
```

```
        Me.FilterOn = True
    End If

    Me.Mayor.SetFocus

    End Sub
```

After the user indicates that she wants to edit the items in the list, the process opens `frmMayorUpdate` because it is the form specified as the value for the `List Items Edit Form`. The `Form_Open` event looks at the `cboCity` field in `frmContactMayor` and stores the text of that field in `strText`. The code then inserts the city that doesn't have a value associated with the mayor's name into `tblMayors`. With the record inserted, the code makes a copy of the Recordset of the form, uses the `FindFirst` method to locate that record, and moves to it using the `Bookmark` property. Finally it sets the focus on the Mayor name field, so that entering the required data is easy for the user.

Of course, you could accomplish that with a lot less code, as shown in the following snippet:

```
    Private Sub Form_Open(Cancel As Integer)
    DoCmd.RunCommand acCmdRecordsGoToNew ' insert a new record
    Me.City = Forms("frmContactMayor")!cboCity.Text
    Me.txtMayor.SetFocus
    End Sub
```

This code simply goes to a new record on the form and copies the text from `cboCity` to the City field. An advantage of this method is that you can then define the Mayor name field in `tblMayors` as required and let Access determine whether the data entered by the user is valid. Then you don't need the `Form_BeforeUpdate` check to make sure the user entered something in the Mayor name field.

Now that you've worked through this example, take a moment to think about related business rules. This scenario has some obvious issues that would have to be addressed, such as the potential to have multiple cities with the same name, the opportunity for people to use different spellings of the same city, and the need to be able to rename a city or mayor. But it does provide a fairly elegant process to allow users to add values.

If you prefer to write code (and most developers do), another way exists to allow the users to update the list of valid values available in a combo box. It provides the means for you to validate the value and saves you from having to create another form. It's the `Not In List` event, which you look at next.

Not In List()

The `Not In List` event triggers when the `Limit To List` property is set to `Yes` and the user enters data that is not in the list. It occurs independently of the settings for `Allow Value List Edits` and `List Items Edit Form` properties, so you can use it to control how your application responds when invalid data is entered in a combo box.

Because combo boxes are usually based on a lookup table, the following example offers the user a chance to add a value that is not in the list. To provide a friendlier dialogue with the user, it also demonstrates how to create a custom message box such as the one shown in Figure 14-12. As you can see, the user tried to use "Entertainment" as the main category. Because it isn't in the list, he's asked if he would like to add it.

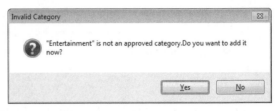

As a refresher, you can use the `Limit To List` property to control what happens when a user enters data into a control. If the value is set to `No`, it places no restrictions on what is entered. If the value is set to `Yes`, several things can be triggered, including the following:

FIGURE 14-12

➤ The user is limited to what is in the list.

➤ If other data is entered, users are asked to choose from the list.

Entering other data can trigger the `NotInList` event.

Because combo boxes are typically based on a lookup table, the following example provides code to offer the user a chance to add a value that is not in the list. It also creates a custom message box.

```
Private Sub cboMainCategory_NotInList(NewData As String, Response As Integer)
On Error GoTo Error_Handler
Dim intAnswer as Integer
intAnswer = MsgBox("""" & NewData & """ is not an approved category. " & vbcrlf _
      & "Do you want to add it now?", _
      vbYesNo + vbQuestion, "Invalid Category")

Select Case intAnswer
    Case vbYes
        DoCmd.SetWarnings False
        DoCmd.RunSQL "INSERT INTO tlkpCategoryNotInList (Category) " & _
            "Select """ & NewData & """;"
        DoCmd.SetWarnings True
        Response = acDataErrAdded
    Case vbNo
        Msgbox "Please select an item from the list.", _
            vbExclamation + vbOkOnly, "Invalid Entry"
        Response = acDataErrContinue
End Select
Exit_Procedure:
    DoCmd.SetWarnings True
    Exit Sub
Error_Handler:
    MsgBox Err.Number & ", " & Err.Description
    Resume Exit_Procedure
    Resume
End Sub
```

The `NotInList` event comes with two parameters:

➤ `NewData As String`: Holds the value that is not found in your list.

➤ `Response As Integer`: Provides three intrinsic constants:

➤ `acDataErrContinue`: Suppresses the standard error message.

➤ `acDataErrAdded`: Suppresses the standard error message, and refreshes the entries in the combo box.

➤ `acDataErrDisplay`: Displays the standard error message.

The `NotInList` event property is literally asking, "This value is not in your table, so what should I do?" The example starts by telling Access to display a message box notifying the user that the category is not in the list. You use the `vbYesNo` constant to provide buttons to get the user's answer and the `vbQuestion` constant to display the Question icon in the message box.

The user can choose Yes or No. If Yes (`vbYes`) is selected, the code adds the new value using the `INSERT INTO` SQL command that appends `NewData` to the specified lookup table. Because it is an append query, the standard append query warnings are triggered. `Docmd.SetWarnings False` turns off these warnings, and later you use `Docmd.SetWarnings True` to turn them back on.

Next, you need to set the `Response`, one of the intrinsic constants for the message box. If the user has responded Yes, `acDataErrAdded` automatically refreshes the combo box. If the user chooses No, `Response` is set to equal `acDataContinue`, which allows the user to continue without adding the item to the list. Either of those constants (responses) suppresses the default Access message. The point here is that by creating custom messages boxes you provide a more informative and professional user interface.

Field List

One of the values for `Row Source Type` that hasn't been mentioned yet is `Field List`. Setting the `Row Source Type` to `Field List` makes the values displayed in the combo box be the actual names of the fields (rather than the data contained in the field) found in the table or query specified in the row source. The `Field List` value is most commonly used when you're going to allow the user to select field names to build a custom filter. Of course, Access 2010 already provides some powerful ways to filter a form, so using these built-in methods may be a better alternative.

But if your form has several fields, a drop-down field finder might help users quickly get to the fields that they are looking for. To create such a tool, first add an unbound combo box to a form. In the combo box properties, set the `Row Source Type` to `Field List`. Then, in `Row Source`, enter the table or query that is used for your form. In the `AfterUpdate` event of the combo box use the following code:

```
Private Sub cboSearchFields_AfterUpdate()
    Dim strFieldChoice as String
    strFieldChoice = Me.cboSearchFields.Value

    DoCmd.GotoControl strFieldChoice

End Sub
```

The user can select the field from the combo box and be taken straight to that field. This code assumes that the `Name` property of the controls on your form are the same as the names of the fields in your `Row Source`. However, that probably isn't the case because you've implemented good naming conventions so the controls have prefixes such as `txt`, in which case you'll have to interpret the names. The following `Select Case` statement is an example of how to do that:

```
Private Sub cboSearchFields_AfterUpdate()
    Dim strFieldChoice as String
    strFieldChoice = Me.cboSearchFields.Value

    Select Case strFieldChoice
        Case "CustomerFirstName"
            strFieldChoice = "txtCustomerFName"
        Case "CustomerLastName"
            strFieldChoice = "txtCustomerLName"
    End Select

    DoCmd.GotoControl strFieldChoice

End sub
```

The user will see the easy-to-interpret term `CustomerFirstName` but the code in the `Select Case` statement switches the value to equal the actual `Name` property of the control: `txtCustomerFName`.

Synchronizing Two Combo Boxes Using AfterUpdate()

Synchronizing combo boxes (often called cascading combo boxes) has become rather popular. The value selected from the first combo box updates the second combo box so that it contains only records related to the item selected in the first combo box. In the following example (`ComboBox.accdb` in the chapter download), the row source of the first combo box (`cboMainCategory`) is set to `tlkpCategory` and the second combo box (`cboSubCategory`) needs the row source to display the values from `tlkpSubCategory` where the foreign key for each subcategory matches the values of the `MainCategoryID`. This is a common function when a one-to-many relationship exists between two tables. In other words, each main category can have many subcategories (as one sales rep has many customers) but only certain subcategories are valid for a given main category.

One way to synchronize the combo boxes is to add the following snippet of code to the `AfterUpdate` event of the first combo box (`cboMainCategory`):

```
Private Sub cboMainCategory_AfterUpdate()
' bind data to the second combo box based on the value selected
If IsNull(Me.cboMainCategory) Then
    Me.cboSubCategory.RowSource = ""
Else
    Me.cboSubCategory.RowSource = _
        "SELECT  SubCategoryID, SubCategoryName " _
        & "FROM tlkpSubCategory " _
        & "WHERE MainCategoryID = " & Me.cboMainCategory
End If
End Sub
```

Although the `row source` of `cboSubCategory` is changed dynamically, you can set the initial value of `cboSubCategory` to equal nothing. This ensures that the user cannot select a value from the second combo box unless he selects a value in the first combo box. If the user can scroll through records on the form, you'll also want to use this code in the form's `On Current` event to make sure that the row source of the second combo box is reset every time the record changes. For that, you use the following snippet:

```
Private Sub Form_Current()
' bind data to the second combo box based on the value selected
' leave second combo box empty if there is nothing in the first combo box
If IsNull(Me.cboMainCategory) Then
    Me.cboSubCategory.RowSource = ""
Else
    Me.cboSubCategory.RowSource = _
        "SELECT  SubCategoryID, SubCategoryName " _
        & "FROM tlkpSubCategory " _
        & "WHERE MainCategoryID = " & Me.cboMainCategory
End If
End Sub
```

Of course, you can add a myriad of other enhancements, such as having the drop-down lists display automatically. But for now, just focus on the functionality of synchronizing combo boxes. Figure 14-13 shows the property configuration for the second combo box, `cboSubCategory`.

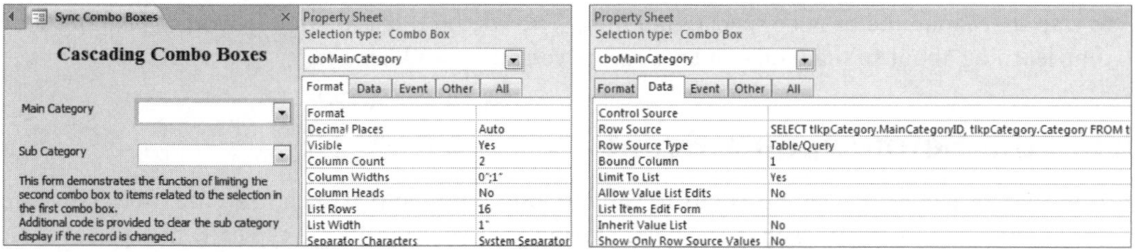

FIGURE 14-13

Although only the value of the subcategory is displayed, two fields are listed in the Row Source. And if you open the Row Source Query Builder, you will see that all three fields of the table, `tlkpSubCategory`, are included in the query. You can understand why including the foreign key from `tlkpCategory` is critical for the query because that is the field that links the two combo boxes and provides the filter for the second combo box list. Comparing the SQL statement for the row source to the query behind it is a good way to learn what makes this work so that you can apply the principles elsewhere. You can also use this example to demonstrate that the value for the Column Count can be based on the Select statement in the Row Source (two fields) or on the underlying query (three fields). The critical part is to ensure that the bound columns and column widths match the field configuration.

An alternative method for handling synchronized combo boxes is to code the row source of the second combo box to point to the value in the first combo box. If the name of the form with the combo boxes is `frmMain`, for example, instead of writing the preceding code, you could just make the Row Source of `cboSubCategory` the following:

```
Select SubCategoryID, SubCategoryName From tlkpSubCategories Where i
MainCategoryID = Forms!frmMain!cboMainCategory
```

One of the easiest ways to create that type of Select statement is to use the Query Builder for the Row Source. After you have the correct properties, the trick is to make sure that the `cboSubCategory` field is refreshed with the new set of valid values. A simple `Me.cboSubCategory.Requery` statement can work. For this example, you would put that code in the `cboMainCategory_AfterUpdate` event and also in the `Form_Current` event.

The downside to this alternative method is that if you rename `frmMain`, you must remember that you hard-coded the name in the `cboSubCategory` row source and that will have to be updated to the form's new name.

Regardless of the method, you can use cascading combo boxes for a multitude of purposes. This example was simple, and you can easily modify and incorporate it into complex scenarios. Remember that you can add additional rows to the row source and use them to auto-fill text boxes or as links to other objects. You can also display additional fields in the combo box to assist users in selecting the correct record. Keep in mind that the `List Width` can be wider than the control width, so you have ample room to briefly display data.

Combo boxes are a great way to help speed up the data entry processes for your user. In Access 2010, `Allow Value List Edits` and `List Items Edit Form` enable you to eliminate some of the code that was used to capture data-entry errors. Of course, you can still use the `Not In List` event to trap user input and provide special handling. The combo box is definitely worth spending some time learning about so that you can leverage its versatility and benefits.

Using the BeforeUpdate Event

You can use the `BeforeUpdate` events to validate user input, and as such, they are used most often on the form or record rather than the field. During data entry, users are typically allowed to fill in all the information for one record before they are prompted to resolve erroneous or missing information. But that's not always the case, so this section explains both approaches.

The choice between using the `Form_BeforeUpdate` event or the `field_BeforeUpdate` event is often based on the type of validation that's needed. In general, you use the `field_BeforeUpdate` event for required data or when the field value does not depend on other values that are entered on the form. The following code example shows a test for `FieldOne`, a required field.

Available for download on Wrox.com

```
Private Sub FieldOne_BeforeUpdate(Cancel as Integer)
If Trim(FieldOne.Value & "") = "" Then
    MsgBox "You must provide data for field 'FieldOne´.", _
        vbOKOnly, "Required Field"
    Cancel = True
End If

End Sub
```

code snippet code 59166_ch14_CodeSnippets.txt Before Update Event

The `cancel = True` statement prevents the user from exiting the control until a value has been entered. Using the `Trim` function while appending an empty string to the control's value, and testing it against an empty string, prevents the user from trying to leave the control empty or simply pressing the spacebar.

You want to use the `Form_BeforeUpdate` event if your form is structured in such a manner that valid values for one field depend on the value entered in another field. The following code snippet shows a case where the value in `FieldTwo` is required only when a value is entered in `FieldOne`. You'll recognize that this code does not address any aspects of preventing input unless a criterion is met. That is a different business rule — one that is often handled by enabling and disabling controls.

Available for download on Wrox.com

```
Private Sub Form_BeforeUpdate(Cancel As Integer)
If (IsNull(Me.FieldOne)) Or (Me.FieldOne.Value =  "") Then
    ' No action required
Else
    If (IsNull(Me.FieldTwo)) or (Me.FieldTwo.Value = "") Then
        MsgBox "You must provide data for field 'FieldTwo´, " & _
            "if a value is entered in FieldOne", _
            vbOKOnly, "Required Field"
        Me.FieldTwo.SetFocus
        Cancel = True
        Exit Sub
    End If
End If

End Sub
```

code snippet code 59166_ch14_CodeSnippets.txt Before Update Event

Because the user may have been on a field other than `FieldTwo` when she attempted to leave or save the record, `SetFocus` is used to move the cursor to the field that has the error. The `Cancel = True` statement prevents the record from being saved. Otherwise, the user may get multiple error messages and be able to address only the last message displayed. The `Exit Sub` statement isn't essential, but it's a good coding technique to include the `Exit Sub` statement at any point where you are reporting an error. And, in many cases, you may come back to this code to add another validation check.

So, your choice of `Form_BeforeUpdate` versus `field_BeforeUpdate` depends on the type of validation performed. Use the `field_BeforeUpdate` when you want to give the user immediate feedback about invalid data. Use the `Form_BeforeUpdate` when you have to perform cross-field validation checks.

The next example uses the `On Click` event of a command button. You need a simple form for data entry. On the Property Sheet, set the form's properties as shown in the following table.

PROPERTY	VALUE
Allow Data-Entry	Yes
Allow Edits	No
Allow Deletions	No

Make sure that the command button is the last control in the tab order, just before navigating to the next new record. Now add the following snippet of code to the command button's `On Click` event:

```
Private Sub cmdCloseForm_Click()

Dim intAnswer As Integer
intAnswer = MsgBox("Do you want to save this record?", _
    vbYesNo + vbQuestion, "Save or Cancel"

Select Case intAnswer
    Case vbYes ' run through the validation
        If (IsNull(Me.FieldOne)) or (Me.FieldOne.Value = "") Then
            MsgBox "You must provide data for field "FieldOne".", _
                vbOKOnly, "Required Field"
            ' direct user to empty field and exit sub
            Me.FieldOne.SetFocus
            Exit Sub
        End If

        If (IsNull(Me.FieldTwo.Value)) or (Me.FieldTwo.Value = "") Then
            MsgBox "You must provide data for field 'FieldTwo´.", _
                vbOKOnly, "Required Field"
            Me.FieldTwo.SetFocus
            Exit Sub
        End If

    Case vbNo ' give user a way out.
            Me.Undo
End Select

DoCmd.Close acForm, Me.Name

End sub
```

code snippet code 59166_ch14_CodeSnippets.txt Private Sub cmdCloseForm_Click()

This is similar to the `Form_BeforeUpdate` example. In this case, when the user clicks the `Close` button, he is asked whether he wants to save the record. If he selects Yes, the code runs through the steps in the `Select Case` process and stops the form's `Close` operation only if a field is empty. In that case, the focus is set to the field in error and the code exits the procedure (`Exit Sub`). If the user selects No, the changes to the record are undone using `Me.Undo` so that no changes are saved. If the process makes it successfully through the `Select Case` checks or if the changes are undone, the form closes as expected. Keep in mind that if a method other than this `Close` button is used to close the form, this validation process will not occur. Of course, you could institute processes to cover contingencies.

One more point about testing for data in the field: The examples use `IsNull`, and a test for the empty string, and trimming and concatenating the empty string. Because Access trims spaces off of data entered on the form, you're not required to test for a single space entered in a field. The code used in the `field_BeforeUpdate` example is just a technique used to simplify validations as well as ensure that Access behaves the way you expect it to.

Saving E-mail Addresses Using the Textbox AfterUpdate Event

Access 2010 is smarter about the way it stores website and e-mail addresses than prior versions. Data in a hyperlink field is automatically evaluated and tagged. The value is tagged with `http` for websites or `mailto` for e-mail addresses.

In previous versions, the Hyperlink data type stored e-mail addresses as Web addresses (`http://customeremail@msn.com`, for example), so when you clicked the link, it opened Internet Explorer and tried to find the website — not at all helpful. (One way to fix this is to right-click the link, select Edit Hyperlink, and change `http` to `mailto` by selecting e-mail Address in the dialog box. Be sure to copy the e-mail address first because you have to add it again.)

However, you want the user to add an e-mail address and have it correctly stored so that she can later click the link and open a new e-mail message. The following code ensures that the initial input is stored in the correct format. You can try it with a simple form to add customers and e-mail addresses; add this code to the `AfterUpdate` event of the `EmailAddress` field, `txtEmailAddress`.

```
Private Sub txtEmailAddress_AfterUpdate()

If Not IsNull(Me.EmailAddress) Then
    Me.EmailAddress = Replace(Me.EmailAddress, "http://", "mailto:")
End if

End Sub
```

The first line checks to see whether an e-mail address exists. If data is in the e-mail address field, it uses the `Replace` function to replace `http` with `mailto`. The code makes this change on-the-fly without the user even knowing.

This works great for sending e-mail to only one person. What if you need to s‾ ' one e-mail to many people? Assume there is a Contacts table and that e-mail address‾   ‾ed in a field with a Text data type rather than as a hyperlink. On your form, you can add a list box named `lstContacts`, as shown in Figure 14-14.

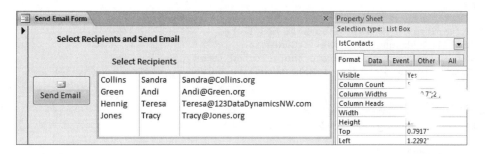

FIGURE 14-14

The list box `RowSource` would equal `tblContacts`, so the column count and column width need to be set to display the first name, last name, and e-mail address for each record. You need to set the list box property named `Multi Select` (on the Property Sheet's Other tab), which has three options:

➤   `None`: Select one item at a time from the list.

➤   `Simple`: Select blocks of items from the list by selecting one item and then holding down the Shift key while highlighting the other items.

➤   `Extended`: Select multiple items by holding down the Ctrl key and then randomly selecting items.

For this example, use `Extended`.

Next, you need a command button named `cmdSendEMail`. Add the following code to its `On Click` event.

```
Private Sub cmdSendEMail_Click()

Dim emName As String, varItem As Variant
Dim emailSubject as String
Dim emailBody as String

emailSubject = "Confirmation Email"
'note the carriage return line feeds to insert a blank line between
'the greeting and the message body. Also, there is no need for the
' & at the beginning of the second and third lines because we used a
' comma after the greeting - just before the close quote on the first line.

emailBody = "Dear Customer, " & vbCrLf & vbCrLf & _
    "We are sending this email to let you know that your request has been " & _
    "confirmed. Please allow 2-3 weeks for shipping."

On Error GoTo cmdSendEMail_Click_error

'if there are no selected items (Contacts) in the list, exit
If Me!lstContacts.ItemsSelected.Count = 0 Then
Exit Sub

For Each varItem In Me!lstContacts.ItemsSelected
    'char(34) adds quotes to Me!lstContacts.
    'Then add a comma to separate the selected items
    emName = emName & Chr(34) & Me!lstContacts.Column(4, varItem) & Chr(34) & ","
Next varItem

'remove the extra comma at the end
emName = Left$( emName, Len(emName) - 1)

'send the message
DoCmd.SendObject acSendNoObject, , , emName, , , emailSubject, emailBody, _
    True, False

cmdSendEMail_Click_error:
    If Err.Number = 2501 Then
        MsgBox "You just cancelled the Email. You'll have to start over.", _
            vbCritical, "Alert!"
```

```
    ElseIf Err.Number > 0 then
        Msgbox "Error sending email." & vbCrlf & Err.Description, _
            vbCritical, "Send Error"
    End If

End Sub
```

This code starts by declaring the e-mail name (emName), subject of the e-mail (emailSubject), and the e-mail body (emailBody) as String, and a variable to use the items in the list as Variant (varItem). Next, it initializes the subject and body variables with string text. The first If statement checks the count of the number of selected items in the list, and if the count is zero, exits the routine.

The For Each loop processes each of the items the user has selected. Because Multi Select is set to Extended, the user can use the Ctrl or Shift keys with the mouse click to select items in sequence or randomly.

With tblContacts as the list box's Row Source, each field defined in tblContacts becomes a column in the list box. You can use the Column property to access the value of each column in the list box. (This applies to multicolumn combo boxes as well.)

> *As with most arrays in VBA, the index for the* Column *property starts at zero; thus, the first field in* tblContacts *is the 0 column in the list box. In this example, the e-mail address is the fifth field defined in* tblContacts*, so in code this would be referred to as* .Column(4).

When building emName, a comma separator is added for each selected item in the list box. That leaves you with an extra comma that you have to strip off after all the e-mail addresses have been collected.

With all the items collected, use DoCmd.SendObject with the following arguments to create the e-mail:

```
DoCmd.SendObject acSendNoObject, , , emName, , , emailSubject, emailBody, _
    True, False
```

Selecting acSendNoObject means that the e-mail will not have an attachment because no object (form/report) exists to send. After that, the commas are the place markers for the following nine arguments:

```
[ObjectName], [OutputFormat], [To], [Cc], [Bcc], [Subject], [Message], _
[EditMessage], [TemplateFile]
```

As in the example, [ObjectName] and [OutputFormat] can be left blank; [To] will be emName (the selected items from the list box); [Cc] and [Bcc] can be left blank; [Subject] will be the emailSubject variable; [Message] will be emailBody; [EditMessage] is True just in case you need to edit the message; and [TemplateFile] is False.

Your users now have the option to send an e-mail to one contact or many contacts by simply selecting the recipient(s) from the list box. Figure 14-15 shows an e-mail created by this example.

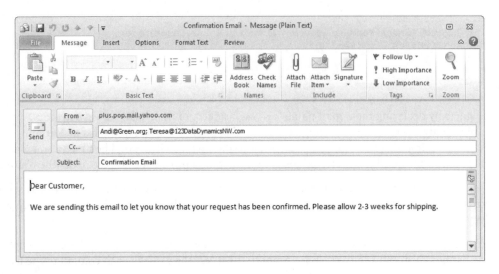

FIGURE 14-15

You'll recall that this example uses an e-mail address from a text field. That is an important distinction because if you use it with a Hyperlink field type, the address line will look something like the following:

```
TO: Teresa@DataDynamicsNW.com#mailto:Teresa@DataDynamicsNW.com#
```

Most mail clients interpret this as one long string, and won't treat it as a valid e-mail address. You can overcome this by processing the hyperlink e-mail address using the following syntax in a calculated field in a query:

```
Left(Replace(CStr([EmailHyperLink]),"mailto:",""),InStr _
(Replace(CStr([EmailHyperLink]),"mailto:",""),"#")-1)
```

This precludes the need for keeping an e-mail address in two different fields — one text and one hyperlink. Simply use the hyperlink field and convert it to text when you need to perform VBA operations against it.

Outputting to PDF

A common challenge for Access developers has been to have a way to send data or output to a PDF file format. Sure, you could do it, but it wasn't easy. Previous versions required the developer to obtain some third-party software (CutePDF, for example) and then to build creative workarounds.

Now Access 2010 has streamlined the process by providing the bridge between Access and PDF utilities, particularly if you download Microsoft's free add-in "Microsoft Save as PDF or XPS." Instead of working with complicated code, you'll have a Save As PDF button on the Ribbon. Along with PDF, you probably discerned that this add-in also offers the option to save in XML Paper Specification (XPS) file format. To take advantage of this, you need to download and install the SaveAsPDFandXPS.exe file. A link to the Web is provided in the Access Help files. You can find it by typing **XPS** or **PDF** in the Search text box or by going to Microsoft.com and searching for `SaveAsPDFandXPS.exe`.

People will still need a PDF viewer to open PDF files. But viewers are commonly available as free downloads, such as the Adobe Reader. Windows Vista or higher is required to view XPS files, but here again, a viewer may become available.

To work with PDF and XPS file formats programmatically, Access has two constants. They are named in the following table.

FILE TYPE	CONSTANT
PDF	acFormatPDF
XPS	acFormatXPS

To see all the constants, open the Object Browser and search for `acFormat`.

Both `DoCmd.SendObject` and `DoCmd.OutputTo` use these constants in their arguments to define the format. The following code snippets show three different ways to use the PDF file format. Minor differences exist in the functionality. For example, notice that using `OutputTo` allows you to specify the export quality.

Available for download on Wrox.com

```
DoCmd.SendObject acSendReport, "MyReportName", acFormatPDF, [To], [Cc], [Bcc], _
    [Subject], [MessageText]

Docmd.OutputTo acOutputReport, _
    "MyReportName", acFormatPDF, , False, , , acExportQualityScreen

Docmd.OutputTo acOutputReport, _
    "MyReportName", acFormatPDF, , False, , , acExportQualityPrint
```

code snippet code 59166_ch14_CodeSnippets.txt Output To PDF

OpenArgs

What if you want to check for conditions or set certain properties when a form is opening? You can use the `OpenArgs` property of the form to pass parameters to the form when you open it. The `OpenForm` method's seventh (last) parameter supplies the value for `OpenArgs`, as shown in the following statement:

```
DoCmd.OpenForm "FormName", , , , , , "OpenArgs value"
```

In this case, the value of the `OpenArgs` property would be `"OpenArgs value"`.

Because the `Open` event triggers whenever a form opens, you can include the `OpenArgs` parameter on the `OpenForm` method to provide information that can be used even before the user sees the form.

An excellent application of this feature is to ensure that the form is opened by code and only under specific conditions. For example, you may have a form that should be opened only by certain users.

Because users can open the form from the Navigation Pane, opening a form is possible for any user — unless you have implemented programmatic restriction. One approach is to use the following code in the form's OnOpen event to prevent it from being opened from the Navigation Pane.

```
Private Sub Form_Open(Cancel As Integer)

If Me.OpenArgs() <> "Valid User" Then
    MsgBox "You are not authorized to use this form!", _
        vbExclamation + vbOKOnly, "Invalid Access"
    Cancel = True
End If
End Sub
```

code snippet code 59166_ch14_CodeSnippets.txt OPENARGS

If a user opens this form from the Navigation Pane, he will see the message, You are not authorized to use this form! The Cancel = True statement prevents the form from opening.

For a user to gain access to this form you must have code in your application that, after the user has been approved, allows the form to open. For example, a form named frmRestricted would need your code to execute the following statement (be sure to specify other parameters as appropriate):

```
DoCmd.OpenForm "frmRestricted", , , , , , "Valid User"
```

Another time to use OpenArgs might be when you automatically populate information in the form you're opening. Suppose you have a combo box that requires the user to select a valid value. If the user enters an undefined value, you may want to pop up a form to collect information about the value just entered — you might want to pass the text that the user entered to the form that you're opening so it is populated in the appropriate field on the pop-up form. Clearly you can utilize the OpenArgs property for a variety of purposes.

 You may prefer the new List Items Edit Form *property, discussed earlier in the chapter, overwriting your own code to pop up a form to collect a new value for the combo box.*

Be aware that after the form is opened, the value of OpenArgs does not change on subsequent executions of the OpenForm method. For that reason, you may want to check to see whether the form is open before you execute OpenForm. The form's IsLoaded property can tell you whether a form is already open.

IsLoaded()

Numerous situations exist in which you might want to know whether a form is open, or loaded. The following scenario helps illustrate when and why to use the IsLoaded property. In this situation, a user may have several forms open, including frmEvent, which lists the names of everyone scheduled to participate in an event. Say that one of the participants cancels, so the user opens a participant form and clicks a command button (cmdCancel) to remove that participant from the event. Because the event form is already open, the data that it displays cannot be updated without some action being taken. One approach is to include code behind cmdCancel on the participant form to see whether the event schedule form is open by using the IsLoaded property. If the form, frmEvent, is not open, the regular cancellation process continues. If frmEvent is open, the appropriate actions — such as closing the event schedule form or requerying the event form after canceling the appointment — should also be included in the code behind cmdCancel. The following snippet is an example of code that you could use in this scenario.

Available for download on Wrox.com

```
If frmEvent.IsLoaded Then
    frmEvent.Requery   ... 'add additional actions

End If
```

code snippet code 59166_ch14_CodeSnippets.txt ISLOADED()

Consider another example: Perhaps you want users to be able to open a form in a specific way, such as only from a specified form, and definitely not from the Navigation Pane. In that case, you may also first want to determine whether the form is already open. The following example uses the IsLoaded property to see whether a particular form is open before it continues code execution. In the code, CurrentProject refers to the open database and for illustration purposes, frmEvent is used again:

Available for download on Wrox.com

```
Private Sub cmdCancel_Click()
    If Not CurrentProject.AllForms("frmEvent").IsLoaded Then

        Msgbox "Cannot cancel while 'frmEvent´ form is open.", _
            vbInformation + VBOkOnly, "Cancel Invalid"
        Exit Sub

    End If
End Sub
```

code snippet code 59166_ch14_CodeSnippets.txt Example using ISLOADED()

As you can see, the IsLoaded property is a convenient and useful way to determine whether a form is open.

On Timer ()

The On Timer event property can identify a process that can be triggered at timed intervals. It is used in conjunction with the TimerInterval property, which stipulates the frequency of the event trigger. When specifying the value for the TimerInterval property, the time is entered in milliseconds (1/1000 of a second), so entering 5000 will trigger the event at five-second intervals.

You may be wondering when you might use a timer. How about to close an application's splash screen (a form that displays for a few seconds as the application opens and then is automatically closed) or to close a message that you only want to display for a few seconds? For instance, you could display your company logo and contact number during the few seconds that it takes for an application to start. Of course, you don't want to leave the splash screen open for too long — four seconds seems like a reasonable time. Assume that the application has an AutoExec macro that runs when the database opens and that one of the actions includes a macro to open the splash screen.

To set the timer for any form, open the form's Property Sheet to the Event tab. Scroll down to `Timer Interval`. The property default is 0; for this example, you change it to 4000, the equivalent of four seconds. Then in the `OnTimer` property, select `Event Procedure` and open the IDE to add the following code.

```
Private Sub Form_Timer()

    DoCmd.Close acForm, Me.Name

End Sub
```

code snippet code 59166_ch14_CodeSnippets.txt ON TIMER()

When the splash screen (your form) opens, the `Timer Interval` starts counting down. When the timer reaches the specified interval time, four seconds, the code runs. In this event, `DoCmd.Close` closes the splash screen. This scenario has worked well in the past, but it can cause problems if the database is opened in disabled mode by Access 2010. If the VBA is disabled, the timer event code never runs and the splash screen is not closed. To avoid risking that situation, you can close a splash screen by using a macro for the `OnTimer` event. (One of the reasons that I mention this is because you may work with MDB files that use VBA to close a splash screen. If so, you need to either replace the code or ensure that the databases are opened fully enabled, from a trusted location, and/or are digitally signed. You will find information about these topics in Chapter 25.)

To create the macro to close the splash screen, set the `OnTimer` property to a macro by clicking the ellipsis and selecting the `Macro Builder`. In the Action column, select `Close`; the lower pane displays the `Action Arguments`. For the `Object Type`, select `Form`; from the `Object Name` list, select the form that is used as the splash screen; and for `Save`, select `No`. From the Close group on the menu bar, select `Save As`, on the first line enter a name for the macro, and then click OK.

Another example of using the `OnTimer` event is in a multi-user environment where the users are recording meetings and setting scheduled times for the clients of the Sales staff. Obviously, knowing when salespeople are available and not booking them twice for the same time period is crucial. Because several people have the potential to be booking appointments at the same time, the form that displays and records the appointments needs to be requeried constantly. For this situation, the form's `Timer Interval` is set to six seconds (6000) and the form's `Timer` event contains the following code:

```
Private Sub Form_Timer()

Me.Requery

End Sub
```

code snippet code 59166_ch14_CodeSnippets.txt On Timer() Example #2

This code allows the form to update on its own rather than requiring the user to click an update button. Because you need to get additions and deletions, the form uses Requery instead of Refresh, which would retrieve only changes to existing records. The main form consistently displays the appointment time blocks, and the subform uses a continuous form to show the number of available openings for each wave for every scheduled date. The Timer event runs a query to refresh the data for the subform. When an appointment is booked, the number for the respective date and wave is decreased. And, thanks to the Timer event, the display will be updated for any user who has the schedule form open. To see the details for any day, users merely double-click the record selector to open the appointment schedule to review or change an appointment.

Keep in mind that the Timer event can create a significant performance hit. Also, if users are manually entering data, likely better alternatives exist — two seconds wouldn't be adequate for data entry. However, in situations where you are merely displaying information, such as the number of appointments or openings in a time slot, then a short timer interval can be an effective mechanism to update data in open forms.

Late Binding

Another timing issue that can have significant impact on performance is whether the form is using early or late binding. Basically, this refers to when the record (or Recordset) is created for a form or other object. Late binding typically involves filtering, which reduces the size of the Recordset and also allows the developer greater control of the record source.

When you add fields to your form, the text boxes that are created become bound text box controls. That is, the table or query fields are bound to those text box controls and when the form opens, the data from your table or query binds to the controls on your form to display data. If the form has only a few controls or is a lightweight form, you might not notice a performance hit when the form loads. But loading all the possible records behind a complex form that has numerous controls, combo boxes, subforms, and complicated criteria can create a drastic slowdown.

One option is to load the controls on demand or after receiving criteria to filter the data rather than when the form opens. The following code snippet uses the Form_Open event to set the RowSource and SourceObjects of a combo box, list box, and subform to an empty string (" "). Obviously, if the intent is for these to be unbound objects, saving the form without record sources for those controls is better. But a form may inadvertently have been saved with values stored for the controls, so the following example demonstrates how to remove the values. Speaking of saving the form, a technique commonly used with subforms is to save the SourceObject as an empty string to prevent the subform from attempting to acquire data as the form opens.

Available for download on Wrox.com

```
Private Sub Form_Open()
Me.cboMyComboBox.RowSource = ""
'Or
Me.lstMyListbox.RowSource = ""
'Or
Me.fsubMySubform.SourceObject = ""
End sub
```

code snippet code 59166_ch14_CodeSnippets.txt Late Binding

After the form opens, you need a way to fill the RowSource. Common techniques are to initiate the process from a command button or by selecting a value from a combo box or list box.

Another method is to use the option group control to load data to other controls. The option group contains controls that include radio buttons, check boxes, and toggle buttons. Each radio button, check box, or toggle button (depending on the type of option box controls you chose) can be assigned a value that is set whenever that control is selected. You can use that numeric value in a Select Case statement to populate the list box or subform.

In the next example, you populate the list box with a list of forms and reports in your database by selecting a numeric value from the option group. You can use the lists for several purposes, even as the basis for a switch-board (menu form), as shown in Figure 14-16. To get started, you need a table to hold the names of the forms and reports that are in the database. Some developers use the hidden system tables that store the object names. Although that's functional, it isn't pretty because they return the actual object names, which the user might not recognize. Providing the user with concise yet descriptive names rather than having them decipher terms that start with tags such as frm or rpt is much better.

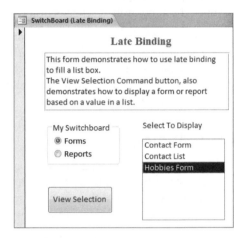

FIGURE 14-16

So, create the table tblMyObjects with the following fields:

➤ userObjectName: The name of the form or report that the user will see.

➤ devObjectName: The actual name of the form or report.

➤ devObjectCode: The code number (created by you) assigned to that object. For this example, 1 = forms and 2 = reports.

Your table should resemble the one used in the query shown in Figure 14-16. Then, you need to populate the table with data. (That will be a manual process, unless you just want to follow along using the LateBinding.accdb file that's included with the download for this chapter.)

Next, create two queries using all the fields in tblMyObjects. Name the first query qryFormName, where devObjectCode = 1, and name the other query qryReportName, where devObjectCode = 2. Based on those criteria, qryFormName will retrieve all the forms and qryReportName will retrieve all the reports. Because the first row contains the ID field, you must clear the Show check box so that userObjectName is the first visible field. To display the names alphabetically, set the Sort order for this field to be Ascending. Each query has the same four fields; the critical differences are the name of the query and the criteria. Because these queries are the foundation for several more steps, confirming that your query looks similar to the example in Figure 14-17 might be prudent.

You'll use these queries to populate a list box to display forms and reports that a user might want to use. Although the queries use all four fields, only the userObjectName field will be displayed. You use the devObjectCode for selecting the items and the devObjectName to programmatically open the object. You'll start the process by creating an unbound form named frmSwitchboard with an option group and a list box. (Figure 14-16, shown earlier, showed the switchboard form with the option group named grpSwitchboard labeled My Switchboard and the list box displaying user-friendly names of selected forms.)

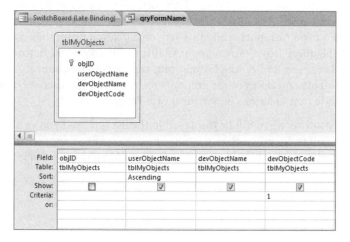

FIGURE 14-17

Begin by adding an option group to the form. The Option Group Wizard prompts for label names. On the first line type **Forms** and on the second line type **Reports**. Next, select Forms as the default option. You then can assign values that match the criteria from the queries that you created: Assign Forms a value of 1 and Reports a value of 2. You'll use these values to write code for the option group's AfterUpdate event. You can create additional buttons for other types of actions, or create custom groups of forms and reports, such as by department. The final question from the wizard is what to name the caption for the group. Name it **My Switchboard**.

Now, open the control's Property Sheet and change the name from frame0 to grpSwitchboard. You need to add code to the AfterUpdate event, but first create an unbound list box that the code will populate. So, add a list box to the form but close the wizard without answering any questions. That creates an unbound list box. Use the Property Sheet to rename this lstItems and to add the following code to the grpSwitchboard AfterUdpate event.

Available for download on Wrox.com

```
Private Sub grpSwitchboard_AfterUpdate()
Dim strRST as String        'RowSourceType
strRST = "Table/Query"
Me.lstItems.RowSourceType = strRST

Select Case Me.grpSwitchboard.Value
    Case 1
        Me.lstItems.RowSource = "qryFormName"
    Case 2
        Me.lstItems.RowSource = "qryReportName"

End Select

End Sub
```

code snippet code 59166_ch14_CodeSnippets.txt Switchboard Form

This code sets the row source type to Table/Query for the list box `lstItems`, which enables you to use queries to populate the display. If `grpSwitchboard` has value 1 selected, the results from `qryFormName` are shown. If the value 2 is selected, the data from `qryReportName` is displayed. If you add additional objects or options, they need similar code. This method is great for viewing a list of forms or reports, but it lacks the capability to open them as you would from a switchboard. Before having the capability to open a form or report, you must set some column properties on the list box so that the values from the query (row source) are available to the command button. Again, open the Property Sheet for `lstItems` and on the Format tab, set the column count to 3 and the column widths to `1";0";0"`. This correlates to the columns for the name the user sees, the actual name of the object, and the code that identifies it as a form or a report.

Now, you have an option group that controls what will be displayed in the list box, and you've also stipulated that the default is to select Forms. So now, when `frmSwitchboard` opens, it appears that Forms are selected, but nothing is listed in the list box. You rectify that by adding the following code to the form's `Open` event.

```
Private Sub Form_Open(Cancel As Integer)
 'When the form opens, load the list box with information
 'based on the default option group selection.
Call grpSwitchboard_AfterUpdate
End Sub
```

code snippet code 59166_ch14_CodeSnippets.txt Switchboard Form Example #2

Finally, you add functionality to open a form or report by creating a command button that will open whichever object is selected. Add the command button to the form and close the wizard without answering any questions (because this will open both forms and reports, you'll write your own code). Use the Property Sheet to rename it `cmdOpenObject`. For the `On Click` event of `cmdOpenObject`, add the following code:

```
Private Sub cmdOpenObject_Click()
Dim varCode as Variant
Dim varObjName as Variant

' Make sure that an item is selected before attempting to display it.
If Me.lstItems.ItemsSelected.Count = 0 Then
    MsgBox "Please select items to display.", vbInformation + vbOKOnly, _
        "List Items Required."
    Exit Sub
End If

varCode = Me.lstItems.Column(2)
varObjName = Me.lstItems.Column(1)

Select Case varCode
    Case 1 'open the form
        DoCmd.OpenForm varObjName
    Case 2 'open the report in preview mode
```

```
        DoCmd.OpenReport varObjName, acPreview
    End Select

    End Sub
```

---

code snippet code 59166_ch14_CodeSnippets.txt Switchboard Form Example #3

The process is predicated on an item being selected from the list, so this code starts with the IF statement and message box. After the item is selected, you can extract the data necessary to display a form or report. To do that, start by declaring two variables — one for the devObjectCode (varCode) field and one for the devObjectName (varObjName) field (the actual name of the object). After setting those variables, you evaluate varCode with a Select Case statement and use DoCmd to open a form or report using the name from the varObjName variable. In keeping with standard Windows practice you may want to also launch the form or report by allowing the user to double-click the form or report name. To do this, add the following code to the list box control's On Dbl Click event:

```
Private Sub lstItems_DblClick(Cancel As Integer)
    Call cmdOpenObject_Click
End Sub
```

You would also want to include additional error trapping, such as for reports with no data. Figure 14-18 shows the form in Design view with the lstItems Property Sheet open. (This chapter's download code includes this example, LateBinding.accdb.)

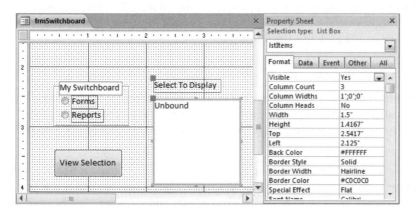

FIGURE 14-18

On Click(): Open a Form Based on a Value on the Current Form

Opening a form based on a value stored on another form is a common practice. The functionality applies to a myriad of tasks, from listing all the orders for one customer to gaining a bigger picture by comparing the total purchases of one customer to other customers in the region. It also works well for drilling into details, such as searching a contact list and then clicking a record to see the detail information about that person.

For this example, you drill into data to get information about the orders of one customer. You'll use two forms, `frmCustomer` and `frmOrder`, which display information about customers and orders, respectively. You may want to use the Northwind database to work through this exercise. For now, just say that you already have the two forms, so you just need a way to integrate their operations. All it takes is a command button (`cmdShowOrders`) on `frmCustomer` and some VBA code.

The pieces that must be tied together are the field names that correspond between `frmCustomer` and `frmOrder`. Typically, the table for each of these entities contains the field called `CustomerID` with an AutoNumber data type. You also need the name of the control that is bound to the `CustomerID` field on `frmCustomer`; in this case, that's called `txtCustomerID`. On `frmCustomer`, add a command button. Close the Command Button Wizard when it opens and use the Property Sheet to name the button `cmdShowOrders`. For the `On Click` event, include the following code snippet:

Available for download on Wrox.com

```
Private Sub cmdShowOrders_Click()
If Not Me.NewRecord Then
    DoCmd.OpenForm "frmOrder", _
        WhereCondition:="CustomerID=" & Me.txtCustomerID
End If
End Sub
```

code snippet code 59166_ch14_CodeSnippets.txt On Click()

If the tables do not follow good naming conventions, you may need to include brackets around the field names. Such is the case with the Northwind database, where the space in the field name requires brackets, so the line would look like the following:

```
DoCmd.OpenForm "frmOrder", _
    WhereCondition:="[Customer ID]=" & Me.txtCustomerID
```

You can add this code configuration to any form to have it open another form to the related record(s). Again, the critical factor is the dependency or relationship between the record sources. You will recognize this type of relationship on the subform Property Sheet, using Link Child Fields and Link Master Fields.

The line `If Not Me.NewRecord Then` references the `NewRecord` property, which is a Boolean value. It signifies whether the user is on the new record of the form. `NewRecord` is more than just a new record — it is the form's property, because in Access, all records are added on the New Record. You check the `NewRecord` property because when a customer is newly entered there obviously should not be any existing orders; thus, no need exists to open the Orders form.

The `OpenForm` method opens the form called `frmOrder` and issues a `Where` clause to specify which records to display in the form. That clause is often called a filter because it limits the form's record source to only those records that meet the criteria. In this example, the criteria restrict the data to those with customer IDs that match the value in the text box called `txtCustomerID`. For clarification, the field name on the left of the equal symbol (=) refers to the field on the opened object. The control name on the right refers to a control on the calling object. In plain English this says to open the Order form to show the orders for the current customer on the Customer form.

Suppose that each order has one invoice printed for it. When you are viewing the Order record, you can print the invoice for the order. The code is nearly identical, except that a Report is being opened in Print Preview:

```
Private Sub cmdShowInvoice_Click()
If Not Me.NewRecord Then
    DoCmd.OpenReport "rptInvoice", WhereCondition:="OrderID=" & Me.txtOrderID, _
    View:=acViewPreview
End If
End Sub
```

Another way to open a form to a specific record is to use the approach *query by form*; that is, to use a query as the record source of the form that is being opened. *Query by form* is a common method by which the criteria for any particular field in your query is set to a control on the main form. You do it by adding criteria to the query using the syntax `Forms!frmName!ControlName`. The first part of that expression stipulates the Forms collection, the second specifies the name of the object to use (a form, in this case), and the last part is the control name that will have the criteria. Now you see how important it is to follow naming conventions — if you don't rename text box controls, they will likely have the same name as the field that is in the record source.

Figure 14-19 shows the portion of the query grid with the criteria used to filter the records as you did previously with the command button `cmdShowOrders`. The query is saved as `qryCustomerOrders`. You could use it as the record source of the form `frmOrder` and it would open to display the orders for the customer selected on the form `frmCustomer`.

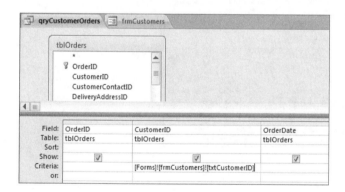

FIGURE 14-19

The following code shows two ways to use queries to filter data (with one table) using one form.

```
Docmd.OpenForm "frmOrder", "qryCustomerOrders", , acFormPropertySettings, _
acWindowNormal
```

or

```
' use the FilterName instead of WhereCondition
Docmd.OpenForm "frmOrder", FilterName:= "qryCustomerOrders"
```

code snippet code 59166_ch14_CodeSnippets.txt Two ways to use queries to filter data

The first line of code leaves the record source for `frmOrder` set to `tblOrders` (set in the form properties). It then uses the saved query named `qryCustomerOrders` as the `WhereCondition`. `qryCustomerOrders` is based on `tblOrders`, and includes all the fields. In `qryCustomerOrders`, the `CustomerID` field needs the criteria `Forms!frmCustomer!txtCustomerID`. That field is the critical link between the customer and the order.

The second example uses the `Docmd.OpenForm` string but instead of using the `WhereCondition` argument, it uses the `FilterName` argument. Using a query (`qryCustomerOrders`) for the `FilterName` actually overrides a form's record source (in this case `tblOrders`).

Multiple Form Instances

Situations occur in which the user needs to compare two or more records from the same table. For example, you may need to compare Order 1 to Order 2 or Supplier 1 to Supplier 2 or Supplier 1 to Supplier 2 and to Supplier 3. You can accomplish this task by opening the same form multiple times.

Suppose a database consultant is creating an Access solution for a client. The consultant is in a bind and needs to subcontract parts of the project to one of her fellow developers. She checks her database to view her contact list. She opens the contact list form (`frmContactList`, see Figure 14-20) and selects two of the records (or contacts) from her list so that she can compare their specialties to find the best match for both the client and project.

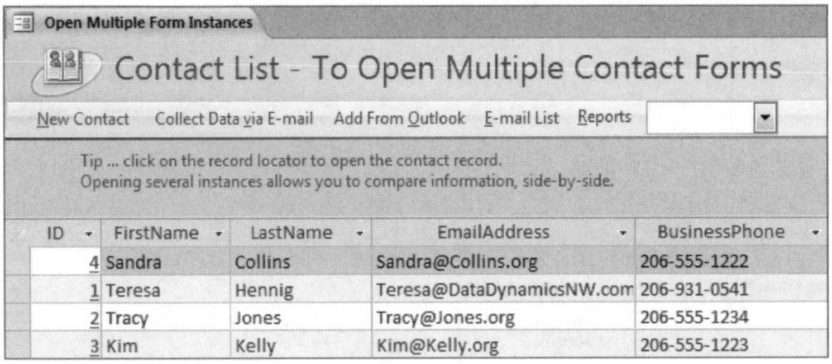

FIGURE 14-20

The form that's used to view the details is named `frmContactDetails` and it is opened twice so that the consultant can do a side-by-side comparison of the candidate's strengths as relayed by the Notes field (see Figure 14-21). (The figure looks a bit crowded, but most screens display two complete records.)

Opening the same form multiple times is referred to as *multiple instances* because every time the same form is opened, Access has to create or instantiate a new instance of the form. The default process is to allow one instance of a form and merely change the record source, so it requires a little code and some preplanning to show multiple instances of the same form.

For this example, use the file `MultiFormInstance.accdb` (in the download for this chapter). The exercise starts with a datasheet form, but you can achieve the same functionality using a regular form. The critical part is to have two forms, one for your list and the other to open multiple times to show and compare details. This example also demonstrates using a drill-through procedure to open the details form. Again, this works equally well for opening forms or reports.

FIGURE 14-21

The code can be used wherever you require this type of functionality. First you create a new module and a global variable to hold the form objects in a collection:

```
Option Compare Database
Option Explicit

Private mcolFormInstances As New Collection
```

> In the collection name, `mcolFormInstances`, m *is for module level and* `col`
> *represents collection.*

The collection holds the forms as they are created. Next, you create a function that allows the user to open the same form multiple times:

Available for download on Wrox.com

```
Function OpenFormInstance(strFormName As String, Optional _
strWhereCondition As String)
'Declare the form name
Dim frm As Form
```

```
Select Case FormName
    Case "frmContactDetails"
        Set frm = New Form_frmContactDetails
    Case Else
        Debug.Assert False
End Select

If WhereCondition <> "" Then
    frm.Filter = WhereCondition
    frm.FilterOn = True
End If
'make the form visible
frm.Visible = True
' Need to add a reference to the form so that it doesn't
' immediately close when the form variable goes out of scope.
mcolFormInstances.Add frm

End Function
```

code snippet code 59166_ch14_CodeSnippets.txt Multiple Instances Of A Form

The function begins by declaring two parameters, FormName and WhereCondition. FormName will hold the name of the form you need to create. WhereCondition will contain a string expression that allows the form to display the correct record. You'll call the function from the Contact form frmContactList and fill these parameters later.

A variable is declared for the form object:

```
Dim frm as Form
```

The Select Case statement evaluates the value in the FormName variable. If the value equals frmContactDetails, then the variable frm is set to equal a new Contact Details form. To use this function for another form, such as to review details about the projects that a contact has worked on, just insert another case in the Select Case statement before the Case Else.

An If..Then statement evaluates the value of the WhereCondition parameter. Because there's always a value for the WhereCondition, the form's filter property equals its value. With a value being supplied to the filter property, you need to turn on the filter with the following line of code:

```
frm.FilterOn = True
```

Adding the form to the module level collection is how you will continue to display the record after another record is selected — in other words, add the form to the collection or it will revert to displaying a single instance of the form. That's because when the frm variable goes out of scope, it loses its value, and the initial instance of the form and its record are gone. So you make the form visible and add it to the collection:

```
frm.Visible = True
mcolFormInstances.Add frm
```

Now go to frmContactList and examine the OpenFormInstance function. With frmContactList open in Design view, you use the ID field's On Click event to place the OpenFormInstance function. You also use the ID field in the expression for the `WhereCondition` parameter. At least four ways exist to make this function work. Three of the possibilities use code, as the following examples show, and the fourth uses an embedded macro.

```
Private Sub ID_Click()
'1st example
Dim FormName As String
Dim WhereCondition As String
FormName = "frmContactDetails"
WhereCondition = "[ID]=" & Me.ID
'Or
'WhereCondition = "[ID]=" & Screen.ActiveControl
Call OpenFormInstance(FormName, WhereCondition)

'2nd example
'Call OpenFormInstance("frmContactDetails", "[ID]=" & Screen.ActiveControl)

'3rd example
'Call OpenFormInstance("frmContactDetails", "[ID]=" & Me.ID)

End Sub
```

code snippet code 59166_ch14_CodeSnippets.txt Use ID field in expression for WhereCondition Parameter

All three code examples are basically the same in that the `FormName` equals the Contact Details form (`frmContactDetails`) and the `WhereCondition` gets its value from the ID field.

The code shows two options for the `WhereCondition` expression. The first says, "Let the ID field of the Details form equal the ID field from the main form." The second is slightly different: "Let the ID field of the Details form equal the value from the Active control (ID field) from the main screen (main form)." Use the style of `WhereCondition` and `Call` that is appropriate for your scenario. You need use only one. As a rule you will want to use the method the specifically calls out the form control. Using the `Screen.ActiveControl` method is only appropriate when the code is used in an event for the active control.

Notice that you don't use the `Docmd.OpenForm` to open the details form. Instead, the form is instantiated by declaring the form object and setting it to equal the form specified in `FormName`. The Filter properties are set to accept the expression from the `WhereCondition`, the form is made visible, and the form instance is added to the collection that was created to hold each instance of this form.

As mentioned, the fourth method uses a macro. This example uses the same function, `OpenFormInstance`, to open multiple instances of the forms. To create a new macro, select Macro on the Ribbon's Create tab. You should have a macro object tab named Macro1. Right-click that tab and select Save. Change the name to `dt` (for drill-through). With the blank macro still open, click the `Conditions` and `Macro Names` buttons in the Ribbon. Those columns, which are hidden when you first open a new macro, now display, as shown in Figure 14-22.

FIGURE 14-22

Start with the Action column and select StopMacro. That stops the macro from running when a condition is met. Next, create named macros for each of the forms you want to drill to. (The process and details are coming up in a moment, but at the end of the exercise, your macro should look similar to the one in Figure 14-23.)

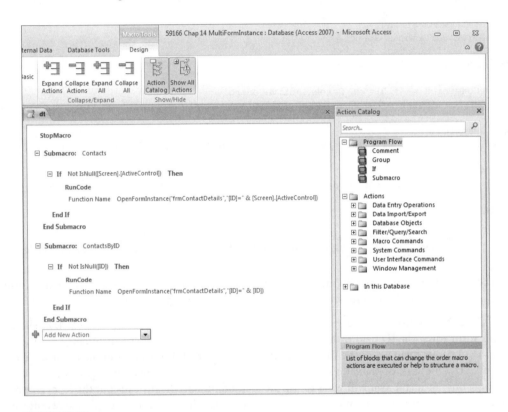

FIGURE 14-23

Briefly, you start by naming the next macro Contacts. In the Condition column, supply an expression that, when evaluated, will equal True. If the condition is True, then perform the action specified in the Action column (RunCode). RunCode requires arguments or action arguments to run the code. In this case, you provide the function name OpenFormInstance and fill in the parameters just like the ones in the code behind.

With the following steps, you create macros that provide two approaches to drill into the details.

1. The first example uses the active control as the record ID to drill into data. In the Macro Name column, type **Contacts**. For the condition, type:

    ```
    Not IsNull([Screen].[ActiveControl])
    ```

2. The Action column has a drop-down list; select RunCode.

3. The lower pane helps prompt for action arguments. Click on the ellipsis to open the Expression Builder and then select the function that you created, OpenFormInstance.

4. The Code Builder assists with syntax, but the key is to include the where clause as you did in VBA. Alternatively, you can type the arguments directly into the Arguments field. The completed argument looks like this:

```
OpenFormInstance("frmContactDetails","[ID]=" & [Screen].[ActiveControl])
```

5. The second example matches the record ID, so name the macro ContactsByID. The condition is:

```
Not IsNull([ID])
```

6. The action will again be to run code to open an instance of the form frmContactDetails where the ID fields match. Here's the argument:

```
OpenFormInstance("frmContactDetails","[ID]=" &[ID]
```

The great thing about the macro is that you can have many submacros under one roof. You could have dt.Contacts, dt.Orders, dt.Products, and so on, all living in the same macro named dt. Because each of the arguments uses the OpenFormInstance function, using the macro to organize or keep track of all the forms needing that functionality is easier. Instead of opening the code behind, you only need to set the Property Sheet for that event to the submacro name. Just remember that for every form that is added to the macro, you must change the Select Case statement in the OpenFormInstance function to add a Case statement for the new form, as shown in Figure 14-24.

```
Option Compare Database
Option Explicit
'This sample demostrates how to use multiple instances of a form.

'Declaring global variable to create collection
'to hold multiple instances of a form.
Private mcolFormInstances As New Collection

Function OpenFormInstance(FormName As String, Optional WhereCondition As String)
'Declare the Form Object
Dim frm As Form
Select Case FormName
    Case "frmContactDetails"
        Set frm = New Form_frmContactDetails
    Case "fsubContactDetails"
        Set frm = New Form_fsubContactDetails
    Case "ThirdFormName"
        Set frm = New Form_ThirdFormName
    Case Else
        Debug.Assert False
End Select


'set the filter properties on the form.
If WhereCondition <> "" Then
    frm.Filter = WhereCondition
    frm.FilterOn = True
End If

'Now make the form visible.
 frm.Visible = True

    ' Need to keep a reference to the form so that it doesn't immediately
    ' close when the frm variable goes out of scope.
 mcolFormInstances.Add frm
End Function
```

FIGURE 14-24

The macro name identifies each macro within the macro group. In the Property Sheet for the ID field's On Click event, select the name of the macro instead of selecting Event Procedure. The Property Sheet offers auto-complete for macro names so as soon as you type dt, you get a list of all the named macros in the dt macro group. See Figure 14-25.

FIGURE 14-25

 Remember that a macro group often contains several macros but it's still called a macro; each named action or series of actions in the group is also called a macro. The terminology can be a bit confusing, but macros are still likely to evolve into popular developer tools.

Displaying Data in TreeView and ListView Controls

One powerful feature of Access development is the capability to add an ActiveX control to a form or report. ActiveX controls are additional components that provide their own user interface, properties, and methods. Adding a control such as TreeView, ListView, or Calendar (having a Calendar control is no longer necessary; a control property called Show Date Picker displays a calendar date selection tool for controls formatted for dates) is a great way to add functionality to your applications with minimal effort on your part. ActiveX controls are not without cost, however. You must install them on each computer to use them. In many cases, this means you must have a license to distribute a particular control to other computers.

 The TreeView and ListView ActiveX controls are not available in 64-bit Access at this time).

The Microsoft TreeView control is used to display data that exists within a hierarchy of information. A hierarchy can involve any data contained within a one-to-one or one-to-many relationship. For example, in the Northwind database, Customers have Orders, and Orders have line items that are known as Order Details. This section shows you how to add a TreeView control to a form and how to populate and display the information based on user interaction with it. You'll also take a look at the `ListView` control, and see an example of responding to an event in the `TreeView` control to fill the `ListView` control.

Suppose you are tracking students and classes for a small college. Classes at the school are categorized into departments. In this example, you display the departments along with their classes in a `TreeView` control, and the students in a given class in a `ListView` control.

To begin, create a new blank form. The form does not need to be bound to a table or query because you will populate data in the `TreeView` control. After you create the form, click the `ActiveX Controls` button on the Ribbon. The Insert ActiveX Control dialog box displays, as shown in Figure 14-26. For this example, you use the `TreeView Control` and `Microsoft ListView Control, version 6.0` control from the included list of ActiveX controls. Name the controls `tvwClasses` and `lvwStudents`, respectively.

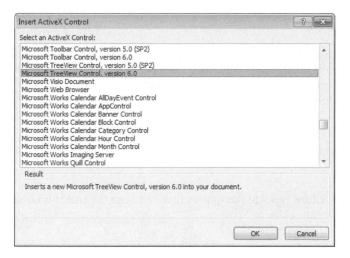

FIGURE 14-26

In the dialog box, select the desired control to add it to the form. ActiveX controls have properties that are displayed in the standard Access properties window, but many also have another set of custom properties that were added by the author of the control. Figure 14-27 shows the custom property dialog box for the `TreeView` control.

You can include images in a `TreeView` or `ListView` control by using another ActiveX control called `Microsoft ImageList Control, version 6.0`. `ImageList` is a storage area for pictures that the `TreeView` uses when it displays the data. You won't use images in this example.

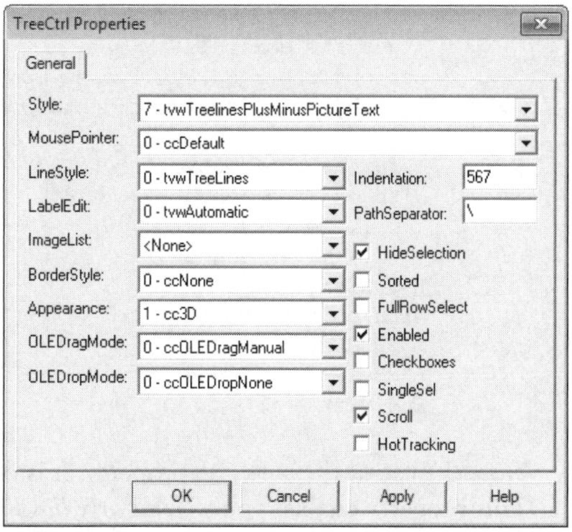

FIGURE 14-27

The next step is to populate the data in the `TreeView` control. Each item of data in a `TreeView` is called a node and is stored in the `TreeView Nodes` collection. The following code demonstrates the addition of a data node to the collection of `TreeView` nodes:

```
tvx.Nodes.Add Key:="C105", Text:="Acme Supply Co.", Image:= 1, SelectedImage:=2
```

The node is defined with a unique key of `C105`, a display name of Acme Supply Co., and is set to use the image with the key of 1 by default, and the image with the key of 2 when selected. If you use images, the image indexes are defined in a corresponding `ImageList` control.

The `Key` *property of every node is of type Text, it must start with a letter, and it must be unique.*

Filling the TreeView Control

During the `Form_Load` event procedure in this example, the `TreeView` is populated with one node for every department in the Departments table, along with the classes that are in the department. Here's how. First you declare object variables for the `TreeView` and `ListView` controls. You use these objects to work with the controls on the form.

```
Dim objTree       As TreeView
Dim objList       As ListView
Dim objItem       As ListItem
Dim objParentNode As Node
Dim objChildNode  As Node
```

Next, create the `Form_Load` event procedure and add the following code to use the controls on the form and provide some formatting.

```
Private Sub Form_Load()
    ' fill the treeview
    Dim rsDept As DAO.Recordset
    Dim rsClasses As DAO.Recordset

    ' get the controls
    Set objTree = Me.tvwClasses.Object
    Set objList = Me.lvwStudents.Object

    ' format the controls
    With objTree.Font
        .Size = 9
        .Name = "Segoe UI"
    End With
    With objList.Font
        .Size = 9
        .Name = "Segoe UI"
    End With
```

Note the use of the `.Object` property. It is defined by Access to return the object for the control. This property enables you to use *early binding* for the Object Model in an ActiveX control. Binding works the same here as it does for other objects. Essentially, early binding loads the data when a form loads and late binding delays attaching to the data, which typically allows for a smaller Recordset and takes less time to process.

If you've used the `ListView` or `TreeView` controls in the past, you may notice that some tabs are missing from the custom property dialog box for the `TreeView` control. Access 2010 no longer includes the components that provide the Font Property Sheet, which is why you added code to format the control.

Now loop through the departments and add a node to the `TreeView` control:

```
' get the departments
Set rsDept = CurrentDb.OpenRecordset( _
    "SELECT * FROM tblDepartments ORDER BY Department")

' loop through the departments
While (Not rsDept.EOF)
    ' add the department node
    Set objParentNode = objTree.Nodes.Add(, , _
        "DPT" & rsDept("DepartmentID"), rsDept("Department"))
```

Here you're adding a node for each department with a key value of `DPT` & `rsDept("DepartmentID")`. Each node on the `TreeView` control needs to have a unique key value. By concatenating the value of a primary key field (`DepartmentID`) with a unique abbreviation for the table (`DPT`), you can ensure that each node has a unique key value. You'll re-use this key later to build relationships with other nodes. For this example, `tblDepartments` is the parent table. The relationships are based on the primary and foreign key relationships of the tables as shown in the `WHERE` clause of the next snippet of code.

It's time to add the related classes. You loop through another Recordset to get the classes for the current department, and add a new node that is a child of `objParentNode` by specifying the `tvw-Child` relationship argument to the `Nodes.Add` method:

```
' get the classes in the selected department
Set rsClasses = CurrentDb.OpenRecordset( _
    "SELECT * FROM tblClasses WHERE Department = " & _
    rsDept("DepartmentID") & " ORDER BY ClassName")

' add the classes to the treeview
While (Not rsClasses.EOF)
    Set objChildNode = objTree.Nodes.Add(objParentNode, tvwChild, _
        "CLS" & rsClasses("ClassID"), rsClasses("ClassName"))
    rsClasses.MoveNext
Wend
rsDept.MoveNext
Wend
```

The only thing left to do now is some cleanup:

```
rsClasses.Close
rsDept.Close
Set rsDept = Nothing
Set rsClasses = Nothing
End Sub
```

In this example, you're working with a small number of departments and classes so you're filling everything when the form is loaded. If you have a lot of nodes to add to the TreeView, filling all the data when the form loads might take a while. To resolve that problem, you might choose to load the classes for a department when a node is selected, which is known as *delay loading* or *loading on-demand*.

Along with properties and methods, ActiveX controls can also provide events such as NodeClick for the TreeView. Access does not know anything about these events, so you must add them using the Visual Basic Editor. To delay loading the classes in the TreeView, add the following event, which will then be called when you click a node in the TreeView:

```
Private Sub tvwClasses_NodeClick(ByVal Node As Object)
    Dim objNode    As Node

    ' get the node object
    Set objNode = Node

    If (objNode.Children = 0 And objNode.Parent Is Nothing) Then
        ShowClasses Node
    End If

End Sub
```

This code makes sure that the selected node does not already have any children. It also checks the Parent property of the Node object to make sure that classes are added only when a department is selected. For root or parent nodes that do not have a parent node of their own, the Parent property will be set to Nothing.

Here's the ShowClasses procedure:

```
Private Sub ShowClasses(pNode As Node)
    Dim rsClasses As DAO.Recordset
    Dim lngDept    As Long

    ' parse the department ID from the selected node
    lngDept = CLng(Mid(pNode.Key, 4))

    ' get the classes in the selected department
    Set rsClasses = CurrentDb.OpenRecordset( _
        "SELECT * FROM tblClasses WHERE Department = " & _
        lngDept & " ORDER BY ClassName")

    ' add the classes to the treeview
    While (Not rsClasses.EOF)
        Set objChildNode = objTree.Nodes.Add(pNode, tvwChild, _
            "CLS" & rsClasses("ClassID"), rsClasses("ClassName"))
        rsClasses.MoveNext
    Wend

    rsClasses.Close
    Set rsClasses = Nothing
End Sub
```

Filling the ListView Control

After you've filled the `TreeView` control, you want to display the students in a given class. To accomplish this, use the `ListView` control that you added to the form earlier. But first, you must configure the `ListView`. Begin by opening the Property Sheet for the `ListView` control, and change the `View` property to `lvwReport`.

The values for the `View` property probably look familiar. That's because the list of files in a Windows Explorer window is a `ListView`. The Explorer's Details view is called the Report view in the `ListView` ActiveX control. The Report view enables you to add your own columns to the `ListView` control.

Now add the following columns on the Column Headers tab of the `ListView` property dialog box. Use the Insert Column button in the dialog box (see Figure 14-28) to do so.

INDEX	TEXT	WIDTH
1	Class	2160.00
2	First Name	1440.00
3	Last Name	1440.00
4	Major	1440.00

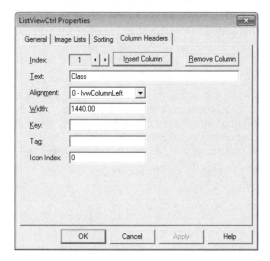

FIGURE 14-28

To fill the `ListView`, add the following code in the `NodeClick` event for the `TreeView`. If a department is selected, the names of all the students in all classes for that department display. If a class is selected, the names of its students display.

```
Private Sub tvwClasses_NodeClick(ByVal Node As Object)
    Dim rstStudents As DAO.Recordset
    Dim objNode      As Node
    Dim strSQL       As String
    Dim lngID        As Long

    ' get the node object
    Set objNode = Node

    ' parse the ID from the node Key property
    lngID = CLng(Mid(objNode.Key, 4))
```

Earlier you saved the ID field along with a table abbreviation in the Key for the node. The preceding code parses the value of the primary key field from the Key so that you can use it in a WHERE clause to get the classes for the selected class or department. Next, you look at the Key to determine whether a department or class was selected and create the appropriate SQL statement:

```
    ' get the students in the selected class or department
    If (objNode.Key Like "DPT*") Then
        strSQL = "SELECT * FROM qryStudents WHERE DepartmentID = " & lngID
    ElseIf (objNode.Key Like "CLS*") Then
        strSQL = "SELECT * FROM qryStudents WHERE ClassID = " & lngID
    End If

    ' open the Recordset
    Set rstStudents = CurrentDb.OpenRecordset(strSQL)
```

Now it's time to fill the ListView. For this, use the ListItems collection of the ListView. To create an entry in the ListView, use the ListItems.Add method. This returns a ListItem object that you'll use to add ListSubItems. You use the Add method of the ListItems collection to add the first column to the ListView. Subsequent columns are added to the ListSubItems collection.

```
    ' fill the listview
    With objList
        .ListItems.Clear
        While (Not rstStudents.EOF)
            Set objItem = .ListItems.Add(, , rstStudents("ClassName"))
            objItem.ListSubItems.Add , , rstStudents("FirstName")
            objItem.ListSubItems.Add , , rstStudents("LastName")
            objItem.ListSubItems.Add , , Nz(rstStudents("Major"), "Undeclared")
            rstStudents.MoveNext
        Wend
    End With

    ' cleanup
    rstStudents.Close
    Set rstStudents = Nothing
    Set objNode = Nothing
End Sub
```

When this is all said and done, you should have something that looks like the form in Figure 14-29.

Although the task of creating the TreeView control is completed, you could add many other features to create a more robust tool. For example, using drill through, you could open a Students detail form when you select a student in the ListView. You could add an e-mail control using the check boxes in the ListView to facilitate e-mailing grades or sending information about an upcoming exam or lecture. You can also write code to sort the items in the ListView control. With minimal programming, adding ActiveX controls to an application can give it an extra level of professionalism and pizzazz that many users will appreciate.

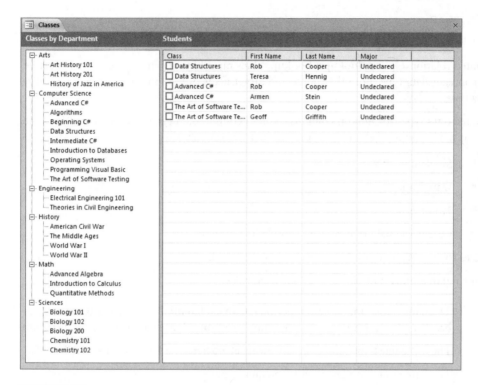

FIGURE 14-29

Web Forms

One of the most significant improvements you will find in Access 2010 is its ability to publish to the Web. While you cannot use VBA with your Web forms, it is well worth mentioning this exciting new feature.

In order to easily publish your database to the Web you must take the following into consideration:

➤ **SharePoint Services:** You will need a SharePoint Server that is exposed to the Internet if you want to fully maximize Web publishing capabilities.

➤ **Macros only:** You cannot use any VBA code behind your forms that are to be published to the Web.

➤ **Limited events:** Not all form control events are supported. Events that are currently supported are:

  ➤ AfterUpdate

  ➤ OnApplyFilter

➤ OnChange

➤ OnClick

➤ OnCurrent

➤ OnDblClick

➤ OnDirty

➤ OnLoad

➤ **Limited relationships for lookups:** Lookup tables must have a primary key and it must be long integer data type. Both the source and target fields of the lookup must be long integer data type.

➤ **Limited data types for lookup columns:** Not all column data types are supported for Web lookups. The lookup field must be one of the following data types:

➤ Single line of text

➤ Date/Time

➤ Number

➤ Calculated field that returns a single line of text

➤ Tables for the Web must have no more than 220 fields.

➤ Control names must not violate the following rules:

➤ The name must not contain a period (.), an exclamation point (!), a set of square brackets ([ ]), a leading space, or a non-printable character such as a carriage return

➤ The name must not contain the following characters: / \ : * ? " " < > | # <TAB> { } % ~ &

➤ The name must not begin with an equal sign (=)

➤ The name must be from 1 through 64 characters long

SUMMARY

The new features in Access 2010 make creating complex solutions much easier and faster than before. In this chapter, you explore many facets of VBA programming within the form environment. You examined new features and investigated examples of how they might be used and how to leverage them with VBA. You also walked through examples of creating and implementing complex scenarios, such as showing multiple instances of a form and the `TreeView` control and `ListView` control.

Forms are exciting because they are the primary user interface. They are your primary tool in helping users enter, search, and report data. Access 2010's interactive reports are also winners, and you tackle them in the next chapter.

15

Enhancing Reports with VBA

WHAT'S IN THIS CHAPTER?

➤ How new features for reports can help increase productivity

➤ Descriptions of the events available for reports

➤ How to use code to add additional functionality to reports

Because of their rich printed view, reports have long been one of the more widely used features in Access. This chapter takes an in-depth look at reports in Access 2010. It starts from the beginning, so if you're already familiar with creating reports in Access, you might want to skip to the sections titled "New in Access 2007" or "New in Access 2010."

The chapter also looks at several ways that you can enhance your reports by adding VBA behind them. You'll explore the various events that are available for reports and sections, and then move into some common uses for those events. Along the way, you'll see some issues that you should look out for as you're designing reports. Finally, you'll examine several new features in reports in both Access 2007 and Access 2010, including Layout view and Report view.

When you write code behind a form, there are certain things to consider, such as the flow of the application, searching for data, data entry, and validation. While reports in Access 2010 are still read-only, they have been greatly enhanced to allow for some of the form-type scenarios that you might have created in the past such as search, sorting, and filtering.

INTRODUCTION TO REPORTS

Reports in Access are designed to provide a view of data in a table or query whose initial purpose is to be printed. That said, beginning with Access 2007, and on into Access 2010 — new views have been added to reports that take them to the next level and provide interactivity that was not available in previous versions.

How Reports Are Structured

Several different components make up a report. Perhaps the most important are the various sections and group levels that are defined in a report.

Sections are used to display data and other controls such as labels or combo boxes. The following table describes the types of sections in order.

SECTION TYPE	DESCRIPTION
Report Header	Typically displays report titles or similar information. Prints once at the top of the report.
Page Header	Prints at the top of each page.
Group Header	Typically displays unique data for a group or aggregate data such as a Sum or Average. Prints at the top of each group level. This section can be repeated when the data in a group spans multiple pages. (You can have a maximum of 10 groups in a report.)
Detail	Displays records in a report.
Group Footer	Displays summary information for a group level. Prints at the bottom of each group level.
Page Footer	Prints at the bottom of each page. Often used to display page numbers.
Report Footer	Prints once at the end of the report.

One thing that sets reports apart from forms is the capability to group data. Grouping enables you to create aggregates or to view related data in a hierarchical fashion using group levels. Let's say you are tracking sessions for a conference and the attendees for each session. Using a report, you can group by the session as well as the time of the session, and display the attendees for each session.

Reports also support sort levels in the hierarchical data. A sort level is the same as a group level, but without a header or footer section. Data within a group or across the report is sorted by the specified field. You can create a maximum of ten group and sort levels in a report. These levels are stored in GroupLevel objects in the GroupLevel property of the report.

The GroupLevel property of the Report object is not a collection; it's an indexed property. Because it includes an index parameter, it acts like a collection, but does not have methods normally associated with collections such as Add, Item, Count, and Remove.

You can add a subreport to a report. A subreport can show related data in a hierarchy, or you can use subreports to build dashboard-style reports.

New in Access 2007

Before we take a look at some of the new features related to reports in Access 2010, let's take a look at some of the features that were changed for reports in Access 2007.

Reports were among the most improved areas in Access 2007. Several new features have been added to make reports both easier to create and more powerful. For starters, *Layout view* allows you to design reports while you are viewing your actual data. Many of the tasks of creating a report, such as formatting, sorting and grouping, and adding totals are handled in Layout view while your data is onscreen. As a result, you can accomplish many design tasks without having to switch between Design view and Print Preview. Later on, we'll take a quick look at improvements that were made to Layout view in Access 2010.

A report opened in Print Preview is really just an image, so you cannot easily search for data or sort or filter content. Access 2007 introduced *Report view*, which provides a new view of the data in a report that rivals that of forms.

Sorting and grouping is another area that has been enhanced in Access 2007. The sorting and grouping dialog box used in previous versions of Access has been replaced with the new Group, Sort, and Total pane, which enables you to quickly create group levels and sort levels.

Creating reports has also been made easier using the Layout view feature. Layouts are groups of aligned controls that resize and move in conjunction with one another. Layouts have been greatly improved in Access 2010, so we'll take a closer look at Layout view in the next section.

Layouts also enable you to add gridlines that grow or shrink with the data. These are much easier than creating lines in previous versions of Access. The Line and Rectangle controls are still available if you require more control over the placement of lines. Figure 15-1 shows a report with a tabular layout that has gridlines.

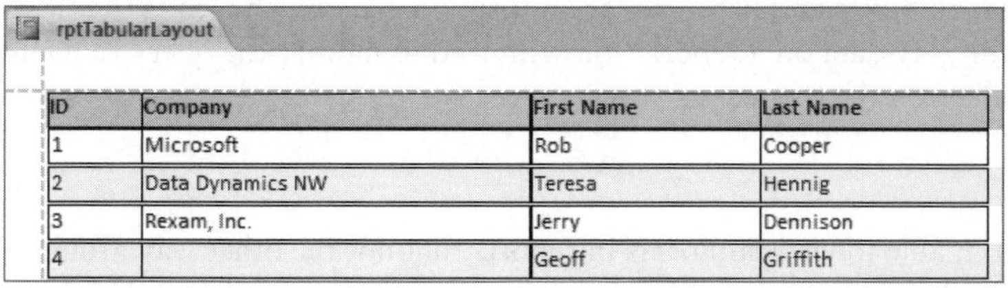

ID	Company	First Name	Last Name
1	Microsoft	Rob	Cooper
2	Data Dynamics NW	Teresa	Hennig
3	Rexam, Inc.	Jerry	Dennison
4		Geoff	Griffith

FIGURE 15-1

New in Access 2010

Access 2010 adds some additional improvements to features that were added for reports in Access 2007. Let's take a look.

Enhancements to Layout View

Layout view was first introduced in Access 2007, and creates a more WYSIWIG approach to design-ing forms and reports. Originally, there were two types of layouts you could create: stacked and tabular. Access 2010 greatly improves the experience of designing objects in Layout view by removing previous limitations.

These new improvements are things such as:

➤ **Adding controls in Layout view:** Previously you could only add text boxes and image controls in Layout view.

➤ **Merging and splitting cells:** Controls can span multiple rows or columns.

➤ **More control over the placement of controls:** You can drop a control virtually anywhere within a layout.

➤ **Easier to insert and delete rows and columns:** New menu commands have been added to simplify these tasks.

➤ **Support for new Office themes:** You can use themes to apply a consistent style to both forms and reports.

Web Reports

Much of what is new in Access 2010 can be used to build applications for Access Services, and reports are no exception. Reports in an Access Services application enable you to create a report, publish it to an Access Services site, and send the URL of the report to end users for viewing. This is powerful, but there are a couple of things you should be aware of.

First and foremost, unlike forms, reports do not support events or macros for custom logic in the report. This means there is no programmability for reports in Access Services. When you create a Web report in Access 2010, no events will be listed in the Property Sheet for the report or controls on the report for this reason.

Second, reports only support a few types of controls. The supported controls are text box, check box, label, and hyperlink. Combo boxes and list boxes are not supported, which means that if you want to use a lookup field to display data on a report, you will need to modify the query to include the lookup table to display values on the report.

SubReports in Forms

For quite some time, we've been able to view subforms in reports, but not the other way around. Reports have never been able to be viewed as a subform on a form — that is, until now. Using Access 2010, you can set the `SourceObject` property of a subform control on a form to the name of a report. This was largely done to enhance the new navigation control in Access 2010, but you can use your own reports in subform controls without a navigation control as well.

You can also add reports to a subform control in an Access Services application.

Detecting Whether a SubReport Is Opened in a Form or Report

Once you've started to use subreports in your subforms, it might be necessary to determine whether a report is open in a subform. To determine this, the `Subform` object in the Object Model now includes a `Report` property. The following code shows how to determine whether a report is open in a subform control.

```
Private Function IsSubreport(objSubform As SubForm) As Boolean
    On Error Resume Next
    IsSubreport = (Not objSubform.Report Is Nothing) And (Err = 0)
    On Error GoTo 0
End Function
```

code snippet ReportsChapter.accdb

Now that reports can be hosted in a subform control in Access 2010, it may also be necessary to determine whether the object in the subform control is actually a subform. The following code shows how to do this:

```
Private Function IsSubform(objSubform As SubForm) As Boolean
    On Error Resume Next
    IsSubform = (Not objSubform.Form Is Nothing) And (Err = 0)
    On Error GoTo 0
End Function
```

code snippet ReportsChapter.accdb

Both of these functions work by testing the object inside the subform control. In the case of a subreport, we're testing the new `Report` property of the `Subform` object. In the case of a subform, we're testing the `Form` property. Also notice that both functions include inline error handling. This is because Access throws a runtime error if the `Form` or `Report` properties of the `Subform` object are invalid.

The following sample code shows how to use these functions:

```
Private Sub cmdTest_Click()
    If (IsSubform(Me.NavigationSubform)) Then
        MsgBox "The name of the subform is: " & Me.NavigationSubform.Form.Name
    Else
        MsgBox "The specified subform control does not contain a subform."
    End If

    If (IsSubreport(Me.NavigationSubform)) Then
        MsgBox "The name of the subreport is: " & Me.NavigationSubform.Report.Name
    Else
        MsgBox "The specified subform control does not contain a subreport."
    End If
End Sub
```

code snippet ReportsChapter.accdb

Improved Conditional Formatting

Conditional formatting for controls in Access 2007 and previous versions allowed up to three defined conditions and the default condition. With conditional formatting in Access 2010, you can now have up to fifty conditions defined for a text box or combo box.

Having the opportunity to add more conditions may eliminate the need for complex logic in code. This is a big win, but it doesn't stop there. In addition to being able to add more than three conditions, there are also new options available for conditional formatting in Access 2010.

If you've used conditional formatting in Excel 2007 or Excel 2010, you may be familiar with data bars. Data bars are a way to apply formatting to a control based on the entire data set. For example, let's say that you have a report that shows number of sales for the month. You could apply data bar formatting to show the person with the highest figures. This type of visualization can make reports easy to understand and very interesting. Figure 15-2 shows data bars on a report in Access 2010. The first data bar includes the text in the control, and the second omits the text and only displays the data bar.

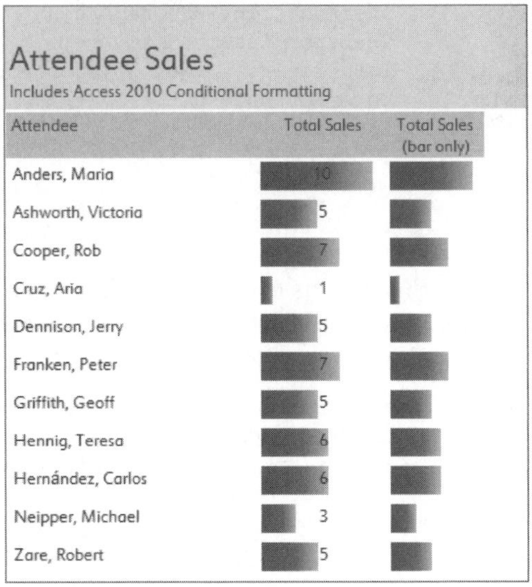

FIGURE 15-2

CREATING A REPORT

There are many ways to create a report in Access 2010, including the following:

➤ **Using Report Designer:** Using the Report Designer gives you the most control over creating reports. You can place any type of control on the design surface and bind the report to a table, query, or SQL statement. The Report Designer also enables you to add VBA code behind the report.

➤ **Using Layout view:** The Report Designer offers a powerful way to create reports. However, as you design your reports, you may frequently need to switch between Print Preview and report design because data from the tables is not shown at design time. Layout view, as mentioned earlier, was created to solve this. With Access 2010, you can add different types of controls, apply formatting, and add sorting, grouping, and totals, all while viewing the actual data from a table or query.

➤ **Using Report Wizard:** The Report Wizard walks you through a report creation process with a number of options from which to choose. The options include data settings such as data source; grouping and sorting; and formatting options, such as layout, orientation, and style. Using the wizard is also an easy way to create reports using multiple tables.

➤ **Programmatically:** You can also create reports with code. Access provides a method on the `Application` object called `CreateReport` that can be used to create a report. This method is largely used when you want to create reports using your own mechanism for gathering input from the user.

➤ **Using Quick Reports:** Click the Report button in the Ribbon's Create tab to create a new report with a tabular layout. The report includes common elements such as header and footer sections, and a count of the number of records.

You'll see more about working in Layout view later in this chapter.

WORKING WITH VBA IN REPORTS

This is a book about VBA, so let's talk about code. More specifically, you'll explore some examples that use specific events and properties such as `CanGrow` and `CanShrink`, and then move into some of the more common types of reports that you can create with just a little VBA. Let's start with some of the basics.

To add a module to a report, simply add an event handler for an event such as `Open`, or set the `HasModule` property of the report to Yes.

Control Naming Issues

As you add controls, or even when you name fields, there are a few things to keep in mind that make the process of creating queries, forms, and reports much easier. The first is to avoid the use of spaces or punctuation in field and control names. Spaces may make your field names easier to read, but they are not user-friendly when it comes to queries or code. Consider a field named `Last Name` with a space in the middle. This field name must be bracketed when used in a query. Without the space, brackets are not required (although Access may add them). It turns out that brackets are also required when you refer to the field in code, so instead of referring to the field like this:

```
Me!LastName
```

you must refer to it like this:

```
Me![Last Name]
```

As you can see, using the space in the name makes it harder to read and write in code. Instead, don't use spaces in names; use the `Caption` property of a field or label control to change the text that is displayed.

Another issue that causes problems is circular references. A circular reference occurs when a control uses itself in an expression. Say, for example, you drag a field named `LastName` to a report, and then decide to change the `ControlSource` property for the control to:

```
=Left([LastName], 1)
```

Unless you rename this control, the `LastName` control will try to use `LastName` in the expression, which is itself an expression — in other words, a circular reference. To avoid circular references, be sure to rename the control when you modify the `ControlSource`. In this example, you might consider renaming `LastName` to `txtLastName`.

The Me Object

The Me keyword is used in class modules in VBA. For forms and reports, Me returns the current form or report object. For a standalone class module, the Me object returns the current running instance of the class. This is particularly useful for writing generic code. For example, if you have a procedure that changes the caption of a report based on the user who is currently logged on, and you want to write the routine so it can be used on any report, you might write this:

```
Public Sub SetReportCaption(objReport as Report)
    ` Set the report caption to the user name
    objReport.Caption = Environ$(`USERNAME")
End Sub
```

To pass a Report object from the report that is currently opened, pass the Me keyword as the parameter for the procedure. The following example uses the new Load event for a report to set the caption:

```
Private Sub Report_Load()
    SetReportCaption Me
End Sub
```

IMPORTANT REPORT EVENTS AND PROPERTIES

The following sections examine the most common events on reports that you will need to use in the course of developing your applications. These events occur when opening a report, when you work with sections and controls, and when you close a report. You can find a more comprehensive list of report events and the order in which they fire in Appendix A.

Opening a Report

The Open, NoData, Load, and Current events are important events that are necessary to implement many Access solutions. The Load and Current events were added to reports in Access 2007.

Open Event

The first event that fires when you open a report is the Open event. It's fired before Access fetches the data for the report, which means that you can dynamically create or alter the query for the report based on user input or the state of controls on another form or report in the database.

You can also cancel the Open event. If you set the Cancel argument of the event to True, Access stops loading the report, no further events fire, and the report is not displayed onscreen. This is useful when you want to ensure that the application is in a certain state before opening the report. For instance, you might want a particular user logged in or a particular form open before opening the report.

If you have a report and you want it to display data from the last 30 days of sales, for example, you can modify the report's RecordSource property when the report is opened to restrict the data:

```
Private Sub Report_Open(Cancel As Integer)
    Me.RecordSource = `SELECT * FROM [Orders] WHERE [Order Date] > Date()-30"
End Sub
```

That can be more efficient than changing the `Filter` property of the report.

Other cases in which you might use the `Open` event include:

➤ Creating a query for the report based on data from a table or displayed on a form

➤ Setting the sort order of a report based on the selection in a form

➤ Filtering the data in the report based on the user who is currently logged on to the computer

NoData Event

If the report is not cancelled in the `Open` event, Access runs a query specified in the report's `RecordSource` property to fetch the data needed by the report. If that query returns no records, either because data has not been entered or because the `WHERE` clause in the query resulted in no rows being returned, Access fires the `NoData` event. If the query does return data, the `NoData` event is not fired.

You can create an event handler that tells Access what to do if there is no data for your report. Often, you'll want to display a message to the user telling her that no data was found. Alternatively, you may want to open a form to allow the user to change the filter or to add new data to a table.

To not display the report if there is no data available, set the `Cancel` argument of the event to `True`. That tells Access to stop loading the report. The report is closed, and only the `Close` event fires.

For example, let's say that you have a report that lists the customers who have ordered a particular product during the current month. You want to notify users if they run the report, but no customers ordered the product this month. The following code displays a message and then cancels the report:

```
Private Sub Report_NoData(Cancel As Integer)
    ` Add code here that will be executed if no data
    ` was returned by the Report's RecordSource
    MsgBox `No customers ordered this product this month. ` & _
            `The report will now close.`
    Cancel = True
End Sub
```

Load Event

After Access has fetched the data and created the controls on your report, the `Load` event fires. It enables you to interact with controls on your report before the report is displayed. The `Load` event was added to reports in Access 2007.

Unlike the `Open` event, the `Load` event is not cancellable. You can perform actions inside the `Load` event, but Access continues to load the report regardless of any logic in your event handler.

Some suggested uses for the `Load` event include:

➤ Display calculated values in unbound controls using the data in your report's Recordset.

➤ Change default values for controls on your report.

Now that reports support both the `Open` and `Load` events, the question comes up as to which one to choose. To create or modify the query on which your report is based, use the `Open` event handler.

This event fires before the query does, giving you a chance to customize the data provided to the report.

To interact with a control on your report, you must use the `Load` event handler. When the `Open` event fires, Access has not yet created the controls on your report.

Current Event

Forms in Access have always had a `Current` event. Every time you move to a new record, the `Current` event fires to notify your form that the selected record has changed. You can use the `Current` event to apply custom formatting to a field, or to hide or show controls based on data in the form.

Until Access 2007, reports were not interactive. You could open a report, view it on the screen, and print it, but you couldn't interact with it, and you certainly couldn't move from record to record. With Access 2007 and Access 2010, you can browse from record to record, click in individual rows in your report, and drill down into the data. With the new interactivity, Microsoft added the `Current` event so that your code can know when a user has clicked into a row on your report.

There is one difference between the `Current` event in a report and the `Current` event in a form. When you open a form, the `Current` event fires toward the end of the opening sequence of events because controls receive focus in forms and records are activated as a result. That is not the case with reports. Controls do not receive focus by default when you open a report, and the `Current` event does not fire. You can use the `Load` event of the report to set focus to a control, which will cause the `Current` event to fire when the report is opened. Naturally, because this event fires when a record on the report receives focus, it does not fire in Print Preview.

 Use the `SetFocus` *method of a control to set focus to it in the* `Load` *event.*

Section Events

Each section in an Access report has many events that may be fired. You probably won't use most of these events in your applications, but it's great to have them all available if you need them.

Here you'll explore the `Format`, `Retreat`, `Paint`, `Print`, and `Page` events. You can find a more comprehensive list of report events and the order in which they fire in Appendix A.

Format Event

The `Format` event is fired when Access is laying out a section for a printed page. It fires after Access has determined that the data in the section will begin on a given page, but before the section is actually formatted.

Because the event fires before formatting occurs, you can add code to the `Format` event that changes the way Access formats the section. You can test the contents of the controls in the section, and you can set values into unbound controls.

The `Format` event is cancellable, which means you can tell Access to not display a report section.

This event is not fired when laying out a section for display on the screen. Format *is fired only when Access is preparing to interact with a printer driver. In other words, it does not fire in Report view or Layout view.*

You can use the Format event to customize section properties and controls. Suggested uses for the Format event handler include:

➤ Dynamically displaying page numbers

➤ Creating dictionary-style headers

For example, let's say you have a report that lists all products that are available for ordering. You want to ensure that items that are out of stock are not listed in the report. You add code to the Format event handler for the Detail section to cancel formatting the item, like this:

```
Private Sub Detail_Format(Cancel As Integer, FormatCount As Integer)
    ` Add code here to affect the formatting of the section
    If Me!ItemStatus = "Out Of Stock" Then
        Cancel = True
    End If
End Sub
```

When you cancel the Format event, the section is not printed. Cancelling the Format event also prevents the Print event from firing for the section.

Retreat Event

The Retreat event is a partner to the Format event; if you don't have a Format event handler, you do not need a Retreat event handler. Retreat fires whenever Access determines that a formatting operation needs to be undone. It is not commonly used, but it's a bit tricky.

Retreat is fired for a section when the Format event has already been fired for the section, and Access determines that the content for the section will not fit on the current page.

For example, you may have set the KeepTogether property on a section to True, to request that the entire section be placed together on the same page. If, while formatting the section, Access determines that the entire section cannot fit on the page, it fires the Retreat event to notify your code that the formatting needs to be done all over again. This enables you to undo any actions you may have performed in the Format event (remember, Format is fired before the actual formatting is done).

This is important if you have code in the Format event handler that assumes a linear progression. You can put code into the Retreat event handler to undo whatever you did in the Format event handler.

Here's an example that shows how this works. You have a report that sequentially numbers each detail section item in the report. Access fires the Format event to notify your code that a new detail section is being formatted. Your Format event handler increments a variable and then sets that value into an unbound text box in the section. The first 50 items fit fine on page one: The Format event has been fired 50 times and you have not yet seen a Retreat event because everything fits.

The 51st time through, Access again fires the `Format` event to tell your code that it will begin to format a new item. Your `Format` event handler increments the variable to 51, and sets the unbound text box, just as it has successfully done 50 times before. When your event handler finishes, Access begins actually formatting the section, and that's when it discovers that the section doesn't fit on page one, and needs to be placed on page two instead. Access fires the `Retreat` event to notify your code that this section is being "unformatted."

Access now knows that this section needs to appear on the next page. So what does it do? When it's time to put the section on page two, Access fires the `Format` event again! Access doesn't know what you may want to do during formatting, so it always tells you when it begins formatting a section. If you don't have code to handle the `Retreat` event, what's going to happen? When the `Format` event is fired for this section for page two, the line counter is incremented (this time from 51 to 52), and 52 is dutifully put in the unbound text box on the report. Yikes! Your user will look at the report and wonder what happened to row 51.

To fix this, all you need to do is handle the `Retreat` event. You can put code into the `Retreat` event handler to decrement the page number variable. When Access figures out that row 51 doesn't fit on page one, it fires the `Retreat` event; in the event handler, you subtract one from the line counter variable, setting it back to 50. Now you are prepared for the `Format` event that Access will fire when formatting the item for page two.

If you do something in the Format event handler, do the opposite in the Retreat event handler.

Paint Event

The `Paint` event was added to reports in Access 2007 and is fired whenever a section needs to be drawn on the screen. Access paints various items in a given section at different times. For example, the background and foreground colors and items are painted separately. Calculated controls are also painted separately, and each section paints its own calculated controls. As you might imagine, the `Paint` event fires multiple times for a given section.

The `Paint` event applies to the screen, not the printer. `Paint` events fire when paging through a report on the screen, not Print Preview.

Because the `Format` event does not fire in Report view, the `Paint` event can be used for conditional formatting of controls in that view.

Print Event

The `Print` event is fired after Access has finished formatting a section for printing, but before it is sent to the printer. The `Print` event handler is passed two parameters:

➤   `Cancel`: Set to `True` to cancel sending the section to the printer.

➤   `PrintCount`: Reports how many times the `Print` event handler has been called for the section item. Typically, this is set to 1, meaning this call is the first time the handler has been called by the layout engine.

The following code shows you how to accumulate totals at the bottom of each page:

```
Dim curTotal As Currency

Private Sub Detail_Print(Cancel As Integer, PrintCount As Integer)
    If PrintCount = 1 Then
        ` accumulate the total for the page
        curTotal = curTotal + Me!ItemAmount
    End If
End Sub

Private Sub PageHeaderSection_Print(Cancel As Integer, PrintCount As Integer)
    ` reset the total at the beginning of the page
    curTotal = 0
End Sub

Private Sub PageFooterSection_Print(Cancel As Integer, PrintCount As Integer)
    ` Display the total at the bottom of the page
    Me!txtPageTotal = curTotal
End Sub
```

Suggested uses for the Print event handler include:

➤ Printing totals such as a count at the bottom of each page

➤ Printing a record more than once

➤ Tracking when reports are printed

Page Event

The Page event is fired after a page has been formatted for printing, but before the page is actually sent to the printer. You can place code in the Page event handler to adorn a page with borders or watermarks.

To draw a border around the pages of your report and display a "Confidential" watermark, for example, you add code to the Page event handler to use the Line method of the report to draw a line for the border, and use several report properties to draw the watermark text in the center of the page, like this:

```
Private Sub Report_Page()
    Dim strWatermarkText As String
    Dim sizeHor As Single
    Dim sizeVer As Single

    With Me
        ` Print page border
        Me.Line (0, 0)-(.ScaleWidth - 1, .ScaleHeight - 1), vbBlack, B

        ` Print watermark
        strWatermarkText = `Confidential"

        .ScaleMode = 3
        .FontName = `Segoe UI"
```

```
            .FontSize = 48
            .ForeColor = vbRed

          ` Calculate text metrics
            sizeHor =.TextWidth(strWatermarkText)
            sizeVer = .TextHeight(strWatermarkText)

          ` Set the print location
            .CurrentX = (.ScaleWidth / 2) - (sizeHor / 2)
            .CurrentY = (.ScaleHeight / 2) - (sizeVer / 2)

          ` Print the watermark
            .Print strWatermarkText
        End With
    End Sub
```

code snippet ReportsChapter.accdb

Closing a Report

The `Unload` and `Close` events are necessary to implement many Access solutions.

Unload Event

The `Unload` event is fired when someone (your user, VBA code, or a macro) attempts to close the report. It is the first event fired during the shutdown sequence, and report data and report controls are still available to your code in this event handler.

Because the `Unload` event is cancellable, you can add code to the event handler to decide whether you want to allow the user to close the report. If you do not want the report to close, simply set the `Cancel` argument to `True`. Most likely you will also want to display a message box or some other form of user feedback to let your user know why you are prohibiting the report from closing.

Close Event

The `Close` event is the last event fired by a report. It allows you to clean up after the report, or prepare another object that you want to work with after the report is closed. This event is fired after the report has closed. You cannot interact with any report controls or data from this event. If you need to work with report controls, use the `Unload` event handler instead.

REPORT PROPERTIES

There are many properties on a report you can use to add some interesting features to your reports. Let's look at a few of these properties and some scenarios for using them with VBA. You can find a more comprehensive list of properties for reports and sections in Appendix A.

Section Properties

As you might expect, the properties on the Section object include members such as CanGrow and CanShrink and formatting properties such as AlternateBackColor. They're interesting, but there are a few properties that are not available in the Property Sheet that you'll want to look at a little closer.

WillContinue

A section's WillContinue property indicates whether the section will break onto the next page. It's useful for displaying a string such as "Continued on the next page" in a label at the bottom of the page.

This property is not available to reports opened in Report view or Layout view.

HasContinued

The HasContinued property is the opposite of the WillContinue property. It indicates whether a section has continued from the previous page. This is useful for displaying a string such as "(continued)" in a section at the top of the page.

This property is not available to reports opened in Report view or Layout view.

ForceNewPage

The ForceNewPage property sets page breaks on a report. You can use it to force a page break after a group level to keep related data on a single page. A good example of this is invoices, where you want the invoice for a single customer to print on a single page.

KeepTogether

You are already aware of two KeepTogether properties: one for the Section object and one for the GroupLevel object.

The KeepTogether property of a Section object attempts to prevent a section from printing across multiple pages. Keep in mind that some sections are so large that this is not always possible. This property is a Boolean value. If it is set to Yes, and the section cannot be completely printed on the current page, printing starts at the top of the next page. If it is set to No, the section is allowed to break across pages as needed to fill the entire page.

The KeepTogether property for a GroupLevel object controls how sections within a group are kept together. This is not a Boolean property, but instead has three values: No, Whole Group, and With First Detail. The default value is No, and it does not attempt to keep any of the sections that make up a group on the same page. With First Detail will make sure that the group header will print on the same page as the first Detail section in the group, while any other Detail sections and the group footer are allowed to be on the following pages. The Whole Group setting attempts to keep all sections in the entire group on the same page. Obviously, with larger groups that may not be possible, but in those cases; the group header would always start on a new page. That may not be the case if you have multiple small groups that will fit onto the same page.

The `KeepTogether` property for a `GroupLevel` object controls how sections within a group are kept together. This is not a Boolean property, but instead has three values:

➤ `No`: The default value. No attempt is made to keep any of the sections that make up a group on the same page.

➤ `Whole Group`: Attempts to keep all sections in the entire group on the same page. Obviously, that's not possible with larger groups, but in those cases the group header would always start on a new page. That may not be the case if you have multiple small groups that will fit onto the same page.

➤ `With First Detail`: Ensures that the group header prints on the same page as the first Detail section in the group, while any other Detail sections and the group footer are allowed to be on the following pages.

RepeatSection

When a group header section prints its controls, the data in the section is not displayed on more than one page. If the group extends to more than one page, this may be confusing for users reading the report. To solve this problem, use the `RepeatSection` property. It repeats the group header section on each page the section spans. A good example of this is a company directory where you want to list employees grouped by department. By using the `RepeatSection` property, you can display the department information at the top of each page if the entire group does not fit on a single page. This property applies only to group header sections.

Control Properties

Most of the built-in Access controls have two properties that are used by Access to customize how the control is displayed on a report: `CanGrow` and `CanShrink`. Report sections also have these properties, except for the Page Header and Page Footer sections, which are always displayed.

Memo fields can store a large amount of data — up to 65,535 characters in the Access user interface, and up to 1GB if you use DAO! While you probably won't have that much to display on a report, the pure fact that they can vary greatly in size can cause some design challenges for display. One record may contain a large amount of data in a memo field, and the next record may contain a very small amount of data. So how do you design report controls to accommodate for something that is not a fixed size?

Enter the `CanGrow` and `CanShrink` properties. These properties have been around for some time, and are very useful in designing reports.

The `CanGrow` property, as its name suggests, determines whether a control can grow (in height) to fit its data. Controls that are below a control that has grown are pushed down to follow the larger control. The `CanShrink` property determines whether a control can shrink (in height) to fit its data. Width of a control is not affected by these properties.

WORKING WITH CHARTS

Charts are useful tools for both forms and reports. They enable you to visually display aggregate data in trends or compared with other data. There are two types of charts you can use on reports. The first is created using the Microsoft Graph OLE Object and can be inserted using the Insert Chart button on the Design tab in the Report Designer. The other is a PivotChart, which can be created using a form. That form can subsequently be used as a subreport on a report to display the chart. The PivotChart object is more flexible and contains a rich Object Model that you can use from Access. While a discussion of this Object Model is beyond the scope of this book, there are some useful things you can do using PivotCharts such as display a chart in a group for a subset of records in a hierarchy.

Both types of charts can display related data using the LinkChildFields and LinkMasterFields properties.

COMMON REPORT REQUESTS

There's a lot that you can do with some imagination and a little VBA code behind your reports. Let's take a look at some of the more common types of reports you can create by adding VBA.

Changing the RecordSource at Runtime

There are many times when you might want to change the data for the report when it opens. For example, if the report is bound to a large table in a SQL Server, you might want to restrict the number of columns and records that are returned in a query at runtime.

Changing the record source for the report can only be done in the Open event of the report by simply setting the RecordSource property. If you try to set the RecordSource property in the Load event, it will fail to bind in Report view and you will get a runtime error in Print Preview.

The following code shows you how to connect to an external data source using a SQL statement and retrieve data.

Available for download on Wrox.com

```
Private Sub Report_Open(Cancel As Integer)
    Dim strSQL        As String
    Dim strConnection As String

    ' create the connection string
    strConnection = "ODBC;DRIVER=SQL Server;" & _
                    "SERVER=<YourServerName>;" & _
                    "DATABASE=<YourDatabaseName>;" & _
                    "Trusted_Connection=Yes"

    ' create the SQL statement that uses the server
    strSQL = "SELECT Company, FirstName, LastName " & _
             "FROM tblConfAttendees " & _
             "IN '' [" & strConnection & "] " & _
```

```
                    "WHERE Company='Microsoft'"

        ' Change the record source
        Me.RecordSource = strSQL
    End Sub
```

> *The preceding code sample uses a copy of the* tblAttendees *table from this chapter. The table in the external data source has been renamed to* tblConfAttendees.

Gathering Information from a Form

There may be times when you want to retrieve some information from a form to provide data to a report. For example, you may want to provide the user with a form to create a filter for the report. You can use the OpenForm method with the acDialog argument to open the form in the report's Open event. acDialog opens the form in a modal view and stops subsequent code from executing. This also prevents the report from opening until the form is closed.

The following is an example of this technique. The code opens a form that contains a unique list of company names in a combo box. When a company is selected, the form is hidden, which runs the remainder of the code in the report. This example also shows you how you can change the record source for a report at runtime.

```
    Private Sub Report_Open(Cancel As Integer)
        Dim strCompany As String

        ` open the form
        DoCmd.OpenForm `frmFilterReport", acNormal, , , , acDialog

        ` get the company
        strCompany = Nz(Forms(`frmFilterReport")!cboCompanies, ``")

        ` set the recordsource for the report
        If (Len(strCompany) > 0) Then
            Me.RecordSource = `SELECT [Last Name], [First Name], Company ` & _
                              `FROM tblAttendees ` & _
                              `WHERE Company = `` & strCompany & ```"
        Else
            Me.RecordSource = `SELECT [Last Name], [First Name], Company ` & _
                              `FROM tblAttendees"
        End If

        DoCmd.Close acForm, `frmFilterReport"
    End Sub
```

Changing the Printer

The `Printer` object was introduced in Access 2002 and greatly simplified changing printer settings or the printer itself for reports. To change the printer for a report, you must open the report in Print Preview, and then change the report's `Printer` property. You cannot change the `Printer` property from the `Open` event of a report, so you'll have to create a form that allows the user to select a printer, and then select a list of reports to send to the printer.

Start by creating a form with two list boxes, named `lstPrinters` and `lstReports`. Set the properties of `lstReports` shown in the table that follows.

PROPERTY NAME	VALUE
RowSource	SELECT Name FROM MSysObjects WHERE Type=-32764 ORDER BY Name;
MultiSelect	Extended

For this example, you use the `MSysObjects` system table to retrieve the list of reports in the database. There are other ways to accomplish that task, but this will suffice.

Before getting into the bulk of the code, you need a variable declaration. Add the following line of code to the declarations section of the form:

Available for download on Wrox.com

```
Private objPrinter As Printer
```

code snippet ReportsChapter.accdb

Next, fill in `lstPrinters`, the list box that will contain the list of installed printers on the computer. To do so, add the following code to the `Load` event of the form:

Available for download on Wrox.com

```
Private Sub Form_Load()
    ` fill the list of printers
    For Each objPrinter In Printers
        Me.lstPrinters.AddItem objPrinter.DeviceName
    Next
End Sub
```

code snippet ReportsChapter.accdb

This code uses the `Application` object's `Printers` collection property. This property contains a collection of all printers installed on the computer. When you run this code, `lstPrinters` should contain the list of all printers on your computer.

Now, you need to be able to print the selected reports. Add a command button to the form named `cmdPrint` with the following code. Also add a checkbox named `chkSendToPrinter`.

```
Private Sub cmdPrint_Click()
    Dim varItem   As Variant
    Dim strReport As String

    ` loop through the selected printers
    For Each varItem In Me.lstReports.ItemsSelected
        ` open the report in print preview
        strReport = Me.lstReports.ItemData(varItem)
        DoCmd.OpenReport strReport, acViewPreview

        ` set the printer
        If (Not IsNull(Me.lstPrinters)) Then
            Set objPrinter = Application.Printers(Me.lstPrinters.Value)
            Set Reports(strReport).Printer = objPrinter

            ` if the check box on the form is checked,
            ` send the report to the printer
            If (Me.chkSendToPrinter) Then
                DoCmd.OpenReport strReport, acViewNormal
            End If

            ` close
            DoCmd.Close acReport, strReport
        End If
    Next
End Sub
```

code snippet ReportsChapter.accdb

This code iterates through the `ItemsSelected` property of the `lstReports` list box and opens each report in Print Preview. It gets a `Printer` object for the printer that was selected in `lstPrinters`. Then, it sets the `Printer` property of the `Report` object to `objPrinter` and conditionally sends it to the printer. Finally, you close the report for cleanup.

Dictionary-Style Headings

Phone books and dictionaries typically add the first entry and last entry at the top of the page to make it easier to find information. You can accomplish this on your reports by adding some code in several different sections. The code uses the `Format` event to create listings at the top of each page. Because this event does not fire for reports open in Report view, you'll need to open the report in Print Preview to see the effect.

The report you'll create is a listing of the attendees for the conference. It is grouped by the first letter of the last name. Figure 15-3 shows part of the report.

You'll modify the report to add two text boxes to the Page Header section. The first control, named `txtFirst`, will be hidden and store the first entry on each page by setting the `ControlSource` property to the last name of the attendee. The second control, named `txtLast`, will be visible and display the attendee entries.

	Last Name	First Name	Company
A			
	Afonso	Pedro	Comércio Mineiro
	Anders	Maria	Alfreds Futterkiste
	Angel Paolino	Miguel	Tortuga Restaurante
	Ashworth	Victoria	B's Beverages
	Accorti	Paolo	Franchi S.p.A.
B			
	Brown	Elizabeth	Consolidated Holdings
	Bennett	Helen	Island Trading
	Bertrand	Marie	Paris spécialités
	Braunschweiger	Art	Split Rail Beer & Ale
	Berglund	Christina	Berglunds snabbköp
	Batista	Bernardo	Que Delicia
	Buchanan	Steven	
	Bergulfsen	Jonas	Santé Gourmet

FIGURE 15-3

The trick is to force Access to do two passes on the report because you need to determine the last attendee on the page and subsequently display it on the top of the page. To do this, use the `Pages` property in the Page Footer. To calculate the number of pages in the report, Access will format the report twice. You also need a report footer section to run some code. Add a text box to the page footer with the following expression:

```
="Page " & [Page] & " of " & [Pages]
```

Now you'll start adding the code. First, add two variables. The first is a flag to indicate whether you are on the first or the second pass. The second will be used to store the last name of the attendee when you get to the bottom of each page.

```
Dim blnFirstPass As Boolean
Dim astrLastNames() As String
```

code snippet ReportsChapter.accdb

Next, add code to the `Open` event of the report. It sets up the array and initializes the flag.

```
Private Sub Report_Open(Cancel As Integer)
    ` start the first pass
    ReDim astrLastNames(0)
    blnFirstPass = True
End Sub
```

code snippet ReportsChapter.accdb

Save the last name of the last attendee on the page. This is the value you want to display at the top of the page. For this, add the following code in the Format event of the Page Footer section:

```
Private Sub PageFooterSection_Format(Cancel As Integer, FormatCount As Integer)
    ` Resize the array
    ReDim Preserve astrLastNames(UBound(astrLastNames) + 1)
    ` Save the Last Name of the last attendee on the page
    astrLastNames(Me.Page - 1) = Me![Last Name]
End Sub
```

code snippet ReportsChapter.accdb

Now you need to display the first entry and the last entry on the page in the Page Header section. Add the following code to the Format event of the section:

```
Private Sub PageHeaderSection_Format(Cancel As Integer, FormatCount As Integer)
    ` Make sure we are not on the first pass
    If (Not blnFirstPass) Then
        Me.txtLast = Me.txtFirst & ` - ` & astrLastNames(Me.Page - 1)
    End If
End Sub
```

code snippet ReportsChapter.accdb

Finally, you set the blnFirstPass flag to False to indicate that the first pass is complete. Add the following code to the Format event of the Report Footer section. The Report Footer is the last formatted section in the report so it's a good place to reset the flag.

```
Private Sub ReportFooter_Format(Cancel As Integer, FormatCount As Integer)
    ` first pass is complete
    blnFirstPass = False
End Sub
```

When you run the report, it should look something like the one shown in Figure 15-4.

Shading Alternate Rows

The ability to set alternating colors for sections was included with Access 2007, so the technique shown here is no longer required for many scenarios. However, you might choose to shade the alternate row color based on the current group level, and for that you still need code. The following example shows you how to combine different section events to provide custom shading based on the group level.

With the sessions and attendees example in mind, imagine you are creating a report brochure that is grouped by day so that you can quickly see the sessions on a given day. In the brochure, you want to shade the presentations on Monday in gray, Tuesday in blue, and Wednesday in yellow. You can accomplish this as follows.

	Last Name	First Name	Company	Rovelli - Zare
R				
	Rovelli	Giovanni	Magazzini Alimentari Riu	
	Rancé	Martine	Folies gourmandes	
S				
	Sergienko	Mariya	Northwind Traders	
	Snyder	Howard	Great Lakes Food Market	
	Simpson	Patricio	Cactus Comidas para llev	
	Steel	John	Lazy K Kountry Store	
	Saveley	Mary	Victuailles en stock	
	Suyama	Michael		
	Sommer	Martín	Bólido Comidas preparad	
	Schmitt	Carine	France restauration	
	Saavedra	Eduardo	Galería del gastrónomo	
T				
	Tonini	Daniel	La corne d'abondance	
	Trujillo	Ana	Ana Trujillo Emparedado	
	Thorpe	Steven	Northwind Traders	
	Tannamuri	Yoshi	Laughing Bacchus Wine	

FIGURE 15-4

Start by declaring a variable to store the shaded color:

```
Private lngShadingColor As Long
```

code snippet ReportsChapter.accdb

Next, add code to the Format event of the GroupHeader section to set the color based on the day:

```
Private Sub GroupHeader0_Format(Cancel As Integer, FormatCount As Integer)
    ` Set the alternate row color based on date
    Select Case Weekday(CDate(Me.txtSessionDate))
        Case vbMonday
            lngShadingColor = &HECECEC
        Case vbTuesday
            lngShadingColor = &HD6DFEC
        Case vbWednesday
            lngShadingColor = vbYellow
    End Select
End Sub
```

code snippet ReportsChapter.accdb

Finally, add the following code to the `Format` event of the `Detail` section to shade the rows. You use a `Static` counter variable to count the rows and then use the `Mod` operator to determine whether the counter value is divisible by two. When it is not divisible by two, you apply the shading.

```
Private Sub Detail_Format(Cancel As Integer, FormatCount As Integer)
    Static intCounter As Integer

    ` reset the counter
    If (Me.Detail.BackColor <> lngShadingColor And _
        Me.Detail.BackColor <> vbWhite) Then
        intCounter = 1
    Else
        intCounter = intCounter + 1
    End If

    If (intCounter Mod 2 = 1) Then
        Me.Detail.BackColor = lngShadingColor
    Else
        Me.Detail.BackColor = vbWhite
    End If
End Sub
```

code snippet ReportsChapter.accdb

A last note about this code: In both Access 2007 and Access 2010, you can just set the `AlternateBackColor` property for the `Detail` section instead of adding code to the `Format` event of the `Detail` section. Access defines the alternate row as the second row. The preceding code defines the alternate row as the first row for a slightly different effect, as shown in Figure 15-5.

10/25/2006			
11	10:00 AM	VBA Debugging	Expert insight for debugging code in VBA.
14	11:00 AM	New Report Events	Reports in Access 2007 support many of the events that their Form counterparts have enjoyed for years. Come to
15	1:00 PM	Programming with Class: Class Modules in Access	What benefit do class modules provide over standard
16	2:00 PM	You Talking to Me?	Learn the ins and outs of using the 'Me' keyword in VBA.

FIGURE 15-5

The Format and Print events do not fire in Report view. There you must use the new Paint event for a section.

Conditional Formatting of a Control

Access includes a feature called Conditional Formatting that enables you to change formatting properties of a control based on an expression. This is a powerful feature that is made more powerful in Access 2010 by allowing more than three conditions for a control. Even with more conditions, there may still be times where you want to use code for conditional formatting. For example, you may want to set properties that are not available in conditional formatting such as gridlines or visibility.

The following example sets the BackColor property for a control called AvgOfRating based on its value. It calls a routine from the Paint and Format events to achieve the same effect in Report view or Print Preview.

Available for download on Wrox.com

```
Private Sub SetControlFormatting()
    If (Me.AvgOfRating >= 8) Then
        Me.AvgOfRating.BackColor = vbGreen
    ElseIf (Me.AvgOfRating >= 5) Then
        Me.AvgOfRating.BackColor = vbYellow
    Else
        Me.AvgOfRating.BackColor = vbRed
    End If
End Sub

Private Sub Detail_Format(Cancel As Integer, FormatCount As Integer)
    ` do conditional formatting for the control in print preview
    SetControlFormatting
End Sub

Private Sub Detail_Paint()
    ` do conditional formatting for the control in Report view
    SetControlFormatting
End Sub
```

code snippet ReportsChapter.accdb

Creating a Progress Meter Report

Progress meter reports are an interesting way to display status as a percentage of a given value. In the conference application, for example, you could ask the attendees to rate each session on a scale of 1 to 10, and enter the data in a table called tblSessionRatings. Aggregate the data using the following query:

```
SELECT tblSessionRatings.Session,
    tblSessions.Title,
    CDate(CLng([Start Time])) AS SessionDate,
    Avg(tblSessionRatings.Rating) AS AvgOfRating
FROM tblSessions
RIGHT JOIN tblSessionRatings
    ON tblSessions.ID=tblSessionRatings.Session
GROUP BY tblSessionRatings.Session, tblSessions.Title, CDate(CLng([Start Time]))
ORDER BY tblSessions.Title,
    CDate(CLng([Start Time])),
    Avg(tblSessionRatings.Rating) DESC;
```

Figure 15-6 shows the query's result.

Session	Title	SessionDate	AvgOfRating
3	Creating Forms and Reports	10/23/2006	3.5
7	Creating Forms and Reports	10/24/2006	7
1	Introduction to Microsoft Access	10/23/2006	7
5	Introduction to Microsoft Access	10/24/2006	8.5
2	VBA Debugging	10/23/2006	6
6	VBA Debugging	10/24/2006	4.5
11	VBA Debugging	10/25/2006	8
4	What's New in Access 2007	10/23/2006	4.5
16	You Talking to Me?	10/26/2006	10

qrySessionRatings

FIGURE 15-6

This data is valuable, but you can make it stand out by using a report. Because you're working with a fixed scale (1–10), you can display the rating as a percentage of 10. To do so, you create the report based on the query and add two rectangle controls to the Detail section of the report. Name the rectangles `boxInside` and `boxOutside` and position `boxInside` inside `boxOutside` as the names suggest. For each average rating, you'll resize the width of `boxInside` to a percentage of the width of `boxOutside`.

You cannot resize controls in Report view, so you'll add code to the `Load` event of the report to hide the rectangles if the report is not opened in Print Preview. Add the following code to the `Load` event:

Available for download on Wrox.com

```
Private Sub Report_Load()
    If (Me.CurrentView = AcCurrentView.acCurViewPreview) Then
        Me.boxInside.Visible = True
        Me.boxOutside.Visible = True
    Else
        Me.boxInside.Visible = False
        Me.boxOutside.Visible = False
    End If
End Sub
```

code snippet ReportsChapter.accdb

Next, to resize the width of `boxInside`, add the following code to the Detail section's `Format` event:

Available for download on Wrox.com

```
Private Sub Detail_Format(Cancel As Integer, FormatCount As Integer)
    Dim lngOffset As Long

    ` Calculate the offset between boxOutside and boxInside for effect
    lngOffset = (Me.boxInside.Left - Me.boxOutside.Left) * 2

    ` size the width of the rectangle and subtract the offset
    Me.boxInside.Width = (Me.boxOutside.Width * (Me.AvgOfRating / 10)) - lngOffset
End Sub
```

code snippet ReportsChapter.accdb

This code divides the average rating by the maximum rating (10) to get a percentage, and then multiplies that percentage by the width of the outside rectangle to set the width of the inside rectangle. For effect, `boxOutside` is slightly offset from `boxInside` so that it looks like there is a border around `boxInside`. Therefore, you calculate this offset and multiply it by 2 to achieve the padding on both sides. The offset represents the difference between the `Left` property of `boxInside` and the `Left` property of `boxOutside`. Figure 15-7 shows the report.

Session Ratings		
Title	**Session Date**	**Avg. Rating**
Introduction to Microsoft Access	10/23/2006	3.5
	10/24/2006	7.0
VBA Debugging	10/23/2006	7.0
	10/24/2006	8.5
Introduction to Microsoft Access	10/23/2006	6.0
	10/24/2006	4.5
	10/25/2006	8.0
VBA Debugging	10/23/2006	4.5
Creating Forms and Reports	10/26/2006	10.0

FIGURE 15-7

 Data bar conditional formatting in Access 2010 provides similar functionality but only allows one color for the values. By creating your own progress bars, you can add additional styles and formatting to the rectangle controls.

LAYOUT VIEW

If you've designed reports in Access in the past and found that you had to frequently switch between Design view and Print Preview, then Layout view is for you. The primary advantage of using Layout view is its speed in creating something that gives you a sense of how the report will look onscreen or in print. That's because Layout view is a combination of Design view and Browse view, giving you a live view of the data while you perform certain design type tasks, including the following:

➤ Adding and renaming controls

➤ Grouping and sorting

➤ Adding totals

➤ Formatting controls and sections

➤ Applying an Office theme

➤ Adding new fields

➤ Adding controls to layouts and formatting layouts

➤ Binding the record source

➤ Changing the record source

➤ Changing many other properties

➤ Applying conditional formatting to a text box or combo box

As you can see, there's a lot that can be accomplished in Layout view, all while viewing the live data in the record source to give you a better perspective of the end result. There are, however, a few tasks that cannot be accomplished using Layout view:

➤ Adding code or setting the `HasModule` property

➤ Changing the orientation

➤ Changing the height of a section

Because Layout view is the only way to create forms and reports for Access Services applications, the improvements are intended to go a long way toward being able to build powerful objects for the Web. Even if you're not building an application for Access Services, the changes to Layout view in Access 2010 make creating reports even easier and can save quite a bit of time.

REPORT VIEW

As mentioned at the beginning of this chapter, Access 2007 introduced a new interactive view for reports called Report view. It is the default view for new reports created in both Access 2007 and Access 2010 and gives you much of the same functionality that you've enjoyed with forms, including the capability to search, sort and filter, and even copy! Let's look at some ways you can use all that new functionality.

Considerations When Designing for Report View

Before you start switching all of your existing reports to use Report view, there are a few things to consider.

Where Are All My Pages?

The first thing you'll notice about Report view is that there aren't any pages. A report open in Report view is really one big page that you scroll like a continuous form. Because of this, calculations that depend on the `Page` or `Pages` properties of the report may return unexpected results.

Events

As mentioned earlier, the `Format` and `Print` events don't fire in Report view. That's because those events are used with individual sections as a report is printed.

Because reports opened in Report view are not printed, there is a new `Paint` event to use with sections in Report view. As you learned earlier in the "Paint Event" section, `Paint` fires multiple times for a single section because of the way that controls are drawn on reports. When a section is being painted, it is too late to hide it, so you cannot dynamically hide sections on a report open in Report view. That's why the `Paint` event handler does not include any arguments.

Controls

With this newfound interactivity, you might be tempted to add other controls you wouldn't normally add to a report such as a command button. To maintain the rich printed view, you'll want to hide those controls when the report is printed. To do so, check the `CurrentView` property of the report, or change the `DisplayWhen` property of the control to `Screen Only`. That displays the control in Report view but hides it in Print Preview.

Text box and combo box controls have a new property called `DisplayAsHyperlink`. It's similar in concept to the `DisplayWhen` property in that it determines how information or data is displayed for screen versus print. `DisplayAsHyperlink` can be used to format data as a hyperlink in screen views such as Report or Layout, but not printed views. The result is that fields displayed as hyperlinks include formatting such as underlines and link colors onscreen, but print without those embellishments.

See the table that follows for the values of this property.

VALUE	DESCRIPTION
If Hyperlink	Formats text as a hyperlink if it is recognized as a hyperlink. This is the default.
Always	Text is formatted as a hyperlink in all views.
Screen Only	Text is formatted as a hyperlink, but not in printed views.

Interactivity

The capability to search, sort and filter, and copy data makes reports much easier to use than in previous versions. In addition to the standard Access functionality, you can add your own interactivity in reports that has only been available in forms in the past. Using some of these features, it is possible to create great reports that act in much the same way as read-only forms, but have the additional benefit of a great printed view.

Hyperlinks

Now that reports are interactive, you can click on hyperlinks in a report to open a Web browser or another object in the database. For instance, you can use a report to list information about one of the conference sessions from earlier examples, and include the link on the report to more information on the session's website.

Drill-Down/Click-Through

By using a hyperlink or the `Click` event of a text box or command button, you can provide drill-down functionality in a report to view detailed information. The templates in Access 2010 frequently use this technique. For example, when you click on the name of a session on a report, you can open a form or another report that shows the attendees for the session and their ratings. The "Query by Report" section coming up includes an example of this.

Multiple Report Instances

Sometimes you might want to show multiple instances of a report to display different pieces of data. A common example is to change the filter or sort for a given report. Because modules behind forms and reports are class modules, you can create new instances of them using syntax such as this:

```
Dim objMyReport as Report_rptMyReport
Set objMyReport = New Report_rptMyReport
objMyReport.Visible = True
```

With interactive reports, you can enable this scenario in your solutions as a part of the drill-down/click-through scenario. Using multiple report instances is another way to enhance the user experience to provide different views of the same report.

 You can find more information about using forms as class modules in Chapters 8 and 14. The concepts introduced for forms also apply to reports.

Query by Report

Another feature that forms have always enjoyed is the capability to create a query that uses a control on a form as criteria in the query. The technique is known as *query by form*, and much has been written about it over the years. With the advent of Report view in Access 2007, reports also can take advantage of this useful feature. Because controls on reports can also receive focus (in Report view), you can now refer to controls on reports as criteria in a query.

Consider the conference tracking application. You have a report that lists the attendees and you want to open another report that you can print as an invoice for the items they purchased. By clicking on an attendee's name, you can run a query something like this:

```
SELECT tblAttendeeSales.Attendee,
       tblAttendeeSales.Quantity,
       tblItems.ItemName,
       tblItems.NormalPrice,
       tblItems.ConferenceDiscount
       tblAttendees.Company,
       tblAttendees.Address,
       tblAttendees.City,
       tblAttendees.[State/Province],
       tblAttendees.[ZIP/Postal Code]
FROM tblAttendees
INNER JOIN (tblItems INNER JOIN tblAttendeeSales ON tblItems.ItemID =
tblAttendeeSales.ItemID) ON tblAttendees.ID = tblAttendeeSales.Attendee
WHERE tblAttendeeSales.Attendee = [Reports]![rptAttendeesDirectory]![ID] OR
[Reports]![rptAttendeesDirectory]![ID] Is Null
```

This query uses the data from three tables to create the invoice. Note the WHERE clause of the query that uses the reference to the ID control on the report called rptAttendeesDirectory. The invoice report is bound to this query so all you have to do from the directory report is open the invoice report as follows:

```
Private Sub Last_Name_Click()
    ` open the invoice
    DoCmd.OpenReport `rptSalesInvoice", acViewReport
End Sub
```

The query uses the ID for the current record on the report to display a single invoice record.

SUMMARY

This chapter provided a closer look at reports and some of the features that make them different from forms. You saw various methods for creating reports and some of the different events you can use with reports and sections. In addition, you learned some ways to extend reports by adding just a small amount of VBA code — in many cases, it doesn't take much code to make reports more interesting, just a solid knowledge of how reports work and when events fire.

The chapter also presented an in-depth look at some of the new features for reports in both Access 2010 as well as Access 2007, and how you can use these features to make report creation easier and to extend the user experience around working with reports.

16

Customizing the Ribbon

WHAT'S IN THIS CHAPTER?

➤ How to create custom ribbons for your solutions

➤ Adding your own functionality to the Access ribbon

➤ Using callback routines written in VBA to extend the functionality of your custom ribbons

➤ Tips for Ribbon development

Unless you've used Access 2007, the first time you open Access 2010, you'll notice that things are different. The familiar menu bar and toolbars have been replaced with the Ribbon. The new interface may appear a bit daunting, but it's only a matter of time until you've learned where commands are located and are more comfortable with it.

This chapter provides a brief look at the Ribbon in Access 2010 and discusses some of the design goals of the Ribbon that you can apply to your applications. Then comes the fun stuff: customization. You start by examining the types of objects you can create in a custom ribbon, and then use what you learn to create two sample applications with different design goals: a ribbon that integrates with the Access Ribbon, and another to replace the Access Ribbon. As you'll soon see, the Ribbon is highly customizable, which can help you create new and exciting interfaces for your own applications.

Ribbon customizations are written in XML. Even if you've never written XML or are just getting started with XML, don't worry — it's straightforward and easy to understand. This chapter offers you the information and tools you need to customize the Ribbon (and learn a little about XML at the same time).

RIBBON OVERVIEW

The Ribbon, the new interface that appears at the top of the majority of the applications in both Office 2007 and Office 2010, is designed to provide easier access to those tools that you use most. No longer are the most common commands buried under several layers of menus or hard-to-discover toolbars. Microsoft has added a Home tab in each of the Office applications that support the Ribbon, and it contains the most commonly used tools in that application.

The Ribbon is supported in all applications for Office 2010. Figure 16-1 shows the Home tab in Access 2010.

FIGURE 16-1

Each group of controls in a tab in the Ribbon is, appropriately enough, called a *group*. The Home tab in Access contains a group to change views (Views), a group to access the clipboard (Clipboard), groups to work with data (Records, Sort & Filter, and Find), and a group to work with formatting (Text Formatting).

The Access 2010 Ribbon includes three additional default tabs:

➤ **Create:** Replaces the Insert menu in previous versions of Access. Use it to create the different types of objects in your database such as Forms and Reports.

➤ **External Data:** Replaces the Get External Data and Import menu items on the File menu in previous versions. It contains the tools that enable you to import and export data.

➤ **Database Tools:** Replaces much of the Tools menu in previous versions of Access.

You may also notice that there seem to be fewer controls or items available in the Ribbon when compared to previous Access menus and toolbars. That's because many of the tools are available only in a particular mode. These tools are said to be *contextual* — that is, they only apply under the context of a particular task.

CUSTOM MENU BARS AND TOOLBARS

If you built custom menu bars and toolbars in previous versions of Access, you might wonder what happens to those in Access 2010. Well, don't worry — you can still use them in Access 2010, although their appearance may be different than what you are used to.

Custom Menu Bars

Custom menu bars that you created in previous versions of Access will appear as a menu bar as long as you have set the `Allow Full Menus` property to `No`. In previous versions of Access, this property appears in the Startup dialog box under the Tools menu. If you have not set this property, custom menu bars will appear on a separate tab in the Ribbon called Add-Ins.

Shortcut Menu Bars

The shortcut menu bars that you created for forms in previous versions of Access will continue to work in Access 2010. They will appear on the context menu, not in the Ribbon. However, the tools for creating toolbars and menu bars have been removed. Unfortunately this means there is no way to create a new shortcut menu bar unless you write code or use a previous version of Access.

The following code (which requires a reference to the Microsoft Office 14.0 Type Library) creates a shortcut menu with two button controls. For more information about the `CommandBar` Object Model, please visit the MSDN website at `http://msdn.microsoft.com`.

Available for download on Wrox.com

```
Public Sub CreateShortcutMenu(strName As String)
    Dim objCommandBar As Office.CommandBar
    Dim objCommandBarControl As Office.CommandBarControl

    ` create the shortcut menu
    Set objCommandBar = Application.CommandBars.Add(strName, msoBarPopup)

    ` create a control
    Set objCommandBarControl = objCommandBar.Controls.Add(msoControlButton)
    objCommandBarControl.Caption = "Button1"
    objCommandBarControl.OnAction = "=MsgBox(`Button1´)"

    ` create another control
    Set objCommandBarControl = objCommandBar.Controls.Add(msoControlButton)
    objCommandBarControl.Caption = "Button2"
    objCommandBarControl.OnAction = "=MsgBox(`Button2´)"

    ` Cleanup
    Set objCommandBarControl = Nothing
    Set objCommandBar = Nothing
End Sub
```

code snippet RibbonSamples.accdb

RIBBON CUSTOMIZATION USING THE OPTIONS DIALOG BOX

The majority of this chapter is about writing your own customizations for the Ribbon that you can include in applications for Access 2010. However, this is not the only way to create a customization. New in Office 2010 is the ability to create a ribbon customization in the Access Options dialog box, as shown in Figure 16-2.

On the right side of the dialog box, you can create new tabs and groups, and add built-in controls. This is useful for creating ribbons where existing commands are used, but this does not allow you to create custom buttons or controls that call your own code. For this, you'll need to write your own customizations as described in the remainder of this chapter.

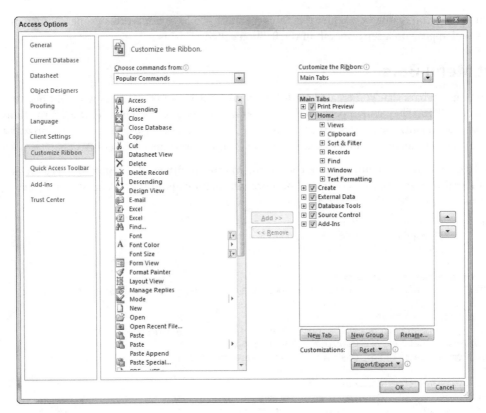

FIGURE 16-2

RIBBON CUSTOMIZATION

Because you could customize your applications by creating custom menu bars and toolbars in previous versions of Office or Access, you want similar functionality for the Ribbon. Microsoft has created a rich customization model that enables you to create your own ribbons for use in your applications. Ribbon customizations are written in XML, and must conform to a specified schema that can be downloaded from the Microsoft website. To find the download, search www.microsoft.com/downloads for "2010 XML Schema Reference."

SAVING A CUSTOM RIBBON

Because you'll probably want to test your custom ribbon as you build it, let's start by talking about how to use ribbon customizations in Access. The primary way to use a custom ribbon is with a special table named USysRibbons. This section explains how you can create this table.

Access loads ribbon customizations from a `USysRibbons` table, which contains the fields shown in the table that follows:

FIELD NAME	DATA TYPE	DESCRIPTION
RibbonName	TEXT	Contains the name of a ribbon that you use in your application. You can specify the name of a ribbon for a form, report, or database.
RibbonXml	MEMO	Contains the XML definition for the ribbon customization.

Alternatively, you can create this table using the following SQL statement in a DDL query:

```
CREATE TABLE USysRibbons
(
    RibbonName TEXT (255) PRIMARY KEY,
    RibbonXml MEMO
);
```

code snippet RibbonSamples.accdb

You can also create application-level ribbons using a COM Add-in. Chapter 20 provides more information about writing a COM Add-in to customize the Ribbon.

To define multiple ribbons in your application, simply add a new record to the `USysRibbons` table.

There is yet another way to create the `USysRibbons` table for use in your databases: by creating a database called `Blank.accdb`. When you create a new blank database in Access 2010, Access first looks for a file named `Blank.accdb` in the Office\Templates directory. If it finds one, it creates a copy of the file for your new Blank Database. If this file contains a `USysRibbons` table, your new database automatically includes the table.

The `USysRibbons` table should be local to the database you are customizing. Ribbon customizations are not loaded if the `USysRibbons` table is linked in another database.

SPECIFYING THE CUSTOM RIBBON

Once you write a ribbon customization, you need some way to display it for your database, form, or report. That's where the new `Ribbon Name` property (in the Current Database group of the Access Options dialog box) comes in. To set the ribbon for a database, you just set this property to the name of a ribbon in the USysRibbons table. Your custom ribbon displays when you re-open the database.

For form and report ribbons, set the Ribbon Name property on the Other tab of the form or report Property Sheet.

Defining a Ribbon Using XML

Before jumping in to write the XML, there is one change to make to your Access environment. By default, any errors that may be caused by the XML are not displayed. Instead, the customization may fail without warning and not load. To see the errors, you must enable the Show Add-In User Interface Errors option in the General section of the Client Settings group of the Access Options dialog box.

You can write XML using a text editor such as Notepad, or an integrated development environment (IDE) such as Visual Studio or XML Spy. The examples in this chapter use Microsoft Visual Web Developer 2008 Express Edition, which at the time of this writing is freely available for download using the Microsoft Web Platform Installer from the Microsoft website, www.microsoft.com/express/Web/.

Many IDEs such as Visual Web Developer provide auto-completion, or IntelliSense, when an XML Schema (XSD) is available. Because the XML you write here is based on a schema, the process is greatly simplified.

Using the Ribbon Schema

The schema file for ribbon customizations is called customui14.xsd. Using Visual Web Developer, the first thing to do is create a new XML file. Once the file is created, click the button in the Schemas property to open the Schemas dialog box. Click the Add button on the right of the dialog box to browse to the customui14.xsd XML schema that is included in the 2010 Office System: XML Schema Reference. Figure 16-3 shows the schema file added to the dialog box.

> *You can save the step of adding the schema by copying* customui14.xsd *to* %programfiles%\Microsoft Visual Studio 9.0\Xml\Schemas *or* %programfiles(x86%)\Microsoft Visual Studio 9.0\Xml\Schemas *if you are running 64-bit Windows.*

Writing the XML

Once you point Visual Web Developer to the schema, you're ready to start writing. The *root node* of a ribbon customization is:

```
<customUI xmlns="http://schemas.microsoft.com/office/2009/07/customui">
```

> *A root node is the node at the top of an XML document. There is one, and only one, root node in any given document.*

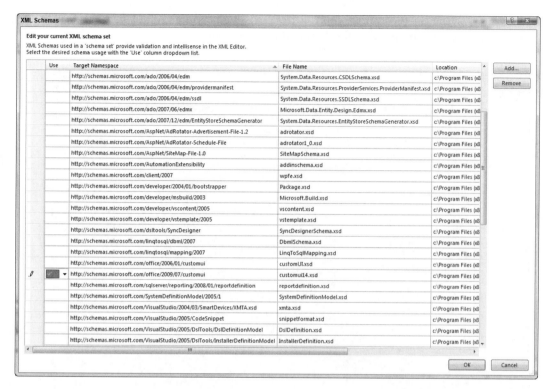

FIGURE 16-3

The namespace specified by the `xmlns` attribute is known as the default namespace. It defines the elements and attributes used when you write a ribbon customization. Within a customization, you can create a Ribbon, modify commands in the Quick Access Toolbar, or modify the Office Backstage. You'll look at customizing the Office Backstage in Chapter 17.

Next, tell the XML that you are creating a ribbon by adding the `ribbon` tag to define it:

```
<ribbon startFromScratch="true">
```

The `startFromScratch` attribute tells Access whether to display the built-in Ribbon. Use the following XML to create an empty ribbon for your database, as shown in Figure 16-4.

```
<customUI xmlns="http://schemas.microsoft.com/office/2009/07/customui">
    <ribbon startFromScratch="true"/>
</customUI>
```

Later in this chapter, you'll build two solutions — one that is incorporated into the Access Ribbon and one that you build from scratch.

Adding Tabs and Groups

Controls such as buttons, drop-downs, and checkboxes are organized into tabs and groups in the Ribbon. Tabs appear at the top of the Ribbon and contain groups. You can define your own tabs and groups, or you can incorporate controls from existing tabs and groups. Tabs are defined using the `tab` element and groups are defined using the `group` element.

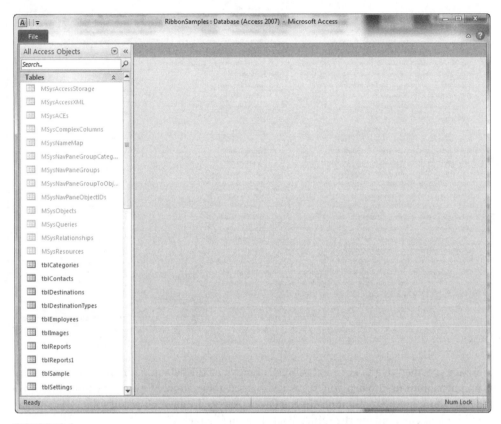

FIGURE 16-4

Here's an example. Say you want to add a tab with one group to the existing Ribbon. The following XML adds a new tab called `My Tab` at the end of the existing tab set. Start with the `customUI` node and the `ribbon` node that you saw in the previous section:

Available for download on Wrox.com

```
<customUI xmlns="http://schemas.microsoft.com/office/2009/07/customui">
    <ribbon startFromScratch="false">
```

To define tabs, you first add a `tabs` node under the `ribbon` node to say that you are defining a tab set:

```
<tabs>
```

Next, add the tab using the `tab` node as follows:

```
<tab id="tabMyTab" label="My Tab">
```

Add the group below the tab:

```
<group id="grpMyGroup" label="My Group"></group>
```

Now, finish the XML by adding the end nodes:

```
          </tab>
        </tabs>
      </ribbon>
    </customUI>
```

code snippet in table USysRibbons in RibbonSamples.accdb

Notice that the `tab` and `group` nodes include attributes named `id` and `label`. All controls that you add to your ribbon including tabs and groups must have an `ID` attribute, which is a string that is unique throughout the ribbon and cannot contain spaces. Add this XML to the `RibbonXml` field of the `USysRibbons` table.

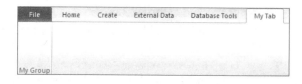

FIGURE 16-5

Assign the XML the name **My First Ribbon** in the `RibbonName` field and then set the `Ribbon Name` property in the Access Options dialog box to the same name: My First Ribbon. When you've completed these steps, you should have something that looks like the ribbon shown in Figure 16-5.

Congratulations! You've just written your first custom ribbon!

> *For the remainder of this section, the* `customUI` *and* `ribbon` *nodes are omitted in the XML. Except where noted, each of the following examples should include these nodes.*

If you are using an IDE that provides IntelliSense, you may have noticed an attribute in the `tab` node called `insertBeforeMso` or `insertAfterMso`. You can use these attributes to set the position of a tab relative to an existing tab in Access. For example, here's the XML that will move the My Tab tab to the beginning of the Ribbon instead of the end:

```
<tabs>
    <tab id="tabMyTab" insertBeforeMso="TabHomeAccess" label="My Tab">
        <group id="grpMyGroup" label="My Group"/>
    </tab>
</tabs>
```

code snippet in table USysRibbons in RibbonSamples.accdb

The first tab always receives the focus after a tab is switched. Imagine that your My Tab tab appears before the Home tab, and you open a form in Design view. Forms and reports in Design view display a contextual tab that enables you to work with the design surfaces. When you close the form, focus is given back to the first tab — in this case, the custom My Tab. You'll see more about contextual tabs shortly.

 Any attribute that ends with Mso *refers to items provided by Office. For example,* imageMso *refers to images that are included in Office. This attribute is discussed later in the chapter.*

It is also possible to add a new group to an existing tab by specifying the idMso attribute. You can use this attribute to refer to tabs, groups, and even controls that are provided by Office. (More on re-using groups and controls later.)

The following XML adds the group called My Group after the Clipboard group in the Home tab:

Available for download on Wrox.com

```
<tabs>
  <tab idMso="TabHomeAccess">
    <group id="grpMyGroup" label="My Group" insertAfterMso="GroupClipboard"/>
  </tab>
</tabs>
```

code snippet in table USysRibbons in RibbonSamples.accdb

Figure 16-6 shows the result.

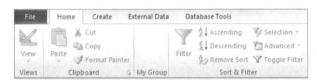

FIGURE 16-6

Fun, huh? Wait, it gets better!

You can also choose to include an existing group in another tab. For example, the Clipboard group contains the familiar controls for Cut, Copy, and Paste, which are pretty useful, so say you want to include that group in your tab. The following XML adds the Clipboard group and two custom groups to My Tab:

Available for download on Wrox.com

```
<tabs>
  <tab id="tabMyTab" label="My Tab">
    <group id="grpMyGroup1" label="First Group"/>
    <group idMso="GroupClipboard"/>
    <group id="grpMyGroup2" label="Second Group"/>
  </tab>
</tabs>
```

code snippet in table USysRibbons in RibbonSamples.accdb

The result of this ribbon is shown in Figure 16-7.

Now let's take a look at contextual tabs.

Contextual Tabs

FIGURE 16-7

As mentioned earlier, a contextual tab is designed to appear for a specific task. For example, contextual tabs are used in Access for designing objects, setting margins on a report, or working with relationships. You can define contextual tabs for forms and reports by setting the Ribbon Name property of the form or report.

Contextual tabs work slightly different from regular tabs. To define a contextual tab, you use the `contextualTab` node, which contains a `tabSet` node. The tab set for contextual tabs is defined by Access and must be specified using the `idMso` attribute `TabSetFormReportExtensibility`.

Here's what it looks like:

Available for download on Wrox.com

```xml
<customUI xmlns="http://schemas.microsoft.com/office/2009/07/customui">
  <ribbon startFromScratch="false">
    <contextualTabs>
      <tabSet idMso="TabSetFormReportExtensibility">
        <tab id="tabMyCTab" label="My Contextual Tab">
          <group id="grpMyGroup" label="Group1"/>
        </tab>
      </tabSet>
    </contextualTabs>
  </ribbon>
</customUI>
```

code snippet in table USysRibbons in RibbonSamples.accdb

Contextual tabs receive the focus when the object is opened, and are hidden when the object loses focus. They are not given focus when you switch back to the form or report.

You design contextual tabs to give context or meaning to specific forms or reports. Use a tab if you have functionality that you want to be available throughout your application. The `Caption` property of a form or report is used as the title of the tab set in the window, as shown in Figure 16-8.

Adding Controls

There is a wide range of controls that you can use in your customizations. Because you've already examined tabs and groups, the XML that follows only describes the controls. To use these controls in the ribbon, you need to include `tab` and `group` nodes in addition to the `customUI` and `ribbon` nodes.

The solutions that you build later in this chapter will use these controls, including two of the more interesting controls: galleries and dynamic menus.

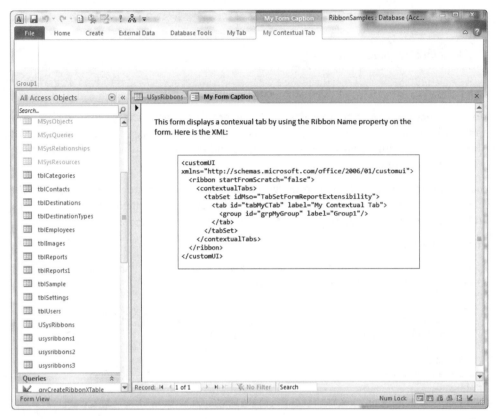

FIGURE 16-8

Menus and Menu Separators

A menu control is a container for other types of controls and is specified using the menu node. You can specify the size of the menu control in the ribbon using the size attribute. You can also specify the size of items in the menu using the itemSize attribute. Possible values for both attributes are normal, shown in Figure 16-9, and large, shown in Figure 16-10.

The following XML defines a large menu with three buttons and two menu separators:

Available for
download on
Wrox.com

```
<menu id="mnuSample" label="Sample Menu" size="large" itemSize="large">
    <menuSeparator id="msep1" title="Separator 1"/>
    <button id="btnSample1" label="Button1"/>
    <button id="btnSample2" label="Button2"/>
    <menuSeparator id="msep2" title="Separator 2"/>
    <button id="btnSample3" label="Button3"/>
</menu>
```

code snippet in table USysRibbons in RibbonSamples.accdb

You can use the `menuSeparator` node inside a `menu` node to add a menu separator. The `title` attribute of the `menuSeparator` sets the text for the menu separator.

FIGURE 16-9

Buttons, Toggle Buttons, and Split Buttons

The vast majority of controls you use will be buttons. As with menus, buttons are available in two sizes: `normal` and `large`. To create a button in your customization, use the `button` node as shown in the following XML:

```
<button id="btnSample" label="Sample Button"/>
```

You can use a toggle button to reflect a state such as on or off, or true or false. An example of the toggle button in Access is the Bold button. To create a toggle button, use the `toggleButton` node as shown in the following XML:

```
<toggleButton id="tglNormal"
    label="toggleButton (size=normal)`"/>
```

Split buttons are a new control that you can use in either Office 2007 or Office 2010. They contain a menu and either a button or a toggle button. The effect is similar to that of a menu, but there is a button that is included in the ribbon as well. The following XML shows how to create a split button with a button:

Available for download on Wrox.com

```
<splitButton id="sb1">
    <button id="b2" label="button in splitButton"/>
    <menu id="mnu2" label="menu in splitButton">
    <button id="b3" label="splitButton > menu > button"/>
    <button id="b4" label="splitButton > menu > button"/>
    </menu>
</splitButton>
```

FIGURE 16-10

code snippet in table USysRibbons in RibbonSamples.accdb

The different types of buttons are shown in Figure 16-11.

To run your own code when a button or toggle button is clicked, handle the `onAction` callback. To get the pressed state for a toggle button using code, handle the `getPressed` callback. Callback actions are discussed later in the "Writing Callback Routines and Macros" section.

button (size=normal)	onAction (macro)	Open Form3			
Save (re-used)	Open Form1	toggleButton (size=normal)	button	toggleButton	button (in
onAction (macro)	Open Form2	button (in splitButton) ▾	(size=large)	(size=large)	splitButton) ▾
		Button Samples			

FIGURE 16-11

Check Boxes

As with a toggle button, a checkbox is used to show true or false, or on or off. To create a checkbox in your customization, use the `checkBox` node, as shown in the following XML:

```
<checkBox id="chkSample" label="Sample Checkbox"/>
```

You can use a checkbox control by itself or inside of a menu control. The appearance of a checkbox in a menu is different from a checkbox outside of a menu, as shown in Figure 16-12.

To run your own code when a checkbox is checked, handle the `onAction` callback. To get the checked state for a checkbox using code, handle the `getPressed` callback.

FIGURE 16-12

Combo Boxes and Drop-Downs

The Ribbon offers two types of controls for listing multiple items — the combo box and the drop-down. There are a couple of differences between these two controls. First, you can type text into a

combo box control but not into a drop-down. Also, although both combo box and drop-down controls contain `item` nodes for their items, the drop-down control can also contain buttons, as shown in Figure 16-13.

The `size` attribute is not available for these controls, but you can set their width using the `sizeString` attribute. The width of the control is set to the width of the

FIGURE 16-13

text specified in this attribute. For example, if you set the `sizeString` to WWWWW, the width of the control is sized to fit the literal string WWWWW.

To create a combo box in your customization, use the `comboBox` node, as shown in the following XML:

```
<comboBox id="cboSample" label="Sample Combo Box"/>
```

To create a drop-down in your customization, use the `dropDown` node:

```
<dropDown id="ddnSample" label="Sample Drop Down"/>
```

The following XML shows a combo box control with three items:

```
<comboBox id="cboSample" label="comboBox">
    <item id="item1" label="item1"/>
    <item id="item2" label="item2"/>
    <item id="item3" label="item3"/>
</comboBox>
```

code snippet in table USysRibbons in RibbonSamples.accdb

Drop-downs and combo boxes in ribbon customizations can be very useful. For example, to provide a mechanism to log in to your application, you can create a drop-down control to display a list of user names that the user can select. Or, you might want to list the days of the week for a filter. Because that list is static, the drop-down control in a ribbon might be a good place to display it. You'll see an example of the latter when you build your first solution.

To run your own code when an item is selected, handle the `onAction` callback. You can fill the items in a combo box or drop-down using three callback functions: `getItemCount`, `getItemLabel`, and `getItemID`.

Edit Boxes and Labels

Edit boxes also allow text to be typed in the ribbon. You create an edit box using the `editBox` node. The control enables you to limit the amount of text that is typed in the edit box using the `maxLength` argument, as shown in the following XML:

```
<editBox id="txtEditSample" label="editBox" maxLength="5" onChange="onEditChange"/>
```

code snippet in table USysRibbons in RibbonSamples.accdb

Figure 16-14 shows what the ribbon looks like when too much text is typed in an `editBox` control.

As the name implies, the `labelControl` node is used to display static text in the ribbon. You might use this control to display messages to your users, such as status information, or the current date. The following XML uses the `labelControl` node to display static text:

FIGURE 16-14

```
<labelControl id="lblSample" label="Sample Label"/>
```

To run your own code when the text is updated in an edit box control, handle the `onChange` callback. To dynamically get the text for a label control, handle the `getLabel` callback.

Separator

A `separator` node is used to provide separation between controls. The separator control appears as a vertical line between controls in the ribbon and is created with the following XML:

```
<separator id="sepMySeparator"/>
```

DialogBoxLauncher

Let's say that you have many choices or options to display to the user — perhaps user settings that are part of your application — but you don't necessarily want to show them all in the ribbon. You might choose to use a form to collect all the related information from the user, and still decide to show the more common options in the ribbon. To make it easy to get to the full set of options, you can use a dialog box launcher in the ribbon to open a form in your database. By using the dialog box launcher, you can avoid having a separate `button` node in the group to open the form.

Use the `dialogBoxLauncher` node to create a launcher in a group. It requires a `button` node that is used to handle the click action taken by the user. The dialog box launcher adds a small button in the bottom of the Other Controls group label, as shown in Figure 16-15.

FIGURE 16-15

The following XML shows a dialog box launcher that displays a message box when clicked:

```
<dialogBoxLauncher>
    <button id="btnDlgLauncher" onAction="=MsgBox(`Open a dialog here´)"/>
</dialogBoxLauncher>
```

code snippet in table USysRibbons in RibbonSamples.accdb

Grouping Controls

There are a few additional types of controls that can be used to group other controls. A `box` control is used to group controls either horizontally or vertically. A `buttonGroup` control is used to group

FIGURE 16-16

button type controls and adds some style to the group. Buttons inside a `buttonGroup` do not support the size attribute for large buttons. You also can use a `separator` to display a vertical line between controls for separation. Each of these controls is shown in Figure 16-16.

Here's the XML for the grouping control ribbon:

```
<group id="grpMiscSample" label="Other Controls">
    <box boxStyle="horizontal" id="boxHorizontal">
        <button id="boxButton1" label="inside horizontal box" size="large"/>
        <button id="boxButton2" label="inside horizontal box" size="large"/>
    </box>
    <separator id="sep1"/>
    <box boxStyle="vertical" id="boxVertical">
        <button id="boxButton3" label="in vertical box"/>
        <button id="boxButton4" label="in vertical box"/>
        <button id="boxButton5" label="in vertical box"/>
    </box>
    <separator id="sep2"/>
    <buttonGroup id="bgrp1">
        <button id="boxButton6" label="button 6"/>
        <button id="boxButton7" label="button 7"/>
    </buttonGroup>
    <buttonGroup id="bgrp2">
        <button id="boxButton8" label="button 8"/>
        <button id="boxButton9" label="button 9"/>
    </buttonGroup>
    <buttonGroup id="bgrp3">
        <button id="boxButton10" label="button 10"/>
        <button id="boxButton11" label="button 11"/>
    </buttonGroup>
    <dialogBoxLauncher>
        <button id="btnDlgLauncher" onAction="=MsgBox(`Open a dialog here´)"/>
    </dialogBoxLauncher>
</group>
```

code snippet in table USysRibbons in RibbonSamples.accdb

AutoScaling

If you had a complex ribbon containing lots of controls in Office 2007, the Ribbon would display scroll buttons on the left or right that allowed you to see the other controls. Scrolling can make an application difficult to use, so Office 2010 introduces a new attribute on the `group` element called `autoScale`. When the `autoScale` attribute is set to `true`, the Ribbon will dynamically size controls in the group to allow them to fit on screen. When this happens, you may see buttons with the `itemSize` set to `large` be resized to `small`, or controls may even collapse into a split button at runtime.

Writing Callback Routines and Macros

Now that you've looked at the different types of controls you can create in a ribbon customization, it's time to make them do some work! Callbacks were mentioned with nearly every control, but what is a callback? A callback is nothing more than a routine that is called when the Ribbon asks for information, or when an action is performed.

Callbacks enable you to respond to actions, such as when a button is clicked or when an item is selected in a drop-down. In addition, they enable you to update controls in the Ribbon itself.

In Access, you can handle a callback in three ways: with a macro, an expression, or VBA code. Naturally, using VBA provides the most flexibility and control, and you'll want to use that in most cases. The following sections explore each of these in the context of clicking a button in the ribbon.

Using Expressions

The easiest way to respond to the `onAction` callback is to use an expression, but the choices for the expressions you can call are a bit limited. We show using an expression for the `onAction` callback here for completeness. Use the following XML to display a message box when the user clicks on a button:

```
<button id="btnOnActionExpression" label="Expression"
        onAction="=MsgBox(`onAction-Expression`)"/>
```

code snippet in table USysRibbons in RibbonSamples.accdb

Using Access Macros

As an alternative to using an expression, you can call an Access macro from the `onAction` callback. Using macros, you can create portions of the application that are available when the database is disabled. For more information about disabled mode, please see Chapter 25.

To specify an Access macro, simply use the name of the macro in the `onAction` attribute, as shown in the following XML:

```
<button id="btnMacro" label="onAction (macro)" onAction="mcrLargeButton"/>
```

code snippet in table USysRibbons in RibbonSamples.accdb

Using VBA

You'll probably want to write most of your callbacks using VBA. As you would expect, you have much more control and flexibility over the ribbon by writing code than by using a macro.

 You can also specify the name of a user-defined function in your code using syntax as you would an expression as shown earlier.

```
<button id="btnOnActionVBAExpression"
        label="VBA UDF Expression"
        onAction="=YourFunction()"/>
```

To use VBA in the `onAction` callback, you simply give the name of the subroutine in the `onAction` attribute, but there are some extra steps. In VBA (or other languages such as C# or C++), the callback routine must match a particular *signature*. A signature is the declaration of the routine including its parameters and return type. The `onAction` callback for a button control has the following signature:

```
Public Sub MyRoutine(ctl As IRibbonControl)
```

In this example, `MyRoutine` is the name of a subprocedure that you specify in the `onAction` attribute. The `IRibbonControl` parameter is passed to your code by the Ribbon, and represents the control that was clicked. To use this parameter, you need to add a reference to the Microsoft Office 14.0 Object Library.

The `IRibbonControl` object has three properties: `Context`, `Id`, and `Tag`. The `Context` property returns the `Application` object for the application that contains the Ribbon. In this example, that is Microsoft Access. The `Id` property contains the `Id` of the control that was clicked. The `Tag` property is like the `Tag` property for a control in Access — it can be used to store extra data with a `Ribbon` control. The value of the `Tag` property is specified using the `tag` attribute for a control.

Say, for example, that you have two buttons in a ribbon. The first button opens a form named `Form1`, and the second button opens a form named `Form2`. You can open these forms with a separate `onAction` callback for each button. In this case, you just want to open forms, so you'll take a different approach.

Because the Ribbon gives you both the `Id` and `Tag` property for a control, you can open the form using the data that you're given. One method is to determine the `Id` of the control and open the appropriate form, as shown in the following code:

```
Sub DoOpenForm(ctl As IRibbonControl)
    Select Case ctl.Id
        Case "btnForm1": DoCmd.OpenForm "Form1"
        Case "btnForm2": DoCmd.OpenForm "Form2"
    End Select
End Sub
```

As you can see, if you reuse this code for many buttons, it can quickly grow quite large. But, by using the `tag` attribute, you can specify the name of the form to open with the control, as illustrated in the following XML:

```
<button id="btnForm1" label="Open Form1" onAction="onOpenForm" tag="Form1"/>
<button id="btnForm2" label="Open Form2" onAction="onOpenForm" tag="Form2"/>
```

This means you can write the following code to open a form:

Available for download on Wrox.com

```
Public Sub OnOpenForm(ctl As IRibbonControl)
    DoCmd.OpenForm ctl.Tag
End Sub
```

code snippet RibbonSamples.accdb

Of course, there will be times when you want to pass extra data or perform extra tasks while opening a form that might require additional code. By combining these techniques, you could use the name of the form as the control `Id`, and pass an `OpenArgs` value to a form in the `tag` attribute, like this:

```
Public Sub DoOpenForm2(ctl As IRibbonControl)
    DoCmd.OpenForm FormName:=ctl.Id, OpenArgs:=ctl.Tag
End Sub
```

The Ribbon allows this type of flexibility depending on the needs of your application.

More Callback Routines

Determining when a button is clicked is useful, but there are many other callbacks that you can use in your customizations to provide a rich experience for your users. As mentioned in some of the other control types, the `onAction` callback is used to notify you that something has happened. In many of those cases, the signature for the routine you write with that callback is different from the signature for a button. You'll take a look at these in a moment.

If you've looked through the schema or the attributes of the controls, you may have noticed that there are a lot of attributes that begin with the word "get." These attributes are also callbacks. When the Ribbon needs to determine the state of a control or the items in a control, it asks your database for that information if you have implemented the appropriate callback. The information is subsequently relayed back to the Ribbon using the callbacks. Take a closer look, starting with the `onAction` callback for a `checkBox`.

Checking a Checkbox

The signature for the `onAction` callback for a button provides only the control that was clicked. For a checkbox, you also want to know whether it was checked. Because the `IRibbonControl` object does not provide a property for this, the signature for this callback is different. To take an action when a checkbox is checked (or *pressed* as the Ribbon refers to it), use the following callback signature:

```
Sub OnPressed(ctl As IRibbonControl, pressed As Boolean)
```

In this case, if the checkbox is pressed, the `pressed` argument will be `True`. Otherwise, it will be `False`. You might use this callback to show or hide portions of your user interface.

Determining Whether to Preselect a Checkbox

Let's say that you want to determine whether a checkbox is pressed when the Ribbon is loaded. To do this, you can handle the `getPressed` callback. The signature for that callback is the same as the `onAction` callback for a checkbox:

```
Sub OnGetPressed(ctl As IRibbonControl, ByRef pressed As Boolean)
```

`ByRef` is the default modifier for a parameter in Visual Basic and VBA, meaning that even if you don't specify `ByRef`, this modifier is implicitly defined. In effect, these two signatures are identical. To set the pressed state of a checkbox, set the `pressed` argument before leaving the routine, as shown in the following code:

```
Sub OnGetPressed(ctl As IRibbonControl, ByRef pressed As Boolean)
    If ctl.Id = "chkMyCheckBox" Then
        ` Code to determine whether the check box should be pressed
        pressed = True
    End If
End Sub
```

> *Most of the `get` callbacks follow this pattern — they return a value using a `ByRef` parameter rather than using a function procedure.*

Filling a Combo Box or Drop-Down

The `comboBox` and `dropDown` nodes enable you to add items using XML, but there may be times when you need to fill them dynamically. To display a list of employees from a table called `tblEmployees` in a

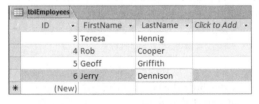

FIGURE 16-17

dropDown, for example, you want a way to fill the control at runtime because the data in an employee table may change. The sample Employees table is shown in Figure 16-17.

To do this, there are three callback attributes to handle. The first one that is called is `getItemCount`. It determines the number of items in the combo box or drop-down. The next one that is called is `getItemLabel`.

It sets the label for a given item that appears in the combo box or drop-down. The last callback is `getItemID`. It sets the unique ID for an item in the list. Note that these callbacks are called when the tab containing the drop-down receives focus. They may not necessarily run when the Ribbon loads.

These last two callbacks are called once for each item that is created when you set the count in
`getItemCount`. So if `getItemCount` returns four items, then `getItemLabel` and `getItemID` are
called four times. The following XML defines these attributes:

```
<dropDown id="ddnEmployees" label="Employees"
          getItemCount="OnGetItemCount"
          getItemLabel="OnGetItemLabel"
          getItemID="OnGetItemID">
</dropDown>
```

code snippet in table USysRibbons in RibbonSamples.accdb

To fill the drop-down list, you want to read data from the Employees table. For that you need a
Recordset — more specifically, you need a Recordset that is available from all three callbacks. So,
start with a module-level Recordset declaration:

```
Dim rst As DAO.Recordset
```

The first callback that's called is `getItemCount`, so open the Recordset from there:

```
Public Sub OnGetItemCount(ctl As IRibbonControl, ByRef Count As Variant)
    Select Case ctl.ID
        Case "ddnEmployees"
            ' open the Recordset and return the count
            Set rst = CurrentDb.OpenRecordset("tblEmployees")
            Count = rst.RecordCount
    End Select
End Sub
```

code snippet RibbonSamples.accdb

Now you need to set the label and the ID in that order. First, the label:

```
Public Sub OnGetItemLabel(ctl As IRibbonControl, index As Integer, _
    ByRef Label As Variant)

    If ctl.ID = "ddnEmployees" Then
        If Not rst.EOF Then
            ' set the label text
            Label = rst("FirstName") & " " & rst("LastName")
        End If
    End If
End Sub
```

code snippet RibbonSamples.accdb

Next, the ID. Because this is the last routine called before getting the next item, you'll move to
the next record in the Recordset here. When you reach EOF, you'll close the Recordset and destroy
the object.

```
Public Sub OnGetItemID(ctl As IRibbonControl, index As Integer, _
    ByRef ID As Variant)

    If ctl.ID = "ddnEmployees" Then
```

```
          ` make sure you are not at EOF
          If Not rst.EOF Then
              ` set the id using the ID field in the table
              ID = "EmployeeID" & rst("ID")

              ` get the next employee
              rst.MoveNext

              ` cleanup when you are at EOF
              If rst.EOF Then
                  rst.Close
                  Set rst = Nothing
              End If
          End If
      End If
  End Sub
```

code snippet RibbonSamples.accdb

The drop-down created using this code and XML is shown in Figure 16-18.

FIGURE 16-18

 Use an ID that is relevant for the item being added. As you'll see in the next section, you are not given the text for the item that is selected, only its ID.

Selecting an Item in a Combo Box or Drop-Down

The callback specified by the `onAction` attribute is called when an item is selected in a combo box or drop-down. Its signature is as follows:

```
Public Sub OnSelectItem(ctl As IRibbonControl, selectedId As String, _
                        selectedIndex As Integer)
```

As you can see from the signature, you are given the ID for a selected item and its index in the list, but not its value. Therefore, you should use an ID value that pertains to the selected item so that you can infer the item given its ID. In other words, if you are displaying a list of employees in a combo box in the ribbon, consider including the ID of the employee as part of the ID attribute for the item in the combo box. This will help you determine which employee was selected later.

For the Employees example, you first want to modify the XML to specify the `onAction` attribute:

```xml
<dropDown id="ddnEmployees" label="Employees"
        getItemCount="OnGetItemCount"
        getItemLabel="OnGetItemLabel"
        getItemID="OnGetItemID"
        onAction="OnSelectItem">
</dropDown>
```

code snippet in table USysRibbons in RibbonSamples.accdb

Next, you write the callback routine, as follows. Because you used the ID value from the table in the ID string for the item, the code just needs to parse it out of the `selectedId` argument.

```vba
Public Sub OnSelectItem(ctl As IRibbonControl, _
        selectedId As String, _
        selectedIndex As Integer)

    Dim lngID        As Long
    Dim strFirstName As String
    Dim strLastName  As String

    ` parse the ID from the ID string
    lngID = CLng(Replace(selectedId, "EmployeeID", ""))

    ` get the first and last name
    strFirstName = DLookup("FirstName", "tblEmployees", "ID = " & lngID)
    strLastName = DLookup("LastName", "tblEmployees", "ID = " & lngID)

    ` Display a message to the user
    MsgBox "Welcome, " & strFirstName & " " & strLastName
End Sub
```

code snippet RibbonSamples.accdb

 If you use the items from a table that has an `AutoNumber` *field where the values are sequential, you can probably just use the* `selectedIndex` *argument.*

Disabling a Control

Disabling a control is similar to setting the checked state of a checkbox. To disable a control, use the `getEnabled` attribute, like this:

```xml
<button id="btnForm1" label="Open Form1" tag="Form1"
  onAction="onOpenForm" getEnabled="OnGetEnabled"/>
```

code snippet in table USysRibbons in RibbonSamples.accdb

Here's the code to handle the callback:

```
Public Sub OnGetEnabled(ctl As IRibbonControl, ByRef Enabled As Variant)
    Select Case ctl.Id
        ` disable the Form3 button
        Case "btnForm3": Enabled = False
        Case Else: Enabled = True
    End Select
End Sub
```

code snippet RibbonSamples.accdb

You might disable a control depending on the specific user, application state, state of data, or any number of reasons.

You can hide a control using the `getVisible` *callback, but the Office guideline is to disable a control rather than hide it. This is to prevent the Ribbon from jumping around as controls are shown or hidden.*

Displaying Images

The Ribbon is graphical in nature so it makes sense that there are a few ways you can load images into your controls. Images can be an important part of an application. They can be used to provide status or state, or help give it a polished look. Perhaps, more importantly, images provide visual cues to users that may help make an application easier for them to use.

You can use three techniques to load images in your application's ribbon, and they're discussed in the following sections.

imageMso Attribute

The easiest way to use images in your application is to use those provided by Office. The `imageMso` attribute on a control specifies an image that is provided by Office. You can use any images provided by any application in Office. For example, here's how you might include images from Outlook in your application:

```
<group id="grpOutlook" label="Outlook">
    <button id="btn17" label="FollowUpComposeMenu" imageMso="FollowUpComposeMenu"/>
    <button id="btn18" label="CalendarInsert" imageMso="CalendarInsert"/>
    <button id="btn19" label="ChartInsert" imageMso="ChartInsert"/>
    <separator id="sep4"/>
    <button id="btn20" label="NewTaskNumbered" imageMso="NewTaskNumbered"/>
    <button id="btn21" label="NewContactNumbered" imageMso="NewContactNumbered"/>
</group>
```

code snippet in table USysRibbons in RibbonSamples.accdb

You can download the list of control IDs from the Microsoft website or get them from inside an Office application (as explained in the section "More Ribbon Tips" at the end of the chapter).

Figures 16-19, 16-20, 16-21, and 16-22 show some of the `imageMso` attributes you can specify in your Access applications. This is only a small subset of what is available to you.

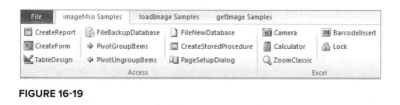

FIGURE 16-19

FIGURE 16-20

FIGURE 16-21

loadImage Callback

Using images that are included with Office is an easy way to use images in your applications. But if you are developing an application, there are likely many more times where you want to use your own images. To do so, the Ribbon provides a callback called `loadImage`, which is called whenever an image is requested via the `image` attribute. To provide a single function for this task, the attribute is defined on the custom UI node, as demonstrated in the following XML:

FIGURE 16-22

```xml
<customUI xmlns="http://schemas.microsoft.com/office/2009/07/customui"
    loadImage="OnLoadImage">
  <ribbon startFromScratch="true">
    <tabs>
      <tab id="tabLoadImageSamples" label="loadImage Samples">
        <group id="grpBMP" label="BMP">
          <button id="btnLoadImage1"
                  label="News"
                  image="news.bmp"
```

```
                              size="large"/>
                <button id="btnLoadImage2"
                        label="Reminder"
                        image="bell.bmp"
                        size="large"/>
            </group>
          </tab>
        </tabs>
      </ribbon>
    </customUI>
```

code snippet in table USysRibbons in RibbonSamples.accdb

The `image` attribute is the name of an image file that is passed to the `loadImage` callback. You can use BMP, GIF, or JPG files for your images. The following code implements the `loadImage` callback to load images in an `Images` subdirectory of the directory from which the database is currently opened. This means you can distribute images as a part of your application and load them dynamically.

```
Public Sub OnLoadImage(imageName As String, ByRef image)
    Dim strPath As String
    strPath = CurrentProject.Path & "\images\" & imageName

    ' return the image
    Set image = LoadPicture(strPath)
End Sub
```

code snippet RibbonSamples.accdb

In this case, the `image` argument must return an object of type `IPictureDisp`. The easiest way to create one is to use the `LoadPicture` function.

getImage Callbacks

If you have a table in your database that stores the names of images for your application, you might choose not to implement the `loadImage` callback because you want to read it from a table. To load the image for this scenario, you can use the `getImage` callback for a control. The sample table of images is shown in Figure 16-23.

FIGURE 16-23

Using this table, let's define a few buttons to display images.

```
<group id="grpGetImage" label="getImage Samples">
    <button id="btnGetImage1" label="Test" getImage="OnGetImage" size="large"/>
    <button id="btnGetImage2" label="News" getImage="OnGetImage" size="large"/>
    <button id="btnGetImage3" label="Bell" getImage="OnGetImage" size="large"/>
</group>
```

code snippet in table USysRibbons in RibbonSamples.accdb

Now, implement the getImage callback to read from the table as follows. For demo purposes, the DLookup function is used. If you had a lot of images in this scenario, a Recordset would probably give better performance.

```
Public Sub OnGetImage(ctl As IRibbonControl, ByRef Image)
    Dim strPath As String
    Dim strImageName As String

    ` get the image name from the table
    strImageName = Nz(DLookup("ImageFileName", "tblImages", _
        "ControlId = `" & ctl.Id & "`"), "")

    ` build the path
    strPath = CurrentProject.Path & "\images\" & strImageName

    ` make sure the file exists
    If Len(Dir(strPath)) = 0 Then
        Exit Sub
    End If

    ` return the image
    Set Image = LoadPicture(strPath)
End Sub
```

code snippet RibbonSamples.accdb

The size of an image displayed in the normal *size is 16 x 16 (pixels) while* large *images are 32 x 32.*

Refreshing Ribbon Content

The ribbons that you've built so far have been fairly static in nature. You were able to read data from tables and display dynamic content, but upon making selections, you took actions in forms and reports. But perhaps you'd like to update other content in the Ribbon itself upon selection — to provide a welcome message to a user, to show status information about a particular piece of data, or even to show something fun like a clock. The following sections describe how to update items in the Ribbon itself.

onLoad Callback

When the Ribbon loads, it calls the onLoad callback if one has been specified. This callback gives you a copy of an IRibbonUI object that can be used to refresh content in the Ribbon itself. Once you have stored a copy of the Ribbon object, you can refresh content using either its Invalidate or InvalidateControl method.

The onLoad callback has the following signature:

```
Public Sub OnRibbonLoad(ribbon As IRibbonUI)
```

Dynamically Setting Text for a Button Control

There have been lots of solutions for building a clock on a form over the years. Most involve using a `Timer` event of a form and a label or text box to display the current time. To update that example for the Access 2010 Ribbon, use a `button` node to display an image. While the button won't do anything in particular, you might use it to stop the `Timer` or to open the Windows Date and Time applet in the Control Panel.

Start with the XML for the `USysRibbons` table:

```xml
<customUI xmlns="http://schemas.microsoft.com/office/2009/07/customui"
          onLoad="OnRibbonLoad">
  <ribbon startFromScratch="false">
    <tabs>
      <tab idMso="TabHomeAccess">
        <group id="grpClock" insertBeforeMso="GroupViews" label="Clock">
          <button id="btnClock" getLabel="OnTick" size="large"
                  imageMso="StartAfterPrevious"/>
        </group>
      </tab>
    </tabs>
  </ribbon>
</customUI>
```

code snippet in table USysRibbons in RibbonSamples.accdb

The `onLoad` attribute for the `customUI` node stores a copy of the Ribbon. Also notice that you are going to implement the `getLabel` callback for the button because you want the label text to change with each `Timer` event.

Next, implement the callbacks. First, the `onLoad` callback. To store a copy of the Ribbon, declare a `Public` module level variable of type `IRibbonUI`:

```vba
` This should appear in the declarations section of a module
Public gobjRibbon As IRibbonUI

Public Sub OnRibbonLoad(ribbon As IRibbonUI)
    Set gobjRibbon = ribbon
End Sub
```

code snippet RibbonSamples.accdb

Then implement the `getLabel` callback (named `OnTick`). This routine sets the `Label` argument to the current time using the `Now()` function. It also makes sure that the form that contains the `Timer` event is open. In this case, the form is bound to the `USysRibbons` table.

```vba
Public Sub OnTick(ctl As IRibbonControl, ByRef Label)
    ` timer form
    If (Not (CurrentProject.AllForms("frmUSysRibbons").IsLoaded)) Then
        DoCmd.OpenForm "frmUSysRibbons", , , , , acHidden
    End If

    ` label
```

```
        If ctl.ID = "btnClock" Then
            Label = Now()
        End If
    End Sub
```

Finally, because this is a clock, you need a timer, so create a form named `frmUSysRibbons` with a `TimerInterval` property of `1000`. That fires the `Timer` event every second. Then, create the `Timer` event for the form as follows:

```
    Private Sub Form_Timer()
        ` Invalidate the clock every second to update the ribbon
        gobjRibbon.InvalidateControl "btnClock"
    End Sub
```

By calling the `InvalidateControl` method, you're asking the `btnClock` control to redraw itself. Because this button implements the `getLabel` callback, the `OnTick` routine is called every time the `Timer` event fires for the form. That gives you the clock tick effect and creates the ribbon shown in Figure 16-24.

Use the `Invalidate` method to refresh all controls in the Ribbon.

FIGURE 16-24

CREATING AN INTEGRATED RIBBON

You've examined the different ways in which you can define ribbon customizations using tabs, groups, and controls. Now let's take a look at two scenarios for which you'll customize the Ribbon.

First, you'll create a Report Manager that integrates with the Access Ribbon. The Report Manager provides users with a nice way to view a list of reports that are in the database and provide them with a means to open a report. Second, you'll create your own contextual tab that you can use from a report to add some custom filtering.

Let's get started!

The sample database that implements the Report Manager is available with the code download for this chapter.

Building the Report Manager

The first scenario has two parts — the Report Manager and the custom filtering for the report. The Report Manager consists of a table to store information about reports, the XML for the Ribbon, and two callback routines.

Creating the Reports Table

To manage your reports, you'll create a table that contains the name and a friendly name for each report. To prevent the user from seeing the actual names of the reports, you'll show the friendly names in the menu. Both fields are defined as Text fields. Figure 16-25 shows the sample reports table named `tblReports`.

ID	ReportName	FriendlyName	Click to Add
1	rptContactsByLocation	Contacts by Location	
2	rptEmployees	Employee List	
3	rptOrdersByEmployee	Orders by Employee	
4	rptContacts	Contact List	
* (New)			

FIGURE 16-25

Using dynamicMenu

Next, write the XML that will fill the menu. Because the number of reports may change throughout development, use the `dynamicMenu` control in the ribbon. If your users create their own reports in the application, this allows their reports to appear in the menu as well, as long as they add an entry to `tblReports`.

Content for the `dynamicMenu` control is provided using the `getContent` callback, which is a required attribute. Here's the XML for the Report Manager control:

```xml
<customUI xmlns="http://schemas.microsoft.com/office/2009/07/customui">
  <ribbon startFromScratch="false">
    <tabs>
      <tab idMso="TabDatabaseTools">
        <group id="grpReportManager" label="Report Manager"
               insertBeforeMso="GroupMacro">
          <!-- Report Manager button -->
          <button id="btnReportManager"
                  label="Report Manager"
                  size="large"
                  tag="frmReportManager"
                  onAction="OnOpenForm"
                  imageMso="FormulaMoreFunctionsMenu"/>
          <separator id="sep1"/>
          <!-- Dynamic report menu to view reports -->
          <dynamicMenu id="dmnuReports" label="Reports"
                       getContent="OnGetReportList"
                       imageMso="ViewsReportView"
                       size="large"
                       invalidateContentOnDrop="true"/>
        </group>
      </tab>
    </tabs>
  </ribbon>
</customUI>
```

code snippet in table USysRibbons in RibbonSamples.accdb

The `dynamicMenu` node also defines an attribute called `invalidateContentOnDrop`. This attribute tells the Ribbon to call the `getContent` callback when the user opens the drop-down menu. Setting it to `true` ensures that the control always has the latest content.

Notice that comments in the XML help make it more readable. XML comments appear between the `<! –` and `– >` characters. This XML also includes a button to open a form that is bound to `tblReports`. This makes it easy to add reports to the Report Manager.

Writing the Callbacks

Finally, add the callback routines. Implement the `getContent` callback to fill the `dynamicMenu`. Start by declaring the routine with the following signature:

Available for download on Wrox.com

```
Public Sub OnGetReportList(ctl As IRibbonControl, ByRef content)
```

Next, add the declarations and open a Recordset for the reports table:

```
Dim rst As DAO.Recordset
Dim strMenu As String
Dim strID    As String
Dim strSQL   As String

strSQL = "SELECT * FROM tblReports ORDER BY FriendlyName"

` open the reports table
Set rst = CurrentDb.OpenRecordset(strSQL)
```

Then start to build the XML for the `dynamicMenu`. This XML should contain a `menu` node, which can subsequently include items such as buttons, checkboxes, split buttons, and toggle buttons. You also need to include the namespace for the Ribbon, as shown in the following code:

```
` build the menu
strMenu = "<menu xmlns='http://schemas.microsoft.com/office/2009/07/customui'>"
```

Now, loop through the reports and add `button` nodes for each report in the Recordset.

```
` loop through the reports
While Not rst.EOF
    ` get the ID for the button by replacing any spaces with empty spaces
    strID = Replace(rst("ReportName"), " ", "")

    ` Append the button node
    strMenu = strMenu & GetButtonXml(strID, _
            rst("FriendlyName"), _
            "OnOpenReport", _
            rst("ReportName"))

    ` Get the next report in the table
    rst.MoveNext
Wend
```

Close the menu node, do some cleanup, and return the menu content:

```
` close the menu node
strMenu = strMenu & "</menu>"

rst.Close
```

```
        Set rst = Nothing

        ` return the menu string
        content = strMenu
    End Sub
```

The callback refers to a helper function called `GetButtonXml`, which is defined as follows:

```
Private Function GetButtonXml(strID As String, _
        strLabel As String, _
        strAction As String, _
        Optional strTag As String = "")

    ` builds the XML for a button
    GetButtonXml = "<button id='" & strID & "`" & _
                    "       label='" & strLabel & "`" & _
                    "       onAction='" & strAction & "`"

    ` add the tag attribute
    If Len(strTag) > 0 Then
        GetButtonXml = GetButtonXml & "        tag='" & strTag & "`"
    End If

    ` close the node
    GetButtonXml = GetButtonXml & "/>"
End Function
```

To use the `OnOpenReport` callback that is called when you click a button in the menu, add the following code:

```
Public Sub OnOpenReport(ctl As IRibbonControl)
    ` opens the report in report view
    DoCmd.OpenReport ctl.tag, acViewReport
End Sub
```

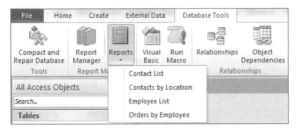

FIGURE 16-26

Great! You are ready for testing. Add the XML you created earlier to a `USysRibbons` table and set the Ribbon Name property for the database. When you select the Database Tools tab, you should have a ribbon that looks like the one shown in Figure 16-26.

If you add or remove reports from `tblReports`, the menu should grow or shrink accordingly.

Building the Custom Filter Interface

A new view was added for reports in Access 2007 called Report View. It provides interactive reports that allow sorting and filtering like never before. In previous versions of Access, you might create a form to provide custom filtering for a report. In this section, you'll create a contextual tab in the Ribbon to provide a different filtering experience for a specific report.

Creating the Report

For this report, use a simple contacts report that includes the company name and the last name for a given contact. The easiest way to create this table is to use the Contacts table template on the Create tab of the Ribbon. The sample table is named `tblContacts` and has fields named `Company` and `Last Name`. These are the fields that you'll use for the filter.

Building the Contextual Tab

This filter only applies to the contacts report, so you'll use a contextual tab that will appear in the ribbon when the report is opened and has focus. Inside the tab, you'll include two `dropDown` controls — one for the `Company` field, and one for the `Last Name` field. To make the callbacks as flexible as possible, store the name of the field that is filtered with the appropriate drop-down in the tag attribute. Create the following XML to define the ribbon.

```
<customUI xmlns="http://schemas.microsoft.com/office/2009/07/customui">
  <ribbon startFromScratch="false">
    <contextualTabs>
      <tabSet idMso="TabSetFormReportExtensibility">
        <tab id="tabReportFilter" label="Filter Report">
          <group id="grpReportFilter" label="Filter Report">
          <!--
            Company dropdown: The tag attribute is the field that
            will be filtered
          -->
          <dropDown id="ddnCompany" label="Company" tag="Company"
                    getItemCount="OnGetItemCount"
                    getItemLabel="OnGetItemLabel"
                    getItemID="OnGetItemID"
                    onAction="OnReportFilter"
                    sizeString="Microsoft Corporation">
          </dropDown>
          <!--
            Last Name dropdown: The tag attribute is the field that
            will be filtered
          -->
          <dropDown id="ddnLastName" label="Last Name" tag="LastName"
                    getItemCount="OnGetItemCount"
                    getItemLabel="OnGetItemLabel"
                    getItemID="OnGetItemID"
                    onAction="OnReportFilter"
                    sizeString="Microsoft Corporation">
          </dropDown>
          <!-- Toggle Filter button -->
```

```
            <separator id="sep1"/>
            <toggleButton idMso="FilterToggleFilter" size="large"/>
          </group>
        </tab>
      </tabSet>
    </contextualTabs>
  </ribbon>
</customUI>
```

code snippet in table USysRibbons in RibbonSamples.accdb

The filtering interface gives the user the capability to choose the company name or last name for a given contact to filter the report. To make it easy to turn the filter on or off, the Toggle Filter button from Access is included. The `idMso` attribute for this button is `FilterToggleFilter`.

Writing the Callbacks

To provide the data for the drop-downs, you implement the `getItemCount`, `getItemLabel`, and `getItemID` callbacks you saw earlier. For this, you need a Recordset. Start by declaring a `Recordset` object in the declarations section of the module:

```
Private rst As DAO.Recordset
```

Now, implement the callbacks. Because the `tag` attribute stores the name of the field, you can use that in your callback code:

Available for download on Wrox.com

```
Public Sub OnGetItemCount(ctl As IRibbonControl, ByRef Count)
    Dim strSQL As String

    ` get the unique data from tblContacts
    strSQL = "SELECT DISTINCT [" & ctl.tag & "] FROM tblContacts"

    Set rst = CurrentDb.OpenRecordset(strSQL)
    Count = rst.RecordCount
End Sub

Public Sub OnGetItemLabel(ctl As IRibbonControl, Index As Integer, ByRef label)
    If Not rst.EOF Then
        label = rst(ctl.tag)
    End If
End Sub

Public Sub OnGetItemID(ctl As IRibbonControl, Index As Integer, ByRef id)
    If Not rst.EOF Then
        id = "id" & rst(ctl.tag)
        rst.MoveNext

        If rst.EOF Then
            rst.Close
            Set rst = Nothing
        End If
    End If
End Sub
```

code snippet RibbonSamples.accdb

Figure 16-27 shows the ribbon when you open the Company drop-down.

Finally, you need to filter the report when the item is selected. For that, you implement the `onAction` callback:

Available for download on Wrox.com

FIGURE 16-27

```
Public Sub OnReportFilter(ctl As IRibbonControl, _
        selectedId As String, _
        selectedIndex As Integer)

    Dim strFilter As String
    Dim strName   As String

    strName = Mid(selectedId, 3)
    strFilter = "[" & ctl.tag & "] = `" & strName & "`"

    ` filter the report
    Screen.ActiveReport.Filter = strFilter
    Screen.ActiveReport.FilterOn = True
End Sub
```

code snippet RibbonSamples.accdb

The resulting ribbon should look like Figure 16-28. When you select an item in either drop-down, the report is filtered accordingly. This filter is not cumulative — that is, it does not append criteria to use the AND or OR operators. To refresh the controls when new contacts are added, you can implement the `onLoad` callback for the Ribbon and invalidate the drop-down controls as demonstrated later in the section "Refreshing Ribbon Content."

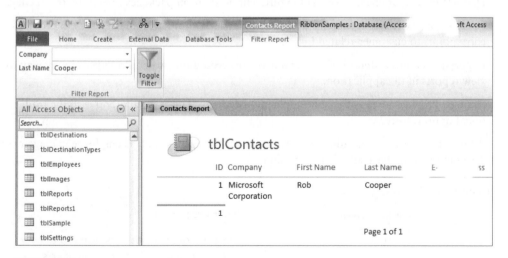

FIGURE 16-28

CREATING A RIBBON FROM SCRATCH

In this second scenario, you'll design a ribbon customization for an application to be used in a travel agency. The application provides tools that are useful for someone working in a travel agency, and the users are not concerned with building databases. As such, the goal for this application is to provide a more off-the-shelf experience. As with any application of this nature, your ribbon should replace the Access Ribbon.

By now, the techniques for building the ribbon should be familiar. You'll build the XML and write the necessary callbacks. Along the way, you'll examine the design decisions made for the application and see some cool stuff such as filling a `dropDown` control with a list of months and a `gallery` control.

 The sample database (`TravelAgencySample.accdb`) that implements the travel agency application is part of the download code for this book.

Defining the Tabs and Groups

Start the ribbon by defining the tabs and groups that you want to build. That provides some organization to the ribbon and helps you fill in the controls in the coming sections. The application will have the following tabs:

➤ **Home:** Contains the most common functionality in the application such as travel information.

➤ **Destinations:** Contains galleries of the different destination packages offered by the agency.

➤ **Customers:** The travel agency wouldn't be what it is without customers! This tab provides entry points to customer-related forms.

➤ **Reports:** Contains a Report Manager like the one you built earlier. Provides an easy way to view reports in the application.

➤ **Settings:** Provides a way to change application settings. This is an alternative to the traditional options form.

➤ **Administration:** Contains administrative tasks for the agency such as employee management. This tab will only be available for certain users.

Now let's flush out the groups in each tab:

TAB	GROUP LABEL	GROUP DESCRIPTION
Home	Flight	Contains controls that work with flight travel such as booking, schedules, and delays.
	Cruise	Provides controls to book a cruise and a destination gallery.

TAB	GROUP LABEL	GROUP DESCRIPTION
	Hotel	Provides controls to find or book a hotel.
	Rental Cars	Contains controls to book a rental car.
	Login	Provides a means to log in to the travel agency.
Destinations	Location	Contains galleries that display destination packages.
	Activity	Provides tools to look for destinations by activity.
Customers	Customer	Provides controls to view customer information.
	Marketing	Contains controls that send marketing materials such as e-mail or brochures to a customer.
Reports	Report Manager	Contains the Report Manager group that you just created.
Settings	Setting	Provides a way to change application settings directly from the ribbon.
Administration	Employee	Contains tools that manage employees.
	Data	Provides tools to re-link tables or export data.
	Security	Provides custom and built-in security tools for the application.

Not listed here is an additional group called Home. It is the first group in each tab and provides an easy way to get back to the startup form for the application.

Define the tabs and groups with XML:

```
<customUI xmlns="http://schemas.microsoft.com/office/2009/07/customui"
 loadImage="onLoadImage">
  <ribbon startFromScratch="true">
    <tabs>
      <tab id="tabHome" label="Home">
        <group id="grpHomeHome" label="Home">
          <button id="btnHomeHome" size="large" label="Home"
                  imageMso="BlogHomePage" tag="frmHome"
                  onAction="OnOpenForm"/>
        </group>
        <group id="grpTravelFlight" label="Flight"></group>
        <group id="grpTravelCruise" label="Cruise"></group>
        <group id="grpTravelHotel" label="Hotel"></group>
        <group id="grpTravelCar" label="Rental Cars"></group>
        <group id="grpHomeLogin" label="Login">
          <button id="btnLogin" size="large" label="Login"
                  imageMso="Lock"/>
```

```
            <button id="btnLogout" size="large" label="Logout"
                    imageMso="PrintPreviewClose"/>
        </group>
    </tab>
    <tab id="tabDest" label="Destinations">
        <group id="grpDestHome" label="Home">
            <button id="btnDestHome" size="large" label="Home"
                    imageMso="BlogHomePage" tag="frmHome"
                    onAction="onOpenForm"/>
        </group>
        <group id="grpDestLocations" label="Location"></group>
        <group id="grpDestActivity" label="Activities"></group>
    </tab>
    <tab id="tabCustomers" label="Customers">
        <group id="grpCustHome" label="Home">
            <button id="btnCustHome" size="large" label="Home"
                    imageMso="BlogHomePage" tag="frmHome"
                    onAction="onOpenForm"/>
        </group>
        <group id="grpCustomer" label="Customer"></group>
        <group id="grpMarketing" label="Marketing"></group>
    </tab>
    <tab id="tabReports" label="Reports">
        <group id="grpReportsHome" label="Home">
            <button id="btnReportsHome" size="large" label="Home"
                    imageMso="BlogHomePage" tag="frmHome"
                    onAction="onOpenForm"/>
        </group>
        <group id="grpReportManager" label="Report Manager"></group>
    </tab>
    <tab id="tabSettings" label="Settings">
        <group id="grpSettingsHome" label="Home">
            <button id="btnSettingsHome" size="large" label="Home"
                    imageMso="BlogHomePage" tag="frmHome"
                    onAction="onOpenForm"/>
        </group>
        <group id="grpSettings" label="Settings"></group>
    </tab>
    <tab id="tabAdmin" label="Administration">
        <group id="grpAdminHome" label="Home">
            <button id="btnAdminHome" size="large" label="Home"
                    imageMso="BlogHomePage" tag="frmHome"
                    onAction="onOpenForm"/>
        </group>
        <group id="grpEmployees" label="Employees"></group>
    </tab>
    </tabs>
  </ribbon>
</customUI>
```

code snippet in table USysRibbons in TravelAgencySample.accdb

The `loadImage` callback is included on the `customUI` node to define a single function to retrieve all images in the `image` attribute. Add the code for the `OnLoadImage` callback as follows:

```
Public Sub OnLoadImage(imageName As String, ByRef image)
    Dim strPath As String
    strPath = CurrentProject.Path & "\images\" & imageName

    ` return the image
    If Dir(strPath) <> "" Then
        Set image = LoadPicture(strPath)
    End If
End Sub
```

code snippet TravelAgencySample.accdb

This XML also includes the `Home` group and button as well as the `Login` and `Logout` buttons.

Building the Home Tab

With your tabs defined, it's time to start filling them in with controls. Use the Home tab in Access as the design principle for the application's first tab, also called Home. This tab contains the tools that might be used commonly in a travel agency.

Building the Flight Group

The Flight group contains controls to book or search for flights as well as other flight-related data such as airport information, flight delays, or weather. For this project, each of these controls will be implemented as a `button`. While they do not include the `onAction` or `tag` attributes, you could add those to open a form defined in the application as demonstrated earlier.

Here's the XML for the Flight group:

```
<group id="grpTravelFlight" label="Flight">
    <button id="btnBookFlights" label="Book Flight" size="large"
            imageMso="OutlookGlobe"/>
    <button id="btnFindFlights" label="Find Flight" size="large"
            imageMso="ZoomClassic"/>
    <button id="btnFlightSched" label="Flight Schedules" size="large"
            imageMso="CalendarInsert"/>
    <button id="btnFlightDeals" label="Today's Deals" size="large"
            imageMso="AccountingFormat"/>
    <separator id="s1"/>
    <button id="btnAirportInfo" label="Airports" imageMso="RmsNavigationBar"/>
    <button id="btnFlightDelays" label="Flight Delays" imageMso="Risks"/>
    <button id="btnTravelWeather" label="Travel Weather"
            imageMso="PictureReflectionGalleryItem"/>
</group>
```

code snippet in table USysRibbons in TravelAgencySample.accdb

Notice that you're using images that were built into Office for each of the controls. The ribbon defined by this XML is shown in Figure 16-29.

Building the Cruise Group

FIGURE 16-29

The Cruise group contains three controls: `button` to book a cruise; `gallery`, which displays the cruise destinations; and `dropDown`, which lists the months of the year (although you could use it to display a list of cruises that are sailing in a particular month).

You'll fill both the `gallery` and `dropDown` controls using callbacks.

You might wonder why you'd use code to fill the list of months instead of a static list of months in the XML. The reason is so that you can fill the list using the `MonthName` *function in VBA. That function returns the localized name of the month depending on the user interface language for Microsoft Office. Using it enables you to build applications that display well in other languages.*

Writing the XML

Here's the XML for the Cruise group:

Available for download on Wrox.com

```
<group id="grpTravelCruise" label="Cruise">
    <button id="btnBookCruise" label="Book Cruise" size="large"
            image="cruise6.bmp"/>
    <gallery id="galCruiseDestinations" label="Destinations"
            size="large" imageMso="PictureReflectionGallery"
            columns="3" rows="3" itemHeight="80" itemWidth="80"
            getItemCount="onGetItemCount"
            getItemLabel="onGetItemLabel"
            getItemImage="onGetItemImage"
            getItemID="onGetItemID"
            onAction="onSelectDestination">
    <button id="btnCruiseDestinations" label="All Cruise Destinations"/>
        </gallery>
    <dropDown id="ddnFindByMonth" label="Find by Month"
            getItemCount="onGetItemCount"
            getItemLabel="onGetItemLabel">
    </dropDown>
</group>
```

code snippet in table USysRibbons in TravelAgencySample.accdb

Gallery controls provide a few additional attributes that you should be aware of. The first are the `columns` and `rows` attributes. They define the number of columns and rows in the gallery when it is dropped down. Next are the `itemHeight` and `itemWidth` attributes. These define the height and width of images in the gallery.

Filling the gallery is similar to filling the dropDown control that you saw earlier. In addition to the getItemCount, getItemID, and getItemLabel callbacks, you also use the getItemImage callback to fill the images from a table.

A button node is included in the gallery. It will display a single button at the bottom of the gallery control.

Writing the Callbacks

To fill both the gallery and the combo box, add the callbacks shown in the following code snippets. First, add the getItemCount callback. Here, you're returning a hard-coded value of 12 for the number of months for the drop-down, while the number of destinations for the gallery comes from a query called qryDestinations.

Available for download on Wrox.com

```
Public Sub OnGetItemCount(ctl As IRibbonControl, ByRef Count)
    Dim strSQL As String

    Select Case ctl.id
        Case "ddnFindByMonth": Count = 12 ` number of months
        Case "galCruiseDestinations":
            ` Open the Recordset for cruises. Use a query because
            ` you store a relative path to the image in the table.
            strSQL = "SELECT * FROM qryDestinations" ` WHERE DestinationType = 2"
            Set rstDestinations = CurrentDb.OpenRecordset(strSQL)

            ` return the recordcount
            rstDestinations.MoveLast
            rstDestinations.MoveFirst
            Count = rstDestinations.RecordCount
    End Select
End Sub
```

code snippet TravelAgencySample.accdb

Next, add the getItemLabel callback. Note the use of the MonthName function for the drop-down.

Available for download on Wrox.com

```
Public Sub onGetItemLabel(ctl As IRibbonControl, Index As Integer, ByRef Label)
    Select Case ctl.id
        Case "ddnFindByMonth"
            Label = MonthName(Index + 1)
        Case "galCruiseDestinations"
            ` return the label from tblDestinations
            Label = rstDestinations("Destination")
    End Select
End Sub
```

code snippet TravelAgencySample.accdb

Then, add the getItemImage callback. You aren't concerned with images for the drop-down so you only return an image for the gallery.

```
Public Sub onGetItemImage(ctl As IRibbonControl, Index As Integer, ByRef Image)
    Select Case ctl.id
        Case "galCruiseDestinations"
            ` return the image
            If Dir(rstDestinations("ImagePath")) <> "" Then
                Set Image = LoadPicture(rstDestinations("ImagePath"))
            End If
    End Select
End Sub
```

code snippet TravelAgencySample.accdb

Finally, return an ID for the gallery using the getItemID callback.

```
Public Sub onGetItemID(ctl As IRibbonControl, Index As Integer, ByRef id)
    Dim strID As String

    Select Case ctl.id
        Case "galCruiseDestinations"
            ` use the ID field in the control id
            strID = "qryDestinationsID" & rstDestinations("DestinationID")

            ` return the ID
            id = strID

            ` get the next destination
            rstDestinations.MoveNext

            ` cleanup when you reach the end
            If rstDestinations.EOF Then
                rstDestinations.Close
                Set rstDestinations = Nothing
            End If
    End Select
End Sub
```

code snippet TravelAgencySample.accdb

When the ribbon loads, it calls these callbacks to fill the gallery and the drop-down. The drop-down contains the list of months; the gallery is displayed in Figure 16-30.

 The image files for this project are included in the download code for this chapter.

Galleries are cool! There's an onAction callback when an item is selected in the gallery. In this case, you'll open a form that is filtered to the item that was clicked. The onAction callback is implemented in the following code:

```
Public Sub OnSelectDestination(ctl As IRibbonControl, selectedId As String,
selectedIndex As Integer)
    Dim lngID As Long

    ` parse the ID number from the ID string
    lngID = CLng(Replace(selectedId, "qryDestinationsID", ""))

    ` open the destinations form
    DoCmd.OpenForm "frmDestinations", , , "DestinationID = " & lngID
End Sub
```

code snippet TravelAgencySample.accdb

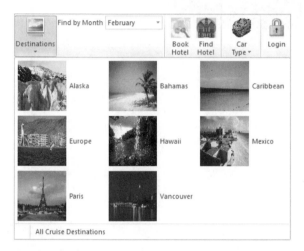

FIGURE 16-30

Selecting an item in the gallery opens the form shown in Figure 16-31.

Building the Hotel Group

The Hotel group contains only two buttons: one to book a hotel, and one to find a hotel. Here's the XML for the group:

```
<group id="grpTravelHotel" label="Hotel">
    <button id="btnBookHotel" label="Book Hotel" size="large"
            image="HotelKey.bmp"/>
    <button id="btnFindHotel" label="Find Hotel" size="large"
            image="Dublin 43.bmp"/>
</group>
```

code snippet in table USysRibbons in TravelAgencySample.accdb

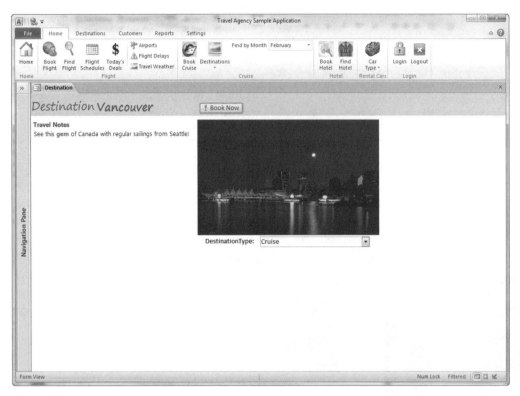

FIGURE 16-31

Building the Rental Cars Group

The Rental Cars group contains a single gallery control. This one is filled using item nodes, as shown in the following XML:

```
<group id="grpTravelCar" label="Rental Cars">
    <gallery id="galRentalCars" label="Car Type" size="large"
             rows="3" columns="1" itemHeight="80" itemWidth="80"
             image="SportsCar3.bmp">
        <item id="itemCar1" label="Sports Car" image="SportsCar1.bmp"/>
        <item id="itemCar2" label="Sports Car" image="SportsCar2.bmp"/>
        <item id="itemCar3" label="Sports Car" image="SportsCar3.bmp"/>
        <item id="itemCar6" label="Sports Car" image="SportsCar4.bmp"/>
        <item id="itemCar4" label="Camper" image="Camper1.bmp"/>
        <item id="itemCar5" label="Van" image="Van1.bmp"/>
    </gallery>
</group>
```

code snippet in table USysRibbons in TravelAgencySample.accdb

This XML creates the ribbon shown in Figure 16-32.

Building the Settings Tab

For the Destinations and Customers tabs, you've implemented button controls so let's skip the details of building those tabs. (For the full implementation of those tabs, see the USysRibbons table in the sample database that's included in the code download for this book. The Reports tab contains the Report Manager you built in the previous solution.)

This brings you to the Settings tab. For this project, you want to store application settings in a table called tblSettings. The table has two fields — SettingName and SettingValue — both of which are defined as Text. In this table, you'll add one option for demonstration: to determine whether today's flight deals are displayed when the application opens. You might use this option to open a form at startup to show the flight deals for the day.

FIGURE 16-32

 If the custom ribbon is active, you may need to close the database and re-open it to create the table. You can return to the Access Ribbon by holding down the Shift key when opening the database.

Start by creating the table and adding one record. Figure 16-33 shows the table with the setting added.

Next, add the XML for the Settings group. As you might expect, you're

FIGURE 16-33

storing the name of the setting in the tag attribute of the check box. You're also including a dialogBoxLauncher control as described earlier in the chapter.

```
<group id="grpSettings" label="Settings">
    <checkBox id="chkSettingFlightDeals" label="Show Flight Deals"
            getPressed="OnGetSetting"
            onAction="OnChangeSetting"
            tag="SHOW_FLIGHTDEALS"/>
    <dialogBoxLauncher>
        <button id="btnSettingsLauncher" tag="frmSettings" onAction="OnOpenForm"/>
    </dialogBoxLauncher>
</group>
```

code snippet in table USysRibbons in TravelAgencySample.accdb

Now implement the callbacks. Use the `OnGetSetting` callback to read from the table to determine whether the checkbox should be pressed.

Available for download on Wrox.com

```
Public Sub OnGetSetting(ctl As IRibbonControl, ByRef pressed)
    ` get the setting value from tblSettings
    Dim varValue As Variant
    varValue = DLookup("SettingValue", "tblSettings", _
        "SettingName = `" & ctl.Tag & "`")

    If varValue = -1 Then
        pressed = True
    Else
        pressed = False
    End If
End Sub
```

code snippet TravelAgencySample.accdb

You also implement the `OnChangeSetting` callback to update the setting in the table when the checkbox value is changed:

Available for download on Wrox.com

```
Public Sub OnChangeSetting(ctl As IRibbonControl, pressed As Boolean)
    ` Update tblSettings with the new value. The setting name
    ` is stored in the tag attribute.
    Dim strSQL As String

    ` build the SQL statement
    strSQL = "UPDATE tblSettings SET SettingValue = " & pressed
    strSQL = strSQL & " WHERE SettingName = `" & ctl.Tag & "`"

    ` update the table
    CurrentDb.Execute strSQL
End Sub
```

code snippet TravelAgencySample.accdb

As you click the checkbox, the value in the table should be updated. If you leave it checked, and then close and re-open the database, it should be checked when you switch to the Settings tab.

Building the Administration Tab

Although you generally want to disable items rather than hide them, the Administration tab brings up an exception. In this case, you want to completely hide the Administration tab if the user is not a

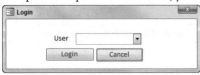

FIGURE 16-34

Manager. The setup is straightforward: a table of users named `tblUsers` that contains three fields — `ID`, `UserName`, and `RoleName`. Start by creating the table and entering some data in it. Next, create a login form, as shown in Figure 16-34. The combo box on the form should contain all three fields with only the `UserName` column displayed.

To change visibility at runtime depending on the role name, you also need to implement the `onLoad` callback on the `customUI` node. Start by changing the `customUI` node in the XML as follows:

```
<customUI xmlns="http://schemas.microsoft.com/office/2009/07/customui"
        loadImage="onLoadImage" onLoad="onRibbonLoad">
```

code snippet in table USysRibbons in TravelAgencySample.accdb

Update the declaration for the Administration tab as shown:

```
<tab id="tabAdmin" label="Administration" getVisible="OnGetVisible">
```

code snippet in table USysRibbons in TravelAgencySample.accdb

Next, implement the `onLoad` callback routine to store a copy of the Ribbon.

```
` This should appear in the module declarations section
Public gobjRibbon As IRibbonUI

Public Sub onRibbonLoad(ribbon As IRibbonUI)
    ` save a copy of the ribbon for future invalidation
    Set gobjRibbon = ribbon
End Sub
```

code snippet TravelAgencySample.accdb

To determine whether the tab should be made visible, implement the `getVisible` callback as shown. This code uses the `Column` property to check the third column in the combo box to determine whether the user is a `Manager`.

```
Public Sub OnGetVisible(ctl As IRibbonControl, ByRef Visible)
    If ctl.id = "tabAdmin" Then
        ` check the login form to determine visibility.
        ` if the form is closed, just return false.
        If Not CurrentProject.AllForms("frmLogin").IsLoaded Then
            Visible = False
            Exit Sub
        End If

        ` The combo box on the login form contains the role:
        ` this can be either Manager or Employee. Show the tab
        ` if it is Manager, otherwise hide it.
        If Forms!frmLogin!cboUsers.Column(2) = "Manager" Then
            Visible = True
        Else
            Visible = False
        End If
    Else
        Visible = True
    End If
End Sub
```

code snippet TravelAgencySample.accdb

Finally, add code to the Login button on the form to invalidate the Administration tab.

```
Private Sub cmdLogin_Click()
    ` invalidate the admin tab to determine visibility
    gobjRibbon.InvalidateControl "tabAdmin"
End Sub
```

code snippet TravelAgencySample.accdb

To test the callbacks, select different users from the combo box to show and hide the tab.

MORE RIBBON TIPS

Here are a few tips to keep for writing ribbon customizations. They can help you in creating your applications, as well as in providing additional polish to your solutions.

➤ **Prevent the Ribbon from loading:** You want to prevent the Ribbon from loading when testing or developing, for instance, when you are developing a ribbon from scratch but you are also developing forms and reports. With a custom ribbon, the form design tools are not available. You can hold down the Shift key as you would to prevent the startup form from loading to prevent your custom ribbon from loading.

➤ **Find existing controls:** Office provides a lot of controls that you can use in your applications. So many, in fact, it begs the question, how do you find them all? You can download the List of Control IDs from the Microsoft website, but it turns out that Office provides this information for you in the Customize group of the Options dialog boxes. To get the control ID for the Toggle Filter button, simply hover over an item in the list, as shown in the Access Options dialog box in Figure 16-35. The ID for the control appears in parentheses.

➤ **Use** screenTip, superTip, **and** description: Use these additional attributes for controls to customize the tooltip or descriptive information for a given control. The description attribute is only valid for controls in a menu node with the itemSize attribute set to large.

➤ **Set keyTips:** A keyTip is the accelerator key or keys for a given control. If not set, the Ribbon assigns keyTips for you such as Y01 or Y02. For keyTips that are more user friendly, set the keyTip attribute. You can also implement the getKeyTip callback for many controls, which would enable you to create a mapping table for control IDs and keyTips.

Setting Focus to a Tab

One piece of functionality that was difficult to do regarding ribbon customizations in Office 2007 was to programmatically set the focus to a particular tab. This was a common request for Access applications to be able to determine which tab should have the focus for different scenarios. You can now set focus to a tab that you have defined the following line of code for in Office 2010:

```
gobjRibbon.ActivateTab "TabName"
```

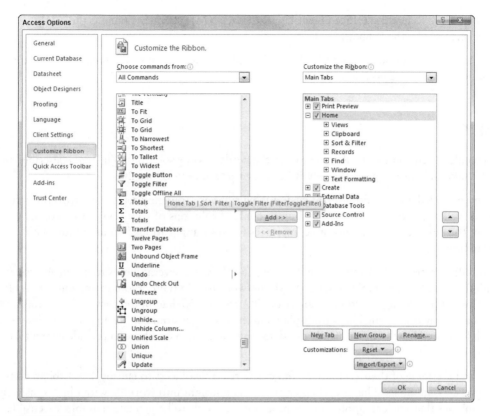

FIGURE 16-35

In this case, gobjRibbon is defined as an object of type IRibbonUI and is typically saved in the onLoad callback for the Ribbon.

Additional Resources

There has been a lot of excitement generated about customizing the Ribbon, and Microsoft has provided an incredible amount of documentation, including an entire MSDN developer center dedicated to the Ribbon! There are examples, documentation, tools, and videos, all related to building custom ribbons. Here are some of the resources that the authors have found to be indispensable when writing customizations (all of these are available from the Ribbon Developer Center):

➤ **Office Ribbon Developer Center:** http://msdn.microsoft.com/office/tool/ribbon/default.aspx

➤ **List of Control IDs:** Provides the list of Office controls that you can use in your own customizations, hide altogether, or specify as the imageMso attribute of your own control.

➤ **Office 2010 Reference: Office Fluent User Interface XML Schema:** Contains the XML Schema used by the Ribbon.

➤ **UI Style Guide for Solutions and Add-Ins:** Provides guidelines for developing ribbon customizations for your applications.

SUMMARY

You can completely customize the Ribbon to suit the needs of your solutions. The tools described in this chapter take full advantage of the new Ribbon user interface in Office 2010.

This chapter provided an in-depth look at customizing ribbons. You explored the controls that are available, as well as put them to use in building a couple of solutions of your own. By customizing the Ribbon, you can create new, innovative interfaces for your applications that are in line with today's standards.

The extensibility story for the Ribbon is quite large, and there are several pieces to it. For Access, it starts with the USysRibbons table, and the XML that you store in there. From there, you can implement callback routines that give you the power of VBA that you've had in the past with controls and command bars. You also learned how to display images in your customizations to give your interface a fresh look, and how to dynamically use data from tables in a database to provide content to the Ribbon.

Now you can take some of these techniques and create reusable objects to encapsulate Ribbon controls by using class modules. The next chapter provides an insight into working with objects, as well as new techniques that you can apply to your programming style to help create reusable, extensible applications of your own.

17

Customizing the Office Backstage

WHAT'S IN THIS CHAPTER?

➤ Types of controls and layouts for controls

➤ How to customize the Office Backstage in your applications

➤ Custom scenarios designed for the Office Backstage for Access applications

The File menu has been replaced in Office 2010 with a new user interface called the Backstage, which is intended to provide document-centric functionality for an application. For example, the Backstage view for Access 2010 includes commands that allow you to compact a database, add a database password, create a new database, save objects, or print. The Backstage also contains commands that apply to the application as a whole such as Help, Options, and Exit. The Backstage takes up the entire screen, making it a good place to draw attention to information that is important to an application.

The Ribbon was first introduced as a part of Office 2007, and with it, a new technique for user-interface development using XML. Office 2010 extends this capability by allowing you to customize the Backstage view as well. Similar to the Ribbon, you can hide and show built-in commands as well as add your own functionality.

In this chapter, we take a look at creating customizations for the Office Backstage view, including controls and callbacks that are specific to the Backstage and designing column layouts. You'll also see some specific scenarios for customizing the Backstage for use in an Access application to provide rich experiences for users.

INTRODUCING THE OFFICE BACKSTAGE

With its full-screen view and availability, the Office Backstage can add interesting new experiences to your applications. We've often written applications where some type of administration was needed for the database. This might be for administering users, or the location of a back-end database. Because this functionality really applies to the database as a whole, the Backstage is an intuitive place to put this functionality.

Before we go into creating your own customizations, let's take a quick look at the different parts of the Backstage, as well as the Backstage view in Access 2010 so that you can become familiar with it.

Access 2010 Backstage

The Backstage view for Access 2010 is where you'll go to open or close a database, create a new database, save a copy of the database, print objects, or to change Access Options. The default view of the Backstage when no database is open is shown in Figure 17-1.

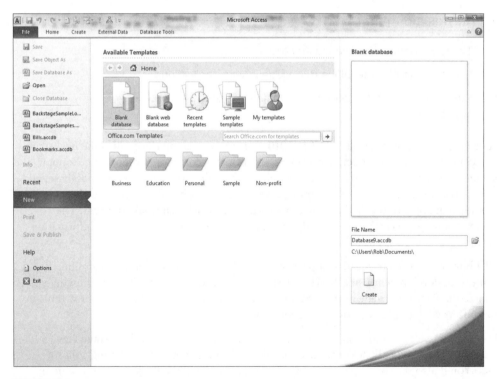

FIGURE 17-1

By default, the Backstage also shows the last four files that have been opened in Access, as well as a Recent tab that shows more recent files. The Recent tab also allows you to pin the databases that you use frequently to the top of the list, as shown in Figure 17-2.

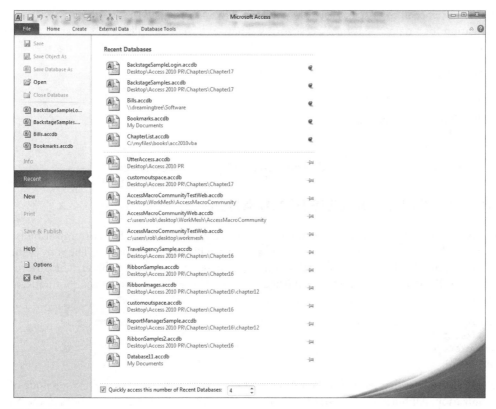

FIGURE 17-2

The Save & Publish tab in the Backstage contains commands that you can use to save a copy of the database, convert the database, create a template, or publish a database to Access Services.

Parts of the Backstage

Before going into building customizations for the Backstage, you should be familiar with the different parts of the Backstage and how it is organized. At the highest level, there are two primary entry points that you can add for users in the Backstage: buttons and tabs. Buttons in the Backstage are sometimes referred to as *fast commands* because they are intended to provide a single command and then return back to the database or main Access window.

Tabs allow you to provide additional controls such as groups, buttons, labels, edit boxes, drop-down controls, and so on. Controls in tabs can be organized into two columns called, appropriately enough, the first column and the second column. You'll learn more about designing column layout in the Backstage later in this chapter.

Uses for the Backstage in Custom Applications

As you've seen, the Backstage view takes up the entire screen when shown. This makes it a great place to add rich functionality to an Access application. You could put your entire application navigation experience in the Backstage, although I wouldn't recommend it. It's still much easier to build navigation for a database using Access forms. That said, there are plenty of scenarios that you might want to consider using the Backstage for in Access 2010:

➤ About page

➤ Application information

➤ Warnings and notifications

➤ Application options

These scenarios and more will also be described in detail later in this chapter.

WRITING A BACKSTAGE CUSTOMIZATION

Customizing the Backstage view is very similar to customizing the Ribbon. The customization is written using XML and stored in the USysRibbons system table in your database. The root element and namespace for a Backstage customization is also the same as that of the Ribbon. The difference, however, is that the Backstage is customized using the backstage element under the root node, as shown here:

```
<customUI xmlns="http://schemas.microsoft.com/office/2009/07/customui">
  <backstage>
  </backstage>
</customUI>
```

For the majority of this chapter, we will omit the root customUI node and the backstage node of the customization. All buttons, tabs, or other controls should appear within these nodes in the XML for the customization.

FIGURE 17-3

Also similar to the Ribbon, the Backstage allows you to write custom code to respond to user actions using callbacks. Because callbacks are discussed in detail in Chapter 16, we won't go into detail about them here. For more information about writing and loading a customization or writing callbacks, please read Chapter 16.

CONTROLS IN THE BACKSTAGE

There are several different types of controls that you can use in the Backstage. Some of these controls are also available in a Ribbon customization so we won't go into detail about these unless they are different from their Ribbon counterparts. Here are the controls that are either unique to the Backstage view, or different from those in the Ribbon in some manner.

Tab

Most of your custom controls for the Backstage will be created in tabs. A tab in the Backstage is functionally equivalent to those in the Ribbon, but they appear different when selected, as shown in Figure 17-3.

Tabs are defined using the `tab` element in the Backstage. The `tab` element can contain two child elements that are used to define columns: `firstColumn` and `secondColumn`. Groups and other controls must be defined in one of these two elements. We'll go into more detail about designing columns later in this chapter.

Group

As you might expect, a `group` element is used to combine controls together in some logical grouping. Unlike the Ribbon, however, groups in the Backstage can contain a `style` attribute that determines how the group appears in the Backstage. There are three values you can assign to the `style` attribute: `normal`, `warning`, and `error`. The warning style will highlight the controls in the group in yellow, and the error style highlights the controls in red. Figure 17-4 shows the differences (although as shades of gray rather than in the colors you'll see on-screen).

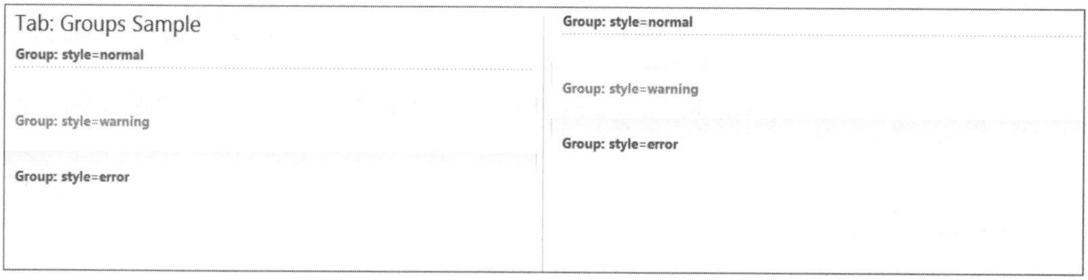

Tab: Groups Sample

Group: style=normal

Group: style=warning

Group: style=error

Group: style=normal

Group: style=warning

Group: style=error

FIGURE 17-4

The following XML defines the Backstage customization shown Figure 17-4 and defines a tab with a label, title, and two columns containing each of these groups.

Available for download on Wrox.com

```
<tab id="t3" label="Groups" title="Tab: Groups Sample">
  <firstColumn>
    <group id="g1" label="Group: style=normal"  style="normal"></group>
    <group id="g2" label="Group: style=warning" style="warning"></group>
    <group id="g3" label="Group: style=error"   style="error"></group>
  </firstColumn>
  <secondColumn>
    <group id="g4" label="Group: style=normal"  style="normal"></group>
    <group id="g5" label="Group: style=warning" style="warning"></group>
    <group id="g6" label="Group: style=error"   style="error"></group>
  </secondColumn>
</tab>
```

code snippet BackstageSamples.accdb

The group element can contain several different types of controls; they are also grouped into different sections. These sections are called the `primaryItem`, `topItems`, or `bottomItems` and are described in the sections that follow.

primaryItem

The `primaryItem` element in a group is used to promote one command as the most important item in the group. A `primaryItem` control can either be a `button` or a `menu`, and the `menu` can contain buttons, checkboxes, toggle buttons, or another menu. The following XML defines a button element as the `primaryItem`.

```
<tab id="t3" label="Groups" title="Tab: Groups Sample">
  <firstColumn>
    <group id="g1" label="Group: style=normal"  style="normal">
      <primaryItem>
        <button id="pb1" label="Primary Button" imageMso="PrintPreviewZoomMenu"/>
      </primaryItem>
    </group>
  </firstColumn>
</tab>
```

code snippet BackstageSamples.accdb

When a `primaryItem` is defined, the label for the group appears indented next to the button, as shown in Figure 17-5.

FIGURE 17-5

topItems

As the name suggests, the `topItems` element defines the controls that will appear at the top of the group. The `topItems` element for a group is also used to keep controls below the group label, but next to the `primaryItem` when a `primaryItem` is used. The button shown in Figure 17-5 is an example of this.

bottomItems

As the name suggests, the `bottomItems` element defines the controls that will appear at the bottom of the group. When a `primaryItem` is defined, controls in the `bottomItems` section appear below the control in the `primaryItem` for the group. The following XML was used to create the `primaryItem`, `topItems`, and `bottomItems` sections, as shown in Figure 17-5.

```
<tab id="t3" label="Groups" title="Tab: Groups Sample">
  <firstColumn>
    <group id="g1" label="Group: style=normal"  style="normal">
```

```
      <primaryItem>
        <button id="pb1" label="Primary Button" imageMso="PrintPreviewZoomMenu"/>
      </primaryItem>
      <topItems>
        <button id="btn10" label="Borderless Button" style="borderless"
                imageMso="PrintPreviewZoomMenu" />
      </topItems>
      <bottomItems>
        <labelControl id="lbl11" label="bottomItems Label"/>
      </bottomItems>
    </group>
  </firstColumn>
</tab>
```

code snippet BackstageSamples.accdb

TaskGroup, Category, and Task

A `taskGroup` in the Backstage is used to organize actions called *tasks*. A task is like a button, but can contain additional descriptive text defined in the `description` attribute of the element and appears as a single item, as shown in Figure 17-6.

The `taskGroup` element in the customization is a container for the `category` element, which in turn defines the `task` element. The XML for the customization shown in Figure 17-6 is shown here:

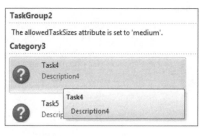

FIGURE 17-6

Available for download on Wrox.com

```
<tab id="t4" label="TaskGroups" title="Tab: TaskGroups Sample">
  <firstColumn>
    <taskGroup id="tg2" label="TaskGroup2"
               helperText=" The allowedTaskSizes attribute is set to 'medium'."
               allowedTaskSizes="medium">
      <category id="c3" label="Category3">
        <task id="task4" label="Task4" description="Description4"
            imageMso="Help"/>
        <task id="task5" label="Task5" description="Description5"
            imageMso="Help"/>
      </category>
    </taskGroup>
  </firstColumn>
</tab>
```

code snippet BackstageSamples.accdb

Both the `group` and `taskGroup` elements contain an attribute called `helperText` that shows additional text below the label of the group.

TaskFormGroup

The `taskFormGroup` element in the customization allows you to define a group of controls that varies between tasks. In fact, this is the difference between the `taskGroup` and `taskFormGroup` elements. The task element inside a `taskFormGroup` can define one or more groups that contain controls whereas the `task` element inside the `taskGroup` element does not.

Let's say that you were building a simple interface for users to choose forms or reports in a database. You might want to show forms in one group and reports in another group. Using the `taskFormGroup` control, you could show a different set of controls altogether including buttons or drop-down controls that define the reports in the application. The XML for such a customization is shown here. This customization defines a single `taskFormGroup` element with three categories: Forms, Reports, and Queries and Search Tools. Each category may contain one or more tasks, and each task may contain one or more groups.

```xml
<tab id="t5" label="TaskFormGroup" title="Tab: TaskFormGroup Sample">
  <firstColumn>
    <taskFormGroup id="tfg1" label="Simple Object Browser"
                   allowedTaskSizes="mediumSmall"
                   helperText="Shows database objects available for viewing.">
      <category id="tfgc1" label="Forms">
        <task id="t10" label="All Forms" imageMso="CreateForm">
          <group id="tfgroup1" label="Client Forms">
            <topItems>
              <labelControl id="lbl1" label="Client forms listed here."/>
            </topItems>
          </group>
          <group id="tfgroup2" label="Web Forms">
            <topItems>
              <labelControl id="lbl2" label="Web forms listed here."/>
            </topItems>
          </group>
        </task>
      </category>
      <category id="tfgc2" label="Reports">
        <task id="t11" label="All Reports" imageMso="CreateReport">
          <group id="tfgroup3" label="Reports">
            <topItems>
              <labelControl id="lbl3" label="Reports might be listed here."/>
            </topItems>
          </group>
        </task>
      </category>
      <category id="tfgc3" label="Queries and Search Tools">
        <task id="t12" label="Queries" imageMso="AdpViewSqlPane">
          <group id="tfgroup4" label="Queries">
            <topItems>
              <labelControl id="lbl4" label="Queries might be listed here."/>
            </topItems>
          </group>
        </task>
        <task id="t13" label="Search Tools" imageMso="PrintPreviewZoomMenu">
          <group id="tfgroup5" label="Search Tools">
```

```
            <primaryItem>
              <button id="btnCustomSearch" label="Custom Search"
                      imageMso="PrintPreviewZoomMenu"/>
            </primaryItem>
            <topItems>
              <radioGroup id="rgSavedSearches" label="Saved Searches">
                <radioButton id="rbSearch1" label="Saved Search 1"/>
                <radioButton id="rbSearch2" label="Saved Search 2"/>
                <radioButton id="rbSearch3" label="Saved Search 3"/>
                <radioButton id="rbSearch4" label="Saved Search 4"/>
                <radioButton id="rbSearch5" label="Saved Search 5"/>
              </radioGroup>
            </topItems>
          </group>
        </task>
      </category>
    </taskFormGroup>
  </firstColumn>
</tab>
```

code snippet BackstageSamples.accdb

Because the `taskFormGroup` allows you to show a separate group of controls for each selected task, the task remains selected after a choice is made. When the Forms task is selected, two groups are displayed, as shown in Figure 17-7.

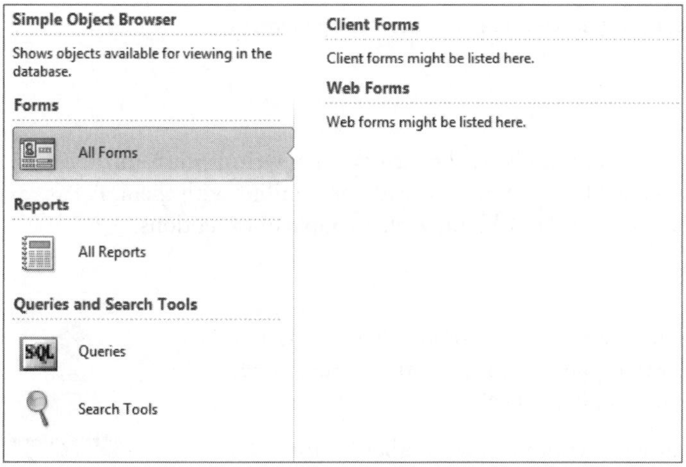

FIGURE 17-7

When the second task of the Queries and Search Tools category is selected, a single group that contains a `button` in a `primaryItem` and a `radioGroup` is displayed, as shown in Figure 17-8. In this example, the `radioGroup` might be used to show saved searches in the database.

FIGURE 17-8

Here are a few rules to keep in mind when you're working with the `taskFormGroup` element:

➤ A `taskFormGroup` element cannot be defined in the `secondColumn` element.

➤ The `taskFormGroup` element must be the only thing in the `firstColumn` element. You cannot define a `taskFormGroup` and a `group` in the same column.

➤ A `firstColumn` element can only have one `taskFormGroup` element.

Button

The `button` element is one of the more commonly used controls when writing customizations, and if you've written customizations for the Ribbon, you may already be familiar with them. A `button` in the Backstage is very similar to a `button` in the Ribbon, with a couple of exceptions.

style Attribute

A `button` element that is not defined as a `primaryItem` also has a `style` attribute that accepts one of three values: `normal`, `large`, and `borderless`. The three types of buttons are shown in Figure 17-9.

FIGURE 17-9

Borderless buttons look really great when combined with other buttons. They feel very lightweight and help reduce some clutter that may occur with many buttons on the screen. The following XML shows four buttons in a `groupBox` element.

Available for
download on
Wrox.com

```xml
<groupBox id="gbSelection" label="Please make a selection">
  <button style="borderless" id="btnChoice1"
          label="First Choice" imageMso="_1"/>
  <button style="borderless" id="btnChoice2"
```

```
                label="Second Choice" imageMso="_2"/>
      <button style="borderless" id="btnChoice3"
                label="Third Choice" imageMso="_3"/>
      <button style="borderless" id="btnChoice4"
                label="Fourth Choice" imageMso="_4"/>
</groupBox>
```

code snippet BackstageSamples.accdb

This customization is shown in Figure 17-10.

 The imageMso *attributes* _0 *through* _9 *can be used to create numbered items for controls, as shown in the previous customization.*

isDefinitive Attribute

The isDefinitive attribute for a button is used to close the Backstage after the button is clicked.

GroupBox

The groupBox control in the Backstage is a container that is used to provide simple grouping of controls. The label attribute of the control specifies the text to use for the control, and any control defined inside a groupBox is indented, as shown earlier in Figure 17-10.

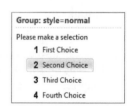

FIGURE 17-10

Hyperlink

Another new control available for the Backstage is the hyperlink control. As you might imagine, a hyperlink is used to navigate to a website that you specify using the target attribute of the control. The hyperlink control appears as a simple label with an underline. When you hover over the control, the cursor changes to the hand icon as you would expect for a hyperlink. The hyperlink control is defined using the following XML:

```
<hyperlink id="lnk1" label="Bing" target="www.bing.com"/>
```

The hyperlink element also defines the onAction attribute, which allows you to run a callback routine but have a control that acts like a hyperlink.

ImageControl

Because the Ribbon is highly visual, it makes sense that images are a big part of the story for defining customizations for the Ribbon. Likewise, images are also highly customizable in the Backstage. Like the Ribbon, you can dynamically assign the image for a button or other controls in the Backstage; however, the Backstage also has a specific control for displaying images called the imageControl.

The image control is shown by default in the top-right corner of the Info tab in the Backstage when a database is open, and displays the object that was previously onscreen, as shown in Figure 17-11.

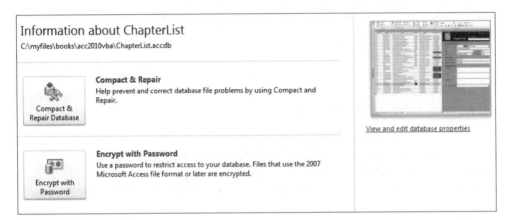

FIGURE 17-11

You can also customize the image displayed using the `imageControl` using the `getImage` callback for the control. We'll take a closer look at providing an image in the control dynamically later in this chapter.

LayoutContainer

You can do some pretty interesting things using the new `layoutContainer` control in the Backstage. As the name suggests, this control is used to define the layout of controls in the container. The `layoutChildren` attribute of the control can be either horizontal or vertical, and the controls can be nested to create multiple levels of controls in a very specific manner.

For example, let's say that you wanted to create something that looks like a telephone number pad. Using the `layoutContainer` control, you could create a grid consisting of borderless buttons to get the effect you were looking for. Here is the customization that creates this layout:

```
<group id="g6" label="Enter PIN"   style="normal">
  <topItems>
    <layoutContainer id="lc15" layoutChildren="vertical">
      <layoutContainer id="lc11" layoutChildren="horizontal">
        <button id="tel1" style="borderless" imageMso="_1"/>
        <button id="tel2" style="borderless" imageMso="_2"/>
        <button id="tel3" style="borderless" imageMso="_3"/>
      </layoutContainer>
      <layoutContainer id="lc12" layoutChildren="horizontal">
        <button id="tel4" style="borderless" imageMso="_4"/>
        <button id="tel5" style="borderless" imageMso="_5"/>
        <button id="tel6" style="borderless" imageMso="_6"/>
      </layoutContainer>
```

```
        <layoutContainer id="lc13" layoutChildren="horizontal">
          <button id="tel7" style="borderless" imageMso="_7"/>
          <button id="tel8" style="borderless" imageMso="_8"/>
          <button id="tel9" style="borderless" imageMso="_9"/>
        </layoutContainer>
        <layoutContainer id="lc14" layoutChildren="horizontal">
          <button id="telmult" style="borderless" imageMso="MultiplicationSign"/>
          <button id="tel0" style="borderless" imageMso="_0"/>
          <button id="telhash" style="borderless"/>
        </layoutContainer>
      </layoutContainer>
    </topItems>
  </group>
```

code snippet BackstageSamples.accdb

This customization is shown in Figure 17-12.

RadioGroup

The last type of control that is specific to the Backstage is the radio group control, which is defined using the `radioGroup` element. This control allows you to select a single item from a choice of radio buttons. For example, the following XML defines a customization that creates three radio buttons:

Enter PIN		
1	2	3
4	5	6
7	8	9
*	0	

FIGURE 17-12

Available for download on Wrox.com

```
<radioGroup id="rgSavedSearches" label="Saved Searches">
  <radioButton id="rbSearch1" label="Saved Search 1"/>
  <radioButton id="rbSearch2" label="Saved Search 2"/>
  <radioButton id="rbSearch3" label="Saved Search 3"/>
</radioGroup>
```

code snippet BackstageSamples.accdb

The `radioGroup` control also defines callbacks that allow you to create a set of `radioButton` controls dynamically. That is, you can fill the `radioGroup` with a varying number of `radioButton` elements. This scenario is described in more detail later in the chapter.

DESIGNING THE LAYOUT OF COMPONENTS

Now that you've started to see the types of controls that you can use to customize the Backstage, let's take a closer look at how you can lay out the controls using columns.

The `tab` element in the Backstage allows you to create one or two columns for grouping controls. You can define the distribution of the column width for the first column as well as the minimum and maximum width in pixels of each column if you want more control over the widths. Let's take a look at creating columns, and then we'll dive deeper into column widths.

Single-Column Layout

To create a single-column layout, define the `firstColumn` element inside the tab element. In a single column layout, the column is sized to the total width of the tab. The `firstColumn` element can contain a `group`, `taskGroup`, or `taskFormGroup`.

Two-Column Layout

Two-column layouts are created by adding the `secondColumn` element inside the `tab` element. As you might expect, you cannot define the `secondColumn` element without the `firstColumn` element.

Column Widths

The widths of columns are defined as attributes on the `tab` element. The attributes you'll use to define column widths are shown in the table that follows.

ATTRIBUTE NAME	MEANING
columnWidthPercent	Specifies the distribution of columns as a percent.
firstColumnMaxWidth	Maximum width of the first column in pixels.
firstColumnMinWidth	Minimum width of the first column in pixels.
secondColumnMaxWidth	Maximum width of the second column in pixels.
secondColumnMinWidth	Minimum width of the second column in pixels.

To define the distribution of the first column, set the `columnWidthPercent` attribute of the `tab` element. The maximum value of this attribute is 99, which means that the first column will take up 99 percent of the width of the tab. If the content will not fit in the specified width, the `columnWidthPercent` attribute will be ignored. The following customization creates a tab with two columns where the first column will take up 99 percent of the width of the tab.

```
<customUI xmlns="http://schemas.microsoft.com/office/2009/07/customui">
  <backstage>
    <tab id="t1" label="Tab1" title="Tab1" columnWidthPercent="99">
      <firstColumn>
        <group id="g1" label="Column1: Group1"></group>
      </firstColumn>
      <secondColumn>
        <group id="g2" label="Column2: Group2"></group>
      </secondColumn>
    </tab>
  </backstage>
</customUI>
```

code snippet BackstageSamples.accdb

The result of this customization is shown in Figure 17-13.

By contrast, Figure 17-14 shows the result of a customization that sets the `columnWidthPercent` attribute to 50. As you can see, the first column takes up half of the width of the tab.

Tab1		Column2:
Column1: Group1		Group2

FIGURE 17-13

Tab1	Column2: Group2
Column1: Group1	

FIGURE 17-14

Creating a Grid

Earlier we looked at an example of creating a grid using buttons inside a `layoutContainer` control to provide the appearance of a telephone number pad. Here are some other types of grids you might want to create.

Many of the controls in the Backstage allow you to define callbacks for responding to actions or events at runtime. These are useful for providing a rich experience when using the Backstage in your applications. Several controls such as the `comboBox`, `dropDown`, and `radioGroup` also allow you to provide content for the controls using callbacks. Unfortunately, however, the `layoutContainer` does not include callbacks to specify the content inside the container. As a result, to create a dynamic grid bound to data, you'll need to build the customization for the XML when the database opens, and then use the `LoadCustomUI` method of the Access `Application` object to load it. The customizations described in this section show you how to create grid-type layouts for static content. If you have a fixed number of items to display in a table type layout, you could then use other callbacks to set the appearance of items or images without loading the entire customization using `LoadCustomUI`.

Column and Row Span

Column span is when one control spans multiple columns. You can define controls that span columns or rows using the `expand` attribute of controls in Office 2010. The following customization defines edit boxes and buttons that span multiple columns.

Available for download on Wrox.com

```
<group id="grpColSpan" label="Column Span (Edit Boxes)"
       helperText="Demonstrates column spans for controls spanning multiple columns
    <topItems>
      <layoutContainer id="lcV3" layoutChildren="vertical">
        <editBox id="txt1" expand="horizontal" label="Label1"/>
        <layoutContainer id="lcH2" layoutChildren="horizontal">
          <editBox id="txt2" expand="horizontal" label="Label2"/>
          <editBox id="txt3" expand="horizontal" label="Label3"/>
        </layoutContainer>
      </layoutContainer>
    </topItems>
</group>
<group id="grpColSpanBtn" label="Column Span (Buttons)"
```

```
            helperText="Demonstrates column span where a button spans multiple columns.">
    <topItems>
      <layoutContainer id="lcV4" layoutChildren="vertical">
        <button id="b8" label="Button" expand="horizontal"/>
        <layoutContainer id="lcH3" layoutChildren="horizontal">
          <button id="b9" label="Button" expand="horizontal"/>
          <button id="b10" label="Button" expand="horizontal"/>
        </layoutContainer>
      </layoutContainer>
    </topItems>
  </group>
```

code snippet BackstageSamples.accdb

This customization is shown in Figure 17-15.

Column Span (Edit Boxes)		
Demonstrates column spans for controls spanning multiple columns.		
Label1		
Label2	Label3	
Column Span (Buttons)		
Demonstrates column span where a button spans multiple columns.		
Button		
Button	Button	

FIGURE 17-15

Row span is when one control spans multiple rows. You can span multiple rows by setting the
expand attribute of a control to vertical. The button control with the style attribute set to large
also will span multiple rows of buttons as shown in the following customization:

Available for
download on
Wrox.com

```
<group id="grpRowSpan" label="Row Span"
      helperText="Demonstrates a row span where the large button spans multiple rows.">
  <topItems>
    <layoutContainer id="lcH1" layoutChildren="horizontal" expand="neither">
      <button id="b1" label="Large Button" style="large"/>
      <layoutContainer id="lcV1" layoutChildren="vertical">
        <button id="b2" label="Button"/>
        <button id="b3" label="Button"/>
        <button id="b4" label="Button"/>
      </layoutContainer>
      <layoutContainer id="lcV2" layoutChildren="vertical">
        <button id="b5" label="Button" style="borderless"/>
        <button id="b6" label="Button" style="borderless"/>
        <button id="b7" label="Button" style="borderless"/>
      </layoutContainer>
    </layoutContainer>
  </topItems>
</group>
```

code snippet BackstageSamples.accdb

This customization is shown in Figure 17-16.

As you can see, by combining `layoutContainer` controls with the expand attribute, you can create fairly complex layouts for controls.

Row Span

Demonstrates a row span where the large button spans multiple rows.

	Button	Button
Large Button	Button	Button
	Button	Button

FIGURE 17-16

Creating a Table-Type Grid

With its clean visuals, the Backstage provides an interesting place to create a full-screen user interface. For example, you could have a number of image controls or labels that, when placed together, create what appears to be a table — something like the Backstage shown in Figure 17-17.

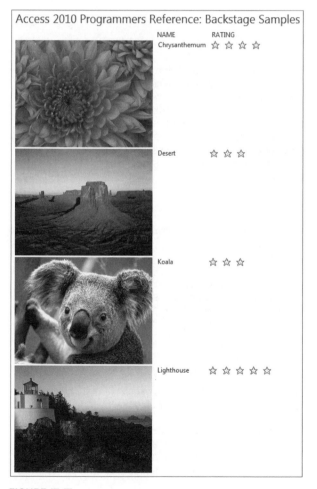

FIGURE 17-17

The customization for this is shown in the code that follows. Notice the use of extra spaces and the `noWrap` attribute of a `label` control to place the labels at their intended positions.

```
<customUI xmlns="http://schemas.microsoft.com/office/2009/07/customui"
         loadImage="OnLoadImage">
  <backstage>
    <tab id="tabImages" label="Images" getTitle="OnGetTitle">
      <firstColumn>
        <group id="grpImages">
          <topItems>
            <!-- Header -->
            <layoutContainer id="lcHeader" layoutChildren="horizontal"
                             expand="neither">
              <labelControl id="lblSpacer" label="                        "
                            noWrap="true"/>
              <labelControl id="lblName"    label="              NAME"
                            noWrap="true"/>
              <labelControl id="lblRating" label="              RATING"
                            noWrap="true"/>
            </layoutContainer>

            <!-- Row: 1 -->
            <layoutContainer id="hlc1" layoutChildren="horizontal" expand="neither">
              <imageControl id="img1" image="Chrysanthemum - copy.jpg"/>
              <labelControl id="lbl1" label="Chrysanthemum"/>
              <layoutContainer id="lcRating1" layoutChildren="horizontal">
                <imageControl id="imgRating1a" imageMso="ShapeStar"/>
                <imageControl id="imgRating1b" imageMso="ShapeStar"/>
                <imageControl id="imgRating1c" imageMso="ShapeStar"/>
                <imageControl id="imgRating1d" imageMso="ShapeStar"/>
              </layoutContainer>
            </layoutContainer>

            <!-- Row: 2 -->
            <layoutContainer id="hlc2" layoutChildren="horizontal" expand="neither">
              <imageControl id="img2" image="Desert - copy.jpg"/>
              <labelControl id="lbl2" label="Desert              "
                            noWrap="true"/>
              <layoutContainer id="lcRating2" layoutChildren="horizontal">
                <imageControl id="imgRating2a" imageMso="ShapeStar"/>
                <imageControl id="imgRating2b" imageMso="ShapeStar"/>
                <imageControl id="imgRating2c" imageMso="ShapeStar"/>
              </layoutContainer>
            </layoutContainer>

            <!-- Row: 3 -->
            <layoutContainer id="hlc3" layoutChildren="horizontal" expand="neither">
              <imageControl id="img3" image="Koala - copy.jpg"/>
              <labelControl id="lbl3" label="Koala              " noWrap="true"/>
              <layoutContainer id="lcRating3" layoutChildren="horizontal">
                <imageControl id="imgRating3a" imageMso="ShapeStar"/>
                <imageControl id="imgRating3b" imageMso="ShapeStar"/>
                <imageControl id="imgRating3c" imageMso="ShapeStar"/>
              </layoutContainer>
            </layoutContainer>

            <!-- Row: 4 -->
            <layoutContainer id="hlc4" layoutChildren="horizontal" expand="neither">
```

```
            <imageControl id="img4" image="Lighthouse - copy.jpg"/>
            <labelControl id="lbl4" label="Lighthouse        " noWrap="true"/>
            <layoutContainer id="lcRating4" layoutChildren="horizontal">
              <imageControl id="imgRating4a" imageMso="ShapeStar"/>
              <imageControl id="imgRating4b" imageMso="ShapeStar"/>
              <imageControl id="imgRating4c" imageMso="ShapeStar"/>
              <imageControl id="imgRating4d" imageMso="ShapeStar"/>
              <imageControl id="imgRating4e" imageMso="ShapeStar"/>
            </layoutContainer>
          </layoutContainer>

        </topItems>
      </group>
    </firstColumn>
   </tab>
  </backstage>
 </customUI>
```

code snippet BackstageSamples.accdb

The customization also defines a `loadImage` callback for the `customUI` element. This callback is used as the global image handler. In this case, we'll load images from a subfolder from the path where the database resides, as shown here:

```
Public Sub OnLoadImage(ImageName As String, ByRef objImage)
    Dim strImagePath As String

    strImagePath = CurrentProject.Path & "\images\" & ImageName

    If (Len(Dir(strImagePath)) > 0) Then
        Set objImage = LoadPicture(strImagePath)
    End If
End Sub
```

code snippet BackstageSamples.accdb

EXTENDING THE EXISTING BACKSTAGE

Unless you are completely replacing the Office Backstage, you might simply want to add functionality to an existing tab or group. Adding content to an existing tab or group in the Backstage is similar to adding a control to a built-in tab in the Ribbon. Using the `idMso` attribute of a control, you can specify where the new control will appear.

Adding a Group to an Existing Tab

The Info tab in the Access Backstage is a great place to consider adding your own group to simply add to the existing tab. One thing you might want to do is to add some contact information in the tab, so that end users can easily send you e-mail. To do this, you'll need to modify the tab with the idMso value of TabInfo, as shown in the following customization:

```
<!-- Extend the Info tab -->
<tab idMso="TabInfo">
  <firstColumn>
    <group id="grpContact" label="Contact Information">
      <topItems>
        <labelControl id="lblContact"
            label="For information about this database, please contact:"/>
        <hyperlink id="lnkContact" label="Rob Cooper" target="mailto:rob"/>
      </topItems>
    </group>
  </firstColumn>
</tab>
```

code snippet BackstageSamples.accdb

This adds an extra group called Contact Information at the bottom of the Info tab, as shown in Figure 17-18.

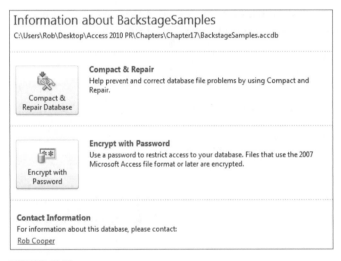

FIGURE 17-18

Adding a Category to an Existing TabFormGroup

Now let's say that you wanted to extend the Save & Publish tab in the Access Backstage to add a task that allows you to save a database in a custom repository. For simplicity, let's say that the repository is defined by a specific file share that is used for version control. To do this, we'll need to extend both the Save & Publish tab, and the task form group inside the tab. Here is the customization that adds a new task to the built-in taskFormGroup element:

```
<tab idMso="TabShare">
  <firstColumn>
    <taskFormGroup idMso="GroupShare">
```

```
<category id="catCustom" label="Repository" insertAfterMso="Share">
  <task id="taskCustom" description="Saves the database to a file repository"
        label="File Repository" imageMso="DatabaseSqlServer">
    <group id="grpRepository" label="Publish to File Repository">
      <primaryItem>
        <button id="btnSave" label="Save" imageMso="FileSave"/>
      </primaryItem>
      <topItems>
        <checkBox id="chkCompressed" label="Compress file"/>
        <checkBox id="chkStorePath" label="Store original path"/>
      </topItems>
    </group>
  </task>
</category>
</taskFormGroup>
</firstColumn>
</tab>
```

code snippet BackstageSamples.accdb

Notice that both the `tab` element and `taskFormGroup` element are extended using the `idMso` attribute. This customization adds a new task form group, as shown in Figure 17-19.

FIGURE 17-19

Adding a Task to an Existing TaskGroup

By now you probably realize that in order to extend an existing tab in the Backstage, you need the name and type of the control that you wish to extend. With this in mind, let's look at how you can add a custom task element to the Print tab to add the Page Setup command in Access in the Backstage.

The name of the tab to extend is `TabPrint`, and the name of the `taskGroup` element to extend is `GroupPrint`. Rather than add a new category to the `taskGroup`, we'll extend the existing category so that it appears seamless. The name of the built-in category is `PrintCategory`. With that, here is the customization:

```xml
<!-- Extend the Print tab -->
<tab idMso="TabPrint">
  <firstColumn>
    <taskGroup idMso="GroupPrint">
      <category idMso="PrintCategory">
        <task id="taskPageSetup" label="Page Setup"
              imageMso="PageSetupDialog"
              isDefinitive="true"
              description="Show the Page Setup dialog"
              onAction="OnShowPageSetup"/>
      </category>
    </taskGroup>
  </firstColumn>
</tab>
```

code snippet BackstageSamples.accdb

This creates a new task in the tab called Page Setup, as shown in Figure 17-20.

You'll also notice that we've included a callback, `OnShowPageSetup`, as part of the customization. This is because the built-in page setup command is defined in the Ribbon and cannot be reused in the Backstage. To work around this limitation, we'll invoke the dialog box using the following code for the callback:

```vb
Public Sub OnShowPageSetup(ctl As _
IRibbonControl)

    On Error GoTo OnShowPageSetup_Error

    DoCmd.RunCommand acCmdPageSetup

    On Error GoTo 0
    Exit Sub

OnShowPageSetup_Error:
    If (Err = 2046) Then
        MsgBox "Please open an object before launching Page Setup", vbInformation
        Exit Sub
    End If
    If (Err <> 2501) Then
        MsgBox "Error " & Err.Number & " (" & Err.Description & _
            ") in procedure OnShowPageSetup of Module basRibbonCallbacks"
    End If
End Sub
```

Print

Quick Print
Send the object directly to the default printer without making changes.

Print
Select a printer, number of copies, and other printing options before printing.

Print Preview
Preview and make changes to pages before printing.

Page Setup
Show the Page Setup dialog

FIGURE 17-20

code snippet BackstageSamples.accdb

BACKSTAGE-SPECIFIC CALLBACKS

So far you've learned about the Office Backstage, and the types of controls you can create. We've also looked at how to create layouts for your controls into columns and groups. Let's take a look at how you can extend the functionality of the Backstage using callbacks. This section will go into callbacks that are specific to the Backstage.

onShow

The onShow attribute of the backstage element specifies a callback that will fire when the Backstage is displayed. This callback is useful when you want to run some code when the user opens the Backstage. For example, you might have an imageControl where the image is set using a callback. If the image is dependent on data in the database, you will likely want to make sure that the image is updated each time. To do this, you'll need to call the InvalidateControl method of the IRibbonUI object as discussed in Chapter 16. The onShow callback for the Backstage is a great place to invalidate controls in the Backstage to make sure they always have the correct values.

The onShow callback is defined using the following customization:

```
<customUI xmlns="http://schemas.microsoft.com/office/2009/07/customui">
  <backstage onShow="OnShowBackstage">
  </backstage>
</customUI>
```

The following code will fire when the Backstage is shown:

```
Public Sub OnShowBackstage(contextObject As Object)
    gobjRibbon.InvalidateControl "imgCurrentUser"
    gobjRibbon.InvalidateControl "lblUserName"
    gobjRibbon.InvalidateControl "rgrpReferences"
    gobjRibbon.InvalidateControl "grpReferences"
    gobjRibbon.InvalidateControl "grpUserInfo"
End Sub
```

code snippet BackstageSamples.accdb

The object passed to the contextObject *parameter of the callback is the* Application *object for the application in question. In our case, it will be the* Access.Application *object.*

onHide

The onHide attribute of the backstage element specifies a callback that will fire when the Backstage is hidden using either the Escape key or a button or task with the isDefinitive attribute set to true. This callback is useful when you want to run some code when the user closes the Backstage. For example, you might want to requery the currently open form or mark a record as having been updated in some manner.

The onHide callback is defined using the following customization:

```
<customUI xmlns="http://schemas.microsoft.com/office/2009/07/customui">
  <backstage onHide="OnHideBackstage">
  </backstage>
</customUI>
```

The following code will fire when the Backstage is hidden:

```
Public Sub OnHideBackstage(contextObject As Object)
    MsgBox "The Backstage has been hidden."
End Sub
```

code snippet BackstageSamples.accdb

getStyle

The getStyle callback lets you specify the style attribute of a group at runtime. For example, let's say that you want to display a message to users if there is a missing reference in the database. There are a few ways you can do this. You can have a label dynamically appear when a reference is missing by using the getVisible callback. However, to show more attention to the issue in the Backstage, you might use the getStyle callback to apply the error style of the group. We look at an example of doing this later in the chapter.

Access applications are often used to track aging of work that needs to occur for a given item. For example, you might have an orders system where an order needs to be placed within a certain amount of time, and the priority of the order may increase the older it gets. Using the getStyle callback, you can show increasing priority the older an item gets.

The signature of the getStyle callback is defined as follows:

```
Public Sub GetStyleCallback(ctl As IRibbonControl, ByRef Style)
```

The values you pass to the Style argument of the callback are defined in the following Enum values:

```
BackstageGroupStyleError
BackstageGroupStyleNormal
BackstageGroupStyleWarning
```

getHelperText

Earlier you saw the helperText attribute of a tab or group element in a customization. The getHelperText callback allows you to set this text dynamically. For example, you could have additional instructions to users depending on the department they belong to. The getHelperText callback is defined here:

```
Public Sub OnGetHelperText(ctl As IRibbonControl, ByRef Text)
```

getTitle

The getTitle callback is used to set the title attribute of a control as defined with the following signature:

```
Public Sub OnGetTitle(ctl As IRibbonControl, ByRef Title)
```

Like the `getHelperText` callback, you might use this callback to provide custom messages to users. Because the title of a tab is affected by this callback, you could also use this to set the title to match the Application Title property of the database. We'll take a look at this scenario later in the chapter.

getTarget

The `getTarget` callback sets the target attribute of a hyperlink control. Let's say that you have a hyperlink in the Backstage that navigates to a specific website for a department depending on the user that is logged in. The base location or URL for the website is the same for all users, but the page or bookmark in the page may vary by user. You can easily change this using the `getTarget` callback, as shown here:

```
Public Sub OnGetTarget(ctl As IRibbonControl, ByRef Target)
```

BACKSTAGE SCENARIOS

Okay. We've made it this far and looked at controls and callbacks for the Office Backstage. It's time to piece this together and create some scenarios that you can use in your Access applications.

Access Runtime Experience

When you open a database in the Access Runtime, certain tabs and buttons are hidden in the Backstage. You can reproduce this with your own Backstage customization with one issue: The only way to remove the recent list of files that appears in the Backstage is to write to the Registry. The following customization will hide everything else with the exception of the Print tab and Exit button as is the case when a database is opened with the Access Runtime or the `/runtime` command-line switch.

Available for download on Wrox.com

```
<!--
   The startFromScratch attribute does not hide tabs in the Backstage,
   so we also need to customize the Backstage.
   -->
<ribbon startFromScratch="true"/>
<backstage>
  <!-- Fast Commands -->
  <button idMso="FileSave" visible="false"/>
  <button idMso="SaveObjectAs" visible="false"/>
  <button idMso="FileSaveAsCurrentFileFormat" visible="false"/>
  <button idMso="FileSaveAsCurrentFileFormat" visible="false"/>
  <button idMso="FileOpen" visible="false"/>
  <button idMso="FileCloseDatabase" visible="false"/>
  <button idMso="ApplicationOptionsDialog" visible="false"/>
  <!-- Tabs-->
  <tab idMso="TabInfo" visible="false"/>
  <tab idMso="TabShare" visible="false"/>
  <tab idMso="TabRecent" visible="false"/>
  <tab idMso="TabNew" visible="false"/>
  <tab idMso="TabHelp" visible="false"/>
</backstage>
```

code snippet BackstageSamples.accdb

Setting the Title of a Tab to the Application Title

Setting the title of an Access application changes the appearance of your application in the Access title bar. This is a nice touch when developing databases and makes them appear more polished. When you set the Application Title property in the Access Options dialog box, you're creating a new property in the `Properties` collection for the database called `AppTitle`. The following code can be used for the `getTitle` callback of a tab in the Backstage to set the title attribute to the `AppTitle` property of the database. If the property is not set, it will set it to the name of the file without the file extension.

```
Public Sub OnGetTitle(ctl As IRibbonControl, ByRef Title)
    Dim strTitle As String

    On Error Resume Next
    strTitle = CurrentDb.Properties("AppTitle")
    On Error GoTo 0

    If (Len(strTitle) = 0) Then
        strTitle = VBA.Left(CurrentProject.Name, _
                    Len(CurrentProject.Name) - InStrRev(CurrentProject.Name, ".") - 1)
    End If

    ' Return the title
    Title = strTitle
End Sub
```

code snippet BackstageSamples.accdb

About Page and Contact Form

Applications often will include a form in the database for displaying contact information or other information about the database such as a list of references or the location of the backend database. Sometimes, you might include a form for collecting information from users such as bug reports, comments, or other suggestions. The Backstage is a nice place to add such a feature.

Let's say that you want to collect certain types of feedback from users: comments, suggestions, and problem reports. To allow the user to make a single choice between the different types of feedback, you might use radio buttons, which only allow one choice. The other thing you'll need is a text box, which can be used to collect the feedback. Here is the customization:

```
<customUI xmlns="http://schemas.microsoft.com/office/2009/07/customui"
        onLoad="OnLoadUI">
    <backstage>
        <!-- About information -->
        <tab id="tabAbout" label="About"
            title="About Access 2010 Programmers Reference"
            insertBeforeMso="FileSave">
            <firstColumn>
                <group id="grp1">
                    <topItems>
```

```
            <labelControl id="lbl1"
                label="By Teresa Hennig, Rob Cooper, Geoff Griffith, Jerry Dennison"
             />
            <labelControl id="lbl2" label="Copyright © 2010 Wiley Publishing"/>
            <hyperlink id="lnk1" label="Published by Wrox"
                        target="http://www.wrox.com"/>
          </topItems>
        </group>

        <!-- Contact information -->
        <group id="grp2" label="Contact">
          <primaryItem>
            <button id="btnSend" imageMso="MailMergeStartEmail"
                    label="Send Feedback" onAction="OnSendFeedback"/>
          </primaryItem>
          <topItems>
            <layoutContainer id="lc2" layoutChildren="horizontal">
              <radioGroup id="rgrpFeedback" label="Type of feedback"
                          expand="neither" onAction="OnSelectFeedbackType">
                <radioButton id="rbtnComment" label="Comment"/>
                <radioButton id="rbtnSuggestion" label="Suggestion"/>
                <radioButton id="rbtnProblem" label="Problem Report"/>
              </radioGroup>
            </layoutContainer>
          </topItems>
        </group>
        <group id="grp3">
          <topItems>
            <editBox label="Feedback" id="txtFeedback" expand="horizontal"
                     onChange="OnUpdateFeedback" getText="OnGetFeedbackText"/>
          </topItems>
        </group>
      </firstColumn>
    </tab>
  </backstage>
</customUI>
```

code snippet BackstageSamples.accdb

This creates a tab in the Backstage, as shown in Figure 17-21.

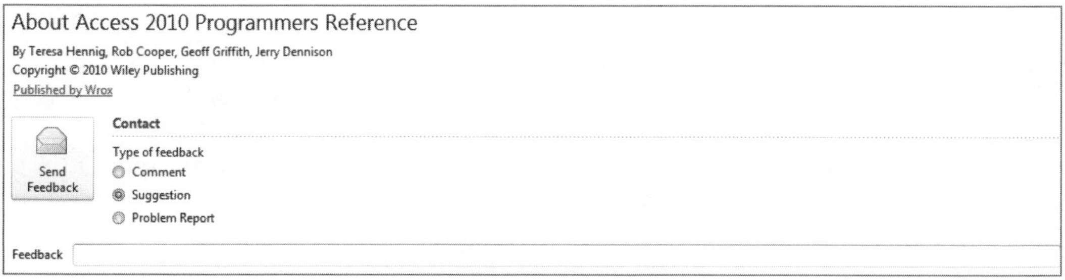

FIGURE 17-21

You'll notice there are a few callbacks we need to define to make this all work. These are described in the following table.

CONTROL ID	CALLBACK	ROUTINE NAME	DESCRIPTION
customUI	onLoad	OnLoadUI	Used to store a copy of an IRibbonUI object for invalidating a control.
btnSend	onAction	OnSendFeedback	Used to send the specified feedback.
rgrpFeedback	onAction	OnSelectFeedbackType	Specifies the type of feedback.
txtFeedback	onChange	OnUpdateFeedback	Specifies the feedback.
txtFeedback	getText	OnGetFeedbackText	Used to clear the text box.

Remember that callbacks are called when the Ribbon or Backstage needs information. In this scenario, we want to specify the type of feedback, and because we can't ask for it directly, we'll use callbacks for the radio group and edit box to store their data. As a result, you'll need a few variables. Start with the following code. The Enum is provided as a convenience to map the indexes for the radioButton controls in the radioGroup.

```
Public Enum FeedbackType
    Comment
    Suggestion
    Problem
End Enum

Public gobjRibbon As IRibbonUI

' used in the About page
Private m_feedbackType As FeedbackType
Private m_feedback      As String
```

code snippet BackstageSamples.accdb

Next, let's look at the callbacks, starting with OnLoadUI, which is used to save the IRibbonUI object. Remember that this is used to invalidate a control.

```
Public Sub OnLoadUI(objRibbon As IRibbonUI)
    Set gobjRibbon = objRibbon
End Sub
```

code snippet BackstageSamples.accdb

In order to determine the type of feedback and the feedback itself, you'll need to respond to callbacks for the radioGroup and editBox controls.

```vba
Public Sub OnSelectFeedbackType(ctl As IRibbonControl, strItemID, lngIndex)
    ' set the type of feedback
    m_feedbackType = lngIndex
End Sub

Public Sub OnUpdateFeedback(ctl As IRibbonControl, strText)
    m_feedback = strText
End Sub
```

code snippet BackstageSamples.accdb

The `OnGetFeedbackText` callback is used to simply clear the `editBox` control.

```vba
Public Sub OnGetFeedbackText(ctl As IRibbonControl, ByRef strText)
    strText = ""
End Sub
```

code snippet BackstageSamples.accdb

Finally, the button will use the callback shown here. In this example, we'll build a string based on the values of the variables that were set from the other callbacks. The code here shows a message box, but you might just as easily choose to send e-mail.

```vba
Public Sub OnSendFeedback(ctl As IRibbonControl)
    Dim strFeedback As String

    If (Len(m_feedback) = 0) Then
        MsgBox "No feedback has been specified.", vbExclamation
        Exit Sub
    End If

    ' sends feedback of a certain type
    Select Case m_feedbackType
        Case FeedbackType.Comment
            strFeedback = "Here is a comment about the software:"
        Case FeedbackType.Problem
            strFeedback = "I'd like to report a problem I am encountering:"
        Case FeedbackType.Suggestion
            strFeedback = "I'd like to make the following suggestion:"
    End Select

    ' add the rest of the feedback from the text box
    strFeedback = strFeedback & vbCrLf & vbCrLf & m_feedback

    ' Send email. We'll use a message box for the example.
    MsgBox strFeedback

    ' clear the textbox and private data
```

```
        gobjRibbon.InvalidateControl "txtFeedback"
        m_feedback = ""
    End Sub
```

code snippet BackstageSamples.accdb

Warning for a Missing Reference

Missing references in a database can cause problems. When Access evaluates expressions, it needs to determine the library that contains the function being used in the expression. When you have a missing reference, Access can't reliably find where a function is defined, and you'll likely see the #Name? error where the value of the expression should be. For this reason, you might consider warning users when a reference is missing in the database.

Much has been written about this topic over the years, so here's a new way to bubble up the issue to users using the Backstage.

There are a few controls that allow you to fill their contents dynamically in the Backstage. These controls are the comboBox, dropDown, and radioGroup controls. Of these, only the contents of the radioGroup control are always visible so we'll go with that one. Here is the customization for the radioGroup.

Available for download on Wrox.com

```
<customUI xmlns="http://schemas.microsoft.com/office/2009/07/customui"
          onLoad="OnLoadUI">
  <backstage onShow="OnShowBackstage">
    <!-- References Tab -->
    <tab id="tabReferences" columnWidthPercent="75" label="References">
      <firstColumn>
        <group id="grpReferences" label="References" getStyle="OnGetStyle">
          <topItems>
            <radioGroup id="rgrpReferences"
                        getItemCount="OnGetReferenceCount"
                        getItemLabel="OnGetReferenceLabel">
            </radioGroup>
          </topItems>
        </group>
      </firstColumn>
    </tab>
  </backstage>
</customUI>
```

code snippet BackstageSamples.accdb

Notice that we've defined the radioGroup inside a group element with the getStyle callback defined. We're going to use this to warn the user if a reference is missing, but we'll get to that shortly.

We first need to define the callbacks that will be used to fill the contents of the radioGroup. Much like dynamically filling the comboBox or dropDown controls, we need to specify how many items there are, followed by their labels. Because we're going to list references in the database, we'll use the References collection in the Access Object Model. The callbacks are as follows.

```
Public Sub OnGetReferenceCount(ctl As IRibbonControl, ByRef Count)
    Count = Application.References.Count
End Sub

Public Sub OnGetReferenceLabel(ctl As IRibbonControl, SelectedIndex As Integer, _
                                ByRef Label)
    Dim ref As Reference
    Set ref = References(SelectedIndex + 1)

    If Not ref.IsBroken Then
        Label = ref.Name
    Else
        Label = "MISSING: " & ref.Name
    End If
End Sub
```

code snippet BackstageSamples.accdb

In this case, `OnGetReferenceCount` simply returns the number of references in the database. `OnGetReferenceLabel` returns the name of the `Reference` to show in the `radioGroup`.

We also need to warn the user if there is a missing reference. To do this, we'll change the style of the group to `BackstageGroupStyleError` when one of the references is missing. Here is the code for the `getStyle` callback for the group:

```
Public Sub OnGetStyle(ctl As IRibbonControl, ByRef Style)
    If (Application.BrokenReference) Then
        Style = BackstageGroupStyle.BackstageGroupStyleError
    End If
End Sub
```

code snippet BackstageSamples.accdb

The customization also defines an `onLoad` callback for the `customUI` element and the `onShow` callback for the Backstage itself. The `onShow` callback will be used to invalidate the group element and the `radioGroup` control to ensure that the list of references is always up-to-date. Add the following line of code to the top of the module:

```
Public gobjRibbon As IRibbonUI
```

These callbacks are defined as follows:

```
Public Sub OnLoadUI(objRibbon As IRibbonUI)
    Set gobjRibbon = objRibbon
End Sub

Public Sub OnShowBackstage(contextObject As Object)
    gobjRibbon.InvalidateControl "rgrpReferences"
    gobjRibbon.InvalidateControl "grpReferences"
End Sub
```

code snippet BackstageSamples.accdb

Custom Database Information

Providing a page in the Backstage to show information such as the database location provides a nice touch. If your database is split into a frontend and backend, you might also want to add the ability to relink tables from here, or to allow users to switch between production and test environments using different back-end databases. Other maintenance tasks such as compacting and backup also fit nicely into this page. You could even include the list of references in the database, as shown in the previous example.

There a couple of other requirements to list before listing the customization. This page will replace the existing Info tab in the Backstage so we'll want to hide that one. Also, to promote the appearance of the tab, we want to make it the first thing that appears in the Backstage. To do this, we'll set the `insertBeforeMso` attribute of the tab element to place the tab before the Save button.

Another requirement is that the application title should appear as the title for the tab. The `getTitle` callback used to define the title is defined in a previous example so we won't list the code here. In addition, the code to relink tables has been written about at length in many places so the customization is intended to show you what you might use in the Backstage.

With these goals in mind, let's create a custom database information page for the Backstage:

```
<customUI xmlns="http://schemas.microsoft.com/office/2009/07/customui"
         onLoad="OnLoadUI">
  <backstage onShow="OnShowBackstage">
    <!-- Hide the built-in Info tab-->
    <tab idMso="TabInfo" visible="false"/>

    <!-- Custom Info Tab -->
    <tab id="tabDbInfo" label="Database Information"
         columnWidthPercent="75"
         firstColumnMaxWidth="800"
         secondColumnMinWidth="200"
         getTitle="OnGetTitle"
         insertBeforeMso="FileSave">
      <firstColumn>
        <!-- Database location -->
        <group id="g1" label="Database Location">
          <topItems>
            <editBox id="txtDbLocation" getText="OnGetDatabaseLocation"
                     maxLength="260" expand="horizontal"/>
          </topItems>
        </group>

        <!-- Relink tables -->
        <taskGroup id="tgrpConnection" label="Database Connection"
                   helperText="Set the database connection"
                   allowedTaskSizes="mediumSmall">
          <category id="c1">
            <task id="t2" label="Production"
                  description="Connect to the production server for deployment."
                  imageMso="DatabaseCopyDatabaseFile"/>
            <task id="t1" label="Test"
                  description="Connect to the test server for application testing."
                  imageMso="CreateTable"/>
          </category>
```

```
            </taskGroup>

            <!-- Maintainence group -->
            <taskGroup id="tgrpUtil" label="Maintainence"
                       helperText="Maintain the database"
                       allowedTaskSizes="mediumSmall">
              <category id="c2">
                <task id="tFileCompactAndRepairDatabase" label="Compact Database"
                      description="Compacts the database for optimal health."
                      imageMso="FileCompactAndRepairDatabase"/>
                <task id="tBackupDb" label="Backup Database"
                      description="Performs a one-time backup of the database"
                      imageMso="FileBackupDatabase"/>
              </category>
            </taskGroup>
          </firstColumn>
        </tab>
      </backstage>
  </customUI>
```

code snippet BackstageSamples.accdb

This should create a customization for the Backstage, as shown in Figure 17-22.

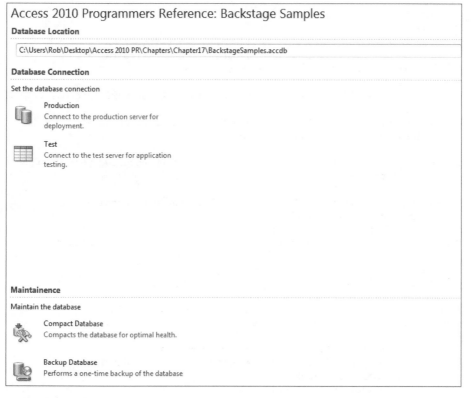

FIGURE 17-22

Let's take a look at the callback used to fill in the `editBox` control that shows the location for the database.

```
Public Sub OnGetDatabaseLocation(ctl As IRibbonControl, ByRef Text)
    Text = CurrentProject.FullName
End Sub
```

code snippet BackstageSamples.accdb

This callback simply returns the full path to the currently open database. Because we're using the `CurrentProject` object, this should work for the MDB, ACCDB, and ADP file extensions.

Creating a Bulleted or Numbered List

Bulleted or numbered lists offer a clear way to provide feedback or instructions to users. You can create a list of instructions in the Backstage using a combination of the `label`, `image`, and `layoutContainer` controls. The trick is to define each image and label in a horizontal layout container, and the entire list in a vertical container. Here is a customization for a simple list of items. We're using the numbers 1 through 3, as mentioned earlier, and the ShapeStar image. Naturally, you can use any image that you like.

```
<tab id="TabWelcome" insertBeforeMso="FileSave" label="Welcome!" title="Welcome!">
  <firstColumn>
    <group id="GrpNumbers" label="Numbers">
      <topItems>
        <layoutContainer id="lcVert1" layoutChildren="vertical">
          <layoutContainer id="lcHorz1" layoutChildren="horizontal">
            <imageControl id="imgN1" imageMso="_1"/>
            <labelControl id="lblStep1"
          label="New here? Be sure to visit the Help page for more information."/>
          </layoutContainer>
          <layoutContainer id="lcHorz2" layoutChildren="horizontal">
            <imageControl id="imgN2" imageMso="_2"/>
            <labelControl id="lblStep2"
      label="Once you're familiar with what to do, start by entering your company
              information."/>
          </layoutContainer>
          <layoutContainer id="lcHorz3" layoutChildren="horizontal">
            <imageControl id="imgN3" imageMso="_3"/>
            <labelControl id="lblStep3"
      label="Lastly, start entering customers and orders, and start using the
              application."/>
          </layoutContainer>
        </layoutContainer>
      </topItems>
    </group>
    <group id="GrpBullets" label="Bullets">
      <topItems>
        <layoutContainer id="lcVert2" layoutChildren="vertical">
          <layoutContainer id="lcHorz4" layoutChildren="horizontal">
            <imageControl id="imgN4" imageMso="ShapeStar"/>
            <labelControl id="lblStep4"
      label="New here? Be sure to visit the Help page for more information."/>
```

```
        </layoutContainer>
        <layoutContainer id="lcHorz5" layoutChildren="horizontal">
          <imageControl id="imgN5" imageMso="ShapeStar"/>
          <labelControl id="lblStep5"
    label="Once you're familiar with what to do, start by entering your company
            information."/>
        </layoutContainer>
        <layoutContainer id="lcHorz6" layoutChildren="horizontal">
          <imageControl id="imgN6" imageMso="ShapeStar"/>
          <labelControl id="lblStep6" label="Lastly, start entering customers
            and orders, and start using the application."/>
        </layoutContainer>
      </layoutContainer>
    </topItems>
  </group>
 </firstColumn>
</tab>
```

code snippet BackstageSamples.accdb

This customization is shown in Figure 17-23.

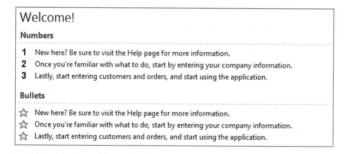

FIGURE 17-23

Welcome Page with Image

Another nice touch of personalization for an application might be to show the user who is logged in. To do this, we'll use the imageControl element in the customization and a set of images on the computer. As you may remember from Chapter 16, there are a few callbacks that you can use to load an image, but we'll use the getImage callback for the control. We also want to display the name of the user and provide a means for locking the application.

FIGURE 17-24

For this, we'll use a label control and a hyperlink control. The hyperlink control will make the action feel like a Web page, but we can run our own code instead of navigating to a URL.

For the login process, we'll build a simple login form, as shown in Figure 17-24.

The login form will simply set a `TempVar` with the ID value of the user that is selected from the combo box. This happens using the following code behind the OK button in the dialog box:

```vba
Private Sub cmdOK_Click()
    ' cache the current user
    If (IsNull(Me.cboUser)) Then
        TempVars.Remove "CurrentUserId"
    Else
        TempVars.Add "CurrentUserId", Me.cboUser.Value
    End If

    DoCmd.Close acForm, Me.Name

End Sub
```

code snippet BackstageSamples.accdb

Here is the customization.

```xml
<group id="grpUserInfo" label="User Info" getVisible="OnGetVisible">
  <topItems>
    <imageControl id="imgCurrentUser" getImage="OnGetCurrentUserImage"/>
    <layoutContainer id="lc1" layoutChildren="horizontal">
      <labelControl id="lblUserName" getLabel="OnGetUserName" noWrap="true"/>
      <layoutContainer id="lcHorz" layoutChildren="horizontal">
        <imageControl id="imgLock" imageMso="Lock"/>
        <hyperlink id="lnkLock" label="Lock"
                   onAction="=MsgBox('Lock the database')" expand="horizontal"/>
      </layoutContainer>
    </layoutContainer>
  </topItems>
</group>
```

code snippet BackstageSamples.accdb

We're going to retrieve the name of the image to use for the ID of the user from a table called `USysRibbonUsers`. Before showing the image, however, let's define the table.

FIELD NAME	DATA TYPE
ID	AutoNumber
FirstName	Text (255)
LastName	Text (255)
UserImageName	Text (255)

The data for the sample database for this chapter (available on Wrox.com) is shown in the table that follows:

ID	FIRSTNAME	LASTNAME	USERIMAGENAME
1	Rob	Cooper	rob.jpg
2	Geoff	Griffith	geoff.jpg
3	Jerry	Dennison	
4	Teresa	Hennig	teresa.jpg

The following code defines the getImage callback that we'll use to display the image and the getLabel callback for the label control.

```
Public Sub OnGetCurrentUserImage(ctl As IRibbonControl, ByRef Image)
    Dim rs As DAO.Recordset

    If (IsNull(TempVars!CurrentUserId)) Then Exit Sub

    Set rs = CurrentDb().OpenRecordset("SELECT * FROM USysRibbonUsers WHERE ID=" & _
                              TempVars!CurrentUserId)

    If (Not rs.EOF And Not rs.BOF) Then
        Set Image = LoadPicture(CurrentProject.Path & "\images\" & _
                    rs("UserImageName"))
    End If

    rs.Close
    Set rs = Nothing

End Sub

Public Sub OnGetUserName(ctl As IRibbonControl, ByRef Label)
    Dim rs As DAO.Recordset

    If (IsNull(TempVars!CurrentUserId)) Then Exit Sub

    Set rs = CurrentDb().OpenRecordset("SELECT * FROM USysRibbonUsers WHERE ID=" & _
                              TempVars!CurrentUserId)

    If (Not rs.EOF And Not rs.BOF) Then
        Label = rs!FirstName & " " & rs!LastName
    End If

    rs.Close
    Set rs = Nothing
End Sub
```

code snippet BackstageSamples.accdb

Figure 17-25 shows the result of the customization.

You can further extend this by refreshing the `imageControl` and `label` using the `onShow` callback for the Backstage. This will ensure that the data in the Backstage is current.

Other Possible Examples

As you can see, there are many possible uses for the Backstage as a part of your application interface. These are but a few possible examples, and there are many others you could come up with.
The following subsections offer a few additional ideas to get you started.

FIGURE 17-25

Administration

Many applications will include an administration form to allow users to perform tasks such as employee or personnel management, or configuring settings such as back-end database location. You can add similar functionality to a new tab in the Backstage and use either the `getEnabled` or `getVisible` callbacks to enable or show the tab for administrative users.

Link Browser

If there are links that are common to your application, you could consider putting them in a central location in the Backstage. The `group` element could be used to group them together in a logical manner.

Reminders

Sometimes you might want to remind people to take action on a certain task. For example, a user might have an order to fulfill, or may need to follow up on a customer that is defined in a record in the database. The Backstage might be an interesting place to display reminders for actions to be taken.

Report Manager

In Chapter 16 we created a Report Manager that allowed you to dynamically display a list of reports to users in the Ribbon. This same scenario could be implemented using the Backstage. Unlike the Ribbon, however, the Backstage does not have the `dynamicMenu` control that we used to show the list of reports. The `comboBox` or `dropDown` controls could be used in its place. If you don't need a place to display reports dynamically, the Backstage still might make a good entry point to display a static set of reports for easy viewing.

SUMMARY

In this chapter you learned how to build upon new user experiences in the Office Backstage. Although the way you write the customizations is similar, the Backstage provides a unique way for interacting with the application. It provides a central location for creating content that is relevant for the whole database, and as such, is a good place to add features such as backup and maintenance as a part of your applications.

Like the Ribbon, there are numerous ways you can extend the Backstage to suit your needs. The callbacks that you define help you provide rich and interactive functionality to the Backstage, and can include data from the database to help make the content meaningful.

The next chapter shows you how you can further build out your Access applications by extending them to work with other applications that are included with Office.

18

Working with Office 2010

WHAT'S IN THIS CHAPTER?

➤ Using Outlook objects in Access using VBA

➤ Creating and sending e-mail with Outlook

➤ Creating Calendar items in Outlook

➤ Using Excel objects in Access using VBA

➤ Getting data from an Excel spreadsheet

➤ Sending Access data to an Excel spreadsheet

➤ Using Word objects in Access using VBA

➤ Creating Word documents

➤ Sending Access data to Word documents

➤ Creating automated mail merges using Word

One of the most powerful features of the Microsoft Office 2010 suite is the interoperability between the various applications. So far, most of the material covered in this book has worked directly within Access and with the Object Model (OM) it provides, but VBA is not specific to Access only. Many of the other Office applications, such as Word, Outlook, and Excel, support VBA and all have their own Object Models that provide the ability to work directly with their respective objects. More importantly, this interoperability provides Access developers with the ability to leverage those Office applications and their features directly from within an Access database application. Similarly, the reverse is true for a developer of Excel spreadsheets; Access features and database data can be used directly from within an Excel spreadsheet application. The idea is that all the features of the entire Office suite of products can be used within any of those products with just a few simple lines of VBA code. This chapter covers the basics of working with the Outlook, Excel, and Word Object Models and provides examples of how you can use their features within your Access database applications.

WORKING WITH OUTLOOK 2010

In today's high-tech world of communication, one of the most common forms of information sharing is e-mail. As you probably already know, Microsoft Office 2010 provides the Outlook application for working with e-mail as well as tracking and managing schedules, tasks, and events. If you're like the authors of this book, you (or more importantly, the users of your applications) probably spend a lot of time in Outlook just reading and writing e-mails, and you may even track the events and tasks of your life in the Outlook Calendar. Wouldn't programmatically creating these sorts of Outlook objects in a database application be nice? The Outlook OM provides this ability to do just that!

Setting References to Outlook

Before you can begin using the Outlook Object Model in a database application, you must first set a reference in the code project to the Outlook OM. To set a reference to Outlook, complete the following steps:

1. From any open database application in Access, press the Ctrl+G key combination to open VBE (the Visual Basic Editor).

2. Choose Tools ➪ Reference. The References dialog box opens.

3. Scroll down and select the Microsoft Outlook 14.0 Object Library option. Click the OK button.

A reference to the Outlook OM is now added to the code project of the database file. You now have everything you need to begin writing VBA code to work with Outlook from Access.

> In Office 2010, the name of the reference to the Outlook OM is "Microsoft Outlook 14.0 Object Library," where the number 14.0 represents the specific major version number of Office 2010. Previous versions of Outlook have a slightly different number in the name, depending on the version of Microsoft Office.

Creating Outlook Application Objects

The first thing to do when working with Outlook is to create an Outlook application object. The `Outlook.Application` object is the top-level object for working Outlook programmatically and provides interfaces to all the Outlook object types. Basically you have two ways to do this: by calling the `New` keyword or by using the `CreateObject` method.

Using the New Keyword

The easiest way to create a new instance of the Outlook.Application class is to use the New keyword to create a new instance of it, as you would any other object in VBA. The following code provides an example of this:

```
Public Function CreateOutlookWithNew() As Outlook.Application

    ' Return a new instance of the Outlook Application object
    Set CreateOutlookWithNew = New Outlook.Application

End Function
```

module OutlookSampleCode in Ch18_Sample.accdb

Using the CreateObject Method

To create a new instance of the Outlook application using the CreateObject method, simply call it with the Outlook.Application name string as the parameter of the method. The following code shows how you can do this:

```
Public Function CreateOutlookWithCreateObject() As Outlook.Application

    ' Return a new instance of the Outlook Application object
    Set CreateOutlookWithCreateObject = CreateObject("Outlook.Application")

End Function
```

module OutlookSampleCode in Ch18_Sample.accdb

New versus CreateObject

The previous two code examples both do the exact same thing — return an instance of the Outlook application object. Both objects work identically and can be used in the exact same manner. The difference between the two is in how the binding of the Outlook.Application class works.

When the New keyword is called in VBA code, the variable is bound to the Outlook.Application object at compile time, which is known as *early binding*. This means that your VBA project knows everything about the Outlook.Application object when the project is compiled. This is why the reference to the Outlook OM is required in the project.

Conversely, the CreateObject method actually returns an Object type that contains the Application class of the specified type. The variable is bound to the Outlook.Application object (or any other Application object created in this manner) at runtime, which is known as *late binding*. This means that the VBA project doesn't need to know anything about the object until it is created at runtime. In fact, in this case, a reference to the Outlook OM is not even required in the project to create the `Outlook.Application` object as an `Object` data type. The following code provides an example of how to do this:

```
Public Function CreateOutlookAsObject() As Object

    ' Return a new instance of Outlook as an Object type
    Set CreateOutlookAsObject = CreateObject("Outlook.Application")

End Function
```

module OutlookSampleCode in Ch18_Sample.accdb

In the previous code, the `Outlook.Application` object is returned packaged as an `Object` data type. You can still call all the same methods that the `Outlook.Application` object supports; the difference is that VBA does not know anything about the object, or its methods, properties, and events until runtime.

New Is Not Always New with Outlook

One other thing to consider about Outlook that differs from other Office applications is that it can have only a single instance running at any given time. This means that when you create a new instance of Outlook and the application is already running, you are actually getting back the instance that is currently running. Although this characteristic probably won't make much of a difference most of the time, it is important to consider and be aware of from a programming standpoint.

Using the GetObject Method

Similarly, a reference to the currently running instance of Outlook, or any Office application, can be retrieved by using the `GetObject` method. Simply call `GetObject` with the name of the particular application class to get. This allows the application to be manipulated programmatically, directly from within the VBA code. The following code provides an example of using the `GetObject` method on the `Outlook.Application` object:

```
Public Function GetOutlookApplication() As Object

    ' Return the running instance of Outlook as an Object type
    Set GetOutlookApplication = GetObject(, "Outlook.Application")

End Function
```

module OutlookSampleCode in Ch18_Sample.accdb

Of course, if Outlook isn't already running on the system, then you will get a runtime error when this code runs.

Working with MailItem objects

The most common task in Outlook is to create and send e-mail items, which you can do quite easily using VBA code in an Access database application. Several methods are available for accomplishing this task.

Creating an E-mail

The most flexible way to create an e-mail message with Outlook is by using the Outlook OM. The Outlook OM exposes several classes and methods for sending basic e-mails, as well as provides additional options and settings to work with the more robust features of Outlook.

Creating an e-mail with the Outlook OM requires taking the following steps:

1. Get an instance of the `Outlook.Application` class.

2. Create a new `MailItem` object.

3. Add the desired settings to the `MailItem`.

4. Call the `Display` method to show the e-mail to the user.

The following VBA function illustrates how easily these steps can be accomplished:

Available for download on Wrox.com

```
Public Function CreateEmailWithOutlook( _
    MessageTo As String, _
    Subject As String, _
    MessageBody As String)

    ' Define app variable and get Outlook using the "New" keyword
    Dim olApp As New Outlook.Application
    Dim olMailItem As Outlook.MailItem  ' An Outlook Mail item

    ' Create a new email object
    Set olMailItem = olApp.CreateItem(olMailItem)

    ' Add the To/Subject/Body to the message and display the message
    With olMailItem
        .To = MessageTo
        .Subject = Subject
        .Body = MessageBody
        .Display    ' To show the email message to the user
    End With

    ' Release all object variables
    Set olMailItem = Nothing
    Set olApp = Nothing

End Function
```

module OutlookSampleCode in Ch18_Sample.accdb

After this function runs, a new e-mail is created and displayed for the user to see. Because the `Display` method was called, the user will see the mail message and have the opportunity to make changes to the message. Of course, the user will be required to send the message manually in this example, per Step 4 above.

Sending an E-mail

Sending a message using the Outlook OM is also possible, but you must consider some Outlook security features when doing so. To send a message using the Outlook OM, simply call the `Send` method from the `MailItem` object. You can modify the previous example to do this by changing the `Display` call to the `Send` method.

```
Public Function SendEmailWithOutlook( _
    MessageTo As String, _
    Subject As String, _
    MessageBody As String)

    ' Define app variable and get Outlook using the "New" keyword
    Dim olApp As New Outlook.Application
    Dim olMailItem As Outlook.MailItem  ' An Outlook Mail item

    ' Create a new email object
    Set olMailItem = olApp.CreateItem(olMailItem)

    ' Add the To/Subject/Body to the message and display the message
    With olMailItem
        .To = MessageTo
        .Subject = Subject
        .Body = MessageBody
        .Send        ' Send the message immediately
    End With

    ' Release all object variables
    Set olMailItem = Nothing
    Set olApp = Nothing

End Function
```

module OutlookSampleCode in Ch18_Sample.accdb

When this code runs, the user gets a security dialog box pop-up message, as shown in Figure 18-1:

This Outlook security feature requires that the user allow the e-mail to be sent from his machine. These features were added to Outlook 2003 to deter the use of malicious code to send e-mail from a user's machine without his knowledge. You find out more about the Outlook security features shortly.

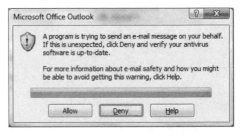

FIGURE 18-1

Adding an E-mail to a Folder

Creating an e-mail with the Outlook Object Model and adding it to a folder requires taking the following steps:

1. Get an instance of the `Outlook.Application` class.

2. Get the namespace and `MAPIFolder` object.

3. Create a new `MailItem` object.

4. Add the desired settings to the `MailItem`.

5. Call the `Save` method to save the e-mail to the folder.

The following block of code illustrates how easily you can create VBA code to complete these steps:

```vba
Public Function SavingEmailToFolder( _
    MessageTo As String, _
    Subject As String, _
    MessageBody As String)

    ' Define app variable and get Outlook using the "New" keyword
    Dim olApp As New Outlook.Application

    ' Define the Namespace object
    Dim olNS As Outlook.Namespace
    Dim olFolder As Outlook.MAPIFolder

    ' Define the email variable
    Dim olMailItem As Outlook.MailItem

    ' Get the NameSpace, Inbox folder, and Add a new mail item
    Set olNS = olApp.GetNamespace("MAPI")
    Set olFolder = olNS.GetDefaultFolder(olFolderInbox)
    Set olMailItem = olFolder.Items.Add("IPM.Note")

    ' Add the To/Subject/Body to the message and display the message
    With olMailItem
        .To = MessageTo
        .Subject = Subject
        .Body = MessageBody
        .Save     ' To Save the Email to the Folder
    End With

    ' Release all object variables
    Set olMailItem = Nothing
    Set olFolder = Nothing
    Set olNS = Nothing
    Set olApp = Nothing

End Function
```

module OutlookSampleCode in Ch18_Sample.accdb

After this function runs, a new e-mail is created and saved in the Inbox folder. It is worth noting that the method used to create the e-mail in this example could also be used in the previous two examples; the only difference here is that you got the Outlook folder explicitly, when the GetDefaultFolder method was called, instead of using the Application object to create the item.

Other MailItem Settings

Before moving on to other Outlook topics, you should note a couple of other useful MailItem object properties. Specifically, the Importance, FlagStatus, and FlagDueBy properties allow you to set the e-mail's importance, status flag, and due date flag for Outlook. The following is an example that you could add to the previous code examples to set these flags.

```
olMailItem.Importance = olImportanceHigh
olMailItem.FlagStatus = olFlagMarked
olMailItem.FlagDueBy = Date + 2
```

Outlook Security Features

Two security dialog boxes were added, originally in Outlook 2003, to prevent malicious code from causing problems for Outlook users. The first dialog box appears when code tries to manipulate addresses in the Contacts folder. The second is the dialog box you saw earlier in Figure 18-1, which is a dialog box that requires the user to allow the VBA code to send an e-mail via Outlook programmatically. Specifically, this is for security purposes and it is important to note that a couple of other methods are also available for sending e-mail. Using other methods, code can be created so e-mail can be sent via Outlook and the user of the application does not have to see these or respond to these Outlook security dialog boxes.

Configuring Outlook Security with Exchange Server

If the application's users are working in an Exchange environment, Exchange provides the capability to configure the Outlook security settings for Exchange Server, via the Security Settings dialog box, to allow mails to be sent automatically without showing Outlook security dialog boxes. By using the Outlook Security Template, Exchange will permit the programmatic sending of e-mail through the configuration of a public folder and custom form stored on the Exchange Server. The advantage of this system is that you don't need to touch the client machines at all. After the form is installed in the public folder on the server, all you need to do is decide which types of programmatic access are needed. This package also provides options to access the address book using the Send method as well as a variety of other types of settings (such as attachment blocking).

The two major disadvantages to this method are that it requires writing code to create a COM Add-in for Outlook *and* it allows programmatic sending of e-mails for all entities with access to the machine. That is, if you allow one application to send e-mails without discretion, you allow *all* applications using the Outlook Object Model to send e-mail without security warnings. Enabling these features on Exchange removes security restrictions that block potential viruses that propagate via e-mail sent from Outlook, so being extremely careful when choosing to modify the Exchange Server security settings is important. If you choose to modify Exchange's security settings for Outlook, make sure that users have virus software for both the client machines and the Exchange Server machine.

Using Redemption to Send E-mail

Another option for preventing the Outlook security dialog boxes involves downloading a third-party DLL called Redemption. The Redemption DLL serves as a wrapper for extended MAPI, another method of creating and sending e-mail messages. Extended MAPI isn't affected by the Outlook security features. The advantage to Redemption is that you can specifically target it to a defined application, so merely having the Redemption DLL present on a system poses very limited security risk.

The major disadvantage is that it must be registered on all machines using the applications that reference it. For single users, Redemption is free. A redistributable Redemption license costs around $200. You can find more information about Redemption on its website at `http://dimastr.com/Redemption`.

Redemption is very easy to use. After you register the DLL on the system, you must set a reference to the Safe Outlook Library in the code project's References dialog box. Then make a few key changes to the preceding code, and users will no longer be presented with the security dialog box. Instead of calling the `Send` method, create a `Redemption.SafeMailItem` object, assign the `MailItem` to it, and then call its `Send` method. The following code sample takes the previous example and modifies it to use Redemption.

```vb
Public Function SendEmailWithRedemption( _
    MessageTo As String, _
    Subject As String, _
    MessageBody As String)

    ' Define app variable and get Outlook using the "New" keyword
    Dim olApp As New Outlook.Application
    Dim olMailItem As Outlook.MailItem  ' An Outlook Mail item

    ' Create a new email object
    Set olMailItem = olApp.CreateItem(olMailItem)

    ' Add the To/Subject/Body to the message and display the message
    With olMailItem
        .To = MessageTo
        .Subject = Subject
        .Body = MessageBody
    End With

    ' Create and send the mail with Redemption
    Set objSafeMail = New Redemption.SafeMailItem
    objSafeMail.Item = olMailItem   ' No need to call Set here
    objSafeMail.Send

    ' Release all object variables
    Set olMailItem = Nothing
    Set olApp = Nothing

End Function
```

module OutlookSampleCode in Ch18_Sample.accdb

If you decide to use this method to bypass the Outlook security dialog boxes, reading more about the Redemption software on its homepage is recommended.

Other Outlook Objects

Creating e-mail messages in Outlook isn't the only way to use Outlook to enhance a database solution. You can manage all meetings, appointments, tasks, and journal items in Outlook using VBA. This section provides a few more examples of creating these kinds of items in Outlook.

Creating Tasks

Scheduling Tasks in Outlook to remind business users to complete an action by a certain date and time is common. You can create Outlook Tasks in a manner similar to how you create an Outlook `MailItem`, but instead using the `TaskItem` object. The steps are as follow:

1. Get an instance of the `Outlook.Application` class.

2. Create a new `TaskItem` object.

3. Add the desired settings to the `TaskItem`.

4. Call the `Save` method to save the Task.

The following function illustrates how to write the code to create a new Outlook Task.

```
Public Function CreateOutlookTask( _
    TaskTitle As String, _
    TaskBody As String)

    ' Define Variables
    Dim olApp As New Outlook.Application
    Dim olTaskItem As Outlook.TaskItem  ' An Outlook Task object

    ' Create the new Task
    Set olTaskItem = olApp.CreateItem(olTaskItem)

    ' Update the new task object with your data
    With olTaskItem
        .DueDate = Date + 2
        .Subject = TaskTitle
        .Body = TaskBody
        .ReminderTime = Date + 1
        .ReminderSet = True
        .Save    ' Save the Task
    End With

    ' Release all object variables
    Set olTaskItem = Nothing
    Set olApp = Nothing

End Function
```

module OutlookSampleCode in Ch18_Sample.accdb

Of course, you could easily replace the preceding call to the `Save` method with a call to the `Display` method. The `TaskItem` object provides many methods and properties for working with Outlook Task objects.

Modifying Tasks

You can modify Outlook Tasks in a similar manner as you would an Outlook mail item, again using the TaskItem object. The difference is that you must get the specific TaskItem object from the Outlook Task folder. The steps to writing this code are as follow:

1. Get an instance of the Outlook.Application class.

2. Get the Namespace object.

3. Get the olFolderTasks folder.

4. Find the TaskItem object.

5. Modify the desired settings for the TaskItem.

6. Call the Save method to save the Task.

The following function illustrates how to write the code to create a new Outlook Task.

```
Public Sub ModifyTaskInOutlook()

    ' Define Variables
    Dim olApp As New Outlook.Application
    Dim olNS As Outlook.Namespace
    Dim olFolder As Outlook.MAPIFolder
    Dim olTaskItem As Outlook.TaskItem   ' An Outlook Task object

    ' Get the Namespace
    Set olNS = olApp.GetNamespace("MAPI")

    ' Get the Outlook "Tasks" folder
    Set olFolder = olNS.GetDefaultFolder(olFolderTasks)

    ' Find the Task by Subject
    Set olTaskItem = olFolder.Items.Find("[Subject] = ""My Task Item""")

    ' Update the new task object with your data
    With olTaskItem
        .DueDate = Date + 3
        .ReminderTime = Date + 2
        .ReminderSet = True
        .Save    ' Save the Task
    End With

    ' Release all object variables
    Set olTaskItem = Nothing
    Set olFolder = Nothing
```

```
        Set olNS = Nothing
        Set olApp = Nothing

    End Sub
```

module OutlookSampleCode in Ch18_Sample.accdb

> *The preceding code could fail to execute properly if a* `TaskItem` *with the specific subject does not exist, or if* `TaskItem` *objects with duplicate subjects exist.*

Of course, you could easily replace the preceding call to the `Save` method with a call to the `Send` or `Display` methods. The `TaskItem` object provides many methods and properties for working with Outlook Task objects.

Deleting Tasks

One last useful thing to do with Tasks is to delete them from the Task folder. To do this, you simply follow the steps from the previous example, except that you call the `Delete` method for the task that you want to delete, instead of calling the `Save` method. The following code illustrates how to do it:

```
Public Function DeleteTaskInOutlook(TaskName As String)

    ' Define Variables
    Dim olApp As New Outlook.Application
    Dim olNS As Outlook.Namespace
    Dim olFolder As Outlook.MAPIFolder
    Dim olTaskItem As Outlook.TaskItem   ' An Outlook Task object

    ' Get the Namespace
    Set olNS = olApp.GetNamespace("MAPI")

    ' Get the Outlook "Tasks" folder
    Set olFolder = olNS.GetDefaultFolder(olFolderTasks)

    ' Find the Task by Subject
    Set olTaskItem = olFolder.Items.Find("[Subject] = " & TaskName)

    ' Delete the Task Item
    olTaskItem.Delete

    ' Release all object variables
    Set olTaskItem = Nothing
    Set olFolder = Nothing
    Set olNS = Nothing
    Set olApp = Nothing

End Function
```

module OutlookSampleCode in Ch18_Sample.accdb

Creating Calendar Items

Creating Outlook Calendar items can be useful and is very easy to do with the Outlook OM. Again, the steps for creating the Calendar item are much the same as those for a `TaskItem` or `MailItem`, but this time you will use the `AppointmentItem` object. The steps are as follow:

1.   Get an instance of the `Outlook.Application` class.

2.   Create a new `AppointmentItem` object.

3.   Add the desired settings.

4.   Call the `Save` method to save the `AppointmentItem`.

The following function illustrates how you can write the code to create a new Outlook Calendar item.

```vb
Public Function CreateOutlookCalendarItem( _
    EventTitle As String, _
    EventLocation As String, _
    EventBody As String)

    ' Define Variables
    Dim olApp As New Outlook.Application
    Dim olAppointment As AppointmentItem     ' An Outlook Calendar Item

    ' Create the new Appointment Item
    Set olAppointment = olApp.CreateItem(olAppointmentItem)

    ' Update the new Appointment with the desired settings
    With olAppointment
        .Start = Date + 1 + TimeValue("19:00:00")
        .End = .Start + TimeValue("00:30:00")
        .Subject = EventTitle
        .Location = EventLocation
        .Body = EventBody
        .BusyStatus = olBusy
        .ReminderMinutesBeforeStart = 120
        .ReminderSet = True
        .Save    ' Save the Appointment
    End With

    ' Release all object variables
    Set olAppointment = Nothing
    Set olApp = Nothing

End Function
```

module OutlookSampleCode in Ch18_Sample.accdb

Again, you could easily replace the preceding call to the `Save` method with a call to the `Send` or `Display` methods. The `AppointmentItem` object provides many methods and properties for working with Outlook Calendar objects.

Creating, Modifying, and Deleting Outlook Items

As you are probably starting to see by now, the steps for creating, modifying, and deleting the various types of Outlook items are much the same. In every example so far, you get the object type (or create it new), and then operate on it in the desired way. Because all Outlook item object types have essentially the same properties, you just set the values you desire and then add, update, or delete the object. Working with any Outlook object is really just that easy!

More Information about Outlook

For more in-depth information about all the Outlook objects, Microsoft provides MSDN library pages for Outlook with the Office Developer's Reference. You can find the online Outlook 2010 Developer's Reference at

    http://msdn.microsoft.com/en-us/library/ee861520(v=office.14).aspx

The Outlook 2010 Object Model is discussed in detail in this reference, including all the various object types, methods, properties, collections, and events, and it provides in-depth examples of how to use each of these items. The Outlook 2010 Developer's Reference is recommended reading if you want to learn more about any of the Outlook objects discussed in this section.

WORKING WITH EXCEL 2010

Although Access provides the capability to create forms and reports, including graphs and tables, you may want to leverage some of the powerful Excel features. Also, users often store their data in an Excel spreadsheet and like to be able to export their data to an Excel spreadsheet. The following section presents several examples of creating VBA code in Access to work with Excel and its various features.

Setting References to Excel

Before you can begin using the Excel OM in a database application, you must first set a reference in the code project to the Excel OM. To set a reference to Excel, complete the following steps:

1. From any open database application in Access, press the Ctrl+G key combination to open VBE (the Visual Basic Editor).

2. Choose Tools ➪ Reference to open the References dialog box.

3. Scroll down and select the Microsoft Excel 14.0 Object Library option. Click the OK button.

A reference to the Excel Object Model is now added to the code project of the database file. You now have everything you need to begin writing VBA code to work with Excel from Access.

In Office 2010, the name of the reference to the Excel OM is "Microsoft Excel 14.0 Object Library," where the number 14.0 represents the specific major version number of Office 2010. Previous versions of Excel have a slightly different number in the name, depending on the version of Microsoft Office.

Creating Excel Application Objects

Several methods exist for creating or getting `Excel.Application` objects. As with Outlook, you can use the `New` keyword, the `CreateObject` method, and the `GetObject` method to accomplish this task. This section provides examples of each.

Using the New Keyword

The easiest way to create a new instance of the `Excel.Application` class is to simply use the `New` keyword to create a new instance of it, as you would any other object in VBA. The following code provides an example of this:

Available for download on Wrox.com

```
Public Function CreateExcelWithNew() As Excel.Application

    ' Return a new instance of an Excel Application object
    Set CreateExcelWithNew = New Excel.Application

End Function
```

module ExcelSampleCode in Ch18_Sample.accdb

Using the CreateObject Method

To create a new instance of the Excel application using the `CreateObject` method, simply call it with the `Excel.Application` name string as the parameter of the method. Note that in this case, every time you call `CreateObject` for the `Excel.Application` class, you get a new instance of Excel, which is different from the `Outlook.Application` class behavior. The following code shows how this can be accomplished:

Available for download on Wrox.com

```
Public Function CreateExcelWithCreateObject() As Excel.Application

    ' Return a new instance of the Excel Application object
    Set CreateExcelWithCreateObject = CreateObject("Excel.Application")

End Function
```

module ExcelSampleCode in Ch18_Sample.accdb

Using CreateObject without References to Excel

Recall that `CreateObject` can dynamically create an `Application` object without requiring a reference to that object type in the code project for the database file. The same is true in the case of an `Excel.Application` object. You can create the `Excel.Application` as the `Object` type and all the methods can be called from that object. The following code is an example of how to create this `Object` type:

Available for download on Wrox.com

```
Public Function CreateExcelAsObject() As Object

    ' Return a new instance of Excel as an Object type
    Set CreateExcelAsObject = CreateObject("Excel.Application")

End Function
```

module ExcelSampleCode in Ch18_Sample.accdb

Using the GetObject Method

To get a currently running instance of Excel you can use the `GetObject` method. Simply call `GetObject` with the name of the particular application class to get:

```
Public Function GetExcelApplication() As Excel.Application

    ' Return the running instance of Excel as an Object type
    Set GetExcelApplication = GetObject(, "Excel.Application")

End Function
```

module ExcelSampleCode in Ch18_Sample.accdb

If Excel isn't already running on the system, you will get a runtime error when this code runs. Also, if multiple instances of Excel are running, you can use the first parameter of the `GetObject` method, the `PathName` parameter, to specify which instance to get.

Showing the Excel Application Window

Being able to show the Excel application window to the user after a new instance of the `Excel.Application` object has been created is often useful. By default, when you create a new `Excel.Application` object via the OM, it is not visible to the user. To show the application window, simply set the `Visible` property of the `Excel.Application` object to `True`. The following code provides an example of how to show the Excel application window:

```
Public Function ShowExcelApplication(xlApp As Excel.Application)

    ' If the xlApp object exists
    If Not xlApp Is Nothing Then

        ' Show the Excel Application Window
        xlApp.Visible = True

    End If

End Function
```

module ExcelSampleCode in Ch18_Sample.accdb

Conversely, sometimes *not* allowing the user to see the Excel application window is useful. Simply set the `Visible` property to the `Excel.Application` object to `False` to hide the application window.

Working with Excel Workbooks

An Excel workbook is really just a simple Excel spreadsheet file, such as an `.xls` or `.xlsx` file. After you create an instance of an `Excel.Application` object, you will typically either create a new workbook or open an existing workbook. This section presents a couple of examples of creating and opening workbooks using the Excel OM.

Creating a New Workbook

To create a new workbook from the Excel OM, use the `Workbooks` collection on the `Application` object. You can create a new workbook by calling the `Add` method of the `Workbooks` collection. The `Add` method takes one optional parameter, the `Template` parameter, which allows specifying the template for the `Workbook`. The following code provides an example of how this can be accomplished:

```
Public Function CreateWorkbookFromOM(xlApp As Excel.Application)

    ' If the xlApp object exists
    If Not xlApp Is Nothing Then

        ' Create a new Workbook using the Add method
        xlApp.Workbooks.Add

    End If

End Function
```

module ExcelSampleCode in Ch18_Sample.accdb

Opening an Existing Workbook

Being able to open an existing workbook and manipulate the data within that file is often handy. To open an existing workbook, simply call the `Open` method from the `Workbooks` collection. The `Open` method is actually quite complex, providing many options for opening the file in various modes. In fact, the `Open` method actually takes 15 parameters, but only the first parameter, the `Filepath` parameter, which is the name path of the file to be opened, is required. The following code provides an example of how to open an existing workbook with the `Open` method:

```
Public Function OpenWorkbookFromOM( _
    xlApp As Excel.Application, _
    strFileNamePath As String)

    ' If the xlApp object exists
    If Not xlApp Is Nothing Then

        ' Open a new Workbook using the Open method
        ' Note - For this code to work properly, the XLS file must exist
        '        at the location specified in the strFileNamePath parameter
        xlApp.Workbooks.Open strFileNamePath

    End If

End Function
```

module ExcelSampleCode in Ch18_Sample.accdb

Saving a Workbook Using SaveAs

After you create or modify an Excel workbook, you must save the work to save the changes to the file. When creating a brand-new file, using the `SaveAs` method of the `Workbook` object to save the new Excel file is best, because it allows the user to specify the location of where to save the file. To get the workbook, the `Item` method of the `Workbooks` collection allows the `Workbook` object to be specified by name string or the ordinal position number (which is a 1-based array, because you are using Excel). The `SaveAs` method is quite complex and actually takes 12 optional parameters, but most importantly, it is the first parameter, the `Filename` parameter, that allows the developer to specify the location in which to save the current file. The following code provides an example of saving a new spreadsheet to a specified location:

```
Public Function SaveAsWorkbook( _
    xlApp As Excel.Application, _
    strFileNamePath As String)

    ' If the xlApp object exists
    If Not xlApp Is Nothing Then

        ' If the Workbook exists
        If xlApp.Workbooks.Count = 1 Then

            ' Save the new Workbook using the SaveAs method
            xlApp.Workbooks(1).SaveAs strFileNamePath

        End If
    End If

End Function
```

module ExcelSampleCode in Ch18_Sample.accdb

Note that if the file already exists at the location specified, a couple of things happen depending on the mode of the `Excel.Application` object. If the `Excel.Application` object is visible, then the user is prompted to overwrite the existing file. But if the `Application` object is not visible, it is your responsibility to figure out how to handle saving when a file already exists. That is, depending on the case, you may or may not want to overwrite the file. In some cases the file cannot be overwritten, such as when it is marked as Read-Only or it is currently open by another user. Although exploring all the events that can arise when using file operations on existing files is beyond the scope of this chapter, having some error-handling code around these types of save methods is always a good idea.

Saving a Workbook Using Save

In addition to the `SaveAs` method, Excel also provides the simpler `Save` method. The `Save` method saves the current file to its current location. The `Save` method does not take any parameters either, so using it is very easy. If the file is new and has not been saved before, calling the `Save` method will save the new file in the user's default documents folder. The following code provides an example of calling the `Save` method on a new spreadsheet:

```
Public Function SaveWorkbook(xlApp As Excel.Application)

    ' If the xlApp object exists
    If Not xlApp Is Nothing Then

        ' If the Workbook exists
```

```
        If xlApp.Workbooks.Count = 1 Then

            ' Save the Workbook using the Save method
            xlApp.Workbooks(1).Save

        End If
    End If

End Function
```

module ExcelSampleCode in Ch18_Sample.accdb

Closing a Workbook

After you have completed all changes and saved the workbook, closing workbooks when you're done with them is always a good idea. To close a workbook, simply call the `Close` method for the `Work-book` object. The `Close` method takes three optional parameters: `SaveChanges`, `Filename`, and `RouteWorkbook`, but to close the `Workbook` with the default options, you do not need to specify any parameters. As with the `SaveAs` method, the exact behavior of `Close` is dependent on the exact mode of the `Excel.Application` object. The following code provides an example of a function to close a workbook:

**Available for
download on
Wrox.com**

```
Public Function CloseWorkbook(xlApp As Excel.Application)

    ' If the xlApp object exists
    If Not xlApp Is Nothing Then

        ' If the Workbook exists
        If xlApp.Workbooks.Count = 1 Then

            ' Close the Workbook
            xlApp.Workbooks(1).Close

        End If
    End If

End Function
```

module ExcelSampleCode in Ch18_Sample.accdb

Working with Sheets in Excel

Each workbook in Excel is a collection of sheets, which are the actual spreadsheet objects. The `Sheets` collection for the `Workbook` object allows the developer to work with and manipulate the various sheets in the `Workbook`. The `Sheets` collection provides many methods and properties, a few of which you explore in this section.

Activating an Existing Sheet

When you work with Excel worksheets programmatically using VBA code, the sheet is typically activated and then manipulated as the active sheet. In most cases, when you open or create a

`Workbook` object, existing sheets will already be in the workbook, and the last one used will be activated by default. The `Sheets` collection `Item` method allows the user to specify the worksheet by name string or ordinal number (which is a 1-based array, because you are using Excel) and then the `Activate` method can be called to make that worksheet the active one. The following code provides an example of activating a specific sheet by name string:

Available for download on Wrox.com

```
Public Function ActivateSheetByName( _
    xlApp As Excel.Application, _
    strSheetName As String)

    ' If the xlApp object exists
    If Not xlApp Is Nothing Then

        ' If the Workbook exists
        If xlApp.Workbooks.Count = 1 Then

            ' Activate the specified sheet
            xlApp.Workbooks(1).Sheets(strSheetName).Activate

        End If
    End If

End Function
```

module ExcelSampleCode in Ch18_Sample.accdb

Creating a New Sheet

Creating a complete new sheet, in case you do not want to use an existing worksheet in the file, is also possible. To create a new worksheet, call the `Add` method from the `Sheets` collection from the `Workbook` object. The `Add` method takes four optional parameters: `Before`, `After`, `Count`, and `Type`, which can be used to manipulate the position and options for the new sheet, but you can create a new sheet without having to use any of these options. After you create it, you can name it to any name you desire by setting the `Name` property for the sheet. The following code example illustrates how to create a new worksheet in this manner:

Available for download on Wrox.com

```
Public Function CreateNewSheet( _
    xlApp As Excel.Application, _
    strSheetName As String)

    ' If the xlApp object exists
    If Not xlApp Is Nothing Then

        ' If the Workbook exists
        If xlApp.Workbooks.Count = 1 Then

            ' Define a Sheet variable as Object type
            Dim oSheet As Object

            ' Create a New Sheet
            Set oSheet = xlApp.Workbooks(1).Sheets.Add
```

```
                oSheet.Name = strSheetName

            End If
        End If

    End Function
```

module ExcelSampleCode in Ch18_Sample.accdb

In this example, the new sheet is created and then renamed. When a sheet is created in this manner, it is automatically set as the active sheet object.

If you want to rename any sheet, simply set the sheet's Name property with the desired value. But, you should consider that not all characters are allowed in sheet names and modifying the name can fail if the string violates the sheet naming requirements.

Deleting a Sheet

You can also delete a sheet from a workbook programmatically using the Excel OM. To delete a worksheet, simply call the Delete method for the sheet. The following code provides an example of deleting a sheet by name string:

Available for download on Wrox.com

```
    Public Function DeleteSheetByName( _
        xlApp As Excel.Application, _
        strSheetName As String)

        ' If the xlApp object exists
        If Not xlApp Is Nothing Then

            ' If the Workbook exists
            If xlApp.Workbooks.Count = 1 Then

                ' Delete the specified sheet
                xlApp.Workbooks(1).Sheets(strSheetName).Delete

            End If
        End If

    End Function
```

module ExcelSampleCode in Ch18_Sample.accdb

As with saving a workbook, many events can occur when you delete a sheet. Having some error-handling code for problems that might arise when deleting a worksheet is generally a good idea.

Working with Data in Excel

Working with data in Excel really is useful both going to and from Excel. Sometimes getting the data from an Excel spreadsheet is useful. Other times sending data from Access to an Excel spreadsheet is useful. And, even other cases exist where you just want to manipulate the cell settings directly in the worksheet. Whatever the task, the Excel OM makes working with data and settings on the cell level easy, by using the `Cells` collection for the `Sheet` object. The `Cells` collection provides a number of methods and properties for working with individual `Cell` objects. You explore a few of these objects in this section.

Getting Data in a Cell

To get the data directly from a cell, you have a couple of ways to access the `Cell` object. The `Item` method of the `Cells` collection allows the cell to be specified by ordinal number or by row and column position number (which are both 1-based arrays, because you are using Excel). The `Value` property of the `Cell` object gets and sets the data value for the cell. The following example function returns the value from the specified cell:

```
Public Function GetDataFromCell( _
    xlApp As Excel.Application, _
    iRow As Integer, iCol As Integer) As String

    ' If the xlApp object exists
    If Not xlApp Is Nothing Then

        ' If the Workbook exists
        If xlApp.Workbooks.Count = 1 Then

            ' Get the ActiveSheet object
            Dim Cell As Object
            Set Cell = xlApp.Workbooks(1).ActiveSheet.Cells(iRow, iCol)

            ' Return the Cell Value
            GetDataFromCell = Cell.Value

        End If
    End If

End Function
```

module ExcelSampleCode in Ch18_Sample.accdb

Modifying Data in a Cell

Similarly, you can also add or modify the data in a cell by setting the `Value` property of the `Cell` object. The following code provides an example of setting the data in a specified cell:

```
Public Sub SetDataInCell( _
    xlApp As Excel.Application, _
    iRow As Integer, iCol As Integer, strNewValue As String)

    ' If the xlApp object exists
    If Not xlApp Is Nothing Then

        ' If the Workbook exists
        If xlApp.Workbooks.Count = 1 Then

            ' Get the ActiveSheet object
            Dim Cell As Object
```

```
            Set Cell = xlApp.Workbooks(1).ActiveSheet.Cells(iRow, iCol)

            ' Set the Cell Value
            Cell.Value = strNewValue

        End If
    End If

End Function
```

module ExcelSampleCode in Ch18_Sample.accdb

Modifying Settings for a Cell

You can modify specific cell settings through the various `Cell` object properties. For example, to modify the font settings for the cell, the `Cell` object provides the `Font` property. The `Font` object contains a number of other properties and methods for working with specific font settings. For example, you could adjust the font size setting for a cell by setting the `Size` property of the `Font` object. The following code provides an example of setting the font size:

Available for download on Wrox.com

```
Public Sub SetFontSizeForCell( _
    xlApp As Excel.Application, _
    iRow As Integer, iCol As Integer, iNewSize As Integer)

    ' If the xlApp object exists
    If Not xlApp Is Nothing Then

        ' If the Workbook exists
        If xlApp.Workbooks.Count = 1 Then

            ' Get the ActiveSheet object
            Dim Cell As Object
            Set Cell = xlApp.Workbooks(1).ActiveSheet.Cells(iRow, iCol)

            ' Set the Font Size for the Cell
            Cell.Font.Size = iNewSize

        End If
    End If

End Sub
```

module ExcelSampleCode in Ch18_Sample.accdb

Although this code is not exactly how you set all properties of a cell, it provides a good example of how to set cell properties. Unfortunately, this book doesn't have room to discuss all the various `Cell` object settings, but you can set most properties using this type of code. Also, it is worth noting that you can set the properties for all the cells for the entire worksheet in one operation by modifying the properties of the `Cells` collection of the worksheet.

Using CopyFromRecordset

To make a very easy task of copying large amounts of data from a `Recordset` into an Excel sheet, the `Cells` collection provides the `CopyFromRecordset` method. `CopyFromRecordset` copies all the records in the specified `Recordset` object into the cells of the specified `Sheet` object. The `CopyFromRecordset` method takes three parameters: `Data`, `MaxRows`, and `MaxColumns`, but only the first, the `Data` parameter, is required. The following code provides an example of using the `CopyFromRecordset` method:

Available for download on Wrox.com

```
Public Sub CopyDataFromQuery( _
    xlApp As Excel.Application, _
    strQueryName As String)

    ' If the xlApp object exists
    If Not xlApp Is Nothing Then

        ' If the Workbook exists
        If xlApp.Workbooks.Count = 1 Then

            ' Create Recrodset Object from the Query
            Dim rsQuery As DAO.Recordset
            Set rsQuery = Application.CurrentDb.OpenRecordset(strQueryName)

            ' Get the Cells object
            Dim Cells As Object
            Set Cells = xlApp.Workbooks(1).ActiveSheet.Cells

            ' Copy the Data from the Query into the Sheet
            Cells.CopyFromRecordset rsQuery

        End If
    End If

End Sub
```

module ExcelSampleCode in Ch18_Sample.accdb

Although this example specifies a query name as the parameter for this subroutine, this name could be either a table or query name, because you are calling the `OpenRecordset` method to create the `Recordset` object.

 If the query called with the `OpenRecordset` method is an action query (`Update`, `Insert`, `Delete`, and so on), this code will fail. For the `OpenRecordset` method to succeed, the query must return a set of records.

Using TransferSpreadsheet

Access also provides a method for automatically creating a new workbook file from a table or query in the database. This method is called `TransferSpreadsheet` and is a member of the `DoCmd` object. The `TransferSpreadsheet` method imports or exports data from several file formats. The `TransferSpreadsheet` method takes seven optional parameters, but to create a new `Workbook` object from a query, you only need the first four. These parameters are `TransferType`, `SpreadsheetType`, `TableName`, and `FileName`. These parameters represent the type of transfer to be completed (import or export), the type of spreadsheet used or to be created, the table name in Access, and the filename to be used, respectively. The following code provides an example of exporting data to a new Excel spreadsheet programmatically:

```
Public Sub UseTransferSpreadsheet(strTableName As String, strFilePath)

    'Use TransferSpreadsheet to create an Excel Workbook
    DoCmd.TransferSpreadsheet _
        acExport, _
        acSpreadsheetTypeExcel9, _
        strTableName, _
        strFilePath

End Sub
```

module ExcelSampleCode in Ch18_Sample.accdb

Note that when using `TransferSpreadsheet` to create new workbooks, if the file already exists at the specified path, the operation will fail.

More Information about Excel

For more in-depth information about all the Excel objects, Microsoft provides MSDN library pages for Excel with the Office Developer's Reference. The online Excel 2010 Developer's Reference is located at

```
http://msdn.microsoft.com/en-us/library/ee861528(v=office.14).aspx
```

The Excel 2010 Object Model is discussed in detail in this reference, including the object types, methods, properties, collections, and events, and it provides in-depth examples of how to use each of these items. The Excel Developer's Reference is recommended reading if you want to learn more about any of the Excel objects discussed in this section.

WORKING WITH WORD 2010

Although Access provides the capability to create robust reports, which can include page numbers and all kind of different formatting in the same manner as a Word docuement, you still may want to leverage Word features in your Access application. Also, users often want to be able to create new or edit existing documents that contain customer-specific data in a generalized template. This section discusses several examples of creating VBA code in Access to work with Word and its various objects and features.

Setting References to Word

Before you can begin using the Word Object Model in a database application, you must first set a reference in the code project to the Word Object Model. To set a reference to Word, complete the following steps:

1. From any open database application in Access, press the CTRL+G key combination to open VBE (the Visual Basic Editor).

    2.   Choose Tools ⇨ Reference. The References dialog box opens.

    3.   Scroll down and select the Microsoft Word 14.0 Object Library option and click the OK button.

A reference to the Word Object Model is now added to the code project of the database file. You now have everything you need to begin writing VBA code to work with Word from Access.

> *In Office 2010, the name of the reference to the Word OM is "Microsoft Word 14.0 Object Library," where the number 14.0 represents the specific major version number of Office 2010. Previous versions of Word have a slightly different number in the name, depending on the version of Microsoft Office.*

Creating Word Application Objects

You have several methods for creating or getting `Word.Application` objects, just as with Excel and Outlook. As with Excel, you can use the `New` keyword, the `CreateObject` method, and the `GetObject` method to complete this task. This section provides some examples of creating `Word .Application` objects.

Using the New Keyword

The easiest way to create a new instance of the `Word.Application` class is to use the `New` keyword to create a new instance of it, as you would any other object in VBA. The following code provides an example of this:

```
Public Function CreateWordWithNew() As Word.Application

    ' Return a new instance of an Word Application object
    Set CreateWordWithNew = New Word.Application

End Function
```

module WordSampleCode in Ch18_Sample.accdb

Using the CreateObject Method

To create a new instance of the `Word.Application` object using the `CreateObject` method, simply call it with the `Word.Application` name string as the parameter of the method. It is worth noting that in this case, every time you call `CreateObject` for the `Word.Application` class, you get a new instance of Word, which is different from the `Outlook.Application` class behavior, but the same as every other Office 2010 program. The following code shows how to do it:

```
Public Function CreateWordWithCreateObject() As Word.Application

    ' Return a new instance of the Word Application object
```

```
Set CreateWordWithCreateObject = CreateObject("Word.Application")

End Function
```

module WordSampleCode in Ch18_Sample.accdb

Using CreateObject without References to Word

Recall that `CreateObject` can dynamically create an `Application` object without requiring a reference to that object type in the code project for the database file. The same is true in the case of a `Word.Application` object. The `Word.Application` can be created as the `Object` type and all the methods can be called from that object. The following code is an example of how to create the `Object` type:

```
Public Function CreateWordAsObject() As Object

    ' Return a new instance of Word as an Object type
    Set CreateWordAsObject = CreateObject("Word.Application")

End Function
```

module WordSampleCode in Ch18_Sample.accdb

Using the GetObject Method

You can get a currently running instance of Word by using the `GetObject` method. Simply call `GetObject` with the name of the particular application class to get:

```
Public Function GetWordApplication() As Word.Application

    ' Return the running instance of Word
    Set GetWordApplication = GetObject(, "Word.Application")

End Function
```

module WordSampleCode in Ch18_Sample.accdb

If Word isn't already running on the system, you will get a runtime error when this code runs. Also, if multiple instances of Word are running, you can use the first parameter, the `PathName` parameter, of the `GetObject` method to specify which instance to get.

Showing the Word Application Window

Being able to show the Word application window to the user when a new instance of the `Word.Application` object has been created is often useful. By default, when you create a new `Word.Application` object via the OM, it is not visible to the user, as it is with any Office 2010 program except Outlook. To show the application window, simply set the `Visible` property of the

`Word.Application` object to `True`. The following code provides an example of how to show the Word application window:

```
Public Sub ShowWordApplication(wdApp As Word.Application)

    ' If the wdApp object exists
    If Not wdApp Is Nothing Then

        ' Show the Word Application Window
        wdApp.Visible = True

    End If

End Sub
```

module WordSampleCode in Ch18_Sample.accdb

Conversely, sometimes *not* having the user see the Word application window is useful. Simply set the `Visible` property of the `Word.Application` object to `False` to hide the application window.

Working with Document Objects

After an instance of Word has been created, you need to get a `Document` object to start working with data in Word. The Word `Documents` collection from the `Word.Application` object provides a number of methods and properties for working with Word documents. You can create a new document object or open one from an existing file format that Word recognizes. This section provides several examples of working with `Document` objects in Word.

Creating a New Document

To create a new document within an instance of Word, simply call the `Add` method from the `Documents` collection. The `Add` method takes four optional parameters (`Template`, `NewTemplate`, `DocumentType`, and `Visible`) for specifying the options for creating the new document. But, to just create a new blank document, call the `Add` method without any parameters. The following code provides an example of creating a new document in Word:

```
Public Sub CreateNewWordDocument(wdApp As Word.Application)

    ' If the wdApp object exists
    If Not wdApp Is Nothing Then

        ' Create a new document in Word
        wdApp.Documents.Add

    End If

End Sub
```

module WordSampleCode in Ch18_Sample.accdb

Opening an Existing Document

Opening an existing Word document to begin working with its data is often preferable, as there are only two options for getting a document object: creating a new document or opening an existing document. To open an existing document, simply call the Open method from the Documents collection. The Open method is actually very versatile and provides many options for opening the file in various modes. The Open method takes a whopping 16 parameters, but only the first parameter, the FileName parameter, the file name path to the document to open, is required. The following code provides an example of how to open an existing workbook with the Open method:

Available for download on Wrox.com

```
Public Sub OpenWordDocument( _
    wdApp As Word.Application, _
    strFileNamePath As String)

    ' If the wdApp object exists
    If Not wdApp Is Nothing Then

        ' Open an existing Word document file
        ' Note - For this code to work properly, the file must exist
        '        at the location specified in the strFileNamePath
        wdApp.Documents.Open strFileNamePath

    End If

End Sub
```

module WordSampleCode in Ch18_Sample.accdb

Saving a Document Using SaveAs

After you create or modify a Word document, you must save the work to persist the changes to file. When you create a brand-new file, using the SaveAs method of the Document object to save the new Word document is probably best. The Item method of the Documents collection allows a specific Document object to be specified by name string or the ordinal position number (which is a 1-based array, because you are using Word). The SaveAs method is also quite complex and actually takes 16 optional parameters. It is the first parameter, the FileName parameter, which allows the developer to specify the location in which to save the current file. The following code provides an example of saving a document to a specified location:

Available for download on Wrox.com

```
Public Sub SaveAsDocument( _
    wdApp As Word.Application, _
    strFileNamePath As String)

    ' If the wdApp object exists
    If Not wdApp Is Nothing Then

        ' If the Document exists
        If wdApp.Documents.Count > 0 Then

            ' Save the new Document using the SaveAs method
```

```
            wdApp.ActiveDocument.SaveAs strFileNamePath

        End If
    End If

End Sub
```

module WordSampleCode in Ch18_Sample.accdb

Note that, just like with Excel, if the file already exists at the location specified, a couple of things could happen depending on the mode of the `Word.Application` object and the parameters specified with the `Open` method. Although exploring all the events that can arise when using file operations on existing files is beyond the scope of this chapter, having some error-handling code around these types of `Save` methods is always a good idea.

Saving a Document Using Save

In addition to the `SaveAs` method, Word also provides a simpler `Save` method. The `Save` method saves the current file to its current location. The `Save` method does not take any parameters either, so using it is very easy. If the file is new and has not been saved before, calling the `Save` method will save the new file in the user's default documents folder. The following code provides an example of calling the `Save` method on a `Document` object.

```
Public Sub SaveDocument(wdApp As Word.Application)

    ' If the wdApp object exists
    If Not wdApp Is Nothing Then

        ' If the Document exists
        If wdApp.Documents.Count > 0 Then

            ' Save the Document to its current location
            wdApp.ActiveDocument.Save

        End If
    End If

End Sub
```

module WordSampleCode in Ch18_Sample.accdb

Closing a Document

After you have completed all changes and saved the document, closing the document is always a good idea. To close a document, simply call the `Close` method for the `Document` object. The `Close` method takes three optional parameters: `SaveChanges`, `OrignalFormat`, and `RouteDocument`, but to close the `Document` with the default options, you do not need to specify any parameters. As with the `SaveAs` method, the exact behavior of `Close` depends on the exact mode of the `Word.Application` object. The following code provides an example of a function to close a document:

Available for download on Wrox.com

```
Public Sub CloseDocument(wdApp As Word.Application)

    ' If the wdApp object exists
    If Not wdApp Is Nothing Then

        ' If the Document exists
        If wdApp.Documents.Count > 0 Then

            ' Close the Document
            wdApp.ActiveDocument.Close

        End If
    End If

End Sub
```

module WordSampleCode in Ch18_Sample.accdb

Working with Data in Word

After a document is open in Word, you can begin working with its data. The `Content` member of the `Document` object provides the ability to work the text and the text formatting in the document. This section describes some common methods for working the `Content` object.

Adding Text to a Document

Adding data to a document is a very common operation in Word and is quite simple to do. To set the text for the document, set the `Text` property of the `Content` object to the desired `String` value. The following code provides an example of setting the data in a Word document.

Available for download on Wrox.com

```
Public Sub SetDataToDocument( _
    wdApp As Word.Application, _
    strData As String)

    ' If the wdApp object exists
    If Not wdApp Is Nothing Then

        ' If the Document exists
        If wdApp.Documents.Count > 0 Then

            ' Set the Data in the Document
            wdApp.ActiveDocument.Content.Text = strData

        End If
    End If

End Sub
```

module WordSampleCode in Ch18_Sample.accdb

Adding Data to the Ends of a Document

The Content object also provides a couple of methods for inserting data into either end of a Word document. The InsertBefore and InsertAfter methods of the Content object allow a string to be inserted into the respective position. Both of these methods only take one parameter — the Text parameter, which is a String object containing the data to be inserted. The following code provides an example of inserting text to the end of the document, using the InsertAfter method:

Available for download on Wrox.com

```
Public Sub InsertDataToEndOfDocument( _
    wdApp As Word.Application, _
    strData As String)

    ' If the wdApp object exists
    If Not wdApp Is Nothing Then

        ' If the Document exists
        If wdApp.Documents.Count > 0 Then

            ' Insert the Data to the end of the Document
            wdApp.ActiveDocument.Content.InsertAfter strData

        End If
    End If

End Sub
```

module WordSampleCode in Ch18_Sample.accdb

Formatting Text in a Word Document

Formatting a particular section of text by underlining it or bolding it, for example, is often useful. To do this, you select the specific range of text and then apply the desired format property for the selected text. To select a specific range of text, use the Range method for the Document object. The Range method takes two optional parameters — the Start and End positions. Then to format the text, simply set the desired text format property to the required value. The following code shows an example of how to select a text range and then underline it in a Word document.

Available for download on Wrox.com

```
Public Sub UnderlineText( _
    wdApp As Word.Application, _
    iStart As Integer, _
    iFinish As Integer)

    ' If the wdApp object exists
    If Not wdApp Is Nothing Then

        ' If the Document exists
        If wdApp.Documents.Count > 0 Then

            ' Underline the specified Range
            wdApp.ActiveDocument.range( _
```

```
            Start:=iStart, End:=iFinish).Underline = wdUnderlineDashHeavy

        End If
    End If

  End Sub
```

module WordSampleCode in Ch18_Sample.accdb

Automating Mail Merges

One of the last features to mention about Word is the ever-popular Word mail merge. A mail merge allows the user to create a set of standardized documents from a form template and a set of records. This can be very useful when you have to create the same standardized document for a set of records, such as a "Payment Overdue" letter for your customers. To complete this task, you open the data source for the mail merge, then add the mail merge fields, and finally execute the merge itself. After you complete these steps, you save and close the document that has been created.

To open the data source, call the OpenDataSource method from the MailMerge object on the Document object. Then, when the data source has opened, create the merge Fields by calling the Add method of the Fields collection, specifying field names that are to be merged to the document. After adding the merge fields, simply call the Execute method of the MailMerge object and the mail merge will be executed. The following code example shows how to create a mail merge automatically using VBA code:

Available for download on Wrox.com

```
Public Sub DoMailMerge(strFileSavePath As String)

    ' Create new Word App, add a document and set it visible
    Dim wdApp As New Word.Application
    wdApp.Documents.Add
    wdApp.Visible = True

    ' Open the data set from this database
    wdApp.ActiveDocument.MailMerge.OpenDataSource _
        Name:=Application.CurrentProject.FullName, _
        OpenExclusive:=False, _
        LinkToSource:=True, _
        Connection:="TABLE Customers", _
        SQLStatement:="SELECT Customers.* FROM Customers;"

    ' Add fields to the mail merge document
    Dim oSel As Object
    Set oSel = wdApp.Selection
    With wdApp.ActiveDocument.MailMerge.Fields

        oSel.TypeText vbNewLine & vbNewLine
        .Add oSel.range, "First_Name"
        oSel.TypeText " "
        .Add oSel.range, "Last_Name"
```

```
              oSel.TypeText vbNewLine
              .Add oSel.range, "Company"
              oSel.TypeText vbNewLine
              .Add oSel.range, "Address"
              oSel.TypeText vbNewLine
              .Add oSel.range, "City"
              oSel.TypeText ", "
              .Add oSel.range, "State"
              oSel.TypeText " "
              .Add oSel.range, "Zip"
              oSel.TypeText vbNewLine
              oSel.TypeParagraph
              oSel.TypeText "Dear "
              .Add oSel.range, "First_Name"
              oSel.TypeText ","
              oSel.TypeText vbNewLine
              oSel.TypeParagraph
              oSel.TypeText "We have created this mail just for you..."
              oSel.TypeText vbNewLine
              oSel.TypeText vbNewLine
              oSel.TypeText "Sincerely," & vbNewLine & "John Q. Public"
              oSel.TypeText vbFormFeed

        End With

        ' Execute the mail merge and save the document
        wdApp.ActiveDocument.MailMerge.Execute
        wdApp.ActiveDocument.SaveAs strFileSavePath

        ' Close everything and Cleanup Variables
        Set oSel = Nothing
        wdApp.ActiveDocument.Close False
        Set wdApp = Nothing

    End Sub
```

module WordSampleCode in Ch18_Sample.accdb

Using OutputTo

In addition to using VBA to create a mail merge, you can export data from an Access database to Word with the OuputTo method. The OutputTo method of the DoCmd object allows a set of data in Access to be output to a specific file type. The OutputTo method takes eight optional parameters, but really, you only need the first four: ObjectType, ObjectName, OutputFormat, and OutputFile, to output your data to an RTF file format. You specify the type of object to export, the object name to export, the file format to export to, and the output file location. The following code provides an example of how to use the OutputTo method to create a file that can be opened in Word.

```
Public Sub OutputToWord(strFilePath As String)

    ' Output the Report to RTF format for Word
    DoCmd.OutputTo acOutputTable, "Contacts", acFormatRTF, strFilePath

End Sub
```

module WordSampleCode in Ch18_Sample.accdb

More Information about Word

For more in-depth information about all the Word objects, Microsoft provides MSDN library pages for Word with the Office Developer's Reference. The online Word 2010 Developer's Reference is at:

```
http://msdn.microsoft.com/en-us/library/ee861527(v=office.14).aspx.
```

The Word Object Model reference discusses all the various object types, methods, properties, collections, and events, as well as provides in-depth examples of how to use each of these items. The Word Developer's Reference is recommended reading if you want to learn more about any of the Word objects discussed in this section.

SUMMARY

This chapter explored a variety of examples using VBA to transfer information between Microsoft Access and other Office applications. This chapter outlined working with the Outlook, Excel, and Word applications included in Microsoft Office 2010. Although this chapter presented a limited number of examples, it covered the basics of working with each of these application's Object Models, and you should now have the ability to begin working with and understanding these objects with ease. Although the code included in this chapter might not perform all the exact operations desired for your applications, the concepts, methods, and code samples included within this chapter provide a strong starting point for further development with the Microsoft Office 2010 suite of products.

19

Working with SharePoint

WHAT'S IN THIS CHAPTER?

➤ A discussion of the Access 2010 features that integrate with SharePoint 2010

➤ An overview of the new Access Web Application features

➤ A discussion about how to build traditional Access database applications that use SharePoint as a data source

➤ How to import, export, and link to SharePoint lists using Access 2010

➤ Code samples for building VBA code that uses the Access Object Model to work with SharePoint

With the release of Office 2010 comes the release of two major SharePoint 2010 (version 4.0) products: SharePoint Foundation 2010 and SharePoint Server 2010. SharePoint Foundation continues to provide the framework for building SharePoint sites and has a number of new and interesting features for this release. However, the SharePoint Server 2010 release, with its brand-new suite of products and, specifically, the Access Services product, is really what has Access developers raving. Access 2010, combined with Access Services for SharePoint, allows the developer to build a new type of Access application, known as an Access Web Application, which runs directly in a Web browser. And, of course, the addition of this new type of Access-SharePoint application and the related features are in addition to all the features that were previously available for working with SharePoint. This chapter describes the features of Access 2010 that integrate with the SharePoint 2010 products.

SHAREPOINT 2010

One of the fastest-growing business software products in the Microsoft family, SharePoint, is one of the hottest technologies for site management available today. Flexible and easy to use, SharePoint provides users with simple site creation and design features, robust content management, and a powerful security model for business data. Before delving directly into the discussion of the feature integration between Access 2010 and SharePoint 2010, this section discusses some of the basics and requirements for SharePoint 2010.

What Is SharePoint?

At its highest-level description, a SharePoint site is nothing more than a website designed to allow users to quickly build, collaborate on, and communicate information. But a SharePoint site is more much more than just a website; it is a framework for a living digital library that allows users to create many different Web interfaces to share information, from many different data sources, by allowing the creation of pages, lists, subsites, data views, charts, document libraries, blogs, applications, and so much more. Users can build full Web applications directly from their browser to retain information, and then show that information in the form of lists, reports, charts, document libraries, and so on. The Office 2010 major document types, such as Word documents and Excel workbooks, can be opened, edited, and versioned directly on the server, allowing users to seamlessly collaborate on documents. As for Access 2010, some of the most powerful database applications can be built and integrated directly into SharePoint with extremely minimal effort from the developer. SharePoint 2010 is truly a powerful tool for building and managing a website, and best of all, SharePoint Foundation 2010 is free if you already have Windows Server!

SharePoint 2010 Requirements

SharePoint 2010 has two basic, but major requirements to consider, as follow:

➤ **Windows Server 2008 64-bit edition:** The heaviest requirement, SharePoint 2010 needs a 64-bit edition of Windows Server, which requires an x64 machine.

➤ **SQL Server 2005 or 2008 64-bit edition:** For single-server deployments, SQL Server Express Editions will work; however, server farm deployments require the full version of SQL Server.

If you do not have a copy of Windows Server 2008, evaluation copies are available at `http://microsoft.com/windows/default.mspx`. The evaluation allows full access to the product for 180 days. You can download SQL Server Express Edition for free from the Microsoft website at `www.microsoft.com/express/database/`, which should be sufficient for testing purposes on a single server, but you can download evaluation copies of full SQL Server as well, if required.

SharePoint 2010 Versions

After you have access to a Windows Server machine with SQL Server, SharePoint can be deployed. As mentioned earlier, SharePoint has a number of different flavors, but there are essentially two major SharePoint products, as follows:

➤ **SharePoint Foundation 2010:** Previously known as Windows SharePoint Services (WSS), SharePoint Foundation is the base framework for the SharePoint technologies and provides everything necessary to start building and hosting a SharePoint site. It is also a requirement for full SharePoint Server 2010.

➤ **SharePoint Server 2010:** Previously known as Microsoft Office SharePoint Server (MOSS), SharePoint Server is a massive collection of additional services, tools, applications,

Web parts, and tons of other SharePoint-related items that provide huge improvements on top of SharePoint Foundation. Specifically, SharePoint Server 2010 provides the new Access Services feature, which is very important for Access 2010.

For more information about the different versions of SharePoint, and all of the features that are supported by each version, go to: `http://sharepoint2010.microsoft.com/Pages/default.aspx`.

Access Services on SharePoint Server

New to SharePoint Server 2010, Access Services is a set of tools that allows the creation of a completely new type of SharePoint application: Access Web Applications. These applications run directly in the Web browser and do not require that the user have Access or the Access Runtime installed to run, but can be run directly from Access if desired. And, best of all, they can be designed and built directly in Access 2010, using many of the features that you are already familiar with. Because Access Services is installed by default with SharePoint Server 2010, nothing else is required to start building Access Web Applications, after the SharePoint Server is up-and-running. This chapter discusses the basics of building Access Web Applications in Access 2010, but Access Services on SharePoint has much more to offer. For more information about Access Services and all the features that it provides, see the SharePoint homepage at `http://sharepoint2010.microsoft.com/Pages/default.aspx`.

ACCESS FEATURES OVERVIEW

The Access 2010 features that integrate with SharePoint 2010 are quite extensive, but break out into two basic categories: features available on the SharePoint Server and the features used from within an Access application. Most of these features were available in the Access 2007, except for the new Access Web Application features and a few related items. This section provides a brief description of all the Access 2010 features for SharePoint 2010 that this chapter covers.

SharePoint Features in Access 2010

The first category of features to discuss is the SharePoint features that are available in Access 2010. The Access 2010 client provides the ability to work with a number of SharePoint features, some new and some previously existing. The following list provides the name and brief description of each of these features, as well as the version of Access in which the feature was introduced.

➤ **Access Web Applications:** New to Access 2010, Access Web Applications can be built and deployed to SharePoint Server 2010 directly from the Access client. These applications are different from and in addition to traditional Access database applications that contain linked tables to SharePoint. Access Web Applications provide a number of additional features and benefits, not available with SharePoint otherwise.

➤ **Importing from SharePoint:** Introduced in Access 2003, Access provides the ability to import SharePoint lists and data into tables in an Access database. When using the Access database (ACCDB) file format, Access supports calculated, complex data, attachment fields, and even append-only memo fields imported from SharePoint. Several methods are available for importing tables, both in the GUI and via code.

➤ **Linked Tables to SharePoint:** Introduced in Access 2003, the SharePoint ISAM (Indexed Sequential Access Method) allows Access to create connections to specific lists on the site. These linked tables can be taken offline, modified, and then resynchronized at a later time, if the user of the application does not always have a direct connection to the server.

➤ **Export Data to SharePoint:** Introduced in Access 2003, Access database applications can migrate their tables and data to SharePoint, to store and manage the data on the server. This creates linked tables in the database to the SharePoint lists and removes the original tables and data from the database file.

➤ **Save & Publish Database to SharePoint:** Introduced in Access 2007, this feature enables users to upload Access databases to a document library on the SharePoint server. Then users can open the application in the Access client from the document library, so that they can use the application from any location where they have a connection to the SharePoint site.

➤ **SharePoint Table Templates:** Introduced in Access 2007, SharePoint Table Templates enable the user to create new predefined tables directly on a SharePoint site and create the corresponding linked table in the database application.

➤ **SharePoint Application Templates:** Introduced in Access 2007, Access 2010 provides two special Access database application templates are invoked when the Open with Access feature is used for the Issues or Tasks SharePoint list types. Instead of just creating simple linked tables to the list, a new fully functional Access database application is created, including several forms and reports, with tables that are linked to the SharePoint list.

➤ **Workflow Integration:** Introduced in Access 2007, Access provides direct access to the SharePoint Workflow configuration UI, providing the capability to start Workflows from within the Access client and displaying a list of all active tasks for an owner. These features are not discussed further in this chapter.

➤ **SharePoint Object Options:** Introduced in Access 2007, SharePoint-related database objects have entry points to their corresponding SharePoint features directly on the context menu for the Navigation Pane in Access. These features are not discussed further in this chapter.

The features listed in this category are really the bulk of the features for working with SharePoint. Most of this chapter discusses these features more in-depth; but first, examine the overview of the Access features that are available in SharePoint 2010.

Access Features in SharePoint 2010

The second category of features to discuss is the Access features that are available in SharePoint 2010. Both SharePoint Foundation and SharePoint Server 2010 support all of these features, except for Access Services, which is only supported in SharePoint Server 2010. The following list provides the name and brief description of each of these features, as well as the version of SharePoint in which the feature was introduced.

➤ **Access Services:** New to SharePoint Server 2010, Access Services (XAS) allows the creation and use of Access Web Applications, a new type of SharePoint application that can be built in Access 2010.

➤ **Access Web Datasheet:** Introduced in SharePoint 2.0, the Access Web Datasheet enables the user to edit SharePoint lists in the Access Datasheet directly within a browser window. It also provides the Datasheet task pane for interacting with both Access and Excel.

➤ **Open with Access:** Introduced in SharePoint 2.0, when Access is installed on the client machine, the Open with Access button appears on the Actions menu of a SharePoint list, allowing the user to open a list in a new instance of an Access database. The list can be either imported or linked.

➤ **Access Views on SharePoint:** Introduced in SharePoint 3.0, when an Access database application has been published to SharePoint, the option of publishing links to the forms and reports to the SharePoint View menu is available. When the user selects one of these published view links from the menu, the published Access database application is invoked and the object opens directly in Access.

Although these features might not seem like a lot, SharePoint 2010 provides greater integration with Access than ever before. Each of the preceding items is discussed in this chapter. But first, you'll explore the SharePoint 2010 features available in Access 2010.

SHAREPOINT FEATURES IN ACCESS

The first set of features to discuss is the features for SharePoint 2010 available in Access 2010, as noted in the earlier feature overview. Although not every single SharePoint feature in Access 2010 is described, the bulk of the major features are discussed in the first two-thirds of this chapter.

Access Web Applications

As mentioned earlier, SharePoint Server 2010 supports a brand-new type of application, called an Access Web Application. This is made possible by the Access Services product that has been released with SharePoint Server 2010. Access 2010 supports building these applications, as you would any other database, but they are a different type of application and do not support all the features available in traditional Access database applications. However, these new Access Web Applications provide a number of features that are not possible using Access alone, most notably the ability to run the application in the Web browser without requiring that Access be installed. This section describes the basics of Access Web Applications and how to build and deploy them to SharePoint Server 2010.

Traditional Apps versus Web Apps

As mentioned earlier, the Access Web Application is a completely new type of SharePoint application and is much different than the tradition Access application with linked tables to a SharePoint list. In the case of versions of Access prior to 2010, an Access database would store the information for the linked table directly in the database, and standard queries, forms, reports, macros, and VBA code could interact with the linked table, as it would with any other table. Although this capability is still possible in Access 2010, the Access Web Application objects are much different.

Access Web Application Design Basics

Access Web Applications are different from traditional Access SharePoint applications in a number of ways. Primarily, the database file itself must be set to be a Web database and all database objects in the Access Web Application are Web objects, which differ from normal Access database objects, though some exceptions exist, as we will discuss in the next section. Also, and possibly more importantly, standard Access Web Applications cannot use VBA code in the Web forms and reports. Event manipulation is limited strictly to macros. In many cases, the designers of the Web objects differ from the traditional Access designers, and how the objects are created and what controls can be used will be different as well. Finally, and most importantly, the Access Web Application actually lives on the SharePoint server, and the database used to create the application can be recreated (rehydrated) at any time by opening the application in Access 2010. Any updates made when the application has been rehydrated need to be synchronized with the server before users will see the updates. To make a long story short, the differences between Access Web Applications and traditional database applications are extensive. The following sections discuss the basics of building Web applications and each of their corresponding objects.

Hybrid Web Application Design Basics

The introduction of the Access Web Application also provides the opportunity for another type of application, loosely termed as a *hybrid Web application*. Access Web Applications technically still allow the creation of normal Access queries, forms, reports, macros, modules, and linked tables to other data sources in the Web database, but these client objects cannot be run on the Web browser or the SharePoint server. These client objects can only be used from the original, or rehydrated, database. Also, it is important to note that no matter what, Web databases cannot have local tables in them. Even though these objects cannot be run from the SharePoint server, the ability to rehydrate the application from the SharePoint server and then run the database file from the client is still a powerful feature in itself as it indirectly provides a method for centrally managing and distributing a traditional Access application. Hybrid applications are a powerful result of a combination of Access Web Application and traditional Access database application features.

Getting Started with Web Apps

Two methods exist for creating an Access Web Application from the Access 2010 client. The first is to simply create a new Web database, as you would any other database, but selecting the Web database option in the Access Backstage. The second is to create a database from one of the included Web database templates. This section provides instructions for creating Web databases using both methods.

Creating a New Web Application Database

You can create a brand-new, empty Access Web Application database from the Access 2010 Backstage. The following are the steps required to create a new blank Web Application database:

1. Start Access 2010 from the Windows Start menu. The Access 2010 Backstage opens.

2. From the New options, click on the Blank Web database option under the list of Available Templates in the middle panel of the Backstage.

3. On the right panel of the Backstage, type in the name for the new Web database, and optionally specify a location, and then click the Create button.

The new blank Access Web Application database is created and is ready for you to begin building the application. Although this is probably the simplest method for creating a Web Application database, you may find building the actual application from one of the premade Access Web Application templates to be easier.

Creating a Web Application from Template

Creating an Access Web Application from a template is just as easy as creating a blank Web database and can be accomplished directly through the Access Backstage. The following steps describe how to create a new Web database from an existing template:

1. Start Access 2010 from the Windows Start menu. The Access 2010 Backstage opens.

2. From the New options, click on the Sample Templates option in the middle panel of the Backstage. A list of available sample templates appears in the center panel of the Access Backstage.

3. Click on any of the templates that have the words *Web Database* in the name to select it. After you select the template, the template's details appear on the right panel of the Access Backstage.

4. On the right panel of the Backstage, type in the name for the new Web database, and optionally specify a location, and then click the Create button.

The new Access Web Application database will be created from the template and be ready for you to use or even to extend the existing functionality. The beauty of the template is that the application is ready to go right out-of-the-box, without any modification necessary. However, if you want to build a custom application, you will likely end up modifying the template after it has been created. Either way, the template is always a good starting point.

Creating Web Tables

After you have a Web database file created, you can begin building new Web tables that will be migrated to SharePoint lists when the Web application is published. However, creating Web tables is somewhat different than creating traditional tables because no Design view exists for Web tables. Also, Web tables do not allow PivotTable or PivotChart views, so you only get the Datasheet view. This section discusses several important aspects of building Web tables in Access 2010.

Creating a New Web Table

All tables created in a Web database, except for linked tables, are Web tables automatically. Web databases do not allow the use of local tables. But, creating Web tables is not really any different than creating any other table in a traditional Access database application. The following list walks through the steps required for creating a new Web table:

1. After opening the Web database in the Access 2010 client, click on the Create tab of the Ribbon to open it.

2. Click the Table button on the Create Ribbon; it is the only option in the Tables group.

The new table will be created and opened in Datasheet view. You are now ready to begin adding fields and data to the new Web table.

The Web Table Designer

The Datasheet View is the Layout Designer, and only designer, for Web tables in Access 2010. The Table Tools Ribbon group provides two Ribbons: The Fields Ribbon and the Table Ribbon. These two Ribbons contain all the options available for creating and modifying Web tables in Access 2010. As their names suggest, the Fields Ribbon is for working with the field options for a table and the Table Ribbon is for working with the table-level options. One new item to note here is that Web tables have several new events that can have macros applied to them. Also, the Property Sheet is not available for Web tables; instead, there is a properties dialog box with four options for setting the table's properties. The simple design of the Datasheet View Table Designer makes quickly building Web tables very easy, because all the options are right in front of you.

Adding Fields to a Web Table

After a new Web table has been created, you must add fields to it to store the actual data in the table. By default, all Web tables have an `AutoNumber` field named `ID`, which is the primary key for the table, and modifying that particular field is not recommended, and impossible through the Access UI. Complete the following steps to add a new field to a Web table:

1. Open the Web table in Datasheet View. This enables the Table Tools Ribbon tabs.

2. Click on the Fields tab of the Table Tools Ribbon group to select it.

3. The Fields Ribbon provides the Add & Delete group for adding fields to the table. Click on any of the buttons for the field types to add it to the form.

After you click an option, the new field is added directly after the field that is currently selected, or the end of the table. Also, the column header will automatically be selected for editing, so that the user can quickly modify the column name. The data type and other properties for the field can be set by selecting any of the options on the Table Tools Fields Ribbon. After the desired field options have been set, the field is ready for use.

Removing Fields from a Web Table

Sometimes removing a field from a Web table is also helpful, especially if the table was created from template and all the fields in the template are not required for the task. The Table Tools Fields Ribbon also provides an option for removing existing fields from a Web table. Complete the following steps to remove a field from a Web table:

1. Open the Web table in Datasheet view. This enables the Table Tools Ribbon tabs.

2. Click on the Fields tab of the Table Tools Ribbon group to select it.

3. Click on the column header of the field you want to delete to select it. This enables the Delete button on the Table Tools Fields Ribbon.

4. Click the Delete button in the Add & Remove group on the Fields Ribbon. The field is deleted from the table.

Always use caution when deleting a field from a table. After the field has been deleted, it is gone forever, along with any data stored in the field. Making a backup of the table when deleting a field as a result of a design change is always recommended, and always do so when the field already contains data.

Data Macros

New to tables in Access, Web tables support several data events and each of these events can have a macro assigned to it. After the Web table has been published to the SharePoint server, these macros then get converted to Workflows on SharePoint to provide the proper functionality. However, to provide this support, not all macro actions are supported for Data Macros. To add a macro to a table event, complete the following steps:

1. With the Web table open in the Access client window, click on the Table Tools Table Ribbon tab to select it.

2. On the Table Tools Table Ribbon, click on the desired table event to select it. This invokes the Macro Designer for the table event.

3. Add any desired macro logic. Although only a limited set of macro options is available, all of these options are supported for the table when it is migrated to a list on SharePoint.

4. After all the functionality has been added to the macro, simply close the macro and choose Yes to save the changes.

Now the Data Macro has been added to the table. When the event is fired, the actions in the macro execute. Although not all macro actions are available, these macros can still be quite powerful for working with data as it enters or leaves the table. See Chapter 4 for an in-depth description of Data Macros, how to build them, and the specifics of the features they support.

Working with Relationships

Relationships in an Access Web Application are somewhat tricky to work with, because no relationship designer exists for Web Applications. When creating relationships in a Web Application, using the Lookup Wizard is recommended only to ensure that the lookup is created properly, though creating and manipulating the relationship through VBA code is also possible. And, when doing so, it is important to realize that all lookups must include the AutoNumber field that is the primary key for the lookup table. Also, be aware that although cascade deletes are supported, cascade updates are not. Although cumbersome to work with, the Lookup Wizard is the best method for building and working with relationships between tables in an Access Web Application.

Linking to Other Data Sources

The only other types of tables supported in an Access Web Application are ODBC-linked tables; local tables are not supported in any form. However, if you need local storage, it is possible to create a second Access database with all the tables needed and then create linked tables in the Web Application database to the second Access database. Although the Web Application won't be able to use those tables from the SharePoint server (that is, in the browser), when the application is run locally through the Access client, the linked tables contained within the application will be accessible to objects within the application. However, it is important to note that anyone who will be using the Web Application with linked tables from the Access client will also need permissions and access to the data sources that the linked tables link to.

To link to an external data source in an Access Web Application, complete the following steps:

1. With a Web database open in the Access client, click on the External Data Ribbon tab to select it.

2. For an Access database, click the Access button on the Ribbon in the Import & Link group. This opens the Get External Data dialog box.

3. Browse to the database to link to by clicking the Browse button and selecting the database in the File Open dialog box. The full filename and path appears in the File Name text box in the Get External Data dialog box.

4. After choosing the database file, select the Link to the data option, which is the second bullet in the dialog box. Then click the OK button to launch the Link Tables dialog box.

 If you do not select the Link to the data option and try to import the tables directly into the Web database, the wizard will run, but you will get a failure at the end, noting that Web compatibility issues exist. However, you may import objects other than tables into the Web database; only tables cannot be imported.

5. After the Link Tables dialog box opens, click on any of the tables that you want to link to. After selecting all the desired tables, click the OK button. The wizard completes and the linked tables are created.

Although you can use linked tables only when the Access Web Application is run through the Access client, they are a powerful feature for allowing Web Applications to work with data sources other than just the SharePoint lists.

Creating Web Queries

The next object in an Access Web Application is the Web Query object. Much like Access Query objects, Web Queries can be used to gather data from the various SharePoint lists in a Web Application. After the Web Application has been migrated to the SharePoint server, these query objects are moved and exist as views on SharePoint. At first glance, Web Queries seem exactly the same as Access Queries, but in reality, they are quite different in a number of ways. This section discusses Web Queries and how to create them in Access 2010.

Creating a New Web Query

You create a Web Query in the same manner as you do a normal Access Query object, except that it can only be created in a Web database. The following steps describe how to create a new Web Query in Access 2010:

1. With a Web database open in the Access client, click on the Create Ribbon tab to select it.

2. Click the Query button under the Queries group in the Ribbon. A new Web Query will be created and opened in the Web Query Designer.

All Queries created in a Web database using this method will be Web Queries by default. Best of all, after you have a Web Query object, you can begin designing the query in the Web Query Designer much like you would a standard Access Query object.

The Web Query Designer

The Access 2010 Web Query Designer is very similar to the Access Query Object Designer, with a few minor differences. When you open a Web Query in Design view, you have all the standard query design tools available: the field list, the Property Sheet, the Show Table dialog box, the Query Tools Design Ribbon, and most importantly, the design grid that you can work with the fields of the query. So, in those respects, the Web Query Designer is exactly the same.

However, a few differences exist between the Web Query Designer and the Access Query Object Designer. The most significant is that Web Queries only have the Design View and Datasheet View modes available, and no SQL View designer is available. Also, to conform to SharePoint, a number of options are not available in Web Queries. The top of this list is that only SELECT queries can be created for Web Queries, but only simpler SELECT queries are supported. For example, SELECT DISTINCT, data aggregation, union, and other types of more complex SELECT queries are not supported. All other query types, such as UPDATE, APPEND, DELETE, and all others are *not* allowed, because they are not supported on SharePoint. However, you can always create local Query objects in the database to perform these types of tasks, which is discussed next. Those two items are really the major, but not the only, differences between creating Web Query objects and Access Query objects in Access 2010, so if you are already familiar with creating Access Query objects, creating Web Queries in Design View will be a snap.

Access Query Database Objects

As part of the hybrid Web application, local Access Query objects are supported in a Web database. As mentioned earlier, these local objects can be of any type supported by Access, such as APPEND or DELETE, so local Access Query objects can be used when these kinds of tasks are required. The Create Ribbon provides the Client Queries button for creating local Query objects in the Web database. However, as with all non-Web objects in a Web database, the local Query functionality can only be run when the application is open in the Access client, and not from the SharePoint site or browser.

Creating Web Forms

The next object in an Access Web Application is the Web Form object. Web Forms attempt to provide much of the same functionality found in standard Access Form objects, such as multiple item forms. After the Web Application has been migrated to the SharePoint server, these Web Form objects are moved and exist as forms on the SharePoint server that can be run from the browser. This section discusses the basics of Web Forms and how to create them in Access 2010.

Although this section discusses the basics of Web Forms in Access 2010, it is only a brief overview of the object type and how it relates to an Access Web Application. For more information about designing Web Form objects, see Chapter 14 in regard to building forms.

Creating a New Web Form

You can create a Web Form in the same manner you do a normal Access Form object, except that it can only be created in a Web database. The following steps describe how to create a new Web Form in Access 2010:

1. With a Web database open in the Access client, click on the Create Ribbon tab to select it.

2. Click any of the various Form buttons under the Forms group on the Create Ribbon, except for the items under the Client Forms button. A new Web Form is created and opens in the Web Form Layout Designer.

All forms created in a Web database using this method will be Web Forms by default. And, after the Web Form has been created, you can begin designing the form in the Web Form Layout Designer, just like you would any other standard Access Form object.

The Web Form Designer

The Web Form Layout Designer is much like the standard Form Layout View Designer in Access 2010, with some differences. When you open a Web Form in Layout View mode, all the standard form design tools are available: the Field List, the Property Sheet, the Form Layout Tools Ribbons, and most importantly, the design surface of the form that you can work with to visually design the form. So, in those respects, the Web Form Layout Designer is exactly the same.

At the same time, a number of differences exist between the Web Forms and standard Access Form objects. Because Web Forms are eventually going to become Web pages, the controls that can be used in Web Forms are different than standard Access Form object controls, in some cases. Also, you may find that the events for these Forms, and the controls that can be used, are much different than standard Access Forms. Probably the most important item to note is that no support exists for VBA code in Web Forms. Only a limited number of macros are supported. Finally, Access 2010 only supports Layout View and Form View modes for Web Forms, so PivotTables, PivotCharts, and the Design View Designers are not allowed in Web Forms. Other than these major differences, designing the Forms using the Access 2010 Layout Designer is much like building standard Access Form objects.

Access Form Database Objects

As part of the hybrid Web application, local Access Form objects are supported in a Web database. These local Form objects can be of any type and use all standard Access Form functionality and controls, so they can be used when this kind of functionality is required. The Create Ribbon provides the Client Forms button for creating Access Form objects in the Web database. However, as with all non-Web objects in a Web database, the Access Forms can only be run when the application is open in the Access client, and not from the SharePoint site or browser.

Creating Web Reports

The next object in an Access Web Application is the Web Report object. Web Reports also attempt to provide much of the same functionality found in standard Access Report database objects. Again, after the Web Application has been migrated to the SharePoint server, these Web Report objects are moved and exist as views on the SharePoint server that can be run from the browser. This section discusses the basics of Web Reports and how to create them in Access 2010.

 Although this section discusses the basics of Web Reports in Access 2010, it is only a brief overview of the object type and how it relates to an Access Web Application. For more information about designing Web Report objects, see Chapter 15 in regard to building reports.

Creating a New Web Report

You can create a Web Report in the same manner you do a normal Access Report object, except that it can only be created in a Web database. The following steps describe how to create a new Web Report in Access 2010:

1. With a Web database open in the Access client, click on the Create Ribbon tab to select it.

2. Click either the Report or Blank Report buttons under the Reports group on the Create Ribbon. A new Web Report is created and opened in the Web Report Layout Designer.

All reports created in a Web database using this method will be Web Reports by default. After the Web Report has been created, you can begin designing the report in the Web Report Layout Designer, just like you would any other standard Access Report object.

The Web Report Designer

Just like with Web Forms, the Web Report Layout Designer is much like the standard Report Layout View Designer in Access 2010, again with some differences. When you open a Web Report in Layout View mode, all the standard report design tools are available: the Field List, the Property Sheet, the Report Layout Tools Ribbons, and most importantly, the design surface of the report. Again, in those respects, the Web Report Layout Designer is exactly the same.

But, just like with Web Forms, a number of differences exist between the Web Report and the standard Access Report objects. Because Web Reports eventually become SharePoint views, the controls that you can use in Web Reports are much more limited than the standard Access Report object controls. Also, Web Reports and their controls are much different, and much more limited, than standard Access Report objects. Web Reports do not support any events what-so-ever, and again, the same rules for macros and VBA code for Web Forms also applies to Web Reports. Finally, all Web Report objects require a data source that is Web compatible, before you can save them to the Web database. Other than these major differences, designing Web Reports using the Access 2010 Layout Designer is much like building standard Access Report objects.

Access Report Database Objects

As part of the hybrid Web application, local Access Report objects are supported in a Web database. These local Report objects can be of any type and can use all standard Access Report functionality and controls. The Create Ribbon provides the Client Reports button for creating standard Access Report objects in the Web database. However, as with all non-Web objects in a Web database, you can only run the Access Reports when the application is open in the Access client, and not from the SharePoint site or browser.

Creating Web Macros

Finally, the last type of Web database object to discuss is the Web macro object. Web macro objects are basically exactly the same as local Access macro objects. When the Web Application is migrated to the SharePoint, these Web macro objects exist on the server and can be used from objects in the browser. In fact, the Data Macro features in the Access 2010 release were specifically created to add support for these features in the Access Web Application. And these Web macros are created directly within the new Access 2010 Macro Designer, so the design experience is exactly the same as standard Access macro objects.

 For more information about designing and building Web macro and Data macro objects in Access 2010, see Chapter 4.

Creating a New Web Macro

You create a Web macro in the same manner you do a normal Access macro object, except that it can only be created in a Web database. The following steps describe how to create a new Web macro in Access 2010:

1. With a Web database open in the Access client, click on the Create Ribbon tab to select it.

2. Click the Macro button under the Macros & Code group on the Create Ribbon. A new Web macro will be created and opened in the Macro Designer.

All macros created in a Web database using this method will be Web macros by default. And, after the Web macro has been created, you can begin designing the macro in the Access 2010 Macro Designer, just like you would any other standard macro object.

Access Macros and VBA Modules

Finally, also as part of the hybrid Web application, local Access macros and VBA code module objects are supported in a Web database. These local macro objects are no different than normal macro objects in a standard database application and can use all standard Access functionality that macro objects normally provide. The Create Ribbon provides the Client Objects button for creating standard Access macro, module, and class module objects in the Web database. However, as with all non-Web objects in a Web database, these objects can only be executed when the application is open in the Access client, and not from the SharePoint site or browser.

Publishing to Access Services

After the design and implementation of the Web application has been completed, it is ready to publish to SharePoint Server 2010. It is important to remember that Access Services (that is, SharePoint Server 2010) is required on the server, before the Web application can be published to it. Publishing and running the application from a SharePoint server provides many benefits:

- ➤ Centralized application management.
- ➤ Server and data management tools and services.
- ➤ A centralized distribution location that can be accessed from anywhere in the world with an Internet connection.

This section discusses the basics of publishing a Web Application to SharePoint Server 2010 using Access 2010.

Publishing an Application Using Access 2010

Actually publishing the Access Web Application to the SharePoint server is very easy, as Access 2010 provides all the tools necessary to do the work to publish the Web Application. When the Web Application is published, all the Web objects in the Web database are created as new objects and live on the SharePoint server. The Web database is moved to the server, and can be re-created at any time, based upon the current settings for the application that are on the SharePoint server. That means that all users can create a current ACCDB version of the Web Application directly from the SharePoint server, use and/or modify it (if they have permissions), and republish any changes for all other users to see immediately.

To publish a Web application to SharePoint 2010 Server, complete the following steps:

1. With a Web database open in the Access client, click on the File Ribbon tab to open the Access Backstage.

2. On the left pane of the Backstage, click on the Save & Publish option. The various options for saving and sharing database files open.

3. In the middle pane, click the Publish to Access Services option. The Publish to Access Services options open in the right pane of the Backstage.

4. Optionally, run the Web Compatibility Wizard to check for any possible compatibility errors by clicking the Run Compatibility Checker button.

 If this is the first time an application is being published to SharePoint, we highly recommended always running the Web Compatibility Wizard first to ensure the application does not have any outstanding problems the first time it is pushed up to SharePoint. If the Wizard returns errors, these should be fixed in the application before publishing to SharePoint, and the Wizard should be rerun to ensure the fixes did not cause additional errors.

5. Input the URL to the SharePoint Server 2010 server and provide a Site Name for the new application.

6. Click the Publish button to create the new site on the SharePoint server.

If any errors occurred during the creation process, a message appears, providing options for viewing the errors. Otherwise, the Web Application will have been successfully published to the SharePoint server and is now ready for use.

The Web Compatibility Wizard

One feature that is very helpful when building Access Web Applications is the Web Compatibility Wizard. Before publishing any Web Application, running the Web Compatibility Wizard to flag and repair any possible problems is always recommended. Running the wizard is easy to do, as described in the previous section and only takes a few minutes of your time. If any issues are present, a message appears and the Web Compatibility Issues button (next to the Run Compatibility Checker button) becomes enabled for viewing the errors. Again, resolving all errors before publishing the Application to SharePoint is highly recommended and, in some cases, is required. The Web Compatibility Wizard is easy to use and designed to ensure your Web Applications will publish to SharePoint without a problem.

> **THE WEB COMPATIBILITY WIZARD MAY NOT CATCH ALL PROBLEMS!**
>
> There are some cases in which the Web Compatibility Wizard may not be able to flag all problems with the application before moving it to SharePoint. The Wizard does not check the data in an application before moving it to SharePoint and it maybe truncated or not moved at all, if the data is not supported on SharePoint. Also, there are some cases with more complex forms and reports, where issues may not be properly assessed by the wizard, and in particular, around the area of subforms and subreports. For this reason, we always recommend fully testing and manually checking the functionality and data of a Web Application every time it has been published to SharePoint.

Working with the Web Application

After the Web Application has been published to the SharePoint server, it lives on the server as a SharePoint application. Users can begin using the application directly from the SharePoint site, in their browser, as they would with any other Web application. This section discusses the basics of running the application from SharePoint, rehydrating the Web Application into an ACCDB file, modifying the application in Access, and synchronizing changes to the application with the SharePoint server.

Running from the Browser

To run a published application from SharePoint in the browser, complete the following steps:

1. Open the browser and type in the URL for the location that the Web Application was published to, for example:

   ```
   http://MySharePointServer/AssetsWebApp
   ```

2. The browser automatically navigates to the default page (similar to a startup form) for the application. If the application does not specify a default page, the user will be taken to a page showing a list of the application objects, which is generated by SharePoint.

After the browser has navigated to the default page for the Access Web Application, simply use the application as you would any other Web application in your browser. Running Access Web

Applications from the SharePoint server is just that simple for users and does not even require that Access be installed on the client machine. Users just run the application in their browser directly from the SharePoint site.

Rehydrating a Web Application

After the Access Web Application has been published to SharePoint, the physical ACCDB file can be re-created at any time directly from the Web server, which is called rehydrating the application. In the case that the application uses local database objects, rehydrating the application and running from the Access client will be required to use that particular functionality in the application. To rehydrate an Access Web Application, complete the following steps:

1. Go to the start page for the Access Web Application on the SharePoint server in your browser.

2. On the Options menu, choose the Open with Access option. This opens the Access program and creates a local copy of the Access Web Application in an ACCDB database.

After the Web Application has been rehydrated, you can run it as you would any other Access database application in the Access client. Also, the rehydrated database provides the user with the opportunity to make changes to the application and to synchronize those changes with the SharePoint server from any machine, which is discussed next.

Modifying a Web Application

Modifying an Access Web Application after it has been published to the SharePoint server is extremely easy to do and one of the key benefits of using Web Applications. The point to consider is the centralized management aspect of the Web Application. Because the definition of the application lives on the SharePoint server, that is the current working copy of the application. It can be rehydrated into an ACCDB file for modification at any time, on any machine with Access 2010 installed, and by any user with permissions to the SharePoint site.

After the application opens in the Access client, you can modify all of its objects, just as with any other standard database. When you've completed all modifications to the application, the application must be synchronized with the SharePoint server to persist the changes to the server. To synchronize an Access Web Application with SharePoint Server 2010 using Access 2010, complete the following steps:

1. With the Web Application open in the Access client, click on the File Ribbon tab to open the Access Backstage.

2. On the left pane of the Backstage, click on the Save & Publish option. The various options for saving and sharing database files appear.

3. Click the Sync Changes button and the changes will be synchronized with the SharePoint server.

Synchronizing changes to an Access Web Application is just that simple. Remember running the Web Compatibility Wizard just before and every time changes to a site will be published is always recommended. Working with Access Web Applications using Access 2010 could not be any easier!

Access Web Application Summary

Using Access Services on SharePoint Server 2010 to host Access Web Applications is a new and powerful type of SharePoint application. Access 2010 provides all the tools necessary for designing, publishing, and running Web Applications. For more information about Access Services and building Access Web Applications in Access 2010, see the Access homepage on Microsoft's website at `http://office.microsoft.com/en-us/access/default.aspx`.

Linked Tables to SharePoint

Both MDB and ACCDB files support the creation of linked tables to SharePoint lists. These linked tables provide the database with virtual tables for working with SharePoint lists and their data directly from within an Access database application. The SharePoint ISAM provides the interface for Access to connect directly to SharePoint. You can use SharePoint linked tables just like native Access tables, except you cannot modify the schema in Access or through VBA code and the actual data in the table is stored on the SharePoint site. SharePoint linked tables also support an offline mode where the data is copied to the Access database file temporarily, so that users can access and modify the SharePoint data without being connected to the site. SharePoint linked tables can be extraordinarily useful in building traditional Access database applications for groups that already collaborate using a SharePoint site.

Several methods exist for creating linked tables to a SharePoint list. You can create linked tables through the Access UI in the exact same manner used for creating linked tables in a Web Application, as described earlier. The Get External Data Wizard can be used to add a linked table to SharePoint, or any other data source, manually to a database via the Access UI. For developers, an Object Model exists for dynamically creating linked tables to a SharePoint list, which is done through the `TransferSharePointList` function. Although both ACCDB and MDB files support linked tables to SharePoint, some differences exist between the two formats in how certain SharePoint data types can be used. If you're using the MDB file format, take great care when designing SharePoint list schema, because several SharePoint data types are unsupported in this format.

SharePoint Linked Tables in an ACCDB

Linking tables to SharePoint in an ACCDB file provides unmatched support compared to any other linked data source supported by Access 2010. SharePoint linked tables in an ACCDB support all SharePoint data types, including multiple value fields, attachment fields, append-only fields, Rich Text fields, and Calculated fields. Moreover, SharePoint lists can be taken offline, so that the application and its data can be used without even requiring a connection to the SharePoint server; a feature not found with any other linked table type in Access.

Probably the biggest difference between importing and linking tables to SharePoint lists is that all lookup tables are automatically created as linked tables when the primary linked table is created. Additionally, Person or Group field types in the SharePoint list are treated as lookup fields to their corresponding list. For that reason, whenever linking tables to SharePoint, the database always links to the User Information List by default when linking to any other SharePoint list, which is discussed shortly. The following table explains the mapping between SharePoint 2010 data types' and the data types support by an ACCDB file.

SHAREPOINT TYPE	ACCDB TYPE	MODIFICATION DESCRIPTION
Single Line of Text	Text	No change.
Multiple Lines of Text	Memo	Rich Text setting is persisted into the imported table. Enhanced Rich Text is not fully supported.
Choice	Text	Values for the choices are also imported into the Row Source property for the field.
Number	Number	Double precision; no change.
Data and Time	Date/Time	No change.
Currency	Currency	The Format and DecimalPlaces properties are persisted.
Lookup	Number	Lookup tables are automatically pulled down.
Yes/No	Yes/No	No change.
Person or Group	Number	Treated as a lookup field to the Person or Group list.
Hyperlink or Picture	Hyperlink	Data is imported as a link to the image file.
Calculated	Varies	Dependent upon the type that the column returns. The field continues to be calculated, even when in offline mode.
Multiple Value Fields	Varies	Complex data field of the same type. The values for the choices (if a static list) are also imported into the Row Source property for the field. If the choices are a lookup, then the lookup table is pulled down as well.
Attachment	Attachment	No change.
Multiple Lines of Text — Append Only Fields	Memo	The AppendOnly property is set to True (the opposite of when importing). The column history is persisted in the linked table and the ColumnHistory function can be used against this field.

Using linked tables to SharePoint in an ACCDB database solution allows users the richest linked table experience possible in a traditional Access database application.

SharePoint Linked Tables in an MDB

Although the older Access MDB file format supports SharePoint linked tables very well, it does have a few limitations. Primarily, the MDB file format does not support complex data and attachment fields in the same manner as the ACCDB file format. The following table describes how SharePoint data types map to the MDB file format data types when linked.

SHAREPOINT TYPE	ACCESS TYPE	MODIFICATION DESCRIPTION
Single Line of Text	Text	No change.
Multiple Lines of Text	Memo	The Rich Text setting is persisted into the imported table and supported when using Access with the MDB file.
Choice	Text	The values for the choices are also imported into the Row Source property for the field.
Number	Number	Double precision — No change.
Data and Time	Date/Time	No change.
Currency	Currency	The `Format` and `DecimalPlaces` properties are persisted.
Lookup	Number	Lookup tables are automatically pulled down.
Yes/No	Yes/No	No change.
Person or Group	Number	Treated as a lookup field to the Person or Group list.
Hyperlink or Picture	Hyperlink	The data is imported as a link to the image file.
Calculated	Varies	Dependent upon the type that the column returns. The field continues to be calculated.
Multiple Value Fields	Memo	Because complex data is not supported in the MDB file format, the data is imported as a comma-separated list for each of the values selected.
Attachment	Yes/No	Because attachment fields are not supported in an MDB, the field is converted to a `Yes/No` field. The value of the field corresponds to whether the record had an attachment in the original SharePoint list.
Multiple Lines of Text — Append Only Fields	Memo	Because no `AppendOnly` property exists in an MDB table field, there is nothing in the Access UI for the user to see. However, the `AppendOnly` property is enforced when data is edited, and thus the column history is also persisted in the linked table. The `ColumnHistory` function is available when using Access 2007 and higher, although the function generates a compile error in previous versions of Access.

When used in an MDB database application, linked tables to SharePoint lists still provide an ample amount of support and functionality for SharePoint features. However, using the ACCDB file format is still the preferred method for working with linked tables to SharePoint lists.

Creating Linked Tables with VBA Code

Although creating linked tables in the Access UI is quick and easy, you may find times when creating linked tables to SharePoint lists with VBA code is useful instead. Fortunately, Access supports creating linked tables programmatically through the `TransferSharePointList` function. Because a few options are available for creating linked tables programmatically, the following section examines the `TransferSharePointList` method a little more.

TransferSharePointList Object Model

The `TransferSharePointList` method allows a developer to either import or link to a SharePoint list programmatically, directly from VBA code within an Access database application. `TransferSharePointList` is a member of the `DoCmd` class, which is a member of the `Application` object. `TransferSharePointList` takes up to six arguments, three of which are required. The following table describes each of these arguments.

PARAMETER	DESCRIPTION
TransferType	Requires a member of the enumeration type `AcSharePointListTransferType`. Two options are available: `acImportSharePointList` and `acLinkSharePointList`.
SiteAddress	The full URL path to the SharePoint site. This parameter is required.
ListID	The Name or the GUID of the list to be transferred. This parameter is required.
ViewID	The Name or the GUID of the view that should be imported. This means that imported data can be pre-filtered by a specific list view on SharePoint before pulling the data into Access. This parameter is optional and not available for when the `acImportSharePointList` option is chosen for the transfer type. If not specified, all the fields on the SharePoint site will be retrieved.
TableName	The name of the new linked table in the database. This parameter is optional and not available for when the `acImportSharePointList` option is chosen for the transfer type. If not specified, the name of the SharePoint list will be used for the new table in the database.
GetLookupDisplayValues	When `False`, any lookup fields will contain the IDs to the list to which the lookup is tied. When `True`, the actual display values will be imported. This parameter is optional and not available for when the `acImportSharePointList` option is chosen for the transfer type.

The `TransferSharePointList` method does not return any values.

Creating a SharePoint Linked Table in Code

To create a linked table to a SharePoint list, the `TransferSharePointList` method must be called with all the parameters set to the appropriate values. The following code illustrates a subroutine that creates a linked table to a hypothetical SharePoint list:

```
Sub LinkSharePointList()

    ` Call TransferSharePointList to link to SharePoint
```

```
Application.DoCmd.TransferSharePointList _
  acLinkSharePointList, _
  `http://MySharePointSite/`, _
  `Tasks`, _
  `{E3908E5d-C32A-4D60-9D55-24A2761E5450}`, _
  `LinkedTasksList`, _
  False

End Sub
```

code snippet module ExampleCode in Ch19_Sample.accdb

Of course, your code must specify the proper URL, GUID, and list name for the specific SharePoint list to be imported. When viewing data or updating data in linked tables to a SharePoint list, remember that the data will have to be pulled down from the SharePoint site and then pushed back up again if a change or addition occurs. This presents the possibility for performance issues in an Access database application, because in most cases, query processing needs to be done on the Access client.

Query Processing for SharePoint Data

The client-server chapter outlines several common performance problems that can occur when linked tables are used in an Access application. SharePoint applications are no stranger to performance issues. Unfortunately, because SharePoint uses an ISAM to read and write data, queries created in Access are processed locally, which can lead to possible performance issues. No support exists for making the SharePoint site process Access queries on the server to increase performance. Fortunately, one saving grace is in the fact that any table can be linked to a specific view for the SharePoint list.

As you'll see in the Chapter 21, the client-server chapter, in many cases Access needs to pull down all the data in a table from the data source when processing queries locally, and possibly even multiple times! If a large number of users are using the SharePoint server or if the lists contain large amounts of data, processing a query may result in huge network bandwidth consumption. The best method for reducing this traffic is creating views that reduce the data set and query processing required by the application, and then creating a linked table to those views directly. That way, the SharePoint server processes the query to create a particular view locally, and then only the data contained in the view — not the entire data set — is transferred across the network. When possible, linking to SharePoint views helps reduce network traffic and improves the overall application performance.

Offline Mode for SharePoint Linked Tables

Another commanding feature for SharePoint linked tables in the ACCDB file format is Offline mode. Offline mode enables users of a database application with linked tables to a SharePoint server to move the tables and data into an offline state where they can interact, modify, add, and delete data in the SharePoint list, without having to actually be connected to the SharePoint server. After the table is synchronized, all data modifications are persisted to the corresponding SharePoint lists. And in the case that a record conflict exists, a conflict resolution wizard appears so that the user can resolve any data conflicts. The Offline feature is exceedingly useful when a user needs access to SharePoint data when no Web or network connection is available. Essentially, the Offline feature enables SharePoint linked database applications to run in any environment, regardless of an Internet connection to the SharePoint site.

Data Storage during Offline Mode

When a table is linked to a SharePoint list, all the data stored in the list resides on the SharePoint site. When a linked table is taken offline, all the data in the list is brought down and stored in the database locally. If the user adds, modifies, or deletes data within the list while it is offline, a record of the changes is stored in the Access database. When the linked tables are switched back into Online mode with the SharePoint site again, the data is synchronized and all the changes are propagated to the list on the server. However, the data is never removed from the Access database file. The only way to remove the data stored in the file after a database has been taken offline is to compact and repair the database file.

Offline Mode Data Synchronization Model

One item to consider is multiple users working with the same SharePoint list in different database applications. If both users take the application offline and modify the same record in different ways, what happens when the data is synchronized with the server? The model for synchronizing data on SharePoint is this: When the linked table is synchronized or moved back into an online state, its current data is synchronized, and any records containing different data will overwrite the existing data in the SharePoint list. That is, the last changes synchronized are always the current data stored in the SharePoint site, overriding any previous data. This may cause a problem when many people are using the same list, and a previous record is overwritten by another person. Fortunately, if a record is modified while an application is offline, the person synchronizing the list is presented with the conflict resolution dialog box. If nothing else, this forces users to make a conscious decision about which data to use when synchronizing the SharePoint list data.

Using Offline Mode via the Access UI

The External Data tab on the Ribbon makes working with Offline mode options for a database through the Access user interface easy for users. The Work Online/Work Offline button simply toggles the tables in the database between online and offline mode. Simply clicking this button causes it to perform its corresponding task, which is dependent upon the current online/offline state of the database application.

Discarding Changes to an Offline Linked Table

When a list has been taken offline and the user of the application has modified the data in the offline table, all the changes made can be discarded before synchronizing the data for the list again by using the Discard Changes button on the Ribbon's External Data tab. However, it is important to realize that discarding the changes to a list is an all-or-nothing operation. If the user chooses to discard changes, all additions, modifications, and deletions are undone and then removed from the database completely. No way exists for the user to choose to discard only selected changes in the list.

Caching List Data for SharePoint Linked Tables

Caching SharePoint list data locally in the database file is also possible. The Cache List Data button is available on the External Data tab, which toggles the caching feature on and off. When the list data is cached locally, the table still behaves as if it were online and any changes made are immediately persisted to the SharePoint site. The major difference here is that when data is pulled down from the SharePoint site, it is cached locally, so that queries made against the linked table don't always need to pull down the full data set from the server. Caching list data in the local database file can substantially improve application performance, especially when working with lists that contain large amounts of data and/or when data in a list is frequently queried. After the application has the data cached locally, it continues to behave this way until the Do Not Cache List Data button is clicked. The Cache List Data and Do Not Cache List Data are actually the same button on the Ribbon, but the text on the button changes depending on the data caching mode.

Using Offline Mode via Code

Access also provides the capability to toggle between Online and Offline modes through VBA code. The RunCommand method now exposes a command to toggle both the Offline status for a list and data caching, which makes invoking either of these features easy.

VBA Code for Offline Mode

The acCmdToggleOffline is a member of the AcCommand enumeration. The RunCommand method accepts AcCommand members to perform specific operations in the Access user interface. Here's an example of a simple function to take the SharePoint lists offline:

```
Sub ToggleOffline()

    ` Toggle the tables between online and offline modes
    Application.RunCommand acCmdToggleOffline

End Sub
```

code snippet module ExampleCode in Ch19_Sample.accdb

VBA Code for Caching Mode

acCmdToggleCacheListData is also a member of the AcCommand enumeration. As its name suggests, the acCmdToggleCacheListData option enables a developer to programmatically control whether the list data is cached. The following example is similar to the last, except the cached data mode is being toggled instead of the Online mode:

```
Sub ToggleCacheData()

    ` Toggle the Cached Data mode for Online lists
    Application.RunCommand acCmdToggleCacheListData

End Sub
```

code snippet module ExampleCode in Ch19_Sample.accdb

Using either the Access UI or code to work with Offline mode is simple. The Offline mode feature is handy when application users cannot access the SharePoint site. But for users to be able to use all of these new Offline features, the application must first be set up on the SharePoint site, which is discussed in the next section.

Migrating a Database to SharePoint

Access 2010 continues to provide support for migrating a traditional Access database application to a SharePoint server. The External Data Wizard provides the ability to bulk create, upload data, and create linked tables to the new SharePoint lists using the Export Data to SharePoint Wizard. This export process moves all the tables and their corresponding data to a SharePoint server. The wizard also offers a few other options during the migration process. When the migration process is completed, the application still continues to be a traditional Access database application, the only difference is that the tables, and possibly the database file itself, have been stored on a SharePoint site.

Using the Export to SharePoint Wizard

For traditional Access database applications, you invoke the Export to SharePoint List Wizard by clicking the SharePoint List button in the Export group, under the More options, on the External Data Ribbon. When an application is migrated, the user has the option to publish the database to the SharePoint site in a document library so that it can be shared with other users. The forms and reports in the database have the option of being advertised on the View menu for the corresponding SharePoint lists, discussed later in this chapter. Finally, any features in an Access application that do not support being moved to a SharePoint site are written out to the Move To SharePoint Issues table that is created after the application is migrated.

The Export Data to SharePoint Wizard is basically a one-step process. The user inputs the full URL path to the SharePoint site and clicks the Next button. The Access application moves the tables and data to the SharePoint site and the last page of the wizard enables the user to see the details that occurred during the migration process. When the Access database is migrated, a backup copy of the original database is created automatically, in case any problems occur during the process. The Export Data to SharePoint Wizard makes migrating an existing database to SharePoint as smooth as possible.

When migrating an existing application to a SharePoint site, you must be aware that some data type conversion happens because Access data types do not map directly to the SharePoint data types. Additionally, certain Access features are not supported when an application has tables linked to SharePoint. You need to be aware of both of these items before moving an application because the data type conversion can cause data precision loss, and unsupported features will not be migrated.

Data Type Conversion

Access databases offer a wide variety of data types for table fields. When developing a database, you will probably take great consideration over the types of data that will be stored in each of the table fields. The type of data is typically determined by the known range in values for the data and the format the data will need to be stored in. For example, if a particular database field is used to store the rating for a hotel or restaurant, which accepts integers 0 through 10, the developer may choose the Number data type with the Field Size property set to Byte. Although setting the Field Size property to Double would work just as well here, it requires that each field be 8 bytes in size instead of 1 byte, and the database field would take more physical disk space than is really necessary.

When designing database applications that will use linked tables to SharePoint lists, consider that you will be working with the SharePoint data types, and not the Access data types. When you export the tables and link them to SharePoint, they are converted to lists that reside on the SharePoint server, and some Access data types do not map directly to SharePoint data types, and thus may not be supported. The following table describes the Access 2010 data types and how they map to SharePoint 2010 when migrated.

ACCESS TYPE	SHAREPOINT TYPE	CONVERSION INFORMATION
AutoNumber	Number or Text	AutoNumber fields are not supported on SharePoint. Long Integer AutoNumber fields are converted to Number fields. Replication ID AutoNumber fields are converted to Text. One field required by SharePoint, called ID, is added to each table and is the primary key for the list. It is automatically populated with sequential numbers for each record, much like an Access AutoNumber field.
Attachment	Attachment	No change.
Currency	Number	Converted to a Number with the FieldSize property set to Double. The Format property is persisted in the linked table. However, because Currency is a fixed precision, scaled number whereas the Double is a floating-point number, some records may be modified because of rounding when the conversion is performed. Starting with a Double, if it is known that the database will be migrated to SharePoint, is always best.
Date/Time	Date or Time	No change.
Hyperlink	Hyperlink	No change.
Lookup (Number)	Number	No type conversion is made. However, lookup values may be regenerated because the lookup field may be switched to the SharePoint list's ID field if the lookup is to the primary key for the table before it is upsized.
Memo	Memo	No change.
Number	Number or Text	Byte, Integer, Long Integer, Single, Double, and Decimal field sizes are all converted to a Double field size when pushed up. The Replication ID number is converted to a Text field type. There may be a loss of data when moving a Decimal field to Double because Decimal fields can hold 12 bytes of data and a Double can hold only 8 bytes. Additionally, a Decimal field is a scaled number field, and a Double is a floating-point number. Some records may be modified because of rounding when the conversion is performed.

ACCESS TYPE	SHAREPOINT TYPE	CONVERSION INFORMATION
OLE Object	Not Exportable	OLE fields are not supported for migration to SharePoint and the field and data are not included in the linked table.
Text	Text	The Field Size property is set to 255.
Yes/No	Yes/No	No changes are made to Yes/No fields.

Probably the most important data type conversions are Decimal and Currency. Because no concept exists of any number type larger than a Double on SharePoint, Decimal format numbers are converted to Double format. Decimal fields have a higher precision than Double fields because they have four additional bytes in which to store numbers. Decimal and Currency field types are both scaled integers, but a Double is a floating-point number. Even though the Double type can store a wider range of numbers, a Double loses precision as the numbers get very large or very small. The Decimal and Currency field types are specifically designed to be more precise and to not lose precision as they get larger or smaller. Although some cases exist when a Decimal or Currency field size is necessary, most of the time the Double field size is sufficient to store the data that is required.

The data type conversion aspect of migrating the tables in a database to SharePoint is important to consider before migration takes place, and really should be considered during the design phase of the application. In most cases, there should not be too many problems with converting data types, but you must remember AutoNumber, Currency, Decimal, OLE Object, and Replication ID field data types can cause problems, not only with the data stored in the table, but also in how the field is used in code. Be sure to fully test the application when data conversion has taken place in a database after migrating to SharePoint.

Database Changes When Migrating to SharePoint

In addition to the modification of the data types in table fields, a few other changes are made to a database when migrated to SharePoint. As mentioned previously, some fields cannot be migrated at all, which results in a linked table without the field added, which can cause problems in the application. Similarly, you must consider some other changes made to tables and relationships when migrating your Access solutions.

When a native Access table is migrated to a SharePoint list, some new fields are added to the table. They are used by SharePoint in one way or another and every list on SharePoint must have these fields. The following table describes the fields that are added to the table when migrating.

FIELD NAME	FIELD TYPE	DESCRIPTION
ID	AutoNumber	Added as the primary key for the field. This is the only AutoNumber field allowed in the table and is required by SharePoint. The field is Read-Only.
Content Type	Text	Used by SharePoint to describe the content for internal information. The field is Read-Only.

continues

(continued)

FIELD NAME	FIELD TYPE	DESCRIPTION
File Type	Text	Used by SharePoint to describe the file type for internal information. The field is Read-Only.
Attachments	Attachment	Stores any attachments that are added to the record. This is the only Attachment field that can be in a list. Any other Attachment fields in the table are removed.
Workflow Instance ID	Text	Stores the information used by the Workflow feature to describe the Workflow information tied to the record. The field is Read-Only.
Modified	Date/Time	Stores the time for when the record was last modified. The field is Read-Only, but updated automatically whenever the record is modified.
Modified By	Number	A lookup into the User Information list to the site user who last modified the record. The field is Read-Only, but updated automatically whenever the record is modified.
Created	Date/Time	Stores the time for when the record was created. The field is Read-Only.
Created By	Number	A lookup into the User Information list to the site user who created the record. The field is Read-Only.
URL Path	Text	Relative path from the site to the record used by SharePoint internally. The field is Read-Only.
Path	Text	The relative path from the site to the list used by SharePoint internally. The field is Read-Only.
Item Type	Text	Type of SharePoint item the record represents. The field is Read-Only.
Encoded Absolute URL	Text	Full URL path to the record used by SharePoint internally. The field is Read-Only.

The ID field is the interesting addition to the table. If the table already has an ID field, the original field is renamed to _ID and converted to a number field. The new ID field will be the new primary key field in the table, and the old _ID field will no longer be the primary key, if it was the key previously. One might assume this operation would cause a problem if the table had fields that were lookups to the original ID field because when the records are pushed up to SharePoint, they may get renumbered when the new values for the ID field are generated, if there is a system relationship between the primary key and foreign key fields. Fortunately, Access is smart enough to take care of this before it becomes a problem. When lookup tables are pushed up to a SharePoint site, the new primary key values are updated for the foreign key fields. Thus, the data in the original database will be consistent when pushed up, although the original values may be different. However, hardcoded values to ID fields, such as lookup fields, will not be updated, so that is important to consider. The important thing here is that the relationship between the two tables is not broken when migrated to a SharePoint site, although the tables, and possibly even the data, may be modified slightly.

Features That Do Not Migrate to SharePoint

Some features cannot be migrated when the application tables are moved to a SharePoint site, including field properties, enforced relationships, and other linked tables. Some of these features are extremely common, so it is important for you to be aware.

The Move to SharePoint Issues Table

When a feature cannot be migrated to SharePoint, Access tries to discard the feature. Any item that is discarded has a record added to the Move to SharePoint Site Issues table. This errors table contains several fields, each of which describes information about the problematic feature. The following table describes the purpose of each of the fields in the Move to SharePoint Site Issues table.

FIELD NAME	DESCRIPTION
Issue	Problem that may be caused by the feature not being migrated
Reason	Explanation of why the feature cannot be moved to SharePoint
Object Type	Type of object the feature belongs to
Object Name	Name of the database object
Field Name	Name of the field affected
Property Name	Property name for the field, if it exists

When the Export Data to SharePoint Wizard completes the migration process, the last page of the wizard denotes whether any errors occurred by showing an error icon. Simply open the Move to SharePoint Site Issues table to see more information about each of the errors that occurred.

Table Feature Not Available on SharePoint

Several table-related features also cannot be migrated to a SharePoint list. Some field properties cannot be migrated, referential integrity is not supported, and linked tables to other data sources are not supported. The following is a list of features that cannot be exported to a SharePoint list:

➤ Binary table fields

➤ AutoNumber table fields

➤ Referential integrity — cascading updates

➤ Join types between tables (although they can be re-created after the table is upsized)

➤ Read-Only tables

➤ Linked tables to other data sources

➤ Default Value table field property

➤ Input Mask table field property

➤ Validation Rule table field property

➤ Validation Text table field property

➤ Unicode Compression table field property

➤ Unique indexes for indexed fields

➤ Smart Tags table field property (although it can be re-created after the table is upsized)

➤ Text Align table field property (although it can be re-created after the table is upsized)

Several of these features are common to Access solutions, but most of the time they are not critical to the application. The impact of data type conversion is minimal in most applications. Any changes made to the database are practically negligible. Overall, the Move to SharePoint feature is incredibly powerful yet simple to use. Access makes the complicated process of exporting database tables to SharePoint as easy as possible for the Access developer.

Publishing a Database to SharePoint

Another extremely useful feature for working with SharePoint, and the predecessor of Access Web Applications, is the ability to Publish a traditional Access database application to a SharePoint document library. This feature allows the database application file to be stored in a document library on the SharePoint site, and is much different than publishing a Web Database to Access Services on SharePoint 2010.

When publishing a traditional Access database application to SharePoint, the actual database file is stored in the document library of the SharePoint site, and only the tables of the database application get converted to SharePoint lists, all other objects remain local to the database file. Also, publishing a traditional database application is supported by SharePoint versions 2.0 and higher, not just SharePoint 2010 Server, as is the case with Web Applications. After the database has been published, all users of the application can access the database file directly from the SharePoint site. The Publish to SharePoint feature for traditional database applications also enables links to be added to the SharePoint views menu, to help better advertise the database application to users of the site. Publishing traditional Access database applications to SharePoint provides a powerful platform for application distribution and data management.

Publishing a Traditional Database Application

You can use the Publish feature in a traditional database application, much in the same manner you can use it for a Web application. To publish a traditional database application to a SharePoint site using Access 2010, complete the following steps:

1. With a Web database open in the Access client, click on the File Ribbon tab to open the Access Backstage.

2. In the left pane of the Backstage, click on the Save & Publish option. The various options for saving and sharing database files open.

3. In the middle pane, click the Save Database As option. The Save Database As options appear in the right pane of the Backstage.

4. In the right pane of the Backstage, click on the SharePoint option at the end of the list. Then click the Save As button. This invokes the Save to SharePoint dialog box.

5. On the Save to SharePoint dialog box, input the URL to the SharePoint Server 2010 server and provide a name for the file. Then click the Save button. The database will be published to the document library on the SharePoint site.

When the database is published to the SharePoint site, the PublishURL database property is set with the URL to the document library storing the application. The next time the database is published, it will automatically be published to the same SharePoint library.

The PublishURL Property

After a database has been published and a local copy of the database is opened, the user sees the Publish option in the Message Bar to automatically republish the database to the same document library. This option enables the user to quickly republish a database when changes have been made to it. The PublishURL database property is used to determine whether and where the database is published; it can be accessed with just a single line of VBA code. The following is an example function that returns PublishURL if it exists:

```
Function GetPublishURL() As String

  On Error GoTo errFailed

  ` Return the PublishURL
  GetPublishURL = CurrentDb.Properties(`PublishURL").Value
  Exit Function

errFailed:

  ` If there is an error, the PublishURL does not exist
  GetPublishURL = `"
  Exit Function

End Function
```

code snippet module ExampleCode in Ch19_Sample.accdb

You can programmatically add, modify, or remove this property just as easily. For example, you may not want the user to see the Publish bar when he opens the database, so you could add some code to automatically clear this property when the database opens. The key is to simply manipulate the PublishURL property whenever necessary, directly from VBA code in the database application.

 The PublishURL property is only set for traditional Access database applications that have been published to a SharePoint server. This property is not set or valid for Access Web Applications.

Opening in Read-Only Mode

When a database is opened from a SharePoint document library, the user is prompted to open in either Read-Only or Edit modes. If Read-Only mode is chosen, Access behaves in one of two ways, depending on whether the application's tables are local or linked. Read-Only mode can mean major differences in how the application functions and should definitely be considered when opening the database file from SharePoint.

Read-Only Mode for Local Tables

If the tables are local to the database file, opening the database from SharePoint in Read-Only mode does not allow the user to add, modify, or delete any data in the application. Because the file is Read-Only, local tables cannot be written to, which is why the data cannot be changed. The application can still be used in other ways — for example, the user can still perform other operations such as running code, viewing forms and reports, or exporting objects; the user is just is not able to make any changes to the actual application data or structure of the database file.

Read-Only Mode for Linked Tables

The behavior is totally different if the application has linked tables to another location, such as a SharePoint site or SQL Server. If the published database has linked tables to a data source that is writable by that user, data modification is allowed in Read-Only mode! This is often counterintuitive at first because people tend to associate the Read-Only status with being able to change nothing. In reality, although the database file is Read-Only, the data store is not, so modifications can easily be made. Keep this in mind when publishing traditional Access database applications so that you do not inadvertently allow or disallow users from modifying data in the published application.

Opening in Edit Mode

The other option available from the SharePoint site, when invoking a database application from a document library, is the option to open the database in Edit mode. Edit mode enables the user to make any changes to the database objects or data without discretion, but requires that the physical database file be downloaded to the local machine to make these changes. After downloading the file, the user can make any desired changes and quickly republish the database using the Publish bar, so that all users will be able to see the changes to the application.

In some cases, the developer may want to deter the user from republishing the database to the SharePoint site. As mentioned earlier, you can remove the PublishURL property using VBA code. Here is a quick example of a subroutine to remove the PublishURL property value setting:

```
Sub ClearPublishURL()

    On Error GoTo errFailed

    ` Remove the PublishURL property to deter users from publishing
    CurrentDb.Properties.Delete `PublishURL"
    Exit Sub

errFailed:

    ` There was an error, the property was not present
```

```
    Exit Sub

End Sub
```

The previous two code examples both do some error checking to ignore errors if the `PublishURL` property does not exist in the database. Of course, you can add your own error-handling code for these situations as desired. The important point here is that you can delete the `PublishURL` database property by calling the `Delete` method of the `Properties` collection for the `CurrentDb` object, and when the property is not present in the database, the user will not see the Publish bar in Access.

Opening Published Databases with VBA Code

Access provides the `OpenCurrentDatabase` method to open a database in the Access client, which includes databases that have been published to SharePoint or other websites. The `OpenCurrentDatabase` method is a member of the `Application` object and takes three parameters, two of which are optional. The following table describes those parameters.

PARAMETER NAME	PARAMETER DESCRIPTION
`filePath`	The full name and path or URL string to the database to be opened. Required.
`Exclusive`	The `Boolean` value that determines whether the database should be opened in `Exclusive` mode. Optional, and if not specified, the default value is `False`.
`bstrPassword`	The password string on the database that is to be opened. Optional, and if not specified, it is an empty string. If the database does have a password, the user is still prompted if this parameter is not passed through.

`OpenCurrentDatabase` can be useful for spawning a new instance of an application using VBA code. The following is one example of how to open a database from a SharePoint site:

```
Sub OpenDatabaseFromSite()

    ` Define variables
    Dim accApp As New Access.Application

    ` Open the database from the SharePoint site
    accApp.Visible = True
    accApp.OpenCurrentDatabase _
        `http://MySharePointSite/Database.accdb"

    ` Clean up
    Set accApp = Nothing

End Sub
```

One other method for opening a published database application using VBA code is by calling the `FollowHyperlink` method with a URL to the database location. The `FollowHyperlink` method is also a member of the `Application` object and takes a single parameter, which is the full URL to the page or other object to open. Here's an example of a subroutine to open a database using `FollowHyperlink`:

Available for download on Wrox.com

```
Sub FollowLinkToDatabase()

    ` Open the database from the SharePoint site
    Application.FollowHyperlink _
        `http://MySharePointSite/Database.accdb"

End Sub
```

code snippet module ExampleCode in Ch19_Sample.accdb

No matter which method you choose, Access is sure to make writing code to open a published database easy for you.

ACCESS FEATURES ON SHAREPOINT

SharePoint 2010 has several entry points for working with Access 2010 features: Access Services, the Access Web Datasheet, the Open with Access button, Import from SharePoint, and Access Views on SharePoint. New to SharePoint Server 2010 is the release of Access Services, a brand-new SharePoint product for building Access Web Applications, which is the major new feature for Access with SharePoint. The Open with Access and Access Views on SharePoint features were introduced in SharePoint 3.0 with Access 2007. And finally, the Access Web Datasheet and Import from SharePoint were both available in SharePoint 2.0 with Access 2003 release. All of these features provide many benefits for providing a rich experience to users of both SharePoint and Access 2010. The new Access Web Application feature has already been discussed earlier, so take a look now at the other features available on SharePoint 2010 and see how they can benefit traditional Access database applications.

SharePoint 2.0 Shows Access Features

Access 2003 was the first release of Access to support any SharePoint integration. This SharePoint support was provided by the `owssupp.dll`, which is installed and registered on the default installation of Microsoft Office System 2003. After this DLL was installed, the Access Web Datasheet could be used from within Internet Explorer to edit SharePoint lists. Importing from or linking to a SharePoint list could be completed by using the Access Web Datasheet task pane options.

The same is true with versions of Access today. By default, the `owssupp.dll` is installed in the Office program files directory when Microsoft Office 2010 Professional is installed. However, if desired, you can choose not to install the `owssupp.dll` component during the installation process by selecting the Not Installed option for the Microsoft Office Access Web Datasheet Component.

No Install on First Use option exists — the `owssupp.dll` *component is either installed or it is not. Of course, if not installed, you can always add the DLL at a later time.*

Access Web Datasheet

Probably one of the most well-known Access features on SharePoint, the Access Web Datasheet allows users to edit SharePoint lists in a datasheet grid on the Web Form. Users can add, modify, or delete data stored on the SharePoint server directly from their Internet browsers. The benefits to the user are a rich data editing experience and the capability to add, modify, and delete multiple records at the same time, in a single view. The Access Web Datasheet feature has two components: the Access Web Datasheet and the Access Web Datasheet task pane.

Edit in Datasheet

Edit in Datasheet is a feature that is used by people editing a list through the SharePoint user interface. In SharePoint 2010, clicking the Actions menu reveals a button called Edit in Datasheet (when Access is installed on the machine). When you click that button, the page refreshes and the list displays in the Access Web Datasheet grid.

Although Edit in Datasheet is a UI feature that is integrated directly into the SharePoint site, a developer can still force the datasheet to be used when a SharePoint page is navigated to. Shown in the SharePoint Create View page, the All Lists section provides an option called Datasheet View. When you create a view with that option, the list is always shown in the Access Web Datasheet. Anyone navigating to the view will see the list in the datasheet and can use the Access Web Datasheet's rich editing capabilities. Of course, this requires that the user has Access installed on the client machine. Otherwise, the user will be required to navigate to another view for the list to view the data and will not be able to open the list in the Web Datasheet view.

Additionally, you can set any view created on SharePoint as the default view for any given SharePoint list. A standard list is created with the All Items view as the default view. The All Items view is simply a list of all the items stored in the list, hence its name. However, you can specify any view — datasheet or otherwise — as the default view for any SharePoint list by selecting the Default View option in the view's details. Setting a datasheet view as the default view means anyone who navigates to the page will see the SharePoint list in the Access Web Datasheet.

Datasheet Task Pane

One feature tied directly to the Access Web Datasheet is the Access Web Datasheet task pane. Collapsed by default, the pane appears on the right side of the Web Datasheet for any SharePoint list. It exposes three entry points for features related to Access — importing, linking, and creating Access views for the SharePoint list — as well as four entry points for Excel features for creating charts, pivot tables, querying a list, and printing a list. Only the Access-related features are discussed in this section, but it's definitely worth noting the Excel features provided by the task pane — just another way Microsoft Office provides seamless integration between Office applications!

Track This List in Access

The Track this List in Access feature is a quick link that enables the user to open the list in a new or existing database. Choosing this option always creates a SharePoint-linked table in the database to the original list. This feature is designed as an easy way to create a SharePoint-linked table in an Access database, directly from the SharePoint list.

Introduced in Access 2003, the Track this List in Access link option was originally called Create Linked Table In Access. Access 2003 users will see the Create Linked Table In Access link in the task pane for both SharePoint lists. However, Track this List in Access and Create Linked Table In Access perform the same functionality: A linked table is created in a new or existing database.

When a user creates a SharePoint list in an Access database using Track this List in Access, Access uses the credentials of the user who is logged into the SharePoint site. If the SharePoint site uses NT Authentication, the next time the SharePoint-linked table is accessed in the database, the current Windows user's credentials are needed to retrieve or update the data in the list. If the credentials are not valid, the user is prompted for a username and password. In cases when the list is linked to an external SharePoint site that uses credentials different from the current Windows user's, the user is always required to input credentials for the SharePoint site containing the list for the linked table.

Export to Access

The Export to Access link in the Web Datasheet task pane provides the user with a quick interface for exporting SharePoint list data to a database file. As with Track this List in Access, the Export to Access link enables the user to choose either a new or an existing database file. This is one of many entry points for the Importing from SharePoint feature in Access, the details of which were discussed previously in this chapter. Clicking the Export to Access link automatically exports the SharePoint list to a local table in an Access database. The user has the option of choosing an existing database or a new database. Be sure to keep in mind the data conversion features discussed previously, when exporting a SharePoint list to an Access table; not all SharePoint data types are always supported, especially in the MDB file format.

Report with Access

The Report with Access link in the Web Datasheet task pane provides the user with an entry point for quickly creating Access views. As with the preceding two links in the task pane, the user has the option to create a new or choose an existing database. After the user selects the database file, a new linked table is created in the database for the SharePoint list. In addition, a new report is created and opened in Layout view mode for the user to work with. Clicking the Report with Access link is equivalent to creating a link to a SharePoint table, selecting it in the Navigation Pane, and then creating a new report based upon the linked table.

Open with Access

Introduced originally in Access 2007, the Open with Access button is available on the SharePoint Actions menu for SharePoint 2007 (version 3.0) or later. The Open with Access feature enables the user to create a linked table to a SharePoint list or to simply import the list directly. When a user chooses Open with Access for specific types of SharePoint lists, Access creates a database application template based upon the SharePoint list. As you will see shortly, these templates provide a nice simple example of exactly how an Access application can be created against a SharePoint server. The Open with Access button provides a highly visible entry point for creating linked tables in a database to a given SharePoint list.

Understanding the differences between linking to the list and importing the list is important. When the tables are linked to a SharePoint list, which is the default behavior for Open with Access, any changes made to the data in the table are pushed up to the SharePoint server. On the other hand, because an imported table resides in the new database, changes to the imported table or its data remain in the local database, and the SharePoint list remains unaffected. See the earlier discussion about the differences between importing tables and linking tables to SharePoint, and the repercussions both options have on the data and data types provided by the SharePoint list.

Access Application Templates for SharePoint

Originally introduced in Access 2007 for use with SharePoint 2007, Access provided three custom application templates that were traditional SharePoint applications corresponding to three distinct SharePoint list templates. Specifically, these Access applications mapped the SharePoint Contacts, Tasks, and Issues Tracking lists. When the Open in Access option is chosen for any of these standard SharePoint lists, and the linked tables option (the default) is chosen, the new database is created as a fully functioning Access application that is linked to SharePoint, complete with forms and reports. These templates are designed to provide an example, as well as a starting point, for creating traditional Access database applications that are bound to a SharePoint data source.

Today in Access 2010, only two of those original three still exist, as the release of the new Access Web Application features are slowly replacing these traditional Access applications linked to SharePoint. Specifically, only the Tasks and Issues SharePoint list types are still supported by this feature. The original Contacts template, which was released in Access 2007, is no longer included, but has instead been replaced by the new Contacts Web Application. This section will discuss both the Tasks and Issues templates for SharePoint, as it relates to Access 2010.

How It Works

When a user clicks the Open with Access button for one of these SharePoint list types, the Open in Microsoft Access dialog box appears, requesting the name and path for the database, as well as whether the SharePoint tables should be linked or imported. If the user selects the linked table option and enters a new database name (which is the default), then the Access SharePoint template will be invoked, and the Access application will be created. However, if the user chooses an existing database for the linked tables, only the tables and data will be linked into the existing database and the Access template will not actually be created. For the import option, with either a new or existing database name, only the tables and data for the SharePoint list are imported, so the template is not created in this case either.

Access SharePoint Tasks Template

The Access SharePoint Tasks template enables the user to work with the standard SharePoint Tasks list and data in a simple Access database application. The Tasks employs the User Information list as a lookup table for the Assigned To field in the Tasks list. That means the users of the SharePoint site can be assigned to the task, just like the SharePoint Tasks application template works. The list can even be configured to automatically send the user an e-mail to inform him when a new task has been assigned.

 The User Information list cannot be updated from an Access database because that would modify the users of the SharePoint site itself. You must add all users through interfaces available via the SharePoint site.

The Tasks application has several more forms and reports, such as a User Information list form and a Tasks List form, which provides the functionality for the Tasks application. Double-clicking any Task or User record opens in their respective List form opens the record in a details form, providing the user with access to all the fields in the SharePoint list for viewing or modification when allowed. The Tasks database application that is created from template when opening the Tasks list in Access is a great example of creating a traditional database application that uses SharePoint to store its data.

Access SharePoint Issue Tracking Template

The Access SharePoint Issue Tracking template is the more complex of the two templates, and is designed to show off the features of the ACCDB file format. This template is actually much different than the Issues Web Application template that is included with Access 2010, mainly in the fact that it is linked to SharePoint site lists, instead of being a true Access Web Application. The Issue Tracking template demonstrates working with Multi-Valued Lookup, Append Only, and Column History fields in a traditional Access database application that uses SharePoint as its data source. The Issue Tracking database application is another great example of how a traditional Access database application can be developed against SharePoint lists, without having to create a full Access Web Application.

Using the AppendOnly Property

Append Only fields are available in SharePoint linked tables as well as native Access tables. To provide the Append Only functionality, the Issue Tracking application for SharePoint employs the `AppendOnly` property on the `Memo` field type. When the `AppendOnly` property is set to `True`, any change to the data is concatenated on the previous value, instead of replacing the previous value. This property is an excellent way to ensure that the history of the data in a table's field is preserved in the database.

In the SharePoint Issues template, type a few words into the New Comment box on the Comments tab of the Issues Details form and close the form. Repeat this several times. You should notice that a bunch of different values are stored in the History field in this form. If the `Comments` field in the `Issues` table is viewed directly, the user sees only the most recent entry for the fields and no previous entries. The same is true when the field data is retrieved via code — only the most recent data entered into the field will be returned.

Using the ColumnHistory Method

The `ColumnHistory` method is a member of the `Application` object. It enables you to retrieve the full data history for an Append Only field. The `AppendOnly` field property is available only for the `Memo` data type and can be set to `True` in the table properties. The `ColumnHistory` method takes three parameters: `TableName`, `ColumnName`, and `QueryString`, each of which is required.

`TableName` obviously takes the name of the table that contains the Append Only field and the `ColumnName` is the name of the Append Only field itself. However, the `QueryString` parameter is really the where condition for the SQL statement, without the WHERE SQL keyword. This type of parameter is common in functions throughout the Access Object Model and is often referred to as the filter string. Using the `ColumnHistory` function requires all three parameters be passed to the function, which means that the field data history can be returned for only one record at a time.

For example, the `ColumnHistory` method could be called to retrieve the `ColumnHistory` string of a given record in the `Comments` field of the `Issues` table:

Available for download on Wrox.com

```
Function GetCommentHistoryForRecord(iRecordId As Integer) As String

    ` Return the ColumnHistory data for the `Comments` field
    GetCommentHistoryForRecord = _
        Application.ColumnHistory( _
            `Issues`, _
            `Comments`, _
            `[ID]=` & iRecordId)

End Function
```

code snippet module ExampleCode in Ch19_Sample.accdb

As in the SharePoint Issues database case, you can tie the `ColumnHistory` function directly to the `RecordSource` property of a Text Box control in a form or report. Because the function is marked as a safe macro, `ColumnHistory` will run when tied to the `RecordSource` for the control, without requiring that code be enabled in the application. In the Issue Details form, the `TableName` parameter actually is passed as the `RecordSource` property for the form. The `TableName` parameter accepts any table or query that returns a `Memo` field type. The `ColumnHistory` method is quite powerful when you're working with Append Only fields in either a SharePoint list or native Access tables.

Creating SharePoint Templates with NewCurrentDatabase

The `NewCurrentDatabase` method is a member of the `Application` object. In Access 2003 and earlier, this method took only one parameter — the filename and path to the new database that is to be created. In Access 2010 (and 2007), `NewCurrentDatabase` takes five parameters. In addition to creating a new database, you can also create a database from an application template, a database linked to a SharePoint list, or even one of the built-in SharePoint templates linked to a SharePoint site. The following table describes each of the parameters available for `NewCurrentDatabase`.

PARAMETER	DESCRIPTION
filePath	Required. The full name and path for the database that will be created. If the database already exists, the `NewCurrentDatabase` method will fail.
FileFormat	The version of database that will be created, as defined by the `AcNewDatabaseFormat` enumeration. Three database version types are available: Access 2007 file format (ACCDB), Access 2002–2003 file format (MDB), and Access 2000 file format (MDB). Optional; if not supplied, the database created will be the default file format selected in the Access Options on the Popular tab. The same is true if the Default Format member of the enumeration is passed. However, ACCDT database templates can only be created databases in the ACCDB file format.
Template	The full file path to the Access Database Template (ACCDT) file. This can be either a standalone database template or a template for an application linked to SharePoint. Optional, but if supplied, a new database from the template will be created in the instance of Access.
SiteAddress	Specifies the URL path to the SharePoint site that a new database or template will be created and linked to. The parameter should be passed in the format `http://MySharePointSite`. Optional; if passed with the `Template` and `ListID` parameters, it will create a SharePoint database template linked to the new database.
ListID	Specifies the Name or the GUID list ID for the list on the SharePoint site. Optional; if passed with the `Template` and `SiteAddress` parameters, it creates a SharePoint database template linked to the new database. If specified as a GUID, the format should be a `String` such as: `{5604F321-4F9F-481B-AF53-C1D795EE2398}`.

These parameters provide all the information needed to create new databases, databases with linked tables to SharePoint, and databases from templates. Here's an example of creating the Access SharePoint Issues templates linked to a SharePoint site:

```
Sub CreateSharePointLinkedTemplate()

    ` Define Variables
    Dim accessApp As New Access.Application

    ` Create a new copy of the Access SharePoint Issues template
    accessApp.Visible = True
    accessApp.NewCurrentDatabase _
        `C:\SharePointTemplate.accdb", _
        acNewDatabaseFormatAccess2007, _
        `C:\Program Files\Microsoft " & _
        `Office\Templates\1033\Access\WSS\1100.accdt", _
        `http://MySharePointSite/`, _
        `{5604F321-4F9F-481B-AF53-C1D795EE2398}`

    ` Clean up
    Set accessApp = Nothing

End Sub
```

code snippet module ExampleCode in Ch19_Sample.accdb

Of course, the URL and the GUID used in the last two parameters of this `NewCurrentDatabase` call need to be updated to the specific SharePoint site settings before the code works with your site.

 A quick method for getting the GUID for a given SharePoint list is to decipher it from the URL. The list's List Settings page shows the GUID for the list in the Address bar for Internet Explorer. However, the non-hexadecimal characters are encoded in the URL, and you must reconstruct the GUID, removing any encoded characters.

Although you can create the Access SharePoint templates with linked tables to SharePoint sites, only specific templates corresponding to the specific list types will work in this case — the `1100.accdt` file corresponds to the SharePoint Issue Tracking list and the `107.accdt` corresponds to the SharePoint Tasks list. Although these template filenames seem arbitrary, the numbers actually correspond to the SharePoint list template ID for which they will be created. That's how the Open with Access feature maps the particular list type to the correct Access database template.

Open with Access for Non-Template Linked Lists

Using Open with Access for any SharePoint list types other than the Issues or Tasks lists and choosing linked tables simply creates new linked tables in a new database or, if chosen, an existing database. When completing this operation, the user always gets two lists: the primary list from which the Open with Access option was invoked and the User Information list, which describes information about the users of the SharePoint site. These linked tables are standard SharePoint linked tables and are discussed further later in this chapter.

As noted earlier, the `NewCurrentDatabase` Object Model allows creation of a database with tables linked to a SharePoint site. To do this, simply call `NewCurrentDatabase` without the `Template` parameter. The following code illustrates the creation of a new database with tables linked to SharePoint:

Available for download on Wrox.com

```
Sub CreateSharePointLinkedDatabaseTemplate()

    ` Define Variables
    Dim accessApp As New Access.Application

    ` Create a new instance of the Access SharePoint Issues template
    accessApp.Visible = True
    accessApp.NewCurrentDatabase _
      `C:\SharePointTemplate.accdb`, _
      acNewDatabaseFormatAccess2007, , _
      `http://MySharePointSite/`, _
      `{5604F321-4F9F-481B-AF53-C1D795EE2398}`

    ` Clean up
    Set accessApp = Nothing

End Sub
```

code snippet module ExampleCode in Ch19_Sample.accdb

As with the first `NewCurrentDatabase` code example, you must update the URL and the GUID to the specific SharePoint site and list settings before this code will work with your SharePoint site.

Importing from SharePoint

An exceptionally useful feature in Access is the capability to import table data and schema directly from a SharePoint list. A number of methods are available for importing this information, such as the Export to Access link in the Web Datasheet Task pane and the Open with Access feature, as noted earlier. Using VBA code, importing data from a SharePoint list programmatically is easy. Also, a couple of approaches exist for importing data directly from SharePoint within the Access client. This section explores importing SharePoint list schema and data into an Access database.

Importing from SharePoint 2010 into an ACCDB

Fortunately, Access supports most of the data types that SharePoint 2010 (version 4.0) supports. However, some differences exist about how data is imported for certain types of fields, such as Lookup or Person or Group type fields. Additionally, a number of fields are not shown in either the Default view or the Column Settings page that are imported along with the rest of the fields in the list. When importing lists from SharePoint, understanding how these fields are treated by Access and exactly what fields in the table are created is important.

Because a couple of SharePoint data types are converted during import, take a look at how Access treats each of the types. The following table describes the data types for SharePoint and the Access type that the SharePoint type is imported as.

SHAREPOINT 2010 DATA TYPE	ACCESS DATA TYPE (TO ACCDB)
Single Line of Text	`Text` — No change.
Multiple Lines of Text	`Memo` — The standard Rich Text setting is persisted into the imported table. However, SharePoint provides two types of rich text: Rich Text and Enhanced Rich Text. Enhanced Rich Text fields support some HTML tags that are not supported by Rich Text fields in Access. The normal Rich Text fields are recommended when creating a SharePoint list that will be used with an Access database solution.
Choice	`Text` — The values for the choices are imported into the `Row Source` property for the imported field, and the `RowSourceType` property is set to `Value List`.
Number	`Number` — Double precision; no change.
Data and Time	`Date/Time` — No change.
Currency	`Currency` — The `Format` and `DecimalPlaces` properties are persisted.
Lookup	`Memo` — The display values for the lookup are inserted into the imported table instead of a second lookup table being created.
Yes/No	`Yes/No` — No change.

SHAREPOINT 2010 DATA TYPE	ACCESS DATA TYPE (TO ACCDB)
Person or Group	`Memo` — The display values for the lookup are inserted into the imported table instead of a second lookup table being created.
Hyperlink or Picture	`Hyperlink` — The data is imported as a link to the image file.
Calculated	For Access 2010, `Calculated` — No change. Access 2007 ACCDB files are dependent upon the type that the column returns. After the field has been imported, only the display values for the `Calculated` field are imported and the table in Access no longer calculates this field.
Multiple Value Fields	Complex data fields of the same type.
Attachment Fields	`Attachment` — No change.
Append Only Fields	`Memo` — With the `AppendOnly` property set to `False`. Only the value for the last edit is persisted during the import.

In addition to any tables created by the user, a standard custom template includes a number of additional fields that are imported automatically: `ID`, `Encoded Absolute URL`, `Item Type`, `Path`, `URL Path`, and `Workflow Instance ID`. The `ID` field is imported as an `AutoNumber` field and can be used for the primary key for the table. The rest are imported as `Text` fields.

The ACCDB file format supports importing the schema and data from SharePoint well. Almost every SharePoint field type is supported, except for Enhanced Rich Text, in the same format in which it's stored on SharePoint. Although MDB database files also support importing tables from SharePoint 2010, a developer should be aware of several more data conversions when importing a SharePoint list.

Importing from SharePoint 2010 into an MDB

Although the Access MDB file formats do support importing SharePoint 2010 (version 4.0) lists, a few more field types will be converted when imported. For example, complex data and attachments are not supported in the MDB file format and therefore cannot be imported into an MDB as those data types. The following table compares the SharePoint data types to the Access data types after conversion when importing into an MDB file.

SHAREPOINT 2010 DATA TYPE	ACCESS DATA TYPE (TO MDB)
Single Line of Text	`Text` — No change.
Multiple Lines of Text	`Memo` — Rich Text setting is not persisted into the imported table because it is not supported in the MDB file format.

continues

(continued)

SHAREPOINT 2010 DATA TYPE	ACCESS DATA TYPE (TO MDB)
Choice	`Text` — Values for the choices are also imported into the Row Source property for the imported field.
Number	`Number` — Double precision; no change.
Data and Time	`Date/Time` — No change.
Currency	`Currency` — The `Format` and `DecimalPlaces` properties will be persisted.
Lookup	`Memo` — Display values for the lookup are inserted into the imported table instead of a second lookup table being created.
Yes/No	`Yes/No` — No change.
Person or Group	`Memo` — Display values for the lookup are inserted into the imported table instead of a second lookup table being created.
Hyperlink or Picture	`Hyperlink` — Data is imported as a link, or a link to the image file.
Calculated	Dependent upon the type that the column returns. After the field has been imported, only the display values for the `Calculated` field are imported and the table in Access no longer calculates this field.
Multiple Value Fields	`Memo` — Because complex data is not supported in the MDB file format, the data is imported as a comma-separated list for each of the values selected.
Attachment Fields	`Yes/No` — Because `Attachment` fields are not supported in an MDB, the field is converted to a `Yes/No` field. The value of this field corresponds to whether the record had an attachment in the original SharePoint list.
Append Only Fields	`Memo` — With the `AppendOnly` property set to `False`. Only the value for the last edit is persisted during the import.

When importing into an MDB from a SharePoint 2010 list, multiple value fields are converted to `Memo` data type fields and a loss in granularity occurs for each individual option that was selected. Still, the full data set that was stored in the original multiple value field is present, only it is now grouped in the new `Memo` field and each individual value is separated by commas. Probably the biggest loss in functionality when importing into an MDB is the `Attachment` field conversion, because that particular field is converted to a `Yes/No` field type in Access. Otherwise, not much of a difference exists between importing into an ACCDB file and an MDB file. Even with these field conversions, importing data from SharePoint into an MDB file is extremely easy.

Importing from SharePoint Using VBA Code

Aside from being able to import data into Access from the SharePoint entry point, a developer can also import a SharePoint list programmatically using VBA code from within Access. The

`TransferSharePointList` method allows a developer to either import or link to a SharePoint list programmatically. `TransferSharePointList` is a method of the `DoCmd` class, which is a member of the `Application` object. `TransferSharePointList` takes up to six arguments, three of which are required. The following table describes each of these arguments.

PARAMETER	DESCRIPTION
TransferType	Requires a member of the enumeration type `AcSharePointListTransferType`. Two options are available: `acImportSharePointList` and `acLinkSharePointList`.
SiteAddress	The full URL path to the SharePoint site. This parameter is required.
ListID	The Name or the GUID of the list to be transferred. This parameter is required.
ViewID	The GUID of the view that should be imported. This means that imported data can be pre-filtered by a specific list view on SharePoint before pulling the data into Access. This parameter is optional and not available for when the `acImportSharePointList` option is chosen for the transfer type. If not specified, all the fields on the SharePoint site will be retrieved.
TableName	The name of the new linked table in the database. This parameter is optional and not available for when the `acImportSharePointList` option is chosen for the transfer type. If not specified, the name of the SharePoint list will be used for the new table in the database.
GetLookupDisplayValues	When `False`, any lookup fields will contain the IDs to the list to which the lookup is tied. When `True`, the actual display values will be imported. This parameter is optional and not available for when the `acImportSharePointList` option is chosen for the `TransferType`.

Importing SharePoint data into an Access database is extremely easy to do. Just remember that when importing data, only the first three parameters (the non-optional parameters) to the `TransferSharePointList` method must be supplied; otherwise, an error message is raised when the code runs. Here's an example of a simple subroutine for importing a list from SharePoint:

Available for download on Wrox.com

```
Sub ImportSharePointList()

    ' Call TransferSharePointList to import the data
    Application.DoCmd.TransferSharePointList _
        acLinkSharePointList, _
        `http://MySharePointSite/`, _
        `Tasks`

End Sub
```

code snippet module ExampleCode in Ch19_Sample.accdb

Writing code for a single import operation may not be cost effective or the easier way for a user to import SharePoint lists into a database. In addition to the entry points for creating an import table in Access from the SharePoint site, a user interface is also available for importing a SharePoint list from within the Access UI.

Importing through the Access User Interface

Although this section of the chapter is devoted to discussing operations that are available on a SharePoint site, let's briefly discuss the import options available directly in the Access client. Importing data into Access is simple and fast, and the import operation parameters can even be saved for future imports. When any database is open in the Access client window (and the standard Ribbon options have not been disabled), the user sees a tab called External Data. That tab allows the user to work with all different kinds of Import (and Export) options and provides a collection of all of these entry points. You can import a SharePoint list with just a few simple clicks using the features that the Access user interface provides. Complete the following steps to import a SharePoint list into Access 2010 using the Access UI:

1. Open any normal database in the Access client window. Note, this cannot be an Access Web database, because they do not allow local tables.

2. Click the External Data tab on the Ribbon to select it.

3. On the External Data tab, click on the More button in the Import & Link group. A Ribbon flyout menu appears with several more options; click on the SharePoint List option. This invokes the Get External Data Wizard.

4. On the Get External Data Wizard, provide the URL to the SharePoint site you want to import the table from. For example, enter a URL in the format:

   ```
   http://www.MySharePointSite.com/
   ```

5. After entering the URL, select the Import radio button to specify importing the table, which is not selected by default. Then click the Next button on the wizard.

6. The second page of the wizard simply allows you to select any lists on the site to import or link. Ensure Import is selected and then click OK.

7. The last page of the wizard enables you to save the import steps if desired. Otherwise, click the Close button; the focus returns to the Access client window.

The new tables are imported from the specified SharePoint site and are now ready for use. If any problems occurred during the import, an Import Errors table will be created with a list of the problems that were encountered. Also, we recommend saving the steps involved in importing a list that will be imported regularly. In this manner, importing the same job next time will only take a few seconds, and you can even schedule the task so that it runs at incremental times.

Access Views on SharePoint

The last Access feature for working with SharePoint is the Access Views on SharePoint feature. An Access view is a form or report that is advertised on the SharePoint view menu for any given list. These views are invoked from the SharePoint list and open the database object in the Access client when selected. Views are a great way to show off a traditional database application that is linked to a SharePoint list.

There are two methods in the SharePoint UI for opening the Create View page for a list:

➤ Select List ➪ Create View on the list's main page.

➤ Select Settings ➪ Create View for the list.

The Create View page is the starting point for making any view for a SharePoint list. When Access is not installed on the machine, four options are available for creating new views on the Create View page: Standard View, Calendar View, Datasheet View, and Gantt View. The Datasheet view utilizes the Access Web Datasheet. It does not work when users try to open the view until Access is installed on the client machine. All other view options on the Create View page should be viewable when created, even if Office or Access is not installed.

When Access is installed on the machine, the Create View page shows one additional option: Access View. When the user selects that option, a new instance of Access opens, prompting the user to choose a save location for a new database. Then the Create Access View dialog box opens, enabling the user to choose a specific form factor for a new form or report for the view. The option he chooses has a link created from the SharePoint view menu to the view in the database. Whenever the user selects the view, the machine launches the Access database and opens the particular form or report.

If the default view for a list is set to an Access view, the Access database launches automatically any time a user navigates to the list. That's a good way to force people to use a particular Access application to view and modify data for a SharePoint list. However, users of the site who do not have Access 2007 or higher installed may have problems viewing the list, so be sure to use this feature cautiously.

Because the database created from the SharePoint Access View option is saved on the local machine, publishing the database to a document library on the SharePoint site is always a good idea so that other users have access to the database. When the list is published, a dialog box asks whether the view links in the SharePoint views menu should be updated. If these are updated when the list is published, the view link redirects the user to the database stored in the document library. Views are a powerful way to provide users with the rich view options that Microsoft Office Access offers.

Advertising Access Views on the View Menu

Creating an Access view from the SharePoint View menu is extremely easy, although it is somewhat cumbersome if the user wants to create multiple views for the list. In most cases, it is far more likely that the database creator wants to design the views for the application long before the SharePoint list has even been created. Fortunately, Access provides developers with the capability to create these views programmatically.

When a database application is migrated to a SharePoint site with the Move to SharePoint wizard, each table in the database has a corresponding SharePoint list created if the check box is selected for that particular table in the wizard. Additionally, all the forms and reports in the database have the chance to be advertised on the View menu for the new SharePoint lists. The form or report will be shown if the `RecordSource` property contains a reference to the list and the `DisplayOnSharePointSite` property is set to `FollowTableSetting`.

Using the DisplayOnSharePointSite Property

One of the conditions for advertising the view on SharePoint is that the `DisplayOnSharePointSite` property is set. That property is available for both forms and reports and you can set it directly through the Property Sheet in Access. It has two possible values: Follow Table Setting and Do Not Display, which are self-explanatory. If you choose the Follow Table Setting option, the view displayed is dependent on the table's `DisplayViewsOnSharePointSite` property setting.

Much like the `DisplayOnSharePointSite` property for forms and reports, each table has a `DisplayViewsOnSharePointSite` property. It also has two possible settings: Follow Database Setting and Do Not Display. Needless to say, the Do Not Display option causes any form or report tied to the list not to be displayed automatically. Otherwise, there is a database property setting to have these views displayed on SharePoint.

The `DisplayAllViewsOnSharePointSite` property is the database property that determines whether the forms and reports in the database are advertised in the SharePoint list's View menu. This property is not shown in the normal database properties of the `CurrentDb` object. To see it, in the Access client choose File ➪ Manage ➪ Database Properties. If the `DisplayAllViewsOnSharePointSite` property is set to 1, all the views for forms and reports will be advertised if the corresponding properties for the form or report object and the table object are set to display the views.

You can also determine the `DisplayAllViewsOnSharePointSite` property setting by using a bit of VBA code. As mentioned previously, this property cannot be retrieved from the `Properties` object from the `CurrentDb` object. To get the object's value, you need to do something slightly different: Retrieve the value from the `UserDefined` properties in the database document. The following function is an example of how the `DisplayAllViewsOnSharePointSite` property can be retrieved in code:

```
Function GetSharePointPropertySetting() As String

On Error GoTo errHandler

    ` Define Variables
    Dim db As DAO.Database
    Dim doc As DAO.Document
    Dim prp As DAO.Property

    ` Get the property from the custom properties
    Set db = Application.CurrentDb
    Set doc = db.Containers!Databases.Documents!UserDefined
    Set prp = doc.Properties(`DisplayAllViewsOnSharePointSite")

    ` Return the value
```

```
    GetSharePointPropertySetting = prp.value
    GoTo CleanUp

errHandler:

    ` If an error is encountered, the property was not present
    GetSharePointPropertySetting = `0"

CleanUp:

    ` Clean up
    Set prp = Nothing
    Set doc = Nothing
    Set db = Nothing
    Exit Function

End Function
```

code snippet module ExampleCode in Ch19_Sample.accdb

Similarly, if the database does not already have this custom property set, or if the property needs to be set programmatically, you can create a subroutine to set it. Here's an example of how to set `DisplayAllViewsOnSharePointSite`, or any custom property, programmatically:

```
Sub SetSharePointPropertySetting(iValue As Integer)

    On Error GoTo errHandler

    ` Define Variables
    Dim db As DAO.Database
    Dim doc As DAO.Document
    Dim prp As DAO.Property

    ` Get the property from the custom properties
    Set db = Application.CurrentDb
    Set doc = db.Containers!Databases.Documents!UserDefined
    Set prp = doc.Properties("DisplayAllViewsOnSharePointSite")

    ` Return the value
    prp.value = iValue
    GoTo CleanUp

errHandler:

    ` If an error is encountered, the property was not present, so create it
    Set prp = db.CreateProperty( _
        `DisplayAllViewsOnSharePointSite", dbLong, iValue)
    doc.Properties.Append prp

CleanUp:

    ` Clean up
```

```
        Set prp = Nothing
        Set doc = Nothing
        Set db = Nothing
        Exit Sub

    End Sub
```

code snippet module ExampleCode in Ch19_Sample.accdb

This code is easy to create if you need custom document properties for the database. Whether you're using the Access UI or VBA code to set the `DisplayAllViewsOnSharePointSite` property, it is sure to be simple and quick.

SUMMARY

Microsoft Windows SharePoint Server 2010 is more powerful than ever and integrates with Access 2010 like never before. Access developers now have the capability to leverage much of the rich tool set that SharePoint provides by developing Access Web Applications that harness centralized application management, data management, and application distribution features provided by the SharePoint technology.

Aside from just the new Access Web Applications, the other, pre-existing SharePoint features are also extremely simple to incorporate into an Access application, traditional application or Web application. The Access Web Datasheet enables users to edit multiple records in the SharePoint list directly from their Web browsers. They can export or link SharePoint list data to an Access database quickly with features such as the Open with Access button or the Web Datasheet task pane. Access supports importing and linking to more SharePoint data types than ever before, and the entry points are very easy to find on SharePoint. Developers creating or migrating existing Access solutions can easily perform this operation using the Move to SharePoint functionality. Users can publish databases to a SharePoint site, allowing them to be used in Access applications in the same manner as working with other Office documents on a SharePoint server. And last, but not least, you can create Access Views that invoke Access applications automatically when the user selects the view from the SharePoint site.

With all of these features, running SharePoint Server 2010 with Microsoft Office 2010 Professional is a compelling business scenario. Both developers and users can take advantage of the integration between SharePoint and Access at a low cost. Be sure to consider using SharePoint technologies to leverage your Access database solution when it is a viable option for your customers.

20

Working with .NET

WHAT'S IN THIS CHAPTER?

➤ An Overview of .NET and Visual Studio 2010

➤ Creating .NET applications that use Access databases

➤ Automating Access using .NET and COM Interop Services

➤ Creating .NET Add-ins for Access 2010

➤ Creating Managed Code Libraries that can be called from VBA code in an Access application.

Simply put, .NET (pronounced "dot-net") is Microsoft's current software development platform for its Windows operating system. .NET provides a unified development platform and interface for all of Microsoft's current assemblies, tools, and languages. This includes many methods for working with Access 2010 databases and the client application itself, both directly and indirectly through the use of other libraries and code. This chapter is devoted to discussing a few of the major integration points between .NET and Access 2010 and will provide some code examples about how to implement these features.

Although this chapter does cover a number of the more common features, it is far from a complete reference of the .NET integration points with Access. We recommend that you read more about any of the topics covered here, or other any other .NET- and Access-related topics, on the free MSDN Library online at `http://msdn.microsoft.com`. The MSDN Library is Microsoft's definitive development handbook for any and all of its code and libraries that are open to developers. And, best of all, the online version is completely free and is only a few browser clicks away!

OVERVIEW

One of the most underutilized, underrated, and misunderstood features of Access 2010 is its ability to integrate with .NET in so many different ways and the sheer power each of these methods provides. This chapter will discuss the following integration points between .NET and Access 2010:

➤ **Using Access databases:** ACCDB and MDB files can be used by .NET applications simply as a database. The database can have standard SQL commands issued against it to provide the application with a mechanism for storing data.

➤ **Automating Access with .NET:** Access 2010, along with the other Microsoft Office applications, provides a PIA (Primary Interop Assembly) for automating the client application and its features via .NET code. This allows .NET developers to have code access to things such as the Access Object Model as you would when creating an Access application with VBA code.

➤ **Creating COM Add-ins for Access:** Access 2010 allows for the use of COM (Component Object Model) Add-ins directly within the client application. COM Add-ins are a very popular template for creating Add-ins for COM applications, can be either generic or specific to the application, and are often used to link the functionality from two different COM applications together.

➤ **Using .NET code in Access:** VBE (Visual Basic Editor) supports referencing COM assemblies and using them within VBA code. Almost any .NET assembly can be compiled to a COM component with a bit of work. This means that a developer can create custom code in .NET, utilizing all of its tools and features, and then call that code from VBA in an Access Application.

Each of these integration points is different and thus their features all provide different benefits and have different drawbacks, depending on their uses. While these are the major direct integration points between .NET and Access 2010, this is not the limit of features between Access and .NET. The following sections of this chapter will discuss each of these four integration points in-depth, but first, some of the basics of Visual Studio and .NET need to be defined to begin discussing how these two platforms integrate.

Example Files

All of the code examples that are included in this chapter are available for download from the Wiley website. We highly recommend that you use these files in conjunction with the material found in this chapter. To download the files for this chapter, go to:

```
www.wiley.com/WileyCDA/WileyTitle/productCd-0470591668.html
```

This link will take you to the Web page for this book, so select the download tab on this page to download any of the sample files.

VISUAL STUDIO .NET 2010

In addition to the monumental release of Office 2010, Microsoft has also released its latest and great version of Visual Studio and .NET 4.0 with the release of Visual Studio 2010. Visual Studio 2010 is Microsoft's IDE (Integrated Development Environment) for designing, building, testing, debugging, releasing, and maintaining .NET applications. Visual Studio 2010 comes in several different flavors, depending on which set of tools are required for your project, but unfortunately most are not free. The Visual Studio 2010 Express Editions are the only free version of Visual Studio provided by Microsoft, but these will provide all of the tools necessary for working with Access 2010, although, this will also require that you have Access 2010 and its PIA installed to implement some of these integration points. The examples in this chapter will assume that the user has both Microsoft Office 2010 Professional (or higher) as well as one of the Visual Studio 2010 Express Editions installed.

This section will discuss how to get and set up the various Visual Studio 2010 .NET Express Editions. Then we will discuss some basic .NET terminologies and technologies to provide some basic definitions. And finally, there will be some brief examples of creating a project, writing some code, and then building, executing, and debugging that code. Once you understand these basics of working with .NET, the following sections will discuss each of the four major integration points between .NET and Access. But first, let's take a look at Visual Studio 2010.

 Although the examples in this book use and refer to both VS 2010 and Office 2010, older versions of VS and Office support interoperability. If you are using an older version of Office or VS, most of the features discussed in this chapter will still be available. Refer to your specific product's documentation on the Microsoft website for more information.

Getting Visual Studio 2010

It's very easy to get the Visual Studio 2010 Express Editions. Simply download any of them directly from Microsoft's Visual Studio Express downloads page at:

```
www.microsoft.com/express/Downloads/
```

Once at the Visual Studio home page, choose the Products option from the menu, and then select the Visual Studio 2010 option from the submenu. This will take you to the Visual Studio 2010 home page. From this page, you should see options for downloading the Visual Studio 2010 Express Editions. Choosing any one of these options will provide instructions for completing the download and installing the product.

Note that there are multiple flavors of the Express Editions available for download. For this chapter, we assume that both the Visual Studio C# (pronounced *cee-sharp*) and Web Developer versions are installed. However, if you want to use Visual Basic .NET, which is often more familiar to VBA programmers than C#, you should install that version of the Visual Basic edition of Visual Studio Express as well. Any and all of the Express editions can be installed side-by-side without discretion, including major versions of Visual Studio (as with Access), which is just another one of the beauties of the Visual Studio product line.

In addition to providing a download version, Microsoft provides a direct Web installation service for installing the 2010 Express editions, as it did with Visual Studio 2008, which means that you won't have to manually download and then perform a separate installation. Also, you can purchase any of the retail versions of Visual Studio, which often come on a DVD and can be installed directly from the disk. This saves you the download time, which can be quite extensive because the installation package is over 2 gigabytes in size for full Visual Studio 2010 Pro, and the Visual Studio

Express edition ISO (which includes all versions) is almost 700 megabytes. The good news is, with so many options available, getting a copy of Visual Studio should be a breeze.

Installing Visual Studio 2010

Once the Visual Studio installation package has been started, the user will have several options available during the setup process. While it is beyond the scope of this book to discuss all available options for the Visual Studio setup process, we recommend that you select the Complete installation option when prompted. This will ensure that all options are available for use when needed and can save you the time and headache in the future of having to set up pieces of Visual Studio down the road. The Visual Studio setup will most likely take several hours, so most people want to minimize the number of times they have to endure this process. Not to worry, though — once the Visual Studio installation has been completed, the power that these tools provide is well worth the wait!

Installing Visual Studio before Access

One other thing to consider about setting up a machine to develop with both .NET and the Office 2010 system is the order in which the components were added to the machine. We recommend that the user install Visual Studio first and then install Microsoft Office (or Access, depending on the version chosen) because this will make a difference in the Office installation options. If .NET is detected on the system, then a complete installation of Office will install the interop assemblies for .NET. Once these tools have been installed, you can begin developing .NET applications with the functionality supplied by any of the supported Office applications.

Installing Access before Visual Studio

If Access, or Office, is installed prior to installing .NET or the Visual Studio package, the .NET tools for Office will not be installed. In this case, you can go back and reinstall the Office .NET components once Visual Studio has been installed to the machines. This can be accomplished by running the original Office setup program again from the disk or network location, or by modifying the setup options for Office in Programs under the Windows Control Panel. When going back through the Office installation, simply select the Custom option and manually select the .NET components for installation. Also, choosing a Complete installation of Office in the options will have the same effect. However, in either case, the Visual Studio tools will have to be installed prior to the .NET tools for Office being installed. Once the .NET tools for Office have been installed, you can begin working with the Access PIA and other supported Office features in .NET.

.NET Terminology

Before you begin writing some .NET code, it is important to discuss some basic terminology used in .NET and define what each of these items are. The following is a list of these .NET terms to be aware of:

➤ **Assembly:** A versioned piece of compiled code, usually compiled into a single file, such as a DLL or EXE. Assemblies can be, and in most cases are, self-describing by providing metadata about the assembly directly within the assembly.

➤ **Class:** A class represents a custom, user-defined object that can include data members, methods, and events, specified by the developer. A class in Visual Basic .NET is essentially the same as it is in Access, and Visual Basic .NET supports both class modules and standard modules. In C#, all code must be defined inside of a class, and every object in C# is a class, or defined as part of one.

➤ **Namespace:** A logical grouping and versioning of classes in an assembly, providing a mechanism for both organizing functionality within an assembly and defining which object should be used when compiling and executing code. Namespaces also allow for two classes with the same name to be used in the same block of code because the namespace is used to reference the correct object and defines which version of the object should be used.

➤ **.NET Framework 4.0:** A latest and greatest collection of namespaces, classes, and assemblies that make up the basis of the .NET language and its components. These are all of the components that are included with .NET by default, and almost all code written in .NET will utilize the framework in one way or another. Version 4.0 has been released with Visual Studio 2010.

➤ **Common Intermediate Language (CIL):** Previously known as the MSIL (Microsoft Intermediate Language), the CIL is a set of ordered byte-code that is, in turn, interpreted and executed by the CLR (Common Language Runtime). By default, when an assembly is compiled in .NET, no matter which language is used, the code is converted to CIL code to be executed by the CLR when the assembly is called, which helps the code be platform-independent, another nice feature of .NET. And, it is also possible to generate a direct executable by selecting the compilation options in Visual Studio, but the default options are recommended in most cases.

➤ **Common Language Runtime (CLR):** The base of the .NET Framework, the CLR is responsible for executing all .NET CIL assemblies. As such, all CIL assemblies can be platform-independent, but this also requires that the CLR package be platform-specific. For a language to be managed by the CLR, it must be compilable to CIL code and must adhere to the Common Language Specification (CLS).

➤ **Common Language Specifications (CLS):** The CLS defines a set of common software language features and a common type system that must be supported by .NET-managed languages. Some languages, such as C#, can also define types that are not defined or supported within the CLS, but in this case, such code will not be executable by the CLR. The developer will need to compile code not supported by the CLS to an executable binary file, which will be platform-dependent.

➤ **Global Assembly Cache (GAC):** A global directory on the machine where .NET assemblies can be installed so that they can be called from any other code executing on the machines. By default, when executing code that references a separate assembly, the CLR first checks the current directory for the assembly, and if not found there, secondarily checks the GAC for the assembly. The GAC directory created by the .NET Framework installation package is found at `%windir%\Assembly`. Because assemblies are versioned in .NET, different versions of the same assembly (same name) can exist in the GAC folder. In that case, the code project will specify the specific assembly version that should be used for the reference.

> ➤ **Primary Interop Assembly (PIA):** A managed code assembly that provides an API (Application Program Interface) to a COM type library. PIAs are typically provided by the author of the type library and can be referenced like other assemblies in a .NET code project. Microsoft Office installs a number of PIAs, such as `Microsoft.Interop.Access.dll` and `Microsoft.Interop.Excel.dll`, which are used by .NET to work directly with their respective Office applications.

> ➤ **Interface:** Used by some programming languages to define a contract that an implementing class must adhere to. An interface is implemented to specify custom, user-defined functionality for a particular class type, which is the interface itself. The properties, methods, and events required by an interface must be implemented in any class that derives from it, so that all callers of the interface class can do so uniformly.

> ➤ **Constructor:** A special method of a class, used by some programming languages (but not VBA), that is called when a new instance of it is created. The constructor always has the same name as the class it is defined in and does not specify a return type. The *Default Constructor*, which is the most basic constructor and is always included with a compiled assembly, does not include any parameters. If not explicitly defined by the developer in code, an empty default constructor will be created when the code is compiled (though not shown in the source code). Optionally, multiple constructors for a class can be specified by implementing *Overloaded Constructors*, which are constructors with parameters added to the method.

While these are the definitions of just a few of the terms used when referring to .NET topics, this should provide a pretty good basis of knowledge for .NET and the basic concepts and components it provides. For more about .NET, there is a plethora of information related to .NET and all of its components, which can found on the MSDN Library website.

Writing Code in Visual Studio 2010

Visual Studio (VS) 2010 provides all of the tools needed to build and deploy software applications using .NET. The first time you start VS, you will be presented with a dialog box to choose the default settings. Depending on which language you are most comfortable with, you must choose the appropriate option. For the purposes of this book, I will be using C# development settings, but any option you choose will be fine; this simply sets the IDE settings and hotkeys, which can always be changed later using the VS Options dialog box. Once you have chosen your settings, you will be taken to the Visual Studio 2010 Start Page, shown in Figure 20-1.

Much like VBE, the VS IDE has a Code Window, Object Browser, a Project Pane, IntelliSense, Code Completion, and built-in debugging tools. Although VS also provides a host of other tools and features not found in VBE, the look and feel of the application is similar enough to VBE that the coding experience is much the same. But, before you can start coding, the first thing to do is to create a new project.

Creating a New Project

VS uses the concept of a Solution file, which is a project file to store information about all of the code projects, files, and other project data, used for a given software project. Additionally, each Solution file contains the Project files for each code project in the solution. Although it is possible to open and edit code files in Visual Studio without a Solution or Project file loaded, you cannot build or execute to debug those files in VS without these, so we recommend that you create Solution and Project files for any code you create in Visual Studio. The Solution is named with the file extension `.sln`, and the raw data is stored as XML data in the file. The SLN file extension gets registered in Windows to VS when installed, so double-clicking any SLN file will open the code project in VS. The Project file will have a file extension according to the name of the .NET language used, but for C# the extension of Project is `.csproj`. Fortunately, VS will do all the work to build and maintain the Solution and Project files for you, as long as you use the VS IDE to make all modifications to the project and code settings.

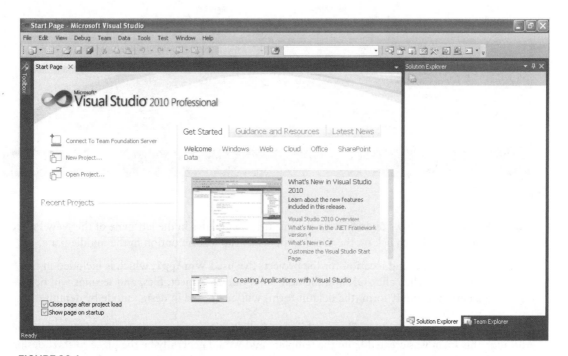

FIGURE 20-1

To create a new Solution in VS 2010 complete the following steps:

1. From the VS Start Page, select the File menu and choose the New option, and click the Project . . . option.

2. The New Project dialog box will be opened, as shown in Figure 20-2, which provides a list of all of the templates available for VS, and is showing Installed Templates by default.

 Notice in the Installed Templates pane that there are options for the Office Project templates, which proves that the .NET tools for Office have been installed and registered with VS.

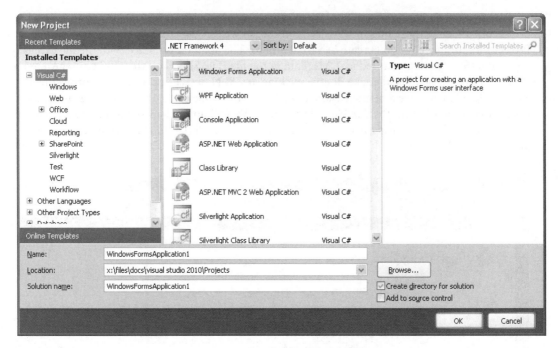

FIGURE 20-2

3. Select the Windows option under the Installed Templates in the left pane of the New Project dialog box. Then click on the Windows Forms Application option in the middle pane.

4. Choose a name and location for the project; I've used **WinApp1**, which is included in the sample files. Then click OK and the new Solution, CS Project, files, and settings will be created and the Form1 form (the default form) will be opened in design mode by default.

You have now created a Solution file and the base Projects files to start writing a .NET application. Although this form was created from the template and would generally be the place to start designing the .NET Windows application, we will start by looking at the Program.cs file.

The Program.cs File

All .NET programs have a Main function, which is the main entry point to the program that is called by the CLR when the application is executed. For C# projects, this method is created by default in the Program.cs file and the method signature for this function is:

Available for download on Wrox.com

```
Static int Main(string[] args)
{
    // Program code here
}
```

code snippet Program,cs in WinApp1 sample files

However, the string array parameter is optional, and is not included by default in the Windows Application template in VS 2010, but can be included if you wish to accept command-line parameters in your program. Also, by default in the Windows Application template, `Main` returns `void`, which is nothing, but could be modified to return an integer, as shown above, to the Windows Shell as an error code, as all standard Win32 and Win64 applications do. Finally, this function must be marked with, and adhere to the requirements of, the `Static` keyword. All code execution within the application will descend from the call to the `Main` method, so the `Progam.cs` file is the start point for any C# application.

Writing Code in C#

Although writing code in .NET is well beyond the scope of this book, there are a few basics we should discuss. The following sections provide some basics about coding in C# for programmers who are familiar with Visual Basic or VBA only.

Defining Namespaces

In C#, all code is written inside of classes, which are in turn, inside of namespaces. Notice that the `Main` method is inside of the `Program` class, which is inside of the `WinApp1` namespace, the name that I gave the project when it was created. This namespace separates the `Program` class from all other `Program` classes inside of the solution file. Also, when the code is compiled to binary, it will be given a `CLSID` (Class ID) that is a `GUID` (Globally Unique ID) that separates these bits from any other binaries with the namespace `WinApp1`. The following code is an example of a namespace declaration:

```
namespace WinApp1
{
    // Code your classes here
}
```

code snippet Example.cs in WinApp1 sample files

Defining Classes

Classes can be declared inside of a namespace in C#. The following is an example of a class declaration:

```
public class Example
{
    // Code data members, methods, and events here
}
```

code snippet Example.cs in WinApp1 sample files

Classes can have an access modifier of `Public`, `Protected`, `Private`, or `Internal`, depending on the level of code access desired. They may also be modified with several other keywords, such as `Static`, to apply the desired setting to the class.

Defining Constructors

All classes have constructors, whether written or not, that are called when a new instance of the class is created, assuming it allows new instances to be created. A constructor is declared by providing an access modifier, the name of the class, and optionally, any desired parameters (for overload constructors); however, the default constructor takes no parameters. Constructors are used to execute any user-defined code required for the class, when the new instance of the class is created. The following is an example of the default constructor for the Example class:

```
public class Example
{
    // The Default Constructor for the Example class
    public Example()
    {
        // Your code here
    }
}
```

code snippet Example.cs in WinApp1 sample files

Defining Variables

Both classes and methods can have variables defined within them. Class-level variables are global to the class, while method-level variables are local to the function only. Class-level variables are declared by providing an access modifier, data type, the variable name, and a semicolon to end the statement. The following is an example of a class-level variable declaration, which is of string data type:

```
public class Example
{
    // Example of a global variable in a class
    public string ExampleDataMember;
}
```

code snippet Example.cs in WinApp1 sample files

Class-level variables can act as properties for the class, but C# also provides get and set methods for a data member, which can be used to control code flow when setting or getting a value, which is similar to properties in VBA classes. The following is an example of creating get and set methods for a data member of a class in C#:

```
public string ExampleProperty
{
    get { return _exampleProperty; }
    set { _exampleProperty = value; }
}
private string _exampleProperty;
```

code snippet Example.cs in WinApp1 sample files

Defining variables in the method is much the same, except that you do not need to specify the access modifier because only code inside of the method will have access to the variable, and it will be destroyed once the method has been exited. The following is an example of defining a few variables inside of a method:

```
int Count;
long SomeNumber = 123456789;
string Data = "New String Data";
object Temp = new object();
```

Defining Methods

Classes can also have user-defined methods to execute some specific code when called. Methods are functions that can take parameters and return values. A C# method is declared much like a function in VBA. The following is an example of a method named `HelloWorld`, which takes no parameters, and returns a `string` object, in this case the literal value `Hello World`:

```
public string HelloWorld()
{
      return "Hello World";
}
```

code snippet Example.cs in WinApp1 sample files

Instantiating Objects

Classes, Structs, and other data types that are not primitive types in C# will typically need to have a new instance created before the object can be used. The syntax for this statement is: the variable name, followed by the equal sign, the `new` keyword, the name of the constructor method to use, and constructor parameters, and terminated with a semicolon to complete the statement. The following is an example of creating a new instance of the `Example` class declaration described previously:

```
Example myExampleClass = new Example();
```

code snippet Program.cs in WinApp1 sample files

Setting Properties

Once an instance of a class has been created, you can set its properties much as you would in VBA. The variable name plus a period is used to specify which instance of the class to use. When the period is pressed, you will see the IntelliSense in VS work, and it will show a list of properties and methods that are available. The statement is completed by selecting the property name to use, the equal sign (assignment operator), the value you wish to assign to the property, and ended by a semicolon. The following is an example of setting the `ExampleProperty` in our `Example` class:

```
myExampleClass.ExampleProperty = "Some string value";
```

code snippet Example.cs in WinApp1 sample files

Calling Methods

Calling methods in C# are also much the same as in VBA. The variable name, followed by a period, followed by the method name, plus any parameters for the method are finished by a semicolon to specify the call. Optionally, if the method returns a value, the assignment operator (equal sign) can be used to assign the return value to another variable. The following example shows the `HelloWorld` method being called from our `Example` class, and the return value is assigned to a `string` variable:

```
string s = myExampleClass.HelloWorld();
```

code snippet Program.cs in WinApp1 sample files

Using Statements

Finally, the `using` keyword in C# has several meanings, but the most common is when it is used to include other libraries in a given code file. Although there must be a reference to any external library used in the project file, the main system components of .NET are included by default because they are already in the GAC. The using statement can be placed at the top of the file to specify the namespace of an external library, and then the object within that namespace can be called by name within your code. The following is an example of a using statement found at the top of the code file, outside of the namespace:

```
using System.Collections.Generic;
```

code snippet Program.cs in WinApp1 sample files

Because the `System.Collections.Generic` namespace using statement has been added to the code file, you can call any of the classes in this namespace, such as the `List` or the `Queue` classes, by name within the code file. However, it is also worth noting that because there is a reference to this namespace in the Project file, the using statement is not required, and these classes could be referenced in code by prefixing the class name with the namespace. For example, the following code uses the namespace to reference the `List` class:

```
System.Collections.Generic.List<string> myList;
```

code snippet Program.cs in WinApp1 sample files

Adding Items to the Project

Now that you know the basics of writing code in VS, adding items to the project is very easy. VS 2010 provides a ton of tools and templates, so when adding new items, you have a lot of predefined options to choose from. Of course, you can always select from an existing item on the machine that you want to add as well. To add a new item, simply right-click on the Project file in the Solution Explorer pane, on the right side of the VS window, and choose Add; then click the New Item option. This will invoke the Add New Items dialog box, which is much like the New Project dialog box. From there you can select from any of the existing templates, ranging from various class files to plain old text files. Once the new item has been added, it will be shown in the Solution Explorer pane, under the selected project.

Building the Project

Once ready, the code project will need to be compiled so that the binaries can be distributed to and executed by users. To build the project and compile the code, choose the Build Solution option from the Build menu. The project will be compiled to an executable set of binaries. However, it is important to remember that, by default, these files are compiled to the CIL code and thus will require the user to have the correct .NET Framework version installed on their machine to properly run these executables. Once the project has been compiled, you can find the executable file under the project folder's `bin\Debug` directory. After compiling our sample project and looking in that folder, you should see a `WinApp1.exe` file. Also, there will be a file named `WinApp1.vshost.exe`, which is used by VS for debugging and not necessary for use with the application. Compiling a project in Visual Studio could not be any easier!

Executing the Binaries

Once you have the compiled binary file, you can simply double-click it to run it as you would any other executable file. In the case of our application, once it is run, the `Form1` form will be opened because that is what the `Main` function specifies. Closing the form will simply exit the form and the `Application` object; then finally, the `Main` function will be exited and the program's execution will be complete. .NET applications look, feel, and act just like any other standard Windows application, and all created with just a few mouse clicks!

Debugging Code in Visual Studio 2010

One of the largest and most powerful features of VS 2010 is the integrated debugger. The VS debugger allows the developer to debug code very quickly and effectively, using the tools built directly into the VS IDE. This section describes the basics of using the VS 2010 debugger.

Executing Code with the Debugger

Once you have the code ready to go and it compiles correctly, you can begin debugging directly within the VS IDE. Choosing the Start Debugging option on the Debug menu will begin execution of the code in the debugger. Also note that you could also push the play button on the debug tool bar, or even press the F5 key. Once the Start Debugging option has been selected, VS will compile the project, if necessary, and then start the application and open the appropriate debugging windows in the VS IDE.

Setting Breakpoints

Once you begin debugging code, you will definitely want to set some breakpoints to halt code execution at certain points. As in VBE, to set a breakpoint, click the left-hand strip of the code window. A red circle will be added if a break point is allowed on that particular line of code. The next time that line of code is reached during code execution, the debugger will halt on that line, just before executing it, until the person debugging provides additional input. Once execution has been halted, the user has the ability to inspect variables and the current state of the program and machine. The user has several options for continuing execution once a breakpoint has been hit, as described in the following sections.

Stepping Into Code

The first and probably most used option when setting a breakpoint is the Step Into option. The Step Into option can be found on both the Debug menu and toolbar. This option allows the developer to move to the next line of code executed, regardless of the location of the code. This option is often used to walk a piece of code line-by-line or to move into a method.

Stepping Over Code

The Step Over option allows the developer to move to the next line of code in the file. The Step Over option is also found on both the Debug menu and toolbar. If the line stepped over was a method call or contains operations in a different file location, the debugger does not take the user into the method or move away from the code that it is currently on. The debugger simply moves to the next line of code in the current location, executing the entire previous line of code, and any other code that is called as a result of it, without halting until the following line of code is reached.

Continuing Code Execution

Another common option used is to continue normal code execution from the current location, which is the Continue option. The Continue option can be found on both the Debug menu and toolbar, and it is the same play button as used to start the debugger.

Resetting Code Execution

One very nice feature of both VS 2010 and VBE 2010 is the ability to move the current code execution pointer to different locations in code in the debugger. While not always supported and dependent upon the specific code being debugged, the user has the ability at a breakpoint to drag the current code execution pointer to the desired location in code and begin executing from there. The current location pointer is the little yellow arrow found on the left-hand strip of the code window where breakpoints are placed.

Using Conditional Breakpoints

Finally, one last feature to mention about debugging in VS 2010 is the ability to set conditions on breakpoints. To set a Conditional Breakpoint, first set the breakpoint as you normally would by clicking on the left-hand strip of the code window and then right-click on the breakpoint and choose the Condition option. This will invoke the Breakpoint Condition dialog box where you can specify an expression to be used to decide whether or not to break at that breakpoint. This can be extremely useful when having to debug loops with lots of iterations or blocks of code that are hit a large number of times, effectively allowing the developer to specify the exact program state in which to stop the code execution.

The MSDN Library

Although the tutorial has discussed many of the basics of Visual Studio .NET 2010 and how to write code using C#, this really is only the very beginning of the subject. We highly recommend that you view the MSDN library if you want to learn more about using C#, VS, and .NET. The MSDN Library contains tons of tutorials from novice to advanced; discusses all of the objects in Access, .NET, and every other Microsoft development tool in-depth; provides literally thousands of code samples; and so much more. And the MSDN Library online is completely free and probably the most powerful resource that Microsoft has to offer Windows developers. You can find the MSDN Library at `http://msdn.microsoft.com`.

USING ACCESS DATABASES IN .NET

Now that the basics of building .NET applications with C# have been laid out, we can begin looking at how you can use .NET with Access. The first method to discuss, and often overlooked by .NET developers, is the ability to build .NET applications that use an Access database as a data storage mechanism for the application. Access database files are extremely easy to build, manage, and distribute, and are extremely cost-effective because they are essentially free to make (once you've purchased Access), and extremely lightweight in comparison to many other database products that require a server to be installed to a machine. Access databases can also provide more flexibility and better query performance compared to a medium to large XML file, and Access databases provide a lot of features that can be used in the application. Of course, Access has its limitations as well — for example, the 2 gigabyte file size limit or lack of user-level security in ACCDB files. In most cases, however, for a small- to medium-sized .NET application, Access databases can be extremely useful and will work well for both client- and Web-based .NET applications.

Working with ADO.NET

Built into the .NET Framework, the ADO.NET (ActiveX Data Objects for .NET) Library enables the developer to connect to and execute commands against a wide variety of data sources, such as an Access database, SQL Server, or even an Excel spreadsheet. These commands are often in the form of SQL statements, so executing commands in ADO.NET is not all that much different than executing queries in Access. VS provides a Query Designer tool from the Server Explorer pane much like Access' Query Designer, or SQL statements can even be created in Access and the SQL can be copied to code and modified to run accordingly. Using ADO.NET does not require much more than setting a few properties and calling a few methods, as you will see in this section.

Also, one thing to consider about ADO.NET is that it is much like the ADO libraries included with Access (although there are major, fundamental differences between the two), so if you are familiar with ADO already, picking up ADO.NET should be a snap. The material contained in Chapter 12 and Appendix C in regards to using ADO may also be useful with this section and learning more about using ADO.NET. Using ADO.NET, a developer can easily implement an Access database in any .NET application.

Adding Using Statements

ADO.NET uses the OLE DB Provider Library in .NET, which is part of the BCL (Base Class Library) and is included in the GAC by default, so no special references are required for the project. However, to be able to call the ADO classes by name, without having to prefix those names with the

System.Data.OleDb namespace, two using statements will be added to the top of the code files that ADO.NET code is used in. The following is an example of adding these two using statements:

```
using System.Data;
using System.Data.OleDb;
```

code snippet AdoExample1.cs in AdoClientExample sample files

Creating an OleDbConnection Object

There are actually a couple of different methods for connecting to a data source, but the most common is by creating an OleDbConnection object. The OleDbConnection class is used to create the physical connection to the data source and stores all of the data settings for the connection. When creating a connection to an Access data source, all you have to do is create a new instance of the OleDbConnection object, and specify the connection string and, optionally, any specific properties that are desired, and presto, the object will be ready to go. The follow code example shows how this can be implemented, along with an example connection string to an Access database:

```
// Create a new instace of the OLEDB Connection Object
OleDbConnection cn = new OleDbConnection();

// Set the connection string for the database
// Note: This code requires that the path to the database exists,
// and that user name and password for the database are
// correct (Admin and blank are the defaults).
cn.ConnectionString =
        "Provider=Microsoft.ACE.OLEDB.12.0;" +
        // This is a full path to the DB
        "Data Source=C:\\test.mdb;" +
        "User ID=Admin;Password=;";
```

code snippet AdoExample1.cs in AdoClientExample sample files

Notice that in the preceding connection string is a standard ADO connection string to an Access database. In this case, we have supplied the four minimum requirements for this string: the provider, the data source path, the user, and the password. However, there are many more options available for the connection strings. For more information about ADO connection strings and the valid settings for an Access database, see Chapter 12 or the MSDN Library.

Maintaining Connections

Before commands can be executed on a connection, the connection must first be opened. The Open method is used to open the connection object, which does not take any parameter, although it requires that the ConnectionString property be previously set; otherwise, it will throw an error on open. The following is an example of calling the Open method, using the previous connection declaration:

```
// Open the Connection
cn.Open();
```

code snippet AdoExample1.cs in AdoClientExample sample files

Similarly, you should always close a connection as soon as you are done using it. To close the connection, simply call the Close method; it does not take any parameters. The following example shows how to implement the Close method:

```
// Close the Connection
cn.Close();
```

code snippet AdoExample1.cs in AdoClientExample sample files

Creating an OleDbCommand Object

The OleDbCommand object is used to execute commands against an OleDbConnection object's data source. To create an OleDbCommand object, simply create a new instance of it using the default constructor. The following code example shows you how to create a new OleDbCommand:

```
// Create a new instance of the Command object
OleDbCommand cmd = new OleDbCommand();
```

code snippet AdoExample1.cs in AdoClientExample sample files

Once a new instance of the OleDbCommand class has been created, the connection and command text will need to be specified so that the command may be executed on the connection. To set the connection for the command, simply set the Connection property of the OleDbCommand object to the new OleDbConnection object created earlier. The following code provides an example of how to implement this:

```
// Set the Connection
cmd.Connection = cn;
```

code snippet AdoExample1.cs in AdoClientExample sample files

Then, to set the command text for the command, simply set the CommandText property of the OleDbCommand to the desired SQL statement. All of the specific options that are supported for the CommandText property will be specific to the data source, but in general for Access, it can be the name of a table or query, or a custom SQL statement. The following is an example of setting the `CommandText` property:

```
// Set the CommandText
cmd.CommandText =
    "SELECT [tblContacts].[FirstName] FROM [tblContacts] ;";
```

code snippet AdoExample1.cs in AdoClientExample sample files

Alternatively, it is worth noting that the `Connection` and `CommandText` property settings for the `OleDbCommand` could have been passed when the object was instantiated, using one of the `OleDbCommand` object's overloaded constructors. The following code basically condenses the creation of the `OleDbCommand` object and the setting of the `CommandText` and `Connection` properties into one statement:

```
// Create the Command object with the Connection and SQL
OleDbCommand cmd =
    new OleDbCommand(cn, "SELECT [FirstName] FROM [tblContacts] ;");
```

code snippet AdoExample1.cs in AdoClientExample sample files

Executing Commands Against a Database

Now that the command has been created and the connection has been established, all that is left to do is to execute the command. However there are several options for doing so. For the purpose of this chapter, we will discuss three options: the `ExecuteReader` method for commands that return records, the `ExecuteNonQuery` method for executing action queries, and `OleDbDataAdaptor` to fill the results of a query into a `DataSet` object.

The ExecuteReader Method

The `ExecuteReader` method is used when the command issued to the database returns a set of records, such as a `SELECT` query. The `ExecuteReader` method optionally takes a command behavior parameter and returns an instance of an `OleDbDataReader` object containing the results of the executed SQL statement. The `OleDbDataReader` can only be used to read data and cannot be used to update data, nor can it be used to execute SQL statements which update data. The following code shows an example of calling the `ExecuteReader` method:

```
// Execute the row returning command
OleDbDataReader dr = cmd.ExecuteReader(CommandBehavior.Default);
```

code snippet AdoExample1.cs in AdoClientExample sample files

The `OleDbDataReader` object will allow the user to walk through the resulting record set, one record at a time. This can be accomplished by calling the `Read` method. The first time the `Read` method is called, the current record cursor is moved to the first record and each additional call moves it to the next record, until the end of the data set is reached. The `Read` method returns a `Boolean`, which is `True` if a value was read. The `GetValue` method for the `OleDbDataReader` object takes a field name or index and returns the value of that field, for the current record that the data reader is pointing to. The following is an example of adding all of the records returned from the previous command to a `List` object:

```
// Read out all of the records and insert them into the results List
List<string> results = new List<string>();
while(dr.Read())
{
    // Get the value from the FirstName column
    results.Add(dr.GetValue("FirstName"));
}
```

code snippet AdoExample1.cs in AdoClientExample sample files

The ExecuteNonQuery Method

The `ExecuteNonQuery` method is used to execute SQL statements against the database that do not return a set of results, but rather modify the data or perform some function, such as an `UPDATE` or `INSERT` query or even a stored procedure. The `ExecuteNonQuery` method does not require any parameters and returns an integer of the number of rows affected by the SQL statement. The following is an example of calling the `ExecuteNonQuery` method:

```
// Create the Command object with the Connection and
// INSERT SQL Statement
OleDbCommand cmd = new OleDbCommand(
    "INSERT INTO [tblContacts] ([FirstName]) VALUES (\"Some Name\"); ",
    cn);

// Execute the SQL statement
int rowsAffected =  cmd.ExecuteNonQuery();

// Check to make sure the rows affected is correct
If(rowsAffected != 1)
{
    // Report an error
}
```

code snippet AdoExample1.cs in AdoClientExample sample files

The OleDbDataAdaptor Object

Finally, sometimes it is much more useful to just fill a `DataSet` object with the entire set of data, without needing to directly access each record separately. The `DataSet` object is extremely versatile in .NET and can be used in conjunction with a wide variety of other .NET objects, such as a `DataGrid` control. The `OleDbDataAdaptor` object can be used to fill the `DataSet` object by simply calling the `Fill` method. The following code provides an example of filling the `DataSet`, using the `OleDbDataAdaptor` class:

```
// Create the Command object with the Connection and SQL
OleDbCommand cmd =
```

```
    new OleDbCommand("SELECT [FirstName] FROM [tblContacts] ;", cn);

// Create the Data Adaptor object and set the Command object to it
OldDbDataAdaptor da = new OleDbDataAdaptor(cmd);

// Create a new DataSet object and fill it with the data
DataSet ds = new DataSet();
da.Fill(ds);
```

code snippet AdoExample1.cs in AdoClientExample sample files

The `DataSet` object will now be filled with all of the results gathered from the command object. Using the `OleDbDataAdaptor` to fill the `DataSet` object can save you the time and effort of having to write to code to manually fill the `DataSet` one record at a time.

Working with SQL

One final thing to consider when working with ADO.NET commands is that the SQL statements that are valid are slightly different than Access SQL statements. The SQL statements that are used by ADO must be ANSI SQL-92–compliant. This means that any SQL statement issued by the `OleDbCommand` object that does not conform to this SQL standard will generate an exception, and although there are a number of exceptions, in most cases, Access SQL and standard SQL will be interchangeable. And, you can force Access to generate ANSI SQL-92 statements in any database, by selecting the that option in the Access Options dialog box, though it is not selected by default.

Types of .NET Applications

There are basically three types of .NET applications: Client applications, Web applications, and Mobile applications. Although each type has its own special purpose, ADO.NET can be used with each of these. For the purposes of this section, we will discuss the differences and considerations when using Access databases for Client applications and for Web applications only. These are the only two types of .NET applications that support using ADO.NET with Access databases.

Unfortunately, there is no OLE DB ADO.NET provider in the .NET Compact Framework, which is the framework used to build Mobile applications, so traditional Access databases are not supported here. However, mobile devices have some support for a database format known as Pocket Access. Although often confused for a Mobile version of Access, this product is not directly related to Microsoft Office Access in any way. Thus, this chapter will not provide any further discussion of building databases for Mobile applications.

Building Client Applications

The first kind of .NET application to consider is a Windows client application, which functions much like traditional Access applications. This is the kind of application that is installed directly to the user's machine and the code executed lives on the user's machine. While using ADO.NET is the same for either case, you should be aware of certain issues when using Access databases with the application architecture for .NET client applications.

Database File Permissions

The most important thing to consider when deploying .NET applications, which use Access databases, is that any user working with the application will potentially need permission to write to the database file via the .NET application. These permissions are based on the permission for the application user's Windows account. For example, if the user needs to write new records to the database through the course of code execution in the .NET application, Windows file system must grant the user write permission to write these records to the database file. If the Windows user does not have the proper permissions, the write operation on the database file will fail and cause problems for the .NET application.

Beyond the obvious reasons, this is important to consider because of the user permission model changes introduced with Windows Vista, and currently in use in Windows 7. This security model is much stricter than in previous versions of Windows, and for very good reasons that we don't have time to delve into in this book. The important thing to consider here is that user accounts no longer have write permissions to the `Program Files` folder, among other folders and Windows permissions settings, with versions of Vista and higher. For this reason, it is very important to consider where to deploy database files to when building .NET client applications with Access databases.

Deciding on a Database Location

The key to deciding the database location is to understand how any given database will be used. In most cases, you'll probably want each individual user to have his or her own separate database, which is easy to do with Access because any given database file can be copied and pasted to create a new instance of it. In this case, you will probably want to deploy the database file to the user's `AppData` folder. The `AppData` folder, although hidden by default, is the standard location for putting local data files for the user. For Windows Vista and 7, this folder path is similar to the following:

```
C:\Users\<User Name>\AppData\Local\<Application Name>\
```

Note that the `<User Name>` corresponds to the user's Windows account name and that `<Application Name>` corresponds to your .NET application's name. This situation also deters one user from potentially having access to another user's database(s) and data, which is always a good security measure.

Conversely, some cases may require that all users of the application on the machine share the same database file. In this situation, we recommend that you use a custom file directory or the `ProgramData` folder, which is hidden by default, but `User` accounts do not have permissions to write to this folder directly. Typically a subfolder is created within this folder and the `Users` group is granted permissions to write to this folder so that the database can be placed here and updated by all users on the machine. This path is typically something like:

```
C:\ProgramData\<Application Name>\
```

The permissions will need to be set appropriately when the application is installed on the machine. And using this method is not really recommended because it will be possible for any user to modify the data in the database or the database itself, which could cause application problems. Whenever possible, stick with putting databases in the user's `AppData` folder; it can save a lot of permissions headaches and security issues.

Manually Setting Permissions

Finally, if worst comes to worst, you can always manually set permissions on any file or folder when the application is installed. For databases that any Windows user account should be allowed to modify, you should assign the Windows `Users` group `Read`, `Write`, and `Execute` permissions in most cases. These are typically set during installation because the user installing the application will be an administrator on the machine and will already have permission to make these kinds of modifications. But, really, this could be done at any time after the application has been installed, as long as the user has the proper permissions. Manually setting permissions is usually a last resort to solving database permissions issues.

Expanding Environment Variables

Depending on what kind of deployment script is used for a .NET application, you may not always know exactly where the database files live on a given machine. Fortunately, .NET provides a static `Environment` class to provide the developer with an object to work with common environment settings that change from machine to machine. Specifically, the `ExpandEnvironmentVariables` method takes a string, which contains data including one or more environment variables, and then returns the same string with the full paths on the current machine in place of the environment variable. For example, the following code calls the `ExpandEnvironmentVariables` method, with the environment variable `%windir%`:

```
string s = Environment.ExpandEnvironmentVariables("%windir%");
```

code snippet EnvVars.cs in AdoClientExample sample files

After this line of code has been executed, the variable `s` will contain a path like `C:\Windows`, or whatever the actual path to the Windows directory is for that specific machine.

Setting Environment Variables

Unfortunately, you may find that the Windows environment variables are somewhat lacking because there are really only a few by default. The good news is that the `Environment` object also allows the developer to set environment variables using the `SetEnvironmentVariable` method, which takes the name of the variable, the value of the variable, and the target of the variable. The following provides an example of using the `SetEnvironmentVariable` method to create an environment variable:

```
Environment.SetEnvironmentVariable(
        "Name",
        "Value",
        EnvironmentVariableTarget.Machine);
```

code snippet EnvVars.cs in AdoClientExample sample files

Note that this method is also used to modify or delete environment variables as well, so be careful about overwriting existing variables. Environment variables can be a great way to keep track of the location of databases, and other application files, in your .NET client applications.

Building Web Applications

The other type of .NET application that can use an Access database is an ASP.NET Web application. ASP.NET is the Web programming language, which consists of ASP.NET, the mark-up language code for creating pages, visual controls, and other such Web items, and a scripting language, or the code behind the page, which can be written with any supporting .NET language, such as C# or even Visual Basic .NET. The code portion of the ASP.NET language is really the true power of it because this allows essentially any .NET object to be used when building the logic for the Web application. In this case, for example, an ADO.NET data wrapper for an Access database can be implemented to provide a mechanism for data storage in the Web application. However, there are some things to consider when building ASP.NET Web applications that use Access databases, a few of which we will discuss in this section.

Creating an ASP.NET Web Application

Several templates are available in Visual Studio 2010 for creating ASP.NET Web applications. The template titled ASP.NET Web Application is a good place to get started building ASP.NET applications and is the template that is used for this example. In the New Project dialog box, click the ASP. NET Web Application template, choose a project name and location, and click OK, and a new ASP.NET Web application will be created from the template.

 If you are using any of the Express Editions of VS 2010, you will need to download the Web Developer Express version, if it is not already installed on your machine, to create .NET Web applications.

Code Execution

The first thing to understand about ASP.NET applications, which is different from some Web programming languages, is that most of the time, code is executed on the server and then the result is sent to the client browser, and in this case, not executed on the client machine. This also means that there is no direct method built into ASP.NET applications to know who is running the code, and in most cases code is running anonymously. That is not to say that you cannot program this functionality into a website, but probably in a lot of cases, you want to show data to a user, without forcing the user to log in to the website first.

So, that raises the question of which Windows user account is actually connecting to the database when the IIS (Internet Information Server, the Web server for Windows) executes code requesting data. By default, the ASPNET account is a Windows user account that executes the ASP.NET code and is used for determining file permissions on the server machine when users access the website anonymously. So the important thing to remember when using an Access database with an ASP.NET Web application is that this account, and any other required user accounts, have file access permissions to the database file(s) for the application. Again, if anonymous website users will need to make modifications to the database file in the Web application, ensure that the ASPNET account has the proper WRITE file permissions when deploying the application.

The App_Data Folder

The good news is that .NET and IIS do most of the work for you when creating, deploying, and running ASP.NET applications that use Access databases as a data source. Upon creating the ASP.NET Web Application template, you will notice that the App_Data folder is created. This folder is special because WRITE permissions are automatically enabled for this folder, allowing files such as Access databases, XML, Text, or any other type of file that requires WRITE permissions. The best practice is to use this folder as the folder for storing Access database files in an ASP.NET Web application.

Setting Permissions

Although the App_Data folder is the preferred location for an Access database, it is by no means required. The beauty of the Access databases is that they use file system-level tools to work with the database file, so they can be anywhere that the Windows file system has access to. This means that you can basically create any folder desired on the Web server to store the Access database.

 We recommend against putting Access database files used for the Web application in any location that is accessible to anonymous users of the website, for security purposes.

Again, the key to using Access database files is that the file system and the user of the ASP.NET application (which is typically the ASPNET account) have the proper permissions set for the database file. If you have physical access to the database server, this should not be a problem. Simply place the files in the desired location, and then you can always manually set the permissions for the files or the folder, using the Windows permissions tools, such as the Security tab of the file's Properties dialog box. Also, IIS provides a nice interface for setting file and folder permissions for ASP.NET Web applications, in addition to the Windows Properties dialog box. No matter which method you choose, setting the file permissions for Access databases in a Web application should be pretty easy to do if you have direct access to the Web server machine.

Working with Third-Party Web Hosts

However, oftentimes, a third-party Web host is used by individuals or businesses that do not have the means to manage a Web server or in-house hosting themselves. In this case, the owner of the ASP.NET application may not have direct access to the actual machine the application is hosted on, so there are a couple of things to consider when building and deploying Access databases with Web applications in this situation:

➤ **.NET versions:** The most important thing to consider is the version of .NET the Web host supports. Although all versions of .NET provide some support for working with Access databases, not all versions of .NET support all functionality available in .NET 4.0 for connecting to Access databases. When building code, you can always target the appropriate version of the .NET Framework in the Project properties if necessary. It is always a good idea to know what versions of .NET your third party host supports, before deploying the Web application.

➤ **File permissions:** The owner of the application may not have direct access to the machine the database files are hosted on. In this case, the Web host often provides an interface for setting file permissions for user accounts. Many hosts even have specific tools for setting permissions for Access databases. Worst case scenario — most Web hosts allow FTP access to the files directly, so the owner should have the capability to set permissions from within an FTP client when connected to the server.

➤ **File locations:** Because Web hosts often have multiple subscribers running from a single server, they assign folders to users based on some custom logic, which differs from host to host. Be careful when using file paths in code as they might be different when deployed to the Web server. The MapPath function is extremely useful for building file paths on a Web server, which is discussed in the next section.

Other than those few items, writing ASP.NET applications that run on third-party Web servers is not very different at all!

The Server.MapPath Method

Finally, the last item to discuss when building ASP.NET Web applications is the Server.MapPath method. The MapPath method returns the full physical path, based on a virtual path supplied by the parameter. When implementing the connection to an Access database using ADO.NET, the connection string requires that you supply the full file path (on the server machine) to connect to the database file. It is always best to utilize the Server.MapPath function when building connection strings for databases that will be used in ASP.NET applications. In this manner, you can develop code that does not require any pre-knowledge of the exact, full path location of the database file on the server. The following code provides examples of using the MapPath function to get the full path to a database:

```
// Get the Full Path to the Database File
string strDatabasePath = Server.MapPath("~/App_Data/Test.accdb");
```

code snippet MapPathExample.cs in AdoWebExample sample files

In the previous code example, the physical path to the Test.accdb file is placed in the strDatabasePath variable after the code has been executed. Now, no matter where the database is located on the machine, you can specify the strDatabasePath variable in the connection string, and the actual file path can be mapped at runtime. Also, it is important to note that the Server object is a member of the System.Web .Services.WebService class, which should be inherited by the class this call is being implemented in.

Other Methods of Using Access Databases

Finally, it should be noted that there are other components in .NET that can connect to Access databases, and the material described in this chapter is by no means the full extent of using Access databases with .NET. For example, you could use the LINQ feature in .NET to link to a DataSet object that has data fetched from an Access database. Also, the OleDbDataAdaptor class has a number of features for abstracting the use of various data sources, such as an Access database. And these are just a couple of examples of how Access databases can be used in .NET applications, but really, the options are limitless! For more information about using Access databases and other features in

.NET that support them, see the information and tutorials found in the MSDN Library at
`http:/msdn.microsoft.com`.

AUTOMATING ACCESS WITH .NET

The next method to discuss for using .NET to work with Access is automating the Access program
in a .NET Windows application. The Access 2010 program itself is a COM application and allows
.NET code to work with it through the use of the Access PIA and COM Interop services. In fact,
this is not only true for Access, but it is true for most of the Office 2010 applications. Writing .NET
code to work with the Access program allows the developer to control and manipulate the program
and its features, by writing code to execute the desired operations, in the same manner that you
would automate the various Office applications in VBA code. This section will discuss how to set up
a .NET project to automate Access 2010.

 *Chapter 18 discusses other Office applications using VBA code in Access 2010,
but that information could be used in conjunction with the material in this section to automate other Office 2010 applications using .NET.*

For this example, create another new application using the Windows Forms Application template
project in VS 2010 to begin building the code explained here. We will use this new project to
illustrate how to implement automating Access 2010 directly from a .NET Windows application.
Although this section is short, keep in mind that most of this book is about VBA programming
and almost anything that can be done in VBA code can also be in .NET code using the techniques
described here.

The Access PIA

The Access 2010 PIA is included and installed with the .NET tools for Office 2010, which are
installed when Office is installed. Once a reference has been set to the Access 2010, you can begin
using the Access `Application` object, and other objects included with Access, as you would in VBA
code. In particular, for Access 2010, you will need to set a reference to the Microsoft Access 14.0
Object Library. This will include all of the libraries necessary for working directly with the Access
2010 program.

Setting References

To add a reference to the Microsoft Access 14.0 Object Library, follow these steps:

   1.   In the Solution Explorer pane, on the right side of the Visual Studio window, right-click
           the References folder and choose the Add Reference option. This will invoke the Add Refer-
           ence dialog box.

2. In the Add Reference dialog box, click the COM tab and select the Microsoft Access 14.0 Object Library from the list of components. Then click OK. PIA references to DAO, ADODB, Microsoft.Office.Core, and VBIDE will be added to the project.

Now that you have a reference to the Access 2010 PIA for the .NET project, you have the ability to use Access objects in your code and are ready to start coding the application.

Creating Code to Automate Access

To begin using Access and its objects in the application's code once the reference to the PIA has been added, there are a couple of steps to complete first. This section discusses the steps needed to create the actual C# code to automate Access 2010.

Add Using Statements

To begin writing code against the Access 2010 PIA, you will need to add two using statements, to include the libraries, the top of the Form1.cs file created by default in the Windows Forms Application project template. Open the Form1.cs code in VS and add the following using statements at the top of the file:

```
using Microsoft.Office.Core;
using Access = Microsoft.Office.Interop.Access;
```

code snippet Form1.cs in AutomateAccessExample sample files

Notice that we added an alias named Access for the Access Interop namespace. This enables you to call Access in your C# code, as you could in VBA code, and to make it simpler when building the code.

The Access Application Object

The next thing to do is to create an instance of the Access.Application object. Once you have a valid Access.Application object, you can begin automating all of that functionality available in Access 2010, such as calling up the Access Object Model to open a new database. To provide a variable for the Application object, create a data member for the Form1 class by adding the following code just inside of the open bracket for the Form1 class:

```
public Access.Application accApplication;
```

code snippet Form1.cs in AutomateAccessExample sample files

Now that you have data storage for the Access.Application in the Form1 class, you need only to create a new instance of it to start using it.

Creating an Instance of Access

To create a new instance of the `Access.Application` class, simply call the new keyword for the `Application` object. This can be accomplished in almost any method anywhere in code. However, even though a new instance of Access has been created in the background (as you can tell by examining your Task Manager), it will not be directly visible to the Windows user until commanded to be visible. To show the instance of the Access 2010 program to the user, set the `Visible` property of the `Application` object to the value of `true`. Add the following code to the `Form1` class to provide a method for opening Access programs for the user to see:

```
public void OpenAccess()
{
    if (accApplication != null)
    {
        accApplication.Quit();
        accApplication = null;
    }

    accApplication = new Access.Application();
    accApplication.Visible = true;
}
```

code snippet Form1.cs in AutomateAccessExample sample files

Notice that this method first checks to see if an instance of Access already exists in the `accApplicaton` variable, and if so, then closes the current instance before creating the new instance of Access and setting it visible for the user to see.

Calling the Access Object Model

Now that the code has opened an instance of Access that the user can see, write a little more code to call up some functionality in the Access Object Model. For example, you could open the Open Database file dialog box so that the user can choose a database to open in that instance of Access. To implement this code, call the `RunCommand` method with the `acCmdOpenDatabase` parameter. Add the following method to the `Form1` class to implement this functionality:

```
public void PromptOpenDatabase()
{
    if (this.accApplication == null)
    {
        this.OpenAccess()
    }

    // Show the Open Database dialog for the user to open a database
    this.accApplication.RunCommand(Access.AcCommand.acCmdOpenDatabase);
}
```

code snippet Form1.cs in AutomateAccessExample sample files

Notice that this method also checks to see if there is an instance of Access already running, and if not, creates one, before trying to call the `RunCommand` method. You're almost done now; the only thing left to do is to tie the `Form1` code into the code you just created to call the Access Object Model.

Calling Access from the Windows Form

The last thing to do is to actually call the code to automate Access from the Windows `Form1` control in the project. From the Toolbox pane, drop a button control on to the Form in the visual designer. Then press the F4 key to open the VS Properties pane (just like in Access). Set the `Text` property for the button to: **Open Database in Access**. Then double-click the button in the designer to automatically create a click method for the button control. You will be taken to the new `Click` event method for the button. Add the following line of code to the method:

```
this.PromptOpenDatabase();
```

Available for download on Wrox.com

code snippet Form1.cs in AutomateAccessExample sample files

Once this call to the `PromptOpenDatabase` method, which you created in the previous step, is placed behind the `Click` event, any time that button is clicked on the `Form1` form, the code will be executed and Access will be opened and will prompt the user to select a database file.

Running the Automated Application

Now that all of the code necessary for this example is ready, let's test it to make sure it is actually working. From the Debug menu in VS 2010, click the Start Debugging option. This will build the project and start running the application in debug mode. The `Form1` form will be opened. Click the button and presto — Access 2010 opens and the Open Database dialog box is presented to the user!

Congratulations, you have now successfully created a .NET Windows forms application that automates the Access 2010 program. Although this is only a simple and limited example of the functionality that is possible when automating Access 2010, most of this book is dedicated to discussing the various techniques for using VBA code to automate Access and thus will apply here as well. And, as always, the MSDN Library will provide a complete list and code examples for using the Access PIA with .NET, which can be found at `http://msdn.microsoft.com`.

CREATING COM ADD-INS FOR ACCESS

The capability to create .NET Add-ins, which can be used directly from within the Access client, is another important aspect of using .NET with Access. In the beginning, the Office Developer Edition for Office 2000 and Office XP allowed you to create COM Add-ins using the Visual Basic Editor. This functionality still remains in Visual Studio 2010. Unfortunately, the Express Editions of Visual Studio 2010 do not include the required project type to create COM Add-ins, but if you have Visual

Studio 2010 Pro or higher, you should have the COM Add-in templates already included. This section will discuss the basics of using COM Add-ins with Access 2010.

The Benefits of COM Add-Ins

Add-ins in .NET are custom controls that can be used within a specific program, such as Access, to provide some custom functionality for the program. COM Add-ins offer several features for Access:

- ➤ They enable code to run when Access starts.
- ➤ They enable code to run when Access shuts down.
- ➤ The current instance of the Access can be interacted with using a COM Add-in.
- ➤ COM Add-ins can be used to extend the Ribbon.

To provide an example of how to implement this functionality, this section will provide the steps for building a COM Add-in. Consider that there is no entry point for Access' Workgroup Administrator dialog box included in the Access user interface, but it can be opened from the RunCommand object. Because the COM Add-in has code access to the currently running instance of Access, you could easily write a COM Add-in that extends the Access Ribbon to display a button to open the Workgroup Administrator dialog box. For this example, we will implement a COM Add-in to open the Workgroup Administrator dialog box, just to prove how easy it is to do!

Creating a New COM Add-In Project

To start, create a new Add-in project using the Visual Studio 2010 template. Complete the following steps:

1. Launch Visual Studio 2010 from the Start menu.

2. From the File menu, choose the New option and click Project. The New Project dialog box opens.

3. From the Installed Template pane, select the Extensibility option under Other Project Types.

4. Click the Shared Add-in option from the list of templates, and choose a location and click OK. An example of this is shown in Figure 20-3. This launches the Shared Add-in Wizard. Click Next to continue.

5. The opening page of the Shared Add-in Wizard dialog box just tells some basics about the wizard, so just click the Next button.

6. On Page 1, select Create an Add-in using Visual C#. Alternatively, you could choose Visual Basic or C++, but this example will show C#. Then click the Next button.

7. On Page 2, clear the checkboxes for all Application hosts with the exception of Microsoft Access. You just want to create an Add-in for Access only. Then click the Next button.

8. On Page 3, type **Show Workgroup Administrator Add-in** for the name of the Add-in. Optionally, provide a description and then click the Next button.

9. On Page 4, select both checkboxes to load the Add-in when Access is launched and to make it available to all users. The Add-in will be loaded to provide the entry point as soon as Access is started. Then click the Next button.

10. On Page 5, just click the Finish button. Visual Studio will promptly create the new Add-in solution.

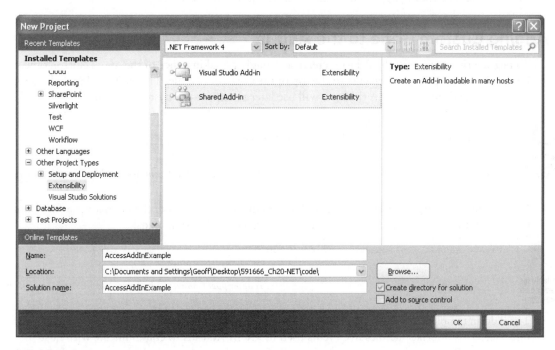

FIGURE 20-3

Creating an Add-in project actually creates two Visual Studio projects. The first is the Add-in project itself, and the second is a setup project that creates a `setup.exe` and an MSI file for distributing the Add-in to users. The MSI file can be used to install the Add-in on other computers. Congratulations, you have successfully created an Access Add-in setup project and you are now ready to begin building the Add-in.

Setting References to the Access PIA

Before you start writing code, there's one more thing to do. As mentioned earlier, the COM Add-in receives an instance of the `Access.Application` object. Because COM Add-ins are generic in the sense that they can run against a number of host applications, the `Application` object is given to you as an object type and is not strongly typed. Working with a strongly typed object would be easier, so cast the object type to an instance of the `Access.Application` object, which is defined in the Access PIA. Start by adding a reference to the Microsoft Access 14.0 Object Library:

1. In the Solution Explorer pane on the right side of the Visual Studio window, right-click on the References folder and choose the Add Reference option. This invokes the Add Reference dialog box.

2. In the Add Reference dialog box, click the COM tab, select the Microsoft Access 14.0 Object Library from the list of components, and then click OK. PIA references to DAO, ADODB, Microsoft.Office.Core, and VBIDE will be added to the project.

Now that you have a reference to the Access 2010 PIA for the project, you have the ability to use Access objects in your code and are ready to start coding the Add-in.

Adding Custom Code to the Add-In

To begin writing code for the Add-in, create a strongly typed instance of the Application object. First, add the following statements to the top of the Connect.cs file. This code will include the Access PIA and the Office PIA that you will use later to expose the custom ribbon.

```
using Microsoft.Office.Core;
using Access = Microsoft.Office.Interop.Access;
```

code snippet Connect.cs in AccessAddInExample sample files

Next, change the applicationObject declaration (near the bottom of the Connect.cs file) from type object to Access.Application so that the variable declaration reads:

```
private Access.Application applicationObject;
```

code snippet Connect.cs in AccessAddInExample sample files

The Add-in template created a class called Connect, which implements the IDTExtensibility2 interface. This interface defines five events used by COM Add-ins to communicate with host applications. The OnConnection method is called when Access starts, which provides the application member object for the program that was started. Change the first line of code in the OnConnection method to use a strongly typed application object by adding an explicit cast to the Access.Application class, as shown in the following example:

```
applicationObject = (Access.Application)application;
```

code snippet Connect.cs in AccessAddInExample sample files

Now, when you call the applicationObject in the Add-in, it will be strongly typed to the Access.Application class, thus providing IntelliSense to all available properties, methods, and events of the class.

Adding Support for the Ribbon

To implement a button for the Add-in in the Access Ribbon, there are a few things that are required to be added to the Add-in code. Complete each of the items in this section to implement a Ribbon button for the Access Add-in.

Inheriting IRibbonExtensibility Interface

The first thing to do to add support for the Ribbon is to include the IRibbonExtensibility interface with the Add-in class. To do this, the Connect class must inherit the IRibbonExtensibility interface, and by default, it does not. To accomplish this task, simply modify the Connect class declaration to include the IRibbonExtensibility interface, as shown in the following code:

Available for download on Wrox.com

```
public class Connect :
    Object, Extensibility.IDTExtensibility2, IRibbonExtensibility
```

code snippet Connect.cs in AccessAddInExample sample files

Adding the Ribbon XML

Next, the Ribbon XML needs to be included. This example will use a resource file to store the Ribbon XML so it can be retrieved at runtime. This Ribbon XML will add a group and one additional button, named Workgroup Administrator, to the Database Tools tab in the Access Ribbon.

 There are multiple methods for including Ribbon XML. Chapter 16 provides more information about building custom Ribbons in Access 2010.

To create the resource file to store the Ribbon XML in, complete the following steps:

1. From the Solution Explorer pane, right-click on the AccessAddInExample project, select the Add option, and click the New Item button. This will invoke the Add New Item dialog box.

2. Click the Resources File in the list of templates and type **wrkgadm.resx** as the file name. Then click the Add button and the new RESX file will be created and opened in the Visual Studio resource designer.

3. Add an item in the resource string table: In the field under the Name column, type **rbnWrkGadm**, and for the Value field, add the following Ribbon XML:

```
<customUI
xmlns="http://schemas.microsoft.com/office/2009/07/customui">
  <ribbon>
    <tabs>
      <tab idMso="TabDatabaseTools">
        <group id="grpWrkGadm" label="Workgroup Administrator">
          <button id="cmdWrkGadm"
                  label="Workgroup Administrator"
                  size="large"
                  onAction="showWrkGadm"
                  imageMso="DatabasePermissionsMenu"/>
        </group>
      </tab>
    </tabs>
  </ribbon>
</customUI>
```

The above code uses the XML namespace for the Office 2010 Ribbon. To work with the Ribbon in Access 2007, use the XML namespace:
`http://schemas.microsoft.com/office/2006/01/customui.`

The resource file is now ready to go, as it includes the Ribbon XML for the Add-in. Close the resource designer and complete one more step to finish implementing a custom Ribbon button for the Add-in.

Add the GetCustomUI Method

The `IRibbonExtensibility` interface defines one other method, named `GetCustomUI`, which must be implemented to in the `Connect` class. This method is called when the host application asks for XML for the Ribbon. Add the following code to the `Connect` class to implement the `GetCustomUI` method for the Add-in's `Connect` class:

Available for download on Wrox.com

```
public string GetCustomUI(string RibbonID)
{
    return wrkgadm.rbnWrkGadm;
}
```

code snippet Connect.cs in AccessAddInExample sample files

Create the Code for the Add-In

Finally, the Ribbon XML defined an `onAction` attribute for the button. It tells the button the name of the method to call when clicked — in this example, the method name is `shwWrkGadm`. For this Add-in to show the Workgroup Administrator dialog box, call the `RunCommand` method of the `Access.Application` object, with the `acCmdWorkgroupAdministrator` parameter. To implement the `shwWrkGadm` method in the Add-in, add the following code to the `Connect` class:

Available for download on Wrox.com

```
public void showWrkGadm(IRibbonControl control)
{
    applicationObject.RunCommand(
        Access.AcCommand.acCmdWorkgroupAdministrator);
}
```

code snippet Connect.cs in AccessAddInExample sample files

Congratulations — believe it or not, the new Add-in is ready to go. Simply build the solution and the Add-in code will be compiled and placed into the Setup project, which will be packaged up and ready for distribution. You are now ready to allow users to install and begin using the Add-in.

When building the project, always make sure to rebuild both the Add-in project and the setup project so that the setup files include the latest build of the Add-in.

Installing the COM Add-In

Once the Setup project has been built, two files will be created: `setup.exe` and the Add-in MSI (Installer file). To install the Add-in, simply run the `setup.exe` by double-clicking it in Windows Explorer. This will launch the Installation Wizard. There are only a few options for the installation, but it is good to choose the Everyone option (so that everyone using Access will be able to use the Add-in) when deciding which users to install the Add-in for. (That option is not selected by default.) Once the wizard has finished, the Add-in will be ready to use the very next time you start Access.

Running the COM Add-In

To test out the Add-in, start Access 2010 from the Windows start menu. In the Access Backstage, create a new Blank MDB database. The database should be an MDB because the Workgroup Administrator dialog box is not available for ACCDB files. Alternatively, you could just open an existing MDB file. The key here is that an MDB file is open in the current session of Access.

Once the MDB file has been opened, click the Database Tools tab of the Ribbon to show it. You should now see an available button named Workgroup Administrator. When the button is clicked, it will open the Workgroup Administrator dialog box. Creating custom Add-ins for Access 2010 is just that simple using Visual Studio 2010!

USING .NET CODE IN ACCESS

The final method to discuss in using .NET with Access is building Access applications that call .NET code from VBA. Because most .NET assemblies can be created to be COM-compatible, this is extremely easy to do! To implement this, there are really two parts to think about here: first, to create the library in .NET that will be used in your VBA code, and second, creating the VBA code to call the .NET assembly. For this example, a stack class will be created and then called from VBA code to show how this can be accomplished. This section covers the basics of how to implement .NET assemblies that can be called directly in VBA code.

Creating a Managed Library in .NET

The first step in calling .NET code from Access is to create the managed library that will be called. However, what makes managed libraries different from standard Windows .NET applications is that, in most cases, a managed library is actually compiled to a DLL file. That DLL file can in turn be consumed by Access and its code can be called from VBA. Complete the following steps in this section to create a managed library using VS 2010.

Creating a Managed Class Library Project

The first thing to do is to create a new project from the Class Library template in Visual Studio. To accomplish this, complete the following steps:

1. Launch Visual Studio 2010 from the Start menu.

2. From the File menu, choose the New option and click Project. The New Project dialog box will be invoked.

3. On the New Project dialog box, click the Windows option to show the Windows template project options. Click the Class Library option from the list of Visual C# templates.

4. Choose Name (we used `ManagedCodeExample`) and Location for the new project and click OK. The new Class Library solution and all its files will be created.

5. Rename the `Class1.cs` code file to `Stack.cs` by right-clicking on the file in the Solution Explorer and choosing the Rename option from the context menu. This will be the main code file for the project.

Once the new project has been created, you will now be ready to begin coding the managed library.

Coding a Managed Class

There are a couple of items to take care of when building the library. For this example, you will create a `Stack` class for `String` data types because VBA does not provide any such data structure. To accomplish this task, you will need to do four things: Create the class name and attributes, create the constructor, declare the data members, and define the class methods. Each of these steps is explained in the following sections.

Adding Using Statements

Because you will be using the `InteropServices` namespace, add the follow using statement to the top of the `Stack.cs` file:

```
using Sytem.Runtime.InteropServices;
```

code snippet Stack.cs in ManagedCodeExample sample files

Creating an Interface for the Class

For the library to be callable from COM, you must create and implement an interface object that the `Stack` class will inherit and adhere to. This interface will expose all of the data members and methods to COM, so COM knows how to call the .NET code. Inside of the `ManagedCodeExample` namespace of the `Stack.cs` file, add the following code to define an `IStackBuilder` interface for the `Stack` class:

```
[ComVisible(true)]
public interface IStackBuilder
{
    int Count { get; }
    void Clear();
    string Peek();
    string Pop();
    void Push(string Data);
}
```

code snippet Stack.cs in ManagedCodeExample sample files

Note that the preceding `interface` code has an attribute of `ComVisible`, which is set to `true`. This is required so that the `interface` object may be referenced by COM. Now that the interface has been defined, the `Stack` class may implement it, as you will see next.

Choosing a Class Name

Next, choose a class name to be used to call the class from VBA code. This will be the data type for the object in VBA, which is all a class really is. For this example, use the name `Stack` as the class name. Also, add the `ComVisible(true)` and `ClassInterface(ClassInterfaceType.None)` attributes to the `class` declaration. And finally, the `Stack` class must inherit the `IStackBuilder` interface that you created in the previous section. To accomplish this modification, change the class declaration code in the `Stack.cs` file to the following:

Available for download on Wrox.com

```
[ComVisible(true)]
[ClassInterface(ClassInterfaceType.None)]
public class Stack : IStackBuilder
```

code snippet Stack.cs in ManagedCodeExample sample files

Creating the Data Members

Next, let's create two data members for our class: one to store the actual `Stack` object, and the other to return the `Count` property of the stack. Add the following variable declarations to the `Stack` class, just inside the class declaration:

Available for download on Wrox.com

```
// Storage for the Stack data
private Stack<string> _stack;

// Get Only! Returns the current Count of the Stack
public int Count
{
    get { return _stack.Count; }
}
```

code snippet Stack.cs in ManagedCodeExample sample files

Notice that the `Count` data member has only a `get` method because the `Count` is actually returned from the underlying stack data member and is not settable in this manner. The `Count` will automatically be incremented as data is added to the `stack`.

Creating the Constructors

Now that you have your data members, you can create the default constructor for the `Stack` class. The constructor will do one simple thing: create a new instance of our underlying stack data member. The following code provides an example of how to create this constructor:

Available for download on Wrox.com

```
public Stack()
{
        this._stack = new Stack<string>();
}
```

code snippet Stack.cs in ManagedCodeExample sample files

> *Note that to be creatable by COM, the class must provide a public default constructor.*

Now, whenever a new instance of the `Stack` class is created, our underlying stack member will be assigned a new instance of the `Stack`.

Creating the Methods

Finally, the last thing to do to create the `Stack` class is to add the four standard methods of a stack: `Clear`, `Peek`, `Pop`, and `Push`. Each of these methods will simply call the underlying method in our `_stack` data member. Add the following code to expose these methods from the `Stack` class:

```
public void Clear()
{
    this._stack.Clear();
}

public string Peek()
{
    return this._stack.Peek();
}

public string Pop()
{
    return this._stack.Pop();
}

public void Push(string Data)
{
    this._stack.Push(Data);
}
```

code snippet Stack.cs in ManagedCodeExample sample files

After these four members have been implemented, the `Stack` class is ready to go! You have essentially just wrapped the `Stack` class to make it a stack of strings that can be used in VBA. The data type could have just as easily been `object` to make it usable for any VBA data type, or you even could have wrapped the `List` or the `Queue` class just as easily. Essentially all .NET assemblies can be used with VBA code.

Signing the Managed Assemblies

For the managed `Stack` class to be usable from VBA code, the DLL must be signed. Visual Studio will take care of the process to sign the DLL when it is built, but you must first supply the project files with an SNK (Strong Name Key) file to sign the assembly with. If you do not have this already, it's okay — you can generate one very easily by using the Visual Studio 2010 tools.

Creating an SNK File

To create an SNK file, simply open the Visual Studio Command Prompt found under the Visual Studio Tools directory, which is found under the Microsoft Visual Studio 2010 directory on the Windows Start menu. The Visual Studio Command Prompt already has all of the VS tools and environment variables set up so you do not have to worry about knowing all of the exact paths to the tools callable from the command line. To create a new SNK file for the project, execute the following command in the Visual Studio Command Prompt:

```
sn -k `c:\ManagedCodeExample.snk"
```

A new SNK file will be created under the C: drive root directory. The SNK file is now ready to be added to the project, so copy it into the ManagedCodeExample project directory.

Setting the Project's SNK File

When the project is compiled, the resulting DLL (or other assembly) can be signed, if specified to do so in the project properties. This is required if you plan to distribute the DLL in raw form to the users of the application. To apply the SNK file to the project settings, complete the following steps:

1. In the Solution Explorer pane, right-click the ManagedCodeExample project file, just under the Solution file, and choose the Properties option from the context menu. This will open the project properties page.

2. On the left side of the project properties page, click the Signing tab that is all the way at the bottom. This will open the Code Signing dialog box for the project.

3. Check the Sign the assembly checkbox. This will enable several options.

4. From the pull-down menu, choose the SNK file option (if it is already part of the project files) or otherwise, choose the Browse option and browse to the SNK file.

5. Make sure the Delay Sign Only checkbox is *not* selected. Then click Save and close the project properties page; the SNK file has been added to the project.

Now that the SNK file has been applied to the project, any time the project is compiled, the signature will be added to the output assembly.

Building the Managed Class

Now that the code for the managed library is completely written, all you have to do is build the code and it will be ready for deployment. From the Build menu, choose the Rebuild Solution option and the debug flavor of the project will be built. Once the project has finished compiling, go to the bin/Debug directory found inside of the project directory. You should see a DLL file in this folder named, for this example, ManagedCodeExample.dll. This DLL file contains the Stack code that you created in the previous step.

Creating a COM Type Library for the Assembly

Finally a COM Type Library, will need to be created for the managed library so that the DLL can be referenced by COM applications. To create a type library file for the DLL, simply copy the built DLL file to the C: drive root, open the Visual Studio Command Prompt again, and issue the following command:

```
regasm /tlb `c:\ManagedCodeExample.dll"
```

A new TLB file will be created for the DLL assembly, under the C: drive root, which can be consumed by Access to add a reference to our new managed library.

Deploying the Managed Class

Now that you have the DLL file, it can be freely distributed to any person who wants to use the managed `Stack` class in their VBA or other supporting code projects. But, it is important to note that the user of this DLL and any user of an application that uses this DLL, must have the .NET Framework 4.0 (for this example) installed on his or her machine for this code to work correctly. Also, the DLL will have to have the TLB file created and registered on each machine it is used on, to be callable from COM, which is typically done during the Access applications setup process. And remember, to be able to actually use this DLL, the client machine must have .NET 4.0 runtime installed. Other than that, distributing a COM callable DLL files created in .NET is as easy as copying the files to the desired location and registering the type library!

Calling a Managed Library from VBA

Now that you have built the managed library and have the DLL and TLB file, the only thing left to do is to implement the code in an Access application. This section discusses the steps required to reference and call the managed `Stack` class code. Complete the steps in this section to implement the managed code in Access.

Choosing a Database

The first thing you need is an Access application to create some VBA code in. Any old Access application will do and for this example, you will just use a new blank database. Once you have created a new blank database, open in it Access, create a new form in Design View, and drop a button control on it. Cancel the Command Button Wizard and then hit the F4 key to open the Property Sheet. For the `OnClick` event, choose the Code Builder option to open VBE. Once VBE is open, you can add a reference to the managed code library and then begin calling it in VBA code.

Setting References

The first thing to do is to copy the DLL and TLB files into the same directory as the Access database, so that you always know where they are located relative to the Access application. Of course, once they have been moved to the new location, the DLL will need to have a new TLB file generated, per the steps above. Now that VBE has been opened, add a reference to the TLB file by completing the following steps:

1. On the VBE Tools menu, click on the References option. This opens the References dialog box.

2. In the Reference dialog box, click the Browse button and browse to the TBL file. Then click the Open button to add a reference to the TBL file to the Access project.

3. Click OK to close the References dialog box.

A reference is now set and the managed library in the code project for the Access application and the `Stack` class is ready to begin coding.

Calling the .NET Code from VBA Code

Now that the managed library has been referenced, VBA code can be created in the project to utilize that code. For example, the following VBA code for the `OnClick` event for the Button control could be used to implement the `Stack` class:

Available for download on Wrox.com

```
Dim stk As New Stack
Dim str As String

stk.Push "Geoff"
stk.Push "Rob"

str = stk.Pop   ` str=Rob
str = stk.Pop   ` str=Geoff
```

code snippet ManagedCodeExample.accdb in ManagedCodeExample sample files

Congratulations — you have now successfully implemented a .NET managed library in an Access application. Building Access applications that use .NET managed code is a great way to use .NET objects in places where they are not otherwise included with VBA. Additionally, using .NET allows the creation of custom, user-defined classes and other data types that would not be possible in VBA alone. Calling .NET code from VBA is a simple yet extremely powerful way to leverage .NET in your Access applications.

SUMMARY

Using .NET with Access 2010 is extremely powerful and easy to do, and there are a number of distinctly different methods available for doing so. This chapter reviewed the basics of Visual Studio 2010 and how to create, code, build, and debug .NET applications. To put this knowledge of Visual Studio to good use, this chapter reviewed the four basic methods for using .NET with Access. Access databases can be used by both .NET Windows and Web applications. Windows client applications can automate Access to provide the Access program and its functionality from within the parent application. COM Add-ins can be created for Access 2010 to provide custom functionality from within the Access client application. And finally, .NET assemblies can even be called and executed directly from VBA code. The possibilities for using .NET and Access together are limitless!

21

Building Client-Server Applications with Access

WHAT'S IN THIS CHAPTER?

- ➤ Building client-server applications using Access 2010 and SQL Server

- ➤ Creating a connection to SQL Server from an Access application

- ➤ Analyzing and optimizing the performance of an Access application connected to SQL Server

- ➤ The differences between using the ACCDB/MDB and ADP file formats against SQL Server

- ➤ Implementing both bound and unbound form and report objects to a SQL Server data source

- ➤ Building forms and reports in ADPs

Access 2010 makes it easy to create applications that interact with other data source formats and enterprise-level database servers. Unfortunately, the easiest methods are not always the best, and incorrect choices can have serious long-term effects on the design, stability, maintenance, and overall success of a project. A thorough understanding of how Access interacts with other databases and the various alternatives that are available for developers is critical to making the best design decisions for any given application.

Chapters 11 and 12 cover working with many of the objects discussed throughout this chapter. Appendixes B and C also provide more in-depth details about the specific objects, methods, and properties used in this chapter. All of these chapters can be used in conjunction with the material found here and are recommended reading as part of learning about client-server applications.

DATABASE APPLICATION EVOLUTION

In a typical business environment, Access database applications tend to sprout up because some individual or small group needs functionality and creates an Access database to implement a viable solution. Other people or groups notice the application's usefulness and decide to use the solution as well. Someone may even split the data tables into a back-end database and link the tables in a front-end application, so that large numbers of users can use a local copy on their machines and connect to the tables stored on a central server. Before long, what began as a personal database application is now shared on the network server, contains hundreds of megabytes of business data, is used on a daily basis by 50 or so people, and requires 2 or 3 people just to maintain and administrate the database. The application has become an unintended, albeit critical, piece of the company's business process.

The solution is cost effective. So another database is created for a different problem, and then a third database, and so on until there are hundreds of applications all over the network, some in use, some dead, and maybe even some that were never even completed. Many IT workers cringe at a mere whisper of the words "Access database" because these applications become difficult to track, maintain, and support. Where does all this data come from? Who has access to the data? Who backs up the data? Who developed this application? Who is maintaining and supporting this database? These are just some of the questions to ask when thinking about how to deal with large numbers of Access databases in a business environment.

Fortunately, there are some easy answers to these tough questions that allow users the flexibility of creating Access database applications and save IT the headache of having to support and maintain all of the data. If the data is stored in a controlled, centralized location, an IT department can effectively manage the database and control which users can view/modify the data. In this case, the more ideal solution would be to use a database server as the centralized location, enabling both developers and administrators to leverage the server's features to help them with their tasks. Fortunately, Access provides the capability to create front-end applications to connect to separate, back-end data sources of many different types. Applications that connect to remote data sources are referred to as the client-server application architecture, which we will discuss throughout this chapter.

CLIENT-SERVER APPLICATIONS

A normal Access application, one with only local tables, is known as a *file-server* application. In this model, all processing occurs on the local client machine regardless of where the file is physically stored. The idea is that the local machine's or network server's file system will accept commands from the ACE (Access Connectivity Engine) database engine, that are made directly from Access to manipulate the data within the database file. This is the key difference between a file-server and a client-server application.

In the *client-server* application model, an application residing on the local machine requests data from a data server that is completely separate from the client application. Often there are many copies of this front-end, client application that are connecting to and retrieving data from a single, or a few, remote data sources. At a minimum, the term "client-server" implies the design of the application is separated into at least two components: a client-side application that allows the user to interact with the data stored in the database, and a server that is responsible for maintaining data and executing requests from the client application. This type of application design can yield great performance and maintenance benefits, especially when large numbers of users are frequently interacting with the data.

Although it's tempting to think that simply moving your Access database application tables to a Microsoft SQL Server 2008 database server will make the program a client-server application, in reality, that's only the beginning. It is more accurate to say: Moving the data to SQL Server provides the potential for a client-server application. The application still needs to take advantage of that potential for most of the benefits to be realized. And, depending on the application, designing client-server applications may also yield a few drawbacks. For reasons discussed later in this chapter, it is not uncommon for an application to be slower immediately after migrating the data from the local file to a SQL Server, or other server, database. Regardless of the application format chosen, significant performance, security, maintenance, and storage benefits can be realized through the careful planning of the design of any Access database solution.

Using the Sample Files

This chapter defines techniques for creating client-server applications that store data in a SQL Server database. These SQL Server–specific examples use Microsoft SQL Server Express Edition 2008 as the database server, installed on the local machine. If you do not have SQL Server Express 2008 installed, you can download it for free from Microsoft. The SQL Server Express binaries and samples can be found at:

```
http://www.microsoft.com/express/Database/
```

In addition, the database used for the examples in this chapter is included with the download files for the book. The `Sample.SQL` script, included with these files, will build the sample SQL database used in the examples in this chapter when executed in SQL Server Management Studio. The sample files for this chapter can be downloaded from this book's Web page at Wrox.com.

SQL SERVER EXPRESS EDITION 2008

If you do not have SQL Server installed, but want to use the sample files or try the examples in this chapter, Microsoft SQL Server Express Edition 2008 can be downloaded and installed for free. Just navigate to `http://www.microsoft.com/express/Database/` and follow the links. Be sure to download SQL Server Management Studio Express as well because it provides a visual interface for working with the SQL Server toolset.

Installing SQL Server Express 2008 requires that the .NET Framework 2.0 or greater be installed on the machine prior to the server installation. For the examples in this chapter, the SQL Express 2008 with Runtime and Advanced Services package is used. Installation instructions are provided on the Microsoft website.

After you've installed SQL Server, you may want to make a few modifications to the server's configuration. By default, network connections from the TCP/IP connections are disabled. Complete the following steps to enable TCP/IP connections:

1. From the Windows Start menu, invoke the SQL Server Configuration Manager. The configuration manager will be invoked. In the left pane in the manager, select SQL Server 2008 Network Configuration ➪ Protocols for SQLEXPRESS.

2. Notice that TCP/IP connections are marked as disabled. This means that incoming connection requests from the network will be denied. To enable network connections, right-click the TCP/IP option on the right side of the screen and select the Enabled option. A message tells you that changes will take effect after the server is restarted. Click OK and you return to the configuration manager.

   In addition to enabling the TCP connections in SQL Server Express, the Windows Firewall setting may also need to be configured to accept incoming TCP connections. Consult Windows Firewall help if this is the case.

3. In the left pane, select the SQL Server 2008 Services option again and in the right pane, right-click SQL Server and choose Stop. This stops the SQL Server services. Right-click the SQL Server option again and choose Start to restart the server, applying the changes for network connections. Then exit the configuration manager program, as the SQL Server is now configured correctly.

Installing the Sample Database

Once the SQL Server has been installed and configured, the machine is ready to add the sample database to the system.

1. From the Windows Start menu, navigate to the Microsoft SQL Server 2008 folder and click on the SQL Server Management Studio Express option.

2. The Connect to Server dialog box will be invoked. By default, the name of the SQL Server is *machine name*\SQLEXPRESS. Input the Server Name and click the Connect button. Management Studio Express is connected and you are ready to create the sample database.

3. In Object Explorer, right-click the Databases folder and choose New Database. Type **NorthwindCS** for the database name in the New Database dialog box and then click OK. A new empty database with the name NorthwindCS is created. Now you're ready to import all of the objects and data in the Sample.SQL file included in this chapter's download files.

4. From the File menu, choose Open and browse to Sample.SQL. This action prompts you to connect to SQL Server again, so click the Connect button again.

5. Sample.SQL will be open for viewing in the main document window of Management Studio. Click the Execute button on the SQL Editor's toolbar to create the sample database. The script runs and the new database table schema, data, and other objects are created. The sample database is ready for use on the new SQL Server. Now you can get down to business.

Choosing the Correct File Format

Many misconceptions exist regarding the differences between the Access Project (ADP) file format and the various Access database (ACCDB and MDB) file formats. Even before ADP files were available (introduced in Access 2000), many developers did not fully understand how MDB files worked or how to optimize their usage in a client-server environment. Although even serious design mistakes can still provide acceptable performance when there is not a large amount of data in the database, as the data grows, the inefficient design becomes more and more detrimental to the application's performance and reliability.

Microsoft Office Access 2010 provides the Access Connectivity Engine (ACE) — also called the Access database engine. If you've used previous versions of Access, you are probably very familiar with ACE's predecessor, the Jet database engine. ACE is a privatized version of the Jet database engine with a number of feature enhancements. Using ACE, Access 2010 supports creating the following file formats: ACCDB (Access 2007 file format), MDB (Access 2000 and 2002–2003 file formats), ADP (Access Project), MDE (Access Complied MDB database), ACCDE (Access Complied ACCDB database), MDA (Access MDB Add-in), ACCDA (Access ACCDB Add-in), and ACCDC (Access Signed CAB file). This section discusses some of the differences between the ACCDB/MDB and ADP file formats.

THE ACCDB/MDB FILE FORMAT

Since its inception in 1992, the Jet (Joint Engine Technology) database engine has been the backbone for every Access version up until the Access 2007 release. One of the main reasons Jet has been so successful is that it has been available since Microsoft Windows 3.0. Originally released as a part of Access, it was eventually separated and shipped with Microsoft Windows as a system component. This meant that any ODBC (Open Database Connectivity) or compatible development environment could employ the Jet database engine without requiring that Access be installed on the system. For example, VBA code (or other programming languages) can make use of a Jet MDB file format database without requiring that Access be installed — and many do! Even today, ADO.NET can be used to connect to MDB file format databases without a hitch, providing a simple and free database system for many different programming environments.

Access 2010 ACE supports most of the features that Jet provided in the 2000 and 2002–2003 MDB file formats. While data in certain legacy formats can still be edited via Access 2010, it should be noted that 2000 and 2002–2003 MDB files are the only two legacy MDB file formats still fully supported for database design by Access 2010. The ACCDB file format continues to be the primary database file format and supports the new features of Access 2010, such as the new macros. While ACCDB file format is essentially the same as the MDB file format (plus a lot more system tables), there are some key differences. The following are features that the ACCDB file format supports, but are not supported for MDB files:

➤ Calculated fields in tables

➤ Web application components, such as Web Forms and Web Reports, and Data Macros

➤ Conditional branching in macros

➤ A number of macros added after the 2003 MDB file format

➤ Complex Data and Attachment field types for tables

➤ Complex Data fields for linked tables to SharePoint lists

➤ Append-only Memo field types

➤ Database file encryption

➤ The Access 2007 Import/Export specifications

➤ Some of the newer features in Forms and Reports, such as the Anchor properties

Additionally, there are several features supported in MDB, but not in ACCDB, including:

➤ User-level security and the Workgroup Database (MDW) files

➤ Database file encoding

➤ Digital signatures (2003 MDB file format only)

On the other hand, MDB and ACCDB file format databases are similar in that they store all of the data, database objects, VBA modules, and database properties directly in a single file structure. Starting with Access 2000, all non-data objects are stored in a single record of a database system table used by Access. Upon opening a database file, Access searches for this record and loads the VBA project and all other objects employed by the database application.

In addition to storing the table data directly within the file, the MDB and ACCDB file formats support linking tables to external data sources such as ODBC, SQL server tables, SharePoint lists, other MDB/ACCDB files, Excel Workbook files, and so on. These linked tables are used to connect to the back-end data source, completing the client-server application architecture. The Access Object Model, DAO, and ADO components all support working with linked tables to develop robust database client-server applications. Also, Access provides the ADP file format specifically for building client-server applications with SQL Server, which will be discussed shortly. But first, let's explore a little more about linked tables and MDB and ACCDB files.

Linking to External Data

Access 2010 supports connecting to a wide variety of external data source types using linked tables. Although a few of these sources are read-only, many external data sources are fully updatable from an Access database. This is because each different data source uses a separate and distinct method to connect to the actual data file. The ISAM (Indexed Sequential Access Method) drivers are generally used for connecting to other desktop or file-based data sources, such as Excel, text, and HTML. On the other hand, ODBC data source vendors typically supply connection utilities for use with their specific database products, specifically to provide an API for working with their data source. For most ODBC data sources, the client machine is required to have the relevant utilities installed, before the front-end application can connect to the data source. For example, even though Access ships with an ODBC driver for Oracle, the Oracle client utilities still need to be installed on the machine for the ODBC driver to be of any use to an Access application. No matter which ODBC data source you decide to use, Access makes it very easy to set up a DSN to the data server.

Creating a DSN via Access

Access 2010 makes it very easy to create linked tables to many different types of ODBC data sources, and even provides a boot strap for creating Windows DSN files directly from the Access UI. Although this is not the only method for creating a DSN, the following steps outline a very common method for creating a connection to a SQL Server Express database, using the Access ODBC Database Wizard:

1. To create a link to an external data source from an Access ACCDB file, select the External Data tab on the Ribbon. In the Import group, click ODBC Database option. This will open the Get External Data — ODBC Database Wizard.

2. In the wizard, choose Link to the data source by creating a linked table (the second radio button in the list) and then click OK. This will invoke the Select Data Source dialog box, which enables you to create links from the current database to other supported ODBC databases.

3. You can select a pre-existing data source name (DSN) connection or create a new data source. For now, open the Machine Data Source tab and click the New button. The Create New Data Source dialog box will be opened.

On Windows Vista or 7, you may get a warning that you are not able to create system DSN connections because of how Access is run and/or the permission level of the Windows account. The warning should provide instructions so that you can create a user DSN.

The path contained here determines the location in the Registry where the connection information will be stored. User-specific data source locations are stored in the following registry key and are available only to the current user:

```
HKEY_CURRENT_USER\Software\ODBC\ODBC.INI
```

Machine data sources are available for all user profiles and are stored in the following registry location:

```
HKEY_LOCAL_MACHINE\SOFTWARE\ODBC\ODBC.INI
```

Odd but true: HKCU Registry entries use the proper case of Software *for that node, while HKLM Registry entries use an uppercasing of* SOFTWARE *for that node. However, the registry is case-insensitive, so it would be okay to make these consistent, although you will see the different cases when viewed from the Windows Registry Editor.*

4. To create a system DSN connection on Windows Vista, you must be logged into an Administrator account or Access will need to be run as an administrator. For now, choose User Data Source, and click the Next button. The next Create New Data Source page will open.

5. At this point, the screens and options presented vary depending on what drivers are present on the machine and which drivers you choose. For now, select the SQL Native Client option from the list, click Next, and then click Finish to bring up the dialog box information specific to SQL Server.

6. Enter **TestDSN** for a name and, optionally, the description for the connection. You can type in the name of your SQL Server or you can select it from the list box. The name of the SQL Server is typically `machine name\database server` — for example: MyMachineName\ SQLServerExpress. Also, a default SQL Server can be configured for the machine, and in that case, you can enter the value (local) to reference the default instance of the SQL Server on the machine. Click Next and the next page of the wizard will be opened.

7. Enter the necessary security credentials to log into the server. The credentials will depend on how the particular SQL Server is configured. If the steps shown earlier were used to install the SQL Server, choose the option to use NT Authentication for the Windows User Account. If your server administrator has specified users using SQL Server authentication, select the proper option and type in the proper username and password. Click Next to continue.

8. The last setting to change is the default database. The default database can be selected on a per-connection basis and different connections can reference different databases on the same server. The default database selection determines the database context for which commands are issued against the server. For example, if code is called to select records from a table in the `NorthwindCS` database, but the default database is the master database used by SQL Server, the query results in an error because the table doesn't exist in the master database. Always specify a default database other than the master database to help prevent any accidental, unwanted modifications to the database.

9. For this example, select the `NorthwindCS` database (which you created earlier) from the default database list and then click Next. The remaining default option settings should be fine, so click Finish to complete the wizard. All of the options selected for the new connection will be displayed.

10. Click the Test Data Source button to ensure that the connection is working correctly. If the connection is working, the dialog box displays the message: TESTS COMPLETED SUCCESSFULLY. Click OK to close the dialog box.

11. You are returned to the Select Data Source dialog box, which now shows a new data source called TestDSN, the connection you just created. If new links are needed for this connection in the future, the existing DSN can be used instead of creating another one from scratch. Select the TestDSN option from the Select Data Source dialog box.

12. Then click OK. The Link Tables dialog box opens showing all of the available objects in the database for the DSN connection that was just created. The names and types of objects depend on the data source, but in this case, you should see the NorthwindCS tables, assuming you are using the NorthwindCS database provided in the sample files.

13. Select the dbo.Orders table object and click OK. A link to the dbo.Orders table is created and is shown in the Navigation Pane. This new link is created directly to the NorthwindCS database on SQL Server and any changes made to the data are reflected in updates to the data on the server. At this point, the new linked table is available to view, bind to a form or report, reference in code, or use in any other way a normal table can be used, except for modifying the schema of the table.

Because the table is linked and the actual structure and data reside on the SQL Server, changes to the design of the table must be completed from the SQL Server database. Design permissions do not affect the data permissions directly, only the schema. However, the user must also have credentials to modify the data in the table(s); otherwise data modification will be impossible, made possible by the SQL Server security model. In short, an Access database application with linked tables to another data source has only as much permission as the user's account credentials, provided in the connection string, have to that particular data source.

DSN Connection Types

There are two primary DSN connection types available on the Windows platform: a DSN file and a machine DSN. A DSN file is a text file that contains all of the relevant connectivity information (including the username and, optionally, the password) for the data source and can be easily moved around from machine to machine or deployed with an installation package. A machine DSN stores the connectivity information in the registry, and therefore is specific to only that machine, which can prove much more difficult to set up without direct access to the machine itself.

Access handles these DSN types differently depending on which is chosen. With a file DSN, Access stores the connectivity information directly in the database file and only retrieves the connection information from the file the first time the connection is made for that instance of the database application. That really means that Access does not need to re-query the DSN each time a table or view is accessed. With a machine DSN, Access must query the registry to retrieve the connectivity information with each time the connection to data source is used. Although this will have a small impact on the overall performance of a database application, in terms of security, the machine DSN is more secure because it cannot be moved from machine to machine as easily.

Using ACE with ODBC Data Sources

Because ACE, and its predecessor, Jet, send information across the network to the data source during the execution of an Access application, it's important to consider exactly when and how much data is being transferred. You should understand that the bandwidth of the network connections, the current load on the data server, and amount of data being transferred across the network all directly affect the overall performance of an Access client-server application. Fortunately, SQL Server provides the tools necessary to help analyze these sorts of operations between the Access application and the SQL Server, and using these tools to analyze and make updates to the application can, in some cases, lead to vast improvements in application performance.

The SQL Server Profiler Tool

Before delving into the intricacies of how ACE (and Jet) sends and retrieves data specifically from SQL Server, it is important to mention the SQL Server Profiler tool. The SQL Server Profiler tool can help determine when and how much data is being transferred across a network. The Profiler provides a breakdown of the commands and data sent to and from SQL Server.

USE THE SQL SERVER PROFILER TO SPY ON ACCESS

If the full version of Microsoft SQL Server 2008 is installed, the SQL Server Profiler tool can be used to watch commands that are sent to SQL Server. The Profiler allows creation of a Trace Session, which logs every command sent to the server, as well as some performance information.

A new session of the SQL Server Profiler can be started from the SQL Server Management Studio. Choose Tools ⇨ SQL Server Profiler to launch the program. Once the Profiler tool is opened, choose File ⇨ New Trace to create a new tracing session. You are prompted to connect to the SQL Server that contains the database to which your Access application is linked, and to enter custom properties. If you just want to view the SQL commands that Access issues to the server, accept all the default values and choose Run to start the Profiler session.

After a tracing session has been established with the database, every command sent from Microsoft Access to the SQL Server will be captured and shown in the trace window, along with a variety of performance information.

To view the results of a SQL command that is listed in the trace window, simply highlight that command and copy the SQL text from the lower half of the trace window. You can then paste the SQL into a new query in SQL Server Management Studio, or create a SQL Pass-through query in your Microsoft Access database. Run the query to see the results that Access received when it ran the query.

Linked-Table Performance Considerations

When a linked table is opened in a database application, Access retrieves the primary key information for the table as well as a few records, if any exist. For example, double-click the dbo.Orders table in the Navigation Pane, and Access sends the following query to the NorthwindCS database:

```
SELECT `dbo`.`Orders`.`OrderID` FROM dbo_Orders;
```

This query provides Access with a full list of the unique record identifiers for the existing records contained within the table. Once Access has been sent this information from SQL Server, each of the records contained in the table can be retrieved for viewing or data processing. To gather a few of the records from the table, Access issues another query to the SQL Server, which would be similar to the following:

```
declare @P1 int
set @P1=3
```

```
exec sp_prepexec @P1 output, @P1 int, @P2 int, @P3 int, @P4 int,
@P5 int, @P6 int, @P7 int, @P8 int, @P9 int, @P10 int,
`SELECT `OrderID`, `CustomerID`,`EmployeeID`, `OrderDate`,
`RequiredDate`, `ShippedDate`, `ShipVia`, `Freight`, `ShipName`,
`ShipAddress`, `ShipCity`, `ShipRegion`, `ShipPostalCode`,
`ShipCountry`
FROM `dbo`.`Orders`
WHERE `OrderID` = @P1 OR `OrderID` = @P2 OR `OrderID` = @P3 OR
`OrderID` = @P4 OR `OrderID` = @P5 OR `OrderID` = @P6 OR `OrderID`
= @P7 OR `OrderID` = @P8 OR `OrderID` = @P9 OR `OrderID` = @P10´,
10249, 10251, 10258, 10260, 10265, 10267, 10269, 10270, 10274,
10275;
select @P1
```

Using the SQL Server Profiler tool, you can see this operation occur, including the full and exact text used by Access to retrieve the first few records, as shown above. Otherwise, ACE performs all of this functionality under the covers and it is never directly shown to the user (or developer) of the Access application.

In the preceding command, the `sp_prepexec` stored procedure prepares a SQL statement for use by subsequent queries and accepts parameter input to retrieve the first few rows (those with `OrderID` 10249-10275). After that statement runs, Access can use the `sp_execute` procedure to retrieve small batches of rows at a time, as shown by the following, and above, statement:

```
exec sp_execute 3, 10280, 10281, 10282, 10284, 10288, 10290, 10296, 10309, 10317,
    10323
```

The exact query text used is specific to the back-end database server and is handled by the ODBC driver for the DSN. Although the specifics are different, ACE uses the same overall process for retrieving first the primary key information, and then retrieving batches of rows based on the primary key information, in this case, a list of OrderID field values for the first set of rows.

Query Performance Considerations

When opening a query instead of a table, these actions are performed for each table in the query. In this situation, Access usually does the following:

1. Requests primary key data for each table separately.

2. Joins the key data locally on the client machine.

3. Requests all needed field data from each table separately based on the key field.

4. Joins the requested data together in a local `Recordset` and displays it to the user.

Compound Key Performance Considerations

If a query has compound primary keys defined for each table, Access may end up pulling down a lot of data that needs to be joined locally before it even begins to retrieve the data that will eventually be returned in the query result. If the application has a table with thirteen fields, but twelve of these fields comprise a compound primary key, Access will end up bringing down the twelve primary key fields twice: once to get the primary key data by itself and again for a second time to get data to be returned in the query result. Needless to say, using compound key fields in ODBC data sources can force the Access application to have a lot of overhead, but there is still hope for reducing the expense of compound keys.

Increasing DSN Performance

Under certain circumstances, Access will have the primary key joining done on the server. Unlike the previous example in which Access retrieved all the primary key data for each table and joined it locally, if *all* the tables in a particular query are based on the same DSN, Access can sometimes pass a WHERE clause to join the data on the server. For example, if you create a local query in an ACCDB file based on linked `Products`, `Suppliers`, and `Categories` tables from the `NorthwindCS` database on the SQL Server, and all three tables are based on the same DSN, a query similar to the following is executed by Access on the SQL Server:

```
SELECT `dbo`.`Products`.`ProductID`, `dbo`.`Categories`.`CategoryID`, `dbo`.`
    Suppliers`.`SupplierID`
FROM `dbo`.`Categories`, `dbo`.`Products`, `dbo`.`Suppliers`
WHERE ((`dbo`.`Products`.`CategoryID` = `dbo`.`Categories`.`CategoryID`) AND
    (`dbo`.`Products`.`SupplierID` = `dbo`.`Suppliers`.`SupplierID`))
```

This allows the join for `CategoryID` and `SupplierID` to be created and executed on the server instead of the client machine. The benefit is that only the primary key data that is necessary for the join will be passed over the network and brought down to Access. Although this is not as ideal as having all query processing happen on the server, it can dramatically improve performance depending on how the tables in the application are structured and joined, and more importantly, how much overall data transfers can be reduced.

 The most important element here is that all tables must be based on the exact same DSN connection. Even if two tables are from the same SQL Server database, but one table uses a file DSN and the other uses a different DSN, a less efficient process is used. Also, more efficient processing is not guaranteed even when the same DSN is used and depends on other factors, but data joins on the SQL Server cannot be completed if there is more than one DSN used for the tables being joined.

Increasing ODBC Performance

When dealing with a client-server environment, the most important factor to remember is to bring data across a network only if, and when, it is needed. However, pulling data across the network is not the only consideration for the performance of a client-server database application. There are three main contributors to performance degradation in a client-server environment:

➤ The time consumed processing on the server

➤ The time consumed processing on the client

➤ The time and bandwidth consumed moving records across the network

All three areas should be examined closely to detect bottlenecks or other performance degradation issues in a client-server application.

Server Resource Considerations

Insufficient server resources are rarely the cause of problems for Access client-server applications. In most cases, it is far more likely that shifting more processing to the server can increase performance. If query processing time on a server seems longer than expected, make sure that the application's table indexes are properly set and optimized. If locking issues occur, changing to the optimistic locking model and ensuring all connection are only open for edits when the editing is actually necessary, may help improve performance as well. Also, it is always good to consider the design of tables and queries in the application, to make sure they are not over-processing or gathering too much unnecessary data. Creating a proper relational database design can reduce performance issues due to improper database design. Unless there is a very large number of users working with the application at any given time, database servers, such as SQL Server, will typically have no problems handling the load from an Access client-server application, even when there are a great deal of clients connecting to the SQL Server.

Client Machine Resource Considerations

Unlike server resources, insufficient client resources are frequently the source of performance issues in an Access client-server database application. When joins are performed locally, queries can cause Access to bring down a lot of records simply to create a join before the requested data is retrieved, and will tend to be slow if there are inadequate resources on the local machine when this occurs. All other considerations being equal, the more RAM on the client machine, the faster the query is likely to run locally. Also, the greater the network bandwidth available, the faster the processing will seem to the user on the client machine, as the data will be pulled down more quickly. Whenever possible, we recommend that you shift as much processing of queries to SQL Server to reduce performance issues.

Network Performance Considerations

An all too common problem in a client-server application is when the tables for an ODBC data source are linked to a local table, (a table that resides in the local database) or a table from a different data connection. When queries containing joins between multiple tables from different sources are processed, the data for the join fields is always pulled down from the remote tables and joined locally. Then Access issues another request to fetch the records for the final result. The same is true with data sources that use an ISAM interface for the connection, such as linking to an Excel worksheet, text file, or other supported ISAM data source. Links to ODBC data sources that use ISAMs to manipulate data always consider each table a separate connection, even if they are contained in the same DSN file, such as two separate sheets in an Excel workbook. In the case of SharePoint, the ISAM has no way to join tables, even if they are on the same SharePoint server, because each table is considered a separate ODBC connection. Always try to minimize queries that use joins between different data sources and use server-side processing when possible to help reduce network traffic and improve application performance.

The second, and also very common, problem is that networks are often the cause of the bottlenecks for a client-server application because of the vast amount of data Access may retrieve for local joining. When the table contains large amounts of data and the keys need to be joined locally, Access can pull down tens or even hundreds of megabytes of data before returning a result that may consist of just one single record. In an environment where network bandwidth is low, such as a WAN or a dial-up environment, joining locally can be devastating to the application's performance. Unfortunately, this problem can be extremely difficult to overcome. One possible solution is to move any local data that requires large joins with server data, to the server first, and then shifting as much query processing to that server, to reduce the overall amount of records that would otherwise be pulled down to create the join and resulting data set.

Pass-Through Queries

Often overlooked, pass-through queries are an easy way to improve performance of a front-end, client application. Pass-through queries are processed entirely on the server and, as such, are a good technique for transferring data processing to the server. Unfortunately, there is no graphical user interface for creating the SQL statements of a pass-through query in Access, and probably more importantly, the data they return is read-only. However, SQL Server 2008 and many other products have built-in tools that are similar to the Access Query Builder and can generate SQL statements just as Access would, which can be used in the pass-through query. It is important to note that in Access 2010, SQL pass-through queries require that the database have code enabled before they can be run, which means that they will not work in disabled mode. Pass-though queries are a great way to help shift the processing of queries to SQL Server and hopefully improve overall client-server application performance.

Pass-Through Query Uses

Because pass-through query data is not updatable, those queries are not as useful for forms. On the other hand, pass-through queries are perfect for list boxes, combo boxes, and reports. Because report data does not need to be updatable, and tends to be based on multiple tables that potentially require joins to be processed locally, converting report Record Source properties from local queries to pass-through queries can realize dramatic performance benefits.

Creating a Pass-Through Query

Creating a pass-through query is extremely simple if you know how to write the proper SQL. On the Ribbon's Create tab, click the Pass-Through button in the Query menu. Because there is no graphical user interface, the SQL text is specific to the ODBC data source the query will run against. The following SQL can be used as a pass-through query against the NorthwindCS sample database:

```
SELECT dbo.Orders.OrderID, dbo.Customers.CompanyName,
    dbo.Customers.ContactName, dbo.Orders.OrderDate,
    dbo.Products.ProductName, dbo.[Order Details].Quantity
```

```
FROM dbo.Orders
INNER JOIN
    dbo.Customers ON dbo.Orders.CustomerID =
    dbo.Customers.CustomerID
INNER JOIN
    dbo.[Order Details] ON dbo.Orders.OrderID =
    dbo.[Order Details].OrderID
INNER JOIN dbo.Products ON
    dbo.[Order Details].ProductID =
    dbo.Products.ProductID
```

code snippet Query PassThroughJoins in Ch21_SampleACCDB.accdb

Access does not parse or validate the SQL text of a pass-through query in any way. Instead, the SQL text is sent (passed through) to the specified ODBC data source as-is and Access attempts to create a `Recordset` from whatever results are returned.

Note that when opening a SQL Pass-Through query, the user is prompted to select the DSN connection unless you set the query's connection property (through the Property Sheet in Query Design mode). But remember that there is a security issue to consider because the connection information is stored in plain text in this property. If the connection does not use NT Authentication, the `UserName` and `Password` properties for the ODBC connection are visible to anyone with access to the query.

Pass-through queries should be used whenever possible to help reduce network traffic and shift query processing to the server. Pass-through queries can result in huge improvements in the efficiency of Access applications that use linked tables to ODBC data source in an ACCDB/MDB file format.

THE ADP FILE FORMAT

Unlike Access ACCDB and MDB database files, ADP (Access Project) files are client-server applications by definition. ADPs were created specifically for working with SQL Server–based data sources, while still providing the rich features and flexibility of an Access application. The ADP file itself contains only the forms, reports, and other non-data objects such as the VBA project. The tables and queries for the application are stored on the SQL Server. Instead of opening a database and retrieving the VBA project stored in it, the VBA project is opened directly, and then Access connects to the SQL Server described by the connection properties stored in the ADP file.

ADPs neither use nor depend on the ACE or Jet database engines. Instead, ADO (ActiveX Data Objects) tools are used to connect to SQL Server, which is used as the database engine. All table and query objects, as well as all data, are stored on the server. After opening an ADP and connecting to the SQL Server, Access retrieves a list of server objects that the user has permission to view or execute and then displays the names in the Tables and/or Queries tabs in the Navigation Pane.

When you double-click on a table or query in an ADP, Access sends a simple SELECT statement to retrieve all of the object's records. Data processing happens on the server, and Access handles only the set of records returned and the presentation processing on the client side. If a SQL statement is specified as the Record Source for a form, report, or control, the SQL statement is sent as-is to the server.

Although ADP files make it easier to shift processing to the server, this won't help performance much if an application is repeatedly bringing down entire tables of data from the server, every time it needs to complete an arbitrary operation. It is important to limit the amount of data that is being pulled down by the application and the frequency with which the data is retrieved or updated. One common way to limit the data is to use `Recordset` objects and retrieve and modify records only when necessary. When a form or report is tied to a table or query, Access issues a command to the database server to modify the records and retrieve the data again *every time* the object is opened or modified. The `Recordset` object can be applied to the form or report, and updates or requeries to the data source can be completely controlled by the application's developer, through the use of VBA code. Of course, this requires more application design, coding, and testing, but the increased performance may be well worth the effort.

Using ADPs to Link to Data

ADP files are specifically designed to work with SQL Server and cannot be bound directly to any other type of data source. They are so tightly bound with and optimized for use with SQL Server that all data processing is done on the server, which can greatly improve performance. Fortunately, SQL Server has the capability to also link to other data sources, so if you need data from sources other than SQL Server, chances are that SQL Server can connect to it, thus providing the opportunity for using data sources aside from only SQL Server in an ADP application.

Linked Servers in SQL Server

SQL Server can store connection information, known as a linked server, in a system table in the SQL Server Master database. An alias is defined when the linked server is created and can be used to reference the server's connection details. The alias can be used from other SQL Server objects such as views, functions, and stored procedures. Views based on linked servers can be created programmatically or through the user interface in an ADP. Linked servers can be created directly through one of the SQL Server client tools, such as SQL Management Studio Express, or through the Access UI.

Creating Linked Servers with Access

To create a new linked-server view connection to a SQL Server, open the `Ch21_SampleADP.adp` file included with the download files for this chapter. Once this ADP file has been opened, complete the following steps:

1. Go to the Select File ➪ Server ➪ Link Tables to invoke the Link Table Wizard. The Link Table Wizard opens.

2. The Linked Server option should be selected by default. To continue, ensure the Linked Server option is selected and click Next. The Select Data Source dialog box opens.

3. From this point, the pages of the wizard vary depending on which data source you choose. To create a new link to another SQL Server, select +New SQL Server Connection.odc and

click Open. The Data Connection Wizard opens. Choose the SQL Server option and click Next. The wizard will request the name of the SQL Server.

4. Enter the name of the SQL Server to be linked, enter the necessary security credentials (in this case, you are using NT Authentication), and click Next to continue. A dialog box opens showing the databases and tables on the SQL Server.

5. Select the NorthwindCS database from the list of databases on the SQL Server in the Data Connection Wizard dialog box. Click Finish and the new SQL Server is linked. The dialog box closes, returning you to the Linked Table Wizard dialog box.

6. At this point, Access needs to know which view to use, so select the objects to create views against. In this case, select the Table:Orders table from the left list, click the > button to move the table to the right list, and click Finish. A new view data source file is created in your My Data Sources folder in My Documents.

Unfortunately, the wizard does not always function as well as one might like. It's generally good for creating links to other SQL Server data sources, but less reliable with other data sources. Sometimes Access creates the linked server, but not any views that use it. And even in some cases, Access won't be able to create the linked server at all. Fortunately, it is not too complicated to create the linked servers programmatically.

Creating Linked Servers with VBA Code

Linked Servers can be created by writing some ADO code to execute a SQL command to create the link. The `CurrentProject` object is the instance of the code project that is currently loaded in Access. It exposes the `Connection` object that can be used to specify the SQL Server to which the ADP is connected. The `Connection` object's `Execute` method can be used to execute commands accepted by the SQL Server. An application can link to a SQL Server by calling `Execute` with the proper SQL statement. Here's an example of linking to a SQL Server data source:

Available for download on Wrox.com

```
Dim strCommand As String

` Create the command to link to the SQL Server
strCommand = _
    "EXEC sp_AddLinkedServer " & _
    "@server='RemoteServerAlias', " & _
    "@srvproduct='', " & _
    "@provider='SQLOLEDB', " & _
    "@datasrc='<Machine Name>\<Instance Name>'"

` Execute the SQL command
CurrentProject.Connection.Execute strCommand
```

code snippet module SampleCode in Ch21_SampleADP.adp

`RemoteServerAlias` is the name to use when referencing the linked server in queries. Then `RemoteServerName` is the actual name of the remote network server that is being linked to. In the case of a SQL Server Express Edition installation (created at the beginning of this chapter), the format is *<machine name>*\sqlexpress. After creating the linked server, you can execute another SQL statement to create the other database objects by writing a few lines of code, such as the following:

```
Dim strCommand As String

` Create the SQL Statement to create a view object on the server
strCommand = _
  `Create View ViewName as ` & _
  `Select ShipperID, CompanyName, Phone ` & _
  `From RemoteServerAlias.NorthwindCS.DBO.Shippers;`

` Execute the SQL command
CurrentProject.Connection.Execute strCommand
```

code snippet module SampleCode in Ch21_SampleADP.adp

This code uses a standard SQL statement to create a new view object. Because all processing occurs on the server, the statement that is passed as the parameter for the Execute method is then, in turn, passed directly to SQL Server and not executed on the client machine. Therefore, any statement that can be processed on the SQL Server can be issued through the Execute method.

Query Options on SQL Server

The three types of query objects in SQL Server that can be used from an ADP are: views, stored procedures, and functions. Each of these types has its own unique strengths that can be leveraged in an ADP application.

SQL Server Views

Views on SQL Server can be thought of as virtual tables. Views can be used in the same manner as regular tables or query objects. The benefit of views is that they can be based on more than one source table and can be limited to include only the fields needed for a particular action. In general, views are similar to an Access Query object.

Although you can generally update, delete, and insert records into a view, if the view is based on multiple tables, there may be limitations on the type of actions a view can be used for — for example, when a SQL statement attempts to insert a record into a view based on multiple tables. The SQL statement generates an error because SQL Server doesn't always know what needs to be done to add a record to a view with multiple underlying tables.

This behavior can be modified on the SQL Server side by adding *triggers*. A trigger is conceptually similar to having a VBA event procedure for a table or other SQL Server object. Instead of running VBA code, triggers are written in SQL Server specific Transact-SQL (T-SQL) query syntax. For instance, it's possible to define a trigger for a view so that the actual inserts are handled by the trigger and don't generate a SQL Server error. Although the creation of SQL Server triggers is outside the scope of this book, you should be aware of their existence and know there is plenty of documentation on the Web about working with them.

Additionally, ADPs have a built-in mechanism for adding records to views based on two tables by adding the new records to the source tables directly and bypassing the view. This can sometimes have unexpected side effects for developers who are used to the regular SQL Server behavior. Even if a view is updatable (perhaps because a trigger has been added), Access attempts to update the view's source tables. If a user has permissions to a view, but not the view's source tables, a permissions error is generated when Access attempts to update the underlying table.

Fortunately, changing a view property can modify this behavior. While in Design mode for a view, right-click the background in the upper half of the design area and select Properties. To allow Access to update the view directly, instead of attempting to update source tables, select the "Update using view rules" checkbox.

SQL Server Stored Procedures

Unlike views, a stored procedure is a set of one or more SQL statements that can be executed on the server. However, Stored Procedures are not updatable directly from Access and cannot be used as a data source by other view objects. On the other hand, they can be created on the SQL Server and can be used to run update queries with complex logic, which regular views cannot do. Although the data returned from stored procedure objects is read-only in Access, it can appear to be updatable from the user interface of an ADP, if programmed to do so. Fortunately, Access is capable of working around the read-only restriction by updating the source tables directly. More savvy SQL developers often use Store Procedures to improve server performance and can be a great asset in a client-server application.

SQL Server Functions

Functions are a sort of cross between views and stored procedures. Unlike stored procedures, functions can be used as a data source in another query object, in the same manner as a view. Unlike a view, the data set returned by a function is not updatable. When opening a function from the user interface, Access can update the data in some cases by updating the source tables directly, similar to the method used to update a Stored Procedure. Functions tend to be useful in situations that call for returning a single value or a read-only `Recordset` object as part of another query.

ACCDB/MDB VERSUS ADP

The ACCDB/MDB and ADP file formats each have benefits and tradeoffs when connecting to SQL Server (or other data sources). It is important to consider these tradeoffs while designing the application before implementation occurs. It is not uncommon for an Access application to start out as an ACCDB or MDB and then eventually have the tables, queries, and data migrated to SQL Server once the application reaches critical mass. Along with this migration comes the cost for completing this work, which is dependent on the initial design of the application and the developer is faced with the choice of using the ACCDB/MDB or the ADP file format to build the front-end, client application. The following sections provide some information to consider before choosing one format over the other when building the client application that will connect to the SQL server.

Recordset Differences

ACCDB and MDB files use a Dynaset `Recordset` by default. Dynaset-type `Recordset` objects have the ability to see changes by other users in near real time. However, it's an expensive `Recordset` to maintain in terms of resource and network usage. If a user moves to the first record in a given table, then to the last record, and then back to the first, Access requeries the first record from the back-end database for updated values, instead of reusing the value that was previously pulled down. In addition, updates to the `Recordset` are committed immediately, so that other connected `Recordset` objects can see the updates immediately. While this may be useful for applications that have multiple users constantly accessing the same records, it means that a lot of data is pushed across the network. In effect, ACE maintains a rolling `Recordset` that contains just the records being viewed, along with a small buffer of records outside the current viewable set.

With an ADP, Access maintains an updatable snapshot `Recordset`. The user can scroll through the records and make changes, but those changes are not committed to the server until the query is rerun. The main benefit to this approach is that there is much less network traffic and, once the records are brought down, the user can move between records without being required to constantly requery large amounts of data. However, if an application is required to have many records that are to be displayed simultaneously and needs to be continuously updated by multiple users, then ACCDB/MDB files may be preferred, since to perform this functionality, the ADP will be required to continuously requery its current view. Although these methods allow the user to see the changes in near real-time, in an ADP, this functionality will require some custom code be created.

The other difference for `Recordset` objects is that ACCDB and MDB files use ACE, which is tightly bound with DAO objects, so the DAO `Recordset` objects are preferred. For ADP files, using ADO code is preferred, because ADO objects are used to connect to the SQL Server by Access. Although DAO can be used in an ADP in some limited cases, ADO is much more natural to use and is universal between an ACCDB/MDB and an ADP file, as well as other true ODBC data sources, because Access uses ADO to connect to these data sources, and DAO object types are not supported in most cases. The important thing to consider here is that the DAO `Recordset` and ADO `Recordset` objects are quite different and not directly interchangeable. For this reason, some database developers make the argument that all Access database code should be done in ADO, so that when the ACCDB grows large enough to be upsized to SQL Server, very little code has to be changed to update the application. Still, many people have a personal preference for using one Object Library over the other (usually because they are more familiar with one than the other) and will base their format choice on that preference. Although there is not necessarily a right or wrong choice here, if the application will use SQL Server as the back-end data source, it is probably easier in the long run to develop the application using ADO when possible.

Security Differences

With MDB, but not ACCDB or ADP, files, Access developers are able to enforce user-level security using the ACE database engine on almost all database objects, including forms and reports. However, using an ADP, user-level security features of SQL Server can be leveraged for the tables, views, and data in the database. Once tables and queries have been moved, SQL Server becomes the primary enforcer of security for those objects. But, there is no user-level security at the ADP file level for controlling permission to forms or reports. Instead, data access is controlled at the server level. The primary security mechanism at the ADP file level is to add a VBA project password or to convert the file to an ADE file, which strips away the source code. If the application is properly designed, there is no need for user-level security because logging in can be controlled through SQL Server permissions.

Local Data Storage

The inability to store local table and query objects in an ADP file is probably the biggest complaint developers have when moving from an ACCDB/MDB file format to the ADP environment. Unlike the ACCDB/MDB file format, every table and view in an ADP is stored on the SQL Server, and there is no way to have these stored locally in the ADP file itself. This is not as big a limitation as it may seem at first because there are still methods for storing data on the local machine if that's truly necessary.

The three primary methods to utilize local machine storage for tables, views, and data connected to an ADP are the following:

➤   Run SQL Server on the local machine. SQL Server can store tables, views, and data locally and can link to other SQL Server databases across the network.

➤   Have a separate ACCDB/MDB file on the local machine. As mentioned earlier, Access does support ADO, so the database can be accessed programmatically.

➤   Store XML (Extensible Markup Language) data locally. The XML data source could be connected to via code as well.

Even in an ADP, it is possible to store data on the local machine, just not in the ADP file itself.

Each of these options involves tradeoffs, but can be a suitable solution depending on the scenario. The best option for a given scenario usually depends on how the locally stored data needs to be used. For serious local number crunching, using SQL Server on the local machine provides a powerful database server for the application, but at the expense of more resource usage requirements. Alternatively, XML files consume few processor resources, but are more difficult to update and manipulate and may require large amounts of file space and consume lots of RAM, depending on how the XML is loaded. Additionally, XML file security is limited to the security of the network, so anyone with access to the directory can view the data. Using ACCDB/MDB files to store local data for an ADP uses fewer system resources than using SQL Server does, and can be easier to update than XML. But, it still requires more code in the application to connect and manipulate the database. The best option of these three will be dictated by the requirements and design of the actual Access application.

Sharing Application Files

Although Access supports opening ACCDB/MDB files over the network, and it is common to share applications from a central network location, this is not a true client-server application. Sharing ACCDB/MDB files over the network usually works well when only a small number of users are working with the database and they are not using it simultaneously. This greatly reduces the complexity added when creating an application that has both a front-end and back-end database, since users simply open it from the network location. But, this will often lead to other issues, such as record locking problems, as the number of users of the application grows. This functionality is made possible through the use of the ACE database engine, which can issue commands that are accepted by network file storage interfaces. However, to be a true client server application, designed to support larger multi-user scenarios, a front-end database file should be installed on each user's local machine and linked to SQL Server or to tables in back-end ACCDB/MDB file stored in a network location.

Because ADP files don't use ACE, the same instance of an ADP file cannot be opened by multiple users over a network. For ADPs, the only solution is to distribute a copy of the ADP file to each user, which can be run directly from their local machine. This is actually the essence of the client-server scenario: The front-end application is run on the client machine, while the back-end database handles all of the data and processing.

CONTROLLING THE LOGON PROCESS

The elegant way to handle logon errors when starting a client-server application is to control the logon process to the back-end database. Undoubtedly the client-server application will run into network or database server connectivity issues at some point in its lifecycle. If the connection process is not controlled at startup, users may get an unpleasant and confusing error message, and it will be difficult to control reconnection in the same session if the network/server becomes disconnected. Controlling the logon process from the beginning makes it quite easy to store the supplied username and password information for connecting to the data source without having to ask the user for security credentials again at a later time, if needed. The exact process and code needed to log in will vary depending on whether the ADP or ACCDB/MDB file format is used to create the application, but the following sections will explore both options.

Controlling Login for ACCDB/MDB Files

A graceful way to control the login process is to create a startup form in the application to prompt the user for his credentials. If the application uses SQL security and does not store user credentials explicitly, users may be prompted for credentials from the server when trying to read or manipulate objects in the application when Access first tries to use the table or view. Fortunately, it is easy to create a custom startup login form that prompts the user for their username and password.

In the case of linked tables in an ACCDB file, you will likely need code to create, or will already have created, a DSN to store connection information for the linked tables. The following code illustrates how to programmatically create a DSN:

```
Public Sub CreateNewDSN()

    ` Define Variables
    Dim strDSNName As String
    Dim strDriverName As String
    Dim strDescription As String
    Dim strServer As String
    Dim strDatabase As String

    ` This is the DSN name to use when
    ` referencing the DSL in your code
```

```
    strDSNName = "TestDSN"

    ` The name of the ODBC Driver used for the connection
    strDriverName = "SQL Server"

    ` This is the optional description to use
    ` in the ODBC Driver Manager program
    strDescription = "Test DSN Description"

    ` In the case of SQL Server, use the following
    ` line of code to specify the SQL Server to connect to
    strServer = "<machine name>\<sqlexpress>"

    ` Then name the Default database on the server
    ` used for this DSN. If not specified, SQL Statements
    ` may end up getting executed against the master database
    strDatabase = "NorthwindCS"

    ` Create the DSN
    DBEngine.RegisterDatabase _
      strDSNName, strDriverName, _
      True, "Description=" & strDescription & _
      Chr(13) & "Server=" & strServer & _
      Chr(13) & "Database=" & strDatabase

End Sub
```

code snippet module ExampleCode in Ch21_SampleACCDB.accdb

Once the DSN has been created, it can be referenced in code to create and refresh linked tables. The following code demonstrates how to create linked tables based on a DSN created using the previous code:

```
Public Sub CreateLinkedTable()

    ` NOTE: This code requires the DAO object library to work.
    ` If you are using the SampleACCDB.accdb sample file, then this
    ` reference should already be present. When unsure, check the
    ` VBA project references under Tools -> References menu option
    ` in the VBA editor and make sure a reference is set to:
    ` 1. Access 2007: Microsoft Office 2007 Access database engine
    `    Object Library
    ` 2. Access 2003 and older: Microsoft DAO 3.6 Object library

    ` Define Variables
    Dim strConnection As String
    Dim daoTableDef As DAO.TableDef

    ` This must reference an existing DSN
    Const strDSNName = "TestDSN"

    ` The application name can be used for tracing and
    ` troubleshooting the source of problems on the server.
    ` This can be anything, but usually the more specific the better.
```

```
        Const strAppName = `Microsoft Office Access 2007"

        ` The database where the table resides on SQL Server
        Const strDatabase = `NorthwindCS"

        ` User name for logging into the database server. This could be
        ` captured by a logon form and stored in a global variable.
        Const strUserName = `sa"

        ` Password for logging in to the database server. This could
        ` be captured by a logon form and stored in a global variable.
        Const strPassword = `password"

        ` Then name of the table on the remote server
        Const strRemoteTableName = `Customers"

        ` The name of the table we want create in the local file
        ` that links to the Remote Table
        Const strLocalTableName = `dbo_Customers"

        ` This will build the ODBC connection string for our new table
        strConnection = _
          `ODBC;" & _
          `DSN=" & strDSNName & `;" & _
          `APP=" & strAppName & `;" & _
          `DATABASE=" & strDatabase & `;" & _
          `UID=" & strUserName & `;" & _
          `PWD=" & strPassword & `;" & _
          `TABLE=" & strRemoteTableName

        ` This creates a new table object and adds it to the local
        ` database.  If your tables already exist, then you would
        ` skip this code and use code to refresh the links, instead
        Set daoTableDef = CurrentDb.CreateTableDef( _
                        strLocalTableName, _
                        dbAttachSavePWD, _
                        strRemoteTableName, _
                        strConnection)
        CurrentDb.TableDefs.Append daoTableDef

        ` Clean up
        Set daoTableDef = Nothing

    End Sub
```

code snippet module ExampleCode in Ch21_SampleACCDB.accdb

Alternatively, if the tables already exist in the database and the links only need to be refreshed, the DAO `TableDef` object exposes the `RefreshLink` method to easily refresh any linked tables. The following code could be used to refresh a linked table:

```
    Sub RefreshTable()

        ` Define Variables
```

```
Dim daoTableDef As DAO.TableDef

` The name of the local linked table to refresh
strLocalTableName = `dbo_Customers"

` This will build the ODBC connection string for our new table
strConnection = _
    `ODBC;DSN=TestDSN;APP=Microsoft Office Access 2007;" & _
    `DATABASE=NorthwindCS;UID=sa;PWD=password;TABLE=Customers"

` This code assumes that the linked table object have
` already been created and only need to be refershed.
Set daoTableDef = CurrentDb.TableDefs(strLocalTableName)
daoTableDef.Connect = strConnection
daoTableDef.RefreshLink

` Clean up
Set daoTableDef = Nothing

End Sub
```

code snippet module ExampleCode in Ch21_SampleACCDB.accdb

 In the previous two code examples, the connection string used the user name "sa" and password "password" to connect to the SQL server, which is the default administrator account created for SQL server, but not the ideal method for connecting, since it may be blocked. You should use the specific user's credentials in the connection string in most cases.

Controlling the Login Process for ADPs

Because Access Projects don't allow storing tables in the ADP file, it is necessary to reconnect only the ADP to the SQL Server database, and not the individual objects themselves. The OpenConnection method can be called to connect an ADP application to a specific SQL Server. The first parameter of the OpenConnection method takes a standard OLE DB connection string, specifying the server, database name, security option, and optionally, the username and password. The following code provides an example of reconnecting an ADP to SQL Server:

```
Public Sub ConnectADP()

` Define Variables
Dim strConnect As String

` Required - This is the network name of the SQL Server.
` `(local)` can be used to reference a default SQL Server
` installation on the local machine.
Const strServerName = `<machine name>\sqlexpress"

` Required - The database you want the ADP to be based on.
```

```
    Const strDBName = "NorthwindCS"

    ` Optional - The SQL Server user name.
    ` Not required if using NT Authentication.
    Const strUserName = "sa"

    ` Optional - The password for the user.
    ` Not required if using NT Authentication.
    Const strPassword = "password"

    ` Use this flag to signify whether the connection string should
    ` contain a username and password or use integrated security.
    Const boolUseIntegratedSecurity = True

    ` This is the full connection string for the ADP. The Provider,
    ` Data Source, and Initial Catalog arguments are required.
    strConnect = _
        "Provider=SQLOLEDB.1" & _
        ";Data Source=" & strServerName & _
        ";Initial Catalog=" & strDBName

    `Add the necessary argument if using NT Authentication
    If boolUseIntegratedSecurity Then
        strConnect = strConnect & ";integrated security=SSPI"

    Else ` Add the user and password if using SQL Server Security
        strConnect = strConnect & ";user id=" & strUserName & _
            ";password=" & strPassword
    End If

    ` Open the connection. If there is already an existing connection
    ` open then this will change it.
    Application.CurrentProject.OpenConnection strConnect

End Sub
```

code snippet module SampleCode in Ch21_SampleADP.adp

Unfortunately, one of the limitations of the OpenConnection method is that the advanced connection properties, such as Application Name or Connect Timeout, cannot be set programmatically. In addition, because Access does not expose these properties, there is no convenient method for changing them after the initial connection is made. The properties that cannot be specified are the properties located on the Advanced and All tabs of the Data Link Properties dialog box. To open the Data Link Properties dialog box, open any ADP file, and choose File ➪ Server ➪ Connection.

If a connection cannot be established with the SQL Server and the code generates an error, it is useful to have a convenient method for specifying an alternate server, which may not even be known when the application is developed. One way to establish a different connection is to use a UDL (Universal Data Link) file to store the connection information about the SQL Server, which is very easy to update later and does not directly require coding by a developer. However, the

`OpenConnection` method does not accept UDL files as a parameter directly, so code is needed to retrieve the connection information by using a regular ADO Connection object to open the UDL file:

```
Sub ConnectToAlternateServer()

` Define Variables
Dim cnnTest As ADODB.Connection

` Open the connection from the UDL file
Set cnnTest = New ADODB.Connection
cnnTest.Open CurrentProject.Path & `\AlternateConnection.udl;"

` Pass the connection string of the ADO connection to the ADP.
Application.CurrentProject.OpenConnection _
                         cnnTest.ConnectionString

` Test the connection
If CurrentProject.IsConnected = False Then
  ` Error - Failed to Connect
End If

` Clean up
cnnTest.Close
Set cnnTest = Nothing

End Sub
```

code snippet module SampleCode in Ch21_SampleADP.adp

It is easy to make custom UDL files through the Windows interface. Simply create a new blank text file, rename the extension to `.udl` and then double-click the file to open it. Because the file does not contain any UDL data, the Data Link Properties dialog box opens. Then, simply set all of the desired properties for the data source and click OK to save the UDL data to the file. The connection string in the UDL file is identical to the connection string used in the previous code samples, only it is prefixed with the `[oledb]` string to denote the data source provider. An example of this string is as follows:

```
[oledb]
; Everything after this line is an OLE DB connection string
Provider=SQLOLEDB.1;
Integrated Security=SSPI;
Persist Security Info=False;
Initial Catalog=NorthwindCS;
Data Source=<machine name>\SQLEXPRESS
```

code snippet file AlternativeServer.udl

This string can even be typed directly into a blank text document and then renamed with the extension `.udl` to create the UDL file. The benefit to using the UDL file is that it is extremely easy to transfer from one machine to another, and is independent of any application that uses it. The application could even create a UDL file by parsing the ADP's connection string and writing the data to a local file in the proper structure. Really, the possibilities for dynamically creating UDL files are limitless.

Finally, there is one more step to make the UDL file work seamlessly with the ADP application. If the ADP is closed in a normal fashion, the connection information is stored in the ADP file and Access will attempt to reconnect the next time the ADP is opened. Access attempts to reconnect before any code in the ADP has a chance to run, so it is impossible to trap any errors that occur. Fortunately, you can prevent an ADP from trying to connect on startup by clearing the connection string when the ADP is closed. Calling `OpenConnection` with an empty string kills the existing connection, so place the following line of code on the `close` event for the last form to be closed in the application:

```
CurrentProject.OpenConnection `"
```

Calling the `OpenConnection` method with an empty string not only closes the current connection, but it also clears the connection information from the file so that the ADP will open in a disconnected state the next time around. This enables you to run code and reconnect the ADP in your own fashion.

One trick that some developers employ is to run the code from the `Close` event of the initial logon form. If you hide the logon form once the user has logged in, instead of closing it, this guarantees that the code will run no matter how the ADP was closed. The only exception to this is when an abnormal closure of the application occurs, such as a power failure or perhaps because the application froze or crashed. In such cases, the previous connection information will still be present in the ADP because the database was not shut down through the normal processes. This will actually cause two logon prompts the next time the ADP is opened: the default Access prompt and then the one presented by the application's code. Although it is an unfortunate side-effect under these circumstances, the hope is that in most cases, this method will work seamlessly for the user of the application.

BINDING ADO RECORDSETS

Tables and views in an ADP do not provide enough flexibility for controlling a `Recordset` for a form. Often it is extremely useful to build a `Recordset` in code and then bind it to the desired object. `Recordset` objects can be bound to combo boxes, list boxes, forms, and reports in ADP files. This section explores how to create and bind `Recordset` objects using ADO.

Binding to a Form, ComboBox, or ListBox

The code and methods used for binding forms, combo boxes, and list boxes are basically the same. They all have a `Recordset` property that can be assigned an active ADO `Recordset` object. Typically, the `Recordset` is bound to the form during the `Form_Open` event, but can be set at any time while the form is open. The following is an example of binding a form to a `Recordset` object:

Available for download on Wrox.com

```
Sub BindRecordset()

    ` Define Variables
    Dim rsRecordSet As New ADODB.Recordset
```

```
Dim cnConnection As New ADODB.Connection
Dim frmForm As New Form
Dim strConnection As String

` Create the Connection string
strConnection = _
    `Provider=SQLOLEDB.1;Data Source=<machine name>\sqlexpress` & _
    `;Initial Catalog=NorthwindCS;user id=sa;password=password`

` Open the connection
cnConnection.Open strConnection

` Open the Recordset
rsRecordSet.Open _
            `Products`, _
            cnConnection, _
            adOpenKeyset, _
            adLockOptimistic

` Bind the Recordset to the form
Set frmForm.Recordset = rsRecordSet

` Clean up
Set rsRecordSet = Nothing
Set cnConnection = Nothing

End Sub
```

code snippet module SampleCode in Ch21_SampleADP.adp

The code for binding a Recordset to controls such as a ComboBox or a ListBox control is virtually identical to this, except the Row Source property is set for these controls, instead of the Record Source property of the form.

Binding to a Report

Reports are not nearly as easy to dynamically bind to an active Recordset as forms, list boxes, and combo boxes. Also, binding an ADO Recordset is not possible with ACCDB and MDB files. The key difference between binding an ADO Recordset object to a report is that the Recordset must be a Shaped Recordset, meaning that it must be created by using the MSDataShape (Microsoft Data Shaping services for OLE DB) provider or the Microsoft Client Data Manager (Microsoft.Access .OLEDB.12.0) provider.

For example, the Invoices report in the Ch21_SampleADP.adp file is based on the Invoices view stored on SQL Server. However, if you try to bind a simple ADO Recordset based on the Invoices view to the Invoices report in the same manner as for a form, an error is raised or some unpredictable behavior occurs. Instead, a starter shape is needed and can be created by calling the shape object for the report. For instance, the SQL statement for the shape can be retrieved by calling the following code from the VBE Immediate window:

```
?reports![Invoices].shape
```

Remember that the report must be open in the Access client window, or this call will fail. The result that will be returned will be similar to the following SQL statement:

```
SHAPE (SHAPE (SHAPE (SHAPE {SELECT `CustomerName`, `OrderDate`,
`OrderID`, `ShippedDate`, `Salesperson`, `ProductName`,
`UnitPrice`, `Quantity`, `ExtendedPrice`, `Discount`, `Freight` FROM `dbo`.`
    Invoices`} APPEND i
CALC((Year(OrderDate)*4+(Month(OrderDate)-1)\3)\1) AS __G0) AS
rsLevel0 COMPUTE rsLevel0, ANY(rsLevel0.OrderDate) AS __COLRef1,
ANY(rsLevel0.OrderID) AS __COLRef2, ANY(rsLevel0.ShippedDate) AS
__COLRef3, ANY(rsLevel0.Salesperson) AS __COLRef4,
ANY(rsLevel0.Freight) AS __COLRef5, Sum(rsLevel0.[ExtendedPrice])
AS __Agg0 BY CustomerName AS __COLRef0, __G0) AS rsLevel1 COMPUTE
rsLevel1 BY __COLRef0) AS RS_9229
```

There's one more step to take before the report will render correctly. Although the previous SQL is valid, if you use this code to bind a Shaped Recordset to the Invoices report, the report generates an error and some fields may display as #Name? or #Error. The reason for this error is that the fields are aliased as names such as __COLRef1 in the SQL statement, but the text box bound to the field in the report is expecting the actual field name for the control. Because field names are not defined in the SQL, the error is generated. Fortunately, there are two ways to fix the problem:

➤ Modify the Control Sources for the broken fields in the report by changing the Control Source property of the text boxes with aliased fields to something such as __COLRef1. This fixes the problem by using the alias defined in the SQL statement, instead of the original field name the control was bound to.

➤ Modify the SQL statement to use the correct field names by changing the references to field aliases like __COLRef1 to the proper field names that the control sources reference in the report. This is the preferred method because using this method does not force the report to be modified in any way. For example, the SQL statement can be modified to:

```
SHAPE (SHAPE (SHAPE (SHAPE {SELECT `CustomerName`, `OrderDate`,
`OrderID`, `ShippedDate`, `Salesperson`, `ProductName`,
`UnitPrice`, `Quantity`, `ExtendedPrice`, `Discount`, `Freight` FROM `dbo`.`
    Invoices`} APPEND
CALC((Year(OrderDate)*4+(Month(OrderDate)-1)\3)\1) AS __G0) AS
rsLevel0 COMPUTE rsLevel0, ANY(rsLevel0.OrderDate) AS OrderDate,
ANY(rsLevel0.OrderID) AS OrderID, ANY(rsLevel0.ShippedDate) AS
ShippedDate, ANY(rsLevel0.Salesperson) AS Salesperson,
ANY(rsLevel0.Freight) AS Freight, Sum(rsLevel0.[ExtendedPrice]) AS
__Agg0 BY CustomerName AS CustomerName, __G0) AS rsLevel1 COMPUTE
rsLevel1 BY __COLRef0) AS RS_9229
```

Now, if the code is run to bind this SQL statement to the Invoices report, the names will match and the report will display as expected. Once the proper shape SQL is known, it can be used to bind the Shaped Recordset to the Invoices report. To use the previous SQL to bind the Shaped Recordset to a report, clear the report's Record Source property and add the following code to the report's Open event:

```
Private Sub Report_Open(Cancel As Integer)

    ` Define Variables
    Dim rsRecordSet As New ADODB.Recordset
```

```
Dim cnConnection As New ADODB.Connection
Dim strSQL As String
Dim strConnect As String

` Create the connection string
strConnect = _
  `Provider=Microsoft.Access.OLEDB.10.0;" &_
  `Data Provider=SQLOLEDB.1;" & _
  `Data Source=<machine name>\SQLEXPRESS;" & _
  `Initial Catalog=NorthwindCS;" & _
  `integrated security=SSPI"
  ` or use `;user id=sa;password=password"

` Open the connection
cnConnection.Open strConnect

` Create the SQL statement for the shape
strSQL = _
  `SHAPE (SHAPE (SHAPE (SHAPE ` & _
  `{SELECT `"CustomerName"`, `"OrderDate"`, `"OrderID"`, ` & _
  `"`"ShippedDate"`, `"Salesperson"`, `"ProductName"`, ` & _
  `"`"UnitPrice"`, `"Quantity"`, `"ExtendedPrice"`, ` & _
  `"`"Discount"`, `"Freight"` FROM `"dbo"`.`"Invoices"`} ` & _
  `APPEND CALC((Year(OrderDate)*4+(Month(OrderDate)-1)\3)\1) ` & _
  `AS __G0) AS rsLevel0 COMPUTE rsLevel0, ` _
  `ANY(rsLevel0.OrderDate) ` & _
  `AS OrderDate, ANY(rsLevel0.OrderID) AS OrderID, ` & _
  `ANY(rsLevel0.ShippedDate) AS ShippedDate, ANY(rsLevel0.Salesperson) ` & _
  `AS Salesperson, ANY(rsLevel0.Freight) AS Freight, ` & _
  `Sum(rsLevel0.[ExtendedPrice]) AS __Agg0 BY CustomerName ` & _
  `AS CustomerName, __G0) AS rsLevel1 COMPUTE rsLevel1 ` & _
  `BY CustomerName) AS RS_9229"

` Open the new Recordset based upon the shape
rsRecordSet.Open _
  strSQL, _
  cnConnection, _
  adOpenKeyset

` Set the Recordset to the Report
Set Application.Reports("Invoices").Recordset = rsRecordSet

` Clean up
Set rsRecordSet = Nothing
Set cnConnection = Nothing

End Sub
```

code snippet module SampleCode in Ch21_SampleADP.adp

Unfortunately, binding `Recordset` objects to reports is often more trouble than it is worth. If you have a lot of reports, you should bind the reports' Record Source property and let Access do the shaping. For forms and combo or list boxes, binding `Recordset` objects can be an effective means of quickly connecting to remote data sources on-the-fly without relying on linked tables or queries.

Using Persisted Recordsets

While bound `Recordset` objects can be useful, sometimes an application needs the same `Recordset` data in multiple forms, and thus the data must be retrieved multiple times. When the data usage is read-only and seldom changes, a quick and easy method for caching the data locally is by using Persisted Recordset objects. This also improves overall performance and reduces network traffic because the data is temporarily stored locally and isn't pulled down every time the data is requested. Persisted Recordsets can be extremely effective when read-only data is frequently accessed.

In an ACCDB or MDB file, there is always the option of storing data locally in tables. Even though local tables are easy to populate by appending data from a linked ODBC table, it is not as convenient as when the data has been retrieved via an ADO `Recordset`. Moreover, storing the data in a local table cannot be done in an ADP file because all of the tables, views, and data must reside on the SQL Server.

Fortunately, the ADO Object Model allows for a simple method of saving data to a local XML file and quickly recreating it as an ADO `Recordset` when needed. This often overlooked and underutilized feature of ADO can dramatically reduce network traffic to increase application performance when used correctly. The best scenarios for using Persisted Recordsets is when data is read-only and rarely changes, and is used in multiple locations and/or is frequently accessed throughout an application.

Persisting the Data to XML

You can create a Persisted Recordset very easily using ADO. Simply create an ADO `Recordset` (using ADO 2.6 or later) and call the `Save` method to persist the data to an XML file. The `Save` method for the ADO `Recordset` object enables you to save the current structure and data in the `Recordset` to two different file formats, defined by the `PersistFormatEnum`. The following code is an example of saving a `Recordset` for the Invoices table as XML:

Available for download on Wrox.com

```
Sub SaveRecordSetAsXML()

    ` Define Variables
    Dim rsRecordSet As New ADODB.Recordset

    ` Create the recordset. A separate ADO connection object can
    ` be created, but the following code uses the current ADP
    ` connection for simplicity. Use a keyset cursor and
    ` adLockBatchOptimistic locking when possible
    rsRecordSet.Open
            `Invoices",
            CurrentProject.Connection,
            adOpenKeyset,
            adLockBatchOptimistic

    ` The save the Recordset structure and data to an XML file
    rsRecordSet.Save
```

```
                        CurrentProject.Path & "\Invoices.xml", adPersistXML

     ` Clean up
     rsRecordSet.Close
     Set rsRecordSet = Nothing

   End Sub
```

Once saved, the XML file can be opened in Notepad or a Web browser such as Microsoft Internet Explorer. The XML file contains both the table's structure, in the form of XSL data, and actually data from the view. This XML could be used by other applications if needed. Not only is it useful for creating Persisted Recordsets, but calling the Save method is also a great method for creating custom XML files, based on the data stored on SQL Server.

Loading the XML Data

Loading an XML file into a Recordset object is just as easy to do as saving it. The Open method for the ADO Recordset accepts the path to an XML file as the first parameter. This is convenient for reloading a Recordset quickly, with little code. The following code provides an example of loading a Recordset with XML data:

```
Sub LoadRecordSetWithXML()

   ` Define Variables
   Dim rsRecordSet As New ADODB.Recordset

   ` Load the Recordset structure and data from an XML file
   rsRecordSet.Open CurrentProject.Path & "\Invoices.xml"

   ` Open the Invoices report
   DoCmd.OpenReport "Invoices", acViewReport

   ` Set the Recordset
   Set Application.Reports("Invoices").Recordset = rsRecordSet

   ` Clean up
   rsRecordSet.Close
   Set rsRecordSet = Nothing

   End Sub
```

Saving a Recordset object as XML data and reloading it when needed can be an efficient way to reduce network traffic, lighten the server processing load, and store data locally for an ADP file.

WORKING WITH UNBOUND FORMS

Probably in more cases than not, it is desirable to directly control the way users manipulate data on any given form. It is extremely useful for security and data control to automatically disallow the manipulation of data, unless it is done explicitly through the application's UI. The most common way to do this is to use unbound forms and manually bind the `Recordset` to the form as needed. Because `Recordset` modifications are not persisted to the server until explicitly called, the data that a user sees in a form is a copy, and if modified, does not result in a change in the data on the server. This differs from the behavior of a form that has its Record Source set to a database object. A bound form is one that has the Record Source set to a SQL statement, query, or table. Any changes made to the data on the form will be saved to the server, as soon as the record is committed.

When to Use Unbound Forms

There are a lot of reasons to use unbound forms in Access for both ADP and ACCDB/MDB files. Sometimes there is just no other easy way to get the fine-grained control of data without writing tons of code behind the form and carefully developing a model for the events in the form. Using an unbound form and setting the Record Source to a `Recordset` object can be much easier for controlling the data in the form. Typical scenarios include the following:

➤   The ADO `Recordset` is updatable, but becomes read-only when bound to a form.

➤   There is a trigger on a multi-table SQL Server view to allow insertion of new records.

➤   SQL Server application role security for data access is implemented.

➤   DAO `Recordset` objects are required for the application in an ADP.

➤   The ADO `Recordset` object needs to be updatable in an ACCDB/MDB.

➤   Server-side `Recordset` objects need to be utilized.

➤   Total control of an object's behavior is required.

For example, an ADO `Recordset` is completely updatable when using the `Recordset` directly, but it becomes read-only when bound to a form. Another example is a trigger for a multi-table view to handle insertions, but errors are raised when trying to insert a new record from a form or when you simply want to completely disallow insertion from that form. In such cases, using an unbound form can provide the necessary flexibility and data control for the application.

The primary drawback to using unbound forms is that there is no built-in method for displaying data automatically, without having to write code to explicitly set the Record Source in the form. It's possible to add ActiveX controls to an Access form that will allow datasheet-type functionality. It is much more difficult, however, to replicate the functionality of some types of forms, such as datasheets, using an unbound form and tying it to a `Recordset` object. Fortunately, for forms that display single records at a time, unbound forms can be very effective.

Although it takes more code to have an unbound form than a bound one, the code itself is not that complicated. Once a basic unbound form is created and some simple, reusable code is written, it can be copied and pasted for easy reuse in the future. As a general rule, DAO is used in an ACCDB or MDB file and ADO would be used for an ADP.

Creating Unbound Forms

It is usually easier to create a normal form and then convert it to an unbound form than it is to create an unbound form from scratch. When the form is bound, you can use built-in form design tools to drag-and-drop fields to build the forms to the desired layout. This technique minimizes the chance for misspelling a field name and decreases creation time. Once the controls for displaying the data have been added to the form, the form can be converted to an unbound form by clearing the Record Source property.

To keep things simple, the following examples will illustrate creating a form based on the Customers table in the sample `NorthwindCS` SQL Server database. Because the forms are unbound, an ADO Recordset can be used, and the code will be the same for both the ADP and ACCDB/MDB files. The following sections walk you through the creation of an Access form in an ADP and its conversion to an unbound form, that is connected to a SQL Server table via a `Recordset` object.

Modifying the Design of the Form

There are several properties that are set for a form when switching it to an unbound form. Because the record selectors and navigation buttons won't be usable when the form is unbound, those properties should be set to **No** on the Format tab of the Form Properties dialog box. Also, the Record Source property, which can be found on the Data tab of the form's Property Sheet, needs to be cleared.

This example attempts to simulate the behavior of a bound form by using an unbound form and adding some buttons to provide an interface with which the user can interact. For this example, nine command buttons will be added to the form with the following names and captions to expose the functionality that will be replicated in the unbound form:

NAME	CAPTION
btnEdit	Edit
btnSave	Save
btnCancel	Cancel
btnNew	New
btnFirst	First
btnPrevious	Previous
btnNext	Next
btnLast	Last
btnExit	Exit

At this point, if the form is opened in Form view, the text boxes are blank because there is no record source defined for the form. Next, the methods needed to make the form work will be defined in the way that the user would want to interact with the data in the form.

Creating the Recordset

Now that the basic form has been created, you can add code to give it functionality. Add the following code to the general declarations section of the form's code module:

```
Option Compare Database
Option Explicit

` Global Variables
Const g_strTableName = `Customers"
Dim g_rsFormSource As ADODB.Recordset
Dim g_cnSQLServer As ADODB.Connection
Dim g_bAddNewMode As Boolean

Private Sub PopulateFields()

   ` Check to be sure the recordset is not in a BOF or EOF state.
   ` If it is then do nothing
   If Not g_rsFormSource.BOF And Not g_rsFormSource.EOF Then
      Me.txtCompanyName.SetFocus
      Me!txtCompanyName.Text = g_rsFormSource.Fields(`CompanyName")
      Me.txtContactName.SetFocus
      Me!txtContactName.Text = g_rsFormSource.Fields(`ContactName")
      Me.txtContactTitle.SetFocus
      Me!txtContactTitle.Text = g_rsFormSource.Fields(`ContactTitle")
      Me.txtCustomerID.SetFocus
      Me!txtCustomerID.Text = g_rsFormSource.Fields(`CustomerID")
      Me.txtFax.SetFocus
      Me!txtFax.Text = g_rsFormSource.Fields(`Fax")
      Me.txtPhone.SetFocus
      Me!txtPhone.Text = g_rsFormSource.Fields(`Phone")

      ` Lock the fields on the form
      Me!txtCompanyName.Locked = True
      Me!txtContactName.Locked = True
      Me!txtContactTitle.Locked = True
      Me!txtCustomerID.Locked = True
      Me!txtFax.Locked = True
      Me!txtPhone.Locked = True
   Else
      ` Throw an error
   End If

   ` Set focus to the Exit control
   Me.btnExit.SetFocus

   ` Reset the buttons on the form
   Me.btnCancel.Enabled = False
   Me.btnEdit.Enabled = True
   Me.btnExit.Enabled = True
   Me.btnFirst.Enabled = True
   Me.btnLast.Enabled = True
   Me.btnNew.Enabled = True
   Me.btnNext.Enabled = True
```

```
    Me.btnPrevious.Enabled = True
    Me.btnSave.Enabled = False

    ` Reset the g_bAddNewMode flag
    g_bAddNewMode = False

End Sub
```

code snippet module Form_Customers in Ch21_SampleADP.adp

The `PopulateFields` subroutine will be used in several events to populate the fields on the form. Next, add the following to the `Open` event of the form:

```
Private Sub Form_Open(Cancel As Integer)

    ` For simplicity, we will use the built-in connection of the ADP.
    ` If connecting to a different SQL Server or an ACCDB/MDB,
    ` then the connection string will need to be supplied here.
    Set g_cnSQLServer = New ADODB.Connection
    g_cnSQLServer.ConnectionString = _
        CurrentProject.BaseConnectionString
    g_cnSQLServer.Open

    ` Create the Recordset and move to the first record
    Set g_rsFormSource = New ADODB.Recordset
    g_rsFormSource.Open_
                g_strTableName, _
                g_cnSQLServer, _
                adOpenDynamic, _
                adLockOptimistic
    g_rsFormSource.MoveFirst

    ` Populate the text boxes on the form with data
    PopulateFields

End Sub
```

code snippet module Form_Customers in Ch21_SampleADP.adp

When the form is opened now, data should be seen in the form, because this event method will load it automatically from the data source.

Adding Code to Navigate the Recordset

Although the form can now display custom data from a `Recordset`, it does not yet have much functionality because there is no method to allow users to move through records or to change any data. It is time to add code to some of the buttons created earlier to provide such functionality. Add the following code to the `Click` event of the `btnFirst` button:

```
Private Sub btnFirst_Click()

    ` Move to the first record
    g_rsFormSource.MoveFirst
```

```
        PopulateFields

End Sub
```

code snippet module Form_Customers in Ch21_SampleADP.adp

Then add the following code to the btnPrevious button:

```
Private Sub btnPrevious_Click()

    ` Check to see if the recordset is already before the
    ` beginning. If so, then do nothing.
    If g_rsFormSource.BOF Then
      Exit Sub
    End If

    ` Moce to the previous record
    g_rsFormSource.MovePrevious

    ` Test for BOF again after moving the recordset
    ` If it is, then reverse the move and do nothing
    If rsTest.BOF Then
      rsTest.MoveNext
      Exit Sub
    End If

    ` Repopulate the controls with data from the previous
    PopulateFields

End Sub
```

code snippet module Form_Customers in Ch21_SampleADP.adp

Then add the following code to the btnNext button:

```
Private Sub btnNext_Click()

    ` Check to see if the recordset is already beyond the
    ` end of the Recordset. If so, then do nothing.
    If g_rsFormSource.EOF Then
      Exit Sub
    End If

    ` Move to the next record
    g_rsFormSource.MoveNext

    ` Test for EOF again after moving the recordset
    ` If it is, then reverse the move and do nothing
    If g_rsFormSource.EOF Then
      g_rsFormSource.MovePrevious
      Exit Sub
    End If

    ` Repopulate the controls with the next record
```

```
        PopulateFields

    End Sub
```

code snippet module Form_Customers in Ch21_SampleADP.adp

And finally, add the following code to the `btnLast` button:

```
    Private Sub btnLast_Click()

        ` Move to the Last record in the set
        g_rsFormSource.MoveLast
        PopulateFields

    End Sub
```

code snippet module Form_Customers in Ch21_SampleADP.adp

After adding this code, the form's user should be able to click the Next, Previous, First, and Last buttons to scroll through the records without generating any errors. However, the text boxes are locked so the user can't make any changes at this point.

Enabling Records for Editing

Although an edit-type button is not absolutely necessary, it simplifies the coding necessary to keep track of changes. Otherwise, code would be needed each time the `Recordset` is moved to compare values and see if anything needs to be updated. Using the following method, nothing is updated until the user clicks the Save button.

To enable the user to start making modifications to data in the form, the Edit button should be implemented by adding the following code to the `btnEdit` button's `Click` event:

```
    Private Sub btnEdit_Click()

        ` Only allow edits if there is a current record.
        ` Note that the CustomerID Field does not get unlocked,
        ` because it is a Primary Key Field.
        If Not g_rsFormSource.BOF And Not g_rsFormSource.EOF Then
            Me!txtCompanyName.Locked = False
            Me!txtContactName.Locked = False
            Me!txtContactTitle.Locked = False
            Me!txtCustomerID.Locked = True
            Me!txtFax.Locked = False
            Me!txtPhone.Locked = False
        End If

        ` Sets focus to the Company Name field
        Me.txtCompanyName.SetFocus

        ` Enable and disable buttons accordingly
        Me.btnSave.Enabled = True
```

```
    Me.btnCancel.Enabled = True
    Me.btnEdit.Enabled = False

End Sub
```

code snippet module Form_Customers in Ch21_SampleADP.adp

To enable saving modifications to data made in the form, the Save button should be implemented by adding the following code to the btnSave button's Click event:

```
Private Sub btnSave_Click()

    ` Check if this is for new Record or change to existing
    If g_bAddNewMode = True Then
        g_rsFormSource.AddNew
    End If

    ` Update the recordset with the new data
    ` Be prepared to handle any errors that may occur
    g_rsFormSource.Fields(`CompanyName") = Me!txtCompanyName.Text
    g_rsFormSource.Fields(`ContactName") = Me!txtContactName.Text
    g_rsFormSource.Fields(`ContactTitle") = Me!txtContactTitle.Text
    g_rsFormSource.Fields(`Fax") = Me!txtFax.Text
    g_rsFormSource.Fields(`Phone") = Me!txtPhone.Text

    ` Update the Recordset
    g_rsFormSource.Update

    ` This command refreshes the newly added record
    If g_bAddNewMode = True Then
        g_rsFormSource.MoveLast
    End If

    ` Repopulate the data and lock fields
    PopulateFields

End Sub
```

code snippet module Form_Customers in Ch21_SampleADP.adp

To allow users to cancel a pending modification without saving it, implement the Cancel button by adding the following code to the btnCancel button's Click event:

```
Private Sub btnCancel_Click()

    ` Check if the recordset is in an add new state,
    ` and ask the user to save the record
    If g_bAddNewMode Then
        ` Prompt to save
```

```
    End If

    ` Repopulate the data and lock fields
    PopulateFields

End Sub
```

Once all of this code has been added, users should be able to modify existing records and have them updated. The last button that needs to be enabled to allow new record creation is the New button. To enable the user to add new records via the form, implement the New button by adding the following code to the `Click` event of the `btnNew` button:

Available for download on Wrox.com

```
Private Sub btnNew_Click()

    ` Set the boolAddNewMode flag to true
    g_bAddNewMode = True

    ` Clear the current data from the controls and unlock
    ` In this case the CustomerID is autogenerated
    Me.txtCompanyName.SetFocus
    Me!txtCompanyName.Text = ""
    Me.txtContactName.SetFocus
    Me!txtContactName.Text = ""
    Me.txtContactTitle.SetFocus
    Me!txtContactTitle.Text = ""
    Me.txtCustomerID.SetFocus
    Me!txtCustomerID.Text = "(New)"
    Me.txtFax.SetFocus
    Me!txtFax.Text = ""
    Me.txtPhone.SetFocus
    Me!txtPhone.Text = ""

    ` Unlock all of the text controls (except txtCustomerID)
    Me!txtCompanyName.Locked = False
    Me!txtContactName.Locked = False
    Me!txtContactTitle.Locked = False
    Me!txtFax.Locked = False
    Me!txtPhone.Locked = False

    ` Set focus to a field
    Me!CompanyName.SetFocus

    ` Enable the save/cancel buttons
    Me.btnSave.Enabled = True
    Me.btnCancel.Enabled = True
    Me.btnEdit.Enabled = False

End Sub
```

Additionally, it's often helpful to supply a button that allows the user to check if any data has been modified before the form is closed and the changes are lost. To implement the Close button for the form, add the following code to `Click` event for the `btnExit` button to close the form:

```
Private Sub btnExit_Click()

    ` Check if the recordset is in an add new state,
    ` and ask the user to save the record
    If g_bAddNewMode Then
        ` Prompt to save
    End If

    ` Close the form
    DoCmd.Close acForm, Me.Name, acSaveNo

End Sub
```

code snippet module Form_Customers in Ch21_SampleADP.adp

Now the form is fully functional for the user and behaves as a normal, single-item form would, except this one uses code to control the records instead of a query or table tied to the Record Source property. This difference allows you to control all data in the form and protects it by limiting what the user is allowed to do. None of this code is overly complex and it can be modified to behave differently depending on the particular needs, but I hope you get the general idea.

Controlling program and data flow can be essential to building a client-server application that protects the data in the database. Controlling data in a client-server application is also useful for improving overall application performance. Not only is it simple, but it requires only a few lines of code, and can be done in such a way that the user gets the same functionality provided by bound Access forms. The `Recordset` object provides enough rich functionality that you can easily protect and manipulate data at desired intervals.

SUMMARY

The ability to create rich client-server applications is a powerful feature that continues to be available in Access 2010. With careful planning and design, client-server applications can perform splendidly in the right environment. By evaluating the possible problems with the client-server scenarios, the proper steps can be put in place to ensure the optimal performance for the application. And properly utilizing the features of any of the supported file formats, be it ACCDB, MDB, or ADP, is the key to providing a solid feature set for your client-server application. Whatever the scenario for your application, Access 2010 is sure to make it very easy to build robust client-server database solutions.

22

The Access 2010 Templates

WHAT'S IN THIS CHAPTER?

➤ A discussion about each of the different kinds of templates in Access 2010

➤ A review of the previously existing standalone database and Field templates for Access 2010

➤ A discussion about the new Web templates and Application Parts features introduced in Access 2010

➤ How to create templates using the Save As Template feature available in Access 2010

➤ A discussion of the ACCDT file format

Microsoft Access 2010 marks another significant release for the Access templates. Not only has the Access team continued to build new templates to expand their depth of built-in database applications, but they have added several new features to expand the template feature set in Access 2010. Leveraging the Access 2010 templates not only reduces the cost of application development, but also greatly enhances any database application. And, best of all, not only can you build applications from templates and application parts, you can also build your own templates to distribute to friends, customers, or even the world using some of the new features of Microsoft Office online with Access 2010!

ACCESS 2010 TEMPLATE FEATURES

The template features available in Access 2010 have changed in a number of ways, compared to Access 2007 and earlier versions. The following list outlines the major template features that are new in Access 2010:

➤ **New database templates:** A set of new templates has been released with Access 2010. The 2010 database templates are designed to be fully functional database applications right out-of-the-box, leveraging many of the features new in Access 2010. These include both standalone databases and the new Access Web applications that work with SharePoint 2010.

➤ **Application parts:** Completely new to Access 2010, application parts are a collection of one or more tables, queries, forms, reports, and macros that encompass a specified set of features.

➤ **Support for Access theming:** Access 2010 templates now support the Access Theme features.

➤ **Support for Access 2010 features:** Of course, the 2010 templates provide support for the new features of Access, such as data macros.

In addition to these new template features, there have been a number of changes to the previously existing templates features, which were introduced in Access 2007. The following is a list of changes from Access 2007 to Access 2010 templates:

➤ **The Access 2010 Template Collection:** Many of the Access 2007 database templates have been replaced with newer 2010 versions that include many of the new features of Access 2010.

➤ **The Field templates have moved:** The Access Field templates now have their own Ribbon. The Table Tools Fields Ribbon hosts all of the old Field templates, plus many new Field template types now in Access 2010.

➤ **Save As Template is included in Access 2010:** The Save As Template feature, which was previously part of the ADE (Access Developer Extensions), is now part of the Access 2010 client.

These changes really complement the evolution of the Access 2007 templates and round out the template features for Access. This chapter is devoted to discussing the Access 2010 template features, how to create templates from existing applications, and an overview of the ACCDT file format structure.

ACCESS 2010 TEMPLATES TYPES

Microsoft Access 2010 actually has three different types of database application templates: standalone database applications, Access templates for SharePoint applications, and Access Web applications. While there is not much difference from the application user's perspective, each type of template has its own unique features.

Standalone Database Templates

The simplest of the templates, standalone database templates create Access database applications as new files that contain all of the database objects (namely the tables) within the output database file. The template file can be used over and over again to create any number of database applications and can be created within just a few seconds, which is the true power of templates. While the Access 2010 standalone templates provide fully functioning database applications that work right out-of-the-box, they can also be a great place to start building a new application, and don't require that you start completely from scratch. Templates can also be a great place to learn how to utilize many of the features of Access because the person that will create a database from the template has full access to all of the objects and code included in the resulting database.

Instantiating a Standalone Template in Access 2010

Creating a template in Access 2010 is easy no matter which type of template you employ. To create a standalone template in Access 2010, complete the following steps:

1. Start Access 2010 from the Windows Start Menu icon in the All Programs menu, under the Microsoft Office folder.

2. When the Access window opens, you will see the new Access 2010 Backstage. On the left panel, choose the New tab to see a list of available options for creating new databases in the center window.

3. Click the Sample Templates option to open a list of Sample templates in the Access main window.

4. Click any template option that does not contain the word "web" in the name to select the template.

5. Click the Create button on the right pane. Voilà, a new database application is created from the template and is ready to use!

In addition to the sample database templates included with the Access 2010 product, you can download templates from Microsoft Office Online at:

http://office.microsoft.com/en-us/templates/CT101527321033.aspx?av=ZAC

Microsoft Office Online is a free service offered as part of the Office product and provides additional template content that is not only created by Microsoft, but by the general public as well.

Community Templates

Starting with the Access 2010 release, Microsoft Office Online now supports community uploading and sharing of Access templates in an effort to promote the sharing of Access database applications. The hope is that there will one day be thousands of Access database template applications to choose from. For more details about community templates, see the Microsoft Office Online website Information at:

http://office.microsoft.com/en-us/templates/CH101923331033.aspx

Access Web Application Templates

New to Access 2010, Access Web applications employ the new XAS (Office Access Services), which is built on top of SharePoint 2010. The primary difference between these Access Web applications and the Access standalone applications is where the data is stored. As noted, a standalone database contains the tables that store the data housed in the Access database application. With Access Web applications, the tables and data are actually stored on an XAS Server and the ACCDB file contains only linked tables to this data.

Access Web applications are similar to, but different than, normal Access database applications. These applications still have tables, forms, reports, queries, and macros. However, the database objects (forms, reports, queries, and so on) are different types of objects, known as Web objects.

Access Web applications can also contain data macros, which can be used with SharePoint 2010. Chapter 19 discusses more about SharePoint and XAS services and how these relate to Access Web applications.

Creating an Access Web application is essentially the same as creating a standalone database template, with one extra step. After you create a Web application template, it needs to be migrated to an XAS Server. Although the application can be used without prior migration, it won't be a true Web application until it is run on XAS services.

Templates for SharePoint Applications

Finally, let's discuss Access templates that work with built-in WSS (Windows SharePoint Services) template applications. Included in WSS are several applications that, when the Open in Access feature on SharePoint is used, create full Access applications with simple linked tables to the SharePoint server. These types of templates (and applications) are much different than the Access Web application templates because these applications contain normal Access forms, reports, queries, and macros, and have only linked tables to the SharePoint lists. These templates are also discussed more in Chapter 19 in the discussion of SharePoint.

APPLICATION PARTS

New to Access 2010, Application Parts are designed to increase productivity in building applications by providing different collections of common objects used in database applications. The collections can contain one or more objects and can be made up of tables, queries, forms, reports, macros and/or modules, and when applied to a database, create a new set of database objects that encompasses the Application Parts' defined objective. While a large number of these parts pertain to different types of forms, there are also some quick objects that are the basic building blocks for many different types of database applications — for example, the Contacts or Issues Application Parts. Simply click the desired part from the Application Parts menu on the Create Ribbon and the part will be added to your database in just a few seconds. Quickly building database applications in Access has never been easier!

TABLE FIELD TEMPLATES

The Access Field templates feature had an overhaul in the Access 2010 release. Introduced originally in Access 2007, the UI (user interface) for the Field templates was the Field List pane, found on the right side of the Access program window. In Access 2010, the Field templates have been promoted to their own Ribbon.

The Fields Ribbon is a new Ribbon added to the Table Tools group that exposes the Field templates, along with many other new and old features for working with table fields. Specifically, the Field templates are found in the Add & Delete group on this Ribbon, most of which are under the More Fields menu button. To add any of these fields to a table, simply open the table in datasheet mode and click on the desired Field template. A new field will be created in the table without any effort!

SAVE AS TEMPLATE

Now included in Access 2010, Access users can create custom Access Database Template (ACCDT) files from their own database applications using the Save As Template feature. Originally created as part of the Access 2007 ADE tools, the Save As Template feature is provided to allow Access developers to create their own templates to distribute to their customers. And the Access 2010 release takes this feature light-years ahead by now allowing the general public to submit their templates for distribution on Office online. Best of all, the Save As Template feature included in Access 2010 can create Access templates in a couple of seconds with just a few button clicks.

Creating ACCDT Files

To create a new template from an existing database application in Access 2010, complete the following steps:

1. Open the desired database application, which the new database template is to be created from, in Access 2010.

 This database must be able to be opened in Exclusive-Mode for the Save As Template feature to work correctly.

2. Once the database has been opened, click the File tab on the Ribbon to open the Access 2010 Backstage.

3. In the Left column of the Backstage, click the Save & Publish tab.

4. Choose the Save Database As option, and select Template as the database file type. This will open the Create New Template from This Database dialog box. This dialog box contains a handful of options, as shown in Table 22-1.

TABLE 22-1: The Create New Template Options

OPTION NAME	DESCRIPTION
Name	Name of the template as it will be shown in the Access Backstage for the template's title.
Description	Optional. The description for the template as it will be shown in the Access Backstage for the template's title.

continues

TABLE 22-1 *(continued)*

OPTION NAME	DESCRIPTION
Category	Optional. The category where the template will be shown in the Office Backstage.
Icon	Optional. The icon to be used for the Template.
Preview	Optional. Name and full path to the preview image to be used for the template file. The supported formats are PNG, JPG, GIF, and BMP image files.
Primary Table	Optional. For the Application Parts features. The default table prompt when inserting the template into an existing application from the Application Parts Ribbon.
Instantiation Form	Optional. For the Application Parts features. The default form opened for further editing when inserting the template into an existing application from the Application Parts Ribbon.
Application Part	`True` or `False`. Used to create user-defined application parts.
Include Data	`True` or `False`. Used to specify the inclusion of the data in the database along with the template.

5. Once the desired properties have been set, click OK. The template will now be created at the following location:

```
C:\<User Folder>\Application Data\Microsoft\Templates\Access\<template name>
.accdt
```

The ACCDT file is now ready for use. In fact, the next time you open the Access Backstage, the template will be shown under the chosen category for the template.

Features Not Supported in ACCDT Files

The primary things to consider when creating a template from an existing database are the features in Access that are not supported by the ACCDT file format. As a general rule, any feature supported in the ACCDB file format is also supported in the ACCDT file format, with a few exceptions. Here are the database features that are not supported in ACCDT:

➤ Creating a database file format other than the ACCDB file format

➤ Creating multiple database files from a single instantiation of an ACCDT file

➤ Data Access Page database objects

➤ User-Level security (also not supported in ACCDB files)

➤ Database passwords

➤ Replication information or any replication features

➤ Linked tables to any other data sources

➤ VBA Project property settings (other than the defaults in a new database)

➤ VBA Project passwords

➤ Database encryption or database encoding

➤ Custom command bars (although custom Ribbons are supported when the USysRibbons table is used)

➤ PivotTable and PivotChart definitions for tables and queries, but PivotChart definitions are supported for forms

➤ Import and export specifications (new or older formats)

This list is not really that long considering all of the features available in an Access database application. Every feature in Access, except those noted, is available in the ACCDT format and can be applied when a new database is created from the template file!

Deploying ACCDT Files

Once an ACCDT file has been created, the next step is to deploy the new template file. There are several ways to accomplish this, but simply distributing the ACCDT file is quite easy to do. The ACCDT file can be transferred via e-mail, copied from machine to machine, or even placed into a setup routine using the Package Solution Wizard.

Once a user is in possession of an ACCDT file, several options are available for creating new databases from that template:

➤ Double-clicking the ACCDT file to invoke Access and show the template information in the Access Backstage

➤ Choosing the template file from the File Open dialog box

➤ Placing the ACCDT file into one of the recognized template folders so that it shows up in the Access Backstage automatically with the rest of the templates included with Access

➤ Using the `NewCurrentDatabase` Object Model method to create the database from template

Using any of these methods to create a template is quite simple to do and sufficient to create a new database application from template, as you will see next.

Opening a Template Using the Access UI

Probably the easiest way to create a database from an Access template is to have the user open the template file in the Access Backstage and then click the Create button on the Preview pane. The user can open a template file in the Backstage Preview pane in three ways.

➤ Double-click the ACCDT file.

➤ Browse to the ACCDT from the Open File menu.

➤ Select a template from the Backstage's Sample templates categories.

Double-Click

Users can open a template by navigating to the template file using Windows Explorer, and then double-clicking the ACCDT file. That file format is registered as a known file type and associated with Access, so the default command is to open the file in Access. When the file is invoked, Access opens to the Backstage, with the template information shown in the Preview pane on the right side of the Access window. A user need only click the Create button, and a new instance of the database is created from the template. This is equivalent to invoking the template from a Windows command line. For example, the user could call the command:

```
"C:\Program Files\Microsoft Office\Office14\MSACCESS.EXE" "C:\test.accdt"
```

Use the Open Dialog Box

The second method for opening a template in the Preview pane is to browse to the template by clicking the File Ribbon tab on the top left of the Access client window and selecting the Open option in the Backstage. As you probably already know, this invokes the Open dialog box, but it is important to notice that the dialog box is not filtered on the ACCDT file format by default. In the Files of Type list control for the file filter, click the down arrow and choose the Microsoft Office Access Database Templates (*.accdt) filter option. Once this filter is set, the ACCDT files in any given directory will be displayed in the open dialog box, and when chosen, the template opens in the Backstage Preview pane.

Selecting Templates by Category

The Access Backstage is shown in the Access client window by default when Access is invoked without a database. By default, all of the template categories are shown under the New tab of the Backstage. Select the Sample templates category and the templates that are installed on the local machine are displayed. Similarly, the My templates category displays any template in the local user's template folder, which we discussed earlier. Click on any template and it will be selected in the Preview pane. Once selected, a user need only click the Create button and a new database will be created from the template.

Showing Custom Templates in the Backstage

As you have already seen, custom templates can be shown in the Access Backstage under any of the various categories by placing the ACCDT file in the proper folder. In fact, there are two locations on the client machine where placing an ACCDT will cause it to show up in the Access Backstage:

➤ **Access template folder:** This is where all of the templates included in the Access product box are placed when the Access program is installed. If the default installation location is chosen for Access 2010, this folder can be found at:

```
%ProgramFiles%\Microsoft Office\Templates\1033\Access
```

Typically, this maps to the location `C:\Program Files\Microsoft Office\Templates\1033\Access` directory.

The folder named 1033, shown in the previous path, refers to English versions of Microsoft Access. If the version you are using is anything other than English, then the number for this folder name will be different.

➤ **The user's Application Data folder:** Hidden by default in Windows. On versions of Windows prior to Vista and Server 2008, this directory is something like:

```
C:\Documents and Settings\<user name>\Application Data\Microsoft\Templates
```

On Windows Vista, Server 2008, and Windows 7 or higher, this directory is:

```
C:\Users\<user name>\AppDate\Roaming\Microsoft\Templates
```

The last thing to consider when showing a custom template in the Office Backstage is the name of the category that will be displayed. When creating a custom template, you are given a choice of several different categories to choose from to help define the type of application template. This category will determine how your template is shown in the Access Backstage. Leveraging the proper category is a great way to get your template noticed when it is most needed!

Using the Access Object Model to Create Templates

The `NewCurrentDatabase` Object Model method now provides the capability to create new databases from a template in an automated fashion. In the case of creating a database from a template file, `NewCurrentDatabase` is called with three parameters: the new database name path, the database format, and the name and path to the ACCDT file. As mentioned earlier, templates can create only ACCDB file format databases, so the second parameter to the `NewCurrentDatabase` call will be ignored if it is any file format other than ACCDB. The following is an example of some code to create a database from a custom template:

```
Application.NewCurrentDatabase _
    "C:\test.accdb", _
    acNewDatabaseFormatAccess2007, _
    "C:\my custom template.accdt"
```

The `Template` (third) parameter is of `Variant` type, not `String` type. That's because there is support to create templates linked to a SharePoint list using the last two parameters in the `NewCurrentDatabase` method call (discussed in Chapter 19). When creating a database from a SharePoint template, the user can pass the ID number of the template instead of the path to the template file.

THE ACCDT FILE FORMAT

The structure of the ACCDT file format is different from any Access database file formats. The Microsoft Office Open XML file format schema defines the ACCDT file structure. ACCDT files are collections of text, XML, images, and a few other miscellaneous files packaged into a single file that is consumable by Access. When a user invokes a template, Access retrieves the database objects and settings from the ACCDT file, creates a new database, and then builds the database objects that are specified in the ACCDT file. This section discusses the structure of the ACCDT file format in depth.

Essentially, the ACCDT file format is a hierarchical structure that contains a set of files describing how the data files contained in the file package are related, as well as a collection of data files that store the actual data. That structure is then compressed into a single file using the ZIP file format, and its extension is renamed `.accdt`. Figure 22-1 provides a diagram of the file structure hierarchy for the ACCDT file format.

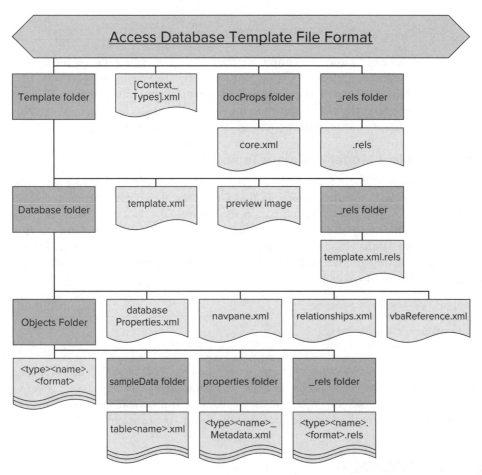

FIGURE 22-1

The ACCDT format stores all of the supported objects that can be created from a template, but unfortunately, not all Access features are supported. Before you look at which features are not supported, explore how each of the objects in the file relates to the template. Understanding the parts of the file format will help you discern why certain features aren't supported in a custom template.

The ACCDT File Parts

Decompressed, the ACCDT file can be thought of as having four levels of data within the file:

1. The root, or the first level, contains data about the types of files contained in the file, metadata about the specific template, and the location of the actual data in the file.

2. The second level, which could be considered the data root level, stores the template's preview image, the template settings, a folder containing the objects in the database, as well as a description of how the parts of the database are defined.

3. The third level, considered the database level settings, contains all of the information about the database properties, the Navigation Pane settings, the system relationships, and the VBA project references as well as a folder containing all of the database object information.

4. The fourth, and last, level contains all of the information about the database objects defined in the database solution, as well as any sample data that those objects contain.

Each of these files plays an integral role in describing how the resulting database will be created when the template is invoked. The following sections examine each of these files in greater depth.

The Template's Root Folder

The files contained directly in the root of the template's folder are used to describe the metadata about the template file itself. These are the file-level properties for the template and contain information about the template itself. All of the files listed in the root level of the structure are required to be in the template. The Table 22-2 describes each of these in more detail.

TABLE 22-2: The Template Root Folder Content

OBJECT NAME	DESCRIPTION
`[Content_Types] .xml`	Describes the types of data files that are stored within this template file. More accurately, the content types XML file knows the extensions of all of the files stored within the template file itself. For example, viewing the contents of the file reveals XML nodes like this: `<Default Extension="txt" ContentType="text/plain" />`. Certain file types, such as `.exe`, are not allowed in an Office Open XML file format. When the package is opened, the extensions are verified and if there are any additional or undefined extension types in the file that are not described by the content types, the entire package is invalidated for security purposes.

continues

TABLE 22-2 *(continued)*

OBJECT NAME	DESCRIPTION
`docProps` folder	Contains the `core.xml` file that describes the template's file-level properties. It can contain any nodes that a developer wants to include, but three specific nodes are reserved for string data about the template. When the template file is opened in the Backstage, the following properties stored in `core.xml` are shown: ➤ `dc:title`: The name of the template, which will be shown in the Preview pane. It's also the default database name when the template is opened in the Backstage. ➤ `dc:decription`: A short description about the template, which is also shown to the user in the Preview pane. ➤ `cp:category`: This is the category of the template, which will be defined by the individual developer. This string will be displayed in the Preview pane. Additionally, this is the string used for the category name of the template for the Backstage.
`template` folder	Contains all of the files used to create the particular database from the template. Everything in this folder is specific to the database that will be created. This is the second level of the structure and will be discussed further in the following section.
`_rels` folder	Contains all of the `.rels` files that describe the relationships of the files within this file package. The root level of the template file structure hierarchy is a single file called `.rels` that relates the other three objects: the `CoreDocumentProperties` metadata for the file, which maps to `core.xml`; the `PreviewImage` property for the file, which maps to the preview image stored in the template folder (remember that the types of file for this image must be defined in the `[Content_Types].xml` file); and the Template data for the file, which maps to `template.xml` in the template folder. All `*.rels` files always describe the relationships of the objects contained within the file package. Although the root of the template file contains only one RELS file, deeper levels of the file may have multiple RELS files for describing each of the different database objects, which you will see shortly.

Each of these objects is pretty straightforward and should be easy to understand. Each is required for the ACCDT file format and if any are missing, the template file will be invalidated. Although this metadata is required for the file, none of the information defines anything about the database created from the template. The real meat of the resulting database is based on the objects contained in the `template` folder.

The Template Folder

The `template` folder, found in the root of the template file structure, holds all of the objects and data that will be used to create the new database. Once again, there is a `_rels` folder for describing the relationships to the files in the template folder hierarchy. In addition, the `template.xml` file contains information about how the database should be created, and the database folder itself contains all of the information about the database objects that will be created. The following sections briefly describe these objects.

Probably the most important file here is `template.xml` because it contains settings that affect the database. The settings in this file mainly affect localization, and need to be changed only if the raw files contained in the ACCDT file are changed after the file is generated by the Save As Template feature. That means that if you always use Save As Template to create your template files, there will never be a need to modify any of the settings in any of the files contained here or elsewhere within the ACCDT file.

Preview Image

Although it is not directly used by the template to create a database, the preview image is stored in the template folder. It is usually named something like `preview.jpg`, but that name is not required. Remember that the preview image name and path is defined by the file in the `.rels` file contained in the root for the template. Also, the type of the preview image must be described in the content types XML file. For Access 2010, the JPG, BMP, GIF, and PNG image file formats are supported for the preview image in templates.

template.xml

The `template.xml` file contains metadata about the format of the template file itself. There are six supported tags in this XML file:

➤ `TemplateFormat`: The version number of the ACCDT file format.

➤ `RequiredAccessVersion`: The minimum version of Access that is supported for the template. This number corresponds to the major build of Access. The lowest value this number can be is `12`, but for templates created in Access 2010, it should be `14`, if Access 2010 features are used in the application. This tag differs from the `TemplateFormat` tag because the major build of Access will be a number of `12` or higher, and it may contain new features that are not supported by previous versions of the ACCDT file format or Access.

➤ `FlipRightToLeft`: By default, the Right-To-Left (RTL) setting is turned off (set to `0`). However, for some languages, such as Arabic, the standard is to read from the right to the left and users prefer to use computer applications that way as well. Setting this tag to `1` turns on the RTL setting in the database created from the template, and all of the controls on forms and reports are reversed.

➤ `PerformLocalizationFixup`: Because these templates are text files, it is possible to modify them (changing the text for a form's label control, for example) after they have been created. The problem is that the text in the label may then be clipped because the size of the label may not have been updated. If `PerformLocalizationFixup` is set to `1`, the Access Name Fixup feature is executed during database creation from template and all of the `Label` controls in the database will be resized, along with a few other actions as well. This setting affects two different features:

　➤ **Name Maps in the template:** The Access Name Fixup feature updates all controls, tables, and fields so that the controls still map to the proper objects.

➤ **Label controls:** The Size-to-Fit feature is applied to all of the labels in forms and reports, except when the label is in a tabular layout or when the `Tag` property for the label includes `;DoNotResize;` (note that the label is wrapped in semicolons).

➤ `PerformFontFixup`: When this value is set to `1`, the Font Fixup feature is run when the database is created. It simply resizes labels in case the template's font settings were modified after the template was created. Font Fixup resizes labels to make sure that they are the correct size for the new font and that no text gets cut off. If this tag is set to `0`, Font Fixup will not run.

➤ `VariationIdentifier`: Defines the ID of the variation of the template and is used internally by Microsoft. Variations are used to create different versions of a template object for a specific locale, based on the language settings for the target database.

Database Folder

The `Database` folder contains all of the information about all of the database objects and settings that will be set when the new database is created. It is really the next major piece to the template and it's covered in detail a little later in the chapter.

_rels Folder

You have already seen the `_rels` folder, which can be found in the root of the template file itself. As mentioned before, the `.rels` files describe the relationships to the objects contained within the template. In this particular `_rels` folder, you'll find the `template.xml.rels` file, which describes information about the template object relationships to the files contained in the ACCDT file package. For each relationship tag in this XML file, there are three attributes:

➤ `Target`: Contains the path, starting from the template folder as the root, to the particular object in the ACCDT file.

➤ `Id`: Contains information about the name of the object that the relationship is pointing to.

➤ `Type`: The namespace of the object in the relationship that is being referenced.

The `.rels` files can be thought of as describing information about the structure of the ACCDT file format. For examples, each database object file in the `Database` folder, whether text or XML, needs to be defined in `template.xml.rels` contained in the `_rels` folder.

The Database Folder

The `Database` folder is where most of the database settings and properties are stored. It has five objects — four XML files and the `objects` folder. These XML files describe the database properties, VBA Project references, the table relationships, and the Navigation Pane settings. The `objects` folder contains the rest of the information about the template, which will be discussed in depth a little later in this chapter. The following sections describe each of the XML files in detail.

databaseProperties.xml

The `databaseProperties.xml` file is used to store all of the database-level properties that need to be set on the database when it is created. Any properties that are set when a new database is created will be there, but if additional properties need to be set or to override the default database settings, nodes can be added to this file. For example, the display form of a database is commonly set to provide an interface for the user when the database is loaded. When this is the case for the database, a property called Startup is set at the database-level. The name of a database-level property can be retrieved in VBA code and seen in the immediate window by calling:

```
?Application.CurrentDb.Properties(X).Name
```

Where X denotes the number of the property. For each Property node contained in the databaseProperties.xml file, there are three attributes that can be set:

➤   Name: The name of the property as it is in the database property's Name object

➤   Type: The type of the value of the property as it is in the database property's Type object

➤   Value: The actual value setting for the property as in the database property's Value object

These attributes are all required for any property settings contained at the database-level or otherwise.

navpane.xml

The navpane.xml file contains most of the information about the Navigation Pane settings and is probably one of the most complex files in the template. It contains all of the structure and data for the four Navigation Pane tables that can be found in any database created or opened by Access 2010. These system tables are called MSysNavPaneGroupCategories, MSysNavPaneGroups, MSysNavPaneGroupToObjects, and MSysNavPaneObjectIDs. All of the data in these tables is required for the database. If navpane.xml is not included or incorrect for the database, there will be a warning that the database's Navigation Pane settings need to be updated when the template is created and will be created automatically.

Trying to read and understand the data contained in navpane.xml is quite difficult because of its complexity. Instead, a quick code sample for creating navpane.xml is included at the end of this section. It contains all of the data necessary for the Navigation Pane tables in the database, which can be applied to the template to create the desired effect.

There are still several Navigation Pane settings that are not contained in the database's system tables. Instead, there are six database-level properties that contain setting information for the Navigation Pane. They're described in Table 22-3.

TABLE 22-3: The Navigation Pane Database Property Settings

PROPERTY	DESCRIPTION
NavPane Category Name	Sets the text shown at the top of the Navigation Pane when the grouping is set to Custom. Not required in the database.
NavPane Category	The default category setting for the Navigation Pane in the database. If not specified, it is created when the database is created from the template file.

continues

TABLE 22-3 *(continued)*

PROPERTY	DESCRIPTION
NavPane Closed	Sets whether the Navigation Pane is expanded or collapsed in the database. If not specified, the pane is expanded by default.
NavPane Width	The width of the Navigation Pane within the Access client. The default width for a new database is used if this property is not specified.
NavPane View By	The View By settings, which can be accessed from the Navigation Pane header's context menu.
NavPane Sort By	The Sort By settings, which can be accessed from the Navigation Pane header's context menu.

The only reason the `navpane.xml` would need to be changed is if the settings were updated after the template is created. The Save As Template feature creates the Navigation Pane settings based on the current settings of the database that is opened in Access at the time the command is executed.

The `Access.Application` object provides the `ExportNavigationPane` method to manually create the `navpane.xml` file. `ExportNavigationPane` takes one parameter, the full file path to the output XML file that will be created. Here's an example of calling this method:

```
Sub CreateNavigationPaneXML(strFilePath as string)

    ExportNavigationPane strFilePath

End Sub
```

The complement of `ExportNavigationPane` is the `ImportNavigationPane` method, which consumes the XML data created by `ExportNavigationPane` and loads the new data into the current database open in Access. `ImportNavigationPane` takes two parameters. The first is the file path to the XML file containing the Navigation Pane XML, which is required. The second, which is optional, is a `Boolean` value of `False` if the data should replace the current Navigation Pane data or `True` if the data should be appended to the Navigation Pane data. Here's an example of importing the Navigation Pane data:

```
Sub CreateNavigationPaneXML(strFilePath as string)

    ImportNavigationPane strFilePath

End Sub
```

relationships.xml

The `relationships.xml` file describes all of the system relationships that need to be created when the new database is created. It represents all of the data that is found in the `MSysRelationships` system table that is stored in the master database. The schema for this XML is not required — it's already known by Access because the structure of the `MSysRelationships` table is known to Access.

If you want to modify this file, you can do so easily by creating the desired relationships in the Access client with the database open. Then call the `ExportXML()` method to create an XML file containing the data for this table. Here's an example of creating a database's system relationships XML file:

```
Sub CreateRelationshipsXML(strFilePath as string)

    Application.ExportXML _
                acExportTable, _
                "MSysRelationships", _
                strFilePath

End Sub
```

vbaReferences.xml

The `vbaReferences.xml` file contains all of the data required for the VBA project references that will be set when the template is created. There is no way to package or create new files to be registered when the template is created, so any project references included in the template must already be available on the machine. For example, if there is a reference to the Outlook 14 Object Library in the VBA Project, then Outlook must be installed on the machine before databases created from the template can be used. Otherwise, the project will have broken references when the template is created.

A database reference can be set in a template in two ways: by GUID or by path. Each VBA reference node can have one of two XML subnodes:

➤ **GUID:** The GUID of the reference as listed in the VBA Project properties. This node looks something like this:

```
<GUID>{9CE720EF-0000-0000-1000-ABCA1020FFED}</GUID>
```

➤ **Path:** The full path to the DLL or other referenced file, as listed in the VBA Project properties. This node will look something like this:

```
<Path>C:\Windows\System32\anyold.dll</Path>
```

These XML nodes correspond to the value of the reference that is to be created. Either one or both properties can be present, but the GUID always overrides the Path parameter when the reference is created in the database. Also, references to other MDB or ACCDB files don't provide a GUID, so they must be referenced by path.

To retrieve the value of either the GUID or Path property for a VBA Project reference, call either of the following code examples in the VBE Immediate window:

```
?Application.References("Access").Path
?Application.References("Access").GUID
```

These calls will return a path String and GUID, respectively, for the Access reference in the VBA Project of a given database. If the Access reference does not exist, this code will throw an error.

The Objects Folder

The final piece to the ACCDT file format puzzle is the `objects` folder. The `objects` folder contains all of the rest of the information about the database objects in the template file as well as any sample data that may be included as XML data in the `sampleData` folder. Once again, there will be a `_rels` folder to describe the structure and a `properties` folder storing some metadata about each of the objects contained in the database. Each of the file objects in the folder represents a different database object.

Depending on the complexity of the database the template is created for, the `objects` folder most likely contains a fair number of files. The file objects in it will be one of two types: text or XML Schema Document (XSD). Each file represents a different and separate database object for the template. Each of these files uses the naming convention:

```
<object type><object name>.<file format>
```

For example, the text file created for the Contacts List form would be named as: `formContactsList.txt`. For forms, reports, queries, macros, and modules, these files are a text file format type. You can create a text files containing data for any one of these objects using the `SaveAsText` method, which is hidden, but part of the Access Object Model. Here's an example:

```
Application.SaveAsText acForm, "Contacts", "C:\formContacts.txt"
```

Although tables can be saved as text using the `SaveAsText` method, they need to be exported differently to work with the ACCDT file. For tables, the file exported will be of type XSD to define the schema of the table. For example, there might be a file called `tableContacts.xsd` included in the template file. An XSD file is a standard way of describing schema in a database table. Still, you can use the `ExportXML` method to export the schema only for a table, by using the following code:

```
ExportXML acExportTable, "Contacts", , "tableContacts.xsd"
```

In this call to `ExportXML`, instead of using the `DataTarget` parameter to specify the output XML file location, the output location to the `SchemaTarget` parameter was passed. (It is possible to pass both parameters simultaneously to output both XML data and schema to two different files.)

 This is a more subtle example of how templates created by later versions of Access may support new features without changing the file format itself (that is, the TemplateFormat *property in* template.xml *still equals* 1, *but the* RequiredAccessVersion *property may be something like* 20). *If the* SaveAsText *method supports exporting the feature to text, then the feature is supported by the ACCDT file format.*

Aside from the database object files themselves, the `objects` folder contains several other objects, as noted earlier in this section. The following sections describe each of those objects in more detail.

Database Object Files

As mentioned in the previous section, the object files in the `objects` folder are the actual database objects that will be created in the database when the template is invoked. The naming convention is the database object type string, followed by the database object's name string, with the extension listed as the file format for the particular objects. The text files represent all the database objects except tables, and the XSD files represent the table schemas in the template.

sampleData Folder

The `sampleData` folder contains any sample data that is to be included with the template for redistribution. The files contained are in the XML file format and have the naming convention:

```
Table<table name>.xml
```

For example, the XML file for the Contacts table would be `TableContacts.xml`. These file names relate directly to the corresponding table XSD file found in the `objects` folder. These files do contain the XSD information for the table as well, but the XML files will not add data or build schema if the corresponding XSD file is not present in the objects folder.

One last item to keep in mind: Data that is contained in value lists in controls on forms or reports is not included in the `sampleData` folder. This is because value list data (other than in a table) is stored directly along with the control definition. In this case, the data stored in the corresponding text file will contain information about the control and any value list that is part of its properties.

Properties Folder

The `Properties` folder holds more XML files that contain more metadata about each of the database objects included along with the template. The naming convention for these files is:

```
<object type><object name>_Metadata.xml
```

By simply viewing any of these XML files, they are quite easy to understand. Each of these files must correspond to a database object contained in the `objects` folder and every database object in the `objects` folder must have a corresponding metadata file in the `Properties` folder. The two supported properties are listed as subnodes of the `AccessObject` XML node that is defined in this file. They are:

➤ `Name`: The name of the object as it will be when the new database is created

➤ `Type`: The database object type of the corresponding database object that will be created when the template is instantiated

These metadata files are required to be present in the ACCDT file format.

_rels folder

As mentioned before, the `.rels` files describe the relationships to the objects contained in the template. In this particular _rels folder, you'll find a `.rels` file that corresponds to each of the database objects contained in the `objects` folder. These files describe information about the template objects' relationships to the files contained in the ACCDT file package. They have the naming convention of:

```
<ACCDT object file name>.rels
```

Where the `ACCDT object file name` corresponds to the object in the template, and each file using the naming convention:

```
<object type><object name>.<file format>
```

For each `relationship` tag in this XML file, there are four attributes, which are described in Table 22-4.

TABLE 22-4: The Attributes for the relationship XML Tags

ATTRIBUTE	DESCRIPTION
Target	Contains the path, starting from the object folder as the root, to the particular properties' XML file in the ACCDT file.
Id	Contains information about the type of relationship the Target path leads to. In this case, the relationship should be metadata because the files in the properties folder are metadata about each of the database objects.
Type	The schema namespace for the metadata object in the relationship that is being referenced.
xmlns	Defines the XML namespace for the relationship schema.

You can think of the `.rels` file as describing information about the structure of the ACCDT file format. Each database object properties file in the `objects` folder, whether text or XML, needs to be defined by one of the files included in this `_rels` folder.

SUMMARY

The new Access 2010 template features are a truly powerful feature set to be leveraged whenever possible in Access. With such a wide variety of different database applications and the number of people submitting to Microsoft Office Online growing every day, the possibilities are endless. Templates reduce the cost of building applications while providing the capability to quickly reuse pre-created database applications and parts. Field templates provide the user with a list of common field types to rapidly build tables and reducing the chance for making mistakes. With the inclusion of the Save As Template feature in Access 2010, any Access user can quickly create his or her own template files and application parts in just a few clicks. And finally, you have learned about how all of this is made possible by the structure and data contained in the ACCDT file format. The Access 2010 templates are an integral part of Microsoft Office platform and are extremely easy to use.

23

Access Runtime Deployment

WHAT'S IN THIS CHAPTER?

➤ A description of the Access 2010 Runtime

➤ Details about getting the Runtime

➤ A discussion about using the Access Runtime

➤ A discussion about deploying the Runtime

➤ A walkthrough of the Package Solution Wizard

Simply put, the Microsoft Access 2010 Runtime allows Access database applications to run on Windows machines even when the Access program itself is not installed. The Access 2010 Runtime redistributable license allows developers to freely distribute the Runtime package, in unlimited quantity, without infringing on any Microsoft licensing rights or requirements, to machines that need to run Access database applications. Although the Access 2010 Runtime does not allow users to use the full Access 2010 program itself, distributing the Access Runtime with database applications can reduce the overall cost of the application for customers who do not already have Access installed. This chapter discusses the details of the Access 2010 Runtime as well as some deployment options.

THE ACCESS 2010 RUNTIME

As part of the Microsoft Office 2010 release, the Access team has provided a 2010 version of the Access Runtime to be distributed with database applications built in Access 2010, or earlier versions. The Access 2010 Runtime supports the new features of Access 2010, as well as providing support for the file formats and database versions supported by Access 2010. As with previous versions of the Access Runtime, the 2010 Runtime License continues to allow the developer to distribute the Access Runtime to an unlimited number of machines, at no additional cost! Best of all, the Access 2010 Runtime is a free download from the Microsoft website.

Why Use the Access Runtime?

When a computer does not have Access installed, running a database application built in Access presents a particular dilemma. Windows machines cannot just run MDB or ACCDB files without specific software for reading and executing the code contained in the actual database file itself. Also, consider that standalone Access is a fairly expensive product, and otherwise, Access only comes with Pro versions of Office or higher, which are even more costly. Often it does not make sense for a user to purchase Access just to run a single, or a few, database applications, especially when the Access program itself won't be used for any other purpose. This is where the Access Runtime comes into play. Redistributing the Access Runtime with a database application can greatly reduce the overall cost for the users running the applications.

Access 2010 Runtime Versions

The Office 2010 release marks a monumental step in Access history; for the first time, a 64-bit version of Access has been created. While the differences to the end user of the application are negligible, this is an important consideration when distributing the Runtime. Remember that 32-bit machines can run only 32-bit versions of the Access 2010 Runtime. While 64-bit versions of Windows can run both the 32-bit and 64-bit versions of the Runtime, Microsoft recommends using the 64-bit version of the Runtime on 64-bit machines. In addition to these Windows version requirements, there are also several considerations when developing applications that will use the Access 2010 Runtime.

While the behavior of an application should not differ between using the 32-bit and the 64-bit Runtimes, there are a number of differences between 32-bit and 64-bit Access that will also affect the Runtime. Most notably, VBA code that is developed in 64-bit Access and calls outside components, such as ActiveX and COM components, must either reference a 64-bit version of the library or use a `Declare` statement to reference the 32-bit version of the library. However, developing database applications on 64-bit Access may result in a number of backward compatibility issues and might not be usable on a 32-bit Windows machine with 32-bit Access. For this reason, Microsoft recommends developing all Access database applications in 32-bit Access, since they should be compatible with both 32-bit and 64-bit versions of Access and Windows.

> *For more information about 64-bit Office, please see Appendix D or the MSDN article on 64-bit Office at:* `http://msdn.microsoft.com/en-us/library/ee691831(office.14).aspx`

Getting the Access 2010 Runtime

There are several methods for getting a copy of the Access 2010 Redistributable Runtime package:

➤ The Access 2010 Runtime package can be downloaded for free from the Microsoft website at:

```
http://www.microsoft.com/downloads/details
.aspx?familyid=57A350CD-5250-4DF6-BFD1-6CED700A6715&displaylang=en
```

➤ The Access 2010 Runtime package can be downloaded from the MSDN downloads site (but this requires an MSDN subscription):

https://msdn.microsoft.com/en-us/subscriptions/securedownloads/default.aspx

➤ The Access 2010 Runtime package is included with the Microsoft Office 2010 tools disks with certain MSDN subscriptions.

Once you have a copy of the Access Runtime package, it can be distributed to users of your application in unlimited quantities, at no cost.

Using the Access Runtime

Invoking the Access Runtime is simple and there are a couple of methods for doing just this. In some cases, the Runtime is invoked automatically, which is discussed shortly. But, there are also two methods for forcing a database application to be opened by the Access Runtime, which can be very useful for building and testing applications that will potentially use the Access Runtime. The first is the ACCDR file format. ACCDR files, which are nothing more than Access database files with the .accdr file extension, automatically use the Access Runtime when it is invoked. The second method is to open the database using the Runtime command-line switch. This is typically accomplished through the use of a Windows shortcut, which can easily be created within Windows and can also be created automatically when the application is installed. Using the Windows shortcut, the target for the shortcut can specify the /runtime switch to automatically open the specified database with the Access Runtime. Using either of these methods to open a database application with the Runtime should be extremely simple to implement for any Access developer.

The ACCDR File Format

The ACCDR file format is nothing more than a renamed ACCDB file. If a .accdb database file extension is changed to .accdr, any time the database is opened, the Access Runtime will be invoked to open the database. The same would be true for the MDB file format, except that the file extension would be .mdr. Although switching the extension for an MDB file to .accdr may work in most cases, it is not guaranteed to work in all cases. It is recommended to use the .mdr file extension to use the Access Runtime for MDB file format databases. If you plan to use the ACCDR extension for the MDB file format database, be sure to thoroughly test the database application to make sure that it is working correctly.

 Renaming a database application extension to .accdr *is a quick way to use and test the Access Runtime against any database application.*

The /Runtime Command-Line Switch

The /runtime command-line switch can be used to invoke the Access Runtime for a database application. Typically, this method is accomplished by creating a Windows shortcut pointing to the database, and the /runtime switch is supplied as the last parameter of the command line. For example, a developer could create a shortcut that has the Target property set to the following:

```
"%ProgramFiles%\Microsoft Office\Office12\MSAccess.exe" C:\Sample.accdb /runtime
```

Notice the `%ProgramFiles%` environment variable in the path to the `MSAccess.exe` executable file. The developer may not always know where Access has been installed on the machine, but a good bet is in the Microsoft Office directory in the machine's Program Files directory, which is where Office programs are installed by default. However, during the installation of Access, the user has the capability to choose almost any directory to install Access to, so the `ProgramFiles` environment variable may not always work. Unfortunately, there is no environment variable that guarantees the path of `MSAccess.exe`. When that's the case, the user may need to manually update the shortcut's path to `MSAccess.exe` to make this scenario work correctly.

Side-by-Side Installations

The Access 2010 Runtime is not directly installed with Office or Access 2010. The Access Runtime can be installed side-by-side with Access 2010, if desired, but it is not required, even to test database applications that will use it. When the Access program is installed on a machine (without a separate version of the Access Runtime installed) and the Runtime is executed, `MSAccess.exe` is actually being called with the Runtime parameters under the covers. That is, the Access 2010 executable already includes all of the Access Runtime functionality and can run in Runtime mode without having to install the Access 2010 Runtime itself.

When the Access Runtime is installed on a machine without a full version of Access installed, the Runtime automatically is used whenever an Access supported file type file is invoked. However, if both Access and the Runtime are installed on a machine, the `MSAccess.exe` executable is used, and not the Runtime, to execute the database application, unless the Runtime is forced, using one of the methods mentioned above. This means that users may have the capability to make changes to a database application that they would not be able to do if the Runtime mode had been enforced. And, of course, the developer of the application may not always know which machines have Access already installed when the application is installed, so I recommend forcing Runtime mode for the application, if that will be the preferred method of database application execution.

Full Access versus the Access Runtime

As you might have already guessed or may have even noticed from past experience, having the Access Runtime installed is not at all the same as having full Access installed. The Access Runtime is a shell program that will execute Access database applications, but it does not provide any of the tools that full Access provides for building these database applications. Many of the objects that you might take for granted in Access, such as the Navigation Pane or the various Ribbons, are not part of the Access Runtime and will not be available to the user of your application when Runtime mode is used. The following is a list of Access tools and features that are *not* included when a database is executed in Runtime mode:

➤ The Navigation Pane/database window

➤ The Access Ribbons, menus, and built-in toolbars

➤ The Backstage options, except Print, Open, Close, Save, and Exit

➤ Customizations to the Ribbon, Quick Access Toolbar, and Backstage (that are not included in a custom Ribbon XML)

- ➤ All of the designers (forms, reports, macros, and so on)
- ➤ All of the designer informational panes (the Property Sheet, Field List, the Grouping Pane, and so on)
- ➤ The Visual Basic Editor
- ➤ Access error-handling dialog boxes
- ➤ Access Help
- ➤ Access hotkeys

For this reason, it is very important that your database applications have solid navigation programmed into them, as well as good error handling. We recommend that you build your own custom Ribbons and Backstage, and provide a custom title, icon, and help files for your application. Just remember that when customers use your application in Runtime mode, they only get what you have programmed into the application, nothing else.

DEPLOYING THE ACCESS RUNTIME

Several options are available for deploying the Access 2010 Runtime. These methods include, but are not limited to:

- ➤ Simply copying the Runtime package onto a machine and installing it manually
- ➤ Using the Access Package Solution Wizard to create the setup script for the particular application, including the Runtime package along with the setup package
- ➤ Developing a custom setup script and including the Access Runtime package along with the application's setup program

All of these are feasible, but the using the Package Solution Wizard is probably the most desirable method of the three options. The Package Solution Wizard is discussed later in this chapter.

Manual Installation of the Runtime

The simplest method for deploying the Access Runtime is to copy it to the machine and install it. You can accomplish this in a number of ways, from using a USB Flash drive to just downloading it from the Microsoft website. One thing to consider when deciding how to deploy the Runtime is that the Access 2010 x64 Runtime package is over 200MB and the x86 version is just under that, which is still fairly large, even by 2010 standards.

Once the Access Runtime package has been copied to the client machines, just double-click the file to start the installation wizard. The default installation steps should be fine; there really isn't much to this wizard except to accept the license agreement, so just complete the installation. The Access Runtime will now be ready to use on the machine — it is just that easy!

The Package Solution Wizard

The Package Solution Wizard is an extremely handy tool for building Access application installation programs; it provides an option for including the Access Runtime along with your custom application installation program. The Package Solution Wizard creates a standard Microsoft Windows Installation package (MSI) file that can perform a number of useful setup tasks, such as deploying Access Runtime, deploying developer-specified application files, adding Windows System Registry keys, and even include digital certificates for the client machine. Employing this wizard greatly reduces the cost and headache of building a streamlined setup process for an Access application. And best of all, other commonly used setup editors can make modifications to this installation package, because the output of the wizard is a standard MSI file.

For the first time in Access' history, Access 2010 includes the Package Solution Wizard directly with the Access program itself, and no longer as a separate Add-in that is not included with the product. The Package Solution Wizard walks you through a series of steps to build the MSI setup file, that are very simple to understand, as opposed to having to write the setup script by hand. Once the installation package settings have been created, they can be saved for future use so that you do not have to go through all of the steps in the wizard each time you want to create a new setup package. Keep in mind, however, that if the files for the application change, the setup script may need to be modified as well. The Package Solution Wizard is the perfect tool for building low cost database application deployment packages, that optionally include the Access Runtime package.

Using the Package Solution Wizard

Because the Package Solution Wizard is a wizard, it is easy to use. It is a series of steps to guide you through creating a standard MSI installation package by providing you with an easy-to-use, step-by-step interface. It is important to note that anything you can do through this wizard can also be done by manually writing a setup script. However, you may find that using the Package Solution Wizard is much simpler and an extremely cost effective solution for building application deployment packages that optionally include the Access Runtime Package.

Starting the Package Solution Wizard

To start the Package Solution Wizard using Access 2010, complete the following steps:

1. Start Access 2010 and open the database file that will have the setup package created for it.

2. Click on the File tab of the Ribbon to open the Backstage.

3. On the Left panel of the Access Backstage, click on the Save & Publish tab. This will show the various Save options for the database.

4. Click the Package Solution tab option in the middle panel of the Backstage, and then click the Package Solution button on the right panel of the Backstage.

The Package Solution Wizard will be opened and ready to begin building the setup package for the database application.

Page 1: Package Solution Wizard Options

The first page of the Package Solution Wizard offers some details about what the wizard is for and a couple of basic options for the new setup program that is to be created. The follow options are included on this page of the wizard:

➤ **The Load Wizard Settings button:** This button allows the user to load any pre-saved setup templates that were previously created by the wizard.

➤ **The Output options:** Allows the user to specify where the setup files will be created.

Target System Requirements for the Setup Package

Be sure to note the system requirement remarks in the second paragraph on the first page of the wizard, warning that the target system for the MSI file to be installed needs to be Windows XP SP2 or higher. The true requirement here is that the target system must have the Microsoft Windows Installer 2.0 or later. The following versions of Windows should meet these requirements: Windows XP (as long as Windows Installer 2.0 is installed, which is included in SP2 and higher), Windows Vista, Windows 7, and Windows 2003 and 2008 Servers.

Starting New or Choosing an Existing Template

Often it is much faster to use an existing setup template that was previously created when the wizard was run for a previous setup package. If an existing template is selected, it can be run without modification. If there is an existing template available, you can apply the template by selecting Load wizard settings from a saved template file button. Choosing an existing template sets all of the options that are defined by that particular template. Most people prefer to make a custom template for each particular database solution, so it can be reused as the database application is updated in the future. But, it is not required to create a setup template for each application, because any template can be applied to any database solution.

Setup templates created by the Package Solution Wizard are nothing more than XML files containing all of the settings needed to create the setup package, with the file extension .adepsws. Once a template is added to the setup template store, it can be applied to any database solution by selecting the template in the Open dialog box and clicking the Open button. Because the template file contains all of the settings as well as the path to the original database that the setup package will be created for, applying a setup template is about a three-click process.

However, the first time the Package Solution Wizard is executed, there will not be any existing setup templates for any database applications, so you will need to create a new setup template before the Load wizard settings button is useful. Once a setup template is created, it can be saved for future use by clicking the Save wizard settings button on the bottom left of the wizard. The Save wizard settings button is on every page of the wizard, so a new template can be created or saved at any time during the use of the wizard.

Page 2: Installation and Shortcut Options

The second page of the wizard allows the user to specify the installation and shortcut options for the setup package. This page is very important, as it is where you can specify to automatically install the Access Runtime. And, you can even specify which version of the Runtime should be used, which will help deter problems arising from users using the wrong version of the Access Runtime with your applications.

The Installation Options

The first section on the second page of the wizard is the Installation Options. These are the basic settings for including the database application file and specifying the system requirements for the application. The following is a list of options that are available on this second page of the Package Solution Wizard:

➤ **File to package:** Required. Specifies the actual database application file that will be inserted into the installer package.

➤ **Root install folder:** Required. Specifies the relative base folder for the application files and folders will be installed on the client machine.

➤ **Install subfolder:** Required. Specifies the name of your program folder that will be created and placed in the Root Installation Folder. All of your application files will be placed in this folder.

➤ **Pre-installation requirements:** These are the requirements for the Access program or the Runtime requirements for the database application that is being installed. This is the location in which you can choose to specify the inclusion of the Access Runtime with the installation package.

The Pre-Installation Requirements

There are three basic options for specifying the Access and/or the Runtime pre-installation requirements for the database application being installed with the setup package:

➤ **Require Microsoft Access 2010 to be installed:** This option is very straightforward; if Access 2010 is on the machine, allow the application to be installed; otherwise deny installation.

➤ **Require and download the Access 2010 Runtime, if not installed:** This option forces the user to download the Access 2010 Runtime from the Microsoft Office website during installation of the application. This is not recommended, as the user may find it difficult to know exactly which version of the Access Runtime to get, but it may be a good option for advanced users. The benefit here is that the overall size of the final setup package will be greatly reduced.

➤ **Require nothing and include the Access Runtime:** This is the recommended option if you plan to have customers use the Access Runtime. This method will allow you to have full control over which version of the Access Runtime is installed for an application. Because there are now x86 and x64 flavors of the Runtime, you may need to create two separate setup packages for your applications, one for each flavor, if 64-bit Access is required.

Shortcut Options

The shortcut options specify which shortcuts should be created automatically when the database application is installed on the client machine. Custom functionality can be specified for the shortcuts, such as custom icons, startup macros, and command options. The following is a list of each of the shortcut options:

➤ **Install Locations:** Specifies the option of creating Windows shortcuts to the database application on the Start menu, the Desktop, or both.

➤ **Shortcut name:** The name that will be used for the shortcuts.

➤ **Icon:** The icon file that will be used for the shortcuts.

➤ **Startup macro:** Name of the macro that will be run when the database solution is launched from the shortcut.

➤ **VBA Command value:** Command-line arguments to be specified with the database solution.

 A shortcut name must be specified before the Next button is enabled to move to the next page of the wizard, regardless of whether or not a shortcut option is selected. This can be somewhat confusing if you do not choose to add shortcuts with the setup package, and in this case, supplying any name is fine, as it will not be used when shortcuts are not selected.

Command-Line Options

Table 23-1 describes the available command-line switches for Access that can be specified in the VBA Command value text box of the second page of the Package Solution Wizard. To use any of these options, place the switch and any required parameters in the VBA Command value text box. Also, it should be noted that placing text in the Startup macro text box automatically adds the /x switch and the macro's name to the command line for the shortcuts that will be created during setup of the database Application.

TABLE 23-1: Access Command Line Switches

SWITCH	DESCRIPTION
/runtime	Forces the application to always open in Runtime mode. If both Access and the Access Runtime are installed on the machine, then, by default, the application will use the full version of Access, but in Runtime mode. Of course, this switch is not required if the database solution is installed as an ACCDR file, as discussed above.
/excl	Forces the application to always open in Exclusive mode. By default, the application opens in Shared mode without the switch.
/ro	Forces the application to always open in Read-Only mode.
/user	Specifies the user name for a database that is secured by User-Level security. This must be followed by the particular user's name string, such as BackupUser. This setting has no effect for an ACCDB file because User-Level security is not supported.

continues

TABLE 23-1 *(continued)*

SWITCH	DESCRIPTION
/pwd	Specifies the password for a particular user of a database that is secured by User-Level security. This must be followed by the particular password string, such as `Password`. This setting has no effect for an ACCDB file because User-Level security is not supported.
/x	Executes a named macro on startup of the application. The switch must be followed by the name string of a macro that exists in the Access application. Note: Another way to run a macro when the application is invoked is to use the `AutoExec` macro. Any macro named `AutoExec` in the database is executed automatically when the database is launched and does not require this switch to be set.
/wrkgrp	Specifies a custom `System.MDW` file for the Workgroup file to be used for the MDB file format database solution. If this is set for the shortcut, you most likely need to include a custom `System.MDW` file with the application, which can be done on the third page of the wizard. Setting this switch has no effect for an ACCDB file.
/cmd	Specifies any command-line arguments that the application needs during startup. All strings that come after this switch on the command line are passed into Access and can be used from VBA code at any time.

Page 3: Additional Files and Registry Keys

The third page of the wizard allows additional files to be included in the setup package, as well as specifying any registry keys that should be created when the installation package is run.

Additional Files

The Additional Files section is used to specify other files that should be included in the setup package, such as custom `System.MDW` files, images, or other files that the database application needs to function properly. To add an additional file to the setup package, click the Add button. The Open File dialog box is displayed and files can be selected, which will be added to the setup package, upon creation. Once a file has been added, a subfolder can be specified for the install root in which to install the file to. Clicking the Remove button removes a selected file from the setup package that is listed in the Additional Files section.

Additional Registry Keys

The Additional Registry Keys section is used to create specific registry keys when the package is installed. Clicking the Add button creates a new record for the registry key. The following values can be set for custom registry keys:

➤ **Root:** The key's root in the registry

➤ **Key:** The registry key that will be created

➤ **Name:** Name of the key to be created

➤ **Type:** Data type of the key's value

➤ **Value:** Value of the key that will be created

Selecting an existing key in the Additional Registry Keys group and clicking Remove will remove the key from the installation package options. Once all of the additional files and registry keys have been selected for the setup package, continue to the next page of the wizard by clicking the Next button.

Page 4: Additional MSI File Settings

The fourth and final page of the wizard allows the final settings for the database application to be specified. This page has five categories of additional settings — General Properties, Feature Information, Add/Remove Program Information, MSI File Properties, and Advanced Options — each of which are explained in the following sections.

General Properties

The General Properties section allows three properties of the MSI package to be specified, which the client machine will see when the setup package is installed:

➤ **Product Name:** Required. The name that will appear in the installation dialog box windows.

➤ **Install Language:** Required. The target language for the package.

➤ **Microsoft Software License Terms:** Specifies a specific EULA file in the RTF format that the user will be required to agree to when the package is installed.

The Microsoft Software License Terms option is not required, but if chosen, will be shown during installation and is a nice touch to personalize an application's installation package.

Contrary to the name, the Microsoft Software License Terms option can be used to specify any End User License Agreement (EULA) and does not necessarily have to be the Microsoft Licensing Terms.

Feature Information

The Feature Information section is used to specify the feature title and description and is required for the setup package. This information will be shown in the Custom installation options screen of the setup package, where the installation options are broken down by component. Because there is no way to break out each of the package items in the Package Solution Wizard, there will only be one option in the Custom installation screen — to install everything.

Add/Remove Programs Information

The Add/Remove Programs Information section is used to specify the options that will be used by the Windows System Add/Remove Programs feature. Although not required, this information is displayed within the Add/Remove Programs dialog box and can be useful to the user for more information about the setup package. The following list describes each option:

➤ **Publisher:** Name of the publisher of the software to be shown in the Add/Remove Program properties for the install solution.

➤ **Product Version:** You can specify the version of the package being installed by the wizard. This version number can include the Major, Minor, and Build numbers for the package.

➤ **Contact Person:** Name of the Person or Entity to contact for more information about the application.

➤ **Help/Support URL:** The URL to any help information available for the product.

➤ **Product Updates URL:** The URL to the location where updated versions of the product will be published.

➤ **Additional Support Info:** Additional support information can be specified here. This information will be shown in the Add/Remove Program properties for this installer package.

File Properties

The File Properties section is used to provide the specific file properties for the MSI setup package to be created. These are the standard properties seen when viewing the file properties in Windows. There are five options available:

➤ **Title:** Required. The title of the MSI package.

➤ **Subject:** The subject matter for the MSI package.

➤ **Author:** The name of the entity that created the MSI package.

➤ **Keywords:** The keywords for the MSI package.

➤ **Comments:** Comment information about the MSI file stored in the file properties.

Advanced Options

The Advanced Options section is used to provide three last options for the MSI file:

➤ **Background Image:** The file path to a custom image to be displayed in the MSI installation wizard pages. The standard size for this image should be 500x400 pixels.

➤ **Product Code:** A GUID that uniquely defines the installation package. A default value is automatically provided, but any GUID value can be used by typing it into this field.

➤ **Upgrade Code:** A GUID that uniquely defines the upgrade package for this installation package. A default value is automatically provided, but any GUID value can be used by typing it into this field.

 There is also a link at the bottom of the Advanced Options section that opens the Access Help to learn more about using products codes.

Finishing the Wizard

Once all of the required fields in the wizard have been completed, the OK button will be enabled, allowing the wizard to be finished and the custom setup package to be created. Click OK to create the custom setup package and finish the wizard. If the data has not been previously saved to a template file, the wizard prompts to save the template before creating the MSI file. After you decide to save or not, the new MSI file is created and the new installation package for the application will be ready for distribution.

It is always a good idea to test new installation packages every time a new MSI package is created. This ensures that the application is still working as expected and gives you a chance to catch any errors before the setup package is distributed to customers, greatly reducing the added cost of customer support that might be required once distributed.

More Information about MSI Files

For more information about any of these options, MSI files in general, or the Windows Installer 2.0 product, be sure to visit the start page for this product at:

`http://msdn2.microsoft.com/en-us/library/aa367449.aspx`

This resource provides tons of useful information about creating and maintaining MSI installer packages. Best of all, it won't cost you a dime to read this plethora of information.

MSI Editing Tools

Many different tools for working with MSI files are available, in both free and paid flavors. Microsoft provides a free tool called Orca that is an MSI editor that is included with the Windows Installer SDK. For more information about the Orca tool, including download location information, or more information about Editing MSI files, go to:

`http://msdn2.microsoft.com/en-us/library/aa370557.aspx`

Install Chaining

One other action that an MSI installation package can perform is called *install chaining*. Install chaining — the capability to cause additional installation packages to run at the completion of the current installation package — is part of the Office Setup Bootstrap. For example, an MSI file could be modified to install a service pack or component update after your application has been installed. Similarly, the package could use install chaining to install an ActiveX control or other auxiliary programs (such as DLLs) that your database solution needs. Install chaining can be extremely useful when other MSI packages need to be installed with your solution. For more information about install chaining, consult the MSI editor's help information or the Microsoft website.

 For more information about the Access 2010 Runtime, the Package Solution Wizard, or Access in general, see the `http://office.microsoft.com/en-us/access/default.aspx` *Web page.*

SUMMARY

This chapter discussed the major highlights of the Access 2010 Runtime, described several options for using the Runtime, and provided several options for deploying the Runtime. The Access Runtime provides the developer with the capability to distribute Access database applications with the free Access Runtime package, thus negating the requirement for users to purchase Access 2010 to run Access 2010 database applications. The Access 2010 Runtime can be easily integrated into any environment; whether it is a manual distribution or via the Package Solution Wizard, deploying the Access Runtime is sure to be a snap!

24

Database Security

WHAT'S IN THIS CHAPTER?

➤ A description of the database security features available in Access 2010

➤ A discussion of security features of the ACCDB file format

➤ A discussion of security features of the MDB file format

➤ Step-by-step instructions for using each of the database security features in Access 2010

➤ VBA Code Samples for manipulating security features programmatically, where possible

Microsoft Office Access 2010 provides a range of security features to meet the needs of most database applications. These security features break down into two categories: database security for the ACCDB file format, which is discussed in the first part of this chapter, and database security for the MDB file format, which is the focus of the second part of the chapter. This chapter discusses the various methods available to secure Access database applications using VBA code in both the ACCDB and MDB file formats, which have some very important differences. Be aware that several of the security features available in the MDB file format are not available in the ACCDB file format. For the ACCDB file format portion of this chapter, you'll examine encrypting databases with passwords and securing code by either compiling the database or locking the modules. For the MDB file format portion, you'll explore shared-level security, user-level security, database encoding, MDE files, and using VBA to manipulate security. There's also a discussion about user-level security and the detachment between the MDW file and the secured database application file. It is important to understand all of the various types of security supported in both file formats and to fully comprehend the implications of the security model that is to be employed in any database application, before actually implementing the security model.

My recommendation is reading this entire chapter before deciding which meth-ods of security are best for any given database application. Also, in general, I recommend only using security methods that are supported going forward in the ACCDB file format, regardless of whether ACCDB or MDB files are used.

Microsoft Office Access 2010 provides application-level security features that protect computers from databases that contain malicious code. These particular security features are covered in Chapter 25.

ACCDB FILE SECURITY

Introduced originally in the Access 2007 release, the ACCDB file format has several features avail-able that are somewhat different than those provided for the MDB file format. This section discusses the security features available for ACCDB files.

ACCDB files have five different forms of database-level security:

➤ **Shared-level security:** Access 2010 offers the "Encrypt with Password" feature to provide a method of shared-level security for databases. Specifically, Access uses a password in com-bination with the RC4 encryption standard to encrypt the contents of a database file. When this security is enabled, the user is required to enter the password before she can open the database and read the contents. In addition, the data in the database is encrypted so that opening a file with a text editor does not reveal the raw data contained in the database. This type of security works well in small workgroups where the password can be shared by several people.

➤ **Compiled database code:** Compiling the VBA code project for a database produces an Access Compiled Database (ACCDE) file. When a database is compiled, the code is transformed into a binary code format, removing the readable code from the file. This means the code in forms, reports, and modules cannot be modified or exported to another database. This method can be used to protect intellectual property rights, as well as to prevent users from modifying the code in the database file.

➤ **VBA project passwords:** Placing a password on the VBA project can prevent unauthorized users from opening or modifying the code in the database, while still enabling distribution of the complete code in the database. This allows authorized personnel to make changes to the code, while keeping unauthorized personnel out. VBA passwords do not secure or protect data in the database in any way, nor does it deter any user from using the database application.

➤ **Package and Sign:** The Package and Sign file feature allows users to create a signed data-base package file for the purpose of securely transferring the database to another user. The receiver of the database package can be assured that the database has not been tampered with and that the database is authentic via the use of a digital signature. This can be used only as a means to verify the database file after it has been transferred. The description of the package feature is covered in Chapter 25.

➤ **Disabled mode:** When Access is open in Disabled mode, all code and unsafe macros in a database are disabled by default and cannot be run until the database is trusted by the user.

In some cases, more than one security method may be applied to a database at the same time to enhance database security. The first three of these security features are discussed in this chapter, and the last two are covered in Chapter 25. Altogether, these features can substantially improve database and application security for both you and the user.

Shared-Level Security for ACCDBs

Shared-level security is a form of security where multiple users shared the same credentials; in the case of Access, this is simply password-protecting a database. Securing a database with a password allows multiple people to share a password to a database. This model works well for small groups, where all users are allowed to have access to any and all of the data contained in the database file, and there is no need to track who has made changes to the data. For example, the Marketing department may need to communicate data statistics through a series of reports created in an Access database solution, in which all of the Marketing employees have full access to the database. Because several departments in the company share the same network resources, however, Marketing wants to prevent unauthorized users, such as Development department employees, from viewing this data until it is released publicly. The shared-level security model is perfect for this situation because all data in the database is okay to be viewed by the entire authorized user group. Meanwhile, this model prevents unauthorized users from seeing the data. Shared-level security is very easy to understand and implement in Access 2010.

Data Encryption Is Key

In versions of Access prior to Access 2007 (i.e., the ACCDB file format), simply password-protecting a database was considered very insecure for one reason: The data in the password-protected database file was stored in plain text in the file. Therefore, anyone who had access to the database file could open it in a text editor and see the data in the file, rendering the database password ineffective for protecting data from all types of attacks. The missing piece to this security puzzle was data encryption. If the database file is encrypted, an intruder will not see any plain text when viewing the raw data in the file. By definition, encryption obscures data files in such a way that they appear to be incomprehensible, random sets of information, and decoding the data without the proper security key is virtually impossible using methods other than brute force. Data encryption in an Access database is critical to making the shared-level security model work correctly. Thus, the "Encrypt with Password" feature was introduced as part of the ACCDB file format in Access 2007.

Encrypt with Password

In Access 2010, the "Encrypt with Password" option supports adding both a case sensitive password and file encryption for a database file as a single feature. When applying a password to an ACCDB file, Access encrypts the data contained within the file, using the password as the key for the encryption. The benefit to encrypting in this manner is that the key is not contained anywhere within the database file, and only people in possession of the password have access to the data.

Once a password is chosen and the encryption is applied, any user of the database is required to supply the password to open the database file in Access. If the database file is opened in a text or binary viewer, the real data contained in the file is completely obscured and will look like random garbage data. Thus, password-protecting the database file will deter intruders that are not in possession of the password.

However, it is important to note that as the number of users in possession of the database password increases, the less effective this type of security will become. It is extremely easy for any individual to transfer a password to other parties and is nearly impossible to know exactly who possesses a password at any given time. Because there is no requirement to provide evidence of identity in any other way, anyone with access to the file could potentially view its contents, provided the password is known. Moreover, you cannot distinguish one user from another with this feature, so there is no way to restrict access to particular database objects on a per user basis. We recommend that you restrict access to the database file when possible and frequently change the database password when using the Encrypt with Password security feature where large groups of people will have access to the physical ACCDB file.

Shared-level security is an effective method of securing an ACCDB file, when used properly. The most important considerations when using this method of database file protection are:

➤   Who has access to the password?

➤   Who has access to the ACCDB file?

Encrypt with Password is truly a powerful feature for almost any multiuser database application scenario.

Using the Access UI to Password Protect

Setting up a database password via the Access 2010 user interface (UI) is probably the fastest method of applying a password to an Access application. Before enabling this feature and always before changing the password, we highly recommend that you back up the original database file and save a copy of the password in a secure location, in case the password is lost in the future. To encrypt the database with a password:

1.   Open the database in Exclusive mode. To open in Exclusive mode:

    a.   Start the Access 2010 program.

    b.   From the File tab on the Ribbon, choose the Open option to invoke the Open dialog box.

    c.   In the Open dialog box, navigate to the database file you want to secure and then click on that file. Once a database file is selected in the dialog box, the Open button will be enabled.

    d.   Notice that the Open button has a down-arrow image on it. This is the Open Options menu for the file. Choose the Open Exclusive option.

The database will now be opened in Exclusive mode, so that you can set a password and encrypt the file.

 Opening a database in Exclusive mode requires that the database file is not open or locked by any other users or programs.

2. Once the database is open in Exclusive mode, the Encrypt with Password feature can be selected on the Info tab of the Access 2010 Backstage. Click the File Ribbon and choose the Encrypt with Password option on the Info tab. This will invoke the Set Database Password dialog box.

3. Type the password into both the Password and Verify text boxes. Then click OK.

4. At this point, you may receive a warning dialog box, depending on the features used in the database file; just click the OK button.

5. Close out of the Access program.

The database file will now be encrypted and protected with the database password. The next time the encrypted database file is opened in Access, the user is prompted to enter the database password in the Password dialog box.

In addition to the initial time required to set up the encrypted database (which is minimal), there may be a slight decrease in performance when using the database. This is because data contained in the database needs to be decrypted when read, and then re-encrypted when data is added or modified. That is the price you pay for the added security that is provided by the Encrypt with Password feature.

Using the Access UI to Remove a Password

The Access UI can also be used to remove a password from the database file, provided the password is known. To decrypt the database, follow these steps:

1. Open the database in Exclusive mode.

2. Click the File Ribbon option and choose the Decrypt Password option on the Info tab. This will invoke the Unset Database Password dialog box.

3. Type the password into the Password text box. Then click OK.

4. Close out of the Access program.

The database file will now be decrypted and the password protection will be completely removed. All people with access to the file will have full access to the contents of the database once again.

Using Code to Encrypt with Password

There are also several methods in which the Encrypt with Password feature can be applied to a database file through code. Using VBA code, a developer has three libraries at his disposal to implement this feature: DAO, ADO, or the Access OM (Object Model). This section will discuss writing VBA code for each of those options.

Using DAO to Set the Database Password

Creating VBA code to use DAO to add, modify, or remove a database password is easy and it can be done with just a few lines of code. DAO provides the `NewPassword` method, which can be called from the `Database` object to set the database password. As with the Access UI, the database must be opened in Exclusive mode to complete this operation. The DAO code to set the database password for an ACCDB file is exactly the same as it is to set the database passwords for an MDB file. The following `SetDatabasePasswordDAO` subroutine is a short example of a procedure you could write to employ DAO to change the database password:

Setting a database password with DAO

```
Public Sub SetDatabasePasswordDAO( _
    strDatabasePath As String, _
    strOldPassword As String, _
    strNewPassword As String)

    ` Define Variables
    Dim db As DAO.Database
    Dim wrk As Workspace

    ` Open the database
    Set wrk = CreateWorkspace("myWorkspace", "admin", "", dbUseJet)
    Set db = wrk.OpenDatabase(strDatabasePath, True, False, _
        "MS Access;PWD=" & strOldPassword)

    ` Set the Password
    db.NewPassword strOldPassword, strNewPassword

    ` Clean up variables
    db.Close
    Set db = Nothing
    wrk.Close
    Set wrk = Nothing

End Sub
```

module Sample ACCDB Code in Ch24_AccdbSample.accdb

Using DAO to Set Encryption Options

When encrypting a database, the encryption is performed by calling into a Cryptographic Service Provider (CSP) that is registered by Windows. The CSP uses a specified encryption algorithm and key length to encrypt the specified data. By default, Access uses the Microsoft Base Cryptographic Provider v1.0 for database encryption. The default encryption algorithm is RC4. These options can be changed in DAO by executing the `SetOption` method of the `DBEngine` object. The three option values for database encryption are shown in the following table.

OPTION VALUE	DESCRIPTION
`dbPasswordEncryptionAlgorithm`	Used to change the encryption algorithm. Access only supports stream ciphers such as RC4.
`dbPasswordEncryptionKeyLength`	Key length for the encryption algorithm. Set to 0 to use the default key length for the algorithm as defined by the CSP.
`dbPasswordEncryptionProvider`	Changes the Cryptographic Service Provider (CSP). Valid CSP names can be found in the Registry.

SetOption changes settings for the current session in Access. When Access is closed, the database engine reverts to the default settings. SetOption does not affect the database that is currently open. Instead, the setting is reflected after calling another method on DBEngine.

The following code demonstrates how to change the CSP and encrypt the current database by setting the database password:

Setting a database password with a custom CSP

```
Sub SetPasswordAndCSP( _
        strOldPassword As String, _
        strNewPassword As String)

    Dim dbs As DAO.Database

    'Get the current database
    Set dbs = CurrentDb

    'Change the CSP
    DBEngine.SetOption dbPasswordEncryptionProvider, _
        "Microsoft Enhanced RSA and AES Cryptographic Provider"

    'Now, set the password
    dbs.NewPassword strOldPassword, strNewPassword

    'You could also choose to compact a database or
    'create a new database once the CSP was set

    'Cleanup
    Set dbs = Nothing
End Sub
```

module Sample ACCDB Code in Ch24_AccdbSample.accdb

A runtime error will be generated if the dbPasswordEncryptionProvider *value is set to an invalid CSP name.*

Using ADO to Set the Database Password

It is also possible to use ADO code to set or unset the database password. In this case, you can use the ALTER DATABASE PASSWORD SQL command to accomplish this task. To do this using ADO, simply create an ADO connection to the database file, open the file in Exclusive mode, and execute the ALTER command on the database. The following code illustrates an example of how this could be accomplished.

Setting a database password with ADO

```
Public Sub SetDatabasePasswordADO( _
    strDatabasePath As String, _
    Optional pOldPassword As Variant, _
    Optional pNewPassword As Variant)

    ' Define Variables and Constants
    Const cProvider = "Microsoft.ACE.OLEDB.12.0"
    Dim cnn As ADODB.Connection
    Dim strCommand As String

    ' Create the SQL Command to change the password
    strCommand = _
        "ALTER DATABASE PASSWORD " & _
        pNewPassword & " " & pOldPassword & "; "

    ' Create the connection object
    Set cnn = New ADODB.Connection
    With cnn

        ' Set Exclusive mode
        .Mode = adModeShareExclusive
        .Provider = cProvider
        .Properties("Jet OLEDB:Database Password") = pOldPassword

        ' Open the Connection
        .Open "Data Source=" & strDatabasePath & ";"

        ' Execute the Alter Database Password command
        .Execute strCommand

    End With

    ' Clean up on exit
    cnn.Close
    Set cnn = Nothing
End Sub
```

module Sample ACCDB Code in Ch24_AccdbSample.accdb

Using the Access OM to Set the Password

The Access 2007 Object Model also provides the capability to open the Set Database Password dialog box through VBA code. You could call the RunCommand object with the acCmdSetDatabasePassword parameter, which opens the Set Database Password dialog box in the instance of Access, so that the user can simply enter the password and click OK. This will not work for a database that is currently open in Access when calling the RunCommand function, because applying a password requires that the database be opened in Exclusive mode. However, it is possible to create a new instance of Access in code to open a database in Exclusive mode and which calls the RunCommand function to allow the user to apply a database password to a database file. The benefit of using the `RunCommand` option is that it allows the user to add the password using the built in Access UI so you do not have to create any additional UI for this operation. The following code creates a new instance of the Access application class, opens the specified database, and then opens the Set Database Password dialog box:

Setting a database password using the Access OM

```
Sub SetDatabasePasswordRunCmd(strSourcePath As String)

    ' Define Variables
    Dim accApp As New Access.Application

    ' Open the Source database in Exclusive mode
    accApp.OpenCurrentDatabase strSourcePath, True

    ' Invoke the "Set/Unset Database Password" dialog
    accApp.DoCmd.RunCommand acCmdSetDatabasePassword

    ' Cleanup Variables
    accApp.Quit acQuitSaveNone
    Set accApp = Nothing

End Sub
```

module Sample ACCDB Code in Ch24_AccdbSample.accdb

Also, it is worth noting that there are possible errors that could occur from the examples in this section. One important error to consider is that if the database is already open or locked by another source, then opening the database file in Exclusive mode will be impossible and will cause an error. If you plan to use any of the code listed, please consider adding some basic error handling, as these examples provide only a basic outline of the required code to complete the functionality, and not necessarily to handle any errors that could occur.

Regardless of the method chosen, enabling the Encrypt with Password feature produces the same result, an encrypted database file that is password-protected. In every case, setting a database password, either programmatically using ADO or DAO, or through the Access UI, is a snap, as shown in the preceding code. Adding shared-level security to a database file is easy to do and can be a great way to improve data security.

Securing VBA Code in ACCDB

Developers generally want to secure their code for a multitude of reasons, from protecting intellectual property to preventing other people from viewing or modifying the original code. Fortunately, Access 2010 provides two features for protecting the VBA code contained in an ACCDB file:

➤   Password protecting the VBA Project for the database

➤   Creating an ACCDE file, which removes the source code text from the original ACCDB file

In this section, we examine both methods of protecting the code in an ACCDB file.

Locking the VBA Project

The Visual Basic Editor (VBE) application built into Access provides a password-protection feature to block the code from being viewed by unauthorized users. This protection allows you to leave the original code in the database file while concealing the code by preventing it from being viewed without the password. It also protects the code from being modified, which ensures consistent application behavior and prevents code tampering by unauthorized users.

The project password can be set while viewing the VBA project in VBE. When a project has a password, that password must be entered by the user before the Visual Basic code can be opened. The password is requested only once each time that database is opened, and it is only requested if there is an attempt to access the code using the VBE. Setting a password for the VBA project also prevents others from changing the `HasModule` property for forms and reports, because Access needs to open the VBA project before it can add or remove code.

 Setting a password and locking the project from viewing does not prevent users from changing event properties on Forms or Reports. Specifically, a user can still remove the [Event Procedure] setting from a form's event property, causing the code to not be executed. Obviously, this could be disastrous if the code executes a critical action when that event occurs. Although users are able to clear the [Event Procedure] setting, they cannot add any new code to the form, reports, or modules.

To prevent users from making form or report changes or changing the properties on events, Access provides the alternative option to generate an ACCDE (a compiled database) file from a database. This is the second method listed previously for securing the code project for an ACCDB file, which we discuss in greater detail shortly.

Protecting the VBA Project

The VBA project can be locked from viewing by adding a password to the VBA project and selecting the Lock Project option. To lock the VBA project in Access 2010, complete the following steps:

 We highly recommend backing up the database file and saving a copy of the password in a secure location before the password is added to the VBA project. If the password is lost, the VBA project can never be opened again.

1. Open the database file in Exclusive mode.

2. Open VBE and select the database application's VBA project in the Project Explorer (the task pane on the top-left side of the VBE window).

3. Select the Tools menu and choose the "*project-name* Properties" option (*project-name* refers to the name of the project in the specific database that is open). The VBA project's Properties dialog box is opened.

4. Select the Protection tab. Then select the Lock project for viewing checkbox option.

5. Specify a password in the Password text box, and re-enter the password in the Confirm Password text box control.

6. Click OK to save the password and apply the protection to the VBA project.

7. Exit the Access program.

To verify that the module password has been set, reopen the database and try to open the VBA project. If you try to open VBE and select the project, the Password dialog box is invoked, requesting the password to view the code and project.

Removing Protection from the VBA Project

To remove the password protection on the VBA project, simply clear the Lock project for viewing checkbox in the project's Properties, which was checked when the project was initially locked. Although this doesn't delete the password, it removes the protection. Otherwise, deleting the password from the Password and Confirm password text boxes removes the password completely from the VBA project. Complete the following steps to remove the VBA project password for a database:

1. Open the database file in Exclusive mode.

2. Select the Tools menu and choose the "*project-name* Properties" option (*project-name* refers to the name of the project in the specific database that is open).

3. The project's Project Properties dialog box is invoked. Select the Protection tab.

4. Clear the Lock project for viewing checkbox control.

5. Clear the data from both the Password and Confirm Password text box controls.

6. Click OK to apply and save the changes and remove the protection to the VBA project.

7. Exit out of the Access program.

It isn't necessary to remove the project password to allow the VBA code to remain unlocked. Setting the password, but not selecting the Lock project for viewing checkbox, will provide password protection for the VBA project properties settings only. Anyone using the database will still be able to view and modify the code without being prompted for the VBA project's password.

Creating an ACCDE File

The second (and safer) method for protecting the code in an Access database is to create an ACCDE file that can be distributed to users, instead of the original database file with all its code. An ACCDE file is created from an existing ACCDB file. Creating the ACCDE file will compile the VBA project code to a binary module and removes all of the text source code from the resulting ACCDE database file, so that the original source code will never be visible to any user of the database. Another benefit to compiling is that the code gets optimized and can provide faster execution in some cases. The compile process also compacts the database automatically. An ACCDE database file prevents users from ever seeing the code in the application as well as modifying the database or code without the developer's explicit permission.

It is important to understand that when the ACCDE file is created, it will not be possible to import, export, create, modify, or rename any forms, reports, macros, or modules in the ACCDE file itself. Therefore, the original ACCDB file used to create the ACCDE file should be retained in a secured location, in the likely case that the database application will require changes or updates in the future. If the application is modified in the future, a new ACCDE file will need to be created and distributed to the users of the application to effect the changes.

 If your project contains references to other databases, you must make ACCDE files for the referenced databases and update the References to them in the primary application's VBA project before an ACCDE file can be made from the current project.

Using the Access UI to Create an ACCDE File

To make an ACCDE file from an ACCDB file using the Access 2010 UI, complete the following steps:

1. Open the Database file in Exclusive mode.

2. Click on the File Ribbon to go to the Access Backstage.

3. Click on the Save & Publish tab in the left panel of the Backstage.

4. Click the Save Database As option in the middle panel.

5. Click the Make ACCDE option in the right panel, under the Advanced options and click the Save As button. This will open the Save As dialog box.

6. Choose a name and location for the resulting ACCDE file, and then click Save button.

The database will now be compiled and the new ACCDE file is created at the specified location. Once this file is created, there is no way to undo this — creating an ACCDE file is a one-way process. As mentioned, any modifications required to the application after the ACCDE file is created must be made to the original ACCDB file and then a new ACCDE file will need to be created to replace the prior file.

Using VBA to Create an ACCDE

Although making an ACCDE through the Access UI is fast and easy, there are times when the developer may want to automate the process through a button click. Perhaps the application is updated constantly, and once regular modifications are complete, the developer wants to click a button to create the new ACCDE file that will be distributed to users.

In Access 2010, there is only one undocumented method for creating ACCDE files programmatically. In versions of Access 2007 and earlier, you were able to use the `acCmdMakeMDEFile` option with the `RunCommand` method to invoke the Access UI to create an ACCDE file, but it seems that this option is no longer usable in Access 2010. That leaves the undocumented system command 603 as the only method for programmatically creating an ACCDE file.

Using SysCmd 603 to Create an ACCDE

More savvy Access developers may recall the undocumented `SysCmd` option 603, which, in versions of Access prior to 2007, creates an MDE from an MDB file. Although still officially undocumented by Microsoft, Access 2010 will create an ACCDE file using system command 603. The `SysCmd` object takes three parameters: the command option and then two arguments that are dependent on the specified command option. In the case of system command 603, the second parameter is the full name and path to the ACCDB database file, and the third parameter specifies the path to where the new ACCDE file is to be created. The following code is an example of a single function to create an ACCDE file programmatically using the `SysCmd` method:

Available for download on Wrox.com

Using SysCmd 603 to create an ACCDE

```
Public Sub MakeAccdeSysCmd( _
    strACCDBPath As String, _
    strACCDEOutputPath As String)

    ' Create a new instance of Access
    Dim app As New Access.Application

    ' Set the Automation Security to Low
    app.AutomationSecurity = MsoAutomationSecurity.msoAutomationSecurityLow

    ' Call SysCmd with option 603 to create an ACCDE
    app.SysCmd 603, strACCDBPath, strACCDEOutputPath

End Sub
```

module Sample ACCDB Code in Ch24_AccdbSample.accdb

ACCDB Security Summary

This concludes the discussion about security in the ACCDB file format. So far you've learned about database encryption with a password, locking the VBA project, and compiling and removing the VBA source code by creating an ACCDE file. These database security methods provide a good level of protection when used appropriately.

The VBA code in a database solution can be secured by locking the VBA project or fully compiling and removing the VBA code by creating an ACCDE. This protects your code from being viewed or stolen, and deters code tampering. Shared-level security uses a password as a key for encrypting the database file to protect the data in the application. Password protecting the database blocks unauthorized users from viewing the database within Access. By encrypting the ACCDB file, an unauthorized user cannot view the contents of the database file using a text or binary reader.

Using one or a combination of these methods can provide a fairly robust security model for any database application. Best of all, each of these methods can be implemented quickly and easily using any of the variety of methods mentioned previously.

MDB FILE SECURITY

To provide legacy support for the MDB file format, Access 2010 and ACE (the Access Connectivity Engine) continue to maintain the security features available in previous versions of Access and Jet (the Joint Engine Technology Database Engine, the predecessor to ACE). For the Access legacy MDB file formats, there are six security features that can be used to secure a database. In most cases, several different methods can be applied to the same database to secure the file in multiple ways. Following is a synopsis of each of the MDB file format security features:

➤ **Shared-Level security:** Access 2010 supports creating database passwords for MDB files, as previous versions of Access did. As with ACCDB files, the database password for an MDB is established by setting a password on a database, and after it is applied, the user must enter the password before the database can be opened in Access. However, in contrast to an ACCDB, an MDB file will not be encrypted, so the data contained in the file is not obscured in any way, leaving it susceptible to Text or Binary readers. Fortunately, password security in MDB files can be combined with database encoding and/or user-level security to provide additional security protection.

➤ **User-Level security:** User-level security is established by defining user or group permissions in a workgroup information file (an MDW file) and defining database object permissions based on those users or groups. User-level security enables you to grant permissions to specific database objects for a specific user and/or group. This can be useful when you have a number of users working in the application and each user needs specific permission to some objects, but must be locked out of other objects. Types of object-level access include adding, deleting, or updating table data, each of which can be established independently of other permissions, based on the credentials supplied by the user at login. Permissions to the database, queries, forms, reports, and pages can also be applied to specific users. This method requires much more planning and possibly more long-term maintenance than other methods, so be sure to have a clearly defined plan for how users are to interact with the application when implementing this method of database security.

➤ **Database encoding:** This method is typically combined with shared-level security or user-level security to enhance database security. It is important to note that database encoding is *not* database encryption, which is only available for ACCDB files. Even though the data is obscured with the database encoding feature, there is no guarantee of complete security or encryption for the data in the file.

➤ **Compiled database code:** As with the ACCDB file format, the VBA code project for an MDB file can be compiled and have the source code removed to produce an MDE (the Access compiled database file format) file. When the database is compiled, the code is converted to a binary format and the readable source code is removed from the database file completely.

Additionally, forms, reports, or modules cannot be modified or exported. This method for securing VBA code protects intellectual property rights and prevents users from making modifications to the code, forms, reports, pages, or modules contained in the MDE file.

➤ **VBA project passwords:** VBA passwords for MDB files are exactly the same as for ACCDB files. This method is typically used when you want to distribute the database with its original source to permit authorized personnel to make changes to the code in the database, if necessary. VBA project passwords prevent unauthorized users from viewing or modifying code in the database file.

➤ **Digital signatures:** Digital signatures enable the developer to digitally sign the VBA code project of a database file. Once a certificate is trusted by the user, code will be enabled in the database without having to set Macro Security to Low when opening the application. The database must be signed with one of two types of digital certificates, and a distributable public key certificate is applied on the client machine to trust the digital certificate. The Microsoft Office System 2010 includes a tool that enables you to create a Self-Cert, which is a certification that can be issued by the developer to the user to allow the user to trust specific database files. Access VBA projects can also be signed certificates issued by a third-party known as a CA (Certificate Authority). CAs specialize in researching and affirming the identity of the developer issuing the certificate, and these are considered the most secure types of certificates. However, obtaining a CA certificate may be expensive and time consuming, and the company applying must make guarantees about its identity and how the certificate will be used. Digital signatures are discussed in-depth in Chapter 25.

Most of these security methods can be applied to a standalone, a front-end, or a back-end database without discretion. In most cases, you'll probably want to use a combination of these security features to get the desired level of protection. The level of security requirements for any database application should be clearly known and understood by the developer of the application, once the initial requirements for the application have been gathered. Adding security to a database application as an afterthought can often be difficult and in some cases, may not even be possible.

 Remember that it is always better to plan security from the beginning than to add it at the end. The security requirements help dictate the application design as well as help uncover weak areas in the application.

Keep in mind that several of the security features that are available in the MDB file format are not available in the ACCDB format. Be sure to adequately plan for and consider all of the security concerns, and how the application will move forward in the future, before beginning the implementation of any of these methods. Mistakes and bad assumptions about how the application will be used and what data needs to be stored can be extremely costly to repair once the initial implementation is completed.

Shared-Level Security for MDBs

ACE supports only one form of shared-level security for an MDB file: a database password. Setting a database password is a simple solution to protecting a database from being opened by any network user who has access to the location of the database file. Theoretically, this method of security is most effective in situations where any person in possession of the password is permitted to insert, delete, or update the data in the database, as well as update any of the objects (forms, reports, and so forth) in the database, without discretion.

Setting a Password for an MDB File

When shared-level security is applied to an MDB file format database, the user is prompted for a password each time the database is opened. In addition, any code or process trying to access the database is required to supply a password to connect to the database. Shared-level security only protects the MDB file on which the password is set and is considered a database-wide setting. When the correct password is entered, the user gains full access to the database file, including all data and all objects contained in that database.

Remember that the Access UI is identical for applying a password to either an ACCDB or an MDB, but the feature itself is very different between the two file formats. In the ACCDB file format, applying a password also automatically encrypts the data in the file. That's not the case in an MDB; adding a password only prompts the user for the password when opening the file in Access, but the data stored in the file remains unaffected, so any person with physical access to the file can still open it in a text or binary file reader and view the data stored with little effort. If you plan to apply a password to an MDB file, we recommend that you encode the data to help obscure it.

In addition, we highly recommend that you make a complete backup of the database before setting the database password in case there is a problem later. Although adding a database password is easy to do via the Access UI, there may be cases where you want to use programmatic methods to change the passwords. Access provides several options for setting the database password using VBA code.

Using the Access UI to Set the Database Password

Just like setting a database password for an ACCDB, the password for an MDB can also be applied through the Access UI. Shared-level security is added to a database from the Ribbon's Database Tools tab. The Set Database Password option is available if the database does not already have a password. The Unset Database Password option is available if the database has a shared-level password applied. Use the following steps to set the database password:

 You should always back up the database file and save a copy of the password in a secure location before the password is added to database in case the password is lost in the future.

1. Open the database in Exclusive mode.

2. The Set Database Password button is found on the Info tab of the Access 2010 Backstage. Click the File Ribbon and choose the Set Database Password option on the Info tab. This will open the Set Database Password dialog box.

3. Type the password into both the Password and Verify text boxes. Then click OK.

4. At this point, you may receive a warning dialog box. Depending on the features used in the database file, just click OK.

5. Close out of the Access program.

Once the password has been applied to the database file, any user who tries to open the file in Access will be prompted to supply a password.

Using VBA Code to Set the Database Password

There are three possible ways to automate the process of adding or modifying a database password. The password can be set using DAO code, ADO code, or the Access OM. Fortunately, the code for setting the password for an ACCDB file is exactly the same as for an MDB file. Please consult the code samples in the "Shared-Level Security for ACCDBs" section earlier in this chapter for code examples to set the database password programmatically.

Encoding an MDB File

Encoding the data in the database obscures the data such that it will be much more difficult to decode the data in the database and the raw file data will not show plain-text data in the database file. However, encoding data does not provide the same level of security as the database encryption feature of the ACCDB file format and is susceptible to being decoded. This is why the feature has been deprecated in the ACCDB file format and the Encrypt with Password feature was added. If you are using this feature, we highly recommend that you move to the ACCDB file format and use the Encrypt with Password feature instead.

Using the Access UI to Encode an MDB

To make an encoded MDB file using the Access 2010 UI, complete the following steps:

1. Open the database file in Exclusive mode.

2. Click the File Ribbon to go to the Access Backstage.

3. On the Info tab of the Backstage, click the Users and Permissions button and select the Encode/Decode Database option. This invokes the Encode Database As dialog box.

4. Choose a name and location for the resulting MDB file, and then click Save.

The encoded database will now be created at the specified location. Once this file is created, you can simply decode the database by doing this same procedure. When the database is already encoded, you will just be asked to specify a location to save the decoded database instead.

Securing VBA Code for MDBs

As with the ACCDB file format, the MDB file format supports protecting the VBA source code in an Access database solution. You can secure VBA code in an MDB file format in Access 2010 by locking the VBA project or creating an MDE file from the database. These methods are exactly the same as those for securing the VBA project in an ACCDB file, with the exception of some naming.

The information applying to the ACCDB file format also applies to the MDB file format, with a few minor differences. The following sections cover the differences between securing the code in an MDB and an ACCDB, so it may be useful to consult the earlier section "Securing VBA Code in ACCDB" in conjunction with this section.

Locking the VBA Project

As with an ACCDB file, locking the VBA project is a good way to protect the code within the Access database solution, while allowing the developer to retain the code in the actual distributed database file. This operation is exactly the same in both the ACCDB and the MDB file formats. For more information about locking the VBA project in an MDB file using Access 2010, please see the section "Locking the VBA Project" in the ACCDB file format discussion earlier in this chapter.

Creating an MDE file

The predecessor of the ACCDE compiled database file format is the MDE file format. The MDE and ACCDE file formats are essentially the same from a compiled code standpoint. The VBA code in the database is compiled to a binary format, and the text source code is removed from the VBA project in both cases. However, the ACCDE format supports the database features in the ACCDB file format and the MDE file format is used to support the legacy MDB file format.

Creating an MDE file from an MDB file using Access 2010 requires that the MDB file be opened in Exclusive mode when generating the MDE file. Also, if the MDB database file format is older than the Access 2002 MDB format, the database will have to be converted forward to the Access 2002–2003 MDB file format. Otherwise, creating an MDE is essentially the same as creating an ACCDE when done through the Access UI.

Using the Access UI to Create an MDE File

As with an ACCDE file, once the MDE file is created, it is not possible to import, export, create, modify, or rename any forms, reports, pages, macros or modules in the MDE file itself. Therefore, the original database that the MDE was created from should be retained in case the application requires changes in the future.

To make an MDE file from an MDB file using the Access 2010 UI, complete the following steps:

1. Open the Database file in Exclusive mode.

2. Click the File Ribbon to go to the Access Backstage.

3. Click on the Save & Publish tab on the left panel of the Backstage.

4. Click the Save Database As option in the middle panel of the Backstage.

5. Click the Make MDE option under the Advanced options on the right panel of the Backstage and click the Save As button. The Save As dialog box will be opened.

6. Choose a name and location for the resulting MDE file; then click Save.

The database will now be compiled and the new MDE file is created at the specified location. Once this file is created, there is no way to undo this — i.e. creating an MDE file is a one-way process.

Using VBA to Make an MDE

As discussed previously, there is now only one method that can be used to programmatically create ACCDE files: using system command 603. You can use the code listed previously for creating ACCDE files to create an MDE file as well. Simply change the extension of the output file to `.mde` ; it is that simple. Because the code is exactly the same, please see the previous section "Using VBA to Create an ACCDE" for information about how to programmatically create an MDE file. Of course, any file conversion forward to the 2003-03 MDB file format that may be necessary should be completed before the MDE file is created, otherwise the MDE file may not function properly.

User-Level Security

Access 2010 does provide legacy support for user-level security in the MDB file format. However, this model of security was deemed insecure by Microsoft and has been deprecated beginning in Access 2007 with the introduction of the ACCDB file format. As such, the discussion of user-level security topics in this edition of the *Access Programmer's Reference* has been limited to feature overviews only and focuses on information about where to find the features and the OM for user-level security. For more information about implementing these features, consult the *Access 2007 VBA Programmer's Reference* (the predecessor to this book) for an in-depth discussion of user-level security and how to implement this model.

User-Level Security Overview

The most robust form of security provided for the MDB file format is user-level security. This model enables granting permissions to groups of users and/or to specific users for each object in a database. Objects include tables, queries, forms, reports, and macros, as well as the database itself. There are two main database components in the user-level security model:

- ➤ The MDW file (the workgroup information file)
- ➤ The MDB file (Access database) that is to be secured

The distinction, detachment, and dependency between the MDW file and the secured database will be clarified shortly.

Planning User-Level Security

Because user-level security provides such granular permissions to database objects, implementing this security can be quite complex. Thorough planning and documentation will be invaluable to setting up and maintaining user-level security over the lifetime of an Access database application. It's important to get the design right the first time — it will be costly to change the model during implementation or after initial development is complete.

Notes about Other Security Methods

User-level security does not override shared-level security. User-level security requires the user to log on to use a database in Access. However, if the user opens a shared-level protected database, the user also must have the password to that database. As with shared-level security, user-level security does not encode the data or prevent it from being viewed using tools other than Access.

The MDW File

The workgroup information for each of the users and groups in the User-Level security model is stored in the MDW file. Every ACE database session requires loading some workgroup information for any given database file. By default, Access has a blank `System.mdw` file with two groups (Admins and Users) and one user account (Admin). The Admin user's password is set to blank by default and every normal session with Access uses this account by default. Access automatically tries to log into all databases as the Admin user whenever a new Jet/ACE session is started, unless directed to log in with different credentials. If Access cannot log in as the Admin user using a blank password, the Login dialog box is displayed to request user credentials. ACE grants/denies permissions to the various database objects based on the user and group security IDs defined for each entity in the workgroup, which are stored in the MDW file. The permissions applied to each specific database object for each security ID is stored in the MDB database file.

The information stored in the MDW uniquely identifies an individual Access user and the user groups to which a given user belongs. New users and groups can be added to the MDW, but the file itself does not contain any information about the database that is being secured; it only stores the security IDs for each user and group. The secured database knows nothing about the users or groups defined in the workgroup; it only knows what permissions are defined for any given security ID. Because of the distinction between the MDW and the secured database, a single MDW can contain many different user and group security IDs that can be used for multiple database solutions.

As previously mentioned, every ACE and Jet database session requires information from an MDW file. A default system MDW file is created for each Windows user account when a database is opened if there is no default `System.mdw` file present. The default location for this file on Windows 7 and Windows Vista is:

```
C:\Users\<user name>\AppData\Roaming\Microsoft\Access\System.mdw
```

Or, for older versions of Windows, the default location is:

```
C:\Documents and Settings\<user name>\Application Data\Microsoft\Access\
System.mdw
```

The Access application is joined to this MDW by default if no other MDW is explicitly specified, meaning that the information contained in `System.mdw` is used when databases are opened. By default, the Admin password in the default `System.mdw` is set to blank, which is why there is no password prompt when opening normal, non-secured databases in Access. For this reason, it is extremely important to understand that if the default `System.mdw` file is modified, then the user for that Windows user account will always be prompted to log on when opening *any* database, which can become extremely confusing. Also, if this MDW becomes corrupted or the password is lost, you won't be able to open any databases created from the MDW file ever again. It is highly recommended that you never modify the default `System.mdw` file, and always create a new MDW file when implementing user-level security.

 The MDW file is not used by Access until an MDB file is opened. If no MDW file is explicitly specified, the default joined MDW file that is currently set for Access is used (which is the `System.mdw` *by default). However, the* `/wrkgrp` *command-line switch can be used when Access is started to explicitly specify the path to the MDW file to use with the particular MDB file. These techniques are discussed later.*

The Database to be Secured

The second component of user-level security is the MDB database file that is being secured. The permissions set for a user in the MDW file authorize the actions that can be taken on objects in the MDB file. The object types that can have permissions set include the database, tables, queries, forms, reports, and macros. Each object, regardless of type, has its own set of permissions. That is, each table in a database has a set of permissions distinct from other tables in the database. Therefore, it is possible to permit a particular group or user to have read-only access to some objects while allowing other groups or users to have full access to all objects in the database.

Permissions are granted to the user cumulatively. Members of a group receive all of the permissions granted to the group, as well as their own specific set of permissions. If a user is granted permissions that exceed any of the permissions of the groups that the user belongs to, that user receives the additional individual permissions, as well as the most permissive authority from each of the groups to which the user belongs. Because the combinations can become very complex and seemingly endless, the cumulative permission effect shows why it is important to define the appropriate permission model for users and groups when designing the database solution, prior to creating the MDW file. The following table lists the different permission types provided by ACE for the MDB file format.

PERMISSION	OBJECTS	ACTIONS
Open/Run	Database, Form, Report, Macro	Open a database, form, or report, or run a macro in a database.
Open Exclusive	Database	Open a database with exclusive access.
Read Design	Table, Query, Form, Report, Macro	View tables, queries, forms, reports, or macros in Design view.
Modify Design	Table, Query, Form, Report, Macro	View and change the design of tables, queries, forms, reports, or macros; or delete them.
Administer	Database, Table, Query, Form, Report, Macro	For databases, set a database password, replicate a database, and change startup properties. For tables, queries, forms, reports, and macros, users have full access to these objects and data, including the ability to assign permissions.
Read Data	Table, Query	View data in tables and queries.
Update Data	Table, Query	View and modify, but not insert or delete, data in tables and queries.
Insert Data	Table, Query	View and insert, but not modify or delete, data in tables and queries.
Delete Data	Table, Query	View and delete, but not modify or insert, data in tables and queries.

The owner of the database or of an object in a database always has all permissions to that database or object in the database, regardless of any other permission settings.

Working with User-Level Security

The three methods for securing a database application with user-level security are as follows:

➤ Use the User-Level Security Wizard to help build the security model.

➤ Use the Access UI to set database permissions manually.

➤ Use the support provided in VBA, including using DAO, ADO, ADOX or some combination thereof.

These are all fairly large topics that are only outlined for legacy support of these features. Use of the user-level security feature is not recommended, as it is deemed insecure by Microsoft.

Using the User-Level Security Wizard

The User-Level Security Wizard is perhaps the easiest method for implementing user-level security in an Access database application. The wizard walks through the steps necessary to secure the database, including setting up user and group accounts. The wizard also provides a predefined set of default groups with common permission settings based on the group type. The wizard will automatically create everything necessary for securing the database, greatly reducing the cost in time to set up the database security manually.

The User-Level Security Wizard cannot be used while a database has shared-level security or if the project has been locked from viewing (both discussed earlier). Both need to be disabled prior to running the wizard. These options can easily be added after the wizard has completed its work.

Access 2010 still provides the User-Level Security Wizard for the MDB file format. To launch the User-Level Security Wizard, go to the Info tab in the Access 2010 Backstage. The User-Level Security Wizard option can be found on the Users and Permissions button sub menu. Simply click this button to launch the wizard.

Using the Access User Interface

There are many steps involved in creating and using user-level security using the Access user interface. Although it can be much more cumbersome to set up user-level security using the Access 2010 UI, it does provide two pieces that the wizard does not: fine-grained control about how to define users and groups and the capability to assign specific database objects to users and groups. The User and Group Permissions dialog box and the User and Group Accounts dialog box allow the developer to set any all permissions and account settings for any object in the MDB file.

Access 2010 still provides the User and Group Permissions dialog box and the User and Group Accounts dialog box. Both of these options can be found in the Access 2010 Backstage, on the Users and Permissions button sub menu found on the Info tab. Also, while there is no way to open it through the Access 2010 UI, the Workgroup Administrator dialog box can be invoked by calling the RunCommand method with the acCmdWorkgroupAdministrator option. This can be called from VBE in the Immediate window with the following code:

```
RunCommand acCmdWorkgroupAdministrator
```

Using these three security dialog boxes, you can effectively manage your legacy user-level secured databases via the Access 2010 UI.

User-Level Security Using DAO

User-level security can be modified using DAO code. Users and Groups are collections of the Database Engine Workspace. The DAO.PermissionsEnum enumeration defines the appropriate numeric values for setting permissions. This section covers the various options for setting permissions using user-level security.

The following declarations are used in the procedures that show how to use DAO to set up user-level security in this section.

```
` Define Global Constants
Const cUser = `Admin"
Const cPW = `"
```

It is important to realize that the code contained through the rest of this section could modify the currently loaded MDW file for the Access session, which is *not* recommended. This means that if a custom MDW file was not specified for the database currently open in Access, then running the code in this section will modify the System.mdw file, which is *not* recommended. The sample MDB and MDW files included with this chapter should be used when running this code for testing and learning purposes so that your default System.mdw file does not get modified inadvertently.

> *I cannot stress enough how important it is to properly back up the* System.mdw
> *or any other MDW file that is used with a database application, before making
> any modifications to the user-level security settings, and every time modifica-
> tions will be made to these settings. If a mistake is made or the MDW becomes
> unusable for any reason, you may never be able to open ANY database applica-
> tion created with that MDW file ever again!*

Adding Groups

The Append method of the DAO Groups collection will add a group to the MDW file. Adding a group only adds the group to the MDW file; it does not set any specific permissions for the group. To add a new group, create an object of type `Group`, set the properties for it, and then call `Append` with `Group` as the parameter. The following block of code shows how to add a `Group` to the `Groups` collection.

Adding group account permissions with DAO

```
Public Sub AddGroupDAO( _
    strGroupName As String, _
    strGID As String)

    ` Define variables
    Dim ws As Workspace
    Dim grp As New Group

    ` Create a workspace object for the database
    Set ws = DBEngine.CreateWorkspace(`DAOWS", cUser, cPW)

    ` Set Group properties
    grp.Name = strGroupName
    grp.PID = strGID

    ` Append the Group to the Groups Collection
    ws.Groups.Append grp

    ` Clean up
    ws.Close
    Set ws = Nothing

End Sub
```

module modUserLevelSecurityDAO in MDB-SampleCode.mdb

Removing Groups

To drop a group, simply call the `Delete` method from the `Groups` collection. Dropping a group does not remove the users contained in the group from the MDW file; it only removes the group itself. The `Delete` method takes one parameter, the group name. The following code shows how to drop a `Group` using DAO code.

Removing group account permissions with DAO

```
Public Sub RemoveGroupDAO(strGroupName As String)

    ` Define variables
    Dim ws As Workspace

    ` Create a workspace object for the database
    Set ws = DBEngine.CreateWorkspace(`DAOWS", cUser, cPW)

    ` Delete the Group from the Collection
    ws.Groups.Delete strGroupName

    ` Clean up
```

```
        ws.Close
        Set ws = Nothing
    End Sub
```

Adding Users

Users can be added using DAO by calling the Append method of the Users collection. As with groups, adding users to the MDW does not modify the original database in any way, only the MDW file. Also, it does not provide any specific permission for the user; that will have to be added separately. To add a new user, create an object of type User, set the properties for it, and then call the Append method for the Users collection. The follow code provides an example of adding a new User to the Users collection.

Available for download on Wrox.com

> ### Adding user account permissions with DAO

```
Public Sub AddUserDAO( _
    strUserName As String, _
    strPassword As String, _
    strPID As String)

    ` Define variables
    Dim ws As Workspace
    Dim usr As New User

    ` Create a workspace object for the database
    Set ws = DBEngine.CreateWorkspace(`DAOWS", cUser, cPW)

    ` Assign the properties to the user
    usr.Name = strUserName
    usr.Password = strPassword
    usr.PID = strPID

    ` Append the User to the Users Collection
    ws.Users.Append usr

    ` Add the user to the `Users" group - Access requirement
    AddUserToGroupDAO strUserName, `Users"

    ` Clean up
    ws.Close
    Set ws = Nothing
    Set usr = Nothing

End Sub
```

Removing Users

To drop a user, simply call the `Delete` method from the `Users` collection. The `Delete` method takes one parameter: the username that is to be deleted. The following code provides an example of removing a `User` object with DAO.

Removing user account permissions with DAO

```
Public Sub RemoveUserDAO(strUserName As String)

    ` Define variables
    Dim ws As Workspace

    ` Create a workspace object for the database
    Set ws = DBEngine.CreateWorkspace(`DAOWS", cUser, cPW)

    ` Delete the User from the collection
    ws.Users.Delete (strUserName)

    ` Clean up
    ws.Close
    Set ws = Nothing

End Sub
```

module modUserLevelSecurityDAO in MDB-SampleCode.mdb

Adding Users to Groups

Once a `User` has been added to the MDW file, you will need to explicitly assign permissions to the `User`, so that they may begin using the account. This can be done in one of two ways: the first, by adding a `User` to a `Group` that already has permission set for it, or the second, by assigning specific permissions directly to the `User` account. It is preferred in most cases to assign the user to a group, so that the administrator of the application doesn't have to worry about maintaining permission levels for every single user, just the security groups.

To add a `User` to an existing `Group` object, get an object for that group by calling the `CreateGroup` method for the `User` object, which added the user account to the group. Then call the `Append` method of the `Groups` collection for that `User` object. The following code provides an example of adding a `User` to an existing `Group` using DAO code.

Adding user account permissions to a Group with DAO

```
Public Sub AddUserToGroupDAO( _
    strUserName As String, _
    strGroupName As String)

    ` Define variables
```

```
        Dim ws As Workspace
        Dim grp As Group
        Dim usr As User

        ` Create a workspace object for the database
        Set ws = DBEngine.CreateWorkspace(`DAOWS", cUser, cPW)

        ` Get the User object to add to the Group
        Set usr = ws.Users(strUserName)

        ' Get the Group object for the specified group
        Set grp = usr.CreateGroup(strGroupName)

        ' Append the Group changes Groups Collection
        usr.Groups.Append grp

        ` Clean up
        Set usr = Nothing
        Set grp = Nothing
        ws.Close
        Set ws = Nothing

    End Sub
```

module modUserLevelSecurityDAO in MDB-SampleCode.mdb

Removing Users from Groups

Inevitably a User account will need to be removed from a Group. To drop a specific User from a Group, call the Delete method from the Users collection of that Group object. This will not delete the User account altogether; this will just remove it from the specified Group. The following code provides an example of removing a User from a Group.

Available for download on Wrox.com

Removing user account permissions from a group with DAO

```
Public Sub RemoveUserFromGroupDAO( _
    strUserName As String, _
    strGroupName As String)

    ` Define variables
    Dim ws As Workspace
    Dim usr As User

    ` Create a workspace object for the database
    Set ws = DBEngine.CreateWorkspace(`DAOWS", cUser, cPW)

    ` Delete the User from the Group in which it belongs
    ws.Groups(strGroupName).Users.Delete strUserName

    ` Clean up
```

```
      ws.Close
      Set ws = Nothing

  End Sub
```

Setting Permissions for the Database

Understanding the detachment between the MDW file and the MDB file that is being secured, consider that although users and groups are maintained through the DB Engine Workspace, permissions are applied to the MDB file as a code, based on the value from the User or Group in the MDW file. You set permissions for the Database object by setting the permissions on the database through the Containers collection from the Database object. Permissions are specified as a Long value of one or more members of the DAO.PermissionsEnum enumeration. The following example shows how to add permissions to a specific Database object using DAO.

Available for download on Wrox.com

Setting database permissions with DAO

```
Public Sub SetPermissionsOnDatabaseDAO( _
    strUserName As String, _
    lngPermissions As Long)

    ` Define Variables
    Dim db As DAO.Database
    Dim con As Container

    ` Get the current database object
    Set db = CurrentDb()

    ` Get the Container object for the DB
    Set con = db.Containers!Databases

    ` Set the User name for the container
    con.UserName = strUserName

    ` Set the user's permissions for the container
    con.Permissions = lngPermissions

    ` Clean up
    Set con = Nothing
    db.Close
    Set db = Nothing

End Sub
```

> *Notice that the* lngPermissions *parameter for the preceding* Sub *is of type* Long *and not* DAO.PermissionEnum. *This is because multiple permission values from the* DAO.PermissionEnum *can be specified by OR'ing the values together into a bitwise combination value for the permission settings, which is discussed in the "Combining Permission Values" section later in this chapter.*

Similarly, one could create a generic method for setting permissions on any container, by slightly modifying the previous code. The following code provides an example of creating a generic method for setting permissions on any object type.

Setting container permissions with DAO

Available for download on Wrox.com

```
Public Sub SetPermissionsOnContainerDAO( _
    strContainer As String, _
    strUserName As String, _
    lngPermissions As Long)

    ' Define Variables
    Dim db As DAO.Database
    Dim con As Container

    ' Get the current database object
    Set db = CurrentDb()

    ' Get the Container object
    Set con = db.Containers(strContainer)

    ' Set the User name for the container
    con.UserName = strUserName

    ' Set the user's permissions for the container
    con.Permissions = lngPermissions

    ' Clean up
    Set con = Nothing
    db.Close
    Set db = Nothing

End Sub
```

module modUserLevelSecurityDAO in MDB-SampleCode.mdb

Setting Permissions for Database Objects

Applying permissions to a specific database object (tables, queries, forms, reports, pages, and macros) adds the permissions only to that object. The type of object must be specified as well as the object's name. To set permissions for an object, first get the object type from the `Containers` collection, then the specific object itself, using the `Documents` collection of the `Container` object. Finally, just set the user and permission values. The following code provides an example of setting permissions for a user for a specific database object using DAO code.

Setting database object permissions with DAO

```
Public Sub SetPermissionsOnObjectDAO( _
    strObjectType As String, _
    strObjectName As String, _
    strUserName As String, _
    lngPermissions As Long)

    ` Define variables
    Dim db As Database
    Dim doc As Document

    ` Get the current database object
    Set db = CurrentDb()

    ` Get the specified Document in the Container
    Set doc = db.Containers(strObjectType).Documents(strObjectName)

    ` Set the User name for the Document
    doc.UserName = strUserName

    ` Set the user's permissions for the Document
    doc.Permissions = lngPermissions

    ` Clean up
    Set doc = Nothing
    db.Close
    Set db = Nothing

End Sub
```

module modUserLevelSecurityDAO in MDB-SampleCode.mdb

Combining Permission Values

As mentioned, in DAO, the `PermissionEnum` object is nothing more than an enumeration of `Long` integer values, each tied to a specific permission settings. Multiple permission settings can be combined as a single permission value by `OR`-ing the permission types together. Using the OR logic to mask the bits together preserves all "1" bits in both of the values being operated on, producing a cumulative effect for the permissions. The following code is an example function, which combines two permission objects into one permissions object, preserving both permission settings that are applied.

Combining PermissionEnum values

```
Public Function CombinePermissions( _
    lngInitialPermissions As Long, _
    lngPermissionToCombine As Long) As Long

    ` Combine the Permissions together
    CombinePermissions = lngInitialPermissions Or lngPermissionToCombine

End Function
```

module modUserLevelSecurityDAO in MDB-SampleCode.mdb

Removing Permission Values

In contrast to combining permissions, it is conceivable that a developer might want to write procedures to remove specific permission values. This can be accomplished by using the AND NOT operators to remove the specified permission values in a bitwise fashion from a given permission value. To do this, the NOT operator flips the bits in the permission to be removed, and then AND logic removes the specific permission type. The following is an example of how a function could be created to remove a specific set of permissions from an existing permission value. However, it is important to note that the result from this example function must be set to the database object to apply the new permission setting to the object itself.

Removing PermissionEnum values

```
Public Function RevokePermissions( _
    lngInitialPermissions As Long, _
    lngPermissionToRemove As Long) As Long

    ` Combine the Permissions together
    RevokePermissions = lngInitialPermissions And Not lngPermissionToRemove

End Function
```

module modUserLevelSecurityDAO in MDB-SampleCode.mdb

Changing the Owner of an Object

To set the owner of a specific database object, simply set the Owner property for that object. It is only possible to change ownership on database objects (tables, queries, forms, reports, pages, and macros), and not on the database or a specific group of containers (database object types). The following code provides an example of how code could be created to change the owner for a specific database object.

Setting the owner for an object using DAO

```
Public Sub ChangeOwnerDAO( _
    strObjectType As String, _
    strObjectName As String, _
    strOwner As String)

    ` Define variables
    Dim db As Database
    Dim doc As Document

    ` Get the current database object
    Set db = CurrentDb()

    ` Get the db object to modify
    Set doc = db.Containers(strObjectType).Documents(strObjectName)

    ` Change the Owner of the Document
    doc.Owner = strOwner

    ` Clean up
    Set doc = Nothing
    db.Close
    Set db = Nothing

End Sub
```

module modUserLevelSecurityDAO in MDB-SampleCode.mdb

User-Level Security Using ADO

ACE also supports using ADO code to set up groups and users and to set up permissions for user-level security. Groups and users are set up using the SQL statements CREATE, ALTER, and DROP, which create, modify, and remove users and groups. The GROUP and USER keywords indicate whether the action is for a user group or user. The ADD and DROP statements add users to a group or remove them from a group. The GRANT and REVOKE statements grant permissions to or remove permissions from a specific object for a group or user. The SELECT, INSERT, UPDATE, and DELETE keywords indicate which permissions are granted or revoked. The following table defines the meaning of these keywords and some additional keyword options.

PRIVILEGE	APPLIES TO	ALLOWS A USER TO
SELECT	Tables, Objects, Containers	Read the data and read the design of a specified table, object, or Container.
DELETE	Tables, Objects, Containers	Delete data from a specified table, object, or Container.

PRIVILEGE	APPLIES TO	ALLOWS A USER TO
INSERT	Tables, Objects, Containers	Insert data into a specified table, object, or Container.
UPDATE	Tables, Objects, Containers	Update data in a specified table, object, or Container.
DROP	Tables, Objects, Containers	Remove a specified table, object, or Container.
SELECTSECURITY	Tables, Objects, Containers	View the permissions for a specified table, object, or Container.
UPDATESECURITY	Tables, Objects, Containers	Allows a user to change the permissions for a specified table, object, or Container.
UPDATEIDENTITY	Tables	Change the values in auto-increment columns.
CREATE	Tables, Objects, Containers	Create a new table, object, or Container.
SELECTSCHEMA	Tables, Objects, Containers	View the design of a specified table, object, or Container.
SCHEMA	Tables, Objects, Containers	Modify the design of a specified table, object, or Container.
UPDATEOWNER	Tables, Objects, Containers	Change the owner of a specified table, object, or Container.
ALL PRIVILEGES	All	Have all permissions, including administrative, on a specified table, object, Container, or database.
CREATEDB	Database	Create a new database.
EXCLUSIVECONNECT	Database	Open a database in exclusive mode.
CONNECT	Database	Allows a user to open a database.
ADMINDB	Database	Administer a database.

It is important to note that the following ADO code examples do not provide any error handling, which is usually recommended for full implementation of security subroutines. Handling basic problems to suit your specific needs enables you to present custom error messages that users can easily understand. For the purpose of this exercise, however, the code is concise. The following declarations are used in the procedures that show how to use ADO to set up user-level security. Also, the example code in this section assumes the following declarations and definitions have been added to the module.

Global declarations for user-level security via ADO

```
Dim strDBPath As String
Dim strMDWPath As String
Dim strAdminUser As String
Dim strAdminPass As String

Enum eObjectTypes
    Database = 1
    Container = 2
    Table = 3
    Other = 4
End Enum

Sub SetGlobals()

    strDBPath = CurrentProject.Path & "\SampleMDB.mdb"
    strMDWPath = CurrentProject.Path & "\SampleMDW.mdw"
    strAdminUser = "Admin"
    strAdminPass = ""

End Sub
```

module modUserLevelSecurityADO in MDB-SampleCode.mdb

Opening an ADO Connection

Before any ADO commands can be executed for a database, a connection to the database must be established first. Any time you connect to a database with ADO code, the username and password, as well as the provider for the connection, must be specified to establish the connection. Then call the Open method to open the connection. The following example function establishes an ADO connection to a data source and returns the Connection object.

Opening a connection to a database with ADO

```
Function OpenConnectionADO( _
    strDatabaseNamePath As String, _
    strMDWNamePath As String, _
    strUserName As String, _
    strPassword As String) As ADODB.Connection

    ' Define variables
    Dim cnn As ADODB.Connection

    ' Open a connection to the database
    Set cnn = New ADODB.Connection
    With cnn
        .Provider = "Microsoft.ACE.OLEDB.12.0"
        .Properties("Jet OLEDB:System database") = strMDWNamePath
        .Open "Data Source=" & strDatabaseNamePath _
```

```
                    & ";User ID=" & strUserName _
                    & ";Password=" & strPassword
          End With

          ` Return the new connection
          Set OpenConnectionADO = cnn

      End Function
```

module modUserLevelSecurityADO in MDB-SampleCode.mdb

The examples throughout the ADO section establish a connection to the database using the OpenConnectionADO function shown in the preceding code. The provider for this connection is Microsoft.ACE.OLEDB.12.0. The database path to be opened by the connection is specified when calling the Open command with the string "Data Source = *your database*". You can choose a specific MDW file by setting a value for the Jet OLEDB:System database connection property. When setting permissions using the GRANT and REVOKE options, it's only necessary to specify the database that will be secured. Otherwise, the data source can be any database.

The SQL statements in the ADO code examples cannot be executed from an Access query.

Adding Groups

To add a new group with ADO, use the CREATE GROUP SQL command. This command takes two parameters: the group name and the group ID.

To add a group name that contains an embedded space, enclose the name in square brackets ([]).

The following code provides an example of adding a new Group to the MDW file using ADO code.

Adding groups with ADO

```
Sub AddGroupADO( _
    strGroupName As String, _
    strGID As String)

    ` Define variables
    Dim cnn As ADODB.Connection
    Dim strCommand As String

    ` Open a connection to the database
```

```
Set cnn = OpenConnectionADO(strDBPath, strMDWPath, strAdminUser, strAdminPass)

` Build the command to create the Group
strCommand = "CREATE GROUP " & strGroupName & " " & strGID & ";"

` Execute the command
cnn.Execute strCommand

` Clean up
cnn.Close
Set cnn = Nothing

End Sub
```

module modUserLevelSecurityADO in MDB-SampleCode.mdb

Removing Groups

When a `Group` is removed, the users are removed from the group, but are not dropped from the MDW file, so those users can still be used for other groups. To remove a `Group`, use the DROP GROUP SQL command. This command takes the group name as the parameter. The following code provides an example of dropping a group using ADO code.

```
Sub DropGroupADO(strGroupName As String)
```

Available for download on Wrox.com

Removing groups with ADO

```
` Define variables
Dim cnn As ADODB.Connection
Dim strCommand As String

` Open a connection to the database
Set cnn = OpenConnectionADO(strDBPath, strMDWPath, strAdminUser, strAdminPass)

` Build the command to drop the Group
strCommand = "DROP GROUP " & strGroupName & ";"

` Execute the command
cnn.Execute strCommand

` Clean up
cnn.Close
Set cnn = Nothing

End Sub
```

module modUserLevelSecurityADO in MDB-SampleCode.mdb

Adding Users

When a user is added, a personal ID must be specified. Also, when a User is added, it should be added to the database Users group to keep the MDW file consistent with the ACE/Jet database engine rule requiring that all Users belong to the Users group. To create a new user, use the CREATE USER SQL command, along with the username, password, and ID. The following code provides an example of creating a new User object using ADO code.

Available for download on Wrox.com

Adding users with ADO

```
Sub AddUserADO( _
    strUserName As String, _
    strPID As String, _
    strPassword As String)

    ` Define variables
    Dim cnn As ADODB.Connection
    Dim strCommand As String

    ` Open a connection to the database
    Set cnn = OpenConnectionADO(strDBPath, strMDWPath, strAdminUser, strAdminPass)

    ` Build the command to create the user
    strCommand = `CREATE USER [` & strUserName & `] [` & strPassword & `] ` & _
                strPID & `;"

    ` Execute the command
    cnn.Execute strCommand

    ` Add the new User to the User Group, per Access integrity rules
    Call AddUserToGroupADO(strUserName, `Users")

    ` Clean up
    cnn.Close
    Set cnn = Nothing

End Sub
```

module modUserLevelSecurityADO in MDB-SampleCode.mdb

Adding Users to Groups

You can add a User to a Group by using the ADD USER SQL command. To use this command, simply specify the username and the group name. The TO SQL operator is used between the User and Group names. The following code provides an example of adding a User to a Group object using ADO code.

Adding user accounts to groups with ADO

```
Sub AddUserToGroupADO( _
    strUserName As String, _
    strGroupName As String)

    ` Define variables
    Dim cnn As ADODB.Connection
    Dim strCommand As String

    ` Open a connection to the database
    Set cnn = OpenConnectionADO(strDBPath, strMDWPath, strAdminUser, strAdminPass)

    ` Build the command to add the user to a group
    strCommand = `ADD USER [` & strUserName & `] TO ` & strGroupName & `;`

    ` Execute the command
    cnn.Execute strCommand

    ` Clean up
    cnn.Close
    Set cnn = Nothing

End Sub
```

module modUserLevelSecurityADO in MDB-SampleCode.mdb

Removing Users

Removing User objects is just as easy using ADO code. Simply use the DROP USER SQL command, along with the username, to remove the user from the MDW file completely. The following code provides an example of removing a User completely from the MDW file using ADO code.

Removing users with ADO

```
Sub DropUserADO(strUserName As String)

    ` Define variables
    Dim cnn As ADODB.Connection
    Dim strCommand As String

    ` Open a connection to the database
    Set cnn = OpenConnectionADO(strDBPath, strMDWPath, strAdminUser, strAdminPass)

    ` Build the command to drop the user
    strCommand = `DROP USER [` & strUserName & `];`

    ` Execute the command
    cnn.Execute strCommand

    ` Clean up
```

```
        cnn.Close
        Set cnn = Nothing

End Sub
```

module modUserLevelSecurityADO in MDB-SampleCode.mdb

Removing Users from Groups

Removing a user from a group does not remove the user from the MDW file, only the Group object. Simply use the DROP USER SQL command along with the username, FROM operator, and the group name. The following code provides an example of removing a User from a Group object using ADO code.

Removing user accounts from groups with ADO

```
Sub DropUserFromGroupADO( _
    strUserName As String, _
    strGroupName As String)

    ` Define variables
    Dim cnn As ADODB.Connection
    Dim strCommand As String

    ` Open a connection to the database
    Set cnn = OpenConnectionADO(strDBPath, strMDWPath, strAdminUser, strAdminPass)

    ` Build the command to drop the user from a group
    strCommand = `DROP USER [` & strUserName & `] FROM ` & strGroupName & `;`

    ` Execute the command
    cnn.Execute strCommand

    ` Clean up
    cnn.Close
    Set cnn = Nothing

End Sub
```

module modUserLevelSecurityADO in MDB-SampleCode.mdb

Modifying a User's Password

The ALTER USER PASSWORD SQL command is used to modify the password for a User object. Although the statement seems to suggest that the password must be known to alter a user's password, if the password is not known, the password parameter can be specified as an empty string. The following code provides an example of modifying the password for a User object using ADO code.

Modifying a user password with ADO

```
Sub AlterUserPasswordADO( _
    strUserName As String, _
    strNewPassword As String, _
    strOldPassword As String)

    ` Define variables
    Dim cnn As ADODB.Connection
    Dim strCommand As String

    ` Open a connection to the database
    Set cnn = OpenConnectionADO(strDBPath, strMDWPath, strAdminUser, strAdminPass)

    ` Build the command to change the password
    strCommand = "ALTER USER [" & strUserName & "] PASSWORD [" & strNewPassword & _
                "] [" & strOldPassword & "];"

    ` Execute the command
    cnn.Execute strCommand

    ` Clean up
    cnn.Close
    Set cnn = Nothing

End Sub
```

module modUserLevelSecurityADO in MDB-SampleCode.mdb

Adding Permissions

Permissions can be applied to both `Group` and `User` objects in ADO using the GRANT SQL command.
The `Permissions` parameter for the GRANT command can be one permission type or many permission
types separated by commas, which is different than the method used to combine permissions for DAO
parameters. Along with the permissions values, the object type must be specified. The following code
provides an example of setting permissions on any object for a specific `User` or `Group` using ADO code.

Adding permissions to users or groups with ADO

```
Sub GrantPermissionsToObjectADO( _
    strUserOrGroupName As String, _
    otObjType As eObjectTypes, _
    strObjectName As String, _
    strPermissions As String)

    ` Define variables
    Dim cnn As ADODB.Connection
    Dim strCommand As String

    ` Open a connection to the database
```

```
    Set cnn = OpenConnectionADO(strDBPath, strMDWPath, strAdminUser, strAdminPass)

    ` Build the command to grant permissions
    strCommand = `GRANT ` & strPermissions & ` ON `
    Select Case otObjType
        Case eObjectTypes.Database:
            strCommand = strCommand
        Case eObjectTypes.Container:
            strCommand = strCommand & `CONTAINER"
        Case eObjectTypes.Table:
            strCommand = strCommand & `TABLE"
        Case eObjectTypes.Other:
            strCommand = strCommand & `OBJECT"
        Case Else
            MsgBox `Object Type Not Recognized"
            Exit Sub
    End Select
    strCommand = strCommand & ` ` & strObjectName & ` TO ` & _
            strUserOrGroupName & `;"

    ` Execute the command
    cnn.Execute strCommand

    ` Clean up
    cnn.Close
    Set cnn = Nothing

End Sub
```

module modUserLevelSecurityADO in MDB-SampleCode.mdb

Removing Permissions

Permissions can be removed from either `Group` or `User` objects in ADO using the REVOKE SQL command. Again, the `Permissions` parameter for the GRANT command can be one permission type or many permission types separated by commas. It also takes the name and type of object to have the permissions removed. The following code provides an example of removing permissions from any object for a specific `User` or `Group` using ADO code.

Available for download on Wrox.com

Removing permissions from users or groups with ADO

```
Sub RevokePermissionsFromObjectADO( _
    strUserOrGroupName As String, _
    otObjType As eObjectTypes, _
    strObjectName As String, _
    strPermissions As String)

    ` Define variables
    Dim cnn As ADODB.Connection
    Dim strCommand As String

    ` Open a connection to the database
```

```
Set cnn = OpenConnectionADO(strDBPath, strMDWPath, strAdminUser, strAdminPass)

` Build the command to revoke permissions
strCommand = "REVOKE " & strPermissions & " ON "
Select Case otObjType
    Case eObjectTypes.Database:
        strCommand = strCommand
    Case eObjectTypes.Container:
        strCommand = strCommand & "CONTAINER"
    Case eObjectTypes.Table:
        strCommand = strCommand & "TABLE"
    Case eObjectTypes.Other:
        strCommand = strCommand & "OBJECT"
    Case Else
        Debug.Print "Object type incorrect"
End Select
strCommand = strCommand & " " & strObjectName & " FROM " & _
            strUserOrGroupName & ";"

` Execute the command
cnn.Execute strCommand

` Clean up
cnn.Close
Set cnn = Nothing

End Sub
```

module modUserLevelSecurityADO in MDB-SampleCode.mdb

User-Level Security Using ADOX

The previous section showed you how to maintain user-level security programmatically using ADO and ACE. Another method to maintain security through VBA code is to use Microsoft ADO Extensions (ADOX) for DDL and Security. ADOX uses an Object Model that supports the `Catalog`, `Group`, and `User` objects. Using ADOX objects, many of the previous ADO functions we created before can be performed without the need to write SQL statements. ADOX provides an Object Model to perform these tasks. That is, rather than having to learn all of the SQL syntax, the methods available in ADOX can simply be called right in VBA code. ADOX also attempts to do some of the work for you. For example, ADOX provides the user and group IDs automatically. Using the ADOX Object Model can greatly reduce the amount of SQL needed to use ADO to work with the user-level security features of the MDB file format.

For more information about ADOX, you can visit the Microsoft Developers Network library. See the article `http://msdn.microsoft.com/library/default.asp?url=/library/en-us/ado270/htm/admscadoxfundamentals.asp`.

SUMMARY

This chapter reviewed the three major security features available in the ACCDB file format. Shared-level security password protects and encrypts the database so that the raw data contained in the file is protected from intruders. Locking the VBA project enables distribution of the code with the database while not allowing unauthorized users to view or make changes to it. And finally, compiling the database to an ACCDE file secures code and prevents any modification by removing all text source code from the database. Used separately or in combination, these features enable a robust security model for ACCDB database solutions.

This chapter also discussed the security features available for MDB file format databases. MDB supports adding a password to the database to implement shared-level security. Creating an MDE database file compiles and removes the text source code from the database, preventing users from making changes to the database code. Encoding the database prevents (or at least seriously challenges) unauthorized users from viewing or manipulating the physical data stored in the MDB file. And, implementing user-level security can enforce and regulate the actions that users and groups can perform for any given database object. Although several of these methods have been deprecated in the ACCDB file format, Access 2010 still supports Access 2002-03 MDB file format databases containing these features.

Although this chapter has provided a great deal of information about database security, this is by no means the end all to information about the subject. The Access help files, the Microsoft knowledge base articles, and the MSDN library all provide useful instructions and guidance about various aspects of Access security and how to secure data and code. Chapter 25 covers more information about macro security, including how the Access program enhances protection for machines from malicious database attacks that use code in database files. And finally, the *Access 2007 VBA Programmers Reference* (Wrox, 2007) and the *Access 2003 VBA Programmers Reference* (Wrox, 2004), the predecessors to this book, also contain more detailed information about the deprecated security features found in previous versions of Access. All of these sources can be very useful for finding out more information about security for Access database files.

25

Access 2010 Security Features

WHAT'S IN THIS CHAPTER?

➤ Managing security settings with the Office Trust Center

➤ Using Disabled mode

➤ Using Automation security

➤ Understanding Macro security in Access 2010

➤ Creating and using digital signatures and certificates

➤ Creating and extracting signed packages

➤ Access Database Engine Expression Service

➤ Understanding Sandbox mode

Now more than ever, you have to concern yourself with the security of your computer systems. One form of security — securing the information contained in and the intellectual property built into your databases — was discussed in Chapter 24.

Another form of security has to do with preventing malicious attacks on your computers — attacks that can delete files, spread viruses, or otherwise disrupt your work. This chapter focuses on the security enhancements built into Access 2010, which help you protect your computer systems and your users' computer systems.

In its efforts to make sure everything is secure, Microsoft had to deal with the fact that an Access database has a lot of power (something Access developers have known all along). And because of this power, someone who chooses to use Access maliciously can make an Access database perform destructive operations. In fact, that is the reason that Outlook does not allow Access database files to be sent as attachments. From a security perspective, an Access database file is essentially an executable.

To curb this power, beginning with Access 2003, Microsoft made changes to Access that meant developers had to do a little more work to make databases as easy to use as they had been with prior versions. But let's face it: If your users use Access to open a database from someone else and that database then attacks their computer, they're more likely to blame Access rather than the database they opened. Their confidence in Access would be right out the window. So, really, the security changes weren't all bad.

But this book is about Access 2010. Beginning with Access 2007, new security features have been added that significantly improve the user experience over that of Access 2003. This chapter explains what these security features are and why they were added. Perhaps more important, it describes the things you can do to make it easy for your users to use your databases in Access 2010. The existing solutions of using a digital signature and Visual Basic scripts still apply, but features such as trusted locations make it even easier. These are not difficult solutions — and once you learn them, they become second nature.

You'll also take a look at Expression Service and Sandbox mode, which are part of the Access database engine. If you installed Access 2003 and found that you had to upgrade to the Jet Engine Service Pack 8, you'll be glad to know that no additional download is required to use wizards or add-ins with Sandbox mode in Access 2010. Because Access 2010 includes the Access database engine, everything you need is already there.

THE OFFICE TRUST CENTER

The Trust Center is a security feature that has been implemented across all applications in Office, including Access. It is not the first feature you'll see when you launch Access 2010 (you'll likely come across Disabled mode first), but it provides several of the key concepts you'll want to know before you explore Disabled mode in more detail.

What Is the Trust Center?

The Trust Center is a centralized feature that you can use to manage security settings for an Office application. In Access, you get to the Trust Center by selecting Options from the File menu, then selecting the Trust Center page. On the Trust Center page, click the Trust Center Settings button to open the Trust Center, shown in Figure 25-1.

Trust Center Features

The Trust Center combines several security and privacy features from previous versions of Office into a common place. Those features include trusted publishers and macro settings. The following sections survey each group in the Trust Center.

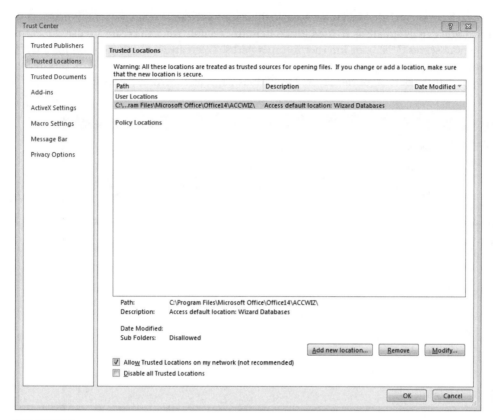

FIGURE 25-1

Trusted Publishers

The Trusted Publishers page (see Figure 25-2) lists the certificates that are installed to the Trusted Publishers certificate store in Windows. Trusted publishers are added when you choose the option to Trust All Documents From This Publisher when opening a database that is signed with a digital signature.

When you trust a certificate from a given publisher, you trust all content for any document or database that you receive from that publisher. You should be certain that you really trust the individual or company before choosing to trust a certificate.

Trusted Locations

Trusted locations are the most exciting feature in the world of security for Office. Having realized some of the issues facing developers and administrators with regard to digital signatures, Microsoft created the concept of a trusted location. A trusted location is exactly what the name suggests — a location that you can designate as trusted for content to execute. You can create a trusted location for local, remote server (UNC), or Internet/intranet paths. To create a trusted location for a UNC or Internet/intranet path, you must select the Allow Trusted Locations on my network (not recommended) option at the bottom of the Trusted Locations page, as shown in Figure 25-3.

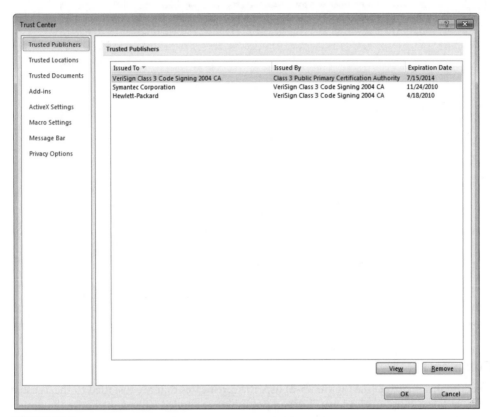

FIGURE 25-2

Opening a database from a trusted location trumps all other security settings, including macro settings. Databases opened from a trusted location always open enabled. Because of this, you must make sure that the locations you mark as trusted really are secure.

By default, Access 2010 includes one trusted location: the `Microsoft Office\Office14\ACCWIZ` directory. The wizards in Access are located in this directory, which is trusted by default to ensure proper operation.

To add a trusted location, click the Add New Location button. That opens the Trusted Location dialog box, as shown in Figure 25-4. You can also choose to trust subfolders of the location. A description can be added that appears in the Trusted Locations group in the Trust Center.

Root folder locations such as `C:`, `\\ServerName\C$`, *or* `http://WebServerName` *cannot be added as trusted locations.*

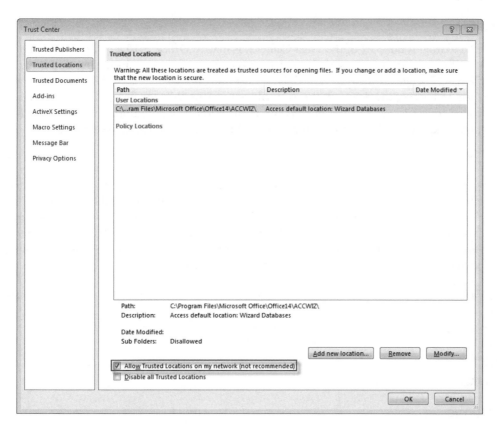

FIGURE 25-3

You can also choose to disable all trusted locations. Doing so forces all databases to open in Disabled mode unless they are digitally signed and the digital signature is trusted.

Trusted Documents

Trusted Documents is a new feature to Office 2010. When a database is opened, its trust state is evaluated and appropriate action is taken. By default, trusted databases bypass most of the security checks and are opened for editing without requiring any security decision by the user

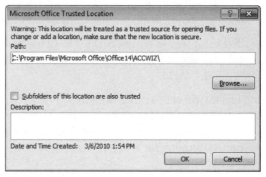

FIGURE 25-4

and with all content enabled. Untrusted databases undergo a multi-layered series of security checks. Once a database has passed these security checks and the user has identified it as a trusted database by allowing editing it is added to the Trusted Documents list, and no further action is required each time the database is subsequently opened. This is true even if new ActiveX content has been added to the database. Trusted files do not bypass virus checking or ActiveX kill-bit checking. The ActiveX kill-bit is set for malicious ActiveX controls as part of Anti-Virus security protocols and is controlled through Policy settings.

File Validation

While File Validation is not part of the Trust Center it is new to Office 2010 (and by extension Access 2010). This new technology automatically scans opening untrusted documents and checks for valid file type. For the most part, File Validation scanning is transparent to the user. If no potential differences in file type are detected, the user will be unaware that any file scanning took place. If a file is found to be suspect, the user may receive notification asking if information about the file may be sent to Microsoft to help improve the tool's ability to detect potential file exploits.

Add-Ins

Add-ins are a great way to enhance the user experience, but they can also be used to introduce malicious code by unscrupulous programmers. Office 2010 has the capability to disable all add-ins. This also includes the built-in Access wizards, but remember that the trusted location trumps this setting as well. If you select the option to Require Application Add-ins to be signed by Trusted Publisher and also Disable all Trusted Locations, you are prompted to run Access wizards. Figure 25-5 shows the prompt when you launch the Form Wizard in this configuration.

FIGURE 25-5

Macro Settings

The macro security settings are controlled by navigating to the Macro Settings in the Trust Center, as shown in Figure 25-6.

The default setting for Access 2010 is Disable all macros with notification. With this setting, the Message Bar is displayed for all databases that are not digitally signed or in a trusted location.

The most secure setting is Disable all macros without notification. With this setting, all databases that are not in a trusted location or haven't been flagged as trusted open disabled. The Message Bar is not displayed.

The least secure setting is Enable all macros. To reinforce the fact that all code will execute, Microsoft includes a warning next to this setting that reads "(not recommended, potentially dangerous code can run)." If you are sure that all the files and add-ins you open are safe, you can select this option, although it is extremely risky.

We highly recommend against using settings that disable or reduce security enhancements. We consider ourselves pretty savvy computer users. We have firewalls and virus software, and a pretty good idea of what to download and whether to open a file that has been downloaded for us. But we won't use these settings ourselves. We would rather have just made the decision to open something that hosed our computer than have it be the result of some setting we chose months ago and then forgot about.

Each Office application has independent control of Trust Center settings for that application.

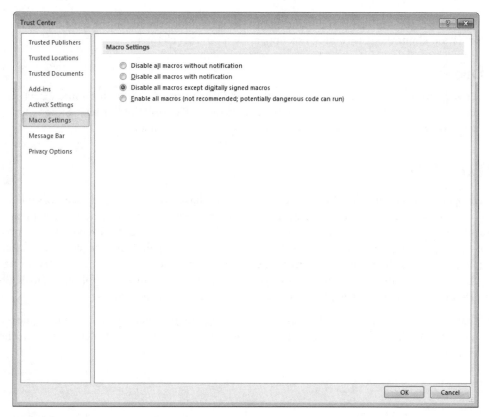

FIGURE 25-6

Message Bar

By default, the Message Bar appears in the Access window when a database is disabled. The Message Bar page in the Trust Center allows you to turn the Message Bar on or off for all applications. You can choose not to see the Message Bar when a database is opened by this setting. This setting trumps the Macro setting: Disable all macros with notification.

There is checkbox at the bottom of the page called Enable Trust Center Logging. With Trust Center logging enabled, Office will log all activity related to the Trust Center to a folder called `%LocalAppData%\Microsoft\Office\TCDiag`. For Access, information will be logged to a file called `ACTCD.LOG`. On Windows Vista and Windows 7, this file was created in `C:\Users\<UserName>\AppData\Local\Microsoft\Office\TCDiag`. The log file includes the following information about each file that is inspected by the Trust Center:

```
--
File Name: "C:\Users\Jerry Dennison\Documents\ Chamber Application.accdb"
Date/Time Opened: 3/7/2010 2:35 PM
Content Type: VBA Macro
Certificate: None
Certificate Signature: None
```

```
Certificate Status: None
Trust Center Decision: Block Content
```

The User Decision entry is added if you make a trust decision about the file in the trust dialog box. More information about the trust dialog box appears later in this chapter.

Privacy Options

Last, the Privacy Options group in the Trust Center includes options to use online content such as help or links. It also provides the opportunity to participate in Microsoft's Customer Experience Improvement Program. It also has a link to Microsoft's Privacy Statement.

DISABLED MODE

If you have opened an existing database in Access 2010, you have probably already seen Disabled mode. It is a standard security feature in Access 2010 that prevents certain content in the database from executing. It's designed to let users securely inspect the content of a database without the possibility of running potentially malicious objects. What is a potentially malicious object? Generally speaking, it is any object that can be used to alter database content, the file system, Registry, or network. In Access, this means VBA code, certain types of queries (action queries, SQL Pass-Through, and Data Definition Language), certain macro actions, and ActiveX controls.

It's pretty easy to notice when code fails to execute. A large piece of functionality in your application doesn't work. As shown in Figure 25-7, the Message Bar is the other way to determine that the database is disabled.

FIGURE 25-7

Unless you change the macro settings, it's worth noting that unless they are digitally signed or in a trusted location, all databases open in Disabled mode. Even empty databases fall into this category.

Why Do We Have Disabled Mode?

Because we live in a time when computer security is becoming more and more critical, Microsoft added the capability to inspect a database without the risk of malicious code running. That is what Disabled mode is all about.

Why all this concern over opening a database, even an empty one? Well, with all the capabilities in Access, add-ins and wizards and whatnot, there must be a way for someone to choose to give you a malicious Access database file. And if there is a way, someone will find it and exploit it.

Take the following lines of code, for example:

```
DoCmd.SetWarnings False
DoCmd.RunSQL `UPDATE msysaccessobjects ` _
& `SET data = Shell(`"c:\windows\system32\notepad.exe""`);"
```

You may test this by entering the above code in the VBA Immediate window using Access 2010, the RunSQL command will then execute the VBA Shell function to determine what the value of the field data should be, and Windows Notepad (C:\windows\system32\notepad.exe) starts.

Of course, Notepad is not likely to cause problems that would result in the destruction of your computer. But there are a lot of destructive programs on your computer — format.com, for example — as well as destructive commands such as DEL that could be run using such a technique.

Those code lines could have been written in an Access macro. That macro could have been named AutoExec, which automatically runs when a database is opened. If the Shell function had called a destructive program instead of Notepad, or if the SQL had contained a destructive command like DEL, data could be destroyed on the computer that opened the database, or worse yet, data could be destroyed on other computers networked to the computer that opened the database. So if you're not paying attention to the databases you open, or worse yet, your users aren't paying attention, well, you have heard about the countless hours spent recovering from viruses. That is nothing compared to the value of data that can be deleted if a hard disk drive is reformatted. And malicious code can do just that.

Enabling a Database

When Access opens a database, it gives certain information, known as *evidence*, to the Trust Center. For Access, the evidence includes the location of the file and the digital signature of the database if it has one. The Trust Center takes the evidence and makes a trust decision based on certain logic. The decision is then given to Access, which opens the database in either Disabled or Enabled mode as needed.

Figure 25-8 illustrates the logic for determining whether a database will open in Disabled mode.

You can leave the content disabled while you examine the data and other objects to determine if you want to enable the content. This is called Sandbox Mode and provides you with a secure method of seeing what is in the database without the risk of executing potentially malicious code.

To enable the database, select Enable Content. The database will then be added to the Trusted Documents list (you may be promted to add it to the list) and its content enabled. If the database contains an Autoexec Macro and has not been enabled, this macro will not be allowed to run and you'll receive the message illustrated in Figure 25-9.

If the database is signed, you can view the details of the source by viewing the publisher's certificate in the Trust Center, as shown in Figure 25-10.

 Only MDB files can be signed. ACCDB files can only be packaged and signed.

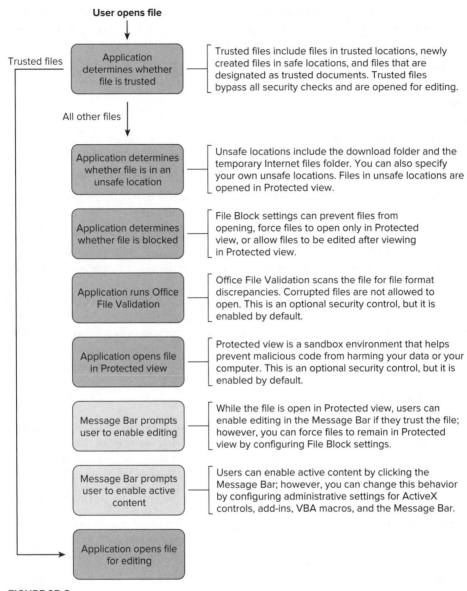

User opens file

Trusted files

Application determines whether file is trusted
— Trusted files include files in trusted locations, newly created files in safe locations, and files that are designated as trusted documents. Trusted files bypass all security checks and are opened for editing.

All other files

Application determines whether file is in an unsafe location
— Unsafe locations include the download folder and the temporary Internet files folder. You can also specify your own unsafe locations. Files in unsafe locations are opened in Protected view.

Application determines whether file is blocked
— File Block settings can prevent files from opening, force files to open only in Protected view, or allow files to be edited after viewing in Protected view.

Application runs Office File Validation
— Office File Validation scans the file for file format discrepancies. Corrupted files are not allowed to open. This is an optional security control, but it is enabled by default.

Application opens file in Protected view
— Protected view is a sandbox environment that helps prevent malicious code from harming your data or your computer. This is an optional security control, but it is enabled by default.

Message Bar prompts user to enable editing
— While the file is open in Protected view, users can enable editing in the Message Bar if they trust the file; however, you can force files to remain in Protected view by configuring File Block settings.

Message Bar prompts user to enable active content
— Users can enable active content by clicking the Message Bar; however, you can change this behavior by configuring administrative settings for ActiveX controls, add-ins, VBA macros, and the Message Bar.

Application opens file for editing

FIGURE 25-8

Modal Prompts

Certain types of files always prompt the user to open them, unless they are opened from a trusted location or are digitally signed. These include ACCDE, MDE, ADP, and ADE files. Those files are opened with a modal prompt for security reasons. ADP and ADE files connect directly to SQL Server, and code executed in these files can also be executed on the server in the form of stored procedures and functions. One primary goal for Disabled mode is to allow you to view the code in a solution without running it. Because VBA source code is removed from ACCDE and MDE files, these files cannot be opened in Disabled mode. For more information about ACCDE and MDE files, please refer to Chapter 24.

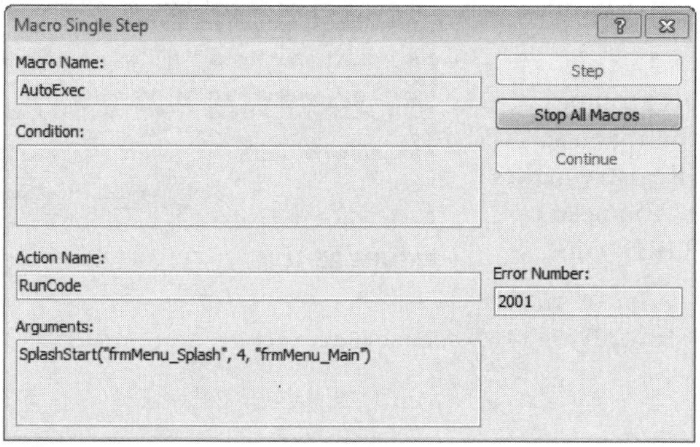

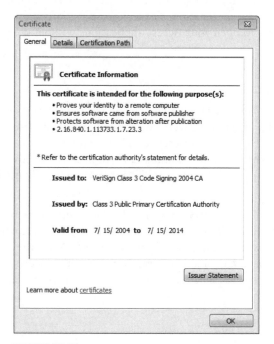

FIGURE 25-9

FIGURE 25-10

You are also prompted when opening a database in the Access Runtime or with the /runtime command-line switch, as shown in Figure 25-11. That's because the Trust Center is not available to users in Runtime mode. There's no way to inspect a database for its safety, so users are given the explicit choice to open the file. This isn't necessarily the optimal solution; after all, when you put your database in front of users, you don't particularly want them to have to respond to this warning every time they open your database. In addition to using trusted locations, we'll describe some options to prevent this, including Visual Basic scripts and digital signatures, later in this chapter.

For security purposes, you can revert to this prompt to open every file from an untrusted location if you so choose. Adding the following value in the Registry makes Access 2010 prompt you to open every file. You need to create the `ModalTrustDecisionOnly` DWORD value because it does not exist by default.

FIGURE 25-11

```
HKEY_CURRENT_USER\Software\Microsoft\Office\14.0\Access\Security\
ModalTrustDecisionOnly = 1
```

AutomationSecurity

The `AutomationSecurity` property was added to the Access `Application` object in Access 2003. It determines how Access behaves when running under automation. The following sections show you how to use the `AutomationSecurity` property to open your Access applications without user interaction.

Opening Remote Databases Programmatically

Access 2010 dramatically improves on Access 2007 in how Disabled mode and trusted locations are handled — by reducing the number of prompts that must be answered before opening a database from an unknown source. That said, it would still be nice if your users didn't have to deal with prompts or disabled content or trusted locations when opening a database. If you work in an environment where you are opening remote databases from VBA code, you'll want (and essentially need) those remote databases to open without issues.

To solve this, you can create a Visual Basic Script file (type VBS) to open a database without getting the security prompt or opening in Disabled mode. The following code temporarily disables security (actually, it effectively enables all code or macros) while the database is being opened. When the script ends, control is turned over to Access and the `AcApp` object is released. Because the security setting is persistent only while the `AcApp` object exists, the macro setting in Access returns to whatever setting was chosen using the Trust Center.

```
Const DATABASE_TO_OPEN = "C:\<FileToOpen>.mdb"
On Error Resume Next

Dim AcApp
Set AcApp = CreateObject("Access.Application")

If AcApp.Version >= 11 Then    ' Set to 11 because this works in Access 2003 as well
    AcApp.AutomationSecurity = 1 ' Enable content (Low security)
```

```
    End If

    AcApp.Visible = True
    AcApp.OpenCurrentDatabase DATABASE_TO_OPEN

    If AcApp.CurrentProject.FullName <> `" Then
        AcApp.UserControl = True
    Else
        AcApp.Quit
        MsgBox `Failed to open `" & DATABASE_TO_OPEN & `".″
    End If
```

Similar code can be used in VBA to open and access a remote database. That is, depending on the reason you are opening the remote database, you may or may not want to switch control to the user (`AcApp.UserControl = True`).

Of course, if you use this VB script for databases that your users open, you cannot specify command-line parameters — for example, `/wrkgrp` to specify a workgroup information file (WIF). If you don't need to specify parameters, this gets around Disabled mode quite easily.

Other Uses for AutomationSecurity

There are several scenarios in VBA code where Access opens a database behind the scenes and can display a prompt to open a database. This is often not desirable because you don't want a dialog box to open while code is running. Examples of this scenario include database conversion using the `ConvertAccessProject` method, and exporting objects using the `TransferDatabase` method. To prevent the prompt from appearing, you can set the `AutomationSecurity` property to 1 (Enable Content) prior to calling the specified method.

The following code demonstrates how to use the `AutomationSecurity` property prior to converting a database not located in a trusted location when using the `ConvertAccessProject` method.

```
    Sub ConvertWithoutPrompt()

        Const SOURCE_DB As String = `\Database8.accdb″
        Const DEST_DB   As String = `\Database8.mdb″

        ` Set AutomationSecurity. This code requires a reference to the
        ` Office 12.0 Object Library
        Application.AutomationSecurity = msoAutomationSecurityLow

        ` Convert an ACCDB to MDB in 2002-2003 format
        Application.ConvertAccessProject CurrentProject.Path & SOURCE_DB, _
            CurrentProject.Path & DEST_DB, _
            acFileFormatAccess2002
    End Sub
```

Macros in Access 2010

Similar to the way that expressions are evaluated for safety in Access, macros in Access 2010 now run in a Sandboxed environment. This means that Access has a list of those macro actions that are safe to execute in Disabled mode. As mentioned in Chapter 4, a safe macro is one that does not perform any of the following tasks:

➤ Change data.

➤ Create or delete objects.

➤ Update or alter the Access user interface.

➤ Access the Windows file system.

➤ Run a SQL statement.

➤ Send e-mail.

Unsafe Actions

Following is a list of actions that are blocked in Disabled mode in Access 2010. If you run any of these actions, an error is displayed while the database is disabled. Unsafe macros are also flagged with an exclamation point warning when created in the macro designed.

```
CopyDatabaseFile

CopyObject

DeleteObject

Echo

OpenDataAccessPage

OpenDiagram

OpenFunction

OpenModule

OpenStoredProcedure

OpenView

PrintOut

Rename

RunApp

RunSavedImportExport

RunSQL

Save

SendKeys

SetValue

SetWarnings

ShowToolbar

TransferDatabase
```

    TransferSharePointList

    TransferSpreadsheet

    TransferSQLDatabase

    TransferText

Nine safe actions are blocked when you set an action argument to a specific value. These are described in the following table.

MACRO ACTION	ACTION ARGUMENT	UNSAFE ARGUMENT VALUE
CloseWindows	Save	No and Yes.
OpenForm	View	Design and Layout.
OpenQuery	View	Design.
OpenReport	View	Design, Layout, and Print.
OpenTable	View	Design.
ExportWithFormatting	Output File	Any. When a filename is specified, this action becomes unsafe.
QuitAccess	Options	Exit and Save All.
RunMenuCommand	Command	See the list of commonly used RunMenuCommand action arguments following this table.
EmailDatabaseObject	Edit Message	No.
EmailDatabaseObject	Template File	Any value specified.

The following commonly used RunMenuCommand action arguments are blocked:

- ➤ InsertObject
- ➤ PasteAppend
- ➤ PasteSpecial
- ➤ Relationships
- ➤ Cut
- ➤ Copy
- ➤ Paste
- ➤ WorkgroupAdministrator

While the list does not include all RunMenuCommand arguments, only a small subset of macro actions are blocked in Disabled mode. Several of the safe actions revolve around navigation, so the actions that remain can still allow an application to be relatively useful. In fact, the majority of the functionality in the new Access templates is implemented using embedded macros so that they can function successfully in Disabled mode. Naturally, for more complex applications you will need to enable the database.

DIGITAL SIGNATURES AND CERTIFICATES

As you now know, databases with digital signatures are exceptions to the macro setting checks. That is, if a database is digitally signed, it can be opened regardless of the macro setting.

Before you tackle creating and using digital signatures, however, let's briefly review ACCDB files. Access 2010 uses the file format called ACCDB. These files include additional features for the Access database engine and are the default file format created in Access 2010, but they do not support digital signatures — at least not in the sense that you were becoming accustomed to in Access 2003. For ACCDB files, Microsoft uses a feature called Signed Packages that enables you to compress a database and sign the compressed file. You'll see more about this feature later in the chapter.

Okay, back to digital signatures. So, what is a digital signature and how do you create one?

You have probably seen various forms of digital signatures or digitally signed programs while browsing the Internet or installing software. Typically you see a security warning dialog box that contains information describing the purpose of the digital certificate used to sign the program, the date and time the certificate was published, and who published it. Some certificates permit you to obtain more information about the program and/or the publisher. After reviewing the information about the certificate, you can accept the certificate or reject it. If desired, you can choose to have that certificate accepted automatically by clicking the Trust all from publisher button as illustrated in Figure 25-12.

FIGURE 25-12

A digital signature is a means to apply a digital certificate to programs, databases, or other electronic documents so that a user of that program, database, or document can confirm that the document came from the signer and that it has not been altered. If the program, database, or document is altered after it has been digitally signed, the signature is invalidated (removed). This feature means that you can be assured that nobody can introduce viruses after the signature is applied.

All of this means that you have to obtain a digital certificate to give your database a digital signature. In a moment, you'll see more about how to obtain a digital certificate, and later, how to sign your database with the digital certificate. But first — a bit more explanation about how digital certificates and digital signatures work with Access.

Microsoft Office 2010 uses Microsoft Authenticode technology to enable you to digitally sign your Access database by using a digital certificate. A person using your signed database can then confirm that you are the signer and that your database has not been altered since you signed it. If that person trusts you, he can open your database without regard to his Access macro security level setting.

You're probably thinking that your database will be altered. After all, that's what a user does when he inserts or deletes data. Because a database is likely to be altered in anticipated ways, a digital signature for an Access database applies to specific aspects of the database rather than to the entire database. Therefore, a database can be updated in the ways you would expect without the signature being invalidated.

More specifically, a digital signature on an Access database covers only objects that could be modified to do malicious things. These objects include modules, macros, and certain types of queries — for example, action queries, SQL pass-through queries, and data definition queries. The signature also applies to the ODBC connection string in queries and properties of ActiveX controls. If any of these types of objects are modified after you sign your database, the digital signature is invalidated (removed).

Types of Digital Certificates

There are two types of digital certificates: commercial and internal. Commercial certificates are obtained through a commercial certification authority (CA) such as VeriSign, Inc. Internal certificates are intended for use on a single computer or within a single organization and can be obtained from your organization's security administrator or created using the Selfcert.exe program, which is described a little later.

Commercial Certificates

To obtain a commercial certificate, you must request (and usually purchase) one from an authorized commercial certificate authority vendor. The vendor sends you a certificate and instructions about how to install the certificate on your computer and how to use it with your Access application.

> *The certificate you need for your Access databases is called a code-signing certificate. Also look for certificates that are suitable for Microsoft Authenticode technology.*

The commercial certificate provides full protection of your database for authenticity. Because the digital certificate is removed if the file or VBA project is modified, you can be sure that your database will not be authenticated if anyone tampers with it.

Likewise, commercial certificates provide protection for users. In the event someone obtains a certificate and uses it for malicious purposes, the commercial authority will revoke the certificate. Then anyone who uses software that is signed with that certificate will be informed of its revocation by the CA.

> *The computer opening a digitally signed program, database, or other electronic document must have access to the Internet to verify the authenticity and status of a commercial certificate.*

Internal Certificates

An internal certificate is intended for use on a single computer or within a single organization. An internal certificate provides protections similar to a commercial certificate in that if the file or VBA project is changed, the certificate is removed, and the database does not automatically open unless Enable all macros is selected as the macro setting.

Internal certificates can be created and managed by a certificate authority within your organization using tools such as Microsoft Certificate Server. You can create a certificate for your own computer using the `Selfcert.exe` tool. Another method of generating a self signed certificate is the `MakeCert.exe` tool which will generate an exportable certificate for use within an organization.

Obtaining a Digital Certificate

As mentioned earlier, you can obtain a certificate from a commercial authority such as VeriSign, Inc. For internal certificates, you can turn to your security administrator or Digital Certificate group, or you can create your own certificate using the `Selfcert.exe` tool.

Be aware that if you create your own certificate, Access still opens a database in Disabled mode when your signed database is opened on a computer other than the one where the certificate was created. This happens because Microsoft considers it to be a self-signed database.

The trouble with self-certification is that the certificate isn't trusted because it is not in the Trusted Root Certification Authorities store. That is, your certificate isn't registered and Microsoft Authenticode technology cannot determine its authenticity — the certificate gets a crosswise look. And the reason for this is that a digital certificate you create can be imitated: Someone can mimic your certificate and sign a database with it. If you have trusted a digital certificate that has been mimicked, a database signed with that certificate will open, and if that database contains malicious code, it could execute that code. This brings up two important issues:

➤ If a certificate you create can be imitated, what kind of security do you really get?

➤ If your certificate won't be trusted on another computer, why bother creating your own certificate?

A certificate is nothing more than a digital document. As with any digital document, it can be copied, replicated, or otherwise imitated. However, Microsoft's Authenticode technology is able to determine authenticity of the certificate if, and only if, it is in a Trusted Root Certification Authorities store.

Using self-certification is a solution that should be considered only if your databases will just be used behind the security of a firewall, with virus software, for protection. If your database, and therefore your certificate, will be made publicly available, such as through the Internet, you will be putting your certificate out where someone could copy it. They could then attach the copy to a database with malicious code and send that database back to you, or worse yet, on to other users who could think the database is from you. If the certificate has been on the computer that is opening the database, that database will be trusted, it will open, and the malicious code will be executed.

If you are interested in acquiring a commercial certificate, the Microsoft Developer Network (MSDN) has a list of root certificate program vendors at `http://msdn.microsoft.com/en-us/`

`library/ms995347.aspx`. When you are looking for a vendor to supply a certificate, you need one that provides a certificate for code signing or that works with Microsoft Authenticode technology.

Using Self-Certification

Now that you have been sufficiently warned about the pitfalls of self-certifying, take a look at how you can self-certify in situations that you believe are secure from hacker attacks.

The question asked in the previous section was: If your certificate isn't going to be trusted on another computer, why bother creating one? The answer is that the certificate isn't trusted unless it is installed on the computer that is opening the signed database. Therefore, the solution is to install your certificate on that computer so that it will be trusted.

Only a few steps are necessary to self-certify and use the certificate for your database as well as use that database on any computer. Some of the steps have to be done only once, and some have to be repeated for each computer that will use your certificate to open your database. First you need to run `Selfcert.exe` to create a certificate on your computer.

Creating a Self-Certification Certificate

To create a certificate for yourself, simply run the `SelfCert.exe` program. This is available from Start ➪ All Programs ➪ Microsoft Office ➪ Microsoft Office 2010 Tools ➪ Digital Certificate for VBA Projects. You can also run this from the Office14 folder. For example, mine is located in `C:\Program Files\Microsoft Office\OFFICE14\SELFCERT.EXE`.

 If `SelfCert.exe` *is not installed on your computer, use the Microsoft Office 2010 installation disk to install it.*

When `Selfcert.exe` starts, the Create Digital Certificate window opens, as shown in Figure 25-13.

Enter a name for your certificate and click OK. This creates a certificate and adds it to the list of certificates for this computer only.

With the certificate created, there are two requirements to use your database on another computer:

1. Sign your database.

2. Create a file from your certificate and install it on the target computer.

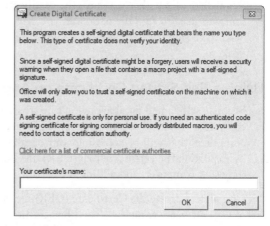

FIGURE 25-13

Signing your database is done through the Visual Basic Editor. Creating a file from your certificate can be accomplished many ways, usually while viewing the certificate details. Installing the certificate on the target computer can be done from Windows Explorer.

 Keep in mind these steps apply only to self-certification. If you use a commercial certificate, you won't have to install your certificate on each computer.

Adding a Certificate to Your Database

To digitally sign your database, you add a certificate to it using the Visual Basic Editor. In the Visual Basic Editor, select Tools ➪ Digital Signature. The dialog box shown in Figure 25-14 opens.

To pick a digital signature to sign your database, click Choose. The Select Certificate dialog box (see Figure 25-15) opens, showing all the code signing certificates on this computer.

Select the certificate you want to use to sign this database and click OK. The name of the selected certificate displays in the Digital Signature dialog box, and a Detail button appears, as shown in Figure 25-16.

FIGURE 25-14

You use the Detail button to get access to an option to create a file from your certificate so you can copy that certificate to another computer. To sign your database now, click OK.

Access 2010 does not automatically re-sign files when a digital signature has been removed. Regardless of whether you have the certificate that was used to sign the database, you will need to re-sign the database if the signature is broken.

FIGURE 25-15

Using a Self-Signed Certificate on Another Computer

Because self-signed databases won't be trusted on another computer, you need to add your self-signed certificate to other computers that will be accessing your databases. You do that by exporting the certificate to a (CER) file, copying the file to the other computer, and adding the certificate to that computer.

One way to create the Certificate (CER) file is to view the details of the certificate from the Visual Basic Editor. Select Tools ➪ Digital Signature to open the Digital Signature dialog box, and click the Detail button. That displays the Certificate Information, as shown in Figure 25-17.

FIGURE 25-16

The bottom of the form shows you have a private key that corresponds to this certificate. The private key is your personal piece of data associated with the certificate and is required to digitally sign a file. For a self-signed certificate, the private key cannot be exported. When you export the certificate, what you are exporting is the public key. The public key is used to uniquely identify a certificate as having been signed by you.

To get to the option that enables you to save the certificate to a file, click the Details tab, shown in Figure 25-18. (Your tab shows actual values in the Value column; they are omitted here for privacy.)

Click the Copy to File button at the bottom of the page to start the Certificate Export Wizard, which will lead you through the process to create a file that you can copy to another computer.

After you create the file, you can take it to another computer and open it. A file of type CER is known to Windows and will show the certificate details, as shown in Figure 25-19.

FIGURE 25-17

Click Install Certificate to start the Certificate Import Wizard.

After the certificate is installed on the computer, the first time you open a database signed with that certificate, the Message Bar appears with the option to trust the publisher. If you select the option to always trust the publisher, databases signed with that certificate will open in Enabled mode.

Signed Packages

As mentioned earlier, Access 2010 does not allow you to digitally sign an ACCDB file using the Digital Signature dialog box. Doing so will result in an error message. Instead, you can package the entire database into a compressed file, which is subsequently signed. The process creates a new file with an ACCDC file extension known as a *signed package*.

FIGURE 25-18

Signed package files can be used as a security feature and a deployment feature. As a security feature, they provide a mechanism to digitally sign a file that can be used to help identify the publisher of the file — just like digital signatures on Access database files. As a deployment feature, they create a file that is smaller than the original with the capability to be opened in Access and verify the publisher of the file.

Creating the Signed Package

Open any ACCDB database file, click the Office button, and select Save & Publish ➪ Save Database As ➪ Package and Sign. The Select Certificate dialog box opens. After you select the certificate you wish to use to sign the package and click OK, you will be asked to provide a location for the package file, as shown in Figure 25-20. (Remember the location for the signed package; you'll use it in the next section.)

Click the Create button to save the package file. Access takes the database file and compresses it into a package with an ACCDC file extension. Then it signs the package file using the certificate you selected in the first step.

FIGURE 25-19

 Because the entire database is packaged, including the data, an ACCDC file represents a digitally signed snapshot of the data at a certain point in time.

Creating the signed package file is only half of the process. The rest is to extract the database from the signed package.

Extracting the Signed Package

Once you have created the signed package, you can extract it simply by double-clicking it or by opening it in Access. When you do so, you see a familiar dialog box, as shown in Figure 25-21.

 *By default, signed packages (.accdc files) will not show up in the Open Files dialog box. You must change the file extension filter to show "Access Signed Package - *.accdc" or "All Files" when you want to select a package.*

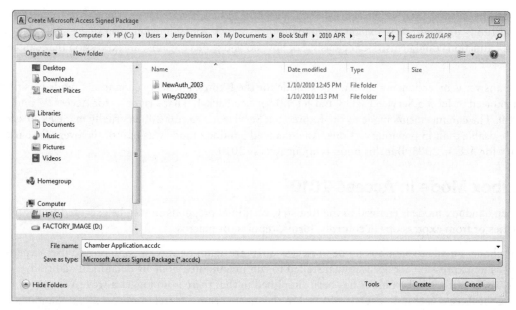

FIGURE 25-20

If you click Open or Trust all from publisher, Access asks you to save the ACCDB file inside the package. This database file is not digitally signed, so it will open in Disabled mode unless you extract it to a trusted location. The database file is no longer associated with the package file. If you change anything in the database, it will not be updated in the package.

Once the database is open, you can use it as you would any other database.

FIGURE 25-21

ACCESS DATABASE ENGINE EXPRESSION SERVICE

The Expression Service has been a part of the Jet database engine for a long time. It is used whenever and wherever expressions are evaluated in Access and also it communicates with the VBA expression service. If you think about all the places in Access that can accept an expression, that's a lot! In terms of security, the surface area for expressions is quite large, so it was not feasible for Microsoft to add expressions to the digital signature for a database. The performance implications of scanning each entry point for an expression would have brought a database to its proverbial knees.

Microsoft takes security very seriously, and it's looking at its software for anything that provides an opportunity for someone to exploit it and maliciously attack your computer. You've seen how the `Shell` function could be used maliciously. So, how do you protect against an expression that can be misused?

The answer is by enhancing the Sandbox mode for the Expression Service. Sandbox mode was first introduced in Jet 3.5 Service Pack 3 and Jet 4.0 Service Pack 1. That's right — for Access 97 and 2000. The enhancements made to the Expression Service for Access 2003 actually made expressions more usable than in previous versions. An enhanced Sandbox mode was half of the overall security story for Access 2003. But this book is about Access 2010.

Sandbox Mode in Access 2010

When Sandbox mode is enabled in the Registry, certain expressions cannot be executed from SQL queries or from expressions in controls, forms, reports, or macros.

The changes made to Sandbox mode in Access 2010 are again by way of an improved user experience. The Expression Service is now installed to run in Sandbox mode by default. In addition, interaction with Sandbox mode has been simplified in that there is no longer a way to change it using the Access user interface. (It was tied to the macro security level in Access 2003.) Sandbox mode is still set in the Registry under HKEY_LOCAL_MACHINE, which means you must be an administrator on the computer to change the setting.

In addition to the other security enhancements already mentioned, Access 2010 always runs in Sandbox mode unless the database is trusted. Even if you change the Sandbox mode value in the Registry to turn it off, unsafe expressions are blocked unless the database is opened from a trusted location or has been explicitly enabled. The idea is that when a database is trusted, all content of the database is trusted including its expressions; until then, potentially malicious content, including expressions, is disabled.

Sandbox Mode Limitations

Sandbox mode blocks VBA functions or commands that could be harmful to a computer. (They're blocked by the Access database engine when they are executed from a SQL query or other expressions in controls, forms, reports, or macros.) The following is a list of functions that are blocked when Sandbox mode is enabled:

AppActivate	CurDir
Beep	CurDir$
Calendar	DeleteSetting
CallByName	DoEvents
ChDir	Environ
ChDrive	Environ$
Command	EOF
Command$	Err
CreateObject	FileAttr

FileCopy	Loc
FileDateTime	LOF
FileLen	Randomize
FreeFile	Reset
GetAllSettings	SaveSetting
GetAttr	Seek
GetObject	SendKeys
GetSetting	SetAttr
Input	Shell
Input$	Spc
InputB	Tab
InputB$	Unload
Kill	UserForms
Load	Width

The Microsoft Knowledge Base has an excellent article that describes the Sandbox mode as well as expressions that are blocked when the Sandbox is enabled at http://support.microsoft.com/kb/294698/. The article also describes how to adjust the Sandbox mode by changing a setting in the Windows Registry, but note that the Registry key for Access 2010 has changed to:

```
HKEY_LOCAL_MACHINE\Software\Microsoft\Office\14.0\Access Connectivity_
Engine\Engines\SandboxMode
```

If you decide to adjust the Sandbox mode, be aware that the Access database engine may be used by services or applications other than Access.

In addition to the functions listed in the list, some properties of ActiveX controls are also blocked. Standard properties such as Name, Value, and Tag are not blocked, but custom properties specific to the control — Day and Month on the Calendar control, for example — may be blocked.

Workarounds

The following sections describe some ways to work around the limitations imposed by Sandbox mode in the Access database engine expression service.

Blocked Functions

If you attempt to call one of the functions in the preceding list from a SQL query, you receive a runtime error indicating that you have used an Unknown Function Name. Calling one of these functions from a control on a form or report displays a #Name? error.

The functions listed are not blocked when executed from your VBA code. So if it is necessary for you to execute one of these functions, you can define a Public function in your VBA code to call from your query, provided that code is enabled in the database.

For example, if you use the `CurDir` function as shown in this SQL statement:

```
SELECT CurDir() AS src FROM Customers;
```

you can write a `Public` function like this:

```
Public Function CurDir ()
    CurDir = VBA.CurDir()
End Function
```

Blocked Custom Properties of ActiveX Controls

If you need to access custom properties of an ActiveX control through the Access database engine, you can create a function as previously described. Alternatively, you can add the ActiveX control to a list of safe controls when your database is loaded or at any time before accessing the property of the control.

To register the control, call `SysCmd 14, <ActiveX Control GUID>`. Be careful to register only ActiveX controls that you are certain cannot do anything malicious.

SUMMARY

Microsoft takes security seriously. Microsoft has also made significant improvements to Access 2010 Security over those from Access 2007 by reducing the number of keystrokes required to enable database content without sacrificing overall security. Sandbox mode helps protect you from malicious attacks on your computer by blocking some functions from SQL queries and other expressions. Because Sandbox mode doesn't affect VBA, you can work around these protections by defining `Public` functions to execute from queries where necessary. You can also use `Public` functions or register ActiveX controls if the properties of those controls are blocked.

You can use the Office Trust Center and Disabled mode to protect you from malicious databases. Both features provide the capability to protect your users and yourself. Because of the power of Access and its increasingly widespread usage, this added protection is a good thing.

You can work around the security warnings in a variety of ways, including trusted locations, using Visual Basic scripts to start your databases or digitally signing the databases you publish. Yes, all this means more effort. But what price do you put on security? It's really a small price to pay for some very effective insurance.

The Access Object Model

By now you've probably read at least a few of the chapters in this book and have realized that there are a lot of tasks you can accomplish by programming in VBA. One concept that should be clear is that to use VBA to manipulate Access, you need some knowledge about the Access object model. It was discussed briefly in Chapter 5, but as a refresher, an object model is a set of objects and collections that programmers use to manipulate a program.

Microsoft Access has a rich object model that you'll use to manipulate forms, reports, queries, macros, and other components of the Access interface. All in all, there are over 5600 members in the entire Access object model, making it a bit too large to fit completely in this appendix. As such, we've included the properties, methods, and events that are used frequently. Much of the information in this appendix can also be found in some form within the Access Visual Basic Reference Help file.

THE APPLICATION OBJECT

All of the objects and collections in the Access object model are children of the `Application` object. Every object and collection is related to the `Application` object through either a direct parent/child relationship or multiple parent/child relationships.

The `Application` object refers to the currently running instance of Access. You can use the `Application` object to apply methods or to set or retrieve properties for the entire Access application. For example, you can use the `Version` property to determine the version of Access that is running. Nearly all code you write in Access utilizes the `Application` object somewhere within the code.

Application Object Properties

The following table lists various properties of the `Application` object. It contains not only string and Boolean properties, but also properties that refer to other objects within the Access object model. Many of those objects are discussed later in this appendix.

PROPERTY	DATA TYPE	DESCRIPTION
AutomationSecurity	MsoAutomationSecurity	Returns or sets an `MsoAutomationSecurity` constant, which represents the security mode Access uses when opening databases.
BrokenReference	Boolean	Returns `True` if the current database has any broken references to databases or type libraries.
CodeData	CodeData	Accesses the `CodeData` object.
CodeProject	CodeProject	Accesses the `CodeProject` object.
CommandBars	CommandBars collection	References the `CommandBars` collection.
CurrentData	CurrentData object	Accesses the `CurrentData` object.
CurrentObjectName	String	Name of the active database object.
CurrentObjectType	AcObjectType Enum	Intrinsic constant used to determine the type of the active database object. See the Object Browser for possible values.
CurrentProject	CurrentProject object	Accesses the `CurrentProject` object.
DBEngine	DBEngine object	Returns the instance of the Access database engine and its related properties and collections.
DoCmd	DoCmd object	Returns the `DoCmd` object, which contains many methods commonly used in Access.
FileDialog	FileDialog object	Represents a common File dialog box such as the Open, Save As, or Browse Folder dialog box.
Forms	Forms collection	Returns the collection of open forms in a database.
IsCompiled	Boolean	Returns `True` if the current Visual Basic project is in a compiled state.

PROPERTY	DATA TYPE	DESCRIPTION
MenuBar	String	Specifies the MenuBar to use for an Access database. The menu bar appears in the Add-Ins tab in the Access Ribbon.
Modules	Modules collection	Returns the collection of open modules in a database.
Printer	Printer object	Returns or sets a Printer object representing the default printer on the current computer.
Printers	Printers collection	Returns the printers installed on the current computer.
References	References collection	Returns the collection of References for the current database.
Reports	Reports collection	Returns the collection of open reports in a database.
Screen	Screen object	Returns the Screen object.
ShortcutMenuBar	String	Specifies the shortcut menu that appears when you right-click on a form, report, or control.
TempVars	TempVars collection	Returns an instance of the TempVars collection. Can be used to maintain temporary data in a collection and pass data between Access macros and VBA code.
UserControl	Boolean	Determines whether the current Access instance was launched via automation.
VBE	VBE object	Returns an instance of the Visual Basic Editor.
Version	String	Returns the current version of Access.
Visible	Boolean	Returns True if the Access window is visible.
WebServices	WebServices object	Returns the WebServices collection for installed services in the current database.

Application Object Methods

The following table lists all of the methods available from the Application object. Any arguments for the methods are also listed.

METHOD	ARGUMENTS	DESCRIPTION
AccessError	ErrorNumber	Returns the error message associated with an Access or DAO error number.
BuildCriteria	Field, FieldType, Expression	Returns a parsed criteria string as it would appear in the query design grid.
CloseCurrentDatabase	None	Closes the current database.
CodeDb	None	Returns a DAO.Database object for a library database or add-in.
ColumnHistory	TableName, ColumnName, QueryString	Returns the column history for an Append-Only memo field. Valid for ACCDB files only.
CompactRepair	SourceFile, DestinationFile, LogFile	Compacts and repairs the specified database. Set LogFile to True to record any corruption found to a log file.
ConvertAccessProject	SourceFileName, DestinationFileName, DestinationFileFormat	Converts the specified database from one version to another.
CreateAccessProject	FilePath, Connect	Creates a new Access Data Project (ADP). Specify the Connect argument to set the ConnectionString for the project.
CreateControl	FormName, ControlType, Section, Parent, ColumnName, Left, Top, Width, Height	Creates a control on a form that is currently open in Design view. Returns a Control object.
CreateForm	Database, FormTemplate	Creates a new form in Design view and returns a Form object.
CreateGroupLevel	ReportName, Expression, Header, Footer	Creates a grouping level on a report.
CreateReport	Database, ReportTemplate	Creates a new report in Design view and returns a Report object.
CreateReportControl	ReportName, ControlType, Section, Parent, ColumnName, Left, Top, Width, Height	Creates a control on a report that is currently open in Design view.

METHOD	ARGUMENTS	DESCRIPTION
CurrentDb	None	Returns a `DAO.Database` object that represents the currently open database.
CurrentUser	None	Returns the name of the current user in the database. Used with user-level security in MDB files.
CurrentWebUser	DisplayOption	Returns the name of the current user in a database that is published to Access Services. Returns an empty string until published.
CurrentWebUserGroups	DisplayOption	Returns the list of groups that a Web user belongs to in a database that is published to Access Services. Returns an empty string until published.
DAvg	Expr, Domain, Criteria	Calculates the average of a set of values in a specified set of records (Domain).
DCount	Expr, Domain, Criteria	Determines the number of records within a set of records.
DeleteControl	FormName, ControlName	Deletes a control on a specified form.
DeleteReportControl	ReportName, ControlName	Deletes a control on a specific report.
DFirst	Expr, Domain, Criteria	Returns the first record from a particular field in a table or query. Because sort order can change, the first record is typically not guaranteed.
DirtyObject	ObjectType, ObjectName	Allows programmatic changes to an object in Layout view.
DLast	Expr, Domain, Criteria	Returns the first record from a particular field in a table or query. Because sort order can change, the last record is typically not guaranteed.

continues

(continued)

METHOD	ARGUMENTS	DESCRIPTION
DLookup	Expr, Domain, Criteria	Gets the value from a particular field from a specified set of records.
DMax	Expr, Domain, Criteria	Determines the maximum value in a specified set of records.
DMin	Expr, Domain, Criteria	Determines the minimum value in a specified set of records.
DStDev	Expr, Domain, Criteria	Estimates the standard deviation across a set of values in a set of records. The standard deviation is calculated for a sample.
DStDevP	Expr, Domain, Criteria	Estimates the standard deviation across a set of values in a set of records. The standard deviation is calculated for the population.
DSum	Expr, Domain, Criteria	Calculates the sum of a set of values in a set of records.
DVar	Expr, Domain, Criteria	Estimates the variance across a set of values in a set of records. The variation is calculated for a sample.
DVarP	Expr, Domain, Criteria	Estimates variance across a set of values in a set of records. The variance is calculated for the population.
Echo	EchoOn, bstrStatusBarText	Specifies whether Access repaints the display screen.
Eval	StringExpr	Evaluates an expression that results in a text string or numeric value.
ExportXML	ObjectType, DataSource, DataTarget, SchemaTarget, PresentationTarget, ImageTarget, Encoding, OtherFlags, WhereCondition, AdditionalData	Allows for export of XML data, schemas, and presentation information.

METHOD	ARGUMENTS	DESCRIPTION
FollowHyperlink	Address, SubAddress, NewWindow, AddHistory, ExtraInfo, Method, HeaderInfo	Opens the document or Web page specified by a hyperlink.
GetHiddenAttribute	ObjectType, ObjectName	Determines whether the specified object is hidden in the Navigation Pane.
GetOption	OptionName	Returns the current value of an option in the Options dialog box.
GUIDFromString	String	Converts a string to a GUID.
HTMLEncode	PlainText, Length	Returns HTML-encoded text for data. Can be used to set data in Rich Text memo fields.
hWndAccessApp	None	Determines the handle assigned to the main Access window by Microsoft Windows.
HyperlinkPart	Hyperlink, Part	Returns information about data stored as a hyperlink data type.
ImportXML	DataSource, ImportOptions	Allows import of XML data and/ or schema information.
IsCurrentWebUserInGroup	GroupNameOrID	Determines whether the current Web user is in the specified Web group. Used for databases published to Access Services.
LoadCustomUI	CustomUIName, CustomUIXML	Loads custom Ribbon extensibility XML.
LoadPicture	FileName	Loads a graphic into an ActiveX control.
NewAccessProject	FilePath, Connect	Creates and sets a new ADP as the active data project.
NewCurrentDatabase	Filepath, FileFormat, Template, SiteAddress, ListID	Creates a new Access database (ACCDB or MDB) in the Access window. Can also create a new database from an Access template.

continues

(continued)

METHOD	ARGUMENTS	DESCRIPTION
Nz	Value, ValueIfNull	Returns zero, a zero-length string, or another value when a value is null.
OpenAccessProject	FilePath, Exclusive	Opens an ADP as the current Access project.
OpenCurrentDatabase	FilePath, Exclusive, bstrPassword	Opens an MDB file as the current database.
PlainText	RichText, Length	Returns unformatted text for the specified rich text.
Quit	Option	Quits Microsoft Access.
RefreshDatabaseWindow	None	Updates the database window after an object has been created.
RefreshTitleBar	None	Refreshes the Access title bar after the AppTitle or AppIcon has been changed via code.
Run	Procedure (up to 30 optional arguments can also follow)	Can be used to carry out a Sub or Function procedure.
RunCommand	Command	Runs a built-in menu or toolbar command.
SaveAsTemplate	Path, Title, IconPath, CoreTable, Category, PreviewPath, Description, InstantiationForm, ApplicationPart, IncludeData, Variation	Saves the specified file as a template or application part.
SetHiddenAttribute	ObjectType, ObjectName, fHidden	Sets the hidden attribute of the specified object in the Navigation Pane.
SetOption	OptionName, Setting	Sets the current value of an option in the Options dialog box.
StringFromGUID	GUID	Converts a GUID to a string.

METHOD	ARGUMENTS	DESCRIPTION
SysCmd	Action, Argument2, Argument3	Can (1) display a progress meter or specified text in the status bar, (2) return information about Access and its associated files, or (3) return the state of a current database object.
TransformXML	DataSource, TransformSource, OutputTarget, WellFormedXMLOutput, ScriptOption	Applies an Extensible Stylesheet Language (XSL) stylesheet to an XML data file and writes the XML to an XML data file.

THE CURRENTDATA OBJECT

The CurrentData object is used to refer to objects stored within the current database by the server application (Access database engine or SQL). It has a variety of properties, described in the following table, that you can manipulate as well as several collections of its own.

PROPERTY	DATA TYPE	DESCRIPTION
AllDatabaseDiagrams	AllDatabaseDiagrams collection	Represents the collection of database diagrams in the SQL Server database.
AllFunctions	AllFunctions collection	Represents all the user-defined functions in the SQL Server database.
AllQueries	AllQueries collection	Represents all of the queries defined in the database. This collection is empty in ADP files.
AllStoredProcedures	AllStoredProcedures collection	References all of the stored procedures in the database.
AllTables	AllTables collection	References all the tables in the database.
AllViews	AllViews collection	References all views in the database.

THE CURRENTPROJECT OBJECT

The CurrentProject object represents the Access project for the database or project that is currently open in Access. The Access project consists of the non-data items such as Forms, Reports, Macros, and Modules. The CurrentProject object has several collections and a number of properties you can use within your application. The following table offers descriptions of those properties.

PROPERTY	DATA TYPE	DESCRIPTION
AccessConnection	Connection	Returns a reference to the currently active ADO Connection object.
AllForms	AllForms collection	Returns a reference to the AllForms collection and its associated properties.
AllMacros	AllMacros collection	Returns a reference to the AllMacros collection and its associated properties.
AllModules	AllModules collection	Returns a reference to the AllModules collection and its associated properties.
AllReports	AllReports collection	Returns a reference to the AllReports collection and its associated properties.
Application	Application object	Returns a reference to the current Application object.
BaseConnectionString	String	Returns the base Connection String for the CurrentProject or CodeProject object.
Connection	Connection object	Returns the currently active ADO Connection object.
FileFormat	AcFileFormat Enum	Returns a constant representing the Microsoft Access version of the specified project.
FullName	String	Returns the full path and name for the CurrentProject object.
ImportExportSpecifications	ImportExportSpecifications collection	Returns the collection of import and export specifications in the database.

PROPERTY	DATA TYPE	DESCRIPTION
IsConnected	Boolean	Determines if the CurrentProject is currently connected to a data source.
IsTrusted	Boolean	Returns True if the current database is opened in enabled mode and can execute code.
IsWeb	Boolean	Returns True if the current database is a Web database for publishing to Access Services.
Name	String	Returns the name of the current database.
Parent	Application object	For the CodeProject object, the Parent property returns the associated Application object.
Path	String	Returns the path to the data location for the Access database (.mdb) or Access project (.adp).
ProjectType	AcProjectType Enum	Determines the type of project currently open through the CurrentProject object.
Properties	Properties collection	Returns a reference to the entire Properties collection for the CurrentProject object.
Resources	SharedResources collection	Returns the collection of shared resources in a database.
WebSite	String	Returns the URL of a database that is published to Access Services.

The following table describes the CurrentProject object's methods.

METHOD	ARGUMENTS	DESCRIPTION
AddSharedImage	SharedImageName, FileName	Adds a shared image to the database.
CloseConnection	None	Closes the current connection between the CurrentProject object and the database specified in the project's base connection string.

continues

(continued)

METHOD	ARGUMENTS	DESCRIPTION
OpenConnection	BaseConnection-String, UserID, Password	Opens an ADO Connection to an existing Access project (.adp) or Access database (.accdb, .mdb) as the current Access project or database.
UpdateDependencyInfo	None	Updates the dependency information for the database.

You've probably noticed that there is some overlap between several objects or methods in the Access and DAO object models, specifically CurrentProject and CodeProject, CurrentData and CodeData, and CurrentDb and CodeDb. Each pair of objects contains the same properties and methods so that they are interchangeable.

Given that they have the same interfaces, how do you know which one to use and when? The short answer is that the Code objects and methods are used to refer to objects in a referenced or add-in database. These are also known as library databases because you can call code from them like a code library. The Current objects are used to refer to objects in the file that is open in the Access user interface. For example, if you have a database called Samples.mdb, and that database contains a reference to a database called VBASamples.mdb, the current database would be Samples.mdb and the code database would be VBASamples.mdb while code is executing in VBASamples.mdb. When code is running in Samples.mdb, the current and the code database both refer to Samples.mdb.

ACCESSOBJECT

The AccessObject object refers to a particular object within any of the following collections: AllDatabaseDiagrams, AllForms, AllFunctions, AllMacros, AllModules, AllQueries, AllReports, AllStoredProcedures, AllTables, and AllViews. This is an all-purpose object that can be used to determine whether an object is dependent upon another object or whether an object is open in the database.

It has its own properties, described in the following table, which you can implement within your code.

PROPERTY	DATA TYPE	DESCRIPTION
CurrentView	AcCurrentView Enum	Returns the current view for the specified Access object.
DateCreated	Date	Returns the date the AccessObject was created.
DateModified	Date	Returns the date the AccessObject was modified.
FullName	String	Sets or returns the full path of the object.

PROPERTY	DATA TYPE	DESCRIPTION
IsLoaded	Boolean	Determines whether the object is currently loaded.
Name	String	Returns the name of the object.
Parent	Object	Returns the collection of which the object is a member.
Properties	AccessObjectProperties collection	Returns the AccessObjectProperties collection for the object.
Type	AcObjectType Enum	Returns the type of the AccessObject.

AccessObject has two methods you can use, as shown in the following table.

METHOD	ARGUMENTS	DESCRIPTION
GetDependencyInfo	None	Returns a DependencyInfo object that represents the database objects that are dependent upon the specified object.
IsDependentUpon	ObjectType, ObjectName	Returns a Boolean value that indicates whether the specified object is dependent upon the database object specified in the ObjectName argument.

THE DOCMD OBJECT

In many regards, the DoCmd object is the workhorse of the Access object model. It carries out tasks such as exporting objects to different formats, opening objects, and manipulating the size of the Access window. It has no properties, but it does have a variety of methods you can utilize within your Access application.

All of the methods carry out an action with the same name as the method, so the following table provides descriptions of those actions, rather than of the methods (which merely call the actions).

METHOD	ARGUMENTS	DESCRIPTION
ApplyFilter	FilterName, WhereCondition	Applies a filter, a query, or a SQL WHERE clause to a table, form, or report.
BrowseTo	ObjectType, ObjectName, PathToSubformControl, WhereCondition, Page, DataMode	Navigates to the specified form or report. Can optionally specify the subform control used to display the form or report.

continues

(continued)

METHOD	ARGUMENTS	DESCRIPTION
Close	ObjectType, ObjectName, Save	Closes the object specified in the ObjectName argument.
CloseDatabase	None	Closes the current database.
CopyObject	DestinationDatabase, NewName, SourceObjectType, SourceObjectName	Copies the specified object to another database (.mdb) or Access project (.adp).
DeleteObject	ObjecType, ObjectName	Deletes the specified object.
Echo	EchoOn, StatusBarText	Turns Echo on or off.
FindNext	None	Finds the next record that meets the criteria specified in the FindRecord action.
FindRecord	FindWhat, Match, MatchCase, Search, SearchAsFormatted, OnlyCurrentField, FindFirst	Finds the first instance of a record that meets the criteria specified by the FindWhat argument.
GoToControl	ControlName	Moves focus to the specified control.
GoToRecord	ObjectType, ObjectName, Record, Offset	Makes the specified record the current record in a table, form, or result set.
Hourglass	HourglassOn	Changes the mouse pointer to an hourglass while the macro or code is running.
Maximize	None	Maximizes the entire Access Application window.
Minimize	None	Minimizes the entire Access Application window.
MoveSize	Right, Down, Width, Height	Moves or resizes the active window.
OpenForm	FormName, View, FilterName, WhereCondition, DataMode, WindowMode, OpenArgs	Opens the specified form in the specified view. Can also be used to filter the data displayed on the form.
OpenModule	ModuleName, ProcedureName	Opens the specified module at the specified procedure.
OpenQuery	QueryName, View, DataMode	Opens the specified query with the specified type of view.

METHOD	ARGUMENTS	DESCRIPTION
OpenReport	ReportName, View, FilterName, WhereCondition, WindowMode, OpenArgs	Opens the specified report in the specified view. Can also be used to filter the data displayed on the report.
OpenTable	TableName, View, DataMode	Opens the specified table in the specified view.
OutputTo	ObjectType, ObjectName, OutputFormat, OutputFile, AutoStart, TemplateFile, Encoding, OutputQuality	Outputs the specified object in the specified file formats.
PrintOut	PrintRange, PageFrom, PageTo, PrintQuality, Copies, CollateCopies	Prints the active object.
Quit	Options	Quits the active Access application.
RefreshRecord	None	Refreshes the currently selected record.
Rename	NewName, ObjectType, OldName	Renames the specified object.
RepaintObject	ObjectType, ObjectName	Completes any pending screen updates for the specified object.
Requery	ControlName	Updates the data in the specified control by requerying the source of the control.
Restore	None	Restores a maximized or minimized window to its previous state.
RunCommand	Command	Runs a built-in Ribbon command.
RunDataMacro	MacroName	Runs the specified named data macro.
RunMacro	MacroName, RepeatCount, RepeatExpression	Runs the specified macro.
RunSavedImportExportSpec	SavedImportExportName	Runs the named import or export specification in the database.

continues

(continued)

METHOD	ARGUMENTS	DESCRIPTION
RunSQL	SQLStatement, UseTransaction	Runs an Access action query by using the corresponding SQL statement.
Save	ObjectType, ObjectName	Saves the specified object.
SearchForRecord	ObjectType, ObjectName, Record, WhereCondition	Allows searching of records including a WHERE clause.
SelectObject	ObjectType, ObjectName, InDatabaseWindow	Selects the specified database object.
SendObject	ObjectType, ObjectName, OutputFormat, To, Cc, Bcc, Subject, MessageText, EditMessage, TemplateFile	Sends the specified Access datasheet, form, report, module, or data access page via e-mail.
SetFilter	FilterName, WhereCondition, ControlName	Applies a filter, a query, or a SQL WHERE clause to a table, form, subform, or report.
SetOrderBy	OrderBy, ControlName	Applies a sort order to a table, form, subform, or report.
SetParameter	Name, Expression	Sets a parameter value for use with the OpenForm, OpenQuery, OpenReport, or RunDataMacro methods.
SetProperty	ControlName, Property, Value	Sets the property to the specified value for a given control. Intended as a safe way to do SetValue in disabled mode.
SetWarnings	WarningsOn	Turns system messages on or off.
ShowAllRecords	None	Removes any applied filter for the table, query, or form.
ShowToolbar	ToolbarName, Show	Displays or hides a built-in toolbar.
TransferDatabase	TransferType, DatabaseType, DatabaseName, ObjectType, Source, Destination, StructureOnly, StoreLogin	Used to import or export data between the current database (.mdb) or Access project (.adp) and another database.

METHOD	ARGUMENTS	DESCRIPTION
TransferSharePointList	TransferType, SiteAddress, ListID, ViewID, TableName, GetLookupDisplayValues	Imports or links data from a SharePoint site into Access.
TransferSpreadsheet	TransferType, SpreadsheetType, TableName, FileName, HasFieldNames, Range, UseOA	Used to import or export data between the current database (.mdb) or Access project (.adp) and a spreadsheet.
TransferText	TransferType, SpecificationName, TableName, FileName, HasFieldNames, HTMLTableName, CodePage	Used to import or export data between a database (.mdb) or Access project (.adp) and a text file.

THE FORM OBJECT

The Forms collection contains all of the open forms associated with the current database. Forms in the database that are not currently open are not in this collection.

The tables that follow list frequently used properties, methods, and events for the Form object.

Form Object Properties

The Form object has a variety of properties, which are described in the following table.

PROPERTY	DATA TYPE	DESCRIPTION
ActiveControl	Control object	Used with the Screen object to determine the control that has the focus.
AllowAdditions	Boolean	Determines whether a user can add a record when using a form.
AllowDataSheetView	Boolean	Determines whether the form can be switched to Datasheet view.
AllowDeletions	Boolean	Determines whether a user can delete a record when using a form.
AllowEdits	Boolean	Determines whether a user can edit and save records when using a form.
AllowFilters	Boolean	Determines whether a user can filter the records when using a form.

continues

(continued)

PROPERTY	DATA TYPE	DESCRIPTION
AllowFormView	Boolean	Determines whether a form can be viewed in Form view.
AllowLayoutView	Boolean	Determines whether a form can be viewed in Layout view.
AllowPivotChartView	Boolean	Determines whether a form can be viewed in Pivot Chart view.
AllowPivotTableView	Boolean	Determines whether a form can be viewed in Pivot Table view.
Application	Application object	Returns the currently active application object.
AutoCenter	Boolean	Determines whether the form will be automatically centered within the Application window.
AutoResize	Boolean	Determines whether the form will be automatically resized to display complete records.
Bookmark	Variant	Used to set a bookmark that identifies a particular record in the form's underlying recordset.
BorderStyle	Byte	Specifies the type of border and border elements for the form.
Caption	String	Specifies text that appears in the Form's title bar.
ChartSpace	ChartSpace object	Returns the PivotChart object for a form in PivotChart view.
CloseButton	Boolean	Specifies whether the Close button on a form is enabled.
ControlBox	Boolean	Specifies whether the form has a control menu (in Form and Datasheet view only).
Controls	Controls collection	Returns the collection of all controls on the form.
Count	Integer	Determines the number of items in a collection.
CurrentRecord	Long	Used to identify the current record being viewed on a form.
CurrentView	Integer	Determines how a form is displayed (Design, Form, Layout, Pivot, or Datasheet view).

PROPERTY	DATA TYPE	DESCRIPTION
Cycle	Byte	Specifies what happens when you press the Tab key while the last control on the form has the focus.
DataEntry	Boolean	Specifies whether a bound form only allows data entry (if True the form opens showing only a blank record).
DefaultView	Integer	Used to specify the opening view for a form.
Dirty	Boolean	True if data has been entered but not saved on a form.
DividingLines	Boolean	Specifies whether dividing lines separate sections on a form.
Filter	String	Used to specify a subset of records to be displayed when a filter is applied to a form.
FilterOn	Boolean	Specifies whether the Filter property of a form is applied.
FilterOnLoad	Boolean	Indicates that a filter should be loaded with the form when the form loads.
FitToScreen	Boolean	Gets or sets whether the width of the form should be reduced to fit the width of the screen.
Form	Form object	Used to refer to the form.
HasModule	Boolean	Determines whether the form has a class module.
HelpContextID	Long	Specifies the context ID of a topic in the custom help file.
HelpFile	String	Returns the name of the help file associated with the form.
Hwnd	Long	Determines the handle of the current window.
InsideHeight	Long	Height in twips of the window containing the form.
InsideWidth	Long	Width in twips of the window containing the form.

continues

(continued)

PROPERTY	DATA TYPE	DESCRIPTION
KeyPreview	Boolean	Specifies whether the form level keyboard event procedures are invoked before a control's keyboard event procedures.
MenuBar	String	Specifies the menu bar to use for a form. The menu bar appears in the Add-Ins tab in the Access Ribbon.
MinMaxButtons	Byte	Specifies whether the Maximize and Minimize buttons are visible on the form.
Modal	Boolean	Specifies whether a form opens as a modal window.
Module	Module object	Used to specify a form module.
Movable	Boolean	True if a form can be moved by the user.
Name	String	Name of the current form.
NavigationButtons	Boolean	Indicates whether navigation buttons and the record number box are displayed on a form.
NavigationCaption	String	Sets or gets the caption for the navigation bar in the form.
NewRecord	Integer	Determines whether the current record is a new record.
OpenArgs	Variant	Determines the string expression specified by the OpenArgs argument of the OpenForm method.
OrderBy	String	Specifies how records on a form should be shortened.
OrderByOn	Boolean	Specifies whether a form's OrderBy property is applied.
OrderByOnLoad	Boolean	Indicates that a sort should be loaded with the form when the form loads.
Orientation	Byte	Specifies the form's orientation (left to right or right to left).
Painting	Boolean	Specifies whether forms are repainted.

PROPERTY	DATA TYPE	DESCRIPTION
Parent	Object	For subforms, returns the main Form object where the subform resides. Throws a runtime error for top-level forms.
Picture	String	Can be used to specify a bitmap on a form.
PictureAlignment	Byte	Specifies where a background picture appears in an image control on a form.
PictureSizeMode	Byte	Specifies how a picture on a form is sized.
PictureTiling	Boolean	Specifies whether a background picture is tiled across the entire form.
PictureType	Byte	Used to specify if the picture is stored as a linked (1) or embedded (0) object.
PivotTable	PivotTable object	Returns the PivotTable object for a form in PivotTable view.
PopUp	Boolean	Specifies whether a form opens in a pop-up window.
Printer	Printer object	Represents the default printer on the current system.
Properties	Properties collection	Collection of all properties of the form.
RecordLocks	Byte	Determines how records are locked and what happens when two users try to edit the same record at the same time.
RecordSelectors	Boolean	Determines whether a form displays record selectors in Form view.
Recordset	Recordset object	Returns the recordset object for the form.
RecordsetClone	Recordset object	Can be used to refer to a form's record-set specified by the form's RecordSource property.
RecordsetType	Byte	Specifies the type of recordset is used within the form.
RecordSource	String	Used to specify the source of the data for the form.

continues

(continued)

PROPERTY	DATA TYPE	DESCRIPTION
RibbonName	String	Name of a custom ribbon to load for the form.
ScrollBars	Byte	Specifies whether scrollbars appear on a form.
Section	Section object	Used to identify a section of a form.
SelHeight	Long	Specifies the number of selected rows or records in the current selection rectangle in a form's datasheet.
SelLeft	Long	Specifies which column is leftmost in the current selection rectangle in the form's datasheet.
SelTop	Long	Specifies which row is topmost in the current selection rectangle in the form's datasheet.
SelWidth	Long	Specifies the number of selected columns in the current selection rectangle in the form's datasheet.
ShortcutMenu	Boolean	Specifies whether a shortcut menu is displayed when you right-click an object on a form.
ShortcutMenuBar	String	Specifies the shortcut menu that appears when you right-click a form.
SplitFormDatasheet	AcSplitFormDatasheet Enum	Specifies whether to allow edits in the datasheet portion of a split form.
SplitFormOrientation	AcSplitFormOrientation Enum	Specifies the location of the datasheet in a split form.
SplitFormPrinting	AcSplitFormPrinting Enum	Specifies whether the form or datasheet portion of a split form will be printed.
SplitFormSize	Long	Indicates the size of the form portion of a split form.
SplitFormSplitterBar	Boolean	Indicates whether the splitter bar is visible between the form and datasheet portions of a split form.
SplitFormSplitterBarSave	Boolean	Specifies whether the location of the splitter bar is saved for a split form.

PROPERTY	DATA TYPE	DESCRIPTION
SubdatasheetExpanded	Boolean	Specifies the saved state of all sub-datasheets within a form.
SubdatasheetHeight	Integer	Determines the display height of a subdatasheet when expanded.
Tag	String	Stores extra information about a form.
TimerInterval	Long	Specifies the interval (in milliseconds) between Timer events on a form.
Toolbar	String	Specifies the toolbar used for a form.
ViewsAllowed	Byte	Specifies whether users can switch between form and datasheet views.
Visible	Boolean	True when the form window is visible.
Width	Integer	Width of the form in twips.
WindowHeight	Integer	Specifies the height of a form in twips.
WindowLeft	Integer	Indicates the screen position in twips of the left edge of the form relative to the left edge of the Access window.
WindowTop	Integer	Specifies the screen position in twips of the top edge of the form relative to the top edge of the Access window.
WindowWidth	Integer	Sets the width of the form in twips.

Form Object Methods

The Form object also has a number of methods you can use within your code. They're described in the following table.

METHOD	ARGUMENTS	DESCRIPTION
Move	Left, Top, Width, Height	Moves the form to the specified coordinates.
Recalc	None	Immediately updates the calculated controls on a form.
Refresh	None	Immediately updates the records in the underlying record source for a form.

continues

(continued)

METHOD	ARGUMENTS	DESCRIPTION
Repaint	None	Completes any pending screen updates for the current form.
Requery	None	Updates the data in the form from the underlying recordset.
SetFocus	None	Sets the focus to the current form.
Undo	None	Resets the value of a form when it has been changed.

Form Object Events

Events are at the core of programming Windows applications. As such, there are a large number of events you'll use within your code behind forms. You will probably use only a handful of these events, but they are all available to you. A Form's events are summarized in the following table.

EVENT	OCCURS
Activate	When the form receives focus and becomes the active window.
AfterDelConfirm	After the user confirms the delete and the records are actually deleted.
AfterInsert	After a new record is added.
AfterUpdate	After changed data in a control or record is updated.
ApplyFilter	When a filter is applied to a form.
BeforeDelConfirm	After the user deletes records but before the delete confirmation dialog box is displayed.
BeforeInsert	When the user types the first character in a new record.
BeforeUpdate	Before changed data in a control is updated.
Click	When a user presses and releases the mouse button over an object.
Close	When a form is closed and removed from the screen.
Current	When the focus moves to a record or when the form is refreshed or requeried.
DblClick	When a user presses and releases the mouse button twice in rapid succession over an object.

EVENT	OCCURS
Deactivate	When a form loses focus to another object.
Delete	When the user presses the Delete key, but before the record is actually deleted.
Dirty	When data has changed on the form, but the current record hasn't been saved.
Error	When a runtime error occurs when the form has the focus.
Filter	When a user chooses the Filter by Form or Advanced Filter/Sort option on the Ribbon.
GotFocus	When the form receives the focus.
KeyDown	When a key is pressed.
KeyPress	When a key is pressed and released.
KeyUp	When a key is released.
Load	When a form is opened and records are displayed.
LostFocus	When the form loses focus to another object.
MouseDown	When the mouse button is pressed.
MouseMove	When the user moves the mouse.
MouseUp	When the mouse button is released.
MouseWheel	When the mouse scroll wheel is moved.
Open	When a form is opened but before the first record is displayed.
Resize	When a form opens and any time it is resized.
Timer	At regular intervals controlled by the form's `TimerInterval` property.
Undo	When the user undoes a change to a control on a form.
Unload	After a form is closed but before it's removed from the screen.

THE CONTROL OBJECT

Within a form, you can have a variety of different controls. You use them to display data from tables, queries, and other data sources such as DAO or ADO recordsets. Every type of control in Access derives from the `Control` object.

Control Object Properties

The `Control` object has quite a few properties, which are described in the following table.

PROPERTY	DATA TYPE	DESCRIPTION
Application	Application object	Returns the currently active Application object.
Form	Form object	Refers to the current form object.
Hyperlink	Hyperlink object	Accesses the properties and methods of a hyperlink object associated with a control.
Name	String	Specifies the name of the control.
Object	ActiveX object	Returns a reference to the ActiveX object associated with a linked or embedded OLE object in a control.
OldValue	Variant	Determines the unedited value of a bound control.
Parent	Object	For controls, usually a form object.
Properties	Properties collection	Returns a reference to the entire collection of properties for the object.

Control Object Methods

The methods you can use with a control object are explained in the following table. For all of these methods, the specified object is the control whose method is being called.

METHOD	ARGUMENTS	DESCRIPTION
Move	Left, Top, Width, Height	Moves the specified object to the coordinates specified.
SetFocus	None	Moves the focus to the specified control.
Undo	None	Resets a control whose value has been changed.

CONTROLS ON FORMS AND REPORTS

There are many properties, methods, and events that are used for controls on forms and reports. The following sections list some of the more commonly used members for different types of controls.

The Attachment Control

The Attachment control was added in Access 2007 for viewing data in the Attachment data type.

Attachment Control Object Properties

The following table describes the properties of the Attachment object:

PROPERTY	DATA TYPE	DESCRIPTION
AttachmentCount	Long	Returns the number of attachments in an attachment control.
CurrentAttachment	Long	Returns the index of the attachment that is currently viewed in the attachment control.
DefaultPicture	String	Returns the path to a picture that will be used when the attachment control is null.
FileName	String	Path to the attachment currently being viewed in the attachment control.

Attachment Control Object Methods

The following table describes the methods of the Attachment object:

METHOD	ARGUMENT	DESCRIPTION
Back	None	Moves to the previous attachment.
Forward	None	Moves to the next attachment.

Attachment Control Object Events

The following table describes the event of the Attachment object:

EVENT	DESCRIPTION
AttachmentCurrent	Fires when attachments are navigated in an attachment control.

The ComboBox Control

Combo boxes are a long-time staple in the Access development toolbox. They are used to look up one or more values in a table or query, and can show multiple columns of data while they are dropped down.

ComboBox Control Object Properties

The following table describes the properties of the ComboBox object:

PROPERTY	DATA TYPE	DESCRIPTION
BoundColumn	Long	Gets or sets the column in the combo box that contains the value.
Column	Variant	Returns data for the specified column in a combo box.
ColumnCount	Integer	The number of columns of data in a combo box.
ColumnHeads	Boolean	Determines whether column headings are displayed.
ColumnWidths	String	Specifies the widths of columns in the combo box.
ItemData	Variant	Returns data at the specified row in a combo box.
LimitToList	Boolean	Determines whether items can be added to the row source of a combo box.
ListCount	Long	Determines the number of items in a combo box.
ListIndex	Long	Returns the row number of the selected item in a combo box.
ListRows	Integer	Gets or sets the number of rows that are displayed when a combo box is dropped.
Recordset	Object	Gets or sets a Recordset object containing the data in a combo box.
RowSource	String	Gets or sets the data that appears in a list box.
RowSourceType	String	Gets or sets the type of data that appears in a list box.

ComboBox Control Object Methods

The following table describes the methods of the ComboBox object:

METHOD	ARGUMENT	DESCRIPTION
AddItem	Item, Index	Adds an item to a value list combo box.
Dropdown		Drops down a combo box.
RemoveItem	Item, Index	Removes an item from a value list combo box.
Requery		Re-executes the table or query that is used in the row source for a combo box.

ComboBox Control Object Events

The following table describes the events of the ComboBox object:

EVENT	DESCRIPTION
Change	Fires when the text inside the combo box control changes.
NotInList	Fires when a value is entered in a combo box that does not appear in the row source.

The CommandButton Control

Command button controls are another long-time staple in Access. They are primarily used to carry out explicit actions in forms.

CommandButton Control Object Properties

The following table describes the properties of the CommandButton object:

PROPERTY	DATA TYPE	DESCRIPTION
AutoRepeat	Boolean	Determines whether the Click event for the command button is fired repeatedly when holding down the button.
Cancel	Boolean	Determines whether the escape key invokes the Click event for the command button.
Caption	String	Gets or sets the text in the command button.
CursorOnHover	AcCursorOnHover	Gets or sets the cursor used when hovering over the command button.
Default	Boolean	Determines whether the enter key invokes the Click event for the command button.
Transparent	Boolean	Determines whether the command button is transparent. Transparent buttons can still be clicked.

The ListBox Control

List box controls are similar to combo boxes in that they can show multiple columns of data. Unlike combo boxes, they display multiple rows at once.

ListBox Control Object Properties

The following table describes the properties of the `ListBox` object:

PROPERTY	DATA TYPE	DESCRIPTION
BoundColumn	Long	Gets or sets the column in the combo box that contains the value of the list box.
Column	Variant	Returns data for the specified column in a combo box.
ColumnCount	Integer	The number of columns of data in a list box.
ColumnHeads	Boolean	Determines whether column headings are displayed.
ColumnWidths	String	Specifies the widths of columns in the list box.
ItemData	Variant	Returns data at the specified row in a list box.
ItemsSelected	_ItemsSelected	Returns the collection of selected items in a list box.
ListCount	Long	Determines the number of items in a list box.
ListIndex	Long	Returns the row number of the selected item in a list box.
MultiSelect	Byte	Determines the method by which multiple items can be selected in a list box.
Recordset	Object	Gets or sets a `Recordset` object containing the data in a list box.
RowSource	String	Gets or sets the data that appears in a list box.
RowSourceType	String	Gets or sets the type of data that appears in a list box.
Selected	Long	Determines whether the specified row is selected.

ListBox Control Object Methods

The following table describes the methods of the `ListBox` object:

METHOD	ARGUMENT	DESCRIPTION
AddItem	Item, Index	Adds an item to a Value List list box.
RemoveItem	Item, Index	Removes an item from a Value List list box.
Requery		Re-executes the table or query that is used in the row source for a list box.

The NavigationButton Control

The navigation button is a new type of control in Access 2010. These controls are used within a navigation control to provide navigation throughout an application. By using the `NavigtionWhereClause` property of the control, you can create multiple buttons for the same form and reports and display different data for the object. This allows you to re-use objects in your applications.

NavigationButton Control Object Properties

The following table describes the properties of the `NavigationButton` object:

PROPERTY	DATA TYPE	DESCRIPTION
Caption	String	Text that appears on the button.
NavigationTargetName	String	Name of the object the button navigates to.
NavigationWhereClause	String	Filter applied to the target form or report.

The NavigationControl Control

The navigation control was added in Access 2010 to provide an easy way to create navigation through an Access database application. There are three components to a navigation control: the control itself, one or more navigation buttons, and the navigation subform. Navigation controls can be oriented horizontally or vertically, and support multiple levels of navigation.

NavigationControl Control Object Properties

The following table describes the properties of the `NavigtionControl` object:

PROPERTY	DATA TYPE	DESCRIPTION
SelectedTab	NavigationButton	Returns the currently selected navigation button.
Span	AcNavigationSpan	Returns or sets the orientation of a navigation control.

The Subform Control

When designing Access forms, you can embed a subform within your main form. The `SubForm` object includes the same properties as the `Control` object. In addition, some of the `SubForm` object's properties are the same as other Access form objects. The following are the properties, events, and methods that are unique to the `Subform` object.

SubForm Control Object Properties

The following table describes the properties of the SubForm object:

PROPERTY	DATA TYPE	DESCRIPTION
Form	Form object	Returns the form associated with the current subform.
LinkChildFields	String	Specifies the field on the subform that links the subform with the master form.
LinkMasterFields	String	Specifies the field on the master form that links the subform with the master form.
Report	Report object	Refers to the report associated with a subreport control.
SourceObject	String	Specifies the form that is the source of the subform.

SubForm Control Object Methods

The following table describes the methods of the SubForm object:

METHOD	ARGUMENT	DESCRIPTION
Requery	None	Updates the controls on the subform by requerying the data source.
SetFocus	None	Moves the focus to the subform.

Subform Control Object Events

The following table describes the events of the SubForm object:

EVENT	DESCRIPTION
Enter	Occurs immediately before the subform receives the focus.
Exit	Occurs immediately before the subform loses the focus to another control or subform.

The TextBox Control

Text box controls are the most commonly used controls in Access. They are used to display data in forms and reports.

TextBox Control Object Properties

The following table describes a property of the TextBox object:

PROPERTY	DATA TYPE	DESCRIPTION
Text	String	Gets or sets the text in a text box control when it has focus.

TextBox Control Object Events

The following table describes events of the TextBox object:

EVENT	DESCRIPTION
Change	Fires when the text inside the text box control changes.
Dirty	Fires when the first edit is made in a text box control.

The WebBrowserControl Control

The Web browser control was added in Access 2010 to provide a native method for browsing Web content in an Access database. Like many controls in Access, the Web browser control includes the ControlSource property, which allows the control to be bound to a field or expression. The field or expression used in the Web browser must evaluate to a URL or an XML string.

WebBrowserControl Control Object Properties

The following table describes the properties of the WebBrowserControl object:

PROPERTY	DATA TYPE	DESCRIPTION
ControlSource	String	Gets or sets the field or expression used for data in the control.
LocationURL	String	Returns the current URL of the Web browser control.
ScrollBars	AcWebBrowserScrollBars	Determines whether to show scrollbars for the Web browser control.
ScrollLeft	Long	Gets or sets the left position in pixels of content in the Web browser control.
ScrollTop	Long	Gets or sets the top position in pixels of content in the Web browser control.
Transform	String	An XSL transformation used to transform XML content in the control. This is typically used to render HTML in the control. The property is the text of the XSLT tself, not a path to an XSLT file.

WebBrowserControl Control Object Events

The following table describes the events of the `WebBrowserControl` object:

EVENT	DESCRIPTION
BeforeNavigate2	Fires before the control navigates to a URL.
DocumentComplete	Fires when the control completes navigation to a URL.
NavigateError	Fires when an error occurs when navigating.
ProgressChange	Fires when the loading progress changes in the control.

OTHER COMMON CONTROL MEMBERS

In addition to the properties, methods, and events for specific controls, there are some commonly used members that appear for multiple controls. The following table lists some of them.

MEMBER NAME	MEMBER TYPE	APPLIES TO	DESCRIPTION
AfterUpdate	Event	Attachment, CheckBox, ComboBox, ListBox, OptionButton, OptionGroup, TextBox, ToggleButton, WebBrowser	Fires after data has been committed in a control.
BeforeUpdate	Event	Attachment, CheckBox, ComboBox, ListBox, OptionButton, OptionGroup, TextBox, ToggleButton, WebBrowser	Fires before data has been committed in a control. This event can be canceled.
ControlSource	Property	Attachment, CheckBox, ComboBox, ListBox, OptionButton, OptionGroup, TextBox, ToggleButton, WebBrowser	Gets or sets the field or expression used for data in the control.
Enabled	Property	Attachment, CheckBox, ComboBox, CommandButton, ListBox, NavigationButton, NavigationControl, OptionButton, OptionGroup, Page, SubForm, TabControl, TextBox, WebBrowser	Gets or sets whether the control is enabled—that is, whether it can receive focus.
Enter	Event	Attachment, CheckBox, ComboBox, CommandButton, ListBox, NavigationButton, NavigationControl, OptionButton, OptionGroup, SubForm, TextBox, ToggleButton, WebBrowser	Fires when a control is entered using the mouse, keyboard, or SetFocus method.

MEMBER NAME	MEMBER TYPE	APPLIES TO	DESCRIPTION
Exit	Event	Attachment, CheckBox, ComboBox, CommandButton, ListBox, NavigationButton, NavigationControl, OptionButton, OptionGroup, SubForm, TextBox, ToggleButton, WebBrowser	Fires when a control is exited using the mouse, keyboard, or SetFocus method. This event can be canceled.
GotFocus	Event	Attachment, CheckBox, ComboBox, CommandButton, ListBox, NavigationButton, NavigationControl, OptionButton, TextBox, ToggleButton, WebBrowser	Fires when a control receives focus. Because there are several ways to receive focus, this event may fire more often than the Enter event of the control.
Locked	Property	Attachment, CheckBox, ComboBox, ListBox, OptionButton, OptionGroup, SubForm, TextBox, ToggleButton	Gets or sets whether the control is locked—that is, whether it can be edited.
LostFocus	Event	Attachment, CheckBox, ComboBox, CommandButton, ListBox, NavigationButton, NavigationControl, OptionButton, TextBox, ToggleButton, WebBrowser	Fires when a control loses focus. Because there are several ways to lose focus, this event may fire more often than the Exit event of the control.
SetFocus	Method	Attachment, CheckBox, ComboBox, CommandButton, Image, ListBox, NavigationButton, NavigationControl, OptionButton, OptionGroup, Page, SubForm, TextBox, ToggleButton, WebBrowser	Moves focus to the specified control.
Visible	Property	Attachment, CheckBox, ComboBox, CommandButton, ListBox, NavigationButton, NavigationControl, OptionButton, OptionGroup, Page, SubForm, TabControl, TextBox, WebBrowser	Gets or sets whether the control is visible.

THE IMPORTEXPORTSPECIFICATION OBJECT

Access 2007 introduced a new technique for creating and managing import and export specifications. If you worked with specifications in previous versions of Access, you'll be glad to know that you can create a specification for each of the supported file types for import and export! No longer are specifications limited to text files. With the addition of this feature, Microsoft has added the `ImportExportSpecification` object and the `ImportExportSpecifications` collection. Obviously, this collection contains `ImportExportSpecification` objects and consists of the standard collection members: `Add`, `Item`, and `Count`.

ImportExportSpecification Object Properties

The following table describes the properties of the `ImportExportSpecification` object.

PROPERTY	DATA TYPE	DESCRIPTION
Application	Application object	Returns the current `Application` object for the specification.
Description	String	Specifies a friendly description for the specification.
Name	String	Specifies the name of the specification.
Parent	Object	Returns the `CurrentProject` or `CodeProject` object for the specification.
XML	String	Specifies the XML representation of the specification.

ImportExportSpecification Object Methods

The `ImportExportSpecification` object's methods are described in the following table

METHOD	ARGUMENTS	DESCRIPTION
Delete	None	Deletes the current specification.
Execute	Prompt	Executes the import or export specification.

THE MODULE OBJECT

The `Module` object refers to either a standard module or a class module within your database.

Module Object Properties

The `Module` object's properties are described in the following table.

PROPERTY	DATA TYPE	DESCRIPTION
Application	Application object	Returns the currently active Application object.
CountOfDeclarationLines	Long	Count of the number of lines in the General Declarations section of a standard or class module.
CountOfLines	Long	Count of lines of code in a standard or class module.
Lines	String	Contains the contents of a specified line or lines in a standard or class module.
Name	String	Returns the name of the standard or class module.
Parent	Object	Usually the Application object.
ProcBodyLine	Long	Contains the number of the line at which the body of the specified procedure begins.
ProcCountLines	Long	Contains the number of lines in a specified procedure of a standard of class module.
ProcOfLine	String	Contains the name of the procedure that contains the specified line in a standard or class module.
ProcStartLine	Long	Identifies the line at which a specified procedure begins in a standard or class module.
Type	AcModuleType Enum	Indicates whether a module is a standard module or a class module

Module Object Methods

The methods for the Module object are listed in the following table.

METHOD	ARGUMENTS	DESCRIPTION
AddFromFile	FileName	Adds the contents of the text file to a module.
AddFromString	String	Adds the contents of the string to a module.
CreateEventProc	EventName, ObjectName	Creates an event procedure in a class module.
DeleteLines	StartLine, Count	Deletes lines from a module.

continues

(continued)

METHOD	ARGUMENTS	DESCRIPTION
Find	Target, StartLine, StartColumn, EndLine, EndColumn, WholeWord, MatchCase, PatternSearch	Finds the specified text in a class module.
InsertLines	Line, String	Inserts a line or group of lines of code in a module.
InsertText	Text	Inserts a string of text into a module.
ReplaceLine	Line, String	Replaces the specified line with a string value.

THE PRINTER OBJECT

Access VBA enables you to manipulate the printers available on your system through code. All available printers are members of the `Printers` collection. You can access an individual printer through the `Printer` object.

Printer Object Properties

The properties of the `Printer` object are explained in the following table.

PROPERTIES	DATA TYPE	SPECIFIES
BottomMargin	Long	Bottom margin for the printed page.
ColorMode	AcPrintColor Enum	Whether the printer should output in color or monochrome mode.
ColumnSpacing	Long	Vertical space between detail sections (in twips).
Copies	Long	Number of copies to be printed.
Dataonly	Boolean	`True` if Access prints only the data and not the labels, borders, gridlines, and graphics.
DefaultSize	Boolean	`True` when the size of the detail section in Design view is used for printing. `False` if the `ItemSizeHeight` and `ItemSizeWidth` properties are used.

PROPERTIES	DATA TYPE	SPECIFIES
DeviceName	String	Name of the printer.
DriverName	String	Name of the driver used by the specified printer.
Duplex	AcPrintDuplex Enum	How the printer handles duplex printing.
ItemLayout	AcPrintItemLayout Enum	Whether the printer lays out columns across and then down, or down and then across.
ItemsAcross	Long	Number of columns to print across a page.
ItemSizeHeight	Long	Height of the detail section in twips.
ItemSizeWidth	Long	Width of the detail section in twips.
LeftMargin	Long	Left margin for the printed page.
Orientation	AcPrintOrientation Enum	Print orientation.
PaperBin	AcPrinterBin Enum	Which paper bin the printer should use.
PaperSize	AcPrintPaperSize Enum	Paper size to use when printing.
Port	String	Port name for the specified printer.
PrintQuality	AcPrintObjQuality Enum	Resolution the printer uses to print jobs.
RightMargin	Long	Right margin for the printed page.
RowSpacing	Long	Horizontal space between detail sections (in twips).
TopMargin	Long	Top margin for the printed page.

THE REFERENCES COLLECTION AND REFERENCE OBJECT

In addition to the various Access objects detailed in this appendix, you can use objects from other applications such as Excel, Word, Outlook, and non-Microsoft programs such as AutoCad and Peachtree Accounting to program in Access. To use these other object models, set a reference to their type libraries. The References collection contains a reference for every external type library you add to the References dialog box within your code.

The properties of the `Reference` object are described in the following table.

PROPERTY	DATA TYPE	DESCRIPTION
BuiltIn	Boolean	Specifies whether a reference points to a default Reference necessary for Access to function properly.
Collection	References object	Returns a reference to the collection that contains an object.
FullPath	String	Specifies the path and filename of the referenced type library.
Guid	String	Returns a GUID that identifies the type library in the Registry.
IsBroken	Boolean	Specifies whether a `Reference` object points to a valid reference in the Registry.
Kind	Vbext_RefKind Enum	Specifies the type of reference that a Reference object represents.
Major	Long	Specifies the major version number of an application you're referencing.
Minor	Long	Specifies the minor version of the application you're referencing.
Name	String	The name of the `Reference` object.

THE REPORTS COLLECTION AND REPORT OBJECT

Microsoft Access contains a `Reports` collection that contains a `Report` object for every open report within your database. Reports that are not currently open in the database are not in the `Reports` collection.

Report Object Properties

The properties of the `Report` object are listed in the following table.

PROPERTY	DATA TYPE	DESCRIPTION
ActiveControl	Control object	Used with the `Screen` object to determine the control that has the focus.
AllowLayoutView	Boolean	Determines whether a report can be viewed in Layout view.

PROPERTY	DATA TYPE	DESCRIPTION
AllowReportView	Boolean	Determines whether a report can be viewed in Report view.
Application	Application object	Returns the currently active application object.
AutoCenter	Boolean	Determines whether the report will be automatically centered within the Application window.
AutoResize	Boolean	Determines whether the report will be automatically resized to display complete records.
BorderStyle	Byte	Specifies the type of border and border elements for the report.
Caption	String	Specifies the caption in the title bar for the report.
CloseButton	Boolean	Specifies whether the Close button on a report is enabled.
ControlBox	Boolean	Specifies whether the form has a control menu (in Form and Datasheet view only).
Controls	Controls collection	Specifies the collection of all controls on the report.
Count	Integer	Specifies the number of items within the Reports collection.
CurrentRecord	Long	Identifies the current record being viewed on a report.
CurrentView	Integer	Determines how a report is displayed (Design view, Report view, Layout view, or Print Preview).
CurrentX	Single	Specifies the horizontal coordinates for the starting position of the next printing and drawing method on a report.
CurrentY	Single	Specifies the vertical coordinates for the starting position of the next printing and drawing method on a report.
Cycle	Byte	Specifies what happens when you press the Tab key while the last control on the report has the focus.

continues

(continued)

PROPERTY	DATA TYPE	DESCRIPTION
DateGrouping	Byte	Specifies how you want to group dates on a report.
DefaultControl	Control object	Can be used to specify the properties of a particular type of control on a report.
DefaultView	Byte	Used to specify the opening view for a report (Report view or Print Preview).
Dirty	Boolean	True if data has been entered but not saved on a form.
DrawMode	Integer	Specifies how the pen interacts with existing background colors on a report when the Line, Circle, or Pset method is used when printing.
DrawStyle	Integer	Specifies the line style when using the Line and Circle methods to print lines on reports.
DrawWidth	Integer	Specifies the line width for the Line, Circle, and Pset methods to print lines on reports.
FillColor	Long	Specifies the color that fills in boxes and circles drawn on reports with the Line and Circle methods.
FillStyle	Integer	Specifies whether circles and lines are transparent, opaque, or filled with a pattern.
Filter	String	Specifies a subset of records to be displayed when a filter is applied to a report.
FilterOn	Boolean	Specifies whether the Filter property of a report is applied.
FilterOnLoad	Boolean	Indicates that a filter should be loaded with the report when the report loads.
FitToPage	Boolean	Gets or sets whether the width of the report should be reduced to fit the width of the page.
FontBold	Boolean	Specifies whether a font appears in bold on a form or report.
FontItalic	Boolean	Specifies whether a font appears in italics on a form or report.

PROPERTY	DATA TYPE	DESCRIPTION
FontName	String	Specifies the font for printing controls on reports.
FontSize	Integer	Specifies the font size for printing controls on reports.
FontUnderline	Integer	Specifies whether a font appears underlined on a form or report.
ForeColor	Long	Specifies the color for text in a control.
FormatCount	Integer	Specifies the number of times the OnFormat property has been evaluated for the current section on a report.
GroupLevel	GroupLevel object	Refers to a particular group level you're grouping or sorting in a report.
GrpKeepTogether	Byte	Specifies whether groups in a multiple column report that have the KeepTogether property set to Whole Group or With First Detail will be kept together by page or by column.
HasData	Long	Specifies if a report is bound to an empty recordset.
HasModule	Boolean	Specifies whether a report has a class module associated with it.
Height	Long	Specifies the height of the report in twips.
HelpContextID	Long	Specifies the context ID of a topic in the custom help file.
HelpFile	String	Returns the name of the help file associated with the report.
Hwnd	Long	Used to determine the handle of the current report window.
KeyPreview	Boolean	Specifies whether the form level keyboard event procedures are invoked before a control's keyboard event procedures.
Left	Long	Specifies the object's location on a report.
MenuBar	String	Specifies the menu bar to use for a report.

continues

(continued)

PROPERTY	DATA TYPE	DESCRIPTION
MinMaxButtons	Byte	Specifies whether the Maximize and Minimize buttons are visible on the report.
Modal	Boolean	Specifies whether a report opens as a modal window.
Module	Module **object**	Specifies a module for the report.
Moveable	Boolean	True if a report can be moved by the user.
MoveLayout	Boolean	Specifies if Access should move to the next printing location on the page.
Name	String	Specifies the name of the report.
NextRecord	Boolean	Specifies whether a section should advance to the next record.
OpenArgs	Variant	Determines the string expression specified by the OpenArgs method of the OpenReport method.
OrderBy	String	Specifies how records on a report should be shortened.
OrderByOn	Boolean	Specifies whether the OrderBy property is applied.
OrderByOnLoad	Boolean	Indicates that a sort should be loaded with the form when the form loads.
Orientation	Byte	Specifies the report's orientation (left to right or right to left).
Page	Long	Specifies the current page number when a report is printed.
PageFooter	Byte	Specifies whether a report's page footer is printed on the same page as the report footer.
PageHeader	Byte	Specifies whether a report's page header is printed on the same page as the report header.
Pages	Integer	Returns information needed to print page numbers on a report.
Painting	Boolean	Specifies whether reports are repainted.

PROPERTY	DATA TYPE	DESCRIPTION
Parent	Object	For subreports, returns the main Report object where the subreport resides. Throws a runtime error for top-level reports.
Picture	String	Specifies a bitmap on a report.
PictureAlignment	Byte	Specifies where a background picture appears in an image control on a report.
PictureData	Variant	Can be used to copy the picture in a report to another object.
PicturePages	Byte	Specifies on which page or pages of a report a picture is displayed.
PictureSizeMode	Byte	Specifies how a picture on a report is sized.
PictureTiling	Boolean	Specifies whether a background picture is tiled across the entire report.
PictureType	Byte	Specifies whether Access stores a report's picture as a linked or embedded object.
PopUp	Boolean	Specifies whether a report opens in a pop-up window.
PrintCount	Integer	Specifies the number of times the OnPrint property has been evaluated for the current section of the report.
Printer	Printer object	Represents the default printer on the current system.
PrintSection	Boolean	Specifies whether a section of a report should be printed.
Properties	Properties collection	Represents the collection of all properties for the report.
PrtDevMode	Variant	Sets or returns the printing device mode information for the report in the Print dialog box.
PrtDevNames	Variant	Sets or returns information about the printer selected in the Print dialog box.
PrtMip	Variant	Sets or returns the printing device mode information for the report in the Print dialog box.
Recordset	Recordset object	Returns the Recordset object for the report.

continues

(continued)

PROPERTY	DATA TYPE	DESCRIPTION
RecordSource	String	Used to specify the source of the data for the report.
Report	Report object	Used to refer to the report associated with a subreport.
RibbonName	String	Name of a custom ribbon to load for the report.
ScaleHeight	Single	Specifies the number of units for the vertical measurement of the page when the Circle, Line, Pset, or Print methods are used when a report is printed.
ScaleLeft	Single	Specifies the units for the horizontal coordinates that reference the location of the left edge of the page when the Circle, Line, Pset, or Print methods are used when a report is printed.
ScaleMode	Integer	Specifies the unit of measurement for coordinates on a page when the Circle, Line, Pset, or Print methods are used when a report is printed.
ScaleTop	Single	Specifies the units for the vertical coordinates that reference the location of the top edge of a page when the Circle, Line, Pset, or Print methods are used on a report.
ScaleWidth	Single	Specifies the number of units for the horizontal measurement of the page when the Circle, Line, Pset, or Print methods are used when a report is printed.
ScrollBars	Byte	Specifies whether scrollbars appear on a report.
Section	Section object	Identifies a section of a report.
Shape	String	Specifies the shape command corresponding to the sorting and grouping of the report.
ShortcutMenuBar	String	Specifies the shortcut menu that appears when you right-click a report.
ShowPageMargins	Boolean	Specifies whether page margins are visible on a report open in Report view.

PROPERTY	DATA TYPE	DESCRIPTION
Tag	String	Stores extra information about a report.
TimerInterval	Long	Specifies the interval (in milliseconds) between Timer events on a report.
Toolbar	String	Specifies the toolbar used for a report.
Top	Long	Specifies the report's top coordinates.
UseDefaultPrinter	Boolean	Determines whether the report uses the system's default printer.
Visible	Boolean	True when the report isn't minimized.
Width	Integer	Specifies the width of the report in twips.
WindowHeight	Integer	Specifies the height of a report in twips.
WindowLeft	Integer	Indicates the screen position in twips of the left edge of the report relative to the left edge of the Access window.
WindowTop	Integer	Specifies the screen position in twips of the top edge of the report relative to the top edge of the Access window.
WindowWidth	Integer	Sets the width of the report in twips.

Report Object Methods

The methods of the Report object are listed in the following table.

METHOD	ARGUMENTS	DESCRIPTION
Circle	flags, X, Y, radius, color, start, end, aspect	Draws a circle, ellipse, or an arc on a report when the Print event occurs.
Line	Flags, x1, y1, x2, y2, color	Draws lines and rectangles on a report when the Print event occurs.
Move	Left, Top, Width, Height	Moves the report to the specified coordinates on the screen.
Print	Expr	Prints text on a Report object using the current color and font.
PSet	flags, X, Y, color	Sets a point on a report object to the specified color when the Print event occurs.

continues

(continued)

METHOD	ARGUMENTS	DESCRIPTION
Requery	None	Updates the data in the report from the underlying recordset.
Scale	flags, x1, y1, x2, y2	Defines the coordinate system for a `Report` object.
TextHeight	Expr	Returns the height of a text string as it would be printed in the current font of a report.
TextWidth	Expr	Returns the width of a text string as it would be printed in the current font of a report.

Report Object Events

Access 2007 introduced a new interactive view for reports called Report view. As a result, many of the events that have existed on forms over the years are now available in reports! The events of the `Report` object are listed in the following table.

EVENT	OCCURS
Activate	When a report receives the focus and becomes the active window.
ApplyFilter	When a filter is applied to a report.
Click	When a user presses and releases the mouse button over an object.
Close	When a report is closed but before it is removed from the screen.
Current	When the focus moves to a record or when the form is refreshed or requeried.
DblClick	When a user presses and releases the mouse button.
Deactivate	When a report loses focus to another object.
Error	When a runtime error occurs when the report has the focus.
Filter	When a user chooses the Advanced Filter/Sort option on the Ribbon.
GotFocus	When the report receives the focus.
KeyDown	When a key is pressed.
KeyPress	When a key is pressed and released.
KeyUp	When a key is released.
Load	When a report is opened and records are displayed.
LostFocus	When the report loses focus to another object.

EVENT	OCCURS
MouseDown	When the mouse button is pressed.
MouseMove	When the user moves the mouse.
MouseUp	When the mouse button is released.
MouseWheel	When the mouse wheel is moved.
NoData	After a report with no data is formatted for printing but before the report is printed.
Open	When a report is opened but before it is displayed on the screen.
Page	After a page is formatted for printing but before the page is printed.
Resize	When a form opens and any time it is resized.
Timer	At regular intervals controlled by the form's `TimerInterval` property.
Unload	After a form is closed but before it's removed from the screen.

THE SCREEN OBJECT

The `Screen` object refers to whatever form, report, or control currently has the focus within the application. You can use the `Screen` object and its properties to manipulate the active window no matter which form, report, or control is currently displayed.

The properties of the `Screen` object are listed in the following table.

PROPERTY	DATA TYPE	DESCRIPTION
ActiveControl	`Control` object	Specifies the control that has the focus.
ActiveDatasheet	`Form` object	Specifies the datasheet that has the focus. This can also be an open table or query.
ActiveForm	`Form` object	Specifies the form that has the focus.
ActiveReport	`Report` object	Specifies the report that has the focus.
Application	`Application` object	References the current Access application.
MousePointer	`Integer`	Specifies the type of mouse pointer currently displayed.
Parent	`Object`	Parent of the object that currently has the focus.
PreviousControl	`Control` object	Specifies the control that previously had the focus.

THE SECTION OBJECT

Every form or report contains several `Section` objects including the header, footer, and detail sections. Each section has a number of properties and methods you can use within your code.

A `Section` object has only one method: `SetTabOrder`. It enables you to programmatically set the tab order for all controls in a section. Calling this method is the equivalent of using the Auto Order button in the Tab Order dialog box.

Section Object Properties

The properties of the `Section` object are described in the following table.

PROPERTY	DATA TYPE	DESCRIPTION
AlternateBackColor	Long	Specifies the alternating row color for a section. It is now easy to change the row color for every other section on a form or report!
Application	Application object	Returns the currently active application.
AutoHeight	Boolean	Indicates whether a section should grow automatically when controls are resized.
BackColor	Long	Specifies the color for the interior of a section.
CanGrow	Boolean	True if you want the section to automatically grow to print or preview all data within the section.
CanShrink	Boolean	True if you want the section to automatically shrink to print or preview only the data within the section (with no extra space).
Controls	Controls collection	References all of the controls within the section.
DisplayWhen	Byte	Controls which sections you want displayed onscreen and in print.
EventProcPrefix	String	Used to get the prefix portion of an event procedure name.
ForceNewPage	Byte	Specifies when sections print on a separate page.
HasContinued	Boolean	Determines if part of the current section begins on the previous page.
Height	Integer	Height (in twips) of the current section.
InSelection	Boolean	Determines if a control on a form is selected.

PROPERTY	DATA TYPE	DESCRIPTION
KeepTogether	Boolean	True if the entire section should print on one page.
Name	String	Name of the current section.
NewRowOrCol	Byte	Specifies whether a section is printed within a new row or column within a multicolumn report or form.
Parent	Object	Refers to the parent of the section (usually either a form, report, or data access page).
Properties	Properties collection	Refers to the entire collection of properties for the section.
RepeatSection	Boolean	Specifies whether the group header is repeated on the next page of a column (when the group spans more than one page or column).
SpecialEffect	Byte	Specifies whether any special formatting applies to a section (such as shadow, sunken lines, or highlight).
Tag	String	Stores extra information about a section.
Visible	Boolean	Specifies whether a section is visible on a form or report.
WillContinue	Boolean	Specifies if the current section continues on the next page.

Section Object Events

There are nine events you can use in your code for the Section object. They're described in the following table.

EVENT	OCCURS WHEN
Click	The user presses and releases the mouse button.
DblClick	The user presses and releases the mouse button twice in rapid succession.
Format	A section is formatted. Does not fire in Report view.
MouseDown	The user presses the mouse button.
MouseMove	The user moves the mouse.

continues

(continued)

EVENT	OCCURS WHEN
MouseUp	The user releases the mouse button.
Paint	A section is redrawn on the screen. Does not fire in Print Preview.
Print	A section is printed. Does not fire in Report view.
Retreat	Access must move back to a section that has already been formatted. Allows you to undo a change to a control that was made in the Format event for the section.

OTHER HELPFUL INFORMATION

There's a lot of information about the Access object model in this appendix. In addition to the basic objects you'll manipulate on a daily basis, there are many other areas of the object model with which you should be familiar. You need to know some of the myriad arguments you can use with some of these objects, as well as the order in which events fire in the different objects. The following sections detail some additional information about programming in Access that may be helpful.

Order of Events

Knowing the order in which events fire is an important aspect of programming with VBA in Access. These order lists can help you decide which events you should choose for your applications. It's also essential to recognize that events do not necessarily fire when actions are triggered using VBA code. For example, if you set a value for a control programmatically, the AfterUpdate event for the control does not fire.

Events that begin with the prefix Before can typically be canceled by setting the Cancel argument of the event to True.

Forms, Controls, and Subforms

Here's the order of events for the opening sequence of a form with controls:

```
Open->Load->Resize->Activate->Current->Enter (control)->GotFocus (control)
```

If there are no controls on the form, the GotFocus event will fire after the Current event. If there is an Attachment control on the form, the OnAttachmentCurrent event will fire before the Form_Current event (as long as it is the first control in the tab order).

The following shows the order of events for the closing sequence of a form:

```
Exit (control)->LostFocus (control)->Unload->Deactivate->Close
```

Subform events fire before main form events because records for a subform are loaded first. Because subforms do not have a form window, they do not fire the Activate event. The following shows the order of events for the opening sequence of a form with a subform:

```
Open (subform)->Load (subform)->Resize (subform)->Current (subform)->
Open->Load->Resize->Activate->Current
```

Reports and Sections

With the introduction of Report view in Access 2007, many of the events that are available to forms are now available to reports. The events that fire, however, are different for a report open in Report view than in Print Preview.

Report View and Layout View

Here's the order in which events fire for the opening sequence of a report in Report view or Layout view:

```
Open->Load->Resize->Activate->GotFocus->Paint (ReportHeader)->Paint (PageHeader)
->Paint (Detail)->Paint (ReportFooter)->Paint (PageFooter)
```

Notice that neither the `Current` event nor control events fire when a report is opened. That's because unlike a form, objects on a report do not receive focus when the report opens. To trigger the `Current` event for a report, click in the Detail section.

The `Paint` event was added in Access 2007 and fires every time Access draws the section in the report. As such, the Paint event can fire multiple times for a given section. The `Format`, `Print`, and `Retreat` events do not fire in Report view or Layout view.

When you close a report in Report view or Layout view, events are fired in the following order:

```
Unload->LostFocus->Deactivate->Close
```

Print Preview

The order of events for a report opened in Print Preview is similar to that for Report view. The primary difference between the two views is the `Format`, `Print`, and `Paint` events. `Paint` does not fire for sections in Print Preview.

```
Open->Load->Resize->Activate->GotFocus->Format (Report Header)->Print
  (Report Header)->Format (Page Header)->Print (Page Header)->Format (Detail)->Print
  (Detail)->Format (ReportFooter)->Print (ReportFooter)->Format (PageFooter)->Print
  (PageFooter)->Page
```

As you can see, a lot of events fire for the given sections on a report! If you try to handle events in Print Preview, you might also notice that the `Format` event can fire for all the sections before the first `Print` event is fired. That's because reports in Access are actually formatted twice on some occasions. Generally speaking, this can occur when a calculation requires other sections further down the page, or even the report itself to be formatted before the calculation is complete. A good example is the expression that returns the current page and page count in the page footer section: `="Page " & [Page] & " of " & [Pages]`.

When you close a report in Print Preview, events are fired in the following order:

```
Unload->LostFocus->Deactivate->Close
```

Records

There are data-related events on forms as well.

Adding Records

There are several events that fire when you add a record using a form:

```
BeforeInsert->Dirty->BeforeUpdate->AfterUpdate->AfterInsert
```

Editing Records

The order of events for editing existing data on a form is as follows:

```
Dirty->Dirty (control)->BeforeUpdate (control)->AfterUpdate (control)
->BeforeUpdate->AfterUpdate
```

Deleting Records

When you delete records, the following events are raised:

```
Delete->BeforeDelConfirm->AfterDelConfirm
```

B

DAO Object Method and Property Descriptions

This appendix provides a detailed alphabetical list of all the objects that DAO supports, including descriptions of their methods, properties, and collections. These descriptions are for reference purposes only, and you should consult the online Help for more in-depth descriptions.

DAO-SUPPORTED OBJECTS

This section outlines the objects that are available in DAO. There have been some changes made to DAO in Access 2007 and 2010, and they're reflected in the descriptions.

ODBCDirect

In addition to the Microsoft Access workspace, previous versions of DAO supported a second type of `Workspace` object called ODBCDirect. ODBCDirect workspaces are used against ODBC data sources, such as SQL Server. Beginning with Office 2007, Microsoft is no longer shipping Remote Data Objects (RDO) that enabled this type of workspace. As a result, ODBCDirect is no longer supported in DAO.

User-Level Security

Beginning with Access 2007, user-level security is no longer supported for new file formats. Thus, you cannot assign permissions to database objects such as tables and queries, or Access objects such as forms and reports in ACCDB files. User-level security is still supported for

MDB files. The DAO object model related to users and groups, however, has been hidden. To view hidden members in an object model, right-click in the Object Browser and choose Show Hidden Members.

Containers Collection

The `Containers` collection contains all of the `Container` objects that are defined in a database (Microsoft Access databases only).

METHOD	DESCRIPTION
Refresh	Refreshes the collection.

PROPERTY	DESCRIPTION
Count	Returns a count of `Container` objects in the collection.

Container Object

The `Container` object contains a collection of `Document` objects that are of the same type. The Containers you are likely to work with the most are Databases, Tables (which also include query objects), Forms, Reports, Scripts (macros), and Modules.

The `Container` object has no methods.

PROPERTY	DESCRIPTION
AllPermissions	(Hidden) Returns a bit field that contains all the permissions that apply to the current user (as identified by the `UserName` property) of the `Container` object, including user-specific and inherited (from group membership) permissions (Microsoft Access workspaces only).
Inherit	(Hidden) Sets/returns a flag that specifies whether new `Document` objects will inherit the default permissions (Microsoft Access workspaces only).
Name	Sets/returns a user-defined name for a DAO object. For an object not appended to a collection, this property is read/write.
Owner	(Hidden) Sets/returns the Container's name (Microsoft Access workspaces only).
Permissions	(Hidden) Returns a bit field that contains the permissions that specifically apply to the current user (or group) of the `Container` object, as identified by the `UserName` property (Microsoft Access workspaces only).
UserName	(Hidden) Sets/returns the name of the user, group, or the owner of the `Workspace` object.

Collections

- ➤   Documents
- ➤   Properties

DBEngine

The DBEngine object is the top-level object in the DAO object model.

METHOD	DESCRIPTION
BeginTrans	Begins a new transaction.
CommitTrans	Ends the current transaction and saves the changes to disk.
CompactDatabase	Copies and compacts a closed Access database.
CreateDatabase	Creates a new Database object and saves it to disk.
CreateWorkspace	Creates a new Workspace object.
Idle	Suspends data processing to allow Access to complete any pending tasks such as memory optimization or page timeouts.
ISAMStats	(Hidden) Returns disk statistics (refer to Chapter 11).
OpenDatabase	Opens an existing database.
RegisterDatabase	Enters ODBC data source connection information in the Registry.
Rollback	Ends the current transaction and cancels any changes made to DAO objects in the workspace.
SetOption	Temporarily overrides Access database engine values in the Registry.

PROPERTY	DESCRIPTION
DefaultPassword	Sets the password used to create the default workspace, when it is initialized. Write-only.
DefaultType	Sets/returns a value that defines the type of workspace that will be used by the next Workspace object to be created. ODBCDirect workspaces are no longer supported.
DefaultUser	Sets the username that is used to create the default workspace when it is initialized.
IniPath	Sets/returns information about the Registry key that contains values for the Access database engine.

continues

(continued)

PROPERTY	DESCRIPTION
LoginTimeout	Sets/returns the number of seconds before an error occurs when you attempt to log on to an ODBC database.
SystemDB	(Hidden) Sets/returns the path to the Workgroup Information File (Microsoft Access workspaces only).
Version	Returns the current DAO version in use.

Collections

- ➤ Errors
- ➤ Properties
- ➤ Workspaces

Databases Collection

The Databases collection contains all open Database objects opened or created within a Workspace object.

METHOD	DESCRIPTION
Refresh	Refreshes the collection.

PROPERTY	DESCRIPTION
Count	Returns a count of Database objects in the collection.

Database Object

The Database object is an open database. With installable indexed sequential access methods (ISAM) such as Text or Excel, it is possible to open a Database object that points to data sources other than Microsoft Access. Many properties or methods listed here apply only to a Database object that has been opened against a Microsoft Access database. These members are noted as such.

METHOD	DESCRIPTION
Close	Closes the database.
CreateProperty	Creates a new user-defined Property object (Microsoft Access workspaces only).
CreateQueryDef	Creates a new QueryDef object.
CreateRelation	Creates a new Relation object (Microsoft Access workspaces only).

METHOD	DESCRIPTION
CreateTableDef	Creates a new `TableDef` object (Microsoft Access workspaces only).
Execute	Runs an action query.
MakeReplica	Creates a new database replica from another replica (Microsoft Access workspaces only).
NewPassword	Changes the password of an existing database (Microsoft Access workspaces only).
OpenRecordset	Creates a new `Recordset` object.
PopulatePartial	Synchronizes changes between a full and partial replica.
Synchronize	Synchronizes two replicas (Microsoft Access databases only).
CollatingOrder	Returns the text sort order for string comparisons and sorts (Microsoft Access workspaces only).
Connect	Sets/returns a value for the source of an open database or a database used in a pass-through query.
DesignMasterID	Returns a 16-byte value that uniquely identifies the database as being the design master in a replica set (Microsoft Access workspaces only).
Name	Sets/returns the database's name.
QueryTimeOut	Sets/returns the number of seconds before an error occurs when a query is executed against an ODBC data source.
RecordsAffected	Returns the number of records affected by the most recent `Execute` method.
Replicable	Sets/returns a value that defines whether a database can be replicated (Microsoft Access workspaces only).
ReplicaID	Returns a 16-byte value that uniquely identifies a database replica (Microsoft Access workspaces only).
Transactions	Returns a value that indicates whether the database supports transactions.
Updatable	Returns a value that indicates whether you can change the `Database` object.
Version	Returns the version of the ODBC driver currently in use.

Collections

➤ Containers

➤ Properties

➤ QueryDefs

➤ Recordsets

➤ Relations

➤ TableDefs

➤ Transactions

Documents Collection

The Documents collection contains all of the Document objects for a specific type of object (Microsoft Access databases only).

METHOD	DESCRIPTION
Refresh	Refreshes the collection.

PROPERTY	DESCRIPTION
Count	Returns a count of Document objects in the collection.

Document Object

The Document object contains information about an instance of an object. The object can be a database, saved table, query, or relationship (Microsoft Access databases only).

METHOD	DESCRIPTION
CreateProperty	Creates a new user-defined Property object (Microsoft Access workspaces only).

PROPERTY	DESCRIPTION
AllPermissions	(Hidden) Returns a bit field that contains all the permissions that apply to the current user (as identified by the UserName property) of the Document object, including user-specific and inherited (from group membership) permissions (Microsoft Access workspaces only).
Container	Returns the name of the Document object's parent Container (Microsoft Access workspaces only).
DateCreated	Returns the date and time that the Document object was created (Microsoft Access workspaces only).
LastUpdated	Returns the date and time of the most recent change that was made to the document (Microsoft Access workspaces only).

PROPERTY	DESCRIPTION
Name	Returns the document's name. This property is read-only.
Owner	(Hidden) Sets/returns a value that specifies the document's owner (Microsoft Access workspaces only).
Permissions	(Hidden) Returns a bit field that contains the permissions that specifically apply to the current user (or group) of the Document object, as identified by the UserName property (Microsoft Access workspaces only).
Replicable	Sets/returns a flag that specifies whether the document can be replicated (Microsoft Access workspaces only).
UserName	(Hidden) Sets/returns the name of the user, group, or the owner of the Document object.

Collection

➤ Properties

Errors Collection

The Errors collection contains all stored Error objects.

METHOD	DESCRIPTION
Refresh	Refreshes the collection.

PROPERTY	DESCRIPTION
Count	Returns a count of the current Error objects.

Error Object

The Error object contains details about data access errors. It has no methods. Each Error object relates to a single DAO operation.

PROPERTY	DESCRIPTION
Description	Default. Returns a descriptive string associated with an error.
Help Context	(Hidden) Returns a context ID for a topic in a Help file.
Help File	(Hidden) Returns a fully qualified path to the Help file.
Number	Returns an error number.
Source	Returns the name of the object that generated the error.

Collections

None.

Fields Collection

The `Fields` collection contains all stored `Field` objects of an `Index`, `QueryDef` (Microsoft Access workspaces only), `Recordset`, `Recordset2`, `Relation`, or `TableDef`. Note that the `Fields` collection of a `Recordset2` object contains the collection of `Field2` objects.

METHOD	DESCRIPTION
Append	Appends a new `Field` object to the collection.
Delete	Deletes a `Field` from the collection.
Refresh	Refreshes the collection.

PROPERTY	DESCRIPTION
Count	Returns a count of `Field` objects in the collection.

Field Object

The `Field` object is a column of data.

METHOD	DESCRIPTION
AppendChunk	Appends data from a string expression to a Memo or Long Binary Field object in a `Recordset`.
CreateProperty	Creates a new user-defined `Property` object (Microsoft Access workspaces only).
GetChunk	Returns all or some of the contents of a Memo or Long Binary Field object in the `Fields` collection of a `Recordset` object.

PROPERTY	DESCRIPTION
AllowZeroLength	Sets/returns a flag that indicates whether you can enter a zero-length string (" ") in a Text or Memo field object (Microsoft Access workspaces only).
Attributes	Sets/returns a value that indicates a `Field`'s characteristics.
CollatingOrder	Returns a value that specifies the sort order for string comparison and sorting (Microsoft Access workspaces only).

PROPERTY	DESCRIPTION
DataUpdatable	Returns a flag that specifies whether the data in the field can be updated.
DefaultValue	Sets/returns the default value of a `Field` object. Read-only for `Field` object in the `Fields` collection (Microsoft Access workspaces only).
FieldSize	Returns the number of bytes actually stored in a Memo or Long Binary Field object in a `Recordset` object's `Fields` collection.
ForeignName	Sets/returns the name of the foreign table involved in a relationship with the field (Microsoft Access workspaces only).
Name	Sets/returns a `Field` object's name. Read-only for `Field` objects in the Fields collection.
OrdinalPosition	Sets/returns the relative position of a `Field` object within the `Fields` collection. Read-only for `Field` objects in the `Fields` collection.
Required	Sets/returns a flag that indicates whether data in the `Field` must be non-Null.
Size	Sets/returns a value that indicates the maximum size, in bytes, of the data for a `Field`.
SourceField	Returns the name of the field that is the original source of the data for a `Field` object.
SourceTable	Returns the name of the table that is the original source of the data for a `Field` object.
Type	Sets/returns a value that indicates the field's data type.
ValidateOnSet	Sets/returns a flag that specifies whether the value of a `Field` is immediately validated when data is entered (Microsoft Access workspaces only).
ValidationRule	Sets/returns an expression that validates the data in a field as it is changed or added to the table (Microsoft Access workspaces only).
ValidateText	Sets/returns a value that specifies the text of the message that displays if the data entered in a Field doesn't satisfy the validation rule (Microsoft Access workspaces only).
Value	Default. Sets/returns the field's actual value.

Collection

➤ Properties

Field2 Object

The `Field2` object is a column of data. The `Field2` object was added in Access 2007 and includes support for multi-value lookup and attachment fields. You can use a `Field2` object anywhere you would normally use a `Field` object, including multi-value lookup and attachment fields, although you won't be able to call the additional properties or methods that are available on the `Field2` object.

METHOD	DESCRIPTION
AppendChunk	Appends data from a string expression to a Memo or Long Binary Field object in a `Recordset`.
CreateProperty	Creates a new user-defined `Property` object (Microsoft Access workspaces only).
GetChunk	Returns all or some of the contents of a Memo or Long Binary Field object in the `Fields` collection of a `Recordset` object.
LoadFromFile	Loads the data in an `Attachment` field from the specified filename. You get runtime error 3259 (Invalid field data type) if you call this method on a non-attachment field.
SaveToFile	Saves the data in an `Attachment` file to the specified filename.

PROPERTY	DESCRIPTION
AllowZeroLength	Sets/returns a flag that indicates whether you can enter a zero-length string (" ") in a Text or Memo field object (Microsoft Access workspaces only).
AppendOnly	Sets/returns a flag that indicates whether a memo field is an append-only field.
Attributes	Sets/returns a value that indicates a `Field`'s characteristics.
CollatingOrder	Returns a value that specifies the sort order for string comparison and sorting (Microsoft Access workspaces only).
ComplexType	Contains a property that returns the collection of `Fields` for a multi-value lookup field.
DataUpdatable	Returns a flag that specifies whether the data in the field can be updated.
DefaultValue	Sets/returns the default value of a `Field` object. Read-only for `Field` object in the `Fields` collection (Microsoft Access workspaces only).
Expression	Sets/returns the expression to use in a calculated column.

PROPERTY	DESCRIPTION
FieldSize	Returns the number of bytes actually stored in a Memo or Long Binary Field object in a `Recordset` object's `Fields` collection.
ForeignName	Sets/returns the name of the foreign table involved in a relationship with the field (Microsoft Access workspaces only).
IsComplex	Determines whether a field is a complex field. Returns True for multi-value lookup fields and Attachment fields.
Name	Sets/returns a `Field` object's name. Read-only for `Field` objects in the `Fields` collection.
OrdinalPosition	Sets/returns the relative position of a `Field` object within the `Fields` collection. Read-only for `Field` objects in the `Fields` collection.
Required	Sets/returns a flag that indicates whether data in the Field must be non-Null.
Size	Sets/returns a value that indicates the maximum size, in bytes, of the data for a `Field`.
SourceField	Returns the name of the field that is the original source of the data for a `Field` object.
SourceTable	Returns the name of the table that is the original source of the data for a `Field` object.
Type	Sets/returns a value that indicates the field's data type.
ValidateOnSet	Sets/returns a flag that specifies whether the value of a `Field` is immediately validated when data is entered (Microsoft Access workspaces only).
ValidationRule	Sets/returns an expression that validates the data in a field as it is changed or added to the table (Microsoft Access workspaces only).
ValidateText	Sets/returns a value that specifies the text of the message that displays if the data entered in a `Field` doesn't satisfy the validation rule (Microsoft Access workspaces only).
Value	Default. Sets/returns the field's value. In the case of a multi-valued lookup field, this property actually returns a `DAO.Recordset2` object that contains the data in the lookup field. You can determine if a field is a multi-valued lookup field by checking the `IsComplex` property.

Collection

➤   Properties

Groups Collection

The Groups collection contains all stored Group objects of a Workspace or User object (Microsoft Access workspaces only). A group is one or more users in the Access security model. Assigning permissions based on groups is often easier than managing permissions to individual users.

This collection is hidden in Access 2010, but can still be used if you are working with an MDB file.

METHOD	DESCRIPTION
Append	Appends a new Group object to the collection.
Delete	Deletes a Group from the collection.
Refresh	Refreshes the collection.

PROPERTY	DESCRIPTION
Count	Returns a count of Group objects in the collection.

Group Object

The Group object is a group of User objects that have common access permissions when a workspace operates in a secure workgroup. This object is hidden in Access 2010, but can still be used if you are working with an MDB file.

METHOD	DESCRIPTION
CreateUser	Creates a new User object (Microsoft Access workspaces only).

PROPERTY	DESCRIPTION
Name	Sets/returns the group's name. Read-only if the group has already been added to the collection.
PID	Sets the group's personal identifier (PID) (Microsoft Access workspaces only).

Collections

➤ Properties

➤ Users

Indexes Collection

The Indexes collection contains all stored Index objects of a TableDef object.

METHOD	DESCRIPTION
Append	Appends a new `Index` object to the collection.
Delete	Deletes an `Index` from the collection.
Refresh	Refreshes the collection.

PROPERTY	DESCRIPTION
Count	Returns a count of `Index` objects in the collection.

Index Object

The `Index` object specifies the order in which records are accessed from a table and whether duplicate records are allowed.

METHOD	DESCRIPTION
CreateField	Creates a new `Field` object (Microsoft Access workspaces only).
CreateProperty	Creates a new `Property` object (Microsoft Access workspaces only).

PROPERTY	DESCRIPTION
Clustered	Sets/returns a flag that specifies whether the index is clustered. The Microsoft Access database does not support clustered indexes, so this property is ignored. ODBC data sources always return False because it does not detect if ODBC data sources have clustered indexes.
DistinctCount	Returns the number of unique values (keys) that exist in the table for the index (Microsoft Access workspaces only).
Foreign	Returns a flag that specifies whether the index is a foreign key in another table (Microsoft Access workspaces only).
IgnoreNulls	Sets/returns a flag that specifies whether records that have Null values also have indexes.
Name	Sets/returns the index's name.
Primary	Sets/returns a flag that specifies whether the index is the primary key.
Required	Sets/returns a flag that specifies whether a `Field` object (or the entire index) can accept Null values. Read-only if the index has been appended to the collection.
Unique	Sets/returns a flag that specifies whether the index keys must be unique.

Collection

➤ Fields

Parameters Collection

The Parameters collection contains all the Parameter objects of a QueryDef object.

METHOD	DESCRIPTION
Refresh	Refreshes the collection.

PROPERTY	DESCRIPTION
Count	Returns a count of Parameters objects in the collection.

Parameter Object

The Parameter object is a defined value supplied to a query. It has no methods.

PROPERTY	DESCRIPTION
Name	Returns the parameter's name. Read-only.
Type	Sets/returns a value that indicates the parameter type.
Value	Default. Sets/returns the parameter value.

Collection

➤ Properties

Recordsets Collection

The Recordsets collection contains all open Recordset objects in a Connection or Database.

METHOD	DESCRIPTION
Refresh	Refreshes the collection.

PROPERTY	DESCRIPTION
Count	Returns a count of Recordset objects in the collection.

Recordset Object

The Recordset object represents the records in a base table, or those that result from executing a query.

METHOD	DESCRIPTION
AddNew	Begins a Recordset editing session that creates a new record for an updatable Recordset object.
CancelUpdate	Cancels any pending updates for a Recordset object.
Clone	Creates a new Recordset object that is a duplicate of the original Recordset object.
Close	Closes an open Recordset object.
CopyQueryDef	Creates a new QueryDef object that is a copy of the original QueryDef that was used to create the Recordset object (Microsoft Access workspaces only).
Delete	Deletes the current record in an updatable Recordset object.
Edit	Begins a Recordset editing session.
FillCache	Fills all or a part of a local cache for a Recordset object that contains data from a Microsoft Access-connected ODBC data source (Microsoft Access-connected ODBC databases only).
FindFirst	Locates the first record in a dynaset- or snapshot-type Recordset object that matches the specified criteria and makes that row the current row (Microsoft Access workspaces only).
FindLast	Locates the last record in a dynaset- or snapshot-type Recordset object that matches the specified criteria and makes that row the current row (Microsoft Access workspaces only).
FindNext	Locates the next record in a dynaset- or snapshot-type Recordset object that matches the specified criteria and makes that row the current row (Microsoft Access workspaces only).
FindPrevious	Locates the previous record in a dynaset- or snapshot-type Recordset object that matches the specified criteria and makes that row the current row (Microsoft Access workspaces only).
GetRows	Retrieves the specified number of rows from a Recordset object.
Move	Moves the Recordset's current cursor position to the specified row.
MoveFirst	Moves the Recordset's current cursor position to the next row in the Recordset and makes that row the current row.
MoveLast	Moves the Recordset's current cursor position to the last row in the Recordset and makes that row the current row.

continues

(continued)

METHOD	DESCRIPTION
MovePrevious	Moves the `Recordset`'s current cursor position to the previous row in the Recordset and makes that row the current row.
OpenRecordset	Creates a new `Recordset` object.
Requery	Refreshes the data in a `Recordset` object by requerying its data source.
Seek	Locates the record in an indexed table-type Recordset that matches the specified criteria for the current index and makes that row the current row (Microsoft Access workspaces only).
Update	Saves all data changes made via a Recordset during an editing session.

PROPERTY	DESCRIPTION
AbsolutePosition	Sets/returns a Recordset's relative row number.
BOF	Returns a flag that indicates whether the current record position is before the first record in a `Recordset` object.
Bookmark	Sets/returns a bookmark that uniquely identifies the current record in a Recordset.
Bookmarkable	Returns a flag that indicates whether a `Recordset` object supports bookmarks.
CacheSize	Sets/returns the number of ODBC data source records that will be locally cached.
CacheStart	Sets/returns a value that specifies the bookmark of the first record in a dynaset-type `Recordset` object that contains data to be locally cached from an ODBC data source (Microsoft Access workspaces only).
Collect	(Hidden) Returns a field's actual value.
DateCreated	Returns the date and time that the `Recordset` object was created (Microsoft Access workspaces only).
EditMode	Returns a value that indicates the current Recordset editing state for the current record.
EOF	Returns a flag that indicates whether the current record position is after the last record in a `Recordset` object.
Filter	Sets/returns a value that specifies the records that will be included in a Recordset that is created from the current `Recordset` object (Microsoft Access workspaces only).
Index	Sets/returns the name of the current `Index` object in a table-type `Recordset` object (Microsoft Access workspaces only).

PROPERTY	DESCRIPTION
LastModified	Returns a bookmark that specifies the most recently added or changed record.
LastUpdated	Returns the date and time of the most recent change that was made to the Recordset or to a base table on a table-type Recordset (Microsoft Access workspaces only).
LockEdits	Sets/returns a value indicating the type of locking that is in effect while editing the Recordset.
Name	Returns the first 256 characters of the Recordset's SQL statement.
NoMatch	Returns a flag that indicates whether one of the find methods (FindFirst, FindPrevious, FindNext, FindLast, or Seek) found the record it was looking for (Microsoft Access workspaces only).
Parent	Hidden. Returns a Database object against which the Recordset was created.
PercentPosition	Sets/returns a value that indicates the current row's approximate position, based on a percentage of the records in the Recordset.
RecordCount	Returns the number of records accessed (so far) in a Recordset or the total number of records in a table-type Recordset.
Restartable	Returns a flag that indicates whether a Recordset object supports the Requery method.
Sort	Sets/returns the sort order for records in a Recordset (Microsoft Access workspaces only).
Transactions	Returns a flag that indicates whether the Recordset supports transactions.
Type	Sets/returns a value that indicates the Recordset type.
Updatable	Returns a flag that indicates whether you can change the Recordset's definition.
ValidationRule	Sets/returns an expression that validates the data in a field as it is changed or added to the table (Microsoft Access workspaces only).
ValidationText	Sets/returns a value that specifies the text of the message that displays if the data entered in a Field doesn't satisfy the validation rule (Microsoft Access workspaces only).

Collections

➤ Fields

➤ Properties

Recordset2 Object

The `Recordset2` object represents the records in a base table, or those that result from executing a query. The `Recordset2` object was added in Access 2007 to support multi-valued lookup fields and attachment fields.

METHOD	DESCRIPTION
AddNew	Begins a Recordset editing session that creates a new record for an updatable `Recordset` object.
CancelUpdate	Cancels any pending updates for a `Recordset` object.
Clone	Creates a new `Recordset` object that is a duplicate of the original `Recordset` object.
Close	Closes an open `Recordset` object.
CopyQueryDef	Creates a new `QueryDef` object that is a copy of the original `QueryDef` that was used to create the `Recordset` object (Microsoft Access workspaces only).
Delete	Deletes the current record in an updatable `Recordset` object.
Edit	Begins a Recordset editing session.
FillCache	Fills all or a part of a local cache for a `Recordset` object that contains data from a Microsoft Access-connected ODBC data source (Microsoft Access-connected ODBC databases only).
FindFirst	Locates the first record in a dynaset- or snapshot-type `Recordset` object that matches the specified criteria and makes that row the current row (Microsoft Access workspaces only).
FindLast	Locates the last record in a dynaset- or snapshot-type `Recordset` object that matches the specified criteria and makes that row the current row (Microsoft Access workspaces only).
FindNext	Locates the next record in a dynaset- or snapshot-type `Recordset` object that matches the specified criteria and makes that row the current row (Microsoft Access workspaces only).
FindPrevious	Locates the previous record in a dynaset- or snapshot-type `Recordset` object that matches the specified criteria and makes that row the current row (Microsoft Access workspaces only).
GetRows	Retrieves the specified number of rows from a `Recordset` object.
Move	Moves the Recordset's current cursor position to the specified row.
MoveFirst	Moves the Recordset's current cursor position to the next row in the Recordset and makes that row the current row.

METHOD	DESCRIPTION
MoveLast	Moves the Recordset's current cursor position to the last row in the Recordset and makes that row the current row.
MovePrevious	Moves the Recordset's current cursor position to the previous row in the Recordset and makes that row the current row.
OpenRecordset	Creates a new `Recordset` object.
Requery	Refreshes the data in a `Recordset` object by requerying its data source.
Seek	Locates the record in an indexed table-type Recordset that matches the specified criteria for the current index and makes that row the current row (Microsoft Access workspaces only).
Update	Saves all data changes made via a Recordset during an editing session.

PROPERTY	DESCRIPTION
AbsolutePosition	Sets/returns a Recordset's relative row number.
BOF	Returns a flag that indicates whether the current record position is before the first record in a `Recordset` object.
Bookmark	Sets/returns a bookmark that uniquely identifies the current record in a Recordset.
Bookmarkable	Returns a flag that indicates whether a `Recordset` object supports bookmarks.
CacheSize	Sets/returns the number of ODBC data source records will be locally cached.
CacheStart	Sets/returns a value that specifies the bookmark of the first record in a dynaset-type `Recordset` object that contains data to be locally cached from an ODBC data source (Microsoft Access workspaces only).
Collect	(Hidden) Returns a field's actual value.
DateCreated	Returns the date and time that the `Recordset` object was created (Microsoft Access workspaces only).
EditMode	Returns a value that indicates the current Recordset editing state for the current record.
EOF	Returns a flag that indicates whether the current record position is after the last record in a `Recordset` object.
Filter	Sets/returns a value that specifies the records that will be included in a Recordset that is created from the current `Recordset` object (Microsoft Access workspaces only).

continues

(continued)

PROPERTY	DESCRIPTION
Index	Sets/returns the name of the current Index object in a table-type `Recordset` object (Microsoft Access workspaces only).
LastModified	Returns a bookmark that specifies the most recently added or changed record.
LastUpdated	Returns the date and time of the most recent change that was made to the Recordset or to a base table on a table-type Recordset (Microsoft Access workspaces only).
LockEdits	Sets/returns a value indicating the type of locking that is in effect while editing the Recordset.
Name	Returns the first 256 characters of the Recordset's SQL statement.
NoMatch	Returns a flag that indicates whether one of the find methods (`FindFirst`, `FindPrevious`, `FindNext`, `FindLast`, or `Seek`) found the record it was looking for (Microsoft Access workspaces only).
Parent	Hidden. Returns a `Database` object against which the Recordset was created.
PercentPosition	Sets/returns a value that indicates the current row's approximate position, based on a percentage of the records in the Recordset.
RecordCount	Returns the number of records accessed (so far) in a Recordset or the total number of records in a table-type Recordset.
Restartable	Returns a flag that indicates whether a `Recordset` object supports the `Requery` method.
Sort	Sets/returns the sort order for records in a Recordset (Microsoft Access workspaces only).
Transactions	Returns a flag that indicates whether the Recordset supports transactions.
Type	Sets/returns a value that indicates the Recordset type.
Updatable	Returns a flag that indicates whether you can change the Recordset's definition.
ValidationRule	Sets/returns an expression that validates the data in a field as it is changed or added to the table (Microsoft Access workspaces only).
ValidationText	Sets/returns a value that specifies the text of the message that displays if the data entered in a `Field` doesn't satisfy the validation rule (Microsoft Access workspaces only).

Collections

➤ Fields

➤ Properties

 The Fields *collection of the* Recordset2 *object contains* Field2 *objects, not* Field *objects as in the* Fields *collection of a* Recordset *object.*

Properties Collection

The Properties collection contains all of the Property objects associated with a DAO object.

METHOD	DESCRIPTION
Append	Appends a new user-defined Property object to the collection.
Delete	Deletes a user-defined Property object from the collection.
Refresh	Refreshes the collection.

PROPERTY	DESCRIPTION
Count	Returns the number of items in the Properties collection.
Item	Default. Returns an individual Property object, either by name or numeric index.

Property Object

The Property object is an attribute that defines an object's characteristics or behavior. It has no methods.

PROPERTY	DESCRIPTION
Inherited	Returns a flag that specifies whether a Property object is inherited from an underlying object.
Name	Sets/returns a property's name. Read-only for built-in properties.
Type	Sets/returns a value that indicates the property's data type.
Value	Default. Sets/returns the property's actual value.

Collection

➤ Properties

QueryDefs Collection

The QueryDefs collection contains all QueryDef objects of a Database (Microsoft Access workspaces).

METHOD	DESCRIPTION
Append	Appends a new QueryDef object to the collection.
Delete	Deletes a QueryDef from the collection.
Refresh	Refreshes the collection.

PROPERTY	DESCRIPTION
Count	Returns a count of QueryDef objects in the collection.

QueryDef Object

The QueryDef object is a stored definition of a query in a Microsoft Access database.

METHOD	DESCRIPTION
Close	Closes an open QueryDef object.
CreateProperty	Creates a new user-defined Property object (Microsoft Access workspaces only).
Execute	Runs an action query.
OpenRecordset	Creates a new Recordset object.

PROPERTY	DESCRIPTION
CacheSize	Sets/returns the number of records retrieved from an ODBC data source that will be cached locally.
Connect	Sets/returns a value that indicates the source of an open database used in a pass-through query or a linked table. Read-only.
DateCreated	Returns the date and time that the QueryDef object was created (Microsoft Access workspaces only).
KeepLocal	Sets/returns a flag that specifies whether you want to replicate the query when the database is replicated (Microsoft Access workspaces only).

PROPERTY	DESCRIPTION
LastUpdated	Returns the date and time of the most recent change that was made to the QueryDef (Microsoft Access workspaces only).
LogMessages	Sets/returns a flag that specifies whether the messages returned from a Microsoft Access–connected ODBC data source are recorded (Microsoft Access workspaces only).
MaxRecords	Sets/returns the maximum number of records to return from a query against an ODBC data source.
Name	Sets/returns the QueryDef name. Read-only.
ODBCTimeout	Returns the number of seconds to wait before a time-out error occurs when a QueryDef is executed against an ODBC data source.
RecordsAffected	Returns the number of records affected by the most recent Execute method.
Replicable	Sets/returns a value that defines whether a query can be replicated (Microsoft Access workspaces only).
ReturnsRecords	Sets/returns a flag that specifies whether an SQL pass-through query to an external database returns records (Microsoft Access workspaces only).
SQL	Sets/returns the SQL statement that defines the query.
Type	Sets/returns a value that indicates the type of QueryDef.
Updatable	Returns a value that indicates whether you can change the QueryDef object.

Collections

➤ Fields

➤ Parameters

➤ Properties

Relations Collection

The Relations collection contains stored Relation objects of a Database object (Microsoft Access databases only).

METHOD	DESCRIPTION
Append	Appends a new Relation object to the collection.
Delete	Deletes a Relation from the collection.
Refresh	Refreshes the collection.

PROPERTY	DESCRIPTION
Count	Returns a count of `Relation` objects in the collection.

Relation Object

The `Relation` object is a defined relationship between fields in tables or queries (Microsoft Access databases only).

METHOD	DESCRIPTION
CreateField	Creates a new `Field` object (Microsoft Access workspaces only).

PROPERTY	DESCRIPTION
Attributes	Sets/returns a value that defines the relation's characteristics.
ForeignTable	Sets/returns the name of the foreign table in a relationship (Microsoft Access workspaces only).
Name	Sets/returns the relation's name. Read-only if the relation has already been added to the collection.
PartialReplica	Sets/returns a flag that indicates whether that relation should be considered when populating a partial replica from a full replica (Microsoft Access databases only).
Table	Sets/returns the name of a `Relation` object's primary table (`TableDef` name or `QueryDef` name). Read-only if the relation has already been added to the collection (Microsoft Access workspaces only).

Collections

➤ Fields

➤ Properties

TableDefs Collection

The `TableDefs` collection contains all stored `TableDef` objects in a database (Microsoft Access workspaces only).

METHOD	DESCRIPTION
Append	Adds a `TableDef` object to the collection.
Delete	Deletes a `TableDef` object from the collection.
Refresh	Refreshes the objects in the collection.

PROPERTY	DESCRIPTION
Count	Returns a count of `TableDef` objects in the collection.

TableDef Object

The `TableDef` object is the stored definition of a table, linked or otherwise (Microsoft Access workspaces only).

METHOD	DESCRIPTION
CreateField	Creates a new `Field` object (Microsoft Access workspaces only).
CreateIndex	Creates a new `Index` object (Microsoft Access workspaces only).
CreateProperty	Creates a new user-defined `Property` object (Microsoft Access workspaces only).
OpenRecordset	Creates a new `Recordset` object.
RefreshLink	Refreshes the connection for a linked table (Microsoft Access workspaces only).

PROPERTY	DESCRIPTION
Attributes	Sets/returns a value that defines the `TableDef`'s characteristics.
ConflictTable	Returns the name of the conflict table that contains details about the records that conflicted during synchronization (Microsoft Access workspaces only).
Connect	Sets/returns a value that indicates the source of a linked table. This setting is read-only on base tables.
DateCreated	Returns the date and time that the `TableDef` object was created (Microsoft Access workspaces only).
KeepLocal	Sets/returns a flag that specifies whether you want to replicate the table when the database is replicated (Microsoft Access workspaces only).
LastUpdated	Returns the date and time of the most recent change that was made to the table (Microsoft Access workspaces only).
Name	Sets/returns the table's name. This property is read-only on linked tables.
RecordCount	Returns the number of records in the table.
Replicable	Sets/returns a flag that specifies whether the table can be replicated (Microsoft Access workspaces only).

continues

(continued)

PROPERTY	DESCRIPTION
ReplicaFilter	Sets/returns a value within a partial replica that specifies which subset of records will be replicated to the table from a full replica (Microsoft Access databases only).
SourceTableName	For linked tables sets/returns the name of the remote table to which the table is connected (Microsoft Access workspaces only). This property is read-only for base tables.
Updatable	Returns a flag that indicates whether you can change the table definition.
ValidationRule	Sets/returns an expression that validates the data in a field as it is changed or added to the table (Microsoft Access workspaces only).
ValidationText	Sets/returns a value that specifies the text of the message that displays if the data entered in a Field doesn't satisfy the validation rule (Microsoft Access workspaces only).

Collections

➤ Fields

➤ Indexes

➤ Properties

Users Collection

The Users collection contains all stored User objects of a Workspace or Group object (Microsoft Access workspaces only). This collection is hidden in Access 2010, but can be used when working with MDB files.

METHOD	DESCRIPTION
Append	Appends a new User object to the collection.
Delete	Deletes a User from the collection.
Refresh	Refreshes the collection.

PROPERTY	DESCRIPTION
Count	Returns a count of User objects in the collection.

User Object

The User object is a user that has access permissions when a workspace operates in a secure workgroup (Microsoft Access workspaces only). This object is hidden in Access 2010, but can be used when working with MDB files.

METHOD	DESCRIPTION
CreateGroup	Creates a new User object (Microsoft Access workspaces only).
NewPassword	Changes the password of an existing User object (Microsoft Access workspaces only).

PROPERTY	DESCRIPTION
Name	Sets/returns the user's name. Read-only if the user has already been added to the collection.
Password	Sets the password for a User object (Microsoft Access workspaces only).
PID	Sets the personal identifier (PID) for a User object (Microsoft Access workspaces only).

Collections

➤ Groups

➤ Properties

Workspaces Collection

The Workspaces collection contains all active, unhidden Workspace objects of the DBEngine object.

METHOD	DESCRIPTION
Append	Appends a new Workspace object to the collection.
Delete	Deletes a persistent object from the collection.
Refresh	Refreshes the collection.

PROPERTY	DESCRIPTION
Count	Returns a count of Workspace objects in the collection.

Workspace Object

The Workspace object defines a named user session.

METHOD	DESCRIPTION
BeginTrans	Begins a new transaction.
Close	Closes a workspace.

continues

(continued)

METHOD	DESCRIPTION
CommitTrans	Ends the current transaction and saves the changes to disk.
CreateDatabase	Creates a new Database object and saves it to disk.
CreateGroup	(Hidden) Creates a new Group object (Microsoft Access workspaces only).
CreateUser	(Hidden) Creates a new User object (Microsoft Access workspaces only).
OpenDatabase	Opens a specific database in a workspace.
Rollback	Ends the current transaction and cancels any changes made to DAO objects in the workspace.

PROPERTY	DESCRIPTION
IsolateODBCTrans	Sets/returns a value that specifies if multiple transactions involving the same Access-connected ODBC data source are isolated (Microsoft Access workspaces only).
LoginTimeOut	Sets/returns the number of seconds before an error occurs when you attempt to log on to an ODBC database.
Name	Sets/returns the workspace name.
Type	Sets/returns a value that specifies the type of workspace being used.
UserName	(Hidden) Sets/returns the name of a user, group, or the owner of a Workspace object.

Collections

➤   Connections

➤   Databases

➤   (Hidden) Groups

➤   Properties

➤   (Hidden) Users

UNDOCUMENTED TOOLS AND RESOURCES

Several Access-specific utilities and object methods are shipped with Microsoft Access 2010. These utilities and methods are not very well documented by Microsoft or are not documented at all. Nonetheless, you can use them to help you develop and maintain your DAO applications.

Utilities ISAMStats

Microsoft Access 2010 contains an undocumented DBEngine method called ISAMStats, which returns various internal statistics. You use ISAMStats to get statistics about different operations. For example, to determine which of several queries will run faster, you can use ISAMStats to return the number of disk reads performed by each query.

Each of the ISAMStats options maintains a separate statistics counter that records the number of times its metric occurs. To reset the counter, set the Reset argument to True. The syntax is as follows:

```
lngReturn = DBEngine.ISAMStats(StatNum [, Reset])
```

where StatNum is one of the following values:

STATNUM VALUE	DESCRIPTION
0	Number of disk reads.
1	Number of disk writes.
2	Number of reads from cache.
3	Number of reads from read-ahead cache.
4	Number of locks placed.
5	Number of locks released.

You must call ISAMStats twice: once to get a baseline statistic and once (after the operation to be analyzed) to get the final statistic. Then you subtract the baseline statistic from the final one to arrive at the statistic for the operation under test. The following examples demonstrate two ways to use ISAMStats:

Method 1

```
Call DBEngine.IsamStats(0, True)
Set rs = db.OpenRecordset(`qryGetOverdueAccts", dbOpenSnapshot)
Debug.Print `Total reads: ` & DBEngine.IsamStats(0)
```

In this example, the first call resets the ISAMStats counter. The code then opens a Recordset using a query you want to test. The last line retakes the statistics and prints it.

Method 2

```
lngBaseline = DBEngine.IsamStats(0)
Set rs = db.OpenRecordset(`qryGetOverdueAccts", dbOpenSnapshot)
lngStatistic = DBEngine.IsamStats(0)
Debug.Print `Total reads: ` & lngStatistic -lngBaseline
```

In Method 2, ISAMStats is not reset, but its return value is stored in a variable. The code then opens the Recordset. The third line retakes the statistic after the operation, while the fourth and final line calculates the actual statistic.

Methods DAO.PrivDBEngine

The unsupported `PrivDBEngine` object enables you to connect to an external database that uses a different Workgroup Information File to the one currently being used. You can open an Access database without having to create another instance of Access. `PrivDBEngine` only allows access to DAO objects, such as `TableDefs`, `QueryDefs`, `Recordsets`, `Fields`, `Containers`, `Documents`, `Indexes`, and `Relations`.

```
Dim dbX As PrivDBEngine
Dim wsX As Workspace
Dim dbe As Database

`Return a reference to a new instance of the PrivDBEngine object
Set dbe = New PrivDBEngine

`Set the SystemDB property to specify the workgroup file
dbe.SystemDB = strWIFPath

`Specify the username (this could be any valid username)
dbe.DefaultUser = strUserName

`Specify the password
dbe.DefaultPassword = strPassword

`Set the workspace
Set wsX = dbe.Workspaces(0)

`Open the secured database
Set dbe = ws.OpenDatabase(strDBPath)
```

The `PrivDBEngine` object does nothing more than create a new instance of the Access database engine. You can get the same functionality by doing the following:

```
Dim dbe As DAO.DBEngine
Set dbe = CreateObject(`DAO.DBEngine")
```

The following table lists the `CreateObject` argument for different versions of the Jet or Access database engine.

JET/ACCESS VERSION	ARGUMENT	EXAMPLE
3.0	DAO.DBEngine	Set dbe = CreateObject(`DAO.DBEngine")
3.5	DAO.DBEngine.35	Set dbe = CreateObject(`DAO.DBEngine.35")
3.6	DAO.DBEngine.36	Set dbe = CreateObject(`DAO.DBEngine.36")
12.0	DAO.DBEngine.120	Set dbe = CreateObject(`DAO.DBEngine.120")
14.0	DAO.DBEngine.120	Set dbe = CreateObject(`DAO.DBEngine.120")

Recordset.Collect

The DAO `Recordset` and `Recordset2` objects expose a hidden, undocumented property named `Collect`. Although `Collect` is a property, it behaves like the `Recordset` object's `Fields` collection, but it's faster because it doesn't need a reference to the `Field` object. Be aware that `Recordset .Collect` only returns a field's value; it doesn't expose any other properties. You can use this property by passing it a numeric item number, or a field name, just like the `Fields` collection. For example:

```
Set rs = db.OpenRecordset(`tblCustomers")
Debug.Print `CustID: ` & rs.Collect(0)
Debug.Print `CustomerNo: ` & rs.Collect(`CustomerNo")
```

Recordset.Parent

The undocumented `Recordset.Parent` property is an object reference to the database to which the Recordset belongs. This may be especially useful in situations where you have several `Database` objects in the same application.

DAO FIELD TYPES

The following table lists the constants in the DAO `DataTypeEnum` and their corresponding data types in the Access Table designer.

DAO DATATYPEENUM	CONSTANT VALUE	ACCESS FIELD TYPE
dbAttachment	101	Attachment
dbBigInt	16	Cannot create in Access, but can be used by linked tables
dbBinary	9	Cannot create in Access designer but can be created in DAO
dbBoolean	1	Yes/No
dbByte	2	Number, Field Size=Byte
dbChar	18	Cannot create in Access, but can be used by linked tables
dbComplexByte	102	Number, Field Size=Byte
dbComplexDecimal	108	Cannot create in DAO but can create in Access designer
dbComplexDouble	106	Number, Field Size=Double

continues

(continued)

DAO DATATYPEENUM	CONSTANT VALUE	ACCESS FIELD TYPE
dbComplexGUID	107	Number, Field Size=Replication ID
dbComplexInteger	103	Number, Field Size=Integer
dbComplexLong	104	Number, Field Size=Long Integer
dbComplexSingle	105	Number, Field Size=Single
dbComplexText	109	Text
dbCurrency	5	Currency
dbDate	8	Date/Time
dbDecimal	20	Cannot create in DAO but can create in Access designer
dbDouble	7	Number, Field Size=Double
dbFloat	21	Cannot create in Access, but can be used by linked tables
dbGUID	15	Number, Field Size=Replication ID
dbInteger	3	Number, Field Size=Integer
dbLong	4	Number, Field Size=Long Integer
dbLongBinary	11	Number, Field Size=OLE Object
dbMemo	12	Memo
dbNumeric	19	Cannot create in Access, but can be used by linked tables
dbSingle	6	Number, Field Size=Single
dbText	10	Text
dbTime	22	Cannot create in Access, but can be used by linked tables
dbTimeStamp	23	Cannot create in Access, but can be used by linked tables
dbVarBinary	17	Cannot create in Access, but can be used by linked tables

OPENRECORDSET CONSTANTS

You'll use a variety of constants when writing VBA code. The following tables list just a few of the constants you might use when opening a DAO Recordset.

> *A runtime error occurs if you attempt to use* dbOpenTable *in the following Microsoft Access workspace situations:*
>
> ➤ *When the Recordset is based on a* QueryDef
>
> ➤ *When the* Source *argument refers to an SQL statement or* TableDef *that refers to a linked table*

The following table lists the constants that can be specified for the Type argument.

CONSTANT	DESCRIPTION
dbOpenTable	Returns an editable data set consisting of records from a single local table only. Cannot be used with linked tables (Microsoft Access workspaces only).
dbOpenDynaset	Returns an editable data set consisting of pointers to records in a table or query. Can be used on multiple local and linked tables (Microsoft Access workspaces only).
dbOpenSnapshot	Returns a read-only data set consisting of a copy of records in a table or query. Can be used on multiple local and linked tables (Microsoft Access workspaces only).
dbOpenForwardOnly	Returns an editable data set consisting of records in a table. Use this option when you only need to move through the data set in one pass and in one direction — forward (Microsoft Access workspaces only).

The following table lists the constants that can be specified for the Options argument.

> *The* dbInconsistent *and* dbConsistent *constants are mutually exclusive. Similarly you cannot supply a* LockEdits *argument on a Recordset whose* Options *argument is set to* dbReadOnly. *If you attempt to do so, a runtime error occurs.*

CONSTANT	DESCRIPTION
dbAppendOnly	Signifies that you can add new records, but not edit or delete them (Microsoft Access dynaset Recordsets only).
dbSQLPassThrough	Signifies that the SQL statement will be passed directly to a Microsoft Access-connected ODBC data source for processing (Microsoft Access snapshot Recordsets only).
dbSeeChanges	Triggers a runtime error if another user attempts to change data that you're currently editing (Microsoft Access dynaset Recordsets only).
dbDenyWrite	Locks all the underlying tables so other users can only view the data. They cannot add, edit, or delete records while the lock is in place (Microsoft Access Recordsets only).
dbDenyRead	Completely locks all the underlying tables so other users cannot even view the data (Microsoft Access table Recordsets only).
dbForwardOnly	Creates a forward-only Recordset (Microsoft Access snapshot Recordsets only). This option is provided for backward compatibility only, and you should use the dbOpenForwardOnly constant in the Type argument instead of this option.
dbReadOnly	Creates a read-only Recordset, preventing users from making changes to the data (Microsoft Access only). You can use dbReadOnly in either the Options argument or the LockEdits argument, but not both. If you attempt to do so, a runtime error occurs. This option is provided for backward compatibility only, and you should use the dbReadOnly constant in the LockEdits argument instead of this option.
dbInconsistent	Allows inconsistent updates (Microsoft Access dynaset and snapshot Recordsets only). An inconsistent update is one in which you can update all the columns in a multi-table Recordset unless referential integrity rules prevent it.
dbConsistent	Allows only consistent updates (Microsoft Access dynaset-type and snapshot-type Recordset objects only). A consistent update is one in which you can perform only those updates that result in a consistent view of the data. For example, you cannot update the many side of a one-to-many relationship unless a matching record exists in the one side.

The following table lists the constants that can be specified for the LockEdits argument.

 You cannot supply a LockEdits *argument on a Recordset whose* Options *argument is set to* dbReadOnly. *If you attempt to do so, a runtime error occurs.*

CONSTANT	DESCRIPTION
dbReadOnly	Creates a read-only Recordset, preventing users from making changes to the data. You can use dbReadOnly in either the Options argument or the LockEdits argument, but not both. If you attempt to do so, a runtime error occurs. Setting dbReadOnly in the Options argument is provided for backward compatibility only. You should use it in the LockEdits argument instead.
dbPessimistic	Uses pessimistic locking for changes made to the Recordset in a multi-user environment. Pessimistic locking is where the entire data page that contains the record you're editing is locked (made unavailable to other users) as soon as you issue the Edit method, and remains locked until you issue the Update method (this is the default setting for Microsoft Access workspaces).
dbOptimistic	Uses optimistic locking for changes made to the Recordset in a multi-user environment. Optimistic locking is where the entire data page that contains the record you're editing is locked (made unavailable to other users) as soon as you issue the Update method and remains locked until the data is written to the table (this is the default setting for Microsoft Access workspaces). You use optimistic locking when manipulating ODBC databases or when the LockEdits property is set to False.

ADO Object Model Reference

This appendix describes each of the ActiveX Data Objects (ADO) provided by the various ADO object models available in Access 2010. The ActiveX Data Objects (ADO) Object Model was designed to allow data access for a wide variety of data formats. The ADO object model isn't overly complicated and can be implemented quite easily in your VBA code. Descriptions of each of the ADO objects, properties, methods, and associated collections have been provided.

 The availability of each collection, event, method, and property is dependent on the functionality supported by each particular ADO data provider. Not all objects are supported by every provider, and functionality may be slightly different depending on the exact version of ADO being used. This section will primarily address Microsoft's Object Linking and Embedding Database (OLE DB) provider for ACE in Access 2010.

 For more information about the enumerations mentioned in the following tables, see "The ADO Enumerations" section later in this appendix.

THE CONNECTION OBJECT

The Connection object represents a unique session to a particular data source. The Connection object has collections, methods, and properties associated with it.

Properties of the Connection Object

The following table describes each of the properties of the Connection object.

PROPERTY	DATA TYPE	DESCRIPTION
Attributes	Long	Generic property indicating one or more characteristics of the Connection object.
CommandTimeout	Long	Configures the timeout value for the Execute method of the Connection.
ConnectionString	String	The default property value. Specifies a data source. Pass in a connection string containing a series of argument = value statements separated by semicolons.
ConnectionTimeout	Long	Specifies how long to wait before terminating the attempt and generating an error.
CursorLocation	Long	Specifies the cursor location. Specified as a member of the CursorLocationEnum. The default is adUseServer.
DefaultDatabase	String	Sets or returns the string that resolves to the name of a database available from the provider.
IsolationLevel	Long	Specifies the isolation level. Specified as a member of the IsolationLevelEnum. The default is adXactReadCommitted.
Mode	Long	Specifies the mode for the connection. Specified as a member of the ConnectModeEnum. The default is adModeUnknown.
Provider	String	Sets or returns a string value representing the provider name. If no provider is specified, the property will default to MSDASQL (Microsoft OLE DB Provider for ODBC).
State	Long	Specifies the connection state. Specified as a member of the ObjectStateEnum. The default is adStateClosed.
Version	String	Reads the version from the ADO implementation.

Methods of the Connection Object

The Connection object also provides several methods useful for connection to and working with a data source. Those methods are described in this section.

The Connection.BeginTrans Method

The BeginTrans method begins a new transaction. Once called, the provider will no longer commit changes until CommitTrans or RollbackTrans is called to end the transaction. The method does not take any parameters or return any values.

The Connection.Cancel Method

The `Cancel` method cancels the execution of a pending `Open` or `Execute` method. The method does not take any parameters or return any values.

The Connection.Close Method

The `Close` method closes the connection to the data source. The method does not take any parameters or return any values.

The Connection.CommitTrans Method

The `CommitTrans` method saves any changes made during the current transaction and ends the transaction. The method does not take any parameters or return any values.

The Connection.Execute Method

The `Execute` method executes an SQL command, or a provider-specific command, on the connection. This method has the following three parameters.

PARAMETER	DATA TYPE	DESCRIPTION
CommandText	String	The SQL statement, specified query, stored procedure, or provider-specific text as the command to execute on the source.
RecordsAffected	Long	Optional. Returns the number of records affected by an operation after the `Execute` method is called.
Options	Long	Optional. Specifies how the data provider should interpret the `CommandText` parameter. Can be specified by a single or bitmask combination of the `CommandTypeEnum` and/or the `ExecuteOptionEnum` values.

Returns a reference to a `Recordset` object containing any resulting data from the command, if the command is row returning, otherwise null.

The Connection.Open Method

The `Open` method establishes the connection to the data source. This method has the following four parameters.

PARAMETER	DATA TYPE	DESCRIPTION
ConnectionString	String	Optional. A string representing the full connection string to the data source. ADO supports only five arguments in this connection string: `Provider`, `File Name`, `Remote Provider`, `Remote Server`, and `URL`. The `Provider` and `File Name` arguments cannot be used together.

continues

(continued)

PARAMETER	DATA TYPE	DESCRIPTION
UserID	String	Optional. Contains the username for secured data sources.
Password	String	Optional. Contains the password for the specified username.
Options	Long	Optional. Specified as one of the ConnectOptionEnum values, which determines how the Connection object should return: synchronously (the default) or asynchronously.

This method does not return any values.

The Connection.OpenSchema Method

The OpenSchema method obtains database schema information from the provider. This method has the following three parameters.

PARAMETER	DATA TYPE	DESCRIPTION
Schema	Long	Specified as one of the SchemaEnum items, describing the schema type. There are 41 options in the SchemaEnum enumeration, but only three of these options are required to be supported by OLE DB: adSchemaColumns, adSchemaProviderTypes, and adSchemaTables.
Restrictions	Variant	Optional. Composed of an array of Constraint Columns for each of the values in the SchemaEnum items selected in the Schema parameter to limit the results of the query.
SchemaID	Long	Required if the Schema parameter is set to adSchemaProviderSpecific to assert that the provider schema is not defined by OLE DB.

Returns a reference to a read-only Recordset object with schema information about the data source.

The Connection.RollbackTrans Method

The RollbackTrans method cancels any changes made in the current transaction and ends the transaction. The method does not take any parameters or return any values.

Collections of the Connection Object

The Connection object has two collections, Errors and Properties, which are described in this section.

The Connection.Properties Collection

The ADO `Connection` object `Properties` collection contains a set of `Property` objects for each specific property supported by the ADO data provider for a specific instance of a connection. See the section of this appendix, titled "The Properties Collections," for a complete listing of the methods and properties of the `Properties` collection and the `Property` object.

The Connection.Errors Collection

The `Errors` collection contains all `Error` objects created as a result of provider-related failures or other errors that occur during command execution on the connection. Any operation that involves an ADO object can generate errors. When an ADO operation generates an error, the `Errors` collection is cleared of all previous `Error` objects and a new set of `Error` objects can be added to the `Errors` collection for that operation.

Properties of the Errors Collection

The two properties of the `Errors` collection are summarized in the following table.

PROPERTY	DATA TYPE	DESCRIPTION
Count	Long	Returns the number of `Error` objects stored in the `Errors` collection.
Item	String or Long	References a specific member of the `Errors` collection by name or ordinal number.

Methods for the Errors Collection

The following table describes the two methods of the `Errors` collection.

METHOD	DESCRIPTION
Clear	No Parameters. Removes all `Error` objects from the `Errors` collection.
Refresh	No Parameters. Updates the `Errors` collection to encompass all current `Error` objects.

THE ERROR OBJECT

The `Error` object is used to store the particular details about any given error that has occurred and been logged by the ADO provider. The `Error` object contains only properties to store information about any given error; there are no methods or collections as part of this object.

Properties of the Error Object

The following table describes each of the properties of the `Error` object.

PROPERTY	DATA TYPE	DESCRIPTION
Description	String	The default property value. Contains the text of the error.
HelpContext	Long	Context ID of a topic in the Help file.
HelpFile	String	Name and location of the Help file.
NativeError	Long	A Long value used to retrieve the database-specific error information for an Error object.
Number	Long	The error constant value.
Source	String	Specifies the object that raised the error.
SQLState	Variant	A five character error code specifying an error during the processing of an SQL statement.

THE COMMAND OBJECT

The ADO Command object is designed to provide an interface for executing commands or operations against a given data source. The specific methods and properties that are supported will be dependent upon the ADO provider and data source type, but in general, the object model provides the following properties, methods, and collections.

Properties of the Command Object

The following table lists the various properties of the Command object.

PROPERTY	DATA TYPE	DESCRIPTION
ActiveConnection	String or Connection	Indicates which Connection object the Command object uses.
CommandStream	Stream object	Stream used as the input for the Command object.
CommandText	String	Indicates the text of the Command being executed.
CommandTimeout	Long	Sets the number of seconds a provider will wait for a command to execute.
CommandType	Long	Specified as a CommandTypeEnum value. Defines the type of command.
Dialect	GUID	Contains a GUID that represents the dialect of the command text or stream.

PROPERTY	DATA TYPE	DESCRIPTION
Name	String	Identifies the `Command` object as a method on the associated `Connection`.
NamedParameters	Boolean	Indicates whether parameter names are passed to the provider.
Prepared	Boolean	`True` if the provider should compile a version of the `Command` before execution.
State	Long	Specifies if the `Command` object is open, closed, or in the process of connecting, executing, or retrieving information.

Methods of the Command Object

There are only three simple methods of the `Command` object, which are detailed in this section.

The Command.Cancel Method

The `Cancel` method cancels the execution of a pending asynchronous method call to the `Execute` method. The method does not take any parameters or return any values.

The Command.CreateParameter Method

The `CreateParameter` method creates a `Parameter` object for the given `Command` object with the specified five parameters: `Name`, `Type`, `Direction`, `Size`, and `Value`. This method has the following five parameters.

PARAMETER	DATA TYPE	DESCRIPTION
Name	String	Optional. The `Parameter` object's name.
Type	Long	Optional. The data type of the `Parameter` object, specified as one of the `DataTypeEnum` members.
Direction	Long	Optional. The direction type of the `Parameter` object, specified as one of the `ParameterDirectionEnum` members.
Size	Long	Optional. The maximum length of the `Parameter` object.
Value	Variant	Optional. The actual value of the `Parameter` object.

Returns a new `Parameter` object with the specified settings.

The Command.Execute Method

The Execute method executes the command stored in the CommandText property. This method has the following three parameters.

PARAMETER	DATA TYPE	DESCRIPTION
RecordsAffected	Long	Optional. Returns the number of records affected by an action query or stored procedure after the Execute method has been called.
Parameters	Variant	Optional. An array of values used as the parameters specified in the CommandText or CommandStream objects.
Options	Long	Optional. Specifies how the data provider should interpret the CommandText or CommandStream properties of the Command object. Can be specified by a single or bitmask combination of the CommandTypeEnum and/or the ExecuteOptionEnum values.

Returns a reference to a Recordset object containing any resulting data from the command, if the command was row returning, otherwise null.

Collections of the Command Object

The Command object has two collections, the Parameters and the Properties collections, which are described in the following table. Each of these collections is described in the following sections.

COLLECTION	DESCRIPTION
Parameters	Contains all the Parameter objects used for stored queries and stored procedures.
Properties	Contains all the Property objects for the current command object.

The Command.Parameters Collection

The Command object has a Parameters collection associated with it that contains all of the Parameter objects for that Command object. The Parameters collection does not contain any sub-collections, only two properties and three methods, which are described next.

Properties of the Parameters Collection

The Parameters collection contains two properties that provide information about the current state of the collection.

PROPERTY	DATA TYPE	DESCRIPTION
Count	Long	Returns the number of Parameter objects stored in the Parameters collection.
Item	String or Long	References a member of the Parameters collection by name or ordinal number.

Methods of the Parameters Collection

There are three methods for the `Parameters` collection, each described in this section.

The Parameters.Append Method

The `Append` method appends a `Parameter` object to the end of the `Parameters` collection. When creating new `Parameter` objects, always use the `Command.CreateParameter` to create those new `Parameter` objects. This method has one parameter.

PARAMETER	DATA TYPE	DESCRIPTION
Object	Object	The `Parameter` object to be appended to the `Parameters` collection. Although the type is `Object`, a `Parameter` type should be provided.

This method does not return any values.

The Parameters.Delete Method

The `Delete` method removes a `Parameter` object, at the specified index, from the `Parameters` collection. This method has one parameter.

PARAMETER	DATA TYPE	DESCRIPTION
Index	String or Long	References the specific member of the `Parameters` collection that is to be removed by name or ordinal number.

This method does not return any values.

The Parameters.Refresh Method

The `Refresh` method updates the `Parameters` collection to encompass all current `Parameter` objects. The method does not take any parameters or return any values.

The Command.Properties Collection

The `Properties` collection of the `Command` object contains all of the `Property` objects for a specific instance of an ADO command. See the section "The Properties Collections" later in this appendix for a complete listing of the methods and properties of the `Properties` collection and the `Property` object.

THE PARAMETER OBJECT

The `Parameter` object is used with the `Command` object to provide the values for parameters of a database command, such as the parameters to a stored procedure that will be executed against an SQL Server database. The `Parameters` object has one method, one collection, and a handful of properties, which are described in the section that follows.

To create new `Parameter` objects in code, use the `Command.CreateParameter` method to create a new `Parameter` object with the desired name and properties for the particular `Command` object that will use those parameters. Then use the `Append` method of the `Parameters` collection to add the newly created `Parameter` object to the `Command.Parameters` collection. Once completed, the parameter will be part of the command and will be used when the `Command.Execute` method is called.

Properties of the Parameter Object

The following table describes the various properties of the `Parameter` objects. All properties are read and write, unless otherwise specified.

PROPERTY	DATA TYPE	DESCRIPTION
Attributes	Long	Read-only. A bitmask of one or more `ParameterAttributesEnum` values. The default value is `adParamSigned`.
Direction	Long	A value from the `ParameterDirectionEnum` object to specify the direction of the `Parameter`.
Name	String	Specifies the name of the `Parameter` object.
NumericScale	Byte	Specifies the number of decimal places to which numeric values are resolved.
Precision	Byte	Specifies the maximum number of digits used to represent values for a `Parameter` object.
Size	Long	Specifies the maximum size, in either bytes or characters, of the `Parameter` object.
Type	Long	A value from the `DataTypeEnum` object to specify the data type of the `Parameter` object.
Value	Variant	The default property. Specifies the actual value of the `Parameter` object.

Methods of the Parameter Object

The only method available for the `Parameter` object is `AppendChunk`, described in this section.

The Parameter.AppendChunk Method

The `AppendChunk` method is used to append large amounts of binary or text data to the `Parameter` object in smaller chunks. If called, the `Parameter.Attributes` property must be set to `adParamLong`. The first time this method is called, it overwrites any existing data that may already be stored in the `Parameter` object. All subsequent calls will append data. This method has one parameter.

PARAMETER	DATA TYPE	DESCRIPTION
Data	Variant	The data to be appended to the `Parameter` object.

This method does not return any values.

Collections of the Parameter Object

There is one collection for the `Parameter` object, which is the `Properties` collection.

The Parameter.Properties Collection

The `Properties` collection of the `Parameter` object contains all of the `Property` objects for a specific instance of an ADO parameter. See the section "The Properties Collections" later in this appendix for a complete listing of the methods and properties of the `Properties` collection and the `Property` object.

THE RECORDSET OBJECT

The `Recordset` object is used to read or manipulate data in an ADO data source. It represents the set of records from a table or the results of an executed command, such as a query. All `Recordset` objects consist of records (rows), which are made up of `Record` objects, and fields (columns), which made up of `Field` objects. Depending on the functionality supported by the ADO provider, some `Recordset` methods or properties may not be available, but in general, the following items are supported.

Properties of the Recordset Object

The following table describes the properties of the `Recordset` object. All fields are read and write, unless otherwise noted in the description.

PROPERTY	DATA TYPE	DESCRIPTION
AbsolutePage	Long	Gets/sets the page the current record of the `Recordset` is on. Setting this will move the cursor to the top of the chosen page. If the cursor is not pointing at a valid record when accessing this property, a value from the `PositionEnum` will be returned.
AbsolutePosition	Long	Read-only. Specifies the position of the current record in the `Recordset`. If the cursor is not pointing at a valid record when accessing this property, a value from the `PositionEnum` will be returned.
ActiveCommand	Variant	Read-only. References to the `Command` object that created the `Recordset`.

continues

(continued)

PROPERTY	DATA TYPE	DESCRIPTION
ActiveConnection	String or Connection	Specifies the Connection object used to retrieve the Recordset.
BOF	Boolean	Read-only. True when the cursor is at the beginning of the file and the position before the first record.
Bookmark	Variant	Gets/sets a cursor to allow returning to a specific record in the Recordset.
CacheSize	Long	Specifies the maximum number of records ADO caches on the server.
CursorLocation	Long	Defines if the cursor service is client-side or server-side. Specified as a member of the CursorLocationEnum.
CursorType	Long	Defines the type of cursor used to access the query results. Specified as a member of the CursorTypeEnum.
DataMember	String	Specifies the name of the data member that will be retrieved from the Recordset that is referenced by the Recordset .DataSource property.
DataSource	Object	Specifies an Object containing a set of data that will be represented as a Recordset object.
EditMode	Long	Read-only. Defines the editing status for the current record. Specified as a member of the EditModeEnum.
EOF	Boolean	Read-only. True if the cursor is currently at the end of the file in a position after the last record in the Recordset.
Filter	Variant	Gets/sets a filter for the Recordset. Valid values can be a criteria String, an array of bookmarks, or one of the FilterGroupEnum values.
Index	String	Gets/sets the name of the current index for the Recordset.
LockType	Long	Specifies the lock type of the Recordset, as one of the values of the LockTypeEnum.
MarshalOptions	Long	Specifies which records are transferred back to the server as a value of the MarshalOptionsEnum.
MaxRecords	Long	Specifies the maximum number of records returned by the query.
PageCount	Long	Read-only. The number of pages in the Recordset.

PROPERTY	DATA TYPE	DESCRIPTION
PageSize	Long	Specifies the number of records per page in the Recordset.
RecordCount	Long	Read-only. Returns the number of records in the Recordset. Supported only when client-side cursors are used.
Sort	String	Specifies a comma delimited string of field names that a Recordset object is to sort on. Any field names with spaces should be enclosed in square brackets and the entire string should be enclosed in double quotes.
Source	String or Command	A query string or a reference to a Command object that is the data source of the Recordset.
StayInSync	Boolean	True if the child record needs to be kept updated. Applies only to hierarchical Recordset objects.
State	Long	Read-only. Returns the current state of the Recordset as a bitwise mask of one or more ObjectStateEnum members.
Status	Long	Read-only. Returns the status of bulk operations for the Recordset, as a bitwise mask of one or more RecordStatusEnum.

Methods of the Recordset Object

The Recordset object has a number of methods that can be used to manipulate the data or the object itself. This section provides a detailed list of each method, its description, any parameters, and the return values of the Recordset object.

The Recordset.AddNew Method

The AddNew method adds a new record to an updatable Recordset with the specified parameters. The following is a description of the two optional parameters.

PARAMETER	DATA TYPE	DESCRIPTION
FieldList	Variant	Optional. This can be a single field name, a comma-delimited string of field names, or the ordinal position of the fields in a record. Field names must be enclosed in double quotes or square brackets.
Values	Variant	Optional. This will be a single value or a comma delimited list of values, depending on the values supplied to the FieldList parameter. When multiple values are used, they must match the order of the names in the FieldList parameter.

This method does not return any values.

The Recordset.Cancel Method

The `Cancel` method cancels the execution of a pending asynchronous method call. The method does not take any parameters or return any values.

The Recordset.CancelBatch Method

The `CancelBatch` method cancels execution of the last pending batch update for the `Recordset`. If canceling the update fails, warnings will be sent to the `Connection.Errors` collection, which should be checked after calling this method. The following is a description of the one parameter.

PARAMETER	DATA TYPE	DESCRIPTION
AffectRecords	Long	Optional. Defines which records are to be affected by the `CancelBatch` method, as a member of the `AffectEnum`. `adAffectAll` is the default.

This method does not return any values.

The Recordset.CancelUpdate Method

The `CancelUpdate` method cancels changes to the current record or discards the row if it is a new `Record`. Changes cannot be canceled if the `Recordset.Update` method has already been called. The method does not take any parameters or return any values.

The Recordset.Clone Method

The `Clone` method creates a new reference to the `Recordset` that allows navigation independently from the original `Recordset`, although they remain the same data and all changes made will be visible to all clones. The following is a description of the one parameter.

PARAMETER	DATA TYPE	DESCRIPTION
LockType	Long	Optional. Specifies which type of lock to use for the new reference to the `Recordset` created by the `Clone` method. Specified as a member of the `LockTypeEnum`, but only two of the five possible values are accepted: `adLockReadOnly` and `adLockUnspecified`.

This method does not return any values.

The Recordset.Close Method

The `Close` method closes the `Recordset` object but does not delete it from memory. The `Open` method can be called later to reopen the `Recordset`, which can even be reopened in different modes. To release the `Recordset` from memory, set it to `Nothing` after calling `Close`. `Close` may discard data or throw an error if batch updates are in progress, so calling Update, UpdateBatch, Cancel, and/or CancelBatch methods before calling Close is recommended. The method does not take any parameters or return any values.

The Recordset.CompareBookmarks Method

The CompareBookmarks method compares the position of two cursors in the same Recordset and returns a value from the CompareEnum describing the relative position of the first bookmark in relation to the second. The following is a description of the two parameters.

PARAMETER	DATA TYPE	DESCRIPTION
Bookmark1	Variant	The Bookmark position that is being compared.
Bookmark2	Variant	The Bookmark position in which Bookmark1 is being compared.

Returns a value from the CompareEnum, as a Long integer, to describe the result of the comparison.

The Recordset.Delete Method

The Delete method marks the current Record in the Recordset for deletion. If the Recordset is in immediate update mode, the record will be removed immediately. If the Recordset is in client-side, batch optimistic updating mode, the record can be manipulated after being marked for deletion, until moving away from the record. In this case, the record will be lost to the Recordset, but not be deleted from the database until UpdateBatch is called, and the deletion can be rolled back by calling the CancelBatch method. For this reason, the Delete method can throw errors, so be sure to check the Connection.Errors collection after calling Delete. The following is a description of the one parameter.

PARAMETER	DATA TYPE	DESCRIPTION
AffectRecords	Long	Optional. Defines which records are to be affected by the Delete method, as a member of the AffectEnum .adAffectCurrent is the default value.

This method does not return any values.

The Recordset.Find Method

The Find method moves the current record cursor to the next record with matching criteria, from the specified start position in the Recordset. If the search fails, the cursor will point to BOF or EOF. The following is a description of the four parameters.

PARAMETER	DATA TYPE	DESCRIPTION
Criteria	String	The criteria to match for the search. This must contain exactly one search field, one comparison operator, and a search value. The only supported comparison operators are: =, >, >=, <, <=, <>, and LIKE. The value can be a number, string, or date. Strings must be enclosed in single quotes or pound signs, while dates must be enclosed by pound signs. Some examples are: `"Pages > 100"`, `"[First Name] = #Geoff#"`, `"Address LIKE '* Baker St'"`, or `"ModifiedDate < #09/01/2009#"`.
SkipRecords	Long	Optional. Specifies the number of records to skip before starting the search. The default is zero, which means start at current record.
SearchDirection	Long	Optional. Specifies the search direction, as a member of the `SearchDirectionEnum`. `adSearchForward` is the default.
Start	Variant	Optional. Specified as a `Bookmark` object, or as a member of the `BookmarkEnum` object to specify the start position of the current search. `adBookmarkCurrent` is the default value.

This method does not return any values.

The Recordset.GetRows Method

The `GetRows` method returns a copy of the specified data from the `Recordset` in a two-dimensional, variant array, where the first dimension is the fields and the second dimension is the records. The following is a description of the three optional parameters.

PARAMETER	DATA TYPE	DESCRIPTION
Rows	Long	Optional. Specified as a value of the `GetRowsOptionEnum`, which contains only one value, `adGetRowsRest`, which is, needless to say, also the default option.
Start	Variant	Optional. Specified as a `Bookmark` object, or as a member of the `BookmarkEnum` object to specify the start position of the current search. `adBookmarkCurrent` is the default value.
Fields	Variant	Optional. Used to specify the names of the fields to be returned. This can be a single field name, a comma-delimited string of field names, or an array of ordinal positions of the fields for the `Recordset`. Field names must be enclosed in double quotes or square brackets. By default, all fields of the `Recordset` will be returned.

This method returns a copy of the data as a two-dimensional `Variant` array object.

The Recordset.GetString Method

The `GetString` method returns the `Recordset` data in a comma-delimited `String` format, based upon the specified parameters. The following is a description of the five optional parameters.

PARAMETER	DATA TYPE	DESCRIPTION
StringFormat	Long	Optional. Specifies the string format to be used when converting the `Recordset` data to a string. Specified as a member of `StringFormatEnum`, which contains only one value, `adClipString`, which is the default.
NumRows	Long	Optional. Specifies the maximum number of rows to be returned by `GetString`. The default is all rows.
ColumnDelimiter	String	Optional. Specifies the character to be used to delimit the `Fields` in the return string.
RowDelimiter	String	Optional. Specifies the character to be used to delimit the `Records` in the return string.
NullExpr	String	Optional. Specifies a string to be used in place of null in the returned string. The default is an empty string.

Returns a delimited `String` containing a copy of the `Recordset` data.

The Recordset.Move Method

The `Move` method moves the current record cursor to the specified location in the `Recordset`. The `Recordset.Update` method will be called implicitly if the current record is modified. Call `Recordset.CancelUpdate` to discard changes before calling the `Move` method. The following is a description of the two parameters.

PARAMETER	DATA TYPE	DESCRIPTION
NumRecords	Long	Specifies the number of records to move the current record cursor. A positive value specifies moving forward and a negative value specifies moving backward, if the `RecordSet.CursorType` supports backward moving cursors.
Start	Variant	Optional. Specified as a `Bookmark` object, or as a member of the `BookmarkEnum` object to specify the start position of the current search. `adBookmarkCurrent` is the default value.

This method does not return any values.

The Recordset.MoveFirst Method

The `MoveFirst` method moves the current record cursor to the first record in the `Recordset`. The `Recordset.Update` method will be called implicitly if the current record is modified. Call

`Recordset.CancelUpdate` to discard changes before calling the `MoveFirst` method. The method does not take any parameters or return any values.

The Recordset.MoveLast Method

The `MoveLast` method moves the current record cursor to the last record in the `Recordset`. The `Recordset.Update` method will be called implicitly if the current record is modified. Call `Recordset.CancelUpdate` to discard changes before calling the `MoveLast` method. The method does not take any parameters or return any values.

The Recordset.MoveNext Method

The `MoveNext` method moves the current record cursor to the next record in the `Recordset`. If the current record cursor is at the last record in the set, then `EOF` will be `TRUE` after calling `MoveNext`. The `Recordset.Update` method will be called implicitly if the current record is modified. Call `Recordset.CancelUpdate` to discard changes before calling the `MoveNext` method. The method does not take any parameters or return any values.

The Recordset.MovePrevious Method

The `MovePrevious` method moves the current record cursor to the previous record in the `Recordset`. If the current record cursor is at the first record in the set, then `BOF` will be `TRUE` after calling `MovePrevious`. The `Recordset.Update` method will be called implicitly if the current record is modified. Call `Recordset.CancelUpdate` to discard changes before calling the `MovePrevious` method. The method does not take any parameters or return any values.

The Recordset.NextRecordset Method

The `NextRecordset` method returns the next `Recordset` in a compound command statement or stored procedure that returns multiple result sets. All edits to the current `Recordset` should be completed before calling `NextRecordset`. The parameter returns the number of records affected by the next command or operation. This method has one optional parameter.

PARAMETER	DATA TYPE	DESCRIPTION
RecordsAffected	Long	Returns the number of records affected by an operation only. It will not return a count of the records used by a `Select` statement to generate the data set.

Returns a `Recordset` of the next `recordset` in a compound command.

The Recordset.Open Method

The `Open` method opens a `Recordset` in the specified mode. A good practice is to call `Close` after calling `Open` on a `Recordset`, once you have finished using that data of course. The following is a description of the five optional parameters.

PARAMETER	DATA TYPE	DESCRIPTION
Source	Variant	Optional. Specifies the data source of the `Recordset`. Can be one of the following: A `Command` object, an SQL command string, the name of an object in the database, a URL specifying a data source, a filename containing a persisted `Recordset`, or a `Stream` object containing a `Recordset`.
ActiveConnection	Variant	Optional. Defines the connection to a data source. Specified as a connection string or `Connection` object.
CursorType	Long	Optional. Defines the type of cursor used for the `Recordset`. Specified as a member of the `CursorTypeEnum`. `adOpenUnspecified` is the default.
LockType	Long	Optional. Defines the type of lock to use for the `Recordset`. Specified as a member of the `LockTypeEnum adLockUnspecified` is the default.
Options	Long	Optional. Specifies how the data source should be interpreted. Can be specified by a single or bitmask combination of the `CommandTypeEnum` and/or the `ExecuteOptionEnum` values.

This method does not return any values.

The Recordset.Requery Method

The `Requery` method re-executes the command that generated the `Recordset`. The following is a description of the one optional parameter.

PARAMETER	DATA TYPE	DESCRIPTION
Options	Long	Optional. Specifies how the command should be re-executed. Specified as a value of the `ExecuteOptionEnum`. `adOptionUnspecified` is the default.

This method does not return any values.

The Recordset.Resync Method

The `Resync` method re-fetches the data and updates the values to the specified values for the current `Recordset`. This will only work on a client-side `Recordset` that is not read-only. The following is a description of the two parameters.

PARAMETER	DATA TYPE	DESCRIPTION
AffectRecords	Long	Optional. Defines which records are to be affected by the Resync method, as a member of the AffectEnum. adAffectAll is the default value.
ResyncValues	Long	Optional. Defines how the Recordset is to be synchronized by the Resync method, as a member of the ResyncEnum. adResyncAllValues is the default value.

This method does not return any values.

The Recordset.Save Method

The Save method writes the Recordset contents to a persisted file or Stream object. The Recordset must be open when calling Save and it will wait until any pending asynchronous operations are complete before the save is performed. The following is a description of the two optional parameters.

PARAMETER	DATA TYPE	DESCRIPTION
Destination	Variant	Optional. Can be specified as a String that is a filename and path or as a Stream object. If nothing is specified for this parameter the first time Save is called, the data will be saved to the Recordset.Source location or throw an error.
PersistFormat	Long	Optional. Defines the data format to be persisted, as a member of the PersistFormatEnum. adPersistADTG is the default value.

This method does not return any values.

The Recordset.Seek Method

The Seek method searches a server-side Recordset using the indexes and sets the current record cursor to the record with the specified criteria. Used as a faster way to search for another record, but the ADO provider must support indexes to implement this method. The following is a description of the two parameters.

PARAMETER	DATA TYPE	DESCRIPTION
KeyValues	Variant	One or more indexes and values stored in a Variant array as the criteria for the record to find.
SeekOption	Long	Optional. Defines how the seek is to be performed. Specified as a member of the SeekEnum. adSeekFirstEQ is the default.

This method does not return any values.

The Recordset.Supports Method

The Supports method returns a Boolean value used to determine if the Recordset supports a particular type of cursor, property, or method, based upon the specified parameter. This method has one parameter.

PARAMETER	DATA TYPE	DESCRIPTION
CursorOption	Long	A bitwise mask of one or more CursorOptionEnum members to check.

Returns a Boolean value specifying if the provided option is supported by the provider.

The Recordset.Update Method

The Update method writes pending changes in the current record to both the Recordset and the data source. This method has two parameters.

PARAMETER	DATA TYPE	DESCRIPTION
Fields	Variant	Optional. Specifies the names of the fields to be updated. This can be a single field name, a comma delimited string of field names, or an array of ordinal positions of the fields for the Recordset. By default, all fields of the Recordset will be updated.
Values	Variant	Optional. Specifies the values of the fields in the Fields parameter to be updated. Can be a single value or an array of values, but must correspond to the fields provided in the Fields parameter.

This method does not return any values.

The Recordset.UpdateBatch Method

The UpdateBatch method writes all pending asynchronous changes in a Recordset to the database when batch optimistic updating is in use. This method has one parameter.

PARAMETER	DATA TYPE	DESCRIPTION
AffectRecords	Long	Optional. Defines which records are to be affected by the UpdateBatch method, as a member of AffectEnum. adAffectAll is the default value.

This method does not return any values.

Collections of the Recordset Object

The Recordset object contains only two collections: Fields and Properties.

The Recordset.Fields Collection

The `Fields` collection of the `Recordset` object contains all of the `Field` objects for a specific instance of a `Recordset`. See the section "The Fields Collection" later in this appendix for specific details about the `Fields` collection and the `Field` object.

The Recordset.Properties Collection

The `Properties` collection of the `Recordset` object contains all of the `Property` objects for the `Recordset`. The section "The Properties Collections" later in this appendix provides a complete listing of the methods and properties of the `Properties` collection and the `Property` object.

THE RECORD OBJECT

The `Record` object represents a row from a `Recordset` or any object returned by a data provider. A `Record` object contains data as a row and allows the user to easily access and manipulate that data. All `Record` objects have fields for each of the columns in the table, and each individual piece of data is placed in its corresponding field. Depending on the functionality supported by the ADO provider, some `Record` methods or properties may not be available, but in general, the following properties, methods, and collections are supported.

Properties of the Record Object

The following table describes the properties associated with a `Record` object.

PROPERTY	DATA TYPE	DESCRIPTION
ActiveConnection	Variant	The `Connection` object used to retrieve the data for the `Record` object.
Mode	Long	The permissions for modifying the `Record` object. Specified as a member of the `ConnectModeEnum`.
ParentURL	String	The Parent URL for the `Record` object.
RecordType	Long	The type of `Record` object. Specified as a member of the `RecordTypeEnum`.
Source	Variant	The source of the data contained in the `Record` object.
State	Long	The state of the `Record` object. Specified as a member of the `ObjectStateEnum`.

Methods of the Record Object

The `Record` object has seven methods for working with the `Record` objects in a `Recordset`.

The Record.Cancel Method

Cancels the asynchronous operation from a call to CopyRecord, DeleteRecord, MoveRecord, or Open methods of the Record object. An error will be generated when calling this method unless the Options parameter of the Execute method is set to either the adAsyncExecute or adAsyncFetch constant. This method does not have any parameters and no return value.

The Record.Close Method

Closes an open Record object. Record objects can be reopened at a later time after closing and closing a Record object does not remove it from memory. To remove the Record from memory, set it equal to Nothing. If there are pending asynchronous operations for the Record, call Update or CancelUpdate before calling close; otherwise an error will be generated. This method does not have any parameters and no return value.

The Record.CopyRecord Method

Copies a Record object, or copies a file or directory (and its contents) to another specified location. By default this method does not overwrite or allow recursive copy, but the Options parameter can be set to do so. This method has six parameters.

PARAMETER	DATA TYPE	DESCRIPTION
Source	String	Optional. Specifies the URL of the file or directory that is to be copied. If not set, then the default value will be the file location of where the Record resides.
Destination	String	Optional. Specifies the URL of the file or directory where the copy will be created. If not set, the default value will be the current directory.
UserName	String	Optional. The user account to use to gain access to the destination location, if required.
Password	String	Optional. The password for the user account.
Options	Long	Optional. Specifies the options to use during the copy. Specified as a member of the CopyRecordOptionsEnum. The default value is adCopyUnspecified.
Async	Boolean	Optional. Specify True if the operation can be asynchronous. False is the default.

Generally returns a String value that is the file or directory path to the destination, but its exact value will be specific to the ADO provider.

The Record.DeleteRecord Method

Deletes the Record object, or deletes a file or directory represented by the Record object. After deleting a Record, changes will not be visible immediately to the Recordset. The best practice is to call the `Update`, `Requery`, or `Resync` methods, or to close and reopen the `Recordset`, to ensure the deletion has been persisted to the data source and `Recordset` object. This method has two parameters.

PARAMETER	DATA TYPE	DESCRIPTION
Source	String	Optional. Specifies the URL of the file or directory that is to be deleted. If not set, then the default value will be the file location of where the Record resides.
Async	Boolean	Optional. Specify True if the operation can be asynchronous. False is the default.

Generally returns a `String` value that is the file or directory path to the deleted data, but its exact value will be specific to the ADO provider.

The Record.GetChildren Method

Retrieves the child data associated with the `Record` object. This method does not have any parameters. Returns a new `Recordset` object with each `Record` representing a child record of the current `Record` object.

The Record.MoveRecord Method

Moves a specified file or directory, represented by the `Record` object, to the specified destination. This method has six parameters.

PARAMETER	DATA TYPE	DESCRIPTION
Source	String	Optional. Specifies the URL of the file or directory that is to be moved. If not set, then the default value will be the file location of where the Record resides.
Destination	String	Optional. Specifies the URL of the file or directory where the data is to be moved. If not set, the default value will be the current directory.
UserName	String	Optional. The user account to use to gain access to the destination location, if required.
Password	String	Optional. The password for the user account.
Options	Long	Optional. Specifies the options to use during the copy. Specified as a member of the MoveRecordOptionsEnum. The default value is adMoveUnspecified.
Async	Boolean	Optional. Specify True if the operation can be asynchronous. False is the default.

Generally returns a `String` value that is the file or directory path to the moved data, but its exact value will be specific to the ADO provider.

The Record.Open Method

Opens an existing `Record` object, or creates a new file or directory represented by the `Record` object. This method has seven parameters.

PARAMETER	DATA TYPE	DESCRIPTION
Source	Variant	Optional. Specifies the data source of the `Record` to be opened. Can be one of the following: a `Command` object, a SQL command string, the name of an object in the database, a URL specifying a data source, a filename containing a persisted `Record`, or another `Record` object.
ActiveConnection	Variant	Optional. Defines the connection to a data source. Specified as a connection string or `Connection` object.
Mode	Long	Optional. Specifies the connection mode to the object being opened. Specified as a bitwise combination of one or more members of the `ConnectModeEnum`. The default value is `adModeUnknown`.
CreateOptions	Long	Optional. Specifies if the `Record` object should be opened or created new. Specified as a bitwise combination of one or more members of the `RecordCreateOptionsEnum`. The default value is `adFailIfNotExists`.
Options	Long	Optional. Specifies the open options for the `Record`, if open is selected in the `CreateOptions` parameter. Specified as a member of the `RecordOpenOptionsEnum`. The default is `adOpenRecordUnspecified`.
UserName	String	Optional. The user account to use to gain access to the source location, if required.
Password	String	Optional. The password for the specified user account.

Collections of the Record Object

The `Record` object has two collections, the `Fields` and `Properties` collections, which are described in the sections that follow.

The Record.Fields Collection

The `Fields` collection of the `Record` object contains all of the `Field` objects for a specific instance of a `Record`. See the section "The Fields Collection" later in this appendix for specific details about the Fields collection.

The Record.Properties Collection

The `Properties` collection of the `Record` object contains all of the `Property` objects for the `Record`. The section "The Properties Collections" later in this appendix provides a complete listing of the methods and properties of the `Properties` collection and the `Property` object.

THE FIELDS COLLECTION

The `Fields` collection contains all the `Field` objects of a `Recordset` or `Record` object. The `Fields` collection allows you to retrieve information about the field as well as data within the field. The following sections describe the properties and methods for the `Fields` collection.

Properties of the Fields Collection

The `Fields` collection supplies two properties: `Count` and `Item`, which are detailed in the following table.

PROPERTY	DATA TYPE	DESCRIPTION
Count	Long	The number of `Field` objects in the `Record` or `Recordset` object.
Item	Field	References the individual `Field` objects by name of ordinal number.

Methods of the Fields Collection

The `Fields` collection has six methods for working with this collection. Each of these methods is outlined in this section.

The Fields.Append Method

The `Append` method will create the `Field` object from the parameters specified and then append it to the collection. This method has five parameters:

PARAMETER	DATA TYPE	DESCRIPTION
Name	String	Specifies the unique name of the `Field` object.
Type	Long	Specifies the data type of the `Field` to be appended. Specified as one of the `DataTypeEnum` members. `adArray`, `adChapter`, or `adEmpty` are invalid here.
DefineSize	Long	Optional. Specifies the length of the new `Field` in bytes (or characters). If larger than 255, the field will be treated as though it has variable length.

PARAMETER	DATA TYPE	DESCRIPTION
Attrib	Long	Optional. Specifies the Field attributes. Specified as a bitwise combination of one of more members of the FieldAttributeEnum. The default is adFldUnspecified.
FieldValue	Variant	Optional. The actual value to be stored in the new Field object.

This method does not return any values.

The Fields.CancelUpdate Method

The CancelUpdate method cancels any pending changes or operations to the Record object. The method does not take any parameters or return any values.

The Fields.Delete Method

The Delete method removes a Field object from the Fields collection. After calling the Delete method, you should call the Update or the CancelUpdate method to complete or reverse the change. This method has only one parameter.

PARAMETER	DATA TYPE	DESCRIPTION
Index	String or Long	References the specific member of the collection that is to be removed by name or ordinal number.

This method does not return any values.

The Fields.Refresh Method

The Refresh method updates the Fields collection and persists any pending changes for the Recordset object only. This method does not have any effect for the Fields collection of the Record object; instead, use the Update method for the Fields collection when working with the Record object. The method does not take any parameters or return any values.

The Fields.Resync Method

The Resync method is used to re-fetch all of the data for the data source and updates the OriginalValue, UnderlyingValue, and Value properties for the Field object. This method has only one parameter.

PARAMETER	DATA TYPE	DESCRIPTION
ResyncValues	Long	Specifies which values can be overwritten when synchronizing. Specified as a member of the ResyncEnum. adResyncAllValues is the default value.

This method does not return any values.

The Fields.Update Method

The Update method updates the Fields collection and persists any pending changes. This is the method that should be used to persist updates to the Record.Fields collection, instead of the Refresh method. The method does not take any parameters or return any values.

THE FIELD OBJECT

The Fields collection contains Field objects. Each object represents an individual Field within a Fields collection from an ADO Record or Recordset object.

Properties of the Field Object

The properties for the Field object are described in the following table.

PROPERTY	DATA TYPE	DESCRIPTION
ActualSize	Long	Returns the actual size of the value of the Field.
Attributes	Long	Describes certain characteristics of the Field.
DataFormat	Object	Used to specify the format of the data in the Field.
DefinedSize	Long	Describes the defined size for the Field.
Name	String	Contains the name of the Field.
NumericScale	Byte	Number of digits allowed to the right of the decimal point for a numeric Field.
OriginalValue	Variant	Stores the original value for the Field.
Precision	Byte	Defines the precision for numeric data.
Status	Long	Determines whether the field has been successfully added to the collection. Specified as a member of the FieldStatusEnum.
Type	Byte	Lists the data type for the Field.
UnderlyingValue	Variant	Lists the most recently retrieved value for the Field.
Value	Variant	Contains the value for the Field.

Methods of the Field Object

The Field object has two methods, which are outlined in detail in this section. These methods apply only to String or Binary Field types and may not be supported by all ADO providers.

The Field.AppendChunk Method

This method appends large amounts of `String` or `Binary` data to the `Field` in smaller chunks. If called, the `adFldLong` members of the `Field.Attributes` must be set to `True`. The first time this method is called, it overwrites any existing data that may already be stored in the `Parameter` object. All subsequent calls will append data. This method has one parameter.

PARAMETER	DATA TYPE	DESCRIPTION
Data	Variant	The `String` or `Binary` data to be appended to the `Field` object.

This method does not return any values.

The Field.GetChunk Method

The `GetChunk` method fetches a portion of the data from a `Field` object. The first call starts from the beginning of the data and each additional call starts from the previous end point in the data. If the `Field` is empty, then `Null` will be returned. This method has one parameter:

PARAMETER	DATA TYPE	DESCRIPTION
Size	Long	Specifies the number of `Bytes` or `String` characters to be returned by each call to `GetChunk`.

This method returns a Variant with the specified portion of the data value from the `Field`.

Collections of the Field Object

The only collection of the `Field` object is the standard `Properties` collection.

The Field.Properties Collection

The `Properties` collection of the `Field` object contains all of the `Property` objects for the `Field`. The section "The Properties Collections" later in this appendix provides a complete listing of the methods and properties of the `Properties` collection and the `Property` object.

THE STREAM OBJECT

The ADO `Stream` object provides the ability to read, write, and manage a stream of binary or text data. The ADO `Stream` object was added in version 2.5, so be aware that not all ADO providers support the `Stream` object. The `Stream` object has only properties and methods; it does not have any events or collections. This section outlines the properties and methods for the ADO `Stream` object.

Properties for the Stream Object

The following table lists the all of the properties of the Stream object.

PROPERTY	DATA TYPE	DESCRIPTION
CharSet	String	Specifies the character set for the stream.
EOS	Boolean	True if the cursor position is at the end of the stream.
LineSeparator	Long	Specifies the characters used as the line separator in the stream. Specified as a member of the LineSeparatorEnum.
Mode	Long	Specifies the permissions for modifying data in the Stream object. Specified as a member of the ConnectModeEnum.
Position	Long	Specifies the cursor position in the Stream.
Size	Long	Specifies the current size in bytes of the Stream.
State	Long	Specifies the current state of the Stream object. Specified as a member of the ObjectStateEnum.
Type	Long	Specifies the type of data stored in the Stream object. Specified as a member of the StreamTypeEnum.

Methods for the Stream Object

The Stream object has 13 methods for manipulating a particular stream. Each of these methods is outlined in this section.

The Stream.Cancel Method

The Cancel method for the Stream object cancels the execution of a pending Open method call. The method does not take any parameters or return any values.

The Stream.Close Method

The Close method for the Stream object closes the Stream. The Stream can be reopened at a later time after closing, with different properties if desired. To remove a Stream object from memory, set it to Nothing. The method does not take any parameters or return any values.

The Stream.CopyTo Method

The CopyTo method copies data from one Stream object to another Stream object. A text Stream can be copied into a binary Stream, but not binary into text. The CharSet property for the destination Stream can be different than the source Stream. This method has two parameters.

PARAMETER	DATA TYPE	DESCRIPTION
DestStream	Stream	The Stream being copied to.
NumChars	Long	Optional. The number of characters or bytes in the source Stream. The default is –1, which copies all data.

This method does not return any values.

The Stream.Flush Method

The Flush method writes all remaining data in the Stream buffer. This method is rarely called because the Stream continuously flushes itself, but this method is typically called before closing the Stream to ensure all data has been written. The method does not take any parameters or return any values.

The Stream.LoadFromFile Method

The LoadFromFile method is used to load a persisted data set from a file into the Stream object. All existing data in the Stream will be overwritten and the cursor will be set to the start of the data. This method has one parameter:

PARAMETER	DATA TYPE	DESCRIPTION
FileName	String	Specifies the full name and path to the file that will be loaded into the Stream object.

This method does not return any values.

The Stream.Open Method

The Open method is used to open a new Stream object. The new Stream can be an already existing Stream, a Stream that has been previously closed, or a completely new Stream object. This method has five parameters.

PARAMETER	DATA TYPE	DESCRIPTION
Source	Variant	Optional. Specifies the source Stream to be opened. Can be a URL, another Stream, or an open Record. The default is to create a new Stream object.
Mode	Long	Optional. Specifies the permissions for modifying data in the Stream object. Specified as a member of the ConnectModeEnum. The default is adModeUnknown.

continues

(continued)

PARAMETER	DATA TYPE	DESCRIPTION
OpenOptions	Long	Optional. Specifies the options for opening the Stream object. Specified as a member of the StreamOpenOptionsEnum. The default is adOpenStreamUnspecified.
UserName	String	Optional. The user account to use to gain access to the source location, if required.
Password	String	Optional. The password for the specified user account.

This method does not return any values.

The Stream.Read Method

The Read method is used to read the specified number of bytes, or a complete binary file, from the Stream object. This method has one parameter.

PARAMETER	DATA TYPE	DESCRIPTION
NumBytes	Long	Optional. Specifies the number of bytes to read from the Stream object. Can either be the actual number of bytes to be read *or* as a member of the StreamReadEnum. The default is adReadAll.

This method returns a Variant object containing the data that was read from the Stream.

The Stream.ReadText Method

The ReadText method is used to read the specified number of characters, or a complete text file, from the Stream object. This method has one parameter.

PARAMETER	DATA TYPE	DESCRIPTION
NumBytes	Long	Optional. Specifies the number of bytes to read from the Stream object. Can either be the actual number of bytes to be read or as a member of the StreamReadEnum. The default is adReadAll.

This method returns a String object containing the text that was read from the Stream.

The Stream.SaveToFile Method

The SaveToFile method is used for saving the contents of a Stream object to a local file. Calling this method does not alter the Stream in any way. This method has two parameters.

PARAMETER	DATA TYPE	DESCRIPTION
FileName	String	The name and path of the file to save the data.
SaveOptions	Long	Optional. Specifies the options for saving the file. Specified as a member of the SaveOptionsEnum. The default is adSaveCreateNotExist.

This method does not return any values.

The Stream.SetEOS Method

The SetEOS method sets the current location cursor as the end of the Stream object. Any data beyond the current position will be truncated and lost. The method does not take any parameters or return any values.

The Stream.SkipLine Method

The SkipLine method is used to move the cursor from the current position to the position just after the next line separator in the Stream object. The method does not take any parameters or return any values.

The Stream.Write Method

The Write method is used to write binary data to a Stream object. When calling this method, it is very important to consider the current position of the cursor in the Stream object. To append data to the end of the Stream, use the Position property to move to the end of the Stream object. If Write is called and the cursor is at the beginning or in the middle of the Stream, the data in the Stream will be overwritten and any existing text that was longer than the written text will be left. In this situation, it is a good idea to then call SetEOS to truncate any data after the current position. For a text Stream, use the WriteText method instead of this one. This method has one parameter.

PARAMETER	DATA TYPE	DESCRIPTION
Buffer	Variant	The binary data to be written to the Stream.

This method does not return any values.

The Stream.WriteText Method

The WriteText method is used to write text data to a Stream object. When calling this method, it is very important to consider the current position of the cursor. To append data to the end of the Stream, use the Position property to move to the end of the Stream object. If WriteText is called and the cursor is at the beginning or in the middle of the Stream, the data in the Stream will be overwritten and any existing text that was longer than the written text will be left at the end. In this situation, it is a good idea to then call `SetEOS` to truncate any data after the current position. For a binary `Stream`, use the `Write` method instead of this one. This method has two parameters.

PARAMETER	DATA TYPE	DESCRIPTION
Data	String	The text data to be written to the `Stream`.
Options	Long	Optional. Specifies the options for writing to the `Stream`. Specified as a member of the `StreamWriteEnum`. The default is `adWriteChar`.

This method does not return any values.

THE PROPERTIES COLLECTIONS

There are many `Properties` collections built into ADO, all of which contain individual `Property` objects representing the dynamic properties of a given object. Depending on the version of ADO being used, the objects that expose a `Properties` collection will vary, but in general, ADODB supports the `Properties` collection for the `Connection`, `Command`, `Parameters`, `Recordset`, and `Field` objects. Additionally, ADOX supports the `Properties` collection for the `Table`, `Column`, and `Index` objects. The structure of these `Properties` collections and their `Property` objects is essentially all the same and is described in this section.

The Properties Collection

The `Properties` collection contains all of the `Property` objects for a specific instance of its given object. The `Properties` collection has two properties and one method, described in the subsections that follow.

Properties of the Properties Collection

The two properties of the `Properties` collection are summarized in the following table.

PROPERTY	DATA TYPE	DESCRIPTION
Count	Long	Returns the number of `Property` objects stored in the `Properties` collection.
Item	String or Long	References a specific member of the `Properties` collection by name or ordinal number.

Methods of the Properties Collection

The following table describes the one method of the `Properties` collection.

METHOD	DESCRIPTION
Refresh	No Parameters. Updates the `Properties` collection to encompass all current `Property` objects.

THE PROPERTY OBJECT

Each Property object represents an individual, dynamic property designed to provide information about a specific ADO object. The Property object consists of four individual property values and does not have any methods or collections.

Properties of the Property Object

The Property object is built from four property values, each of which is designed to provide a piece of information about a dynamic property of a particular ADO object. The values of these properties will vary depending on the ADO object, the data provider, and the specific use of the Property.

PROPERTY	DATA TYPE	DESCRIPTION
Attributes	Long	A Long value that indicates characteristics of the property that are provider-specific.
Name	String	A String that identifies the property.
Type	Integer	An Integer that specifies the property data type.
Value	Variant	The default property value. A Variant that contains the property setting.

THE ADO ENUMERATIONS

The ADO object has many different enumerations to represent lots of different parameter options and property values throughout its object model. The following section describes each of the ADO enumeration objects discussed previously throughout this appendix. However, this is not a complete list of ADO enumerations. For a complete listing of all the ADO enumeration objects, see the MSDN library at www.msdn.microsoft.com.

The AffectEnum Members

The AffectEnum is used in conjunction with the AffectRecords parameter of the Recordset.CancelBatch, Recordset.Delete, and Recordset.UpdateBatch methods.

MEMBER	VALUE	DESCRIPTION
adAffectAll	3	Specifies all records in the Recordset, including those hidden by a filter.
adAffectAllChapters	4	Specifies all records in all child Recordset objects for that Recordset.
adAffectCurrent	1	Specifies the current record only.
adAffectGroup	2	Specifies only the filtered records in the Recordset.

The BookmarkEnum Members

The `BookmarkEnum` is used in conjunction with the `Start` parameter of the `Recordset.Find`, `Recordset.GetRows`, and `Recordset.Move` methods.

MEMBER	VALUE	DESCRIPTION
adBookmarkCurrent	0	Specifies the current record in the `Recordset`.
adBookmarkFirst	1	Specifies the first record in the `Recordset`.
adBookmarkLast	2	Specifies the last record in the `Recordset`.

The CommandTypeEnum Members

The `CommandTypeEnum` values can be used in the `Options` parameter of the various `Execute`, `Open`, and `Requery` methods. For the `Execute` method, these values can be used in combination with the `ExecuteOptionEnum` when specifying values for the `Options` parameter.

MEMBER	VALUE	DESCRIPTION
adCmdFile	256	The argument is the filename of a persistently stored `Recordset`.
adCmdStoredProc	4	The argument is the name of a stored procedure.
adCmdTable	2	The argument is the name of a table.
adCmdTableDirect	512	The argument is the name of a table. This option cannot be combined with `adAsyncExecute`.
adCmdText	1	The argument is a command or the name of a stored procedure.
adCmdUnknown	8	The type of command is unknown.
adCmdUnspecified	-1	Hidden. No command type is specified.

The CompareEnum Members

The `CompareEnum` is used to describe the relative position of one bookmark to another in a `Recordset`.

MEMBER	VALUE	DESCRIPTION
adCompareEqual	1	Specifies that the bookmarks have an equal position.
adCompareGreaterThan	2	Specifies that the first bookmark is after the second.
adCompareLessThan	0	Specifies that the first bookmark is before the second.
adCompareNotComparable	4	Specifies that the bookmarks are not comparable.
adCompareNotEqual	3	Specifies that the bookmarks are not equal and not ordered.

The ConnectOptionEnum Members

The ConnectOptionEnum has only two values that can be used in the Options parameter of the Connection.Open method.

MEMBER	VALUE	DESCRIPTION
adConnectUnspecified	-1	Opens a synchronous connection to the data source, returning only when the connection has been established.
adAsyncConnect	16	Opens an asynchronous connection to the data source, returning immediately, regardless of whether the connection has been established.

The ConnectModeEnum Members

The ConnectModeEnum is used to specify the permissions for the Connection, Record, Recordset, and Stream objects' mode.

MEMBER	VALUE	DESCRIPTION
adModeRead	1	Specifies read-only permissions.
adModeReadWrite	3	Specifies read/write permissions.
adModeRecursive	4194304	Is bit-masked with other members of the ConnectModeEnum to propagate sharing restrictions to all sub-records of the current Record. Can be used with adModeShareDenyNone only when combined with other members, otherwise an error.
adModeShareDenyNone	16	Specifies allowing others to open a connection to this object in any permission mode.
adModeShareDenyRead	4	Specifies preventing others from opening a connection to this object with read permissions.
adModeShareDenyWrite	8	Specifies preventing others from opening a connection to this object with write permissions.
adModeShareExclusive	12	Specifies preventing others from opening any connection to this object.
adModeUnknown	0	Specifies that the permissions have not been set or are undetermined.
adModeWrite	2	Specifies write-only permissions.

The CopyRecordOptionsEnum Members

The `CopyRecordOptionsEnum` is used to describe the options to be used during a `Record` copy.

MEMBER	VALUE	DESCRIPTION
`adCopyAllowEmulation`	4	If the copy fails because the destination is a different server or uses a different provider than the source, then the source provider should attempt to simulate the copy by using the `Upload`, `Download`, and `Delete` methods.
`adCopyNonRecursive`	2	Specifies copying the directory and the files in it, but not subdirectories.
`adCopyOverWrite`	1	Specifies overwriting the existing file or directory at the destination.
`adCopyUnspecified`	-1	Specifies the basic copy options, but does not allow overwrite or recursive copy.

The CursorLocationEnum Members

The `CursorLocationEnum` is used in conjunction with the `Recordset.CursorLocation` property.

MEMBER	VALUE	DESCRIPTION
`adUseClient`	3	Specifies using a client-side cursor that is supplied by the local cursor library.
`adUseClientBatch`	3	Obsolete. Same as using the `adUseClient` member.
`adUseNone`	1	Obsolete. Specifies using no cursor service.
`adUseServer`	2	Specifies using the cursor supplied by the ADO provider or database server.

The CursorOptionEnum Members

The `CursorOptionEnum` is used in conjunction with the `CursorOption` parameter of the `Recordset.Supports` method.

MEMBER	VALUE	DESCRIPTION
`adAddNew`	16778240	Supports the `AddNew` method.
`adApproxPosition`	16384	Supports the `AbsolutePosition` and `AbsolutePage` properties.

MEMBER	VALUE	DESCRIPTION
adBookmark	8192	Supports the Bookmark property.
adDelete	16779264	Supports the Delete method.
adFind	524288	Supports the Find method.
adHoldRecords	256	Supports fetching records and changing the cursor position without having to save pending changes.
adIndex	1048576	Supports the Index property.
adMovePrevious	512	Supports the GetRows, Move, MoveFirst, and MoveLast methods.
adNotify	262144	Supports Recordset events.
adResync	131072	Supports the Resync method.
adSeek	2097152	Supports the Seek method.
adUpdate	16809984	Supports the Update method.

The CursorTypeEnum Members

The CursorTypeEnum is used in conjunction with the Recordset.CursorType property and the Recordset.Open method.

MEMBER	VALUE	DESCRIPTION
adOpenDynamic	2	Specifies a dynamic cursor with both forward and backward scrolling. All changes made to the Recordset are visible to other users.
adOpenForwardOnly	0	Specifies a forward-only, static cursor. Improves performance for one-pass operations. Changes are not visible to other users.
adOpenKeyset	1	Specifies a keyset cursor. All changes are visible to other users, except additions by other users are not visible in the current Recordset.
adOpenStatic	3	Specifies a static cursor. This is a forward and backward scrolling cursor in an unchangeable copy of records in the Recordset.
adOpenUnspecified	-1	The cursor type is not specified.

The DataTypeEnum Members

The `DataTypeEnum` values are used for `Type` property of `Parameter` and `Field` objects.

MEMBER	VALUE	OLE DB TYPE	DESCRIPTION
adArray	8192	None	Always combined with another `DataTypeEnum` value. Denotes an array of the other data type. Not valid for ADOX.
adBigInt	20	DBTYPE_I8	An 8-byte signed integer type.
adBinary	128	DBTYPE_BYTES	A `Binary` type.
adBoolean	11	DBTYPE_BOOL	A `Boolean` type.
adBSTR	8	DBTYPE_BSTR	A null-terminated Unicode string.
adChapter	136	DBTYPE_HCHAPTER	A 4-byte type, used to identify rows in a child rowset.
adChar	129	DBTYPE_STR	A `String` type.
adCurrency	6	DBTYPE_CY	A `Currency` type.
adDate	7	DBTYPE_DATE	A `Date` type.
adDBDate	133	DBTYPE_DBDATE	A `Date` type in the format YYYYMMDD.
adDBTime	134	DBTYPE_DBTIME	A `Time` type in the format HHMMSS.
adDBTimeStamp	135	DBTYPE_DBTIMESTAMP	A `Date/Time` type in the format YYYYMMDDHHMMSS plus the fraction of seconds (in billionths).
adDecimal	14	DBTYPE_DECIMAL	A `Decimal` type with fixed precision.
adDouble	5	DBTYPE_R8	A double-precision floating point type.
adEmpty	0	DBTYPE_EMPTY	An empty type value.
adError	10	DBTYPE_ERROR	A 32-bit integer to represent an error code value.

MEMBER	VALUE	OLE DB TYPE	DESCRIPTION
adFileTime	64	DBTYPE_FILETIME	A 64-bit integer to represent the number of 100 nanosecond intervals since January 1, 1601.
adGUID	72	DBTYPE_GUID	A GUID type.
adIDispatch	9	DBTYPE_IDISPATCH	A pointer to an IDispatch interface on a COM object. Not supported by ADO.
adInteger	3	DBTYPE_I4	A 4-byte signed integer.
adIUnknown	13	DBTYPE_IUNKNOWN	A pointer to an IUnknown interface on a COM object. Not supported by ADO.
adLongVarBinary	205	None	A Long binary type.
adLongVarChar	201	None	A long String type.
adLongVarWChar	203	None	A long null-terminated Unicode String type.
adNumeric	131	DBTYPE_NUMERIC	A fixed precision numeric type.
adPropVariant	138	DBTYPE_PROP_VARIANT	An Automation PROPVARIANT type.
adSingle	4	DBTYPE_R4	A single-precision floating-point type.
adSmallInt	2	DBTYPE_I2	A 2-byte signed integer.
adTinyInt	16	DBTYPE_I1	A 1-byte signed integer.
adUnsignedBigInt	21	DBTYPE_UI8	An 8-byte unsigned integer.
adUnsignedInt	19	DBTYPE_UI4	A 4-byte unsigned integer.
adUnsignedSmallInt	18	DBTYPE_UI2	A 2-byte unsigned integer.
adUnsignedTinyInt	17	DBTYPE_UI1	A 1-byte unsigned integer.
adUserDefined	132	DBTYPE_UDT	A user-defined variable type.
adVarBinary	204	None	A Binary type.
adVarChar	200	None	A String type.

continues

(continued)

MEMBER	VALUE	OLE DB TYPE	DESCRIPTION
adVariant	12	DBTYPE_VARIANT	An Automation Variant type. Not supported by ADO.
adVarNumeric	139	None	A Numeric type.
adVarWChar	202	None	A null-terminated Unicode character string type.
adWChar	130	DBTYPE_WSTR	A null-terminated Unicode character string type.

The EditModeEnum Members

The EditModeEnum is used to specify the editing state of a Record or a Recordset object.

MEMBER	VALUE	DESCRIPTION
adEditAdd	2	Specifies that the AddNew method has been called and the current record in the copy buffer is a new record that has not been saved to the database.
adEditDelete	4	Specifies that the current record has been deleted.
adEditInProgress	1	Specifies that data in the current record has been modified, but not yet saved.
adEditNone	0	Specifies that no editing operation has occurred.

The ExecuteOptionEnum Members

The ExecuteOptionEnum values can be used in the Options parameter of the various Execute and Requery methods. The value can be a bitmask combination of one or more members in the CommandTypeEnum when specifying a value for the Options parameter.

MEMBER	VALUE	DESCRIPTION
adOptionUnspecified	-1	Hidden. The command is not specified.
adAsyncExecute	16	The command executes asynchronously. This option cannot be combined with adCmdTableDirect.
adAsyncFetch	32	The rows that remain to be retrieved after those specified by the CacheSize property are to be retrieved asynchronously.

MEMBER	VALUE	DESCRIPTION
adAsyncFetchNonBlocking	64	The main thread never blocks while retrieving data, so if the requested row has not been retrieved, the current row automatically moves to the end of the file. This setting is ignored if the adCmdTableDirect option is used, or if you open a Recordset from a stream that contains a persistently stored RecordSet.
adExecuteNoRecords	128	The CommandText argument is a command or stored procedure that does not return records.
adExecuteStream	1024	Return the results of a command operation as a Stream object (used with Command.Execute only).
adExecuteRecord	2048	Hidden. The CommandText argument is a command or stored procedure that returns a single row as a Record object.

The FieldAttributeEnum Members

The FieldAttributeEnum is used to specify the attributes for a field object. The value can be specified as a bitwise combination of one or more of these members.

MEMBER	VALUE	DESCRIPTION
adFldCacheDeferred	4096	Specifies that the provider should cache the data values.
adFldFixed	16	Specifies that the Field has fixed-length data.
adFldIsChapter	8192	Specifies that the Field is a chapter value with a child Recordset.
adFldIsCollection	262144	Specifies that the Field is a collection of resources.
adFldIsDefaultStream	131072	Specifies that the Field contains a default stream.
adFldIsNullable	32	Specifies that the Field accepts null values.
adFldIsRowURL	65536	Specifies that the Field contains a URL that names a resource from the data store for the Record.
adFldKeyColumn	32768	Specifies that the Field is the primary key or part of the primary key.
adFldLong	128	Specifies that the Field is a long binary field that can use the AppendChunk and GetChunk methods.

continues

(continued)

MEMBER	VALUE	DESCRIPTION
adFldMayBeNull	64	Specifies that the `Field` can have null values.
adFldMayDefer	2	Specifies that the `Field` values are returned only when the `Field` is explicitly accessed, and not returned when the entire record is requested.
adFldNegativeScale	16384	Specifies that the `Field` will allow negative scale values.
adFldRowID	256	Specifies that the `Field` stores a row identifier used only to identify this row.
adFldRowVersion	512	Specifies that the `Field` uses a time/date stamp for version updates.
adFldUnknownUpdatable	8	Specifies that the provider cannot determine if data can be written to the `Field`.
adFldUnspecified	-1	Specifies that the `Field` does not specify attributes.
adFldUpdatable	4	Specifies that data can be written to the `Field`.

The FieldStatusEnum Members

The `FieldAttributeEnum` values can be a bitwise combination of one or more of these members to specify the status and the operations that caused the `Status` property to be set.

MEMBER	VALUE	DESCRIPTION
adFieldAlreadyExists	26	Specifies that the `Field` already exists.
adFieldBadStatus	12	Specifies that the status value sent from the ADO to the OLE DB provider was invalid.
adFieldCannotComplete	20	Specifies that the operation could not be completed by the server of the data source.
adFieldCannotDeleteSource	23	Specifies that a tree was moved to a new location, but the source could not be deleted.
adFieldCantConvertValue	2	Specifies that the data cannot be stored or fetched without data loss due to conversion.
adFieldCantCreate	7	Specifies that a `Field` could not be added due to a provider limitation.

MEMBER	VALUE	DESCRIPTION
adFieldDataOverflow	6	Specifies that a data overflow occurred for the `Field` due to the data returned by the provider.
adFieldDefault	13	Specifies that the default value for the `Field` was used when the value was set.
adFieldDoesNotExist	16	Specifies that the `Field` provided does not exist.
adFieldIgnore	15	Specifies that this `Field` was not set when the record was created.
adFieldIntegrityViolation	10	Specifies that the `Field` cannot be modified because it is a derived entity.
adFieldInvalidURL	17	Specifies that there are invalid characters in the data source URL.
adFieldIsNull	3	Specifies that the provider returned a `VARIANT` value of type `VT_NULL`.
adFieldOK	0	Specifies that the `Field` was added or deleted without error.
adFieldOutOfSpace	22	Specifies that the provider is unable to obtain enough storage to complete a move or copy.
adFieldPendingChange	262144	Specifies that the `Field` has been modified and is pending a call to `Update` or `CancelUpdate` to complete.
adFieldPendingDelete	131072	Specifies that a `Delete` call is pending a call to `Update` or `CancelUpdate` to complete.
adFieldPendingInsert	65536	Specifies that the `Append` method added a `Field` to the `Fields` collection and is pending a call to `Update` or `CancelUpdate` to complete.
adFieldPendingUnknown	524288	Specifies that an unknown source caused the `Field` to be modified and is pending a call to `Update` or `CancelUpdate` to complete.
adFieldPendingUnknownDelete	1048576	Specifies that an unknown source caused the `Field` to be deleted and is pending a call to `Update` or `CancelUpdate` to complete.

continues

(continued)

MEMBER	VALUE	DESCRIPTION
adFieldPermissionDenied	9	Specifies that permission to modify the `Field` or data has been denied.
adFieldReadOnly	24	Specifies that the `Field` is read-only.
adFieldResourceExists	19	Specifies that the provider could not complete the operation because an object already exists at the destination and it is unable to overwrite the object.
adFieldResourceLocked	18	Specifies that the provider could not complete the operation because the data was locked.
adFieldResourceOutOfScope	25	Specifies that a source or destination is outside the scope of the current record.
adFieldSchemaViolation	11	Specifies that the value violated the schema constraints for the `Field`.
adFieldSignMismatch	5	Specifies that the value fetched by the provider was signed but the `Field` value was unsigned, or the reverse.
adFieldTruncated	4	Specifies that the data was truncated when fetched from the data source.
adFieldUnavailable	8	Specifies that the provider could not determine the value when fetching the data.
adFieldVolumeNotFound	21	Specifies that the provider could not locate the storage volume.

The FilterGroupEnum Members

The `FilterGroupEnum` values can be used to specify a filter for the `Recordset.Filter` property.

MEMBER	VALUE	DESCRIPTION
adFilterAffectedRecords	2	Only displays records changed by the previous call to the `CancelBatch`, `Delete`, `Resync`, or `Update` methods for the `Recordset` object.
adFilterConflictingRecords	5	Only displays the records that failed the last batch update for the `Recordset`.

MEMBER	VALUE	DESCRIPTION
`adFilterFetchedRecords`	3	Only displays the records in the current cache.
`adFilterNone`	0	Removes any applied filters and all underlying records are shown.
`adFilterPendingRecords`	1	Displays changed records that have not yet been saved.

The GetRowsOptionEnum Members

The `GetRowsOptionEnum` is used in conjunction with the `Rows` parameter of the `Recordset` `.GetRows` method.

MEMBER	VALUE	DESCRIPTION
`adGetRowsRest`	-1	Retrieves all records from the provided starting point to the end of the records.

The LineSeparatorEnum Members

The `LineSeparatorEnum` is used to describe the characters used as the line separator in the `Stream` object.

MEMBER	VALUE	DESCRIPTION
`adCR`	13	Specifies a carriage return.
`adCRLF`	-1	Specifies a carriage return and a line feed.
`adLF`	10	Specifies a line feed.

The LockTypeEnum Members

The `LockTypeEnum` values are used to specify the type of lock to be used for the `Recordset` `.LockType` property and the `Recordset.Open` method.

MEMBER	VALUE	DESCRIPTION
`adLockBatchOptimistic`	4	Specifies using optimistic batch update mode, which is required for calling the `BatchUpdate` method.
`adLockOptimistic`	3	Specifies optimistic locking in a record-by-record manner. This type of locking only locks records after the `Update` method is called.

continues

(continued)

MEMBER	VALUE	DESCRIPTION
adLockPessimistic	2	Specifies pessimistic locking, in a record-by-record manner. The type of locking ensures successful editing of the records, usually achieved by immediately locking records directly at the data source, once they have been edited.
adLockReadOnly	1	Default. Specifies that the data is read-only.
adLockUnspecified	-1	No type of lock is specified.

The MarshalOptionsEnum Members

The MarshalOptionsEnum is used in conjunction with the Recordset.MarshalOptions property, which defines how records will be transferred from the client back to the server.

MEMBER	VALUE	DESCRIPTION
adMarshallAll	0	Specifies returning all records to the server.
adMarshallModifiedOnly	1	Specifies returning modified records only.

The MoveRecordOptionsEnum Members

The MoveRecordOptionsEnum is used to describe the options to be used when calling the MoveRecord method.

MEMBER	VALUE	DESCRIPTION
adMoveAllowEmulation	4	If the move fails because the destination is a different server or uses a different provider than the source, then the source provider should attempt to simulate the move by using the Upload, Download, and Delete operations.
adMoveDontUpdateLinks	2	Specifies not updating hypertext links of the current Record object. Not supported by all ADO providers.
adMoveOverWrite	1	Specifies overwriting the existing file or directory at the destination.
adMoveUnspecified	-1	Specifies the basic copy options, but does not allow overwrite.

The ObjectStateEnum Members

The ObjectStateEnum is used in conjunction with the State properties of the Recordset, Record, and Stream objects.

MEMBER	VALUE	DESCRIPTION
adStateClosed	0	Specifies that the object is closed.
adStateConnecting	2	Specifies that the object is connecting to a data source.
adStateExecuting	4	Specifies that the object is executing an operation.
adStateFetching	8	Specifies that the object is fetching data.
adStateOpen	1	Specifies that the object is open.

The ParameterAttributesEnum Members

The ParameterAttributesEnum values are used to specify the Attributes property of Parameter object.

MEMBER	VALUE	DESCRIPTION
adParamLong	128	Specifies that the parameter allows long binary data.
adParamNullable	64	Specifies that the parameter allows null values.
adParamSigned	16	Default. Specifies that the parameter allows signed values.

The ParameterDirectionEnum Members

The ParameterDirectionEnum values are used to specify the Direction property of the Parameter object.

MEMBER	VALUE	DESCRIPTION
adParamInput	1	Default. Specifies an Input parameter.
adParamInputOutput	3	Specifies that the parameter is both Input and Output.
adParamOutput	2	Specifies an Output parameter.
adParamReturnValue	4	Specifies that the parameter is a return value.
adParamUnknown	0	Specifies that the direction is unknown.

The PersistFormatEnum Members

The `PersistFormatEnum` has two values that can be used in the `PersistFormat` parameter of the `Recordset.Save` method.

MEMBER	VALUE	DESCRIPTION
`adPersistADTG`	0	Specifies the Microsoft Advanced Data TableGram (ADTG) format.
`adPersistXML`	1	Specifies the Extensible Markup Language (XML) format.

The PositionEnum Members

A `PositionEnum` value can be returned as an error code to describe the current state of the cursor position when it does not point to a valid record. When the `Recordset.AbsolutePage` property is accessed and the cursor is *not* pointing to a current record, a value from the `PositionEnum` will be returned. When the cursor is *not* pointing to a valid record when the `Recordset.AbsolutePosition` property is called, a member from the `PositionEnum` will be returned.

MEMBER	VALUE	DESCRIPTION
`adPosBOF`	-2	The current record cursor is at the beginning of the file, before the first record.
`adPosEOF`	-3	The current record cursor is at the end of the file, after the last record.
`adPosUnknown`	-1	The current position is unknown, the `Recordset` is empty, or is not supported by the ADO provider.

The RecordCreateOptionsEnum Members

The `RecordCreateOptionsEnum` is used to open options for the `Record` object.

MEMBER	VALUE	DESCRIPTION
`adCreateCollection`	8192	Specifies creating a new `Record` object determined by the `Source` parameter. The `adCreateCollection` can be combined with `adOpenIfExists` or `adCreateOverwrite` to open or overwrite.
`adCreateNonCollection`	0	Specifies creating a new `Record` of type `adSimpleRecord`. Can be combined with `adCreateOverwrite`.

MEMBER	VALUE	DESCRIPTION
adCreateOverwrite	67108864	Specifies overwriting the existing Record or data at the location specified by the Source parameter. Can be combined with the adCreateCollection, adCreateNonCollection, or adCreateStructDoc members. Cannot be used together with adOpenIfExists.
adCreateStructDoc	2147483648	Specifies creating a new Record of type adStructDoc.
adFailIfNotExists	-1	Specifies failing if the Source parameter references non-existent data or is invalid.
adOpenIfExists	33554432	Specifies opening the existing record or data at the location specified by the Source parameter, instead of creating a new record. Can be combined with adCreateCollection, adCreateNonCollection, and adCreateStructDoc.

The RecordOpenOptionsEnum Members

The RecordOpenOptionsEnum is used to describe the open options for a Record.

MEMBER	VALUE	DESCRIPTION
adDelayFetchField	32768	Specifies fetching the fields for the Record only when necessary.
adDelayFetchStream	16384	Specifies fetching the stream for the Record only when necessary.
adOpenAsync	4096	Specifies opening in asynchronous mode.
adOpenExecuteCommand	65536	Specifies that the Source parameter contains command text that should be executed.
adOpenOutput	8388608	Specifies that the Source parameter contains a script that should be executed and the output should be opened. Only valid for non-collection records.
adOpenRecordUnspecified	-1	Specifies that no open options are selected.

The RecordStatusEnum Members

The RecordStatusEnum is used in conjunction with the Recordset.Status property, which is used to describe the current status of a bulk operation. These can be returned as a single value, or a bit-wise combination of multiple options.

MEMBER	VALUE	DESCRIPTION
adRecCanceled	256	The operation was canceled and the record was not saved.
adRecCantRelease	1024	The existing record was locked and was not saved.
adRecConcurrencyViolation	2048	Optimistic concurrency was in use and the record was not saved.
adRecDBDeleted	262144	Specifies the record has already been deleted from the data source.
adRecDeleted	4	Specifies the record was deleted.
adRecIntegrityViolation	4096	The integrity constraints were violated by the user and the record was not saved.
adRecInvalid	16	The bookmark is invalid and the record was not saved.
adRecMaxChangesExceeded	8192	Too many pending changes, the record was not saved.
adRecModified	2	The record has been modified.
adRecMultipleChanges	64	The record was not saved, because multiple records would have been affected.
adRecNew	1	Specifies that the record is new.
adRecObjectOpen	16384	A conflict with an open storage object occurred and the record was not saved.
adRecOK	0	The record was successfully updated.
adRecOutOfMemory	32768	An out-of-memory error occurred and the record was not saved.
adRecPendingChanges	128	The record is referring to a pending insert or other change and was not saved.
adRecPermissionDenied	65536	The user has insufficient permissions, so the record was not saved.

MEMBER	VALUE	DESCRIPTION
adRecSchemaViolation	131072	The record violates the schema of the database, so it was not saved.
adRecUnmodified	8	The record was not modified.

The RecordTypeEnum Members

The RecordTypeEnum is used to specify the type of Record object.

MEMBER	VALUE	DESCRIPTION
adCollectionRecord	1	Specifies the Record has child nodes.
adRecordUnknown	-1	Specifies that the type of Record is unknown.
adSimpleRecord	0	Specifies that the Record does not have child nodes.
adStructDoc	2	Specifies that the Record is a COM structured document.

The ResyncEnum Members

The ResyncEnum has only two values that can be used in the ResyncValues parameter of the Recordset.Resync and Fields.Resync methods.

MEMBER	VALUE	DESCRIPTION
adResyncAllValues	2	Overwrites all values. Pending updates are canceled.
adResyncUnderlyingValues	1	Overwrites underlying values; pending updates are not canceled.

The SaveOptionsEnum Members

The SaveOptionsEnum is used to specify the save options for the Stream object.

MEMBER	VALUE	DESCRIPTION
adSaveCreateNotExist	1	Specifies creating a new file.
adSaveCreateOverwrite	2	Specifies overwriting an existing file.

The SchemaEnum Members

The SchemaEnum can be used in the Schema parameter of the Connection.OpenSchema method; however, not all members are supported by the ACE (or Jet, for previous versions of Access) OLE DB Provider. The following table includes the constraint columns' mapping.

MEMBER	VALUE	DESCRIPTION	CONSTRAINT COLUMNS
adSchemaAsserts	0	Returns the constraints defined in the catalog. Not supported by ACE.	CONSTRAINT_CATALOG CONSTRAINT_SCHEMA CONSTRAINT_NAME
adSchemaCatalogs	1	Returns the catalogs that are accessible from the database. Not supported by ACE.	CATALOG_NAME
adSchemaCharacterSets	2	Returns the character sets defined in the catalog. Not supported by ACE.	CHARACTER_SET_CATALOG CHARACTER_SET_SCHEMA CHARACTER_SET_NAME
adSchemaCheckConstraints	4	Returns the check constraints (validation rules) defined in the catalog.	CONSTRAINT_CATALOG CONSTRAINT_SCHEMA CONSTRAINT_NAME
adSchemaCollations	3	Returns the sort orders defined in the catalog. Not supported by ACE.	COLLATION_CATALOG COLLATION_SCHEMA COLLATION_NAME
adSchemaColumnPrivileges	13	Returns the privileges on columns that are available to, or granted by, a given user. Not supported by ACE.	TABLE_CATALOG TABLE_SCHEMA TABLE_NAME COLUMN_NAME GRANTOR GRANTEE
adSchemaColumns	4	Returns the columns of tables and views that are accessible to a given user.	TABLE_CATALOG TABLE_SCHEMA TABLE_NAME COLUMN_NAME
adSchemaColumnsDomainUsage	11	Returns the columns that are dependent on a domain that is owned by a given user. Not supported by ACE.	DOMAIN_CATALOG DOMAIN_SCHEMA DOMAIN_NAME COLUMN_NAME
adSchemaConstraintColumnUsage	6	Returns the columns used by referential constraints, unique constraints, check constraints, and assertions.	TABLE_CATALOG TABLE_SCHEMA TABLE_NAME COLUMN_NAME

MEMBER	VALUE	DESCRIPTION	CONSTRAINT COLUMNS
adSchemaConstraintTableUsage	7	Returns the tables that are used by referential constraints, unique constraints, check constraints, and assertions for a given user. Not supported by ACE.	TABLE_CATALOG TABLE_SCHEMA TABLE_NAME
adSchemaCubes	32	Returns information about the available cubes (multidimensional data) in a schema (or the catalog, if the provider does not support schemas). Not supported by ACE.	CATALOG_NAME SCHEMA_NAME CUBE_NAME
adSchemaDBInfoKeywords	30	Returns a list of provider-specific keywords.	None
adSchemaDBInfoLiterals	31	Returns a list of provider-specific literals (quotes and escape characters) used in text commands.	None
adSchemaDimensions	33	Returns information about the dimensions in a cube; one row per dimension. Not supported by ACE.	CATALOG_NAME SCHEMA_NAME CUBE_NAME DIMENSION_NAME DIMENSION_UNIQUE_NAME
adSchemaForeignKeys	27	Returns the foreign key columns defined in the catalog.	PK_TABLE_CATALOG PK_TABLE_SCHEMA PK_TABLE_NAME FK_TABLE_CATALOG FK_TABLE_SCHEMA FK_TABLE_NAME
adSchemaHierarchies	34	Returns information about the hierarchies available in a cube dimension. Not supported by ACE.	CATALOG_NAME SCHEMA_NAME CUBE_NAME DIMENSION_UNIQUE_NAME HIERARCHY_NAME HIERARCHY_UNIQUE_NAME

continues

(continued)

MEMBER	VALUE	DESCRIPTION	CONSTRAINT COLUMNS

`adSchemaIndexes`	12	Returns the indexes defined in the catalog.	`TABLE_CATALOG`
			`TABLE_SCHEMA`
			`INDEX_NAME`
			`TYPE`
			`TABLE_NAME`

`adSchemaKeyColumnUsage`	8	Returns the columns that are defined in the catalog as keys.	`CONSTRAINT_CATALOG`
			`CONSTRAINT_SCHEMA`
			`CONSTRAINT_NAME`
			`TABLE_CATALOG`
			`TABLE_SCHEMA`
			`TABLE_NAME`
			`COLUMN_NAME`

`adSchemaLevels`	35	Returns information about the levels available in a cube dimension. Not supported by ACE.	`CATALOG_NAME`
			`SCHEMA_NAME`
			`CUBE_NAME`
			`DIMENSION_UNIQUE_NAME`
			`HIERARCHY_UNIQUE_NAME`
			`LEVEL_NAME`
			`LEVEL_UNIQUE_NAME`

`adSchemaMeasures`	36	Returns information about the available cube measures. Not supported by ACE.	`CATALOG_NAME`
			`SCHEMA_NAME`
			`CUBE_NAME`
			`MEASURE_NAME`
			`MEASURE_UNIQUE_NAME`

`adSchemaMembers`	38	Returns information about the available cube members. Not supported by ACE.	`CATALOG_NAME`
			`SCHEMA_NAME`
			`CUBE_NAME`
			`DIMENSION_UNIQUE_NAME`
			`HIERARCHY_UNIQUE_NAME`
			`LEVEL_UNIQUE_NAME`
			`LEVEL_NUMBER`
			`MEMBER_NAME`
			`MEMBER_UNIQUE_NAME`
			`MEMBER_CAPTION`
			`MEMBER_TYPE`

`adSchemaPrimaryKeys`	28	Returns the primary key columns defined in the catalog.	`PK_TABLE_CATALOG`
			`PK_TABLE_SCHEMA`
			`PK_TABLE_NAME`

MEMBER	VALUE	DESCRIPTION	CONSTRAINT COLUMNS
adSchemaProcedureColumns	29	Returns information about the columns in stored procedures. Not supported by ACE.	PROCEDURE_CATALOG PROCEDURE_SCHEMA PROCEDURE_NAME COLUMN_NAME
adSchemaProcedureParameters	26	Returns information about the parameters and return codes of stored procedures. Not supported by ACE.	PROCEDURE_CATALOG PROCEDURE_SCHEMA PROCEDURE_NAME PARAMETER_NAME
adSchemaProcedures	16	Returns the procedures defined in the catalog. Not supported by ACE.	PROCEDURE_CATALOG PROCEDURE_SCHEMA PROCEDURE_NAME PROCEDURE_TYPE
adSchemaProperties	37	Returns information about the available properties for each level of the cube dimension. Not supported by ACE.	CATALOG_NAME SCHEMA_NAME CUBE_NAME DIMENSION_UNIQUE_NAME HIERARCHY_UNIQUE_NAME LEVEL_UNIQUE_NAME MEMBER_UNIQUE_NAME PROPERTY_TYPE PROPERTY_NAME
adSchemaProviderSpecific	-1	Returns schema information for a provider that defines its own non-standard schema queries.	Provider specific
adSchemaProviderTypes	22	Returns the base data types supported by the provider.	DATA_TYPE BEST_MATCH
adSchemaReferential-Constraints	9	Returns the referential constraints (relationships) defined in the catalog.	CONSTRAINT_CATALOG CONSTRAINT_SCHEMA CONSTRAINT_NAME
adSchemaSchemata	17	Returns the schemas (database objects) that are owned by a given user. Not supported by ACE.	CATALOG_NAME SCHEMA_NAME SCHEMA_OWNER

continues

(continued)

MEMBER	VALUE	DESCRIPTION	CONSTRAINT COLUMNS
adSchemaSQLLanguages	18	Returns the levels of ANSI SQL confor-mance, options, and dialects supported in the catalog. Not sup-ported by ACE.	None
adSchemaStatistics	19	Returns the catalog statistics.	TABLE_CATALOG TABLE_SCHEMA TABLE_NAME
adSchemaTableConstraints	10	Returns the table constraints (validation rules) defined in the catalog.	CONSTRAINT_CATALOG CONSTRAINT_SCHEMA CONSTRAINT_NAME TABLE_CATALOG TABLE_SCHEMA TABLE_NAME CONSTRAINT_TYPE
adSchemaTablePrivileges	14	Returns the privileges on tables that are avail-able to, or granted by, a given user. Not sup-ported by ACE.	TABLE_CATALOG TABLE_SCHEMA TABLE_NAME GRANTOR GRANTEE
adSchemaTables	20	Returns the tables and views defined in the catalog.	TABLE_CATALOG TABLE_SCHEMA TABLE_NAME TABLE_TYPE
adSchemaTranslations	21	Returns the character translations defined in the catalog. Not sup-ported by ACE.	TRANSLATION_CATALOG TRANSLATION_SCHEMA TRANSLATION_NAME
adSchemaTrustees	39	Returns the users and groups defined in the catalog.	None
adSchemaUsagePrivileges	15	Returns the USAGE privileges on objects that are available to, or granted by, a given user. Not supported by ACE.	OBJECT_CATALOG OBJECT_SCHEMA OBJECT_NAME OBJECT_TYPE GRANTOR GRANTEE

MEMBER	VALUE	DESCRIPTION	CONSTRAINT COLUMNS

`adSchemaViewColumnUsage`	24	Returns the columns included in views. Not supported by ACE.	`VIEW_CATALOG`
			`VIEW_SCHEMA`
			`VIEW_NAME`

`adSchemaViews`	23	Returns the views defined in the catalog.	`TABLE_CATALOG`
			`TABLE_SCHEMA`
			`TABLE_NAME`

The SearchDirectionEnum Members

The `SearchDirectionEnum` is used in conjunction with the `SearchDirection` parameter of the `Recordset.Find` method.

MEMBER	VALUE	DESCRIPTION
`adSearchBackward`	-1	Specifies searching backward toward the beginning of the `Recordset`. The record cursor is positioned at BOF if a match is not found.
`adSearchForward`	1	Specifies searching forward toward the end of the `Recordset`. The record cursor is positioned at EOF if a match is not found.

The SeekEnum Members

The `SeekEnum` is used in conjunction with `SeekOption` of the `Recordset.Seek` method.

MEMBER	VALUE	DESCRIPTION
`adSeekAfter`	8	Seek to a key just after where a match occurred.
`adSeekAfterEQ`	4	Seek to a key equal to or just after where that match occurred.
`adSeekBefore`	32	Seek to a key just before where a match occurred.
`adSeekBeforeEQ`	16	Seek to a key equal to or just before where a match occurred.
`adSeekFirstEQ`	1	Seek the first key matching.
`adSeekLastEQ`	2	Seek the last key matching.

The StreamOpenOptionsEnum Members

The `StreamOpenOptionsEnum` is used to describe options for opening a `Stream` object.

MEMBER	VALUE	DESCRIPTION
adOpenStreamAsync	1	Specifies opening in an asynchronous mode.
adOpenStreamFromRecord	4	Specifies opening an open `Record` object.
adOpenStreamUnspecified	-1	Specifies using the default for the source type.

The StreamReadEnum Members

The `StreamReadEnum` is used to define how much data should be read from the `Stream` object.

MEMBER	VALUE	DESCRIPTION
adReadAll	-1	Specifies reading from the current position to the end of the `stream`.
adReadLine	-2	Specifies reading from the current position to the end of the line.

The StreamTypeEnum Members

The `StreamTypeEnum` is used to describe the type of `Stream` object.

MEMBER	VALUE	DESCRIPTION
adTypeBinary	1	Specifies that the `Stream` is binary data.
adTypeText	2	Specifies that the `Stream` is text data.

The StreamWriteEnum Members

The `StreamWriteEnum` is used to specify adding a line separator onto the end of the text data that will be written to the `Stream` object.

MEMBER	VALUE	DESCRIPTION
adWriteChar	0	Specifies not adding a line separator to the end of text.
adWriteLine	1	Specifies adding a line separator to the end of text.

The StringFormatEnum Members

The `StringFormatEnum` is used in conjunction with the `StringFormat` parameter of the `Recordset.GetString` method.

MEMBER	VALUE	DESCRIPTION
adClipString	2	Specifies delimiting columns with the `ColumnDelimiter` parameter and delimiting rows with the `RowDelimiter` parameter, and defines a substitute for `Null` with the `NullExpr` parameter.

64-Bit Access

For the first time in the history of Microsoft Office, the Microsoft Office 2010 system is available in both 32-bit and 64-bit versions. This is a significant move on the part of Microsoft to take full advantage of the larger memory space offered in the 64-bit operating system environment. This appendix discusses the pros and cons of both versions and gives you better insight into which version is best for your needs.

INTRODUCING THE 64-BIT VERSION OF MICROSOFT OFFICE 2010

With the introduction of the new 64-bit version of Microsoft Office 2010, a new version of Microsoft Visual Basic for Applications, known as Microsoft Visual Basic for Applications 7.0 (VBA 7), is being released to work with both 32-bit and 64-bit applications. This appendix addresses only the 64-bit changes. Using the 32-bit version of Office enables you to use existing solutions built into previous versions of Microsoft Office without modification.

With VBA 7, you must update existing Windows Application Programming Interface (API) statements (such as `Declare` statements) to work with the 64-bit version. You must also update address pointers and display window handles in user-defined types that are used by the API declaration statements.

This discussion will primarily center on the impact of the 64-bit version as it applies to Microsoft Access 2010 and its application of VBA. But, installation of either the 32-bit or 64-bit versions is an all or nothing proposition and applies to all Microsoft Office applications. You cannot install a 64-bit version of Access and 32-bit version of Word on the same system.

By default, the 32-bit version of Office 2010 will be installed, even on 64-bit systems. You must explicitly select the Microsoft Office 2010 64-bit version option during installation.

32-BIT TO 64-BIT ACCESS 2010 COMPARISON

The most significant difference between 32-bit and 64-bit Access is memory addressing. Applications built with the 64-bit version of Access 2010 can reference larger address spaces and utilize significantly more physical memory than ever. This can mean a potential reduction in system resource overhead spent moving data in and out of physical memory.

In addition to the ability to refer to specific locations (also known as *pointers*) in physical memory that your application uses to store data or to store programming instructions, you can also use addresses to reference display window identifiers (known as *handles*). Whether you are using a 32-bit or 64-bit operating system (and/or corresponding Access 2010 version) will determine the size (in bytes) of the pointer or handle you can address.

There are two major issues you will have to deal with when you run existing solutions with 64-bit Access 2010:

➤ **Native 64-bit processes in Access 2010 cannot load 32-bit binaries.** This is expected behavior when you incorporated existing Microsoft ActiveX controls and existing add-ins. You can also expect this behavior with third-party ActiveX controls and add-ins that are not specifically designed for 64-bit architecture.

➤ **Prior versions of VBA do not have a pointer data type.** Because of this, developers used 32-bit variables to store pointers and handles. These variables now truncate 64-bit values returned by API calls when using *Declare* statements.

THE VBA 7 CODE BASE

VBA 7 is a new code base. It replaces earlier versions of VBA. VBA 7 exists for both the 32-bit and 64-bit versions of Access 2010. There are now two compilation constants you may use with VBA 7: VBA7 and Win64. The VBA7 constant helps ensure the backward compatibility of your code by testing where your application is using VBA 7 or a previous version of VBA. The Win64 constant is used to test whether code is running as 32-bit or 64-bit. We examine how to incorporate both of these constants later in this appendix.

ACTIVEX CONTROL AND COM ADD-IN COMPATIBILITY

There is a potentially very significant drawback to using 64-bit Access 2010. Existing 32-bit ActiveX controls (both Microsoft-supplied and third-party) are not compatible with 64-bit Access 2010. There are three possible solutions:

➤ Generate a 64-bit version yourself (possible, if you have the source code).

➤ Contact the vendor for an updated version.

➤ Search for an alternative solution (i.e., a similar 64-bit ActiveX control provided by a different vendor than the original 32-bit version you were using).

API COMPATIBILITY

Using VBA and type libraries allows you to provide a tremendous amount of flexibility when creating Access 2010 applications. Sometimes, however, you must communicate directly with the computer's operating system and other components (such as when you manage memory or process or work directly with the user interface elements such as windows or controls, or when modifying the Windows Registry). In these situations, your best option is to use external functions that are embedded in *dynamic-link library (DLL)* files. You accomplish this in VBA by making *API* calls using `Declare` statements. Making API calls is discussed in greater detail in Chapter 9 of this book.

 Microsoft provides a Win32API.txt file that contains approximately 1,500 Declare statements plus a tool for cutting and pasting the Declare statement into your code. Unfortunately, these statements are for 32-bit systems. You will need to convert any of these statements to 64-bit versions before using them in your 64-bit application.

`Declare` statements are used to incorporate API calls into your code. They will take on one of two types: *subroutine* or *function*. A subroutine cannot provide a return value when called, but a function may provide a return value when called. The following is an example of incorporating an API element of either type:

```
[Public|Private] Declare [Function|Sub] Name Lib "LibraryName" Alias "AliasName" _
    (argument list)
```

Replace the placeholder (*Name*) with the actual name of the procedure from the DLL library and replace the placeholder *LibraryName* with the name of the DLL file that contains the sub or function you wish to incorporate. The `Alias` argument is optional and allows you to assign your own name to the sub or function for use later in your application. It is useful to use an alias to prevent possible confusion in your code. The (*argument list*) must contain the parameters and data types that are to be passed to the procedure.

Here's an example of incorporating an API function for opening and replacing a subkey in the Windows Registry:

```
Declare Function RegOpenKeyA Lib "advapi32.dll" (ByVal KEY AS Long, ByVal SubKey _
    As String, NewKey As Long) As Long
```

In Microsoft Visual C or Visual C++ the previous example will compile correctly for both 32-bit and 64-bit systems. This is because HKey is defined as a pointer and its size directly reflects the platform it is compiled on.

Prior versions of VBA, however, do not have a pointer data type so the long data type was used. Because the long data type is always 32-bit, it would break on systems using 64-bit memory space. The upper 32 bits of memory space would either be truncated or would overwrite other memory addresses. This behavior would cause unpredictable results or even system crashes.

VBA 7 resolves these issues by containing a true pointer data type: LongPtr. This new data type now enables you to write your Declare statement correctly:

```
Declare PtrSafe Function RegOpenKeyA Lib "advapire32.dll" (ByVal hKey As LongPtr, _
    ByVal lpSubKey As String, phkResult As LongPtr) As Long
```

Note that we are calling the 64-bit version of the DLL and that the arguments are slightly different. You will also notice a new PtrSafe attribute; when you combine this new attribute with the LongPtr data type in your Declare statement your code will work on either 32-bit or 64-bit systems (provided the DLL is also compatible with 64-bit). The PtrSafe attribute indicates to the VBA compiler that the Declare statement is specifically targeted for the 64-bit version of Access 2010. If you do not include this Declare statement in a 64-bit system, you will get a compile-time error when you attempt to compile the code. The PtrSafe attribute is optional on a 32-bit version of Access 2010. This allows backward compatibility for Declare statements in code for existing applications built with prior versions of VBA.

The following table provides important information on the new attribute qualifier, data types, conversion operators, and functions you may need to help ensure your 64-bit code will function properly.

TYPE	ITEM	DESCRIPTION
Qualifier/attribute	PtrSafe	This attribute is required on 64-bit systems. It indicates that the Declare statement is 64-bit compatible.
Data type	LongPtr	This variable data type is 4 bytes on 32-bit versions and 8 bytes on 64-bit versions of Access 2010. We strongly recommended that you declare a pointer or a handle for new and existing (legacy) code using this data type when running on a 64-bit installation of Access 2010. This data type is only supported in VBA 7 on both 32-bit and 64-bit systems.
Data type	LongLong	This is a new 8-byte data type, which is available only on 64-bit versions of Access 2010. You can assign numeric values to this data type but not numeric types. This will avoid truncation.
Conversion operator	CLngPtr	Converts a simple expression to a LongPtr data type.
Conversion operator	CLngLng	Converts a simple expression to a LongLong data type.
Function	VarPtr()	Variant converter. Returns a LongPtr data type on 64-bit systems, and a Long data type on 32-bit systems.
Function	ObjPtr()	Object converter. Returns a LongPtr data type on 64-bit systems, and a Long data type on 32-bit systems.
Function	StrPtr()	String converter. It returns a LongPtr data type on 64-bit systems, and a Long data type on 32-bit systems.

Declare statements without the PtrSafe *attribute are assumed incompatible with the 64-bit version of Access 2010.*

Earlier, we mentioned two new conditional compilation constants: VBA7 and Win64. If you want to ensure backward compatibility with prior versions of Access, use the VBA7 constant to prevent 64-bit code from being run in the earlier version. If you are writing an application that could run on either platform, you will want to use the Win64 constant. For example, the following code will conditionally compile on a VBA 7 application on either a 32-bit or 64-bit version of Access 2010:

```
#If Win64 Then
      Declare PtrSafe Function FunctionName Lib `User32" (ByVal N As LongLong) _
   As LongLong
#else
      Delcare Function FunctionName Lib `User32" (ByVal N As Long) As Long
#End If
```

while the following will compile on a 32-bit system for either Access 2010 or a prior version of Access:

```
#If VBA7 Then
      Declare PtrSafe Sub FunctionName Lib `User32" (ByVal N As Long)
#else
      Delcare Sub FunctionName Lib `User32" (ByVal N As Long)
#End If
```

If you write 64-bit code that you intend to run on a prior version of Access, you will want to use the VBA7 conditional compilation constant. But, if you write 32-bit code in Access 2010, that code will work in prior versions of Access without needing the compilation constant. If you want to ensure that you are using the correct statement for either 32-bit or 64-bit versions, you will need to use the Win64 conditional compilation constant.

DEALING WITH LEGACY CODE

For existing applications written for prior versions of Access that you wish to migrate to the Access 2010 platform, you may need to modify some of your code to allow for the differences between earlier versions of VBA and VBA 7. The following is an example of modifying existing VBA code.

Existing VBA code

```
Declare Function SHBrowseForFolder Lib `shell32.dll" Alias `fSHBrowseForFolder" _
    (lpBrowseInfo As BROWSEINFO) As Long

Public Type BROWSEINFO
      hOwner As Long
```

```
            lngRoot As Long
            strDisplay As String
            strTitle As String
            lngFlags As Long
            lptPFN As Long
            lptParam As Long
            lngImage As Long
    End Type
```

New VBA code

```
#If VBA7 Then `For use with VBA7
Declare PtrSafe Function SHBrowseForFolder Lib `shell32.dll" Alias _
    `fSHBrowseForFolder" (lpBrowseInfo As BROWSEINFO) As Long

Public Type BROWSEINFO
        hOwner As LongPtr
        lngRoot As Long
        strDisplay As String
        strTitle As String
        lngFlags As Long
        lptPFN As LongPtr
        lptParam As LongPtr
        lngImage As Long
End Type

#Else  `For use with prior versions of VBA
Declare Function SHBrowseForFolder Lib `shell32.dll" Alias `fSHBrowseForFolder" _
    (lpBrowseInfo As BROWSEINFO) As Long

Public Type BROWSEINFO
        hOwner As Long
        lngRoot As Long
        strDisplay As String
        strTitle As String
        lngFlags As Long
        lptPFN As Long
        lptParam As Long
        lngImage As Long
End Type
#End If
```

PERFORMANCE AND THE 64-BIT ENVIRONMENT

There are significant performance gains to be had using the 64-bit version of Office 2010 provided the machine has sufficient physical memory to take full advantage of the 64-bit hardware and OS. These gains are not limited to Access 2010 but can be seen in other Office products. This is especially true when working with very large data sets or numeric values. The following experiment was performed using the same database on both the 32-bit and 64-bit versions of Access 2010. The test machine has 7GB of memory (more than can be addressed using 32-bit architecture). A series of trials were run whereby 100,000 records were programmatically added to an empty table and the time required was noted. The table was deleted, the database was compacted between trials, and the average time required was calculated. A second set of trials was performed whereby 1,000,000 records were added to the empty table and the time required. The following table shows the average time required for each operation on each platform and the percentage faster the 64-bit version is over the 32-bit version.

RECORDS ADDED	32-BIT	64-BIT	% FASTER
All Trials	115.56	54.41	112
100,000	53.35	48.15	11
1,000,000	551.06	98.25	461

Note that there wasn't a large increase in performance when adding 100,000 records on either platform because the overall memory requirement for that number of records was within the capability of both the 32-bit and 64-bit systems. The real difference is found when adding 1,000,000 records. The 32-bit system had to keep moving data from physical memory to virtual memory but the 64-bit system didn't — a very significant improvement in performance.

Utilizing the 64-bit operating system environment by installing the 64-bit version of Office 2010 can allow you to see significant performance gains but at a cost. Legacy systems that use 32-bit ActiveX or COM objects will not work on the 64-bit platform without creating or finding 64-bit versions of those objects. This will be difficult until more vendors create 64-bit versions of the more popular ActiveX controls (such as `TreeView` and `ListView`). If your applications require the use of a lot of ActiveX controls, then you will probably want to install the 32-bit version of Access 2010 until more of these controls are available in 64-bit versions.

E

References for Projects

Throughout this book you have seen type libraries or object libraries, such as those described in Chapter 17, used to enhance functionality through VBA code. You know how libraries can provide access to functions that manipulate the Windows System Registry or retrieve and send data to other applications.

In addition to using libraries supplied with Microsoft Office, you can acquire type libraries to help simplify a variety of programming tasks. Like Microsoft Office libraries, other vendors' libraries provide classes to manipulate objects — the QuickBooks libraries are provided in the QuickBooks Software Development Kit (SDK), for example. These libraries provide classes you can use to create objects that contain data that is returned from a QuickBooks data file through an XML access method.

Acquiring libraries can be a cost-effective way to get more work done in less time. Of course, there's always the tradeoff between what you pay for a library and the effort that may be required to learn how to use it, and the time and effort you spend writing your own functions. And don't forget the effort you have already put into writing your own code. After all of the "bold, test, and swears" you put into your routines, you really must consider creating code libraries from your code.

This appendix describes techniques for using references to libraries in your projects, including how to reference libraries provided by others and why the order of your reference list can be important. It also discusses the types of libraries available (DLLs and ActiveX controls, for example).

This appendix also discusses procedures for referring to the References class and why you would want to. It describes some correct techniques for writing code that will go into your own code libraries. And it suggests ways to avoid missing libraries and what to do when they go missing.

TYPES OF REFERENCES

You can add references to many types of libraries from your Access projects. Library types include the following: type or object libraries (OLB, TLB, and DLL), ActiveX controls (OCX) and references to other Access databases (ACCDB, ACCDE, MDB, and MDE), Access add-ins (ACCDA and MDA), and Access Projects (ADP and ADE).

An object library or type library generally provides functionality for access to other applications or adds functionality to use in your Visual Basic code. For example, Microsoft Office exposes its Component Object Model (COM) through the Microsoft Office Object Library DLLs. These include the Microsoft Access 14.0 Object Library, Microsoft Excel 14.0 Object Library, and Microsoft Word 14.0 Object Library, to name just a few.

ActiveX controls usually include controls that you can add to your user interface. They can display data on forms or provide an access method to data through a form with little or no extra programming. For example, DBI Grid Tools 2.0's ctGrid control displays a grid of data, a two-dimensional table that looks similar to Access's datasheet view. It has properties to indicate which data to display, adjust colors of cells, and add icons and much more, all without programming. The control also enables more functionality through Visual Basic when a reference is made to the Grid Tools DLL.

Access add-ins provide enhanced functionality to Access as a whole. For example, the New Form Wizard provided with Access is an add-in. By creating an ACCDA or MDA file from Access, you can create your own add-ins for Access.

By setting a reference to an Access database or project, you can access routines to create your own code library. Those routines can then be used with all of your applications. This is discussed more in the section "Building Code Libraries" later in this appendix.

ADDING REFERENCES TO YOUR PROJECTS

You know that you can automate Office applications by adding a reference to one of the libraries that comes with Microsoft Office, such as Microsoft Office 14.0 Object Library. Here are the steps necessary to add a reference, as well as what it means when you do:

1. Press ALT+F11 to open the Visual Basic Editor and select Tools ➪ References to display the References dialog box.

2. The Available References list includes items that have been registered to the Windows System Registry. To add one of these libraries to references for your project, check the box to the left of its name. When you close and reopen the References dialog box, any libraries you have checked are listed above all unselected libraries.

3. Many application installation packages handle registering libraries for you. If the library you want to use does not appear in the list of Available References, there are two ways to use the library:

   ➤ **Use the Browse button.** Click the Browse button to open a file selection dialog box. Select the type of library you want from the drop-down list for Files

Of Type. Browse to the folder that contains that library and select the library.

➤ **Register the library yourself using REGSVR32.** To run REGSVR32, select Run from the Windows Start menu. In the Open box, enter **REGSVR32** followed by the full file specification of the library you want to register. For example:

```
REGSVR32 `C:\Program Files\Common Files\Microsoft\Office14\MSOCFU.DLL"
```

After you register a library, you need to close and reopen the References dialog box to get the library to display in the Available References list.

Reference Order Is Important

One of the reasons for adding references to your project is to make additional classes available so you can declare variables in your code and manipulate objects of those classes. But you must be aware that the name of a class in one library does not have to be unique from the names of classes in other libraries.

A classic example of this occurs when you include references to both DAO (Data Access Objects) and ADO (ActiveX Data Objects). Both libraries have a `Recordset` class. (You can use the Object Browser, which is discussed in the next section, to see when a class occurs in more than one library.)

In situations in which there is a duplication of class names, Access determines which class to use by searching sequentially the list of libraries listed in the Available Libraries list. Unfortunately, the compiler won't always tell you that you have the wrong reference. If you refer to a property or method that is not available for the class you have used in your variable declaration, the compiler will report the problem. Otherwise, you'll discover the problem only when you test your code.

If you have libraries that have classes with the same names, you can get Access to choose the class you want by changing the Priority of the library in the list. Use the Priority buttons (to the right of the Available References list) to move the selected library up or down in the list. Move the library containing the class you want higher than libraries containing the same class name.

You can also avoid problems with duplicate class names by making a specific reference to the library that contains the class you want to use. For example, if you reference both the ADO and DAO libraries, and you want to declare a variable for the `Recordset` class of ADO, you can declare your variable using the following syntax:

```
Dim rsADO as ADODB.Recordset
```

To declare a variable for the DAO `Recordset` class, you can use the following syntax.

```
Dim rsDAO as DAO.Recordset
```

Using this syntax does not eliminate the need to have the reference to the library in your Reference list, but it prevents any confusion about which library you are referring to in your variable declaration. In addition, it has the added benefit of ensuring that code continues to use the correct library if a new library with a duplicate class name is added later in the development cycle.

The Object Browser

After you have added a reference to a library, the classes contained in that library are available for viewing in the Object Browser. To see the Object Browser in the Visual Basic Editor, select View ⇨ Object Browser or press F2.

When you select an item in the Classes list, its properties and methods (also known as the "members" of the class) display in the right pane. Select an item in the right pane and more specific information about that item displays in the bottom pane.

You can specify which of the referenced libraries you want to browse by selecting it from the libraries drop-down list at the top-left of the Object Browser. This is the list that starts with `<All Libraries>`.

If you are looking for a particular class, property, method, or declared constant, you can specify a portion of the string to search for in the text box below the libraries drop-down, and then click the Search icon (the binoculars) to find it. If `<All Libraries>` is selected, search results may appear in one or more libraries.

BUILDING CODE LIBRARIES

In addition to the four types of reference libraries (OLB, TLB, DLL, and OCX), a set of library types is often overlooked. These types include:

➤ **MS Access databases:** ACCDB, ACCDE, MDB and MDE

➤ **MS Access add-ins:** ACCDA and MDA

➤ **MS Access Projects:** ADP and ADE

With these types of references, you can develop your own code libraries that contain routines to share in all of your applications. An example might be something like a common error-handling routine.

Because you can use these routines over and over, you can justify putting a little more effort into them. Take error handling, for example. Generally, you develop code to display a message to the user requesting that the user report the error to you. Have you ever seen a user use your application and expose an error you hadn't found in testing? He clicks OK on the message without giving it a second thought. You ask why he didn't wait to review the message, and he says, "Oh, that happens all the time. I was told to just ignore it."

Suppose that instead of depending on the users to call in report errors, you write routines to track the errors in a table. Then you could investigate what is happening. Perhaps your tables could even maintain some trace data to help discover what causes the problem. Suppose you also realize that the main reason errors don't get reported is that it is too difficult for the user to report them. So you add some functionality that builds an e-mail message for the user to send through Outlook.

Of course, there are always so many things to do when building the current application that you don't have time for tasks like these. But if you could find the time to write these routines and then reuse them in all of your applications, wouldn't that be worthwhile? That's what code libraries are for.

> **SECURITY**
>
> To prevent other users from reading your source code, you can compile the database into an ACCDE or MDE. That removes all the editable code and compresses the database. See Chapter 25 for more information.
>
> If you are going to make an ACCDE or MDE from a database that uses a reference to your code library databases, those databases must be made into ACCDEs or MDEs as well. Remember that if you create an ACCDE or MDE file, you *must* hold on to the ACCDB or MDB file that was used to create the file. You cannot recover source code from an ACCDE or MDE file.

Using CurrentDB versus CodeDB

One thing to consider when developing code libraries is that CurrentDB refers to the database that is open in the Access user interface. If you want your code library project to refer to objects that are in its own database, you need to use CodeDB. Likewise, there are the CurrentProject and CodeProject properties and CurrentData and CodeData properties, so be sure that you are setting a reference to the correct objects.

For a more detailed explanation about the differences between CurrentDb and CodeDb, please refer to Appendix A.

Working with References Programmatically

There are a few techniques that make working with Access references easier. And there are a few techniques that you should be aware of to avoid problems when using references to your own code libraries. These techniques are discussed in this section.

The Reference Object

The Access Application object includes the References collection, which can be used for a number of purposes. The References collection contains the list of references in the database. You can determine the number of references in the project using the following:

```
Application.References.Count
```

You can determine if a reference is missing by checking the BrokenReference property of the Access Application object. This property returns True if there is a missing reference. From there, you can walk through the References collection to find the missing reference:

```
Dim ref As Reference

If Application.BrokenReference Then
    For Each ref in Application.References
        If ref.IsBroken then
            Debug.Print ref.name & ` is broken."
        End if
    Next Ref
End If
```

You can add references at runtime using the `AddFromFile` or `AddFromGUID` methods. For `AddFromFile`, you simply specify the full path to the library file. For `AddFromGUID`, the reference library must be registered in the Windows System Registry and you must know the exact GUID for that library, in addition to the major and minor version. The simplest way to find the GUID is to manually add the reference, and then check the `GUID` property of the Reference object for the specified reference.

Running a Procedure from a Library Database

Say you have an `Errors.mdb` file that contains the `HandleError` procedure. You can call that procedure using the `Call` statement in Visual Basic like this (depending on the parameters needed in the routine, of course):

```
Call Errors.HandleError _
(Err. .Number, Err.Description, Err.Source)
```

You can also use the `Application.Run` method:

```
Application.Run("Errors.HandleError", _
Err.Number, Err.Description, Err.Source)
```

The qualifier does not have to be the same as the name of the MDB. In this example, Errors *was used to qualify where the* HandleError *procedure is located. You can change the name of the qualifier by changing the* Name *property of the project. To change the project name, open the Properties dialog box using the Tools menu in the Visual Basic Editor.*

Compiling to Validate References

An easy way to be sure that the references in your project are not broken is to use the Debug ➪ Compile menu option. It quickly finds declarations that use classes that are not available to your project.

For best results with this technique, use `Option Explicit` for every module to be sure that you are declaring all variables. The compiler will tell you if you have not declared a variable even before you attempt to run the code. And, because all variables must be declared, if any variables reference classes or object types from a library that has gone missing, the compiler lets you know.

To include the Option Explicit statement for new modules that you create, check Require Variable Declaration in the Options dialog box in the Visual Basic Editor.

Be aware that if you are using late binding to an `Object` variable that the type will not be checked until the code is executed. That means that until a procedure is run, you may not know that a variable has been defined using a class from a missing library. You can avoid having the users find these problems later by checking the `IsBroken` property of the references in your application during startup. That would be a good routine to write and put into your code library so that you can use it with all of your applications.

Fixing Broken References

If your code suddenly stops working after you have installed your database on another computer, it's a good idea to inspect the references. One of the first things to check for is a MISSING referenced type library in the References dialog. To fix the missing references, open the Visual Basic Editor's References dialog box and update the references.

 You typically run into two problems here. First, if you have delivered the database as an ACCDE or MDE, you cannot modify references. And second, the library you are referencing doesn't exist on the computer. In either case, the most likely solution is to get the library into the right place on the computer. For that, see the following section, "Avoiding Broken References."

When you have fixed missing references, it's a good idea to compile the module using Debug ⇨ Compile — that is, if you're not working with an ACCDE or MDE. Compiling helps ensure that the library on the new computer matches the one on the computer where you did your testing by indicating that the library has the same classes and type definitions you used in your code.

If you have a broken or missing reference, compiling may report an error incorrectly. In particular, you may find that Visual Basic functions (for example, Right or UCase) are reported as undefined. If this occurs, fix the missing references first, and then proceed with other fixes.

Avoiding Broken References

Can you claim that you've never had a problem delivering an application to one of your users? Then you've probably never used references. Either that, or you are one of the fortunate developers who develops on a machine with a configuration that is identical to your users'. But even if the machine is identical, you can still run into problems if you have taken the time to develop a code library. You know what we mean — the one you forgot to take with you when you went to the user's machine to install your database.

Of course the first thing to do to avoid broken references is to be sure that you are delivering all of the components that go with your application. And don't forget those DLLs that you acquired from a vendor to improve the features in your application. And just delivering them isn't all that there is to it; you need to be sure you've installed those DLLs in the right folder and that they are registered properly.

So how do you know what the right folder is? When Access searches for referenced libraries, it first searches based on the file specification provided when the library was added. If the library is not found, it follows these steps:

1. Access searches for a RefLibPaths key in the following location in the Microsoft Windows Registry: HKEY_LOCAL_MACHINE\Software\Microsoft\Office\14.0\Access.

2. If the key exists, Access checks for the existence of a value name that matches the name of the referenced file. If it finds a matching value name, Access loads the reference from the path specified in the corresponding value data.

3. If Access doesn't find a `RefLibPaths` key, it searches for the referenced file in the following locations in order:

    ➤   Application folder containing the application (the folder where `msaccess.exe` is located).

    ➤   Current folder.

    ➤   System folders (the System, System32, and SysWOW64 folders located in the Windows folder).

    ➤   Windows folder.

    ➤   PATH environment variable. For more information about environment variables, see Windows Help.

    ➤   The folder that contains the Access database, and any subfolders located in that folder.

If Access still can't find the reference after performing this search, you must fix the reference manually.

When running your code, classes from referenced libraries are not checked until the procedure that declares a variable using one of those classes is executed. In your StartUp procedure, you can walk through the References using the technique previously mentioned and use the `IsBroken` property to find broken references. If you find a broken reference you can inform your user with a meaningful message instead of letting an error pop up from Visual Basic.

References in Access 2010 64-bit

For the first time, a 64-bit version of Office is available with Office 2010. This can create some issues as far as references are concerned because code compiled for one platform cannot be run by a process running in the other platform. In other words, if you have a reference to a library (DLL, OLB, TLB, OCX, MDE, or ACCDE) that was compiled for 32-bit Windows, it cannot be loaded in the 64-bit version of Access 2010. The reverse is also true — a library compiled for a 64-bit version of Windows cannot be loaded in the 32-bit version of Access 2010. For more information about 64-bit considerations for MDE and ACCDE files, please see Appendix D.

So let's say that you are running Access 2007 and have a reference to `actives.tlb` which is located in `C:\Windows\System32` on 32-bit Windows. When Access 2010 is released, you upgrade to the 64-bit version of Access 2010. This file exists in this path on the machine running 64-bit Windows, except now the reference is a 64-bit version. Now, think for a moment about how VBA loads references. Since the path exists, VBA will try to load it, only it will fail — silently. There is no error and no missing reference. As such, the code to check the `BrokenReference` or `IsBroken` properties will not work because the reference was never set. Except for the fact that the code won't compile, it's as if the reference never existed.

So, how do you work around this issue? If you're not running in an MDE or ACCDE file, the easiest thing to do might be to maintain a list of references in a table, and make sure they are set correctly when your database opens.

Considerations When Upgrading to Access 2010

There are a few considerations you should take into account when upgrading to Access 2010, and the references in your database are one of them. Here are some of the questions to consider for your databases that have non-standard references when upgrading:

➤   Am I upgrading to the 32-bit version of Access 2010, or the 64-bit version?

➤   Are the databases I'm referencing available?

➤   Does my database reference an MDE or ACCDE? If so, it may need to be recompiled in the 64-bit version of Access 2010.

RESOURCES

A number of commercially available products provide libraries for you to reference from your Access projects. You can also find many shared libraries or libraries that are available as shareware. Here are a few resources to get you started. We have not tried all of the controls and libraries found, so we can't endorse all of them.

➤   Compatibility Between the 32-bit and 64-bit Versions of Office 2010 (`http://msdn` `.microsoft.com/en-us/library/ee691831(office.14).aspx`)

➤   UtterAccess (`http://www.utteraccess.com/links/index.php3`): A great online forum for many things related to Access.

➤   FMS Inc. (`www.fmsinc.com/products`): Quite a number of ActiveX controls and add-ins for Microsoft Access.

➤   The Access Web (`www.mvps.org/access/resources/products.htm`): With many resources including ActiveX controls and beyond.

➤   DBi Technologies Inc. (`www.dbi-tech.com`): Solutions::PIM, Solutions::Schedule, and many more, tested with Microsoft Access.

➤   ID Automation (`www.idautomation.com/activex`): Barcode ActiveX control and DLL designed for Office programs.

➤   Intuit Developer Network (`www.developer.intuit.com`): Software Development Kit (SDK) to work with data in QuickBooks.

You should also be aware that many libraries and ActiveX controls that are designed for Visual Basic programming languages can be used by Access. Contact the vendor to find out.

Reserved Words and Special Characters

As with most spoken languages, programming languages also have some words and symbols that have special meanings. In general, words that have specific meanings to a program are called *reserved words*, and they should not be used to name fields, objects, and variables. Reserved words have a specific meaning to Microsoft Access and to the database engines, both Access Connectivity Engine (ACE) and it's predecessor Jet database engine. For your convenience, we have compiled some lists of reserved words — for Access and for some of the more common interfaces, including Visual Basic for Applications (VBA), Visual Basic (VB), SQL Server, and Open Database Connectivity (ODBC) drivers.

You may want to use these lists as a baseline for creating your own lists. Depending on how your application interfaces with other programs, it may be prudent (and necessary) to avoid using words that have specific programmatic meanings to those programs as well. If you are going to be working with other programs such as SharePoint or .NET, you will also want to get the current list of reserved words for those programs — as well as for Visual Basic.

To compile a list of reserved words, you might consider that a more comprehensive list will allow your program to work with more programs and avoid conflicts as new features and interfaces are added. With that in mind, you might begin with the list of all the properties of database objects, and keywords from VBA and VB, as well as names from any third-party or user-defined functions that are used in your applications. Keep in mind that the list of reserved words for any program is likely to change as features are added. It isn't just with the release of a new version — service packs and updates can also add new reserved words.

You might wonder why Access doesn't always prevent you from using reserved words — at least those specific to Access. In many cases it does, but it is not something that you should rely on. Access will create an error message when select reserved words are used as field names, but it is not always easy to decipher the cause of the error message and not all reserved words will prompt an error message. For example, it is far from intuitive that the following error message may have been triggered by the use of a reserved word:

```
The wizard was unable to preview your report, possibly because
a table needed by your report is exclusively locked
```

Consequently, a developer may unnecessarily spend time troubleshooting the wrong problem. When you are working with an application that uses reserved words, particularly as the names of tables or fields, you should rename the database objects if it is at all possible and feasible to do so. If it isn't possible to rename them, then be sure to enclose the names in brackets when they are called in code or in queries. Here's an example showing the name of the table in brackets because the term `tableName` is a reserved word:

```
SELECT fieldX

FROM [tableName]
```

When writing code, it is often handy to use the IntelliSense feature and just select from the available list of objects and actions. This requires the use of `Me.` (pronounced "me dot") rather than `Me!` (pronounced "me bang"). However, if the name of a field is a reserved word that could also be the object's property, the code will not compile. The debugger will stop and highlight the problem object, as shown in Figure F-1. In this instance, merely changing the syntax to use `Me!` instead of `Me.` will allow the code to compile. You cannot avoid the problem simply by not compiling the code because that will merely ensure that if the application reaches that part of the code when it is running, the code will break and stop the application. (You will find additional discussion of using the bang and dot operators in Chapter 7.)

FIGURE F-1

When writing or modifying code, we recommend the practice of debugging directly after making changes to a function or module. This enables you to catch errors promptly and prevents them from being repeated or compounded. And when you are making changes, particularly to the names of objects, it is helpful to use search and replace utilities, which are designed to find and replace the word(s) throughout an application, including the code project (the VBA). Some utilities offer different features and reporting capabilities that may be beneficial to your specific needs. The Access news groups and MVP websites are great resources for learning about these types of tools. Although some are free, you may find that the features and benefits provided by some of the commercial software make it worth the price.

It is clear that if reserved words are causing a problem with a database, it is worth enforcing naming conventions. Implementing a comprehensive naming policy can help you avoid most of the problems associated with using reserved words. Appendix G discusses the principles and benefits of some of the popular naming conventions.

WHAT ARE THE SOURCES OF RESERVED WORDS?

In addition to the lists of reserved words that are directly associated with Access, ACE, and VBA, there are also words that have special meaning to ActiveX Data Objects (ADO), OLE DB, ODBC, and any DLL (dynamic-link library) referenced in your application. These should be treated as reserved words for your application. Just by setting a reference to a type library, an Object Library, or an ActiveX control, all the reserved words for the referenced items become reserved words for the Access application. And the list keeps growing; as we mentioned earlier, built-in function names and user-defined names also become reserved words. As you create interfaces to work with other programs and development languages, such as SharePoint, Excel, .NET, and Visual Basic, you will want to be cautious and avoid their reserved words as well.

It can get even more complicated because the reserved words for a given application can vary depending on the mode that the ACE is running. This is determined by whether ACE is called from Microsoft Access, the Microsoft OLE DB Provider for ACE, a Data Access Object, or the Microsoft Access ODBC driver. Whether ACE is running in ANSI mode or non-ANSI (traditional) mode also determines some reserved words. This can mean that a query that works under one scenario may fail when the database application is opened in a different mode. (You can find more information about ANSI modes with respect to Access databases online from Microsoft.com, Access support forums, and other websites.) With all these variables, you can see the attractiveness of taking the conservative approach to avoid conflicts.

You can also find lists of reserved words by using the online help feature in Access, by searching for reserved words on the Internet, and by pouring through reference books. Regretfully, no single source will be comprehensive or tailored specifically to your needs. And, given the dynamically changing environment, even the lists published by authoritative sources cannot be assumed to be complete as programs and features are constantly changing. This is yet another endorsement for implementing naming conventions, as following a naming convention can help ensure that you do not inadvertently run into conflicts with reserved words

The potential lists of reserved words can seem a bit overwhelming. That is why this appendix not only contains a table of reserved words but also lists some of the other words that we think should be considered when creating master lists of words to avoid. The table is a compilation of words from a variety of sources, including the reserved words for ANSI mode; we hope that it gives you a solid foundation and significantly reduces your research time. Please keep in mind that it is not an exhaustive list and that it does not include additional words associated with third-party add-ins. Allen Browne's Access MVP website (`http://allenbrowne.com/AppIssueBadWord.html`) has a compilation of reserved words that generously includes the source, such as SQL, Access, Jet, and so forth. Allen also offers a utility that will check your application for usage of reserved words.

RESERVED WORDS WITH ERROR MESSAGES

You might wonder why you can't simply use a tool that will check against your custom list of reserved words and give you a timely and specific error message as you are creating your tables and adding fields. Although that seems like a great idea, it wouldn't be easy to implement. The Access team recognizes the merit in the concept, however, and has instituted an automatic check for a limited number of terms that are commonly used in both VBA and as field names. At this time, the list contains only six words:

Name	Value	Text
Date	Year	Month

Nonetheless, the seed has been planted, so to speak.

Keep in mind that you might circumvent this built-in check if you are creating a table in code. Access performs the check and generates the appropriate error message (see Figure F-2) when you are creating a new table in the Access UI. However, it won't trigger the error if you create a table using `CreateTableDef` or the `CREATE TABLE` statement.

FIGURE F-2

RESERVED WORD LIST

If you're ambitious, you might be tempted to try to compile your own list of reserved words by combining lists from the most common sources. Be aware, however, that some of the lists were incomplete when initially published, and that additional words should be included in the lists as new objects or actions are added. Given those caveats, you'd still want a list that is a compilation of words from Access, ACE, MS Query SQL, and ANSI-92 and any third-party add-ins that you use.

Searching Access help for "Reserved Words" leads you to an explanation and list of words reserved for use in SQL statements, whether they are used by Access, ACE, Jet, or other applications. To be more inclusive, it lists words that have specific meaning to select other programs even if they have no special meaning to ACE or Jet. You'll still need to add the lists of special characters and ASCII characters and their names.

As you can see, there is no easy way to consolidate everything into one tidy list. And, even if you do have a comprehensive list, it can be helpful to know why you should avoid certain words and characters as well as how to use them when you need to. We've provided the following three lists that you can use as the foundation for your custom lists: the compilation of words to avoid (reserved words), a list of special characters, and a list of other ASCII characters.

Following is the list of words and terms that are reserved by Access or by programs and languages commonly used with Access. We've included a few words that have been reported to cause problems, so that you can avoid using them, too.

ABSOLUTE	ACTION	ACK
ADD	ALLOCATE	ALPHANUMERIC
ALTER	ALTER TABLE	AND
ANY	APPLICATION	ARE
AS	ASC	ASSERTION
ASSISTANT	AT	AUTHORIZATION
AUTOINCREMENT	AVG	BAND
BEGIN	BEL	BETWEEN
BINARY	BIT	BIT_LENGTH
BNOT	BOOLEAN	BOR
BOTH	BS	BXOR
BY	BYTE	CAN
CASCADE	CASCADED	CASE
CAST	CATALOG	CHAR
CHAR_LENGTH	CHARACTER	CHARACTER_LENGTH
CHECK	CLOSE	CLUSTERED
COALESCE	COLLATE	COLLATION
COLUMN	COMMIT	COMP
COMPACTDATABASE	COMPRESSION	CONNECT
CONNECTION	CONSTRAINT	CONSTRAINTS
CONTAINER	CONTAINS	CONTINUE
CONVERT	CORRESPONDING	COUNT
COUNTER	CRCREATE	CREATEDATABASE
CREATEDB	CREATEFIELD	CREATEGROUP
CREATEINDEX	CREATEOBJECT	CREATEPROPERTY
CREATERELATION	CREATETABLEDEF	CREATEUSER
CREATEWORKSPACE	CROSS	CURRENCY
CURRENT	CURRENT_DATE	CURRENT_TIME
CURRENT_TIMESTAMP	CURRENT_USER	CURRENTUSER

CURSOR	DATABASE	DATE
DATETIME	DAY	DC1
DC2	DC3	DC4
DEALLOCATE	DEC	DECIMAL
DECLARE	DEFAULT	DEFERRABLE
DEFERRED	DELETE	DESC
DESCRIBE	DESCRIPTION	DESCRIPTOR
DIAGNOSTICS	DISALLOW	DISCONNECT
DISTINCT	DISTINCTROW	DLE
DOCUMENT	DOMAIN	DOUBLE
DROP	ECHO	ELSE
EM	END	END-EXEC
ENQ	EOT	EQV
ERROR	ESC	ESCAPE
ETB	ETX	EXCEPT
EXCEPTION	EXCLUSIVECONNECT	EXEC
EXECUTE	EXISTS	EXIT
EXTERNAL	EXTRACT	FALSE
FETCH	FF	FIELD
FIELDS	FILLCACHE	FIRST
FLOAT	FLOAT4	FLOAT8
FOR	FOREIGN	FORM
FORMS	FOUND	FROM
FS	FULL	FUNCTION
GENERAL	GET	GETOBJECT
GETOPTION	GLOBAL	GO
GOTO	GOTOPAGE	GRANT
GROUP	GROUP BY	GS
GUID	HAVING	HOUR

IDENTITY	IDLE	IEEEDOUBLE
IEEESINGLE	IF	IGNORE
IMAGE	IMMEDIATE	IMP
IN	INDEX	INDEXCREATEDB
INDEXES	INDICATOR	INHERITABLE
ININDEX	INITIALLY	INNER
INPUT	INSENSITIVE	INSERT
INSERTTEXT	INT	INTEGER
INTEGER1	INTEGER2	INTEGER4
INTERSECT	INTERVAL	INTO
IS	ISOLATION	JOIN
KEY	LANGUAGE	LAST
LASTMODIFIED	LEADING	LEFT
LEVEL	LEVEL* MIN	LF
LIKE	LOCAL	LOGICAL
LOGICAL1	LONG	LONGBINARY
LONGCHAR	LONGTEXT	LOWER
MACRO	MATCH	MAX
MEMO	MIN	MINUTE
MOD	MODULE	MONEY
MONTH	MOVE	NAK
NAME	NAMES	NATIONAL
NATURAL	NCHAR	NEWPASSWORD
NEXTNO	NONCLUSTERED	NOT
NOTE	NTEXT	NUL
NULL	NULLIF	NUMBER
NUMERIC	NVARCHAR	OBJECT
OCTET_LENGTH	OFF	OFOLEOBJECT
OLEOBJECT	ON	ONLY

OPEN	OPENRECORDSET	OPTION
OR	ORDER	ORIENTATION
ORORDEROUTER	OUTPUT	OVERLAPS
OWNERACCESS	PAD	PARAMETER
PARAMETERS	PARTIAL	PASSWORD
PERCENT	PIVOT	POSITION
PRECISION	PREPARE	PRESERVE
PRIMARY	PRIOR	PRIVILEGES
PROC	PROCEDURE	PROPERTY
PUBLIC	QUERIES	QUERY
QUIT	READ	REAL
RECALC	RECORDSET	REFERENCES
REFRESH	REFRESHLINK	REGISTERDATABASE
RELATION	RELATIVE	REPAINT
REPAIRDATABASE	REPLICATION	REPORT
REPORTS	REQUERY	RESTRICT
REVOKE	RIGHT	RIGHT SPACE
ROLLBACK	ROWS	RS
SCHEMA	SCREEN	SCROLL
SECOND	SECTION	SELECT
SELECTSCHEMA	SELECTSECURITY	SESSION
SESSION_USER	SET	SET SUM
SETFOCUS	SETOPTION	SHORT
SI	SINGLE	SIZE
SMALLDATETIME	SMALLINT	SMALLMONEY
SO	SOH	SOME
SPACE	SQL	SQLCODE
SQLERROR	SQLSTATE	STDEV
STDEVP	STRING	STX

SUB	SUBSTRING	SUM
SYN	SYSNAME	SYSTEM_USER
TAB	TABLE	TABLEDEF
TABLEDEFS	TABLEID	TABLEID*
TEMPORARY	TEXT	THEN
TIME	TIMESTAMP	TIMEZONE_HOUR
TIMEZONE_MINUTE	TINYINT	TO
TOP	TRAILING	TRANSACTION
TRANSFORM	TRANSLATE	TRANSLATION
TRIM	TRUE	TYPE
UNION	UNIQUE	UNIQUEIDENTIFIER
UNKNOWN	UPDATE	UPDATEIDENTITY
UPDATEOWNER	UPDATESECURITY	UPPER
US	USAGE	USER
USING	VALUE	VALUES
VAR	VARBINARY	VARCHAR
VARP	VARYING	VIEW
VT	WHEN	WHENEVER
WHERE	WITH	WORK
WORKSPACE	WRITE	XOR
YEAR	YES	YESNO
ZONE		

WHAT ARE SPECIAL CHARACTERS?

Special characters are those that are interpreted by Access, SQL Server, and VBA as field type delimiters, as the introduction of a comparison function, or other instructions. Therefore, special characters and control characters (ASCII values 0 through 31) should not be used as part of the name of a database field, object, variable, procedure, or constant. (Okay, we do concede that there are different guidelines for naming VB procedures, variables, and constants than for naming database objects and fields. But it seems sensible to combine the two sets of rules and apply them to both situations.)

If you look at the list of special characters, it is obvious why some should be avoided. For example, the . (period) can return unexpected results when used with a reserved word. For example, given a field Name in table Students, the syntax Students.Name would return the value of the table's Name property instead of the value in the Name field.

Similarly, putting an apostrophe in a field name causes the VBA to choke as it interprets the single quote as the beginning or end of a string. Because the ' is being used as an apostrophe, there is nothing to close the string until VBA comes to the next apostrophe — which is likely meant to start another string. You can see how this creates a ripple effect.

In addition to the following two lists of characters to avoid, there are a couple of seemingly innocent things that can turn into gotchas:

➤ Do not put spaces in field names. For example, field names such as 2ndPhoneand Area Code could cause unexpected hiccups. If you insist on separating words, use the underscore (a grudgingly acceptable option).

➤ Do not start field or column names with numeric characters.

Remember that an object or field name cannot begin with a space. Access immediately advises you of the error if you try to put certain special characters in a field name. Figure F-3 shows the error message generated by trying to create a field name with a leading space. Notice, however, that Access accepts other special characters within the field name. This may create a false sense of well-being because, as pointed out earlier, a name containing a special character requires special treatment throughout the application.

FIGURE F-3

Special characters not only wreak havoc in code, but they can also cause problems if they are within text and memo fields. Most of these special characters will put the brakes on a word search, and an application that has been working smoothly for months may suddenly throw error messages when the user runs a search on a text field. For example, a search for a business named Mike's Steak n Spirits, will likely stop a search. The apostrophe causes the SQL interpreter to respond as though a string has been initiated or ended. One solution is to use code to prevent users from entering special characters into text and memo fields. See the code example at the end of this appendix.

Special Characters To Avoid

KEY	ASCII	NAME
,	44	Comma
.	46	Period
;	59	Semicolon
:	58	Colon
`	96	Grave (open single quote, backtick)
'	39	Apostrophe (single quote)
"	34	Quote (double quote)
?	63	Question mark
/	47	Solidus (slash)
>	62	Greater than
<	60	Less than
[	91	Left square bracket
]	93	Right square bracket
{	123	Left curly brace
}	125	Right curly brace
\	92	Reverse solidus (backslash, whack)
|	124	Vertical bar (pip, pipe)
~	126	Tilde
!	33	Exclamation mark
@	64	Commercial at
#	35	Number sign (pound, hash)
$	36	Dollar sign
%	37	Percent

continues

(continued)

KEY	ASCII	NAME
^	94	Caret
&	38	Ampersand
*	42	Asterisk
(	40	Open parenthesis
)	41	Close parenthesis
=	61	Equal sign
+	43	Plus sign

ASCII Characters to Avoid

You often see the term ASCII, but its full name is seldom spelled out, so here it is in plain English: American Standard Code for Information Interchange. Computers are number-driven, and ASCII code is the numeric representation of characters or actions. The first 32 ASCII characters are actions or nonprinting characters, which is why using any of these characters as the name of an object or function would be interpreted as an instruction and could initiate unexpected actions. Most developers recognize ESC, CAN, NUL, LF, CR, and TAB as commands, but many of the other ASCII characters have been forgotten. The following table, then, has a dual purpose. It's a handy reference for knowing what characters to avoid, and it's a useful resource for when you want to include an action such as inserting a carriage return and line feed in your VBA. The character names have been incorporated into the list of words to avoid.

Ascii Characters 0 Through 31

DEC	HX	OCT	CHAR	FUNCTION
0	0	000	NUL	Null
1	1	001	SOH	Start of heading
2	2	002	STX	Start of text
3	3	003	ETX	End of text
4	4	004	EOT	End of transmission
5	5	005	ENQ	Enquiry
6	6	006	ACK	Acknowledge

DEC	HX	OCT	CHAR	FUNCTION
7	7	007	BEL	Bell
8	8	010	BS	Backspace
9	9	011	TAB	Horizontal tab
10	A	012	LF	NL line feed, new line
11	B	013	VT	Vertical tab
12	C	014	FF	NP form feed, new page
13	D	015	CR	Carriage return
14	E	016	SO	Shift out
15	F	017	SI	Shift in
16	10	020	DLE	Data link escape
17	11	021	DC1	Device control 1
18	12	022	DC2	Device control 2
19	13	023	DC3	Device control 3
20	14	024	DC4	Device control 4
21	15	025	NAK	Negative acknowledgement
22	16	026	SYN	Synchronous idle
23	17	027	ETB	End of transmission block
24	18	030	CAN	Cancel
25	19	031	EM	End of medium
26	1A	032	SUB	Substitute
27	1B	033	ESC	Escape
28	1C	034	FS	File separator
29	1D	035	GS	Group separator
30	1E	036	RS	Record separator
31	1F	037	US	Unit separator

Web Objects

Web applications have some additional rules for reserved words and special characters. The following are some of the special rules for web object names.

➤ Must be from 1 to 64 characters in length.

➤ Cannot contain a period (.), exclamation point (!), square brackets ([]), leading space, or non-printable character such as a carriage return.

➤ Cannot begin with an equal sign (=).

➤ May not contain any of the following characters: / \ : * ? " < > | # <TAB> { } % ~ &.

➤ Tables cannot have any of the following names:

AppImages	Report Definitions	WFTemp
ComMd	Solutions	Workflow
Docs	WebParts	
Lists	Webs	

You'll notice that these are much like the guidance for other objects, and that the first two bullets apply across the board.

Bonus Code Example

It's sometimes beneficial to prevent users from entering certain characters as they type data into a form. By setting the form's `KeyPreview` property to `Yes`, an event procedure can be used to essentially ignore the entry of selected characters. This is accomplished by using an event procedure on the control's `OnKeyPress` property.

The following example prevents the database from entering a period, apostrophe, or ampersand in the text box `txtBusinessName`.

```
Private Sub txtBusinessName_KeyPress(KeyAscii As Integer)

   Select Case KeyAscii
     Case 46, 39, 38 ' Period, apostrophe, ampersand
     KeyAscii = 0
   End Select
End Sub
```

If someone enters `Traci & Brandi's Travels`, the table will actually store `Traci Brandis Travels`. The specified ASCII characters are replaced with the ASCII character 0; which effectively eliminates the character because the ASCII character 0 is null. You will notice that only the character is eliminated, so unless you include additional code you will have two spaces between the words wherever the "&" was deleted. This code snippet can be modified to fit many situations and an infinite combination of characters. You can use the ASCII character numbers listed in the "Special Characters to Avoid" table earlier in the appendix to customize the code snippet to prevent other characters from being stored in the database. You will also want to incorporate error trapping; as you've seen in numerous examples throughout the book.

Naming Conventions

The logic of using a naming convention is about as easy to grasp as the logic of standardizing an alphabet or language. Both structures are intended to make communication easier. In addition to providing standards, they also allow plenty of opportunities for customization. Adopting a naming convention provides for consistency, can avoid conflicts with reserved words, and sets the framework for building strong code that is more easily read and interpreted by the original developer and by other developers. You may as well count on someone else trying to interpret your code, whether it is someone on your team, a technical consultant, or someone who inherits your project.

Using a naming convention also helps prevent conflicts that can occur when several objects have the same name. For clarity and ease of use, a name should have only one meaning within an application.

When you are new to Access or to writing code, it is the perfect time to become familiar with the most common naming conventions and to start developing your own protocols. This appendix includes some guidance for naming objects and provides tables of the most commonly accepted names used in VBA. It also provides some guidelines for working with macros.

As you adopt, adapt, and create your own conventions, you will benefit from being familiar with standard naming conventions. Becoming fluent with the prefixes, abbreviations, and terms will help you to read and interpret code used in Access, VBA, and macros, whether it is in help files, books, and sample applications, or when collaborating with others.

THE BENEFITS OF USING A NAMING CONVENTION

As previously indicated, the use of naming conventions is voluntary, and you can certainly create applications without applying naming conventions. However, conventions can save you a lot of time and money. They can prevent needless frustration by making it easier and faster to read and interpret code, whether it is code that you wrote last week or last year, or code from another developer.

Naming conventions offer many benefits in that they are like sharing a common language. Following are some of the most common benefits of using a naming convention:

➤ They make object names more informative so developers can quickly understand an application's structure and code.

➤ They provide a standardized vocabulary for team efforts.

➤ They minimize conflicts when adding third-party products.

➤ They allow code, tools, and code libraries to be shared across various platforms.

➤ They group objects and facilitate various sort options.

➤ They can provide self-documenting program code.

➤ They enhance search and replace capabilities.

➤ They enable you to learn, modify, and incorporate code from others, including from magazines, reference books, the Internet, and peers.

Naming conventions should be incorporated at the beginning of the design process. In addition to establishing rules for objects within your Access application, you also need to consider the path and filenames for objects with which your application will interface. Establishing naming conventions takes a little extra time upfront, but naming conventions provide an immediate payoff; and the benefits are compounded as the application grows, becomes more complicated, interfaces with other applications, and is used by other developers.

Many developers are careful about naming tables, forms, fields, and even the controls that they build. But all too often, the controls that a wizard builds are left with their original names such as `Command65` or `Text58`. Because those names do not indicate what the control really does, they can create confusion and unnecessary conflicts, particularly if code is added to one of the control's events. One solution is to let the wizards do their stuff, and then promptly rename the object so that all future references to it will automatically use the correct name. Please remember that if the wizard generated the code, the name of the object needs to be changed both in the object's property and in VBA. That means you need to open the VBA Editor and update the name of the control within the code.

A BRIEF HISTORY

Currently, the most common naming conventions used in Access applications, Microsoft product documentation, and reference books are based on the Hungarian notation created by Charles Simonyi when he worked at Microsoft in the 1980s. In the Access world, Greg Reddick and Stan Leszynski further developed and popularized the naming convention. Greg published the Reddick VBA (RVBA) Naming Conventions at `www.xoc.net/standards/rvbanc.asp`. The Leszynski Naming Conventions (LNC) and development style continue to be referenced in several books and have been incorporated in various websites. Because URLs frequently change, a search is probably the best bet for finding a publication of the LNC.

The critical part is to recognize that the Hungarian notation is pretty much universally recognized, if not adopted, and that it continues to be adapted to keep up with technology. Some tags are becoming obsolete and new ones are continuously added. Although some tags may be retired, there are still programs using them, so it is handy to know where to find a translator, which, in this case, is a table of tag definitions.

THE FUNDAMENTALS OF THE HUNGARIAN CONVENTION

The Hungarian convention has a very straightforward design. It dictates that a name may contain up to five parts, and that the parts are combined in the order of prefix(es), tag, base name, qualifier, and suffix:

A *prefix* precedes a tag to provide clarification. It can describe one or more important properties with one or two lowercase characters.

A *tag* is considered by some to be the critical, non-optional element. A tag should be unique and easily differentiated from similarly named tags. A tag is typically three (occasionally four) lowercase characters that identify what the object is — a table, form, or text box, for example. The tag is usually a mnemonic abbreviation, such as tbl, frm, and txt or the first letter of each word from multiword items. Exceptions can occur for a number of reasons, such as: The tag has already been assigned for a different purpose, a tag was adopted from another program, and of course, it isn't always easy to create an intuitive three-letter abbreviation.

The *base name* is a descriptive name that defines the particular object. This could be the layman's term used to concisely identify the subject. Use proper case and be brief but clear.

A *qualifier* is an extension that indicates how the object is being used. Qualifiers should be title case and as short as practical, without sacrificing comprehension. For example, the qualifier Avg may be added to a query name to indicate that the query calculated the qryStudentGradeAvg (or qsumStudentGradeAvg).

A *suffix* is rarely needed. Its purpose is to differentiate object names that could otherwise be identical. The suffix is written in title case or as a number and should be as short as practical. For example, a series of queries that calculate the average grade for each grade (see the need to make a distinction?) could be named qryStudentGradeAvg4, qryStudentGradeAvg5, and qryStudentGradeAvg6, indicating the average for the fourth grade, the fifth grade, and the sixth grade class, respectively. And, although many developers avoid using the underscore, some developers like to separate the suffix by using one, as in qryStudentGradeAvg_4.

Although it isn't necessary for an object name to contain all of the parts, nearly every name will contain a tag and a base name. For example, here's the name for a table: tblStudent. You can quickly see that it conforms to the rules — there are no spaces, the tag is all lowercase, and the base name is title case. That is a fairly universally accepted format. Remember, object names should never include special characters or spaces (an exception being the underscore, as noted above). Other guidelines that you may want to follow are covered in the "Rules for Creating Names — Adding the Personal Touch" section later in this appendix.

The flag is the optional sixth part to a name. A flag affects where an object appears in lists and is effective for grouping items at the beginning or the end of a list. The following table describes common flags.

FLAG	DESCRIPTION
_ (underscore)	Causes the item to be listed before numbers and letters. Often used for items under development.
zh	Indicates a system object used for development and maintenance, but it is a hidden object.
zs	Indicates a system object used for development and maintenance but should not be seen by the end user, but not hidden.
zt	Indicates a temporary object that is created programmatically, such as a query built by code, and not preserved after it has been run.
zz	Denotes an object that you are no longer using and that is waiting to be deleted.

Remember that object names should not include special characters (except underscore) or spaces.

RULES FOR CREATING NAMES — ADDING THE PERSONAL TOUCH

Developers tend to have an independent streak, which often means that we like to do things our own way. Thankfully, development is a creative process, so typically there are multiple ways to achieve the desired results. That's also the case with naming conventions. Even if you choose to adopt existing standards, there are plenty of opportunities to incorporate your own preferences and come up with a system that is easy for you to remember, implement, and share. But before you start customizing things, it's still a good idea to understand the basic rules and principles of naming conventions. The following sections provide information to help you to both work with existing standards and create your own. You may find that a combination works best.

Starting with the Basics

Naming conventions apply to application objects, such as forms, reports, controls, queries, and user-defined objects, as well as to Access Connectivity Engine (ACE) (and to the predecessor Jet) objects such as Containers, databases, fields, `queryDefs`, `tableDefs`, and workspaces.

Consistency is the key. As stated earlier, it's best to determine your naming conventions before you create the first object in your database so that you can apply them consistently throughout your application. Remember that even when following an established naming convention, there will be plenty of situations that challenge your interpretation of how to apply it.

Next, think KISS (Keep It Short and Simple). Although Access allows up to 64 characters for each object name, no one wants to type or read names that are that long. Plus, your application may need to interface with other programs that are more restrictive in name length. If your object names aren't compatible with those programs, you could be in for a lot of extra work. So, although field names can be up to 64 characters, it is not necessarily a good thing to use very long names.

The following are some basic rules and guidelines that apply to both the name and the elements of objects:

➤ Names can contain up to 64 characters (but shorter is better, while still being descriptive, as previously discussed).

➤ Use complete words or consistently apply easy-to-interpret abbreviations. You might use FName and LName for FirstName and LastName, for example, or in a table with company details you might have field names of CoName, CoAddress, and so on.

➤ Names can consist of any combination of letters and numbers. For example, in tables with multiple address lines, it's common to see Address1 and Address2.

➤ Be aware: While spaces and some special characters are technically acceptable, they are known to create problems in table and field names. Field names cannot include a period (.), exclamation point (!), accent grave (`), or brackets ([ ]). We strongly advise you to avoid spaces and characters; they will require special handling (such as wrapping each name in brackets []) if you are going to customize and add code to work with these objects. You can learn more about special characters in Appendix F.

If you change the name of an object, remember that the name also needs to be updated in any code, modules, or other objects that reference it. This is why it's best to start off right!

➤ Do not begin a name with a leading space. We take this a step further to strongly recommend against using spaces in names (they can cause undue problems with program integration and some programming actions. For readability, we recommend using CamelCase, where you capitalize the first letter of each word — such as, tblCharityEvents.

➤ Do not include control characters ASCII values 0–31. The list is provided in Appendix F.

➤ Don't duplicate the name of a property or other element used by DAO.

➤ Avoid a series of uppercase letters — these typically indicate official abbreviations, such as USA. An exception would be if you consistently use an acronym for a lengthy table name in your application.

➤ Use singular rather than plural names, for example `LastName` for a field or `txtState` for a text box.

➤ Include the base name of the object(s) that it is built on, when practical and logical. This can be particularly helpful if there are multiple objects with similar names, such as a field name that appears in several tables. In that case, you might use `EventCity` for the field City in the table `tblEvent`.

➤ List multiple base objects left-to-right in descending order of importance, such as `tblStudentClass` for a table that joins records from `tblStudent` with records from `tblClass`.

You may also notice that although it is more common to list terms (table names) in the order of Parent-Child, some people choose to join the words alphabetically. You may also want to establish a specific policy for naming junction tables.

➤ A name should use CamelCase construction for the base. It is preceded by a lowercase, three-letter tag, as in `tblStudentClass`, `lblClassDate`, or `intQuantity`.

When you are the sole developer on a project, you may have the latitude to establish the naming conventions. If you are collaborating with others or combining objects from several projects, planning ahead and agreeing on naming conventions can prove to be invaluable. You will need to consider the types of tables, relationships, and objects that will be needed.

Some Additional Thoughts about Other Objects

If you are going to customize existing conventions or create your own, there are several other things that you will want to consider. The following are some of the more common objects that you'll want to have rules for handling.

Variables and Routines

The body of a variable or routine name should use mixed case and should be only long enough to describe its purpose. For example, `Dim intFormCount As Integer` returns the number of open forms.

Functions

Function names will typically begin with a noun as they return a value. Some developers add a prefix `fnc` or `f`, to add clarity and make them easier to locate, but this is a personal preference and it can make the functions more awkward to read in code. Avoid using `fn_` because that is the prefix that SQL Server uses for functions. Using `fncDisplayUnexpectedError`, for example, makes it clear that this is a function and not the name of a field that contains captured error messages.

Constants

The base name of a constant is often UPPERCASE_WORDS with underscores (_) between words. Prefixes such as g and m can be very useful in understanding the scope of a constant. For example, in the string for a new line character `gstrNEW_LINE`, the g indicates that it is global to the entire application and the s indicates that it's a String. This also provides an opportunity to point out a source of future confusion if prefixes can have multiple meanings. The s could also stand for single, so we see an immediate benefit of using `str` for string.

Constants should be prefixed by the scope prefixes m or g for module or global, respectively. A constant is indicated by appending the letter c to the end of the data type, or it can have the generic tag `con`. For the constant `gintcDiscount`, g is the scope, `int` indicates the data type, c means it's a constant, and the base name is `Discount`. Although `conDiscount` could also name the same constant, it conveys less information because it uses the generic tag. `mdblcPI` indicates module level (`m`), double (`dbl`) constant (`c`), with the base name `PI`.

Classes

A class defines a user-defined object. Because this creates a new data type, you may want to establish a new tag for the object. You can add a base name to the tag to spell out the abbreviation indicated by the tag. There are several examples throughout the book and download files. You may find it helpful to know that many developers use the class base name by itself, without any prefix or tag.

Arrays and Collections

An array is a variable that can store multiple values. In a *fixed array*, the number of rows and columns are specified; in a *dynamic array*, the dimensions can be established in the procedure calling the array. Arrays often use the tag a, such as `aintFontSizes` or `astrFields`.

Collections are groups of objects, such as the forms collection or a collection established to allow multiple instances of a single form. `col` is often used as a prefix to indicate a collection. For example, `mcolFormInstances` is a module-level collection allowing multiple form instances.

You may see this as a divergence from the norm of using singular names, but because arrays and collections are inherently plural, it's okay to use plural names.

Attachments

The attachment data type, added in Access 2007, allows you to store attachments within your Access database. As you add the file to the database, you can specify a name that best suits your users and your application — this will not affect the location or name of the original file. Although the rules for naming attachments are more lenient, we recommend that you use short, easy-to-interpret names that follow good naming standards.

Macros

A macro automates a task. It can be used alone or in a macro group, also called a macro. Macro is one of the objects listed in the Navigation Pane. Each macro and macro group should have a unique name that clearly describes the action that it performs. We recommend following standard naming procedures, including avoiding reserved words and special characters.

A good example of a macro name is `AutoExec`. Because it's often employed at startup, it is the most commonly used macro for an Access database. You learn more about macros in Chapter 4.

Web Objects

Because the names of web objects, particularly web forms and reports, are typically displayed in the browser's address box, many people choose user-friendly names without tags and use an underscore instead of a space. For example, a web report might be named `Sales_Report` instead of `rptSalesReport`. Arguably, both the underscore and space are outside our previously stated recommendations for naming local objects. But, as we mentioned, the names of web objects are often seen by the end user, so you may need to take that into account. This is a relatively new area, and you may find that the naming convention applied will vary greatly depending on the project and they will certainly grow over time.

MORE DOS AND DON'TS

By now, you'd think that all the basics have been covered, but of course, there is always more. So, just for good measure, here are a few more dos and don'ts:

➤ When creating a new tag, stick to existing rules and styles for length, case, and so forth.

➤ Don't repurpose an existing tag. Either create a new unique tag or find an existing tag that fits the purpose.

➤ Before creating a new tag, review existing tags to search for one that covers the situation.

➤ Avoid using ID as a prefix or suffix except for primary and foreign key fields. By default, these will cause Access to create an index on the field.

➤ Because ADO, ADOX, and DAO share some of the same tags, it is a good idea to fully qualify the library name. In addition to avoiding confusion, explicitly naming the library will make the code run faster. For example, to specify that it is an ADO record set, you might write:

```
Dim rst As ADODB.Recordset
```

And to specify that you are using ADOX, you might write:

```
Dim idx As ADOX.Index
```

TABLES OF TAGS

From working with the examples in this book, you are probably familiar with the prefixes and tags for the most frequently used objects. And, you've likely noticed some variations in the style and preferences of various authors and contributors. Although we've been emphasizing the benefits of consistency, we also see the value of exposing you to a variety of acceptable standards as a means to help you establish your own conventions.

For your convenience, we've compiled terms and tags from a multitude of sources and are providing them in a companion file that can be downloaded for this appendix. They are by no means all-inclusive listings of all the tags currently in use or that have been used, and new tags will continue to be generated as programs evolve and as developers create their own objects. That being said, the hope is that having this reasonably comprehensive list will save you valuable research time while you are trying to select the right tag or trying to decipher the meaning of a tag that is used in code that you have inherited. And, because you can download the file, you can easily search, sort, and customize the lists to best suit your needs.

STANDARDS

Throughout the book, we've pulled together reference material, sharing our expertise and experiences, and encouraging you to take the try-it, like-it, modify-as-appropriate approach. That methodology is particularly fitting for the lists and guidelines in these appendixes. With that in mind, here are a few reminders:

➤ Rules and guidelines change over time, so your naming conventions may need to be updated as you work with new versions and additional programs.

➤ There's an overwhelming supply of reference material with varying degrees of quality and applicability.

Some of the more reliable sources for additional or updated information on naming conventions, reserved words, and special characters will likely be found by searching Microsoft and www.mvps.org. Although it might seem that the most of Microsoft's articles are related to .NET, there are several that are relevant to Access development.

The most critical factor is that you consistently implement and follow some standard.

The Access Source Code Control

The Access Source Code Control (SCC) is a tool distributed separately from Access to allow developers to track the changes during the development of Access database applications. Source code controls can be effective for versioning and protecting software and any changes made to it, especially when there are multiple users accessing and updating the same code for long periods of time. Because there is no mechanism built directly into Access to version the changes made to a database, installing the SCC can provide systematic versioning for an Access database development project.

Three pieces are required to use the SCC with Access:

➤ Microsoft Access (any version after and including Access 2000).

➤ The Access Source Code Control component (which is included in the ADE).

➤ A source code control program, such as Microsoft Visual Source Safe (VSS); both versions 6.0a and 2005 will work.

Unfortunately the Access SCC Add-in does not include a source code control program, but it does give the user the capability to use Access with any standard source code control program. A standard source code control program is defined as any SCC provider that is registered to Windows as a standardized source code control provider in the Windows Registry. While many different source code control applications are available, the examples in this appendix use the Access SCC Add-in with Microsoft Visual Source Safe 2005 (MS VSS), the latest release of the MS VSS available with the Microsoft Visual Studio .NET 2010 product.

 Although the Visual Studio team is recommending using Team Foundation Server as a SCC over VSS for .NET development projects, the Access team is still recommending the use of VSS with the Access SCC Add-in features.

GETTING THE ACCESS SCC

The Access SCC component is a free but separate download available from the Microsoft Office website. The Access 2010 SCC Add-in can be downloaded from here:

```
http://www.microsoft.com/downloads/details
.aspx?displaylang=en&FamilyID=586912a5-3809-44ef-ac55-43d36ecab9de
```

INSTALLING THE ACCESS SCC

Once you have downloaded the Access 2010 SCC Add-in from the Microsoft website, installing the tool is a snap. Just double-click on the downloaded file to run the installer. Follow the steps on the installation wizard and complete the process, and the Access SCC component will be installed automatically.

If an SCC program, such as VSS 2005, is already installed on the machine when the ADE is installed, Access will be ready to use the Access SCC tool without any further modification. If that's your situation, you can just skip right to the section "Using the Access SCC," because you are ready to go!

However, if a source code control program, such as VSS 2005, was not already installed on the system when the SCC Add-in was installed, then a few steps are necessary to set up the SCC control program so that it can be used with the Access SCC tools.

 If the SCC Add-in is installed prior to installing a source code control program, every time Access is invoked, an error message — "you don't have a source code control program installed" — will be shown. The message asks if Access should continue to show the message when Access is started. Clicking the No button suppresses the message and you will not lose any functionality such as the capability to associate an SCC program with Access.

Installing an SCC Program

The first thing to do to is to get an SCC program installed on your machine. Again, this can be any standard source code control program, as long as it is registered in Windows and implements the MSSCCI provider. As mentioned before, for this example, we will be using VSS 2005, but there are also a multitude of free source code control tools available that will work equally well, assuming they support the MSSCCI provider implementation.

To set up VSS 2005, run the setup.exe program. Follow and complete the steps for the setup wizard. Using the default install options for VSS is fine; it needs only to be registered as the default SCC program. Once VSS is installed, there are a couple of setup items to take care of before it can be used with the Access SCC tools.

Registering an SCC Database

First you need to register an SCC database for VSS to use. Start the Visual SourceSafe Administrator program from the Windows Start menu. If you have a preexisting database, choose File and then choose Open SourceSafe Database. Otherwise, to make a new SCC database, select File and choose the New Database option. In either case, the Add SourceSafe Database Wizard dialog box will be invoked. Complete the following steps for the wizard:

1. Click the Next button on the first page of the wizard.

2. The second page requests the location of the SCC database. If one already exists, supply the full name and path of the database. Otherwise, choose a new location for the new database, and click Next.

3. On the third page, enter a name for the new database and click Next.

4. The fourth page requests the source code control model to use for the project. Either model can be used, so choose the model that works best for your situation, and then click Next. (More information about either model can be found in the MS VSS help files.)

5. The last page of the wizard — you're done. It was just that easy to register a database! Click Finish, and the new database is set up and ready to use.

Adding Users

The second item of business is to add users to the database if the SCC project will be used by multiple people. By default, the user of the account that installed the VSS program is added to the users' list automatically. To add other user accounts for the database, simply select Users and choose the Add User option to open the Add User dialog box. Add any desired users to the database and then the setup of the database will be complete and you are ready to begin adding Access database applications to the SCC project.

Be sure to note that any users added to the database will also need network access to the database created by the wizard. Also, the users will need to set up VSS on their local machine and then add the database to the VSS client.

After the users have been added, you can close the Visual SourceSafe Administrator program. You are ready to begin using the Access SCC tools with your Access databases.

USING THE ACCESS SCC

Once VSS 2005, or another SCC control program, and the ADE are installed, you're ready to begin using the Access SCC tools. The SCC add-in has a new, custom Ribbon tab, Source Control, which is shown in the Access window when a database is open. This tab is the user interface for working with the SCC features. In this section, you'll see how each of the Source Control options works with the VSS source control database.

Adding a Database to the SCC

To begin using the Source Control Ribbon features for any given database, you must first add the database to the source code control project. The following steps add a database to the SCC:

1. On the Source Control Ribbon, click the Add Database to SourceSafe button to open the Log On To Visual SourceSafe Database dialog box. Use your user name and password. (Note: Your default user name is your Windows user account name and a blank password.) Then click OK to log in and continue.

2. You're prompted for a location to add the database to. Each database that is checked into the SCC database should be separate from all other databases, and it's recommended that you choose a location folder to help separate the projects in a logical manner. Click OK when you're done.

3. The Add Objects to SourceSafe dialog box opens. By default, all objects in the database are selected, so just click OK and the entire database will be added. Of course, you could easily deselect any database objects that are not to be stored in the SCC database.

You are ready to begin using the SCC to version your database project. Once the database has been checked in, a new Check Out Data bar is shown, which is new to Access 2010, to quickly allow the user to check out the objects in the database. From now on, when the database is opened in the Access client, you can check out, check in, modify, and sync the database project with just a few button clicks.

Modifying SCC Databases

Now that the database has been added to the SCC database, notice that all of the objects in the Navigation Pane have a lock icon to denote that they are checked in and locked by the SCC. Right-click any of these objects and you'll see some new options added to the context menu for that database object. These allow the user to work with the various options available for the SCC project.

The user cannot modify the database objects until they are checked out. To check out an object, right-click on the object in the Navigation Pane and choose the Check Out option. The object is checked out and can now be modified. Once all changes have been completed, the object can be checked in from the corresponding option on the Navigation Pane's context menu called Check-In.

Note that there is an Undo Check-Out option available. If it is selected, all of the current changes for the database object will be discarded and the currently checked in version of the object will be restored to the local database. This undo option is provided to enable you to disallow any changes that have been made. However, this is an all-or-nothing proposition; there is no way to undo only specific changes made to the database object using the Undo Check-Out option.

Creating a Database from the SCC

If you do not have a copy of a database that's checked in to your source safe project to work on, you can easily create one from the SCC project. Just open the Office Backstage (without a database open) and select the New from SourceSafe option on the New tab. The Log On To Visual

SourceSafe Database dialog box opens. Enter a user name and password and click OK. The Create Local Project Form SourceSafe dialog box is opened. Navigate to the database you want to create a local copy of, select it, and click OK. A new database registered to the SCC project is created and you are ready to begin working with the database project.

THE ACCESS SCC OPTIONS

To work with the features supplied by the SCC provider and the SCC Add-in for Access, go to the Source Control Ribbon tab. Because the database is already registered in an SCC project, all of the options on this tab should be enabled, except for Add Database to SourceSafe for obvious reasons. When working with a database object, for actions such as checking out and checking in changes, click the object name in the Navigation Pane and then click the desired action in the Ribbon. The Navigation Pane is the interface for selecting database objects to use to work with in the Source Code Control program. Each of the available options for the SCC Add-in is described in the following table.

SCC OPTION	DESCRIPTION
Add database to SourceSafe	Adds a new database project to the source code–controlled database. If the current instance of the database is already checked into the SCC database, this option is disabled.
Create from SourceSafe	Closes any currently open database, creates the selected database from the SCC data, and opens the new database in the current instance of Access. Note: A New from SourceSafe option is available on the Office Backstage.
Check In	Checks in the current version of the database that is open in the Access client. To check in an object, select the object in the Navigation Pane and click the Check In button in the Ribbon. This option is also available in the Navigation Pane's context menu for the object. This invokes the Check In Objects dialog box, which allows one, many, or all database objects to be checked in.
Check Out	Checks out objects that are currently locked for editing. Access will prompt to automatically check out when changes are made to any locked object. To manually check out an object, select the object in the Navigation Pane and then click the Check-Out button on the Ribbon. This option is also available in the Navigation Pane's context menu for the object.
Undo Check Out	Discards any pending changes to the objects, restores the database project to the last checkpoint version, and marks the objects as checked in.
Latest Version	Synchronizes the database project to the current checkpoint in the SCC database. The option to get one, many, or all of the current project items is available. Note: If any items in the project are already checked out, they will either need to be checked in or discarded before those objects can be synchronized. This option is also available in the Navigation Pane's context menu for the object.

continues

(continued)

SCC OPTION	DESCRIPTION
Add Objects to SourceSafe	Adds one or many objects to the SCC database. Note: Some objects, such as modules, are not automatically added to the SCC project when they are saved. If an object has been added to the database project, but not to the SCC database, use the Add Objects to SourceSafe to add the objects to the SCC. This is the only way an object can be added to the SCC project if it is not automatically added when the object is created.
History	Displays the change history for a database object. To view the history for an object, select the object in the Navigation Pane and click the History button. The History Options dialog box opens; to see the full history, simply click OK. The full history of the changes displays in the History dialog box and you can view each version using the SCC program.
Share Objects	Shares the current version of a project to create a new subproject or branched version of the project. If a branch of the project is created, changes made in one branch are not propagated to other branches or versions of the SCC project.
Properties	Describes some of the basic details about the object settings in the SCC database. The path to the object, type of object, and current status of the object are provided here.
Differences	Provides the capability to view the differences between two objects in the SCC database. To view the differences between two objects, select the object in the Navigation Pane and click the Differences button. The Differences Options dialog box opens, and you can select which two files should be compared. This option is also available in the Navigation Pane's context menu for the object.
Run SourceSafe	Invokes MS VSS directly from the instance of Access. This opens the SCC database for the current code project in the VSS Explorer window.
Refresh Status	Updates the status of all of the objects in the SCC database. If new changes have been made from another user of the SCC project, those changes are propagated to the current instance of Access.
Options	Invokes the Source Code Control Options dialog box for the SCC Add-in.

The Source Code Control Options dialog box allows five basic options to be set for the SCC Add-in. The Options dialog box also exposes an entry point into the SourceSafe Options dialog box. These five options allow the user to do the following:

➤ Choose to automatically get the latest versions of objects when a database is checked in.

➤ Specify if the database objects should be automatically checked in when the database or Access is closed.

➤ Specify if the objects should be added to the SCC database when they are created in Access.

➤ To automatically remove objects from the SCC database when they have been deleted from the database in the Access client.

➤ To automatically get the updated status of all objects when the database is opened.

Clicking the Advanced button in this dialog box provides another dialog box with some of the more granular options provided for the SCC Add-in, via the SourceSafe Options dialog box. If you want to add a custom object editor for the SCC Add-in, for example, it can be chosen from the Advanced SourceSafe Options dialog box. This dialog box also provides a few more options for managing the SCC database settings.

If a program other than Microsoft Visual SourceSafe 2005 is used, the options available should be similar to the items discussed here because the SCC must be registered and implement the MSSCCI provider for Windows. Also, all of the other functions of an SCC program other than VSS should be very similar and should not affect the behavior of the previously discussed Access SCC options, which could cause the Access SCC to fail if not ensured.

SUMMARY

As you have seen, the Access SCC component can be very useful for developing Access database applications for either a single person or a team of developers. The Access SCC component is a free tool to allow the versioning of an Access database and its objects during the development process. The Access SCC component will work with any standard source code control program which implements the MSSCCI provider and provides the required functionality supported by the Access SCC. The Access SCC provides a rich and powerful versioning feature set for any database project. For more information about the Access Source Code Control Add-in, see the `http://Office.Microsoft.com` website.

Tips and Tricks

Gaining technical competence is only one part of the equation for becoming a successful Access developer, and most of this book has been focused on helping you learn solid skills for writing and modifying code, including macros. But you also need to consider the user's perspective in order to deliver, intuitive solutions that are easy to maintain and modify. In this appendix, we share several of our favorite tips, tricks, and techniques. When you work with the download files for this appendix, you'll see that most of the examples are contained in the Chamber application. And, as an extra bonus, we've collected a few tips from other esteemed developers and colleagues. In addition to augmenting your developer toolbox, these will also provide wider variety in style and techniques.

VISUAL INTERFACE STANDARDS

As with many areas of life, appearances can make a lasting impression. The way an application looks can have a significant impact on its success — so much so, that a poorly designed UI, in looks and/or functionality, can essentially sabotage a project, no matter how great the underlying code and concepts. On the other hand, an intuitive, clean, user-friendly UI can earn invaluable user buy-in and even off-set other shortcomings. Rather than leaving you to learn on your own, we have drawn from our cumulative years of experience as developers and consultants to share some recommendations that will help your applications present a desired level of professionalism and polish.

Use Businesslike Colors

Consider using a theme or style and then limit the number of colors. If you want your applications to look like they fit right into the Windows environment, use the venerable Windows Standard color scheme, meaning gray. You should actually make the colors of your forms adapt to the Windows scheme automatically.

For the background color of almost everything (forms, buttons, read-only text boxes, and so on), use the Windows default Background Form color. The numeric color value is -2147483633. Use white for the background of changeable fields. In Access 2007, you can now see the names of the Windows colors in the drop-down list instead of their numbers. And, to help you view and use shades of selected colors, we've also provided a color-blending tool, which is discussed later in this appendix.

> *Magic numbers: Access color properties use regular, positive numbers for normal static colors. All the "Windows" colors (that change automatically when the Windows scheme changes) are negative numbers.*

To test your colors and make sure they aren't hard-coded to a certain color, change your Windows color scheme to something completely different and look through your forms to make sure all the colors remain consistent.

Use red sparingly. You can use red (255) for the Fore Color of the Exit button and any dangerous buttons you might have, but don't use it anywhere else. If you overuse it, it loses its special purpose as a warning or danger color.

Provide a Well-Marked Exit

Provide an easy but safe exit from most of your forms (screens). Almost every form should have an Exit button, and always in the same place, such as the lower-right corner. Depending on the length of the form and variations in screen resolutions, you may also want to consider placing an Exit button at both the top and bottom of the form. It should call a function that asks users if they really want to exit the application. This provides a quick exit and reinforces the practice of following procedures. Of course, you should not put an Exit button on a form that is in the middle of a series of steps where the user needs to complete a particular action before exiting, such as in the middle of a wizard or in a pop-up form where they can modify detailed information.

You can call the following code from the On Click event of the Exit button. It can be placed in any module. The function DisplayUnexpectedError is described in Chapter 7.

Available for download on Wrox.com

```
Sub ExitProgram()
On Error GoTo Error_Handler

Dim response As Variant
If MsgBox("Are you sure you want to exit " & "My Application" _
    & "?", vbOKCancel, "My Application") = vbOK Then

  DoCmd.Quit
End If

Exit_Procedure:
  Exit Sub

Error_Handler:
  DisplayUnexpectedError Err.Number, Err.Description
  Resume Exit_Procedure
  Resume

End Sub
```

code snippet CS 1 in appI_Tips_Code.txt

This allows your users a chance to stay in the application in case they didn't mean to exit. By aborting the exit routine, they can continue to work; and avoid wasting saving valuable time waiting for the application to reopen and then to navigate back to the process that they were working on.

Watch Your Punctuation

Most Access applications are used in a business setting so it's best to keep a professional tone in the message boxes, forms, and reports. Proper punctuation is especially important because it shows a level of polish and thoroughness.

For example, you should use exclamation points very sparingly. And you should always end sentences and statements with periods. Keep in mind that the placement or lack of punctuation can change the meaning of a statement. If you keep your punctuation correct and your tone businesslike, your users will perceive your application as a professional business tool and asset.

Use Consistent Button Placement & Shortcut Keys

Be consistent with button placement, size, and color. Close (a form or report) and Exit (the application) buttons should always be in the same places on forms. The "drill-down" form the user opens by double-clicking on a row should also be available by clicking the left-most button (Detail) at the bottom of the form, as shown in Figure I-1. The key is position control buttons so that they are convenient (for the user) and consistently placed.

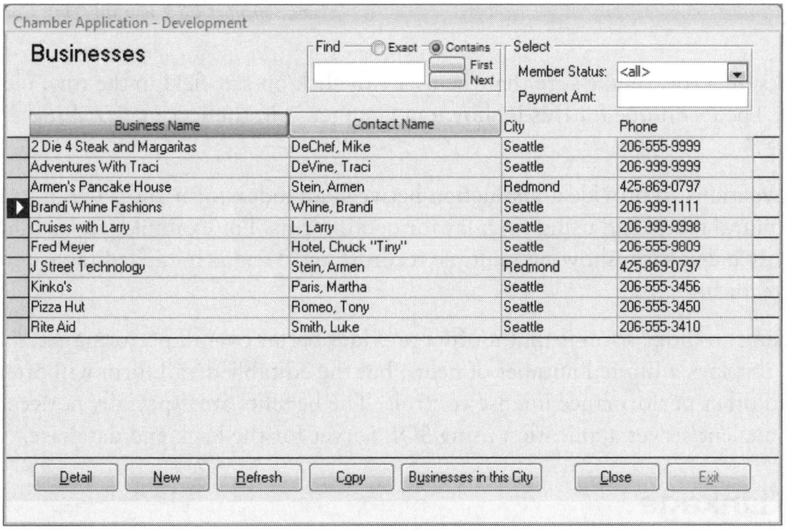

FIGURE I-1

Also, you should provide shortcut or Alt keys for your buttons. It's easy: In the `Caption` property of each button, add an ampersand (&) before the letter you want to use for the Alt key combination. Try to be consistent across all your forms, and make sure that you don't use the same letter for two different buttons. This simple step can be a tremendous time saver, especially for those who prefer keystrokes to mouse moves.

Hide Higher-Level Forms

Hide previous forms as you drill down, unless the next one is directly related to the previous one and you open the next one in Dialog mode. Be careful if you let the user click between multiple open forms; the user may get lost or take actions you didn't plan for in your code. This is even more important with the default tabbed form interface because simply maximizing a form won't hide the tabs for the other visible forms. See the daisy-chaining topic later in this appendix for a method that displays only one form at a time.

Use Read-Only "Index" Forms

When your user needs to open a table or Recordset to modify data, don't just dump the user straight into the detail form in which the first record is always displayed. Not only is this unprofessional, but it forces the user to navigate to the desired record, and it increases the potential for the user to change the wrong record.

Alternatively, we suggest using a read-only index form that shows all the records in continuous form with the Windows Background color instead of a white background. When the user double-clicks on a row or clicks the Detail button, you can open the specified detail record by setting the `Where Condition` on the `OpenForm` command to the key of the selected record, like this:

```
DoCmd.OpenForm FormName:="frmBusiness", _
    WhereCondition:="BusinessKey = " & Me!BusinessKey
```

Available for download on Wrox.com

code snippet CS 2 in appI_Tips_Code.txt

If you allow double-clicks on a row, make sure that the user can click on any field in the row, plus the record selector itself. The technique for this is shown in Chapter 7, in the section "Drilling Down with Double-Click."

You can use naming conventions to provide a distinction between an index form and a detail form by giving index forms a plural name and using singular for detail forms. For example, you can have `frmBusinesses` (read-only index form showing multiple records) and `frmBusiness` (editable detail form showing only one record).

Another advantage of using an index form is that it often provides better overall performance. An index form typically displays a limited number of fields; but the editable detail form will often include combo boxes and other performance intense controls. The benefits are especially noticeable if you are working with a client/server application using SQL Server for the back-end database.

Check Your Table Linkage

We are working under the premise that you are using a split database with the UI in the frontend and connecting to data files in the backend. And you know that you can't always control if or when files are moved. So, rather than risk alarming the user with a message about invalid tables, we recommend checking the table links every time the database is started.

There are some common routines on the Internet or in other books to check table links, or you can write your own. Either way, your application will look a lot more professional if you handle your linked tables before the user sees a problem.

Translate Default Delete Messages

You may also want to replace the messages Access gives you when you delete records with a friendlier version of your own. You can confirm deletions for each record or for a whole group, and you can prevent the default Access messages from appearing. This takes a bit more work, but it's more professional. (See Chapter 7 for more information about using the `Delete` and `Before Delete Confirm` events.) Use wording such as: `Are you sure you want to delete product Grilled Tenderloin?`

Showing your own message before deleting a record is especially helpful when you have enabled cascade deletes in back-end relationships. You may want to use wording such as:

```
Are you sure you want to delete business Mike's Steak & Margaritas? This will also
delete all the payments and records associated with this business.
```

By using your own friendly warning messages instead of the default Access messages, your application will look more professional and be more meaningful to users. A bonus is that you can customize the caption, include your company name, or other relevant instructions. . In situations where it is beneficial to give the user more, you may want to allow them to proceed without prompts/messages, and then provide them with a clear and easy method to undue or otherwise return to a prior state.

Looking Good

Remember that your users can't see your great code or beautiful database structure. They can see only your user interface — the forms and reports in your application. Much of their perception of your application will be determined by how it looks, so it's important to pay special attention to these areas.

Now that you have your applications looking good, let's explore some techniques that you can use to make your applications more powerful and easy to use.

DAISY CHAIN YOUR FORMS

When your user navigates from one form to another, one of your jobs as an application developer is to keep things simple. When users have the ability to click between multiple open forms, they can lose track of their current form, or perform actions that are not handled as intended. A safer approach is to carefully control which forms are visible at any one time.

Controlling the visibility and flow of one form to another is often called *daisy chaining*. There are a few different types of daisy chaining. They involve two main choices: whether to hide the calling form, and whether to open the called form in Dialog mode. For this example, say the calling form is Form A and the called form is Form B.

If Form A needs to be requeried (to have record source updated) after Form B is closed, then open Form B in Dialog mode to have Form A's code wait until the user is finished with Form B. You often see this when Form A is an index form showing multiple records, and Form B is a detail form where the user can create, change, or even delete one of the records.

If Form A provides some contextual information that would be handy for the user to see while Form B is open (such as which record he's currently working with), then you can leave Form A visible while Form B is open. To prevent the user from clicking between the two and possibly obscuring Form B, use your old friend Dialog mode to prevent him from clicking on Form A.

If Form A does not need to be visible while Form B is open or is not requeried when Form B closes, then the easiest form of daisy chaining is to hide Form A when Form B is opened, and make it visible again when Form B closes. This is the most common form of daisy chaining and it works well when traversing menu or "switchboard" forms.

The main VBA components of the "hiding and showing" aspects of daisy chaining code are described in the following sections.

> ## DIALOG MODE (SETS THE MODE FOR SUBSEQUENT FORMS AND REPORTS)
>
> When you daisy chain a form and use Dialog mode, you are committed to using Dialog mode for each level thereafter unless you hide the calling form. That's because a form opened in Dialog mode does not allow any non–Dialog mode form to come to the forefront or to accept input. Also, if you open a report while a form is open and visible in Dialog mode, the report will appear behind the Dialog mode form, and also will not accept any input. One way around this is to open the report using Dialog mode. However, the report will not be maximized even if you specify `DoCmd.Maximize` in its `On Activate` event.

Form A Opens Form B

When Form A opens Form B, Form A also needs to "hide itself." However, to make Form A visible again, Form B needs to remember which form opened it. To remember this, Form A uses a global variable to "pass in" its own name (see the example Form A in Figure I-2). In this example, the user can drill down on a particular business by double-clicking the record or clicking the Detail button.

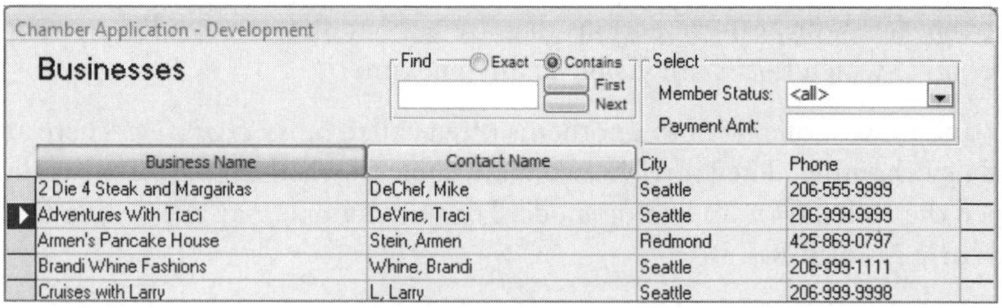

FIGURE I-2

Access 2007 introduced the `TempVars` collection. It is an `Application` collection that can store values that persist while the Access database remains open, and the values are not cleared when code is stopped during debugging. You use `TempVars` like this:

```
Application.TempVars.Add ("MyGlobalVariableName", "MyGlobalValue")
```

Then, when you need to retrieve the value, you can load it into a VBA variable like this:

```
MyVariableName = Application.TempVars("MyGlobalVariableName")
```

One handy feature of the TempVars collection is that you don't need to check if the particular item is already added to set its value. When you use the .Add method for a TempVars item that already exists, the new value just replaces the old value.

The following examples employ a global variable for compatibility with earlier versions of Access, but if you know your application will be running in Access 2007 or later, you could switch to using TempVars.

Here is some example code in frmBusinesses (an index form showing many businesses) to open frmBusiness (a detail form to modify a single business).

Available for download on Wrox.com

```
Private Sub cmdDetail_Click()
On Error GoTo Error_Handler

Dim strLinkCriteria As String

If IsNull(Me!BusinessKey) Then
  EnableDisableControls
  GoTo Exit_Procedure
End If

gstrCallingForm = Me.Name
strLinkCriteria = "[BusinessKey]=" & Me![BusinessKey]
DoCmd.OpenForm FormName:="frmBusiness", _
WhereCondition:=strLinkCriteria
Me.Visible = False

Exit_Procedure:
  On Error Resume Next
  Exit Sub

Error_Handler:
  DisplayUnexpectedError Err.Number, Err.Description
  Resume Exit_Procedure
  Resume

End Sub
```

code snippet CS 3 in appI_Tips_Code.txt

Note that before `frmBusiness` is opened, the name of the current form (`Me.Name`) is loaded into the global variable `gstrCallingForm` using `gstrCallingForm = Me.Name`

Then, after the line to open `frmBusiness`, the current form is hidden using `Me.Visible = False`. At this point, the first form is hidden and only the second (detail) form (B) is visible, as shown in Figure I-3. Although maximizing Form B will essentially hide Form A, this may result in the desired presentation. With the range in monitors and display settings, a maximized form may have excessive white space and other detractions. The show/hide technique is indifferent to monitor size and resolution settings.

Chamber Application - Development				
Business				
Business Name:	Adventures With Traci			
First Name:	Traci	Last Name:	DeVine	
First Name 2:	Brandi	Last Name 2:	Whine	
Street:	123 Forever			
City:	Seattle	State: WA	Zip Code:	98123
Telephone:	206-999-9999	Fax:	206-999-9999	
Email:	Traci@AdventuresOfALifetime.4Fun			
Website:				
Business Type:	TRAVEL AGE	District: BRD		
Member Since:	2004	Status: CUR	☐ Non Profit Flag	

Payments

Date	Amount
▶	

Comments: (Double-click to zoom)

Best adventures that money can buy.

For custom tailored attire, visit Brandi Whine's fashions.

This Week's Promotion:
2 Die 4 Steak and Margaritas
Talk with Mike DeChef and ask for
"the Traci Special"

[Close]

FIGURE I-3

Form B Opens

When Form B wakes up, it has a little housekeeping to do before anything else happens. In the `On Open` event, it needs to remember the name of the form that called it. Later, when Form B closes, it will use that name to make Form A visible again.

```
Private Sub Form_Open(Cancel As Integer)
On Error GoTo Error_Handler

Me.Caption = AppGlobal.ApplicationNameAndDB()
mstrCallingForm = gstrCallingForm
gstrCallingForm = ""

Exit_Procedure:
  Exit Sub
```

```
Error_Handler:
  DisplayUnexpectedError Err.Number, Err.Description
  Resume Exit_Procedure
  Resume

End Sub
```

code snippet CS 4 in appl_Tips_Code.txt

To remember the name, the value in `gstrCallingForm` is placed safely into `mstrCallingForm`:

```
mstrCallingForm = gstrCallingForm
```

This module-level variable (prefix `m`) is declared at the top of Form B's module, like this:

```
Option Compare Database
Option Explicit
Dim mstrCallingForm As String
```

Notice that `gstrCallingForm` is set to an empty string right after its contents are saved into `mstrCallingForm` with the following line of code:

```
gstrCallingForm = ""
```

There is no programming logic that requires this, but it clearly communicates to other programmers that you are completely done using the global variable, so you are clearing its value. It can go back to being an empty string now that it has transferred its contents to the local module variable.

At this point, Form B (the detail form) is ready to continue opening and perform whatever functions it is designed to do. It will remember the name of the calling Form A until it closes.

Form B Closes

During the entire time that Form B (`frmBusiness`) is open, Form A (`frmBusinesses`) remains hidden. However, when the user closes Form B, you need to make sure that Form A becomes visible again. The following code is in the `On Close` event of Form B (the detail form):

Available for download on Wrox.com

```
Private Sub Form_Close()
On Error GoTo Error_Handler

If mstrCallingForm <> "" Then
   Forms(mstrCallingForm).Visible = True
End If

Exit_Procedure:
  Exit Sub

Error_Handler:
If Err = 2450 Then
  ' ignore error if calling form is no longer loaded
  Resume Next
```

```
Else
  DisplayUnexpectedError Err.Number, Err.Description
  Resume Exit_Procedure
  Resume
End If

End Sub
```

code snippet CS 5 in appI_Tips_Code.txt

The operative code here is: `Forms(mstrCallingForm).Visible = True`

This code uses the `Forms` collection (a collection of all currently open forms in the database) to locate the form with the name stored in `mstrCallingForm` and make it visible.

However, two other sections of code are there just for you, the developer. The first is a check to make sure that `mstrCallingForm` actually has a value before attempting to make it visible. This enables you to open Form B directly during development (instead of from Form A), and not have to deal with the resulting error every time Form B closes.

```
If mstrCallingForm <> "" Then
  Forms(mstrCallingForm).Visible = True
End If
```

Along the same lines, the error handler code contains an exception for `Error 2450`, which will occur if the calling form is no longer loaded. Again, this is to allow you, in development mode, to close Form A while Form B is open without seeing an error when Form B closes.

```
If Err = 2450 Then
  ' ignore error if calling form is no longer loaded
  Resume Next
```

When Form B closes and makes Form A visible again, Form B's link in the daisy chain is complete.

When Form A Is a Subform

When Form A (the index) is a subform (subforms can also have their own subforms), you cannot send `Me.Name` into Form B because a subform cannot be made visible or hidden directly. Instead, you need to specify the name of the parent form. So, instead of setting the global variable and making the current form hidden, like this:

Available for download on Wrox.com

```
gstrCallingForm = Me.Name
Me.Visible = False
```

You can use the following code to hide the parent form.

```
gstrCallingForm = Me.Parent.Name
Me.Parent.Visible = False
```

code snippet CS 6 in appI_Tips_Code.txt

Form B will never know the difference. When it closes, Form A's parent form will be made visible again. Later, we'll show you how to use `TempVars` to limit what a user can see or do based on their login or credentials (for Access and/or Windows).

FIND RECORDS

Although Access provides some built-in ways to search for records, they can be confusing for users who are running your application. For example, the binoculars button offers several search options, but most users don't know how to use it properly. As an alternative, you can provide a custom search form, as shown in Figure I-4.

FIGURE I-4

This record-finding technique allows any phrase to be entered in the text box, and then it finds the first (or next) record that contains that phrase anywhere in the displayed fields. Alternatively, the user may change the radio buttons to request an exact match, where the entire field must match the phrase. Exact mode is not used very often, but it can be handy in searching for exact codes or numbers (such as membership or account numbers).

Calling the Record Finder Code

The On Click event of the First button (shown in Figure I-4) includes this code:

```
Private Sub cmdFirst_Click()
On Error GoTo Error_Handler

FindRecordLike "first"

Exit_Procedure:
  On Error Resume Next
  Exit Sub

Error_Handler:
  DisplayUnexpectedError Err.Number, Err.Description
  Resume Exit_Procedure
  Resume

End Sub
```

code snippet CS 7 in appI_Tips_Code.txt

The code really has only one operative line: FindRecordLike "first"

The code behind cmdNext_Click() is almost identical. Instead of using "first" as the parameter for FindRecordLike, it sends in "next" resulting in: FindRecordLike "next".

The following code is for the subroutine FindRecordLike. It is also used in the index form that contains the record finder controls.

```
Private Sub FindRecordLike(strFindMode As String)
On Error GoTo Error_Handler

Call ww_FindRecord(frmCallingForm:=Me, _
    ctlFindFirst:=Me!cmdFirst, _
    ctlFindNext:=Me!cmdNext, _
    ctlSearchText:=Me!txtFind, _
    ctlSearchOption:=Me!optFind, _
    strFindMode:=strFindMode, _
    strField1:="BusinessName", _
    strField2:="LastName", _
    strField3:="FirstName", _
    strField4:="City")

Exit_Procedure:
    On Error Resume Next
    Exit Sub

Error_Handler:
    DisplayUnexpectedError Err.Number, Err.Description
    Resume Exit_Procedure
    Resume

End Sub
```

code snippet CS 8 in appI_Tips_Code.txt

This subroutine accepts a parameter strFindMode of "first" or "next", which it passes directly to the ww_FindRecord procedure. In fact, pretty much all this procedure does is call ww_FindRecord. The interesting part is that the parameters that are passed to ww_FindRecord, many of which are explained in the next section. First, take a look at the parameters strField1, strField2, strField3, and strField4.

You must specify which fields the record finder routine will search. You can do this by sending in up to ten field names. These must be names of fields that appear in the Recordsource for the form. Although they don't technically have to appear on the form itself, it will seem strange to the user to find records containing a phrase that he can't see.

Why not automate the list of fields? It would be possible to use VBA to cycle through all of the fields displayed on the form, using the form's Controls collection, and send their names to the ww_FindRecord procedure automatically. However, you may not want all the fields to be searchable. By sending them yourself, you can control which fields are searched.

This example sends only four field names to be searched, but it could have specified up to ten. Fields 2 through 10 are optional parameters, and are explained later in this chapter.

Record Finder Code

You'll want to make this code as easy as possible to implement and reuse. The key is to pass references to the controls on this form (the text box, buttons, even the form itself) to a reusable Record Finder function. Note that this code has a ww_ prefix (for Wiley-Wrox) to reduce conflicts with any other public procedures.

Available for download on Wrox.com

```
Option Compare Database
Option Explicit

'Record Finder

'Accepts references from a continuous form with Record Finder
'controls, finds the first/next record containing the search
'text in one of the passed-in field names, and repositions the
'form to that record.

Public Function ww_FindRecord(frmCallingForm As Form, _
    ctlFindFirst As Control, _
    ctlFindNext As Control, _
    ctlSearchText As Control, _
    ctlSearchOption As Control, _
    strFindMode As String, _
    strField1 As String, _
    Optional strField2 As String, _
    Optional strField3 As String, _
    Optional strField4 As String, _
    Optional strField5 As String, _
    Optional strField6 As String, _
    Optional strField7 As String, _
    Optional strField8 As String, _
    Optional strField9 As String, _
    Optional strField10 As String)

On Error GoTo Error_Handler

Dim recClone As Recordset
Dim intBookmark As String
Dim strAllFields As String
Dim strSelection As String

' Field delimiter is used to separate concatenated
' field values below. This prevents text from being
' matched across adjacent fields. It may be changed
' to any text value that is unlikely to appear in the fields.
Const FIELDDELIMITER = "@%%@"
```

```
' If there is no string to search for set the focus back to
' the text box.
If ctlSearchText & "" = "" Or strField1 & "" = "" Then
  ctlSearchText.SetFocus
  Exit Function
End If

DoCmd.Hourglass True

ww_FindRecord = False
```

code snippet CS 9 in appI_Tips_Code.txt

The next section of code handles the search if the user has specified the Contains mode. It is the default search and the most flexible because it will find the phrase anywhere in any of the specified fields. You might wonder about the effects of including optional strings that have no values. They will become a ZLS (zero length string) rather than a Null, as a string field cannot be Null.

```
'Test search option
If ctlSearchOption = 1 Then 'Contains search

  ' build string to concatenate all fields together
  strAllFields = "[" & strField1 & "]"
  If strField2 <> "" Then
    strAllFields = strAllFields & " & " & """ & FIELDDELIMITER & _
    """ & [" & strField2 & "]"
  End If

  If strField3 <> "" Then
    strAllFields = strAllFields & " & " & """ & FIELDDELIMITER & _
    """ & [" & strField3 & "]"
  End If

' ----  repeat If Then … End If block for each field. --------

  If strField10 <> "" Then
    strAllFields = strAllFields & " & " & """ & FIELDDELIMITER & _
    """ & [" & strField10 & "]"
  End If

  Set recClone = frmCallingForm.RecordsetClone

  ' if find First button was used
  If strFindMode = "first" Then
    recClone.FindFirst strAllFields & " Like ""*" & _
    Replace(ctlSearchText, """", """""") & "*"""
    If recClone.NoMatch Then
      MsgBox "No matches found.", vbOKOnly, "Record Finder"
      ctlSearchText.SetFocus
    Else
      frmCallingForm.Bookmark = recClone.Bookmark
      ctlFindNext.SetFocus
      ww_FindRecord = True
    End If
```

```
    Else
        ' if find Next button was used
        If strFindMode = "next" Then
          recClone.Bookmark = frmCallingForm.Bookmark
          recClone.FindNext strAllFields & " Like ""*" & _
          Replace(ctlSearchText, """", """""""") & "*"""

          If recClone.NoMatch Then
            MsgBox "No more matches found.", vbOKOnly, _
            "Record Finder"
            ctlFindFirst.SetFocus
          Else
            frmCallingForm.Bookmark = recClone.Bookmark
            ctlFindNext.SetFocus
            ww_FindRecord = True
          End If
        End If
    End If
Else
```

Following is the code for the search if the user specifies Exact mode. It checks the exact contents of each of the specified fields to see if they equal the user's search phrase.

```
'ctlSearchOption = 2 'Exact Search
strSelection = "CStr(" & strField1 & " & """") = """ & _
Replace(ctlSearchText, """", """""""") & """"

If strField2 <> "" Then
  strSelection = strSelection & _
  " OR CStr(" & strField2 & " & """") = """ & _
  Replace(ctlSearchText, """", """""""") & """"
End If

If strField3 <> "" Then
  strSelection = strSelection & _
  " OR CStr(" & strField3 & " & """") = """ & _
  Replace(ctlSearchText, """", """""""") & """"
End If

' ----  repeat If Then ... End If block for each field. --------

Set recClone = frmCallingForm.RecordsetClone

If strFindMode = "first" Then
  recClone.FindFirst strSelection
  If recClone.NoMatch Then
    MsgBox "No matches found.", vbOKOnly, "Record Finder"
    ctlSearchText.SetFocus
  Else
    frmCallingForm.Bookmark = recClone.Bookmark
    ctlFindNext.SetFocus
    ww_FindRecord = True
  End If
```

```
      Else
        ' if find Next button was used
        If strFindMode = "next" Then
          recClone.Bookmark = frmCallingForm.Bookmark
          recClone.FindNext strSelection
          If recClone.NoMatch Then
            MsgBox "No more matches found.", vbOKOnly, _
            "Record Finder"
            ctlFindFirst.SetFocus
          Else
            frmCallingForm.Bookmark = recClone.Bookmark
            ctlFindNext.SetFocus
            ww_FindRecord = True
          End If
        End If
      End If
    End If

    DoCmd.Hourglass False

Exit_Procedure:
    Exit Function

Error_Handler:
    DoCmd.Hourglass False
    DisplayUnexpectedError Err.Number, Err.Description
    Resume Exit_Procedure
    Resume

End Function
```

code snippet CS 11 in appI_Tips_Code.txt

This code incorporates several techniques that we'll explain in the next few sections.

Passing Control and Form References to a Function

The Record Finder function is in a separate module rather than residing behind a specific form. For it to be usable from any index (or search) form in the application, it needs to be able to interact with that form, so in addition to actual parameter values you also pass the following object references from your form:

➤ `frmCallingForm`: The actual form itself, to build a `RecordsetClone` and to set the `Bookmark`

➤ `ctlFindFirst`: The First button, to set focus

➤ `ctlFindNext`: The Next button, to set focus

➤ `ctlSearchText`: The text box with the search phrase, to use for searching and to set focus

➤ `ctlSearchOption`: The radio button group of Exact/Contains, to determine which kind of search to perform

The key thing to remember is that these references are not the actual values. They are pointers to the controls on the original form, so they give you direct access to those controls as if this code were in that form itself.

The rest of the parameters are values, such as the Find mode (first or next matching record) and the names of up to ten fields to search.

Optional Parameters

The Record Finder function uses *optional parameters*, meaning that when you call this function, you can choose whether to specify them. In this example, the optional parameters are `strField2` through `strField10`. Optional parameters are very useful in this case because they give you the flexibility to specify any number of fields to search; in this case we've allowed from 1 to 10. If you didn't use optional parameters in this procedure, you'd have to specify all ten field names every time you called it, sending in empty strings for the ones you didn't need.

Using the RecordsetClone

A `RecordsetClone` is a Recordset based on a form's Recordset, and it provides full search capabilities and a different record cursor. You use a `RecordsetClone` of the form to find a matching record, and then use its `Bookmark` property to position the form to the matching record. You do this using the passed-in `Form` reference, as shown here:

```
Set recClone = frmCallingForm.RecordsetClone
frmCallingForm.Bookmark = recClone.Bookmark
```

code snippet CS 12 in appI_Tips_Code.txt

The reference is passed in as a parameter to this procedure, so the `RecordsetClone` being searched is the same as the Recordset currently displayed on the index form that called the record finder procedure. You'll find explanations and examples of how to use a `RecordsetClone` and the `Bookmark` property in several chapters, particularly in Chapter 11, which covers DAO.

Searching Multiple Fields Using Concatenation

To search multiple fields, the Record Finder function takes a different approach than you might be familiar with. Instead of building a complex SQL string that searches each specified field in the Recordset with `OR` statements, it concatenates all the desired fields from the Recordset into one large string (`strAllFields`). Then it searches the large text field for the search phrase.

There's one problem with this approach. The search phrase may be discovered using the end of one field and the beginning of another. For example, if the fields for City and State are concatenated together, they may look like this: `SeattleWA`. So, a search for "lew" may find a record even if the letters were not all in the same field.

To avoid this problem, use the `FIELDDELIMETER` constant. In our example, it is set to `"@%%@"`, a value that's unlikely to occur in any search phrase. When you concatenate the desired fields together into the one big field, they are separated by this delimiter value, like this: `Seattle@%%@WA`.

Using the `FIELDDELIMETER` constant separates the two words and prevents a search from returning records based on a value created by combining two fields.

Handling Quotes in the Search Phrase

There's a potential problem when the user types a quote (") in the search phrase of an index/search form, as shown in Figure I-5.

Chamber Application - Development				
Businesses	Find ○ Exact ● Contains "tiny" First Next	Select Member Status: <all> Payment Amt:		

Business Name	Contact Name	City	Phone	
2 Die 4 Steak and Margaritas	DeChef, Mike	Seattle	206-555-9999	
Adventures With Traci	DeVine, Traci	Seattle	206-999-9999	
Armen's Pancake House	Stein, Armen	Redmond	425-869-0797	
Brandi Whine Fashions	Whine, Brandi	Seattle	206-999-1111	
Cruises with Larry	L, Larry	Seattle	206-999-9998	
▶ Fred Meyer	Hotel, Chuck "Tiny"	Seattle	206-555-9809	
J Street Technology	Stein, Armen	Redmond	425-869-0797	

FIGURE I-5

Because you build strings using quotes in the code, these "extra" quotes supplied by the user can cause errors. To guard against that, replace each quote in the user's search phrase with two quotes. You learn more about string handling techniques in Chapter 13.

You can use the VBA `Replace` function to replace the quote, as shown in the following line of code:

```
Replace(ctlSearchText, """", """""")
```

This takes every instance of a quote (") in `ctlSearchText` and replaces it with two quotes (""). Then, when you build search strings with it, those doubled-up quotes will "collapse" back into solo quotes. It looks weird, but it works.

Setting Focus from Afar

You can make the `Find` routine more user-friendly and efficient by controlling the focus so that keystrokes make sense. For example, if the user clicks the First button and no match is found, he's probably going to want to change the search phrase to something else. So, you can help by using the following code to set the focus to the Search Text control

Available for download on Wrox.com

```
If recClone.NoMatch Then
   MsgBox "No matches found.", vbOKOnly, "Record Finder"
   ctlSearchText.SetFocus
```

code snippet CS 13 in appI_Tips_Code.txt

Remember that this code is not in the form the user is viewing — you are controlling focus from this procedure using a reference to the control on the index form that called `ww_FindRecord`.

Similarly, to facilitate cycling through all the matching records, we set focus to the Next button when a record is found, and to the First button after no more records are found. That allows the user to continue to press the Enter key on the keyboard to repeatedly loop through all the matching records. This feature is convenient, adding a lot of polish to your applications.

SPLIT YOUR APPLICATION

Developers may have different opinions and preferences about writing code, naming conventions and even the approach to application development, but with very few exceptions they will agree that a database solution should be split into a front-end application (user-interface) and a back-end database (data source). There are countless benefits, and although it may be optional in many circumstances, many times it is the only practical approach. Split files allow each user to have a copy of the application file (one user per file), they allow you to modify and replace the application without touching the data, and they allow you to switch or connect to different back-end files.

Although Access provides a wizard that will split the database, it is easy to do manually. In addition to understanding the concepts and steps involved, knowing how to split a database will help you to manage the database and to work with linked tables. In general, the steps are;

1. Make a backup.

2. Copy your database to another file, named something such as `MyApp_Data.accdb`.

3. Rename the first file to something like `MyApp.accdb`.

4. In the data file, delete all objects except the tables. You can also delete configuration tables that you know will be in the front-end database.

5. In the application file, delete the tables (except any local configuration tables). Then, on the Ribbon's External Data tab, use Import group ⇨ Access, and then choose Link To The Data Source By Creating A Linked Table to link all the tables from the data file. (In earlier versions of Access, you use File ⇨ Get External Data ⇨ Link Tables.)

Now that your database is split, you can relink tables using the Linked Table Manager (located in the Database Tools group on the Ribbon's Database Tools tab), or you can install one of the many Access table relinker functions available on the Internet or in other books. (In previous versions of Access, the Linked Table Manager can be found under Tools ⇨ Database Utilities.) You'll also recall that we recommend confirming linked tables at startup.

DISPLAY INFORMATIVE FORM CAPTIONS

If you don't set your own form captions, Access just displays the form name, a sure sign of a novice developer. You need to, at least, replace the caption with the name of your application. One nice additional touch for the caption is to indicate which back-end database you are currently using. This is a nice way to let the users know if they're using the Production, Training, or Development file.

For this technique, you'll need a table in the back-end database to store system-wide configuration values. In this example, the system configuration table in the backend is named `tsysConfig_System`, and it has a field containing the name of the database (see Figure I-6).

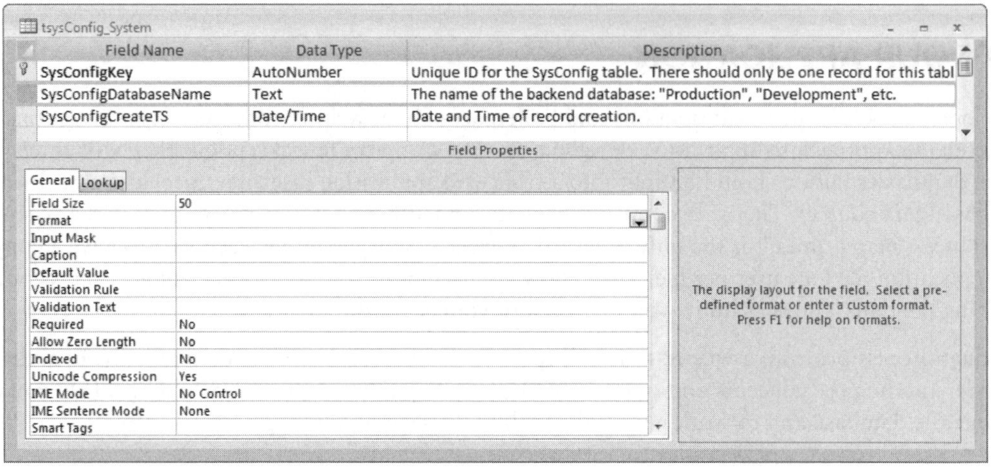

FIGURE I-6

You also need a local table in the frontend to store static values for the application itself, such as the example shown in Figure I-7. In the example, one of the fields is the name (title) of the application, suitable for showing on various forms throughout the system.

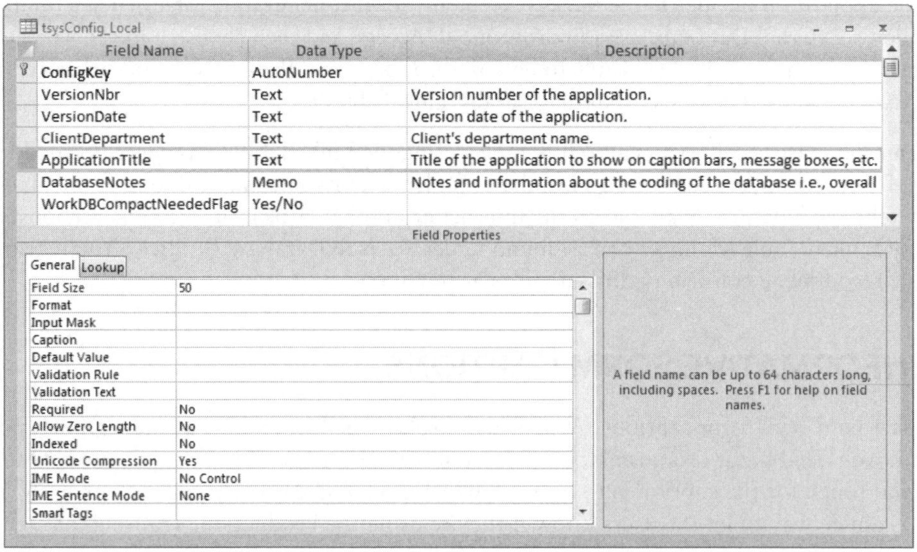

FIGURE I-7

You can use the following code to set the caption. It belongs in the Open event code behind every form:

```
Me.Caption = DLookup("ApplicationTitle", "tsysConfig_Local") _
&" - "& DLookup("SysConfigDatabaseName", "tsysConfig_System")
```

code snippet CS 14 in appl_Tips_Code.txt

When each form opens, you can set Caption to the title of the application, concatenated with the name of the back-end database, as shown in Figure I-8.

By setting the caption of every form, you avoid the rookie move of showing an internal form name such as frmBusinesses. And by using a configuration table to supply

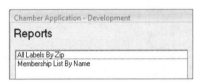

FIGURE I-8

the application name, you avoid hard-coding it in every form. This makes your job a lot easier for each application you develop because you can reuse the code and you only need to change the value in the one configuration table.

Another technique for storing application data that is limited to one value is to create an administrative table that contains only one record. This might be used to manage the company name, address, phone, logo, bank routing, current sales tax rate, and other single values. Unlike other tables, the fields do not need to be related because the critical factor is that it can have only one value at any given time. You can easily create a table with only one record. Simply create a table with the primary key as an Integer data type and both the default value and validation rule as =1. Because it is the primary key, it will not allow duplicate values. Voilà! You have an admin table that provides quick and easy access to edit and use the data.

PRELOAD RECORDS

Sometimes, you'll have a problem when you open a detail form for a new record. If the detail form has a subform with child records, users will encounter an error if they try to enter data into the subform (create a child record) before they have entered data for the parent (master) record, as shown in Figure I-9.

The error occurs because the parent key still contains a Null, and the child record requires a foreign key for the parent Business record. If the foreign parent key in the child record isn't set to Required, you'll have a different problem: The child record will have a Null foreign parent key, making it an orphan record with no parent.

As demonstrated in the Chamber Application, one way to prevent this error is to create an empty record before opening the Detail form. That way, the parent record already has a primary key and can accept related child records. During this preloading operation, you can specify a default name for the new record, such as <New Business>. As shown in Figure I-10, this tells the user that he has created a new record and it allows him to immediately add child records.

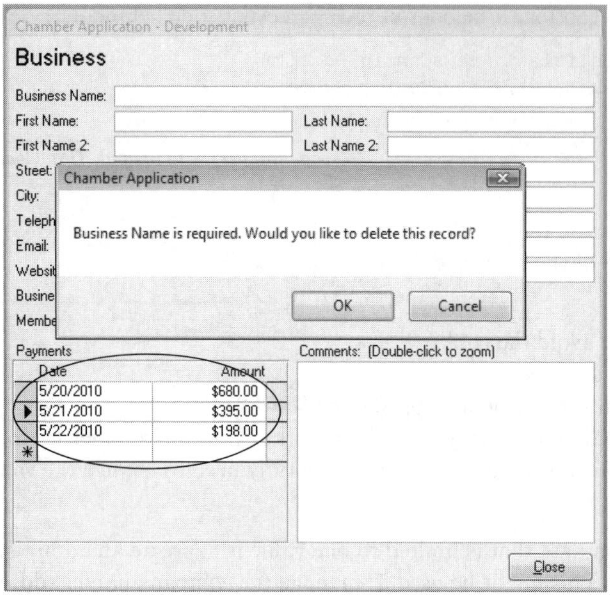

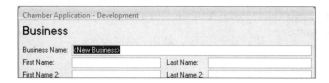

FIGURE I-9

FIGURE I-10

The code to preload the record is in the index form `frmBusinesses` (refer to Figure I-4), in the `Click` event of the New button:

Available for download on Wrox.com

```
Private Sub cmdNew_Click()
On Error GoTo Error_Handler

Dim rs As Recordset
Dim strDocName As String
Dim strLinkCriteria As String

'Open form to new record

gstrCallingForm = Me.Name
strDocName = "frmBusiness"
strLinkCriteria = "[BusinessKey]=" & NewBusinessKey()
Me.Visible = False
DoCmd.OpenForm FormName:=strDocName, _
   WhereCondition:=strLinkCriteria, WindowMode:=acDialog
```

```
'Requery index form to pick up the new record, then
'set the bookmark to this new record.
Me.Requery
Set rs = Me.RecordsetClone
If Me.RecordsetClone.RecordCount > 0 Then

  'If first new record was cancelled, would fail.
  rs.FindFirst strLinkCriteria
  If Not rs.EOF Then
    Me.Bookmark = rs.Bookmark
  End If
End If

Exit_Procedure:
  On Error Resume Next
  rs.Close
  Set rs = Nothing
  Exit Sub

Error_Handler:
  DisplayUnexpectedError Err.Number, Err.Description
  Resume Exit_Procedure
  Resume

End Sub
```

code snippet CS 15 in appI_Tips_Code.txt

Notice that after the Business detail form is closed, the Businesses index form is requeried and then positioned to the new business record so the user gets visual feedback that the newly added record is indeed in the list.

You'll also notice that the Business form is opened with a key specified as NewBusinessKey() that uses the following function to generate the new Business record:

Available for download on Wrox.com

```
Public Function NewBusinessKey() As Long
On Error GoTo Error_Handler
'This function creates a new Business record and returns the key.

Dim db As Database
Dim rec As Recordset
Set db = CurrentDb
Set rec = db.OpenRecordset("tblBusiness")

'Add the record, storing new key value as variable and
'passing it out as the function name
With rec
  .AddNew
  NewBusinessKey = rec!BusinessKey
  !BusinessName = "<New Business>"
  .Update
  .Close
End With
```

```
Set rec = Nothing

Exit_Procedure:
  Exit Function

Error_Handler:
  DisplayUnexpectedError Err.Number, Err.Description
  Resume Exit_Procedure
  Resume

End Function
```

code snippet CS 16 in appI_Tips_Code.txt

We have one more issue to handle. If the user tries to leave the Business Name as `<New Business>`, you should provide a message box to prompt the user to either provide a name or discard the record, as shown in Figure I-11.

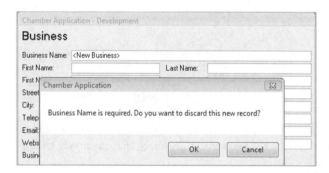

FIGURE I-11

Notice that the message box uses the term `discard` instead of `delete`. As a developer, you know a new empty record was created but the user may not, so using the word "delete" may be confusing. (Remember our comment about polish?) You can do this by using the following code in the `Unload` event of the `Business` form:

Available for download on Wrox.com

```
Private Sub Form_Unload(Cancel As Integer)
On Error GoTo Error_Handler

Dim strSQL As String
Dim bDelete As Boolean

bDelete = False

'If user has not changed preloaded record, or if there is no name,
'delete the record.
If (Me!BusinessName = "<New Business>") Then

  If MsgBox("Business Name is required. Do you want to " _
    & "discard this new record?", vbOKCancel, _
  DLookup("ApplicationTitle", "tsysConfig_Local")) = vbOK Then
```

```
      'Delete the record
      bDelete = True

   Else
      'Yes delete the record, return to the form
      Cancel = True
   End If
End If

If Me!BusinessName & "" = "" Then

   If MsgBox("Business Name is required. Would you like to " _
      & "delete this record?", vbOKCancel, _
      DLookup("ApplicationTitle", "tsysConfig_Local")) = vbOK Then
\
      'Delete the record
      bDelete = True

   Else
      Cancel = True
   End If
End If

If bDelete = True Then
   strSQL = "DELETE * FROM tblBusiness WHERE BusinessKey = " _
      & Me!BusinessKey
   DoCmd.SetWarnings False
   DoCmd.RunSQL strSQL
   DoCmd.SetWarnings True
End If

Exit_Procedure:
   Exit Sub

Error_Handler:
   DoCmd.SetWarnings True
   DisplayUnexpectedError Err.Number, Err.Description
   Resume Exit_Procedure
   Resume

End Sub
```

code snippet CS 17 in appl_Tips_Code.txt

If the user clicks OK, it deletes the record and closes the form. Clicking Cancel, will cancel the Unload event and return you to the record. Keep in mind, that if the parent record is discarded, you will also need to ensure that the child records are deleted or you will be back to the issues related to orphaned child records.

You'll also notice that the code actually uses the word delete in the message (rather than discard as displayed in the message box) if the Business Name is blank. That is because some users may try to delete a record by clearing out the main name field. If you discover records with blank values in a table, that may be what happened. This code recognizes the situation and offers to delete the record.

USE A SPLASH SCREEN

You can display a custom logo (instead of the Access logo) while your Access program loads. Just name a bitmap the same name as your database file (`YourApp.tif`) and put it in the same folder as the database (`.accdb` or `.mdb`). When the file is launched, you'll see the bitmap image instead of the Access startup logo.

Alternatively, if you prefer to remove the Access startup logo, you can create a bitmap image with just one pixel. Here's how: Start Paint, select Image ⇨ Attributes, specify Width = 1 and Height = 1, make sure Pixels is selected in the Units pane, and save the image. It doesn't really matter what color the pixel is because it will hardly be noticeable.

With a fast computer, you probably won't notice your custom logo (or the pixel) because it will only be displayed for a fraction of a second. So, you need another splash screen inside your application. The first screen of your application should always be a splash screen that shows the application name and version, the client's company name, and your company name. This single feature says, "This is a professional application." You could use a logo (either yours or your client's) and some basic application information, as shown in Figure I-12.

FIGURE I-12

Example code for displaying the Splash screen for a specified number of seconds (3 or 4 seconds seems like a good duration) can be found in the Microsoft Knowledge Base article 101374.

POP-UP MEMO WORKSPACE FORM WITH SPELL CHECK

Sometimes it may be helpful to provide users with more room to enter long text into a memo field. Instead of using the built-in Access zoom feature, you can include a "workspace" feature to zoom into a memo field, allow the user to select to either "OK" (accept) or "Cancel" (delete) his changes, and even spell-check the text. This zoom feature and workspace is shown in the Comments memo field in Figure I-13.

The following code is in the double-click event of the memo field on `frmBusiness`:

Available for download on Wrox.com

```
Private Sub BusinessComments_DblClick(Cancel As Integer)
On Error GoTo Error_Handler

Workspace Me.ActiveControl, Me

Exit_Procedure:
  Exit Sub

Error_Handler:
  DoCmd.SetWarnings True
  DisplayUnexpectedError Err.Number, Err.Description
```

```
        Resume Exit_Procedure
        Resume

    End Sub
```

code snippet CS 18 in appl_Tips_Code.txt

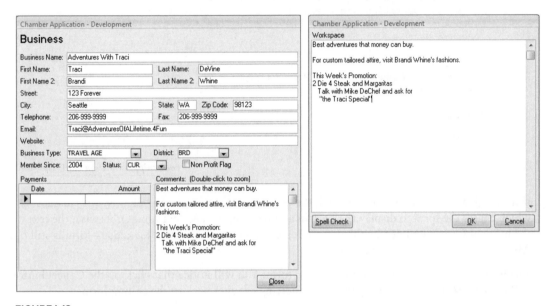

FIGURE I-13

The Workspace procedure, which is in a standalone module such as basGlobal, uses the following code:

```
Sub Workspace(ctl As Control, CallingForm As Form)
On Error GoTo Err_Workspace

CallingForm.Refresh
'Save any data which may have been entered into memo field

Set gctlWorkspaceSource = ctl

If ctl.Locked Or Not ctl.Enabled Then
  DoCmd.OpenForm "frmWorkspace", WindowMode:=acDialog, _
    OpenArgs:="ReadOnly"

Else
  DoCmd.OpenForm "frmWorkspace", WindowMode:=acDialog
End If

If IsLoaded("frmWorkspace") Then
  gctlWorkspaceSource = Forms.frmWorkspace.txtWorkspace
  DoCmd.Close acForm, "frmWorkspace"
End If
```

```
Exit_Workspace:
  Exit Sub

Err_Workspace:
  Select Case Err
    Case 3163 'Too much data for field
      MsgBox "The field is too small to accept the amount " _
        & "of data you attempted to insert. As a result, " _
        & "the operation has been cancelled.", vbExclamation, _
      DLookup("ApplicationTitle", "tsysConfig_Local")
      Resume Next

    Case Else
      MsgBox Err.Number & ", " & Err.Description
      Resume Exit_Workspace

  End Select
End Sub
```

code snippet CS 19 in appI_Tips_Code.txt

If the original text box control is locked, the Workspace form is passed OpenArgs of "ReadOnly", which causes the form to display the data in a grayed out, locked text box. Otherwise, the text on the original form is updated by the Workspace text, providing that the Workspace form is still open. After that, the Workspace form is closed.

The following code is behind the Workspace form. You will notice that clicking the Cancel button will close the Workspace form without transferring changes back to the calling form.

```
Option Compare Database
Option Explicit

'Note: Choose one mode; Uncomment the spell check mode you want to support:
'Const conSpellCheckOption = 0 'No Spell Checking
Const conSpellCheckOption = 1 'Spell Checking

Private Sub cmdCancel_Click()
On Error GoTo Error_Handler

  DoCmd.Close ObjectType:=acForm, ObjectName:=Me.Name

Exit_Procedure:
  Exit Sub
Error_Handler:
  DisplayUnexpectedError Err.Number, Err.Description
  Resume Exit_Procedure
  Resume
End Sub
```

code snippet CS 20 in appI_Tips_Code.txt

> *Options, options: This code is written so that you, the programmer, can decide whether spell-checking will be available. You can turn it off entirely using a value of 0. It is good to note that the spell-check and cancel functions are independent of each other.*

If OK is clicked, the `Workspace` form is merely hidden, as the following code shows. It was opened in Dialog mode, so the calling code was paused until now.

```
Private Sub cmdOK_Click()
On Error GoTo Error_Handler

    Me.Visible = False

Exit_Procedure:
  Exit Sub
Error_Handler:
  DisplayUnexpectedError Err.Number, Err.Description
  Resume Exit_Procedure
  Resume
End Sub
```

code snippet CS 21 in appI_Tips_Code.txt

If the spell-checking option is enabled, the spell check may be performed:

```
Private Sub cmdSpellCheck_Click()
On Error GoTo Error_Handler

    Dim intTemp As Integer

    intTemp = fnCheckSpelling(Me!txtWorkspace)

Exit_Procedure:
  Exit Sub
Error_Handler:
  DisplayUnexpectedError Err.Number, Err.Description
  Resume Exit_Procedure
  Resume
End Sub
```

code snippet CS 22 in appI_Tips_Code.txt

To support the standard usage of the F7 key to check spelling, this code traps the F7 keystroke and, if the spell-checking button is enabled, runs its code:

```
Private Sub Form_KeyDown(KeyCode As Integer, Shift As Integer)
On Error GoTo Error_Handler

    If KeyCode = vbKeyF7 Then
      KeyCode = 0
```

```
        If Me!cmdSpellCheck.Visible And Me!cmdSpellCheck.Enabled Then
          Me.cmdSpellCheck.SetFocus
          Call cmdSpellCheck_Click
        End If
      End If

  Exit_Procedure:
    Exit Sub
  Error_Handler:
    DisplayUnexpectedError Err.Number, Err.Description
    Resume Exit_Procedure
    Resume
  End Sub
```

code snippet CS 23 in appI_Tips_Code.txt

When the `Workspace` form loads, the option constant determines whether the Spell Check button is visible. Then the text from the original form is loaded into the `Workspace` text box, and the whole thing is locked down if the original text box was locked. Here's the code:

Available for download on Wrox.com

```
Private Sub Form_Load()
On Error GoTo Error_Handler

Dim ctl As Control

  'Setup SpellChecker Options
  If conSpellCheckOption = 0 Then
    'Spell Checker is OFF
    Me!cmdSpellCheck.Visible = False
  Else
    'Spell Checker is ON
    Me!cmdSpellCheck.Visible = True
  End If

  'Import data into workspace form
  Me!txtWorkspace = gctlWorkspaceSource

  If Me.OpenArgs = "ReadOnly" Then
    Set ctl = Me!txtWorkspace
    With ctl
      .EnterKeyBehavior = False 'Sets to Default / No new line
      .Locked = True
      .BackColor = vbButtonFace
    End With
    Set ctl = Nothing

    Me!cmdSpellCheck.Enabled = False
  End If

Exit_Procedure:
  Exit Sub
Error_Handler:
  DisplayUnexpectedError Err.Number, Err.Description
```

```
      Resume Exit_Procedure
      Resume
   End Sub
```

This is just the normal form caption setting as described earlier in this appendix:

```
   Private Sub Form_Open(Cancel As Integer)
   On Error GoTo Error_Handler

      Me.Caption = DLookup("ApplicationTitle", "tsysConfig_Local") _
      & " - " & DLookup("SysConfigDatabaseName", "tsysConfig_System")

   Exit_Procedure:
      Exit Sub
   Error_Handler:
      DisplayUnexpectedError Err.Number, Err.Description
      Resume Exit_Procedure
      Resume
   End Sub
```

When the Workspace text box receives focus, you make sure that the insertion point jumps to the end of the text instead of highlighting the whole field. This prevents the user from inadvertently changing the entire field.

```
   Private Sub txtWorkspace_GotFocus()
   On Error GoTo Error_Handler

      Dim varX As Variant

      ' jump to end of existing text instead of leaving it
      'all highlighted.
      varX = Len(Me!txtWorkspace.Text & "")
      If Not IsNull(varX) And varX > 0 Then
        Me!txtWorkspace.SelStart = Len(Me!txtWorkspace)
        Me!txtWorkspace.SelLength = 0
      End If

   Exit_Procedure:
      Exit Sub
   Error_Handler:
      DisplayUnexpectedError Err.Number, Err.Description
      Resume Exit_Procedure
      Resume
   End Sub
```

When the Spell button is clicked, the text on the `Workspace` form is checked for spelling errors, as shown in Figure I-14.

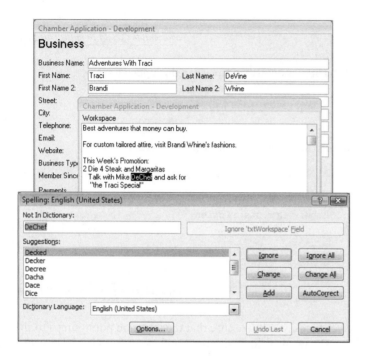

FIGURE I-14

The following code is in the `Spell Checking` module:

```
Option Compare Database
Option Explicit

Public Function fnCheckSpelling(ctl As Control) As Boolean
On Error GoTo Error_Handler

    'This procedure checks the spelling of the text in the
    'passed-in control ctl.

    DoCmd.Hourglass True
    'This function is meant for textbox controls only.
    Select Case ctl.ControlType
      Case acTextBox
        If Not ctl.Enabled Or ctl.Locked Then
           'Text in control cannot be updated.
          GoTo Exit_Procedure
        ElseIf IsNull(ctl) Then
           'Nothing to check
           GoTo Exit_Procedure
        End If
      Case Else
```

```
        GoTo Exit_Procedure
    End Select

    ctl.SetFocus
    ctl.SelStart = 0
    ctl.SelLength = Len(ctl.Text & "")
    If ctl.SelLength <> 0 Then
      DoCmd.Hourglass False
      RunCommand acCmdSpelling
      ctl.SelLength = 0
      fnCheckSpelling = True
    End If

Exit_Procedure:
    On Error Resume Next
    DoCmd.Hourglass False
    Exit Function
Error_Handler:
    DoCmd.Hourglass False
    DisplayUnexpectedError Err.Number, Err.Description
    Resume Exit_Procedure
    Resume
End Function
```

code snippet CS 27 in appl_Tips_Code.txt

By adding an area for users to enter text in a larger window and check the spelling, you make your application more powerful and easy to use. Plus, when you add this capability, you don't have to make memo field text boxes as large, thereby saving valuable real estate on your forms. You may be wondering if it matters what order you check to see if the control is enabled or locked. It doesn't matter; as we'll demonstrate by reversing the order in an upcoming example.

DETERMINE THE USER NAME

You'll often need to identify the current user. This may be used to determine what activities they are allowed to do or to log data about who created and changed records. There are two user names that you'll be concerned with: the current Access user and the current Windows user. You can store this type of data using a `TempVar`, as discussed later in this appendix.

The Current Access User

The current Access user is determined using the built-in `CurrentUser` function. However, if you are not using Access security and requiring the user to log in with a User Name and Password, this user name will always be the default Access user of Admin. Because this doesn't provide a definitive identification, you may need to know the name of the user that is currently logged into the PC — also known as the current Windows user.

The Current Windows User

The following steps will allow you to identify the current Windows user. First, in the module declaration section, include this code:

```
Global Const ERRORMOREDATA = 234
Global Const ERR_SUCCESS = 0

Private Declare Function WNetGetUser Lib "mpr" Alias _
    "WNetGetUserA" (ByVal lpName As String, _
    ByVal lpUserName As String, lpnLength As Long) As Long
```

code snippet CS 28 in appI_Tips_Code.txt

Then, create a function with this code:

```
Public Function WinUserName() As String
Dim lUserNameLen As Long
Dim stTmp As String
Dim lReturn As Long

Do
    ' Set up the buffer
    stTmp = String$(lUserNameLen, vbNullChar)

    lReturn = WNetGetUser(vbNullString, stTmp, lUserNameLen)

' Continue looping until the call succeeds or the buffer can't fit any more data
Loop Until lReturn <> ERRORMOREDATA

If lReturn = ERR_SUCCESS Then
    WinUserName = Left$(stTmp, InStr(1, stTmp, vbNullChar, _
        vbBinaryCompare) -1)
End If

End Function
```

code snippet CS 29 in appI_Tips_Code.txt

You can use this Windows username anywhere you like, including displaying it on forms, using it to allow or disallow certain features, or including the username whenever a record is changed or created.

CONTRIBUTOR TIPS

The real value of a tip is realized when you match the right tip to the specific situation, exactly when you need it. So, to give a broader perspective, we've added this section to share a few tips that have been contributed by esteemed colleagues. As you'll experience when collecting code and files from others, you may discover a wide variety of styles, formatting, and naming conventions. The files that support this section use the contributor's styles and conventions. Their primary purpose is to demonstrate the tip and functionality. Rather than invest in fancy formatting, we kept the forms relatively plain in appearance to make them easier to customize and assimilate into your own files. We ask that when so this reads We ask that when you use the code and modules in your applications and demos, you retain the credit and notations of the original authors.

Need Data in Columns: IIF Queries to the Rescue

One of the issues that you have may have to solve is to provide a report with the totals in columns, not in rows. In other words, provide a report that looks familiar to those accustomed to working with Excel. Actually, this type of report is quite often asked for and side-stepped. A common tendency is to think that cross-tab queries should easily fit the bill, but we quickly find that they have limitations and introduce challenges of their own.

With thanks to Garry Robinson, Access MVP and editor of `http://www.vb123.com/kb`, we'll show you how to use an `IIF` statement in combination with a query to essentially group and sum data from a table and display the results (that is, totals for products by regions) across columns in a query. The table and query results used for our example are shown in Figure I-15. We encourage you to follow the process using the IifQueries database that is included with the download files for this appendix.

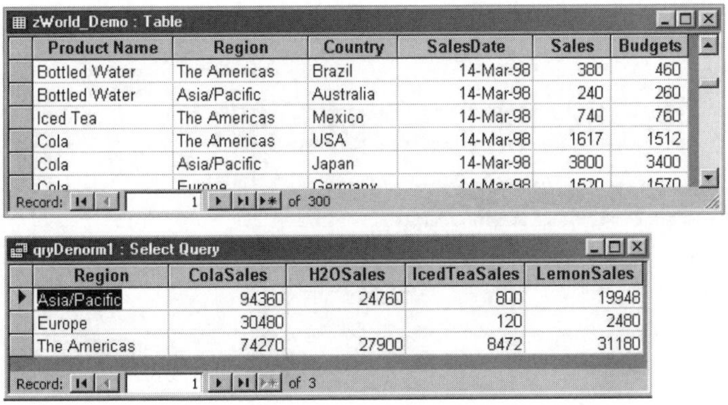

zWorld_Demo : Table

Product Name	Region	Country	SalesDate	Sales	Budgets
Bottled Water	The Americas	Brazil	14-Mar-98	380	460
Bottled Water	Asia/Pacific	Australia	14-Mar-98	240	260
Iced Tea	The Americas	Mexico	14-Mar-98	740	760
Cola	The Americas	USA	14-Mar-98	1617	1512
Cola	Asia/Pacific	Japan	14-Mar-98	3800	3400
Cola	Europe	Germany	14-Mar-98	1520	1570

Record: 1 of 300

qryDenorm1 : Select Query

Region	ColaSales	H2OSales	IcedTeaSales	LemonSales
Asia/Pacific	94360	24760	800	19948
Europe	30480		120	2480
The Americas	74270	27900	8472	31180

Record: 1 of 3

FIGURE I-15

The IIF Query Solution

Although it may not be the best fit for every situation, the method that seems to work in most scenarios is to use `IIF` functions in conjunction with a consolidation query (aka Group By or Totals query). The Design view of the completed query is shown in Figure I-16. First you need to set up the columns in a normal query as follows:

Available for download on Wrox.com

```
SELECT Region,
IIf([ProductName]="Cola",[Sales],Null) AS ColaSales
FROM WorldDemo;
```

code snippet CS 30 in appI_Tips_Code.txt

This will return all rows from the table, but in the column known as ColaSales, it will return the Sales result only if the ProductName for that row is Cola. For other rows such as for the products, Bottled Water or Iced Tea, the ColaSales column will return a null value. This step starts the process so that when you convert the ordinary query to a consolidation query (using the ∑ button), you can total all the values in the ColaSales column and you will get only the totals rows of data for Cola sales, as shown in both the following SQL statement and in the Design view of the query, shown in Figure I-16.

```
SELECT Region,
Sum(IIf([ProductName]="Cola",[Sales],Null)) AS ColaSales,
FROM WorldDemo
GROUP BY Region;
```

code snippet CS 31 in appI_Tips_Code.txt

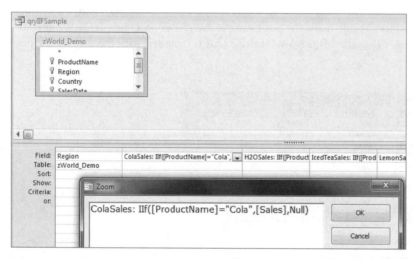

FIGURE I-16

Taking the IIF Statement a Little Further

Now that you have the totals for Cola sales, you can copy the column in Design view and paste it to create a column for each of the other ProductNames. Next, replace the value inside the quote with the specific product name. So when you change the line that begins with `IIf([ProductName]="Cola"` to begin with `If([ProductName]="Iced Tea"` you will be able to sum the Iced Tea totals, and so on.

This approach also allows other consolidation function options that are not available when you use crosstab queries. For example, you can calculate product totals from different columns in the raw data, and you can use different consolidation functions in the same query. The following SQL shows product totals by quarter for Cola Sales and Budgets, and it also shows the maximum sale in each region during that period.

```
SELECT Region, Format([SalesDate],"yyyy-q") AS Quarter,
Sum(IIf([ProductName]="Cola",[Sales],Null))
AS ColaSalesTotal, Sum(IIf([ProductName]="Cola",[Budgets],Null)) AS ColaBudgetTotal,
Avg(IIf([ProductName]="Cola",[Sales],Null)) AS ColaSalesMax
FROM WorldDemo
GROUP BY Region, Format([SalesDate],"yyyy-q");
```

code snippet CS 32 in appl_Tips_Code.txt

In addition to this example, the IifQueries database also includes an example that is even more powerful; it uses your own functions to provide the group by column for the query. As you can see, the technique of combining IIF functions and consolidation queries provides functionality and flexibility because it can deliver the customized column-based queries and reports that many managers are used to.

TempVars

Since TempVars were introduced with Access 2007, they have grown in popularity as developers realize how valuable they can be for providing quick yet durable solutions. They bring a new level of flexibility and simplicity to working with variables throughout your application. In case the earlier example wasn't enough to prompt you to try TempVars, we wanted to share some of the experiences and enthusiasm of Steve Schapel, Access MVP.

Creating a TempVar

As you learned earlier, it takes only one line of code to create a TempVar object and set its value. For example, to create a TempVar object named MyName and set its value to my name, use:

```
TempVars!MyName = "Steve"
```

They can also be created in a macro, using the SetTempVar action. And once created, they are available throughout the application. Whether a TempVar is created in VBA or in a macro, it is accessible to all VBA procedures and all macros. The TempVar stays in memory until the application is closed, unless it is explicitly cleared.

To clear the value from a TempVar, you remove or delete the TempVar itself. They can be removed using a RemoveTempVar macro action (there is also a RemoveAllTempVars action), or in code using:

```
TempVars.Remove MyName     ' Deletes the TemVar MyName
```

or:

```
TempVars.RemoveAll    ' Deletes all TempVars in the application
```

To re-set the value of an existing TempVar, you can use the same line of code as above. For example, if I decide to go incognito, I can change my name use the following code:

```
TempVars!MyName = "Traci"
```

code snippet CS 33 (group) in appl_Tips_Code.txt

Compared with Global Variables

As you can tell a lot of the functionality that `TempVars` offer is similar to that provided by global variables. The key is to leverage the differences. `TempVars` can be:

➤ Created and removed whenever you need them, within the code where they will be used.

➤ Used directly in, and exchanged between, macros or VBA procedures.

➤ Directly used in query criteria.

➤ Used within calculated fields in a query.

➤ Used in the Control Source of calculated controls on a form or report.

➤ Used either alone or as part of an expression in Property settings (e.g. `[TempVars]![RegRef]` in the Default Value property of a combo box).

➤ Used to store text or numeric data. But because they are always Variant data type, they are limited in scope and functionality compared with VBA variables.

This adds up to a recipe for quick and effective solutions to a number of application development tasks. We'll use a couple of examples to illustrate how `TempVars` can be used.

Using TempVars to Identify Application Users

In an application that is used by the headquarters of an organization and several regional offices, the regional offices are only allowed to see the data applicable to their own region. There is also some functionality that is only applicable to the headquarters staff.

Each region is identified by a three-character code that is stored when people log in to the application. This region code is assigned to a `TempVar` named `RegRef`, on the Open event of the application's startup form, like this:

```
TempVars!RegRef = DLookup("[RegionCode]", "RegionLookup", "Active <> 0")
```

It is not important for the details of the code snippets here to be fully understood because they implement requirements that are peculiar to a specific application. However, they help to illustrate a concept. And, although this is not a gargantuan application, the `TempVars!RegRef` is used in 47 places in the code. And that is just one of many `TempVar` objects that are used. The following snippets and queries should give you even more ideas for leveraging `TempVars`.

Available for download on Wrox.com

```
' - Writes a user-entered email address as the default email address for the
' region represented by the TempVar
dbs.Execute "UPDATE RegionLookup SET BaseEmail = '" & Me.EmailTo & _
  "' WHERE RegionCode = '" & TempVars!RegRef & "'", dbFailOnError

' - A combo box requires a different Row Source if the user is from headquarters
If TempVars!RegRef = "NLO" Then    ' headquarters
Me.AreaCode.RowSource = "SELECT … FROM…"
Else    ' do something else
End If

' - A control on a form is only visible if the user is from headquarters
Me.AdminRegion.Visible = ((Me.StatsOut = 2) And (TempVars!RegRef = "NLO"))
```

```
' - A Recordset is created by using the TempVar in the WHERE clause of a SQL
' statement to filter the data that is returned
Set rst = dbs.OpenRecordset("SELECT OneField, AnotherField" & _
" FROM People INNER JOIN Personnel ON People.PersonID = Personnel.PersonID" & _
" WHERE Personnel.RegionCode = '" & [TempVars]![RegRef] & "'"

' - The data returned to a subform is restricted according to the user region, or
' not restricted if the user is headquarters
    Me.Personnel_sub.Form .RecordSource = "SELECT * FROM Personnel" & _
" WHERE (PersonID = " & Me.PersonID & ")" & _
" AND ((RegionCode = TempVars!RegRef) OR (TempVars!RegRef = 'NLO'))"
```

code snippet CS 34 in appI_Tips_Code.txt

As you can see, using `TempVars` can save a lot of time and code. But the crowning jewel may be that with no further effort, we also have direct access to the value of the `TempVar`, as shown in the queries in Figures I-17 where it is used as criteria and then as a calculated expression; and Figure I-18 where it is used in the Control Source for a control on a report.

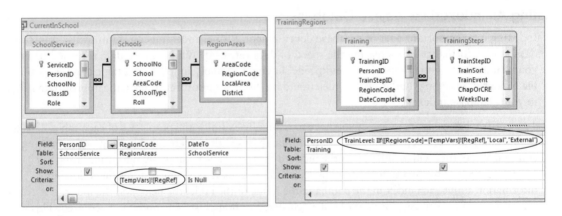

FIGURE I-17

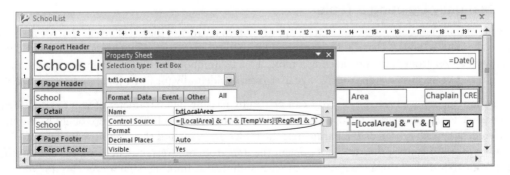

FIGURE I-18

And now that you've seen how easy and quick it is to use `TempVars`, we encourage you to reinforce your learning and follow-up by exploring the bonus example in the download file that uses `TempVars` in a process that allows users to print or preview a report or create and e-mail a PDF.

Tips for Tables and Colors

The longer you work with databases, the more you'll appreciate tools that make it easier to maintain and manage them, whether they document the structure, protect the data, or help on the creative side.

Dane Miller, Utter Access VIP and veteran Access developer has generously shared five of his favorite tips that cover those topics. They are best learned in action, so we'll limit this discussion to briefly describe the functionality and benefits. You'll learn more from the documentation that we've incorporated into the forms and modules that are in the companion database, HandyDeveloperTools (provided in both accdb and mdb format).

You'll immediately notice that HandyDeveloperTools is about function not fashion; it is for developers not end-users. The forms serve as navigation and documentation. Being relatively stark, they can easily be tailored to be assimilated into your own developer toolbox.

Listing All Indexed Fields in a Database

Indexing is an important part of database development. Proper indexing can significantly improve database performance by increasing the speed of data retrieval. While having data returned from your database is advantageous, on the flip side, having too many indexes on a table can take a notable toll when inserting, updating, and deleting data. So it is important to have the appropriate fields in your database indexed.

To identify what fields are indexed, you have to manually examine the properties of each table. This is both tedious and time consuming, especially for databases with numerous tables. But, we're offering a convenient tool that will identify all of the indexed fields in a given database: the custom function `ListIndexes()`. This function creates a table called `tblIndexList`, which stores the following information about each index in the database: the name of the table, the field, and the index, if it is a primary or foreign key, the type of index (clustered or non-clustered), and if it is required. This `ListIndexes` function can be especially handy when you take over maintenance of an existing database as it will not only help you to enhance performance, but also to learn about the database structure.

Prohibit Manually Deleting a Table

As developers, we not only have to design an application that satisfies the users' needs, but we also need to take steps to ensure that data are secure. One method that can assist with preserving the data is to prevent a user from manually deleting a table. This technique comes in handy more often than you might expect because it stops the average user from accidentally (or intentionally) deleting a table.

The function `StopManualTableDelete()` can be run by passing in a parameter of YES or NO. When YES is passed as the parameter, the code is applied to all the tables and they can no longer be manually deleted. When NO is used as the parameter, the tables are reset and they can now be deleted manually again. Of course, this does not prevent the user from inadvertently deleting the data itself, but that's an area that can be better addressed with audit trails, limiting what a user can do, and backup processes.

Scripting Access Tables

Sometimes a developer might want to re-create all the tables and their relationships in a database automatically via code. The ability to do this can prove especially beneficial when two developers are working on the data normalization aspects of an application but using different versions of Access. By converting the table structure to text, each developer can start with an identical file structure and have minimal risk of conversion issues.

The function `fn_JetSQLScript()` will export the table structure to a text file and save it in the same folder as the "calling" database. The text file can then be passed to another developer who can paste the contents into a module and then run it to re-create all the tables and relationships.

> ### TIMELY TIP FOR UPGRADING AND MIXED PLATFORM ENVIRONMENTS
>
> Talk about a timely tip — if you are upgrading files or working in an environment with multiple versions of Access, this one tip about converting tables to and from text can more than pay for this book, and save you from hundreds of hours of needless frustration.

Implementing Audit Trail Capabilities

Traditionally, tracking and recording changes to data in a database has involved copious lines of custom code, but now you can use Access 2010 data macros to do a lot of that work. But data macros might not meet your needs, and they won't work with prior versions of Access. So we've provided a tool that is simple to implement and uses just two class modules: `clsAudit` and `clsAuditCollection`. After importing these modules, you can get set up and be able to track changes to data within an Access database by adding as little as five lines of code to a form.

The changes to the data are stored in a hidden table within the current database, or you can specify that the audit changes be stored within an external database by merely pointing the code to the location of the external database — for example, `C:\MyFolder\TrackerDb.mdb`. You'll find an example of that in the code on the On Current event of the form `frmCaptureAuditChanges`. The hidden table stores information such as the name of the form that was used to change the data, the Recordsource of the form, the primary key of the record, the name of the Windows user (if you have custom security, the name of that logged-on user), the name of the field that the data was stored in, the previous data value, the new data value, and the time of the change.

Color Blender

For the final tip in this group, we'll move the focus from the backend to the application. As we mentioned at the beginning of this appendix, developers not only need to manage what happens behind the scenes of an application but we also need to provide an attractive user interface (UI). And picking the right colors and blend of these colors is important for styling your application. The new styles can help, but we've provided another option that gives you flexibility, control, and consistency when selecting colors — the `Color Blender`.

With the `Color Blender`, as shown in Figure I-19, we've created code that allows you to pick two colors from a palette and pass these colors to a control on the form. You then choose a number from one to ten and click the `Blend` button. The two colors are transitioned and blended to meet each other, and the various color outputs are displaced on the form with their associated Access color number.

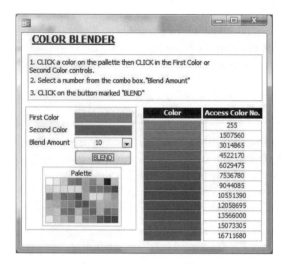

FIGURE I-19

This is a handy item to add to your developer toolbox. In addition to giving you a convenient way to view and select colors, you can also explore the code behind the form to learn about the techniques, and apply them in your solutions. As a reminder, the companion download file, HandyDeveloperTools has a form demonstrates how to implement each of the tips in this section.

That takes us to the final section in this appendix, an example of how to leverage Access Services. There again, we'll take a similar approach of briefly describing the functionality and benefits in the book and providing the bulk of the material in download files.

Access Services 2010 in Action: Screencast Tutorial Database Project

Access Services in SharePoint 2010 provides new opportunities to develop Web-based applications from Access 2010. It is such a new and dynamic art that we turned to an industry leader, Larry Strange of Access Hosting, for an example that will continue to evolve as the technology matures.

This solution uses a series of forms and reports that demonstrate how you can take advantage of this new functionality. All of the tables, forms, and reports have been published to a SharePoint 2010 Server with Access Services installed and are available for public viewing at `http://www.access2010tutor.com` (Please logon as User: **AH\tutor** and Password: **tutor**). Keep in mind that one of the beauties of a Web-based application is that they are exactly that — Web-based — so Access is not required in order to use an Access Web app.

It could take several chapters to thoroughly cover all of steps as things that you need to know to create a successful and dynamic Web application, so obviously we can't cover it in this appendix. But we have done something even better: Although we limit the book to a brief discussion of the key features and benefits, we direct you to online material — both in the book's companion files at Wrox.com and to relevant websites.

With the exploding popularity of screencast tutorials, this seemed like the perfect way to demonstrate how to use Access Services to solve a growing need. So, in addition to learning about Access Services, you'll also see how you can use recording software, such as Camtasia Studio, to create a set of compelling training and support resources. Our example reflects the real-world scenario, where AccessHosting.com uses screencasts to support their customers and provide visual answers to frequently asked questions. To do this efficiently, they created an Access 2010 Web database template to store, update, and display their library of screencast tutorials.

The Web Database

We'll briefly describe the structure here, but your benefit will come from exploring the Web objects as they are hosted online, and from downloading the companion database. With the database, you can examine the forms, reports, and macros. As you copy, modify, and work with the objects, they serve both as a learning tool and the basis for your own solution.

There are two tables in the database container: tutorials and products; the structure of the Tutorials table is shown in Figure I-20. The Tutorials table includes fields to support the formal title of the tutorial, production notes, the date it was published, the product it covers (a lookup list populated from the products table), the playback URL, and the production status (a lookup inside field properties). The playback URL is an externally hosted link to an 800x600 screencast produced with Camtasia Studio.

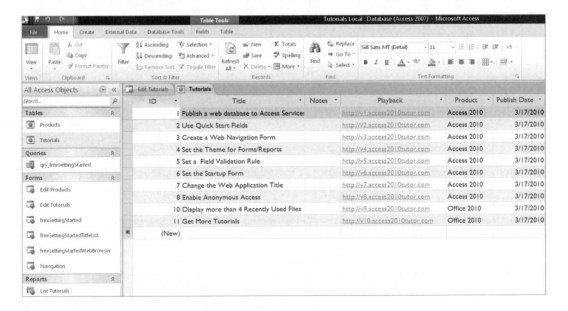

FIGURE I-20

One of the remarkable aspects of this application is that it provides the necessary functionality with just a handful of forms and reports. The main database objects include:

➤ **Tutorial Add/Change/Delete Form:** This simple Web-based form provides an easy way to update the records in the table directly from the browser.

➤ **Products Add/Change/Delete Form:** This form updates the products list, which populates choices in the products field of the tutorial table.

➤ **Tutorial List Report:** This report lists all of the titles currently available in the Tutorials table.

➤ **Tutorial Playback Form:** This is the most complex form in the project and consists of two subforms, one that displays query results from the Tutorials table and another that holds the new Web browser control and enables playback of the tutorial content URL. The first sub-form loads the list of tutorials (visible) and their associated playback URL (invisible). When a topic is clicked, the strVideoName variable is set to the correct playback URL and the Web browser subform begins playing the tutorial. Playback can be stopped and started by the embedded Flash player or by simply clicking another tutorial topic in the list.

As you are investigating how to create and modify the forms and reports, you'll also want to gain an understanding of the macro logic. The macro events drive the strVideoName variable, which instructs the Web control where to find the screencast content associated with each tutorial. There are two macros defined, an OnLoad macro to set up the URL when the playback form is first loaded, and an OnClick macro (shown in the following code) to change the playback URL when a title is selected from the Title List subform.

```
SetTempVar
Name   strVideoName
Expressoin =[Forms]![frm.GettingStarted]![sfrmTitleList]![Playback]
BrowseTo
        Object Type  From
        Object Name  frmGettingStartedWebBrowser
Path to Subform Control   frmGettingStarted.sfrmContent
Where Condition
Page
Data Mode  Edit
```

code snippet CS 35 (macro) in appI_Tips_Code.txt

The navigation form, shown in Figure I-21 in the Browser view, provides an administrative dashboard by rolling up the Add Tutorials form, the Add Product form, and the List Tutorials Report under a unified tabular view. This form is also set as the default form to be loaded when an authenticated user visits the site. To see how to create a form like this, you can play the "Create a Web Navigation Form" screencast from http://www.access2010tutor.com. (Please logon as User: **AH\ tutor** and Password: **tutor**).

Benefits to the End User

By using Access Services, you can effectively turn all (or selected) reports and forms into Web applications, such as the one shown in Figure I-22 (Browser view). With Web applications, the only client requirements are a compatible browser (Safari, IE, Firefox, Chrome), Adobe Flash, and a high-speed Internet connection. That's enough for most applications, but you can also redirect from a high level domain name to any form or report, creating shortcuts to specific features. One example of this would be creating a top level domain that redirects the user to content that is optimized for playback on mobile devices.

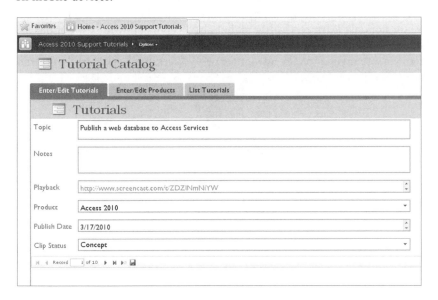

FIGURE I-21

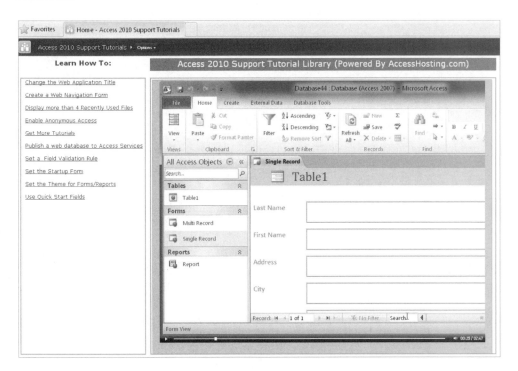

FIGURE I-22

You can download the template database, `Tutorials Local.accdb`, from the appendix files so that you can work with, modify, and use it as a model to create your own solutions. You can also see this project in action at `http://www.access2010tutor.com` (Please logon as User: **AH\tutor** and Password: **tutor**). New tutorial topics are added weekly to this growing library of screencasts. So it is an excellent resource for not only learning the basics, but also keeping up with new options as the technology grows. And when you are ready to experiment with publishing your own files (or modifications to this template), you are invited to take advantage of an Access Services Hosting offer for a free 30-day trial of Access Services at `http://www.accesshosting.com`.

INDEX